DEBATES ON U.S. HEALTH CARE

DEBATES ON U.S. HEALTH CARE

Editors

Jennie Jacobs Kronenfeld
Arizona State University

Wendy E. Parmet
Northeastern University School of Law

Mark A. Zezza
The Commonwealth Fund

Los Angeles | London | New Delhi
Singapore | Washington DC

Los Angeles | London | New Delhi
Singapore | Washington DC

FOR INFORMATION:

SAGE Publications, Inc.
2455 Teller Road
Thousand Oaks, California 91320
E-mail: order@sagepub.com

SAGE Publications Ltd.
1 Oliver's Yard
55 City Road
London, EC1Y 1SP
United Kingdom

SAGE Publications India Pvt. Ltd.
B 1/I 1 Mohan Cooperative Industrial Area
Mathura Road, New Delhi 110 044
India

SAGE Publications Asia-Pacific Pte. Ltd.
3 Church Street
#10-04 Samsung Hub
Singapore 049483

SAGE REFERENCE

Publisher: Rolf A. Janke
Acquisitions Editor: Jim Brace-Thompson
Assistant to the Publisher: Michele Thompson
Production Editor: Tracy Buyan
Reference Systems Team: Leticia Gutierrez,
        Laura Notton, Anna Villasenor
Typesetter: Hurix Systems Pvt. Ltd.
Proofreader: Bonnie Moore
Indexer: Julie Sherman Grayson
Cover Designer: Bryan Fishman
Marketing Manager: Carmel Schrire

MTM PUBLISHING, INC.

Editorial and Book Development Services,
New York City; www.mtmpublishing.com
Publisher/President: Valerie A. Tomaselli
Vice President, Book Development: Hilary Poole
Additional Research and Writing: Tim Anderson
Copy Editor: Jason Miller
Editorial Assistants: Anna Luciano, Meghan McHugh

Printed in the United States of America.

Library of Congress Cataloging-in-Publication Data

Debates on U.S. health care / editors, Jennie Jacobs Kronenfeld, Wendy E. Parmet, Mark A. Zezza.

p. cm. — (A Sage reference publication)

Includes bibliographical references and index.

ISBN 978-1-4129-9602-0 (cloth)

1. Medical policy—United States. 2. Medical economics—United States. 3. Public health—Moral and ethical aspects—United States. I. Kronenfeld, Jennie J. II. Parmet, Wendy E. III. Zezza, Mark A.

RA395.A3.D433 2012

362.10973—dc23

2012023367

SFI Certified Sourcing
www.sfiprogram.org
SFI-00453

12 13 14 15 16 10 9 8 7 6 5 4 3 2 1

CONTENTS

ABOUT THE EDITORS

Jennie Jacobs Kronenfeld is a professor in the Sociology Program in the School of Social and Family Dynamics, Arizona State University. Her research areas are medical sociology and aging and the life course with a special focus on health policy, health care utilization, and health behavior. She has recently published *Medicare* by Greenwood Press (2011) and serves as the editor of the research annual *Research in the Sociology of Health and Health Care* published each year by Emerald Press. She is co-editor of Health and Associate Editor In Chief of *American Journal of Health Promotion.* Her current research interests in addition to health policy include research on gender and health, and research on aspects of obesity as linked to social factors.

Wendy E. Parmet is George J. and Kathleen Waters Matthews Distinguished Professor of Law and Associate Dean for Academic Affairs at Northeastern University School of Law, where she is also Director of the Program on Health Policy and Law. She is the author of *Populations, Public Health, and the Law,* published by Georgetown University Press in 2009 and with Professor Patricia Illingworth, *Ethical Health Care,* published by Prentice Hall in 2005, as well as numerous articles in medical, legal, and public policy journals on public health law, health care access, bioethics, and disability law. Professor Parmet has served as counsel on several major court cases involving health care access. She received her JD from Harvard Law School and her BA from Cornell University.

Mark A. Zezza, PhD, currently works at the Commonwealth Fund as a Senior Policy Analyst. His main issues of interest relate to payment and delivery system reform, with a focus on the development of accountable care organizations. Dr. Zezza joined the Commonwealth Fund from the Engelberg Center for Healthcare Reform at the Brookings Institution, where he managed projects evaluating and providing implementation support to health-reform initiatives on accountability payment models, health information technology, and quality measurements. Prior to Brookings, Dr. Zezza was Associate Director at the Lewin Group, working as a member of the State Healthcare Reform team to analyze the economic and coverage effects of various reform proposals. From July 1999 through 2006, Dr. Zezza worked at the Centers for Medicare & Medicaid Services analyzing and helping to operationalize various Medicare payment systems. He holds a BS in Math and Psychology from Dickinson College, an MA in Economic Policy Analysis from the University of Maryland, Baltimore County and a PhD in Public Policy from the same institution.

ABOUT THE CONTRIBUTORS

E. Kathleen Adams, PhD, is a health economist with over 25 years experience in applied health services research. She is Professor at the Rollins School of Public Health at Emory University where she teaches public finance in the Department of Health Policy and Management and completes research on the effects of health policy on low-income and vulnerable populations.

Ellie Andres, MPH, is a researcher in the Department of Health Policy at the George Washington University School of Public Health and Health Services. Her research focuses primarily on health care access and quality for vulnerable populations, such as immigrants and children.

Tishra Beeson, MPH, is a researcher in the Geiger Gibson Program in Community Health Policy, in the Department of Health Policy at the George Washington University School of Public Health and Health Services. She conducts research on Federally-Qualified Health Centers and other safety-net providers with a focus on expanding access to primary care services in underserved communities. Ms. Beeson received her master's degree in public health from Oregon Health and Science University and is currently a doctoral student in public health at the George Washington University.

Lilliana L. Bell, MHA, is a Research Program Manager in the Department of Health Services Research, Management and Policy in the College of Public Health and Health Professions at the University of Florida. She serves as the Research Program Manager for the evaluation of Florida's Section 1115 Research and Demonstration Waiver program. Ms. Bell is also an Adjunct Assistant Professor in the Bachelor of Applied Science in Health Services Administration program at Santa Fe College in Gainesville, Florida.

Carl Berdahl graduated with honors from the Yale University School of Medicine in 2012, and he now works as an emergency medicine resident at Los Angeles County Hospital/USC. His research interests include health services, resource utilization, disparities, and public health.

Dhrubajyoti (Dru) Bhattacharya, JD, MPH, LLM, is the Director of the health policy and law track for the MPH program at Loyola University Chicago; Assistant Professor of Health Policy in the Department of Preventive Medicine and Epidemiology, Loyola University Stritch School of Medicine; and also serves as a Visiting Professor of Law at Loyola University Chicago School of Law. He received his LLM from Georgetown University Law Center and his MPH from Johns Hopkins Bloomberg School of Public Health.

Julia Bienstock is a law student at Fordham University School of Law. She has studied international health systems and has worked at the National Health Law Program and the Legal Aid Society's Health Law Unit. She is currently a staff member of Fordham's *Urban Law Journal*.

Joel C. Cantor, ScD, is the director of the Center for State Health Policy and professor of public policy at Rutgers University in New Brunswick, New Jersey. He has authored numerous studies of health insurance regulatory policy, health care delivery system performance, and access to care for low-income and minority populations. Cantor received his doctorate in health policy and management from the School of Public Health, Johns Hopkins University.

Kathleen Carey, PhD, is a Professor in the Department of Health Policy and Management at the Boston University School of Public Health where she teaches Health Economics and conducts research in health economics and health care policy. She also holds an appointment as an economist with the VA Center for Health Outcomes, Quality and Economic Research.

David W. Carlson is with PharmaMetrics, Inc.

Crystal Wiley Cené, MD, MPH, is Assistant Professor at the University of North Carolina (UNC) at Chapel Hill. She completed her medical degree at the Brody School of Medicine at East Carolina University and internship and residency at the Yale University Primary Care Internal Medicine Residency. She also completed her master's in Public Health and a

3-year General Internal Medicine Fellowship at Johns Hopkins University. Dr. Cené is a practicing general internist and physician-researcher at UNC.

Marcelo Coca-Perraillon is a PhD student in the department of Health Studies at the University of Chicago. Before joining the University of Chicago, he was a researcher at the National Bureau of Economic Research (NBER) in Cambridge, Massachusetts.

William S. Custer is Director of the Center for Health Services Research in the J. Mack Robinson College of Business at Georgia State University. Dr. Custer's research has investigated a wide range of topics including the sources of health insurance coverage, employment-based health insurance, health plan cost management initiatives, and health insurance regulation.

Corey Davis, JD, MSPH, is a Staff Attorney with the National Health Law Program and the Network for Public Health Law. His writing on the intersection of law and public health has appeared in publications including the *American Journal of Public Health*, the *American Journal of Bioethics,* and the *Clearinghouse Review Journal of Poverty Law and Policy*. He is licensed to practice law in Pennsylvania, New Jersey, and numerous federal courts.

Aubrey M. Denmon is a doctoral student in the Department of Sociology at the University of Georgia. She holds a master's degree in Public Health from the University of Georgia, and a Bachelor of Arts from Agnes Scott College. Her current research focuses on illness narratives among college students.

Diane Dewar is the Associate Dean for Academic Affairs at the School of Public Health and Associate Professor in the Departments of Health Policy, Management and Behavior and Department of Economics at the University at Albany, State University of New York. Her research focuses on the economic evaluation of programs and treatments for vulnerable populations and those with chronic conditions. She is the author of *Essentials of Health Economics,* a text geared toward noneconomists.

R. Paul Duncan, PhD, is the Malcolm and Christine Randall Professor and Chair of the Department of Health Services Research, Management and Policy in the College of Public Health and Health Professions at the University of Florida. Dr. Duncan is also the Director of the Florida Center for Medicaid and the Uninsured, where his work is focused on health insurance, the uninsured, Medicaid, and state program evaluations.

Leonard M. Fleck, PhD, is Professor of Philosophy and Medical Ethics in the Center for Ethics and Humanities in the Life Sciences, College of Human Medicine, Michigan State University. He is the author of *Just Caring: Health Care Rationing and Democratic Deliberation,* as well as 90 articles and book chapters on a range of issues in medical ethics and health care policy. He is also one of the editors for the forthcoming volume *Fair Rationing at the Bedside.*

Seth Freedman is an Assistant Professor at the Indiana University School of Public and Environmental Affairs and was a Robert Wood Johnson Scholar in Health Policy Research at the University of Michigan from 2010 through 2012. He received his PhD in Economics from the University of Maryland. His research interests are in health economics and health policy, particularly competition and financial incentives in provider markets.

Bianca K. Frogner, PhD, is an assistant professor in the Health Services Management and Leadership Department in the School of Public Health and Health Services at The George Washington University. As a health economist, her areas of research have included modeling the growth of health care spending, international health systems comparisons, trends in health care workforce as it relates to technology, and other topics in health care financing. She received her BA from University of California, Berkeley and PhD from Johns Hopkins Bloomberg School of Public Health.

Barry Furrow is a Professor of Law and Director of the Health Law Program at the Earle Mack School of Law at Drexel University. He publishes books and articles in the area of patient safety, medical liability reform, and bioethics generally.

Elise Gould is Director of health policy research at the Economic Policy Institute. She has authored a chapter on health in *The State of Working America 2008/09,* coauthored a book on health insurance coverage in retirement, published in venues such as *The Chronicle of Higher Education, Challenge Magazine,* and *Tax Notes,* and academic journals including *Health Economics, Journal of Aging and Social Policy, Risk Management & Insurance Review, Environmental Health Perspectives,* and *International Journal of Health Services.* She holds a master's in Public Affairs from the University of Texas and a PhD in Economics from the University of Wisconsin.

Linda Grant is Professor of Sociology and a faculty affiliate of the Institute for Women's Studies at the University of Georgia. She previously taught at Southern Illinois University–Carbondale, where she held a cross appointment with the School of Medicine. Her research has focused on the impact of gender on careers in medicine and academic science. She holds a PhD degree in Sociology from the University of Michigan–Ann Arbor.

Allyson G. Hall, PhD, is an Associate Professor and Associate Director of the Florida Center for Medicaid and the Uninsured in the Department of Health Services Research, Management and Policy in the College of Public Health and Health Professions at the University of Florida. Dr. Hall is also the Director of the Florida Office on Disability and Health. Dr. Hall's research centers around issues related to access to care for vulnerable populations including those who are low-income or live with a disability.

Randy Haught is a Senior Director at the Lewin Group. He has 20 years of experience in data analysis and microsimulation modeling of health care financing and policy-related issues. Mr. Haught has extensive experience in modeling the impact of the Patient Protection and Affordable Care Act and other health care reform proposals on major stakeholder groups including governments, business, providers, and households.

B. Jessie Hill is a Professor of Law at Case Western Reserve University. Her teaching and scholarship focus on constitutional law, civil rights, reproductive rights, and law and religion. She is a frequent lecturer and consultant on reproductive rights issues.

David Himmelstein has practiced primary care internal medicine and taught health policy research at Harvard Medical School. Since 2009, he has been a Professor of Public Health at City University of New York. He has authored more than 100 articles on various health policy topics, many of them with Dr. Steffie Woolhandler.

Michael Hochman is a general internist and a fellow in the Robert Wood Johnson Foundation Clinical Scholars program at the University of California, Los Angeles, and the Veterans Administration of Greater Los Angeles. He has published original medical research about comparative effectiveness research as well as other topics. Dr. Hochman has also written about medical topics for the *Boston Globe* and several other lay media publications.

Jason Hockenberry is an Assistant Professor in the Department of Health Policy and Management, Rollins School of Public Health, Emory University. He was previously a faculty member at the University of Iowa Department of Health Management and Policy, where he taught courses on health insurance and managed care and health economics. His primary research focus is on the impacts of provider human capital, technology diffusion, and policy on the quality and efficiency of health care.

Jill R. Horwitz is Professor of Law and Co-Director of the Program in Law and Economics at the University of Michigan Law School. She also holds appointments at the University of Michigan School of Public Health, Ford School of Public Policy, University of Victoria Department of Economics, and the National Bureau of Economic Research. Her scholarly interests focus on health policy, as well as the legal regulation of health care organizations, nonprofit law, law and economics, and tort law.

David Howard is a professor in the Department of Health Policy and Management at Emory University. A health economist by training, Dr. Howard's research focuses on the impact of evidence on use of technology and the cost and value of cancer treatment and screening. Dr. Howard received his PhD in Health Policy from Harvard University.

Patricia Illingworth teaches in the Department of Philosophy, the College of Business Administration and in the Law School at Northeastern University. She has held fellowships at Harvard Law School and Harvard Medical School. She is the author of *Us Before Me: Ethics and Social Capital for Global Well Being* and *Trusting Medicine: The Moral Costs of Managed Care* and co-editor of *Giving Well: The Ethics of Philanthropy, Ethical Health Care* and *The Power of Pills*.

Peter D. Jacobson, JD, MPH, is Professor of Health Law and Policy, and Director, Center for Law, Ethics, and Health, at the University of Michigan School of Public Health. He teaches courses on health law, public health law, and health care regulations. Jacobson's current research includes projects on public health entrepreneurship, safety net services, and how state and federal laws influence public health preparedness. In 1995, he received an Investigator Award in Health Policy

Research from the Robert Wood Johnson Foundation to examine the role of the courts in shaping health care policy. Jacobson's most recent books are *Law and the Health System* (coauthored with Lawrence O. Gostin, Foundation Press, 2005), and *False Hope vs. Evidence-Based Medicine: The Story of a Failed Treatment for Breast Cancer* (coauthored, Oxford University Press, 2007).

David K. Jones, MSPH, is a doctoral student at the University of Michigan, joint with the Department of Health Management and Policy in the School of Public Health and the Department of Political Science. His dissertation examines political and policy issues surrounding the implementation of the Affordable Care Act.

Jennifer M. Kerner, MPH, is a Political Science Doctoral Student at the University of New Mexico, Albuquerque. She received her master's in Public Health from Indiana University, Bloomington where her research focused on violence as a public health issue. Her current research interests include transitional justice, politics of violence, and international relations, specifically with regard to the African continent.

Patricia G. Ketsche is an associate professor in the Institute of Health Administration at Georgia State University. Dr. Ketsche focuses her research on financing and organization of health care in the United States with a particular interest in studying the intersection between public and private financing mechanisms.

Simeon Kimmel is an MD/PhD student at Harvard Medical School and the Harvard Graduate School of Arts and Sciences where he studies medicine and medical anthropology respectively. He has completed three years of medical school and is in his first year of graduate school.

R. Tamara Konetzka is Associate Professor at the University of Chicago, Department of Health Studies. She conducts research in health economics, aging and long-term care, quality of care, hospital markets, and Medicare and Medicaid policy, focusing on the interplay between economic incentives and quality of care. Professor Konetzka holds a PhD in health economics and health policy from the University of North Carolina at Chapel Hill and completed a post-doctoral fellowship at the University of Pennsylvania.

Elizabeth Weeks Leonard is a professor at the University of Georgia School of Law, where she teaches health care law and tort law. She has published numerous book chapters and articles on health care financing and regulation, public health law, and health care reform. Professor Leonard received her BA from Columbia University and JD from the University of Georgia.

Katy Mahraj received her Master of Science in Information, focused on health informatics, from the University of Michigan School of Information and Graduate Certificate in Health Informatics from the University of Michigan School of Information and School of Public Health in 2012. She earned her Bachelor of Arts summa cum laude from Harvard University in 2008. Currently, she is a health information analyst at Altarum Institute, a nonprofit health research and consulting company, in Alexandria, Virgina.

Thomas R. Marshall completed his PhD at the University of Minnesota and now teaches at the University of Texas at Arlington. His work focuses on the impact of public opinion on policymaking. Currently he is researching public opinion and health care, particularly public opinion toward smoking and health-related issues. His most recently published book is *Public Opinion and the Rehnquist Court* (2008).

Danny McCormick, MD, MPH, is an Assistant Professor of Medicine at Harvard Medical School, Director of the Division of Social and Community Medicine in the Department of Medicine at the Cambridge Health Alliance and co-director of the Harvard Medical School Fellowship in General Medicine and Primary Care. He received his internal medicine training at the Boston City Hospital and his general medicine fellowship training at the Massachusetts General Hospital/Harvard Medical School. He also holds an MPH from the Harvard School of Public Health. He is a health services researcher with an interest in access to and quality of care for underserved populations and practices primary care internal medicine at a public hospital affiliated community health center. He served as a Robert Wood Johnson Foundation Health Policy Fellow in Washington, D.C., and as a staff member of United States Senate Committee on Health Education Labor and Pensions under Senator Edward M. Kennedy.

Benjamin Mason Meier is an Assistant Professor of Public Policy at the University of North Carolina at Chapel Hill. Dr. Meier's interdisciplinary research, at the intersection of international law, public policy, and public health, examines legal frameworks for global health. Working collaboratively across UNC's Department of Public Policy and Gillings School of Global Public Health, he has written and presented extensively on the development of rights-based public health policy pursuant to state, national, and international law. He received his PhD in Sociomedical Sciences from Columbia University, his JD and LLM in International and Comparative Law from Cornell Law School, and his BA in Biochemistry from Cornell University.

Tom Miller is a resident fellow at the American Enterprise Institute, where he focuses on health policy. He was a member of the National Advisory Council for the Agency for Healthcare Research and Quality from 2007 to 2009 and previously served as a senior health economist for the Joint Economic Committee. He is a coauthor of *Why ObamaCare Is Wrong for America.*

Dinushika Mohottige is a fourth year medical student at the University of North Carolina (UNC) School of Medicine in Chapel Hill. She received her MPH at the UNC Gillings School of Global Public Health in 2008, and completed a Bachelor of Arts in Public Policy at Duke University.

Alan C. Monheit is Professor of Health Economics at the School of Public Health, University of Medicine and Dentistry of New Jersey, a research professor at the Rutgers Center for State Health Policy, and a research associate of the National Bureau of Economic Research. Dr. Monheit is editor of *Inquiry: The Journal of Health Care Organization, Provision, and Financing,* a member of the National Academy of Social Insurance, and a fellow of the Employee Benefits Research Institute. His research interests include the relationship between employment and health insurance, the uninsured population, health insurance reform, the distribution of health spending, and the determinants of population health.

Elaine Morrato, DrPH, MPH, CPH, has over 20 years of experience in health outcomes research with a focus on the diffusion and clinical translation of pharmaceutical innovation and policy. She is an Assistant Professor in the Department of Health Systems, Management & Policy in the Colorado School of Public Health, University of Colorado Denver and Assistant Director for the Children's Outcomes Research Program. Dr. Morrato has a career development award to study the diffusion of comparative effectiveness evidence into clinical practice and serves on the Key Function Committee for Comparative Effectiveness Research for the National Institutes of Health Clinical and Translational Science Awards.

Shayla Nagy graduated with honors from Johns Hopkins University in 2012 with a bachelor's degree in Neuroscience. During this time she was a health economics intern at both the Brookings Institution and the Aspen Institute, and worked on maternal and child health policy at the Maryland State Medical Society.

Dylan Nelson is a researcher in the Department of Health Policy at the George Washington University School of Public Health and Health Services, with particular interests in payment reform, population health, and disparities in care.

Brenda Ohta, PhD, MSG, MSW, CPHQ, is a Senior Director for NYU Langone Medical Center administratively responsible for the departments of Care Management; Integrative Health Programs; Language, Cultural and Disability Services; and Ethics Consultation. Dr. Ohta holds an appointment as Adjunct Associate Clinical Professor at the NYU Silver School of Social Work, teaching in the graduate program on subjects related to hospital and health system policy. Her areas of research and program development focus on the impact of social determinants of treatment variation and patient care for older adults, factors affecting health care utilization, and the development of care management models to support patient care across the continuum.

Stephen T. Parente, PhD, is the Minnesota Insurance Industry Chair of Health Finance in Carlson School of Management and the Director of the Medical Industry Leadership Institute at the University of Minnesota. As a Professor in the Finance Department, he specializes in health economics, health information technology, and health insurance.

Kavita Patel is a Fellow and Managing Director of Delivery System Reform and Clinical Transformation at the Engelberg Center for Health Care Reform at the Brookings Institution. She was previously Director of Policy for the White House Office of Public Engagement and Intergovernmental Affairs and the Deputy Staff Director for the Senate HELP Committee, under the leadership of the late Senator Edward Kennedy. Dr. Patel is a board-certified physician with expertise covering delivery system reform, access, coverage, and quality.

Jodyn E. Platt, MPH, is a doctoral student in the Health Services Organization and Policy Program at the University of Michigan School of Public Health. She received her MPH in health policy from the University of Michigan in 2005. Her research interests include science and technology studies, public health and health services systems, and public health genetics.

David Randall, PhD, currently serves as Executive Director of the Consumer Driven Health Care Institute based in Washington, D.C. Randall has testified before both U.S. House and Senate committees of Congress on a variety of health policy issues and has extensive experience as a former top insurance regulator, legislative staff member, health care lobbyist, consultant, and executive. He received his PhD in political science (policy analysis and administration) from Kent State University and wrote his doctoral dissertation on the politics of Medicaid contracting and privatizing.

Marsha Regenstein, PhD, is a professor in the Department of Health Policy at the George Washington University School of Public Health and Health Services. Dr. Regenstein's work focuses on vulnerable populations, the safety net, quality of care and health care disparities.

Sara Rosenbaum, JD, is the Harold and Jane Hirsh Professor of Health Law and Policy, George Washington University School of Public Health and Health Services. A nationally respected expert in health law and policy for over 35 years, Professor Rosenbaum is best known for her work in public and private health insurance and health care for medically underserved populations.

Daniel B. Rubin is a law student at the University of Michigan Law School as well as a graduate student in the Ph.D. program in Health Services Organization and Policy, in the Department of Health Management and Policy, The University of Michigan School of Public Health. Before coming to the University of Michigan he received undergraduate training in neuroscience at Oberlin College, and a master's degree in Bioethics from Case Western Reserve University.

Shenae K. Samuels, BS, is a Master of Public Health student in the College of Public Health and Health Professions at the University of Florida concentrating in Public Health Management and Policy. Ms. Samuels is a Graduate Assistant for the Florida Office on Disability and Health at the University of Florida and has interned at the Centers for Disease Control and Prevention's National Center for Chronic Disease Prevention and Health Promotion as a Public Health Summer Fellow.

Ronald Sandler is an Associate Professor of Philosophy and the Director of the Ethics Institute at Northeastern University. His primary research areas are ethical theory, environmental ethics, and ethics and emerging technologies. Sandler is author of *Character and Environment: A Virtue-Oriented Approach to Environmental Ethics*, *Nanotechnology: The Social and Ethical Issues*, and *The Ethics of Species*.

Anthony L. Schlaff is the Director of the Public Health Program and Professor of Public Health and Community Medicine at Tufts University School of Medicine. He received a BA in history from Yale University, an MD from Columbia College of Physicians and Surgeons, and an MPH from Harvard University. He is board certified in Internal Medicine and Preventive Medicine and has been a part-time clinician through most of his career. His academic interests are in the intersection of medicine and public health and in the use of public health methods to address the social determinants of health.

Kevin Seitz has over 40 years of experience in the administration of public and private health insurance programs. Over the years he has served as a hospital billing caseworker, legislative analyst, director for social services and Medicaid spending, director of Michigan's Medicaid program, president/CEO of the Blues' HMO in Michigan, and executive vice president at Blue Cross Blue Shield of Michigan. Seitz is an adjunct professor at the University of Michigan School of Public Health.

Barbara Sheer, PhD, FNP, FAANP, is Professor Emeritus at the University of Delaware and a consultant at Nurse Consultant Associates (NCA). She has been actively involved in nurse practitioner (NP) movement for the past 40 years, was a Public Health Policy Fellow, and has held national and international positions in NP organizations. Among those positions were President of American Academy of Nurse Practitioners, Chair of the National Alliance of Nurse Practitioners, Chair of the American Academy of Nurse Practitioner Fellows, Chair of Communications and Core Steering Group Member for the International Council of Nurses Nurse Practitioner/Advanced Practice Nursing Network.

Topher Spiro is the Managing Director of Health Policy at the Center for American Progress. He has worked on health care reform at both the federal and state levels, working to draft the Affordable Care Act as deputy staff director for health policy on the U.S. Senate Committee on Health, Education, Labor, and Pensions, and has also served as a health policy director for the Rhode Island Healthcare Reform Commission.

Sally C. Stearns is with the University of North Carolina at Chapel Hill.

Neera Tanden is President of the Center for American Progress and one of our nation's leading experts on comprehensive health care. She has previously served as a senior policy advisor for health reform at the Department of Health and Human Services, working to pass the Affordable Care Act, and has also served as a policy director for the Obama-Biden and Hillary Clinton presidential campaigns.

Marianne Udow-Phillips, MHSA, is the director of the Center for Healthcare Research & Transformation, a health policy center based at the University of Michigan with a mission to promote evidence-based care delivery, improve population health, and expand access to care. From 2004 to 2007, Udow-Phillips served as director of the Michigan Department of Human Services, which handles Medicaid eligibility and all public assistance programs. Udow-Phillips is an adjunct professor at the University of Michigan School of Public Health.

Steffie Woolhandler is a primary care physician and health policy researcher. She began her career at Harvard Medical School, where she was Professor of Medicine, and currently serves as Professor of Public Health at the City University of New York.

Ruqaiijah Yearby is a Professor of Law and Associate Director of the Law-Medicine Center at Case Western Reserve University School of Law. In 2000, Professor Yearby earned her Master of Public Health from Johns Hopkins and her law degree from Georgetown, where she was on the Dean's List. Bridging the gap between numerous disciplines, her work has been cited in *The Oxford Handbook of Bioethics* (2007), Barry Furrow et al., *Health Law: Cases, Materials and Problems* (6th ed., 2008), Michele Goodwin, *Black Markets: The Supply and Demand of Body Parts* (2006), and in the written testimony of Professor Vernellia Randall before the United States Senate Judiciary Subcommittee on Human Rights and the Law (Dec. 16, 2009).

Cynthia Zeldin is an MPH candidate in the Department of Health Policy and Management at the Rollins School of Public Health, Emory University. She is also the Executive Director of Georgians for a Healthy Future, a nonprofit consumer health advocacy organization based in Atlanta. She holds an MA from the George Washington University and a BA from Emory University.

Kai Zheng, PhD, is Assistant Professor in Information Systems and Health Informatics jointly appointed in the School of Public Health Department of Health Management and Policy and School of Information at the University of Michigan. His research draws on techniques from information systems research and human–computer interaction to study the use of information, communication, and decision technologies in patient care delivery and management. He is the recipient of the 2011 American Medical Informatics Association New Investigator Award that recognizes early-career achievements in health informatics and significant scholarly contributions.

PREFACE

Reforming the health care system has occupied a major place in the public discourse long before President Obama signed the Patient Protection and Affordable Care Act (ACA). Since the ACA became law, national anxiety and heated political exchanges seem only to have intensified. The debates presented in this volume are designed to help readers make sense of the issues that trigger these arguments and arrive at judgments with the facts at their fingertips and a clearer understanding of what's at stake.

The book is divided into three sections: Philosophical, Political, and Legal Debates; Economic and Fiscal Debates; and Quality of Care Debates. In each of these sections, critical issues are considered in a Point-Counterpoint format. The editors of each section selected the debate topics with two main things in mind: to ensure that the general issues surrounding health care reform are comprehensively discussed and to analyze the most contentious aspects of the ACA, in an effort to lay out the pros and cons in an analytical and objective manner.

While the authors strongly make the case for each side, the Point and Counterpoint sections taken together will give the reader a well-rounded sense of the entire issue, allowing for an appreciation of both sides. It's possible that a reader might see the merits of the argument made on the Point side of the debate and then feel the same way about the Counterpoint. Often the validity of the conclusions of one side will not preclude the validity of those on the other—this represents just how complex and difficult these issues are to confront and solve. The goal is careful consideration of all aspects of health care reform—from all perspectives.

That said, it is worth pointing out that the authors do, indeed, have strong points of view. Nonetheless, some authors contributed both Point and Counterpoint sides of particular debates; they were willing and able to set those views aside momentarily to explore aspects of the debate with which they may not personally agree.

The introductions to each chapter aim to introduce these conflicting points of view. Written in an effort to contextualize each debate, they help to summarize the positions taken by the author and indeed will offer readers a road map into the Point and Counterpoint. The introductions invoke considerations for readers to be alert to as they reason through the arguments presented in each chapter.

Each of the three sections also has an introduction, taking all the debates into account and connecting them together analytically. The editors, in these introductory essays, also offer historical context both in general terms and in terms of the current reform efforts under the ACA. Reading the section introductions alone will help to demystify much of the debate surrounding health care reform in the United States.

One particular point of complication—something seemingly very simple—is the name of the 2010 reform measure. You will see different titles and acronyms that are generally used to signify the reform measure in total. The Patient Protection and Affordable Care Act was originally passed by the Senate in December of 2009. In order for it to get approval from the House, it was amended by Health Care and Education Reconciliation Act of 2010 (HCERA), which was passed by the House on March 21. Together these bills constitute the reform measure and collectively are generally referred to as the Affordable Care Act. In both the media and the political arena, the acronym ACA often is used as an umbrella term for both pieces of legislation, and we have done so here.

The complexities surrounding the name of the measure reflect the difficult, even tortured, deliberations that Congress and the executive branch went through on their path to reform. The measure itself is a reflection of the conflicting interests and values embodied in the American public—all manifested in the political and philosophical arena—surrounding health care reform in general and the ACA in particular. These forces are still at play and, according to many analysts the ACA is simply one more step on the long road that United States is on to develop an equitable and efficient health care system.

Philosophical, Political, and Legal Debates

Introduction

On March 23, 2010, President Barack Obama signed the Patient Protection and Affordable Care Act (ACA) into law. For those watching the White House signing ceremony that day, it might have seemed as if the nation's perennial debates over health reform had finally been resolved. After decades of political stalemate, Congress had passed, and the president had signed, far-reaching health-reform legislation that, its advocates promised, would make health insurance newly available to over 30 million uninsured Americans, while at the same time "bending the cost curve" and decelerating the cost of care.

Any impression that the battles over health reform were over was illusory. The debates leading up to the ACA's passage were highly partisan and unusually rancorous. The summer before the act's passage, opponents charged that Democratic supporters of reform were trying to impose resource-limiting "death panels" on older Americans. When the president addressed a joint session of Congress in support of his reform proposal in September 2009, Republican congressman Joe Wilson (SC) defied decorum by interrupting the speech with a shout of "You lie!" After Senator Ted Kennedy of Massachusetts, a long-time champion of health reform died and was replaced by Republican Scott Brown, thereby denying Democrats a filibuster-proof majority in the Senate, it seemed as if health reform would once again fail. Only after congressional Democratic leaders agreed to invoke a procedure that permitted health reform to bypass the Senate's filibuster rule was the ACA enacted. The result was a messy, highly partisan, and far-from water-tight piece of legislation.

The ACA's potential political and legal pitfalls soon became apparent. Shortly after President Obama signed the act, Republican governors and attorneys general began filing lawsuits, challenging the law's constitutionality. At first, most legal commentators gave the suits little chance of success. But by the fall of 2010, when federal district judge Roger Vinson of the Northern District of Florida found that the ACA's minimum coverage provision, the so-called individual mandate was unconstitutional, that consensus began to erode (*State of Florida v. Dep't of Health & Human Services*, 716 F. Supp. 2d 1120). Less than a month later, sweeping gains in the 2010 midterm elections by Republicans who vowed to repeal the act highlighted the ACA's political vulnerability.

In fall 2011 the Supreme Court agreed to decide the constitutionality of both the individual mandate and another key provision expanding Medicaid coverage to all citizens whose income is less than 133 percent of the Federal Poverty Level. Riveting oral arguments were held over three days in March—an exception to the Court's practice of hearing arguments in a single day. During the arguments, many of the justices appeared to be skeptical of, if not downright hostile to, the ACA. When the arguments were over, many Court watchers and much of the public expected the Court's five Republican-appointees to strike down the individual mandate. On June 28, 2012, the Supreme Court surprised the nation with its ruling in *National Federation of Independent Business v. Sebelius*. As expected, the Court's decision was split, but not in the ways that were anticipated. Chief Justice John Roberts joined the four Democratic appointees to the high Court in concluding that the individual mandate was a constitutional exercise of Congress's power to levy taxes. The Chief Justice, however, agreed with his four fellow Republican appointees that the mandate could not rest upon Congress's power to regulate interstate commerce, as the mandate, in the majority's view, did not regulate commercial activity, but rather it compelled activity. Nevertheless, because an act of Congress is constitutionally valid as long as it rests on one constitutionally valid source of authority, the mandate survived, albeit under the taxing authority.

More surprising, perhaps, was the Court's seven–two decision finding that Congress had unconstitutionally coerced the states by tying the ACA's Medicaid expansion to a state's receipt of its prior Medicaid funds. Although the seven justices who reached this decision did not agree on a single majority opinion, they suggested that because Medicaid constitutes a very large share of the states' budgets and the expansion was different in kind than past expansions of Medicaid, the ACA did not give states a meaningful choice as to whether or not to expand their Medicaid programs. This lack of a choice, the justices concluded, failed to respect the sovereignty of the states. For four of the justices, this infirmity was sufficient to strike down the Medicaid expansion in toto. But Chief Justice Roberts, along with Justices Stephen Breyer and Elena Kagan, concluded that the Medicaid expansion could survive as long as it was viewed as optional for the states. When their votes were joined with those of the four justices who found the Medicaid expansion wholly constitutional, the provision was left to stand as a state option.

Despite the Court's ruling, as this volume goes to press, the ACA's fate remains uncertain. The Court's decision effectively returned the debates over the ACA, and health reform more broadly, to the political process. What will happen there in the 2012 presidential and congressional elections, as well as in the years to come, remains uncertain.

What is not in doubt is that the problems plaguing the U.S. health care system will continue to demand solutions. Despite its technological prowess, the American health care system is deeply troubled. In 2009 about 50 million Americans lacked health insurance; many others were underinsured. At the same time, Americans spent far more per capita, and a higher percentage of their gross domestic product (GDP), on health care than did people in other developed countries. For all that money, they experience relatively poor health outcomes. In 2010 the Central Intelligence Agency (CIA) estimated that life expectancy in the United States was worse than in 50 other countries in the world, including in some far-less wealthy nations such as Jordan or Greece.

The ACA's proponents claim that it will improve the health care system, but they admit that it will not end all of its problems. Even if the ACA is fully implemented in 2014, millions of Americans will remain uninsured. Moreover, although the act provides for pilot programs designed to slow the cost of care, no one believes that the ACA alone will solve the problem of rising health care costs, a problem that will only deepen as the population ages. Likewise, although the ACA provides support for research and initiatives designed to improve the quality of health care, quality will remain a daunting problem. And if the ACA is repealed as many Republicans urge, the problems it was designed to address—the increasing numbers of uninsured, the rapid rise of health care costs, and questionable quality of care—will remain in urgent need of resolution. The one certainty is that the health reform process, and the debates over it, will continue.

The section begins by looking at foundational debates that underlie almost all discussions of health reform, but are often not expressed. As the chapters illustrate, reaching a consensus over health reform is difficult not only because the debates touch upon some of the most fundamental issues regarding human health and the relationship between individuals and society but also because there are strong, often compelling, arguments to be made on each side of the debate.

Consider the simple but critical question raised in the chapter by Patricia Illingworth and Ronald Sandler: Is health care special? Is it just another good or service, like cell phones or travel, or is there a unique moral significance to health care that warrants it being the focus of a protracted national debate? Critical to that question, is the related but often-overlooked issue analyzed by Anthony Schlaff: Is health care even important to human health? We often think of health care as essential because we assume it is vital to our health and well-being. But is that so? Or, to put it another way, if society wanted to maximize health, would it put more resources into health care, or would it instead emphasize other goods and services, such as education, pollution control, or good housing? Some insight into that question is offered by Ruqaiijah Yearby's chapter on the continuing problem of health disparities. Yearby demonstrates the importance that social forces, including race discrimination and income inequality, play in perpetuating health disparities. These observations do not negate the importance of health care to health; indeed, Yearby shows how discrimination and inequality affect health by influencing access to and quality of health care. But they suggest that effective health reform, at least if it is to achieve equity in health outcomes, requires broader reforms than public debates often suggest.

Other chapters implicitly accept the moral significance and importance of health care, but explore the roles that individuals and governments have in assuring it. For example, in the Point section of their chapter, Benjamin Mason Meier and Dhrubajyoti Bhattacharya observe that international law recognizes a right to health and argue that the United States should respect that right. In their Counterpoint, they note that the recognition of a right to health would stand in stark contrast to the notion of rights accepted in the nation's civic and legal culture.

Seth Freedman and Jill Horwitz continue the exploration of government's role in regard to health by examining the role of the market and the proper focus of government regulation. In the Point section of their chapter, they argue that market competition is often the best device for allocating health care and that government regulation should seek to harness market forces. In the Counterpoint, they examine the many flaws in the health care market, and argue that given its imperfect nature, regulations are often required. Touching upon similar themes, but with a different emphasis, Jones and colleagues debate whether individuals or government should be viewed as bearing the primary responsibility for health. In the Point section, they note the high regard that American culture places on individual autonomy and responsibility and suggest that, as a result, health care decisions should be left primarily to individuals. Likewise, responsibility for staying healthy should be viewed as resting with the individual. In the Counterpart, they explore the social and cultural factors that affect health and question whether individuals can in fact exercise as much control over their health as society may wish to believe. If that is the case, what does it suggest in terms of health-reform policies? Should health reform seek to maximize individual choice or influence the social structures that lead to poor health and costly health care? In their chapter, Steffie Woolhandler, David Himmelstein, Simeon Kimmel, and Carl Berdahl consider the ideal structure of a reformed health care system. They ask whether the United States would be better off having a so-called single-payer style health system, as exists in Canada, or whether such a system would go either too far in restricting individual choice, or not far enough in fundamentally reforming the health care system.

Subsequent chapters focus on several concrete policy issues that arise in health-reform debates. For example, Barry Furrow analyzes the role that malpractice litigation plays in the health care system. In the Point section of his chapter, he presents the case for strong malpractice reform, arguing that lawsuits increase the cost of care while lowering access and quality. In the Counterpoint, he presents evidence suggesting that malpractice suits have played a relatively small role in increasing the cost of care, but are required to ensure that health care providers offer quality care.

Several chapters look at the political and legal issues that have arisen as a result of ACA. Tom Marshall looks at polling data across the decades. In the Point section of his chapter, he offers evidence that a majority of Americans support a wide range of health reforms. In the Counterpoint, he cites data showing the thinness of that support and the political dangers that elected officials face if they attempt to reform the health care system.

Those political dangers have perhaps been most glaring with respect to the ACA's individual mandate. The concept of a mandate— designed to legally compel individuals to carry health insurance and to penalize those who refuse—was originally proposed by conservative health policy analysts and politicians. In 2006 it became a signature feature of a Massachusetts health-reform law championed by Republican governor Mitt Romney. Yet, once the ACA was enacted, the mandate proved to be the act's most politically controversial and constitutionally problematic feature.

Several chapters explore questions pertaining to the mandate. In his chapter, Leonard Fleck looks at the normative arguments for and against the mandate. In the Point section, he provides a "liberal defense" of the mandate, explaining why it is necessary to prevent free riding and essential to maintain the ACA's prohibitions on discrimination by insurance companies. In the Counterpoint, he offers a libertarian critique of the mandate, arguing that it violates the U.S. tradition of individual choice and liberty. Julia Bienstock and Corey Davis, in contrast, explore the constitutional arguments that the Supreme Court considered for and against the mandate. These arguments relate to federalism and whether Congress exceeded the scope of its constitutional authority in enacting the mandate. Although the Supreme Court has rendered its decision, the debates will continue, as will the broader issue that Elizabeth Weeks Leonard engages: whether health reform should be undertaken by the federal government or be left to the states. Should the answer to that question depend upon the particular content of the health-reform policy at issue? The politics of the issue?

In their chapter, Sara Rosenbaum and Tishra Beeson expand upon these questions by looking at a range of barriers to health care and health facing medically underserved populations. In the Point section, they contend that, assuming states opt to go forward with the expansion, the ACA will offer an important step toward solving some of these problems by expanding eligibility for Medicaid and investing in community prevention and services. Some critics of the ACA, however, argue that the law does not go far enough and is likely to be of minimal impact. Thus, in the second half of their chapter, Rosenbaum and Beeson explore the idea that the ACA represents a lost opportunity to assist the medically underserved.

Although all of the debates presented arouse controversy, none do so more than those presented by Jessie Hill in her chapter on the nexus between health reform and reproductive health. Prior to the ACA's passage, arguments over the coverage of abortion threatened to derail the legislation. After its enactment in the winter of 2012, a decision by the Department of Health and Human Services that would have required all employers—even those affiliated with the Catholic Church (although not churches themselves)—to include contraceptive services in the health plans offered to their employees ignited a political firestorm. After a few weeks, the Obama administration announced a compromise policy, under which insurers, but not employers, would have to provide coverage for such services. Whether the compromise serves to quench the fire, only time will tell. But as Hill's chapter shows, the flames could have been anticipated. The debate over the ACA's coverage of birth control implicates the clash of two fundamental principles: religious liberty and gender equality. And it does so in the cauldron in which the culture wars meet health policy debates.

The issues raised by Hill's chapter offer an important clue as to why debates over health reform are both so compelling and so difficult to settle. The issues presented in this volume, and the issues that Americans will continue to debate about health reform, are not simply complex technical questions of policy and economics, affecting almost one-fifth of the U.S. economy. They are that. But technocratic solutions alone will never silence the debates because health reform also implicates important values and beliefs about which American society is deeply divided: When does life begin? What do we owe to those who are sick or dying? Why is health care important? What role should governments play in insuring health? What obligations do individuals have to stay healthy or keep the health care system viable? All of these questions can only be answered by engaging in thoughtful and informed dialog. The chapters that follow present such a discourse.

Wendy E. Parmet
Northeastern University School of Law

Moral Significance of Health Care

POINT: Health care is of special moral significance because it is critical to survival; without health care individuals cannot take advantage of other opportunities and cannot pursue their other goals in life. Because health care is of special moral significance, a just society treats health care differently than other goods that people may want or need.

Patricia Illingworth, Northeastern University School of Law

COUNTERPOINT: Human beings need many goods and services in order to take advantage of opportunities and pursue their goals. Health care is neither intrinsically more important than nor of greater moral significance than many other goods, such as housing, food, and even clothing.

Ronald Sandler, Ethics Institute, Northeastern University

Introduction

Debates over health care reform usually assume that there is something unique, or at least very important, about health care that warrants it being the subject of major political discourse. Indeed, the extensive public discussion dedicated to the subject seems to indicate that there's a fundamental and distinct public good at the core of the debate. Yet is health care truly unique? In this chapter, Patricia Illingworth and Ronald Sandler debate whether there is a special moral significance to health that should inform the discourse and direct public policy.

The Point part of the chapter argues that indeed there is, offering up four arguments supporting this position. The first, espoused in 1983 by the President's Commission for the Study of Ethical Problems in Medicine and Biomedical and Behavioral Research, proposes that health care is special because it underlies people's abilities to take advantage of the full range of opportunities afforded to them. The second argument, proposed in extensive writings by philosopher and ethicist Norman Daniels, extends this idea of opportunity by tying it to justice: health care promotes health, which in turn supports opportunity; and since opportunity is critical to justice, health care is a distinct feature of a just world. The third argument centers on the notion of capabilities: People should be free to fulfill their capabilities—one of which is bodily health—in order to achieve well-being. The fourth argument is founded on the concept of solidarity and proposes that treating health care as a special moral concern enhances the bonds between individuals, which, due to the fact that we are social beings, increases our sense of well-being. In reading the Point, consider the similarities and distinctions among these arguments and whether they are all equally persuasive.

The Counterpoint approaches the debate in two ways, arguing, (1) that health care is not uniquely essential to health, as other factors such as environmental, genetic, and social determinants play important roles in promoting health, and (2) that although opportunity is a critical component of justice, health is not unique in its ability to promote opportunity; in fact, so many factors—such as technological and educational access—promote opportunity that the specialness of health seems impossible. In reading the Counterpoint, consider whether these arguments are convincing. Even if we accept that other goods—like food or shelter—are critical to human opportunity, and even important to health, does that imply that health care should not be regarded as having a moral significance distinct from most other goods?

Americans' extensive consumption of health care and the overdrive of the public debate surrounding it indicates that as a country we are certainly preoccupied with health and health care. Do these trends suggest that our society ascribes a greater significance to health care than it does to most other goods and services? Or is society simply foolhardy in thinking that health care is of greater moral significance than most consumer goods? How can we explain why, as a society, we would have no problem denying a TV set to a poor person, but virtually everyone would think it immoral to deny medical care to someone who might die without it?

Likewise does the recognition that social determinants play a major role in health complicate our analysis of whether health care is morally significant? If a social factor, say education, plays a greater role in determining life expectancy for a population than does access to life-saving surgery, does that diminish the moral importance of such surgery for an individual? Must our ethical analysis be able to consider both the importance of health care to the individual and to the larger society?

Complicating the question further is the perception of the relative importance of some types of health care over others. A critical procedure to prolong life is likely viewed as more of a moral imperative than elective surgery to repair an athletic injury.

Whether or not greater moral significance is placed on some types of health care, the freedom to obtain any type of health care clearly weighs into this debate. Both the Point and Counterpoint acknowledge the importance of liberty as a component of our moral fabric. Indeed personal freedom lies at the base of this debate, since both sides argue against the backdrop of the free enterprise system, our reliance on the marketplace to allocate resources, and the freedom of individuals to make their own economic decisions. If health care is of special moral significance, then it might be an exception to market rules, and indeed many stakeholders in the health care reform discussion would have a problem leaving health care entirely up to the market forces. Does this fact alone matter? Do we even need to have clear and convincing answers regarding the specialness of health care to inform our health-reform debates? Or is the fact that we spend over 17 percent of our gross domestic product on health a sufficient reason for placing health high on the national agenda?

POINT

Typically, the goods that people consume are distributed on the basis of the market: supply and demand. Flashy cars, LCD televisions, and state-of-the-art stereo equipment go to those willing and able to purchase them. Few people object to such a distribution with respect to these consumer goods. Indeed many believe that market distribution is not only economically efficient, it is also morally desirable primarily because of the role it plays in protecting liberty. More specifically, the distribution of goods according to market principles enhances autonomy because if people want a flashy car or the latest gadget they can arrange their lives so that they can purchase those things, while others, with no interest in such items, can arrange their lives so that they can pursue the things they desire.

Leaving the distribution of these goods to the market thus furthers the moral goals of liberty and autonomy. According to this reasoning, everyone is free to have whatever they want; if what they want is luxury items or expensive vacations they only need the money to purchase them. Moreover, the market leaves people free to pursue life paths that will give them the financial wherewithal to purchase the goods they want. On this view, individuals are in the best position to know what they want, and allowing a distribution on the basis of the market is the best way to respect their wishes. We can see that the argument is founded on a concern with autonomy and liberty. It is worth noting that the liberty at issue here is negative liberty: the liberty not to be interfered with.

Health care reform, and government provided health care, are important exceptions to this general market-based distribution. Although few people object to distributing televisions according to market principles, many object to distributing health care on the basis of the market. But given moral arguments that support relying on the market for most goods, it is necessary to show that there is something about health care that justifies treating it as special—a view that can be called the specialness thesis.

The justification for treating health and health care differently has been posed in terms of whether health care is morally special. If health care is morally special, then protecting it—by means of, for example, higher taxes on the wealthy or regulation of the pharmaceutical industry—may be justified. There are many reasons why health care is considered morally special. Some of those reasons are in keeping with a concern for liberty.

The discussion that follows reviews the main arguments that have been offered for thinking that health care is morally special and should be exempt from the usual market-based distribution principles. These include arguments from the President's Commission for the Study of Ethical Problems in Medicine and Biomedical and Behavioral Research, Norman Daniels' opportunities-based analysis, the capabilities approach of Amartya Sen and Martha Nussbaum, and a view based on an understanding of human beings as social animals, which can be called the solidarity argument.

THE PRESIDENT'S COMMISSION

In 1983 the President's Commission for the Study of Ethical Problems in Medicine and Biomedical and Behavioral Research issued an influential volume on access to health care. The Commission argued that health care is special because of its importance in promoting "personal well-being by preventing or relieving pain, suffering, and disability and by avoiding loss of life" (pp. 16–17). In the absence of health care people may not be able to live full lives in which they can enjoy a full range of opportunities. The Commission also discussed the fact that health is different from other goods because many of the health problems people have are not within their control, but are instead the result of factors such as genetics, the environment, and chance. Therefore many of the health problems that people have are undeserved. Although some health conditions may result from lifestyle choices, many do not. Even illnesses associated with lifestyles, such as lung cancer and smoking are highly influenced by social factors such as the effective lobbying efforts of tobacco companies and the legal rights we extend to them to advertise freely.

The Commission stated that because of health care's special nature it ought to be "accessible, in a fair fashion, to all" (p. 18). Despite this the Commission concluded that it was difficult to determine what would constitute an equitable division of health care. The Commission therefore decided that an equitable distribution only required an "adequate level of health care" (p. 20). But even with that caveat the Commission failed to assert that there was a right to health care, arguing only for the more modest position that society has an "obligation" to provide all with an "adequate level of health care" (p. 22).

The Commission's analysis illustrates some of the concerns with liberty discussed earlier. By identifying factors that put health outside the individual's control, such as genetics, the environment, and bad luck, the Commission highlighted how health and health care are different from many other goods, and cannot be left solely to the market. If a person's health is not within their control, their liberty is thusly impaired. In addition, health problems are often unpredictable and distributed randomly without regard to effort, prudence, merit, or coping ability. Although some people might argue that the same is true with respect to socioeconomic status, and the purchasing power it enables, the Commission believed that the case was stronger with respect to health. If we add to this the idea that in order to protect against the uncertainties of sickness, we must work together and spread risk among many, the case for treating health care different from other goods is strong.

NORMAN DANIELS' APPROACH

One of the most compelling arguments in support of the view that health care is special comes from philosopher Norman Daniels. Daniels points out that unequal distributions of goods are permissible provided people have an equal opportunity to secure them. The basic format of his argument goes as follows: because health care promotes health, and health is important for opportunity, health care promotes opportunity. Because justice requires access to opportunity, it must also treat health as important. Although Daniels defends this argument on the basis of John Rawls's influential theory of justice, other theories can be used to support the idea.

According to the Constitution of the World Health Organization, health is a state of complete physical, mental, and social well-being and not merely the absence of disease or infirmity. This is a broad definition of health, and one that, although controversial, has been widely used over the years. Yet, it is not the definition that Daniels uses. In order to determine what aspects of health are important for opportunity, Daniels ties health to normal functioning, namely, what behavior and activities are typical for a member of the human species. Impairment to normal functioning is viewed as unhealthy. Daniels connects health to normal functioning because the ensuing needs are objectively ascribable, and there seems to be general public agreement that these needs should be met. In general, it is difficult to achieve our goals without the satisfaction of such needs.

Daniels also advances another view. Impairments to normal functioning reduce the range of opportunities from which people may construct their life plans. So for Daniels health understood as normal functioning is morally special because of the role it plays with respect to protecting a range of opportunities for people, and health care needs are special because they act in the service of normal functioning.

Although few people would quarrel with the idea that health care is important for health and opportunity, many other things, including the social determinants of health, are also important. Some scholars think that social determinants are more important for health than health care. For example, studies show that economic inequality has deleterious effects on health, as does being lonely or being a member of a minority racial group, among other things. If social determinants are important for health, then they too need to be protected for the sake of health and opportunity. For the sake of consistency and justice, they too count as special. Given this line of thinking, many things may count as morally special. Although some people think the multiplicity of opportunity-based needs undermines the specialness thesis, this isn't true. From the fact that health care is not alone in being special, it doesn't follow that health care is not morally special. Food, shelter, equality, and education, among other things, are morally special in part because of the relationship they bear to opportunity. For Daniels, health care is "one among a broader set of health needs" (Daniels, 2008, p. 30) and he accepts that health needs that are met or compromised by the social determinants of health are special. More specifically, Daniels identifies the following as the broad set of health needs required for normal species functioning:

1. Adequate nutrition

2. Sanitary, safe, unpolluted living and working conditions

3. Exercise, rest, and such important lifestyle features as avoiding substance abuse and practicing safe sex

4. Preventive, curative, rehabilitative, and compensatory personal medical services and devices

5. Nonmedical personal and social support services

6. An appropriate distribution of other social determinants of health (Daniels, 2008)

For Daniels then, health care is morally special because it promotes health, which in turn, is morally special because of the role it plays in securing our opportunities. Daniels is right that the same is true for the social determinants of health. Indeed, there are more social determinants of health than Daniels lists, including social capital and equality. The main justification for the special moral character of all lies in their role in establishing our opportunity range from which we choose our life plans.

THE CAPABILITIES APPROACH

The capabilities approach offers another argument in support of the view that health care is morally special. This view sees health care as special because of the role it plays with respect to our capabilities, and human flourishing more broadly. According to this view, supported by scholars like Martha Nussbaum and Amartya Sen, among others, it is important that people have the freedom to choose among capabilities and in this way to achieve well-being. For people, well-being consists in realizing their capabilities. The notion of a capability is complex, but has to do with what a person can be, and do, in a social context, given their particular skills, talents and abilities. In Sen's words:

> *Functionings* represent parts of the state of a person—in particular the various things that he or she manages to do or be in leading a life. The *capability* of a person reflects the alternative combinations of functionings the person can achieve, and from which he or she can choose one collection. The approach is based on a view of living as a combination of various 'doings and beings,' with quality of life to be assessed in terms of the capability to achieve valuable functionings. (Sen, 1993, p. 31)

Although Sen has so far refrained from providing a list of specific capabilities, Martha Nussbaum has offered one. She lists 10 capabilities: a normal life span, bodily health, bodily integrity, senses, imagination and thought, emotions, practical reason, affiliation, other species, play, and control over one's environment. Nussbaum believes governments have an obligation to protect these capabilities.

Nussbaum's second capability specifically identifies health. But other capabilities also implicate health, including mental health. It is difficult, for example, to imagine a satisfying emotional life and affiliations without a modicum of health. People who suffer because of illness may be unable to interact in positive ways with others. For example, if a person is wracked with pain, or preoccupied with her personal survival, she may be unable to interact with others at all. In thinking about whether or not health care is special one would need to consider health broadly, and then consider it with respect to the other capabilities to see what specific health care was important to realize human capabilities.

Being healthy is a capability that people have and societies should protect their capacity for health. On this view, health is special because it is among a select group of important capabilities. Health care is special because it is a means to enable people to be healthy. Capabilities can also be understood as substantial freedoms, such as the ability to live a normal life span and to be healthy. Those who support the capability approach are concerned with the actual freedom to be healthy. Poor health, like poverty itself, should be understood as a deprivation in capability and well-being. It is easy to understand that people who are very sick, and not able to realize the capability of health, are substantially less free than those who are perfectly healthy.

THE SOLIDARITY ARGUMENT

The capabilities approach suggests another reason why health and health care are important. It is widely recognized by philosophers and others that we are social beings, and that our well-being depends to some extent on the well-being of others. This was an important insight of John Stuart Mill. Consider these two passages from Mill's famous book *Utilitarianism*:

> [T]here is this powerful natural sentiment; . . . when once the general happiness is recognized as the ethical standard, will constitute the strength of the utilitarian moralists. This firm foundation is that of the social feelings of mankind—the desire to be in unity with our fellow creatures. (Mill, 1957, pp. 10–11)

Later in *Utilitarianism,* Mill states:

> [T]hey are also familiar with the fact of cooperating with others and proposing to themselves a collective, not an individual, interest as the aim . . . of their actions. So long as they are cooperating, their ends are identified with those of others; there is at least a temporary feeling that the interests of others are their own interests. Not only does all strengthening of social ties, and all healthy growth of society, give to each individual a stronger personal interest in consulting the welfare of others, it also leads him to identify his feelings more and more with their good. (Mill, 1957, pp. 40–41)

Mill, like others before and after him, recognizes the importance of social ties and connections for individual and community well-being. He notes that people want "harmony between their feelings and aims and those of their fellow human beings" (pp. 42–43). We cannot enjoy harmonious relationships with our fellow human beings if we do not respect their basic human dignity and help them when they are suffering.

If we do not treat health care, along with some other things, such as food and shelter, as morally important, people with whom we enjoy social ties will suffer. Instead of watching them suffer, we risk feeling the need to retreat to a place where we cannot observe their suffering, leaving the sick to suffer their fate alone. Treating health care as special allows our social ties to blossom. Denying people health care when they are suffering commits us to living in a world of haves (those who have health care) and have nots (those without), a modern day quarantine.

Studies on mirror neurons show that when we see people in pain we experience it as if we ourselves are also in pain. Marco Iacobini wrote in 2008, ". . . it seems as if our brain is built for mirroring, and that only through mirroring— through the simulation in our brain of the felt experiences of other minds—do we deeply understand what other people are feeling" (p. 126). This in turn gives us our capacity for empathy. Empathy may be, and often is, a precursor to our willingness to help others, which in turn, facilitates trust and social ties. Health care is special in this view because without it people would not be able to have the kind of social connections with others that their very natures depend on and that contribute to their well-being. We can call this the solidarity argument: Unlike the other arguments discussed, the solidarity argument for treating health care as morally special reflects the social nature of people and not their autonomy.

To sum up, health care is special for a variety of moral reasons. It is important for opportunity. People who are sick are unable to enjoy the opportunities available to them. As Daniels points out, the opportunity range of someone who is sick or disabled is reduced. Health care is also important because health is among the important capabilities that all societies should protect. Finally, given the social dimension of human beings, health care may be morally special in order to preserve social ties and maintain well-being.

REFERENCES AND FURTHER READING

Berlin, I. (1969). Two concepts of liberty. *Four essays on liberty.* London, UK: Oxford University Press.

Daniels, N. (2008). *Just health: Meeting health needs fairly.* New York, NY: Cambridge University Press.

Iacobini, M. (2008). *Mirroring people: The science of empathy and how we connect with others.* New York, NY: Picador.

Illingworth, P. (2011). *Us before me: Ethics and social capital for global well being.* New York, NY: Palgrave Macmillan.

Illingworth, P., & Parmet, W. (2005). *Ethical health care.* Upper Saddle River, NJ: Prentice Hall.

Illingworth, P., & Parmet, W. (2012). Introduction. *Special issue on solidarity in bioethics. Bioethics.* US and UK: Blackwell Publishing.

Mill, J. S. (1957). *Utilitarianism.*(O. Piest, Ed.). Indianapolis, IN: Bobbs-Merrill Educational Publishing.

Nussbaum, M. (2001). Adaptive preferences and women's options. *Economics and Philosophy, 17*(1), 67–88.

Preamble to the Constitution of the World Health Organization as adopted by the International Health Conference. (1948). Geneva, Switzerland: World Health Organization.

President's Commission for the Study of Ethical Problems in Medicine and Biomedical and Behavioral Research. (1983). *The ethical implications of differences in the availability of health services, volume one.* Washington, DC: U.S. Government Printing Office.

Ruger, P. (2006). Toward a theory of a right to health: Capability and incompletely theorized agreements. *Yale Journal of Law and the Humanities, 18*, 273–326.

Sen, A. (1993). Capability and well-being. In M. Nussbaum & A. Sen (Eds.), *The quality of life* (pp. 30–53). Oxford, UK: Clarendon Press.

Patricia Illingworth

COUNTERPOINT

The claim that health care is of special moral importance is made in the context of discussions about justice and the institutional distribution of resources. In particular, it is intended to convey that, as a matter of social justice, institutions need to ensure access to health care for members of society in a way that differs from that applied to other goods, that is, in a more equitable manner, even at higher costs, or not by pure market mechanisms. The claim that health care should be treated as a special good (hereafter, *the specialness thesis*) needs to be justified. Proponents of the view need to explain what it is about health care and its relationship to justice that merits affording it special status. While health care is important and justice may well require institutional assurance of at least some health care (or health promotion) for citizens, it is not morally special in the sense intended by proponents of the specialness thesis.

THE STRUCTURE OF THE ARGUMENT FOR WHY HEALTH CARE IS SPECIAL

Health care is not of special moral importance in and of itself. The reason for this is that health care is not an end, but a means. Health care often promotes health, and reliable access to health care can provide psychological benefits related to security and long-term planning. It is good for people to have assurance of health care and to receive health care when needed because of what it does for them physically and psychologically. But health care access and service are not unique in being physically or psychologically good for people. Reliable sources of income, healthy relationships, self-esteem, and stimulating environments are good for people as well. So what is it about health care that is thought to distinguish it in the context of just resource allocations?

The answer provided by proponents of the specialness thesis is that health care stands in a special relationship to health and that health stands in a special relationship to justice. Norman Daniels states: "the answers to these questions [about what makes health care morally special] depend on explaining the special moral importance of health itself, at least from the point of view of justice. Once we can explain why health is of special moral importance, we can explain why special importance is given to meeting health care needs equitably" (Daniels, 2008, p. 29). Daniels is the most prominent and persistent proponent of the specialness of health care. His preferred answer to the question of why health, which he identifies as "normal functioning," is especially morally important is that health is crucial to promoting opportunity and, as a matter of justice, institutions must protect and promote equality of opportunity. Daniels' answer to the question of the special moral importance of health draws on John Rawls' influential conception of justice as fairness in which justice requires that institutions ensure equality of opportunity for citizens. In Rawls' view, fair equality of opportunity applies primarily to competitive contexts, such as employment and education, where position-oriented goods are at stake. However, Daniels argues that the Rawlsian commitment to justice actually requires (or, at least, favors) a broader sphere of equality of opportunity that encompasses the pursuit of life plans and civic participation as well. He then argues that lack of health (or normal functioning) unreasonably restricts the range of possible life plans (that is, opportunities) available to people: "impairments of normal functioning reduce the range of exercisable opportunities from which individuals may construct their 'plans of life' or 'conceptions of the good.' . . . Life plans for which we are otherwise suited, and that we reasonably hope to find satisfying or happiness-producing, are rendered unreasonable by some impairments of normal functioning" (Daniels, 2008, p. 35). Thus, because justice requires protecting people's fair range of opportunities, and lack of health unreasonably restricts people's opportunities, health stands in a special relationship to justice and justice requires health promotion.

The specialness thesis is not tied to a Rawlsian conception of justice. As Daniels argues, the thesis can be modified to accommodate several other theories of justice, including capabilities approaches in which justice requires ensuring that people have the capabilities needed to identify and pursue their own conceptions of the good, as well as opportunity for welfare approaches in which justice requires that people have equal, fair, or adequate opportunities for positive well-being outcomes. In each case, what is crucial is that there is

(1) a special link between health care and health; and

(2) a special link between health and what the theory of justice claims is owed to people (that is, capabilities, opportunities, welfare outcomes, or solidarity).

The discussion that follows considers both claims, focusing on Daniels' particular view, but the discussion can be applied *mutatis mutandis* to the specialness thesis understood through other theories of justice.

IS THERE A SPECIAL LINK BETWEEN HEALTH CARE AND HEALTH?

As mentioned previously, health care is thought to be good because it promotes health, both physical and psychological. Of course, there are many other things that promote health as well—potable water, clean air, exercise, and a nutritious diet, for example. What makes people unhealthy (that is, sick or disabled) is not primarily lack of access to health care. Even focusing on only social—and not genetic—factors, the causes of less than normal functioning are everything from lead paint to stress and unsafe workplaces to particulate pollution. Moreover, "[w]hile medical care can prolong survival and improve prognosis after some serious diseases, *more* important for the health of the population as a whole are the social and economic conditions that make people ill and in need of medical care in the first place" (Wilkinson & Marmot, 2003, p. 7). For these reasons, Daniels has revised his original specialness thesis, which focused on health care, to be more inclusive. His more recent version encompasses "meeting health needs" (2008, p. 30) through health care, public health policies, workplace safety, environmental hazard remediation, consumer protection, and so on.

But even this expansive conception of "meeting health needs" does not capture all the social factors that are relevant to health outcomes. The social determinants of health include socioeconomic factors such as income inequality, social exclusion, workplace organization, family structures, education access, and employment, for example. Therefore, even given a conception of the first part of the specialness thesis—that is, claim (1) on the previous page—which asserts that meeting health needs, and not just health care, stands in the special relationship to health, the thesis is problematic. There are many other social factors that stand in a similarly significant relationship to health and, like meeting health needs, these factors can be affected by institutional policies and change. Meeting health needs does not appear to be special.

In response to this criticism, proponents of a special link between meeting health needs (or public health promotion) and health might argue for a still greater expansion of what counts as "public health promotion" so that it encompasses institutional efforts to address all the social determinants of health. (Daniels at times seems to embrace such an expansion.) However, while this would make claim (1)—that a special relationship exists between promotion of health and health care—true, it would undermine the specialness thesis overall. By extending the specialness thesis to encompass all the social determinants of health, it would follow that the specialness thesis applies to tax policy, education policy, agricultural policy, employment policy, policies that affect familial structures, and so on. But if all of the relevant goods impacted by these policies are special, if they all have the same standing with respect to principles of institutional distributive justice, then none of them is special. Moreover, there are many other considerations, besides health-oriented ones, which are relevant to tax, education, and employment policies that would need to be taken into account when defining goals, evaluating strategies, and implementing programs. Therefore, not only is health care (or health promotion) not a special policy area, consideration of health outcomes do not have special (that is, overriding or unique) justice-oriented significance in other policy contexts.

Thus, claim (1), that there is a special relationship between promotion of health needs and health, appears to be either false or uninteresting. Either it is understood in the more restrictive public health sense, in which case there are other social determinants of health that stand in the same qualitative relationship to health and (collectively) a greater quantitative relationship, or it is understood in the more encompassing sense, in which case so much is counted as being special that the specialness thesis becomes practically insignificant. If everything is special, and needs to be treated as such, then nothing is.

IS THERE A SPECIAL LINK BETWEEN HEALTH AND OPPORTUNITY?

The second part of the specialness thesis—that is, claim (2) on the previous page—asserts a special link between health and what justice implies we owe to people. On Daniels' particular view, the relevant thing that is owed to people is opportunity. So, in evaluating the second part of the specialness claim, given Daniels' Rawlsian conception of justice, the critical question is whether health stands in a special relationship to opportunity for carrying out one's life plans or for full social participation.

Health certainly is relevant to fair opportunity in the sense at issue—that is, reasonable life plans can be rendered unobtainable by a lack of health. However, the same is true of many other goods. For example, in highly technologized nations, reliable access to information technologies is increasingly critical for developing and executing an individual's life plan, as well as for full social (including civic) participation. A lack of access to the Internet and email, for example, can marginalize people from employment opportunities and can constitute a significant barrier to social and civic participation. As a result, lack of access or technological competence can render reasonable life plans unrealizable. Therefore, on the fair opportunity conception of justice that Daniels endorses, we owe people reliable access to information technologies, just as we do health promotion. The same point applies, *mutatis mutandis,* to capabilities and welfare-oriented conceptions of justice. In a highly technologized society, information technology access and competence are capabilities crucial to accomplishing personal and social functionings, and they can be vital to realizing strong social ties, solidarity, and positive life outcomes.

The symmetry, with respect to justice, between information technologies and health promotion can be seen by substituting the relevant terms in Daniels' summary of the case for the specialness thesis. Here, first, is Daniels' more recent formulation of the case that health care is special—that is, the one modified to accommodate non-Rawlsian theories of justice and the broader conception of health promotion:

> (1) Since meeting health needs promotes health (or normal functioning), and since health helps to protect opportunity, then meeting health needs protects opportunity. (2) Since Rawls's justice as fairness requires protecting opportunity, as do other important approaches to distributive justice, then several recent accounts of justice give special importance to meeting health needs. (2008, p. 30)

Here is the version of the argument made analogous to information technology:

> (1) Since meeting information technology needs promotes economic, social and civic functioning, and since economic, social and civic functioning protects opportunity, then meeting information technology needs protects opportunity. (2) Since Rawls's justice as fairness requires protecting opportunity, as do other important approaches to distributive justice, then several recent accounts of justice give special importance to meeting information technology needs.

There are many other goods, in addition to access to information technologies, that promote the sort of social, economic, and civic functioning that protects opportunity—that is, economic means, educational opportunities, and social capital. Moreover, public policies affect access to and distribution of these other goods, just as public health policies do for health. Thus, the second part of the specialness thesis—that there is a special moral relationship between health and opportunity—appears to be false. Meeting technology needs, economic needs, educational needs, and social needs all seem to stand in the same relationship to justice as does meeting health needs. That this is so is not tied to Daniels' particular account of why health matters for justice; it is rather a general point about the relationship between health and justice.

IMPLICATIONS

Both parts of the specialness thesis appear to be false. Meeting health needs does not stand in a special relationship to health, and health does not stand in a special relationship to opportunity (or capabilities, social goods, or well-being outcomes). It is possible to substitute many different goods into the core specialness argument to generate the conclusion that they, like health promotion, are special and therefore warrant exemption from pure market distributions. But then it seems like health promotion is not really very special. It is not uniquely, distinctively, or overridingly important from the perspective of justice. As a result, it should be given the same priority within social institutions as is information technology access and education access, for example. We do not have a special obligation to guarantee equitable access to health promotion that we do not have for these other goods, and we should not treat health promotion costs differently from the costs of promoting these other goods. It does not follow from this that promoting health needs is unimportant. It may be that justice requires aggressive and equitable promotion of all these goods. But it does follow that health promotion should not be treated as exceptional in public policy.

Proponents of the specialness thesis might agree with the claim that health promotion is not the only special good. (As mentioned earlier, Daniels at times seems to endorse this view.) However, the practical significance of recognizing that there is a very broad range of goods which are special in just the same way as health promotion undermines the motivation for and purported implications of the specialness thesis. Since health promotion is not uniquely special, it is subject to the same cost-benefit and cost-effectiveness considerations as are information technology, education, and welfare policies. In each case, the core issue in evaluating a policy is the extent to which the resource (or the practice or institution) it allocates will produce positive opportunity (or capability or well-being) outcomes. The fact that a particular policy is health-oriented rather than employment-oriented, information technology-oriented, or education-oriented is immaterial. A policy is justified to the extent that it effectively uses scarce resources to provide what we owe to people as a matter of justice, be it opportunities or capabilities or well-being. This is true both within and across policy domains.

Because health promotion (including health care) should be held to this same standard of evaluation as other types of opportunity (or capability or outcome) promotion, it is not only acceptable, but required, to trade off health promotion against the other types of opportunity promotion when doing so accomplishes opportunity gains more effectively and efficiently. For example, public policies that pay for medical treatments that have low health or longevity outcomes would merit much lower priority than technology policies that effectively enable people to pursue reasonable life plans (for example, by facilitating educational and employment opportunities). Again, that the one is health-oriented and the other is not is immaterial from the perspective of justice. The upshot of this, with respect to a right or entitlement to health care, is that if people do have a justice-grounded entitlement to health care or health promotion, it is likely more restricted than is often supposed. Justice does not require that people have access to any and all forms of medical assistance available. It requires that they have access to care that is effective and efficient at promoting opportunity or well-being outcomes (evaluated across the population) in comparison to other ways in which these might be promoted. Determining the implications of this for specific policies, practices, and treatments requires detailed social and economic analyses that go beyond the scope of this chapter. But, generally and speculatively, it may be that social institutions ought to provide people with access to basic health care, such as immunizations and primary care, but not to expensive, cutting edge technologies and procedures. This in turn would imply that justice is compatible with substantial health care inequalities.

Individual liberty is valuable and should be protected by public policies. When governments coercively (that is, at threat of punishment for non-compliance) take resources from citizens through taxation, they restrict the liberty of citizens to use those resources as they see fit. This must be justified, either by appeal to the need to protect and promote liberty or by other important values, such as justice. Therefore, public policies that make use of scarce resources coercively obtained from citizens must be evaluated with respect to efficiency and effectiveness, even when the aim of the policies is to promote justice or satisfy what is owed people, be it opportunity, capabilities, autonomy, or well-being outcomes. Because health promotion does not stand in a special relationship to justice, it should be evaluated in the same way as many other types of goods and it should not be privileged within resource-oriented public policy evaluations. The likely practical implication of this is that the right or entitlement to health care access is considerably more restricted with respect to types of health care than is commonly supposed.

CONCLUSION

This counterpoint part of the chapter has made the case that neither health care nor health promotion is of special moral importance—specifically:

a. Health care and health promotion do not stand in a unique or distinctive relationship (either qualitative or quantitative) to health, due to the social determinants of health.

b. Health care and health promotion do not stand in a unique or distinctive relationship (either qualitative or quantitative) to what we owe people as a matter of justice (be it opportunities, capabilities, or well-being), since other goods (such as technology and education access) also promote what justice requires.

c. Health promotion policies should not be afforded privileged status in determining the allocation of scare resources to try to accomplish what we owe to people as a matter of justice.

d. As a result of (c), health promotion policies should be evaluated according to the same standards as are other policies that try to accomplish what we owe to people, including cost-benefit and cost-effectiveness analyses.

e. From (c) and (d) it follows that there is no special right or entitlement to health care.

The foregoing is consistent with the view that justice requires public policies that promote health, including providing substantial access to health care. It is also consistent with the view that health care distribution should not be left to pure market mechanisms. Given the policy evaluation framework defended here, a pure market approach to health care distribution would be justified only if it were the most effective and efficient policy for meeting the demands of justice. This is extremely unlikely, due to existing economic inequalities; it is also unlikely due to the fact that health care does promote health and health does stand in a significant relationship to opportunity, capabilities, and well-being. However, because health care access and health promotion are not of greater moral significance than many other goods whose distribution is also impacted by public policies and the use of scare public resources, the justice-grounded right or entitlement to health care is less robust than is often claimed and justice is compatible with significant inequalities in access to health care.

References and Further Reading

Cohen, J., & Rogers, J. (2000). *Is inequality bad for our health?* Boston, MA: Beacon Press.

Daniels, N. (1985). *Just health care.* Cambridge, UK: Cambridge University Press.

Daniels, N. (2001). Justice, health, and healthcare. *American Journal of Bioethics, 1*(2), 2–16.

Daniels, N. (2008). *Just health: Meeting health needs fairly.* New York, NY: Cambridge University Press.

Marmot, M. (2004). *The status syndrome: How social standing affects our health and longevity.* New York, NY: Times Books.

Rawls, J. (1971). *A theory of justice.* Cambridge, MA: Harvard University Press.

Segall, S. (2007). Is health care (still) special? *Journal of Political Philosophy, 15*(3), 342–361.

Wilkinson, R., & Marmot, M. (2003). *Social determinants of health: The solid facts* (2nd ed.). Geneva, Switzerland: World Health Organization.

Wilson, J. (2009). Not so special after all? Daniels and the social determinants of health. *Journal of Medical Ethics, 35*(1), 3–6.

Ronald Sandler

Health Care and Human Health

POINT: Health care plays a relatively small role in determining human health. Health is more significantly affected by genetics, individual behavior, and a wide range of social determinants, including education, wealth, and the quality of the environment.

Anthony L. Schlaff, Tufts University School of Medicine

COUNTERPOINT: Access to health care and the means to pay for it are critical to ensuring health. Without health care, individuals are more likely to suffer from preventable illnesses and experience premature mortality.

Anthony L. Schlaff, Tufts University School of Medicine

Introduction

Public debates over health policy usually focus on three issues—access, quality, and cost—all in relation to the health care system. The unstated premise of these debates, and indeed of much of U.S. health policy, is that improvements to the health care system are central to improving health. In this chapter, Anthony Schlaff reviews the literature that questions that premise, showing that the relationship between health care and health is far less robust, and perhaps more complex, than is widely believed.

As Schlaff shows, a wide range of studies demonstrate that factors other than health care are important to securing a population's health. For example, long before antibiotics were developed, there was a dramatic decline in deaths from infectious diseases. Scholars attribute these declines not to the treatments of physicians, who really could not do much to help their sick patients before the arrival of antibiotics, but instead to improvements in wealth, nutrition, sanitation, and the establishment of clean water supplies. More recently, in a 1999 paper, *Ten Great Public Health Achievements—United States,* the Centers for Disease Control and Prevention celebrated public health achievements which it credits for expanding the life expectancy of Americans in the twentieth century. Many of these advances did not involve the health care system at all. For example, adding fluoride to the water supply has improved dental health, and engineering improvements and highway safety laws have reduced the risks of death from automobile accidents.

In addition, as Schlaff explains, researchers have noted a fairly strong and ubiquitous association between health and absolute and relative socioeconomic status. People with high socioeconomic status are healthier than are those with a lower socioeconomic status, even when both groups have equal access to health care. Many studies also suggest that health is affected by levels of inequality within a society. Populations in more egalitarian societies have better health outcomes than do their counterparts with the same levels of wealth and income in less egalitarian societies. According to the Central Intelligence Agency's *World Factbook,* the United States ranks fortieth in the world with respect to the Gini index, which measures income inequality, and fiftieth in life expectancy, even below less wealthy nations such as Greece or Jordan.

These findings suggest that health care alone cannot explain disparities in health. To understand why some groups live long and healthy lives and others live shorter and less healthy ones, Schlaff shows, requires a consideration of so-called social determinants of health, the social factors, such as education, income distribution, environmental protection, and even the legal and political systems, that shape the world people live in, the behaviors they engage in, and the health risks they face.

The distinction that Schlaff draws between the role of social determinants and the role of health care in determining human health parallels the widely recognized distinction between public health and medical care. Although health care focuses on treating individual patients, often after they have become ill, public health emphasizes improving the health of communities or populations, generally by preventing disease or illness, or "assuring the conditions in which people can be healthy" as the Institute of Medicine states in its 1988 report, *The Future of Public Health*. Because public health focuses on preventing disease in broad communities, it often seeks to address social determinants; public health may also be considered a social determinant.

Public health interventions often have a more positive impact on more lives than do health services. For example, the provision of clean water to a community may provide greater benefits to its population's health than will the provision of therapy to patients who come down with water-borne diseases. Likewise, more lives can be saved by reducing cigarette smoking than by treating the illnesses caused by smoking.

An appreciation of the importance of social determinants suggests that policies that relate only remotely to health—for example improving K–12 education or reducing wealth disparities—may also reap significant health benefits. For this reason, the World Health Organization (WHO) promotes what is known as Health in All Policies, which considers the health impact of all public policies, not just those designed to address health. Would such an approach be feasible in the United States? Does it risk overemphasizing the importance of health compared to other public goals?

Despite the importance of social determinants to health, U.S. health policy emphasizes the health care system. The United States spends over 17 percent of its gross domestic product on health, more than any other country, but almost all of that money is spent on medical research and clinical treatment. Very little is spent on public health interventions. For example, the 2010 Patient Protection and Affordable Care Act (ACA) significantly expanded access to clinical preventions, also known as secondary prevention, by requiring insurance companies to provide screenings and other preventive services without cost sharing. Indeed, the ACA's advocates emphasized its focus on prevention, suggesting that by preventing illness, the act would save money in the long run. Yet far less money was devoted to so-called primary prevention, upstream interventions that identify and address sources of disease at a population or community level. Indeed, although the ACA authorized $15 billion over 10 years for a National Prevention, Health Promotion, and Public Health Council to coordinate national prevention and public health efforts, that amount represents only 1.5 percent of the ACA's total costs and half of the amount the National Institute of Health spends annually on biomedical research. Moreover, only half of the $10 million the Prevention and Public Health Fund was allocated in fiscal year 2010 was directed to public health activities; the rest was allocated to training primary care doctors and nurses, who presumably can promote secondary prevention. Is that allocation appropriate? Does the United States spend too much on health care and not enough on public health?

Or are the distinctions between health care and social determinants, or health care and public health exaggerated? Schlaff reminds us that modern medicine can have significant population-level impacts on both mortality and morbidity. In addition, health care services offer patients important benefits, such as relief of pain, not ordinarily captured in population health statistics. Health care providers can also influence public health policies and social determinants by gathering information about the nature of a health threat, counseling patients about their behaviors and social influences, and encouraging public policies that are designed to address health threats. In this regard, consider the many different ways that health care providers can address the problem of smoking-related illnesses.

Finally, the fact that neither access to nor spending on health care services explains health disparities does not disprove that a well-designed health care system would do a better job of advancing the health of populations. Perhaps social determinants appear to be more important to population health than health care only because health care has not been as well organized and effective as it might be. In response to that possibility, should health-reform efforts try to enhance the health care system's impact on population health? Can reform efforts achieve that goal while also seeking to restrain the cost of health care? Or does the United States simply pay too much attention, and too many dollars, to health services? Would the nation be better off thinking more about the myriad other social factors that influence health?

POINT

The contribution of health care to population health is almost certainly lower than most laypersons believe. Over 40 years of research and inquiry have yielded an understanding of the determinants of health that recognizes the powerful influences of behavior and environment on the health of a population. This chapter will summarize that literature and discuss its implications for health policy.

BEHAVIOR AND ENVIRONMENT: THE SOCIAL DETERMINANTS OF HEALTH

Three broad categories of inquiry have contributed to our understanding of behavioral and environmental determinants of health: analysis of historical and cross national differences in health, analysis of preventable morbidity and mortality within societies, and analysis of disparities among sub-groups within a society.

Historical and cross-national differences. In his seminal work of 1976, *The Role of Medicine: Dream, Mirage or Nemesis,* Thomas McKeown traced the dramatic increase in life expectancy that occurred in England between the eighteenth century and the mid-twentieth century and noted that most came as a result of changes in behavior and the environment. Reductions in family size, improvements in nutrition, and improved sanitation in the home and community were key factors. Improvements in health followed these changes, but preceded most of the advances in health care that were later credited with the improvement. For example, by 1950, rates of death from tuberculosis had dropped almost 10-fold in Britain, but the first drug used to treat the disease was not introduced until 1947, and highly effective drugs were not widely available until the 1950s. Nutrition and sanitation, not medicine, led to the drop in deaths from tuberculosis. This pattern holds true for other infectious diseases that were the major killers of the pre-modern era. Dramatic drops in death rates preceded the introduction of effective therapy.

Health status among nations varies greatly, with developed nations having significantly better health status than poorer, less developed nations. In comparing nations in the present time, it is harder to separate differences in behavior and environment from the development of health care systems, but even countries with similar access to universal and modern health care have significant differences in health status, suggesting other factors are at play.

Preventable morbidity and mortality. In his 1974 report on the health of Canadians, Marc Lalonde noted that by the second half of the twentieth century most deaths occurred among those over the age of 70, and that most health care was directed at treating the elderly, but that it was the reduction in premature deaths—the drop in deaths before the age of 70—that accounted for the improvements in overall population health that had led to the current state of affairs in Canada. Lalonde further argued that future gains would depend on reducing remaining premature deaths. By focusing on causes of premature death, strategies for improving population health can be identified. For Canada and other modern societies in the late twentieth and early twenty-first centuries, these causes include infant mortality, and injury and suicide in children and young adults. For older adults, the major causes are cardiovascular and cerebrovascular disease, cancers, particularly of the respiratory tract, and chronic respiratory diseases. Lalonde noted the prominent role of behavior—diet, exercise, tobacco, and other drug use—in most of these deaths. Lalonde also mentioned the role of the environment: lack of sanitation systems, pollution, working conditions, and urbanization, as important contributors to premature deaths.

The 1979 U.S. Public Health Service's *Healthy People: The Surgeon General's Report on Health Promotion and Disease Prevention* built on the Lalonde report and developed methodology to quantify the contribution of behavior and environment to health. This method involved calculating the percentage contribution of specific behaviors to causes of death as listed on death certificates, using estimates generated by a review of medical and epidemiologic literature. By multiplying these estimated percentages by the number of deaths of a specific cause, and summing these products for each cause of death that the behavior contributed to, researchers were able to estimate a total number of deaths attributed to each specific behavior. By adding the attributed numbers of deaths across all behavior studies, the researchers estimated that 50 percent of deaths were attributable to behavior. A similar process of attribution, estimating, and calculating was done for other determinants and led to the widely accepted estimates that failures of health care account for 10 percent of preventable mortality, behavior for 50 percent, environment for 20 percent, and biological factors (presumably genetic) for the final 20.

The Lalonde and U.S. Surgeon General's reports, coming just as health care costs were identified as a growing problem for industrialized nations, provided arguments for shifting the focus of governmental health policy away from health care and towards prevention directed at behavioral and environmental causes. Although these studies contributed to our understanding of health determinants, they did not have a dramatic effect on the direction of health policy and health spending in Canada or the United States, which continued to focus on health care services.

DISPARITIES

The study of disparities in health status within populations has generated multiple new avenues of research, which in turn have deepened the understanding of the complexity and importance of social determinants of health. Population health disparities among and within societies are profound and are by and large unexplained by differences in health care, but rather by social, cultural, and environmental conditions. Differences in life expectancy between the healthiest and least healthy nations on Earth are close to 50 years. Within the United States, defined populations with low socioeconomic status or nonwhite ethnicity have life expectancies 20 years less than do affluent whites. Worldwide, the chances of dying between the ages of age 15 and 60 ranges from a low of 8 percent in Sweden to a high of 82 percent in Zimbabwe.

Disparities in health across social class have been observed since the mid-nineteenth century. In the 1980s, two seminal publications from Britain, the Black Report in 1980 and the Whitehall Study in 1987, documented the extent of and persistence of these disparities, with differences in life expectancy between the richest and poorest in society of 20 years persisting for over a century despite the overall rise in life expectancy across all social groups. Since then, disparities in life expectancy of this magnitude have been found wherever they have been studied. They are consistent across time, culture, and levels of development and modernity. The Black Report was so startling because it documented a decade-by-decade persistence in dramatic differentials in mortality throughout a period of time when the underlying causes of death changed significantly, from the infectious to the chronic diseases, and across the time when the British National Health Service (NHS) was implemented, which for all intents and purposes wiped out significant differences in access to and quality of health care afforded to rich and poor. How and why social gradients should be such a consistent and powerful predictor of premature mortality, independent of such powerful changes in social structures, health systems, and biological endpoints, remain questions of debate and study. Death is a biological phenomenon. Any explanation of how economic position and social standing result in death requires a biological mechanism. This, too, is just beginning to be understood.

Thirty years of study since the Black Report have taught us a great deal. Both absolute poverty and relative poverty matter. Regarding absolute poverty: Material want can dramatically affect health. The mechanisms are not difficult to understand. Poverty can lead to poor diets, substandard housing, exposure to violence and the elements, crowding and resultant infections, and environmental exposures. Literacy, which correlates closely with wealth, is also an independent predictor of health status, as is the status of women in society. In particular, women's control of their reproductive destiny, as measured by increased intervals between births, powerfully influences the overall health of society as well as individual social strata within the society.

Gradients of wealth, and of social status, are also powerful predictors of health in every society, regardless of the absolute levels of wealth at top or bottom. All societies show a gradient with health status correlating with social class. For any absolute level of wealth, societies that spread wealth more equitably and that have less fixed social hierarchies have better health status than do those that have larger and more fixed hierarchies. Here the mechanisms are more difficult to understand. Some differences across social gradients are explained by behavior. Members of lower social strata smoke more, drink more alcohol, and engage in less health-seeking behavior. Lower social status affects behavior through a variety of mechanisms. Poorer people have more constraints on their choices, less opportunity for the future hence less incentive to invest in it, greater need to seek alleviation of stress, and less education. When studied carefully, however, behaviors explain only a small portion, often in the range of 15 to 25 percent, of the difference in health outcomes between the richest and poorest groups. Group as well as individual characteristics play a role. For example, poor neighborhoods have a detrimental effect regardless of the income of the individual. Much of the variance in health by socioeconomic gradient remains unexplained, both in terms of which social phenomenon are causal, and in terms of the biological pathways by which they act.

BIOLOGICAL MECHANISMS AND SOCIAL DETERMINANTS

Two biological mechanisms have been proposed that likely explain some, and perhaps much, of how social gradients affect health. The first is chronic stress. The second is gene/environment interactions that occur during fetal and early childhood development.

Lower social status increases chronic stress. Chronic stress in turn has significant biological effects, including an increase in sympathetic nervous system arousal which leads to increases in blood pressure and to a host of neurological and hormonal changes that can result in increased insulin resistance, increased blood clotting activity, and a number of other metabolic changes that increase the risk of cardiovascular disease. (See, for example, P. A. Thoits's 2010 article "Stress and Health," from the *Journal of Health and Social Behavior.*)

As their understanding of genomics increases, researchers are beginning to glimpse the complexity by which the environment influences genetic expression. Although observational studies can lead to conclusions that genetics account for a large part of the variation in disease risk, such studies ignore the potent role that environment can play on influencing gene expression. Identical twins share the same genome, but by the time they are born they have already also shared a common environment for nine months of gestation. Half of their genome—the egg provided by their mother—had also shared an environment for a generation. Because a woman's eggs are formed at birth, they are subject to a host of environmental influences from that time until the pregnancy. Most observational studies of genetic influence have ascribed to genetics any environmental influences that may have had an effect during the mother's life to the time of conception or during gestation.

Some studies now suggest that gene-environment interaction during gestation and early life can have profound effects on how genes are expressed in the living organism. One such area relates to the notion of caloric thriftiness: the extent to which an animal (or human) will tend to hoard calories (i.e., to store them as fat) rather than expend them through activity or through a higher metabolic rate. Increased thriftiness offers a survival advantage through childhood in times of scarcity. In environments of plenty, such thriftiness can lead to obesity, insulin resistance, and a number of other biological processes that increase risk for early cardiovascular mortality. Indeed, in every study across time and place where linked birth/death data is available, low birth weight is correlated with early adult mortality, largely from cardiovascular disease. Low birth weight is of course associated with poverty—with deprivation during gestation. The current hypothesis, not yet proven, is that human genes provide a range of levels of thriftiness, and that during a critical period of gestation a set point is determined in response to the environment of either want or plenty. This makes evolutionary sense. A range that allows humans to determine their thriftiness depending on the availability of calories increases their chance of getting it right, and of surviving. Poor children born into rich societies may, however, be giving their genes a scrambled message. Women at lower levels of social hierarchy may, through a combination of poor nutrition and chronic stress, deliver fewer nutrients to their fetuses, despite plentiful calories, but the children, once in the outside environment, are exposed to a world of caloric density. (For a more detailed explanation of the developmental origins theory by one of its creators, see D. J. P. Barker's 2007 article, "The Origins of the Developmental Origins Theory," in the *Journal of Internal Medicine.*)

The thrifty gene is but one of many gene-environment interactions of early life currently under study that show promise for explaining at least some of the mechanisms by which relative and absolute poverty result in poorer health status and premature death.

EMERGING VISION OF SOCIETAL DETERMINANTS OF HEALTH

The World Health Organization (WHO) has attempted to summarize the growing literature and understanding of the social determinants of health (see Figure 2.1). Unlike the U.S. Surgeon General's report of 1979, the WHO framework does not seek to place numerical value on the degree to which each type of determinant contributes to health, but rather seeks to elucidate the relationships among these determinants.

The emerging understanding of determinants suggests that the categories are neither clear-cut nor distinct. Behavior is highly influenced by the physical, social, and cultural environment, and in fact modifications of the environment have been shown in numerous public health studies to be much more powerful ways to change behavior than education, legal sanction, or other efforts designed to directly influence individual behavior. For example, raising the price of cigarettes

Figure 2.1   World Health Organization Social Determinants of Health Framework

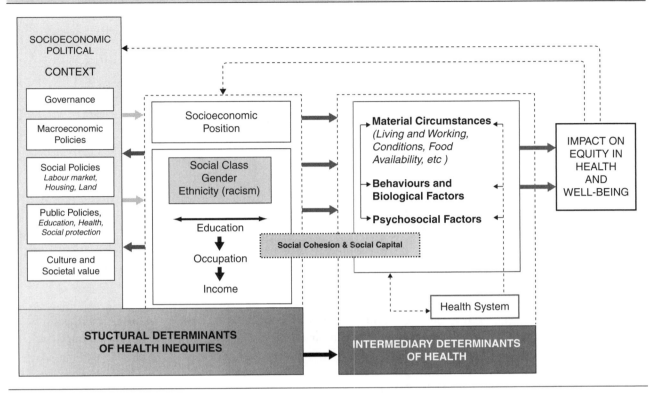

Source: World Health Organization. Reprinted with permission.

is the single most effective strategy known to affect smoking behavior. Conversely, behavior influences environment: for example, the proportion of city residents who drive rather than use public transport for their commute will affect levels of air pollution. As described above, recent studies in genomics and developmental biology suggest that biology is significantly influenced by the environment. Clearly, too, the social-economic and political environment have profound impacts on whether health care is delivered or not.

Thus, any analysis that attributes a percentage of affect on population health to a single category of determinant is of necessity simplifying a model that includes a complex set of inter-dependencies (see Figure 2.2).

Similarly, the policy categories by which governments attempt to affect health can have indistinct borders. Defining health care, and considering it distinct from other determinants, is not easy. For example, partly as a result of educational and public health policies, attitudes towards tobacco use have shifted dramatically in a single generation and have in turn had profound effects on population health. The likelihood that a person will get smoking cessation counseling during health care, and the likelihood that such counseling will be effective, may vary with these cultural attitudes. More profoundly, attitudes regarding race and racism, and the socioeconomic condition of blacks, have changed substantially over a generation. There is no single policy that created this shift in attitude. Nevertheless, it is certain that many policies, made at many levels and over time, contributed to and facilitated this shift in attitudes and circumstances, and these in turn have helped to make health care more available to African Americans. How do researchers measure the independent effects of cultural change, of socioeconomic change, of policy change, and of changes of health care on the overall health status of this or any population group?

Despite the difficulty in determining the specific contribution that policy activities may make on population health, many areas of policy activity are believed to improve human health at the population level. These policies include providing economic and social security, improving living conditions in childhood, providing universal education, creating healthier workplaces and workplace cultures, environmental protection and restriction of use of toxic products, and

Figure 2.2   Causal Interactions Among Determinants of Health

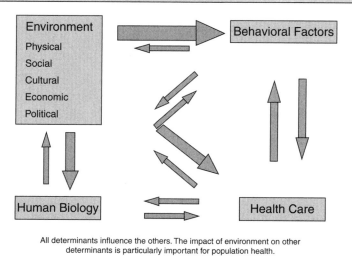

All determinants influence the others. The impact of environment on other
determinants is particularly important for population health.

Source: Created by author.

making efforts to promote healthy behaviors. In addition, increasing citizens' participation in the civic and political life of society has also been postulated to reduce social hierarchy and thereby improve population health, although this relationship is less clearly demonstrated or understood.

CLAIMS OF THE MEDICAL LITERATURE

Although modern health care has advanced dramatically in terms of the scientific knowledge and technical prowess brought to treating disease, these advances can be and often are systematically overstated. The effects of health care are studied in *patients,* a selected group in the sense that they have sought and are able to receive care. The healthy effect attributed to the care may be instead a measure of this selection bias. Even in randomized trials, where selection bias can be at least partly addressed, treatment and control groups that do not reflect the general population may lead to an overstatement of beneficial effects: Those not in the study may not be subject to the same beneficial effect as those who are. Population-based studies that rely on observational designs—comparing people who choose a therapy to those that did not—often have positive findings that are found to be spurious when a true experiment is done.

The most well-known example of this "healthy worker" effect was in the Nurse's Health Study that began in 1976. It had long been observed that women who took hormone replacement therapy (HRT) to protect their bones and prevent hip fractures lived longer than those who did not, and this led most physicians to urge healthy women over 50 to take these medications. When a randomized trial was finally conducted, however, hormone replacement was shown to do more harm than good and possibly to shorten life expectancy. The reason for the discrepancy between the observational and experimental studies is most likely that healthier women, who engaged in many other behaviors to improve health, were more likely to take hormones than were less healthy women. Thus, the cause of taking the medications was thought to be an effect. Rather than the drugs causing the increased life span, it turns out that the taking of the drugs and the increased life span were themselves both caused by something else—the health-seeking lifestyles of the women.

The medical literature often uses proxy measures for population health outcomes, and measures of relative rather than attributable risk, which have the effect (deliberate or not) of inflating or even falsely claiming benefit. In cancer studies, for example, disease-free survival and tumor shrinkage are often used as outcomes of the study even though they may have no relationship to the key measures of interest, quality of life, and overall survival. Relative risk measures the risk of a bad outcome between those who take or do not take a therapy. For instance, the decrease in heart attacks for men at high risk who take medication to lower cholesterol is about 50 percent. The measure of interest for the population, however, is the change in risk that would happen to all men in a particular risk group at the time they are offered treatment. Measured in this way, the drop in risk is 2 percent. Four percent of untreated men will go on to have heart attacks, compared to 2 percent of those treated. The 50 percent decrease in relative risk is better understood as a 2 percent drop in actual risk.

Bailer, in a series of articles on cancer treatment, shows that the age-specific mortality rate for all cancers actually increased from 1950 to 1993. This occurred despite the passage of Medicare in 1965, the dramatic increases in cancer research funding that started in 1971, the drop in cigarette smoking that started in the mid-1960s, and the introduction of scores of new and "proven" cancer treatments during that period.

THE NEED FOR MARGINAL ANALYSIS

The absolute contribution of health care to population health may not be a particularly useful or important question. All wealthy and advanced societies have health care, and there is no chance that any of them will dispense with it. The practical questions, from a policy perspective, are those of marginal analysis and opportunity cost. Given the proportion of a society's wealth that is currently being invested in health care and in other activities that sustain or create health in a population, what should be done with the next or with the last unit of investment? Should a society invest more in health care, at the expense of other investments; or should it invest less, allowing resources that currently go to health care go to other activities? Because other societal activities, such as investment in education and economic development, can also have a powerful effect on population health, the answer to such questions depends on the marginal utility of the next unit of investment in health care (i.e., how much health does the next dollar buy?) and on the relative value of alternative investments.

To answer the question of where the next dollar of health expenditure should go—to health care or to other activities—it is crucial to know what those other activities are, and to what extent they contribute to population health. As was noted above, determinants of health besides health care have been grouped into categories of behavior, environment, and biology. Environment can be further subdivided into physical, socioeconomic, and cultural environments. Broadly speaking, there are three arenas of societal activity, other than health care, that can have impact on these determinants. They are public health activities, policy activities in arenas other than health (e.g., housing and education), and societal structures and systems that are not themselves caused by or immediately affected by specific policies or actions. This latter category includes such things as the demographics, culture, and belief systems of a society. Although this category is by definition not immediately affected by policy, they are worth considering because they can be affected by policy efforts directed over a longer period of time.

Challenges to conducting comparative marginal analysis of health care and other activities. No cost-effective analysis can adequately compare the cost and health outcomes of health care to those of education, income redistribution, economic, and other policy. First, health care is not a single thing but, rather, a complicated mix of technologies and services with highly variable values. Cost-effectiveness analyses on many medical procedures have been done and the dollars spent per life vary widely. The methods and models of cost-effectiveness themselves are complex, and different assumptions can lead to widely disparate results even for the same service. Nevertheless, it is possible to make some generalizations. Some interventions, such as vaccines and certain types of counseling, are actually cost saving. Many preventive measures, such as screening for and treating hypertension, cost in the range of $10,000 to $50,000 per life saved. These are ranges that are widely regarded as being worthwhile. Some highly technical procedures cost upward of $300,000 per life saved, but even some extraordinarily expensive surgeries, if done on the right sub-groups of patients, can be surprisingly cost-effective. Some procedures and medical activities have no life-saving value whatsoever, or are even harmful, again in part depending on who is receiving the service.

The health care market is complex and highly subsidized and regulated. For these reasons, prices and charges for health care services are a poor marker of their true value, and there is no reliable metric for determining the value of health care. Not only are different medical services of greatly different value but also some services that are currently provided are actually harmful (i.e., they have negative value), and yet individuals and society seek out and pay for these services. Conversely, other medical services of extraordinarily low cost and high value are not being provided. For example, far fewer flu vaccines are given than an economic analysis would suggest should be.

Though cost-effectiveness data exist on at least some health care services, it is even more difficult to measure the effectiveness, as it pertains to *health*, of a marginal unit of other services and policies, whether they be in education, housing, poverty reduction, or a myriad of other societal activities known to have population health benefits. This is at least in part because of the interdependency of the social determinants of health. Although it is possible to calculate the total health benefit that would accrue to the United States if every group had the same health status as a relatively rich and empowered reference group, it is not known which policies would contribute to improved health in specific quantities, nor what would be unintended consequences of many such policies. Education, income, and neighborhood of residence all matter and are all subject to change, but they are interdependent. Which ones should be addressed in order to have an effect on the others? How should society intervene? These questions are subject to both scientific and political controversy. There are no metrics to show what the cost-effectiveness for health status would be on the areas of social policy that would do the most to improve health.

What might a marginal analysis of health care reveal? Although it is not possible to give a definitive answer on the correct policy approach to reducing health based on a marginal analysis, the thought experiment says that in the United States today a complete analysis would likely yield the result that too many resources are put into health care, and that population health would be better served by spending the next dollars on other forms of social policy. The conclusion of that experiment would likely be that resources currently directed to health care would be better spent on other activities. At the very least, society would do well to divert resources from medical services that are actually harmful.

Perhaps the best evidence comes from comparing overall national spending on health. The United States pays twice as much for health care as any other nation on earth—including those that provide universal health care—and yet has worse health statistics. Sixteen percent of the entire U.S. economy goes into health care, and it is clear that much of what that system does is harmful, of no value, or of exceedingly small marginal benefit. Estimates suggest that 30 percent or more of U.S. health care is unnecessary or wasteful. And so, though there are still people who do not get sufficient care, and there are some types of care that it would be better to have more of, the overwhelming evidence suggests that on balance the United States would do better with less. Furthermore, in comparing countries that have universal health care but otherwise have high degrees of social and economic inequity (e.g., England) to those that have less inequity and invest heavily in other social programs (e.g., the Scandinavian countries), the latter countries do better on all measures of health status. The benefits that the Scandinavian countries gain over England through economic and social equity appear to be greater than the benefits that England gets over the United States by virtue of its universal access to health care.

In the United States, despite its private system, approximately half of the spending on health care comes from government, and this percentage has been rising steadily. This is of critical importance in a time when government spending is significantly constrained. The two greatest costs of state and local governments are health care and education. The greatest domestic costs at the federal level are health care, and anti-poverty/income support programs. Given the realities of U.S. politics today and for the foreseeable future, more health care means less funding for education, for anti-poverty programs, and for income redistribution: the very policies that would likely have the most positive impact on population health.

The other evidence suggesting that a marginal shift in priorities from health care to social spending comes from the analysis of the disparities within the United States. Although the specific effects of education, income, and environment cannot be disaggregated, researchers can look at them collectively and calculate the health impact of socioeconomic gradients overall. In 2007, Stephen Woolf and others calculated the lives that would be saved each year if all adults aged 18 to 64 in the United States had the same health status as those who had at least one year of college education. They calculated that approximately 370,000 deaths would be averted. It is unlikely that policymakers could save anywhere near that number by increasing or improving health care.

Health care itself might contribute to increased social gradients. How? Although medicine has its share of low-wage workers, a large proportion of the workforce are professionals—doctors, nurses, technicians, and social workers—who earn more than the median income, and health care is becoming more and more capital-intensive, generating concentrated wealth. Furthermore, health care charges are regressive—poor individuals and families who are privately insured pay as much for health insurance (or see as great a wage deduction) as do the rich, and the rich get a better tax break. The lost wages that poor communities pay for health care get transferred to the wealthy communities where doctors, nurses, and health care administrators and entrepreneurs live, thus potentially increasing wealth disparities which in turn have an overall negative impact on health.

The contextual nature of marginal analysis. It is important to note that the calculations and conclusions of a marginal analysis depend completely on the context in which the analysis is done—because the marginal benefits and costs of anything will depend on exactly what else is being done in a particular time and place. It may be correct that the marginal cost of health care in the United States is too high to justify—but this might not have been true in the past, and may not be true in another country—particularly one that has very little health care and devotes scant resources to it. And as noted above, this may be true for much of the care delivered in the United States today—but not necessarily all of it.

CONCLUSION

Health care is but one of many determinants of population health. Socioeconomic factors, behavior, and environment all play a role and are likely more important determinants of the overall health of a society. A marginal analysis of investments in social policy would likely suggest that resources be shifted from health care to other policy arenas and societal sectors.

REFERENCES AND FURTHER READING

Bailer, J. C., & Gornik, H. L. (1997). Cancer undefeated. *New England Journal of Medicine, 336*(22), 1569–1574.

Barker, D. (2007). The origins of the developmental origins theory. *Journal of Internal Medicine, 261*(5), 412–417.

Black, D., Morris, J. N., Smith, C., & Townsend, P. (1982). The Black report. In P. Townsend & N. Davidson (Eds.), *Inequalities in health.* Harmondsworth, UK: Pelican Books.

Bodenheimer, T. S., & Grumbach, K. (2009). *Understanding health policy: A clinical approach* (5th ed.). New York, NY: McGraw-Hill.

Coffield, A. B., Maciosek, M. V., McGinnis, J. M., Harris, J. R., Caldwell, M. B., Teutsch, S. M., et al. (2001). Priorities among recommended clinical preventive services. *American Journal of Preventive Medicine, 21*(1), 1–9.

Evans, R. G., Barer, M. L., & Marmor, T. R. (Eds.). (1994). *Why are some people healthy and others not? The determinants of health of populations.* New York, NY: Transaction Publishers.

Graham, H. (2007). *Unequal lives: Health and socioeconomic inequalities.* Buckingham, UK: Open University Press.

Hofrichter, R. (2003). *Health and social justice: Politics, ideology, and inequity in the distribution of disease.* San Francisco, CA: Jossey-Bass.

Irvine, E. J. (2004). Measurement and expression of risk: Optimizing decision strategies. *American Journal of Medicine, 117*(Suppl. 5A), 2S–5S.

Lalonde, M. (1974). *A new perspective on the health of Canadians.* Ottawa, Ontario, Canada: Minister of Supply and Services.

Marmot, M. G., Shipley, M. J., & Rose, G. (1984). Inequalities in death—Specific explanations of a general pattern. *Lancet, 1*(8384), 1003–1006.

Marmot, M. G., Smith, G. D., Stansfeld, S., Patel, C., North, F., Head, J., & Feeney, A. (1991). Health inequalities among British civil servants: The Whitehall II study. *Lancet, 337*(8754), 1387–1393.

McGinnis, J. M., & Foege, W. H. (1993). Actual causes of death in the United States. *Journal of the American Medical Association, 270*(18), 2207–2212.

McKeown, T. (1976). *The role of medicine: Dream, mirage, or nemesis?* London, UK: Nuffield Provincial Hospitals Trust.

Solar, O., & Irwin, A. (2007). *A conceptual framework for action on the social determinants of health.* Geneva, Switzerland: World Health Organization. Retrieved from http://www.who.int/sdhconference/resources/ConceptualframeworkforactiononSDH_eng.pdf

Tengs, T. O., Adams, M. E., Pliskin, J. S., Safran, D. G., Siegel, J. E., Weinstein, M. C., & Graham, J. D. (1995). Five hundred life-saving interventions and their cost effectiveness. *Risk Analysis, 15*(3), 369–390.

Thoits, P. A. (2010). Stress and health: Major findings and policy implications. *Journal of Health and Social Behavior, 51*(Suppl. 1), S41–S53.

U.S. Public Health Service. (1979). *Healthy people: The surgeon general's report on health promotion and disease prevention.* Washington, DC: United States Public Health Service.

Woolf, S. H., Johnson, R. E., Phillips, R. L., & Philipsen, M. (2007). Giving everyone the health of the educated: An examination of whether social change would save more lives than medical advances. *American Journal of Public Health, 97*(4), 679–683.

Anthony L. Schlaff

COUNTERPOINT

Since the Canadian Lalonde Report of 1974 and the U.S. Surgeon General's 1979 report, *Healthy People,* most public health scholars have accepted as true that health care adds little to population health. Both reports note that the principle causes of death in developed nations should be largely preventable through behavioral and environmental change. The Surgeon General's report estimates that 10 percent of preventable mortality is due to "inadequacies of health care," with 50 percent attributable to behavior, 20 percent to the environment, and 20 percent to biological factors. These estimates are largely unchallenged, although a generation of scholarship has added greatly to the understanding of the complex interaction of these classes of determinants.

Before relegating health care to a minor role in population health, however, it should be noted that there has never been nor will there be a controlled experiment to measure the contribution of health care. The literature on determinants of population health has added richly to researchers' understanding of the effects of the socioeconomic environment, acting both directly and through behavior, on population health. Interestingly, the absolute wealth of a society and the equitable distribution of that wealth emerge as two of the greatest positive predictors of population health. Modern wealthy societies are those that, not coincidently, also provide a great deal of health care, and it is those wealthy societies that are most equitable that tend to provide that health care most equitably (i.e., to most of the population). Therefore, wealth and equity are highly correlated with the provision of health care, and all three are correlated with high levels of population health.

Therefore, methods to estimate the potential health consequences of health care are indirect and inferential, often relying on historical trends or cross-national comparisons to tease apart the relative effects of medical care and closely correlated measures of wealth and equity.

THE LIMITED APPLICABILITY OF HISTORICAL ANALYSIS

Although Thomas McKeown noted in 1979 that the dramatic drops in death from infectious disease that occurred in the early twentieth century occurred prior to the introduction of effective therapies, his data also show greater rates of decrease in some of these diseases subsequent to the addition of these therapies. Though the contribution of health care to the drop in mortality from 1900 to 1950 might be relatively modest in comparison to the effects of other factors *at that time,* the relevant question for social policy is to ask what contribution medical care makes to reduced premature mortality and to lengthening of healthy life *now.* The answer is not necessarily the same as it was for the past. A controlled experiment is not possible: Researchers are not going to deliberately reintroduce poor nutrition and unsanitary water and sewage disposal systems to modern societies (though it is worth remembering our advances in these arenas). In a society with modern infrastructure and with relatively low "naturally occurring" premature mortality, the relative contribution of health care to reductions in the *remaining* preventable and premature mortality is likely to be far higher than was true in the past. In effect, as society has greatly reduced the effect of the environment on health status, further efforts in the same domain become subject to the law of diminishing returns, and other interventions, including health care, increase in relative importance.

Health care has changed dramatically as well in the 60 years that have elapsed since the first half of the twentieth century. Some of these changes have included medical advances that have targeted diseases whose prevalence has risen and contributed a greater degree to premature mortality. Just because health care offered relatively modest gains in comparison to environmental change for infectious disease does not mean that the same is true for a society whose deaths are caused by cancer, heart disease, strokes, chronic respiratory disease, and diabetes. And, though these chronic diseases are indeed caused in large part by behavior, they also are amenable to effective and relatively new medical treatments. In addition, although treatments of chronic disease may have had limited efficacy in the past, research and experience have increased and improved the medical interventions that can be directed at these conditions.

MORE RECENT HISTORICAL STUDIES

Several more recent studies of historical changes suggest that health care does have a significant effect on population health. In Australia, Korda and colleagues noted a drop in avoidable mortality from 1968 to 2001 of approximately

70 percent. His research team grouped causes of avoidable mortality into those amenable to health care, those caused by ischemic heart disease, and those amenable to health policy interventions. They found that 54 percent of the reduction in avoidable deaths among women was in those causes amenable to health care. For men the figure was 32 percent.

Taiwan implemented universal access to health care in 1996. In the decades leading up to this law, preventable deaths fell at a rate of approximately 2/3 of 1 percent per year. In the three years after the law's implementation, the rate of decrease averaged nearly 6 percent per year, with the bulk of the drop occurring in the very young and very old, the specific populations most affected by the law.

Costa Rica provides perhaps the most persuasive case example of the effect of improving health care to an entire population. In the early 1990s Costa Rica recreated its health system, developing a model of universally accessible primary care. Despite its relative poverty, the effect was dramatic. After implementation, Costa Rica's childhood mortality dropped 13 percent in four years, and the adult mortality dropped 4 percent. These trends have continued, and the country now has life expectancy and other health status indicators comparable to countries with much higher per capita income. Along with Cuba, another low-income country that has invested heavily in universal primary care, Costa Rica is an outlier on the otherwise consistent relationship between a country's wealth and health.

POPULATION EFFECTS OF SPECIFIC HEALTH SERVICES

It is also possible to directly measure the effect of specific medical interventions on defined clinical populations, and by estimating the size of these clinical populations, the population health effect of these medical interventions can be surmised. By summing these separate effects across those medical interventions that are known to have a significant positive impact on large clinical populations, researchers can estimate at least some of the contribution that health care makes to population health. Using this method, it appears that health care contributes more to population health than more indirect methods suggest.

U.S. mortality. Clinical preventive services are perhaps those most likely to have a positive population effect. The U.S. Preventive Services Task Force (USPSTF) has determined that approximately 50 preventive services are of benefit. The USPSTF analysis is particularly helpful because these services have been evaluated at the population level. In 2001 researchers at the Partnership for Prevention conducted an analysis to determine the numbers of lives that could be saved if these services were provided to the entire population. The researchers estimated benefits based on known patient adherence rates: population effect would be even higher if services were not only offered to all but also accepted. The researchers found that four services could each save over 500,000 quality-adjusted life years (QALYs): childhood immunizations, hypertension screening and treatment, cholesterol screening and treatment, and tobacco screening and cessation counseling. Two others, cervical cancer and colorectal cancer screening, could save between 300,000 and 400,000 QALYs, and three, influenza vaccination, breast cancer screening, and vision screening in the elderly, could each save between 100,000 and 200,000 QALYs. Together, the universal provision of these six services would save over 3 million QALYs each year.

Thomas Farley, with a team at the New York City Health Department, used a mathematical model, estimating rates of pre-clinical disease in a population and the preventive fraction (the percentage of a disease that could be prevented by universal use of an intervention), to model how many lives could be saved by increased use of effective clinical preventive services. They concluded:

> [T]he all-cause model predicted that every 10 percent increase in hypertension treatment would lead to an additional 14,000 deaths prevented and every 10 percent increase in treatment of elevated low-density lipoprotein cholesterol or aspirin prophylaxis would lead to 8000 deaths prevented in those aged <80 years, per year. Overall, the models suggest that optimal use of all of these interventions could prevent 50,000–100,000 deaths per year in those aged <80 years and 25,000–40,000 deaths per year in those aged <65 years. (Farley, 2010, p. 600)

Curative and treatment services, and not just prevention, may also have significant population effects. For example, cardiovascular disease kills roughly 600,000 people in the United States each year, approximately a quarter of all deaths. If cholesterol-lowering medication was taken by all for whom it was indicated, mortality rates for this condition would fall by roughly 25 percent. This would represent approximately 150,000 fewer deaths, or 6 percent of all deaths. Additional lives are saved by emergency responses to prevent sudden cardiac death, the use of coronary care units to prevent arrhythmia deaths after heart attacks, and the use of anti-clotting and blood pressure–lowering agents both in the hospital and outpatient after heart attacks. Age-adjusted rates of cardiovascular death rates have fallen from 267 to 191 per 100,000 just from 1999 to 2007. This is an almost 30 percent decline. Though much of this reduction is related to reduced rates of smoking, some is attributable to clinical prevention and to care.

Diabetes or impaired glucose metabolism (a precursor to diabetes) affects approximately 15 percent of the population, over 30 million people. Diabetics are at risk for premature death from heart disease and stroke, and significant morbidity from blindness, kidney failure, and amputations. Studies that compare intensive treatment to less intensive treatment show declines in serious endpoints of 10 to 12 percent and reductions in all cause mortality of around 6 percent.

Although health care has failed thus far to have more than modest effects on cancer death rates, with drops of approximately 1 percent per year over the past 20 years, childhood cancers, particularly leukemias, and cervical cancer are important exceptions. Childhood leukemias, which as a group represent 1/3 of cancers of children, used to be almost uniformly fatal. Now, with treatment, five-year survival rates, most of which are cures, are greater than 80 percent for acute lymphocytic leukemia and 50 to 70 percent for various types of acute myeloid leukemia. With the advent of PAP smears and early treatment, cervical cancer death rates fell 70 percent between 1955 and 1972 and continue to drop at approximately 3 percent per year.

Although end-stage kidney failure affects less than 1 percent of the U.S. population, dialysis and renal transplantation now add decades of life to what is without health care a uniformly fatal disease.

Approximately 300,000 out of hospital cardiac arrests occur each year, with a mortality rate of 92 percent and less than 10 percent receiving timely bystander resuscitation. If appropriate health care is given (most importantly by bystanders, requiring that all adults be trained in CPR), the death rate drops by 4 percent. Thus, over 10,000 deaths per year could be prevented by provision of this single medical intervention, if available to all.

Unintentional injuries and homicide together accounted for 142,000, or 6 percent of all deaths, in 2007. All of these deaths are preventable, but many are amenable to medical treatment. The number of lives saved by health care is difficult to estimate. One study that compared death rates for motor-vehicle accidents in rural versus more densely populated areas found a two-fold higher death rate in rural areas, once severity of injury was controlled. The remaining difference was access to timely care. This suggests that the provision of timely health care can have a significant effect on outcomes from trauma. Comparisons of trauma centers and hospitals without specialized units also show a treatment advantage in overall mortality, with one study suggesting a 25 percent drop in death rates due to motor-vehicle injury as a result of the higher quality of the care available.

Mortality in the developing world. The major causes of death in the developing world are infectious diseases. Although the major determinants of diarrheal and respiratory infectious diseases remain social, environmental, and behavioral, there is considerable evidence that a substantial portion of the recent reductions in mortality from the three biggest killers—tuberculosis, malaria, and HIV—comes from medical care. The Global Public Health Achievements Team at the U.S. Centers for Disease Control and Prevention estimates that in the case of tuberculosis the use of directly observed therapy has resulted in 41 million cases cured and 6 million deaths prevented. Within a few years, tuberculosis mortality, approximately 1 million deaths per year, will likely be cut in half from the rates of the 1990s. Malaria deaths have dropped over 20 percent in the past decade as a result of comprehensive strategies that include public health measures but also aggressive treatment of cases and preventive medications given during pregnancy. Similarly, the provision of effective medications to over 5 million persons with HIV/AIDS living in low- and middle-income countries, and in particular prevention of over half of mother-child transmission through the use of medication has contributed to substantial declines in mortality worldwide.

Morbidity. Health care does more than prevent deaths. It reduces suffering and disability as well. Roughly one-quarter of non-elderly adults have one or more of five chronic conditions: asthma, diabetes, hypertension, chronic obstructive pulmonary disease, and congestive heart failure. Quality ambulatory care directed at these conditions can prevent hospitalizations. Rates of hospitalization can vary across communities by as much as four-fold, and analyses suggest that half or more of this variation is due to lack of access to care.

Blindness is one of the most significant causes of morbidity in the United States. According to a report by the Eye Diseases Prevalence Workshop Group, almost 1 million adults, or 0.78 percent of the population, are blind. Even greater numbers have significantly impaired vision. Much of this is preventable or treatable. Cataracts account for 8.7 percent of blindness in whites and 37 percent in blacks. Over 1 million cataract operations are done each year in the United States. Glaucoma, a treatable cause of blindness, accounts for 6.4 percent of blindness in whites and 26 percent in blacks. The differences in rates between whites and blacks for these two conditions in themselves suggest how much of this disability is prevented or reversed by health care, as much of the difference in rates of blindness are due to the lower levels of access to early care available to blacks. Macular degeneration and diabetic retinopathy, two of the other major causes of blindness, are also treatable with health care.

Many elderly become functionally impaired long before death, and many spend their last years of life in a nursing home. Approximately 1.5 million elderly, about 4 percent of the elderly population, live in nursing homes. A variety of health care interventions, including fall-prevention programs, home visiting, and comprehensive community care programs, have been shown to reduce the likelihood of admission to a nursing home.

ACCESS TO HEALTH CARE AND POPULATION HEALTH

Another approach by which the effect of health care can be estimated is to look within populations and to compare those that have insurance to those that do not. Though this approach is also indirect and has the potential for significant confounding, researchers have some fairly sophisticated efforts to tease out the independent effect of care itself on the differential population health outcomes between those with and those without access to health care.

In 2002 the Institute of Medicine's Committee on the Consequences of Uninsurance published *Care Without Coverage: Too Little Too Late*. The committee undertook an extensive literature review to determine the independent contribution of health-insurance status on health outcomes. Although the IOM study had many limitations due to the difficulty of separating health insurance status from other important predictors of health such as income, ethnicity, education, and employment, the researchers were able to demonstrate independent effects of health insurance status and the ability to get care with health status. Through a review of over 130 studies, and careful modeling, the IOM found that populations between the ages of 25 and 65 without health insurance had age-adjusted mortality rates 25 percent higher than their insured counterparts, with all known confounders controlled. In total, they conservatively estimate that 18,000 unnecessary deaths occur among the uninsured adults in the United States because of the lack of care associated with lack of insurance. Other authors using similar methodology place these estimates in the range of 75,000 deaths. Using the IOM's more conservative number, this would represent a drop in death rates of approximately 40 per 100,000.

PRIMARY CARE AND THE RIGHT KIND OF CARE

The late Barbara Starfield left a lifetime of scholarship dedicated to studying the attributes and value of primary care. Her work suggests that the kind of care a population gets matters to a variety of population health measures, including all-cause mortality. This in turn suggests first that care itself has an effect on these measures, and second that empirical studies of actual care, as that care is currently given, might underestimate the potential value of care if it were given to an entire population in an optimum manner.

Starfield notes that numerous studies of different kinds are consistent in showing a positive population effect when primary care services are offered at higher rates or in a manner most consistent with the provision of optimum care to a population. Studies that compare geographic areas with higher and lower levels of primary care access show those with higher levels have lower age-adjusted mortality rates, reduced infant-mortality rates, and increased rates of self-reported good health. When known confounders are controlled for, mortality rates remain 2 to 5 percent lower. These studies are supported by others that compare individuals within a community. Those who get the primary care are those that have better health and contribute to the higher population health measures.

Importantly, the availability and provision of primary care to poor and other underserved populations appears to have a protective effect against the effects of socioeconomic deprivation. Unlike many public health interventions that improve the health of an entire community but appear to benefit the rich more than the poor (thus unintentionally increasing disparities), the provision of primary care appears to have a greater beneficial effect for the poor compared to the rich, thus reducing disparities.

Most of these studies of primary care are natural experiments and subject to considerable confounding even when efforts are made to control for them. The example of Costa Rica suggests, however, that an intervention to increase the provision of primary care, done at the population level, has a significant causal effect in improving population health.

THE COMPLEXITY OF THE DETERMINANTS OF HEALTH AND THE POTENTIAL UNDERVALUING OF HEALTH CARE

In describing the interaction between social and behavioral determinants of health, scholars refer to a web of causation. This term raises a critical point. The studies that show that behavior and social factors have an effect on a large number of deaths do not imply that the presence or absence of any particular behavior or social circumstance was *sufficient* to cause a death. What causes a death need not be the same thing that prevents it. The Surgeon General's report can be true—that 60 or 70 percent of preventable deaths might be due to behavior and environment. Nevertheless, though one strategy to prevent those deaths might be to change those behavior and environmental determinants, it is in theory possible to prevent each and every one of the premature deaths by intervening at a subsequent point, by interfering with the biological pathway that leads from environment and behavior to the end points of disease and death.

Put another way, the determinants of health need not add up to 100 percent. Every preventable illness might be delayed through modifications of behavior and the environment—but each individual will eventually be subject to a disease that leads to death through biological mechanisms, and irrespective of what preventive strategies regarding behavior and environment were tried at an earlier point, that disease might still be subject to medical interventions that can extend life and well-being. For those diseases for which such health care is not available, it someday may be.

As a thought experiment, imagine a society where every death was due to one of two things: lung cancer from smoking or cardiovascular collapse that occurred over the age of 100. With the right health care—counseling on tobacco use prevention and cessation, screening, and treatment—a certain amount of those lung cancer deaths could be delayed, some of them late enough that the other cause of death would occur instead. Currently, secondary screening methods and treatment of lung cancer are not particularly effective, and tobacco prevention and cessation counseling is not done as frequently or well as it could be. If, however, the care across the spectrum were good enough, as it is for cervical cancer and as it may someday be for other cancers including lung cancer, most of these deaths could be prevented and people would die of the other cause—old age.

Just because behavior causes a lot of deaths doesn't mean health care isn't—or can't be—critical to dramatic improvements in population health. Every death eventually has to be mediated through biological processes—so there is in theory always a possibility that a biological intervention can interrupt the connection between social cause and biological outcome. For many medical conditions and causes of death, it already does so.

Although researchers recognize the powerful influence of environment and behavior in causing disease, disability, and death, this knowledge does not translate automatically into knowing how to change those influences so as to prevent those outcomes. Society is limited in its technical knowledge and divided politically in regards to what policies it should implement. While researchers and policymakers can and should pursue the science and have the political dialogues that will lead to policies promoting a more healthy environment, the current state of uncertainty regarding what to do in these realms makes health care, when it is shown to be effective at improving population health, the stronger option.

CONCLUSION

Health care is not the single most important determinant of population health. Nevertheless, those that see health care as a minor determinant overstate their case. Historically, there has been a discrepancy between the amount of resources that the industrialized nations devote to health care, at the expense of investments in other health promoting policy. This has led to rhetoric that attempts to correct this imbalance by marginalizing and even demonizing medicine. This section seeks to correct the overly broad generalizations that come from that rhetoric. Health care may not be the single most important determinant, and there may be times and places, as argued in the first half of this chapter, where an over-investment in health care crowds out other important health-promoting policy opportunities. Society risks, however, letting this understandable rhetoric cause it to undervalue the important contribution that health care makes to population health.

This contribution is significant and substantial. Society should also remember its ethical obligation to provide health care to its members. Regardless of the preventive opportunities taken or missed earlier in life, all members of society are subject to illness and death. Many of these illnesses can be prevented or delayed by clinical interventions as well as by environmental or behavioral ones. Many can be treated with interventions that reduce suffering and provide comfort and dignity. Some even prolong survival—by decades for some individuals and by smaller but measurable amounts for those afflicted with certain illnesses. Medicine may not live up to its full potential, but if universally available and properly done, it could likely add more to population health than it does today. Finally, continued research and experience suggest that promising new treatments and technologies may in the future contribute even more to population health.

Although society could do more to be critical of unnecessary and harmful health care, and to be aware of the opportunity to use other policies and investments to improve health, it should nevertheless continue to give importance to and invest in health care of proven value and to increase and improve the provision of such services to the entire population.

REFERENCES AND FURTHER READING

Bindman, A. B., Grumbach, K., Osmond, D., Komaromy, M., Vranizan, K., Lurie, N., & Stewart, A. (1995). Preventable hospitalizations and access to health care. *Journal of the American Medical Association, 274*(4), 305–311.

Clark, D. E. (2003). Effect of population density on mortality after motor vehicle collisions. *Accident Analysis and Prevention, 35*(6), 965–971.

Coffield, A. B., Maciosek, M. V., McGinnis, J. M., Harris, J. R., Caldwell, M. B., Teutsch, S. M., et al. (2001). Priorities among recommended clinical preventive services. *American Journal of Preventive Medicine, 21*(1), 1–9.

Congdon, N., O'Colmain, B., Klaver, C. C., Klein, R., Muñoz, B., Friedman, D. S., et al. (2004). Causes and prevalence of visual impairment among adults in the United States. *Archives of Ophthalmology, 122*(4), 477–485.

Evans, R. G., Barer, M. L., & Marmor, T. R. (Eds.). (1994). *Why are some people healthy and others not? The determinants of health of populations.* New York, NY: Transaction Publishers.

Farley, T. A., Dalal, M. A., Mostashari, F., & Frieden, T. R. (2010). Deaths preventable in the U.S. by improvements in use of clinical preventive services. *American Journal of Preventive Medicine, 38*(6), 600–609.

Global Public Health Achievements Team, CDC. (2011). Ten great public health achievements: Worldwide, 2001–2010. *Morbidity and Mortality Weekly Report, 60*(24), 814–818.

Institute of Medicine, Committee on the Consequences of Uninsurance. (2002). *Care without coverage: Too little, too late.* Washington, DC: National Academy Press.

Korda, R. J., & Butler, J. R. (2006). Effect of healthcare on mortality: Trends in available mortality in Australia and comparisons with Western Europe. *Public Health, 120*(2), 95–105.

Lalonde, M. (1974). *A new perspective on the health of Canadians.* Ottawa, ON, Canada: Minister of Supply and Services.

Lee, Y. C., Huang, Y. T., Tsai, Y. W., Huang, S. M., Kuo, K. N., McKee, M., & Nolte, E. (2010). The impact of universal national health insurance on population health: The experience of Taiwan. *BMC Health Services Research, 10,* 225.

McKeown, T. (1976). *The role of medicine: Dream, mirage, or nemesis?* London, UK: Nuffield Provincial Hospitals Trust.

McNally, B., Robb, R., Mehta, M., Vellano, K., Valderrama, A. L., Yoon, P. W., et al. (2011). Out-of-hospital cardiac arrest surveillance—Cardiac arrest registry to enhance survival (CARES), United States, October 1, 2005–December 31, 2010. *Morbidity and Mortality Weekly Report, 60*(8), 1–19.

Starfield, B., Shi, L., & Macinko, J. (2005). Contribution of primary care to health. *The Milbank Quarterly, 83*(3).

U.S. Preventive Services Task Force. (2002). *The guide to clinical preventive services: Report of the United States Preventive Services Task Force.* McLean, VA: International Medical Publishing, Inc.

U.S. Public Health Service. (1979). *Healthy people: The surgeon general's report on health promotion and disease prevention.* Washington, DC: Author.

Wagner, E. H., Sandhun, N., Newton, K. M., McCulloch, D. K., Ramsey, S. D., & Grothaus, L. C. (2001). Effect of improved glycemic control on health care costs and utilization. *Journal of the American Medical Association, 285*(2), 182–189.

Xu, J., Kochanek, K. D., Murphy, S. L., & Tejada-Vera, B. (2010). Deaths: Final data for 2007. *National Vital Statistics Reports, 58*(19). Hyattsville, MD: National Center for Health Statistics.

Anthony L. Schlaff

Health Care as a Human Right

POINT: By reengaging long-standing debates on the "moral commitment" of government to secure the health of every American, the 2010 Patient Protection and Affordable Care Act (ACA) draws on an internationally recognized conception of a positive human right to health, which asserts a government obligation to realize the "highest attainable standard of physical and mental health" through policies that ensure the availability, accessibility, acceptability, and quality of health care.

Benjamin Mason Meier, University of North Carolina at Chapel Hill
Dhrubajyoti Bhattacharya, Loyola University

COUNTERPOINT: Health care is not a right in the same sense that, for example, freedom of expression is a right. Such a legal obligation stands in stark contrast to the American tradition of negative rights, a tradition of restraining government infringements on individual liberties without fulfilling positive entitlements.

Benjamin Mason Meier, University of North Carolina at Chapel Hill
Dhrubajyoti Bhattacharya, Loyola University

Introduction

The Universal Declaration of Human Rights (UDHR), issued by the United Nations in 1948, was in great part a reaction to the atrocities of World War II. The declaration articulates the rights of individuals and their relationship to states. These rights fall into two basic categories: civil and political rights, which are covered in Articles 2 through 21 of the Declaration and are often called first-generation rights; and economic, social, and cultural rights, which are covered by Articles 22 through 29 and are often referred to as second-generation rights. As the chapter explains, these rights have been codified in a series of international agreements, such as the International Covenant on Civil and Political Rights, which generally recognizes first-generation rights, and the International Covenant on Economic, Social and Cultural Rights, which focuses on second-generation rights.

Broadly speaking, civil and political rights are those that concern individuals' control over their own lives. They often function in the negative sense, meaning that they declare the right of an individual not to be prevented from doing something (e.g., joining an association) or not to be treated in a certain way (e.g., being tortured or enslaved). The protection of these *negative rights* usually entails that the state refrain from interfering in the individual's liberty. Economic, social, and cultural rights are different because they require that an individual have something, such as a job, an education, or—most importantly for the purposes of this chapter—health care. Thus, these rights are often referred to as *positive rights,* because they compel the state to take a particular action, rather than refrain from taking it.

The distinction between positive and negative rights, however, is not always clear cut. Although many civil rights compel the state to not do something, some require that positive action be taken (e.g., the right to a fair trial). Likewise, some economic, social, and cultural rights require that the state take no action (e.g., the right to free choice of employment).

The right to health care, which is covered under Article 25, is a second-generation right that is primarily positive in nature, compelling the state to take action to ensure for the individual, in the words of the Article, "a standard of living adequate for the health and well-being of himself and of his family, including . . . medical care and necessary social services."

Although the language of the UDHR itself is quite straightforward, in the real world guaranteeing human rights can be anything but. Though some rights are solely influenced by the state (e.g., the right to a nationality), many—especially positive ones—are impacted by a variety of actors, both public and private. Health is certainly one of those cases, as human health is influenced not only directly by individual decisions but also by the actions, or inactions, of health care providers and insurance companies, as well as other factors, such as the environment, economic circumstances, and level of education.

The degree to which individuals can sustain their health depends in no small part on the level of development in their country. Thus, international law obligates states to recognize the right to health—but not to guarantee that it is attained immediately. In other words, the right to health is subject to progressive realization. Nations that recognize the right are obligated to work toward its fulfillment, but there is no agreed-upon level of services that must be provided.

In the chapter that follows, Benjamin Mason Meier and Dhrubajyoti Bhattacharya look to international law as a backdrop for debating whether or not health is a fundamental human right in the United States. As discussed below, the 2010 Patient Protection and Affordable Care Act (ACA) was influenced by the belief of President Barack Obama and his supporters that health is, indeed, a fundamental right of U.S. citizens. In the Point half of the chapter, Meier and Bhattacharya argue that, though the United States has resisted the expansion of many positive rights, the country is a signatory of the UDHR, which clearly includes the right to health in its obligations. In the Counterpoint, however, the authors note that historically the United States has asserted the primacy of first-generation rights over second-generation ones, and that the ACA is consequently "an affront" to these principles, as it seems to deny the rights of the free market while growing the welfare state.

Expanding slightly on the question of whether human health is a right, one might ask whether or not the United States is already addressing it as such. Given that there were about 50 million uninsured Americans at the time of the ACA's passage, the answer to that question might seem obvious—no, the United States is not currently respecting the universal right to health. However, if as noted above, the "right to health" is understood in the context of progressive realization—the obligation to work toward a goal, rather than to achieve it immediately—then the ACA can be construed as a positive affirmation of the U.S. commitment toward the right to health.

On the other hand, the right to health can also be understood to require considerably more effort than the ACA promises. Achieving the right to health, not simply a right to health care, would require not only increased access to services but also the creation of conditions that make health possible. Observance of that level of right to health could arguably include a far greater government investment in clean air and water, to workplace safety, and to maternal and infant care, among many other things. As you read this chapter, consider the broader policy implications of this right to health. How would U.S. policy change—indeed, would it change—if the United States pursued the right to health in this broader definition? Would greater adoption of international law norms demand substantial changes in U.S. health policy? If the right to health is understood as meaning "the right to the conditions that make health possible," has the term then been stretched to the point of meaninglessness?

Finally, when reading this chapter, consider the fact that rights often conflict. If the existence of the right to health is accepted, how is it to be reconciled with rights to individual choice (e.g., under an insurance mandate system)? What if the right to health conflicts with the right to the free practice of religion? Do these conflicts provide a basis for rejecting the right to health, or can these rights be reconciled—and, if so, how?

POINT

During the second presidential debate in October 2008, then-Senator Barack Obama was pressed to address the specific question "Is health care in America a privilege, a right, or a responsibility?" Focusing on inequities in access to care, Obama responded:

> Well, I think it should be a right for every American. In a country as wealthy as ours, for us to have people who are going bankrupt because they can't pay their medical bills—for my mother to die of cancer at the age of 53 and have to spend the last months of her life in the hospital room arguing with insurance companies because they're saying that this may be a pre-existing condition and they don't have to pay her treatment, there's something fundamentally wrong about that.
> . . . We have a moral commitment as well as an economic imperative to do something about the health care crisis that so many families are facing. (Second Presidential Debate, 2008)

In explicitly referring to a "moral commitment" by which health care should be a right for every American, Obama acknowledged an internationally recognized conception of a right to health, a right that asserts a government obligation to realize the "highest attainable standard of physical and mental health" through policies that ensure the availability, accessibility, acceptability, and quality of required health care.

Following the presidential election, national debates, and legislative considerations, President Obama signed the Patient Protection and Affordable Care Act (ACA) into law on March 23, 2010, establishing the most expansive reform of the U.S. health care system in decades. Though such reforms remain unfinished, this most recent effort to reform health care policy in the United States reflects an evolving debate on the development of a human right to health under international law and the implementation of these rights-based norms through U.S. health care policy.

The human right to health signifies an imperative to respect, protect, and fulfill health for each individual through prescribed government obligations. Guaranteed under international law, the right to health has evolved through the development of a progressive series of United Nations (UN) treaties and interpretive documents. In the implementation

Figure 3.1 The Development of an International Human Right to Health and U.S. Health Care Policy

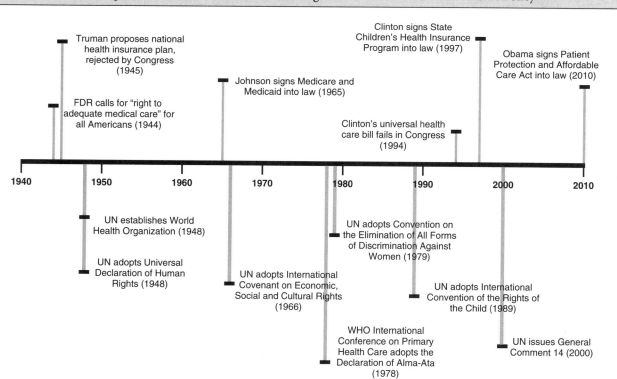

Source: Created by author.

of this international right to health, a rights-based approach to health care has increasingly framed reforms of U.S. health care policy. Recognizing the failure of market-based approaches to health care—the United States spends far more on health care but achieves far worse health outcomes than other developed nations—the ACA represents a comprehensive effort to reign in rising costs and improve equitable outcomes, bringing the United States closer to other nations in realizing a right to the highest attainable standard of health.

HUMAN RIGHTS AS A BASIS FOR JUSTICE

Employing human rights under international law as a means to the public's health, the right to health provides a powerful normative framework to advance justice in health. Construing health disparities as "rights violations" offers international standards by which to frame government responsibilities and evaluate conduct under law, shifting from the rhetoric of social justice to the enforcement of legal obligations. With all human rights thought to be indivisible, interdependent, and interrelated—with freedoms and entitlements of equal importance—the right to health is of equivalent moral standing with all other rights. Viewing health as the right of every individual, a categorical imperative necessary for a life with dignity, the human rights framework implicates government duties to ensure the health care necessary to realize those rights.

As such, a human rights–based approach identifies rights-holders (individuals) and their entitlements and corresponding duty-bearers (government) and their obligations, and works to strengthen the capacities of rights-holders to make their claims and improve the capacities of duty-bearers to meet their responsibilities. Pursuant to a rights-based approach to health, the individual rights-holder demands that the government duty-bearer respect, protect, and fulfill health through policies (e.g., law reforms, budget allocations, or program evaluations) to assure that health is available, accessible, acceptable, and of sufficient quality.

A RIGHTS-BASED APPROACH TO HEALTH

In this process, individuals make claims on national governments to respect their rights by refraining from direct violations and discriminations, to protect their rights by guarding against interference by third parties, and to fulfill their rights by adopting measures to achieve universal care. By linking rights with correlated duties, the human rights framework

Figure 3.2   A Rights-Based Approach to Health

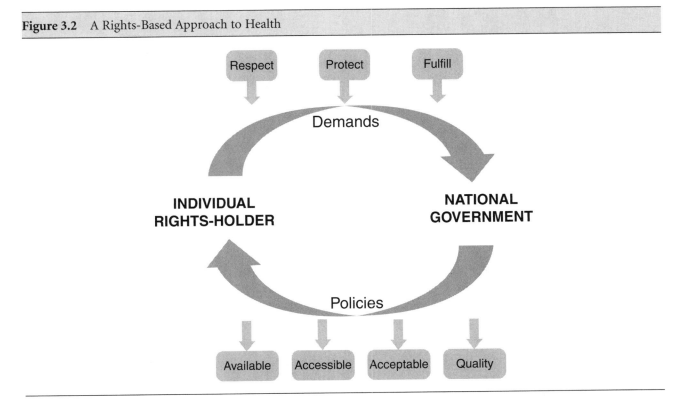

directly connects health demands with the policies necessary to realize an interconnected set of negative freedoms and positive entitlements through health care policy.

As a framework for governance, this rights-based approach to health structures the legal and policy environment, integrates core principles into policy and programming, and strengthens accountability for international norms. These principles shape policymaking decisions by delineating individual rights and framing associated government duties in realizing the right to health through health care policy. Developing these principles as a means to global justice, the U.S. government has sought to influence the evolution of the right to health under international law.

THE EVOLUTION OF THE RIGHT TO HEALTH IN INTERNATIONAL LAW

The international codification of a human right to health emerged, as with all modern human rights, in the context of World War II. On January 6, 1941, President Franklin Delano Roosevelt announced to the world that the post-war era would be founded upon four "essential human freedoms": freedom of speech, freedom of religion, freedom from fear, and freedom from want. Reflecting contemporaneous understanding of the most crucial threats to human dignity, it was the final of these "Four Freedoms," freedom from want, that introduced a state obligation to provide for the health of its people, with Roosevelt couching these rights in the American discourse of freedom.

The Four Freedoms became the basis by which the United States came together with leading members of the international community to create a new system of human rights under international law, with social and economic rights serving to prevent deprivations like those that had taken place in the Great Depression and the war that followed. In the aftermath of the war, the 1945 Charter of the United Nations became the first international legal document to recognize universal human rights as a normative basis for global governance. To define a collective set of interrelated rights for all peoples, the UN proclaimed the Universal Declaration of Human Rights (UDHR) on December 10, 1948, including in it a right to health by which "Everyone has the right to a standard of living adequate for the health and well-being of himself and of his family, including food, clothing, housing and medical care and necessary social services."

Supporting the UDHR's expansive vision of social welfare for public health, states established the World Health Organization (WHO) as a means to realize rights-based global health policy. The preamble of the WHO's constitution declared that "the enjoyment of the highest attainable standard of health is one of the fundamental rights of every human being," defining health positively to include "a state of complete physical, mental, and social well-being and not merely the absence of disease or infirmity." To meet this expansive rights-based vision of "complete" health through corresponding government obligations, the WHO constitution held that "governments have a responsibility for the health of their peoples which can be fulfilled only by the provision of adequate health and social measures."

With the UN codifying the social and economic obligations of the UDHR in the 1966 International Covenant on Economic, Social and Cultural Rights (ICESCR), elaborating a "right of everyone to the enjoyment of the highest attainable standard of physical and mental health," states explicitly defined government obligations to progressively realize "conditions which would assure medical service and medical attention to all in the event of sickness." Providing influential U.S. support for this budding international consensus on health care obligations, the WHO International Conference on Primary Health Care adopted the 1978 Declaration of Alma-Ata, by which the international community recognized the broader obligation of primary health care as a global objective, reinforcing government commitments to realize health through the fulfillment of health care and social systems.

This evolving right to health was clarified in 2000 by the UN Committee on Economic, Social and Cultural Rights (CESCR), whose General Comment on the ICESCR interprets the right to health as an "inclusive right extending not only to timely and appropriate health care but also to the underlying determinants of health." Specific to health care, General Comment 14 outlined government obligations to assure that all health care services should be made available, accessible (physically and economically), acceptable, and of sufficient quality. As a means to structure rights-based facilities, goods, and services for health, these obligations include, at a minimum, "the provision of equal and timely access to basic preventive, curative, rehabilitative health services and health education; regular screening programmes; appropriate treatment of prevalent diseases, illnesses, injuries and disabilities, preferably at community level; the provision of essential drugs; and appropriate mental health treatment and care" (CESCR, 2000, article 12.2[d]).

Developed through the evolution of international law, the international right to health now offers a normative framework for setting national health care policy to guarantee universal health care. Despite its lack of an explicit recognition under the U.S. Constitution, statutory law, or treaty ratification, the United States has expressed its commitment to the right to health: in its vote and consistent support for the UDHR; through its member status, funding, and participation with the WHO; and as a signatory to the ICESCR, the Convention on the Elimination of All Forms of Discrimination Against Women, the Convention on the Rights of the Child, and a wide range of international instruments recognizing the right to health. Based on the global legitimacy endowed by these international treaties, declarations, and institutions, the right to health is seen to have equal standing with all human rights and is understood to present binding obligations on all national governments, requiring governments to implement the highest attainable standard of health through universal access to health care.

RIGHTS AND HEALTH CARE REFORM

Notwithstanding U.S. support for these human rights obligations under international law, the evolution of the international right to health was largely avoided in domestic health care policy discourse due to a perceived ideological tension between individual liberty and health equity—a uniquely American position that finds human rights relevant only to freedoms against state intrusion. As a result, the policy implementation of the right to health long remained uncertain in the United States, until recently leaving it the only developed nation without universal health care coverage.

Whereas legislation in the United States did not seek to develop universal health care policy prior to World War II, President Roosevelt's 1944 State of the Union address expressed his desire for a new U.S. conception of rights, calling for a "second Bill of Rights" that would entitle every American to the "right to adequate medical care and the opportunity to achieve and enjoy good health." Seeking to carry out this vision following Roosevelt's death, President Harry S. Truman in 1945 became the first U.S. president to propose a national health insurance plan, outlining a comprehensive, prepaid medical insurance program to be realized for all Americans through the Social Security system. Although these early U.S. efforts did not succeed in bringing about universal health care or an explicit recognition of the right to health—with the United States diverging from the progressive post-war experiences of European nations—such efforts did influence incremental congressional efforts to expand public involvement in health care through the 1943 Emergency Maternal and Infant Care Act, which ensured that the spouses and children of low-ranking servicemen would receive health care; the 1948 Hospital Survey and Construction Act, which provided federal funds to build hospitals in underserved communities on the condition that these new hospitals offer a certain amount of free care; and the 1956 Civilian Health and Medical Program of the Uniformed Services, which extended federal health care benefits to dependents of those serving in the military.

During the civil, labor, and elder rights movements of the 1950s and 1960s—as activists rallied against the inequities of market-based health insurance—a growing demand for universal health care presented an opportunity for the reemergence of policy reforms founded upon the human right to health. Building upon President John F. Kennedy's repeated invocation of the plight of the elderly uninsured, President Lyndon B. Johnson finally succeeded in 1965 in pressing Congress to establish Medicare and Medicaid, progressive health insurance expansions enacted over the strong opposition of the Republican Party, American Medical Association (AMA), and other business interests. Although this vocal opposition proved a significant political challenge, President Johnson reiterated his commitment to establishing Medicare in private conversations with Vice President Hubert Humphrey:

> I'll go a hundred million or a billion on health or education. I don't argue about that any more than I argue about [Mrs. Johnson] buying flour. You got to have flour and coffee in your house and education and health. I'll spend the goddamn money. I may cut back some tanks. But not on health. (Blumenthal & Morone, 2008, p. 2385)

Viewing health as an imperative to be realized regardless of cost, President Johnson's rights-based vision drove his staunch advocacy for health care reform. Although such policy reforms did not provide comprehensive coverage for all Americans, the enactment of Medicare (covering the needs of the elderly through federal payment for care) and Medicaid (providing for the indigent through matching federal contributions to state health programs) offered the first formal government recognition of a positive right to health for the most vulnerable members of society. Following this limited congressional effort to expand access to health care, with health care reform finding deep political and popular support, advocates looked to state legislatures to expand coverage for all. Yet, despite sporadic state advances to reform health care policy, these piecemeal efforts lacked the effectiveness and inclusiveness that could only be provided by congressional recognition of a universal right to health care.

By the 1970s already described as a "national health care crisis," escalating health care costs (and rising disparities in health care outcomes) led the Richard Nixon and Jimmy Carter presidential administrations to renew federal health care reform efforts. Addressing this crisis in access to quality health care, Senator Ted Kennedy of Massachusetts promoted health care as a fundamental right for all Americans, arguing in moral terms that

> I am shocked to find that we in America have created a health care system that can be so callous to human suffering, so intent on high salaries and profits, and so unconcerned for the needs of our people. American families, regardless of income, are offered health care of uncertain quality, at inflated prices, and at a time and in a manner and a place more suited to the convenience and profit of the doctor and the hospital than to the needs of the patient. Our system especially victimizes Americans whose age, health, or low income leaves them less able to fight their way into the health care system. (Furrow, 2011, p. 458)

Proposing universal health care as the means to realize this right, Senator Kennedy introduced the 1971 Health Security Act, which aimed to establish a "single-payer" health care system to provide government health insurance for all Americans. In response, President Nixon offered a compromise proposal that would have expanded health care coverage through private employers and offered government subsidies for the poor (an approach similar to those later adopted by Presidents Bill Clinton and Obama); however, the Democratic Party opposed this effort in favor of a single-payer approach, leading to a stalemate in health care policy and the entrenchment of Republican opposition to all health care reform efforts. Even within the Democratic Party, President Carter's 1977 proposal to control costs through a phase-in plan for national health insurance met with resistance from congressional Democrats, who favored a national health insurance system. With the 1980 election of President Ronald Reagan, the prospects for national universal health care reform were drastically diminished, as conservative ideology preempted any discussion of expanding health care access.

Given the unrelenting rise in insurance costs and health disparities, President Clinton's 1993 policy effort to enact universal health care coverage seemed poised to succeed in a political environment receptive to an overhaul of U.S. health care policy. Seeking consensus around an incremental, market-oriented means to realize universal care, President Clinton sought to avoid the rhetoric of a rights-based approach to policy reform. This incremental attempt to address health care ultimately proved disastrous to reform efforts, as Republican lawmakers and interest groups scaled back their support for the individual elements of reform, retrenching in general opposition to any government involvement in health care. Abdicating reform efforts to an increasingly divided Democratic Party—divided between those who preferred more public involvement through a single-payer system and those who preferred more limited, market-based reforms—universal health care policy faltered. Much like previous attempts to achieve comprehensive reform, proponents had to settle for small, tailored efforts to expand care for specific vulnerable populations, as seen in the 1997 State Children's Health Insurance Program, which provided comprehensive coverage for the children of select working families.

Following another decade of inaction, the second presidential debate of 2008, elevating the right to health care as a principal justification for universal health care reform, appeared initially to herald a change in the parameters of the national health care debate; however, these hopeful assertions on the right to health never advanced beyond rhetoric and never drew upon international human rights law in developing national health care policy.

THE ACA AS A LANDMARK FOR RIGHTS-BASED HEALTH CARE POLICY

Though the 2010 ACA was neither presented nor developed as means to implement the right to health, the ACA nevertheless furthers government efforts to address multifaceted rights-based imperatives, building from a long line of past health care and public health policies to realize underlying determinants of health. In parallel with the international legal obligations of the human right to health, the United States has implemented this right through policies for the (1) reduction in infant mortality and healthy development of children, (2) improvement in environmental and industrial hygiene, (3) prevention and control in response to epidemics, and (4) creation of conditions that ensure access to medical services for all. Addressing the healthy development of the child, a combination of social, medical, and educational interventions have contributed to a sharp drop in infant mortality rates—from 30 deaths per 1,000 live births in 1950 to under 10 deaths in 2006. Through environmental and occupational health and safety standards, a vast network of government agencies is responsible for monitoring environmental and industrial hygiene, including the Food and Drug

Administration, the Environmental Protection Agency, Food Safety and Inspection Service, Centers for Disease Control and Prevention, Department of Health and Human Services, the Ministry of Agriculture, and the Occupational Safety and Health Administration. With every state developing legislation to govern the prevention, control, and treatment of communicable and noncommunicable diseases, the country has made notable progress in extending preventive measures and epidemic responses through its public health system. And, as this history has shown, the ACA is only the most recent and most expansive effort to meet the federal government's final discrete obligation to implement the right to health: assuring access to medical care for all.

Given that the United States has long sought to progressively realize all these facets of the right to health, why is the term "right to health" so controversial in contemporary public policy discourse? In one sense, the right to health has become conflated with a right to health care, which consequently reduces the broader debate about measures to secure population health to a singular determination as to whether governments may (or ought to) guarantee access to medical care for the individual through private health insurance, a proxy for access to care. This narrow perspective minimizes the legitimate progress in the United States to implement the right to health, as well as the expansive role of the ACA in fulfilling multiple facets of the right to health. Within the context of these broader obligations, this section discusses four key rights-based aspects of health care policy under the ACA: (1) fulfilling universal and equitable access, (2) protecting from harm through obligatory participation, (3) expanding the social safety net, and (4) prioritizing public health prevention.

The right to health unequivocally affirms universal access to care by requiring conditions that assure medical service and attention in the event of illness "to all," implicitly seeking equity through universal access to market-based health insurance. The ACA identifies exorbitant costs as the primary obstacles to universality, creating a rights-based measure of progress through the assurance of minimal health care for all. Beyond universality, equity implicates safeguards to narrow gaps in health access and outcomes. In a society plagued by health disparities across a broad spectrum of indicators—sex, race, geography, education, and income, to name a few—an equitable system must contemplate the social determinants of, and structural impediments to, realizing health care for all. Identifying disparities in outcomes is a necessary but insufficient determination that often overlooks the existing distribution of resources, both monetary and social, coupled with the unavailability of equal opportunities in education and employment, particularly for impoverished and minority communities. These overlooked factors exacerbate existing health disparities by constraining individual opportunities to engage in healthy lifestyles and behaviors, which in turn are limited by individual, social, and environmental resources. Insufficient funds, lack of social capital, and unsafe or underdeveloped communities affect the healthy environment for all, as seen, for example, in the quality and quantity of food choices, the ability to rely on neighbors and community organizations for resources and support, and the opportunities that exist for physical activity. Equity, therefore, does not demand an accounting of people as patients, but as participants in and adherents of a social contract to secure the health and prosperity of fellow individuals.

The right to health is built on a conception of justice that demands a minimum level of health care for every individual to flourish, and in doing so, recognizes the harm of third-party interference or negative externalities from those who would take advantage of a universal system without contributing to it. In 2008, Congress estimated the aggregate cost of providing uncompensated care to the uninsured to be $43 billion, an amount that providers pass on to private insurers, who in turn pass it on to insured families in the form of higher premiums, increasing annual premiums by over $1,000 per family. Howsoever one chooses to characterize this uninsured population, its reluctance or inability to purchase insurance has not shielded insured consumers from bearing the expenditures associated with treatment and care of the uninsured in the event of illness. By requiring each individual to purchase insurance (creating an "individual mandate"), government protects everyone from these negative externalities by employing a collective response to the impact of the nonparticipation by the uninsured, shielding the insured from the actions of the uninsured and recognizing that liberty can (and ought to be) restrained when its exercise harms others. The individual mandate to purchase health insurance enables every individual to realize a right to care by securing the full participation of all individuals. Thus, the ACA promotes justice through obligatory participation and safeguards against "free riding," with equitable cost sharing through subsidies for those who cannot afford coverage, as this restraint on individual liberty is intended to fulfill the government's obligation to prevent the harms of third-party interference as a means to ensure access to care.

By expanding the social safety net, the ACA seeks to increase the availability of insurance, and thus realize the highest attainable standard of health for all. Against a backdrop of over 50 million uninsured Americans, as reported in a 2011 study from the Centers for Disease Control and Prevention, the creation of a system that enables everyone to attain a basic level of health care services has become a moral imperative. In the absence of social insurance through the federal government, the expansion of market-based insurance coverage is intended to create a safety net to ensure immediate access to care. Under the ACA, individuals who would otherwise be unable to afford private insurance (up to 133 percent of the federal poverty level in 2014) will soon become eligible for Medicaid (assuming their states expand Medicaid eligibility), and primary care providers (e.g., family medicine, general internal medicine, pediatrics) will soon receive increased resources to care for these vulnerable individuals. Though inadequate funding and attention to social determinants of health continue to exacerbate health disparities, particularly among low-income and minority populations, the expansion of health insurance coverage will begin to rectify this injustice, if still neglecting many investments in prevention that are necessary to completely address these underlying determinants of health.

Prevention is a vital component of a rights-based approach to health, explicitly recognized through international legal obligations to realize the "prevention, treatment and control of epidemic, endemic, occupational and other diseases" pursuant to the human right to health. Although it fails to completely address the underlying determinants of health, the ACA expands from this narrow definition of enumerated diseases to include broader initiatives to promote community health and individual well-being through, among other policies, the mandatory nutrition labeling of standard menu items at chain restaurants and the enhanced data collection and analysis of health disparities through federally supported or conducted health programs (which will disaggregate data on the basis of race, ethnicity, sex, primary language, and disability status). Above and beyond such specific policy initiatives, the ACA establishes a National Prevention, Health Promotion and Public Health Council, whose purpose is to provide recommendations to the president and Congress concerning the most pressing issues and the necessary changes in federal policy to achieve national wellness, health promotion, and public health goals. This multi-sectoral Council seeks to influence the myriad of human activities that bear some influence, directly or indirectly, on population health. Seeking to support structures and environments that facilitate healthy choices, this focus on prevention marks a significant rights-based transition in the national healthcare debate—from individual health care financing to public health interventions embedded within a complex system of multiple underlying determinants of health. In prioritizing prevention in future policy reforms, evidence-based interventions must focus on the structural forces that extend beyond the traditional purview of health care providers and the biomedical paradigm of morbidity and mortality. With the rise of social epidemiology identifying underlying determinants of health, the identification of insalubrious social forces must become an integral component of broader health policies. Though the ACA takes concrete steps to address these determinants of health, translating research findings into meaningful policy, future reforms will become necessary to ameliorate burdens on vulnerable populations and promote health and well-being for all.

CONCLUSION

By envisioning health care as a public good that is financed and administered at the national level, rights-based advocates in the United States seek to create a powerful normative justification to support the government in providing universal health care and protecting against inequitable market forces, transcending the prevailing American policy narrative to create a rights-based approach to health. Despite the continuing reluctance of the United States to explicitly embrace a right to health—a reluctance driven by political misunderstandings about government obligations under the right to health and false distinctions between positive rights and negative freedoms—the United States has taken preliminary steps to join other developed nations in implementing a rights-based approach to health care. Echoing President Roosevelt's message seventy years later, President Obama stood before the United Nations in 2011 and declared that "freedom from want is a basic human right." Moving forward, advocates of rights-based reforms aim to confront the subjugation of human needs to market forces, constructing a sustainable movement for an ideological shift away from the American model of commodifying needs through the market and toward a collective fulfillment of rights through social insurance.

Notwithstanding the progress of the ACA in facilitating compliance with an international right to health, numerous challenges remain: Many of the ACA's requirements will begin only in 2014, the costs of expanding Medicaid may lead states not to expand their programs in the midst of a fragile economic climate, and individuals may resist the mandate not to procure health insurance. These challenges present formidable obstacles to the ACA, but even as opposition has grown to federal government involvement and spending in public health, advocates have risen to support a rights-based approach to health care in U.S. public policy discourse, pressing state governments to establish publicly financed health care systems to support the ACA. As these complementary state and national policies are enacted and revised in the years to come, the international human right to health will play an instrumental normative role in the ongoing struggle to define the scope and content of government obligations to realize the highest attainable standard of health.

REFERENCES AND FURTHER READING

Blackstone, W. (1976). On health care as a legal right: An exploration of legal and moral grounds. *Georgia Law Review, 10*(2), 391–418.

Cassel, C. (1994). The right to health care: The social contract, and health reform in the United States. *Saint Louis University Law Journal, 39*(1), 53–64.

Chapman, A. (1994). *Health care reform: A human rights approach.* Washington, DC: Georgetown University Press.

Daniels, N. (2009). Is there a right to health care and, if so, what does it encompass? In H. Kuhse & P. Singer (Eds.), *A companion to bioethics* (2nd ed., pp. 46–52). Chichester, UK: Wiley-Blackwell.

Donnelly, J. (1994). International human rights and health care reform. In A. Chapman (Ed.), *Health care reform: A human rights approach.* Washington, DC: Georgetown University Press.

Friedman, E., & Adashi, E. (2010). The right to health as the unheralded narrative of health care reform. *Journal of American Medical Association, 304*(23), 2639–2640.

Furrow, B. (2011). Health reform and Ted Kennedy: The art of politics . . . and persistence. *New York University Law Journal of Legislation and Public Policy, 14,* 445–476.

Gostin, L. (1994). Securing health or just health care? The effect of the health care system on the health of America. *Saint Louis University Law Journal, 39,* 7–43.

Kinney, E. D. (2008). Recognition of the international human right to health and health care in the United States. *Rutgers Law Review, 60*(2).

Leary, V. (1994). Defining the right to health care. In A. Chapman (Ed.), *Health care reform: A human rights approach.* Washington, DC: Georgetown University Press.

Litsios, S. (2002). The long and difficult road to Alma-Ata: A personal reflection. *International Journal of Health Services, 32*(4), 709–732.

London, L. (2008). What is a human-rights based approach to health and does it matter? *Health and Human Rights, 10*(1), 65–80.

Meier, B. (2005). The highest attainable standard: Advancing a collective human right to public health. *Columbia Human Rights Law Review, 37,* 101–147.

Rudiger, A., & Meier, B. M. (2011). A rights-based approach to health care reform. In E. Berachochea, C. Weinstein, & D. P. Evans (Eds.), *Rights-based approaches to public health* (pp. 69–86). New York, NY: Springer.

Second Presidential Debate. (2008, October 7). *The New York Times.* Retrieved from http://elections.nytimes.com/2008/president/debates/transcripts/second-presidential-debate.html

Stone, D. A. (1993). The struggle for the soul of health insurance. *Journal of Health Politics, Policy and Law, 18*(2), 287–317.

United Nations, CESCR. (2000). *General comment no. 14.* Retrieved from http://www.unhchr.ch/tbs/doc.nsf/(symbol)/E.C.12.2000.4.En#15

Weissert, C. S., & Weissert, W. G. (2006). *Governing health: The politics of health policy* (3rd ed.). Baltimore, MD: Johns Hopkins University Press.

Yamin, A. (2005). The right to health under international law and its relevance to the United States. *American Journal of Public Health, 95*(7), 1156–1161.

Benjamin Mason Meier and Dhrubajyoti Bhattacharya

COUNTERPOINT

Asked during the second presidential debate in 2008, "Is health care in America a privilege, a right, or a responsibility?" Senator John McCain, the Republican candidate for president, offered a position in stark contrast to then-Senator Barack Obama's assertion that health should be viewed as a right. Focusing instead on individual liberty and freedom from government intrusion, McCain stated:

> I think it's a responsibility, in this respect, in that we should have available and affordable health care to every American citizen, to every family member. . . . It is certainly my responsibility. It is certainly small-business people and others, and they understand that responsibility. American citizens understand that. Employers understand that. We have got to give people choice in America and not mandate things on them and give them the ability. Every parent I know would acquire health insurance for their children if they could. (Second Presidential Debate, 2008)

In viewing health care as a responsibility, emphasizing the importance of choice in health insurance coverage and rejecting the imposition of government mandates for that coverage, McCain was appealing to an American tradition of individual negative rights, rights that restrain government from infringing upon individual liberties without offering any positive entitlements.

It is often said that the United States has the "best health care system in the world," standing as an unrivaled leader in medical innovation due to its privatized health care system. Realization of a human right to health would undercut this free market and infringe individual liberty to choose among health care options. For this reason, the United States has long resisted the human right to health, subverting its development under international law and rejecting its implementation in domestic health care policy. The Patient Protection and Affordable Care Act (ACA) represents an affront to this American tradition, deviating from U.S. acceptance of international legal obligations and subverting individual self-determination in health care to a federal prerogative that is fundamentally unconstitutional.

LIBERTY AND NEGATIVE RIGHTS IN A FREE MARKET

Within the American conception, there can be no right to health because, at its core, the United States values the normative supremacy of negative rights to the exclusion of positive human rights like the right to health. Unlike negative rights, which are thought to be inherent in nature, positive rights are only possible if they are realized through the affirmative actions of government. Correspondingly, whereas negative rights only require the state to refrain from activities that undermine the dignity of its people—where violating a negative right requires actively causing individual harm or infringing individual freedom—positive rights are violated by omission and can require potentially unlimited forms of assistance and resources from the state. Recognizing the provision of health care as a right will open the door to demands to recognize many other human needs as rights. Fulfilling such an expansive right to health care is thus incompatible with the function of a libertarian "minimalist state," focused solely on respecting negative rights to liberty and property. Where rights are viewed through this negative rights lens, in which government is restrained from intruding on the civil and political rights of the individual rather than required to ensure the individual's economic or social benefit, the progressive realization of a positive right to health cannot be seen as a government obligation.

With this American conception of rights proclaimed in the Declaration of Independence and codified in the U.S. Constitution, such a notion of freedom reflects an inviolable belief that human dignity requires the government to treat each person with equal concern, respect, and in a manner which does not infringe upon his or her personal autonomy. Advancing through the rise of liberal democracies, libertarian philosophy has narrowed human rights to those "natural rights" enjoyed by individuals without burdening the rights of others, such as the right to freedom of speech, freedom of belief, freedom of movement, and freedom to own private property. Whereas natural rights promote the widely accepted American notion of limited government, non-natural positive rights encourage the continued expansion and enlargement of the welfare state through taxation, eventually leading to systems of socialized medicine. Imposing requirements on individuals or businesses to share needed resources to realize a positive right violates their absolute right to property. (Similarly, the right to health stands in opposition to the freedom of health care providers to practice their profession as they choose and may usurp providers' liberty to set the rates they charge for their labor.) In the American tradition, liberty is of paramount importance, and such libertarian ideology resists any weakening of the right to own and transfer one's property through the imposition of government taxation.

As such, positive human rights and demands for social responsibilities like a right to health are in direct opposition to the core market-based ideology at the heart of the U.S. economic system. Where social responsibilities rest solely with individual choice in a free marketplace, no individual can be coerced to redistribute resources to benefit others—ensuring that transactions in the market follow the most efficient path possible, regardless of the distributional consequences to society as a whole. Beyond the strict responsibilities necessary under law, businesses bear only one social responsibility—to use their resources to maximize profit for their shareholders. When voluntary transactions are subverted to further social goals, the efficiencies of the marketplace—and, by extension, an individual's own resources—are degraded. Consequently, whereas other nations have typically considered health care to be a public good, the United States has consistently treated health care as a market good or commodity, framing justice in health through a normative focus on efficiency. Facilitating efficiency through competition, everyone's interests are better served in a free market in which consumers can choose their insurance and health insurance companies can compete for business. This free market for medical care, as the optimal framework to allocate goods, should be maintained because it is responsible for bringing the United States to its position of dominance and affluence within the international community and for motivating the development of America's preeminent medical industry.

Thus, positive rights are normatively antithetical and practically infeasible in the United States. By requiring individuals to provide something for others, either directly or through taxation, such actions transmute this "right" into a "taking" that infringes upon natural rights and weakens inherent liberties. With economic, social, and cultural rights thought to favor equity through redistribution over liberty for individuals, creating obligations that cannot ever be fully met, American notions of individual freedom stand in opposition to these collective interests under international law.

AMERICAN FOREIGN POLICY AND THE INTERNATIONAL PRIORITIZATION OF CIVIL AND POLITICAL RIGHTS

From the inception of the modern human rights era, America's conception of international human rights—extended from the U.S. Constitution to U.S. foreign policy through the United Nations (UN)—has prioritized civil and political rights—those negative rights stemming from a highly individualistic view of human nature, holding freedom to be the most important social good, and serving to protect individuals from government interference. This unique depiction and prioritization of rights has consistently led the United States to influence the international evolution of human rights to support its own negative conception of civil and political rights, and to oppose the broader positive economic, social, and cultural rights initially put forward in the UN by the Soviet Union. As a foundational conflict of the Cold War, the development of human rights divided national foreign policies into two alternative ideological camps, Western capitalist democracies and Soviet communist regimes, with this divide impacting the development of human rights in international law and the implementation of health policy through the World Health Organization (WHO). As a result, the comprehensive vision of rights laid out by states in the 1948 Universal Declaration of Human Rights (UDHR) unraveled quickly along ideological and economic lines, as states moved to codify human rights into legally binding covenants, with the two major superpowers (and their respective spheres of influence) split on both a belief in the substance of economic and social rights and the feasibility of realizing these rights. Led by the United States, Western states advocated for the advancement of legal obligations only for civil and political rights, dismissing positive rights as a basis for a just world and maintaining that the best way to achieve such resource-dependent entitlements was to uphold primarily negative rights, which would assure the capitalist markets and economic growth necessary for "aspirational" social and economic rights.

By upholding its domestic values under international law—stymieing international obligations to realize a human right to health and rejecting the litany of evolving treaties and institutions to support health-related rights—the United States has limited the international legal development of the right to health. In doing so, the United States has long remained suspicious that the WHO would seek to advance a rights-based program of "socialized medicine" at the expense of American notions of liberty and capitalism in the medical marketplace. As a WHO member state, the United States sought to influence WHO health programming and human rights participation to focus on guaranteeing only civil and political rights, discouraging the WHO from addressing health care organization and thereby reducing Soviet opportunities to criticize the United States for its failure to guarantee a right to health. When the Soviet states temporarily withdrew from WHO in the 1950s in protest of this U.S. influence, an unchallenged United States succeeded in constraining the WHO's efforts to advance a human right to health in international law. Even after the Soviet states returned to the WHO, seeking to advance socialist medicine through the Declaration of Alma-Ata's rights-based focus on "primary health care," the 1980 election of President Ronald Reagan (and with it, conservative opposition to the WHO's regulatory activities) ultimately closed any international opportunity for the WHO to codify a rights-based approach to health care that differed from the U.S. conception of rights.

DEFEAT OF HUMAN RIGHTS IMPLEMENTATION IN U.S. HEALTH CARE REFORM EFFORTS

Whereas other industrialized countries have concluded that health care is an essential obligation to their peoples and have created taxpayer-funded public or public-private systems to provide for health care needs, the United States has diverged from health care models of other nations, and any international frameworks that have arisen under the human right to health have not been implemented through U.S. health care policy. In every previous instance in which rights-based health policy has been proposed prior to the ACA, the majority of lawmakers and the American people have rejected those policies on grounds rooted in U.S. traditions of liberty and market justice. Given the prevailing American view of health care as a market commodity, as opposed to a public good and a human right, rights-based social movements have rarely led to political mobilization, with nonmarket health-reform efforts faltering repeatedly.

Although the United States was poised to join European nations in the enactment of universal health care policy in the aftermath of World War II, the 1946 midterm elections delivered control of the U.S. Congress to the Republican Party, breaking up the "New Deal coalition" and subsequently leading to the abandonment of proposals to establish a comprehensive health insurance system. Reflective of these shifting sentiments, an anti-Communist aversion to "socialized medicine" became a hallmark of U.S. health policy, leading to the defeat of President Harry S. Truman's proposal for national health insurance and the rise of congressional opposition to international efforts to implement the right to health. Contributing to this shift in the U.S. health policy debate, physician groups and other health care business interests aligned in opposition to comprehensive health care reform, with the American Medical Association (AMA) objecting vigorously to government interference in private medical practice. Spending an unprecedented $1.5 million (in 1945 dollars) to lobby Congress against intrusions in the free market for medicine, the AMA explicitly linked President Truman's national health plan to the threat of Communism. This well-funded campaign against a nationally recognized right to health care extended from national to international forums, with U.S. advocates arguing for "personal freedom" over "socialized medicine" in the UN and at international health policy conferences. This growing political and organizational opposition to the right to health led to a 20-year impasse in health policy reform—with few advancements in international law for health and without any assumption of legal obligations by the U.S. government.

The movements that established Medicare and Medicaid were the first initiatives to break this health reform deadlock, coming about during the course of international negotiations on the ICESCR and placing ideological demands on the national government for a minimum level of medical care for specific vulnerable population groups. In building political support for these rights-based entitlements, however, such policies came to be seen as facilitating rights to individual choice in medical care, rather than duties on the government to realize health on an equitable basis. With universal access to care a political impossibility where inequalities of wealth, income, and resources are morally accepted, opponents successfully contended that requiring equality of access to health care in the United States would limit medical advancements and result in the rationing of care. Instead of viewing a right to health as a means to equal access, the medical profession argued that the right to health should be interpreted as a negative right for individuals to have free choice within the health care system, as they do within the overall market-based system. Any policy efforts to provide universal health coverage were viewed as stifling this freedom of choice in medicine.

This American aversion to a rights-based approach to health care led President Bill Clinton, in advocating for health insurance reforms in the early 1990s, to avoid human rights discourse and focus instead on market-based rationales for insurance-policy reform. In doing so, the Clinton administration pursued a managed-competition approach to health reform—with policy discourse that was primarily free market–oriented, emphasizing the economic effects of reform on corporations, small businesses, employers, insurance companies, and health care providers. Given the longstanding conceptualization of health care as a commodity in American society, the policy debate rarely focused on the actual effects of the U.S. health care system on the health of the American people, downplaying the proposal's public health benefits to advance discourse on economic considerations and cost/benefit analysis in the medical marketplace. Working exclusively through private-sector reforms—explicitly avoiding government provision of care through a "single-payer option," and thereby hoping to avoid the label of "too much big government"—the Clinton administration's complex, managed-competition approach was nevertheless viewed as excessive government interference, emboldening opponents against government intrusion and failing to galvanize supporters in favor of health care reform. As the focus of debate shifted from reforming health care to reducing government intrusion, policy efforts collapsed where there was no normative justification for increasing the role of government in the health care market. When next the George W. Bush administration sought to increase access to health care, expanding Medicare's reimbursement for pharmaceutical coverage under the 2003 Medicare Modernization Act, the policy was not framed in the language of rights and was widely viewed as a tailored response to the political mobilization of the AARP and the financial interests of the Pharmaceutical Manufacturers Association (PhRMA).

Leading up to the 2008 presidential election, numerous proposals—even a constitutional amendment in support of universal health care and in recognition of a right to health—were met with abject failure in Congress. With an aging U.S. population increasingly relying on the federal health care system, the establishment of a formidable elderly voting bloc afforded a rare opportunity for the expansion of the government health care system, as individuals over sixty increasingly voted on the basis of health care policy and presented an occasion to shift political support in favor of a rights-based approach to health care reform. But as the presidential campaign progressed, this rights-based movement lost political traction, as policymakers increasingly directed their attention to a uniquely "American solution," one based on the outright rejection of the government health care models of other countries. As in the past, health care was treated as a market commodity, leaving out any government obligation to secure equitable access as a public good and allowing the policy discourse to be dominated by claims for consumer choice and "fair" competition in the insurance marketplace. Even President Obama, the purported proponent of a rights-based approach to health care reform, offered his support for health care policy proposals largely in the language of commodified health care, suggesting that the government's participation in the marketplace would introduce needed "competition" to combat select market failures. As a result, any normative vision of a positive right to health or government obligation for health care was abandoned in favor of economic arguments, grounded in notions of individual liberty, leaving the ACA as an incremental policy reform for the management of the health insurance market.

THE ACA AS AN AFFRONT TO LIBERTY

In the United States, all legal authority must emanate from the U.S. Constitution. Finding that the Constitution's substantive limits on congressional authority preclude the implementation of a right to health in domestic policy, this section explains how (1) the Constitution prevents recognition of an international human right to health, (2) the international health-related obligations undertaken by the United States are narrowly tailored to meet economic and security needs, and (3) the ACA infringes the individual liberty of all citizens, including health care providers, to make decisions about health care.

Under Article II, Section 2 of the U.S. Constitution, an international obligation becomes national law only upon its ratification by a two-thirds majority of the Senate. To date, the United States has not ratified the International Covenant on Economic, Social and Cultural Rights (ICESCR) or any other relevant human rights treaties that recognize a right to health. Although President Jimmy Carter signed the Convention on the Elimination of All Forms of Discrimination Against Women (CEDAW), which has a provision on a woman's right to health, the Senate has failed to ratify this treaty despite multiple committee hearings on its content and scope. Because the United States has never ratified an international treaty that articulates a right to health, the U.S. government is not subject to any binding international law with respect to the adoption of health care policy. Even where the United States becomes engaged in health-related issues through partnerships with other countries or international organizations, such efforts are strictly construed outside of the jurisdiction of international law. For example, although the United States and the WHO executed a 2011 "memorandum of understanding" to collaborate in enhancing global alert and response systems for public health emergencies, the United States specified that this agreement did not bind the U.S. government under international law. Without recognizing the legal authority of international law, the United States is under no obligation to implement a human right to health based upon treaties that it has not ratified.

Where the United States has ratified health-related treaties, agreeing in limited terms to be bound by international law, it has done so in adherence with overarching principles that prioritize national economic and security interests over public health burdens. As an example of the prioritization of these national interests, the 2005 International Health Regulations (IHRs), the only recent health-related treaty to be ratified by the United States, seek specifically to prevent disease-related threats to national security while avoiding unnecessary interference with traffic and trade. In prioritizing national security, the IHRs view public health measures as a means to free trade, rather than an end of international law; focus on identifiable threats to the safety of the population; and do not mandate that states take measures beyond securing the immediate health and safety of the population. Whereas a human rights framework conceptualizes health as a right and an end in itself, the IHRs recognize health only to the extent that it is instrumental to alleviating threats to trade, traffic, and security. Focusing only on identified threats, the IHRs do not address public health prevention or health care inequalities, requiring that government measures be taken only once an outbreak or related health threat creates a "public health emergency of international concern." Though states are required to notify the WHO of these outbreaks, they are not required to assist states that lack the capacity to respond promptly to such risks, with purely discretionary collaboration and assistance encouraged "to the extent possible." In contrast to this example of U.S. endorsement of a treaty whose overarching purpose is to secure national security, the United States has not ratified the Framework Convention on Tobacco Control (FCTC), adopted by the WHO to address the particular public health burdens of the global tobacco epidemic. Because the FCTC seeks only to protect individuals from the health consequences of tobacco consumption—through educational, economic, and other social interventions to lower the prevalence of consumption and exposure—these measures are not a response to imminent threats to population safety. Although the measures contemplated by the FCTC may be laudable from a human rights perspective, U.S. reluctance to ratify this international treaty is consistent with U.S. commitments that prioritize trade and security.

Finally, in seeking to implement international human rights standards through national policy, the ACA ultimately amounts to unconstitutional coercion, supplanting the individual liberty and self-determination of both health care providers and patients. Marginalizing health care providers, the ACA has increased Medicaid reimbursement payments but expanded Medicaid coverage (in states that expand Medicaid eligibility) for individuals making up to 133 percent of the federal poverty level, pressing health care providers to serve an increasing number of patients at unsustainable costs. Extending the 1940s advocacy of the AMA, this conceptualization of physician freedom has been rekindled by Senator Rand Paul, the Kentucky Republican who has forcefully suggested that a right to health care is a means to the "conscription" and "slavery" of health care practitioners. At the level of the individual patient, the ACA's efforts to expand access to health care do not justify infringing upon the fundamental liberty and self-determination of an individual to secure his or her own health and well-being. Such freedom from governmental intrusion is in direct conflict with the ACA's individual mandate, which places a duty on every citizen to contribute to a government initiative to extend health benefits to every other citizen.

This is illustrated in the ACA's "Shared Responsibility Payment," which enumerates the income levels and attendant penalties for individuals who refuse to purchase insurance coverage. The coercion explicit in these penalties is an affront to the overarching conception of a free society, and the suggestion that such requirements are vital to fund the initiative does not amount to a compelling governmental interest to secure public health at the expense of the fundamental rights of each and every citizen. Compounding the harm of this mandate that individuals purchase health insurance, penalizing an individual for not taking a specific action, the ACA also seeks to mandate individual lifestyles. For example, the ACA holds individuals accountable for certain lifestyles and behaviors (e.g., discriminates by allowing for premium rate variation based on tobacco use) but not others (e.g., being overweight, drinking alcohol, having unsafe sex with multiple partners, taking drugs, having a history of traffic infractions, or engaging in any other risky behavior)—denying individual liberty in the pursuit of happiness. With the U.S. legal system premised upon individual liberty as a safeguard against governmental intrusion, the ACA's paternalistic approach to health care reform unjustly coerces individual behavior in ways antithetical to the American libertarian tradition.

CONCLUSION

To the extent that the ACA has implemented a right to health through U.S. policy, it represents an anomaly in the American health care policy narrative, an assault on liberty under the auspices of a "right" that has never before found resonance in the United States. Distorting the free market for health care, such an approach undermines the uniquely American approach that prioritizes individual negative rights over collective welfare benefits. In reforming public policy, it will be necessary to reconcile this rights-based approach to health with the for-profit business model, acknowledging market freedoms that are at the heart of the American normative framework and health care system. As the United States seeks to reconcile this debate and interpret the tradition of liberty in the health care market, the U.S. Supreme Court has agreed to review a constitutional challenge to the ACA, with this challenge capable of reversing policy efforts to expand health care access by infringing individual liberty to make health care decisions free from government coercion.

REFERENCES AND FURTHER READING

Beam, C. (2009). Med school: What the 1965 Medicare debate can teach us about health care reform. *Slate*. Retrieved from http://www.slate.com/id/2222296

Blendon, R. J., & Benson, J. M. (2011). The public's views about Medicare and the budget deficit. *The New England Journal of Medicine, 365*(4), e8.

Bloche, G. (2005). Is privatisation of health care a human rights problem? In K. De Feyter & F. Gomez (Eds.), *Privatisation and human rights in the age of globalization* (p. 209). Oxford, UK: Intersentia.

Blumenthal, D., & Morone, J. (2008). The lessons of success—Revisiting the Medicare story. *The New England Journal of Medicine, 359*(22), 2384–2389.

The Democrats' second 2008 presidential debate. (2007, June 3). *The New York Times*. Retrieved from http://www.nytimes.com/2007/06/03/us/politics/03demsdebate_transcript.html

Epstein, R. A. (2003). Let the shoemaker stick to his last: A defense of the "old" public health. *Perspectives in Biology and Medicine, 46*(3), S138–S159.

Fos, P. J. (2011). *Epidemiology foundations: The science of public health.* San Francisco, CA: Jossey-Bass.

Fried, C. (1976). Equality and rights in medical care. *Hastings Center Report, 6*(1), 29–34.

Friedman, M. (1970, September 13). The social responsibility of business is to increase its profits. *New York Times Magazine,* pp. 122–126.

Hidalgo, J. (2010). *A glance into Costa Rica's health care system.* Retrieved from CATO Institute website: http://www.cato-at-liberty.org/a-glance-into-costa-ricas-health-care-system

Hoffman, B. (2003). Health care reform and social movements in the United States. *American Journal of Public Health, 93*(1), 75–85.

Kesler, C. (2008). *The nature of rights in American politics: A comparison of three revolutions.* Retrieved from Heritage Foundation website: http://www.heritage.org/Research/Reports/2008/09/The-Nature-of-Rights-in-American-Politics-A-Comparison-of-Three-Revolutions

National Prevention Council. (2011). *National prevention strategy.* Washington, DC: U.S. Department of Health and Human Services, Office of the Surgeon General.

Nocera, K. (2011). *Rand Paul: "Right to health care" is slavery.* Retrieved from Politico website: http://www.politico.com/news/stories/0511/54769.html

Parmet, W. (2002). After September 11: Rethinking public health federalism. *Journal of Law, Medicine, and Ethics, 30*(2), 201–211.

Pellegrino, E. (1999). The commodification of medical and health care: The moral consequences of a paradigm shift from a professional to a market ethic. *Journal of Medicine and Philosophy, 24*(3), 243–266.

Sade, R. (2000). Medical care as a right: A refutation. In R. M. Veatch (Ed.), *Cross-cultural perspectives in medical ethics* (2nd ed.). Sudbury, MA: Jones and Bartlett.

Second Presidential Debate. (2008, October 7). *The New York Times.* Retrieved from http://elections.nytimes.com/2008/president/debates/transcripts/second-presidential-debate.html

Shapiro, I. (2010). *Health care rights and wrongs.* Retrieved from CATO Institute website: http://www.cato-at-liberty.org/health-care-rights-and-wrongs

Starr, P. (1995). What happened to health care reform? *American Prospect, 20,* 20–31.

Benjamin Mason Meier and Dhrubajyoti Bhattacharya

Individual and Societal Responsibility for Health

POINT: Individuals are in the best position to maintain their own health, not the government. Moreover, individuals should have the autonomy to decide which health care services they want and which they do not. It follows that it is an individual's responsibility, not the government's, to choose and to pay for health care services.

David Jones, University of Michigan School of Public Health and University of Michigan Department of Political Science
Jodyn Platt, University of Michigan School of Public Health
Daniel B. Rubin, University of Michigan School of Public Health and University of Michigan Law School
Peter D. Jacobson, University of Michigan School of Public Health

COUNTERPOINT: The fundamental causes of health and disease lie beyond the reach of individual control. Whereas individual choices about smoking, eating, and physical activity affect individual health, social, political, and economic contexts powerfully shape de facto options and opportunities for health and health care.

David Jones, University of Michigan School of Public Health and University of Michigan Department of Political Science
Jodyn Platt, University of Michigan School of Public Health
Daniel B. Rubin, University of Michigan School of Public Health and University of Michigan Law School
Peter D. Jacobson, University of Michigan School of Public Health

Introduction

At some point in their lives, almost everyone will experience health problems. Often, society will bear some of the economic costs associated with those illnesses and injuries. It's no surprise, then, that the question of responsibility for human health is an ongoing theoretical debate. In this chapter, authors David Jones, Jodyn Platt, Daniel Rubin, and Peter Jacobson examine who is ultimately responsible for health—the individual or the state?

Few people would argue in an absolutist way that either individuals or the state have no role to play in health. Almost everyone agrees that a sensible, and ethically justifiable, health policy requires a balance between individual and social responsibility. This debate is really about where society should fall on the continuum, with libertarians and conservatives placing a greater weight on individual responsibility, and liberals and progressives wanting a larger role for the government.

In the Point section, the authors note that concepts of autonomy and responsibility are fundamental ideals in the United States. Whether they play out in our understanding of private property, reward for individual enterprise, or free-market competition, these ideals are essential to America's notion of itself, and they certainly influence any discussion of health care. The authors quote the liberal philosopher John Stuart Mill, who in *On Liberty,* wrote, "The only freedom which deserves the name is that of pursuing our own good in our own way. . . . Each is the proper guardian of his own health, whether bodily, or mental or spiritual."

However, there is no guarantee that all individuals will make good choices to protect their own health. Indeed, the very ideal of individual autonomy also must make room for the fact that individuals are free to smoke, drive unsafely, eat fast food, or make any of a myriad of choices that may negatively impact their individual health. Opponents of health care reform efforts during the presidential administrations of both Bill Clinton and Barack Obama strongly objected to what they saw as attempts to enforce an unacceptable level of state control over individual health choices—the battle over mandated health insurance is a perfect example of this conflict. Investing in health insurance is widely assumed to be a good choice, but is it the proper role of the state to force this choice to be made?

In the Counterpoint, the authors note that human health is quite different from, say, commercial goods whose success or failure can be determined by the market. The poet John Donne wrote that "no man is an island"; certainly individual health does not exist in a vacuum. People live in communities—and families, employers, and neighbors can all be impacted by an individual's health problems. The state therefore has not only moral but also practical reasons to invest in the health of the larger community.

This chapter broaches a number of broad, thematic questions worth consideration. For example, the argument for individual responsibility usually assumes a certain level of competence among adults. But what about children? There is broad agreement that the state has some level of responsibility to protect its youngest citizens, but how far should that responsibility extend? Consider also the severely ill, the aged, or the developmentally disabled, who are less able to care for themselves. Does the state have a larger role to play in their health? What is gained and what is lost when the state assumes that responsibility?

Further, the question of individual responsibility tends to assume that health outcomes are the result of individual choices, but that is not always the case. What about people who are born with particular genetic conditions? In their case, society has not "caused" the problem. But, then again, can anyone say that individuals are responsible for their own genes? More fundamentally, how should society decide when individuals are responsible for their own health conditions? Does it tend to assign responsibility—which can sometimes be a euphemism for *blame*—based on social values? For example, does society believe that a skier is responsible for his or her injuries? An alcoholic? Is there a danger that social stigma and discrimination affects perceptions as to when individuals are and are not responsible for their health conditions?

Given the above, how can society decide whether a particular issue or problem belongs on one side or another of the continuum? Should that decision be decided based on pragmatic reasons (whether individuals or the state can prevent or handle the problem more effectively/efficiently) or moral ones?

POINT

The debate over U.S. health policy is characterized by divergent understandings of the roles and responsibilities of the state versus the individual. Concerns about individual self-determination lead to calls for limiting state paternalism and promoting individual autonomy and responsibility. Three arguments support this individualistic approach. First, U.S. political culture is grounded in the language of individual freedoms and checks against state power. Preserving health and paying for one's own health care needs is an individual moral responsibility. Second, the health care system is more efficient when it relies on individuals instead of government. Market competition results in lower costs and higher levels of quality. Third, maintaining health is an individual responsibility because individual lifestyle behaviors are a major factor in the leading causes of death and illness. Individuals have the freedom to choose whether to exercise, eat well, be screened regularly, and seek medical treatment when necessary.

Autonomy as an American ideal. The language of individual autonomy and personal responsibility pervades the history, culture, and laws of the United States. American political culture is rooted in models of liberalism that emphasize limiting state power for the sake of individual freedom. Key principles of American conservatism derive from classical liberal aims: to promote free markets, to reward individual enterprise, and to protect private property. To varying degrees, conservatives protective of private interests and libertarians suspicious of government power share an impulse to constrain the reach of the state. In politics and civil society, the conflict between social and individual responsibility remains central to debates about health and health care, even as federal, state, and local governments have played a more active role in health. With respect to an individual's responsibility for health, the philosopher John Stuart Mill epitomized the classical liberal perspective when he said, "The only freedom which deserves the name is that of pursuing our own good in our own way, so long as we do not attempt to deprive others of theirs, or impede their efforts to obtain it. Each is the proper guardian of his own health, whether bodily, or mental or spiritual. Mankind are greater gainers by suffering each other to live as seems good to themselves, than by compelling each to live as seems good to the rest" (1863, p. 10).

Any improvement in health care must come through privatization, rather than new government programs. Libertarian ideals of individual autonomy run deep among many Republican and independent voters, as well as among many within the Tea Party movement. Republicans view free-market competition in health care markets as a critical mechanism for assuring access, while the somewhat less mainstream American Libertarian Party calls for the total deregulation and dismantling of government involvement. Party members propose disbanding agencies such as the Food and Drug Administration (FDA). Republican Congressman Ron Paul (TX) favors repealing all health-related laws, including those for physician licensure. He argues that deregulating the insurance and physician markets would create efficient and effective competition.

These arguments co-exist with an implicit expectation of personal responsibility. Withdrawing the social safety net gives back to individuals their freedom and responsibility to participate in a system of health care based on free-market principles. Though government may play a role in developing the health infrastructure, it should do so merely as a procurement agent using private-sector competition to assure efficiency. Libertarianism places great faith in the power of individuals to create a fair and good society. In contemporary politics, this translates to a staunch rejection of government paternalism and a reliance on the private sector (i.e., ownership, exchange of goods and services in the free market) to provide individuals with the freedom to promote their own health and well-being. In this sense, the role of government is to be an arbiter of a robust health care market, rather than its architect.

Efficiency. Economic efficiency is a primary concern for libertarians and is predicated on the existence of competitive markets with a variety of companies responding to the dynamics of supply and demand. The behavior of consumers of health care will be similar to their behavior with regard to any other market goods, and therefore will benefit from laissez-faire economic policies. These policies force individuals to be the principal bearers of the cost of health care, just as they are the principal bearers of the cost of food and transportation. In health insurance markets, the well-known eight-year RAND Health Insurance Experiment demonstrated that requiring individuals to be financially accountable for at least part of their health care costs reduced the utilization of care, albeit for both unnecessary and necessary care.

Effectiveness. Individuals are in a better position to effectively maintain their own health than are government and social programs. Both the onset and management of most of the leading causes of mortality and morbidity are driven by individual-level decisions and behaviors, such as tobacco use, diet, and exercise. Observing that not everyone will assume responsibility for their own health and some will knowingly take risks that may jeopardize their health, John H. Knowles opined that, "One man's freedom in health is another man's shackle in taxes and insurance premiums" (p. 59). Libertarians suggest that one mechanism for assuring personal responsibility is to couple personal behavior choices with personal insurance premiums. This approach provides an incentive for healthy behaviors and expects people to accept the consequences of their unhealthy ones. For example, nonsmokers should be rewarded with lower premiums, as should those who lose weight through diet and exercise. Government may provide information and knowledge to guide such health decisions, but it cannot be expected to make those decisions for individuals. Indeed, only with both personal autonomy and individual responsibility can optimal health be achieved.

The courts have also supported the view that individuals must bear the responsibility for their own health. For example, in the 2003 case *Pelman v. McDonald's Corporation*, the plaintiffs claimed that McDonald's deceived the public about the adverse health effects of the fast food it serves. The plaintiffs argued that McDonald's ought to be held accountable for the rise in obesity among minors. Ruling for McDonald's, Judge Robert Sweet articulated the tension between individual and governmental responsibilities for the well-being of citizens:

> The issue of determining the breadth of personal responsibility underlies much of the law: where should the line be drawn between an individual's own responsibility to take care of herself, and society's responsibility to ensure that others shield her? Laws are created in those situations where individuals are somehow unable to protect themselves and where society needs to provide a buffer between the individual and some other entity. (*Pelman v. McDonald's Corp.*, 237 F. Supp. 2d 512, at 516)

Judge Sweet also drew on American cultural norms. In his opinion, he asserted that Americans believe that, with the freedom to choose among products in a free-market society, comes the individual responsibility to accept the consequences of one's decisions:

> This opinion is guided by the principle that legal consequences should not attach to the consumption of hamburgers and other fast food fare unless consumers are unaware of the dangers of eating such food. . . . [T]his guiding principle comports with the law of products liability under New York law. As Sir Francis Bacon noted, "Nam et ipsa scientia potestas est," or knowledge is power. Following from this aphorism, one important principle in assigning legal responsibility is the common knowledge of consumers. (*Pelman v. McDonald's Corp.*, 237 F. Supp. 2d 512, at 517)

In sum, today's conservative perspective on health is that the American values of individualism and free enterprise achieve the best outcomes in health and health care decision making. By directly purchasing their health care and acting in their own best interests, individuals may take responsibility for assuring their own health.

EXAMPLES

This section highlights three examples to demonstrate how the libertarian perspective has been applied in specific political debates and to specific policy issues. As will be seen, an agreement over the principle of individual responsibility does not always lead to an agreement over policy.

Health insurance. Opponents of government involvement have long used libertarian arguments to quell sweeping changes. For example, in 1961, Ronald Reagan, the soon-to-be governor of California, spoke on behalf of the American Medical Association (AMA) against a proposal to expand Social Security by including guaranteed health insurance for seniors (what was eventually signed into law by President Lyndon B. Johnson in 1965 as Medicare). Reagan warned that such socialized medicine would eventually infiltrate every aspect of the health care system and lead to a country devoid of freedoms. This was powerful rhetoric during the Cold War and it continues to be effective.

Opponents of the Clinton administration health-reform proposals in the early 1990s argued similarly that "the Clinton Administration [was] imposing a top-down, command-and-control system of global budgets and premium caps, a superintending National Health Board and a vast system of government-sponsored regional alliances, along with a panoply of advisory boards, panels, and councils, interlaced with the expanded operations of the agencies of Department of Health and Human Services and the Department of Labor, issuing innumerable rules, regulations, guidelines, and standards" (Moffit, 1993). In other words, according to critics, the reform was another attempt to expand the role of government and decrease personal autonomy. The policy argument running parallel to this ideological argument was that not only was the role of government inappropriate in the Clinton plan but also that it was likely to be ineffective. Instead of increasing accountability and strengthening competition, the plan's reliance on government programs would insulate consumers from the consequences of their choices and thus weaken markets and drive up costs.

President Barack Obama faced similar issues while promoting his own health care reform plan. Shortly after his inauguration, health-reform debates focused on whether the bill would include an individual mandate and a so-called public option, a government-run health insurance plan to compete with plans sold by private insurance companies. The requirement that all individuals purchase insurance is one of the most controversial provisions in the reform law that was ultimately passed, the Patient Protection and Affordable Care Act (ACA), though many other of its provisions raise critical questions about the role of government. For example, many Republican leaders support the creation of health insurance exchanges as long as they are run by the states instead of the federal government. Utah was the first Republican-led state to create an exchange, and it varies significantly in structure and purpose from the exchange set up in Democrat-led states such as a Massachusetts. Although not fully compliant with ACA, leaders in Utah have chosen to focus their exchange exclusively on employees of small businesses. Rather than using the exchange as a government tool to expand Medicaid coverage and provide subsidies to the nonworking poor, it is set up as a marketplace with the goal of increasing competition, driving down costs, and increasing quality. Conservative states such as Utah allow any plan participate in the exchange (a clearinghouse model), as opposed to some states which are setting high standards for who is allowed to sell plans (an active purchaser model). The objective of the clearinghouse approach is that consumers, rather than government, will be the best judges of what plans should survive in a competitive marketplace.

Debates over rationing.   The question of whether Medicare should pay doctors for the time they spend consulting with elderly patients about end-of-life issues raises persistent ethical questions about the government's role in health care. This issue sparked a fierce national debate that played out in town hall meetings throughout the summer and fall of 2009 in response to proposed health-reform legislation. Ultimately, ACA did not allow Medicare to make such payments and administrative attempts to authorize reimbursement for this service have not been successful.

The bill that emerged from the House of Representatives in July 2009 provided Medicare coverage for optional end-of-life consultations. Within days, House Republican leader John Boehner (R-OH) warned, "This provision may start us down a treacherous path toward government-encouraged euthanasia if enacted into law." As dramatic as this claim was, it was a Facebook posting from 2008 Republican vice-presidential candidate Sarah Palin on August 7 that brought intense media focus to this issue. She wrote, "The America I know and love is not one in which my parents or my baby with Down syndrome will have to stand in front of Obama's 'death panel' so his bureaucrats can decide, based on a subjective judgment of their 'level of productivity in society,' whether they are worthy of health care. Such a system is downright evil" (Palin, 2009). Many conservatives portrayed the issue of rationing medical care as emblematic of the potential for government take-over of health care through the reform package. They feared the government would gain too much power to make decisions about what is and is not covered. This is exactly the type of government decision making that libertarians want to avoid. Hence, the danger of rationing is an argument against public insurance. Ironically, the issue of end-of-life consultation was initially framed by a Republican senator, Johnny Isakson (GA), as a matter of personal responsibility. He described his proposal as enabling people "to obtain assistance in formulating their own living will and durable power of attorney" (Rutenberg & Calmes, 2009). In other words, even when people agree on the principle of limited government involvement, they do not necessarily agree on how that principle should be applied to a given policy.

Obesity.   The debate over personal vs. societal responsibility plays a particularly important role in formulating a response to the increasing obesity rates in the United States. Few people dispute that levels of obesity have risen dramatically in recent years. According to the Centers for Disease Control and Prevention (CDC), in 1990 every state had less than a 15 percent rate of obesity. By 2010, 36 states had a prevalence of obesity equal to or greater than 25 percent, of which 12 had a prevalence of obesity greater than 30 percent. There is little agreement about the best way to address rising obesity rates, including the question of whether interventions should be addressed at the individual or societal levels.

Proponents of individual responsibility use three main arguments to explain why the problem of obesity does not justify government intervention. The first echoes the cultural argument described earlier, namely that people should be free to decide what they eat and how much they exercise, understanding that they must live with the consequences. According to this argument, obesity is a personal health issue that requires personal responsibility as a solution. Unlike tobacco use, which can harm others via second-hand smoke, the adverse health effects of eating are limited to the individual. Libertarians also argue that the government has no business regulating the industries that are often blamed for the rising obesity rates, such as fast food restaurants, producers of high-fat snack foods, and drinks high in sugar.

Business leaders concerned with obesity also argue that the obesity problem can be best addressed through industry self-regulation. For example, many businesses and corporations create incentive programs to reward employees who make efforts to lose weight. Steven Burd, CEO of the Safeway grocery store chain, claims that his company has kept health care costs stable through insurance incentives rewarding good behavior. He draws a parallel with the automobile insurance industry, which charges higher premiums for accident-prone drivers and rewards safe drivers with lower premiums.

Another argument against government intervention opposes framing obesity as an epidemic, disease, or problem. Advocates of this stance argue that obesity is not a communicable disease, and the very definition of obesity is problematic and stigmatizes people unfairly. Many people are genetically prone to obesity regardless of what they eat and how much they exercise. By interfering with personal decision making over food and exercise, and thus stigmatizing people who are overweight regardless of their choices, government programs may actually be doing more harm than good. In addition, the argument goes, calling obesity an epidemic creates an urgency that gives government the responsibility to act forcefully. For libertarians, this could lead to an unacceptable, paternalistic role for government.

Finally, libertarians and others who advocate for individual autonomy maintain that government policy and legal tools are ineffective at reducing the incidence of obesity. Because of the vast difference among individuals, it would be impossible to legislate what and how much food people eat and where they buy it.

CONCLUSION

Three arguments explain why health is a matter of individual responsibility. First, the roots of classical liberal notions of individual autonomy run deep in the American psyche. The debates over rationing and the shape of health insurance exchanges are good examples of how classical liberalism continues to influence policy. Opponents of health care rationing argue that a major role for the government is not just bad policy but is actually un-American. Second, the market will be more efficient than government regulation at financing and delivering care. People are the best judges of their own health status and health care needs; if market forces are allowed to work, people will consume the appropriate level of health care.

Third, people have a moral responsibility to care for themselves. This is similar to the argument rooted in classical liberalism, but is even broader. The debate over obesity policy provides a clear lens through which to view this belief. On the one hand, some argue that rising obesity rates is not a problem to be addressed. On the other hand, some argue that individuals have both the responsibility for maintaining their health and of accepting the consequences of their good and bad decisions.

Finally, it is worth noting that those who believe health to be a matter of individual responsibility typically acknowledge that government does have some role to play, but they believe that government's involvement should be as minimal as possible. When it must act, government should seek to reinforce, not undermine, individual autonomy.

References and Further Reading

A much-debated health care proposal. (2009, August 14). *The New York Times.* Retrieved from http://www.nytimes.com/imagepages/2009/08/14/health/policy/14panelgraphic.ready.html

Allen, A. W. (2006, February 25). House panel doesn't buy ban on school vending sweets. *The Spokesman-Review.* Retrieved from http://news.google.com/newspapers?nid=1314&dat=20060225&id=021WAAAAIBAJ&sjid=FfMDAAAAIBAJ&pg=2040,2392448

Arrow, K. J. (1963). Uncertainty and the welfare economics of medical care. *The American Economic Review, 53*(5), 941–973.

Burd, S. (2009, June 12). How Safeway is cutting health-care costs. *The Wall Street Journal*, p. A14. Retrieved from http://online.wsj .com/article/SB124476804026308603.html

Centers for Disease Control and Prevention. (2011). *Obesity and overweight: U.S. obesity trends.* Retrieved from http://www.cdc.gov/ obesity/data/trends.html

Chernew, M. E., & Newhouse, J. P. (2008).What does the RAND Health Insurance Experiment tell us about the impact of patient cost sharing on health outcomes? *The American Journal of Managed Care, 14*(7), 412.

Committee for the Future of the Public's Health in the 21st Century. (2002). *The future of the public's health in the 21st century.* Washington, DC: The National Academies Press. Retrieved from http://www.nap.edu/openbook.php?isbn=030908704X

Committee for the Study of the Future of Public Health. (1988). *The future of public health.* Washington, DC: The National Academies Press.

Epstein, R. A. (2003). Let the shoemaker stick to his last: A defense of the "old" public health. *Perspectives in Biology and Medicine, 46*(3), S138–S159.

Fuchs, V. R. (1998). *Who shall live? Health, economics, and social choice* (Vol. 3). Singapore: World Scientific Publishing.

Gostin, L. O. (2001). Law as a tool to facilitate healthier lifestyles and prevent obesity. *Journal of the American Medical Association, 297*(1), 87.

Gwatkin, D. R. (2001). The need for equity-oriented health sector reforms. *International Journal of Epidemiology, 30*(4), 720.

Hodge, J., Garcia, A., & Shah, S. (2008). Legal themes concerning obesity regulation in the United States: Theory and practice. *Australia and New Zealand Health Policy, 5*(1), 14.

Holmes, S. (1995). *Passions and constraint: On the theory of liberal democracy.* Chicago, IL: University of Chicago Press.

Jacobs, L. R., & Skocpol, T. (2010). *Health care reform and American politics: What everyone needs to know.* New York, NY: Oxford University Press.

Jones, C. (2000). Levels of racism: A theoretic framework and a gardener's tale. *American Journal of Public Health, 90*(8), 1212–1215.

Kersh, R., & Morone, J. (2002). The politics of obesity: Seven steps to government action. *Health Affairs, 21*(6), 142.

Knowles, J. H. (Ed.). (1977). *Doing better and feeling worse: Health in the United States.* New York: Norton.

Libertarian Party. (n.d.). *Healthcare: Making healthcare safe and affordable.* Retrieved from http://www.lp.org/issues/healthcare

McGinnis, J. M., & Foege, W. H. (1993). Actual causes of death in the United States. *Journal of the American Medical Association, 270*(18), 2207.

Mello, M. M., Rimm, E. B., & Studdert, D. M. (2003). The Mclawsuit: The fast-food industry and legal accountability for obesity. *Health Affairs, 22*(6), 207.

Mill, J. S. (1863). *On liberty.* Boston, MA: Ticknor and Fields.

Moffit, R. E. (1993). *A guide to the Clinton health plan: A checklist on vital national issues.* Washington, DC: Heritage Foundation.

Novak, W. J. (1996). *The people's welfare: Law and regulation in nineteenth-century America.* Chapel Hill, NC: University of North Carolina Press.

Oberlander, J. (2003). *The political life of Medicare.* Chicago, IL: University of Chicago Press.

Oliver, J. E. (2006).The politics of pathology: How obesity became an epidemic disease. *Perspectives in Biology and Medicine, 49*(4), 611–627.

Palin, S. (2009, August 7). Statement on the current health care debate [Facebook update]. Retrieved from http://www.facebook.com/ note.php?note_id=113851103434

Parmet, W. E. (2009). *Populations, public health, and the law.* Washington, DC: Georgetown University Press.

Paul, R. (n.d.). *On the issues: Health care.* Retrieved from http://www.ronpaul.com/on-the-issues/health-care

Pelman v. McDonald's Corp., 237 F. Supp. 2d 512 (S.D.N.Y. 2003).

Pew Research Center for the People & the Press. (2011). *Beyond red vs. blue: The political typology.* Retrieved from http://www .people-press.org/typology

Rawls, J. (1999). *A theory of justice.* Cambridge, MA: Belknap Press of Harvard University Press.

Rubin, D. B. (2010). A role for moral vision in public health. *Hastings Center Report, 40*(6), 20–22.

Rutenberg, J., & Calmes, J. (2009, August 13). False "death panel" rumor has some familiar roots. *The New York Times.* Retrieved from http://www.nytimes.com/2009/08/14/health/policy/14panel.html

Sen, A. (2002). Why health equity? *Health Economics, 11*(8), 659–666.

Sunstein, C. R., & Thaler, R. H. (2003). Libertarian paternalism is not an oxymoron. *University of Chicago Law Review, 70*(4), 1159.

David Jones, Jodyn Platt, Daniel B. Rubin, and Peter D. Jacobson

COUNTERPOINT

The promotion of health is a social responsibility and government has an important role because it has effective tools at its disposal. A concern for equity, solidarity, and distributive justice provides a compelling case that the basic health needs of all should be met. This belief is supported by cultural, economic, and egalitarian arguments.

CULTURAL AND MORAL ARGUMENTS

Individuals have a positive human right to health. This view is codified in international accords, such as the United Nations Universal Declaration of Human Rights (1948), which declared that "everyone has the right to a standard of living adequate for [their] health and well-being . . . including food, clothing, housing, and medical care and necessary social services." Society's moral responsibility in this regard trumps the importance of individual autonomy argued for by libertarians. Indeed true autonomy over health may never be possible for some, given the limited range of options available to them.

Socioeconomic status (SES) is a fundamental cause of health outcomes. SES influences individual and group-level access to employment, health care, education, and housing. Low SES can constrain access to knowledge, power, prestige, and social cohesion, each of which affects acute and chronic stress and health outcomes. Those with higher SES, for example, generally have more resources to cope and succeed than do those with lower SES.

A concern for equity is one of the primary moral motivations for viewing health as a social responsibility. As a political ideal, achieving equity in health means providing a fair opportunity for all people to achieve their full health potential. Guided by this principle, the Institute of Medicine (IOM) in the United States defined the mission of public health in its 1988 *Future of Public Health* report as "assuring the conditions in which people can be healthy" (Committee for the Study of the Future of Public Health, 1988, p. 40). As Wendy E. Parmet points out, a common feature of most definitions of public health is the focus on the well-being of people, not individuals.

In 2002, the IOM's follow-up report, *The Future of the Public's Health in the 21st Century,* defined the key players in the public health sector as government, health care providers, academia, community, business, and the media. Working together, these institutions collectively shape the conditions affecting the social determinants of health. The metric for the achievement of equitable opportunities for health and health care among the population is articulated in philosopher John Rawls' notion of distributive justice. According to this concept, the collective good benefits when two conditions are met: First, the least advantaged members of society are better off, and, second, all citizens have an equal opportunity to improve their quality of life. Society, as a collective of individuals, determines what "equal opportunity" means. Solidarity, the notion that people are both part of a collective and autonomous individuals, plays a key role in defining and working toward the common goal of social equity. Public health policy should be targeted at both the individual and social determinants of health.

EFFICIENCY ARGUMENTS

Libertarians view health and health care as objects of the economic marketplace. However, health and health care are distinct from commercial commodities. The nature of the health market leads to inefficiencies and market failures for which individuals cannot be held responsible. A few key points deserve highlighting, including an asymmetry of information and a misalignment of incentives.

One of the economic assumptions of a free market is that purchasers (i.e., patients) have complete information about the services and products they demand. However, in the case of health care, doctors possess technical knowledge not available to most people, so patients typically have no way of assessing the quality of care they receive. They may be able to discern whether their symptoms are improving or worsening, but not necessarily whether such changes are affected by anything their doctor has done. Similarly, it is very difficult for patients to systematically compare practitioners when deciding where to seek care. Reliable information about the quality and costs of providers is difficult to obtain. Also, doctors seldom discuss the costs of suggested treatments or compare the marginal benefits and costs of other treatments.

A misalignment of incentives, on both the demand and supply sides, compounds the lack of information problem. Whereas libertarians use the RAND Insurance Experiment to argue that passing on the costs of health care to individuals decreases utilization, critics highlight the study's finding that sharing costs led to decreased utilization of both necessary and unnecessary care. They counter that people are not good judges of whether the care they have forgone was necessary or not. The information asymmetry described above means that patients often do not question their doctor's recommendations. This can be problematic because providers may have a vested interest in a certain treatment, such as ordering more tests than necessary to protect against liability. That is not to say that doctors are deceitful or recommend harmful care for their financial gain, but rather that their patients are usually unaware of the context in which their doctors make decisions.

EFFECTIVENESS ARGUMENTS

Societal problems require societal solutions. The challenge is that the interaction between social status and health is complex and difficult to parse, though it is clear that health inequalities result from the differences in cumulative exposures to historical, cultural, and political-economic processes and institutions. In other words, disparities can be in part explained by both our social organization and the roles individuals play therein. Equitable social change is best achieved via publicly accountable programs and interventions. At least since the Progressive Era, "well-ordered" capitalist societies have demanded the development of strong regulatory environments assuring the health and trust of the people through measures such as health and safety inspections and licensure. Today, public and private operate rhetorically as separate arenas, though the American economy has never been entirely free of state influence. Rather, government and private interests are harmonized in good governance and social policy. Government has powers available to no other type of organization, including the ability to compel the private sector to make choices that it would not have otherwise made that improve population health.

EXAMPLES

Federal and state governments are highly invested in promoting health, including providing health insurance coverage via Medicare and Medicaid, subsidizing graduate medical education, monitoring public health, supporting clinics and hospitals, and regulating food and drugs, among other investments. The government should play a role in ensuring access to a basic level of services for all. This section highlights three examples demonstrating how this belief in health as a societal responsibility and government as a valuable partner has been applied in specific political debates and to specific policy issues.

Health insurance. One of the fundamental policy debates between those who view health as an individual or societal responsibility is whether and how to ensure that people have health insurance, and how comprehensive this insurance should be. The disagreement over the constitutionality of the individual mandate contained in the 2010 Patient Protection and Affordable Care Act (ACA) is just one example of how contentious such matters can be. The creation of health insurance exchanges in the ACA provides another example of how political philosophy shapes policy preferences. The act gives states the option of creating their own exchanges or allowing the federal government to create a state-based exchange for them. The fact such exchanges are a part of health care reform at all is an example of the debate over the role of government. Many liberals preferred a single-payer system or a public option (i.e., a government-run plan) but compromised with conservatives and accepted that the exchanges could expand coverage while maintaining free-market features.

The vision for the exchange varies depending on one's view of the role of government in health. Whereas conservative policymakers generally establish exchanges to operate as marketplaces with limited government involvement, liberals want the exchanges to take a more active role. Rather than open up the exchanges to any insurance company, some states are more heavily regulating what types of plans are allowed to be sold. An extreme version of this is Vermont's efforts to build its exchange in such a way as to facilitate the establishment of a state-wide single-payer system. Governor Peter Shumlin signed legislation in May 2011 outlining a plan to detach insurance status from employment, standardize fees, and route all payments through a single government entity. The state plans to set up an exchange by the ACA's 2014 deadline and then request federal waivers to transition to the new system by 2017.

Related to the debates over the exchanges are disagreements over how comprehensive the essential benefits packaged required under the ACA should be. Those who would prefer that government stay out of the way of the market argue for a modest set of benefits and that insist people will pay for the level of coverage that is appropriate for their needs. Others cite the market failure arguments mentioned above and call for more comprehensive coverage.

Debates over rationing. The public sector should play the leading role in assuring access to health care. Whereas critics describe this approach as overly reliant on government and giving bureaucrats the power to ration care, health care services in the United States are already rationed in that the poor and uninsured are left to go without. It is better to have explicit rationing based on a (at least somewhat) transparent process than to have a system of implicit rationing based on the results of inherently unfair market forces.

The United States is not the only country to grapple with the question of what comprises basic services and how much of them to cover. Many look to the National Institute for Health and Clinical Excellence (NICE) in the United Kingdom as an example of how to involve government expertise in making such decisions. NICE is an independent organization commissioned to advise the National Health Service by determining whether treatments are funded according to supposedly objective thresholds of value and effectiveness; in other words, they are covered if the outcome is deemed worth the given price. Specifically, an incremental cost-effectiveness ratio (ICER) is calculated to estimate the cost of the procedure for each quality-adjusted life year (QALY) gained.

Much of the debate in the United States about basic services is centered on comparative effectiveness research (CER), which compares multiple methods of preventing, diagnosing, and treating health conditions, rather than looking at them one at a time. Proponents of CER believe that it improves the way clinical research is typically achieved. Some see it as a positive development toward promoting health care that weighs both the costs and benefits, as opposed to the current system, which generally ignores costs even if the benefit gained is marginal. Advocates of this approach have been cautious, settling for incremental advances and taking care not to sound ideological alarms about rationing. This is challenging given that the mere mention of CER is enough to trigger such alarms.

The American Recovery and Reinvestment Act of 2009 allocated $1.1 billion over two years to CER, making it the largest investment in CER to date. The key difference between CER in the United States and NICE in the United Kingdom, is that under CER American agencies have no authority to act on their findings by changing how money is spent. For example, they have no ability to cut Medicare or Medicaid funding for procedures deemed to be cost-ineffective. Still, CER is a positive step for the public sector in its role to improve societal health.

Interestingly, the U.S. government's Agency for Healthcare Research and Quality (AHRQ) describes CER in terms of empowering personal decision making within the context of an inefficient market. As is outlined on the agency's website, "When you shop for a new car, phone or camera, you have lots of information about your choices. But when it comes to choosing the right medicine or the best health care treatment, clear and dependable information can be very hard to find. You deserve the best and most objective information about treating your sickness or condition. With this research in hand, you and your doctor can work together to make the best possible treatment choices." By framing CER as critical to and meaningful for individuals, AHRQ at once recognizes that individual decisions have an impact on population health, and addresses the strategic hope that, when it is framed in this way, libertarians may be less likely to oppose the policy.

Obesity. Although it is true that people who have high-caloric intake and low levels of physical activity are generally more likely to be obese, such factors are often socially constrained because people's choices are limited. In this sense, obesity is a societal issue. For example, it is difficult for residents of downtown Detroit—where high-calorie, high-sodium, and low-fiber processed foods are both widely available and affordable—to make healthy choices when there are so few grocery stores with fresh food available to them. In these food deserts, fast-food restaurants and junk food can seem like the best available option, particularly where gas stations and corner stores accept food stamps.

Those who support government intervention in health care matters advocate spending taxpayer money and increasing the regulation of businesses in order to combat this social problem. In some cases, the strategy is to completely remove options harmful to health, exemplified by efforts in some states to ban vending machines in elementary schools and regulate their content in middle and high schools. Interestingly, this has been framed in terms of individual autonomy, in that it empowers parents to help children make healthier choices. In other cases, the strategy is to increase the availability of information and healthy options, such as mandating menu labeling at restaurants or building foot and bike paths. Providing individuals with more information and options empowers them to make better decisions.

Because obesity has multiple societal-level causes, no single solution is likely to bring about sufficient change. Advocates adopt multi-faceted strategies pushing for change across multiple dimensions. Strategies to reduce obesity involve tailored approaches to working with, for example, schools, the food industry, employers, and health care providers. One of the challenges for public agencies in general, and the federal government in particular, is the competing interests of diverse stakeholders. The government subsidizes the production and marketing of foods high in fat and sodium, while also urging Americans to eat healthier foods. The reduction of smoking rates among youth is often cited as a positive example of behavioral change brought about by a broad strategy of multiple interventions. The diffuseness of the effect of any one intervention, however, makes relying on a cost-benefit analysis for determining action untenable. In the case of obesity policy, the sum is greater than its parts. The decision to implement a single obesity-reducing policy is based as much, or more, on normative values of equity and justice as it is on "hard" evidence.

Achieving equity. One of the key principles animating the view that health is a social responsibility is that, although individual choice is still an important factor in determining one's health, the reality is that not everyone has the same options available to them, and the choices they make from among those options are highly socially determined. Individual autonomy is constrained or enhanced by a complex set of factors known as the social determinants of health. Those living in poverty are less likely to have access to healthy food sources and safe places to exercise. They also face different challenges in securing health insurance and access to health services than do those not in poverty. Those with little education have lower levels of health literacy; that is, even if they are able to access health care, they are less likely to understand and apply their caregiver's advice. Racial and ethnic barriers operate at multiple levels and affect whether a physician understands the cultural context in which care is sought. These and other related inequities are part of cultural, institutional, and personal patterns of implicit and explicit discrimination.

Those who believe health to be a social responsibility argue that, to some extent, total individual autonomy is a fiction. Everyone is socially and economically connected to everyone else. Not only is it unjust to, say, let a poor person go without insurance or necessary care, it is unrealistic to claim that they are the only ones affected by poor health. Health problems that would have been addressed through relatively simple and inexpensive means become increasingly complicated and expensive the longer they are left untreated. These costs are ultimately shifted to insurance companies, leading to higher premiums for those who purchase insurance.

Although there is still debate over how to best go about it, government can play an important role in ensuring a basic level of health care services for all members of society. Information asymmetry and other deficiencies of the health care market lead to implicit rationing of health care services and limit the ability of the private sector to achieve desirable outcomes such as equity and efficiency.

CONCLUSION

Who is responsible for the health and health care of people in the United States? The libertarian perspective assigns accountability to the individual, while the alternative perspective largely ascribes this duty to society at large, with government as the main lever for bringing about societal change. An optimal solution draws from both perspectives. Individual autonomy and personal responsibility are essential cultural values celebrated in America, yet it is important that their limitations be acknowledged. In practical terms, this means recognizing the role and responsibility of government to ensure a basic level of health services.

Health and liberty are inextricably intertwined. Health is more than a biological state; it is a determinant of individual flourishing, without which it is difficult to exercise one's personal freedom. Therefore, individual health is a matter of pressing social concern. In addition, the costs imposed by the treatment of illness and the lost productivity that results from infirmity are borne by the nation as a whole. The ever-present threat of communicable disease is a social concern, as well. McGinnis and Foege attributed more than half of all deaths in 1990 to factors such as tobacco, diet and exercise, and microbial and toxic agents. These so-called "actual causes of death" suggest an active role for government in shaping policy guided by the notion that equity, solidarity, and distributive justice are all integral to the achievement of a healthy population.

In addition to raising questions of public policy, personal health also transcends the level of the individual, because spouses, families, and communities share the burden of illness and infirmity when they support and care for those whom they love. As social beings, human lives are predicated on their connections with others. Physical survival has always been contingent on the successful coordination of individuals. Atomistic individualism is a fiction. The lives people live, the freedoms they enjoy, and the health they experience are all contingent on the relationships they have with others. Although it is crucial to acknowledge the reality of individual rights and responsibilities regarding personal health, people must also recognize that family, society, and public policy all impact their very capacity to exercise these basic rights and responsibilities.

REFERENCES AND FURTHER READING

A much-debated health care proposal. (2009, August 14). *The New York Times.* Retrieved from http://www.nytimes.com/imagepages/2009/08/14/health/policy/14panelgraphic.ready.html

Agency for Healthcare Research and Quality. (n.d.). *What is comparative effectiveness research?* Washington, DC: U.S. Department of Health & Human Services. Retrieved from http://www.effectivehealthcare.ahrq.gov/index.cfm/what-is-comparative-effectiveness-research1

Allen, A. W. (2006, February 25). House panel doesn't buy ban on school vending sweets. *The Spokesman-Review.* Retrieved from http://news.google.com/newspapers?nid=1314&dat=20060225&id=021WAAAAIBAJ&sjid=FfMDAAAAIBAJ&pg=2040,2392448

Arrow, K. J. (1963). Uncertainty and the welfare economics of medical care. *The American Economic Review, 53*(5), 941–973.

Burd, S. (2009, June 12). How Safeway is cutting health-care costs. *The Wall Street Journal.* p. A14. Retrieved from http://online.wsj.com/article/SB124476804026308603.html

Centers for Disease Control and Prevention. (2011). *Obesity and overweight for professionals: U.S. obesity trends.* Retrieved from http://www.cdc.gov/obesity/data/trends.html

Chernew, M. E., & Newhouse, J. P. (2008). What does the RAND Health Insurance Experiment tell us about the impact of patient cost sharing on health outcomes? *The American Journal of Managed Care, 14*(7), 412.

Committee for the Future of the Public's Health in the 21st Century. (2002). *The future of the public's health in the 21st century.* Washington, DC: The National Academies Press.

Committee for the Study of the Future of Public Health. (1988). *The future of public health.* Washington, DC: The National Academies Press.

Daniels, N. (2008). *Just health: Meeting health needs fairly.* New York, NY: Cambridge University Press.

Durkheim, E., & Simpson, G. (1979). *Suicide: A study in sociology.* New York, NY: Free Press.

Gostin, L. O. (2007). Law as a tool to facilitate healthier lifestyles and prevent obesity. *The Journal of the American Medical Association, 297*(1), 87.

Gwatkin, D. R. (2001). The need for equity-oriented health sector reforms. *International Journal of Epidemiology, 30*(4), 720.

Hodge, J., Garcia, A., & Shah, S. (2008). Legal themes concerning obesity regulation in the United States: Theory and practice. *Australia and New Zealand Health Policy, 5*(1), 14.

Jacobs, L. R., & Skocpol, T. (2010). *Health care reform and American politics: What everyone needs to know.* New York, NY: Oxford University Press.

Jones, C. (2000). Levels of racism: A theoretic framework and a gardener's tale. *American Journal of Public Health, 90*(8), 1212–1215.

Kersh, R., & Morone, J. (2002). The politics of obesity: Seven steps to government action. *Health Affairs, 21*(6), 142.

Kirkland, A. R. (2008). *Fat rights: Dilemmas of difference and personhood.* New York, NY: New York University Press.

Light, D. W. (2009). Countervailing power: The changing character of the medical profession in the United States. In P. Conrad (Ed.), *The sociology of health and illness* (pp. 239–248). New York, NY: Worth Publishers.

Link, B. G., & Phelan, J. (1995). Social conditions as fundamental causes of disease. *Journal of Health and Social Behavior, 35,* 80–94.

Mari Gallagher Research & Consulting Group. (2007). *Examining the impact of food deserts on public health in Detroit.* Retrieved from http://www.marigallagher.com/site_media/dynamic/project_files/5_Det-Pages9-120nly.pdf

Marmot, M. (2007). Achieving health equity: From root causes to fair outcomes. *The Lancet, 370*(9593), 1153–1163.

McGinnis, J. M., & Foege, W. H. (1993). Actual causes of death in the United States. *The Journal of the American Medical Association, 270*(18), 2207.

McKinlay, J. B., & Marceau, L. D. (2009). The end of the golden age of doctoring. In P. Conrad (Ed.), *The sociology of health and illness: Critical perspectives* (pp. 213–238). New York, NY: Worth Publishers.

McKinlay, J. B., & McKinlay, S. M. (2009). Medical measures and the decline of mortality. In P. Conrad (Ed.), *The sociology of health and illness: Critical perspectives* (pp. 7–19). New York, NY: Worth Publishers.

Mello, M. M., Rimm, E. B., & Studdert, D. M. (2003). The Mclawsuit: The fast-food industry and legal accountability for obesity. *Health Affairs, 22*(6), 207.

Metzl, J. M., & Kirkland, A. (Eds.). (2010). *Against health: How health became the new morality.* New York, NY: New York University Press.

Mill, J. S. (1863). *On liberty.* Boston, MA: Ticknor and Fields.

Moffit, R. E. (1993). *A guide to the Clinton health plan: A checklist on vital national issues.* Washington, DC: Heritage Foundation.

Moss, M. (2010, November 6). While warning about fat, U.S. pushes cheese sales. *The New York Times.* Retrieved from http://www.nytimes.com/2010/11/07/us/07fat.html?pagewanted=all

National Research Council. (2003). *Unequal treatment: Confronting racial and ethnic disparities in health care* (B. D. Smedley, A. Y. Stith, & A. R. Nelson, Eds.). Washington, DC: National Academies Press.

Novak, W. J. (1996). *The people's welfare: Law and regulation in nineteenth-century America.* Chapel Hill, NC: University of North Carolina Press.

Oberlander, J. (2003). *The political life of Medicare.* Chicago, IL: University of Chicago Press.

Oliver, J. E. (2006). The politics of pathology: How obesity became an epidemic disease. *Perspectives in Biology and Medicine, 49*(4), 611–627.

Parmet, W. E. (2009). *Populations, public health, and the law.* Washington, DC: Georgetown University Press.

Rawls, J. A. (1999). *Theory of justice.* Cambridge, MA: Belknap Press of Harvard University Press.

Rubin, D. B. (2010). A role for moral vision in public health. *Hastings Center Report, 40*(6), 20–22.

Rutenberg, J., & Calmes, J. (2009, August 13). False death panel rumor has some familiar roots. *The New York Times.* Retrieved from http://www.nytimes.com/2009/08/14/health/policy/14panel.html

Sen, A. (2002). Why health equity? *Health Economics, 11*(8), 659–666.

Starfield, B. (2007). Pathways of influence on equity in health. *Social Science & Medicine, 64*(7), 1355–1362.

United Nations. (1948). *Universal declaration of human rights.* Retrieved from http://www.un.org/en/documents/udhr

Whitehead, M. (1992). The concepts and principles of equity and health. *International Journal of Health Services, 22*(3), 429–445.

Zenk, S. N., Schulz, A. J., Israel, B. A., James, S. A., Bao, S., & Wilson, M. L. (2005). Neighborhood racial composition, neighborhood poverty, and the spatial accessibility of supermarkets in metropolitan Detroit. *American Journal of Public Health, 95*(4), 660.

David Jones, Jodyn Platt, Daniel B. Rubin, and Peter D. Jacobson

The Role of the Market in Health Care

POINT: Market competition can lead to the efficient pricing and consumption of health care services.

Seth Freedman, Indiana University School of Public and Environmental Affairs and University of Michigan
Jill R. Horwitz, University of Michigan Law School

COUNTERPOINT: Unregulated free exchange is an inappropriate model for health care because of the numerous and fundamental failures associated with health care markets.

Seth Freedman, Indiana University School of Public and Environmental Affairs and University of Michigan
Jill R. Horwitz, University of Michigan Law School

Introduction

Given the importance of neoliberal economics to the ideological fabric of the United States, it's not surprising that so much of the debate surrounding health care reform focuses on the role of the market. The U.S. economic system relies on the market to distribute most goods and services. But even in well-functioning capitalist economies, government regulation is necessary to ensure that markets function properly. Indeed, the health care industry adheres to numerous market-oriented principles in the delivery of and payment for health care. Nevertheless, government regulation helps to structure the industry. Tension frequently exists over how much regulation, and what type of regulation, is appropriate. These debates continue today.

The health care market, some argue, would be best served by more fully allowing the market to bring efficiency to the production and consumption of health care goods and services, establishing the appropriate level of supply and demand. However, as many see it, the health care market is beset by significant imperfections that prevent it from functioning well. One of the main sources of these imperfections is the insurance industry, itself a product of free enterprise. Purchasing insurance as a means of dealing with an unknowable future can disrupt the theoretical functioning of the market by introducing moral hazard. As the Point states below, "insurance lowers the price that consumers see, causing them to make consumption choices based on these artificially lower prices, and by the usual law of demand, purchase more care at lower prices."

Another market failure relating to health insurance is the phenomenon of adverse selection: In a classic example of this phenomenon, those individuals who are more likely to buy insurance, or pay more for it, are those who know they are likely to need it. This, in turn, relates to another imperfection of the marketplace—asymmetric information; in this case, insurance companies don't have access to full information about their customers and are led to increase costs in an effort to even out their risk. The Counterpoint of this chapter states the most extreme outcome of this asymmetry and adverse selection as such: "When customers have different health risks and know more about their own health status than do insurers, insurers may raise the price so high that nobody will actually buy insurance. This happens because the insurer cannot tell which customers are the highest risks, so insurers must offer the same price to all customers."

Information asymmetry also limits the ability of patients—that is, consumers of health care—to properly value health care products and services. Physicians, nurses, and other providers have specialized knowledge outside the ken of the average patient. How do patients know whether their care is of high quality, or even adequate? Even if their health status improves, how can they know whether it was because of the care they received or because of some other unknown factor? And if they can't determine the quality of their care, how do they act in the rational way a market consumer is expected to—that is, how do they put an economic value on their treatment?

Another classic market failure that affects health care is that of externalities. These occur when the decisions of individuals affect others. For example, an individual's decision to forgo purchasing health insurance may result in a negative externality if that individual has an accident and requires health services that others will pay for. In this case, the externality is closely related to the phenomenon of free-riding. One might argue that the individual who rejects insurance acts as a free-rider, knowing that others will pay for her necessary medical care.

Externalities can also be positive, as in the case of many public goods. As the Counterpoint explains, once these goods are produced, individuals cannot be excluded from enjoying them. Moreover, one person's consumption of such a good doesn't limit the consumption by others. Many public goods relate to health. For example, the control of infectious diseases is a public good. It benefits everyone. Left to their own accord, markets will tend to underinvest in public goods.

Despite these market failures and imperfections, a strong case can be made, as is shown in the Point, for reducing health care regulation and allowing markets to establish appropriate levels of production and consumption. Indeed, some regulations can be seen as obstructive to what many would believe are positive health care outcomes. For instance, government-supplied health insurance and that provided by employers—with what many would say are perverse tax incentives—aggravate the moral hazard problem. And even licensing laws, though addressing to some extent the information asymmetry problem, can limit competition in the provider market, increase cost, and reduce innovation.

Faced with the limitations of the market and the problems introduced by regulation, policymakers are faced with three choices: (1) to remove regulations that interfere with or undermine the efficient functioning of the health care market (the libertarian solution), (2) to enact regulations that attempt to use market principles to improve the functioning of the market (as the Point suggests the Patient Protection and Affordable Care Act did), or (3) conclude that health care should not be treated as a market commodity at all.

Historically, it seems as if the United States has tried all three approaches, sometimes at the same time, and often in conflicting ways. For example, the country has not provided universal health insurance, and has left employer-provided insurance largely unregulated. These approaches seem to point to the policy approach expressed in the first choice above. Yet the United States has used antitrust laws and prospective payment schemes to try to perfect the market, in accordance with the middle approach. The nation has also required uncompensated care in emergency rooms, provided free care in public health clinics, and even instituted a form of universal coverage to veterans in the form of veterans integrated service networks, in accordance with the last option.

Does it make sense to employ all three approaches? Will doing so add to the complexity and dysfunction of the U.S. health care system? Or would such a multipronged approach respond appropriately to not just the complexity of the problems presented by the health care market but also to the ideological and political environment in which health care policy is made?

POINT

Despite imperfections in health care markets, competition can be harnessed to efficiently price and allocate health care. Either on its own or with government intervention, competition can generate prices that signal value and encourage appropriate transactions. Not only does the free market accord with legal tradition but market competition has also been a powerful tool in reducing health care costs, improving quality, and increasing access to care.

Many contemporary legal rights rest on the classical liberal vision of autonomous citizens pursuing their interests, free from improper interference from others and from the state. This conception of autonomous and free actors is particularly dominant in American laws related to bodily integrity. Patients are commonly conceived of as holding the right—indeed, even holding the moral responsibility—to determine the course of their own medical care. As Professor Carl Schneider has noted, in "the law governing medicine—the autonomy paradigm's prominence is plain. It is now a weary commonplace that 'Anglo-American law starts with the premise of thorough-going-self-determination' " (1998). Examples of this focus on individual autonomy abound in U.S. medical law. Consider the laws of informed consent, advance directives, and, more generally, tort law. Indeed, even if a physician's intervention leaves a patient better off, that physician may be found to have committed a battery if she operates on a patient without that patient's consent.

It is a short step from a liberty-based understanding of rights and its expression in health law to an embrace of the free-market exchange of health care goods and services. After all, who better to know whether and how much health service to acquire than the patient herself? This is why, according to the neoclassical model of economics, one can tell whether consumption of a particular good is in someone's best interest simply by observing whether they consume it. If they do, they must value the good. If they don't, they must not.

The idea of fully autonomous and informed patients shopping for medical services in a competitive health care market holds great appeal. In such an ideal world, those on the demand side (patients) would choose how much health care to consume, taking into account how they value health care relative to other goods and services like food, housing, and entertainment. These consumer-patients would only purchase health care services that provide value to them at a level greater than their price. Those on the supply side (providers) would take into consideration their costs of providing treatment and set a price which, if they were operating in a perfectly competitive market, would be set at a level no higher than those costs.

Patients and providers meeting in such a marketplace would exchange an efficient quantity of health care. That is, all transactions that would lead to the patient obtaining a benefit of greater value than the provider's cost of providing treatment would occur. Moreover, a marketplace based on repeat interactions between providers and consumers would lead to high quality; providers would build reputations, allowing consumers to choose only providers with good reputations, thereby allowing only high-quality providers to remain in the market. Such an ideal system would eliminate a great deal of waste, freeing up resources for more valuable purchases.

Many conditions, however, are required if markets are to work according to theory. For example, consumers must be fully informed and rational, all players must have knowledge about the quality of the products being sold, the market must be free from perverse incentives such as the widespread subsidies that lead to too much consumption of a good, and the market must be free of pricing distortions that come from taxes and other regulations.

As health economists have known for years—and behavioral economics has recently reminded us—the world does not always operate as theory suggests. In particular, many complications differentiate real-world markets from this archetype. Markets often do not work smoothly as theorized, and sometimes people do not or cannot know or act according to their own best interest. Challenges to seamless market competition, however, are particularly acute in health care markets.

First and foremost, although individuals may have a fairly accurate idea of their current health status, at what point in the future they will require health care, and what that health care will cost when they do, is unpredictable. As a result of this uncertainty, consumers typically rely on health insurance to pay for care because it allows them to shift their expenditures from a large, potentially unaffordable amount when a health shock occurs to smaller, evenly spaced insurance premium payments. But insurance leads to price distortions. Reliance on insurance also introduces additional parties to the health care transaction, including payers who come to the market with their own interests.

Second, even when a patient knows that he needs care, it is difficult to know which care and how much of it he should buy. The correct treatment is often uncertain, yet decisions often need to be made quickly. Moreover, many health care goods are experience goods, the characteristics of which cannot be observed until consumed—that is, until *after* the patient takes the treatment. And sometimes consumers cannot ascertain the quality of care they have received *even after treatment.* It is often hard to know whether a patient has recovered because of medical skill or some other cause.

Despite these imperfections, market forces can be harnessed to price and allocate health care efficiently. Even in imperfect markets, there is ample room for competition. Accordingly, this chapter discusses areas in which market forces themselves or regulation designed to harness market forces offer powerful tools for improving quality, cost, and access. Relying on Professor Meredith Rosenthal's research on market-oriented health policy interventions, this essay will outline the theoretical justifications for competition and consider the empirical evidence for its effectiveness. On the demand side of the market, the essay will consider market-based incentives that expose consumers to some portion of the price of their care or provide them with information. Also included is a consideration of supply-side market mechanisms in both insurance and provider markets.

In addition, the essay will highlight the use of market mechanisms in the Patient Protection and Affordable Care Act (ACA). Although it may seem odd to highlight a statute authorizing massive government intervention in health insurance and health care markets in an essay on the benefits of competition, one should bear in mind that regulation can take many forms. Sometimes regulation is used to give people what regulators think they need, an approach that undermines markets and can lead to increased inefficiencies. But regulation can also be used to tweak a market that would fail on its own and, thereby, allow the invisible hand to achieve improved outcomes. The essay will focus on those parts of the ACA that were designed to advance this latter goal.

DEMAND-SIDE MARKET MECHANISMS

Health care consumers face many uncertainties, though two seem deserving of particular consideration: (1) how much health care they will need, and (2) how to find a high-quality provider. The first uncertainty leads people to insure against unpredictable costs, allowing them to afford care when they need it. But insurance also induces inefficiently high demand through what is called "moral hazard." Because insurance shields consumers from the true cost of additional care, they will consume more care than they value. In other words, insurance lowers the price that consumers see, causing them to make consumption choices based on these artificially lower prices, and by the usual law of demand, purchase more care at lower prices. The second problem arises because patients have less information than do providers. Although many patients are able to choose their own providers, they do not typically know how to judge their quality in advance (and sometimes even after their care). Market mechanisms can be used to solve both problems.

Insurance, moral hazard, and the consumption of health care. Despite the problem of moral hazard, insurance provides value by allowing people to smooth income across different health states. And, although insurance is not the only way that patients could pay for health care, under the U.S. health care system insurance is the main mechanism by which they access health care.

This reliance leaves the problem of balancing the benefit of insurance and the costs of moral hazard. One way to address the problem would be to assign government regulators to determine which patients receive which treatments. However, such an approach removes treatment decisions from doctors and patients and would ignore individual differences in valuation. Alternatively, a market-oriented approach recognizes the root of the moral hazard problem and alters the incentives faced by patients. Health policy analysts colloquially refer to these approaches as ones that give patients "more skin in the game." Although there are many mechanisms to incentivize patients to demand less care, three are especially significant and worthy of further consideration here: (1) sharing the cost of insurance, (2) altering the tax incentives related to the purchase of insurance, and (3) increasing the incentives for the insured to prevent illness.

Cost-sharing and moral hazard. When patients face prices that rise with the cost of care, they are encouraged to choose only treatments for which the benefits exceed the cost. To this end, the RAND Health Insurance Experiment (1971–1986) tested the effects of various levels of cost sharing on patient demand. It randomized individuals into health plans that differed only in the rate at which patients shared in the cost of their care, and found that individuals facing a higher fraction of the cost of their care consumed less, often with no ill health effects.

There are many forms of cost sharing, all of which can lead to more efficient outcomes than heavier regulatory approaches because they all allow individuals to decide which treatments are most valuable to them. All the forms vary to the extent to which the consumer's price mirrors the actual price of care. Co-payments—small, fixed payments that patients pay when visiting a provider—can alter a patient's choice to visit the doctor, but do not affect decisions about the extent of care to consume once in the physician's office. Deductibles and coinsurance—in which patients pay a fraction of the total price of their care, in the former case the first dollars spent and in the latter case a flat percentage of the price—also change the incentives for a patient to seek care and the amount of care to consume more broadly. However, these plans are typically combined with a maximum expenditure amount beyond which the patient no longer pays, limiting the cost-sharing effects to early spending in an insurance cycle.

At the extreme are insurance plans with high deductibles where the patient absorbs the full cost of care up to a set level. These high-deductible plans can be combined with Health Savings Accounts (HSAs) in which the consumer sets aside pretax earnings to be used in the event of incurring health care costs. These accounts allow consumers to shift wealth from periods when they do not need care to periods in which they do, but they are still utilizing their own funds to pay for care and are therefore responsive to price. This option, however, is only available to those who are employed, and the tax benefits disproportionately go to employees in the higher tax brackets.

Although such incentives seem to work well at reducing spending, they often lead to reductions in care that is valuable as well as care that is of little worth. But market approaches can solve this problem as well. Value-based insurance design has been developed to increase cost sharing for lower-value treatments (e.g., those that show little clinical promise) and to decrease cost sharing for higher-value ones (e.g., those that show high levels of success). These plans attempt to incentivize the utilization of the most effective treatments while still allowing patients to make decisions based on their own interests.

Taxes and insurance. The insurance system has a number of other structural features to encourage consumers to demand too much care. However, these, too, can be addressed by market-based regulation. For example, in addition to individual insurance plans altering the incentives for consuming health care, the tax exclusion for employer-provided health insurance exacerbates the inefficiencies caused by individual health insurance. Because the purchase of health insurance through an employer is tax free for many employees, a dollar in health benefits is more valuable to employees than is a dollar in wages. This structure gives employees the incentive to demand and employers the incentive to provide more compensation in the form of benefits relative to wages. And, as explained above, the more generous the insurance coverage, the larger the incentive a beneficiary faces to consume care. So the current tax treatment of health insurance exacerbates moral hazard by further increasing the level of insurance above what the individual would choose if a dollar of health insurance had the same value as a dollar of wages. These incentives have large effects. Jonathan Gruber and James Poterba, for example, have shown that when self-employed individuals began receiving tax subsidies for purchasing insurance, a 1 percent decrease in the cost of the insurance increased the probability of its purchase by 18 percentage points.

The ACA partially addresses this regulatory distortion by imposing an excise tax on so-called "Cadillac" health plans. The tax is meant to discourage consumers from shielding themselves excessively from the cost of care and, therefore, demanding more care than they value. Beginning in 2018, a 40 percent tax will be charged on the portion of a plan exceeding $10,200 for individuals or $27,500 for families. Many health policy experts have noted that an even more efficient level of health insurance purchase could be achieved if the tax deduction was completely removed, and have advocated for such a policy despite the possibility that fewer people would buy insurance.

Workplace wellness. More and more employers have introduced workplace wellness programs to help employees identify their individual health risks and take steps to address them. These programs typically provide financial incentives for employees to engage in health-promoting activities such as quitting smoking, exercising regularly, eating healthy foods, and decreasing stress. More than half of all large employers already offer some kind of incentive-based wellness program, and the ACA makes it easier for employers to enact or expand them.

Although there are moral justifications for these programs, for example those based on personal responsibility and avoidable illnesses, their underlying economic goal is to prevent employees from externalizing the costs of their unhealthy behaviors onto their co-workers. Because employees are grouped in insurance pools, each employee's health behaviors can raise (or lower) the costs of care for the pool, thus raising (or lowering) the premiums paid by others in the pool. Adjusting premiums according to health behaviors helps internalize some of the costs of employee's unhealthy behaviors by raising the price of unhealthy behaviors like smoking, living a sedentary lifestyle, or overeating.

The role of information in demand for quality and public reporting. In addition to the distortions that arise from the unpredictable need for care and the corresponding need for insurance, health care consumers also face considerable difficulty identifying high-quality medical providers. Quality in health care has many dimensions, making it difficult for consumers to find, interpret, and verify information about a provider's quality. Indeed, unlike more conventional goods, it is difficult to identify quality care. Is it care that satisfies a patient's desires? Is it care that corresponds with professional treatment recommendations? Or care that achieves particular, measurable outcomes?

Moreover, health insurance leads to another trade-off. Although it allows people to purchase the care they need when sick, by limiting the role of price in a consumers' decision-making process, health insurance makes it even more difficult for patients to choose high-quality medical providers. In a typical market, price tends to signal quality. If a seller is competing against other suppliers of a similar good but charges a higher price, it is likely the case that other buyers have revealed a willingness to pay more for that particular seller's product. Health care providers, on the other hand, do not advertise price or compete for patients through price, so price is uninformative to consumers about a provider's quality. Market mechanisms, such as employer efforts to amass quality information, provider report cards, and disease-management techniques, can be useful in addressing the uncertainty regarding the quality of care.

Publicly available quality reports can help create a market in which providers compete through these available quality measures. These reports come in various forms. The nonprofit National Committee for Quality Assurance, for example, accredits high-quality provider organizations and publishes online report cards. In addition, employers have leveraged their role as purchasers to assemble and publish provider-quality information. Through organizations such as The Leapfrog Group, they have sought to improve safety for their employees by making quality information accessible and transparent. Moreover, *U.S. News and World Reports* ranks the country's "Best Hospitals." In 2005 the Hospital Quality Alliance and Centers for Medicare & Medicaid Services launched the Hospital Compare website, which provides self-reported information on compliance with recommended processes for patient treatment. Some states, such as New York, produce annual reports on patient outcomes by hospital and surgeon.

The idea underlying these reports is that armed with such information, patients can decide where to get treatment. Providers will respond by improving their quality to compete for patients. Although patient attention to such reports is growing, there is evidence that few patients know about them or rely on them. However, Ashish Jha and Arnold Epstein have recently shown that public reporting has caused poorly performing surgeons to exit the market. Perhaps this is because the surgeons feared losing market share.

Quality reports must be introduced into the market with care, particularly in terms of adequate risk adjustment. If ratings are not adjusted to account for the seriousness of patients' condition or comorbidities, information-facilitated competition may harm patients. For example, providers might avoid high-risk patients or selectively target the reported measures at the expense of other unreported measures. Therefore, some patients who would have gotten care without report cards may not get care where report cards are used to facilitate patient choice. Nonetheless, several sections in the ACA and the Health Information Technology for Economic and Clinical Health (HITECH) Act encourage or require the production of public information with which consumers can choose providers based on quality. For example, the ACA includes improvements to the Physician Quality Reporting System, which provides incentive payments to providers who report data on quality measures to the Centers for Medicare & Medicaid Services and the public reporting of physician quality information through a new Physician Compare Internet website.

SUPPLY-SIDE MARKET MECHANISMS

Competitive market arrangements are not only helpful in solving problems that cause inefficiencies on the demand side of health care markets where consumers are insured but they are also useful for increasing the availability and quality of care on the supply side. There are myriad examples of market competition—and challenges to effective market competition—on the supply side. Perhaps most obviously, in the case of hospitals and other large providers, the suppliers compete in oligopoly or monopoly markets. It is neither realistic nor desirable to allow more hospitals to enter where there is little need. On the other hand, restricting competition may inflate prices and decrease quality of care.

As in the demand-side discussion above, this section will focus on a few examples in which policymakers have used markets to encourage the efficient provision of accessible, affordable, and quality care on the supply side. First, the section will consider the suppliers of insurance and focus on a critical issue that always confronts health care markets—that many people remain uninsured because they cannot afford health insurance, particularly if they become sick and insurance providers adjust prices to reflect those illnesses. Following is a discussion of the perhaps counter-intuitive idea that private, individual insurance markets based on competition have advantages over alternative policies. Second, the section will turn to medical providers and a discussion of the theoretical and empirical evidence supporting the importance of maintaining a competitive provider market. Despite the advantages of competitive provider markets, there are important flaws in such markets. For example, providers have an informational advantage over patients and insurers, which can lead providers to supply excess care to increase profits. However, as was outlined in the demand-side discussion, market mechanisms can be brought to bear to mitigate these perverse incentives while preserving the benefits of competition.

Insurance markets. Americans obtain their health insurance coverage from various sources, including federal and state governments, employers, and private insurance firms. Most Americans take up employment-based health insurance from the large firms where they work. This makes a great deal of sense. Large groups make insurance more feasible because the risk of unexpected expenditures by a particular individual can be spread over a wide pool of premium payers. But this arrangement leaves those who are ineligible for government-sponsored insurance with few options. Indeed, the vast majority of the uninsured population is made up of those who are employed by small firms, who are self-employed, or who are unemployed. Without the option of group insurance, they must seek coverage from the individual market where there are high premiums partially due to insufficient risk pooling.

Accordingly, one of the central features of the ACA is the implementation of state-based health insurance exchanges. These provide a framework to thicken private insurance markets through statewide risk pooling. By regulating benchmark benefit levels and instituting new rating rules and guaranteed issue requirements, the exchanges prevent insurers from cherry picking the least risky individuals and pricing higher-risk individuals out of the market. In essence, the insurance exchanges allow consumers access to a market in which they can compare like products on the basis of quality and cost.

These regulations provide a structure for a competitive insurance market to function where it had previously been subject to many market failures. At the same time, the system exploits the benefits of a competitive market relative to a government-run single payer. For example, instead of having access to only one insurance plan, individuals will have several plans to choose from and will be able to make independent decisions about which best fits their needs. The limits on preexisting condition clauses and other methods of cherry picking mean that insurers need to compete in a more productive manner for consumers. The new market structures give insurers incentives to compete for consumers by innovating and introducing various types of products to consumers, thereby increasing consumer choice. Finally, because individuals are seeking care from private providers with their own private insurance, the restrictions and wait times associated with some single-payer systems in which regulators can explicitly control the supply of care are avoided. Instead, care decisions are made in the context of the marketplace based on the insurance and provider chosen by the patient.

In addition to the exchanges required by the ACA are alternative approaches to improve individual insurance markets and exploit the advantages of market forces. For example the Patient Choice Act, introduced by Republicans prior to the passage of the ACA, proposed to eliminate the tax benefits of employer-sponsored insurance and provide all individuals and families with a tax rebate to use towards purchasing their insurance. The goal of this plan was to eliminate the distortion of tax-preferred health benefits and stimulate the individual market by subsidizing the costs to insureds of insurance premia.

Despite changes introduced by the ACA, regulatory limits to competition on the supply side of insurance markets persist. For example, some scholars such as Stephen Parente and colleagues have argued that the individual insurance market is limited because it is regulated at the state level and cannot operate across state lines, and not because of inherent problems with the individual market. By simulating national health insurance markets, they have concluded that several million uninsured individuals would take up insurance in a national market, although that insurance might be of low quality. For these and other reasons, the ACA allows states to create health care choice compacts through which insurers can market policies across state lines as long as they offer coverage and affordability similar to what is offered on the exchanges.

All of these market-oriented proposals are aimed at making insurance accessible for individuals who are not offered employer-sponsored health insurance. Similar mechanisms may also be used to separate insurance from employment, and allow everyone to purchase insurance from the open marketplace. As discussed above, the tax-preferred status of employee-sponsored health insurance distorts the level of health care consumed. The employment-based nature of health insurance may also have distortionary effects on the labor market itself. Indeed, a large empirical literature has shown that health insurance affects retirement decisions and decreases job mobility, though it is not clear to what extent the costs of these impacts outweigh the benefits of employer-sponsored insurance. More research in this area and many related policy changes would be needed, but if market mechanisms can be used to make individual insurance markets more efficient, individual markets could potentially become large enough to ease the separation of insurance from employment.

Medical provider markets. There are many kinds of market failures that arise on the provider side of markets for medical care. However, rather than replacing markets with government provision of care or direct regulation of care decisions, regulatory interventions can be used to improve competition in markets, thereby increasing efficiency. In a standard market, firms compete to sell an identical product, leaving suppliers with the single decision of how to price the product. However, in the real world, many markets' products are not identical—in addition to setting prices, firms can differentiate the product they sell.

Health care providers do not provide identical products; the quality and type of care they offer differs a great deal. This raises the question of how competition in health markets affects the level of quality provided. Not surprisingly, economic theory on this question is quite complicated, and often leads to ambiguous predictions. In an unregulated market in which providers set their own prices, a monopolist may under-supply or over-supply quality relative to the socially optimal level. The analysis is simpler when prices are set by a regulator, as is the case for Medicare participating providers. In this case, as long as price exceeds the marginal cost of providing a service, competition unambiguously leads to additional quality. Theory predicts that, when providers lose the ability to compete on price, quality becomes the only relevant margin, and, thus, quality increases to attract patients.

There are important caveats to the theory regarding competition over quality, however. First, in practice, quality signals can be obscured by the complex conditions of markets in the real world. In addition, while this increase in quality may be good for individual patients, it is possible for competition of this sort to lead to quality that, from a social perspective, is too high. For example, competition between hospitals can lead to an arms race, in which they both purchase the newest, most-expensive equipment and spend more on upgrading their facilities than the overall value to patients of the upgrades.

Consistent with theoretical research that has generated mixed predictions, in their extensive review of the empirical evidence regarding competition in health care markets, Martin Gaynor and Robert Town report somewhat mixed results. Among privately insured patients, some studies find that competition improves patient outcomes, while others find the opposite effect or no effect at all. However, most studies of Medicare patients find improved patient outcomes in more competitive hospital markets. Another body of research has found that competition leads to greater capacity and service provision. Finally, hospitals in less-competitive markets tend to charge higher prices as well. That being said, most of these empirical studies are unable to determine the overall cost or benefit to society of these effects.

There has been a long history of regulatory efforts to intervene in provider markets to mimic the incentives offered by competitive markets or ordinary goods. For example, the development of health maintenance organizations (HMOs) and related structures starting in the 1970s was meant to encourage providers to attend to the costs of care by paying providers under capitation arrangements rather than through payments for each service.

Pay for performance and value-based purchasing represent two more recent efforts to harness market forces to improve quality of care. Both concepts rest on a similar and simple premise; rather than paying providers for the provision of a service based on its volume and time regardless of quality and outcomes, as payment systems in the United States have traditionally done, payers should adjust their payments to reward health care providers for meeting quality goals and penalize them when they do not. Research on early pay-for-performance programs have found mixed evidence of their effectiveness in improving care.

Nonetheless, Title III of the ACA includes extensive application of the incentive pay programs to a huge swath of the health care sector. Value-based purchasing ties Medicare payments to quality measures. By shifting payments from the quantity of care to the quality of care, providers face stronger incentives to maximize quality. Additionally, public quality reporting changes the landscape of competition. To compete for patients, providers must enhance their quality.

The ACA also promotes shared savings programs which use financial incentives to encourage Medicare providers to increase quality and control costs. The program allows providers to form groups (known as ACOs or accountable care organizations) to keep some of the financial savings they generate through low-cost and high-quality care. The ACA also experiments with various types of bundled payment systems that aim to work in a similar manner as the Medicare Prospective Payment System (PPS) that focused on episodes of care rather than particular interventions.

Health care markets involve markets for an enormous variety of goods and services, ranging from service and labor markets to product markets, such as markets for pharmaceuticals and durable medical equipment. Despite the failures that characterize these markets to a greater or lesser extent, competition can be an effective way to involve consumer preferences in the creation of accessible and high-quality medical care.

Note: The authors thank Nicholas Bagley and Edward Norton for their helpful comments.

REFERENCES AND FURTHER READING

Akerloff, G. A. (1970). The market for "lemons": Quality and the market mechanism. *The Quarterly Journal of Economics, 84*(3), 488.

Arrow, K. J. (1863). Uncertainty and the welfare economics of medical care. *The American Economic Review, 53*(5), 941.

Dranove, D., & Zhe Jin, G. (2010). Quality disclosure and certification: Theory and practice. *Journal of Economic Literature, 48*(4), 935.

Epstein, R. A. (1997). *Mortal peril: Our inalienable right to health care?* Reading, MA: Addison-Wesley.

Gaynor, M., & Town, R. J. (2011). *Competition in health care markets.* National Bureau of Economic Research Working Paper No. 17208.

Gruber, J., & Madrian, B. C. (2004). Health insurance, labor force participation, and job mobility: A critical review of the literature. In C. McLaughlin (Ed.), *Health policy and the uninsured.* Washington, DC: Urban Institute Press.

Gruber, J., & Poterba, J. (1994). Tax incentives and the decision to purchase health insurance: Evidence from the self-employed. *The Quarterly Journal of Economics, 109*(3), 701.

Hurley, J. (2000). An overview of the normative economics of the health sector. In A. J. Culyer & J. P. Newhouse (Eds.), *Handbook of health economics* (Vol. 1A, pp. 55–118). New York, NY: Elsevier.

Jha, A., & Epstein, A. M. (2006). The predictive accuracy of the New York state coronary artery bypass surgery report-card system. *Health Affairs, 25*(3), 844.

Madison, K. M. (2009). The law and policy of health care quality reporting. *Campbell Law Review, 31*, 215–255.

Manning, W. G., Newhouse, J. P., Duan, N., Keeler, E. B., & Leibowitz, A. (1987). Health insurance and the demand for medical care: Evidence from a randomized experiment. *The American Economic Review, 77*(3), 251.

Newhouse, J. P., & The Insurance Experiment Group. (1992). *Free for all? Lessons from the RAND health insurance experiment.* Cambridge, MA: Harvard University Press.

Parente, S. T., Feldman, R., Abraham, J., & Xu, Y. (2011). Consumer response to a national marketplace for individual health insurance. *Journal of Risk and Insurance, 78*(2), 389.

Pauly, M. V. (1986). Taxation, health insurance, and market failure in the medical economy. *Journal of Economic Literature, 24*(2), 629.

Rosenthal, M. (2009). What works in market-oriented health policy. *New England Journal of Medicine, 360*(21), 2157.

Rothschild, M., & Stiglitz, J. (1976). Equilibrium in competitive insurance markets. *Quarterly Journal of Economics, 90*(4), 629.

Schneider, C. E. (1998). *The practice of autonomy: Patients, doctors, and medical decisions.* New York, NY: Oxford University Press.

Seth Freedman and Jill R. Horwitz

COUNTERPOINT

Market competition is a powerful concept. Allocating goods and services through a decentralized system in which consumers decide what they want to buy and suppliers decide what they want to sell based on market prices can maximize overall well-being. It is generally better for consumers to decide what they want to eat or wear and suppliers to decide what and how much they want to innovate and offer than it is for government to make decisions for them. Indeed, alternative systems in which government officials have allocated goods and services have generated lower standards of living than is the case in market economies.

Not surprisingly, however, market competition does not always work as magically as theory predicts. The inherent and fundamental market failures associated with health care markets mean that unregulated health care markets would lead to many distressing outcomes. Absent government intervention, for example, an even larger percentage of the population than is currently uninsured would be unable to afford health care. Physicians and hospitals would supply and patients would demand excessive and costly medical treatments. The result would likely be lower vaccination rates that would put the population at higher risk of infectious disease outbreaks.

Recognizing the risks of an unregulated health care market, many observers argue that governments should intervene in the provision of health care because health care, and even health itself, is a human right and that it is intolerable for a civilized society to deny its citizens access to it. Correspondingly, Article 25(1) of the Universal Declaration of Human Rights, which was adopted by the United National General Assembly in 1948, states, "Everyone has the right to a standard of living adequate for the health and well-being of himself and of his family, including food, clothing, housing and medical care." Some would go further, arguing that people not only have a right to access to care but also a responsibility to consume it.

Regardless of any philosophical or political justifications for government regulation in health care markets, the economics of those markets offer a compelling justification for extensive government intervention. Accordingly, this essay focuses only on the economic case for rejecting the free-market provision of health care goods.

Why does free-market competition work so well for commodities like clothing, televisions, paperback books, or automobiles but so poorly for health care? One reason is that health care is innately different from these other goods, and these differences generate market failures that are particularly hard to solve. Moreover, the conditions that need to be met for free-market competition to work well do not hold in the health care context. Unlike in well-functioning, competitive markets, health care consumers are not fully informed, all players in the market do not have knowledge about the quality of the goods being sold, health care markets are filled with perverse incentives, and there are multiple price distortions stemming from tax policy and other regulations.

This section will identify and examine the economic failures characteristic of health care markets, and it will argue, on economic terms alone, that these failures make it inappropriate to provide health care through unregulated markets. Such market failures suggest that in health care, unlike in many other markets, the appropriate quantity and quality of product consumed and provided cannot be determined by market forces. The section will proffer several specific examples of the need for extensive regulation of health care markets because of (1) the effects of health insurance, (2) provider market failures, and (3) externalities and other public goods.

Before turning to market failures that arise in health care markets and the promising regulatory interventions that can be implemented to address them, this section will briefly mention one other type of important challenge to reliance on the free-market exchange of goods and services that apply to many markets but may be particularly acute in health care markets. In many cases, decision makers do not act according to the foundational, behavioral assumptions of competitive market theories such as using strict logic rather than "rules of thumb" to make decisions, acting according to consistent valuation of utility over time (i.e., applying consistent discount rates regardless of time frames), and acting so as to maximize wealth.

Both firms and individuals, however, exhibit what is known as nonstandard behavior. For example, they use heuristics to make decisions when faced with incomplete information, have preferences for conducting transactions with particular parties, engage in routinized behaviors, and tend to prefer near-term to long-term income. Such behavior occurs in many markets, but there is good reason to suspect that nonstandard behavior is acute in health care markets given the emotional valence of illness compared to, for example, buying a quart of milk.

To get a sense of how these common behaviors affect health care markets, consider how patients, their families, and medical providers often behave when a patient is diagnosed with a dreaded disease like cancer. Many decisions need to be made quickly and under a great deal of uncertainty and stress, and these decisions depend on the proclivities and experiences of all the parties involved. Physicians will recommend treatment based on the culture of the hospital in which they operate. Patients and family members may ask questions based on the information they recently heard about new treatments. And all of this will be complicated by race, gender, and class relationships among patients, family members, nurses, and doctors.

COMPLICATIONS INTRODUCED BY INSURANCE

In well-functioning competitive markets, consumers know what goods they need, and they have reasonably full information regarding their quality and how to obtain them. Health care, however, is complicated by several types of uncertainty. Unlike with shelter or food, for example, people typically cannot predict how much care they will need in either the short or the long term because both individual health and the development of treatments are uncertain. They may find themselves not needing a physician's services at all beyond routine primary care. Or they may have an expensive emergency room visit or begin to need expensive pharmaceuticals. Or they may be lucky and be diagnosed with a disease just as a new and effective treatment comes along. All that is certain is that the need for health care is inevitable for almost everybody at some point in their lives, and it is commonly too expensive for most people to pay for it out of pocket. This kind of uncertainty means that most health care is paid for with insurance, adding additional layers of complication to the health care market.

Insurance plays an important role by allowing people access to health care when they become sick; however, absent government intervention, private insurance markets have a hard time providing affordable coverage for all consumers who would like to purchase insurance. The failure of private insurance markets stems from two important gaps between the consumer's information and the insurer's information. At the time of purchase, an insurer is sometimes better than or sometimes worse than the consumer at predicting the consumer's likely future medical expenditures. In addition, once insurance has been purchased, it is difficult for an insurer to monitor the amount of care the patient chooses to consume.

The need for risk pooling. The result of these information gaps between insurers and their customers is that the private market has a difficult time providing coverage for many groups of people. First, insurance markets exhibit a classic example of what is called adverse selection. When customers have different health risks and know more about their own health status than do insurers, insurers may raise the price so high that nobody will actually buy insurance. This happens because insurers cannot tell which customers are the highest risks, so they must offer the same price to all customers. At any given price (i.e., premium level), there are likely to be some people (such as the young and healthy) who decide insurance is not worth it. Because their expected need for care is so low, insurance at the offered price is not a good value for them. As these low-risk customers exit the pool, insurers must raise their price to reflect the expected costs of their remaining, higher-risk customers. Facing this higher price, a whole new set of individuals may decide insurance is no longer worth purchasing. This adverse selection "death spiral" can potentially lead to a total collapse of the insurance market.

Alternatively, there are cases where insurers have an advantage in predicting an individual's health care expenditures. In these cases, profit-maximizing insurers (indeed, even nonprofit insurers) have incentives to deny coverage to individuals whose costs are likely to exceed their premium payments. Therefore, insurers have the incentive to provide coverage only to the lowest-risk customers, a practice that is known as "cream-skimming." This leads insurers to charge extremely high prices to higher-risk consumers, precisely the group most in need of insurance.

Both adverse selection and cream-skimming make it difficult for higher-risk groups to obtain coverage in unregulated markets. Regulation has addressed this problem for some people. For example, employer-sponsored insurance programs operate under regulations, known as community rating, that require insurers to offer the same price to all customers, regardless of their health status. In some cases, prices can be differentiated by certain demographic groups or characteristics such as smoking status, but the idea is to limit the ability of insurers to exclude higher-risk individuals by charging them much higher prices.

These interventions have not solved the problem for everybody, even everyone with access to employer-sponsored coverage, inasmuch as community rating accentuates the problem of adverse selection. Because insurers cannot offer lower rates to low-risk customers, some of those customers will not purchase insurance at all or will flee high-coverage plans, forcing overall prices to rise in the most comprehensive plans. Adverse selection and cream-skimming become even more important for individuals without access to employer-sponsored insurance. Because these individuals do not have built-in groups with which to pool risk, they are usually charged much higher premiums than are people with employer-sponsored insurance.

The federal and state governments have intervened directly to provide insurance for individuals with limited access to employer plans. In particular, through Medicare the federal government provides insurance coverage for the elderly and chronically ill, both groups more likely than others to need care. The Medicaid program, which is a joint federal-state program, provides insurance to many who are poor and disabled. States and, under the Patient Protection and Affordable Care Act (ACA), the federal government also operate high-risk pools to provide insurance at affordable levels for those who cannot get coverage elsewhere because of serious medical conditions.

The ACA goes further in providing regulations to prevent the unraveling of insurance markets for individuals and other groups not able to purchase insurance from their employer. For example, the statute requires insurers to offer coverage regardless of individual health status, thus preventing them from barring the highest-risk individuals from the insurance coverage they need. It also provides for risk-adjustment mechanisms so that health insurers do not suffer from attracting a disproportionate share of patients who consume expensive health care. The ACA does this, in part, by requiring many insurers to offer a comparable set of benefits and by requiring transfer payments among insurers to equalize the effects of the health status of enrollees. In its most controversial policy, the ACA also mandates insurance coverage for all individuals. By compelling low-risk individuals to buy insurance and join the insurance pool, the effects of adverse selection can be mitigated and affordable insurance coverage made available for all.

Moral hazard and the patient who demands too much. Health insurance is valuable and desirable. It provides financial protection against the uncertain risk of needing expensive medical care, allowing people to smooth their income over time and pay a small premium in every period, rather than nothing when healthy and a potentially unaffordable amount when sick. In the United States, health insurance is also inextricably linked to access to medical care. Although it is not the only arrangement that allows people to consume health care services when they need them, as a policy matter it is the one most relied upon.

This financial protection and method of accessing care, however, come at a cost. Once insured, consumers no longer face the full price of the care they receive, and they therefore consume more than a standard supply-and-demand analysis would deem an optimal amount. Instead of comparing their valuation of care to its true cost, patients make their choice based on the price they face after insurance. This induces them to consume care they value less than the cost of care— that is, care they purchase only because they have insurance but would not purchase if they were uninsured but still had the funds to pay out of pocket. Though this phenomenon is labeled moral hazard, it is rational for insured patients to consume more of a good that they can purchase for far less than the full price.

This excess demand is not merely theoretical. The RAND Health Insurance Experiment found empirical evidence of this moral hazard effect (Newhouse & The Insurance Experiment Group, 1992). This experiment illustrated that patients demand less care as they face more of its actual cost. Of course, providing the financing to pay for care when it is needed is the point of insurance. But one cost of insurance is that patients demand care that is both necessary and unnecessary because insurance pays for it.

As a result, regulations and insurance design that forces patients (and their physicians) to internalize some of the cost of their care through mechanisms like deductibles, co-payments, and quality regulation are necessary elements of insurance markets. These regulations help society balance the cost of care with the benefits it achieves. While these mechanisms allow consumers to continue receiving the important financial protection of insurance and obtain necessary medical care, they help prevent the inefficient use of care that offers little value relative to its cost.

PROVIDER MARKET FAILURES

Uncertainty and information asymmetries also have important effects on provider markets. In addition to uncertainty over how much health care an individual will need, once care is needed, diagnosis and treatment are uncertain. This is considerably different from typical goods in that, with health care, consumers often do not initially know the true value of what they are purchasing. Moreover, even after a patient purchases and consumes health care, he does not necessarily know its value. Did the patient get better because of the treatment or because he was lucky? Perhaps he was not sick in the first place; the doctor had misdiagnosed him and the intervention did nothing at all. Because the value of health care is difficult to know, it is difficult to assess the costs and benefits of additional treatments.

In addition to such information asymmetries between patients and insurers, the information gaps between patients and providers also affect the quality and quantity of care provided. In fact, unregulated health care markets can lead to lower quality or an excess provision of care.

Because physicians typically hold expert information about health and treatment that patients do not, patients cannot fully monitor the decisions of their physicians. Therefore, physicians may shirk on the quality of care they provide or prescribe unnecessary care for the sake of financial benefits. These issues are compounded by the fact that providers are paid by insurance companies and not directly by consumers. Therefore, even if their goal is to maximize their patients' health, physicians may still face conflicting financial incentives because of their relationship with insurers.

Quality of care. Unlike in markets for other goods, it is difficult for patients to judge the quality of their providers or the care they provide. Physicians and nurses have professional training beyond the reach of patients, and even if patients were able to educate themselves to some degree about medical treatments, it would still be hard for them to find high-quality providers or to judge the care they receive. And because most health care is paid for by insurance and not the patient directly, providers cannot advertise on the basis of price in order to signal quality, as in other markets. One solution to help patients more effectively shop for medical care is to mandate the public release of information about provider quality. State-mandated report cards and public reporting requirements adopted in the ACA follow this approach. But there are limits to this market-based approach. To be useful, the rankings must be accurate. If they do not reflect quality of care, but rather the health status of a provider's patient population or the, potentially inaccurate, reputation of providers, such rankings will not be reliable indicators of quality. Moreover, patients need to have the time and skill to find and interpret the ratings.

The limitations of relying on consumer demand to ensure quality is one reason why regulations often constrain entry into health care markets. Legal constraints, like licensing, certification, and rules governing the patient-provider relationship, prevent untrained providers from entering the business. Licensing, for example, can directly ensure that minimum quality standards are met and indirectly lessen the competitive incentives for physicians to act in their own best interest when doing so might not be best for patients. This makes good sense, inasmuch as society does not want people to be able to perform surgery just because they think they might be good with a knife; nor does it want restaurant owners trying their hand at the hospital business because they think they might make more money. Unregulated markets would put patients at a risk they cannot protect themselves against alone.

Finally, there are a host of legal rules that protect patients that do not apply in other markets. For example, informed-consent laws require providers to spell out the potential consequences of the treatment that patients are about to buy. Several procedures are typically required before treatment is provided, unlike most markets in which we rely on consumers to protect themselves. Similarly, in other labor markets, contractors can simply walk off the job if they wish to quit, particularly if a customer cannot pay their bill. Because we are worried about protecting the health of patients, physicians must continue to provide care to even the most troublesome of patients until either the patient fires the doctor or the physician ensures that the patient has adequate time to find alternative, sufficient treatment.

Quantity of care. Information asymmetries between patients and providers can also have important implications for the quantity of care provided. Physicians often face financial incentives to exploit their informational advantage and order unnecessary tests or choose additional or more expensive treatment options than a fully informed patient would choose in order to generate additional income. These physician incentives are particularly prominent when physicians are reimbursed based on the amount of care provided to the patient, a method known as fee-for-service. Even after a treatment decision is made, it is difficult for patients to monitor whether a doctor's decisions were necessary or not. Whereas consumers, because of advertising, may be tempted to buy more video games than would be good for them, they will generally forgo purchasing games if the prices are higher than the value the consumer places on them.

In health care, however, the patient must rely on the physician's recommendation. Given market incentives, physicians may create unnecessary patient demand, a process known as "supplier-induced demand." Even if physicians have the best interests of their patients at heart, they still face financial incentives to provide excess care in marginal cases. There is evidence that they, perhaps unconsciously, adjust treatment patterns to maintain their incomes.

In response to these financial incentives to provide excess care, government regulators have replaced fee-for-service payment systems in some insurance programs with prospective payment systems. For example, Medicare reimburses hospitals based on a patient's diagnosis instead of the specific treatments administered. Under this system, hospitals face the cost of providing additional treatment, limiting their incentive to prescribe excess care.

However, even prospective payment allows providers to exploit their informational advantage to increase their income through incorrect diagnosing, providing less or less costly care than is medically appropriate, or billing for a high-paying service than was performed (a practice known as "upcoding").

The ACA tries to combat these practices in Medicare by rewarding providers for good patient outcomes and by encouraging providers to bundle services. With bundled payments, Medicare will reimburse a fixed rate for any care a patient receives associated with a particular health problem over a certain length of time, and not just during their hospital stay.

Technology diffusion. In addition to affecting care decisions at the individual level, the intersection of insurance and provider markets can lead to too much investment in health care resources. Because patients pay for care with insurance dollars rather than out-of-pocket dollars, health care providers cannot attract customers by lowering treatment prices. As a result, providers must compete on non-price dimensions such as signals of quality or other characteristics that they believe will be attractive to patients. Though theoretically the net effect of non-price competition on health expenditures, health benefits, and overall social welfare is ambiguous, this type of competition can in some cases lead to excessive provision of medical services or a kind of medical arms race. Hospitals, for example, quickly buy updated equipment or offer new services even when they add little value. Once the hospital has invested in new equipment—for example a new, higher-resolution diagnostic scanning machine—doctors and hospitals have incentives to use the likely more highly reimbursed technology, even when the old technology was as effective or more cost-effective.

Some states have sought to curtail duplicative technology adoption and service provision through Certificate of Need (CON) laws, which require hospitals or other providers to seek state approval before investing in additional hospital beds, new equipment, or new service lines. Although the laws and the level of enforcement vary a great deal, applicants must demonstrate that the new investment will meet a medical need in their community. However, researchers such as Vivian Ho and colleagues have found mixed results on the effects of CON on both quantity and quality of care.

Concentrated markets. Some of the interventions described above result in the structure of health care markets being different from markets for other goods like cars or food. Licensing, certification, government approval to install new equipment, and other restrictions on market entry protect quality and, sometimes, control costs, but one consequence is that medical markets are often oligopolies or monopolies. Because of the lack of competition in these markets, additional regulation is often needed to discipline them and ensure that prices are not inflated by providers with excessive market power. Therefore, antitrust policy monitoring mergers and acquisitions plays an important role in the health care sector.

EXTERNALITIES AND PUBLIC GOODS

The health-related behaviors and investments of individuals affect others as well. Typically, individuals make decisions about whether to utilize a health care good or service in response to only their own well-being, without considering the effect of their choices on society. If the effect of their decisions on others, known as an externality, is positive, the result will be an underinvestment in such goods or services. For example, as will be discussed further, an individual's incentive to be vaccinated for a communicable disease is lowered when others around him have also been vaccinated for the disease.

In addition, many health-related goods are public goods; once they are produced, others cannot be excluded from enjoying them, and one person's consumption does not prevent another from also consuming them. Both externalities and public goods can result in a free-rider problem in which each individual chooses not to engage in a behavior or produce a good because they can freely take advantage of others' choices.

Communicable diseases, vaccines, and public health. Historically, some of the most important improvements in public health have come when government intervened to provide goods that the private market could not sustain. Though health improvements during recent decades have been attributed to advances in medical technology, the most rapid health improvements in the United States occurred during the late 1800s and early 1900s when infectious diseases became far less prevalent. Many factors likely led to this decline in disease but, as David Cutler and Grant Miller have shown, nearly half of mortality declines over this period resulted from public health interventions providing clean water. When cities chose to provide clean water for their populations, infectious disease and, therefore, mortality rates fell drastically. This serves as an important example of government's role in providing health-improving public goods.

The free market often faces free-rider problems in the cases of clean water, air, and sanitation because, inasmuch as private firms cannot prevent others from freely using them, the firms have little incentive to provide them. As in the case of water filtration, direct government financing and provision can solve this collective-action problem. In other cases, price subsidies can spur the market by increasing the individual value of investing in or providing a good with external benefits. For example, the government can subsidize firms that do not pollute and tax those that do.

Some individual health care goods, like vaccines, also have externality and public-good characteristics. The direct benefit of immunization is private, but it also has external benefits because one individual's vaccination decreases his chance of spreading the disease to others. This external benefit is greatest when a high fraction of the population is vaccinated, resulting in what is known as herd immunity, meaning that there are not enough unvaccinated people in the community to enable the disease to take hold. When the external benefit from others' immunization is large, the private benefit of vaccination does not outweigh the cost, and thus no individual has the private incentive to seek immunization. To solve this collective-action problem, government action is required to incentivize or compel immunization. For example, states require children to receive certain immunizations before entering school, and the federal government and some states subsidize vaccines or offer them for free to low-income patients.

Medical education. Medical education is another aspect of health care that is more valuable to society than to the individual. A ready supply of appropriately trained medical professionals may be difficult to obtain without subsidizing medical education. A student may choose to forgo the high debt associated with medical school (or, indeed, other types of medical education, such as nursing or physician assistant school) when she could instead choose to enter the work force more quickly or profitably in another profession. Some argue that within medical education, further subsidies should be provided to train physicians in general fields, as opposed to specialty fields, although with the aging of the population there may be an undersupply of specialty physicians as well.

Regardless, it is widely believed that the United States faces a shortage of primary care providers and an excessive number of specialists that leads to higher costs of care and insufficient levels of preventative care. Primary care providers often earn lower salaries than do specialists, providing a financial incentive for physicians to choose such specialties. The ACA includes several provisions to motivate students to become primary care providers, including doctors, nurses, and other professionals.

Insurance coverage for infants and children. As was discussed earlier, concerns about information asymmetries can motivate government provision of health insurance, but public goods motives are important as well. Particularly in the case of health care for infants and children, access to health care can have positive external effects. Because healthy children are more likely to succeed in school, earn more money, and, therefore, contribute more to overall economic productivity and growth, the state has an interest in supporting children's health. In addition to the private benefit these children obtain from access to care and improved health, the external benefit to others from their increased economic productivity makes such investment more valuable.

This externality argument provides one justification for Medicaid expansions of the late 1980s and early 1990s that focused on providing insurance coverage for pregnant women and infants. Similar justifications support the implementation of the State Children's Health Insurance Program (SCHIP) in 1997, which provided coverage for older children in low-income households.

Purchasing health insurance. Some additional externalities not commonly seen in other markets are associated with the decision to purchase or forgo purchasing health insurance. Although the decision to purchase or forgo purchasing any good affects the market—a consumer's decision to buy a Ford rather than a GM affects the market for Ford cars—such externalities are what economists call "pecuniary externalities." That is, the decision to buy a car has a price effect on the market for cars, but this is the normal way that markets function. The decision to forgo insurance for health care has a different kind of externality, one that leads to allocational inefficiencies. When an individual chooses not to purchase insurance and then has an emergency or becomes ill, it often falls on others to pay for his care. Either through charity care or by taking up government programs, others shoulder the burden of paying for care that could have been paid by a private insurance policy had the individual purchased one when healthy. This provides another argument for mandating insurance coverage for all individuals. With such a government intervention, more individuals would purchase private coverage and be less likely to utilize public resources.

Access to emergency treatment. Sometimes otherwise desirable practices, enforced by government regulation or public pressure, create market failures which, in turn, require additional intervention. For example, the Emergency Medical Treatment and Active Labor Act (EMTALA) requires hospitals that treat Medicare patients, essentially all general hospitals, to stabilize patients who come to their emergency rooms with an emergency condition, regardless of the patient's ability to pay. (These narrowly drawn rules are often reinforced by public pressure to provide free service to the medically indigent.) This legal requirement is unique to health care. Whereas people who do not buy airline tickets are not permitted to fly, under EMTALA the uninsured, poor patient who arrives at the emergency room without money will get emergency treatment, and somebody else will have to pay for that care. Private hospitals, be they nonprofit or for-profit, will take the money out of profits and therefore raise prices to their other customers. Tax dollars will cover the costs at public hospitals. This is an example of a political choice turning medical care into something akin to a public good.

Most Americans support such rules out of social commitments to rescue people in dire need and provide medical care even when patients cannot pay. Others support the requirement because of the externalities that would arise if such patients were turned away, such as lost productivity, additional strain on other social programs, or the harms to society that result from allowing the sick to die because they are poor. Regardless of the justification for providing emergency care to people in need, EMTALA not only involves desirable restrictions on the market behavior of private parties itself, it leads to costs that require further government intervention.

Health care goods are considerably different from other goods. These unique characteristics lead to market failures in insurance and provider markets. Additionally, externality and public-good aspects of many health goods make them difficult to provide in private markets. Because of these difficulties, government intervention is often required to ensure individuals are able to obtain appropriate health care.

Note: The authors thank Nicholas Bagley for his helpful comments.

REFERENCES AND FURTHER READING

Akerloff, G. A. (1970). The market for "lemons": Quality uncertainty and the market mechanism. *The Quarterly Journal of Economics, 84*(3), 488–500.

Arrow, K. J. (1963). Uncertainty and the welfare economics of medical care. *The American Economic Review, 53*(5), 941–973.

Baicker, K., & Chandra, A. (2004, April 7). Medicare spending, the physician workforce, and beneficiaries' quality of care. *Health Affairs* [Web exclusive]. Retrieved from http://content.healthaffairs.org/content/early/2004/04/07/hlthaff.w4.184.short

Cutler, D. M., & Miller, G. (2005). The role of public health improvements in health advances: The twentieth-century United States. *Demography, 42*(1), 1–22.

Cutler, D. M., & Zeckhauser, R. J. (2000). The anatomy of health insurance. In A. J. Culyer & J. P. Newhouse (Eds.), *Handbook of health economics* (Vol. 1A, pp. 563–643). New York, NY: Elsevier.

Dafny, L. S. (2005). How do hospitals respond to price changes? *The American Economic Review, 95*(5), 1525–1547.

Dranove, D., & Jin, G. Z. (2010). Quality disclosure and certification: Theory and practice. *Journal of Economic Literature, 48*(4), 935–963.

Gaynor, M., & Town, R. J. (2011). *Competition in health care markets.* National Bureau of Economic Research, Working Paper No. 17208.

Gruber, J., & Owings, M. (1996). Physician financial incentives and cesarean section delivery. *The RAND Journal of Economics, 27*(1), 99–123.

Ho, V., Ku-Goto, M. H., & Jollis, J. G. (2009). Certificate of need for cardiac care: Controversy over the contributions of CON. *Health Services Research, 44*(2 Pt 1), 483–500.

Hurley, J. (2000). An overview of the normative economics of the health sector. In A. J. Culyer & J. P. Newhouse (Eds.), *Handbook of health economics* (Vol. 1A, pp. 55–118). New York, NY: Elsevier.

Newhouse, J. P., & the Insurance Experiment Group. (1992). *Free for all? Lessons from the RAND health insurance experiment.* Cambridge, MA: Harvard University Press.

Pauly, M. V. (1986). Taxation, health insurance, and market failure in the medical economy. *Journal of Economic Literature, 24*(2), 629–675.

Rothschild, M., & Stiglitz, J. (1976). Equilibrium in competitive insurance markets. *Quarterly Journal of Economics, 90*(4), 629–649.

Zweifel, P., & Manning, W. G. (2000). Moral hazard and consumer incentives in health care. In A. J. Culyer & J. P. Newhouse (Eds.), *Handbook of health economics* (Vol. 1A, pp. 150–183). New York, NY: Elsevier.

Seth Freedman and Jill R. Horwitz

Racial Disparities in Health Status and Accessing Health Care

POINT: Interpersonal and institutional racial biases are the principal reasons for racial disparities in access to health care and in African Americans' health status, and disparities can only be addressed by acknowledging and putting an end to interpersonal and institutional racial bias in the health care system.

Ruqaiijah A. Yearby, Case Western Reserve University School of Law

COUNTERPOINT: The irrational structure of health care, which is based on one's ability to pay rather than on need, is the main cause of racial disparities in health. These will not be equalized until the structure of the health care system is fixed or until African Americans' economic inequalities are addressed.

Ruqaiijah A. Yearby, Case Western Reserve University School of Law

Introduction

In the United States, health is unevenly distributed. According to its 2011 "Health Inequalities Report," the Centers for Disease Control and Prevention (CDC) found significant disparities in health associated with race, socioeconomic status, disability, and gender. Women live longer than men. People with higher socioeconomic status tend to be healthier than people in lower socioeconomic groups. In addition, racial minorities experience higher rates of morbidity. Rates of both asthma and diabetes, for example, are far higher among minority children than among white children. Racial minorities also experience higher rates of HIV infection and heart disease. Even automobile deaths vary by race. According to the CDC, in 2007 the rate of fatal car injuries for all Americans was 14.5 per 100,000; for American Indians and Alaskan Natives, it was 29.1 per 100,000.

The starkest health disparities, however, are between African Americans and Caucasians. Using preliminary data for 2009, Kenneth Kochanek and colleagues reported in 2011's "National Vital Statistics 59" that the life expectancy for white females was 80.9 years; for African American females, it was 77.4; for white men, it was 76.2; for African American men, it was 70.9. Thus a white woman can expect to live a decade longer than an African American man. Equally glaring is the disparity in infant mortality rates: In 2009 the infant mortality rate for African American infants was 2.4 times that of white infants.

In this chapter, Ruqaiijah A. Yearby focuses on the dramatic disparities between the health of African Americans and Caucasians. She reviews a plethora of studies documenting significant racial disparities and examines different causal explanations for their existence. She notes that biology is almost certainly not responsible, inasmuch as the genetic variations between the races are trivial. Instead, the causes of health disparities are socially based.

In the Point section, Yearby considers two types of racial bias that may lead to race-based disparities: interpersonal bias and institutional bias. Interpersonal bias occurs when either conscious or unconscious prejudice against a racial group adversely influences the interactions between individuals. Yearby explains that interpersonal bias remains rampant in the health care system, despite civil rights laws prohibiting discrimination on the basis of race in many health care settings. For example, researchers have reported that physicians are less likely to aggressively treat African Americans for many medical conditions. If civil rights laws have been unsuccessful in combating such discrimination, what policies might be effective? Should health care providers be trained to recognize and overcome their implicit racial prejudices? Should greater efforts be made to ensure cultural competency among health care providers? Should the government adopt more aggressive policies to increase the numbers of minority physicians?

Institutional bias, in contrast, operates through organizational structures that reflect and reinforce racial privilege. According to Yearby, the closing or relocation of hospitals in African American neighborhoods illustrates the impact of institutional bias. Although such closings are often defended on race-neutral grounds, Yearby argues that those defenses can't withstand scrutiny. Instead, she explains, the closings are linked to race, and in turn harm the health of African American communities. What policy options exist for eradicating this and other biases in the health care system?

The Counterpoint focuses on a different explanation: the structure of the health care system. The U.S. health care system, Yearby notes, rations care according to one's ability to pay. Except in the case of emergencies—when the law requires that most hospitals provide care regardless of one's ability to pay—an individual's access to the health care system depends largely on having health insurance. This form of rationing, known as first-dollar rationing, is deleterious to health; many studies have shown that people without insurance receive less health care and suffer worse health outcomes than people who have insurance. Lack of insurance is also associated with race. Yearby notes that people of color make up only about one third of the U.S. population, but more than half of the uninsured. Thus the Counterpoint argues that health disparities can only be eliminated by severing the connection between health care and ability to pay. Can the type of reforms established by the 2010 Patient Protection and Affordable Care Act (ACA) accomplish that goal? What other reforms would be required to ensure that health care is provided on the basis of need, rather than the ability to pay?

All three of the potential causes for health disparities discussed in this chapter—interpersonal bias, institutional bias, and the structure of health care—focus on problems within the health care system as the source of health disparities. But is the health care system the chief villain? Might the roots of health disparities lie outside of the health care system, in the role that race and racism play in the broader society?

The chapter offers some suggestions that this might be the case. For example, Yearby notes that research has shown that a woman's experience with racial prejudice throughout her life, not simply within the health care system, is associated with her going into premature labor. Yearby also cites evidence establishing a positive correlation between perceived racial prejudice and increased cigarette smoking and alcohol use. The CDC has also pointed to environmental factors in minority neighborhoods, such as air pollution or the lack of supermarkets with nutritious food, as the source of some health disparities. Such explanations suggest that deeply entrenched racial bias, both explicit and implicit, in society at large may play a significant role in health disparities.

Likewise, the association between health insurance status and health disparities discussed in the Counterpoint stems not only from the structure of the health care system and its reliance on the ability to pay but also results from the fact that insurance status in the United States is closely associated with income. This, in turn, is unevenly distributed by race. Income is also associated with a broad range of other socioeconomic factors, the so-called social determinants of health, including education and housing. And, in the United States, all of these factors are themselves highly correlated with race. Does this suggest that the problem of health disparities cannot be addressed simply by reforming the health care system? Does the persistence of race-based health disparities provide a rationale for instituting broader-based changes in public policy? What would those look like?

POINT

The U.S. Department of Health and Human Services (HHS) defines health disparities as differences in health between groups of people who have systematically experienced greater obstacles to health based on their racial group, socioeconomic status, or other characteristics historically linked to discrimination or exclusion. Even after the enactment of Title VI of the Civil Rights Act of 1964, which granted minorities a legal right to "equal" access to health care services from providers receiving federal funds, decades of research studies and government reports have shown that racial disparities in accessing quality health care and health status continue to exist. The largest disparity in accessing quality health care and health status in the United States was and remains between African Americans and Caucasians.

Empirical research studies have shown that racial disparities in accessing quality health care and health status have worsened, which according to Professor Rene Bowser has led to significant racial disparities in mortality rates between African Americans and Caucasians (2001). According to the medical literature reviewing national health statistics, "there has been no sustained decrease in black-white inequities in age-adjusted mortality (death) or life expectancy at birth at the national level since 1945" (Levine et al., 2001). In fact, research studies have shown that in 1950, before the end of legalized racial segregation, the life expectancy of 65-year-old African Americans and whites were the same. By 1995 African American mortality rates and mortality ratios when compared to Caucasians for cancer, diabetes, suicide, cirrhosis of the liver, and homicide were higher than they were in 1950. These disparities are also illustrated by government reports.

In 1985 the secretary of HHS issued the landmark *Heckler Report,* which exposed the existence of racial disparities between African Americans and Caucasians in the U.S. health care system. In 2003 the groundbreaking Institute of Medicine (IOM) study *Unequal Treatment: Confronting Racial and Ethnic Disparities in Healthcare* acknowledged the continuation of racial disparities in health status and the access to health care and provided suggestions for the elimination of these disparities. Finally, in 2007, the National Healthcare Disparities Report (NHDR) noted that racial disparities in health status and access to quality health care between African Americans and Caucasians were not getting smaller; instead, the gaps persisted (U.S. Department of Health and Human Services, 2008). In response to these data, the federal government has issued several initiatives to put an end to racial disparities in access to health care and health status.

In 1990 HHS issued the first national health initiative, which provides science-based 10-year national objectives for improving the health of all Americans. One of the main objectives of the first national health initiative, called *Healthy People 2000,* was to reduce health disparities among all Americans. In 1998 President Bill Clinton announced the Initiative to Eliminate Racial and Ethnic Disparities in Health Care that, by the year 2010, was supposed to eliminate racial and ethnic health disparities in six key areas of health status, including infant mortality. In 2000 the *Healthy People 2010* initiative was issued with an objective of eliminating racial disparities in health care. In 2010 the *Healthy People 2020* initiative expanded the goal of eliminating racial disparities in health care to include achieving health equity and improving the health of all groups. In spite of all the research, government reports, and initiatives, health care disparities persist and in some cases have worsened. In 1985, 60,000 excess deaths occurred each year in minority populations. By 2005 an estimated 83,570 African Americans died each year who would not have died if African American death rates were equivalent to those of whites (Satcher et al., 2005).

Scholars and researchers have proposed a panoply of causes for the continuation of racial disparities in access to quality health care and health care status, including cultural differences, insurance status, socioeconomic status, and education levels. Yet many research studies show that, even when all these factors are controlled, racial disparities in health care persist, leaving race as the only plausible explanation for the continuation of disparities. But what does race have to do with it?

Some argue that race means that biological differences cause these disparities in health outcomes; however, race differences account for at most .03 percent of genetic variation (Mak, Cheung, & Ho, 2006). Thus, if race plays a role in racial disparities, genetic research suggests that it is due to the social construction of race, and not biological differences. The social construction of race refers to society's creation of defined racial groups based on physical traits (e.g., skin color) that determine the distribution of resources such as health care and jobs. As Professors David Williams and Pamela Jackson noted, "Race is a marker for differential exposure to multiple disease-producing social factors. Thus, racial [disparities] in health should be understood not only in terms of individual characteristics but also in light of patterned racial inequalities in exposure to societal risks and resources" (Williams & Jackson, 2005). Unfortunately, the significance of societal risks, such as racial bias in causing racial disparities in health care, is often ignored. However, some credible and robust research studies have suggested that racial bias is the chief factor in the continuation of racial disparities in health care. Social psychologists, medical researchers, and legal scholars have suggested that interpersonal and institutional racial biases are the chief causes of racial disparities.

Interpersonal bias is the conscious (explicit) or unconscious (implicit) presence of prejudice in interactions between individuals. Interpersonal bias is best illustrated by the ways in which racial prejudice influence physicians' treatment decisions and the effects of those decisions on African Americans' health status. Institutional bias operates through organizational structures within an institution that "establishes separate and independent barriers" to health care services, which is best demonstrated by hospital closures in African American communities. Even though interpersonal racial bias focuses on interactions between individuals, while institutional bias focuses on interactions between an institution and an individual, both focus on the direct effects of racial prejudice (Grant-Thomas & Powell, 2006). This essay discusses the research studies that support the proposition that interpersonal and institutional racial bias are the central causes of racial disparities in accessing health care and health status and proposes some solutions.

INTERPERSONAL RACIAL BIAS

Prejudice is a negative *pre-judgment* against a person or group. An action based on racial prejudice is *racial bias*, whereas *racism* is racial bias plus power. Interpersonal racial bias is defined as a conscious (explicit) prejudicial action or comment by an individual, who is racist, which harms another person. However, Professor Charles Lawrence notes that this definition fails to recognize the harm caused by an individual, who although unconscious of his or her prejudice, acts as a racist (Lawrence, 1989). The full harm caused by interpersonal racial bias is best captured by social psychology research, which acknowledges both conscious (explicit) and unconscious (implicit) racial prejudice. According to the psychiatrist Joel Kovel, two types of people exhibit interpersonal racial bias: dominative and aversive racists (1984). A dominative racist is one who is conscious of his or her prejudice that members of one racial group, such as Caucasians, are superior and acts out these beliefs. An aversive racist, on the other hand, believes that everyone is equal, but harbors contradicting, often unconscious, prejudice that minorities, such as African Americans, are inferior.

Over four decades of social psychology research suggest aversive racism has become the dominant form of interpersonal racial bias between African Americans and Caucasians in the United States. More recently, medical research studies have begun to study aversive racism in health care by measuring physicians' unconscious prejudicial beliefs about African Americans and the effect of these beliefs on physicians' treatment decisions. Medical research studies show that, instead of relying on individual factors and scientific facts, physicians rely on their conscious and unconscious prejudicial beliefs, which result in disparities in medical treatment, often leading to racial disparities in mortality rates between African Americans and Caucasians.

That African Americans often sense physicians' unconscious racial prejudice against them negatively affects their health by serving as a barrier to health care services. Empirical data show that African Americans' perception of racial prejudice inside the health care system results in delays in seeking care, an interruption in continuity of care, non-adherence to treatment regimens, and reduced health status, while perceptions of racial prejudice outside the health care system increases African Americans' stress level, which is linked to higher rates of infant mortality. Thus, in order to put an end to racial disparities in health care, interpersonal racial bias has to be acknowledged, physicians must be educated about their aversive racism and its effects on patient care, and African Americans need to be taught stress-coping measures to mitigate the health effects of physicians' and society's racism.

Physician's unconscious racial bias. In 1999 the Schulman study of primary care physicians' perceptions of patients found that a patient's race and sex affected the physician's decision to recommend medically appropriate cardiac catheterization. Specifically, African Americans were less likely to be referred for cardiac catheterizations than were Caucasians; African American women were significantly less likely to be referred for treatment than were Caucasian males. One year later, Dr. Calman, a white physician serving African American patients in New York, wrote about his battle to overcome his and his colleagues' racial prejudice, which often prevented African Americans from accessing quality health care (Calman, 2000).

In 2000 van Ryn and Burke conducted a survey of physicians' perceptions of patients. The survey showed that physicians rated African American patients as less intelligent, less educated, and more likely to fail to comply with physicians' medical advice. Physicians' perceptions of African Americans were negative even when those perceptions were contradicted by direct evidence. In 2006 van Ryn repeated this study using candidates for coronary bypass surgery. Again, physicians exhibited prejudicial beliefs about African Americans' intelligence and ability to comply with medical advice. In this study, physicians acted upon these prejudicial beliefs by recommending medically necessary coronary bypass surgery for African Americans less often than they did with Caucasians.

In 2002 and 2006 research showed that, compared to Caucasian patients, African American patients were less likely to receive encouragement to participate in medical decision making and sufficient information from their physicians about their medical condition (Dovidio, Penner, Norton, Gaertner, & Shelton, 2008). Furthermore, the 2003 IOM study found evidence of poorer quality of care for minority patients in studies of cancer treatment, treatment of cardiovascular disease, rates of referral for clinical tests, diabetes management, pain management, and other areas of care due in part to racial bias.

Most recently, a 2008 study by Penner found that physicians subconsciously favor Caucasian patients over African American patients. In this study, physicians' racial attitudes and stereotypes were assessed and then physicians were presented with descriptions of hypothetical cardiology patients differing in race. Although physicians reported not being explicitly racially biased, they held implicit negative attitudes about African Americans; and thus, were aversive racists. This study further showed that Caucasian male physicians tend to exhibit higher levels of aversive racism compared to Caucasian female, African American female, and African American male physicians (Sabin, Nosek, Greenwald, & Rivara, 2009). This is significant because 75 percent of African Americans' medical interactions are with physicians who are not African American. Finally, the stronger the implicit bias, the less likely the physician was to recommend the appropriate medical treatment for African American patients.

Other studies have reported similar findings. For example, in 1996, Gornick published a study regarding racial disparities in the provision of Medicare services. For instance, even after controlling for income, the study showed that physicians treated African American Medicare patients less aggressively than Caucasians who were more likely to be hospitalized for ischemic heart disease; have a mammography; and undergo coronary-artery bypass surgery, coronary angioplasty, and hip-fracture repair. Likewise, a 1998 study conducted by Bach found that African Americans were less likely than Caucasians to receive curative surgery for early stage lung cancer, which is linked to increased mortality rates of African Americans. In fact, Bach found that, if African American patients were to undergo surgery at a rate equal to Caucasians, their survival rate would approach that of Caucasian patients.

According to a study by Harvard researchers that same year, African American Medicare patients receive poorer basic care than did Caucasians who are treated for the same illnesses (Ayanian, Weissman, Chasan-Taber, & Epstein, 1999). For example, the study showed that only 32 percent of African American pneumonia patients were given antibiotics within six hours of admission, compared with 53 percent of Caucasian Medicare patients. Also, physicians were less likely to take blood cultures from their African American patients during the first two days of hospitalization. The researchers noted that other studies had associated the prompt administration of antibiotics and the collection of blood cultures with lower death rates.

In a 1999 study, Hannan evaluated the medical records of patients to ascertain whether there were race and gender differences in the underutilization of coronary artery bypass surgery among patients for whom this procedure was the appropriate intervention. After controlling for disease status, income level, and educational attainment, African American patients were only 64 percent as likely as Caucasians to receive surgery.

Further, even though African Americans have a higher rate of stroke and cerebrovascular death than do Caucasians, African American patients have a lower rate for carotid endarterectomy, a procedure that would greatly reduce fatalities from these conditions (Mort, 1994). A majority of these studies controlled for socioeconomic status, disease status, and education level, suggesting that racial bias in the form of implicit racial bias is one of the central causes of disparities in medical treatment. Research shows that African Americans perceive this implicit bias and respond negatively.

Patients' perception of bias. Data show that African Americans reacted most negatively to physicians who were aversive racists, compared to physicians who were either not racist or were dominative racists (Penner et al., 2010). Patients perceive aversive racists as deceitful, compared to dominative racists, who were clear and honest about their prejudicial beliefs. Studies further found that medical interactions between racially different patients and physicians are characterized by less patient trust, less positive interactions, fewer attempts at relationship building, and less joint decision making (Dovidio et al., 2008). Additionally, surveys of African American patients show that they have less trust in the health care system than do Caucasians. African Americans' perception of racial prejudice outside the health care system also results in negative health outcomes.

Empirical evidence shows that perceptions of racial prejudice result in increased stress that negatively affects health status. In fact, perceived racial prejudice has been associated with poorer health status for African Americans. Several studies have shown a positive correlation between perceived racial prejudice and increased cigarette and alcohol use among African Americans, compared to Caucasians (Jackson, Neighbors, & Williams, 2003). Increased stress from perceived racial prejudice also affects birth outcomes by increasing rates of infant mortality.

During the last century, infant mortality rates in the United States decreased. Nevertheless, the ratio of disparity of infant mortality rates between African Americans and Caucasians has continued, regardless of socioeconomic status, educational levels, or health insurance status. Though it varies somewhat by geographic area, the infant mortality ratio of African Americans is 1.4 to 4.8 times that of Caucasians. Nationally, the rate of African American to Caucasian infant mortality was 2.4 in 2003, a rate that has held steady since 2000. The main cause of death for African American infants is preterm birth and low birth weight, which according to Richard David and James Collins Jr. is caused in part by racial bias (Collins, David, Handler, Wall, & Andes, 2004).

Their study compared birth weights among three groups of women: African American, Caucasians, and Africans who had moved to Illinois. The birth weight of Caucasians and African infants was almost identical, whereas the birth weight of African American infants was substantially less. Researchers suggested that one reason African American mothers have babies who weigh less at birth is that they are subject to stress caused by perceived interpersonal racial bias.

Between African American women who had babies with normal weights at birth (NLBW) and African American women whose babies' birth weight was very low (VLBW), under three pounds, interpersonal racial bias played a significant role. Specifically, African American mothers who delivered VLBW preterm infants were more likely to report experiencing racial prejudice during their lifetime than were African American mothers who delivered NLBW infants at term. Hence, the perception of racial prejudice negatively affects African American health status at birth and throughout adulthood.

Interpersonal racial bias inside and outside the health care system results in racial disparities in medical treatment, which compromises African Americans' health status. Studies have shown that when treatment disparities are eliminated, racial disparities in health outcomes are substantially attenuated or absent. Nevertheless, simply addressing interpersonal racial bias will not completely eliminate treatment disparities when hospitals and quality nursing homes located in predominately African American neighborhoods continue to close, relocate, or provide poor quality care as a result of institutional racial bias.

INSTITUTIONAL RACIAL BIAS

Institutional bias operates through organizational structures and establishes "separate and independent" barriers through the neutral denial of access to quality health care that results from the normal operations of the institutions in a society (Mullings & Schulz, 2006). Not all actions by an institution that disproportionately affect minorities are racially biased. In order to constitute institutional racial bias, the action must reinforce the racial hierarchy of the inferiority of minorities and impose substantial harm on them (Bowser, 2001). Once this occurs, the institution's actions constitute institutional racial bias, even if the actions are seemingly race neutral.

The most poignant examples of institutional racial bias in health care are the closure of hospitals in predominately African American communities and the overconcentration of quality nursing homes in predominately Caucasian neighborhoods. These decisions may seem race neutral. However, medical research and legal scholarship show that closures and the dearth of quality nursing home care in African American communities re-enforce the racial hierarchy that African Americans' health does not matter compared to the health of Caucasians and have resulted in significant harm, including increased mortality rates of minorities. In order to control costs, state and federal regulators have allowed health care institutions to make this decision without balancing the needs of African American communities. Unfortunately, not only have closures failed to control costs, they have also caused racial disparities in accessing health care and health status.

Hospital closures. In the late 1970s, the American Hospital Association published a study surveying hospital administrators to determine the primary reasons for hospital closures or relocations. The survey showed that 27 percent of closures and relocations were because of financial reasons, 23 percent were because the facility was to be replaced by a new one, 14 percent were due to low occupancy rate, 13 percent were because the facilities had become outdated, and 10 percent were because of an inadequate supply of physicians (Clark, 2005). The AMA's survey, in concert with repeated assertions by hospital administrators about fiscal justification, created the perception that hospital closures were beneficial for society and race neutral, and thus such closures and relocations were routinely approved by state and federal regulators. However, that is not the case: Hospital closures increase costs, decrease access to health care, and are significantly linked to race.

The perception that hospital closures reduce excess hospital bed capacity, improve quality care and help save scare public resources is false. Research shows that anticipated benefits from hospital closures never materialize because, as hospitals decrease the number of beds available in African American communities, they increase the number of hospital beds in predominately Caucasian neighborhoods (Clark, 2005). Additionally, the reduction of beds in predominately African American communities with the greatest needs for care compromises African Americans' health by decreasing access to health care, thereby increasing health care costs.

As these hospitals leave predominately African American neighborhoods, the remaining hospitals are left to fill the void, placing great strain on those hospitals' resources and ability to provide quality care. Consequently, the hospitals that do remain to provide care to African Americans gradually deteriorate and provide substandard care. Access to health care is diminished not only because of a reduction of hospital services but also because of physician departures.

Once a hospital has closed or relocated, physicians practicing in the area often follow the hospital to affluent neighborhoods, disrupting primary care services in predominately African American neighborhoods. Evidence shows that primary care physicians often leave after the closure of a neighborhood hospital because the hospital is a critical base for their practice. Moreover, as the number of primary care physicians decreases, African Americans are forced to seek care in emergency rooms and public hospitals, which are often understaffed and not adequately maintained. Lack of access to health services is not the only harm from hospital closures: Patients and minority communities experience humiliation, frustration, and a sense of helplessness. The effect of these closures and physician departures on the surrounding community is best illustrated by California's health care crisis in the 1990s.

Since 1990 more than 70 hospital emergency rooms and trauma centers have closed in California alone (Clark, 2005). As a result, patients have been unable to obtain timely and medically necessary health care. One emergency room physician in California noted that a woman who had a miscarriage was forced to wait in a hospital waiting room for hours with her fetus in a Tupperware dish before she could be seen, while a boy with serious head trauma went without medically necessary services. These two patients and many more were not able to access medically necessary health care because of a shortage of physicians and overburdened emergency rooms, the result of private hospital closures.

Most predominately Caucasian neighborhoods are full of health care services, while many African American neighborhoods are left without health care services and often suffer unnecessary disability and deaths as a result. Moreover, the closures often lead to physician shortages and overburdened emergency rooms, leaving African Americans humiliated, frustrated, and feeling helpless. Thus, hospital closures re-enforce the racial hierarchy that African Americans' lives are less valued than those of Caucasians.

Hospital placement, closures, and removal of services have been linked to race since 1937. In 2006, Alan Sager reported that, as the African American population in a neighborhood increased, the closure and relocation of hospital services increased for every period between 1937 and 2003, except between 1990 and 1997 (Sager & Socolar, 2006). In the Jim Crow era, hospital closures were overtly linked to race. Since the passage of Title VI, hospitals have used fiscal explanations to justify closures and relocations; however, closures and relocations are still significantly correlated with race.

Those who decide to close or relocate a hospital often fail to consider that doing so will deprive predominately African American neighborhoods of health care services and force African Americans to seek care in increasingly overburdened predominately white communities. Though the institutional decision to close a hospital may seem race neutral, research shows that, irrespective of financial concerns, hospital closures remain linked to race and reinforce racial hierarchy.

Quality nursing home care. Similar to those of hospitals, the institutional policies and practices of nursing homes, such as opening facilities in affluent neighborhoods, harm African Americans and widen racial disparities in access to health services. The best quality nursing homes are situated in predominately Caucasian neighborhoods and have a predominately Caucasian population. Just like hospital owners, nursing home owners have cited financial reasons for leaving predominately African American neighborhoods without health care services to relocate to overserviced affluent areas. Those nursing homes that do remain in predominately African American neighborhoods are often underfunded and understaffed, and therefore provide substandard care (Yearby, 2010).

For example, Alden Wentworth, a predominately African American nursing home in Illinois, is part of a chain of 30 for-profit nursing homes. The chain owns three predominately African American nursing homes and 16 predominately Caucasian ones. All three of the predominately African American nursing homes received the lowest quality ranking by the federal government, whereas fewer than half of the 16 predominately Caucasian facilities received that same rating. In fact, the two nursing homes that received the highest quality ratings were predominately Caucasian. However, a 2009 investigation by the *Chicago Reporter* showed that Alden Wentworth had the worst rating a nursing home can receive and that residents were attended by staff less than half the time than were residents at a predominantly Caucasian facility in Evanston operated by the same owner (Yearby, 2010).

CONCLUSION

In sum, race continues to matter in health care even after the passage of civil rights laws like Title VI. Race matters because physicians continue to exhibit conscious and unconscious racial prejudice, which affects their treatment decisions, and health care providers' closures and relocations remain linked to race and re-enforce racial hierarchy. In order to put an end to racial disparities in access to health care and health status, both interpersonal and institutional racial bias need to be addressed.

Recognizing and acknowledging the significance of racial prejudice on racial disparities in accessing health care and health status is the first step to addressing interpersonal racial bias. Second, physicians need to be educated about their subtle, often unconscious, racial prejudice, which affects their medical treatment decisions. In fact, research suggests that making physicians aware of how their unconscious racial prejudice can influence outcomes of medical encounters and sensitizing them to their own unconscious bias can help motivate them to correct their bias (Dovidio et al., 2008). Finally, African American patients need to be educated about the severe health consequences of failing to cope with the stress of perceived racial bias and provided with coping strategies.

In order to put an end to institutional racial bias, both state and federal regulators—the government agencies that regulate health care—need to review institutional plans to close, relocate, or place quality facilities only in predominately Caucasian neighborhoods with an eye toward the disproportionate harm such plans have on African American communities. This review will force hospitals and nursing homes to balance the benefits of closing, relocating, and overconcentrating quality facilities in predominately Caucasian neighborhoods with the detrimental effects on African American communities that result from disruptions of care. By instituting this review, the racial link will be made clearer, and owners will have to mitigate the harmful effects of closing, relocating, and overconcentrating quality facilities in predominately Caucasian neighborhoods by providing transportation to new facilities, coordinating care with the remaining facilities, or improving the provision of care.

Some argue that by focusing on how individuals and institutions make decisions, one fails to understand the structural problems with the health care system that allow institutional and interpersonal racial bias to continue. The structure of the U.S. health care system, which is based on the ability to pay instead of need, prevents minorities, who are disproportionally poor and without health insurance, from accessing health care. However, research shows that even when insurance status, socioeconomic status, and income are controlled for, racial disparities persist (Williams, 1999). Thus, even if addressing interpersonal and institutional racial bias will not change the structure of health care, simply changing the structure of health care will not equalize racial disparities in access to health care and health status.

REFERENCES AND FURTHER READING

Ayanian, J. Z., Weissman, J. S., Chasan-Taber, S., & Ebstein, A. M. (1999). Quality of care by race and gender for congestive heart failure and pneumonia. *Med Care, 37*(12), 1260–1269.

Bach, P. B., Cramer, L. D., Warren, J. L., & Begg, C. B. (1999). Racial differences in the treatment of early-stage lung cancer. *New England Journal of Medicine, 341*(16), 1198–1205.

Bowser, R. (2001). Racial profiling in health care: An institutional analysis of medical treatment disparities. *Michigan Journal of Race & Law, 7,* 79–133.

Calman, N. S. (2000). Out of the shadow: A white inner-city doctor wrestles with racial prejudice. *Health Affairs, 19*(1), 170–174.

Clark, B. (2005). Hospital flight from minority communities: How our existing civil rights framework fosters racial inequality in healthcare. *DePaul Journal of Health Care Law, 9,* 1023–1046.

Collins, J., David, R. J., Handler, A., Wall, S., & Andes, S. (2004). Very low birth weight in African American infants: The role of maternal exposure to interpersonal racial discrimination. *American Journal of Public Health, 94*(12), 2125–2138.

Dovidio, J. F., Penner, L. A., Norton, W. E., Gaertner, S. L., & Shelton, J. L. (2008). Disparities and distrust: The implications of psychological processes for understanding racial disparities in health and health care. *Social Science and Medicine, 67*(3), 478–486.

Gornick, M. E., Eggers, P. W., Reilly, T. W., Mentnech, R. M., Fitterman, L. K., Kucken, L. E., & Vladeck, B. C. (1999). Effects of race and income on mortality and use of services among Medicare beneficiaries. *New England Journal of Medicine, 335*(11), 791–799.

Grant-Thomas, A., & Powell, J. A. (2006). Toward structural racism framework. *Poverty & Race, 15*(6), 3–6.

Hannan, E. L., van Ryn, M., Burke, J., Stone, D., Arani, D., & DeBuonno, B. A. (1999). Access to coronary artery bypass surgery by race/ethnicity and gender among patients who are appropriate for surgery. *Med Care, 37*(1), 68–77.

Jackson, J. S., Neighbors, H. W., & Williams, D. R. (2003). Racial/ethnic discrimination and health: Findings from community studies. *American Journal of Public Health, 93*(2), 200–208.

Kovel, J. (1984). *White racism: A psychohistory.* New York, NY: Columbia University Press. (Originally published 1970)

LaVeist, T. A., Gaskin, D., & Richard, P. (2009). *The economic burden of health inequalities in the United States.* Washington, DC: Joint Center for Political and Economic Studies.

Lawrence, C. R. (1989). The id, the ego, and equal protection: Reckoning with unconscious racism. *Stanford Law Review, 39*(2), 317–388.

Levine, R. S., Foster, J. E., Fullilove, R. E., Fullilove, M. T., Briggs, N. C., Hull, P. C., et al. (2001). Black-white inequalities in mortality and life expectancy, 1933–1999: Implications for healthy people 2010. *Public Health Report, 116*(5), 474–483.

Mak, W., Cheung, R., & Ho, S. L. (2006). Biological basis of the racial disparities and diseases: An evolutionary perspective. In E. V. Metrosa (Ed.), *Racial and ethnic disparities in health and health care* (pp. 73–100). New York, NY: Nova Science Publishers.

Mort, E. A., Weissman, J. S., & Epstein, A. M. (1994). Physician discretion and racial variation in the use of surgical procedures. *Archives of Internal Medicine, 154*(7), 761–767.

Mullings, L., & Schulz, A. (2006). *Intersectionality and health: An introduction, in gender, race, class, and health.* San Francisco, CA: Jossey-Bass.

National Research Council. (2003). *Unequal treatment: Confronting racial and ethnic disparities in health care.* Washington, DC: The National Academies Press.

Penner, L. A., Dovidio, J. F., West, T. V., Gaertner, S. L., Albrecht, T. L., Dailey, R. K., & Markova, T. (2010). Aversive racism and medical interactions with black patients: A field study. *Journal of Experimental Social Psychology, 46*(2), 436–440.

Sabin, J., Nosek, B. A., Greenwald, A. G., & Rivara, A. G. (2009). Physicians' implicit and explicit attitudes about race by MD race, ethnicity, and gender. *Journal of Health Care Poor & Underserved, 20*(3), 896–913.

Sager, A., & Socolar, D. (2006). *Closing hospitals in New York State won't save money but will harm access to care.* Boston, MA: Boston University School of Public Health. Retrieved from http://dcc2.bumc.bu.edu/hs/Sager%20Hospital%20Closings%20Short%20Report%2020Nov06.pdf

Satcher, D., Fryer, G. E., McCann, J., Troutman, A., Woolf, S. H., & Rust, G. (2005). What if we were equal? A comparison of the black-white mortality gap in 1960 and 2000. *Health Affairs, 24*(2), 459–464.

Schulman, K., Berlin, J. A., Harless, W., Kerner, J. F., Sistrunk, S., Gersh, B. J., & Dube, R. (1999). The effect of race and sex on physicians' recommendation for cardiac catheterization. *New England Journal of Medicine, 340*(8), 618–626.

U.S. Department of Health and Human Services. (1985). The report of the secretary's task force on black and minority health. *Morbidity and Mortality Weekly Report, 35,* 109.

U.S. Department of Health and Human Services. (2008). *2007 national healthcare disparities report.* Rockville, MD: Agency for Health Care Research and Quality. Retrieved from http://archive.ahrq.gov/qual/nhqr07/nhqr07.pdf

Van Ryn, M., Burgess, D., Malat, J., & Griffin, J. (2006). Physicians' perceptions of patients' social and behavioral characteristics and race disparities in treatment recommendations for men with coronary disease. *American Journal of Public Health, 96*(2), 351–357.

Van Ryn, M., & Burke, J. (2000). The effect of patient race and socio-economic status on physicians' perceptions of patients. *Social Science & Medicine, 50*(6), 813–828.

Williams, D. R. (1999). Race, socioeconomic status, and health: The added effects of racism and discrimination. *Annals of the New York Academy of Sciences, 896,* 173–188.

Williams, D. R., & Jackson, P. B. (2005). Social sources of racial disparities in health. *Health Affairs, 24*(2), 325–334.

Yearby, R. (2010). African Americans can't win, break even, or get out of the system: The persistence of unequal treatment in nursing home care. *Temple Law Review, 82*(5), 1177–1203.

Ruqaiijah A. Yearby

COUNTERPOINT

Structural racial bias operates at the societal level, denying some groups access to the resources of society while privileging others (Mullings & Schulz, 2006). Structural bias measures how non-race-based factors, such as economic inequalities, indirectly affect racial minorities, whereas interpersonal and institutional biases focus on the direct racial effects of individual or institutional actions (Grant-Thomas & Powell, 2006). Structural racial bias is a result of power relationships between racial groups in which one dominant group holds power over the other and uses its power to secure material and social resources such as health care. The dominant group remains in power because its position in society enables it to retain power, despite the will or aims of the groups it has power over.

The structural bias of health care has created a system in which the allocation of care is based on a given patient's ability to pay, rather than on his or her actual health needs. This allows those with privilege, such as wealthy Caucasians, to obtain the best-quality health care available, while those without privilege, such as poor African Americans, are relegated to substandard hospitals and nursing homes. Thus, differences in income and health insurance status leave African Americans without the privilege of access to quality health care. To end racial disparities in the access to health care and health status, the structure of health care must be based on need, not the ability to pay.

RATIONING

For over 70 years, the United States has rationed health care as a means of allocating scarce resources. During the 1940s penicillin supplies were rationed first to members of the U.S. military; in the 1960s access to scarce dialysis machines was rationed in Seattle based on disease prognosis. The ultimate example of the rationing of health care access in the United States, however, is managed care, which began in the late 1970s (Yearby, 2011).

Managed care organizations used rationing as a means to lower health care costs by limiting access to physicians and mandating primary care gatekeepers and pre-admission or service authorizations. According to several scholars, each of these methods of rationing failed in part because they explicitly limited access to health care, in effect making tragic, and quite public, life-and-death decisions. As a result of public criticism, many of the care limitations once used by managed-care organizations have been discontinued. Perhaps reflecting wisdom gained from past failures, rationing in the United States is no longer explicit. Instead, rationing is implicitly based on one's ability to pay.

A patient's ability to pay for health care is determined by two main factors: health insurance and income. Those who lack private health insurance and the income to pay for health care are often left without access, unless they qualify for government health insurance such as Medicaid. However, providers only use ability to pay when rationing non-emergency health care. Specifically, Americans' access to basic health care services, such as preventative services and care for chronic conditions, are limited based on their ability to pay. Scholars call this first-dollar rationing because access to health care is limited through a denial of coverage for initial services. Under first-dollar rationing, coverage is denied either because of a lack of coverage for basic services or because of high deductibles and coinsurance, even though more expensive, tertiary care is often covered. Other countries, such as Great Britain, use last-dollar rationing to control health care costs. Under last-dollar rationing, "Access to very high-cost services is impeded whereas the initial, or first-dollar, costs of basic care are covered. Hence, although access to primary physician care is open to all, those who are more severely ill and likely to require expensive therapies are more likely to confront rationing" (Lamm, 1992). Most experts agree that last-dollar rationing utilizes resources in a way to maximize the public's health because it provides the most cost-effective health care resources, in turn offering the most benefit to the population.

However, last-dollar rationing does not always improve access to health care. For example, Medicaid coverage governed by last-dollar rationing does not necessarily increase access to health care. Reimbursement rates are so low that some physicians refuse to accept Medicaid patients. Physicians who do accept Medicaid patients often have abnormally long wait times. The result is that some recipients forgo care. Ironically, once an uninsured or Medicaid patient's condition becomes more serious, and the cost of care becomes more expensive, access to health care is gained through the use of emergency rooms in public hospitals. Hence, first-dollar rationing based on ability to pay has resulted in delayed access to health care and a misuse of scarce resources, while last-dollar rationing has not increased access under Medicaid because reimbursement rates are below cost.

Lack of insurance.   In the United States, some 45.7 million people do not have health insurance. There are severe health consequences for adults without insurance. Eleven percent of the uninsured are in fair or poor health, compared to 5 percent of those covered by private health insurance. In fact, studies show that uninsured women with breast cancer are diagnosed later in its development, when treatment is less effective. Increasing the likelihood of serious harm, uninsured men with hypertension are more likely to go without screenings and prescribed medication and to skip recommended doctor visits. Data from the Institute of Medicine's 2002 report, *Caring Without Coverage: Too Little, Too Late,* showed that, on average, the uninsured received only about half the care that privately insured patients received, and the uninsured tended to wait longer and get sicker before seeing a doctor (IOM, 2002).

Moreover, the uninsured are less likely to receive recommended preventive and primary care services, face significant barriers to care, and ultimately face worse health outcomes. Compared to the insured, a larger share of the uninsured are unable to pay their medical bills. In addition, the uninsured report problems procuring dental care, filling prescriptions, and accessing physician care. As has been illustrated by empirical data, rationing by ability to pay leads to the under-treatment of those that are unable to pay such as the uninsured, which results in unnecessary deaths. Unfortunately, those most affected by rationing are racial minorities, who are disproportionately uninsured and already subject to racial inequities in accessing health care.

African Americans are more likely than Caucasians to work in low-wage jobs, and so tend to have reduced access to employer-sponsored coverage. Consequently, minorities are more likely than Caucasians to be uninsured or be covered by Medicaid. In addition to lacking access to health care, minorities disproportionately live in poverty. In 2007 the U.S. Census Bureau reported that 24.5 percent of African Americans were living at the poverty level, compared to 8.2 percent of Caucasians. By 2008 over half of African Americans were poor or near poor, compared with 27 percent of Caucasians (Yearby, 2011).

The result of these factors is that minorities are disproportionately unable to afford health care. Because racial inequities related to health care access already exist, it is important not to exacerbate the problem by limiting minorities' access to health care through rationing. Although not the only cause, current rationing practices result in racial inequities in health, which manifest themselves in two ways: disparate access to health care and increased mortality.

People of color make up one third of the U.S. population, but more than half of the uninsured. Of the 45.7 million nonelderly Americans who were uninsured in 2008, more than half were minorities. Specifically, 21 percent of African Americans are uninsured, compared to 13 percent of Caucasians. Additionally, public health insurance programs like Medicaid disproportionately serve minorities. Minorities are less likely than Caucasians to receive health coverage through their employer because they are more likely to hold low-wage jobs (Yearby, 2011).

Impact on patient health.   Between 2005 and 2006, the largest difference in doctor visits between insured and uninsured populations was seen among African Americans and individuals of two or more races. This racial difference in physician visits is not new. In 1986 a national survey of the use of health care services found that "even after taking into account persons' income, health status, age, sex, and whether they had one or more chronic or serious illnesses, blacks have a statistically significantly lower mean number of annual ambulatory [walk-in] visits and are less likely to have seen a physician in a year" (Blendon, Aiken, Freeman, & Corey, 1989). These are just a few examples of the well-documented racial inequities in access to health care, which have resulted in serious harm. Unable to see a doctor because of their inability to pay for health care, African Americans often forgo care, leading to unnecessary deaths.

A recent research study showed that the uninsured are 1.8 times more likely to die from their injuries from auto accidents and 2.6 times more likely to die from gunshot wounds than are privately insured patients. According to Dietrich Jehle, the first author of the study, uninsured adult patients in general have a 25 percent greater mortality rate for all medical conditions than do insured adults. These results are consistent with several previous research studies, which also found that the uninsured have a higher death rate from trauma injuries due to treatment delays, different care due to receipt of fewer diagnostic tests, and decreased health literacy (Yearby, 2011).

One study further showed that, regardless of insurance status, African American and Hispanic patients had higher mortality rates from trauma injuries and were more likely to die from the injuries than were Caucasian patients. Even though insured African American and Hispanic patients had increased mortality rates compared with insured Caucasian patients, the highest adjusted odds of death were for uninsured African American patients when compared with insured Caucasian patients, suggesting that insurance status has a stronger association with mortality after trauma.

The 2002 IOM Report *Caring Without Coverage: Too Little, Too Late* found that approximately 18,000 people died in that year because they lacked insurance. By 2006 the number of deaths was approximately 22,000. Three years later, another Institute of Medicine study, *America's Uninsured Crisis: Consequences for Health and Health Care,* showed that uninsured adults are more likely than insured adults to die from stroke, cancer, heart failure, and congestive heart failure. Moreover, uninsured adults have significantly worse control of their diabetic conditions than do insured adults and are less likely than insured adults to be aware of their hypertension and, if hypertensive, more likely to have inadequate blood pressure control. Finally, the study found that uninsured adults hospitalized with serious acute conditions are at greater risk than insured adults of higher mortality in hospitals and for at least two years after admission.

Although these data were not broken down into racial categories, when combined with other research studies they suggest that lack of insurance causes increased disability and mortality in minorities. For example, research shows that African Americans are more likely than Caucasians to be uninsured. Additionally, African Americans are more likely than Caucasians to die from heart disease, diabetes, and cancer.

Specifically, government data shows that African American women were 10 percent less likely to have been diagnosed with breast cancer; however, they were 34 percent more likely than non-Hispanic white women to die from the disease (Yearby, 2011). Moreover, in 2005 diabetic African Americans were twice as likely as diabetic Caucasians to be hospitalized, and by 2006 African Americans were 2.3 times as likely as Caucasians to die from diabetes. Additionally, these reports showed that African American men were 2.4 times as likely to die from prostate cancer compared to Caucasian men and had a lower five-year cancer survival rate for lung and pancreatic cancer than did Caucasian men. African American men were 30 percent more likely than white men to die from heart disease.

Not all of the racial inequities in mortality can be attributed to rationing policies. However, the above data suggest that the current structure of the rationing system has a disproportionately negative effect on minorities' access to health care. Yet, before a solution can be crafted, it is necessary to understand why seemingly race-neutral rationing policies are a form of structural racial bias.

BIAS IN RATIONING

This structure of rationing is not rationally related to medical need. Furthermore, this rationing system is ineffective in allocating scarce health care resources, as was illustrated by a recent report estimating that 30.6 percent, or $230 billion, of direct medical expenditures between 2003 and 2006 were excess costs due to health and health care inequities incurred by racial minorities (LaViest, Gaskin, & Richard, 2009). Irrational and ineffective, the rationing system is structured to benefit the privileged.

Specifically, structural bias allows those with privilege, such as wealthy Caucasians, to obtain the best-quality health care available. The privileged obtain access because they are able to afford health insurance or pay for health care that their insurance doesn't cover. Those without privilege, such as minorities, who are disproportionately poor, have limited access to heath care because they do not have health insurance and cannot afford to pay for it. Adding insult to injury, the wealthy, who have health insurance, receive discounts on the cost of health care, negotiated by their insurers, while indigent minorities, who do not have health insurance, are charged more and are increasingly required to pay upfront for the health care services they receive. Unable to afford the full cost of or pay upfront for health care, minorities go without treatment until it is too late, resulting in racial inequities in mortality.

The effect of this structural bias is evidenced by empirical data of the health status and mortality rates of uninsured minorities. Compared to the privately insured, the uninsured tend to be in worse health. In fact, 11 percent of the uninsured are in fair or poor health, compared to 5 percent of those covered by private health insurance. Moreover, 19 years of data show that more African Americans have died from coronary disease, breast cancer, and diabetes than Caucasians, even though more Caucasians than African Americans suffer from these conditions. Perhaps the best example of the structural bias of rationing, however, is the story of Deamonte Driver.

Deamonte Driver died of a toothache because he never received a routine $80 tooth extraction that might have saved his life (Yearby, 2011). Deamonte Driver's family was no different than most working-poor families. His mother worked several jobs, but none provided insurance or paid enough for the family to buy insurance. Deamonte was covered under Medicaid, which covers oral health services. However, he never received the dental care he needed due to a shortage of dentists willing to treat those who cannot afford to pay for health care or who rely on government programs for insurance. By the time his mother was able to locate a dentist, Deamonte was no longer covered by Medicaid and thus did not receive treatment.

Lacking health insurance, Deamonte received all of his care in an emergency room or hospital. Instead of a tooth extraction, his care included two brain surgeries, six weeks of hospitalization, and physical and occupational therapy. On his last day, Deamonte played cards and watched a show on television with his mother. As his mother was leaving, Deamonte asked her to pray for him. The next morning, Deamonte was dead from a brain infection caused by the spread of the bacteria from the abscess in his mouth. Deamonte did not have to die; he was only a 12-year-old boy with a cavity. He died because health care in the United States is provided based on ability to pay, not medical need. Clearly, this is an irrational way to allocate health care resources.

Notwithstanding, the irrationality of the system and its failure to allocate scarce resources, the wealthy remain dominant under the current structure of health care rationing because they can afford unlimited access to basic health care, which keeps them healthy. Whereas, minorities are barred access to health care until their conditions are so bad that the cost of care is astronomical, the care given is not effective, and they die unnecessarily.

CONCLUSION

In order to improve the allocation of scarce health care resources for everyone, the underlying problem of access to basic health care services must be addressed. The 2010 ACA has the potential to provide access to insurance for African Americans by alleviating some of the problems with the allocation of health care based on ability to pay, not need. By providing access to health insurance, African Americans will be able to pay for health care. However, mere access to insurance will not equalize access to health care, as illustrated by *Douglas v. Independent Living of Southern California*, the recent Supreme Court case that challenged cuts in California's Medicaid reimbursement rates, thus threatening Medicaid beneficiaries' equal access to health care. The case brought by California pharmacists, hospitals, and Medicaid beneficiaries argues that state cuts to Medicaid reimbursement rates are so severe that providers will stop treating Medicaid patients, thereby significantly threatening their access to care. Hence, effectively addressing structural racial bias requires that health care be rationed according to need, not ability to pay.

REFERENCES AND FURTHER READING

Blendon, R., Aiken, L. H., Freeman, H. E., & Corey, C. R. (1989). Access to medical care for black and white Americans—A matter of continuing concern. *Journal of the American Medical Association, 261*(2), 278–281.

Braveman, P., Cubbin C., Egerter, S., Williams, D. R., & Pamuk, E. (2010). Socioeconomic disparities in health in the United States: What the patterns tell us. *American Journal of Public Health, 100*(S1), 186–189.

Delgado, R. (2001). Two ways to think about race: Reflections on the id, the ego, and other reformist theories of equal protection. *Georgetown Law Journal, 89*, 2279–2296.

Douglas v. Independent Living Center of Southern California, U.S. __ 132 S.Ct. 1204 (2012).

Franks, P., Muennig, P., Lubetkin, E., & Jia, H. (2006). The burden of disease associated with being African-American in the United States and the contribution of socio-economic status. *Social Science & Medicine, 62*(10), 2469–2478.

Grant-Thomas, A., & Powell, J. A. (2006). Toward structural racism framework. *Poverty & Race, 15*, 3–6.

Hummer, R., & Chinn, J. (2011). Race/ethnicity and U.S. adult mortality: Progress, prospects, and new analyses. *Du Bois Review, 8*(1), 5–24.

Institute of Medicine. (2002). *Caring without coverage: Too little, too late 1–3.* Washington, DC: National Academy Press.

Krieger, N., Chen, J. T., Waterman, P. D., Rehkopf, D. H., & Subramanian, S. V. (2005). Painting a truer picture of US socioeconomic and racial/ethnic health inequalities: The public health disparities geocoding project. *American Journal of Public Health, 95*(2), 312–323.

Lamm, R. (1992). Rationing of health care: Inevitable and desirable. *University of Pennsylvania Law Review, 140*(5), 1511–1523.

LaVeist, T. A. (2005). Disentangling race and socioeconomic status: A key to understanding health inequalities. *Journal of Urban Health: Bulletin of the New York Academy of Medicine, 82*(2), 26–34.

LaVeist, T. A., Gaskin, D., & Richard, P. (2009). *The economic burden of health inequalities in the United States.* Washington, DC: Joint Center for Political and Economic Studies.

Lochner, K., Pamuk, E., Makuc, D., Kennedy, B. P., & Kawachi, I. (2001). State-level income inequality and individual mortality risk: A prospective, multilevel study. *American Journal of Public Health, 91*(3), 385–391.

Macinko, J. A., Shi, L., Starfield, B., & Wulu, J. T. (2003). Income inequality and health: A critical review of the literature. *Medical Care Research Review, 60*(4), 407–452.

Mullings, L., & Schulz, A. (2006). Intersectionality and health: An introduction. In *Gender, race, class, and health: Intersectional approaches* (pp. 3–17). San Francisco, CA: Jossey-Bass.

Williams, D. R., & Collins, C. (1995). U.S. socioeconomic and racial differences in health: Patterns and explanations. *Annual Review of Sociology, 21,* 349–386.

Yearby, R. (2011). Racial inequities in mortality and access to health care: The untold peril of rationing health care in the United States. *Journal of Legal Medicine, 32*(1), 77–91.

Ruqaiijah A. Yearby

Single-Payer Health Care System

POINT: Single-payer systems work well in many countries and can often provide care at lower cost than can the private insurance system.

Steffie Woolhandler and David Himmelstein, City University of New York School of Public Health
Simeon Kimmel, Harvard Medical School
Carl Berdahl, Yale University

COUNTERPOINT: Single-payer insurance is not enough and in fact would entrench an already-broken system. The entire health care delivery system needs reform.

Steffie Woolhandler and David Himmelstein, City University of New York School of Public Health
Simeon Kimmel, Harvard Medical School
Carl Berdahl, Yale University

Introduction

Many advocates of universal health care have long pointed to a single-payer system as the answer to the problems facing U.S. health care, whereas critics of the single-payer approach vociferously disagree. While the Patient Protection and Affordable Care Act (ACA) did not incorporate such a plan into the reforms it instituted, the efficacy of single-payer systems will likely form the core of the ongoing debate on health care reform as the ACA, and even future reforms, take effect.

Proponents of a single-payer system argue that the savings resulting from having one entity in charge of paying health care providers will enable increased coverage and improved outcomes; this position—argued in the Point section of this chapter—is typically supported by policymakers and politicians of a liberal persuasion. Opponents of single-payer systems generally stand firm against the involvement of the government in free enterprise and individual choice in the health care market; this concept—touched upon at the beginning of the Counterpoint section—lies at the root of many conservative objections to a single-payer system. However, the authors of the Counterpoint take the critique of single-payer systems in a decidedly different direction, arguing that the introduction of a single-payer system would be an insufficient reform and that a more wholesale remaking of not just the payment systems employed in U.S. health care, but the delivery of health services, must form the core of health care reform.

The authors—in both the Point and Counterpoint—emphasize this critical distinction between payments and services, between the organization of financing and the organization of delivery. In short, as the authors explain, a single-payer approach consolidates financing, but not necessarily delivery. In fact, in the Canadian health care system, which informs much of the discussion in the Point section, and which provides the model for advocates of a single-payer system, health care providers remain in the private sector, but the payment process is in government hands; likewise, if we think of Medicare as another model for a single-payer system, it too relies on private-sector providers. Conversely, the British National Health Services relies primarily on providers who are government employees; so does the Veterans Administration (VA) system described in the Counterpoint.

Despite this variation in who pays for and who provides health care services, the authors argue that some systems are more efficacious in terms of both reducing costs and improving outcomes. As the Point proposes in its elaboration on the Canadian system, improved health care outcomes are not at all correlated with competition in the payment and insurance market. In fact, Canada outpaces the United States in terms of three of the most common indicators of health outcomes: life expectancy, infant mortality, and maternal mortality. Moreover these health advantages are achieved at significant aggregate savings: Canada spends 35 per cent less per capita on health care than does the United States. And while the United States spends considerably more, it covers fewer individuals. The reasons for this, the authors argue, revolve primarily around the higher administrative costs in the United States, due to its multiple-payer structure. Furthermore, in our fragmented health care system, most payers have limited bargaining power and cannot prevent providers from charging more and more.

On the other hand, a single-payer system, such as that in Canada, eliminates competition in the health insurance market, and in theory competition should lower costs. Additionally, as critics of single-payer systems propound, innovation in health care itself is at risk with a single-payer system as the performance of providers, and hence health care outcomes, might be hurt in a monopolistic payment setting. Incomes of doctors, hospitals, clinics, and research facilities might be limited due to the shrinking of government finances, stifling innovation in the development of new drugs, new surgical procedures, new technologies, and even new and better delivery models.

One innovative delivery approach arising from recent pressures in the U.S. health care market is the accountable care organization (ACO). ACOs seek to consolidate services, not through the public employment of providers, but through creating financial incentives for hospitals and physicians to work together to take care of a population of patients, improving their health outcomes while reining in overuse of services and containing costs. The Counterpoint makes the sound observation that this type of consolidation may not exist even in a single-payer system. The promise that this type of health care organization can deliver better care while reducing costs has been enshrined in the ACA, which funds ACO demonstration projects. However, the fact is that ACOs do not consolidate financing, and ACOs may bill to multiple payers, so we are left to wonder if the potential loss of health care dollars to administrative inefficiency saddles ACOs with the same problems from which the current U.S. system suffers. Are ACOs enough of an innovation? In addition, it is worth asking if ACOs are all that different than the managed care plans that were so reviled in the 1990s. In any case, does the existence of ACOs speak for or against the adoption of a single-payer system? Can't you have ACOs with or without a single payer?

After questioning the efficacy of both single-payer systems and ACOs, the Counterpoint describes the Veterans Administration health system—having undergone sweeping reforms starting in 1995—as the one model in the United States that has successfully improved health outcomes while lowering costs—all achieved with the federal government in charge of both the payment system and provision of care. However, this type of government involvement in health care may be politically palatable only because of the specific population it serves: virtually all politicians and policymakers find it easy to support such a system for U.S. veterans who fulfill one of the most critical roles a government can provide to its citizens. And this raises another crucial question: Is any one-size-fits-all plan acceptable given our political, economic, and government structure? The VA system serves the population it was designed to serve, but as the conservative thinking goes, individual choice interacting with market dynamics helps to create an environment in which quality of care and innovation are rewarded. Veterans who participate in the VA system are in effect beneficiaries of advancements resulting from private investments in health-related industries. If the government ran the entire U.S. health care system—even simply as a single payer, not a single provider—how would that innovation, which is the hallmark of health care in the United States, thrive?

Conservative values such as choice and freedom seem to clash directly with what liberal observers say must be key components in health care—the use of limited financial resources to expand health care to the uninsured and underinsured. The single-payer debate, as elaborated here, helps to illuminate why indeed it is so difficult to arrive at meaningful health care reform in the United States, but it also suggests ways that these seemingly conflicting values might be rebalanced to arrive at models based on sound analysis and reasoning. Indeed, many scholars point to an increasing convergence between systems around the world and even within the United States. Even single-payer systems have moved away from a singular uniform model in recent years. For example, Medicare looks much less like a single-payer model than it did 30 years ago. The prescription drug benefit is really a voucher system, which allows beneficiaries to buy private plans. Moreover Medicare Part C, which allows beneficiaries to buy into private plans, especially managed care plans, is growing in popularity, with many people preferring such plans to traditional Medicare. Canada is also experimenting with privatization of health care, as is Great Britain. With the ACA, the United States is moving toward a more consolidated, or at least regulated, system, while the more uniform systems are increasingly relying on competition. Does this convergence suggest some limits of looking toward a Canadian model? And will it help the United States develop a system that balances potentially conflicting values and serves the purposes and needs of the broadest possible population?

POINT

The United States spends more on health care than any other nation. Canada, a country that is demographically similar, spends 35 percent less per capita and has better health outcomes. The Canadian single-payer health system has saved money through administrative simplification and improved health planning. Similar improvements could be realized in the United States by switching to a Canadian-style single-payer system.

THE U.S. HEALTH SYSTEM

The health insurance system in the United States is comprised of a mixture of private and public programs. Many of the insured obtain private coverage through an employer, while some others purchase private insurance independently. Public programs insure many other individuals. The eligibility for these programs is limited to specific subsets of the population, including children, pregnant women, veterans, the disabled, the impoverished, and the elderly.

In 2009, the patchwork of public and private health insurance providers left 16.7 percent of residents completely uninsured, and, even after implementation of the Patient Protection and Affordable Care Act, many will remain uninsured. Additionally, there is evidence that many insured people are actually "underinsured," meaning that they have such poor coverage that accessing medical care is daunting and paying medical bills often leads to bankruptcy. In the United States, both uninsurance and underinsurance have been associated with death and poor health outcomes.

The chaotic insurance system in the United States requires large-scale administrative staffing by health providers and health insurance companies. Doctors and hospitals collect fees from patients and also from many different insurers, each with its own rules and regulations. Hence, each provider must maintain personnel dedicated to billing. Additionally, each insurance company requires administrative staff to process bills and monitor the appropriateness of payments. In the end, consumers pay a premium for medical services because of the administrative complexity of the system.

Compared to other countries with highly developed economies, the United States relies heavily on market-based competition to encourage efficiency within the health sector, and health planning suffers as a result. For example, market forces encourage (1) the buildup of profitable health services such as high-tech procedures in areas populated by wealthy patients and (2) the closing of unprofitable health services such as primary care, mental health services, and emergency departments in areas populated by low-income patients. While the government exercises some influence over health planning, as a general rule, the health sector is seen as a collection of businesses rather than a system intended to provide services to the population.

While the United States has grown accustomed to its health system, there are alternatives. This chapter examines the Canadian single-payer system as a potential health-reform model.

Single payer is a term used to describe a health care financing system in which one entity, usually a government-run organization, collects virtually all health care dollars and pays virtually all health care costs. Financing health care through a single payer makes it possible to streamline administrative practices, simplify billing, and save money on bureaucracy. In essence, a single health insurance provider could take the place of the tens of thousands of insurance plans in the United States, making life simpler for health care practitioners and administrators, while also making health care better and more affordable.

THE CANADIAN HEALTH SYSTEM

Approximately 97 percent of all Canadians receive insurance through Canadian Medicare, a jointly funded federal/provincial health insurance system. Nearly all other Canadians are covered by federal health services designed for veterans or aboriginal groups. All of these programs provide hospital and physician services. Only dental care, residential (that is, long-term) care, and pharmaceutical costs are not uniformly covered. Many individuals, or their employers, pay for these services out-of-pocket or purchase supplemental insurance through the private market.

As in the United States, delivery of health care involves both public and private organizations. In Canada, most physicians are in private practice, while most hospitals are operated by charities or by local or provincial governments. Because nearly all Canadians are covered under one system of insurance, administrative costs are much lower than in the United States.

The government also exercises far more control over investments in new facilities and programs in Canada. The government takes financial responsibility for its population's health, and it has a vested interest in ensuring that all Canadians have access to quality health care. Primary financing for all major capital projects comes from the province's single payer, and government approval is needed to, for instance, build a new hospital wing or purchase an MRI machine. This provides a very powerful health planning lever that allows investments to be directed to meeting community needs rather than businesses' profits.

THE DIVERGENCE OF U.S. AND CANADIAN HEALTH INSURANCE AND SPENDING

From 1900 until the mid-1960s, health care financing and delivery were similar in the United States and Canada. The private practice of medicine had emerged as the most common way physicians interacted with patients. While doctors in 1900 had little to offer patients in terms of proven therapy, scientific progress soon brought a wave of useful diagnostic and therapeutic technologies. But as medical care became more advanced, it also became less affordable. The United States and Canada dealt differently with the burgeoning need for health insurance.

In the United States, the earliest widespread health insurance took the form of workers' compensation, which protected employees from financial ruin in case of on-the-job injury. During the Great Depression, hospitals encouraged the development of large-scale private health insurance programs. Then, during World War II, the federal government instituted a wage freeze, so employers began to offer health insurance as a means to increase compensation and attract workers. Unions started to bargain with employers for health insurance, and the IRS soon treated employer-paid health insurance as a tax-free benefit. This favorable tax treatment catalyzed the creation of the employment-centered health insurance system that persists in the new millennium.

Following World War II, many middle-class families obtained employer-based health insurance. However, many of the elderly, the unemployed, and the poor relied on limited public programs or charity from hospitals and doctors. In 1965, Congress voted to create Medicare and Medicaid. These programs provided health insurance for the elderly and some of the poor, respectively, thought to be the two most vulnerable populations in need of health insurance. In 2011, Medicare and Medicaid continue to function as essential sources of health insurance for the elderly, the permanently disabled, and the eligible poor, while other vulnerable groups such as the ineligible poor still lack insurance.

In Canada in the 1920s and 1930s, there were several attempts in economically depressed regions to pool resources and provide basic health services for the poor. Doctors and hospitals in the province of Saskatchewan were hit particularly hard during the Great Depression: they had difficulty generating revenue because so many patients were unable to pay for services. By 1933, the Saskatchewan Medical Association officially endorsed a public health insurance program, thereby inviting the government to pay patients' bills. However, the economy soon improved, and momentum for reform slowed until the mid-1940s, when the socialist-leaning Cooperative Commonwealth Federation gained power in Saskatchewan. In 1946, the province passed the Hospital Services Plan, which provided hospital services to its citizens. Inspired by the success of this program, the Canadian federal government passed the National Hospital and Diagnostic Services Act in 1957, granting federal funding to any province that provided hospital services to its residents. By 1961, all provinces were participating. In 1962, Saskatchewan again led the way by adding coverage for physician services. Despite strong physician opposition, including a two-week doctors' strike, the program proved successful, and a Royal Commission appointed by a conservative federal government recommended nationwide adoption of Saskatchewan's program. With the 1966 passage of the federal Medical Care Act, all provinces began to provide physician services as well. This event marked the beginning of Canada's modern single-payer system, under which the government guarantees comprehensive health services for all Canadians.

In the 1960s, when these major health reforms were taking place in the United States and Canada, health expenditures were similar: each nation spent approximately 6 percent of gross domestic product (GDP) per year on health care, and spending was increasing gradually each year. By the 1970s, spending patterns began to diverge, and the United States experienced rapid increases while Canada's spending increased more slowly.

In the economically developed world, the United States soon became the clear outlier in health spending, while Canada's spending progressed at rates similar to those of major western European countries. These trends continue today, despite efforts to slow spending in the United States. In 2010, the United States spent nearly 17 percent of GDP on health care, a share that is about twice the average of other developed nations.

THE UNITED STATES SPENDS MORE AND REAPS NO CLEAR BENEFIT

The United States ranks number one in the world for total health care spending. One might expect that spending the most would buy the best health system. However, the data reveal otherwise.

Both the United States and Canada are members of the Organisation for Economic Co-operation and Development (OECD), an organization consisting of countries with highly developed economies. Standardized health data from the OECD consistently demonstrate that the United States is no better off, and in many cases clearly performs worse than most other OECD nations, despite significantly higher spending.

The United States spends 35 percent more per capita on health care, while it trails Canada every year in the three most commonly cited health outcome measures: life expectancy, infant mortality, and maternal mortality. A joint survey by the two nations' health statistics agencies in 2006 found that Canadians enjoy better access to care, and a review of comparative studies found that quality of care appears at least as good in Canada. Thus, spending more than Canada does not guarantee better health outcomes for the United States.

INCREASED SPENDING IS DUE TO ADMINISTRATIVE COSTS

Health economists have closely studied the differences in health spending in the United States and Canada. Most investigators agree that Canada delivers more total health services per capita. The difference is that each test, treatment, and medication is more expensive in the United States. Higher overhead expenses contribute greatly to the disparity.

By definition, overhead expenses are lost resources that do not contribute directly to an end-product. In the health sector, these are expenses not directly involved with patient care. The United States is relatively inefficient compared to Canada when it comes to administration and, more specifically, tasks related to billing and oversight of care.

Billing in Canada is simple because there is only one organization to bill, whereas in the United States, hospitals and insurance companies require many personnel to support the complex billing system. Additionally, in Canada, the government monitors the appropriateness of care by investigating large-scale trends in the practice of medicine; meanwhile, insurance companies in the United States oversee care primarily at the level of the patient-physician interaction, attempting to deny insurance claims one-by-one. Monitoring each patient encounter is a huge expense, and it inevitably gets passed on to consumers. In this fashion, administrative inefficiency in U.S. hospitals and insurance companies contributes greatly to higher health care expenses. Furthermore, quality of care comes into question in this regard: while some critics of single-payer systems argue that government involvement in health care is intrusive, private health insurers burden health providers much more. A single-payer health system would actually enable doctors and patients to spend more time focusing on health instead of paperwork.

A 2003 study by some of the authors of this chapter examined the discrepancy between administrative expenses in the United States and Canada. According to 1999 data, health administration accounted for 31.0 percent of United States health expenditures versus 16.7 percent of Canadian expenditures. Between 1969 and 1999, administrative workers' share of the American health labor force grew from 18.2 to 27.3 percent, while in Canada it grew from 16.0 to 19.1 percent from 1971 to 1996. During these years, an explosion of administrative expenses occurred in the United States. The investigators concluded that, if the United States were to change to a universal single-payer system and take advantage of new administrative efficiencies, the savings would be substantial enough to provide insurance for all currently uninsured Americans and to upgrade coverage for the underinsured. This conclusion has since been confirmed by both the U.S. Government Accountability Office and the Congressional Budget Office.

Administrative costs in the United States soared in the late twentieth century, and they continue to make medical care expensive. Canada's relative administrative simplicity allows its health sector to function more efficiently; the United States could realize similar benefits if it converted to a single-payer system.

UNINSURANCE AND UNDERINSURANCE HARM U.S. PATIENTS

Numerous studies demonstrate that having insurance is important. In fact, lack of health insurance has been shown to cause 45,000 deaths in the United States each year. Possible reasons that the uninsured have a higher risk of death are that they are less likely to receive preventive care, less likely to receive necessary primary care, and more likely to fall ill to preventable illness than people who are insured. In a country as rich as the United States, it is tragic that so many people die because they lack insurance.

Unfortunately, uninsurance is not the only problem. Some *insured* patients forego necessary medical care because their insurance plans require exorbitant out-of-pocket spending. Thus, these enrollees are "underinsured" because they are unprotected despite being insured. A study by C. Schoen found that 42 percent of all Americans were either uninsured or underinsured. As health spending skyrockets, enrollees are forced to pay more out-of-pocket expenses, and the number of underinsured individuals climbs further. Underinsurance commonly leads to financial ruin when expenses arise, thus also causing more people to default on insurance payments and ultimately become uninsured.

A study by the National Bureau of Economic Research demonstrated that newly insured individuals get healthier. This finding gives hope that transitioning to a single-payer system and guaranteeing coverage for everyone would improve quality of life and save lives.

HEALTH PLANNING IS POOR IN THE UNITED STATES

The United States health system has no coherent system of health planning. Under a single-payer national health plan, the government could work to coordinate health services with the future in mind, funding new programs and facilities based on health needs as is done in Canada. Instead, market forces take the place of health planning in the United States. As a result, medical education produces few primary care doctors and necessary programs and facilities are starved for funds while investment is directed toward already abundant profitable services.

Indeed, the proportion of physicians in primary care specialties is diminishing in the United States. Along with the decline of primary care comes the decline of preventive care. Under a national health system, there could be increased emphasis on maintaining primary and preventive health services. In Canada, about half of all medical school graduates enter training in primary care, and primary care payments to doctors are only modestly lower than payments to specialists. Meanwhile, in the United States, specialists' incomes have soared, encouraging medical students to specialize despite the increasing shortage of primary care physicians. If a coherent sense of health planning existed, the system would encourage doctors to pursue careers that would be most useful to the greatest number of patients.

Another health planning failure in the United States is that resources are distributed unfairly. Because procedure-oriented services are more profitable than primary care, mental health, or emergency services, high-tech facilities have been proliferating. These facilities drive up costs because they specialize in the very procedures that physicians often perform unnecessarily. For example, experts estimate that 40 percent of cardiac stents and nearly a quarter of implanted defibrillators are not needed. Furthermore, patient outcomes are worse at these smaller facilities because they have fewer patients than large institutions, which compromises quality. These new facilities tend to appear in high-income locales because it is relatively easy to generate revenue there. Costly advertising campaigns bring in patients who do not need treatment, and facilities often treat them anyway to maximize their profits. In this fashion, economics are turned upside down, supply drives demand, and medical costs soar. A national health system that stressed health planning would encourage the proliferation of necessary services, not just profitable ones.

While these unnecessary high-cost facilities proliferate, less profitable services are forced to shut down despite community needs. Hospitals and doctors providing primary care, mental health, or emergency services suffer financially when located in low-income areas with few privately insured patients. Many of these facilities have closed because they have been unable to generate enough revenue. As a result, poor areas end up with a paucity of necessary health services, despite having major needs. Under a national health system, the government would work to bring services to those who were underserved, rather than allowing market forces to take them away.

A single-payer system would empower the government to actively engage in real health planning to guarantee access to health services for all, eliminate duplicative services, and coordinate physician training to meet population needs. The United States unfortunately sees the health sector as a collection of profitable businesses rather than a system that should serve the population's needs.

SINGLE-PAYER VERSUS OTHER REFORM OPTIONS

What would a single-payer system look like in the United States? The United States already has a model for a single-payer system. Traditional Medicare, which covers necessary hospital and medical services, acts as a health insurer for most people 65 years and older and for some disabled individuals. In conceptualizing a transition to a single-payer system, it is simplest to envision the expansion of traditional Medicare into a system that would cover all Americans for all medically necessary services, including: doctor, hospital, preventive, long-term care, mental health, reproductive health care, dental, vision, prescription drug, and medical supply costs.

Under a single-payer system, patients would have the ability to choose any doctor, and doctors would have no financial incentive to accept one patient over another. Each bill for patient care would be sent to Medicare, and physicians would be reimbursed for services. Hospitals would receive a yearly global budget for operating expenses, which they would be able to spend as necessary to support services for all their patients. Investments in new health facilities and expensive equipment purchases would be allocated by regional health planning boards, which would seek to distribute resources according to the needs of patients and communities.

The United States wastes huge amounts of money on administrative costs. With the amount that the country already pays for health care, Americans could enjoy universal health coverage. Funding for a single-payer system would be generated in two different ways: (1) replacing the premiums and out-of-pocket spending that individuals and businesses already pay with modest new taxes and (2) recapturing administrative waste by eliminating private insurers and consolidating health insurance under a single payer.

In other words, if all individuals and businesses were to continue paying what they now pay toward to the health sector, under a single-payer system there would be enough money to finance all necessary health services for everyone. The key to financing universal health care is eliminating private insurers and recapturing money that is wasted on administration. Many private insurers spend 20 to 30 percent of their revenue on expenses other than medical services. Traditional Medicare, on the other hand, is much more efficient, spending about 2 to 3 percent on similar expenses. Under a single-payer system, the money currently spent on administrative waste would instead be spent on productive services for patients.

Having a single health insurance entity would also give the United States the opportunity to save money in novel ways. For instance, there would be new leverage to negotiate lower fees when purchasing drugs and medical devices from large corporations, as happens in Canada. Hospitals would no longer have financial incentives to perform unnecessary procedures; on the contrary, they would have incentives to keep costs down so that they could continue to operate within pre-specified global budgets.

Perhaps most importantly, a single-payer health system would guarantee health insurance for everyone. Unemployment would no longer cause loss of insurance, and no one would be uninsured or underinsured. Patients would be able to go to any doctor or hospital. The health insurance system would be designed to keep all people healthy, whether rich or poor. In a country that values equality, access to health care would finally be equal.

The test of time has shown that the private sector has failed to produce a health system that is affordable and effective. A single-payer approach is fiscally responsible, and it would make the country healthier. It is the most promising overarching solution to problems that plague the United States, and it would outperform other reform options that Congress has considered.

THE AFFORDABLE CARE ACT ENTRENCHES A DEFECTIVE SYSTEM

In 2010, Congress passed the Patient Protection and Affordable Care Act (ACA), and President Barack Obama signed it into law. While the bill will extend health insurance coverage to many low-income individuals and protect consumers from some detrimental practices by the private health insurance industry, it fails to enact substantial long-term cost-control measures. Worse still, the law mandates that all Americans not covered by a public program must purchase private health insurance, thereby entrenching a system of private health insurance that is unaffordable and ineffective.

The ACA's cost-containment strategy is unlikely to produce real savings because it relies heavily on making the health insurance market more transparent (e.g., through building insurance exchanges, establishing standardized tiers of plans with similar coverage, and so forth). Unfortunately, the law assumes that informed consumers will choose the most affordable plans, and insurance companies will be forced to compete with one another to reduce the cost of their products. This strategy is unlikely to produce sustainable savings or quality coverage. Over time, it has become clear that insurance companies produce profits not by becoming more efficient but instead by selectively enrolling healthy patients and denying sick patients' claims. Because cherry picking enrollees and denying claims require administrative infrastructure, systemic inefficiency will continue to plague the health sector. ACA regulations do seek to limit such abuses, but private insurance companies with decades of experience gaming the system will quickly find new ways to maximize profits at their enrollees' expense.

The other central tenet of cost savings under the ACA is the idea that unifying physicians and medical services into organizations accountable for costs and outcomes of medical care will produce better health outcomes for less money. These so-called accountable care organizations (ACOs) are held up as a revolutionary idea, but in reality they are nearly identical to health maintenance organizations (HMOs) such as Kaiser Permanente that already exist in the United States. HMOs have not produced dramatic cost savings or improved patient outcomes, and ACOs will not be any different.

The most problematic aspect of the ACA, though, is that it requires Americans not covered by public programs to buy coverage from a private insurer, thereby cementing health insurance as an overpriced, ineffective commodity. True health reform under single payer would guarantee all U.S. residents health insurance from birth to death, provide all necessary medical care, prioritize patients over profits, and cut administrative waste.

A PUBLIC OPTION CANNOT COMPETE EFFECTIVELY WITH PRIVATE PLANS

Some policymakers propose a public health insurance option to heighten competition for private insurance companies. Because profit-driven private health insurance companies naturally seek ways to (1) avoid enrolling high-risk patients and (2) avoid paying for medical care for enrollees who become sick, competition among insurers does not occur on a level playing field. Therefore, if a public option were available, it would quickly become the "dumping ground" for high-risk patients.

Medicare's experience allowing private plans to compete with the traditional Medicare program illustrates this danger. Despite prohibitions on cherry picking, private Medicare plans have avoided high-risk patients through selective marketing, tailoring services to be more attractive to healthier patients (for example, by holding enrollment sessions at night when healthier people are more likely to attend). Like traditional Medicare, a public plan would eventually be comprised of people with health problems who get sick frequently, while the private plans would have mostly healthy enrollees. In the end, the public plan could not afford to charge low monthly fees because of its high concentration of costly patients.

On this skewed playing field, a public plan, despite being more efficient, could not effectively compete with private plans. A better health-reform option would be to guarantee health insurance for everyone in the nation under a single, comprehensive health plan. With single payer, a single insurance pool dilutes risk, administration becomes simpler, and health insurance is affordable.

CONSUMER-DRIVEN HEALTH CARE IS LIKE UNDERINSURANCE

The term consumer-driven health care refers to health insurance plans that require consumers to pay for day-to-day medical expenses, with insurance kicking in once cost reaches a certain level (that is, so-called catastrophic coverage). The idea is that the consumer can set aside money for routine health expenses in a health savings account and pay a low monthly premium for catastrophic health coverage. If each individual has a financial incentive to use less health care, the country as a whole can reduce its health care spending. Studies do show that patients in consumer-driven plans reduce the amount of care that they use; as well as unnecessary care, however, they also forego necessary care, which can be dangerous.

Another problem with consumer-driven health plans is that enrollees with chronic conditions pay major out-of-pocket costs. Even healthy persons are likely to develop a chronic condition while enrolled (since the majority of all Americans have at least one chronic condition), and yet most enrollees have no money in health savings accounts. Consumer-driven plans are also administratively complex, requiring all of the usual paperwork plus the added burden of tracking enrollees' finances to determine when catastrophic coverage kicks in.

In sum, patients in consumer-driven plans forego necessary care, and the plans fail to protect chronically ill patients. Hence those with consumer-driven health plans are underinsured. Furthermore, administrative inefficiency persists. A more efficient single-payer system providing the full spectrum of preventive care, ongoing care for chronic conditions, and catastrophic coverage would better serve enrollees.

CONCLUSION

The United States spends more than any other country on health care without reaping significant benefits. Millions of people are uninsured, millions more are underinsured, health outcomes are mediocre, and market forces take the place of real health planning.

The United States and Canada have similar systems for the *delivery* of health care, but Canada's system for *financing* health care—the single-payer approach—allows for significant administrative savings and better health planning. The free market has failed to produce affordable health insurance or a system guaranteeing health care for all. Switching to a single-payer system would be feasible for the United States, and it would provide savings great enough to guarantee comprehensive health insurance for all U.S. residents.

Changing to a single-payer system would not be the health-reform endgame, but it is a sound choice in terms of economics and public health. It would also build a stronger health system, which would help the nation better address the problems of the future.

REFERENCES AND FURTHER READING

Aaron, H. J. (2003). The costs of health care administration in the United States and Canada—Questionable answers to a questionable question. *New England Journal of Medicine, 349*(8), 801–803.

Al-Khatib, S. M., Hellkamp, A., Curtis, J., Mark, D., Peterson, E., & Hammill, S. (2011). Non-evidence-based ICD implantations in the United States. *The Journal of the American Medical Association, 305*(1), 43–49.

American College of Physicians. (2008). Achieving a high-performance health care system with universal access: What the United States can learn from other countries. *Annals of Internal Medicine, 148*(1), 55–75.

Boden, W. E., O'Rourke, R. A., Teo, K. K., Hartigan, P. M., Maron, D. J., Kostuk, W. J., & Weintraub, W. S. (2007). Optimal medical therapy with or without PCI for stable coronary disease (COURAGE Trial). *New England Journal of Medicine, 356*(15), 1503–1516.

Buntin, M. B., Damberg, C., Haviland, A., Kapur, K., Lurie, N., McDevitt, R., & Marquis, M. S. (2006). Consumer-directed health care: Early evidence about effects on cost and quality. *Health Affairs, 25*(6), w516–w530.

Callahan, D. (2009). *Taming the beloved beast: How medical technology costs are destroying our health care system.* Princeton, NJ: Princeton University Press.

Chalkidou, K., Tunis, S., Lopert, R., Rochaix, L., Sawicki, P. T., Nasser, M., & Xerri, B. (2009). Comparative effectiveness research and evidence-based health policy: Experience from four countries. *Milbank Quarterly, 87*(2), 339–367.

Finkelstein, A., Taubman, S., Wright, B., Bernstein, M., Gruber, J., Newhouse, J. P., et al. (2011). *The Oregon health insurance experiment: Evidence from the first year.* NBER Working Paper Series, Vol. w17190. Retrieved from http://ssrn.com/abstract=1881018

Geyman, J. (2010). *Hijacked! The road to single-payer in the aftermath of stolen health care reform.* Monroe, ME: Common Courage Press.

Guyatt, G., Devereaux, P., Lexchin, J., Stone, S., Yalnizyan, A., Himmelstein, D., et al. (2007). A systematic review of studies comparing health outcomes in Canada and the United States. *Open Medicine, 1*(1), e27–e36.

Hsia, R. Y., Kellermann, A. L., & Shen, Y. (2011). Factors associated with closures of emergency departments in the United States. *The Journal of the American Medical Association, 305*(19), 1978–1985.

Iglehart, J. K. (2000). Revisiting the Canadian health care system. *New England Journal of Medicine, 342*(26), 2007–2012.

Johnson, J. A., & Stoskopf, C. H. (2010). *Comparative health systems: Global perspectives.* Sudbury, MA: Jones and Bartlett Publishers.

Lasser, K. E., Himmelstein, D. U., & Woolhandler, S. (2006). Access to care, health status, and health disparities in the United States and Canada: Results of a cross-national population-based survey. *American Journal of Public Health, 96*(7), 1300–1307.

Lavarreda, S. A., Brown, E. R., & Bolduc, C. D. (2011). Underinsurance in the United States: An interaction of costs to consumers, benefit design, and access to care. *Annual Review of Public Health, 32*(1), 471–482.

McWilliams, J. M. (2009). Health consequences of uninsurance among adults in the United States: Recent evidence and implications. *Milbank Quarterly, 87*(2), 443–494.

Newhouse, J. P. (2004). Consumer-directed health plans and the RAND health insurance experiment. *Health Affairs, 23*(6), 107–113.

Nichols, L. M., Ginsburg, P. B., Berenson, R. A., Christianson, J., & Hurley, R. E. (2004). Are market forces strong enough to deliver efficient health care systems? Confidence is waning. *Health Affairs, 23*(2), 8–21.

Organisation for Economic Co-operation and Development (OECD). (2011). OECD health data: Health care utilisation [Data set]. *OECD Health Statistics.* Retrieved from http://www.oecd-ilibrary.org/content/data/data-00542-en

Orszag, P. R., & Ellis, P. (2007). The challenge of rising health care costs—A view from the congressional budget office. *New England Journal of Medicine, 357*(18), 1793–1795.

Pozen, A., & Cutler, D. M. (2010). Medical spending differences in the United States and Canada: The role of prices, procedures, and administrative expenses. *Inquiry, 47*(2), 124–134.

Redelmeier, D. A., & Fuchs, V. R. (1993). Hospital expenditures in the United States and Canada. *New England Journal of Medicine, 328*(11), 772–778.

Reinhardt, U. E., Hussey, P. S., & Anderson, G. F. (2004). U.S. health care spending in an international context. *Health Affairs, 23*(3), 10–25.

Scanlon, D. P., Swaminathan, S., Lee, W., & Chernew, M. (2008). Does competition improve health care quality? *Health Services Research, 43*(6), 1931–1951.

Schoen, C., Collins, S. R., Kriss, J. L., & Doty, M. M. (2008). How many are underinsured? Trends among U.S. adults, 2003 and 2007. *Health Affairs, 27*(4), w298–w309.

Tuohy, C. H. (1999). *Accidental logics: The dynamics of change in the health care arena in the United States, Britain, and Canada.* New York, NY: Oxford University Press.

Wilper, A. P., Woolhandler, S., Lasser, K. E., McCormick, D., Bor, D. H., & Himmelstein, D. U. (2009). Health insurance and mortality in US adults. *American Journal of Public Health, 99*(12), 2289–2295.

Woolhandler, S., Campbell, T., & Himmelstein, D. U. (2003). Costs of health care administration in the United States and Canada. *New England Journal of Medicine, 349*(8), 768–775.

Woolhandler, S., Campbell, T., & Himmelstein, D. U. (2004). Health care administration in the United States and Canada: Micromanagement, macro costs. *International Journal of Health Services, 34*(1), 65–78.

Woolhandler, S., & Himmelstein, D. U. (1991). The deteriorating administrative efficiency of the U.S. health care system. *New England Journal of Medicine, 324*(18), 1253–1258.

Steffie Woolhandler, David Himmelstein, Simeon Kimmel, and Carl Berdahl

COUNTERPOINT

A shift to a Canadian-style single-payer health care system would achieve important advances in reducing administrative waste and inequity in health care access. However, it would take the existing fragmented, wasteful fee-for-service delivery system and freeze it in place—limiting potential gains in health care quality and cost reduction.

Some critics of single-payer reform see it as too radical a departure from current health financing arrangements, worrying that it would unduly expand the reach of government and disrupt care. They fear that an expansion of government control over health care financing will stifle health insurance innovation that they believe can emerge only in a competitive marketplace. They sometimes even argue that doctors' incomes would decrease and, therefore, fewer highly competent people would be attracted to medicine. Many of these critics hear stories of long waits for specialized surgeries or new technologies that are slow to be adopted in countries with shrinking health care budgets and assume this would be transferred to a U.S. system. Or, they sincerely believe that the American health care system offers the best care in the world, even if it is not the most cost-effective. Other critics of a single-payer system are concerned that too many jobs would be lost if the hefty insurance industry was handed over to a single government payer. Even some who agree as to the merits of the single-payer vision argue that it is not a politically feasible goal because of a flawed democratic process and an overwhelmingly powerful health care industry. They suggest more pragmatic incremental changes can expand and improve care in the interim while providing a springboard towards a single-payer system. While these critiques raise important questions, they hinge primarily on political strategy and political preference rather than on data from existing experiences with a single-payer approach. Given that the political circumstances for health care reform may change, it is important to ask whether a single-payer system would achieve the advantages that proponents claim, or will more thorough reform be necessary to achieve improved access, quality, and decreased cost.

This Counterpoint addresses a central nexus of health-reform debate: Will payment reform alone adequately address the shortcomings of our health care system, or is reform of the health care delivery system also required? Reform that merely changes the payers fails to address key shortfalls in the current health system: it maintains fragmented entities of care and incentives for physicians and hospitals to perform high volumes of tests and procedures. Though a single-payer system would streamline billing and provide equal, universal coverage, eliminating the incentive for providers and hospitals to attract patient populations with private insurance, physicians will confront ongoing fee-for-service incentives and hospitals will continue to compete to provide patients with services that are reimbursed most generously. Meanwhile, these services will be disproportionately distributed—services that are overly abundant in certain areas and hard to access in others. Without delivery system integration and planning, in addition to providing a single payer, it is unlikely that electronic medical records will be shared between practices and institutions, practice guidelines will be implemented and monitored uniformly, and services will be designed specifically commensurate with a geographical population's need. Hence, a Canadian-style single-payer insurance model would not be sufficient; integration of inpatient and outpatient care into nonprofit entities resembling the Veterans Health Administration (VA) is needed to maximize both quality and efficiency.

The fragmentation of health care, which a shift to single-payer would preserve, has led many political and corporate leaders to look to accountable care organizations (ACOs) as a model for reform. An ACO is envisioned as a coordinated group of health care providers who jointly take financial and clinical responsibility for the full range of care for a defined population of patients, accepting accountability for the quality and costs of that care. In the proposed ACO model, payments are linked not only to cost reduction, but also to quality indicators, which are tracked by performance measures (e.g., rates of recommended drugs used in heart failure patients). It is possible to imagine ACOs, single payer, and the VA on a spectrum of health care administrative structures with different ways of distributing economic risk and delivering care. ACOs shift economic risk to physicians with multiple payers reimbursing individual delivery entities. In single payer, the existing delivery system would remain, but the entire population would share risk because everyone is part of a single insurance program. Finally, in a national VA-like system, risk is shared by the population, but the delivery system would be reestablished as a network of nonprofit entities.

ACOs have garnered much attention, most notably in the 2010 Patient Protection and Affordable Care Act (ACA), as the national health-reform law is called, which includes provisions for ACO demonstration projects. Moreover, physicians are currently affiliating with hospitals at an accelerating pace, and independent fee-for-service practice is shrinking. While this trend is mostly driven by the enhanced market clout (that is, the ability to demand higher fees) that doctor-hospital affiliation brings, it sets the stage for ACO-style reimbursement.

ACO advocates envision them as a new way to integrate health care delivery. However, the emergence of competing, profit-driven ACOs is unlikely to improve the U.S. health care system. Fully capitalizing on the promises of improved quality and decreased cost through coordination and teamwork will require integrated nonprofit delivery systems, with physicians paid salaries, and region-wide health planning of capital expenditures. Without macro-level planning and coordination, competition for profit (or a surplus in the case of nonprofit ACOs) will distort ACO priorities and shift resources to plans most adept at gaming the payment system, as hospitals and insurers have done under the current payment arrangement. Performance and quality measures are not sufficient to guarantee fair competition in the face of sophisticated methods of manipulation.

ACCOUNTABLE CARE ORGANIZATIONS: TREATING FRAGMENTATION

Two prominent ACO proponents, Elliot Fisher, Director of the Center for Population Health at Dartmouth, and Mark McClellan at the Brookings Institution, have pointed out that the current fee-for-service payment system incentivizes overuse of tests and procedures. Because a single-payer system would retain fee-for-service payment their arguments hold great relevance. They argue that reform should create groups of health providers who are jointly responsible for the care of a defined population of patients, and accountable for achieving both quality improvements and cost containment that can rein in overuse while upgrading quality.

Though ACOs might take various forms, McClellan and Fisher emphasize (1) a strong base of primary care providers, (2) payments linked to quality improvements with incentives to reduce overall costs, and (3) performance measures that can reliably support improvements that achieve savings. They believe that a wide variety of provider organizational and payment structures could meet these requirements. In fact, Fisher and his colleagues have shown that most patients already receive the majority of their care from a particular hospital and its "extended hospital medical staff," which comprise a natural organizational structure for utilizing quality and performance measures to improve care coordination and quality while also reducing costs.

These arguments and early evidence about the impact of reorienting payment incentives resonate with many politicians, health policy experts, and the general public, who see redundant high technology facilities and neglect of primary care, public health, prevention, and mental health. ACO supporters also properly highlight the need for systemic solutions to problems like poor teamwork, poor public accountability, and variable quality. For these reasons, the 2010 ACA legislation encouraged ACOs.

The adoption of a single-payer system, on its own, would not resolve the fragmentation that ACOs are designed to address. Though a single-payer system would eliminate the multiplicity of payers, it would retain the existing incentives for providers to order more tests and write more referrals and would be unable to reduce the redundant services that ACO critics highlight. Though global budgeting in a single-payer system has effectively controlled hospital spending in other nations, global budgeting would be much more difficult in the United States where expensive diagnostic tests and procedures are often performed outside of hospitals. Arguably, a single payer would merely lock the United States' fragmented and costly delivery system into place.

LIMITS OF ACOs: LESSONS FROM HEALTH-MAINTENANCE ORGANIZATIONS (HMOs)

Though ACO proponents offer useful critiques of fee-for-service health care, the problems that ACOs face illustrate why adoption of a single-payer system, even with the inclusion of ACOs, will fail to provide an adequate solution to the uneven quality, high cost, and inequality in the U.S. health system. ACO advocates closely echo the early backers of the managed care strategy, who identified similar limitations of the then current system. In 1971, Paul Ellwood, the most important proponent of Health Maintenance Organizations (HMOs), argued that the delivery system was too fragmented and the payment system rewarded overuse of services rather than improved quality or reduced cost. While today's ACO proponents endorse a wider array of possible payment models than Ellwood initially envisioned, the managed care plans of the 1980s and 1990s employed many of the strategies described by ACO advocates and the logic of the two models is very similar.

The logic of the ACO/HMO model functions in the following way. First, the ACO model shifts insurance risk to the provider group and away from the insurance company, or under a single-payer system, away from the government. That is, cost overruns are borne by health care providers rather than the insurer. Second, because small clinics and hospitals cannot absorb the potential losses from extremely costly patients, consolidation must occur. For instance, the birth of premature triplets might absorb the entire capitation budget of a small family practice. In a large group, the high costs of the three infants would be spread out over a larger pool. Hence consolidation is essential. Finally, shifting risk to providers creates incentives to deny care to high-risk patients, as occurred under managed care.

Proponents of ACOs point to performance measures and report cards as antidotes to these incentives, the means to protect patients. ACO advocates also suggest that guidelines defining quality standards and risk adjustments to compensate providers enrolling sicker and more complex patients can counter the problematic incentives to avoid high-cost patients and deny high-cost care. The reliability and efficacy of these safeguards and adjustments is crucial to the success of the HMO/ACO model. ACOs and HMOs function similarly enough that a look at the historical experience with HMOs is instructive.

A number of studies have shown the quality of HMO care to be worse than fee-for-service care. In the RAND Health Insurance Experiment, the only randomized trial of HMO care, vulnerable patients assigned to a high-quality HMO had a higher risk of dying than those in fee-for-service care. Furthermore, doctors presented with scenarios where tests and referrals were clearly indicated were more likely to prescribe appropriate care when the patient's insurance was described as fee-for-service rather than as capitation. Depression care has also been shown to be inferior in an HMO setting.

These results show the strong incentives that exist in a capitated system to provide less care than is appropriate. A 1997 survey even found that all physicians who were not paid through capitation and 95 percent of physicians paid via capitation believed that the payment method presented a conflict of interest. Other studies showed that for-profit plans provided lower quality care, yet they came to dominate the HMO market. Ultimately a raft of widely publicized abuses and patient backlash against capitation resulted in many HMOs trying strategies other than capitation. Though ACOs may not fully replicate the earlier HMO incentives and experience, the HMO story provides a cautionary tale. In order to capitalize on improved care by decreasing fragmentation more thorough reforms will be required.

Under closer scrutiny, the promise of large savings from shifting to an ACO model also does not hold up. The Congressional Budget Office calculated in 2008 that if 20 to 40 percent of Medicare patients were to enroll in ACOs, savings over ten years would amount to less than 0.1 percent of total Medicare spending of $6.8 trillion. Moreover, while some ACO proponents have heralded ACO demonstration projects as a success, closer inspection indicates that the apparent overall savings were illusory, reflecting diagnosis coding changes that led to higher risk adjustment scores (and hence payments) rather than real cost cutting. In other words, outcomes were not improved: rather, patients were recategorized in ways that made them appear sicker than they actually were.

The ACO model requires performance measures that provide financial incentive for providers who improve quality and reduce cost. Fisher has acknowledged that developing these measures is challenging. If performance measures and risk adjustment scores can be manipulated by providers within the ACOs, then the model offers little chance for successful cost containment or quality improvement.

Moreover, even if an ACO can achieve coordination, improved quality and lower costs for its own group of enrollees, competition among ACOs might raise costs. ACOs will naturally tailor services to compete for the patients who are profitable under the new incentive system. For instance, diabetes can range from a mild condition controllable with diet and exercise to a serious and expensive condition threatening life and limb. If generous payments are available for diabetic management, ACOs may seek out and aggressively diagnose mild diabetes, while eschewing patients with severe or complicated diabetes. An ACO that successfully sheds its severely affected diabetics onto other insurers will both pocket a large profit and look better on quality measures, while raising costs of other insurers in the area. As envisaged under the ACA, ACOs will compete with one another for financial surplus rather than using savings to improve care for everyone.

The ACO model presents important critiques of fragmented fee-for-service practice, whether financed by multiple insurance companies or by a single government payer. The weaknesses of ACOs, however, reveal important strategies for more thorough health reform. The Veterans Administration (VA) system provides solutions both to the fragmentation that ACOs attempt to address and the high cost and inequality that a single-payer system attempts to solve.

THE VETERANS HEALTH ADMINISTRATION: A MODEL FORWARD

The VA system offers an alternative to both a fragmented fee-for-service single-payer system and ACO-based reform. Like single-payer models, it eliminates complicated networks of payers and incentives to cherry pick healthy patients. It goes further, however, by establishing an integrated payment and delivery system with coordination, central planning, regionalized nonprofit facilities, salaried physicians, and a track record of successful quality improvements, thereby providing solutions to problems that neither single-payer systems nor ACOs alone can solve. The VA's evolution into a model health care delivery system since 1995 provides important lessons for redesigning the U.S. health care system.

Though the VA system was initially designed to provide medical care for military service-related conditions, the rapidly growing cadre of veterans needing medical care after World War I led Congress to extend benefits to a wider group of veterans. In 1924, Congress passed legislation to provide hospital care for indigent veterans without disabilities resulting from their service, which established the system as an important national safety net. When President Hoover consolidated all veterans' benefits programs in a single federal agency in 1930, the modern veterans' health system was established. The system grew dramatically to meet the needs of the 12 million World War II veterans and by the 1950s, the VA affiliated with many university medical schools, added more than 70 new hospitals, and greatly expanded research capacity. The system's growth was also paralleled by increased bureaucratization from a large central administration.

In response to a series of embarrassing quality-of-care incidents in the 1970s and 1980s, as well as pressure from the more activist generation of veterans from the Vietnam War, President Ronald Reagan established a Cabinet-level position for the Department of Veterans Affairs in 1989. By 1994, the VA had become the country's largest health care provider, but it had also become a bloated, dysfunctional system. Kenneth Kizer, the reform-minded undersecretary for health in the Department of Veterans Affairs from 1994 to 1999, has noted that like the rest of the health care system, the quality of care in the VA was variable and fragmented, there was overemphasis on inpatient care, customer service was inadequate, and access was a challenge. Since many of these problems continue to plague the rest of the health care system, the VA's transformation offers important lessons.

Single-payer proponents and detractors can find in the VA's history both a cautionary tale of bloated, dysfunctional government programs and the possibility of rapid change ushered in by a centralized government body. In fact, the VA's transformation most evidently shows how establishing integrated delivery and payment systems along with quality of care measurements can lead to profound, measurable changes in the success of a health system. The government control of the VA was a precondition for these changes, but government control alone is insufficient to account for the VA's success or failure. While a Canadian-style single-payer system would reform the payment system to a single government payer, it would fall far short of the comprehensive reforms that the VA has shown to be possible.

STRATEGIES FOR TRANSFORMING THE VA

During Kizer's tenure at the VA, a series of changes were implemented with the expected goal of providing consistent high-quality, patient-centered, cost-effective care of better value than the private sector. To achieve this, the VA leadership sought to (1) create accountable management structures, (2) integrate and coordinate services, (3) improve quality, (4) align system finances with desired outcomes, and (5) modernize information management. Evidence from many studies suggests that these goals were met.

Prior to 1995, the VA was overly centralized and bureaucratic. The key change was the creation of Veterans Integrated Service Networks (VISNs), tasked with providing adequate primary, secondary, and tertiary VA services to a defined geographical area. As the central operating unit, VISNs provided a structure for the coordination and pooling of resources, preventing duplication and thus maximizing value impossible to replicate with competing ACOs or even with a single-payer system. Standardized metrics were used to quantify performance with the goal of improving care, rather than as a precondition for payments as the ACO model proposes. Finally, rather than centralizing all decision making in Washington, VISNs began to make operational decisions. VISNs together form a coordinated delivery system with central funding. Despite simplifying payment, a single-payer system does not control the delivery system and would provide no method for the degree of geographically based coordination and planning that was crucial to the VA's success.

To counter historical problems with poor care coordination resulting from an inpatient and specialist-dominated historical focus, the VA implemented universal primary care embedded within the VISN networks and leveraged these networks to standardize care. A national formulary was established to promote evidenced-based prescribing, care coordination efforts were enhanced, and hundreds of community-based outpatient clinics were opened. A fee-for-service single-payer system would be unable to integrate and coordinate on such a level because it would fix the current delivery system in place with its skewed fee-for-service incentives.

In order to improve quality of care at the VA, performance measures with public reporting were implemented. Adherence to nationally recognized primary prevention and early recognition recommendations were tracked with a prevention index, while a similar index tracked chronic diseases. In addition, evidence-based clinical guidelines were developed to promote improved clinical performance, offering recommendations for elements as varied as access, wait times, and quality improvements. The VA took a national lead in the patient safety movement with organizational and cultural changes, research, and partnerships. The system's national structure uniquely enabled this effort.

To finance these emerging systems, the VA allocated funds geographically to VISNs rather than to individual hospitals and clinics. Global payments are made based on average expenditures for services adjusted for variables that are specific to different VISNs like the cost of labor and the amount of research and educational activities. Most VA patients are offered services comparable to Medicare's package, while a small percentage, including severely wounded combat veterans receive additional services. Kizer reports that VA spending for basic care patients is significantly less than care under Medicare's Advantage program, a privately administered Medicare benefits program. The adoption of a single-payer system by itself might not be able to replicate the VA's experience. Although it would provide global payments to hospitals, under a single-payer system, outpatient care would continue to be financed and delivered on a fee-for-service basis.

Finally, the VA introduced a systemwide electronic health record. Experts developed and tested modules locally, then knitted them together into a comprehensive system. The VA implemented the electronic health record (EHR) nationwide in 1997, with the final VA centers being included by the end of 1999. The system, which is still considered one of the best EHR systems in use today, included the patient record, clinical reminders and alerts, computerized order entry, and access to real-time data to improve clinical flow. This nationalized EHR is only possible because of the VA's coordinated delivery system.

RESULTS OF THE TRANSFORMATION

There is robust documentation of the improved clinical performance of the VA health system since its transformation. Just a few years after the changes, the VA was superior to fee-for-service Medicare on all performance measures examined between 1997 and 2000 except for one measure in one year. Influenza and pneumococcal vaccination rates drastically improved and variations based on geography were eliminated. As a result, admissions for community-acquired pneumonia decreased by half, while they increased by 15 percent for Medicare patients in the same time. Furthermore, quality of care, preventive care, and chronic disease management have been generally shown to be better in the VA than in managed care organizations. These studies show that the investment in universal primary care and geographical planning paired with the prudent use of technology can produce great achievements. Though a single-payer system may be able to leverage health care spending with reimbursement rates, because independent entities will continue to comprise the delivery system, the incentive schemes are likely insufficient to achieve broad-based reorganization and coordination that the VA has accomplished with joint payment and delivery system control.

Kizer has provided further evidence documenting better cancer prevention, cardiovascular risk reduction, diabetes management, infectious disease prevention, and adherence to evidence-based guidelines, as well as decreased mortality for VA patients when compared to Medicare Advantage patients. In 2011, a study found that cancer care was equal or better when compared to Medicare Advantage patients, including earlier detection. Perhaps most remarkably, racial disparities in care are minimal at the VA, with one study actually finding slightly better outcomes in black veterans relative to whites. These examples document the evolution of the VA into a functioning, integrated health system made possible by its simple payment system and impressive delivery reforms.

As soaring health costs are central to any discussion of health policy, it is most impressive that the VA's superior quality-of-care achievements compared to other systems of care are almost certainly provided at lower cost than those purchased through Medicare, and VA costs appear to have increased at a slower rate. Like single-payer systems, the VA appears to effectively control costs.

LESSONS FROM THE VA

The VA health system was able to make monumental improvements in quality of care in a cost-effective manner. The aspects of the VA that have contributed to its success include its geographic level planning and budgeting; its tradition of fully salaried practice; its embrace of collaborative innovation, as in its information technology development; and its consistent focus on primary care. Moreover, administrative costs in the VA are believed to be only a fraction of those in the civilian sector. This success may also have been facilitated by the VA's thoroughgoing commitment to racial equality and its explicit public accountability (although its direct Congressional oversight is not an unalloyed blessing). These aspects cannot be fully replicated in either ACO or single-payer models.

Many of the problems the VA confronted at the beginning of its transformation in 1995—especially fragmentation and uneven quality—are similar to the challenges that the civilian health care system faces and would remain within a single-payer system. The fact that the VA is a centralized, government-run program is not a sufficient condition for good quality of care, as shown by the VA's poor quality performance before 1995. The same holds for a single-payer system. However, the structure of the VA was a pre-condition for its drastic and rapid transformation. If there were multiple payers but an integrated nonprofit delivery system, risk would be shared unevenly with varying reimbursement rates and resulting incentives to cherry pick patients. Even under a single-payer system, it would be hard to imagine any group of health care services as large as the VA in the private sector implementing such a varied and thorough set of changes in such a short time.

Though a single-payer system would reduce uninsurance and health costs by reforming health care payments, it would leave many of the delivery system inefficiencies and perverse incentives in place. Proponents of ACOs offer profound and often-heard critiques about fragmentation, applicable to the current system and fee-for-service single-payer model. Their proposal, however, also does not go far enough. Creating financial incentives attached to performance measures creates as much an incentive to manipulate measures as it does to change performance. Without centralized planning to account for regional needs based on populations, ACOs will continue to seek surplus in competition with other ACOs instead of designing systems to provide first-rate care for a geographic population.

Though a single-payer system may be able to promote particular provider behaviors and structures of care, its impact would necessarily be limited by the existing delivery system. The VA system incorporates the apt critiques that ACO proponents have raised about coordination and fee-for-service incentives, but goes further with a nonprofit delivery system, salaried physicians, and regional planning of capital expenditures. There is no need to look further than the VA to find a national health system that functions squarely within the U.S. political and cultural traditions.

References and Further Reading

Asch, S. M., McGlynn, E. A., Hogan, M. M., Hayward, R. A., Shekelle, P., Rubenstein, L., et al. (2004). Comparison of quality of care for patients in the Veterans Health Administration and patients in a national sample. *Annals of Internal Medicine, 141*(12), 938–945.

Berenson, R. A. (2010). Shared savings program for accountable care organizations: A bridge to nowhere? *American Journal of Managed Care, 16*(10), 721–726.

Congressional Budget Office. (2008). *Budget options: Volume 1, health care.* Retrieved from http://www.cbo.gov/doc.cfm?index=9925

Ellwood, P. M., Anderson, N. N., Billings, J. E., Carlson, R. J., Hoagberg, E. J., & McClure, W. (1971). Health maintenance strategy. *Medical Care, 9*(3), 291–298.

Fisher, E. S., & Shortell, S. M. (2010). Accountable care organizations: Accountable for what, to whom, and how. *Journal of the American Medical Association, 304*(15), 1715–1716.

Fisher, E. S., Staiger, D. O., Bynum, J., & Gottlieb, D. J. (2007). Creating accountable care organizations: The extended hospital medical staff. *Health Affairs, 26*(1), w44–w57.

Jha, A. K., Perlin, J. B., Kizer, K. W., & Dudley, R. A. (2003). Effect of the transformation of the Veterans Affairs Health Care System on the quality of care. *New England Journal of Medicine, 348*(22), 2218–2227.

Jha, A. K., Shlipak, M. G., Hosmer, W., Frances, C. D., & Browner, W. S. (2001). Racial differences in mortality among men hospitalized in the Veterans Affairs health care system. *Journal of the American Medical Association, 285*(3), 297–303.

Jha, A. K., Wright, S. M., & Perlin, J. B. (2007). Performance measures, vaccinations, and pneumonia rates among high risk patients in Veterans Administration health care. *American Journal of Public Health, 97*(12), 2167–2172.

Keating, N. L., Landrum, M. B., Lamont, E. B., Bozeman, S. R., Krasnow, S. H., Shulman, L. N., et al. (2011). Quality of care for older patients with cancer in the Veterans Health Administration versus the private sector. *Annals of Internal Medicine, 154*(11), 727–736.

Kerr, E. A., Gerzoff, R. B., Krein, S. L., Selby, J. V., Piette, J. D., Curb, J. D., et al. (2004). Diabetes care quality in the Veterans Affairs Health Care System and commercial managed care: The TRIAD study. *Annals of Internal Medicine, 141*(4), 272–281.

Kizer, K. W. (1999). The "new VA": A national laboratory for health care quality management. *American Journal of Medical Quality, 14*(1), 3–20.

Kizer, K. W., Demakis, J. G., & Feussner, J. R. (2000). Reinventing VA health care: Systematizing quality improvement and quality innovation. *Medical Care, 38*(6 Suppl. 1), I7–I16.

Kizer, K. W., & Dudley, R. A. (2009). Extreme makeover: Transformation of the veterans health care system. *Annual Review of Public Health, 30*, 313–339.

Lipsky M., McCray, L., Prottas, J., & Sapolsky, H. (1976). The future of the veterans' health care system. *Journal of Health Politics Policy and Law, 1*(3), 285–294.

McClellan, M., McKethan, A. N., Lewis, J. L., Roski, J., & Fisher, E. S. (2010). A national strategy to put accountable care into practice. *Health Affairs, 29*(5), 982–990.

Pantilat, S. Z., Chesney, M., & Lo, B. (1999). Effect of incentives on the use of indicated services in managed care. *Western Journal of Medicine, 170*(3), 137–142.

Rogers, W. H., Wells, K. B., Meredith, L. S., Sturm, R., & Burnam, M. A. (1993). Outcomes for adult outpatients with depression under prepaid or fee-for-service financing. *Archives of General Psychiatry, 50*(7), 517–525.

Ryoo, J. J., & Malin, J. L. (2011). Reconsidering the Veterans Health Administration: A model and a moment for publicly funded health care delivery. *Annals of Internal Medicine, 154*(11), 772–773.

Ware, J. E., Bayliss, M. S., Rogers, W. H., Kosinski, M., & Tarlov, A. R. (1996). Differences in 4-year health outcomes for elderly and poor, chronically ill patients treated in HMO and fee-for-service systems. *Journal of the American Medical Association, 276*(13), 1039–1047.

Ware, J. E., Brook, R. H., Rogers, W. H., Keeler, E. B., Davies, A. R., Sherbourne, C. D., et al. (1986). Comparison of health outcomes at a health maintenance organisation with those of fee-for-service care. *Lancet, 1*(8488), 1017–1022.

Wells, K. B., Hays, R. D., Burnam, M. A., Rogers, W., Greenfield, S., & Ware, J. E. (1989). Detection of depressive disorder for patients receiving prepaid or fee-for-service care. *The Journal of the American Medical Association, 262*(23), 3298–3302.

Wynia, M. K., Picken, H. A., & Selker, H. P. (1997). Physicians' views on capitated payment for medical care: Does familiarity foster acceptance? *American Journal of Managed Care, 3*(10), 1497–1502.

Steffie Woolhandler, David Himmelstein, Simeon Kimmel, and Carl Berdahl

8

Public Opinion and Health Care Reform

POINT: Majorities of Americans now support a wide variety of health care reforms. Polls show that American public opinion often supports a greater federal role in providing health care even before the federal government enacts such reforms. Since the 1930s public opinion support for health care reform has been surprisingly broad and stable.

Thomas R. Marshall, University of Texas at Arlington

COUNTERPOINT: Public opinion support for health care reform is limited, mixed, and ambivalent. Majority support is usually limited to narrowly targeted and gradual reform. The American public's apparent support for health care reform often ends when the public becomes aware of its drawbacks and costs.

Thomas R. Marshall, University of Texas at Arlington

Introduction

Health care reform may be a contemporary controversy, but it is not a new one. In 1912 former Republican president Theodore Roosevelt ran for another term as chief executive, this time as leader of the Progressive Party. Among the key issues on the Progressive platform that year was the idea of national health insurance, something Roosevelt argued America should adopt (and adapt) from the European model. One hundred years later, health care remains at the top of the political discourse in the 2012 presidential campaign. There is no doubt that Americans spend a great deal of time talking and thinking about health care—in both personal and policy terms—but what do they really think about it?

This chapter, by Thomas R. Marshall, examines the question of whether Americans truly desire an overhaul of the health care system. American opinion seems to be not only divided but also inconsistent: Many people seem to desire reform in theory but reject specific proposals—especially those that might increase costs or limit individual choice. For example, Marshall argues that in 2009 and 2010, the majority of Americans were in support of not only expanding health care and but also expanding the federal government's role in providing it. And yet support for the 2010 Patient Protection and Affordable Care Act (ACA) has been mixed at best. One reason for this seeming inconsistency is that strong feelings on health care cut across the ideological spectrum—in other words, the people who disapprove of the ACA do so for a variety of conflicting reasons. Marshall points out that many polls suggest that mixed feelings about the ACA exist, not because Americans do not support reform, but rather because some feel the ACA went too far, while a roughly equal number believe it did not go far enough.

As Marshall suggests in the Point half of this chapter, the American body politic's apparently schizophrenic view of health care reform has a long history. Whether at the end of the Great Depression in the late 1930s or in the comparatively boom times of the 1980s, one finds similar mixed messages in opinion polls—on the one hand, strong broad-based support for expanded access to health care and for federal spending on it, and on the other a resistance to specific spending increases, as well as to any perceived government intrusion into citizen's personal lives.

History suggests that sweeping reforms, such as the ones attempted by the Bill Clinton presidential administration in the mid-1990s, or the more recent ACA, tend to provoke the greatest opposition. In the chapter that follows, Marshall suggests that narrowly targeted reforms garner the most support. But we may want to ask whether there is a danger that these smaller reforms, by addressing the needs of some constituents, might leave them less willing to embrace further reforms. For example, a majority of senior citizens support Medicare, and perhaps consequently they are especially reluctant to support reforms that might take anything away from them. In other words, is it possible that past incremental reforms, such as the creation of Medicare, might make it more difficult to generate public support for additional reforms?

As you read the chapter, consider why it might be that the American public is so consistently inconsistent. What is it about the nature of health care in particular that inspires such conflicting and yet recurring opinions over time? How should policymakers respond to this inconsistency? Politicians must respond to the needs of their constituencies, and it seems clear that the majority of Americans feel that something should be done about health care. And yet, as Marshall notes in the Counterpoint section, presidents who implement health care reform experience an immediate decline in their support.

Americans seem to want health care reform in theory, but have trouble with it in practice. They believe that the health care system is unfair and that government should do more, but they are troubled by specific proposals and are opposed to reforms that may cost them more or alter their own access to health care. Why is this? Is it because most Americans really do have access to the best health care in the world? (Would they still think that if they knew that the health outcomes in most other wealthy countries are far better than they are in the United States?) Is it because Americans want a better system but not if it requires personal sacrifice, or is it because of an American inclination toward self-reliance? Or is it because they do not trust their leaders, or because they do not understand the health care system?

Although the need for health care is universal, conflicts in the United States about health care do seem to have a unique character. After all, universal health care systems enjoy broad support in most other industrialized countries. As you read, consider why this difference might exist. Are Americans less trusting of government than are the citizens of other countries? Do they have a weaker sense of community? Or is it because they have come to health reform so late, giving powerful private interests time to coalesce around the cause of defeating reform? Or has the country's system of divided government simply made it easier for the opposition to block and complicate the adoption of health-reform proposals?

POINT

For many years, health care reform has been a recurring dispute in American politics. Public opinion polls show that there is a consistent and surprisingly broad public demand for health care reform. Since the dawn of modern public opinion polling in the mid-1930s, majorities of Americans have supported a wide range of reforms, including both broadly written and problem-specific reforms. Typically, public support for health care reform exists well before Congress enacts a reform, and public attitudes are largely unaffected by the back-and-forth of congressional debate. Public support for health care reform is chiefly driven by Americans' personal fears about rapidly rising health care costs. Further, growing numbers of Americans depend on government-subsidized and government-regulated health care plans, and this trend will doubtlessly continue into the foreseeable future. The growing number of Americans who believe that access to high-quality health care is a fairness issue also drives public support for health care reform. The view that Americans believe that health care is simply a private good, one that can be adequately provided by individuals and private employers, is a myth that over the last three-quarters of a century has found little polling support.

PUBLIC SUPPORT FOR HEALTH CARE REFORM

Health care reform does not occur in a vacuum. At the time that the 2010 Patient Protection and Affordable Care Act (ACA) was being debated, nationwide public opinion polls showed that majorities of Americans favored a wide range of specific reforms. Ninety percent of Americans favored tax breaks for small businesses to make coverage for their workers more affordable. Over two thirds of Americans favored new health insurance exchanges, expanding Medicare's prescription drug benefit, and requiring employers to offer health insurance to employees or else pay a penalty. Well over half of Americans favored a federal or state government review of insurance premium increases, increased taxes on families making more than $250,000 a year, a requirement that insurance plans cover all applicants regardless of preexisting conditions, and rules to prevent insurance companies from dropping coverage for people who are sick. Majorities of Americans also favored individual mandates if subsidies were also provided. Indeed, majorities would have gone even further than did the final version of the ACA. Over 60 percent of those polled favored allowing Americans to buy prescription drugs imported from Canada, limiting malpractice awards, and expanding Medicare to cover people 55 to 64 years old who do not have another health insurance plan.

To be sure, not all of the health care reforms debated in 2009 and 2010 were supported by clear majorities. However, a closer examination of the less popular measures does not suggest that Americans oppose health care reform, because many of these less popular measures would actually have cut back on the availability of health care. Only about a third (36 percent) of Americans favored reducing Medicare payments to doctors and hospitals. Only 38 percent favored additional taxes on insurers, drugmakers, and medical-device manufacturers. Only 19 percent favored reducing spending on Medicare. Only a quarter to a third of Americans favored additional taxes on the most expensive health care plans. Public opinion was evenly divided on the "public option" proposal to allow government-offered health insurance plans to compete with private insurance plans. In short, polls in 2009 and 2010 largely showed that Americans favored more, not less health care, and a greater federal role.

Critics of the 2010 health care reform bill argue that no clear majority favored the bill either before or after it was signed into law. However, polls gauging public opinion on the bill as a whole suggest that this view is simply not the case. In the weeks after the ACA became law, public opinion was about evenly divided, with 42 percent to 47 percent of Americans favoring the bill, and between 46 percent and 50 percent opposing it. However, when respondents were given more choices than simply favoring or opposing the bill, a better reading of American public opinion appears. In a March 2010 CNN/ORC Poll, 15 percent of Americans approved of the bill and had no reservations about it, 27 percent approved of the bill but thought it did not go far enough, 31 percent disapproved of the bill but supported a few of its proposals, and 25 percent disapproved of the bill and opposed all of its proposals. A July 2011 Kaiser Health poll reported that a third (33 percent) of Americans favored expanding the law, 20 percent favored keeping the law as it is, 16 percent favored repealing the law and replacing it with a Republican-sponsored alternative, and only 21 percent favored repealing the law and not replacing it at all. In short, many of those who express disapproval of ACA actually favor some of its provisions, and only about a quarter of Americans express complete disapproval.

That many Americans favor a greater federal role in funding and managing health care is not a new development. Since at least the mid-1930s, the American public has supported many specific federal health care reforms. During the 1930s President Franklin D. Roosevelt considered supporting nationwide health care coverage, although he never moved forward on a comprehensive plan. Even so, most Americans favored a greater government role in the health care issues then being debated. In a 1937 Gallup Poll 74 percent of Americans said that the federal government should aid state and local governments in providing medical care for babies at birth. In 1938, 78 percent of Americans said that the federal government should be responsible for providing medical care for people who are unable to pay for it; just 18 percent disagreed. In 1939 even more (84 percent) Americans favored the federal government spending $3 million for clinics to fight cancer.

True, the 2010 ACA reform bill, providing millions of uninsured or underinsured Americans with dependable health insurance, passed nearly three-quarters of a century after these early and modest efforts to improve the nation's health care. Yet support for the ACA reflects public concerns similar to those of the 1930s. Many Americans have long favored a wide variety of federal-level initiatives to improve the nation's health, some of which focus on insurance coverage and some of which do not. For example, since the mid-1960s, majorities have supported a growing number of restrictions on cigarette sales, advertising, and public smoking. At least since the early 2000s the same is true of efforts to curb the obesity epidemic. That most Americans supported many parts of the ACA bill should not be surprising, because public opinion support for better health outcomes is a long-standing pattern across a wide variety of health-related problems.

Health care experts who talk about health care reform usually mean comprehensive health care programs that would provide insurance for all or nearly all Americans. As the examples just above show, however, many proposals for health reform are not sweeping and comprehensive, but rather address one specific health problem. Ignoring public opinion on problem-specific health care reforms leads one seriously to underestimate public-opinion support for narrower health care reform.

A few examples illustrate a recurring pattern. In a 1971 Harris Poll an overwhelming (81 percent) majority of Americans favored President Nixon's major health care initiative to increase federal funds for cancer research. In a 1987 Roper Poll, 71 percent of Americans favored some form of catastrophic health insurance coverage for those on Medicare, a proposal that led to President Ronald Reagan's 1988 Medicare Catastrophic Coverage Act. Even when the measure was repealed in 1989, under pressure from affluent seniors who faced steep surcharges, three-quarters (77 percent) of Americans opposed doing away with the program. A Gallup Poll conducted five months before the plan passed showed that President George W. Bush's 2003 Medicare Modernization Act, which provided a measure of prescription drug coverage under Medicare, enjoyed the support of a 76 percent-to-19 percent margin. Two weeks after the plan passed, it was favored by a 52 percent-to-30 percent margin. On most of these measures public opinion support was not only widespread but also bipartisan.

A similar pattern of broad public support appears on many proposed health care reforms, some of which were enacted by Congress, but others which derived from states or from private lawsuits. For example, in a 1999 Princeton Survey Research Associates/*Newsweek* Poll, by a 72 percent-to-17 percent margin Americans favored allowing people to sue their managed care plans for denying coverage for essential care. By a 90 percent-to-5 percent margin, Americans favored letting HMO patients choose any family doctor or primary care physician they want. In a 1999 *Time*/CNN/Yankelovich Poll, Americans favored by a 77 percent-to-17 percent margin requiring HMOs to pay for emergency medical care even if the patient did not get permission in advance. By a 77 percent-to-18 percent margin Americans said that employers should be required to offer insurance for mental illnesses at the same level as insurance for physical illnesses.

As these examples suggest, Americans favor a wide variety of health regulations that would broaden benefits, even if they increase health care costs. This support goes much further than just regulating HMOs. For example, since at least the 1980s most Americans have supported a mandate requiring employers to cover health care costs for their employees. Public support for an employer mandate illustrates that public-opinion approval of health care reform usually precedes action from the federal government. In this case, majority public support for an employer mandate to provide health insurance for their employees was evident nearly a quarter of a century before the ACA enacted such a mandate.

Yet to look only at polls on currently debated health care reforms is to risk seriously underestimating public support for the government's role in providing health care. Once a health care reform is enacted, Americans usually soon come to accept it, and the program's benefits become a settled expectation in the public mind. Medicare is a good example. During the early 1960s the Medicare plan was stalled in Congress and not until the mid-1960s did it receive majority poll support. Only after President Lyndon Johnson's landslide win in the 1964 presidential election did Congress pass the program. Yet, once passed, Medicare quickly became a widely accepted, if increasingly expensive part of the federal government's health care package. By 1967 a Harris Poll already showed widespread support for Medicare; more than a third (35 percent) of Americans wanted to expand the program, slightly more than half (51 percent) wanted to keep it as is, and only 8 percent wanted to cut back. Nearly half a century later, Americans oppose cutting Medicare to reduce the government deficit. A 2011 Kaiser Family Foundation Poll reported that when Americans were asked what areas Congress might cut to reduce the federal deficit, over half (59 percent) favored no spending reductions on Medicare, 30 percent favored minor reductions, and only 10 percent favored major reductions. Two-thirds (67 percent) of Americans said that the country's budgetary problems could be addressed without reductions in Medicare spending. In a 2011 Pew Research Center survey, 88 percent said that Medicare had been good or very good for the country, and only 10 percent said it had been bad or very bad. As these examples show, once established, Medicare soon became a widely accepted program.

Reforms such as the ACA that aim to provide millions of uninsured or underinsured Americans with dependable health insurance should also not be viewed in isolation. Majorities of Americans have long favored a wide variety of federal-level initiatives to improve the nation's health, some of which focus on insurance coverage and some of which do not. For example, since the mid-1960s poll majorities have supported a growing number of restrictions on cigarette sales, advertising, and public smoking. At least since the early 2000s the same is true of efforts to curb the obesity epidemic. That most Americans supported many parts of the ACA should not be surprising; public-opinion support for better health outcomes is a long-standing pattern across a wide variety of health-related problems.

The history of both comprehensive and problem-specific health reforms shows that the federal government seldom enacts a health care initiative before the emergence of a supportive public-opinion majority. Polls typically show at least majority support for health care reform before Congress and the White House pass a specific bill; often there is a lag of several years between the time when majority poll support exists for a reform and the time when the government acts. As discussed above, even though support for Medicare grew after it was enacted, a majority of Americans supported it before Congress acted. Admittedly, presidents have many reasons to enact health reforms, among them achieving social justice, burnishing their own legacy, and building electoral support for their party. Yet most presidents since the 1930s have also been astute followers of public opinion, and most presidents' health care initiatives have clearly followed, not led, American public opinion.

During the debate over the ACA, public support was fairly stable and was not greatly affected by six months of often quite-contentious Congressional deliberation. Poll support was stable for both the so-called "public option" plan and the individual mandate to purchase health care insurance. The exact wording of poll questions significantly affected public opinion support for these two measures. However, when question wording is taken into account, attitudes on these two measures proved quite stable over time. Support for each of these two measures dropped by only two percent every ten weeks—a very small rate of change.

Admittedly, poll support for comprehensive health care reform sometimes drops once the plan is announced and becomes the subject of a hot political debate. In a widely cited example, Gallup Poll pegged support for President Clinton's comprehensive health insurance proposal as dropping from 59 percent to 43 percent between September 1993 and April 1994. However, this pattern of declining support may have resulted more from the Clinton administration's inept handling of the bill than from any underlying drop in support for better health care insurance coverage. By contrast, Gallup poll support for President Obama's ACA plan was very stable over time, ranging only between 50 percent and 43 percent between September 2009 and March 2010, the months when ACA was being debated. In short, public support for health care reforms, once debated, does not inevitably show a large drop. Dropping support for comprehensive health care reform is largely the result of a regular drop in poll support for any measure that undergoes a highly partisan public debate, and the extent to which poll support falls off varies widely depending on how well organized the plan's supporters are. In the case of problem-specific health care reforms, there is no evidence of falling public support during a public debate.

HEALTH CARE AND PERSONAL CONCERNS

Americans' personal concerns over steadily rising health care costs are both widespread and growing. When Gallup asked Americans about their financial concerns, not surprisingly, health care costs ranked high. In 2011, 60 percent of

Americans said that they were very worried or moderately worried about not being able to pay medical costs for a serious illness or accident. Almost half (48 percent) said they were very or moderately worried about not being able to pay medical costs for normal health care. Since 2001 both figures have risen steadily—from 50 percent to 60 percent on paying for a serious illness or accident, and from 44 percent to 48 percent on paying for normal medical costs.

A growing number of Americans experience difficulty paying for health care. The percentage of Americans who receive employer-provided health care is steadily declining, and the rate of decline accelerates during economic recessions. Between 2008 and 2011 Gallup/Healthways showed the percentage of American adults with employer-based health insurance dropping from 49.2 percent to 45 percent. Employer-based health insurance dropped among all major demographic groups. The percentage of Americans with a government plan rose slightly from 23.4 percent to 25.3 percent. The percentage of Americans who report that they are not covered under any type of health care plan rose from 14.8 percent to 16.6 percent between 2008 and 2011. Among the fastest-growing groups of Americans—Hispanics, low-income, and younger (18 to 29 year old) adults—the percentages of uninsured is much higher: 41.5 percent, 28.6 percent, and 27.6 percent, respectively. Further, as tens of millions of baby boomers reach age 65, retire, and enroll in Medicare, the number of Americans who receive government-provided health care will steadily rise.

By another measure, the percentage of Americans who report that either they or a family member put off medical treatment within the last twelve months because of costs continues to rise—from 19 percent in 2001 to 30 percent in 2010, according to a Gallup Poll. Nor did this rise in delayed medical treatment occur solely among low-income families. Two-fifths (39 percent) of low-income (under $30,000 a year) Americans put off medical treatment because of costs. Yet even 20 percent of high-income ($75,000 a year or more) Americans reported doing so.

Nor do a majority of Americans hold much confidence in health maintenance organizations (HMOs). Between 1999 and 2010 Gallup reported that only between 13 and 19 percent of Americans said that they had a great deal or quite a lot of confidence in HMOs. As noted above, majorities of Americans also supported additional regulations for HMOs. In short, the old system of employer-provided health insurance leaves a large and growing number of Americans with an inadequate health care plan, or even no plan at all.

Not surprisingly, given these attitudes and experiences, many Americans would shift health care costs from the private sector to the government. In a November 2005 Gallup Poll, for example, most (58 percent) Americans said it is the government's responsibility to guarantee affordable health care, versus only 34 percent who disagreed. At least since the early 1970s, most Americans have said that the United States spends too little on improving the nation's health—a view that puts ordinary Americans at odds with most health care experts.

Taken together, economic insecurity and rising costs are doubtlessly sufficient to drive many Americans to support a greater governmental role in providing and regulating health care. However, public support for health care reform is not solely a result of perceived individual self-interest. Over two-thirds of Americans view inequalities in access to health care and inequalities in the quality of care as unfair. Views on fairness help explain public support for government-provided health care, just as does economic self-interest, partisanship, norms of egalitarianism and humanitarianism, and views on the causes of illness. Politicians typically discuss both comprehensive and problem-specific health care reforms in terms of the self-interest of Americans. However, the widely held view that health care is also a fairness issue, not simply a matter of individual self-interest, also increases public support for reform. Not surprisingly, many advocates of health care reform increasingly focus on the concept of fairness and aim to raise public awareness of the large discrepancies in the access and quality of health care. To the extent that these advocates succeed in raising public attention to fairness as a key issue, public support for health care reform is also likely to increase.

CONCLUSION

The debate over health care reform is complex, long running, and ongoing. Passage of the 2010 ACA does not mark the end of history, but only a new stage in America's long-running health care debate. Sometimes this debate focuses on problem-specific health care reforms, and at other times it focuses on comprehensive reform. Sometimes the debate is driven by the election of a new president. Yet the list of key players on health care reform is now numerous and includes academics, foundations, think tanks, state governors and legislators, members of Congress, federal judges, interest groups, health care professionals, and large numbers of ordinary citizens. Whatever future Congresses and presidents decide about the fate of the ACA, the underlying causes that drive demands for health care reform will not change. Most Americans worry about the quality and affordability of their own health care, and there is no reason to believe that these worries will lessen in the foreseeable future. The list of possible future reforms is extensive—among them, medical malpractice, illegal immigrant health care, risk-based health care insurance pricing, obesity, tobacco controls, the importation of cheaper prescription drugs, and how the multitude of ACA requirements will be administered and financed.

Public opinion polling since the mid-1930s shows deep support for health care reform. No evidence exists to support the idea that Americans view health care as a purely private good that can be adequately provided by the private marketplace. Nor have most Americans held that view at least since the mid-1930s when modern public opinion polling began. Poll majorities support a wide variety of policies that would improve access to and the quality of health care. Narrowly tailored, problem-specific reforms clearly win the greatest public approval. Ironically, perhaps the best evidence of broad public support for health care reform lies not in public opinion poll questions. Rather, the best evidence is that, since the 1930s, almost every president has understood this enduring public view and, once elected, pushed forward with one or more health care reforms.

References and Further Reading

Blendon, R. J., & Benson, J. M. (2001). Americans' views on health policy: A fifty-year historical perspective. *Health Affairs, 20*(2), 33–46.

Blendon, R. J., & Benson, J. M. (2011). Public opinion at the time of the vote on health care reform. *New England Journal of Medicine, 362*(16), e55(1–6).

Blendon, R. J., Brodie, M., & Benson, J. (1995). What happened to Americans' support for the Clinton health plan? *Health Affairs, 14*(2), 7–23.

Blumenthal, D., & Morone, J. A. (2010). *The heart of power: Health and politics in the oval office.* Berkeley, CA: University of California Press.

Eisinger, R. (2003). *The evolution of presidential polling.* New York, NY: Cambridge University Press.

Erskine, H. G. (1975). The polls: Health insurance. *Public Opinion Quarterly, 39*(1), 128–141.

Grande, D., Gollusk, S. E., & Asch, D. A. (2011). Polling analysis: Public support for health reform was broader than reported and depended on how proposals were framed. *Health Affairs, 30*(7), 1242–1249.

Jacobs, L. R. (1993). *The health of nations: Public opinion and the making of American and British health policy.* Ithaca, NY: Cornell University Press.

Jacobs, L. R., Shapiro, R. Y., & Schulman, E. C. (1993). Poll trends: Medical care in the United States—An update. *Public Opinion Quarterly, 57*(3), 394–427.

Lynch, J., & Gollust, S. E. (2010). Playing fair: Fairness beliefs and health policy preferences in the United States. *Journal of Health Politics, Policy and Law, 35*(6), 849–887.

Marcovitz, H. (2007). *Health care: Gallup major trends & events.* Broomall, PA: Mason Crest.

Marmor, T. (1973). *The politics of Medicare.* Chicago, IL: Aldine.

Marshall, T. R. (in press). Health care and the growing partisan divide. In W. Crotty (Ed.), *Party polarization in America.* Boulder, CO: Westview Press.

Morone, J. A., & Jacobs, L. R. (2005). *Healthy, wealthy, and fair: Health care and the good society.* New York, NY: Oxford University Press.

Skocpol, T. (1997). *Boomerang: Health care reform and the turn against government.* New York, NY: Norton.

Thomas R. Marshall

COUNTERPOINT

Since the 1930s four American presidents have proposed comprehensive health care bills. Presidents Harry Truman, Richard Nixon, and Bill Clinton failed, while President Barack Obama finally passed the 2010 Patient Protection and Affordable Care Act (ACA). All four efforts share a common experience: Never was there a clear public-opinion majority in support of the respective bills. Public opinion may favor comprehensive health care as a lofty goal, but once it focuses on a bill's specific provisions, support becomes unreliable and ambivalent. Most Americans do not see comprehensive health care reform as improving their own situation. To the contrary, many Americans see large-scale, expensive, federally run health care as undesirable and as violating long-standing American norms, such as individual responsibility and limited government. The debate surrounding the ACA reflects a long-familiar pattern: polarized and closely divided public opinion on the bill itself, falling public approval for the president and Congress, and massive losses for the president's party in the next congressional election. The history of public opinion toward problem-specific health care reforms is more mixed, but also not wholly favorable to reformers.

PUBLIC DOUBTS ON HEALTH CARE REFORM

Most Americans are satisfied with their own health care plans and providers. They understand that privately provided health care better serves themselves and their families. According to Gallup Poll figures between 2001 and 2010, about four-fifths of Americans rated the quality of their health care as excellent or good. About two-thirds rated their health care coverage as excellent or good. Fifty to sixty percent said they were satisfied with the total cost they paid for health care. Not surprisingly, when asked in a 2010 survey which would be better—a government-run health care system or a system based mostly on private health insurance—only a third (34 percent) of Americans preferred the former, and a large majority (61 percent) preferred the latter.

Few Americans see new federal health care rules as helping either themselves or their families. During 2009 and 2010, during and shortly after the ACA was being debated in Congress, Gallup reported that only a fifth (21 to 22 percent) of Americans thought that the bill's passage would mean that "the costs you and your family pay for health care would get better," while nearly twice as many (from 42 to 50 percent) said that their costs would get worse. Americans were equally skeptical that ACA would improve the quality of their own health care: Only 18 to 21 percent said that the quality of their own health care would get better, while between 33 and 39 percent said it would get worse. Only 20 to 24 percent said that under the ACA their own health care coverage would get better, while between 33 and 37 percent said it would get worse. Only 25 percent said that the ACA would lessen the insurance requirements they are required to meet if their care is to be covered, while 46 percent said that such requirements would get worse. On a question as to how the bill would affect "your family's overall health," a fifth (20 percent) said it would get better, a similar percentage (19 percent) said it would get worse, and most (58 percent) said it would not change.

Polling just after the ACA's passage showed no more favorable views on the bill's impact on the country as a whole. Between 30 and 34 percent said that the bill would make the overall quality of health care in the United States better, while between 41 and 44 percent held the opposite view. Two-fifths (40 percent) said it would help improve the overall health of Americans, while about as many (35 percent) said that public health would instead worsen. These consistent results show that as many or more Americans doubted the benefits of comprehensive health care reform.

Nor does passage of a broad-ranging health care reform plan necessarily lead to widespread public support. Gallup Polls taken in 2010 and 2011, *after* Congress passed the ACA, illustrate this pattern. Slightly fewer than half (between 45 and 49 percent) of Americans said that it was "a good thing" that Congress passed the law. In the same polls, even fewer Americans (between 39 and 44 percent) said that the ACA would "improve medical care in the U.S." Kaiser Family Foundation's tracking polls conducted between February 2009 and July 2011 also show declining public support for the ACA during the congressional debate and after the bill was signed on March 23, 2010. The percentage of Americans who said that "the country as a whole will be better off" under the health-reform law fell from 59 to 45 percent between February 2009 and March 2010, and then fell further to 39 percent by July 2011.

The level of skepticism about how well federally run health reform would work is not surprising. Americans are well aware of the failings of federally run programs. In 2011 Americans estimated that, on average, the government wastes slightly 51 cents of every tax dollar it spends on federal programs—a figure that rose from 40 cents on the dollar when Gallup first asked the question in 1979. Further, most Americans recognize that Medicare and Social Security are unsustainable. A 2011 Gallup Poll reported that a third (34 percent) of Americans said that the costs of Medicare and Social Security are already creating a crisis for the federal government, and another 33 percent said that these costs would do so within the next ten years. When President Obama was elected in 2008, only 30 percent of Americans said that they trusted the federal government to do what is right "just about always" or "most of the time." That figure was 78 percent in 1964 when Medicare was debated. By yet another measure, a September 2010 Gallup Poll asked Americans to describe the federal government in a single word or phrase. Almost three-fourths (72 percent) of respondents' descriptions were negative, such as "too big," "confused," or "corrupt." Only ten percent used clearly positive words or phrases. In short, large-scale policy initiatives such as the ACA suffer from Americans' highly negative perceptions of the federal government.

SHALLOW POLL SUPPORT FOR HEALTH CARE REFORM

Poll support for major new federally run health care programs is superficial. Americans prefer health care reform only up to the point that they actually understand what it will cost—or that it will, in fact, cost anything at all. At that point, support drops off sharply. A 2009 national survey asked respondents whether they would support subsidies for the chronically ill, a Medicaid expansion for moderate-income people, or a government subsidy for low- and moderate-income people to buy health care insurance. For all three proposals, public support fell sharply if respondents were told that their income taxes would rise by 5 percent or more. Other polls show similar results. The 2007 Health Confidence Survey reported that 68 percent of Americans said that they would pay 1 percent more in federal income taxes to make sure that all Americans have health insurance, but only 39 percent of Americans would pay 3 percent more, and only 22 percent of Americans would pay 5 percent more.

Poll questions that initially show majority support for a greater federal government role in health care should be interpreted cautiously. Many Americans change their views if presented with conflicting or negative information about what reform might actually mean, or with more choices about how they might receive health care. For example, in a 2006 *ABC News*/Kaiser Family Foundation/*USA Today* survey, 56 percent of Americans at first said that they preferred a "universal" government-run health insurance program that covered everyone, versus the current employer-based system. However, when supporters of government-run health insurance were asked if they would still support a government-run program "if it limited your own choice of doctors," 49 percent of initial supporters switched to opposition. If told that "there were waiting lists for some non-emergency treatments," 40 percent of initial supporters switched to opposition. When told "it meant that some medical treatments that are currently covered by insurance are no longer covered," 64 percent of initial supporters switched to opposition.

That Americans support health care reform as a vague principle, but not in its specifics, is nothing new. As early as the mid-1940s, a careful analysis of poll results showed that half or more of those who at first said they favored a government-run plan also said they would equally or more greatly favor a private insurance one. In a later example, a 2000 survey reported that over half (54 percent) of registered voters said that they favored national health insurance, financed by taxes, that paid for most forms of health care. However, when registered voters were asked whether they favored a national health insurance plan, financed by taxpayers, in which all Americans would get their insurance from a single government plan, support fell to only 38 percent.

What Americans most dislike is a health care reform plan that is mandatory, threatens their own existing coverage, bundles several different proposals into a comprehensive plan, is immediate rather than gradual, or that is the result of a "messy" congressional process. This is, however, exactly what is involved in major (or "comprehensive") health care reform. Further, majorities of Americans prefer reforms that focus on private-sector plans. In a 2007 Gallup Poll, majorities of Americans supported several health reforms that focus primarily on private-sector insurance plans, even though, ironically, these reforms might require a federal mandate to achieve their goals. Among these private-sector-oriented reforms preferred by the public are those that would let workers keep their existing medical plan when they change jobs (86 percent in favor), establish incentives for those who maintain a healthy lifestyle (81 percent in favor), limit medical-malpractice awards (69 percent in favor), and reduce government regulation to encourage more health care insurance providers to enter the system (77 percent in favor). As far back as the 1940s, polling shows that many popular reforms are ones that primarily focus on improving private-sector plans, rather than establishing government-run health insurance.

THE HISTORICAL RECORD OF SUPPORT FOR HEALTH CARE REFORM

Because public support for health care reform is tenuous, superficial, and unstable, it is not surprising that public opinion support usually drops sharply once a comprehensive plan is announced and undergoes a serious public debate. The history of comprehensive health care reform shows that most such plans steadily lost support once debate about them was taken up. President Harry Truman was the first chief executive to propose a comprehensive plan. Among those who said that they had heard or read about the Truman plan, public support fell steadily—from 59 percent in favor in the first Gallup Poll question in November 1945, to only 28 percent in favor in the last poll in November 1950. In 1962 President Kennedy mounted a serious effort to pass a Medicare program that would cover costs for older persons through a Social Security tax. Despite his efforts, public support for the plan dropped from 55 percent to 44 percent during five months of Gallup polling, and the bill died in Congress. President Kennedy's successor, Lyndon Johnson, finally passed the Medicare and Medicaid bill in 1965, apparently enjoying stable poll support from nearly two thirds of Americans, according to the few available polls. It is worth pointing out, however, that the Medicare and Medicaid programs were not truly comprehensive in that they did not regulate existing employer-based health insurance plans.

President Richard Nixon's surprisingly expansive Comprehensive Health Insurance Plan (or CHIP) required employers to cover their employees, limited employee cost sharing, expanded employee benefits, and provided catastrophic health care. However, only 30 percent of Americans favored the Nixon plan, according to a Harris Poll question. Admittedly, the short-lived and ill-fated plan's lack of popularity may have been due, in part, to the president's own anemic approval ratings, then only 26 percent in Gallup Polls.

No president proposed another comprehensive plan. President Bill Clinton unveiled his far-reaching Health Security Act (HSA), which would have required employers to cover their employees, required an expansion of bare-bones plans, and covered most of the uninsured through state-run plans. Between fall 1993, when the plan was announced, and summer 1994, when the plan died in Congress without ever coming to a vote, public support steadily dropped. In September 1994 Americans favored the plan by a 55 percent-to-20 percent margin, with the remainder unsure, mixed, or unfamiliar with the plan. By July 1994 poll support had dropped from 55 percent to 40 percent, and opposition had risen from 20 percent to 56 percent, according to a series of 14 Gallup Polls. The Clinton administration's comprehensive plan witnessed one of the sharpest, but by no means the only, drop in public support for a health-reform plan.

President Obama's plan, the ACA, is the last of these four efforts to reorganize health care under the federal government's control. Though several parts of the complex were popular, many provisions barely achieved 50 percent approval in the polls, and some high-profile provisions were less popular. True, the Obama administration's successful effort to pass the ACA overcame many legislative hurdles. Yet one hurdle that the ACA never overcame was that of rising much above the 50 percent mark in terms of public support. When the ACA finally passed, Gallup Poll pegged its support at only 45 percent. An interesting question, and one that scholars have yet to address, is exactly why the ACA never won clear majority support, even though several of its components were apparently quite popular. Overall, the ACA rated in the polls only about as well as its least popular parts.

The Obama experience is not unique. Over the last three quarters of a century, only four American presidents, Truman, Nixon, Clinton, and Obama, have offered a truly comprehensive health care plan. None of these enjoyed majority poll support once the public debate was underway. Arguably, the short-lived Nixon plan, offered only in the dying weeks of his scandal-plagued presidency, might be discounted. However, 10 of the last 14 presidents apparently understood that comprehensive health care reform is not a winner in the polls. Instead, most presidents offered problem-specific health care reform plans. The answer to the question, why have most Americans never supported comprehensive health care reform, is complex. Part of the answer is that health care reform is usually a low-priority issue to Americans, one that rarely exceeds 10 percent in Gallup Poll's "most important problem" rating. By comparison, over two thirds of Americans typically describe economic issues as the nation's most important issue during periodic recessions. Another part of the answer is that the media constantly alerts the public as to how complex and torturous the congressional process actually is. In addition, public opinion support for health care reform is itself superficial and ambivalent. Moreover, groups opposing comprehensive health care enjoy a steadily better and wider array of methods to raise doubts about a particular plan and thereby reduce public-opinion support. Finally, if a president unveils a comprehensive health care reform plan during a hotly contested presidential campaign, support from the opposition party will, naturally, never be very high.

If no comprehensive plan ever won clear majority support in the polls, what then of problem-specific health care reforms? Indisputably, a majority of Americans have supported many problem-specific reforms over the years. Yet even that support has its limits. Americans seldom support problem-specific remedies that are costly, sweeping, or coercive. For example, many polls show that the ACA's least popular requirement is the "individual mandate" requirement that, by 2014, virtually all Americans must either have a health care insurance plan or else pay a fine. A 2011 Kaiser Family Foundation Poll, for example, reported that 67 percent of Americans believed that the requirement should be repealed.

That Americans oppose comprehensive health care reform plans, while picking and choosing among problem-specific reforms, points to a larger issue about American values. Many Americans do value both equality in access to health care and more affordable health care. Yet in conflict with those beliefs are other long-standing, widely shared American values that oppose government-regulated and government-financed health care. Chief among these are the classical liberal values of individual responsibility and self-reliance, and suspicion toward the federal government. Gallup's polling in 2010 points to this split. When asked which perspective to providing health care the respondent preferred, only a third (34 percent) chose "a government-run healthcare system," while 61 percent chose "a system based mostly on private insurance." Experimental evidence shows that when the public views ill health as a result of unhealthy personal behaviors, such as smoking or over-eating, support for a government remedy drops sharply. Further, many Americans do not see the lack of health insurance as so serious a problem in getting health care as do policy experts.

In short, the debate over health care reform does not occur in a political vacuum. Many Americans do not judge comprehensive health care reform as an isolated issue, but rather as a new set of federal programs and regulations with enormously negative side effects. Just after passage of the ACA, Gallup reported that around three-fifths (61 percent) of Americans said it would worsen the federal budget deficit, while less than a quarter (23 percent) said it would improve the deficit picture. By a closer, 46 percent-to-35 percent margin, Americans said that the ACA would further damage the U.S. economy. That many Americans view comprehensive health care reform from a broader philosophical or policy-oriented view typically works to the disadvantage of broadly written reforms.

THE CONSEQUENCES OF HEALTH CARE REFORM

Polling on specific health care reforms, whether comprehensive or problem-specific, offers only one measure of public opinion. Another useful indicator can be found in the approval ratings of presidents and of Congress during the time in which a health care reform plan is actively under debate. Typically, a president's approval ratings drop during this process, as do those of Congress, suggesting that health care reform is seldom well received. In its poll just before his televised speech on the ACA to a joint session of Congress on September 9, 2009, Gallup put President Obama's approval rating at 54 percent. A few days after President Obama signed the bill, however, Gallup pegged his approval rating at 46 percent—a drop of 8 percent. Other presidents experienced similar drops in their approval ratings. President Clinton's approval ratings fell from 46 percent at the time of his initial speech on health care to Congress in September 1993 to 42 percent in late July 1994 when the HSA bill was finally written off as dead. President Truman's approval ratings stood at 57 percent prior to his special message to Congress on comprehensive health care in April 1949, but fell to 43 percent in August 1950 when his bill was widely conceded to be dead. Apparently, a months-long debate on comprehensive health care reform damages, rather than helps, a president's approval ratings.

Polls on approval ratings for Congress show a similar pattern. When President Obama sent his comprehensive health care bill to Congress, Gallup Poll put Congress's approval rating at an already-anemic 31 percent. By early March 2010, Congress's approval rating dropped to a near-record low of only 16 percent. This sharp drop may be surprising inasmuch as the ACA was, by any standards, a landmark bill of historical importance. Most accounts attribute this drop to a "messy" and visible congressional process of deal-making and high levels of partisan rancor. When the American public becomes better informed and more aware about comprehensive health care reform, both the president and Congress pay a price in falling approval ratings.

That comprehensive health care plans, once debated, lose popularity can be illustrated in yet another way. A president who pushes for comprehensive health care reform, whether successfully or not, suffers heavier-than-usual losses in the next round of congressional elections. After President Clinton's HSA plan failed, Democrats lost 53 U.S. House seats and seven Senate seats in the 1994 midterm election. After President Obama's ACA bill passed, Democrats lost 65 House seats and six Senate seats in the 2010 election. These are the largest midterm congressional losses of the last half-century. To be sure, the president's party typically loses some congressional seats in midterm elections, particularly if the economy is weak, if the president's own approval ratings are low, or if the president's party gained a large number of House seats in the prior presidential election. Even so, attempting to pass an ambitious health insurance plan, whether successfully or not, also helps to explain midterm election losses. Election analysts have paid too little attention to this process, which may occur when well-organized and well-financed opponents of health reform mount effective negative publicity and voter-targeting campaigns throughout both the congressional deliberation stage and the following election. Whatever the exact process, when a president tries to pass a sweeping health-reform bill, what follows is a serious public-opinion backlash.

CONCLUSION

Passage of the ACA does not mark the end of the long-running debate over health care reform. If the ACA survives political challenges, a new era of greater federal oversight of health care standards and plans will emerge. Very likely, access to health care will be more greatly equalized and privately financed plans will slowly be driven out through greater regulations, mandates, cost shifting, and premium increases. Whether the steady rise in health care inflation will be restrained is at best unclear. How American public opinion will react to all this is uncertain, but at least a hint is offered by polling evidence from Canada and Britain. In both of those countries, the government has long regulated and financed most health care services, and far fewer services are paid for by privately financed plans than in the United States.

Gallup polls conducted in 2003 and 2005 in the United States, Canada, and Britain suggest that Canadians and Britons are far from satisfied with their government-financed health care. On some measures, Americans are the most satisfied, and on other measures they are the least. Americans are more satisfied with the quality of national health care, the quality of their own health care, the care provided by hospitals and emergency rooms, and with waiting lists and delays in obtaining medical care. Citizens in all three countries are equally well satisfied with the care provided by nurses and doctors. Americans are less satisfied with pharmaceutical companies, health care costs, and access to care. In short, it is far from certain that a heavily federally regulated health care system would be more popular than the current mixed system of public and private insurance. Indeed, a federally managed health care system may prove much less popular.

References and Further Reading

American National Election Study. (2010). *Trust the federal government 1958–2008*. Retrieved from http://www.electionstudies.org/nesguide/toptable/tab5a_1.htm

Blendon, R. J., & Benson, J. M. (2001). Americans' views on health policy: A fifty-year historical perspective. *Health Affairs, 20*(2), 33–46.

Blendon, R. J., Benson, J. M., & DesRoches, C. M. (1999). The uninsured, the working uninsured, and the public. *Health Affairs, 18*(6), 203–211.

Blizzard, R. (2003). *Healthcare system ratings: U.S., Great Britain, Canada*. Retrieved from http://www.gallup.com/poll/8056/Healthcare-System-Ratings-US-Great-Britain-Canada

Blizzard, R. (2005). *Britons, Americans, and Canadians diagnose healthcare*. Retrieved from http://www.gallup.com/poll/14638/Britons-Americans-Canadians-Diagnose-Healthcare.aspx

Blumenthal, D., & Morone, J. A. (2010). *The heart of power–Health and politics in the oval office*. Berkeley, CA: University of California Press.

Employee Benefit Research Institute. (2007). *Health confidence survey*. Retrieved from http://www.ebri.org/surveys/hcs/2007

Gollust, S. E., & Lynch, J. (2010). *Who deserves health care?* Paper presented at the annual meeting of the American Political Science Association, Washington, DC.

Jacobs, L. J. (2008). 1994 all over again? Public opinion and health care. *New England Journal of Medicine, 358*(18), 1881–1883.

Jacobs, L. J., & Skocpol, T. (2010). *Health care reform and American politics: What everyone needs to know*. New York, NY: Oxford University Press.

Kessler, D. P., & Brady, D. W. (2009). Putting the public's money where its mouth is. *Health Affairs, 28*(5). Retrieved from http://content.healthaffairs.org/content/28/5/w917.full.html

Marshall, T. R. (in press). Health care and the growing partisan divide. In W. Crotty (Ed.), *Party polarization in America*. Boulder, CO: Westview Press.

Morone, J. A. (2011). Big ideas, broken institutions, and the wrath at the grass roots. *Journal of Health Politics, Policy, and Law, 36*(3), 375–385.

Payne, S. L. (1946). Some opinion research principles developed through studies of social medicine. *Public Opinion Quarterly, 10*(1), 93–98.

Skocpol, T. (1997). *Boomerang: Health care reform and the turn against government*. New York, NY: Norton.

Thomas R. Marshall

States' Rights and Health Care Reform

POINT: State health care reform is consistent with the constitutional design and is more likely to produce workable policies that reflect the preferences of voters.

Elizabeth Weeks Leonard, University of Georgia School of Law

COUNTERPOINT: Federal regulation is necessary to manage and coordinate the nationwide health care system and ensure that all individuals have access to essential medical care.

Elizabeth Weeks Leonard, University of Georgia School of Law

Introduction

In the United States, power and authority are divided between the states and the federal government in Washington, D.C. That structure, so central to all of the nation's policies and politics, adds a layer of complexity to debates concerning health reform. It means that observers must always ask not simply what types of health reform the country should have but also whether reforms should be initiated by the states or by the federal government.

As the following debate, written by Professor Elizabeth Leonard, suggests, policymakers can look to the Constitution, Supreme Court decisions, U.S. history, and policy considerations to provide insights as to whether reforms to the health care system should come from the federal government or the states. Unfortunately, none of these sources provide irrefutable answers.

Under the U.S. Constitution, the federal government can only exercise the powers that are explicitly granted to it. As the Tenth Amendment underscores, all other powers are left to the states. This means that the federal government lacks what the states possess: a general "police power" that would allow it to enact laws simply on the ground that they would protect the health or safety of the public.

The lack of a federal police power, however, does not end the constitutional analysis. Although the Constitution grants Congress only limited powers, those powers are robust and can be used to authorize a wide array of federal regulations. Indeed, since the 1930s, when President Franklin Roosevelt's New Deal expanded the role of the federal government in response to the Great Depression, the Supreme Court had interpreted Congress's enumerated powers broadly. These powers, which include the power to regulate commerce among the states and to tax and spend for the general welfare, permit a plethora of federal regulations, many of which aim to protect public health or reform the health care system. Still, as Professor Leonard's Point essay suggests, if the federal system is to remain, and if the states are to continue to be sovereign, Congress's authority must be subject to limits. The Supreme Court echoed that sentiment, concluding in *National Federation of Independent Business v. Sebelius* (2012) that the authority of Congress to regulate interstate commerce did not empower it to mandate that individuals purchase health insurance and that its power under the Spending Clause did not reach so far as to compel states to expand their Medicaid programs. On the other hand, the Court also held that the power of Congress to tax provided constitutional support for the mandate and that the ACA's Medicaid expansion could go forward, albeit as a state option. Thus while limited, congressional authority remains significant. The Constitution's requirements, however, do not tell the whole story about the division of responsibilities regarding health policy between the federal government and the states. History also has much to tell. Alas, it too sends mixed messages. Without question, throughout the history of the United States, most health laws have been state laws. The common saying that public health protection is a "traditional state function" is a truism that happens to be true. Since the founding of the Republic, states have enacted "health laws of every description," including laws that regulate the practice of medicine, provide for the provision of charitable care, and oversee the business of health insurance companies (*Gibbons v. Ogden*, 1824).

History, however, also provides numerous examples of federal health laws. For example, as far back as 1798, Congress established the U.S. Marine Hospital Services to provide for the care of sailors. In the nineteenth century, federal involvement in health protection grew, for example, with the establishment of the Bureau of Chemistry that eventually gave rise to the Food and Drug Administration. By the middle of the late twentieth century, federal regulations pertained to almost every aspect of the health care system. Consider, for example, the laws that govern the Medicare and Medicaid programs; the Food, Drug, and Cosmetic Act, which regulates the sale and distribution of pharmaceuticals; and the Employee Retirement Income Security Act that regulates employer-provided health insurance plans. According to the Centers for Medicare & Medicaid Services (CMS), by 2009, 27 percent of health care dollars were spent by the federal government. If history and practice are any guide, it is hard to say that health care belongs solely to the states.

Yet health reform often has a dual ancestry. Many features of the U.S. health care system that most now take for granted started out as reforms initiated by a single state. Other reforms derived from federal initiatives. Recent history echoes this pattern. The ACA is a complex federal law with several novel features. But many of its provisions, including the controversial individual mandate and a less controversial requirement that restaurants post the calories of their menu items, were borrowed from state-based reforms. Does this history mean that reform should be left to the states? Or that there comes a time when the federal government should, as it so often has, step in and make reforms nationwide?

Policy considerations may offer a different perspective for assessing whether health reform should be left to the states or the federal government. Professor Leonard's Point demonstrates the numerous advantages that states have over the federal government when it comes to health care regulation. Ironically, the very complexity of the health care system may argue for leaving reform to the states, which can "experiment" with multiple, locally tailored approaches. As the health care system becomes more complex, a single, "one-size-fits-all" approach to reform may be doomed from the outset. Nevertheless, as the Counterpoint shows, complexity also presents challenges for states that lack both the fiscal and technical resources of the federal government. There is also a very real question as to whether any state can adequately reform this increasingly interstate, if not global, health care system.

In reading Professor Leonard's chapter, consider how society should decide whether health reform belongs properly to the states or the federal government. Think also about whether the conclusion about the respective roles of the states and federal government might depend upon the specific nature of a health-reform law. In other words, is it possible that some types of health reform should be carried out by the states, while others should be led by the federal government? If so, how should we distinguish between the types of reforms that states should control and the types of reform that should come from Washington? Finally, consider whether popular debates over federalism and health reform are fueled by genuine concerns about the rights of states and the prerogatives of the federal government. Or do proponents and opponents of various approaches to health reform use federalism as yet another weapon to advance their position? In other words, do arguments about the respective roles of the states and federal government mask more fundamental disputes about the role of *any* government when it comes to health?

POINT

Most everyone can agree that the U.S. health care system is in desperate need of reform, but they may not agree on the most pressing problems or the best approach for addressing them. States are in a better position than the federal government to identify and evaluate the key problems and design solutions that represent the broad range of public preferences and priorities. By design, the U.S. Constitution limits the power of the national government and reserves all other power and authority to the states. Consistent with the constitutional design and the intricate, controversial nature of the debate, health care reform should be focused at the state level.

The health-reform debate has brought to the forefront fundamental questions about individual rights and the role of government in people's personal lives. Health care is a highly personal matter generally decided between a patient and physician. To the extent that those physician-patient relationships have been regulated previously, it generally has been at the state level. The range of approaches is amply represented in diverse state laws on medical licensure, health care facility certification and inspection, and insurance market regulation. Federal involvement in health care has, and should continue to be, secondary.

In 2010 Congress passed comprehensive federal health-reform legislation, the Patient Protection and Affordable Care Act (ACA), which represented the most significant reform of the U.S. health care system in a generation. The debate surrounding the ACA awakened a deeply held, well-founded preference for states, rather than the national government, to take primary responsibility for enacting laws that affect the health and well-being of individuals. The text and purpose underlying the U.S. Constitution support this preference. Moreover, state-level reform offers several distinct advantages over the national government in establishing broad social policies, like health care.

LEGAL BASIS FOR STATE PRIMACY IN HEALTH REFORM

Federally mandated health care policy displaces states' constitutional authority and discretion to govern activities and residents within their borders. The U.S. Constitution establishes a federal system, characterized by a central national government and separate state governments. The states are represented in Congress but also operate their own sovereign governments. Under the Constitution, state powers are plenary; any powers not expressly granted to the national government are reserved to the states. Federal powers are limited and enumerated in the Constitution and include, among other powers, the power to regulate commerce among the states, the power to tax citizens to generate revenue, and the power to spend revenue for the general welfare of the country's residents.

The framers of the Constitution deliberately designed the federal system to diffuse power both horizontally among the three branches of government (executive, legislative, and judicial) and vertically among the national and state governments. Courts have repeatedly recognized that regulation of public health, safety, welfare, and morals fall squarely within the powers that the Constitution left to the states, the so-called reserved powers. Moreover, Congress has affirmed states' primary authority for regulating the business of health insurance, specifying that the national government may regulate only to the extent that states do not. In addition, states' long experience with regulating health care providers, health care facilities, and health insurance companies operating within their borders gives them expertise, which the national government lacks.

States are also the last line of defense for individual rights of citizens. An essential function of the federal structure is to protect individual liberty. As Justice Kennedy wrote in his opinion for *Bond v. United States* (2011), "Federalism is more than an exercise in setting the boundary between different institutions of government for their own integrity. State sovereignty is not just an end in itself: Rather, federalism secures to citizens the liberties that derive from the diffusion of sovereign power." Rights protected in the U.S. Constitution operate as a floor, whereas states are free to interpret individual rights more broadly or recognize additional rights not protected by national laws. Over 30 years ago former U.S. Supreme Court Justice William Brennan in fact urged states to expand protection for individual rights to continue the Court's progressive 1960s civil rights jurisprudence. States might do so, for example, by recognizing an affirmative right to health care in their state constitutions or laws, even though the U.S. Constitution does not recognize such a right. Or states might enact a constitutional amendment or statute protecting individuals' right to refuse to participate in a particular health care plan or program, or to purchase health care directly from health care providers rather than insurers. Those state-specific laws are valid, even if they differ from, but as long as they do not conflict with, federal law.

Even when federal health reform does not directly implicate states' reserved powers, states have a role in safeguarding the constitutional rights of their residents. Individuals may claim the right to be free of certain federal regulations and requirements. Though individuals, on their own, can challenge objectionable federal laws, they may have a stronger voice and more power to influence the national debate when speaking through their state representatives in Washington. Accordingly, states' elected and appointed officials may serve as advocates for the rights of their residents.

LIMITS OF FEDERAL ENUMERATED POWERS FOR HEALTH REFORM

States' plenary reserved powers are broader than the federal government's enumerated powers to regulate interstate commerce, lay and collect taxes, and spend for the general welfare. To be constitutionally valid, new federal policies must fit within one of those or another enumerated power. Those three enumerated powers, which are particularly relevant to health care regulation, not only allow but also limit Congress's authority to enact broad, federally mandated health care policy.

One limit on the federal power to regulate interstate commerce is that the authority allows Congress to regulate economic activity of individuals and businesses, but not inactivity. For example, the decision not to participate in a particular health insurance plan, or health care plan or program is best characterized, a majority of the justices explained in *National Federation of Independent Business* (2012), as inactivity and thus outside of the federal commerce power. The Court rejected the federal government's argument that it could regulate the way that people purchase health care because everyone will likely participate in the market for health care at one time or another. "Any police power to regulate individuals as such, as opposed to their activities, remains vested with the states."

Another limit on the commerce power is that Congress cannot ordinarily regulate intrastate, or purely local, activities. The Supreme Court has specified that in order for Congress to reach certain individual actions at the local level, those actions in the aggregate must have a substantial effect on interstate commerce. One individual's decision not to purchase health insurance or to forego medical treatment altogether does not substantially affect interstate commerce. Because a majority of the Court in National Federation of Independent Businesses decided that the individual mandate was not a regulation of existing commercial activity, the issue of aggregation was beside the point. Therefore, the federal government's attempt in the ACA to require the purchase of health insurance exceeded its commerce power. There must be limits on federal commerce power; otherwise, the national government could just as readily require people to eat healthy foods and join gyms because those practices tend to make people healthier and, therefore, decrease health care costs. The federal commerce power does not justify mandatory purchases, nor does it reach those sorts of incidental effects.

The federal government has broad power to lay and collect taxes, but the taxing power does not include the power to impose penalties designed to regulate conduct or punish violations of the law. Due to strong popular opposition to increased federal taxes, the framers of the ACA were careful to avoid calling the payment required by individuals who fail to comply with the individual mandate a "tax." But Congress's label is not controlling if the Court determines, as it did in National Federation of Independent Business, that the law actually functions as a tax.

Opponents of the ACA and supporters of states' rights believe that Congress should not be able to use its taxing power to regulate matters of state concern that are otherwise outside of Congress's authority. In other words, Congress should not be able to avoid constitutional limits on another enumerated power, such as the commerce power, simply by calling the new regulation a "tax." For example, if Congress otherwise lacks authority to compel individuals to purchase health insurance, it should not be able to avoid the limit simply by imposing a federal tax penalty on individuals who refuse. By rejecting this argument, the Supreme Court in *National Federation of Independent Business v. Sebelius* (2012) permitted Congress to extend its authority, using the power to tax as a de facto source of regulatory authority.

The Court's holding also erred, states' rights proponents maintain, in not finding the penalty associated with the ACA's mandate as an impermissible direct tax. Under the Constitution, Congress cannot impose a direct tax (e.g., a tax on property or on a person simply by virtue of his existence, as opposed to a tax on income) unless the tax is fairly apportioned. Fair apportionment means that the amount collected from the citizens of each state must be proportional to each state's population. According to opponents, the ACA's tax penalty on the failure to purchase health insurance should have been found to fail the uniformity and fair apportionment requirements.

Federal spending power is also limited. The spending power has been used to enact broad, nationwide public benefit programs, like Social Security and Medicare. But the federal government has no authority to require states to enact certain programs or to "commandeer" state officials to enforce federal laws. Courts have recognized an extension of the federal spending power, allowing Congress to offer federal funds to states on the condition that they enact certain programs or policies. For example, Congress can condition federal highway funding on states' enacting minimum age requirements for purchase of alcohol. That use of the "conditional spending power" does not constitute unlawful state "commandeering." But the Court long ago recognized that when pressure to participate in a federal program turns to "compulsion," the law violates principles of federalism.

The offer of federal funding conditioned on states' compliance with certain federal requirements or standards does not violate the Constitution as long as states have clear notice of the conditions and can choose freely whether to accept them. These sorts of cooperative approaches may be constitutional if carefully structured, but they remain problematic for federalism because they leave accountability unclear. The federal government implements broad reforms but leaves states bearing the brunt of voters' objections to the cost and operation of the programs once implemented. The Medicaid health care program for low-income and other qualifying individuals and the Children's Health Insurance Program (CHIP) are examples of "conditional spending power" to induce state cooperation. States voluntarily accepted federal funding in exchange for agreeing to implement state Medicaid and CHIP programs in accordance with federal requirements.

Although all 50 states have long participated in the Medicaid conditional spending program, the ACA required states to dramatically expand the number of citizens covered under the program. If states refused to expand Medicaid under the statute, they would lose all federal Medicaid funding for both current and newly eligible beneficiaries. As Chief Justice Roberts explained in *National Federation of Independent Business v. Sebelius* (2012), once states agree to implement federal programs and accept federal funds, the federal government cannot radically change the rules of the game without allowing states the option of declining further participation. Although states may have the legal right to withdraw from federal conditional spending programs, it may be impossible as a practical matter for them to step out of large public-benefits programs, like Medicaid, on which many state residents and the state budget have come to depend. At the time of the Court's decision, Medicaid spending accounted for over 20 percent of state budgets, on average, with the federal government paying 50 percent or more of those costs. Moreover, over the years, states have implemented detailed, interconnected programs and regulations, based on Medicaid. The loss of that significant portion of state budget funding and the practical difficulty of disentangling so many Medicaid-dependent programs left states with no real choice but to accept the ACA's new conditions. That, the Court held, crossed the line from permissible pressure to unconstitutional coercion. For these reasons, the Court was correct in holding that Congress could not compel the states to expand their Medicaid programs. That option must remain with the states, which cannot be coerced by the threat of having significant federal funds withheld.

PUBLIC POLICY REASONS TO PREFER STATE HEALTH REFORM

In addition to the constitutional arguments, there are several public policy reasons to favor state-level health care reform. First, states are in a unique position to serve, as the U.S. Supreme Court has termed, as "laboratories of democracy," designing and testing different approaches to health reform, which approaches can then be adopted by other states or the federal government. For example, many key features of the Massachusetts health-reform plan of 2006 were incorporated into the federal health-reform plan that culminated in the ACA in 2010, including the controversial individual mandate, employer play-or-pay penalties, health insurance exchanges, high-risk insurance pools, Medicaid expansion, and government subsidies. State experimentation allows states to try novel approaches on a smaller scale, with less risk to the entire nation if the experiment fails.

In addition, states have the flexibility to establish health care systems that serve the unique preferences and interests of their citizens, which may not be shared by the nation as a whole. Local preferences, tastes, economies, and priorities vary widely from state to state. Some states are characteristically libertarian, preferring limited government regulation of property, business, and personal liberties. Other states may seek to accomplish various environmental, social justice, and other public policy objectives through active state regulation. Also, priorities may vary depending on the states' demographics. For example, health policy goals for a state with a high percentage of elderly residents may be different from those of a state with a younger population. Likewise, states with high levels of employer participation in offering health insurance plans may require less extensive public health care programs than do states with lower employer participation.

Another reason to favor state health reform is that state government officials and politicians are more accessible and accountable to their constituents than are representatives in Washington, D.C., in part, simply because they have fewer people to represent. Also, local representatives tend to share the tastes and priorities of their constituents and spend more time in the jurisdictions that they represent. Accordingly, state lawmakers are in the best position to gather information and satisfy citizens' particular preferences. States may have different economic conditions and spending priorities, which a uniform national policy could not reflect. State-based reform allows for diverse approaches, rather than one-size-fits-all policymaking. The diversity of approaches among states allows residents the ultimate right to "vote with their feet," by choosing to remain in a state the policies of which they favor, or move away from a state with policies they disfavor.

Social policy issues, like health care, tend to implicate subjective values and may be especially controversial, making it important to facilitate diverse opinions and approaches. With controversial issues like health reform, abortion, or same-sex marriage, it may be beneficial to let ideas percolate up slowly from the states, rather than rushing a broad, federal pronouncement that may generate backlash or ill-fitting solutions. In addition, states may represent more homogenous populations and thereby may face less political opposition than the federal government in adopting particularly controversial or comprehensive health reforms, such as single-payer or universal health care systems. For example, Vermont voted to attempt to implement a single-payer health care system, while a similar proposal was never even considered in Congress. Allowing states, one-by-one, to adopt new policies, could eventually pave the road to consensus for dramatic reforms at the national level.

Allowing different approaches to health care reform from state to state need not lead to a "race to the bottom" of states competing among themselves to provide the fewest benefits and least protections to their residents. Empirical evidence does not support the "race-to-the-bottom" concern; people generally do not move from one state to another simply to obtain public benefits. Often, those individuals most in need of public benefits are often the least able to relocate. A different sort of race-to-the-bottom concern is that businesses and employers may be attracted to states with fewer regulations, but the interests of customers and employees will tend to "check" states' incentives to remove too many protections.

CONCLUSION

The Constitution imposes important limits on federal health policy. Furthermore, federally mandated reforms are not the best approach to health reform, as a policy matter. Under the U.S. Constitution, federal powers are limited and enumerated. All powers not specifically granted to the federal government are reserved to the states. The federal commerce power does not provide adequate authority for board national health reform. The U.S. Supreme Court, however, recently recognized the authority of Congress to tax individual citizens who choose not to maintain a minimum level of health insurance.

Health care regulation has long been recognized as a core component of states' plenary police power to provide for the safety and welfare of their citizens. Moreover, state reform better represents the diverse preferences of individuals across the country. State governments are more accessible and more directly accountable to their citizens. Also, as states design and implement various approaches to health reform, those experiments may be instructive to other states and the national government considering similar proposals.

REFERENCES AND FURTHER READING

Adler, J. H. (2011). Cooperation, commandeering, or crowding out? Federal intervention in state choices in health care policy. *Kansas Journal of Law & Public Policy, 20*(2), 199–221.

Barnett, R. E. (2003). *Restoring the lost constitution: The presumption of liberty*. Princeton, NJ: Princeton University Press.

Bond v. United States, __ U.S. __, 131 S. Ct. 2355 (2011).

Chermerinsky, E. (1995). The values of federalism. *Florida Law Review, 47*(4), 499–540.

Gardner, J. A. (1996). The "states as laboratories" metaphor in state constitutional law. *Valparaiso University Law Review, 30*(2), 475–491.

Hills, R. M. (1998). The political economy of cooperative federalism: Why state autonomy makes sense and "dual sovereignty" doesn't. *Michigan Law Review, 96*(4), 813–944.

Kahn, P. W. (1993). Commentary, interpretation and authority in state constitutionalism. *Harvard Law Review, 106*(5), 1147–1168.

Leonard, E. W. (2010). Rhetorical federalism: The value of state-based dissent to federal health reform. *Hofstra Law Review, 39*(1), 111–168.

Leonard, E. W. (2010). State constitutionalism and the right to health care. *University of Pennsylvania Journal of Constitutional Law, 12*(5), 1325–1406.

National Federation of Independent Business v. Sebelius, __U.S.__, 2012 WL 247810 (U.S. June 28, 2012) (Nos. 11-393, 11-400).

Rodriguez, D. B. (1998). State constitutional theory and its prospects. *New Mexico Law Review, 28*(2), 271–302.

Weil, A. R., & Tallon, J. R. (2008). The states' role in national health reform. *Journal of Law, Medicine & Ethics, 36*(4), 690–692.

Elizabeth Weeks Leonard

COUNTERPOINT

The 2010 Patient Protection and Affordable Care Act (ACA) represents the most significant reform of the U.S. health care system in a generation. Historically, health care has been regulated and financed by a patchwork of federal and state laws, along with business customs and standards. Health care, however, has evolved into a major interstate industry requiring comprehensive federal regulation. The health insurance and health care industries operate nationwide and are not confined to particular states. Although anachronistic state laws currently require insurance companies and health care providers to be incorporated, licensed, and regulated at the state level, in reality, most are national corporations that operate in multiple states. Uniform, coordinated federal regulation is more likely to achieve the goals of controlling health care costs, expanding access to care, and improving quality of care.

The federal government possesses broad powers that clearly authorize it to enact comprehensive, nationwide reforms. In particular, the U.S. Constitution grants the federal government the powers to regulate interstate commerce, and tax and spend for the general welfare. There is a long history of federal health care programs and regulation. Moreover, there are several distinct public policy advantages to centralized, coordinated health reform at the national level.

FEDERAL CONSTITUTIONAL AUTHORITY FOR HEALTH CARE

The U.S. Constitution expressly grants the federal government broad powers to regulate matters that affect the nation as a whole and to enact national health care programs. Specifically, the Commerce Clause empowers the federal government to regulate commerce among the several states and across state lines. The federal taxing and spending power also authorizes the federal government to lay and collect taxes in order to fund national programs. Under the Supremacy Clause, federal law preempts conflicting or contrary state laws. Accordingly, states cannot enact laws that purport to nullify or "opt out" of otherwise valid federal laws or requirements.

COMMERCE POWER

The federal commerce power has been interpreted broadly to allow federal regulation of economic activity, including many aspects of the health care system. Congress has authority to regulate channels of interstate commerce, instrumentalities of interstate commerce, and local activities that have a substantial economic effect on interstate commerce. In addition, Congress has constitutional authority to enact laws that are "necessary and proper" for carrying out other enumerated federal powers, including the commerce power.

Examples of federal laws enacted under the commerce power include regulation of pharmaceutical products, devices, and other controlled substances sold on national markets, under the authority of the U.S. Food and Drug Administration. Also, federal law has long regulated employer-provided health insurance plans, through which the majority of Americans receive their health insurance. Employers and insurance companies specifically sought federal regulation because of the burden and inefficiency of complying with myriad state laws. Accordingly, federal law provides a uniform set of rules for health plans, making it easier and cheaper for employers and insurers to comply. Federal law also ensures that employees can move from one job to another, including jobs in other states, without being denied health insurance or facing discrimination because of preexisting medical conditions. Most of the ACA's insurance reform provisions, such as the ban on preexisting condition exclusions and modified community rating, fall squarely within this tradition and are clearly supported by the Commerce Clause. There was never any serious constitutional question as to their validity.

Although the commerce power extends only to interstate commerce, even economic activity that seems confined to a single state's borders may substantially affect interstate commerce by altering the national market for the particular good or service. This holds true even for such seemingly isolated matters as an individual's own decision whether or not to purchase health insurance. When it comes to health care, no one is an island; everyone in the system, whether insured or uninsured, affects the cost and availability of health care. Health insurers determine premiums based on all the members of a relevant risk pool, spreading the losses among them. Health care providers determine rates, in part, based on the amount of uncompensated care they necessarily provide to indigent patients. Health care is not an industry in which people can effectively choose not to participate. Everyone, sooner or later, will need care. When people need emergency medical care but lack insurance or other means to pay for it, society has chosen to provide that care, regardless of the patient's ability to pay. Congress has codified that societal preference in a law that requires hospitals that accept federal funding to provide at least emergency medical care. Accordingly, individual decisions to forego health insurance, in the aggregate, affect interstate commerce by increasing the cost of health insurance and health care for all. Moreover, if people do not have regular access to preventive and other medical care through health insurance plans, they may become sicker and avoid seeking help until their conditions are acute, at which point they will be even more costly to treat. For these reasons, the Supreme Court should have found that Congress had authority under the Commerce Clause to impose the ACA's individual mandate.

Alternatively, the Court should have concluded that the mandate was authorized by Congress's power to enact laws that are necessary and proper to supporting other constitutionally enacted laws. The Necessary and Proper Clause empowers Congress to enact a law, which might not fit within congressional power standing alone, if the law is an integral part of a larger, complex regulatory program that is valid. Requiring most Americans to purchase health insurance was necessary and proper to the larger regulatory scheme under the ACA. In particular, without the individual mandate, the ACA's ban on preexisting condition exclusions and community-rating requirement would trigger an insurance "death spiral," as may people would wait until they were sick to purchase health insurance. Accordingly, it may be necessary and proper for Congress to require the purchase of health insurance to carry out other reforms, including regulation of health insurance underwriting, rate structures, and coverage requirements.

TAXING AND SPENDING POWER

In addition to the commerce power, federal taxing and spending power authorizes federal regulation and financing of health care. The federal government has the power to lay and collect taxes and spend the revenue of such taxes for the general welfare. Congress has wide discretion to decide which taxes and expenditures serve the general welfare. Promoting a healthy population, expanding access to care, and preventing individuals from falling into poverty because of medical costs certainly promote the general welfare. As long as the federal tax produces some revenue, the tax is not invalid just because it also regulates, discourages, or deters the activities taxed. Taxes, however, cannot operate simply as punishment for unlawful activity, if Congress otherwise lacks authority to regulate the conduct. For example, the Supreme Court long ago held that Congress could not impose a "tax" on unlawful child-labor practices, which were outside of its authority as then interpreted by the Supreme Court to regulate under the Commerce Clause. Requiring individuals who fail to maintain minimum health insurance coverage to pay a monthly tax penalty does not operate as punishment for conduct outside of Congress's authority, as the Supreme Court correctly found in *National Federation of Independent Business v. Sebelius* (2012). The individual mandate operates as a tax because the amount owed to the government will be far less than the price of an individual insurance policy and thus is not a financial "punishment." Also, it contains no scienter requirement, as criminal laws usually do. Finally, the law is collected by the Internal Revenue Service through normal means of taxation.

The Court's decision in National Federation of Independent Business is consistent with its validation of longstanding federal public-welfare programs, like Social Security and Medicare, as legitimate exercises of federal taxing and spending power. The U.S. Supreme Court held that federal welfare spending power is validly exercised as long as there is common benefit, distinguished from local purpose. Accordingly, the federal payroll tax that funds Social Security and the unemployment compensation program under it were expressly upheld. Even opponents of the ACA agree that Congress could use similar taxing and spending power to enact a national health care program in which all Americans could enroll, or "Medicare for All," if political objections could be overcome.

Federal spending power can also be used to encourage state cooperation in enacting federal standards or programs. Examples of cooperative state-federal programs include Medicaid and the Children's Health Insurance Program (CHIP). States that choose to establish Medicaid or CHIP plans that meet federal standards receive federal matching dollars for all state spending on the approved programs. Those sorts of cooperative arrangements allow states flexibility to tailor programs to their localities while ensuring compliance with broad federal standards and assurance of federal financial support. Although the Supreme Court in *National Federation of Independent Business v. Sebelius* (2012) found that Congress could not sanction states that refused to expand their Medicaid programs by withdrawing all of their federal Medicaid funds, the Court did not undermine the federal government's ability to use its spending power to offer states the option of expanding Medicaid. Nor did the Court question the constitutionality of the existing Medicaid program. Moreover, the Court's limitation on Congress's spending power should be read as limited to the unique context of Medicaid, which consumes an inordinate share of state budgets, making the threat of withdrawing Medicaid funds especially coercive. Congress continues to be able to use its spending power to condition other health-related grants of federal funds to the states (e.g., to set up health insurance exchanges).

PUBLIC POLICY REASONS TO FAVOR FEDERAL REGULATION

In addition to the constitutional arguments supporting federal health reform, public policy arguments favor a national approach. First, centralized health reform at the national level facilitates uniformity and equal treatment. Health care is so essential to human existence that its availability and distribution should not vary based on ability to pay or state of residence. All citizens should have access to the same core package of health care services. Uniformity can be achieved effectively only at the national level.

Uniform laws also promote business by making it easier for companies (including employers, insurance companies, and health care providers) to comply with one federal standard, rather than 50 different state laws. Federal regulation also avoids a "race to the bottom" among the states. In order to attract employers and other business opportunities, states may be tempted to alleviate businesses of burdensome regulations, many of which are intended to protect consumers. In order to compete for businesses, states may end up compromising the safety and rights of their citizens. In a different sort of race to the bottom, states also may fear that if they offer generous public benefits to their residents, people will move from other, less generous states to obtain the benefits. In response to this fear, states may elect to offer fewer and fewer public benefits to avoid attracting poor and sick residents from other states. National health benefits and standards eliminate that type of adverse competition among states. Uniform federally defined benefits also are portable, allowing people to move from state to state without losing or having to change their health care plans or programs.

Another reason to favor federal regulation is that the federal government can better achieve efficiencies and broad redistribution of income and benefits. Close to one third of all health care spending in the United States is by the government. The federal government as a purchaser of health care on behalf of the public has the advantage of "economies of scale." Just like any successful business with lots of customers, the federal government can drive a strong bargain and obtain better prices from health insurers, health care providers, pharmaceutical companies, and other suppliers. Moreover, the federal government, as a single purchaser, has to negotiate only one or a few contractual arrangements, reducing the cost of transacting business with those health care providers and suppliers.

Federal regulation also effects large, nationwide "risk pools." Health insurance operates by collecting premiums from all participants while gambling that only some participants will actually require extensive medical care. Accordingly, the premiums of those who use few medical services end up supplementing those who use lots of services. To ensure that they collect enough in premiums to pay the cost of the care provided, insurers need a certain level of healthy participants. As a policy matter, nationwide risk pooling facilitates redistribution of resources to those in greater need, meaning both individuals and states in greater need. The federal government can spread the costs of health care across a broader group of people by bringing a broader, more diverse population into the risk pool. Requiring all individuals across the nation, including young, healthy adults who typically opt out of health insurance, to purchase health insurance and thereby be included in the risk pool, is necessary to maximize the nationwide risk-pooling objective.

Although states have been dubbed "laboratories of democracy," the federal government actually may be in a better position to experiment with different approaches to health reform than states. First, the federal government typically has greater resources, technical expertise, and administrative capacity to gather information and implement reforms. As a pragmatic consideration, the federal government has more capacity to implement major health reforms because it can, at least temporarily, engage in deficit spending, whereas most states require annual balanced budgets. Also, the federal government can exact higher taxes to fund major reforms, without the concern that states face by raising taxes and driving citizens or businesses to flee to another state to avoid the tax increase.

In addition, unlike state-by-state experimentation, which tends to derive from demographic, policy, and fiscal conditions unique to that state, federal experiments can be designed to study and predict the impact of reforms on states across the country. The federal government has a stronger incentive to gather, store, and distribute information relevant to all states, not just the one particular state conducting the experiment. For example, the lessons of Massachusetts's comprehensive health care reform relied on a constellation of factors unique to Massachusetts, which made it difficult for the lessons learned there to inform proposals in other states, such as California, where there is less political consensus, a larger, more heterogeneous population, and lower levels of insured residents as a baseline. Moreover, Massachusetts can readily assess the success or failure of its reforms by observation and has little incentive to collect data and share it with other states. The central government, by contrast, would have a strong interest in assessing the experiments more methodically and making the results more broadly available. In any event, federally led experiments do not have to be national in scale but could focus on certain localities and demographics.

The argument for the importance of state diversity in health reform assumes that individual preferences align with state borders, which is not necessarily true. Just because an individual lives in Kansas does not necessarily mean that she shares more political or social views with other Kansans than with individuals from another state or states. Federal reform, enacted by elected representatives of all 50 states, better represents the diverse views and preferences of the nation as a whole.

A final policy reason to favor federal health reform stems from advances in technology and communication. Health care is increasingly reliant on technology, including electronic medical recordkeeping, electronic imaging, and other forms of communication. In the modern technological era of medicine, the argument for state and local regulation has much less salience than it once did. Moreover, federal regulation allows for widespread data collection and electronic health records interoperability, both of which are essential for improving quality of care and implementing further reforms.

CONCLUSION

The federal government has clear constitutional authority under the commerce power and taxing and spending power to enact comprehensive health care reform. Although Congress may not compel individuals to engage in commerce, health care is a major interstate industry, subject to many other forms of federal regulation under the Commerce Clause. In addition, the federal taxing and spending power authorizes programs that benefit the general welfare of all citizens and has been used previously to enact national programs, such as Medicare and Medicaid. The Court also recognized in *National Federation of Independent Business*, that the individual mandate is constitutional under the taxing power, even if not under the commerce power. Although that case recognized limits on federal power to compel state participation in implementing federal programs, it did not declare the existing Medicaid program or its characteristic federal-state cooperative design unconstitutional.

Moreover, a national approach to health reform ensures uniform standards of essential health care for citizens and uniform regulation of health care providers. The federal government's greater resources, purchasing power, and risk-pooling capabilities also help achieve the goals of reducing health care costs, increasing access to care, and improving quality of care. In the modern technological age, with national markets for health care, there is no longer a compelling case for state-level health reform.

REFERENCES AND FURTHER READING

Chapman, C. B., & Talmadge, J. M. (1970). Historical and political background of federal health care legislation. *Law and Contemporary Problems, 35*(2), 334–347.

Greer, S. L., & Jacobson, P. D. (2010). Health care reform and federalism. *Journal of Health Politics, Policy & Law, 35*(2), 203–226.

Hodge, J. G., Arias, J., & Ordell, R. (2010). Nationalizing health care reform in a federalist system. *Arizona State Law Journal, 42*(4), 1245–1275.

Holahan, J., Weil, A., & Wiener, J. M. (2003). *Federalism and health policy.* Baltimore, MD: Urban Institute Press.

Jacobson, P. D. (2007). The federalist approach to health care and its limitations: Introductory remarks. *Hamline Journal of Public Law & Policy, 30*(1), vii–xvii.

Kinney, E. D. (1999). Clearing the way for an effective federal-state partnership in health reform. *University of Michigan Journal of Law Reform, 32*(4), 899–938.

Mashaw, J. L., & Marmor, T. R. (1995). The case for federalism and health care reform. *Connecticut Law Review, 28*(1), 115–126.

Moncrieff, A. R., & Lee, E. (2011). The positive case for centralization in health care regulation: The federalism failures of ACA. *Kansas Journal of Law & Public Policy, 20*(2), 266–294.

National Federation of Independent Business v. Sebelius, __U.S.__, 2012 WL 247810 (U.S. June 28, 2012) (Nos. 11-393, 11-400).

Rich, R. F., & White, W. D. (1998). Federalism and health care policy. *University of Illinois Law Review, 1998*(3), 861–884.

Super, D. A. (2008). Laboratories of destitution. Democratic experimentalism and the failure of antipoverty law. *University of Pennsylvania Law Review, 157*(2), 541–616.

Elizabeth Weeks Leonard

Liberty and the Individual Mandate

POINT: Individual mandates are an essential tool for providing affordable health insurance to all. In order to keep the costs of premiums affordable, insurance companies need low-risk, healthy individuals to participate in their coverage pools.

Leonard M. Fleck, Michigan State University

COUNTERPOINT: Health insurance mandates violate individual liberty. In a free society, individuals should have a right to decide to stay out of the health insurance market.

Leonard M. Fleck, Michigan State University

Introduction

For decades, Americans have debated whether to recognize a right to health care. With the inclusion in the 2010 Patient Protection and Affordable Care Act (ACA) of a mandate penalizing individuals for not having insurance, the opposite question has taken center stage: Do individuals have a right to *refuse* to have health insurance? Julia Bienstock and Corey Davis explore that question from a legal perspective, looking at the mandate's constitutionality in their chapter, "Federal Authority Over the Individual Mandate." In this chapter, Leonard Fleck focuses on the ethical issues raised by the mandate.

As the chapter notes, the ACA's mandate is morally problematic for several reasons. First, U.S. society generally views individual liberty and autonomy as important values. As a result, it recognizes the rights of noninterference, meaning that individuals have the right to make decisions about how they wish to live their lives, as long as their actions do not harm others. This suggests that individuals should have the right to reject both health care and health insurance, even if they may suffer for doing so. Respect for individual liberty generally counsels a rejection of paternalistic arguments that attempt to justify limiting an individual's autonomy for his or her own good. For this reason, most bioethicists and health professionals accept that competent patients generally have the right to reject medical treatments, even when those treatments are necessary to save their lives. This right, known colloquially as "the right to die," continues after an individual is no longer competent through the recognition of a living will or other form of advanced directive. Does the widespread acceptance of the right to die also support a right to refuse health insurance? Or is there a significant moral difference between the right to reject health care and the right to reject health insurance?

In this chapter, Fleck suggests also that the right of noninterference includes the right to choose with whom to associate. A mandate that requires individuals to join a health insurance pool is potentially troubling in part because it compels individuals to join with others to form a health insurance risk pool. Once in the pool, individuals may provide indirect financial support for health care services, such as birth control, about which they may have strong moral objections. In addition, a mandate effectively redistributes wealth from those who are mostly healthy and relatively prosperous to those who are less so. Although altruism may support such redistribution, respect for individual liberty argues against compelling people to act as good Samaritans.

But does the mandate depend on either paternalism or enforced good Samaritanism for its defense? After all, an individual's decision to forgo health insurance can have significant consequences for others. First, the uninsured often end up needing and receiving health care. When they can't pay for that care, others in the health care system must bear the cost. According to Congress, in 2008, over $43 billion was spent on uncompensated care to the uninsured. Thus, people who reject insurance act either intentionally or unintentionally as "free riders," who benefit from others' prudent investment in health insurance. It was this fact that then-Governor Mitt Romney emphasized in 2006 when he demanded the inclusion of an individual mandate in the Massachusetts health-reform legislation that became a model for the ACA's mandate. Writing in *The Wall Street Journal,* Governor Romney stated, "someone has to pay for the health care that must, by law be provided: Either the individual pays or the taxpayer. A free ride on government is not libertarian." But is an insurance mandate a legitimate response to Governor Romney's observation? Or should we simply stop providing health care to those who cannot afford it? Does our unwillingness to deny people life-saving care provide any insight to the moral dilemma posed by the mandate?

Governor Romney's statement emphasizes the problem of individuals who choose to forego insurance, suggesting that they are acting irresponsibly. But a more subtle defense of the mandate may note that a private health insurance system simply cannot provide adequate coverage to those who need it most without some sort of mandate. Without a mandate, the young and healthy will be less likely to purchase insurance (because it is less valuable to them) than will those who are older or unhealthy. In response to that adverse selection, insurers will have an incentive to deny coverage to people with preexisting conditions. Conversely, if that practice is banned, to ensure that people who need coverage can get it, insurers will raise the cost of their premiums to pay for people with high health care needs. If insurers raise their premiums, however, insurance will become even less attractive to those who are healthy, prompting them to cease their coverage. The result would be a premium-spiral, as the cost of insurance rises continually in response to the narrowing of the risk pool. Eventually the insurance market may erode, as coverage becomes unaffordable to those who need it. This possibility may explain why, prior to the ACA's enactment, insurance companies and conservative policymakers tended to support an individual mandate. They feared that, without a mandate, the private insurance system would collapse, leading the public to demand a government-run insurance system in its place. Thus, prior to 2010, many opponents of government intervention in the health care market supported an individual mandate as a tool for limiting government interference and maintaining a private insurance market.

Government-run insurance programs, however, may also rely upon a mandate. Consider the Medicare program. When Medicare was established in 1965, it consisted of two programs, Part A, which covered hospital costs, and the optional Part B program, which covered physician bills and other outpatient costs. Like Social Security, Medicare Part A is financed by a mandatory payroll tax. Participation in the program is also mandatory for everyone who is 65 and over and receives Social Security retirement benefits. Libertarians question the legitimacy of these Medicare mandates, but proponents argue that the tax is necessary to ensure the program's viability and that the mandate to attain coverage is justified because it helps guarantee that hospitals will be paid for treating patients who are over 65. In effect, Medicare's mandates are designed not to help the individuals to whom they apply, but rather the health care system writ large. Does the fact that the well-established and highly regarded Medicare program relies on mandates offer any insight into whether we should recognize a right to reject health insurance? Or does the fact that Medicare is a government-run program, financed through the tax system, provide an ethically relevant distinction, suggesting that the right to reject insurance only applies to privately run insurance plans? What if Medicare were changed to a voucher program that provided government support for private insurance plans? Would Medicare's mandates cease to be legitimate? If so, is there any way for a nation to recognize both a right to reject health insurance and a right to health care?

POINT

In March 2010 Congress passed the Patient Protection and Affordable Care Act (ACA) in an effort to substantially reform the U.S. health care system. One of the primary goals of this legislation was to reduce significantly the number of Americans without health insurance (roughly 50 million individuals in 2011) as well as the number of Americans with inadequate health insurance (roughly another 25 million individuals). One of the central features of this legislation is what is known as the "individual mandate." This legal requirement obliges nearly every American (there are some exceptions) to carry minimally comprehensive health insurance coverage, either provided by the government or an employer or purchased by an individual. Failure to abide by this requirement would result in a significant tax penalty. This mandate has created much controversy, much of it pertaining to the constitutionality of the mandate itself. The question was resolved by the Supreme Court in June 2012. This essay will address the independent question of whether the individual mandate is ethically and politically justified.

As background, one ought to ask why anyone might believe the individual mandate is morally or politically unjustified. Political scientists describe U.S. society as a *liberal* society which values granting everyone a right to choose the values they would judge would allow them to lead a good life. The understanding is that these liberty rights will be respected so long as an individual does not use his or her liberty to violate the equal liberty rights of others. Thus, U.S. citizens affirm the right of individuals to take many kinds of risks with their health, including smoking, eating a high-fat diet, refusing sound medical advice, and engaging in risky sports, to name but a few. Why should individuals who indulge in these behaviors not be allowed to gamble with both their health and their financial well-being by going without health insurance? That they should be allowed to spend their money on other goods and services seems perfectly congruent with what a liberal society is supposed to accept. True, a liberal society imposes some limits on individual liberty. For example, individuals are required to use seat belts, but few raise any serious objections to the effect that this requirement is especially illiberal. The costs are low, observance is easy, no deep personal values are threatened. The individual mandate, however, is costly for individuals (at least several thousand dollars in many cases), and it is something strongly resisted by political conservatives as a violation of their fundamental political values.

In spite of these objections, the key argument of this essay will be that the individual mandate is both just and justified. The individual mandate is *just* because it requires all who are beneficiaries of the U.S. health care system to pay their fair share of the costs. The individual mandate is *justified* because it is a necessary feature of a reformed health care system that supports fairer approaches to health care cost-containment. In addition, it is justified because it protects individuals who choose to forego buying health insurance because they feel healthy from the potentially devastating and irreversible consequences of their imprudent choices. The individual mandate also protects the integrity of medical practice by diminishing the corrosive effects that a patient's ability to pay can have on the quality of care a physician can provide.

HISTORICAL CONTEXT

Why does the United States have 50 million uninsured individuals? Who are the uninsured? Answering these questions will help in understanding the need for the individual mandate. The most significant fact about the U.S. health care system, politically and economically, is that it is extraordinarily expensive. To be precise, the United States spent a total of about $2.6 trillion on health care in 2010 according to Truffer and others, which represented 17.6 percent of gross domestic product (GDP). By themselves, those numbers are not especially meaningful. In 1960 the United States spent $26 billion on health care, only 5.2 percent of GDP at that time. What is politically and economically troubling is that health care costs have steadily increased at about 2.5 times the core inflation rate in the economy over those 50 years. This has been driven by the steady introduction of costly new medical technologies, an aging population, an increasing burden of chronic illness, and the moral hazard of insurance. This trend is expected to continue far into the foreseeable future. Thus, Truffer and others estimate that in 2019 the United States will spend $4.5 trillion on health care, about 19.8 percent of projected GDP.

The other historical fact that must be noted is that the U.S. private employer–based health insurance system was largely a product of economic aspects of World War II. While a wage freeze was in place during the war, employers were allowed to increase benefits to their employees, including health insurance, an inexpensive benefit at the time. However, when the cost of providing that benefit increased dramatically during the 1980s and beyond, marginal low-wage employers began to rescind that benefit or not offer it all. Reinhardt, a Princeton economist, citing the Milliman Medical Cost Index, notes that in 2011 the average cost of health insurance for a family of four in the United States was $19,343. That a worker who earns $10 per hour makes $20,000 a year readily explains why low-wage workers do not have health insurance. At present only 60 percent of workers in the United States have health insurance through their employers.

Two other groups of uninsured individuals need to be identified. Millions of relatively young people earn enough to afford health insurance but choose to forego it because they believe themselves to be healthy and consider spending several thousand dollars for health insurance to be a waste of money. Likewise constituting a large bloc of the uninsured are individuals with preexisting medical conditions. These are people who want health insurance because they have chronic, costly medical problems, but insurers either refuse to offer them health insurance at any price, or only at an exorbitant price far beyond their means, or at a reasonable price but with exclusions for anything related to their preexisting medical condition. Again, if costly medical advances over the past 50 years had not occurred, such as $100,000 cancer drugs and $200,000 left ventricular assist devices, insurers could offer coverage to patients with preexisting conditions at a reasonable cost. But this is contrary to fact.

Key coordinated elements of the ACA. One of the requirements of the ACA is that insurers may no longer deny health insurance to individuals with costly preexisting medical conditions. For now, insurers may still charge individuals more than the average cost of their policies, but after 2014 the ACA will prohibit that practice. Many philosophers and health policy analysts, such as Norman Daniels and Stuart Altman, would regard such denials as being fundamentally unjust because such individuals would often be faced with a premature death because they could not afford the medical care necessary to save or prolong their lives. Many of these individuals would be described as among the "medically least-well-off" whose health care needs ought to have high priority as a matter of both justice and compassion. But current underwriting practices effectively assign them a low priority or no priority because of the financial losses they represent.

Insurers respond to the charge of injustice by arguing that it was equally unjust to impose the extraordinary costs associated with medical care for these individuals on the rest of their more healthy clients, especially if those clients were free to move to other less costly insurance plans. The virtue of the ACA is that it levels the playing field by requiring all insurers to accept these individuals.

As noted already, the primary goal of the ACA is to reduce substantially the number of Americans without health insurance. However, the vast majority of the uninsured are in relatively low-wage jobs, and few could afford the costs of coverage. Consequently, the ACA includes substantial graduated subsidies to the uninsured up to income levels at four times the federal poverty level for a family of four, about $88,000 in 2011. The general idea holds that no family should have to pay more than 10 percent of its income for health insurance. This would strike many as a reasonable expectation in exchange for insurance coverage. However, a number of studies by Susan Marquis and others demonstrate that generous subsidies are still inadequate to motivate a large portion of the uninsured to spend some of their money for health insurance. The basic problem is that individuals and families in the lower half of the income spectrum have multiple financial needs, relative to which health insurance appears as a poor buy when everyone feels healthy. This is one practical reason why an individual mandate to purchase health insurance is an integral part of the ACA.

THE INDIVIDUAL MANDATE: AN ANTIDOTE TO "FREE RIDING"

There are several variations of the "free-riding" problem that would threaten the stability and fairness of the system for financing health care if there were no individual mandate. Hospitals, employers, and the federal government could all have their legitimate interests unjustly threatened without a requirement that everyone financially capable of purchasing health insurance do so.

Hospitals and free riders. It is a political and moral fact that hospitals will not turn away patients with true emergency health care needs, whether or not those patients are insured or have any ability to pay. This is required by law, specifically the Emergency Medical Treatment and Active Labor Act. The resulting costs are commonly thought of as "being absorbed" by the hospital, but hospitals cannot just absorb costs that patients are unwilling or unable to pay. Instead, they have to be passed along to everyone else who is insured, which translates into higher insurance premiums for insured individuals. Those individuals are then paying "more than their fair share" for their own health insurance and health care. No doubt, some individuals are so near the poverty line that even with government subsidies they cannot pay for any insurance product in the market. They cannot be justly accused of free riding. But other individuals do have the economic capacity to pay for insurance and yet choose not to. These individuals are justly mandated to purchase health insurance.

Insurers and free riders. Again, the ACA would not allow insurers to turn away individuals who wished to purchase health insurance. In the absence of an individual mandate, individuals could simply wait to purchase health insurance until such a time as they were faced with a costly medical problem. The result would be individuals in good health waiting five, ten, or twenty years to purchase health insurance, thereby denying the insurance pool all the money they would otherwise have paid in insurance premiums. Then, faced with an illness requiring $100,000 worth of health care, they could purchase for $6,000 the necessary insurance to cover those costs. In effect, everyone else in the insurance pool would have to absorb that $94,000 in excess expenses as part of *their* insurance premium. This is another version of the free-rider problem. It will strike most individuals who are absorbing those costs as being patently unjust. Individuals who take advantage of the insurance scheme in this way are enjoying the benefits of health insurance without bearing their fair share of the burden of health insurance costs.

Further, if any individuals had the right to buy health insurance in the midst of a health crisis for a tiny fraction of the likely cost, then all individuals (morally speaking) would have that same right. But for everyone to exercise such a right would effectively destroy the insurance pool. No one would rationally want to remain in such a pool if they were going to have to pay to subsidize free-riding behavior. And if there were no insurance pool, everyone would be responsible for paying entirely for the cost of their health care at the time they needed it. In the case of serious illness, these would be costs that only the rich could afford. If only the rich could pay for very costly health care needs, the U.S. health care system would financially collapse. In turn, the vast majority of Americans would have no effective access to costly lifesaving medical care.

Employers and free riders. To be clear, no one expects the dire consequences outlined in the prior paragraph to occur. But these are the sorts of consequences that could occur if everyone had a moral and legal right not to buy health insurance until faced with a costly health crisis. Further, employers who now provide health benefits to their employees would find themselves in the same situation. That is, without an individual mandate, millions of individuals would refrain from buying health insurance until a health crisis. Insurers would have to pass all those excess costs on to employers, some of whom would then be economically forced either to pass those costs to workers or to drop offering health benefits in order to protect their profit margins or market competitiveness (though the ACA includes a weak employer mandate to limit this).

In the policy debates that preceded the passage of the ACA, insurers were strong supporters of the individual mandate. This was more a matter of self-interest than moral concern. If they were going to be forced to accept millions of individuals with costly preexisting medical conditions and those excess costs were not offset by the premiums generated by the mandated enrollment of healthy individuals, they would have to protect their profits by passing along those costs to employers. But if employers balked and insurers lost that business, insurers could be forced to exit that business.

The federal government and free riders. The federal government, too, has its own interests to protect. The individual mandate is supported through the graduated public subsidies mentioned above. If large numbers of employers were to cease offering health insurance as a benefit because of the cost, their employees would be dumped into the individual market for insurance. This could result in a large shift in health care costs from the private sector to the public sector because the federal government would now be responsible for providing some level of subsidy to all these individuals and families who were below 400 percent of the poverty level. Such an eventuality would add substantially to the deficit problem faced by the federal government unless new taxes were imposed that, to be fair, would somehow have to be focused on those employers who had shifted these costs to the federal government.

MINIMIZING INEQUITIES

Employers do have an alternative option to dropping health insurance as a benefit: offering an increasingly "thinner" and less costly package of health benefits. Doing so would involve excluding from coverage some range of costly medical interventions in various clinical circumstances, such as very costly cancer drugs or cardiac interventions, such as the left ventricular assist device. Perhaps worse still, morally speaking, would be adding much more burdensome co-pay requirements for employees, especially with regard to more costly medical interventions. The shift in costs is then to individuals rather than to government. The effect would be one of exacerbating inequities with regard to access to needed health care. Employees at the higher end of the pay scale might be able to bear these costs but employees in the middle range and below would be forced to deny themselves costly but effective life-prolonging health care interventions. In effect, access to needed health care would be determined by ability to pay, precisely the sort of inequity that the health insurance provided by employers was supposed to minimize.

All individuals within a company were supposed to have the same health plan and roughly equal access to needed health care. But if large co-pays are required by a stripped-down health plan, that sort of equity is sacrificed. Such an outcome would also undermine the goals of the ACA, which is supposed to protect against that sort of inequity by requiring that all "qualified plans" offer a list of "essential benefits" determined by a federal board appointed. In effect, this represents a minimal level of health care coverage that all would be expected to have. More comprehensive plans would also be available, but no one would be mandated to purchase any of those plans, nor would the federal government provide any additional subsidies for access to them. Whether such plans represented a "good buy" from the perspective of any individual would be left up to the judgment of that individual. In this respect, congruent with the liberal commitments of U.S. society, individual value judgments are respected. Still, individuals are obligated to have a basic level of health insurance, whether they see it as valuable or not. The critic asks, "How can that be liberal?"

One response to the critic is that a liberal society does not permit individuals to use their liberty to undermine just policies and practices, or to impose injustices on others. Just policies and practices may be seen as the social glue that maintains a stable, mutually respectful society without which individual rights and liberties could not be protected or sustained. A liberal society also seeks to protect the long-term liberty interests of all its citizens, especially its most vulnerable. As has been noted, hospitals are legally obligated to treat individuals with true emergency medical conditions. But individuals who show up in an emergency room with early signs of a treatable cancer (and no ability to pay for care) will typically be turned away because that cancer is not presently life-threatening. They may return when the cancer has advanced, is creating a true medical emergency, and is no longer curable. But this means they will be condemned to a premature death that was avoidable if they had had an earlier ability to pay, something mandated insurance would provide.

This situation is especially morally problematic when the afflicted individual is the spouse or child of an uninsured head of household who imprudently refused to buy insurance in order to, for example, save money for a vacation. In such a situation, hospitals will often provide the needed care out of a sense of compassion. What makes such compassion morally problematic is that the cost of such compassion will be taken from declining charitable care dollars that ought (as a matter of justice) to be reserved for meeting the medical needs of the truly impoverished, as opposed to the truly imprudent.

Liberties also entail responsibilities. No society could sustain itself if there were only liberties and no corresponding responsibilities. The liberty to drive wherever one wishes requires the creation and maintenance of roads through public funding. To pay for some of those roads, tolls are collected. Clever individuals who found an electronic means of bypassing toll booths could hardly justify such behavior as a legitimate exercise of liberty. The U.S. health care system is a roadway that allows its citizens to traverse life more safely around the risks of disease and accident. But it is the responsibility of all who enjoy the benefits of that system to pay for its maintenance. This is what the individual mandate accomplishes.

The individual mandate also protects individuals from the risks of their own imprudence as a result of being uninsured. Such individuals, faced with vague symptoms of some medical disorder, will often be motivated to delay seeking a timely diagnosis. They might hope that the symptoms will simply go away. Sometimes that happens. But at other times the problem worsens and results in permanent health damage. Mandated insurance gives assured access to timely diagnostic care, thereby removing the temptation to make such imprudent choices.

Physician integrity and the individual mandate. The individual mandate serves to protect the medical integrity of physicians—that is, their presumptive obligation to provide timely and competent care to their patients. One of the unfortunate and unjust features of the health care system as it is now is that insured individuals are exposed to enormous variation in the quality of their insurance coverage. That may mean in practice that physicians who have patients with the same medical problem but different insurance coverage may provide substandard care to the patient with inadequate insurance because that patient has no independent ability to pay for care that is outside the ability of that physician to provide in the form of charity. If such care is very costly and likely to yield only marginal benefits, the moral problem is somewhat alleviated. But if the care is costly but very effective, the sort of care that a just society would include in a basic benefit package, then a morally problematic situation arises. The individual mandate, along with a reasonably comprehensive basic benefit package as envisioned by the ACA, prevents those sorts of threats to the ethical integrity of physicians.

The individual mandate: Key to fair cost control. Reasonable cost-containment can be more easily and fairly achieved if virtually all are part of the system for financing health care. This is what the individual mandate seeks to achieve. Individuals who are uninsured and who have no ability to pay for emergency care have no incentive for caring about the cost of health care. They will receive the care they need (in a hospital emergency room) and someone else will have to bear those costs, no matter what they might be. Unfortunately, the same logic often governs the behavior of the well insured *as patients in the hospital.* This will be especially true if they feel that they are being "overcharged" for their care in order to pay for the care of others whom they regard as "taking advantage" of the system. They can then demand "as their right" all manner of very costly care that yields only marginal benefits because someone else will actually bear most of those costs through their insurance. Of course, the net result of such choices will be a further acceleration of health care costs to everyone in the system. In his essays, Uwe Reinhardt has spelled out the self-defeating character of this behavior. The bottom line is that fair health reform requires fair health care cost-containment.

Health care cost-containment will necessarily require some health care rationing, denying individuals what, from some social perspective, is judged to be marginally beneficial, non-cost-worthy health care. As things are now, reasonably well-insured individuals can demand almost everything the health care system has to offer, no matter the cost and no matter how marginally effective. Fojo and Grady, health policy analysts at the National Institutes of Health, call attention to cancer drugs that cost between $50,000 and $130,000 for a course of treatment but that will yield a few additional weeks or months of life. More than 30 such drugs have already been approved by the Food and Drug Administration with many more in development. The heated rhetoric of health reform in late 2009 is evidence that anyone who would advocate excluding these drugs from health insurance packages would be accused of being part of a "death panel." What happens in practice is that the well insured are successful in demanding these drugs. Those costs are simply passed on by insurance companies to employers. Marginal employers increasingly cannot bear such costs, so they simply drop health care as a benefit, thereby increasing the ranks of the uninsured and underinsured. None of these individuals will have any access to these drugs (or most other costly health care interventions, no matter how effective they might be). This is how we currently control health care costs: unfairly.

The uninsured have no say in coverage decisions. But the virtue of an individual mandate is that virtually everyone (as a patient) has a stake in controlling health care costs. No one can be pushed out of the system as a mechanism for controlling costs. If individuals chafe under the cost of the mandate, either as direct payers of premiums or as indirect payers of taxes to underwrite the cost of government subsidies for the economically less well-off, then *all* can be part of a broad public democratic deliberative conversation aimed at controlling costs by identifying health care services in specific clinical circumstances that yield too little benefit at too high a cost. Such a conversation would articulate health care rationing protocols that would apply to all in specific clinical circumstances because all would be part of the health care financing system (fragmented but with a large overlapping core of health services constituting a national benefit package). Assuming a fair and reasonable deliberative process, one not co-opted by special interests, the rationing protocols that emerged from that deliberative process would be fair, transparent, and self-imposed. This is justice as reciprocity, and it would have been made possible as a result of the individual mandate.

Finally, in response to conservative critics and in keeping with U.S. society's liberal foundations, individuals who were averse to what they regarded as the risks associated with the rationing protocols would have the right to buy more costly and more comprehensive health plans (the gold and platinum plans under the ACA). But they would be entirely responsible for paying those additional costs. There would be no subsidies from the federal government or taxpayers whose financial circumstances restricted them to the more basic silver plans. Employers could continue to offer more generous plans, but the likelihood is that employers will either follow the lead of the federal government, or the federal government will tax the value of those excess benefits as income to employees. In either case, both justice and individual liberty would be protected through the working of the individual mandate in a reformed health care system with improved and assured access for all along with fairer and more effective health care cost-containment.

REFERENCES AND FURTHER READING

Aaron, H., Schwartz, W., & Cox, M. (2005). *Can we say no? The challenge of rationing health care.* Washington, DC: Brookings Institution Press.

Bodenheimer, T., & Grumbach, K. (2009). *Understanding health policy: A clinical approach* (5th ed.). New York, NY: McGraw-Hill.

Brennan, P. (2011). The individual mandate, sovereignty, and the ends of good government: A reply to Professor Randy Barnett. *University of Pennsylvania Law Review, 159*(2011), 1623–1648.

Buchanan, A. (2009). *Justice and health care: Selected essays.* New York, NY: Oxford University Press.

Callahan, D. (2009). *Taming the beloved beast: How Medical technology costs are destroying our health care system.* Princeton, NJ: Princeton University Press.

Daniels, N. (2008). *Just health: Meeting health needs fairly.* Cambridge, UK: Cambridge University Press.

Daniels, N., & Sabin, J. (2002). *Setting limits fairly: Can we learn to share medical resources.* New York, NY: Oxford University Press.

Eddy, D. (1996). *Clinical decision making: From theory to practice.* Sudbury, MA: Jones and Bartlett Publishers.

Fleck, L. (2009). *Just caring: Health care rationing and democratic deliberation.* New York, NY: Oxford University Press.

Fojo, T., & Grady, C. (2009). How much is life worth? Cetuximab, non-small cell lung cancer, and the $440 billion question. *Journal of the National Cancer Institute, 101*(15), 1044–1048.

Hunter, N. (2011). Health insurance reform and intimations of citizenship. *University of Pennsylvania Law Review, 159*(6), 1955–1998.

Marquis, S., Buntin, M., Escarce, J., Kapur, K., Louis, T., & Yeglan, J. (2006). Consumer decision making in the individual insurance market. *Health Affairs 25*(3), w226–w234.

Rawls, J. (1993). *Political liberalism.* New York, NY: Columbia University Press.

Reid, T. R. (2009). *The healing of America: A global quest for better, cheaper, and fairer health care.* New York, NY: Penguin Press.

Reinhardt, U. (2011, May 13). Would privatizing Medicare lead to better cost controls? *The New York Times.* Retrieved from http://economix.blogs.nytimes.com/2011/05/13/would-privatizing-medicare-lead-to-better-cost-controls

Syrett, K. (2007). *Law, legitimacy, and the rationing of health care: A contextual and comparative perspective.* Cambridge, UK: Cambridge University Press.

Truffer, C., Keehan, S., Smith, S., Cylus, J., Sisko, A., Poisal, P., et al. (2010). Health spending projections through 2019: The recession's impact continues. *Health Affairs, 29*(3), 522–529.

Leonard M. Fleck

COUNTERPOINT

In March 2010 Congress passed the Patient Protection and Affordable Care Act (ACA) in an effort to put in place substantial reform of the health care system in the United States. The primary goal of the legislation was to reduce substantially the number of uninsured in the United States, which stood at about 50 million in late 2011.

The uninsured are a somewhat heterogeneous lot, which adds to the complexity of the political problem they create. Almost 75 percent of the uninsured are either working full time or are the dependents of full-time workers. Their employers either do not offer health insurance as a benefit or have stopped offering it as a result of the high cost of insurance premiums. Some of the currently unemployed could have health insurance if they had been covered while employed and if they were able to afford the cost of paying the premiums their employers had previously paid. However, being unemployed often makes that option irrelevant. Other uninsured individuals have been denied affordable health insurance because of potentially costly preexisting medical conditions. Finally, an estimated 14 million relatively young and healthy individuals (below the age of 30) deliberately choose to be uninsured (despite being offered the option of purchasing insurance through an employer) because they value using their money for other reasons. In the popular press, these are known as the "young invincibles."

Supporters of the ACA are especially concerned about the welfare of those who are denied affordable health insurance because they have potentially costly preexisting health conditions. Insurers argue that it would be "bad business" to provide health insurance coverage for these individuals because it will be certain that they will command much more in the way of resources than they will provide in the form of paid premiums. Still, most Americans would not want to see these uninsured individuals put out in the proverbial hospital parking lot to suffer and die for lack of ability to pay for needed care. Consequently, one of the central provisions of the ACA requires all insurers to provide affordable (community-rated) coverage for those with preexisting medical conditions.

LIBERTARIANS AND THE INDIVIDUAL MANDATE

Among political philosophers, libertarians are those who would be most opposed to an individual mandate. Libertarians regard individual liberty as the most important social value. They argue that the only sort of moral or political rights individuals ought to have are rights of noninterference, as opposed to positive rights or welfare rights. The right of non-interference means that individuals should be free to live their lives as they wish, in accord with whatever set of values give meaning and direction to their lives, as long as they do not use their rights to interfere in the lives of others. For them, the legitimate role of government (apart from national defense) is to protect those rights of noninterference (as opposed to meeting various welfare needs). What this practically implies is that taxes may only be collected to support national defense and maintain internal social order. If libertarians had the political authority to do so, they would abolish Social Security, Medicare, Medicaid, and every other government program that meets one or another society's welfare need, inasmuch as all these programs must be supported through the coercive collection of taxes.

Clearly then, the individual mandate is incongruent with a libertarian political philosophy. For the libertarian, one fundamental right of non-interference is that of free association. An individual who chooses not to be associated with any health insurance plan should be allowed to live with whatever consequences that choice might involve. The libertarian will not be satisfied to be told that the government is not coercing that individual to join some *particular* plan; the problem is that individuals should not be mandated to join *any* health plan. For the libertarian, an individual's reasons for refusing to purchase health insurance have no relevance at all. The individual might be stingy or hate doctors or prefer home remedies or regard health insurance as a poor buy. No one else needs to accept those reasons as reasonable, but no one, least of all government with its coercive capacities, has the right to require that individual to buy health insurance, contrary to his or her own judgment.

Among the arguments in favor of the individual mandate is that it is economically necessary in order to correct for the higher costs that insurance companies would have to bear because the ACA will require them to accept all comers, no matter their health status, for a premium payment far below the likely costs these patients will generate. From the perspective of political liberals, both justice and compassion justify the imposition of that requirement. From the perspective of libertarians, however, individuals with excellent health status are being "forced to associate" with individuals who are the most medically needy and medically costly. Or, to be more precise, healthy individuals are being forced to subsidize the cost of health care for the medically needy. If healthy, young individuals wish to join such health plans as a result of charitable impulses that well up from within, they ought to be free to make that choice for themselves. But, otherwise, for the libertarian it is both unjust and uncaring to impose unwanted costs associated with the infirm on the young and healthy.

THE "YOUNG INVINCIBLES" AND INSURANCE

The most common reason young and healthy individuals will chafe at the individual mandate is that they are young and healthy. They will not see health insurance as a good buy. On the contrary, what they will imagine is spending several thousands of dollars per year for 20 years that might otherwise have been wisely invested in the stock market or in gold. Supporters of the ACA will point out that some portion of these young invincibles will be afflicted with cancer or some other costly health problem. And, though some of them may be able to pay for the care they require, many others will leave hospitals and physicians with large unpaid bills.

Hospitals may be seen as charitable institutions, but they need to pay their staff and pay for their equipment and supplies. If the young and healthy are unable to pay for the care they need to avoid permanent disabilities or a premature death, the hospital must spread those costs to all other patients who have the ability to pay. This is precisely the sort of redistribution to which libertarians vigorously object to as unjust. These other patients are not asked for their permission to be overcharged. Hospitals, of course, could turn away the foolish young and allow them to suffer or die in the hospital parking lot. This is a conclusion libertarians can accept in the intellectual safety of the philosophy seminar room, as opposed to the trauma and tragedy of the emergency room of the local hospital.

NUDGING VERSUS MANDATING

In *Nudge: Improving Decisions About Health, Wealth, and Happiness* (2008), Thaler and Sunstein, professors of economics and law respectively, argue for an approach to public policy which they label "libertarian paternalism." The idea is to create a social and economic environment in which individuals are "nudged" by features of the environment to freely make choices that are congruent with their best interests, but that they might not have otherwise made. One might imagine the Obama administration abandoning the individual mandate and simply relying on the gradated individual subsidies nudging otherwise reluctant young and healthy uninsured individuals to buy health insurance because the subsidized price makes it a more reasonable buy.

However, from the perspective of libertarians, paternalistic nudges are as objectionable as paternalistic mandates. Any form of governmental paternalism is intrinsically objectionable because government is making a judgment about what is best for individuals who are otherwise perfectly capable of making that judgment for themselves. In addition, the subsidies are problematic for the libertarian because excess taxes or premiums would have to be extracted from other citizens in order to make them possible in the first place. David Gordon of the Ludwig von Mises Institute writes, "Those who wish to preserve liberty must take people's actions as they find them, not substitute for them 'better' or more 'rational' actions, based on an assessment of what people 'really' want."

More generally, libertarians are concerned that the individual mandate represents the proverbial "camel's nose under the tent." If the government can require citizens to purchase health insurance, either to protect the profit margins of insurance companies or to protect the financial viability of hospitals then government could also mandate (or nudge) its citizens to buy American cars in order to protect the financial viability of American car manufacturers. Likewise, if government can mandate (or nudge) individuals to purchase health insurance for their own good, government can also mandate (or nudge) its citizens to eat broccoli (as one judge observed) or to exercise thirty minutes every day, and so on.

CONSERVATIVE CRITIQUES

Political conservatives also offer strong criticisms of the individual mandate. Political conservatives are generally divided into two large groups, *fiscal* conservatives and *social* conservatives. Fiscal conservatives share with libertarians an abhorrence of powerful and expansive government. They want to maximize economic power in the private sector by minimizing the government's economic and regulatory power. For their part, *social* conservatives see government power as an opportunity to impose their social values on society and to reverse what they regard as the dominance of liberal political values. The abortion debate is a prominent example of such an attempted imposition.

Fiscal conservatives and the injustice of the mandate. Both fiscal and social conservatives criticize the ACA in general and the individual mandate in particular, though for different reasons. Havighurst and Richman, law professors, are among the fiscal conservative critics of the individual mandate. They offer an interesting counterargument to the political liberal who regards the present health care system as peppered with injustices. For example, the political liberal will point out that members of the employed middle class with health insurance through an employer will receive a tax subsidy of about 45 percent of the value of that health insurance. This is because health insurance is a tax-free benefit of employment. Hence, middle-class individuals are excused from paying federal income taxes, state income taxes, and Social Security taxes on the value of those plans. It is estimated that this represents a $200 billion tax subsidy, the amount of money government would otherwise have collected if the value of employer-sponsored insurance were taxed as income. This can be fairly seen as "middle-class welfare."

What makes this health insurance subsidy unjust in the eyes of political liberals is that the working uninsured, most of whom are in the lower half of the income scale, would have to pay for health insurance (if they could afford it) with after-tax dollars. They receive no subsidy. This strikes many as grossly unfair, inasmuch as these workers are clearly less well off than the more secure middle class. The ACA can be seen as correcting this injustice by providing explicit subsidies to the uninsured in order to make health insurance more affordable.

Havighurst and Richman, however, see this "subsidy reform" of the ACA as merely compounding the magnitude of the injustices, rather than correcting them. As fiscal conservatives, they are opposed to many kinds of governmental subsidies to many economic activities in the private sector. The traditional conservative reason for such opposition is that such activities distort and undermine the efficiency of private markets. But Havighurst and Richman suggest also that subsidies increase the injustice of the U.S. health care system.

Economists in general agree that the tax subsidies for health insurance have the effect of causing more health insurance to be purchased than would otherwise be the case. A subsidy of 45 percent represents a substantial discount on a desirable good, thereby nudging employees to purchase more comprehensive coverage through negotiations with their employers. That, in turn, subsidizes access to more health care services and more expensive health care services, which in turn creates an upward-spiral of health insurance premiums. Hospitals can confidently over-invest in expensive health technologies, such as radiologic equipment, because those excess costs can be passed on to patients in the form of higher charges, which are passed on to insurers, which are passed on to employers. The net effect, according to Havighurst and Richman, is that doctors, insurers, hospitals, and medical goods providers all become richer at the expense of the working and middle class. This is the case because there are no effective price controls on providers anywhere in the system. The net effect is a hidden, and unjust upward-redistribution of income.

Under ordinary circumstances, economic competition drives prices downward. But hospitals compete on the basis of quality supported by generous funding through the insurance mechanism. The ultimate effect is that, if employers are prevented from raising prices on their goods and services by normal competitive markets, employees must absorb excess health insurance costs in the form of lower wages. Havighurst and Richman see this as a serious injustice, because those who are less well off (workers) are supporting a relatively lavish standard of living for health care providers. Furthermore, it is governmental policy (the tax subsidies) that is facilitating this redistribution of wealth, contrary to the obvious interests of workers.

THE INDIVIDUAL MANDATE AND EXCESS HEALTH INSURANCE

Havighurst and Richman also contend that the ACA, with the help of the individual mandate, only worsens this unjust situation by requiring more workers to sacrifice more of their earnings by buying the excessive health insurance that supports the lavish lifestyles of health care providers and insurers. One of the major provisions of the ACA is that a comprehensive set of "essential benefits" will comprise the benchmark package, relative to which subsidies will be determined. That benchmark package will also serve as a reference point for the health insurance offerings that will be available through the insurance exchanges, which presumably are the insurance plans that would satisfy the insurance mandate.

Again, one of the goals of the ACA is to minimize the number of underinsured individuals, those whose health insurance will be grossly inadequate for covering the costs of more complicated health care problems. From the perspective of the Obama administration, this is a matter of fairness. But for Havighurst and Richman it only expands and reinforces the injustices inherent in the system—effective monopoly pricing ability on the part of providers. Rather than the individual mandates and subsidies and a comprehensive package of essential health care benefits, Havighurst and Richman want a wide open market of health plans from which consumers could choose. Their chief complaint is that "virtually no health plans available to ordinary Americans in the marketplace are designed with their specific interests in mind." Instead, Havighurst and Richman argue, that American health plans "embody the particular values and serve the particular interests of the health care industry and its most affluent customers" (2011b, p. 495).

THE FISCAL CONSERVATIVE ALTERNATIVE

What, then, do fiscal conservatives imagine would be a more just approach to health care reform? In brief, individuals would choose health plans that fit their economic circumstances and interests. If a family could afford no more than $3,000 for a health insurance plan, it could choose a high-deductible health plan, say, a deductible of $10,000. Perhaps such a plan would pay only 50 percent of the cost of a hospital day. What these fiscal conservatives imagine is that, faced with having to pay the first $10,000 for health care needs within a year, individuals would bargain with health care providers for the best deal. In theory, this would serve as a check on the wealth aspirations of health care providers. In practice, when health care is needed, whether to mend a broken leg or to respond to a heart attack, individuals are not in a position to "comparison shop" or to drive a hard bargain.

Moreover, from a libertarian perspective, physicians and all other health providers ought to be free to associate or not with individuals whose health plans might only pay a fraction of their customary fee. In other words, the number of providers available to individuals with low-cost/high-deductible health plans might be very limited (unless there were a provider mandate to accept and treat). Also ethically and politically problematic is that insurance products are generally designed for families. A family with a high-deductible plan and limited financial means would potentially put at risk the well-being of a nonworking spouse and children who have had no say regarding the terms of that plan. It is one thing for an individual to gamble with his or her own health fate by purchasing one of these inexpensive health plans. But a legitimate moral and political question can be raised regarding gambling with the lives and well-being of these others.

High-deductible plans have been the focus of considerable moral criticism. Such plans do cause individuals to refrain from profligate use of the health care system, such as hospital emergency rooms for medical problems that would have resolved harmlessly on their own. But high deductibles also serve as a high barrier to seeking timely and appropriate diagnosis of the early stages of a then treatable, potentially life-threatening medical disorder. Individuals who are financially less well off are vulnerable to the tragic consequences of misjudgment in this regard. Such misjudgments are common because few individuals have the medical training or medical technology to make such judgments correctly on their own. The ACA goes far toward protecting individuals from such misjudgments by not authorizing these plans as meeting "qualifying" standards. This will still strike libertarians as unjustifiably paternalistic. And fiscal conservatives, such as Havighurst and Richman, will still see "qualified" health plans as excessively costly and unfair to workers who would prefer much less expensive health plans.

Havighurst and Richman want insurers to be able to offer low-cost plans that remain so by refusing coverage for expensive but only marginally beneficial health care interventions, for example a cancer drug that costs $100,000 or more for a course of treatment but yields only extra weeks or months of life. They write, "Yet if one can accept that many might be better off taking modest statistical risks with their family's health in order to make mortgage payments, pay energy bills, educate their children, or save for an uncertain retirement, then forcing working people to pay for health care of speculative or only marginal value can reasonably be viewed as unfair" (2011b, p. 507). Though Havighurst and Richman would not mandate such a plan, they would restrict any governmental subsidy (tax or otherwise) to the value of such low-cost plans on grounds of fairness. That is, they would contend that workers would then not be subsidizing through either taxes or insurance premiums the more expensive health tastes (risk aversions) of more well-off citizens or the lavish life styles of health care providers and insurers.

SOCIAL CONSERVATIVES AND THE INDIVIDUAL MANDATE

As was noted earlier, social conservatives also object to the individual mandate, but for reasons quite different from those of fiscal conservatives. Both social and fiscal conservatives will endorse more limited government and safety net programs provided through private organizations. But, in addition, social conservatives will be most concerned about the content of the "essential benefit package" that might be mandated, abortion services in particular. Social conservatives object to the idea of subsidizing through their tax dollars a procedure that they find personally abhorrent.

Though at first it might seem easy to exclude such controversial procedures from essential coverage packages, matters become more complicated as we imagine a larger and larger range of health care services to which various religious or ideological groups might object. For example, some conservative religious practitioners object to a wide range of contraceptive services, including sterilization procedures. Others might object to health services aimed at addressing fertility problems. Still others might object to funding the protease inhibitors and fusion inhibitors used to manage threats to the immune system represented by HIV, the claim being that HIV was God's punishment for deviant sexual behavior. As for coverage for drug and alcohol dependency, it is easy to imagine conflicting religious perspectives. Some religious advocates might see funding such programs as a required religious response, helping those who wanted to help themselves to manage their addictions. But other religious perspectives might see such programs as an inappropriate social safety net that interferes with individuals experiencing the consequences of their "irresponsible choices."

Then there is the controversy surrounding embryonic stem cell research and the emerging field of regenerative medicine. No one can say at present whether this medical research will bear fruit. But, if it does, and if cloned embryonic cells can be used to repair spinal cord injuries, or to repair heart tissue damaged by a heart attack, or to reverse diabetes, then regenerative medicine will have served to radically alter much of traditional medicine. It is difficult to imagine such broad medical interventions being justifiably excluded from an essential benefit package to avoid offending certain religious sensibilities.

The same may prove true with regard to all that is happening in the field of medical genetics, especially in regard to reproductive decision making. We have some capacity now to spare future children debilitating genetic fates associated with cystic fibrosis or Duchenne's muscular dystrophy or dozens of other comparable genetic vulnerabilities through the use of pre-implantation genetic diagnosis. But this medical intervention is also the object of religious objections because of the need to create excess numbers of embryos for genetic analysis before a genetically normal embryo can be identified and implanted.

The individual mandate does not require anyone to use any medical services to which they are deeply opposed on religious grounds. But social conservatives object to the use of either their premium dollars or tax dollars to support insurance for medical interventions to which they object. In the case of the ACA, their objections include using taxes to provide subsidies for purchasing insurance for families below 400 percent of the federal poverty level. The ACA, as it stands now, does permit a limited range of religious exemptions to the individual mandate. But it is a *very* limited range, wholly unsatisfactory to the social conservative. A more expansive range, however, suggested by the examples above, would effectively negate the intent of the individual mandate as well as the adequacy of the essential benefits that are supposed to be assured to all citizens. This is a consequence that social conservatives would seem to welcome.

THE PRAGMATIC CRITIQUE

Other writers have criticized the mandate for reasons that are less overtly moral, legal, or political. Allison Hoffman, a lecturer in law, calls attention to the diverse goals that the mandate is supposed to achieve in a fragmented health care system that will be hostile to achieving those goals. Specifically, one of the main goals of the individual mandate is to effect a redistribution of health and wealth from those who are well off in these regards to those less well off. But the fragmentation of the insurance market into large group, small group, and individual markets (left untouched for political reasons) will mean in practice that disproportionate numbers of those less well off health-wise and wealth-wise will be concentrated in plans provided through the exchanges, which means in practice that the equalizing redistributive effects will be reduced from what could be achieved in insurance plans not fragmented in this way. From her perspective, restoration of the public option in the ACA would go a long way toward promoting the goals of the individual mandate. From the perspective of political conservatives, however, restoration of the public option would represent an unjustified expansion of government control of the health care system.

CONCLUSION

It must be noted that both political liberals and political conservatives appeal to the language of justice to defend or criticize the individual mandate, and, more broadly the goals of the ACA. It would be grievously wrongheaded to dismiss such differences as excess rhetoric. No society can endure as a civil and peaceful society if there are not shared understandings regarding the justness of its policies and practices. Such understandings are never given; they must be forged in the crucible of honest and mutually respectful democratic deliberation.

REFERENCES AND FURTHER READING

Anand, G. (2005). The most expensive drugs: Lucrative niches: How drugs for rare diseases became lifeline for companies. *The Wall Street Journal*, p. A1.

Anderson, G., Reinhardt, U., Hussey, P., & Petrosyan, V. (2003). It's the prices, stupid: Why the United States is so different from other countries. *Health Affairs, 22*(3), 89–105.

Barnett, R. (2010). Commandeering the people: Why the individual health insurance mandate is unconstitutional. *New York University Journal of Law and Liberty, 5*, 581–637.

Engelhardt, H. T., Jr. (1996). Rights to health care, social justice, and fairness in health care allocations: Frustrations in the face of finitude. In *The foundations of bioethics* (2nd ed., pp. 375–410). New York, NY: Oxford University Press.

Gordon, D. (2008). *Nudge: Improving decisions about health, wealth, and happiness. The Mises Review, 14*(2). Retrieved from http://mises.org/misesreview_detail.aspx?control=333

Havighurst, C., & Richman, B. (2006). Distributive injustice(s) in American health care. *Law and Contemporary Problems, 69*(7), 83–101.

Havighurst, C., & Richman, B. (2011a). The provider monopoly problem in health care. *Oregon Law Review, 89*, 847–883.

Havighurst, C., & Richman, B. (2011b). Who pays? Who benefits? Unfairness in American health care. *Notre Dame Journal of Law, Ethics, and Public Policy, 25*, 493–526.

Hoffman, A. (2010). Oil and water: Mixing individual mandates, fragmented markets, and health reform. *American Journal of Law and Medicine, 36*, 7–77.

Kavilanz, P. (2010). *Young invincibles imperil health reform.* Retrieved from CNN Money website: http://money.cnn.com/2010/04/09/news/economy/health_reform_young_invincibles_threat/index.htm

Krugman, P. (2011, September 15). Free to die. *The New York Times.* Retrieved from http://www.nytimes.com/2011/09/16/opinion/krugman-free-to-die.html

Mariner, W., Annas, G., & Glantz, L. (2011). Can Congress make you buy broccoli? And why that is a hard question. *New England Journal of Medicine, 364*(3), 201–203.

Monahan, A. (2011). On subsidies and mandates: A regulatory critique of ACA. *Journal of Corporation Law, 36*, 781–806.

Parmet, W. (2011). The individual mandate: Implications for public health law. *Journal of Law, Medicine and Ethics, 39*(3), 401–413.

Reinhardt, U. (2011, September 16). The role of prices in health care spending. *The New York Times.* Retrieved from http://www.economix.blogs.nytimes.com/2011/09/16/the-role-of-prices-in-health-care-spending.html

Rivkin, D., Casey, L., & Balkin, J. (2009). A healthy debate: The constitutionality of an individual mandate. *University of Pennsylvania Law Review, 158*, 93–118.

Thaler, R. H., & Sunstein, C. R. (2008). *Nudge: Improving decisions about health, wealth, and happiness.* New Haven, CT: Yale University Press.

Leonard M. Fleck

Federal Authority Over the Individual Mandate

POINT: The U.S. Constitution gives the federal government broad powers to regulate interstate commerce, tax and spend for the general welfare, and enact laws that are necessary and proper to support other federal powers. A law that penalizes individuals who do not purchase health insurance falls squarely within the scope of these federal powers.

Julia Bienstock and Corey S. Davis, National Health Law Program

COUNTERPOINT: A federal mandate that penalizes individuals who fail to purchase health insurance exceeds the scope of federal authority. The failure to purchase health insurance is inactivity; Congress's power to regulate interstate commerce has never been construed to encompass inactivity. The necessary-and-proper and the tax-and-spend clauses also do not empower Congress to require individuals to purchase health insurance.

Corey S. Davis, National Health Law Program

Introduction

One of the most controversial provisions of the 2010 Patient Protection and Affordable Care Act (ACA) is the so-called individual mandate. As enacted, beginning in 2014, the mandate will require most U.S. citizens and legal residents to maintain "minimum essential coverage" or pay a penalty that will eventually rise to the greater of $695 or 2.5 percent of taxable income. The penalty will be assessed on individuals' tax returns. Low-income individuals, religious objectors, prisoners, members of Native American tribes, and individuals who obtain a hardship waiver will be exempted from the mandate.

The mandate was designed to support provisions in the ACA that prohibit insurance companies from discriminating on the basis of health status or denying coverage to people with preexisting conditions. Though these reforms will help make insurance available to those who need it most, they can create a perverse incentive that leads healthy individuals to forgo insurance until they need health care. If this so-called adverse selection occurs widely, insurance risk pools will be disproportionately made up of individuals who use a lot of health care services. This will lead to higher premiums, making insurance even less affordable and prompting even more healthy people to go without insurance. The resulting spiral can undermine the insurance system. To prevent this, Congress imposed the mandate, which requires most people to obtain health insurance while they are still healthy.

In this chapter, Corey Davis and Julia Bienstock focus on a critical question that the Supreme Court decided in June 2012: the constitutionality of the individual mandate.

Shortly after President Barack Obama signed the ACA into law, opponents filed lawsuits challenging the act's constitutionality. Although these legal challenges raised many different claims and challenged different parts of the ACA, one of the most serious claims alleged that Congress exceeded its constitutional authority by enacting the mandate. The Counterpoint part of the chapter explores the arguments raised by the states bringing that claim, some of which were accepted and some of which were rejected by the Supreme Court.

As Davis and Bienstock explain, under the Constitution the federal government has limited authority. Critics of the ACA's mandate argued that Congress's power to regulate interstate commerce only permits it to regulate certain economic activity, while the mandate attempts to regulate inactivity. Challengers also argued that the penalty enforcing the mandate is not a tax and is not authorized by Congress's power to tax and spend for the general welfare. In response, supporters of the mandate claimed that Congress's constitutional power is broad and permits it to regulate decisions that have a substantial effect on interstate commerce, including decisions that individuals make about whether or not to pay for their health care through insurance. Defenders of the mandate added that the penalty is a tax and is authorized by Congress's authority over taxation.

In *National Federation of Independent Business v. Sebelius* (2012), the Supreme Court affirmed the constitutionality of the mandate, but not for the reason many had expected. In a closely divided decision, a five-justice majority comprising Chief Justice Roberts and Justices Scalia, Kennedy, Thomas, and Alito concluded that neither Congress's authority to regulate interstate commerce nor its authority to enact laws that are "necessary and proper" to carry out its other powers could sustain the mandate. Critical to these justices was the fact that in their view, the mandate did not regulate commerce; it compelled it. But a different five-justice majority, this time composed of the Chief Justice and Justices Ginsberg, Breyer, Sotomayer, and Kagan, concluded that the mandate was in fact a tax and that Congress had the power to enact it under its constitutional authority to "lay and collect taxes." As a result, the mandate survived the constitutional challenge.

As a result of the Supreme Court's decision, Congress cannot make you buy health insurance but can tax you for not having it. Is this the correct result? Should the Court be the ultimate arbiter on the constitutionality of health reform generally and the individual mandate specifically? Should we leave such critical and contentious questions to five unelected justices? Or by deciding that Congress had the authority to enact the mandate, did the justices return the question to the political system, leaving it to the people of the United States through their elected representatives to decide how to reform their health care system?

POINT

The Patient Protection and Affordable Care Act (ACA), passed by Congress and signed by President Barack Obama in March 2010, seeks to increase access to affordable health coverage and care. The ACA aims to accomplish these goals, in part, by requiring most individuals to purchase health insurance, providing subsidies to those for whom purchasing insurance presents a financial hardship, and requiring those who refuse to purchase insurance to pay a tax penalty. This section presents arguments in support of the view that Congress has the constitutional authority to require a person to purchase health insurance (referred to as the "individual mandate") or else pay what the Supreme Court ultimately concluded was a constitutionally authorized tax.

The first part of this essay briefly discusses the problems with the U.S. health care system that the ACA is designed to address. The second part explains how the ACA addresses these problems through, among other things, requiring all Americans to secure health insurance. The third part reviews the specific provisions in the Constitution that have been argued to support the constitutionality of the individual mandate, including the Commerce Clause, the Necessary and Proper Clause, and the Taxing and Spending authority—the provision the Court ultimately relied on in upholding the individual mandate.

THE AMERICAN HEALTH CARE SYSTEM

In most developed countries, health care is available to all citizens regardless of economic or employment status, either through the direct provision of services or via government-sponsored insurance. In the United States, however, health care is available only to those who are able to pay for services out-of-pocket or who have them paid for by health insurance. The U.S. health care system relies primarily on a combination of public and private insurance to cover the cost of health care. This insurance is typically either provided by the government or purchased through individual employers, although some people purchase it on their own. Unfortunately, a large number of people—approximately 50 million in 2009, according to the Census Bureau—are without any form of health insurance.

Lack of health insurance often translates into limited or no access to health care, with potentially disastrous consequences. The Institute of Medicine has estimated that more than 18,000 uninsured Americans die each year because lack of health insurance prevents them from accessing medical care. Having so many people without insurance also drives up costs for those who do have coverage. The Institute of Medicine estimates that the U.S. economy loses as much as $130 billion each year because of the untreated illnesses of uninsured Americans. Even when uninsured people do receive health care, they are often unable to pay for it. These unpaid costs are shifted to others in the form of higher insurance premiums, higher charges for medical services, and higher taxes. The Congressional Budget Office (CBO) estimated that in 2008 the uninsured shifted $43 billion of health care costs to others.

Health insurance works by spreading risk across a broad range of consumers. In an insurance system with a large number of enrollees, at any given time, most will be healthy and paying more in premiums than the amount spent on their care. But, as the number of insured people goes down, the premiums paid by those still covered goes up as risk is spread across a smaller pool. This causes more healthy people with insurance to cancel their policies, further extending the spiral, resulting in sicker risk pools and higher costs for those purchasing coverage. This is what is happening in the United States and is contributing to the deterioration of the U.S. health care system.

THE ACA AND THE INDIVIDUAL MANDATE

Congress enacted the ACA to improve the health of Americans while reducing the escalating costs of health care. The ACA does this in part by prohibiting insurers from denying coverage to or charging more for individuals with preexisting medical conditions, creating health exchanges through which individuals and families not eligible for employer- or government-sponsored health insurance may purchase coverage and requiring most individuals to carry health insurance. It is largely this last requirement that opponents challenged in the courts.

Under this individual mandate, most citizens will be required to be covered by health insurance that meets certain criteria or pay a penalty that will be collected by the Internal Revenue Service (IRS). The ACA exempts from the mandate undocumented immigrants, American Indians, those with a religious conscience objection, and those who do not meet the income tax filing threshold or for whom affordable coverage is not available. Coverage is considered unaffordable if it exceeds 8 percent of an individual's income. The ACA does not mandate the source of coverage; it may be obtained individually, through an employer, or through public programs such as Medicare or Medicaid.

The individual mandate was included in the law because Congress believed that it was necessary to spread insurance risk across as many consumers as possible in order to keep premiums affordable. The ACA contains several provisions that should enable the poor and sick to gain access to health insurance, including the guaranteed issue provision requiring insurance to be sold, regardless of health condition. As a result, Congress feared that some people would take their chances and drop their health insurance on the assumption that they could simply wait until they need care to purchase insurance. Eventually, this would lead to too many healthy people dropping out of the insurance pool, leaving only the sickest and most expensive people. Thus, Congress concluded that the individual mandate was an integral part of the ACA's larger regulatory scheme.

In June 2012 in *National Federation of Independent Business v. Sebelius*, the Supreme Court decided the constitutionality of the individual mandate. Five justices concluded that the mandate imposed a tax rather than a penalty and was therefore constitutional under Congress's taxing authority. A different set of five justices, however, believed that Congress lacked authority to impose the mandate under the so-called Commerce Clause. The Supreme Court's decision misconstrues the nature of the Commerce Clause, failing to recognize the enormous impact that individuals' decision to forego health insurance has on interstate commerce.

CONGRESS' POWER TO ENACT THE INDIVIDUAL MANDATE

The Constitution grants Congress the power to enact laws in a number of specific areas and to create laws that are "necessary and proper" to carry out the powers granted to it. As discussed in the following, the decision to purchase or not purchase health insurance has a substantial effect on the overall national health care market and as such constitutes interstate commerce, one of the key areas in which Congress is permitted to regulate. In addition, the individual mandate is an essential component of the ACA's broader regulatory scheme. Finally, the individual mandate is sustainable under Congress' independent power to tax and spend for the general welfare.

THE COMMERCE CLAUSE

Article I, Section 8 of the Constitution gives Congress the power "to regulate Commerce with foreign Nations, and among the several States." Though the Supreme Court has placed some limits on Congress's ability to regulate under the Commerce Clause, it has generally adopted an expansive view of those powers. In fact, from 1936 to 1995, the Supreme Court upheld every single law that was challenged on Commerce Clause grounds. Since then, the Court has struck down two laws (not including the ACA) that regulate the private sector under the Commerce Clause. However, the general rule remains the same: Congress has broad power to regulate economic activities that have a substantial effect on interstate commerce.

Historical development of the Commerce Clause. For over 175 years, the Supreme Court has struggled to define the scope of the Commerce Clause. In 1824 the Court decided its first significant Commerce Clause case, *Gibbons v. Ogden*. Aaron Ogden had the right to a state-granted monopoly to operate steamboats in waterways under the jurisdiction of the state of New York. Thomas Gibbons ran steamboats between New Jersey and New York under a license issued by the federal government. Ogden sued, arguing that Gibbons was violating his state-granted monopoly, and the case made its way to the Supreme Court.

The Court had to decide whether the federal law that authorized Gibbons to operate was a valid use of the Commerce Clause. The Court found that it was and therefore New York could not prohibit Gibbons from operating in its waters. The interstate requirement was met because the ships moved between states, and the operation of the steamboat business was considered to be commerce. The Court cautioned, however, that the Commerce Clause authorized Congress to regulate only interstate business.

Following *Gibbons*, the Supreme Court held for many decades that Congress could only regulate interstate business, not local business. For example, in 1895, the Court held that the federal Sherman Antitrust Act could not be used to stop a monopoly in the sugar-refining industry because Congress could not regulate local production of sugar under the Commerce Clause. Eventually, however, the Court began to recognize that the national economy was growing ever more interdependent, and as a result the distinction between commerce and other stages of business such as production and manufacturing was becoming increasingly blurred. This shift was illustrated in the 1942 case of *Wickard v. Filburn.*

In *Wickard,* the Court upheld a law that restricted the amount of wheat an individual farmer could sell by putting quotas on production. Filburn challenged the application of the quota to the wheat he produced for personal consumption, arguing that the law violated the Constitution by effectively requiring him to purchase wheat on the open market rather than grow it himself. The Supreme Court disagreed. In upholding the constitutionality of the law and its application to Filburn's homegrown wheat, the Court deferred to Congress's finding that production of wheat for personal consumption, in the aggregate, has a substantial effect on interstate commerce. This aggregate effect, the Court reasoned, was sufficient to permit Congress to regulate goods that were not, themselves, a part of interstate commerce. Over the next 50 years Congress relied on the Commerce Clause to pass a number of laws, including the worker-protection legislation that was part of the New Deal and the civil rights laws of the 1960s.

Contemporary Commerce Clause doctrine. *Wickard* established Congress's power to regulate local activity that has a substantial effect on interstate commerce, a power that is still recognized today. However, after several decades in which the Supreme Court refused to invalidate any law passed under the Commerce Clause, the Court identified two instances in which Congress had exceeded its Commerce Clause power.

In *United States v. Lopez* in 1995 and *United States v. Morrison* in 2000, the Court found that Congress had stretched the Commerce Clause too far. In *Lopez,* the Court struck down a federal law, the Gun Free Schools Act, which made it a federal crime to carry a gun in a school zone. In *Morrison,* the Court invalidated a portion of the Violence Against Women Act that permitted victims of gender-motivated violence to sue the perpetrator in federal court. In these cases, the Court identified three general categories of regulation in which Congress is authorized to engage under its Commerce Clause power.

First, Congress can regulate the channels of interstate commerce. Second, Congress has the authority to regulate and protect the "instrumentalities" of interstate commerce, and persons or things in interstate commerce. Third, Congress has the power to regulate activities that substantially affect interstate commerce. Though the third category was first articulated in *Wickard, Lopez* and *Morrison* clarified its reach. In both *Lopez* and *Morrison,* the Court concluded that the regulated activities were not economic or commercial in nature and that any economic effect was too attenuated to be regulated under the Commerce Clause.

In 2005, in *Gonzales v. Raich,* the Court sought to further clarify this third category. Angel Raich grew and used medical marijuana, which was legal under California law but illegal under the federal Controlled Substances Act (CSA). Raich filed a lawsuit to stop the federal government from interfering with her right to produce and use medical marijuana, claiming that the CSA was not constitutional as applied to her conduct. The Court had to decide whether Congress could use the Commerce Clause to regulate the local cultivation and use of marijuana and therefore enforce the CSA against Raich. The Court found that it could, explaining that Congress has the power to regulate purely local activities that are part of a class of activities that have a substantial effect on interstate commerce. The activity regulated by the CSA—the cultivation, possession, and distribution of drugs—was "quintessential economic activity," the Court said. Using the same reasoning as the *Wickard* Court, this Court held that even the cultivation of marijuana in Raich's home for her personal consumption had a substantial effect on supply and demand in the national market.

In addition, the Court concluded that Congress could regulate noneconomic local activity if it finds that the failure to regulate that class of activity would undercut the larger regulation of the interstate market in that commodity. The CSA was enacted in order to control the supply and demand of controlled substances in both lawful and unlawful drug markets. The Court thus concluded that the inability to regulate personal consumption would undercut the law's larger regulatory purpose, and therefore the CSA was within Congress's Commerce Clause power.

The Necessary and Proper Clause. Although many of the justices in *Raich* felt that the Commerce Clause was sufficient to regulate the marijuana at issue, in his concurring opinion Justice Scalia relied on the Necessary and Proper Clause to come to that conclusion. Article I, Section 8 of the Constitution not only enumerates Congress's express powers but also gives Congress the authority "To make all Laws which shall be necessary and proper for carrying into Execution . . . all other Powers vested by [the] Constitution in the Government of the United States." This Clause permits Congress, when enacting a broad regulatory statute, to include provisions important to the implementation of the statute even though those provisions might not be constitutional standing alone. Because the CSA is a broad effort to regulate illicit drugs, Scalia explained that regulating the cultivation of marijuana for personal medicinal use is permissible. Unlike the provisions at issue in *Lopez* and *Morrison,* the CSA's broad regulatory scheme could be undercut unless the local activity was regulated.

The individual mandate should have been found to be a constitutional exercise of Congress's Commerce Clause power.

Justice Ginsberg, writing for herself and Justices Breyer, Sotomayer, and Kagan, was correct in concluding that Congress had authority under the Commerce Clause to enact the mandate. It is well established that matters relating to insurance substantially affect interstate commerce and thus the regulation of the health insurance market falls within Congress's Commerce Clause power. In 1944, in *United States v. South-Eastern Underwriters Association,* the Supreme Court held that Congress has the power to regulate the interstate insurance market under the Commerce Clause. Since then, Congress has repeatedly exercised its power to regulate the health insurance industry, both by providing directly for government-funded health insurance through the Medicare Act, and by adopting numerous statutes regulating policies offered by private insurers.

Even if that was not the case, law outside of the insurance area clearly supports the extension of the Commerce Clause to the individual mandate. In *Wickard* and *Raich,* the Court had little problem concluding that personal consumption of wheat and marijuana as part of a broader regulatory scheme would have a substantial influence on price and market conditions and could therefore be regulated under the Commerce Clause. Given these precedents, the individual mandate should have been seen as part of a broader scheme to regulate the health insurance industry.

Opponents of the ACA argued, and five Justices (Roberts, Scalia, Kennedy, Thomas, and Alito) found, that despite this longstanding precedent, the individual mandate is different because it does not regulate an individual's activity in the insurance market but instead attempts to regulate "inactivity." According to these justices, Congress can regulate economic activity that is substantially related to commerce but cannot compel an individual to become active in commerce. However, individuals who forego health insurance do not therefore forego health care. To the contrary, the uninsured still participate in the health care market and, in fact, participate substantially. In a 2011 report, the Congressional Research Service found that the uninsured consumed more than $48 billion in uncompensated care in 2008. Almost all Americans, insured or not, will need some sort of health care in their lifetime—or even in an average year. Individuals may be "inactive" in the sense that they do not intend to engage in the commercial activity of purchasing insurance, but they are certainly not "inactive" in the health care market.

The purpose of the individual mandate is twofold: on the one hand, it helps to ensure that everyone has access to health care; on the other, it ensures that everyone—rich and poor, sick and well, old and young—is in the health care pool to spread insurance risk. As Congress explained in the Act, the ACA and specifically the individual mandate "regulate activity that is commercial and economic in nature: economic and financial decisions about how and when health care is paid for, and when insurance is purchased."

As Justice Ginsberg stated, failure to purchase health insurance is a form of self-insurance. Jack Balkin, a professor at Yale Law School, explains that people make a decision to "self-insure" (i.e., not to purchase insurance) as part of a larger set of individual budget calculations about health care consumption. Buying insurance reflects a choice of one method of dealing with the cost of potential medical expenses. Those who do not buy insurance, and therefore choose to self-insure, resort to other options to finance their medical expenses, such as selling assets or borrowing and going into debt to cover needed health care services.

Because people without insurance, as a class, do not pay for all the health care services that they consume, the economic decision to forego insurance has a substantial and direct effect on health care providers, taxpayers, and the insured population who ultimately pay for the care provided to the uninsured. Unlike in *Lopez* and *Morrison,* the Court did not have to "pile inference upon inference" in order to establish that the economic decision to forego insurance has a substantial effect on interstate commerce.

In addition, the individual mandate is an essential part of Congress's larger health care reform effort and is therefore should have been found constitutional based on the Necessary and Proper Clause. In *Raich,* Justice Scalia made it clear that where Congress has the power to enact a regulation of interstate commerce, "it possesses every power needed to make that regulation effective." Unlike the statutes at issue in *Lopez* and *Morrison,* the individual mandate is part of a broad economic regulation of the national health care market. If Congress had enacted the ACA's other insurance reforms without the individual mandate, healthy individuals would have an incentive to forego insurance coverage, knowing that they could obtain coverage later if and when they become ill. As a result, the cost of insurance would skyrocket, and the larger system of reforms would fail. Thus, without the individual mandate, the ACA would have been unable to decrease health care costs and increase access to health insurance.

The law regarding the Necessary and Proper Clause was clear. A provision, such as the individual mandate, that is rationally related to the exercise of an enumerated power, including the Commerce Clause, should be sustained under the Necessary and Proper Clause unless it violates an independent constitutional prohibition. Although opponents suggest otherwise, there is no fundamental right to be uninsured. The individual mandate, therefore, cannot be a violation of individual liberties protected under the Constitution. The Supreme Court should have found that the mandate was within Congress's power to enact laws in furtherance of its enumerated powers.

THE POWER TO TAX AND SPEND

In addition to enumerating the Commerce Clause, Article I, Section 8 of the Constitution vests Congress with the power to "lay and collect taxes . . . for the common defense and general welfare of the United States." This power to tax is independent of all other power granted to Congress and is in itself sufficient to sustain the individual mandate. The Supreme Court has repeatedly reaffirmed the taxing power's broad reach, and has held that a tax is valid if it serves the general welfare, is reasonably related to raising revenue and does not violate any independent constitutional prohibition.

Subject to some exceptions, the individual mandate requires individuals who fail to purchase health insurance to pay a tax penalty equal to the greater of $695 per year per person (up to a maximum of $2,085 per family) or 2.5 percent of household income per year. This penalty encourages individuals to purchase health insurance, rather than pay the government. As discussed previously, without the penalty, other aspects of the law would increase existing incentives for individuals to delay purchasing health insurance until they needed care, making the health insurance market unworkable.

The individual mandate penalty is a tax. Opponents of the individual mandate and four dissenting justices (Scalia, Kennedy, Thomas, and Alito) argued that, because Congress cited the Commerce Clause and not the taxing and spending authority as the source of its authority for the individual mandate, the government cannot now claim the taxing power as a basis for the mandate. This argument has a certain common-sense appeal, but is not actually supported by law. There are no magic words; a tax cannot be turned into a nontax simply by saying so, and vice versa. The key to determining whether a law creates a penalty or a tax, as Chief Justice Roberts explained in *National Federation of Independent Business v. Sebelius* (2012), is whether it seeks to punish. The mandate does not. In any case, though the tax penalty is referred to as a "penalty" in some parts of the ACA, it is referred to as a "tax" in others.

Regardless of the language used in the law, the mandate imposes a tax. The relevant provision of the ACA places the "penalty" in the Internal Revenue Code and directs the IRS to verify compliance with the mandate. Proof of health insurance must be submitted with the taxpayer's yearly tax return and the penalty is calculated by reference to the taxpayer's household income.

The individual mandate is a constitutional exercise of Congress's taxing power. Even if the penalty is classified as a tax, opponents argue that it is an unconstitutional one. But Congress's authority to impose taxes is extremely broad. Congress may tax activities that it cannot otherwise reach, subject to only a few limitations. The individual mandate must satisfy three requirements to be considered a constitutional exercise of the taxing power. First, as is evident from the text of the Constitution, a tax must seek to provide for the "general welfare." In *Helvering v. Davis* (1937) the Court held that Congress has wide discretion to determine whether a tax measure serves the general welfare. As was discussed earlier, uninsured individuals impose significant costs on society in the form of increased taxes and higher insurance premiums, and the tax serves to keep those people in the insurance pool. These costs are sufficient to establish that taxing uninsured individuals provides for the general welfare.

Second, Supreme Court precedent requires that legislation bear a reasonable relationship to the raising of revenue, even if the revenue actually produced is negligible and secondary to a regulatory purpose. Though the Supreme Court used to strike down taxes on the ground that they were regulatory rather than revenue-raising in nature, it abandoned this distinction decades ago. As Justice Roberts stated, "taxes that seek to influence conduct are nothing new" (*National*

Federation of Independent Business v. Sebelius [2012]). For example, the federal cigarette tax was implemented in large part to discourage smoking. Though Congress may have intended the mandate's penalty to encourage individuals to purchase health insurance, its purpose in enacting a regulatory tax is irrelevant so long as it raises some revenue. The individual mandate will collect revenue from individuals who fail to purchase insurance as part of their income tax. This provision is expected to generate $4 billion annually, according to the nonpartisan Congressional Budget Office (CBO), and thus satisfies the revenue-raising requirement.

Third, the tax, like all other laws, cannot violate another part of the Constitution. The individual mandate does not violate any constitutionally protected right. No one has a right to be free from taxation, and Congress's decision to target individuals who decide to forego insurance is rational, given the impact of their decision on society. Congress could have enacted a statute that imposes a general tax on all citizens to pay for health care reform and then provide a deduction or tax credit for citizens who purchase health insurance. But there is no legal difference between that approach and the tax targeting only citizens who do not purchase health insurance—both fall squarely within Congress's taxing power. The choice of what type of tax to enact is a policy determination that should be left to the legislature, not the courts. Thus, the individual mandate falls within Congress's independent authority to levy taxes.

CONCLUSION

It is clear that Congress has ample authority to regulate the decision to purchase health insurance. The Supreme Court correctly found that the individual mandate is constitutional, enacted pursuant to Congress's powers under its authority to tax and spend for the general welfare. The Court should also have followed its own precedent and found that the Commerce and Necessary and Proper Clauses authorized the mandate.

REFERENCES AND FURTHER READING

Balkin, J. M. (2009). A healthy debate: The constitutionality of an individual mandate for health insurance. *University of Pennsylvania Law Review PENNumbra, 158*(93), 102–106. Retrieved from http://www.pennumbra.com/debates/pdfs/HealthyDebate.pdf

Centers for Medicare & Medicaid Services. (2009). *National health expenditure fact sheet.* Washington, DC: U.S. Department of Health and Human Services. Retrieved from https://www.cms.gov/NationalHealthExpendData/25_NHE_Fact_Sheet.asp

Congressional Budget Office. (2008). *Key issues in analyzing major health insurance proposals.* Retrieved from http://www.cbo.gov/ftpdocs/99xx/doc9924/toc.shtml

DeNavas-Walt, C., Proctor , D. B., & Smith, J. C. (2010). *Health insurance coverage in the United States: 2009.* Retrieved from U.S. Census Bureau website: http://www.census.gov/prod/2010pubs/p60-238.pdf

Dorn, S. (2008). *Uninsured and dying because of it: Updating the Institute of Medicine analysis of the impact of uninsurance on mortality.* Retrieved from Urban Institute website: http://www.urban.org/UploadedPDF/411588_uninsured_dying.pdf

Executive Office of the President, Council of Economic Advisers. (2009). *The economic case for health care reform.* Retrieved from http://www.whitehouse.gov/assets/documents/CEA_Health_Care_Report.pdf

Gibbons v. Ogden, 22 U.S. 1 (1824).

Goldman, T. R. (2011). *Health policy brief: Legal challenges to the Affordable Care Act.* Retrieved from Health Affairs website: http://www.healthaffairs.org/healthpolicybriefs/brief.php?brief_id=49

Gonzales v. Raich, 545 U.S. 1 (2005).

Hall, M. A. (2009). *The constitutionality of mandates to purchase health insurance.* Retrieved from O'Neill Institute for National and Global Health Law at Georgetown University website: http://www.law.georgetown.edu/oneillinstitute/national-health-law/legal-solutions-in-health-reform/Individual_Mandates.html

Hall, M. A. (2011). Health care reform: What went wrong on the way to the courthouse. *New England Journal of Medicine, 364*(4), 295–297. Retrieved from http://www.nejm.org/doi/pdf/10.1056/NEJMp1013234

Helvering v. Davis, 301 U.S. 619 (1937).

Institute of Medicine. (2002). *Care without coverage: Too little, too late.* Retrieved from http://www.iom.edu/~/media/Files/Report%20Files/2003/Care-Without-Coverage-Too-Little-Too-Late/Uninsured2FINAL.ashx

Institute of Medicine. (2003). *Hidden costs, value lost: Uninsurance in America.* Washington, DC: National Academies Press. Retrieved from http://www.nap.edu/catalog/10719.html

Jacobs, L. R., & Skocpol, T. (2010). *Health care reform and American politics: What everyone needs to know.* New York, NY: Oxford University Press.

National Federation of Independent Business v. Sebelius, __U.S.__, 2012 WL 2427810 (U.S. June 28, 2012) (Nos. 11-393, 11-400).

Rosenbaum, S. (2010). A "broader regulatory scheme"—The constitutionality of health care reform. *New England Journal of Medicine,* *363*(20), 1881–1883. Retrieved from http://www.nejm.org/doi/pdf/10.1056/NEJMp1010850?ssource=hcrc

Rosenbaum, S., & Gruber, J. (2010). Buying health care, the individual mandate, and the constitution. *New England Journal of Medicine,* *363*(5), 401–403. Retrieved from http://www.nejm.org/doi/pdf/10.1056/NEJMp1005897?ssource=hcrc

Staman, J., Brougher, C., Liu, E. C., Lunder, E. K., & Thomas, K. R. (2011). *Requiring individuals to obtain health insurance: A constitutional analysis.* Washington, DC: Congressional Research Service. Retrieved from http://www.achp.org/themes/ACPH_Main/files/ Requiring_Individuals_to_Obtain_Health_Insurance_2-1-2011.pdf

United States v. Lopez, 514 U.S. 549 (1995).

United States v. Morrison, 529 U.S. 598 (2000).

United States v. South-Eastern Underwriters Association, 322 U.S. 533 (1944).

Wickard v. Filburn, 317 U.S. 111 (1942).

Julia Bienstock and Corey S. Davis

COUNTERPOINT

The 2010 Patient Protection and Affordable Care Act's (ACA) individual mandate exceeds even the farthest boundaries of the federal government's constitutional authority. As five justices of the Supreme Court correctly concluded, the mandate is not authorized by the Commerce Clause, which can only reach activities that substantially affect interstate commerce. Nor does it fall under the Necessary and Proper Clause, which merely permits Congress to take actions in furtherance of its existing authority. Finally, the majority of the Supreme Court erred in ruling that the mandate is saved by the General Welfare Clause, which does not permit Congress to sidestep the constitutional limits on its authority by simply adding a noncompliance penalty to an otherwise unconstitutional law.

This Counterpoint begins with a brief exposition of the concepts of federalism and liberty as they apply to the citizens and government of the United States. It then walks through the reasons that the authority to enact and enforce the individual mandate is not found in any of Congress's enumerated powers or in the Necessary and Proper Clause, and debunks several arguments that were made by the mandate's supporters. It concludes that, regardless of the positive aspects the mandate may have, the Supreme Court should have found that it is incompatible with the nation's federal system of government and impermissible under the Constitution.

FEDERALISM, LIBERTY, AND INDIVIDUAL RIGHTS

Though it is sometimes said that the Constitution gives certain rights (e.g., the right to freedom of speech or freedom of religion) to the people, this is actually backward. In the United States, it is held as self-evident that all people are born with the rights to life, liberty, and freedom, among others.

We the people of the United States have chosen, as a society, to surrender some of our natural liberty to a democratic government to gain collective safety, security, and well-being. Few seriously argue, for example, that the interests of individual liberty should preclude the government from requiring that restaurants take steps to ensure that food is safely handled or from banning inebriated drivers from the roads. However, the federal government's ability to deprive people of their liberty for the greater good is carefully prescribed by the Constitution, which clearly spells out the circumstances in which Congress is permitted to pass and enforce laws. These limited instances are referred to as Congress's "enumerated powers."

The Constitution safeguards the people from an overreaching federal government by setting out a system in which power is shared between a central federal government and individual state governments. The powers held by the federal government are generally limited to those that can only be meaningfully wielded by a central authority, such as the power to wage war, coin money, and regulate interstate and foreign commerce. All other powers are held by the states and the people within them.

By late 2011 over half the states had joined federal cases challenging the ACA's constitutionality, claiming that the individual mandate is an impermissible encroachment by the federal government into the lives and decisions of ordinary citizens. In addition, by late 2011 at least 17 states had passed legislation officially opposing elements of the law, and 24 states had proposed state constitutional amendments banning its enforcement. Although individuals within these states will now be forced to comply with the individual mandate, a number have declared that they will not be adopting the ACA's now-optional Medicaid expansion, demonstrating that the ACA's requirements remain deeply problematic to our federal structure.

THE INDIVIDUAL MANDATE IS UNCONSTITUTIONAL UNDER THE COMMERCE CLAUSE

One of Congress's key enumerated powers is that to regulate "Commerce . . . among the several states." For roughly the first 150 years of the nation's existence the Supreme Court interpreted the Commerce Clause largely as it had been written, permitting Congress to regulate only activities that constituted commerce and involved more than one state.

This changed beginning in 1937 when then-President Franklin D. Roosevelt, perturbed that the Court continually struck down New Deal legislation he favored, attempted to change the law so that he could increase the number of justices on the Court—new justices that he would appoint. These new justices, presumably, would vote to uphold his initiatives. Although Roosevelt's "court-packing" plan was never adopted by Congress and there is some debate as to the effect it had on the Court's decisions, shortly after the plan was introduced the Court changed course and began to uphold federal laws that it once would have found to be outside the scope of the Commerce Clause.

Due to a series of Supreme Court decisions that began shortly after this "switch in time that saved nine," the federal government today is permitted to regulate activities that "substantially affect interstate commerce," even if the activity in question occurs completely within one state. The Supreme Court subsequently watered down even this requirement by ruling that the "substantially affect" test can be met by aggregating the effects of a number of small activities that would not have any substantial effect standing alone.

This broad interpretation is seen in its most extreme form in the 1942 case of *Wickard v. Filburn* and the 2005 case of *Gonzales v. Raich*. In both of those decisions, the Court upheld a federal law, passed under the authority of the Commerce Clause, that prohibited a person from growing a particular crop (wheat in the case of *Wickard*, marijuana in the case of *Gonzales*) on his or her own land for their own personal consumption. In both cases, the Court found that, because Congress has the authority to regulate wheat and marijuana in the interstate market and the production of those crops for personal consumption would have a substantial effect on that market, Congress can regulate their intrastate production as well.

Supporters of the individual mandate argued that, if the *Wickard* and *Raich* decisions are followed, the individual mandate is clearly authorized by the Commerce Clause. A single person's decision not to purchase health insurance, they argue, is analogous to a single person's decision to plant wheat or marijuana. However, as the Supreme Court rightly determined, the activities in *Wickard* and *Raich* differ from the individual mandate in several important ways.

United States v. Lopez (1995) and *United States v. Morrison* (2000) are clear that the Commerce Clause has limits, even under its current broad interpretation. Neither carrying a gun in a school zone, which was the activity regulated in *Lopez*, nor committing violence against a woman, the subject of the law at issue in *Morrison*, have a close enough connection to interstate commerce to be regulated under the Commerce Clause. After all, almost everything can be described in a way that it can be said to affect interstate commerce, and if such sleight of hand is permitted, the Commerce Clause would become the exception that swallows the rule.

For the ACA's mandate to succeed under the Commerce Clause, it would have had to satisfy two tests: It must regulate an activity, and that activity must substantially affect interstate commerce either alone or when combined with all other similar activity. The Court correctly decided that the individual mandate fails both.

THE MANDATE DOES NOT REGULATE ECONOMIC ACTIVITY

Not buying health insurance is not economic activity. Perhaps realizing this problem, the government and other mandate supporters attempted to conflate the individual mandate, which does not regulate economic activity, with the rest of the act, much of which does. According to this line of argument, because almost everyone will at some point or another require health care regardless of whether or not they are insured, almost everyone will engage in health care–related economic activity.

This may be true, but it is beside the point. The ACA can, and does, regulate a wide variety of economic activities. It provides subsidies for many people to purchase insurance that meets certain requirements, places restrictions of various sorts on the types of insurance that can be offered, and so on. If a person decides to purchase health insurance, or has health insurance purchased for him, all of these provisions apply. But that has nothing to do with the fact that not purchasing insurance is not an economic activity.

A novel and somewhat alarming version of this confusion holds that the decision not to buy health insurance is an "economic decision," and economic decisions, like economic actions, can be regulated under the Commerce Clause. Under this logic, Congress can not only regulate any person any time he does anything with the vaguest connection to interstate commerce, but also any time he *doesn't* do anything with such a connection. The Commerce Clause would become not a limit on Congress's authority, but a blanket license for it to do almost anything. The Supreme Court has never approved anything remotely approaching such a broad reading of the Commerce Clause and declined to do so in *National Federation of Independent Business v. Sebelius* (2012).

THE COMMERCE CLAUSE DOES NOT EXTEND TO INACTIVITY

The main question with which the Supreme Court grappled in *Lopez, Morrison,* and *Raich* was whether the activity in question was economic in nature. In *Lopez* and *Morrison,* the Court decided that it was not; in *Raich,* as in *Filburn,* the Court decided that it was. Both learned commentators and members of the Court disagree as to whether those cases were rightly decided, and what they might mean for the power of the government to regulate economic and quasi-economic activity.

That was not the question raised by the mandate. *National Federation of Independent Business v. Sebelius* did not concern a person who wished to plant wheat, or grow marijuana, or carry a handgun. This case was about people who wish to not be ordered by the government to purchase a product that they neither want nor need—people who want to be free to not engage in any activity at all.

The Commerce Clause, by its very nature, can only regulate activity. Although the Supreme Court had never before stated this directly, that was because there was no need to do so. Until the individual mandate, Congress had never attempted to use the Commerce Clause to force people to engage in commerce. Unlike the laws in *Lopez, Morrison,* and *Raich,* the individual mandate does not target people who are engaging in an activity the government wishes to regulate. Rather, it indiscriminately reaches nearly everyone who lives in the United States.

The Point section of this chapter lays out the broad outlines of the history of the Commerce Clause. From this history comes one inescapable fact: Every instance in which the Commerce Clause was found to have been constitutional involved the regulation of some sort of voluntary activity. Roscoe Filburn, who challenged the federal law in *Wickard,* voluntarily and intentionally partook in the activity of producing wheat. Likewise, Angel Raich, whose case was heard in *Gonzales v. Raich,* voluntarily produced and used marijuana. In contrast, people who do not buy health insurance are not engaging in any activity. In fact, they are exercising their right not to do so.

Some supporters of the individual mandate's constitutionality incorrectly pointed to several cases that upheld provisions of the Civil Rights Act of 1964 (CRA), particularly *Heart of Atlanta Motel v. United States* (1964), as showing that Congress can regulate inactivity. The Civil Rights Act is a landmark legislative enactment that effectively ended (at least in law) the doctrine of "separate but equal." Among other things, the CRA banned racial discrimination in public places, including hotels and restaurants.

The Heart of Atlanta was a whites-only hotel in Atlanta, Georgia. The hotel's owner challenged the CRA, claiming, among other things, that the CRA exceeded Congress's authority under the Commerce Clause. The government countered that restrictions on where nonwhite people can stay significantly affect interstate commerce, and as such Congress can prohibit that kind of discrimination through its Commerce Clause authority.

The Court agreed with the government, finding that since Heart of Atlanta was a business engaged in commerce and many of its clients moved between states the requirements were met and the hotel could be regulated under the Commerce Clause. In a similar case, *Katzenbach v. McClung,* the Court unanimously held that the Commerce Clause also justified the CRA's application to restaurants. Racial discrimination, the Court found, has a substantial effect on interstate commerce, and the fact that any particular restaurant's contribution to interstate trade was minimal was of no substance. The aggregate effect of failing to provide food and shelter to a large group of people had a substantial effect on interstate commerce, and Congress could use the Commerce Clause as a foundation to take steps to address that injustice.

The issues raised in the CRA cases are completely different from the question presented by the individual mandate. Each of the CRA cases involved a business engaged in commercial activity. There is no question that once a company or person voluntarily enters the stream of interstate commerce he or she is subject to regulation under the Commerce Clause. A situation truly analogous to the ACA would be a law that required a person who was not in the hotel or restaurant industry and had no interest in running a hotel or restaurant to open one and to ensure that the new business did not discriminate on the basis of race. But that is not what the CRA did. The CRA cases told us nothing about the constitutionality of the individual mandate.

Similar claims were made about laws such as the Child Support Recovery Act (CSRA), which makes it a federal crime to willfully refuse to pay child support to a person in another state, or to leave a state with the intent to evade a lawful support order. It was claimed that this law, which forces certain people to pay their debts under threat of federal sanction, is directly analogous to the individual mandate. This argument quickly falls apart.

Those subject to the CSRA have, through their own voluntary actions, incurred a debt. They have attempted to avoid that debt by moving out of the state in which the debt was owed. Congress has attempted to make it easier for the children to whom that debt is owed to recover it by preventing deadbeats from being able to avoid their obligations by fleeing across state lines. This is markedly different from the individual mandate, which is a freestanding requirement that affects many who have incurred no debt, have taken no action, and have harmed no one. Nearly everyone is targeted for no reason other than that they exist.

HEALTH INSURANCE IS NOT UNIQUE

The next claim made by some mandate supporters was that, even if it would be unconstitutional to regulate inactivity in other markets, health insurance and the health care market are somehow special. Because of the unique nature of the health care market, this argument holds, federal regulations that are not permissible elsewhere are permissible here. The argument, in other words, was that there is some sort of health care exception to the Constitution. There is not.

This claim was a variation on the health insurance vs. health care confusion discussed above. The premise is that since everyone will access health care at some point, the decision not to purchase health insurance has ripple effects throughout the economy. The aggregation of everyone who hasn't purchased health insurance but needs to access health care affects interstate commerce as the uninsured are forced to pay out of pocket, or have that care paid for by the public purse or written off by the provider. Even if this argument is correct, there is nothing unique about the situation it describes.

There are a large number of activities in which everyone (or nearly everyone) will engage at some point. Everyone must have food. Everyone must have shelter. Nearly everyone consumes education, electricity, gasoline, and so on. As Judge Hudson of the Eastern District of Virginia noted in his 2010 decision striking down the mandate, "the same reasoning could apply to transportation, housing, or nutritional decisions. This broad definition of the economic activity subject to congressional regulation lacks logical limitation." As Chief Justice Roberts wrote in *National Federation of Independent Business v. Sebelius* (2012), "[this] logic would justify a mandatory purchase to solve almost every problem." He added, "People, for reasons of their own, often fail to do things that would be good for them or good for society. Those failures—joined with the similar failures of others—can readily have a substantial effect on interstate commerce." From a constitutional standpoint, there is nothing unique about health care.

The Supreme Court correctly ruled that Congress can no more require that Americans purchase health insurance than it can require that they buy an American car or eat their broccoli.

AN UNCONSTITUTIONAL MANDATE CANNOT BE SAVED BY THE NECESSARY AND PROPER CLAUSE

The Necessary and Proper Clause gives Congress the power to "make all Laws which shall be necessary and proper for carrying into Execution" its enumerated powers. As this language implies, the Necessary and Proper Clause does not grant Congress freestanding authority; it merely permits Congress to take actions in furtherance of an enumerated power.

Some mandate supporters argued that the mandate is necessary to the survival of the ACA, and is therefore permissible under the Necessary and Proper Clause. Without it, supporters claimed, the cost of health insurance will increase as insurance companies are forced to offer insurance to people they previously would have denied. This will drive the cost of insurance up, causing healthier people to drop out. This spiral will feed on itself until the entire system implodes.

This argument had two fatal flaws. The first is that the predicted negative consequences have not materialized. Many of the requirements that supposedly cannot function without the individual mandate went into effect in 2010, a full four years before the mandate is scheduled to come online. These include a provision requiring insurance companies to extend coverage to young adults up to the age of 26 and another that requires that all new insurance plans cover certain preventive services without co-pays or deductibles. A provision that forbids insurance plans from rescinding coverage in most cases also went into effect in 2010, as did the elimination of lifetime limits on benefits and restrictions on annual limits on coverage of essential benefits. Many health plans are also prohibited from denying coverage to people under the age of 19 because of preexisting conditions. None of these changes have caused the health care market to implode. On the contrary, health insurers are doing extremely well: *The New York Times* reported in May 2011 that the "nation's major health insurers are barreling into a third year of record profits."

The second and most important flaw in this argument is that even if the provision is "necessary," it still cannot be saved by the Necessary and Proper Clause. Any laws passed under the authority of the Necessary and Proper Clause must be tied to a specific, enumerated, constitutional power. The only candidate is the Commerce Clause, and the Commerce Clause is not sufficient to support the mandate. As Chief Justice Roberts explained, laws that "undermine the structure of government" created by the Constitution cannot be "proper" (*National Federation of Independent Business v. Sebelius*). Because the mandate exceeds the scope of the Commerce Clause it is impermissible under the Necessary and Proper Clause as well.

THE INDIVIDUAL MANDATE IS UNCONSTITUTIONAL UNDER THE GENERAL WELFARE CLAUSE

The majority of the Supreme Court erred in finding that the individual mandate is saved by the General Welfare Clause that empowers Congress to lay and collect taxes and spend for the "common Defense and general Welfare of the United States." As dissenting justices Scalia, Kennedy, Thomas, and Alito recognized, the penalty imposed on those who do not purchase insurance as required is exactly that, a penalty. Although housed in the tax code, the penalty is not designed to raise revenue but rather to force compliance. Although taxes are permitted to serve a regulatory function, Congress may not sidestep the constitutional limits on its power by passing an otherwise unconstitutional law in the guise of a tax.

When the ACA was being debated, both the president and Congress went out of their way to claim that the proposed penalty was not a tax. They were correct, and the relevant ACA text clearly states that the individual mandate is enacted under the power of the Commerce Clause. The General Welfare Clause is not mentioned. This was a conscious and calculated decision. The penalty was explicitly called a "tax" in earlier versions of the bill in both the House and Senate, but was switched to "penalty" when it became clear that a bill that imposed a tax would be less politically viable. It is abundantly clear that the penalty was never intended to be a tax.

The government changed its mindwhen it saw the writing on the wall regarding the flawed Commerce Clause argument and began to argue that the penalty is, for the purposes of this argument only, a tax. The Court should not have accepted that about-face. The ACA does impose several taxes—on tanning services and on certain "Cadillac" health plans, for example. They are clearly referred to as taxes. As the Supreme Court has noted, where Congress uses "particular language in one section of a statute but omits it in another section of the same act, it is generally presumed that Congress acts intentionally and purposely in the disparate inclusion or exclusion" (*Russello v. United States,* 1983). Not a single lower court agreed with the government that the penalty is a tax, and the Supreme Court should have resisted the temptation as well.

In any event, even if the penalty is a tax, the argument that that fact saves the mandate is unconvincing. The penalty is not the mandate; it is a way of attempting to enforce it. If all that was necessary for an otherwise unconstitutional law to become constitutional was for Congress to affix a tax penalty for noncompliance, there would be almost no limits on federal power. The Supreme Court should not have upheld the mandate under Congress's power to levy taxes.

CONCLUSION

Thomas Jefferson, writing in 1791, described the constitutional limits on Congress as follows: "I consider the foundation of the Constitution as laid on this ground: that all powers not delegated to the United States by the Constitution, nor prohibited by it to the states, are reserved to the states or to the people. . . . To take a single step beyond the boundaries thus specially drawn around the powers of Congress is to take possession of a boundless field of power, no longer susceptible of any definition."

It seems that with every passing decade the United States comes closer to such boundless federal power. By reaffirming that there are limits to Congress's power under both the Commerce and Necessary and Proper Clauses, the Supreme Court in *National Federation of Independent Business v. Sebelius* (2012) reaffirmed critical limits on federal power. However, in upholding the mandate as an exercise of Congress's taxing authority, the Court shirked its obligation to stem the overreach of the federal government and left the door open to even more egregious intrusions into individual liberty in the future.

REFERENCES AND FURTHER READING

Abelson, R. (2011, May 13). Health insurers making record profits as many postpone care. *The New York Times,* p. A1.

Barnett, R. (2010). Commandeering the people: Why the individual mandate is unconstitutional. *NYU Journal of Law and Liberty,* 5(3), 581–637.

Bowen, C. (1986). *Miracle at Philadelphia: The story of the Constitutional Convention.* New York, NY: Little, Brown.

Boyd, J. P. (Ed.). (1950). *The papers of Thomas Jefferson.* Princeton, NJ: Princeton University Press.

Cauchi, R. (2012). *State legislation and actions challenging certain health reforms.* Retrieved from National Conference on State Legislatures website: http://www.ncsl.org/?tabid=18906

Commonwealth ex rel Cuccinell v. Sebelius, 728 F. Supp. 2d 768 (E.D. Va. 2010).

Dean v. United States, 556 U.S. 568 (2009).

Gibbons v. Ogden, 22 U.S. 1 (1824).

Gonzales v. Raich, 545 U.S. 1 (2005).

Heart of Atlanta Hotel v. United States, 379 U.S. 241 (1964).

Katzenbach v. McClung, 379 U.S. 294 (1964).

National Federation of Independent Business v. Sebelius, __U.S.__, 2012 WL 247810 (U.S. June 28, 2012) (Nos. 11-393, 11-400).

Russello v. United States, 464 U.S. 16 (1983).

Somin, I. (2011, August 10). Will the Supreme Court give an unlimited mandate for mandates? [ScotusBlog]. Retrieved from http://www.scotusblog.com/2011/08/will-the-supreme-court-give-congress-an-unlimited-mandate-for-mandates

Staman, J., Brougher, C., Liu, E. C., Lunder, E. K., & Thomas, K. R. (2011). *Requiring individuals to obtain health insurance: A constitutional analysis.* Washington, DC: Congressional Research Service. Retrieved from http://www.achp.org/themes/ACPH_Main/files/Requiring_Individuals_to_Obtain_Health_Insurance_2-1-2011.pdf

United States v. Lopez, 514 U.S. 549 (1995).

United States v. Morrison, 529 U.S. 598 (2000).

Wickard v. Filburn, 317 U.S. 111 (1942).

Corey S. Davis

Underserved Communities and Health Care Reform

POINT: The Patient Protection and Affordable Care Act's health care and prevention investments will help close the gap in health and health care for medically underserved communities and populations.

Sara Rosenbaum and Tishra Beeson, George Washington University School of Public Health and Health Services

COUNTERPOINT: The Patient Protection and Affordable Care Act can be expected to have a marginal impact at best on health and health care for the medically underserved.

Sara Rosenbaum and Tishra Beeson, George Washington University School of Public Health and Health Services

Introduction

Among the more significant reforms instituted by the 2010 Patient Protection and Affordable Care Act (ACA) is the expansion of Medicaid to cover more Americans. In this chapter, Sara Rosenbaum and Tishra Beeson explore whether this expansion, as well as other reforms established by the ACA can be expected to have a significant impact on improving care for America's most vulnerable.

The technical terms for medically underserved communities include Health Professional Shortage Areas (HPSAs), which refers to communities where there is a paucity of doctors, dentists, and other health care providers; Medically Underserved Areas (MUAs), which similarly refers to particular geographical spaces where health care is in short supply; and Medically Underserved Populations (MUPs), which describes people who, due to race, culture, or other factors, face high barriers to obtaining care. Attempts to define, identify, and then serve these communities have a long history.

The Medicaid program was created in 1965 alongside the better known Medicare program that provides health insurance to people over 65, as well as some individuals with disabilities. In contrast to Medicare, Medicaid is a means-tested program. Originally it provided health insurance for a rather limited subsection of the poorest population: individuals who were eligible for the then-existing federal/state welfare program, primarily children, pregnant women, and single parents. (Because Medicaid is a joint state and federal program, eligibility requirements can vary somewhat from state to state.) Over time, Medicaid eligibility has expanded—for instance Medicaid now covers many disabled adults, as well as pregnant women and children under five with family incomes up to 133 percent of the Federal Poverty Level, and all children whose family incomes are up to 100 percent of the Federal Poverty Level. As Rosenbaum and Beeson explain in the Point essay, the ACA provided for the expansion of Medicaid coverage even further, to include all nonelderly citizens whose income is below 133 percent of the poverty level, whether or not they have children. In 2010 the Congressional Budget Office estimated that expansion would cover an additional 16 million persons.

The states that challenged the ACA in court claimed that the Medicaid expansion unconstitutionally coerced them because they could theoretically lose all of their Medicaid funds if they refused to comply with the expansion. Initially, most legal experts regarded this claim as frivolous. The courts have long recognized that Congress can attach conditions when it gives federal money to the states. Moreover, since the New Deal, the Supreme Court had never found a federal spending law to be unconstitutionally coercive. For that reason, every lower court that heard the claim rejected it.

In *National Federation of Independent Business v. Sebelius* (2012), the Supreme Court surprised court watchers by deciding in a 7-to-2 vote that the Medicaid expansion was unconstitutionally coercive on the states. Four justices (Scalia, Kennedy, Thomas, and Alito) concluded that the constitutional infirmity required that the entire Medicaid expansion be struck down. Chief Justice Roberts, however, was joined by Justices Breyer and Kagan in concluding that the Medicaid expansion could be saved by barring the federal government from utilizing the normal power granted the Secretary of Health and Human Services when a state fails to comply with a mandatory Medicaid requirement—namely, withholding existing state funding. Instead, the Chief Justice determined that the appropriate remedy was to limit the Secretary's power to withhold funds only to funds connected with the expansion itself. Justices Ginsburg and Sotomayor, who concluded that the expansion fell within Congress's powers to modify federal Spending Clause programs, acceded to this approach, thereby creating a majority opinion that saved the expansion.

For all practical purposes, the majority ruling means that the mandatory expansion, while still on the books as such, cannot be enforced like other minimum Medicaid requirements. The practical effect is that the states now have the option of expanding or not expanding their Medicaid programs. As Rosenbaum and Beesom explain in the Point section of the chapter, the ACA expands Medicaid on terms that are very favorable to the states. Most will likely opt to take the new federal money and cover all of their citizens with incomes up to 133 percent of the federal poverty level. But some states may not. If that happens, will the ACA be able to fulfill its promise? What other reforms might be required?

Even if states choose to expand their Medicaid programs, the ACA's impact on MUAs and MUPs is very much an open question, as Rosenbaum and Beeson explain in the Counterpoint. A number of structural issues suggest that, whatever its good intentions, the ACA will be inadequate to resolve the existing problems. One issue Rosenbaum and Beeson point to is, somewhat ironically, the ACA's very dependence on Medicaid. Enrollment in the Medicaid program can be complex, and even when Medicaid enrollment is sorted out, it's of limited use in HPSAs, places where medical professionals are in short supply to begin with. Rosenbaum and Beeson further argue that the ACA's continued emphasis on private insurance as the backbone of U.S. health care also seems likely to continue leaving many of the poor underserved. The ACA also does not address the question of immigrants who are "illegal" or "out of status"—a population estimated to be as high as 11 million—who must depend on public hospitals, many of which are closing due to economic pressures.

The closing of public hospitals is not merely an issue to illegal immigrants. Care that in the past was provided free of charge in public facilities is increasingly provided, if at all, in privately run institutions for a fee. Although many people think that emergency rooms must care for all comers, that is not precisely true: Under federal law (as well as the law in many states) emergency rooms are required to screen and stabilize all patients, but after they provide the necessary care, the hospitals are permitted to bill the patients. Fear of being billed presents a major deterrent to obtaining care. Moreover, paying those bills remains a major cause of personal bankruptcy in the United States. This may continue, especially in states that choose not to expand their Medicaid programs.

Considering the political realities that influenced the writing of the ACA, it is worthwhile to consider whether the reform measure could have achieved more than it promises in terms of shoring up health care for underserved populations. Special interests and economic realities create pressures that forced compromise on many of the provisions of the ACA. The Supreme Court's interpretation of the federal government's spending authority imposed other limitations. However, some observers contend that the nation has a moral obligation to offer adequate health care to those who can't afford it, no matter the monetary or political challenges. This chapter explores exactly those issues and helps illuminate what the ACA's innovations hold for the underserved.

POINT

The Patient Protection and Affordable Care Act (Pub. L. 111–148, amended by the Health Care and Education Reconciliation Act, Pub. L. 111–152) (ACA) represents a landmark in the evolution of U.S. health policy. Building on an array of existing laws, including the Social Security Act, the Public Health Service Act, the Employee Retirement Income Security Act, and the Internal Revenue Code, the act puts into place a near-universal system of health insurance coverage (Rosenbaum & Frankford, 2012). When enacted, the ACA was projected to reduce the proportion of uninsured nonelderly Americans to 6 percent, if only citizens and persons lawfully present in the United States are included, and 8 percent if nonlawful residents also are included in the estimates (Congressional Budget Office, 2010). Although the Supreme Court's ruling in *National Federation of Independent Business v. Sebelius* (2012) may result in a slower state adoption of its Medicaid expansion and a higher number of people who remain uninsured, the ACA will still effect a dramatic reduction in the number of Americans lacking health insurance.

Although the ACA is universal in scope and purpose, its most important implications may be felt in communities and populations considered "medically underserved" as a result of elevated levels of poverty, indicators of health care need, and a shortage of primary health care professionals (Health Resources and Services Administration, 2008). It is these populations and communities that are the poorest and face the most significant deficits in health and health care for whom the ACA represents a major step toward redirecting health care resources toward easing these deficits.

BACKGROUND

The closely linked problems of inequality in health and inequitable access to health care are matters of longstanding concern in U.S. health policy (Agency for Healthcare Research and Quality, 2011; Davis & Schoen, 1978; Institute of Medicine, 2002; Raphael, 2003). Since 1975 the federal government has maintained a formal process for designating communities and populations as medically underserved, an outgrowth of initial legislation establishing the community health centers program under the Public Health Service Act (Pub. L. 94–63, Title V). Unlike criteria used to establish eligibility for entitlement programs such as Medicare or Medicaid, the medical underservice designation is ecological in nature and is intended to specify a geographic area or discrete population whose overall characteristics suggest a significant but unfulfilled need for health care. In addition to the community health centers program, numerous federal, state, and local initiatives utilize the MUA/MUP designation process (as it has come to be known) in order to target resources aimed at improving health and health care, as well as its companion, the Health Professional Shortage Area (HPSA) designation process, through which the government directs deployment of National Health Service Corps personnel (Health Resources and Services Administration, 2008).

The MUA designation methodology involves four variables, each of which is weighted to arrive at an overall designation score known as the Index of Medical Underservice (IMU). These variables consist of the ratio of primary medical care physicians per 1,000 people, the infant mortality rate, the percentage of the population with incomes below the poverty level, and the percentage of the population age 65 or over. According to the Health Resources and Services Administration, which oversees the MUA/MUP/HPSA designation process, "the value of each of these variables for the service area is converted to a weighted value, according to established criteria. The four values are summed to obtain the area's IMU score." Even when a particular community does not qualify for MUA/MUP designation under the formula, the chief executive officer of a state may request designation if "unusual local conditions which are a barrier to access or the availability of personal health services" exist (Health Resources and Services Administration, 2012).

What emerges from the designation process is a literal map of health care need for the nation, down to the county, census tract, and market region. All states have areas and populations designated as medically underserved whether through application of the objective formula or by virtue of special designation. Furthermore, the very elements of the formula dictate that, whether urban or rural, communities and populations designated as medically underserved share certain key characteristics. Estimates of the population residing in areas designated as medically underserved place the total resident population at over 96 million people, while the related HPSA designation process (which looks exclusively at the available supply of primary health care professionals in relation to the total population) reveals a population count of 64.5 million. Within this population, some 28 percent, approximately 1.5 times the national average, are uninsured and thus disconnected from the major resource—health insurance—that enables both individual access to health care and the creation of stable and vibrant health care markets capable of attracting and sustaining an adequate supply of health care resources (Rosenbaum, Jones, & Shin, 2009).

Elevated poverty levels mean that communities designated as medically underserved collectively are far more likely to be uninsured and, simultaneously, to be without the ability to pay for even basic health care. The U.S. approach to health insurance has moved beyond treating insurance as a replacement for loss and has grown into a means of financing even routine health care (Mariner, 2010). As such, the widespread absence of health insurance coverage among an impoverished population translates into measures of health care inadequacy at the individual level and exhibits serious spillover effects into families and entire communities (Institute of Medicine, 2002). In poor communities and populations, the lack of coverage is pervasive, with 57 percent of persons with incomes below 133 percent of the federal poverty level (FPL) uninsured during the year, 41 percent uninsured for one or more years, and 35 percent uninsured for two years or more (Collins, Robertson, Garber, & Doty, 2012).

At the individual level, being uninsured is associated with worse health outcomes among adults, the lack of a usual source of care, less appropriate use of health care, and greater disparities in health and health care. Being insured, by contrast, is associated with better access to preventive care, more appropriate management of chronic illnesses and conditions, and improved access to care in emergency situations. Populations that lack access to continuous and stable health insurance coverage and experience worse health status are more likely to have attributes that elevate the risk of medical underservice, including poverty and its closely associated membership in a disadvantaged racial or ethnic minority subgroup (Institute of Medicine, 2002).

DISPARITIES IN HEALTH OUTCOMES ACROSS THE LIFESPAN

Although the overall health of the U.S. population has steadily improved in recent decades, disparities in health outcomes across the lifespan continue to grow in underserved populations. Birth outcomes are poorest among African Americans, with infant mortality rates more than twice those of whites (Nickens, 1995). Furthermore, these disparities persist among poor populations, irrespective of race or ethnicity. In fact, children of low socioeconomic status (SES) are significantly more likely to be low-birth weight than infants born to higher SES families (Parker, Schoendorf, & Kiely, 1994). Similarly, uninsured newborns are significantly more likely to have adverse hospital outcomes than are infants whose parents carry private insurance (Braveman, Oliva, Miller, Reiter, & Egerter, 1989). Moreover, the prevalence of childhood chronic diseases continues to be elevated in underserved populations. Low-income children have higher rates of disease-specific mortality, disability, and co-morbidities (McCarty & Levine, 1999; Wise, Kotelchuck, Wilson, & Mills, 1985).

Children from low-income families are more likely to be in fair or poor health when compared with their more affluent peers, as are African American and Hispanic/Latino children when compared with non-Hispanic whites (Newacheck & Starfield,1988; Children's Defense Fund, 2006). African American and low-income children are more likely to have been diagnosed with asthma than are white and higher-income children, and they are also more likely to have experienced an acute asthma event. Because asthma is the number one cause of missed school days, these particular disparities in childhood asthma outcomes are of great concern. Similarly, low-income children and both Hispanic/Latino and African American children are more likely to be overweight or at risk of being overweight or obese, compared to white children and children from more affluent families (Centers for Disease Control and Prevention, 2006). Moreover, Medicaid-enrolled children are almost six times more likely to be diagnosed with obesity than privately insured children (Mardner & Chang, 2005). The associations between childhood overweight and obesity, and other health issues such as hypertension, cardiovascular risk factors, and diabetes continue to underscore the need to address these gaps in health outcomes for underserved populations (Dietz, 1998).

Throughout adulthood, racial and ethnic minorities face disparities in prevalence and mortality from chronic diseases. Mortality from heart disease, cancer, and HIV/AIDS is higher among African Americans than among any other racial and ethnic group and American Indians experience the highest rates of mortality from liver disease and cirrhosis. Hispanic/Latinos face a disproportionate burden of diabetes, with a mortality rate nearly twice that of non-Hispanic white populations (Smedley, Stith, & Nelson, 2003). Similarly, African American and American Indian/Alaskan Native populations have lower five-year cancer survival rates than do non-Hispanic whites. And among persons living in poor census tracts, the five-year survival rate for all cancers is significantly lower than that of higher-income areas

(Ward et al., 2004). Similarly, disparities in cardiovascular disease tend to be highest among racial and ethnic minority groups. Mortality due to cardiovascular disease is highest in African American populations at all ages, and life expectancy with cardiovascular disease is nearly five years lower for African Americans than for white patients (Mensah, Mokdad, Ford, Greenlund, & Croft, 2005).

DISPARITIES IN ACCESS TO HEALTH INSURANCE AND HEALTH CARE SERVICES

With the growing concern about these substantial disparities in health outcomes among underserved populations, researchers and policymakers have focused their attention on system-level determinants of health status such as access to health insurance coverage and health care services. Several barriers to adequate access to care exist for medically underserved patients, including lack of health insurance, low income, old age, poor health outcomes, insufficient health infrastructure, and an inadequate supply of primary care providers (Hawkins & Rosenbaum, 1993). These factors tend to disproportionately affect medically underserved populations and their access to adequate health insurance coverage and health care services. As a result, Hispanic, American Indian, Alaskan Native, and African American patients are less likely to have health insurance than are whites, and thus have fewer choices among facilities and providers from which to receive their care (Brown, Ojeda, Wyn, & Levan, 2000).

The uninsured are six times less likely than patients with access to health insurance to seek health care for a medical problem (Halle, Lewis, & Seshamani, 2009; Kaiser Family Foundation, 2009). Medically underserved patients often report forgoing or delaying necessary medical or dental care as well as prescription medications. The percentage of people reporting forgoing or delaying care is twice as high for low-income and uninsured patients than for high-income patients and those who are privately insured (Agency for Healthcare Research and Quality, 2010). Even with access to health insurance coverage, medically underserved patients still face significant barriers to receiving essential health care services. Obtaining usual source of care has been linked to improved health outcomes and reduced costs (De Maeseneer, De Prins, Gosset, & Heyerick, 2003). However, African Americans, Latino/Hispanics, patients living in poverty, and uninsured patients report lower than average rates of having a usual source of care (Agency for Healthcare Research and Quality 2010; Mead et al., 2008).

These disparities in access to coverage and services present additional barriers to achieving optimal health, especially for medically underserved patients who bear a disproportionate burden of chronic conditions and co-morbidities. The patterns of underutilization of preventive services and delaying or forgoing essential care among underserved populations demonstrate that these access barriers will continue to exacerbate disparities in health outcomes without substantial system-level reform and interventions (Brown et al., 2000).

DISPARITIES IN QUALITY OF CARE

Beyond access-related barriers, medically underserved patients may also experience disparities in the quality of care they receive—especially within inpatient care settings. In particular, African Americans are significantly less likely than whites to receive preventive screening and counseling services, as well as other recommended care such as follow-up after hospitalization due to mental illness and receipt of beta-blocker medication after a cardiovascular event (Halle, Lewis, & Seshamani, 2009; Schneider, Zaslavsky, & Epstein, 2002). Asian patient populations have higher rates of mortality due to complications during a hospital stay than do white patients, and for those who lack health care insurance the rate of death following complications of care is significantly higher than for privately insured patients (Agency for Healthcare Research and Quality, 2010). Complications during hospitalization are also significantly higher among Medicaid recipients than for patients who have access to private insurance (Dasenbrock, Wolinsky, Sciubba, Gokaslan, & Bydon, 2012). Insurance status can often influence quality measures of care. In cases of cardiac care, Medicaid patients are less likely to be admitted to hospitals with cardiac-catheterization capabilities. Even after adjusting for demographic and facility characteristics, Medicaid patients are less likely to see a cardiologist and to receive recommended treatments such as antiplatelet therapy within 24 hours of admission (Pamboukian et al., 2008). Uninsured patients also face underutilization of cardiac-care procedures such as angiographies, bypass grafting, and angioplasties (Wenneker, Weissman, & Epstein, 1990).

Patient perceptions of their interactions with providers are also important measures of quality. Racial and ethnic minority patients, those with low SES, and patients in poor health status are more likely to rate their clinical visits as less participatory, and minority patients who have a race-discordant relationship with their providers often report lower satisfaction ratings of their care (Cooper & Powe, 2004; Cooper & Roter, 2003). In addition, patients whose primary language is not English are significantly less likely to report satisfactory communication with their provider (Ku & Waidmann, 2003).

CASCADING EFFECTS FOR INDIVIDUALS, FAMILIES, AND COMMUNITIES

Widespread lack of health insurance, coupled with poverty, also elevates family and systemic risks. In what the Institute of Medicine has termed a "cascade of effects," pervasive uninsurance within a community or among a population creates certain types of "causal and temporal relationships" (2002). At the family level, adverse outcomes include adverse economic and financial consequences such as lower earning capacity, a lack of resources to meet other basic needs, and an elevated exposure to bankruptcy. At a broader level, the consequences of widespread underfinancing of health care can be found in less stable health care institutions, the absence of health care resources, and lower overall community health, which in turn limits the "social and economic fortunes" of communities. Indeed, the spillover effects of elevated community uninsurance include compromised access to primary care, emergency medical and trauma care, specialty care, and hospital-based services, both outpatient and inpatient (Institute of Medicine, 2003).

In the absence of a systematic and multipronged intervention, the challenges that arise in addressing the needs of medically underserved communities can be expected to intensify as Americans grow poorer and more uninsured. Between 1999 and 2010, real median household income in the United States declined by 7.1 percent, with declines in evidence across rates, for both U.S. born and foreign-born residents, and in all geographic regions of the country. Consistent with this picture of overall economic decline, the share of income held by the bottom two-fifths of Americans fell to less than 12 percent of aggregated household income (DeNavas-Walt, Proctor, & Smith, 2011). In 2010 the number of uninsured Americans stood at 50 million persons, 18.5 percent of the nonelderly population, more than a 20 percent increase over 2000 levels (Holahan & Chen, 2011).

HOW THE AFFORDABLE CARE ACT RESPONDS TO MEDICAL UNDERSERVICE

The ACA responds to medical underservice through investments at the individual, institutional, and community levels.

Investing in individuals. The ACA invests in individuals through two basic strategies: the expansion of Medicaid to cover the poorest nonelderly Americans; and the establishment of a new, subsidized health insurance market for low and moderate family incomes. The act is projected to reduce the number of uninsured Americans by half by 2019, and the vast majority of the individuals who will gain access to affordable coverage are the very lower-income people who lack it prereform (Collins et al., 2010).

Medicaid expansion. Congress intended that as of January 1, 2014, the ACA would expand mandatory Medicaid coverage in all participating states (all states, the District of Columbia, and the U.S. territories participate in Medicaid) to cover all children and nonelderly citizen adults (and lawfully present immigrants who have been in the country for five years) with family incomes up to 133 percent of the FPL. This reform would have completed a mandatory expansion cycle, begun in the 1980s, which extended coverage to low-income children up to age 6 and pregnant women up to 133 percent of the FPL, and to children ages 6 to 18 with incomes up to 100 percent of the FPL. Income is to be determined in accordance with a modified gross income test that simplifies the process of financial eligibility determinations (ACA §2002).

Until passage of the ACA, mandatory coverage of nonpregnant adults was limited to two categories: caretaker relatives of minor dependent children and nonelderly adults considered disabled under the Social Security Act. Not only was mandatory Medicaid coverage limited but also federal Medicaid law did not even recognize low-income, nonpregnant, nondisabled adults as an optional coverage category unless minor children were present in the home.

Discrimination against adults did not stop at categorical exclusion from Medicaid. Even in the case of adults falling into a recognized eligibility category, states had the discretion (with the exception of pregnant women) to specify financial eligibility standards at levels far below the FPL. In only 15 states did the income eligibility standard for adult categories reach 100 percent of the FPL, and 14 states reported financial eligibility levels below 50 percent of the FPL, with Arkansas at the all-time last place at 17 percent of the FPL (Kaiser Family Foundation, 2012).

The Supreme Court's decision in *National Federation of Independent Business v. Sebelius* (2012) thwarts Congress's expectation that the federal government will be able to enforce compliance with the Medicaid expansion mandate. The Court's ruling bars the Secretary from using the power she otherwise has under Medicaid to withhold existing program funding from states that do not comply with minimum program requirements. Although the Court was careful to reaffirm this ultimate remedy in the case of the current Medicaid program, its holding effectively treats the expansion as a new program and bars the Secretary from sanctioning states that do not implement the expanded coverage by withholding funding from their preexisting programs. In this sense, the ruling has the practical effect of treating the expansion group as optional, although it remains very much on the books as a mandatory coverage group.

Most states, however, will likely choose to accept the ACA's Medicaid expansion, as it is accompanied by a highly favorable financial basis in relation to state program expenditures. In the case of most eligibility categories, the federal financial contribution for covered services furnished to program beneficiaries ranges from 50 percent to 77 percent of total state expenditures. Under the ACA, federal funding for newly eligible children and adults is set at 100 percent for the first two years, declining to 90 percent financing beginning in 2020 and thereafter (ACA §2001). Few states are apt to refuse to cover their uninsured on such favorable terms.

The Medicaid eligibility expansions are accompanied by reforms designed to streamline enrollment and improve retention rates (ACA §1413). Medicaid enrollment historically has been a major challenge as a result of complex application procedures, the unavailability in many states of accessible enrollment points or online enrollment systems, the inability to easily renew coverage at the end of an eligibility period, and extensive documentation requirements related to both income and assets (Cohen-Ross & Cox, 2002). (The ACA eliminates the option of states that accept its funds to use asset requirements, chiefly because the poor have virtually no assets, and the asset test therefore succeeded only in escalating already onerous documentation requirements.) The new eligibility determination and enrollment process emphasizes online, mail, and telephone enrollment, simplified application forms, simplified verification procedures, and coordination with the individual private insurance market established through state health insurance exchanges (ACA §1413). This coordination process is critical, since as a result of minor income fluctuations, an estimated 50 percent of individuals with incomes below 200 percent of the FPL can be expected to transition between Medicaid and state insurance exchanges in a single year (Sommers & Rosenbaum, 2011).

Medicaid's reach into both the child and adult population as a result of the ACA may have an enormous impact on underserved communities. Because low-income persons tend to be concentrated in poor and medically underserved communities, the population-wide reach of the Medicaid expansions can be expected to bring a new infusion of resources into entire communities, as individuals begin to enroll and utilize services.

A subsidized private insurance market through state health insurance exchanges. In order to assist low- and moderate-income people, the ACA establishes state health insurance exchanges. Beginning in January 2014, all qualified individuals (state residents who are legally present in the United States and otherwise uninsured through "minimum essential coverage such as Medicaid or employer-sponsored coverage," ACA §1501) will be legally entitled to secure affordable insurance coverage (ACA §§1311, 1401, and 1402). Qualified health plans sold through state exchanges will be required to cover a range of benefits known as "essential health benefits" (ACA §1302), which consist of 10 separate classes of services including evidence-based preventive screening and immunization coverage without cost sharing (ACA §1001 and 1302). Both advance premium tax credits and cost-sharing reduction-assistance will be available for individuals and families with incomes below 400 percent of the federal poverty level.

Exchanges will be required to satisfy a range of federal requirements, including the use of simplified enrollment through online procedures and the availability of navigators to assist populations to enroll and retain coverage. Qualified health plans also will be expected to meet state and federal standards governing network adequacy, the use of essential community providers" serving hard to reach populations, and health care quality (ACA §1311). In order to ensure universal access to subsidized qualified health plans through exchanges, the act empowers the Secretary of the U.S. Department of Health and Human Services (HHS) to establish and operate an exchange in any state that elects not to operate one or whose exchange is not operational by 2013 (ACA §1321).

Investing in communities. Beyond insurance coverage, the ACA invests in health care access, quality, and health improvement. An $11 billion Community Health Center Trust Fund and a $1.5 billion fund for the National Health

Service Corps (which supplies primary health care professionals to medically underserved communities with primary health professional shortages) are key elements of the Health Care and Education Reconciliation Act, enacted into law simultaneously with passage of the ACA (Pub. L. 111–152). The Community Health Center and National Health Service Corps Fund investments are set to occur between FYs 2011 and 2015 so as to anchor expanded access to primary health care in medically underserved communities in advance of full implementation of the coverage provisions, which are projected to significantly boost use of health care services (Collins et al., 2012; Rosenbaum, Jones, Shin, & Tolbert, 2010).

Investments are made on a mandatory spending basis, as well, in a permanently authorized Prevention and Public Health Fund (ACA § 4002). The fund is slated to make $5 billion available for community health-improvement investments between FY 2010 and 2014, and $2 billion annually thereafter. The fund can be invested in any activity authorized under the Public Health Service Act, such as prevention, wellness, screening programs, prevention research, and other authorized initiatives, including investment in a preventive clinical workforce. As of winter 2012, the HHS had made multiple investments in activities such as community transformation grants (authorized under ACA §4201), the clinical preventive workforce, screening programs for mental illness, substance abuse, and HIV prevention and treatment, as well as initiatives aimed at boosting the public health infrastructure (Department of Health and Human Services, 2012). The ACA also establishes teaching health centers (ACA §5508) in order to increase the training and education of health professionals in health settings located in medically underserved communities (Health Resources and Services Administration, 2012).

The ACA also revises and strengthens the community benefit requirements related to nonprofit hospitals that seek federal tax-exempt status (ACA §9007). Under these revised requirements, hospitals will be required to tie their community investments, a prerequisite to claiming tax-exempt status under the Internal Revenue Code, to "community health needs assessments" that are evidence based, include input from individuals who represent the community as well as persons with expertise in public health, and that prioritize community investments in health and health care in accordance with an implementation strategy. Under the act, the community health-needs assessment must be made widely available through online posting and other means, and with actual investments codified in reports to the Internal Revenue Service (IRS) that are made widely available (26 C.F.R. §301.6104(d)(2)). Through these new requirements, the ACA in essence seeks to harness the resources of the nation's more than 2,900 nonprofit hospitals in order to improve their accountability, which has been extensively explored (Government Accountability Office, 2008).

In order to improve the quality and efficiency of health care delivery, the ACA contains numerous provisions aimed at strengthening health system performance. Utilizing a combination of strategies such as comparative clinical effectiveness reviews (ACA §6301), establishment of a national quality strategy that includes measures aimed at improving health equity and reducing disparities (ACA §3013), and Medicare payment reform, the ACA places an imperative on increasing access to cost-effective community-based services, reducing the use of emergency departments and unnecessary inpatient hospital admissions and readmissions, and reducing medical errors (Furrow, 2011).

In order to ensure that these reforms, as well as the operation of the new exchange system, are targeted at and designed for populations at greatest risk for poor health outcome, the ACA requires reforms in data collection, analysis, and quality that incorporate data on race, ethnicity, primary language, and disability status and that are sufficiently localized to be able to measure patient care and outcome differences within health systems (ACA §4302). In addition, the ACA extends existing civil rights protections aimed at preventing discrimination based on race, national origin, language, and disability, to health insurance exchanges and qualified health plans sold inside exchanges (ACA §1557).

The ACA's system transformation provisions emphasize new approaches to health care delivery through the establishment of a Center for Medicare & Medicaid Innovation, which is required to bring a special focus to health care reform for the nearly 9 million elderly and disabled persons dually enrolled in Medicare and Medicaid who represent some of the highest cost, highest need patients in the United States (ACA §3021; Kaiser Family Foundation, 2011a). Through the use of Medicare "shared-savings" arrangements that permit the federal government to share savings realized from quality and efficiency improvements, the ACA encourages the formation of accountable care organizations, including organizations located in and serving medically underserved communities (ACA §3022; Centers for Medicare & Medicaid Services, 2011).

CONCLUSION

Cumulatively, these reforms in health care financing, organization, and delivery, along with investments in public health improvement activities, can be expected to have a measurable impact on the ACA's millions of direct beneficiaries over time. This impact will be seen in improved measures of health care access to both primary preventive care such as health screenings and immunizations, as well as performance measures related to access to treatment for serious and chronic health conditions that nonetheless are amenable to treatment and management. Measures such as the ability to routinely receive health care, the likelihood of reporting a regular source of health care, and patient satisfaction also can be expected to experience an uptick among the most underserved individuals, as affordable insurance coverage empowers them to establish a stable and ongoing relationship to the health care system.

As importantly, medically underserved communities can be expected to benefit from the combined effects of these investments. As millions gain insurance coverage, entire communities can be expected to improve health care market power. This growing power to shape health care markets will be further enhanced by the direct investments in primary health care reflected in the Community Health Center and National Health Service Corps expansions as well as the Prevention and Public Health Fund's investment in clinical preventive services. As underserved populations become more extensively insured, the clinics and safety net hospitals that anchor these communities will be positioned to grow and expand as their enormous uncompensated care burdens fall. This flourishing of the health care infrastructure for medically underserved populations following a major insurance expansion already has been seen in the long-term growth trajectory of community health centers in the wake of the major Medicaid expansions for children, pregnant women, and (in some states) parents that occurred during the 1980s and 1990s (Rosenbaum & Frankford, 2012). As Medicaid coverage penetrated more deeply into the population, so did the number of health center service sites, the scope of health center services, and the number of clinical and health professionals employed. Estimates are that the ACA's broad insurance expansions, coupled with its jump-start infrastructure investments, will have the same effect, with a projected doubling of health-center capacity between 2010 and 2019 (Ku et al., 2010).

REFERENCES AND FURTHER READING

Agency for Healthcare Research and Quality. (2010). *National health care disparities report.* Washington, DC: U.S. Department of Health and Human Services.

Agency on Healthcare Research and Quality. (2011). *Disparities in health care quality among racial and ethnic minority groups: Selected findings from the 2010 national healthcare quality and disparities reports.* Washington, DC: U.S. Department of Health and Human Services.

Braveman, P., Oliva, G., Miller, M. G., Reiter, R., & Egerter, S. (1989). Adverse outcomes and lack of health insurance among newborns in an eight county area of California, 1982–1986. *The New England Journal of Medicine, 321*(8), 508–513.

Brown, E. R., Ojeda, V. D., Wyn, R., & Levan, R. (2000). *Racial and ethnic disparities in access to health insurance and health care.* Los Angeles, CA: UCLA Center for Health Policy Research.

Centers for Disease Control and Prevention. (2006). National health and nutrition examination survey. In *Improving children's health: Understanding children's health disparities and promising approaches to address them.*Washington, DC: Children's Defense Fund. Retrieved from http://www.childrensdefense.org/child-research-data-publications/data/Childrens-Health-Disparities-Report-2006.pdf

Centers for Medicare & Medicaid Services. (2011). Accountable Care Organizations final rule. 76 *Fed. Reg.* 67702–67988.

Children's Defense Fund. (2006). *Improving children's health: Understanding children's health disparities and promising approaches to address them.* Washington, DC: Children's Defense Fund.

Cohen-Ross, D., & Cox, L. (2002). *Enrolling children and families in health coverage: The promise of doing more.* Washington, DC: The Kaiser Commission on Medicaid and the Uninsured.

Collins, S., Robertson, R., Garber, T., & Doty, M. (2012). The income divide in health care: How the affordable care act will help restore fairness to the U.S. health system. *Issue Brief* [The Commonwealth Fund], *1579*(3).

Congressional Budget Office. (2010). *Letter to the Honorable Harry Reid from Douglas W. Elmendorf.* Washington, DC: Congressional Budget Office.

Cooper, L. A., & Powe, N. (2004). *Disparities in patient experiences, health care processes, and outcomes: The role of patient-provider racial, ethnic, and language concordance.* Washington, DC: The Commonwealth Fund.

Cooper , L. A., & Roter, D. L. (2003). Patient-provider communication: The effect of race and ethnicity on process and outcomes of healthcare. In B. D. Smedley, A. Y. Stith, & A. R. Nelson (Eds.), *Unequal treatment: Confronting racial and ethnic disparities in health care* (p. 552). Washington, DC: National Academies Press.

Dasenbrock, H. H., Wolinsky, J. P., Sciubba, D. M., Gokaslan, Z. L., & Bydon, A. (2012). The impact of July hospital admission on insurance status on outcomes after surgery for spinal metastases. *Cancer, 118*(5), 1429–1438.

Davis, K., & Schoen, C. (1978). *Health and the war on poverty: A ten year appraisal.* Washington, DC: Brookings Press.

De Maeseneer, J. M., De Prins, L., Gosset, C., & Heyerick, J. (2003). Provider continuity in family medicine: Does it make a difference? *Annals of Family Medicine, 1*(3),144–148.

DeNavas-Walt, C., Proctor, B. D., & Smith, J. C. (2011). *Income, poverty, and health insurance coverage in The United States: 2010.* U.S. Census Bureau Current Population Reports P60-239. Washington, DC: U.S. Government Printing Office.

Department of Health and Human Services. (2012). *Search of prevention and public health fund activities.* Retrieved from http://search .hhs.gov/search?q=Prevention+and+Public+Health+Fund&site=HHSgov&entqr=3&ud=1&sort=date%3AD%3AL%3Ad1&outp ut=xml_no_dtd&ie=UTF-8&oe=UTF-8&lr=lang_en&client=HHS&proxystylesheet=HHS&btnG.x=22&btnG.y=9

Dietz, W. H. (1998). Health consequences of obesity in youth. *Pediatrics, 101*(2), 518–525.

Furrow, B. (2011). Regulating patient safety: The patient protection and Affordable Care Act. *University Pennsylvania Law Review, 159,* 1701–1765.

Goetz, E. (2003). *Clearing the way: Deconcentrating the poor in urban America.* Washington, DC: The Urban Institute.

Government Accountability Office. (2008). *Variation in standards and guidance limits comparison of how hospitals meet community benefit requirements* (GAO 08-880).

Halle, M., Lewis, C. B., & Seshamani, M. (2009). *Health disparities: A case for closing the gap.* Washington, DC: Department of Health and Human Services. Retrieved from http://www.healthreform.gov/reports/healthdisparities/disparities_final.pdf

Hawkins, D., & Rosenbaum, S. (1993). *Lives in the balance: The health status of America's medically underserved populations.* Washington, DC: National Association of Community Health Centers, Inc.

Health Resources and Services Administration. (1995). *Medically underserved areas and populations (MUA/Ps): Guidelines for MUA and MUP designation.* Washington, DC: U.S. Department of Health and Human Resources. Retrieved from http://bhpr.hrsa.gov/shortage/muaps

Health Resources and Services Administration. (2008). Designation of medically underserved populations and health professional shortage areas, Notice of proposed rule making. 73 *Fed. Reg.* 11232–11281.

Health Resources and Services Administration. (2012). *Teaching health centers.* Washington, DC: U.S. Department of Health and Human Resources. Retrieved from http://www.hrsa.gov/grants/apply/assistance/teachinghealthcenters

Holahan, J., & Chen, V. (2011). *Changes in health insurance coverage in the great recession, 2007–2010.* Washington, DC: Kaiser Commission on Medicaid and the Uninsured.

Institute of Medicine. (2002). *Care without coverage: Too little, too late.* Washington, DC: National Academies Press.

Institute of Medicine, Committee on the Consequences of Uninsurance. (2003). *A shared destiny: Community effects of uninsurance.* Washington, DC: National Academies Press.

Kaiser Family Foundation. (2009). *Medicaid and the uninsured.* Washington, DC: Author.

Kaiser Family Foundation. (2011a). *Dual eligibles: Medicaid's role for low income medicare beneficiaries.* Washington, DC: Author.

Kaiser Family Foundation. (2011b). *The uninsured: A primer.* Washington, DC: Author.

Kaiser Family Foundation. (2012). *Income eligibility limits for working adults at application as a percent of the Federal Poverty Level (FPL) by scope of benefit package.* Kaiser State Health Facts. Washington, DC: Author. Retrieved from http://www.statehealthfacts .org/comparereport.jsp?rep=54&cat=4

Ku, L., Richard, P., Dor, A., Tan, E., Shin, P., & Rosenbaum, S. (2010). *Strengthening primary care to bend the cost curve: The expansion of community health centers through health reform.* Washington, DC: George Washington University.

Ku, L., & Waidmann, T. (2003). *How race, ethnicity, immigration status and language impact access to care and quality of care among the low income population.* Washington, DC: Kaiser Family Foundation.

Mardner, W. D., & Chang, S. (2005). Childhood obesity: Costs, treatment patterns, disparities in care and prevalent medical conditions. *Thomson Medstat Research Brief.* Ann Arbor, MI: Thomson Medstat.

Mariner, W. K. (2010). Health reform: What's insurance got to do with it? Recognizing health insurance as a separate species of insurance. *American Journal of Law & Medicine, 36*(2–3), 436–451.

McCarty, D., & Levine, H. J. (1999). Needs of people with chronic and disabling conditions. In M. Martinez, B. Lyons, B. Rowland, & D. Lillie-Blanton (Eds.), *Access to health care: Promises and prospects for low-income Americans.* Washington, DC: The Kaiser Commission on Medicaid and the Uninsured.

Mead, H., Cartwright-Smith, L., Jones, K., Ramos, C., Woods, K., & Siegel, B. (2008). *Racial and ethnic disparities in health care: A chartbook.* Washington, DC: The Commonwealth Fund.

Mensah, G. A., Mokdad, A. H., Ford, E. S., Greenlund, K. J., & Croft, J. B. (2005). State of disparities in cardiovascular health in the United States. *Circulation, 111*(10), 1233–1241.

National Association of Community Health Centers and National Health Law Program. (2008). *Serving patients with limited English proficiency: Results of a community health center survey.* Washington, DC: National Association of Community Health Centers.

National Center for Health Statistics. (2010). *Health United States, 2010.* Washington, DC: U.S. Department of Health and Human Services. Retrieved from http://www.cdc.gov/nchs/data/hus/hus10.pdf

National Federation of Independent Business v. Sebelius, __U.S.__, 2012 WL 247810 (U.S. June 28, 2012) (Nos. 11-393, 11-400).

Newacheck, P. W., & Starfield, B. (1988). Morbidity and use of ambulatory care services among poor and nonpoor children. *American Journal of Public Health, 78*(8), 927–933.

Nickens, H. W. (1995). The role of race/ethnicity and social class in minority health status. *Health Services Research, 30*(1), 151–162.

Pamboukian, S. V., Funkhouser, E., Child, I. G., Allison, J. J., Weissman, N. J., & Kiefe, C. I. (2008). Disparities by insurance status in quality of care for elderly patients with unstable angina. *Ethnicity and Disease, 16*(4), 799–807.

Parker, J. D., Schoendorf, K. C., & Kiely, J. L. (1994). Associations between measures of socioeconomic status and low birth weight, small gestational age, and premature delivery in the United States. *Annals of Epidemiology, 4*(4), 271–278.

Raphael, D. (2003). A society in decline: The political, economic, and social determinants of health inequalities in the United States. In R. Hofrichter (Ed.), *Health and social justice: Politics, ideology and inequity in the distribution of disease.* San Francisco, CA: Wiley.

Rosenbaum, S., & Frankford, D. M. (2012). *Law and the American health care system* (5th ed.). Westbury, NY: Foundation Press.

Rosenbaum, S., Jones, E., & Shin, P. (2009). *National health reform: How will medically underserved communities fare?* Washington, DC: George Washington University.

Rosenbaum, S., Jones, E., Shin, P., & Tolbert, J. (2010). *Community health centers: Opportunities and challenges in health reform.* Washington, DC: Kaiser Commission on Medicaid and the Uninsured.

Schneider, E. C., Zaslavsky, A. M., & Epstein, A. M. (2002). Racial disparities in the quality of care for enrollees in medicare managed care. *Journal of the American Medical Association, 287*(10), 1288–1294.

Shin, P., Jones, K., & Rosenbaum, S. (2003). *Reducing racial and ethnic disparities: Estimating the impact of high health center penetration in low-income communities.* Washington, DC: The George Washington University Center for Health Services Research and Policy.

Shin, P., Ku, L., Jones, E., & Rosenbaum, S. (2008). *Analysis of the proposed rule on medically underserved populations and health professional shortage areas.* Washington, DC: The George Washington University.

Smedley, B. D., Stith, A. Y., & Nelson, A. R. (Eds.). (2003). *Unequal treatment: Confronting racial and ethnic disparities in health care.* Washington, DC: National Academies Press.

Sommers, B., & Rosenbaum, S. (2011). Issues in health reform: How changes in eligibility may move millions back and forth between Medicaid and insurance exchanges. *Health Affairs, 30*(2), 228–236.

Ward, E., Jemal, A., Cokkinides, V., Singh, G. K., Cardinez, C., Ghafoor, A., & Thun, M. (2004). Cancer disparities by race/ethnicity and socioeconomic status. *CA Cancer Journal for Clinicians, 54*(2), 78–93.

Wenneker, M. B., Weissman, J. S., & Epstein, A. M. (1990). The association of payer with utilization of cardiac procedures in Massachusetts. *Journal of the American Medical Association, 264*(10), 1255–1260.

Wise, P. H., Kotelchuck, M., Wilson, M. L., & Mills, M. (1985). Racial and socioeconomic disparities in childhood mortality in Boston. *New England Journal of Medicine, 313*(6), 360–366.

Sara Rosenbaum and Tishra Beeson

COUNTERPOINT

Despite its nominal achievements, the Patient Protection and Affordable Care Act (ACA) contains deep flaws that will seriously diminish its effectiveness for individuals while shortchanging the very communities that are in the most desperate need of population investment. The ACA's shortcomings can be seen in the structure of its insurance reforms and the limited nature of its community-level investments.

AN INADEQUATE, UNSTABLE, AND EXCLUSIONARY APPROACH TO HEALTH INSURANCE COVERAGE

Exclusion of persons not lawfully present in the United States. The ACA exacerbates the fundamental problem of the exclusion of individuals not lawfully present in the United States. This population, which government estimates placed at approximately 11 million in 2010, is excluded from Medicaid coverage, even when otherwise eligible, except in medical emergencies (Hoefer, Rytina, & Baker, 2010). The ACA continues this exclusionary practice, and even escalates the problem by banning undocumented persons from access to state health insurance exchanges as well as the premium tax credits and cost-sharing assistance otherwise available to low- and moderate-income people (ACA §1311 and §1401). Because undocumented persons are more likely to reside in lower-income medically underserved communities, this ongoing and intensified exclusion from the public and private health insurance markets leaves these communities with a higher burden of uncompensated care and a greater exposure to populations who experience elevated health risks and yet lack the means to secure more than minimal access to even basic health care. Health care providers such as community health centers and safety net public hospitals, which provide the bulk of care to undocumented persons and families, will continue to bear this responsibility with inadequate resources (National Association of Community Health Centers, 2011).

Some localities contribute to the cost of care in safety net settings because of the importance of the population to the workforce. In others, however, where opposition to undocumented persons is intense, governments have withdrawn or severely scaled back direct aid. For example, state and local infusion into health centers, which reached a zenith of more than $600 million by the mid-2000s, had fallen by more than 40 percent by the end of 2011, a victim of the ongoing state and local economic crisis coupled with antipathy toward expenditures for populations not lawfully present in the United States (Rosenbaum, Shin, & Paradise, 2012).

Continuing reliance on Medicaid. The ACA relied heavily on the expansion of Medicaid in 2014 to cover all citizens (and legal immigrants who were in the United States for five years) whose income was up to 133 percent of the Federal Poverty Level. As the act was written, states that chose not to expand their Medicaid programs risked losing all of their federal money. Although the federal government has never imposed such a draconian penalty on a state for noncompliance with a federal Medicaid requirement, the threat would have been a powerful one, since states rely heavily on federal Medicaid funding. In *National Federation of Independent Business v. Sebelius* (2012), the Supreme Court ruled that this threat was unconstitutional. States cannot lose their preexisting Medicaid funds if they fail to expand their Medicaid program. They can only lose the new money provided by the ACA.

It is uncertain how many states, if any, will decide to reject the federal funds offered under the ACA and fail to expand their Medicaid program. Although the federal government will pay 100 percent of the cost of covering new beneficiaries for two years, states will thereafter have to begin sharing some of the costs (up to 10 percent by 2020). States also worry about the administrative expense of expanding their Medicaid program. As health care costs continue to exact an ever-greater share of state budgets, some states, especially those that challenged the ACA in court and have chosen in the past to keep their Medicaid program relatively restrictive, may decide not to accept the ACA's Medicaid expansion. If so, some percentage of the 16 million who were expected to attain coverage under the expansion, may not. Many of these poor Americans will be left without any insurance options as the tax credits and subsidies provided by the ACA to enable people to purchase insurance on the newly formed health insurance exchanges are not available to people whose income is less than 100 percent of the Federal Poverty Level (ACA §1401) because Congress assumed they would receive their insurance through Medicaid. Ironically, depending on the costs of insurance in their states, some of these individuals may even be subject to the tax the ACA will impose on people who remain uninsured.

Even when Medicaid is available, it is associated with barriers to health care access not found in the commercial insurance market. Certain factors account for Medicaid's association with constrained access to health care, such as the greater clinical and social challenges of Medicaid beneficiaries, their unstable Medicaid enrollment, their concentration in poorer communities where resources are less available to begin with, and the program's perceived administrative challenges. Above all, however, providers report low rates of Medicaid participation (particularly in the case of adult care and specialty care) as a result of the program's historically low payment rates. In 2009, when 74 percent and 88 percent respectively of physicians were accepting new Medicare or commercially insured patients, new patient acceptance rates in Medicaid were measured at 65 percent (Medicaid and CHIP Payment and Advisory Commission [MACPAC], 2011).

Beyond Medicaid's low provider-participation rates, stability of coverage over time has been a major problem. Even small changes in family income or characteristics and living arrangements (e.g., several hours per month of additional paid work resulting in a modest rise in income, a child who turns 18, a marriage) are enough to cause eligibility to cease. Furthermore, federal Medicaid law lacks a continuous enrollment guarantee; that is, each change in income, resources, or living arrangements must be reported, and individuals must undergo a redetermination of eligibility. Failure to report such changes can result in serious sanctions and can subject beneficiaries to liability for payments made during periods of ineligibility. In the case of children, states have the option (which some have taken) to adopt 12-month continuous enrollment policies. No such option exists for adults, and the ACA fails to create one. As a result, high Medicaid eligibility disruption rates—estimates are that more than 40 percent of adults enrolled in Medicaid will experience at least one break in coverage by the end of a 12-month enrollment cycle—can be expected to remain high (Medicaid and CHIP Payment and Advisory Commission, 2011). Although all individuals, even the poorest, are subject to the ACA's "minimum essential coverage" requirements, the number of very poor people who are uncovered at any given time as a result of breaks in eligibility will most likely remain considerable.

Congress's decision to leave the poorest Americans in Medicaid was made in part because the entire Act is incremental in nature, building on the public and private insurance markets that predated passage. At the same time, Congress's decision to bar the very poor from entitlement to premium tax credit and cost-sharing reductions (with the exception of recently arrived legal U.S. residents who are ineligible for Medicaid during the first five years of their U.S. presence) in favor of Medicaid also reflects a desire to exclude the poor from commercial insurance markets, a position strongly taken by the insurance industry during debates over the ACA. With their heavier burden of poor health, the lowest-income Americans represent a risk factor that the industry was not willing to absorb in the newly established commercial market of state insurance exchanges. This desire for risk avoidance in turn leaves the poor segregated into separately financed programs that while characterized by broad coverage and low patient cost sharing (two of Medicaid's most important hallmarks), nonetheless achieves these results through deeply discounted provider financing that leaves beneficiaries inadequately served.

MISPLACED RELIANCE ON THE COMMERCIAL INSURANCE MARKET

The ACA represented an unprecedented opportunity to replace—with a single, unified approach to health care financing—the nation's fractured public and private markets for health insurance, with their high administrative costs and the potential for frequent interruptions in coverage as individuals' and families' economic and social circumstances change. What remains after the ACA is very much what came before—employer coverage for slightly more than half of all nonelderly Americans and their families, Medicaid for most of the poorest people, and a new individual commercial insurance market (with subsidies for low- and moderate-income consumers) operated through state health insurance exchanges. The ACA is an exercise in gap filling rather than a seamless approach to coverage and payment. It secures the future of a health insurance industry that adds to the already excessively high cost of health care in the United States through the use of products that carry high administrative costs and that lack the type of transparency and ease of use that characterize more unified systems found in other wealthy democracies. Indeed, even provisions of the ACA designed to make insurance policies more understandable through the use of simplified explanations of benefits and coverage (ACA §1001) were fiercely resisted by the industry during the period of regulatory implementation by the U.S. Department of Health and Human Services (HHS).

This decision to retain and build on a poorly performing private insurance market was, of course, a concession to the obvious politics of early-twenty-first century America, in which government interventions are met with deep suspicion and fear, and insistence on market solutions for problems as basic as how to allocate health care resources across a population is at an all-time high. The people who will suffer from the effects of the decision to protect the existing insurance market at all cost, and even to strengthen it, will be low- and moderate-income families and the communities in which they live. The retention of a fractured approach to health care financing further impedes the ability of even affluent communities to create the types of powerful markets for health care purchasing that in turn begin to affect the high cost of care in the United States (Elhauge, 2010). But the communities that will be hurt the most by this intensification in health care markets are those that struggled to claim resources to begin with.

This struggle to make a commercial insurance market work in poorer communities is complicated further by two additional considerations. First, private insurers will judge poorer communities more costly to cover, and the price of insurance will remain high. The ACA restructures the insurance market, beginning January 2014, to bar exclusions based on preexisting conditions and require the use of community rating in order to stop premium pricing discrimination against the sick (ACA §1201). The ACA also attempts to regulate the structure and cross-market pricing of commercial offerings so that insurers cannot effectively dump their worst individual and small-employer group risks into state health insurance exchanges and must have an evidentiary basis for what regulators deem to be unreasonable rate increases. But these reforms, as important as they are, cannot paper over the fact that people will be required to buy coverage, even as the cost of a relatively ungenerous "silver level" family policy (with an actuarial rate of only 70 percent) surpasses $12,000 as a result of the high cost of health care coupled with the high cost of commercial health insurance.

Second, the premium tax credits and cost-sharing assistance simply are inadequate. Under the ACA, virtually all legally resident Americans will be required to show evidence of insurance and will face serious tax penalties if they cannot satisfy the minimum coverage requirement. For lower income Americans whose incomes nonetheless exceed Medicaid eligibility levels, or live in states that choose not to expand their Medicaid programs, payment of this penalty (approximately $700) will create impossible choices; it is likely that the penalty will be recouped from lower-income workers' earned income tax credit, which is a lifeline for families who struggle to meet the most basic needs of food and shelter. The concentration of poverty in the United States means that it will be medically underserved communities that bear the brunt of families' struggles to meet the twin demands of health insurance and rent.

This struggle might have been alleviated through more broadly available and generous tax subsidies that make coverage truly affordable for lower income families. But the tax credits are far from adequate, leaving lower-income families facing significant financial exposure. What might this exposure look like?

The Kaiser Family Foundation offers a premium calculator that allows users to calculate individuals' share of premiums in 2014, as well as the value of the premium subsidy that will be available if coverage is purchased through a state exchange. Assuming a 40-year-old parent in a family of four and earning $35,000 (277 percent of the FPL), the calculator projects the cost of a family policy at $12,130 in 2014 in a state with midrange health care costs. The value of the federal subsidy will be $10,742, and the family's share will be $1,388, or about $110 per month for a family living at the edge. In many metropolitan areas, this type of family would not be able to afford the cost of a two-bedroom rental apartment. The additional monthly premium cost, which does not include the family's remaining cost-sharing obligations for co-payments, deductibles, and uncovered health care costs (e.g., eyeglasses for an adult) will be difficult if not impossible to meet. Failure to pay the premium leaves the family uncovered and subject to federal penalties, taken from its earned income tax credit (assuming that the family files for the EITC).

It gets worse. When the family applies for help, it will be told that if income should rise during the year (e.g., through some overtime work or a drop in family size if a child moves out to go to college) the assistance will fall. Furthermore, if the income rise is not reported, the family will face recoupment of the premium assistance, which under the law, could amount to the entire subsidy amount it has received (ACA §1401, amended by Pub. L. 112–9, The Comprehensive 1099 Taxpayer Protection and Repayment of Exchange Subsidy Overpayments Act of 2011).

In sum, the ACA preserves a costly and fragmented insurance market, which not only fails to ensure stability and continuity of coverage but also is highly costly. The people most aided by the ACA's coverage reforms are, of course, the people who do not have coverage today, meaning low- and moderate-income working families without employer coverage. Rather than making coverage affordable, however, the ACA leaves families with significant, ongoing financial obligations that in turn either may deter them from enrolling (at which point they face a penalty) or may leave them exposed to a costly recoupment process should their incomes rise even slightly.

WEAK INVESTMENT IN COMMUNITIES

The community health center and National Health Service Corps investments are important. But they are not enough. Even at expanded capacity, health centers in 2019 will serve a projected 40 million persons. The actual number of people living in medically underserved communities has been estimated at nearly 100 million (Rosenbaum, Jones, Shin, & Tolbert, 2010). The investments fall short of the mark by a factor of more than two. The Public Health Trust Fund, valued at $2 billion annually beginning in 2015 and thereafter, is inadequate to change the health-risk picture for more than a handful of communities over time. Indeed, in the first year of operation, the federal Community Transformation Grant program, which invests Trust Funds into prevention activities, made only 75 awards in a nation of more than 300 million people. Left untouched is the fundamental imbalance in the U.S. health care workforce, which emphasizes specialty training and practice and seriously underinvests in and undervalues primary health care. Congress might have revised federal laws that spend literally billions of dollars in workforce training through Medicare's hospital graduate medical education payment system (GME). Instead, it left the GME system essentially untouched, while failing to adequately finance the alternative workforce training programs authorized under the ACA but not given a special fund similar to the Community Health Centers, National Health Service Corps, and Prevention Trust Funds. Of the funding available through the Prevention and Public Health Fund, $167 million was made available to the recruitment of primary health care professionals, a fraction of what is needed to close the primary health care gap, especially in medically underserved communities (Kliff, 2012).

An improved national focus on quality and efficiency is laudable. But changing the manner in which the U.S. health care system operates requires more than national quality measures. Reform requires real financial investments in quality improvement efforts and a complement of health professionals trained in a new approach to health care practice in which teamwork and early intervention are emphasized. The ACA promises neither. Though the Center for Medicare & Medicaid Innovation represents a first step toward restructuring, its $10 billion spending line over the 2011–2019 period can be charitably characterized as modest, and much of this funding will be invested in health care systems serving more affluent communities, not only those that struggle for resources.

Nor does the ACA change physicians' historic grip on state licensure laws, which preserve the primacy and autonomy of the medical professions while barring entry by other health professionals fully capable of competing for market share. In many states, nursing and other allied professions continue to find themselves constrained from practicing up to the full capacity of their training as a result of restrictive licensure laws (Rosenbaum & Frankford, 2012).

CONCLUSION

In sum, the ACA represents a modest step, at best, toward true investment in medically underserved communities and populations. Medicaid, a program that has achieved much but that faces numerous limitations, is maintained as the centerpiece of coverage for the poor, who as a result will remain either uninsured in states that choose not to expand coverage or segregated within a financing scheme characterized by significant underpayment to providers. The private insurance market is preserved, despite its costs and inefficiencies, and yet the ACA's subsidy scheme, which is absolutely essential to making this costly approach to health care coverage work for low- and moderate-income families, is seriously inadequate. Furthermore, undocumented persons remain entirely excluded, despite their contribution to the economy, their need for health care, and the ongoing burden that their care will impose on economically struggling communities.

Finally, the community-level investments in health care infrastructure, while a modest step forward, are just that. Thousands of communities will remain medically underserved, and the underlying challenges of a realigned health care infrastructure and workforce will remain essentially unaddressed except, perhaps, in health care systems serving the most affluent communities, which do not require government investment in order to begin the long and difficult process of health care reinvention.

REFERENCES AND FURTHER READING

Elhauge, E. (2010). *The fragmentation of U.S. health care: Causes and solutions.* New York, NY: Oxford University Press.

Hoefer, M., Rytina, N., & Baker, B. C. (2010). *Estimates of the unauthorized immigrant population living in the United States: January 2010.* Washington, DC: U.S. Department of Homeland Security.

Kaiser Family Foundation. (n.d.). *Health reform subsidy calculator.* Retrieved from http://healthreform.kff.org/Subsidycalculator.aspx?CFID=78780178&CFTOKEN=73428136&jsessionid=60301aa30837599cb170659193731311e455

Kliff, S. (2012, February 11). The health-care overhaul depends on primary-care doctors. They work more and earn less. Who'd sign up for that? *The Washington Post*, p. G1.

Medicaid and CHIP Payment and Advisory Commission. (2011, March). *Report to Congress on Medicaid and CHIP.* Retrieved from http://democrats.energycommerce.house.gov/sites/default/files/documents/MACPAC_Report_031511.pdf

National Association of Community Health Centers. (2011). *Access endangered: Profiles of the medically disenfranchised.* Washington, DC: National Association of Community Health Centers.

National Federation of Independent Business v. Sebelius, __U.S.__, 2012 WL 247810 (U.S. June 28, 2012) (Nos. 11-393, 11-400).

Rosenbaum, S., & Frankford, D. M. (2012). *Law and the American health care system* (2nd ed.). Westbury, NY: Foundation Press.

Rosenbaum, S., Jones, E., Shin, P., & Tolbert, J. (2010). *Community health centers: Opportunities and challenges in health reform.* Washington, DC: Kaiser Commission on Medicaid and the Uninsured.

Rosenbaum, S., Shin, P., & Paradise, J. (2012). *Community health centers: The challenge of growing to meet primary care need in medically underserved communities.* Washington, DC: Kaiser Commission on Medicaid and the Uninsured.

U.S. Supreme Court. (2012). Brief of the United States: *State of Florida et al. v United States Department of Health and Human Services et al.* (No. 11-400).

Sara Rosenbaum and Tishra Beeson

Abortion and Reproductive Health Services

POINT: Abortion, contraception, and reproductive health services are essential components of women's health care. Women have a fundamental right to access such services.

B. Jessie Hill, Case Western Reserve University School of Law

COUNTERPOINT: Many people believe that abortion and other reproductive health services are morally repugnant. Government taxes should not support such divisive services, and there is no constitutional right to government support for these services.

B. Jessie Hill, Case Western Reserve University School of Law

Introduction

Since the Supreme Court's 1973 decision in *Roe v. Wade,* holding that a woman has the right to an abortion prior to viability, a debate has raged over the use of taxpayer funds to cover reproductive health services. This debate has been especially intense in regard to abortion. In this chapter, Jessie Hill recounts those debates and offers arguments both for and against the legitimacy of a right to government-supported reproductive health services.

As Hill shows, many women rely upon reproductive health services to prevent unintended pregnancy. Women with employer-based health insurance can almost always use that insurance to attain such services. According to the Guttmacher Institute, nine in ten employer-based insurance plans offer a full range of prescription contraceptives. Many women with such insurance, however, have to pay co-pays and other forms of cost sharing for their reproductive health services. As Hill explains, a regulation issued under the authority of the 2010 Patient Protection and Affordable Care Act (ACA) prohibits cost sharing for contraceptive services in new private health insurance plans.

Since the 1970s, when Congress amended the Medicaid statute to require coverage of contraceptive services, millions of women have relied upon government-funded contraceptive services. The Guttmacher Institute reports that in 2008 alone, 7.2 million women received contraceptive services from taxpayer-supported family planning clinics. In addition, millions of poor women have relied upon Medicaid for access to contraceptive services.

Taxpayer support, however, is far less common in the case of abortion. Although most private employer-sponsored insurance plans cover abortion, federal law bans coverage of the procedure in the health insurance plans offered to federal employees. In addition, the Hyde Amendment, enacted in the wake of *Roe v. Wade,* prohibits the use of federal Medicaid funds for abortion services except when the pregnancy endangers the woman's life, or is the result of rape or incest. This limitation on abortion funding was upheld by the U.S. Supreme Court in cases such as *Harris v. McCrae* (1980). Thus, as Hill explains, it is well established that there is no federal constitutional right to taxpayer support for abortions. However, in a few states, such as Massachusetts, the courts have held that the state constitution requires the state to support abortions for Medicaid recipients. All told, 17 states have either opted or been required by their courts to provide such coverage. But, because of federal law, these states must rely solely on their own funds.

In the absence of a constitutional right, legislatures remain free to decide whether or not to provide funding for abortion or contraception. This question can spark heated arguments, as it did during the 2010 congressional debate over health reform. Under the ACA, individuals and small businesses who qualify for tax subsidies may use them to purchase private insurance on the insurance exchanges established by the new law. Many legislators and antiabortion activists were concerned that, because private insurance plans have traditionally offered abortion coverage, the ACA's subsidies would likewise be used to fund the procedure. As Hill explains, abortion opponents generally believe that taxpayers should not be compelled to subsidize a medical procedure that violates their conscience. Opponents note that there is no constitutional right for taxpayer-supported abortions, and that the rights that are recognized in the United States are generally negative rights; that is, they protect individuals from interference from the government. Rights in the United States are seldom positive; they do not establish entitlements to government support. Indeed, although international human rights law may offer strong support for a right to government-supported reproductive health services, the United States has not ratified and does not abide by those international treaties; the United States recognizes few positive rights and does not follow international law in acknowledging a right to health. In response, supporters of reproductive rights point to the importance of reproductive health services, including abortion, to women's health. They also argue, as Hill explains, that the denial of such rights may undermine women's equality.

The controversy over the ACA's treatment of abortion almost killed the health-reform bill. Ultimately, the act was passed only after President Barack Obama signed an Executive Order reaffirming the Hyde Amendment and extending it to the insurance exchanges that will be created under the ACA. In addition, the final version of the ACA contained the so-called Nelson Amendment, which requires private insurance plans offering abortion coverage to collect separate premiums specifically for that coverage and to ensure that claims for abortion services are paid exclusively by private funds. Insurers must establish a financial system to segregate the funds to ensure that federal funds are never mixed with funds related to abortion. Such a complicated system may well lead many, if not most, insurance companies to refuse coverage for abortions.

Since the ACA's passage, both federal and state legislators have proposed additional laws to further restrict abortion funding. Thirteen states have enacted laws restricting abortion coverage in plans offered through the exchanges, and two states prohibit abortion coverage without exceptions. Six states have laws restricting insurance coverage of abortions for insurance plans written in those states; however, such laws have exceptions for life endangerment and provide for abortion coverage through a separate plan or premium. Federal legislators have also introduced bills in Congress to further restrict abortion funding. One such bill, the No Taxpayer Funding for Abortion Act, proposes to prohibit the use of tax deductions for employers who offer insurance plans with abortion coverage. The bill would also prohibit employees from using pretax dollars to pay for insurance premiums for plans that provide abortion coverage. This bill was passed by the House of Representatives in May 2011, but is not expected to pass the Senate.

As Hill's chapter demonstrates, the arguments for and against taxpayer support of abortion can apply to all reproductive health services. Can a right to government-supported reproductive health care exist in the absence of a right to government support for abortion? Can a right to health care for women exist in the absence of a right to government support for reproductive health services? Does the intensity of the debates surrounding these issues represent an argument for rejecting the existence of any positive right to health? Or does the strength of the debate offer a rationale for the proposition that the health of Americans can only be protected if the United States follows other developed nations in accepting a positive right to health care?

POINT

Virtually all women require some form of reproductive health care at some point in their lives. Reproductive health care encompasses not only abortion and contraception but also prenatal care, safe childbirth, and treatment for sexually transmitted infections. Many forms of reproductive health care profoundly impact both maternal and infant health and long-term well-being, as well as men's health; as such, reproductive health care is essential if both individuals and society are to flourish.

The government clearly has a duty not to interfere with women's access to reproductive health services. Going beyond mere noninterference, however, the government should provide affirmative financial support for those services. This view is supported by a number of considerations. First, international human rights law has long recognized the centrality of reproductive health to upholding the values of human dignity, equality, and overall health. Those values are relevant in the American context as well. Second, the U.S. Constitution recognizes as fundamental an individual's right to make decisions about whether and when to bear a child; as such, that right should not be available only to those who can afford to exercise it. Third, women are uniquely burdened by the unavailability of reproductive health care, and the value of gender equality is greatly served by expanding access. Fourth, from a public health perspective, all of society—including men and children—benefit from the availability of such services.

THE USE AND IMPORTANCE OF REPRODUCTIVE HEALTH CARE

In order to assess the arguments in favor of expansive access to and funding for reproductive health services, it is helpful to understand the meaning, scope, and enormous importance of reproductive health care. "Reproductive health care" may be defined as "the constellation of methods, techniques, and services that contribute to reproductive health and well-being by preventing and solving reproductive health problems" (United Nations Population Fund, 1994, 7.2). Reproductive health care thus includes a wide range of counseling and treatment in four separate periods of the reproductive cycle: preconception, pregnancy, childbirth, and post-childbirth. Preconception services include infertility treatment, prevention and treatment of sexually transmitted infections and other reproductive-tract diseases, and family planning and contraception. During pregnancy, women require access to prenatal care or, possibly, abortion. Reproductive health care during childbirth primarily means access to the facilities, medication, and assistance necessary to ensure a safe birthing process, and postnatal care includes any necessary medical attention for mother and child, including breastfeeding support.

Nearly every woman will need reproductive health care at some point in her life. According to the Alan Guttmacher Institute's fact sheet, *Facts on Publicly Funded Contraception in the United States,* the typical woman in the United States spends approximately five years of her life pregnant, postpartum, or trying to conceive, and approximately 30 years trying to avoid becoming pregnant. The Guttmacher Institute also asserts that over 99 percent of those women between the ages of 15 and 44 who have ever had sex have used some method of contraception. Nonetheless, by the age of 45, about half of all American women have experienced an unintended pregnancy, and nearly one third have had an abortion. *Facts on Publicly Funded Contraception in the United States* also states that roughly half of all pregnancies in the United States are unintended. The rate of unintended pregnancies is much lower in other developed countries, however.

Medicaid and Title X of the Public Health Service Act (Title X) are the primary means by which reproductive health care is publicly funded in the United States. According to the Guttmacher Institute, in 2006, Medicaid provided approximately $1.3 billion for family planning and related services, and Title X added another $215 million. That source also reports that, in 2008, there were approximately 66 million women of childbearing age in the United States; of those, 36 million were sexually active and capable of becoming pregnant but did not wish to become so. Of those 36 million, 17.4 million women were sufficiently low income that they relied on publicly funded contraceptive services. Publicly funded centers provide more than contraception, however; they also provide services such as cervical cancer screening; routine gynecological examinations; screening for STIs, including HIV; and counseling for teens about abstinence and sexuality. The Medicaid program also pays for childbirth and prenatal care for qualifying women; it does not, however, pay for any abortions, except those necessary to save the life of the woman, or when rape or incest has occurred. A handful of states also pay for all medically necessary abortions, not just life-saving ones, from their own funds.

THE RIGHT TO REPRODUCTIVE HEALTH CARE: AN INTERNATIONAL PERSPECTIVE

Internationally, there is a growing consensus that access to reproductive health care is a human right. The United Nations–sponsored International Conference on Population and Development (ICPD), held in Cairo, Egypt, in 1994, recognized a right to "safe, effective, affordable, and acceptable" methods of family planning and fertility regulation, as well as a right to access safe pregnancy and childbirth services (United Nations Population Fund, 1994, 7.2). In its report, the ICPD explicitly linked reproductive health and human rights, noting that the right to reproductive health care arises out of the right of couples to control the timing and number of their children, the international right to health, and the right to reproductive and sexual decision making that is free from discrimination and violence. That document also noted the important role of government in designing and supporting family planning and other reproductive health programs. This suggests that both public health interventions and subsidies are needed to realize the right to reproductive health. Not long after the ICPD, moreover, the Fourth World Conference on Women, held in Beijing, China, in 1995, reaffirmed the importance of reproductive health care in the overall context of women's human rights.

Indeed, like many other human rights, reproductive health is vital if human beings are to flourish. Childbearing and childrearing often assume central roles in individuals' lives and even their identities. Undoubtedly, both childbearing and the ability to determine the number and timing of one's children are just as important as other human rights, such as the ability to practice one's religion freely or the right to be free from discrimination on the basis of race.

In fact, reproductive health care rights are intimately connected to many other human rights. Insofar as reproductive health care is an essential aspect of overall health care for women, the right to it is intimately connected to the right to health, which has been recognized by numerous international instruments, including the United Nations' Universal Declaration of Human Rights and the International Covenant on Economic, Social, and Cultural Rights. Moreover, because women primarily bear the burden of seeking reproductive health care, preventing reproductive ailments, and suffering from sexually transmitted infections as well as pregnancy- or childbirth-related injuries, a meaningful right to health helps to vindicate the right to gender equality and nondiscrimination, which are also recognized as international human rights. Finally, the right to decide the number and spacing of one's children may implicate other important rights, such as the right to act according to one's conscience and the right to access information.

Several international human rights instruments proclaim the right of individuals not just to government noninterference with their access to reproductive health care but also to actual attainment of a state of reproductive health. Those instruments imply that the government should strive to make reproductive health services accessible and affordable, as well as engage in public health efforts directed at reproductive health. Given this virtually universal consensus in the human rights realm, the United States should not lag behind other countries. American citizens are entitled to the same human rights as citizens elsewhere. If there is sufficient international consensus that reproductive health care is fundamental, the United States should respect this consensus and work toward providing affordable and accessible reproductive health care for all of its citizens.

The United States is a signatory to some, but not all, of the international human rights instruments that assert reproductive health-related rights. If the United States has not signed onto a treaty, it is not technically binding or enforceable within the United States. For example, the United States has not signed onto the Convention on the Elimination of All Forms of Discrimination against Women, which asserts a right to gender nondiscrimination; nor has it accepted the International Covenant on Economic, Social, and Cultural Rights, which sets forth an affirmative right to health. But the norms of equality and individual autonomy on which those rights are based resonate strongly within the U.S. political and constitutional culture. Moreover, the United States did vote in favor of the Universal Declaration of Human Rights (UDHR), the foundational document of the United Nations. Though not itself a treaty with legally binding effect, the UDHR elaborates the values underlying international human rights laws and includes language supporting the protection of motherhood, the right to health, and the right to privacy—all of which support a right to reproductive health care.

THE FUNDAMENTAL RIGHT TO REPRODUCTIVE HEALTH CARE IN THE UNITED STATES

In the United States, the right to health, including the right to reproductive health, has not been recognized to the same extent, nor in the same manner, as it has been internationally. No significant U.S. legal document specifically trumpets the right to health, much less the right to reproductive health care. Nonetheless, the U.S. Supreme Court has recognized a constitutional right to privacy that specifically includes a broad constellation of rights involving childrearing, childbearing, pregnancy, abortion, and contraception. This right is understood to require, at a minimum, that the government refrain from substantially burdening women's access to reproductive health care.

In the United States, the right to privacy is a fundamental right to make certain important decisions—decisions central to one's identity, personality, and conscience—autonomously and without government interference. In *Griswold v. Connecticut,* decided in 1965, the Supreme Court first recognized the constitutional right to privacy while finding that the Constitution prohibited a state from making it illegal for married couples to use contraceptives. Shortly thereafter, in *Eisenstadt v. Baird* (1972), the Supreme Court extended that decision to unmarried individuals; in 1973, *Roe v. Wade* concluded that the right to privacy—which includes the right to decide whether and when to have a child—also encompassed the right to choose abortion.

Roe v. Wade did not, of course, settle the public controversy over abortion, even if it clarified the constitutional questions. Almost as soon as *Roe* was decided, states began passing laws to test its limits. Though forbidden from banning the procedure outright, states sought to regulate it in ways that often proved burdensome, such as by prohibiting public funding of abortions and by requiring waiting periods, spousal consent, and parental consent for minors seeking abortions. In its 1992 decision in *Planned Parenthood of Southeastern Pennsylvania v. Casey,* the Supreme Court made clear that it would uphold most legal restrictions on abortion, as long as they did not unduly burden a woman's access to the procedure. In addition, the Supreme Court reaffirmed the central holding of *Roe v. Wade* that the Constitution protects a woman's right to choose abortion before the point at which the fetus is viable, or capable of life outside the womb.

There is, therefore, clear precedent within U.S. law for an individual right to access reproductive health care services. Constitutional doctrine, however, has protected only the right to make reproductive choices privately, without government interference; it has not recognized an affirmative right to access services provided by the government or to achieve a state of complete reproductive health. Indeed, in *Maher v. Roe* and *Harris v. McRae,* decided in 1977 and 1980 respectively, the Supreme Court made it clear that the government is not required to pay for abortions—even medically necessary abortions for women who could not otherwise afford them.

The current approach to reproductive rights in the United States is thus different from that under international human rights law in two important ways. First, U.S. constitutional law emphasizes removing government-imposed barriers to reproductive health care, but unlike international human rights law, it does not suggest that individuals have a right to attain a particular standard of health or that the government has any obligation to make services available and accessible. Many scholars have criticized the Supreme Court's understanding of the Constitution as only protecting rights against government interference, arguing that it is not necessary to impose such a limitation. Yet, and although constitutional doctrine does change over time and the Supreme Court could eventually recognize an affirmative right to accessible reproductive health care, the current state of U.S. constitutional law does not accommodate the sort of right that has been recognized by international law. Programs such as Medicaid, Title X, and the ACA demonstrate, however, that the United States has made some progress toward enacting a statutory right to health care even for those who cannot afford it. Much work remains to be done to ensure that all individuals have access to the comprehensive care that they need, however.

Second, the right to access reproductive health care in the United States is grounded in the right to privacy, whereas the international right to reproductive health arises from the human right to health and, to some extent, the right to gender nondiscrimination. Nonetheless, U.S. law has begun to recognize that reproductive health implicates more than privacy. In the *Planned Parenthood v. Casey* decision, for example, the Supreme Court acknowledged that the ability of women to plan their reproductive life is essential to their ability to fulfill their aspirations and achieve social equality. In addition, that opinion spoke of reproductive autonomy as central to human dignity and flourishing. More recently, some courts and scholars have observed that the reproductive rights cases also imply a constitutional right to access medical treatments necessary to protect one's health, without government interference. Given the centrality of reproductive health care services to the overall health of individuals, especially women, at least a minimal right to access reproductive health care without government-imposed obstacles may be understood to follow from the rights to health and gender equality.

Given the fundamental nature of these rights, moreover, it seems profoundly unjust, if not almost nonsensical, to assert that they should be available only to those who can afford them. If individuals are to have a meaningful right to make autonomous reproductive decisions, their exercise of that right should not be limited by their ability to pay. The government cannot avoid placing a thumb on the scale unless it funds all reproductive health care options. Indeed, although reliable studies are few, Henshaw et al. estimate that, due to the legal restrictions on Medicaid funding, roughly one-quarter of women on Medicaid carry pregnancies to term when they would have preferred to have abortions.

REPRODUCTIVE HEALTH CARE AND WOMEN'S EQUALITY

Although U.S. constitutional law does not currently recognize an affirmative right to health, it does recognize a right to gender equality. Meaningful access to reproductive health care is also essential if gender equality is to be realized. Of course, infertility and sexually transmitted infections (STIs) are reproductive conditions that may affect men or women. In many cultures, however, women in heterosexual relationships disproportionately bear the burden of these afflictions. For example, one of the primary methods of preventing the transmission of STIs is the condom, which must be used by the male partner. As a result, a woman generally cannot prevent transmission without her partner's cooperation; she is dependent on him for her protection. This lack of control entails even more significant risks for women in societies in which male promiscuity is accepted and widespread, and among groups of people for whom condom use is socially unacceptable.

In many cultures, the psychological distress and social stigma associated with both infertility and STIs also falls primarily on women. Moreover, because childbearing is exclusively the domain of women, women are uniquely burdened when safe childbirth services and postnatal care are unavailable. In addition, in many cases the responsibility for child care also falls primarily on the mother, both in the immediate postnatal period and beyond. As a result, it is particularly important for women to be able to plan the number and timing of their children, taking into account the other needs and priorities in their lives. Avoiding unwanted pregnancy and childbearing allows women to pursue schooling and careers, putting off motherhood until they are ready.

THE SOCIETAL BENEFITS OF GOVERNMENT-SUPPORTED ACCESS TO REPRODUCTIVE HEALTH CARE

Women are not alone in benefitting from widely available and accessible reproductive health care. Indeed, all segments of society, including men and children, realize positive effects. From a public health perspective, therefore, government subsidy of reproductive health care is a sensible choice.

Access to reproductive health care is fundamental to both maternal and infant health. The emotional costs of unintended pregnancies can be enormous. In addition, women whose pregnancies are unintended are more likely to delay or go without prenatal care, to engage in unhealthy behaviors such as drinking or smoking during pregnancy, to suffer from depression, and to be subjected to domestic violence. They are also less likely to breastfeed and more likely to deliver preterm or low-birth-weight infants.

Access to safe pregnancy-related care is a major reason for the decline in maternal and infant mortality in the developed world. By comparison, according to Glasier, in the developing world, where 99 percent of maternal deaths take place, millions of preventable deaths occur due to a lack of access to safe childbirth and health care during pregnancy. Worldwide, according to the figures compiled by Cohen, somewhere between 340,000 and 550,000 women die each year from causes related to pregnancy or childbirth, making it the most common cause of death among women in the developing world. Singh et al. find that nearly 4 million newborns die each year, mostly from preventable causes; in addition, babies whose mothers die in childbirth are significantly more likely to die themselves before age two than babies whose mothers survive. Due to the enormous costs of unintended pregnancy, Cohen estimates that every dollar spent on providing contraceptive services to women saves $1.40 in health care costs.

As Glasier explains, after pregnancy-related causes, sexually transmitted infections (not including HIV) are the second-most important cause of death of otherwise healthy women in the developing world. Such infections are often passed onto infants through the birthing process. Finally, the World Health Organization (WHO) finds that an estimated 20 million unsafe abortions are performed each year, mostly in countries where abortion is illegal or extremely restricted; this number accounts for 13 percent of maternal deaths, as well as a significant amount of injury and infertility.

Though the U.S. supports reproductive health care to a much greater degree than many developing countries, access to contraception and abortion are still limited. The cost of contraceptives, especially for women who do not have private insurance, can be prohibitive. In addition, Henshaw et al. estimate that the lack of Medicaid funding for abortion delays women's abortions by an average of two to three weeks, as they raise the funds necessary for the procedure. This delay translates into higher risks for the woman. Indeed, Finer, et al. find that nearly three-fifths of women who have an abortion state that they would have liked to have had their abortion earlier, and most of them cite difficulty in making arrangements to access abortion, including raising the money for the procedure.

The federal government has begun to see the value of providing reproductive health services, particularly in light of their cost-effectiveness. In 2011, the Institute of Medicine, a branch of the National Academy of Sciences and an independent advisory organization, issued a report stating that contraceptive services, education, and counseling should be considered a "preventive service" that must be covered by group insurance plans without cost sharing. The report pointed to the effectiveness of contraception and contraceptive counseling at reducing unintended pregnancies and therefore contributing substantially to overall health. Increased contraceptive use is also associated with reduced rates of abortion. The report further noted that the United States would save billions of dollars each year in health care costs due to the reduced rate of unintended pregnancy. In addition, the report recommended coverage of other standard reproductive health services for women, such as screening for gestational diabetes and cervical cancer; counseling about STIs; counseling and screening for HIV; and support for breastfeeding, including counseling and coverage of rental costs for breastfeeding equipment. The Obama administration agreed with the Institute's findings and has promulgated a rule requiring all new insurance plans to cover these services in full.

Finally, it is important to keep in mind that men also require reproductive health care. Men, too, suffer from infertility and STIs; in addition, some reproductive ailments, such as prostate enlargement and prostate cancer, affect only men. The benefits of reproductive health care related to physical well-being and human dignity—including those involving the prevention and management of disease, as well as family planning—may be enjoyed by men, too.

CONSCIENTIOUS OBJECTIONS TO PUBLIC FUNDING OF REPRODUCTIVE HEALTH SERVICES

Opponents of public funding for reproductive health care services sometimes argue that many Americans find these services to be morally objectionable. However, this concern should not bar the funding of vital health services for women. The spending priorities for a democracy should be determined largely by the will of the people; they should not be held hostage to the views of a minority. Recent polling data indicates widespread support for public funding of reproductive health services. For example, a recent Pew Research Center poll from the Polling Report indicates that 86 percent of Americans believe that the government should do more to improve the affordability and accessibility of health care. Eighty-nine percent of Americans believe that health care should be considered a human right. Moreover, the majorities in favor of government-supported health care remain even when reproductive health care is included in the mix. A 2009 survey conducted by the National Women's Law Center, also available at the Polling Report website, demonstrates that 71 percent of Americans favor mandating coverage of reproductive health care by insurance plans; an even larger percentage (77 percent) believe that health plans should cover contraception. According to the Polling Report, polls by CNN and Quinnipiac University indicate that a solid majority of Americans (between 53 and 65 percent) support federal government funding of Planned Parenthood. Such substantial margins demonstrate that public opinion is in favor of bringing the United States more in line with the international human rights community through government-supported access to vital reproductive health services.

A further reason that claims of conscience should not stand in the way of taxpayer support for such services is that government could not function if it could not spend taxpayer funds on activities to which taxpayers objected. Given the substantial religious and ideological diversity in the United States, there is likely someone who objects to virtually every course of action the U.S. government takes. Government would grind to a halt if it had to respect each individual citizen's veto. Indeed, though many taxpayers object on sincere religious or conscientious grounds to the waging of war, or of particular wars, the government is nonetheless entitled to collect taxes from those individuals to support its war efforts. Indeed, the Supreme Court has never held that this kind of government activity violates anyone's First Amendment rights to practice their religion.

Finally, it is important to recognize that claims of conscience do not lie on only one side of the debate. It may be considered a matter of conscience to provide needed health care to indigent individuals, to equip women with the tools for avoiding unwanted pregnancies, and even to terminate a pregnancy that threatens a woman's mental or physical health. And, of course, no woman is coerced by the mere availability of funding for reproductive health services into choosing a service, such as abortion, contraception, or sterilization, that she does not wish to have; similarly, no individual provider is required by public funding to engage in a service she does not wish to provide. Public funding for reproductive health care only increases individuals' freedom and options, allowing each person to act according to his or her conscience.

CONCLUSION

Reproductive health services are essential to women's lives, health, and equality, and they benefit society as a whole. As such, women should have a fundamental right not only to free access to those services without governmental interference, but also to government funding and support of those services. Given the current state of the health care system in the United States, it is not a triviality that every dollar spent on family planning pays for itself, and then some. The international human rights community has already recognized the importance of reproductive health; it is time that the United States caught up and did the same. Indeed, our lives, our health, our futures, and our economy may well depend on it.

REFERENCES AND FURTHER READING

Alan Guttmacher Institute. (2010). *Facts on contraceptive use in the United States.* New York, NY: Author. Retrieved from http://www.guttmacher.org/pubs/fb_contr_use.html

Alan Guttmacher Institute. (2010). *Facts on publicly funded contraception in the United States.* New York, NY: Author. Retrieved from http://www.guttmacher.org/pubs/fb_contraceptive_serv.html

Bandes, S. (1990). The negative constitution: A critique. *Michigan Law Review, 88*(8), 2271–2347.

Cohen, S. (2010). Family planning and safe motherhood: Dollars and sense. *Guttmacher Policy Review, 13*(2), 12–16.

Dickens, B. M., & Cook, R. J. (2011). Conscientious commitment to women's health. *International Journal of Gynecology and Obstetrics, 113*(2), 163–166.

Eisenstadt v. Baird, 405 U.S. 438 (1972).

Fathalla, M. F., & Fathalla, M. M. F. (2011). Sexual and reproductive health: Overview. *Sexual and reproductive health: A public health perspective* (pp. 34–44). Amsterdam, Netherlands: Elsevier.

Finer, L. B., Frohwirth, L. A., Dauphinee, A., Singh, S., & Moore, A. M. (2006). Timing of steps and reasons for delays in obtaining abortions in the United States. *Contraception, 74*(4), 334–344.

Gable, L. (2010). Reproductive health as a human right. *Case Western Reserve Law Review, 60*(4), 957–996.

General Assembly of the United Nations. (1948). *Universal declaration of human rights.* Retrieved from http://www.un.org/en/documents/udhr

Glasier, A., Gulmezoglu, A. M., Schmid, G. P., Moreno, C. G., & Van Look, P. F. A. (2006). Sexual and reproductive health: A matter of life and death. *Lancet, 368*(9547), 1595–1607.

Griswold v. Connecticut, 381 U.S. 479 (1965).

Harris v. McRae, 448 U.S. 297 (1980).

Henshaw, S. K., Joyce, T. J., Dennis, A., Finer, L. B., & Blanchard, K. (2009). *Restrictions on Medicaid funding for abortions: A literature review.* New York, NY: Guttmacher Institute.

Hill, B. J. (2009). Reproductive rights as health care rights. *Columbia Journal of Gender and Law, 18*(2), 501–549.

Institute of Medicine. (2011). *Clinical preventive services for women: Closing the gap.* Washington, DC: National Academies Press.

Maher v. Roe, 432 U.S. 464 (1977).

Mason Meier, B., & Labbok, M. (2010). From the bottle to the grave: Realizing a human right to breastfeeding through global health policy. *Case Western Reserve Law Review, 60*(3), 1073–1142.

The Opportunity Agenda. (2010). *Meta-analysis of public opinion research on reproductive justice.* New York, NY: Author.

Planned Parenthood of Southeastern Pennsylvania v. Casey, 505 U.S. 833 (1992).

Polling Report. (2011). *Abortion and birth control.* Retrieved from http://www.pollingreport.com/abortion.htm

Roe v. Wade, 410 U.S. 113 (1973).

Singh, S., Darroch, J., Ashford, L., & Vlassoff, M. (2009). *Adding it up: The costs and benefits of investing in family planning and maternal and newborn health.* New York, NY: Guttmacher.

Soohoo, C., Albisa, C., & Davis, M. (Eds.). (2009). *Bringing human rights home.* Westport, CT: Praeger.

Soohoo, C., & Goldberg, J. (2010). The full realization of our rights: The right to health in state constitutions. *Case Western Reserve Law Review, 60*(3), 997–1072.

Title X, Public Health Service Act of 1970, Pub. L. No. 91–572, 42 U.S.C. § 300 to § 300a-6 (1970).

United Nations Population Fund. (1994). *Report of the international conference on population and development*, Cairo, September 5–13, 1994. A/CONF.171/13/Rev.1

World Health Organization. (2007). *Unsafe abortion—Global and regional estimates of the incidence of unsafe abortion and associated mortality in 2003*. Geneva, Switzerland: Author.

B. Jessie Hill

COUNTERPOINT

Although women have a right to access reproductive health services when they are paying for them with their own funds, they are not entitled to government-funded services. First, it has long been established that the U.S. Constitution protects individuals only against interference with their liberty; except in very limited circumstances, it does not affirmatively require the government to pay for or to provide access to any health service. Decisions about the allocation of scarce funds generally must be left to the discretion of legislators, not made by federal judges as a matter of constitutional law. International human rights law, which is not limited in this way, is therefore irrelevant to establishing the contours of Americans' fundamental rights.

In addition, reproductive health services are controversial. Using taxpayer money to pay for them arguably violates the conscience of taxpayers. Indeed, polls indicate that a majority of Americans oppose taxpayer funding for abortion. Because funds paid to an entity that provides abortions, such as Planned Parenthood, cannot be easily separated from funds used for other reproductive health services, it is no answer to this objection to argue that taxpayer money should be provided to such organizations to pay for some reproductive health services, but not others.

U.S. CONSTITUTIONAL LIMITS: ABORTION AND CONTRACEPTION

Though the Constitution protects the right to make family planning decisions, including the use of contraception and abortion, there is no constitutional right to receive affirmative, financial government support for those services. The legal precedent is clear that the rights to choose abortion and contraception do not entail a right to the help of the state in accessing or affording them. In addition, international human rights law does not require a different result.

When the U.S. Supreme Court decided, in 1973, that the Constitution protected the right to choose abortion, it attempted to settle an issue that had been highly controversial in U.S. politics. Yet, by many accounts, *Roe v. Wade* only further stoked the controversy over reproductive rights, more deeply entrenched advocates on both sides of the issue, and generated a severe backlash that began shortly after the Supreme Court's decision and continues to this day. Thus, most polls today show Americans to be divided roughly evenly between the pro-choice and pro-life positions. According to Greenhouse and Siegel, however, a Gallup poll from 1972 indicated that prior to *Roe v. Wade*, a clear majority—64 percent of Americans—supported the liberalization of abortion laws.

Following on the heels of cases like *Griswold v. Connecticut* (1965) and *Eisenstadt v. Baird* (1972), which prevented states from making contraceptives illegal, *Roe v. Wade* decided that states could not prohibit, or even substantially limit, abortion before a certain point in the pregnancy. Although the Court designated abortion and contraception to be fundamental rights, it did not hold that states had to affirmatively provide access to those services or subsidize them for persons who otherwise could not afford them. And, indeed, in the wake of *Roe v. Wade*, several states quickly moved to limit the use of Medicaid funds, providing that they could be expended only to reimburse physicians for "therapeutic" abortions—abortions performed for medical reasons. In 1976 the federal government passed the Hyde Amendment, a budgetary act that, in its original form, prohibited the use of federal Medicaid funds to pay for any abortions except when necessary to save the life of the woman. A version of the Hyde Amendment has been in effect ever since. In its current form, the amendment also allows payment for abortions in cases of rape or incest, but it limits life-saving abortions to those cases where the woman's life is endangered by a physical ailment or condition, thereby excluding any mental health conditions. An executive order issued by President Barack Obama in 2010 affirms that the Hyde Amendment still applies under the new health care reform law, the Patient Protection and Affordable Care Act (ACA).

Although pro-choice advocates had challenged both state and federal restrictions on abortion funding very early on, the Supreme Court turned them away in cases such as *Harris v. McRae* (1980) and *Maher v. Roe* (1977). The Court made it clear that the prohibitions on abortion funding did not violate a woman's right to choose an abortion, the right to equal protection of the laws, or the constitutionally required separation of church and state. These decisions left the government free to make a policy choice as to whether to fund abortions, and under what circumstances.

In *Maher v. Roe,* the Supreme Court explained why the government's refusal to fund abortions does not violate a woman's right to choose abortion. The refusal to fund, the Court explained, "places no obstacles absolute or otherwise in the pregnant woman's path to an abortion" (1977, p. 474). Thus, the Court asserted, even in the absence of government funding, a poor woman seeking an abortion remains in the same position as before the restriction was enacted—that is, in need of private funds to pay for her abortion. Even if the state is in some sense favoring childbirth over abortion when it pays for the former but not the latter, thereby influencing the woman's choice, it has not restricted abortion or created any new obstacle to a woman's access. In other words, the state has an obligation under the Constitution not to interfere directly with a woman's choice to seek an abortion, but it has no obligation to make abortion accessible to her. That she cannot afford an abortion, the Court explained in *Maher v. Roe,* is not the state's fault, and the state has no constitutional responsibility to provide her with one free of charge. The same reasoning applies to the state's decision whether to fund contraception and other reproductive health services.

THE DISTINCTION BETWEEN POSITIVE AND NEGATIVE RIGHTS AND THE RELEVANCE OF INTERNATIONAL HUMAN RIGHTS LAW

The Supreme Court's decision in *Maher v. Roe* was not based on novel logic; instead, it drew on the long-standing distinction between "positive" and "negative" rights. It is widely understood that the U.S. Constitution generally protects only negative rights, which may be defined as rights *against* government intrusions on individual liberty. These rights can be contrasted with positive rights, which may be defined as rights *to* something, such as a government-subsidized benefit or other affirmative governmental support. For example, the First Amendment prevents the government from interfering with individuals' ability to speak freely, but it does not require the government to provide paper and pens, printing presses, or Internet access to those who cannot afford such things, even if they are necessary to self-expression. Likewise, Americans have the right to practice their religion freely, but the government is not required to support that right by purchasing mezuzahs or Bibles for indigent individuals. Thus, although states and the federal government subsidize a wide array of reproductive health services for indigent women—including contraception, screening, counseling, prenatal care, and hospital services related to childbirth—they do so based on a judgment that it is a wise policy choice, not because the Constitution mandates it.

Although some international human rights instruments declare that governments are obligated to enforce positive rights by taking affirmative measures to provide access and funding for certain basic human necessities to those who cannot afford them, there is no warrant for extending this approach to U.S. law. The American understanding of constitutional rights is based on the view that classical liberalism requires a limited government that stays out of people's way, except in order to protect them from harm. This understanding finds partial expression in the U.S. constitutional doctrine of state action, which holds that the government must engage in an action in order for the Constitution to apply; the Constitution generally does not apply when the government fails to act or when harm arises from the conduct of private individuals. The liberal view embodied in U.S. constitutional law thus generally understands individuals to have negative rights against certain kinds of government action, but not positive entitlements to government action or government removal of privately imposed barriers to the exercise of constitutional rights.

Several additional considerations support the distinction between negative and positive rights in U.S. constitutional law. Negative rights are more easily enforceable by courts than are positive rights, which may be vague in terms of how much and what kind of support they actually require from the government. For example, recognizing a constitutional right to health would raise questions about how much health care an individual is entitled to receive; whether the government must pay for every physician-recommended treatment, no matter how costly; and whether there is a bare minimum of health care necessary for survival—and if so, how the court should decide what that bare minimum includes. Moreover, because enforcement of an entitlement to something such as health care will undoubtedly have major budgetary implications, conventional wisdom holds that such decisions are best handled by the legislative branch, which is accountable to the people through the democratic process and which is already charged with the task of balancing competing priorities and making judgments about which services are to be publicly funded and how they are to be provided. Making such an entitlement a matter of constitutional law would empower courts to trump well-considered legislative decisions about the expenditure of resources and place those decisions instead in the hands of often unelected, largely unaccountable judges.

In some South American countries, such as Colombia and Brazil, the courts have recognized a positive right to health. Yet some commentators have suggested that the resulting flood of individual claimants seeking payment for expensive drugs and medical interventions has resulted in severe budgetary problems and a greater degree of inequality in access to health care than existed before. For example, Ferraz suggests that in Brazil, administrative chaos has resulted, as public health agencies are required to shift resources and priorities constantly in response to court orders. At the same time, because most individual claimants do not come from the poorest ranks of society but rather from the middle class, enforcement of the right to health does not serve the goal of health equity and may even aggravate existing inequalities.

Three final points about the applicability of international human rights norms are worth considering. First, the United States is not a signatory to any international treaty that enacts a positive right to health, such as the International Covenant on Economic, Social, and Cultural Rights, nor has it signed onto the Convention on the Elimination of All Forms of Discrimination Against Women, with its expansive language regarding gender equality and government-provided access to health care. Although the United States voted to adopt the Universal Declaration of Human Rights, which aspires to adequate health care for all, that document does not itself create any legally binding duties. Second, the U.S. Supreme Court has rarely looked beyond American law and legal precedent to decide the scope of U.S. constitutional rights; and those rare and discrete cases in which it has done so have been highly controversial. Finally, human rights norms protect the right of conscience just as much as they protect other rights, like the right to health. As will be discussed at greater length below, taxpayer funding for controversial reproductive health services may violate individual taxpayers' conscience.

CONSCIENTIOUS LIMITS ON TAXPAYER SUPPORT FOR CONTROVERSIAL REPRODUCTIVE HEALTH SERVICES

One of the most salient areas of differing religious and conscientious beliefs involves the availability of reproductive health services—especially abortion, but also, to some extent, contraception and sterilization. Fortunately, U.S. law has long respected individuals' rights of conscience. By providing protections for individuals who do not wish to participate in controversial medical procedures, numerous laws recognize the harm to individuals' dignity and conscience that arises from being forced to assist in conduct that they find to be morally repugnant, even if that conduct is legal. Thus, the law has long protected health care providers against having to assist in procedures to which they object. Given the division of opinion among Americans over those same procedures, moreover, it follows that they should not be forced to assist in them by paying for them with tax dollars.

THE IMPORTANCE OF INDIVIDUAL CONSCIENCE IN AMERICAN LAW

The United States has a long tradition of protecting conscience. Of course, the importance of religious freedom to the country's history and founding is undeniable: One of the primary reasons why the first colonists fled England and came to America was to practice their religion free from prosecution. The right to religious freedom was quickly enshrined in the First Amendment to the U.S. Constitution. For these reasons, the right to freedom of religion and belief is sometimes referred to as "the first freedom."

There is broad acceptance of the view that to legally compel a medical provider to extend a service, such as abortion, would constitute a violation of her conscience and her right to morally object to that service. Though a requirement to do so may not technically violate the constitutional protections for religious freedom, it may in fact violate other constitutional rights, such as the constitutional right to privacy and autonomy in personal decision making—the same rights protected by *Roe v. Wade*.

Due to the consensus that it is inappropriate to force individual providers to engage in practices to which they are morally opposed, federal law currently contains numerous protections for individual conscience in the reproductive health care arena. Some provisions, for example, clarify that no health care professional can be forced to perform an abortion or threatened with sanctions for refusing to do so. The first laws of this kind, called the Church Amendments, were passed in the 1970s in response to *Roe* and protect health care personnel against being coerced to perform or assist in abortions or sterilizations. In addition, the Church Amendments protect individuals involved in any program funded by the federal Department of Health and Human Services from having to participate in *any* "health service program or research activity" that is contrary to their moral or religious convictions (Church Amendment § 300a–7[d]). This protection is broad enough to include not just abortion but also contraception, sterilization, and many other forms of health care.

THE PUBLIC CONTROVERSY OVER REPRODUCTIVE HEALTH SERVICES

If U.S. law recognizes the right of individual doctors, nurses, and health care workers to avoid assisting in morally objectionable procedures, it should also recognize the conscientious rights of large numbers of taxpayers in this context. Because so many individual taxpayers object to the provision of certain reproductive health services, they should be protected against having to assist in those services through the provision of subsidies. Although each taxpayer's individual contribution may be miniscule in the overall scheme, the injury to conscience exists nonetheless. The only way to avoid that injury is to decline to subsidize highly divisive services.

Congress has already recognized taxpayers' right of conscience to some extent through bans on public funding for abortions. This protection is provided not only by the Hyde Amendment but also by a federal ban on abortion funding for military personnel and their dependents, federal employees and their dependents, and women in federal prisons, except in extremely limited circumstances. Additionally, if a female prisoner can procure an abortion with her own funds, the federal government may expend funds to provide her with an escort, but individual federal workers are entitled to refuse for conscientious reasons to serve in that capacity.

Similarly, the ACA forbids discrimination by federally funded entities against health care providers or facilities based on their refusal to perform or assist in abortions and assisted suicide. In addition, states may prohibit plans that participate in state-sponsored insurance exchanges from covering abortion services. If those plans do cover elective abortion, they must require that the insured individuals pay for them separately, so that no public subsidies are used for that purpose.

Some reproductive health services are extremely controversial in U.S. society. Polls reveal severely divided opinions over the morality of abortion, with a majority of Americans currently stating that they believe abortion is immoral. A 2011 Gallup poll indicates that 49 percent of Americans identify as "pro-choice," while 45 percent are "pro-life." A year earlier, the same survey found 45 percent of Americans to be pro-choice and 47 percent pro-life. Though a majority of Americans support public funding for organizations such as Planned Parenthood, which provides reproductive health care services, a substantial minority (34 percent) favors eliminating that funding. Moreover, even pro-choice individuals may personally find abortion to be morally repugnant. In a 2010 Gallup poll, 50 percent of respondents said abortion was generally morally wrong, and only 38 percent said it was morally acceptable. The margin in 2009 was 56 percent saying abortion was morally wrong to only 36 percent who found it morally acceptable. It is reasonable to assume, then, that some or even many citizens who are pro-choice but who are personally morally opposed to abortion may believe that women should be legally permitted to choose abortion but that they themselves should not have to fund abortions through their tax money. Indeed, when asked directly whether the government should fund abortion for women who cannot afford it, 61 percent of respondents gave an unequivocal "no."

In light of such profound disagreement within a society, many argue that using taxpayers' money to pay for reproductive health care services violates their conscience. Allowing women to access those services with their own resources but declining to pay for them with taxpayer funds is a sensible compromise. It recognizes many people's belief that providing a financial subsidy, however small, for a morally repugnant service is a form of assisting in that service. The compromise of allowing those services to occur but refusing to fund them therefore demonstrates the country's commitment to protecting individual taxpayer conscience. This argument carries particular weight in the case of services that are not, strictly speaking, driven by medical necessity—such as elective abortion or emergency contraception. It is much harder to justify public subsidy of services that do not alleviate illness or injury, but rather reflect personal choices based on social, economic, and other factors. Especially in light of the fact that many taxpayers oppose such interventions based on deeply held religious beliefs, one might argue that the harm caused by this violation of conscience outweighs the benefit to the individual who wishes to choose an abortion for nontherapeutic reasons.

Opponents of public funding also point out that avoiding taxpayer support for such controversial services is the best way to respect the diversity of views on the issue. If taxpayers are forced to pay for services such as abortion and contraception, their consciences are tarnished. If the government declines to use taxpayer funds to support those services, however, no one's conscience is harmed. No one is coerced, and no woman is prevented from accessing the services she needs or desires. Indeed, one empirical study by Haas-Wilson even found that Medicaid funding restrictions have no measurable impact on abortion rates or birthrates (perhaps because of the availability of private sources of funds to pay for the service). Thus, individuals who want to use abortion or emergency contraception may still pay for those services with their own funds. Physicians may still provide them. And citizens are free to support the provision of those services to others who cannot pay, for example by making private donations to Planned Parenthood. Indeed, those contributions will, in most cases, even be tax-deductible. But individuals are not entitled to force the government to use the taxes of those who disagree with them to support such divisive services. Thus, U.S. politics and the U.S. Constitution have struck an eminently sensible balance that respects the ideological and religious differences within a diverse polity.

A decision not to fund reproductive health services is, moreover, a reasonable response to the scientific uncertainty about the mechanism of contraceptive drugs. Many contraceptive drugs and devices, such as intrauterine devices (IUDs) and emergency contraception (the so-called morning-after pill) have the effect of preventing a pregnancy from continuing after fertilization but before the fertilized ovum implants in the uterus. Moreover, though enormous uncertainty remains, recent scientific research has indicated that even regular birth control pills (including combined oral contraceptives, or COCs, and progestin-only pills, or POPs) may work, in some indeterminate number of cases, by preventing implantation of a fertilized egg rather than by preventing fertilization. This is troubling because, although most scientific sources consider pregnancy to begin with implantation, some people hold, often according to their religious beliefs, that life begins at conception—that is, at fertilization. For adherents to the conception view of personhood, such as many Catholics, contraceptive methods that prevent implantation are equivalent to abortion. Thus, although a large majority of the population is morally untroubled by the use of contraceptives, given the existing scientific uncertainty and differing beliefs among Americans, one might argue that the government should refrain from funding drugs and procedures that may turn out to induce abortions.

Finally, proponents of public funding for reproductive health care tend to ignore the fact that money is fungible. Although it is true that organizations such as Planned Parenthood provide a wide range of services, including many non-controversial ones such as screening for sexually transmitted infections and cervical cancers, they also provide abortions. The money that is used to support facilities, personnel, and general overhead for noncontroversial services cannot easily be segregated from funds used to support more controversial services. Thus, the conscientious objections of individual taxpayers cannot be sidelined by the fact that, from a public health perspective, the funding of some services is relatively uncontroversial and desirable.

CONCLUSION

Every government must prioritize the use of limited budget funds. Arguments can be made to support virtually any kind of investment. When a particular use of funds is highly controversial within a society, however, the government should not allocate taxpayers' money to it. By avoiding the funding of reproductive health services, the government will avoid violating the conscience of millions of taxpayers by forcing them to pay for, and thereby assist in, a procedure they find morally repugnant.

REFERENCES AND FURTHER READING

Boonstra, H. S. (2007). The heart of the matter: Public funding of abortion for poor women in the United States. *Guttmacher Policy Review, 10*(1), 12–16.

Church Amendment to the Health Programs Extension Act of 1973, Pub. L. No. 93–45, 42 U.S.C s. 300a-7 (1973).

Eisenstadt v. Baird, 405 U.S. 438 (1972).

Feder, J. (2005). The history and effect of abortion conscience clause laws. *CRS Report for Congress, RS21428,* 1–5.

Ferraz, O. (2010). The right to health in the courts of Brazil: Worsening health inequities? *Health and Human Rights: An International Journal, 11*(2), 33–45.

Greenhouse, L., & Siegel, R. B. (2011). Before (and after) *Roe v. Wade:* New questions about backlash. *Yale Law Journal, 128,* 2028–2087.

Griswold v. Connecticut, 381 U.S. 479 (1965).

Haas-Wilson, D. (1997). Women's reproductive choices: The impact of Medicaid funding restrictions. *Family Planning Perspectives, 29*(5), 228–233.

Harris v. McRae, 448 U.S. 297 (1980).

Hyde Amendment, Pub. L. No. 111–8, H.R. 1105 (1976).

Kaiser Family Foundation. (2010). *Focus on health reform: Access to abortion coverage and health reform.* Retrieved from http://www .kff.org/healthreform/upload/8021.pdf

Larimore, W. L., & Stanford, J. B. (2000). Postfertilization effects of oral contraceptives and their relationship to informed consent. *Archives of Family Medicine, 9*(2), 126–133.

Maher v. Roe, 432 U.S. S.Ct. 464 (1977).

Planned Parenthood of Southeastern Pennsylvania v. Casey, 505 U.S. S.Ct. 833 (1992).

The Polling Report. (2011). *Abortion and birth control.* Retrieved from http://www.pollingreport.com/abortion.htm

Rienzi, M. L. (2011). *The constitutional right to refuse: Roe, Casey, and the fourteenth amendment rights of healthcare providers.* Retrieved from http://papers.ssrn.com/s013/papers.cfm?abstract_id=1749788

Roe v. Wade, 410 U.S. 113 (1973).

Sullivan, D. M. (2006). The oral contraceptive as abortifacient: An analysis of the evidence. *Perspectives on Science and Christian Faith, 58*(3), 189–195.

B. Jessie Hill

Reforming Medical Malpractice Liability

POINT: The fear of medical malpractice causes health care providers to practice defensive medicine, leading to inappropriate health care and higher health care costs. Reform of the malpractice system is essential to providing affordable health care to all.

Barry R. Furrow, The Earle Mack School of Law, Drexel University

COUNTERPOINT: Malpractice claims play only a small role in increasing health care costs. Malpractice suits are based on real injuries, and the volume of patient injuries in U.S. health care is increasing. The real malpractice problem is that not enough suits are brought to create pressure on hospitals and physicians to solve the current epidemic of patient injuries.

Barry R. Furrow, The Earle Mack School of Law, Drexel University

Introduction

Medical malpractice litigation has long been one of the most contentious features of the U.S. health care system. Many health care providers and other critics of medical malpractice law charge that it raises the cost of health care while undermining access and quality. Opponents counter that malpractice litigation is necessary to deter poor care and to compensate the victims of medical negligence. This chapter will examine both perspectives.

Under current law, patients who are injured as a result of a provider's negligence—generally understood to mean a provider's failure to practice as a reasonably competent member of that provider's profession—may bring a civil suit against that provider. In theory, the threat of such suits deters negligent behavior by providers and financially compensates patients for their resulting medical costs, lost wages, and pain and suffering. As will be discussed in this chapter by Barry Furrow, it is highly debatable whether the current system actually achieves these objectives and whether the costs associated with malpractice liability contribute significantly to the nation's overall health expenditures.

In the Point section, Furrow argues that malpractice suits do a bad job of identifying provider negligence and compensating injured plaintiffs. Indeed, most injured patients are never compensated. On the other hand, many providers who were not negligent nevertheless face medical malpractice suits. In addition, the fear of liability may lead providers to order unnecessary tests and procedures, in other words to engage in what is known as "defensive medicine." This may drive up health care costs, making it harder for patients to afford health care. The Point advocates a series of reforms designed to make litigation less expensive and better able to achieve the goals of the malpractice system, including replacing the civil jury system with alternative dispute-resolution practices and shifting the focus of liability from the providers to institutions, such as hospitals.

In the Counterpoint, Furrow argues that litigation is surprisingly effective in identifying and preventing adverse events and compensating injured patients. Moreover, the direct and indirect costs associated with medical malpractice litigation are actually quite low. Escalations in health care costs and malpractice premiums are due primarily to other factors, including, in the case of health care costs, perverse incentives created by payment systems, and in the case of malpractice premiums, fluctuations in investment markets. Although some reforms to the malpractice system may be advisable, these should be focused on improving patient safety, not simply deterring litigation. Indeed the threat of litigation, Furrow argues, may be necessary to prod health care providers to take patient safety seriously.

Traditionally, malpractice law has been state law. Over the last several decades, many states have enacted numerous malpractice reforms. For example, many have shortened the statute of limitations for malpractice claims. As Furrow notes, states have also imposed a variety of other procedural requirements on plaintiffs wishing to sue. They have also replaced joint and several liability with the so-called fair share rule. Joint and several liability allows the plaintiff to recover all damages from each defendant, even if other defendants are also or even more responsible for an injury. In contrast, the fair share rule limits a defendant's liability to the percentage of his or her own responsibility for the injury. Perhaps most importantly, many states have imposed caps on noneconomic damages. In some states, these caps have been found to violate the state constitution; in other states, they have been upheld.

Although medical malpractice liability reform is typically a state issue, some policymakers believe that reform is needed on a national level. Republicans in particular have long argued that significant reforms to the malpractice system, including damage caps, are critical to holding down the high cost of health care. Reflecting that view, in January 2011, Representatives Phil Gingrey (R-GA), David Scott (D-GA), and Lamar Smith (R-TX) introduced into the House of Representatives the HEALTH Act (H.R. 5). This bill would essentially federalize malpractice reforms. It would impose a three-year statute of limitations for such cases, impose a national cap of $250,000 on all pain and suffering damages, and impose limitations on the award of punitive damages. It also would replace joint and several liability with the fair share rule and establish sliding-scale limits on contingency fees for lawyers. The Congressional Budget Office (CBO) estimates that the savings realized by H.R. 5 will result in a 0.5 percent reduction in national health care expenditures. Would you support passage of this bill? Is federal malpractice reform critical to reforming the health care system? Or should malpractice law be left to the states?

Democrats, for the most part, believe that malpractice liability is not a major cause of health care costs and that malpractice reform is not critical to reforming the health care system. Reflecting that perspective, the Patient Protection and Affordable Care Act (ACA), signed by President Barack Obama in 2010, does little to reform the malpractice system. It does, however, contain two provisions related to medical malpractice liability. One authorizes states to engage in malpractice demonstrations; however, some analysts believe the funding levels are too low to allow states to fund alternative compensation systems. The second provision extends federal malpractice protections under the Federal Tort Claims Act to nonmedical personnel in free clinics. Many other provisions in the ACA are designed to improve the quality of care (e.g., by creating incentives for more coordinated care, and funding research on the effectiveness of medical treatments), but they do not address malpractice liability per se. Does this absence of broad malpractice reform measures in the ACA undermine that law's potential to reform the health care system? Or were the ACA's drafters correct in believing that malpractice reform is not a central imperative of health care reform?

As Furrow shows, the debate about malpractice reform arises in large part because of the high number of medical injuries in the United States. The release of *To Err Is Human* by the Institute of Medicine in 1999 gave rise to a new patient safety movement, which emphasizes greater focus on patient safety and injury. Many supporters of that movement believe that malpractice liability conflicts with the movement's goals. For example, the patient safety movement favors disclosure of injuries as a means to promote safety, but many providers contend that they fear disclosing injuries due to the risk of litigation. Patient safety advocates also seek a blame-free culture to promote safety; however, this runs counter to the liability system, which is adversarial. As Furrow points out, some researchers and policymakers suggest the current system places too much emphasis on punishing the provider and that reform should encourage disclosure and help promote education about medical errors.

As you read the chapter, think about the role that medical error plays in the U.S. health care system. Can the patient safety movement make a meaningful reduction in the number of errors? Would the type of malpractice reforms proposed in H.R. 5 abet the patient safety effort? Or would a reduced threat of liability undermine providers' incentive to participate in the patient safety effort? Finally, if significant limitations are imposed on malpractice litigation, what happens to the goal of compensating those who are injured due to provider negligence? Would broader access to health insurance solve part of that problem?

POINT

The world of modern medicine is increasingly risky. The famous Institute of Medicine report *To Err Is Human* concluded that almost 100,000 patient deaths annually were due to medical errors, and the number may be far higher (Kohn et al., 1999). One recent study concluded that patients suffer adverse events in one third of all admissions, many life-threatening or causing severe injuries (Classen et al., 2011).

Medical progress has been one of the driving forces of expanded tort liability, by increasing the risk of harm as the benefits of treatment have also expanded. Doctors can now diagnose and treat cancer, keep premature infants alive, and treat elderly patients who, two decades ago, would not have survived surgery. At the same time, health care cost inflation has naturally increased the size of malpractice jury awards as medical damages have increased far more rapidly than wages. Industrialization in the health care industry has also expanded liability, as more health care is delivered in hospitals, outpatient facilities, and group practices. Although malpractice crises historically have been driven by perceived litigation risks to physicians, all of the institutional players in today's health care system are now exposed to litigation risks.

Medical malpractice suits are a response to these changes. In the United States, health care oversight of patient safety issues is handled by a mixture of public law (such as the federal Medicare program) and private law (civil litigation over patient injuries), along with private organizations—such as the *National Quality Forum*—that disseminate voluntary standards, checklists and other ideas for improvement. Medical malpractice litigation is typically brought in state courts under state law, initiated by individuals seeking compensation for negligent treatment that caused them injury. Injured plaintiffs can recover both economic damages (lost earnings and cost of subsequent medical treatment) and noneconomic damages (pain and suffering). In theory, the possibility of having to compensate injured plaintiffs deters physicians and hospitals from providing negligent treatment and promotes a more intense focus on improving patient safety in hospitals.

Critics charge malpractice suits of being an inefficient and destructive approach to the risks of modern medicine. They allege that such suits occur unpredictably and the costs to defendants can reach millions of dollars. Protection against the risks of a malpractice suit requires that providers carry malpractice insurance. Health care providers buy medical malpractice insurance to protect themselves from medical malpractice claims. Under the insurance contract, the insurance company agrees to accept financial responsibility for payment of any claims up to a specific level of coverage during a fixed period in return for a fee. The insurer investigates the claim and defends the health care provider. This insurance is sold primarily by commercial insurance companies.

Insurance is itself a major driver of the malpractice crises that have occurred periodically over the last few decades. Crises, like those in the 1970s and 1980s, are triggered by rapid increases in premiums for malpractice insurance purchased by doctors and other health care providers. Insurance carriers have gone bankrupt or dropped out of the malpractice market, while others raise their malpractice premiums precipitously to compensate for investment losses. With these rapid rate increases, physicians and hospitals feel the sudden pressure of rapid increases in their annual insurance costs. The most recent crisis in 1999 was precipitated by a sudden escalation in malpractice insurance premiums for most physicians and the limited availability of coverage in some states.

Malpractice suits suffer from a multitude of failings, and the litigation system needs further reforming. The civil jury process accounts for many of these systemic failures—it misses valid claims, while awarding other claims over-generously. An injured patient must find a lawyer willing to take his or her case. Many patient injuries caused by adverse events are relatively minor and therefore do not provide enough financial benefit to motivate a lawyer to accept the case. Malpractice cases are also complicated, requiring expensive expert testimony regarding the standard of medical care as well as the nature and extent of the patient's damages. Tort cases are brought before nonspecialty general civil trial courts, each of which view the case and the range of acceptable remedies in isolation. Such suits are therefore woefully inadequate to the task of compensating patients with real injuries.

Many physicians liken such lawsuits to random strikes of lightning, imposing damages on them for some harms but missing other harms entirely. The threat of being sued demoralizes physicians, driving them to practice defensive medicine or even to leave practice altogether.

Physicians are unlikely to work toward patient safety solutions for fear of being sued. Useful public information about such suits is often hard to come by because defendants are often willing to pay more for a confidential settlement, which means that other injured persons and other health care providers may not receive information about risks and injuries.

Finally, the costs of resolving disputes through the tort system are extremely high. Malpractice suits impose high costs on providers both in insurance premiums and anxiety; and high defensive medical and insurance premium costs end up being passed on to patients, payers, and taxpayers, raising the nation's overall health care bill.

THE CIVIL JURY PROCESS IS UNRELIABLE

Patients indeed do suffer injury from medical adverse events, particularly in hospitals where complex procedures are done. The term *adverse event* refers to injuries that result from medical care. Examples include pneumothorax from central venous catheter placement, anaphylaxis to penicillin, postoperative wound infection, and hospital-acquired delirium (or "sundowning") in elderly patients. An adverse event does not necessarily mean that error or negligence has occurred. Instead, it means only that an undesirable clinical outcome was suffered by a patient due to diagnosis or therapy, not from the patient's underlying disease process. In a malpractice suit, by contrast, the plaintiff must prove that the physician has been negligent; that is, that the physician has failed to follow the standard of care of other physicians in that particular medical specialty. Examples might include a cardiologist who neglected to follow a practice guideline for treating a blocked artery in a patient, or a surgeon who operated on the wrong organ.

The malpractice system fails to meet its goals, in part, because too few patients who suffer harm from adverse events get compensated. That most malpractice claims involve adverse events resulting in severe injury or death suggests that the vast majority of errors go undiscovered. Even when patients know that an adverse event has occurred, they are unlikely to actually file a claim. And, of those claims filed, many will be dropped for lack of evidence, or fail later at trial. Adverse events, after all, are often not caused by the negligence of a physician but may be purely accidental, or due to a unique patient vulnerability, or an undiscovered system error. When a case does go all the way to a trial and verdict, doctors win almost 75 percent of the time. Most valid claims go uncompensated and undeserving claims are often compensated. This failure of tort compensation to align with the intensity of provider error means that the medical malpractice system is a failed model, requiring more reforms and perhaps even replacement by a new administrative model, such as specialized health courts.

One of the reasons for this poor relationship between the merits of a claim and the awarding of compensation is that medical malpractice cases are too complicated for juries, who can be easily confused and are therefore often arbitrary in their awards. Medicine is in many cases an imprecise science, and there is often a lack of clear evidence as to what treatments will work or even what the precise diagnosis is. Given the complex variations in human beings and the difficulties inherent in diagnosing them, patients may suffer harm from health care, without any physician fault. Lay jurors, however, lack the capacity and training needed to evaluate complex medical treatment decisions. As a result, jury decisions are frequently inaccurate; studies have found that juries often do not faithfully perform their assigned task of applying the legal standard of care, frequently misunderstanding instructions, permitting a range of other factors to influence their decisions, and erring in their negligence determinations relative to what experts would decide. Medical malpractice cases also give juries too much leeway. Damages are hard to measure, particularly those related to pain and suffering. The biases of the jury can lead to large verdicts, with unreasonable amounts awarded for such imprecise injuries as "mental anguish." State tort reforms, including caps on noneconomic losses such as for pain and suffering, have helped to reduce the number of frivolous lawsuits and assign a reasonable limit to pain-and-suffering amounts. But they have not completely solved the problem of excessive jury verdicts.

MALPRACTICE SUITS IMPEDE ACCESS TO QUALITY CARE

Physicians are demoralized by the threat of suit, driving them to practice defensive medicine or even leave practice. Doctors feel unfairly singled out when they are sued, and suffer from anxiety and psychological distress as a result of the experience of being unfairly named a defendant. They also practice *defensive medicine,* the provision of inappropriate treatment to avoid being sued. Defensive medicine can also harm the quality of care. One study of physicians in Pennsylvania found that defensive medical practices were widespread among high-risk specialists in that state. Ninety percent reported defensive practices that ranged from ordering excess diagnostic tests, to prescribing more medications than needed, to recommending invasive procedures, such as biopsies, to confirm diagnoses.

Physicians who experience high levels of psychological anxiety may, in response, reduce patients' access to care. Obstetrics and breast cancer detection are two examples where women's health may suffer due to the reluctance of physicians to practice as a result of their concern about litigation. The result is a shortage of physicians in these areas, and without access to gynecologists and obstetricians, women may have to forego early diagnosis and possible detection of serious health problems. High malpractice insurance premiums may also drive physicians out of practice, further reducing patient access to necessary care. Indeed, malpractice suits and ever-rising insurance costs sometimes cause doctors to retire early, further reducing patients' access to necessary care and making it harder for patients to develop relationships with their physicians. Delays in detection of patient health problems are therefore more likely, increasing costs by postponing treatment until patients are sicker and past the point of early treatment and prevention. The U.S. health care system already faces a major shortage of medical professionals, and escalating costs of malpractice insurance and the stresses of being sued will only continue to shift physicians toward safer medical specialties. High premium costs also make it less likely that doctors will open small offices or clinics, thus reducing patients' access to primary care. Doctors who may want to provide free or discounted services are handcuffed by these insurance costs, particularly in lower-paid specialties such as primary care.

TORT LITIGATION UNDERMINES EFFORTS TO IMPROVE PATIENT SAFETY

Supporters claim that malpractice litigation deters poor-quality care, but the facts say otherwise. The failure of malpractice insurers to experience-rate doctors' medical malpractice premiums undermines its deterrent effect. If insurers raised their premium prices based on provider claims experience, those providers who create more patient risks would have to face either higher prices or changes to their practices.

Moreover, malpractice suits retard the development of effective patient-safety efforts. Medical malpractice litigation is often touted as a tool that incentivizes doctors to practice safer medicine. There are two problems with this argument. The first results from the nature of the medical malpractice liability insurance. Insurers typically treat practice specialties the same in designing their premiums for insurance, without making adjustments for the higher malpractice rates of a particular high-risk physician. As a result, though physicians in a specialty may all experience higher costs, the real malpractitioners do not pay more for creating higher risk.

A second problem arises from the fact that most patients injured as a result of negligence do not sue. Too few claims means that the incentives for improvement are too low, and even if these problems were solved it is not clear that either provider or consumer behavior would change. If lawsuits are perceived as largely random, providers will have little incentive to alter their behavior, except to practice defensively across the board at higher cost to patients.

Malpractice laws that place providers at risk for engaging in peer-review risk-management activities, such as root-cause analysis (a systematic analysis of why an adverse event has occurred), could have the perverse effect of detracting from broader patient-safety efforts. One recent study observed that "malpractice laws that place providers at risk for engaging in peer review risk-management activities, root-cause analysis, and the like, could have the perverse effect of detracting from broader patient safety efforts. In turn, that could increase the frequency of adverse events and preventable injuries and, indirectly, increase the volume of malpractice litigation itself" (Greenberg, Haviland, Ashwood, & Main, 2010). Major patient-safety activities require team efforts to assess hazards in hospitals through the collection of information about patient harms, and through constant safety audits. Why should a provider engage fully in such time-intensive activities if the discovery of such adverse events might cause her to be sued? If fear of a malpractice suit leads physicians to avoid safety initiatives, malpractice has created substantial barriers to changes that might reduce patient harm. This will increase the frequency of adverse events and preventable injuries and, indirectly, increase the volume of malpractice litigation itself.

MALPRACTICE LITIGATION IS COSTLY

Malpractice suits inflict high costs. These fall on physicians in the form of lost time, higher overhead costs for insurance, and the psychological pain of being sued. They also lead to higher health care costs to society, as defensive medical and insurance premium costs are passed on to patients and to payers.

Health care costs in the United States are high, the escalation in health care inflation creating large increases in health insurance premiums, subscriber co-payments and deductibles, and other costs. A significant percentage of these cost problems can be blamed on malpractice lawsuits. High jury verdicts have led to increases in the cost of medical malpractice insurance for physicians, with premiums for malpractice liability in some specialties rising above $200,000 a year. These costs, of course, have to be passed on to patients, causing high cost increases for everyone. The overall costs of health care are driven higher by the escalating costs of the adversarial litigation system.

Defensive medicine also pushes up the cost of care. An examination of Medicare hospital spending for patients who had been hospitalized for heart disease concluded that states that had enacted tort reforms had lower health care costs than did those that had not, the assumption being that, in those states, doctors were less likely to practice defensive medicine.

It has been estimated that the costs of defensive medicine range from $55 billion to $200 billion per year. Economists say that the tort liability system has increased physician health care output, largely as the result of increased provision of marginal care due to defensive practices such as unnecessary testing or referral to specialists. Doctors overtest and in some cases overtreat to avoid being sued, and this often unnecessary care raises the costs of health care generally. For example, Kessler and McClellan looked at the decrease in hospital expenditures for elderly patients with serious heart disease after tort reforms were implemented, and concluded that expenditures fell between 5 and 9 percent in response to the lowering of liability risks. Their conclusion as to the cost-effects of medical-practice litigation was that suits had raised hospital costs by 5 to 9 percent. A later study looked at all personal health costs, and concluded that medical liability concerns increased personal health care expenditures by $115 billion in 2004 ($124 billion in 2006 dollars).

Rising health care costs also leads to a decline in health insurance coverage. As the cost of care increases, insurance premiums also increase. A simple economic analysis suggests that, if premium growth exceeds income growth, fewer people can afford insurance. That means that the poor and the near-poor are at the greatest risk of becoming uninsured. Liability driven defensive medical practices therefore contribute to the growth of the uninsured in America.

The loss of insurance adds another cost to defensive medical practices. The uninsured have higher mortality rates due to a lack of access to quality health care. The Kaiser Commission Report on Medicaid and the Uninsured found that the uninsured receive "less preventative care, are diagnosed at more advanced disease states, and once diagnosed, tend to receive less therapeutic care" (Holohan, Cook, & Dubay, 2007). As a result of this lack of access, the uninsured are more likely to die prematurely due to untreated illnesses. Their work productivity suffers, and they have increased health-related work absences. McQuillan et al. conclude that "the increase in health expenditures due to liability concerns, therefore, has added 3.4 million Americans to the rolls of the uninsured" (McQuillan, Abramyam, & Archie, 2007). They further argue that 1,538 premature deaths each year can be blamed on liability effects. By adding the costs of premature deaths and lost productivity due to reduced access to health care from liability driven rising health care expenditures, they arrive at a figure of almost $39 billion.

The total of all this liability impact on health care costs generally can be as high as $191 billion. Even if the liability system has some benefits in terms of safety improvements and deterrence of negligent physician behavior, it is clear that the overall costs to the economy are far too high.

CONCLUSION

We are left with a compensation system that does not compensate and does not deter dangerous behavior. Given these flaws, it would be better to reform the system by eliminating jury trials, setting limits on damages, and making suits harder to bring. A range of reform ideas have been proposed. Serious reforms of tort ligation include alternative dispute resolution, provider early payment programs, and new administrative structures such as health courts or workers' compensation processes.

The simplest reform, though, would be to leave the current litigation process in place, but to create what is called "enterprise liability," which moves the locus of liability from physicians to hospitals and other institutions. The development of tort doctrines, such as corporate negligence, has been valuable in moving the law in this direction, providing powerful financial incentives to push hospital practices toward convergence on validated standards of care. The expansion of this form of liability would spur further litigation-avoidance activities, such as offices of patient safety and quality management, patient-safety compliance officers, and a new emphasis on problem-solving behavior in complex health care settings like hospitals. A renewed internal focus on adverse events driven by the filing of more tort claims, coupled with the patient-safety initiatives and money provided by the ACA will increase pressure to remake obtuse institutions like hospitals. It would also relieve physicians of their burden as the primary target of malpractice litigation, recognizing that it is often the system that created the potential for errors in hospitals.

A second category of reforms include *alternative dispute resolution* (ADR), including arbitration in which a decision is made not by a jury but rather by an arbitrator using documentary evidence in an expedited forum. Such decisions can be overturned only if corruption, fraud, or undue influence is shown or new evidence unavailable at the ADR proceeding is presented. Mediation, however, is more commonly used as an alternative to litigation; it is often offered to patients entering the hospital as an option to litigation if they experience a bad outcome. The parties can agree quickly on a fair sum without the expense of a jury trial, and the plaintiff can receive money quickly to cover her injury costs.

Provider-based early payment approaches have also been proposed, whereby providers would voluntarily agree to identify and promptly compensate patients for avoidable injuries. Under most such proposals, damages would be limited. When the adverse outcome occurred, the patient or provider would file a claim with the insurer, which would decide whether the injury was covered. If so, it would make prompt payment. Disputes would be resolved through the courts or arbitration. The plan as proposed would experience-rate insurance premiums paid by providers, in order to create incentives for the providers to improve the quality of care, thereby reducing their exposure for the adverse outcomes listed. Provider experience under the plan would also be used to strengthen peer review within hospitals.

Major administrative reforms have also been proposed, reducing the role of malpractice litigation by providing an alternative way to compensate patients. A state system loosely based on the workers' compensation model would give physicians and hospitals immunity from torts in exchange for mandatory participation in a state-sponsored, administrative system established to provide compensation to patients who have suffered avoidable injuries. This system has been put into place for obstetric accidents in Virginia, but other states have not chosen to adopt such reforms

Health courts are the latest and most-elaborate reform proposal. Such courts promise to balance the need for patient compensation with the need to improve the accountability and the efficiency of the current liability system. They would use specially trained judges and an avoidability standard. Compensation will be based on expert interpretations of the scientific literature; fast-track decision aids based on precedent will speed up the process, and compensation awards will be based on *ex-ante* guidelines. In the health-court model, providers inform patients at the time of disclosure of an injury that patients can file a compensation claim with the provider or its insurer. A panel of experts, aided by decision guidelines, determines whether the injury was avoidable. That is, would the injury ordinarily have occurred if the best specialist—or an optimal health care system—had been provided? For avoidable injuries, the institution offers full compensation for economic losses plus a scheduled amount for pain and suffering based on injury severity. A voluntary model would allow a patient to reject the compensation offer and file a lawsuit, unless the patient had waived this right as a condition of receiving care.

The current liability system is deeply flawed and reforms are desperately needed to relieve physicians and other providers of unnecessary stress, high costs, and the crippling anxiety that keeps them from engaging in necessary patient-safety initiatives. Hospital-based reforms make the most sense and are the easiest to implement. Here a combination of early offers of payment to patients who have suffered injury, coupled with an efficient mediation system that allows for quick development of the facts and discussion of how to settle the patient's claim, would provide a dramatic improvement in compensation for patients while removing stress from individual physicians and moving the focus to health care systems, which are better equipped to implement safety changes.

REFERENCES AND FURTHER READING

American Tort Reform Association. (2004). *Frivolous lawsuits undermine healthcare system and hurt patients, according to new survey.* Retrieved from http://www.atra.org/show/7748

Biondi, R. S., & Gurevitch, A. (2003). The evidence is in: Noneconomic damage caps help reduce malpractice insurance premiums. *Contingencies, 30.* Retrieved from http://contingencies.org/novdec03/evidence.pdf

Classen, D. C., Resar, R., Griffin, F., Federico, F., Frankel, T., Kimmel, N., & James, B. C. (2011). "Global trigger tool" shows that adverse events in hospitals may be ten times greater than previously measured. *Health Affairs, 30*(4), 581.

Dauer, E. A., Marcus, L. J., & Payne, S. M. (2000). Prometheus and the litigators: A mediation odyssey. *Journal of Legal Medicine, 21*(2), 159–186.

Greenberg, M., Haviland, A. M., Ashwood, J. S., & Main, R. (2010). *Is better patient safety associated with less malpractice activity? Evidence from California.* Santa Monica, CA: RAND Corporation. Retrieved from http://www.rand.org/pubs/technical_reports/TR824.html

Hadley, J., & Holalan, J. (2004). *The cost of care for the uninsured: What do we spend, who pays, and what would full coverage add to medical spending?* Washington, DC: Henry J. Kaiser Family Foundation.

Holahan, J., Cook, A., & Dubay, L. (2007). *Characteristics of the uninsured: Who is eligible for public coverage and who needs help affording coverage?* Washington, DC: Henry J. Kaiser Foundation. Retrieved from http://www.kff.org/uninsured/upload/7613.pdf

Kessler, D. P., & McClellan, M. (1996). Do doctors practice defensive medicine? *Quarterly Journal of Economics, 111*(2), 353–390.

Kohn, L. T., Corrigan, J. M., & Donaldson, M. S. (Eds.). (1999). *To err is human: Building a safer health system.* Washington, DC: National Academy Press. Retrieved from http://www.iom.edu/Reports/1999/To-Err-is-Human-Building-A-Safer-Health-System.aspx

Lakin, S. B. (2003). *Medical malpractice insurance in Missouri: The current difficulties in perspective.* Jefferson City, MO: Missouri Department of Insurance. Retrieved from http://www.citizen.org/documents/Missouri%20Report%20from%20D.%20of%20Insurance%202-7-03.pdf

Marx, D. (2009). *Whack-a-mole: The price we pay for expecting perfection.* Plano, TX: By Your Side Studios.

McQuillan, L., Abramyam, H., & Archie, A. (2007). *Jackpot justice: The true cost of America's tort system.* San Francisco, CA: Pacific Research Institute.

Mello, M. M., Studdery, D. M., & Brennan, T. A. (2003). The leapfrog standards: ready to jump from marketplace to courtroom? *Health Affairs, 22*(2), 46–59.

Mello, M. M., Studdert, D. M., Kachalia, A. B., & Brennan, T. A. (2006). "Health courts" and accountability for patient safety. *Milbank Quarterly, 84*(3), 459–492.

Messerli, J. (2012). *A new frivolous lawsuit statute.* Retrieved from http://www.balancedpolitics.org/editorial-frivolous_lawsuits.htm

Rozovsky, F. A., & Woods, J. R. (Eds.). (2005). *The handbook of patient safety compliance: A practical guide for health care organizations.* San Francisco, CA: Jossey Bass.

Sick of Lawsuits. Retrieved from http://sickoflawsuits.org

Studdert, D. M., Mello, M. M., Sage, W. M., DesRoches, C. M., Peugh, J., Zapert, K., & Brennan, T. A. (2005). Defensive medicine among high-risk specialist physicians in a volatile malpractice environment. *The Journal of the American Medical Association, 293*(21), 2609–2617.

Tancredi, L. R. (1986). Designing a no–Fault alternative. *Law & Contemporary Problems, 49*(2), 277–286.

Tancredi, L. R., & Barondess, J. A. (1978). The problem of defensive medicine. *Science, 200*(4344), 879–882.

U.S. Congress, Office of Technology Assessment. (1993). *Impact of medical malpractice tort reform on malpractice costs* (OTA-BP-H-119). Washington, DC: Government Printing Office.

U.S. Department Health & Human Services. (n.d.). *Glossary.* Gaithersburg, MD: Agency for Healthcare Research and Quality. Retrieved from http://psnet.ahrq.gov/glossary.aspx

Barry R. Furrow

COUNTERPOINT

Malpractice suits respond to real patient injuries, and the frequency of adverse events in hospitals is increasing. Real tort reform requires improvements that allow more adverse events to be discovered and more suits to be filed, particularly against institutional providers like hospitals, to create pressure on hospitals and physicians to control the patient injury epidemic. Sensible reforms would improve patients' ability to sue for even small claims, creating wider access to lawsuits, so that those harmed by poor quality care will receive compensation and health care providers will have more motivation to pay serious attention to the quality of care they offer.

The civil jury process is quite accurate in determining physician negligence. Frivolous claims are rare in malpractice litigation. Some defensive medicine clearly occurs, but the magnitude is hard to prove in light of physician self-reporting, which overstates the level of defensive practices. Because the costs of treatment and testing are paid by insurance, physicians have little incentive not to overtest or overtreat. Physicians and other providers need the spur of liability to push for better patient-safety solutions. The patient-safety movement assumes that medical care exposes patients to a significant risk of adverse events, that these events are preventable and that a "system" perspective is needed to reengineer the health care delivery process. The goal of patient-safety efforts is to identify the causes of patient injury, whether errors or not; identify, design, test, and evaluate practices that eliminate systems-related risks and hazards that compromise patient safety; educate, disseminate, and implement best practices; and maintain vigilance in monitoring and evaluating threats to patient safety.

Physician resistance to patient-safety initiatives is caused by a variety of reasons, including provider resistance to change, and the relative lack of power of hospital administrators and patients to change medical practices. The risk of medical liability is only a small factor in creating such resistance. Finally, malpractice claims play only a small role in increasing health care costs. The costs of defensive medical practices and litigation have been overstated by special interest groups such as insurance companies. The rising costs of U.S. health care is primarily driven by a medical culture of overtreatment and reimbursement systems that pay too much.

Malpractice reform proposals can be evaluated by three tests. First, do they improve the operation of the tort system for compensating victims of medical injuries? Second, will the reforms create incentives for the reduction of medical error and resulting injury to patients? Third, are changes likely to encourage insurers to make malpractice insurance more available and affordable? It is clear that most current reform proposals fail to pass the first two tests. And reform measures that satisfy insurers typically have reduced the ability of injured patients to sue at all, or to recover as much as they might have absent reforms. Sensible reforms, in contrast, would improve patient ability to sue for even small claims, creating wider access to lawsuits, so that those harmed by poor-quality care will receive compensation and health care providers will be more motivated to pay serious attention to the quality of care they offer.

DANGEROUS CARE

The health care system is dangerous, producing high levels of adverse events that impact patients. The famous Institute of Medicine report *To Err Is Human* (Kohn et al., 1999) extrapolated from earlier closed-claim studies to predict almost 100,000 patient deaths annually due to medical errors. A recent study concluded that patients suffer adverse events in one third of all admissions (Classen et al., 2011). This extrapolation may, in fact, have seriously underestimated the incidence of injuries. Other recent studies have confirmed that adverse events occur at higher levels than previously thought.

Frivolous claims are rare in malpractice litigation. Most people with valid claims never file suit, often because they are unaware that their claims are, in fact, valid. Nor is it true that claims that are brought and then dropped before trial, or dismissed after suit is filed, are necessarily false or frivolous claims. It simply takes lawyers time to uncover the facts underlying an injury, which may turn out to be a pure accident and not a medical error of any kind.

The high volume of patient injury due to adverse events suggests that tort reform needs to find ways to discover such events and promote efficient compensation for even minor injuries. Yet the goal of most malpractice reforms is to reduce the total volume of litigation and the severity of the payouts, thereby driving lawyers away from medical malpractice litigation as a well-compensated specialty of law practice. Such reforms are designed to protect doctors from suits, reduce the size of verdicts, and ease insurance company uncertainty, with little regard to the harms suffered by patients. These measures seek to restrict the operation of the tort system in four ways: (1) affecting the filing of malpractice claims (requiring expert affidavits), (2) limiting the award recoverable by plaintiffs (caps on damages), (3) altering the plaintiff's burden of proof through changes in evidence rules and legal doctrine (i.e., abolishing the use of doctrines such as *res ipsa loquitur* that make it easier for plaintiffs to meet their burden of proof), and (4) changing the role of the courts by substituting an alternative forum (i.e., mandated mediation). Eleanor Kinney characterizes such measures as "first generation" reforms (Kinney, 1995).

A study of past tort reforms concludes that such traditional reforms have focused on liability costs, rather than attempting to improve the safety of health care delivery. The most powerful reform in actually reducing the size of malpractice awards has been a dollar limit, or cap, on awards. Caps may take the form of a limit on the amount of recovery of general damages, typically pain and suffering, or a maximum recoverable per case, including all damages, such as California's $250,000 on recovery for noneconomic damages, including pain and suffering. The goal of most malpractice reforms like caps on damages is to reduce the total volume of litigation and the severity of the payouts. Such reforms, as implemented, are defendant- and insurer-friendly, and deliberately ignore or obfuscate the costs to patient safety, reduce or eliminate any fair compensation to harmed patients, and reduce the level of litigation needed to police dangerous medicine. As such, tort reforms have been largely ineffective. More recent patient-safety approaches that encourage innovation in health care risk-reduction may foreshadow a liability system that, in Kachalia and Mello's (2011) words, "fosters, rather than obstructs, progress toward safe and high-quality healthcare."

THE JURY SYSTEM

The jury system is quite accurate in determining physician negligence and allows for localized democratic decision making on medical mistakes. Jury decision making in medical liability cases gives juries a voice and provides ordinary people with an opportunity to speak out in specific cases about the problems with technological, industrialized medicine. Juries are, in fact, very competent decision makers in complex medical cases, in most cases matching the performance of expert panels of physicians. Juries function well in medical liability cases when it comes to evaluating medical errors and harm. Having studied jury verdicts in medical malpractice cases, Neil Vidmar (2009) concluded that "widely held views of irresponsible and incompetent juries held by doctors and by the general public do not stand up to empirical evidence. This is not to say that every jury verdict is correct, but when verdicts for plaintiffs are compared against verdicts for doctors and against alternative criteria, such as ratings by medical professionals and decisions by legal professionals, juries come out reasonably well."

Some changes in damage rules may improve the accuracy and consistency of the fact-finding process. For example, the jury could be given examples of past jury awards in similar cases, or even a schedule of damages to guide their decision making. Generally, however, the American jury process is unique in its ability to apply lay decision making to complex facts and reach an accurate decision.

DEFENSIVE MEDICINE?

Because it is usually self-reported by physicians, the existence of defensive medicine is difficult to prove. Providers certainly overestimate their risks of being sued for malpractice and of losing such suits, and clearly those in some specialties overreact by ordering more tests than good practice would otherwise allow. Such testing, it should be noted, is typically paid for by health insurance, and in rare cases it also provides more clinical evidence to a physician that may prove useful. These factors, taken together, lead to defensive practices. It is hardly the threat of tort alone that drives whatever defensive testing or treatment occurs. Indeed, if the tort system were eliminated tomorrow, many so-called defensive testing and treatment practices would continue, driven by income from insurance and by physicians' desires for medical certainty.

It is estimated that defensive medicine costs around $55 million a year, a figure that does not include the possible benefits of such tests and procedures. In other areas of the law, such as product liability suits, it is clear that the risk of suit has promoted innovation in product safety.

Medical culture, reimbursement systems, and problems with malpractice insurance generally are more responsible for the rising costs of health care than are malpractice claims and the defensive medicine they are alleged to create. Defensive medicine costs have been a minor factor in the escalation of health care costs. Indeed, recent analyses show that the effect of defensive medicine on overall costs is, at best, marginal. The most visible analysis came from the nonpartisan Congressional Budget Office (CBO). In a recent report, the CBO concluded that earlier studies had overstated the benefits of tort reform in reducing health care costs overall. The CBO, using the methodology of earlier studies, found no evidence that restrictions on tort liability reduced medical spending. It also found no difference in per capita health care spending between states with and without limits on malpractice awards. Another recent study found that the effects of tort reforms over a longer time period did not reduce payments for Medicare-covered services.

The most recent balanced assessment of the costs of so-called defensive medicine was conducted by Michelle Mello and her colleagues. They concluded that overall annual medical liability system costs are around 55.6 billion in 2008 dollars, or 2.4 percent of total health care spending. The CBO had already concluded in a 2004 report that rising malpractice premiums were not driving doctors out of business and thus cutting access to care. That report found some instances of reduced access to emergency surgery and newborn delivery due to malpractice litigation, usually in scattered rural areas, but it also found that the most reported shortages of health care providers either could not be substantiated or had no effect on access (Mello et al., 2010). Access problems in rural areas will exist with or without tort reform; indeed, the shortage of health professionals in such areas is a constant issue.

The total assessment of the primary and secondary liability costs of medical malpractice are hard to project. The CBO has calculated that implementation of tort reforms nationally might "reduce total national health care expenditures by about 0.2 percent" (2009). The CBO also noted, however, that tort reform cost-reductions might increase overall patient mortality rates by limiting the rights of patients to sue. Mello's lower-end figure of $55 billion fails to include possible safety benefits, and the authors conclude that the likely benefits of a tort system on provider behavior have proved difficult to measure.

The bottom line is that defensive medicine is not a significant problem, and tort reform has had little effect on provider behavior, while it has clearly had effects on malpractice insurance by making lawsuits harder to bring. What the U.S. health care system faces, then, is a crisis not of the medical-legal system, but of the economics of malpractice insurance, as doctors have seen their premiums skyrocket in recent years. The malpractice insurance market is not consistently profitable and is less stable than are larger insurance markets, such as the one for auto insurance, given the difficulty of determining the actuarial risk of lawsuits. The insurance cycle means that malpractice premiums may jump suddenly, causing pricing shocks for physicians. Understandably upset, physicians often blame the tort system for the problem, rather than placing blame with insurer investment decisions. The crisis can more legitimately be seen as a malpractice insurance premium crisis. Public Citizen, a consumer advocacy group, notes that malpractice insurance rates rise in large part based on the investment market. Medical malpractice "crises" are tied to declining investment income for insurance companies and poor pricing practices in the insurance industry, rather than to increases in medical malpractice filings and awards. More often, the insurance industry covered losses through rapid rate increases, then blamed the lawyers of patients who sought legitimate compensation for negligently caused adverse events.

The problem with dramatic increases in malpractice premiums during recurrent medical malpractice "crises" is that providers can no longer easily pass along added costs to health insurance companies and government payers. Over the years, all health care payers have constrained their reimbursement and have made it more difficult for costs to be passed on to them, leaving physicians to absorb these extra costs. Forced to increase their volume of patients to cover these added costs and maintain their incomes, physicians have less time to talk to their patients. It becomes a vicious circle—injured patients who are disgruntled and angry at the loss of a personal relationship are far more likely to sue than are patients who have a close relationship with their providers.

THE POSITIVE LINK BETWEEN LIABILITY CONCERNS AND PATIENT-SAFETY IMPROVEMENTS

Physicians and other providers need the spur of liability to push for better patient-safety solutions. Physician resistance to patient-safety initiatives is caused by a variety of factors, including provider power and the relative lack of power of hospital administrators and patients to change medical practices. The problem is that providers are often reluctant to adopt patient-safety measures, even such basic measures as regular hand-washing and the use of checklists for complicated procedures. Physicians, in particular, are often arrogant providers, slow to change their practices unless they are under pressure to do so. Without the threat of liability, providers are unlikely to embrace time-consuming patient-safety initiatives. Litigation and increased costs push providers to reduce adverse events in order to reduce liability. It is clear that serious adverse events that inflict serious harm on patients trigger lawsuits. Not surprisingly, patient-safety activities reduce such lawsuits. More liability risks on hospitals and other institutional providers would, in fact, lead them to push more aggressively for patient-safety efforts that would drive down the risk of medical liability over time by making the health care provided in their institutions safer and less prone to harmful error.

Medical liability has been a major force behind today's patient-safety movement and its various manifestations in federal and state law that promotes digital patient-safety records and other safe practices in hospitals today. A recent RAND study found a direct link between improvements in safety and the number of malpractice claims. The study concluded that, without the threat of liability, providers are less likely to embrace time-consuming patient-safety initiatives. Patient-safety initiatives can be sold to physicians as a way to reduce adverse events and therefore their risk of being sued. Physician worries about being honest about their role in patient injury can be calmed through efforts to help them understand how the law creates legal immunities that protect them in many health care settings. Every state has a peer-review immunity statute; these protect physicians who discuss medical errors in hospital committee meetings by keeping their discussions confidential. Lawyers do not have access to committee minutes and discussions and cannot use them in a malpractice suit. As a result, the statutes grant effective protection to physicians engaged in patient-safety activities in hospitals. This means that candid and open discussion about adverse events and errors do not create tort risks; to the contrary, open discussion and admission of errors can lead to patient-safety measures, which in the long run will reduce tort risks.

New and better safety interventions serve to reduce the volume of malpractice litigation. Improvements in safety performance have a proven effect in aligning the interests of patients and providers by reducing harm and the resulting litigation. It seems obvious that—if measures such as checklists, teamwork on safety, and obsessive attention to analyzing adverse events are implemented—fewer adverse events will occur and fewer patients will be injured. The strongest historical evidence of the power of the threat of liability in improving medical safety comes from the long-term effort of the American Society of Anesthesiologists to systematically study and learn from malpractice claims. Its efforts to make anesthesia safer have led to dramatic reductions in patient injury, lowering the organization's insurance costs as well as the costs associated with patient death and injury. Many practice areas, particularly obstetrics, have become safer because of the threat of liability suits and the need to reduce the causes of such suits.

Insurers are also part of the patient-safety solution. When insurers demand patient-safety measures, they help reduce their own claims exposure by reducing the volume of litigation. Some newer safety approaches, such as checklists for complex medical procedures, are easy to mandate. In fact, insurers engage in a variety of risk-rating practices for physicians, increasingly conducting office audits and paying closer attention to the claims history of their insured physicians. It is likely that the malpractice insurance market can be stabilized by more aggressive risk-management activities on the part of medical liability insurers.

The critiques of medical liability are overstated or just plain wrong. Lawsuits are powerful patient-safety tools, and if anything, more lawsuits are needed to capture the full spectrum of adverse events that seriously harm patients. The pressure of higher premiums and increased exposure to the perils of litigation might finally spur real attention to patient-safety improvements. As Hyman and Silver write, "The main problem with the legal system is that it exerts too little pressure on health care providers to improve the quality of the services they deliver. Safe health care is expensive, and the tort system forces providers to pay only pennies on the dollar for the injuries they inflict" (2005). One set of safety reforms would penalize providers for not disclosing adverse events when they are discovered; it is clear that provider anxiety about lawsuits is one reason they are reluctant to disclose information about such events. Providers, however, conceal adverse events for many other reasons as well, including their own shame and desire to appear to be perfect practitioners. Changes in the culture of patient safety require a range of tools, including penalties for failures to disclose (Furrow, 2011).

Medical liability litigation is a critical component of a comprehensive patient-safety solution for the high level of medical adverse events in the U.S. health care system. Litigation should be viewed as a productive patient-safety tool, one with sharp edges that can help increase attention to medical errors that cause death or permanent harm. Litigation can be improved in terms of effective compensation to plaintiffs, and can also be sharpened as a tool for both uncovering adverse events and creating incentives for their elimination from medical practice.

CONCLUSION

Providers are sensitive to bright-line rules of practice and the costs of noncompliance. So are malpractice insurers. Malpractice suits, for all their inefficiencies, serve a range of functions in promoting medical accountability. Tort suits are not frivolous, and awards to plaintiffs are based on jury assessments of defendant error that are confirmed by studies involving medical experts. Tort litigation has changed medical practices for the better. Liability judgments—and the costs of settling such cases, the reputational effects, and the time lost—create incentives to change behavior. The specter of a lawsuit limits certain kinds of conduct and adds financial pressures to other forces that reinforce good medical practice.

Hospitals are "obtuse" organizations; they often make the same mistakes over and over, seemingly unable to learn from them. They are dominated by high-status physicians who are often reluctant to embrace patient-safety initiatives. Adverse events present a twofold challenge: Errors must be discovered, and leadership tools must be created to systematically address their causes. Adverse events in hospitals are more often due to interaction problems and system failures than to individual provider mistakes. And the real level of injury is much higher than is indicated by the Institute of Medicine figure of 98,000 deaths every year due to medical errors, with up to a third of medical admissions experiencing some kind of adverse event. What is needed is a new patient-safety culture. The creation of a safety culture in complex institutions like hospitals will require a leadership focus that is hard to achieve, but pressures from multiple sources are building in hospitals which are increasingly bearing the brunt of new reimbursement and adverse-event disclosure rules. A move toward institutional liability will provide an additional boost toward an obsessive focus on patient safety as a new area of compliance. Enterprise liability proposals have existed in the legal literature since the 1970s. The development of a corporate-negligence doctrine represents a first step toward holding hospitals liable for system mistakes and poor supervision. "Never events" are another regulatory move to capture or prevent medical events that should never happen through required disclosures and threats to deny Medicare reimbursements.

The best way to reduce uncertainty in risk evaluation for both insurers and providers is to impose some version of enterprise liability for an adverse medical event without requiring that "unavoidability" or "unreasonable" criteria be met and without leaving the provider totally in control of whether to make an offer. If an adverse event does occur, it must be disclosed to the patient. Then a provider may tender an early offer, perhaps coupled with mediation, to move the claims process forward rapidly with the plaintiff and the plaintiff's lawyer. If, however, it is discovered that a reportable adverse event has not been revealed, the plaintiff would be entitled to treble damages as an element of the damage claim. Procedural advantages, such as an extension of the statute of limitations, might also be considered. Such real reforms, aimed not at reducing lawsuits but improving safety, offer the promise of improving the quality of care and, incidentally, reducing the number of lawsuits.

REFERENCES AND FURTHER READING

Baker, T. (2005). *The medical malpractice myth.* Chicago, IL: University of Chicago Press.

Baker, T. (2005). Reconsidering the Harvard medical practice study conclusions about the validity of medical malpractice claims. *The Journal of Law, Media & Ethics, 33*(3), 501–514.

Baker, T. (2006). Medical malpractice insurance reform: "Enterprise insurance" and some alternatives. In W. M. Sage & R. Kersh (Eds.), *Medical malpractice and the U.S. health care system* (pp. 267–290). New York, NY: Cambridge University Press.

Blumstein, J. F. (2006). Medical malpractice standard-setting: Developing malpractice "safe harbors" as a new role for QIOs? *Vanderbilt Law Review, 59*(4), 1017–1049.

Chesebro, K. (1993). Galileo's retort: Peter Huber's junk scholarship. *American University Law Review, 42*(4), 1637–1735.

Clark, S. L., Belfort, M. A., Byrum, S. L., Meyers, J. A., & Perlin, J. B. (2008). Improved outcomes, fewer cesarean deliveries, and reduced litigation: Results of a new paradigm in patient safety. *American Journal of Obstetrics and Gynecology, 199*(2), 105.

Classen, D. C., Resar, R., Griffin, F., Federico, F., Frankel, T., & Kimmel, N. (2011). "Global trigger tool" shows that adverse events in hospitals may be ten times greater than previously measured. *Health Affairs, 30*(4), 581–589.

Congressional Budget Office (CBO). (2009, October 9). *Letter to the Honorable Orrin G. Hatch.* Retrieved from http://www.cbo.gov/ftpdocs/106xx/doc10641/10-09-TORT_Reform.pdf

Currie, J., & MacLeod, W. B. (2006). First do no harm? Tort reform and birth outcomes. *The Quarterly Journal of Economics, 123*(2), 795–830.

Danzon, P. (2000). Liability for malpractice. In A. J. Culyers & J. P. Newhouse (Eds.), *Handbook of health economics 1* (pp. 1341–1404). Oxford, UK: North-Holland.

Fogel, R. L. (1986). *Medical malpractice: No agreement on the problems or solutions.* Washington, DC: U.S. Government Accountability Office.

Friedson, A. I., & Kniesner, T. J. (2011). Losers and losers: Some demographics of medical malpractice tort reforms. *IZA Discussion Papers* (5921). Retrieved from http://aifrieds.mysite.syr.edu/Friedson%20Kniesner%20MedMal%208-12-11.pdf

Furrow, B. R. (2011). The patient injury epidemic: Medical malpractice litigation as a curative tool. *Drexel Law Review, 4*(41), 56–61.

Furrow, B. R., Greaney, T. L., Johnson, S. H., Jost, T. S., & Schwartz, R. L. (2008). *Health law: Cases, materials and problems* (6th ed.). St. Paul, MN: Thomson West.

Galanter, M. S. (1983). Reading the landscape of disputes: What we know and don't know (and think we know) about our allegedly contentious and litigious society. *UCLA Law Review, 31*(4), 4–71.

Galanter, M.S. (1996). Real world torts: An antidote to anecdote. *Maryland Law Review, 55,* 1093–1160.

Gawande, A. (2009). *The checklist manifesto: How to get things right.* New York, NY: Metropolitan Books.

Greenberg, M., Haviland, A. M., Ashwood, J. S., & Main, R. (2010). *Is better patient safety associated with less malpractice activity? Evidence from California.* Santa Monica, CA: RAND Corporation. Retrieved from http://www.rand.org/pubs/technical_reports/TR824.html

Grunebaum, A., Chervenak, F., & Skupski, D. (2011). Effect of a comprehensive obstetric patient safety program on compensation payments and sentinel events. *American Journal of Obstetrics & Gynecology, 204*(2), 97–105.

Hillman, R. J., & Allen, K. G. (2003). *Medical malpractice insurance: Multiple factors have contributed to increased premium rates* (GAO-03-702). Washington, DC: U.S. General Accounting Office. Retrieved from http://www.gao.gov/new.items/d03702.pdf

Hyman, D. A. (2000). Medical malpractice and system reform: Of babies and bathwater. *Health Affairs, 19*(1), 258–259.

Hyman, D. A. (2002). Medical malpractice and the tort system: What do we know and what (if anything) should we do about it? *Texas Law Review, 80*, 1639.

Hyman, D. A., & Silver, C. (2005). The poor state of health care quality in the U.S.: Is malpractice liability part of the problem or part of the solution? *Cornell Law Review, 90*(40), 893–993.

Hyman, D. A., & Silver, C. (2006). Medical malpractice litigation and tort reform: It's the incentives, stupid. *Vanderbilt Law Review, 59*(4), 1085–1130.

Jacobson, P. D. (2006). Medical liability and the culture of technology. In W. M. Sage & R. Kersh (Eds.), *Medical malpractice and the U.S. health care system* (pp. 115–154). New York, NY: Cambridge University Press.

Kachalia, A., & Mello, M. M. (2011). New directions in medical liability reform. *New England Journal of Medicine, 364*(16), 1564–1572.

Kinney, E. D. (1995). Learning from experience, malpractice reforms in the 1990s: Past disappointments, future success? *Journal of Health Politics, Politics and Law, 20*(1), 99–135.

Kohn, L. T., Corrigan, J. M., & Donaldson, M. S. (Eds.). (1999). *To err is human: Building a safer health system.* Washington, DC: National Academy Press. Retrieved from http://www.iom.edu/Reports/1999/To-Err-is-Human-Building-A-Safer-Health-System.aspx

Levinson, D. R. (2010). *Adverse events in hospitals: National incidence among Medicare beneficiaries* (OEI-06-09-00090). Washington, DC: U.S. Department of Health and Human Services. Retrieved from http://oig.hhs.gov/oei/reports/oei-06-09-00090.pdf

MacPhail, L. H., & Edmondson, A. C. (2011). The importance of work context in organizational learning from error. In D. Hoffman & M. Frese (Eds.), *Errors in organizations.* New York, NY: Routledge.

McQuillan, L., Abramyam, H., & Archie, A. (2007). *Jackpot justice: The true cost of America's tort system.* San Francisco, CA: Pacific Research Institute. Retrieved from http://www.legalreforminthenews.com/2007PDFS/PRI_2007JackpotJusticeFinal.pdf

Mehlman, M., & Nance, D. A. (2007). *The case against "health courts."* American Association for Justice Working Paper Series. Retrieved from http://ssrn.com/abstract=1785383

Mello, M.M., & Brennan, T. A. (2002). Deterrence of medical errors: Theory and evidence for malpractice reform. *Texas Law Review, 80*, 1595.

Mello, M. M., Chandra, A., Gawande, A. A., & Studdert, D. M. (2010). National costs of the medical liability system. *Health Affairs, 29*(9), 1569–1577.

Public Citizen's Congress Watch. (2007). *The great medical malpractice hoax: NPDB data continue to show medical liability system produces rational outcomes.* Retrieved from http://www.citizen.org/documents/NPDB%20Report_Final.pdf

Sage, W. M. (2003). Understanding the first malpractice crisis of the 21st century. In A. Gosfield (Ed.), *The health law handbook* (pp. 31–32). St. Paul, MN: Thomson West.

Sage, W. M., & Kersh, R. (Eds.). (2006). *Medical malpractice and the U.S. health care system.* New York, NY: Cambridge University Press.

Saks, M. (1986). In search of the "lawsuit crisis." *Law, Medicine & Health Care, 14*(2), 77.

Shurtz, I. (2010). *The impact of malpractice litigation on physician behavior: The case of childbirth.* Retrieved from http://www.biu.ac.il/soc/ec/seminar/data/15_12_10/impact_malpractice_litigation.pdf

Studdert, D. M., Mello, M. M., Gawande, A. A., Gandhi, T. K., Kachalia, A., Yoon, C., et al. (2006). Claims, errors, and compensation payments in medical malpractice litigation. *New England Journal of Medicine, 354*(19), 2024–2033.

Tucker, A. L., & Edmondson, A. C. (2003). Why hospitals don't learn from failures: Organizational and psychological dynamics that inhibit system change. *California Management Review, 45*(2), 55–72.

Vidmar, N. (1995). *Medical malpractice and the American jury: Confronting the myths about jury incompetence, deep pockets and outrageous damage awards.* Ann Arbor, MI: University of Michigan.

Vidmar, N. (2009). Juries and medical malpractice claims: Empirical facts versus myths. *Clinical Orthopaedics & Related Research, 467*(2), 367–375.

Vogus, T. J., Sutcliffe, K. M., & Weick, K. E. (2010). Doing no harm: Enabling, enacting, and elaborating a culture of safety in health care. *Academy of Management Perspectives, 24*(4), 60–77. Retrieved from http://ssrn.com/abstract=1904620

Wells, C. P. (1990). Tort law as corrective justice: A pragmatic justification for jury adjudication. *Michigan Law Review, 88*, 2348–2413.

Widman, A. (2010). Liability and the health care bill: An "alternative" perspective. *California Law Review Circuit, 57*, 60–62. Retrieved from http://www.californialawreview.org/articles/liability-and-the-health-care-bill-an-alternative-perspective

Barry R. Furrow

Economic and Fiscal Debates

Introduction

The Patient Protection and Affordable Care Act (ACA), signed into law by President Barack Obama on March, 23, 2010, introduces a host of innovations designed to deal with two overarching problems in U.S. health care: the high number of uninsured and the spiraling costs of health care. The degree to which the ACA can effectively tackle these problems is the subject of ongoing debates. The range of opinions vary from those who believe that the ACA puts the United States on a path that will eventually transform the nation's health care system into one that provides affordable access to high-quality care for all Americans, to those who believe the ACA will only carry the United States farther away from that vision. Reaching that vision will require systematic changes to how care is paid for and delivered, involving all of the major stakeholders—payers, providers, and patients. In this section, strategies to make those changes, focusing on the provisions in the ACA, are explored from an economic perspective in an effort to demystify the complexities of the problems and their solutions and defuse the combustibility of the rhetoric surrounding these debates.

The Economic Context

It's no revelation that health care in the United States occupies a major share of the country's economy. According to data from the Centers for Medicare & Medicaid Services (CMS), the share of the U.S. gross domestic product (GDP) devoted to health care expenditures was a little over 5 percent in 1960, grew to over 9 percent in 1980, and ballooned by the end of the century to nearly 14 percent; by 2010 that figure had spiked to almost 18 percent. International comparisons also point to the outsized role that health care plays in the U.S. economy. Data from the Organisation for Economic Co-operation and Development (OECD) show that U.S. health care expenditures far surpass that of any other OECD country. Again in terms of GDP share, the United States outspends the next highest country, the Netherlands, at 12 percent, and a group of other countries that spend in the 11 to 11.9 percent range—Austria, Canada, Denmark, France, Germany, and Switzerland—by nearly 50 percent.

Projections for the coming years increase concerns about the future of health care spending. According to CMS, spending on health care will rise from $2.6 trillion in 2010 to $4.6 trillion in 2020 with nearly one in every five dollars spent in this country being used for health care. To be sure, some of the increase expected over the course of the next decade is due to changes instituted by the ACA's efforts to reduce the number of uninsured, either privately through newly established insurance exchanges or publicly through an expansion of Medicaid. CMS projects an annual increase in national health expenditures of 8.3 percent in 2014 alone, the year the ACA brings the exchanges and expansion to Medicaid online. Thus, though the coverage expansion would address the problem of the high number of uninsured, it only amplifies the need to ensure that we are getting the best return on our expenditures. Considering that the United States spends so much more than any other country on health care (whether as a percentage of GDP or on a per-capita basis), one would expect that Americans would have superior access to high-quality care. However, the evidence does not support this: the United States is often fairly mediocre in measures of access to health care and performance relative to other OECD countries.

The fact that health care in the United States comes with such a big economic footprint helps to explain why tackling these problems is so challenging. And the sheer size of the industry is aggravated by the complex structure of the system, which is fractured and decentralized, with many stakeholders at play, often with conflicting goals. Holding costs down, maximizing profits, expanding coverage, ensuring quality care—how does an industry balance all these needs and wishes?

The Debates

The debates presented here describe not just specific issues concerning the ACA, but health care reform in general. They include both the most contentious, high-profile concerns covered vociferously in the media and less discussed but equally important concerns. The goal of these chapters is to illuminate the issue from all angles and perspectives, in an effort to provide the reader with the tools to make his or her own informed judgments.

Expanding coverage. Getting to universal, or near-universal, coverage is one of the lodestars of U.S. health care reform efforts, showing up on presidential agendas at various times for nearly a century. When the ACA was enacted, the problem of the uninsured, indeed, had reached critical proportions, especially when the economic downturn that began in 2007 sent unemployment rates skyrocketing. In 2011, there were over 50 million uninsured in the United States, which is about 6 million more than in 2007 and close to 14 million more than in 2000 (the last year of robust economic growth before the first recession in the 2000s).

Rather than completely revamping the health care system, such as through implementation of a single-payer system, the ACA attempts to maintain the current mixed public-private system, including its large employment-based component. To do this, the ACA developed a complex set of tools designed to fit together and support each other. These include

- the individual mandate, requiring nearly all legal U.S. residents obtain health insurance, the validity of which was upheld in a much-anticipated June 2012 Supreme Court ruling;

- health insurance exchanges and subsidies to support the purchase of insurance through the exchanges for certain individuals and families with incomes below 400 percent of the federal poverty level;

- new regulations on insurers, including a requirement to accept all applicants regardless of preexisting conditions (i.e., guaranteed issue); prohibition against charging higher premiums to offset risks brought on by the guaranteed issue requirement; limits on rescission; elimination of lifetime and annual benefit limits; and requirements to cover certain essential health benefits, to extend coverage to dependent children up to age 26, and to use a certain percentage of premium revenues on medical claims;

- the so-called employer mandate, instituting penalties on certain large employers if any of their workers obtain federal government subsidies for coverage through insurance exchanges; tax credits are also made available for small employers that offer insurance to their employees; and

- an expansion of Medicaid eligibility to most nonelderly people whose incomes are below 138 percent of the federal poverty level; while the validity of this expansion was also upheld in the 2012 Supreme Court ruling, the primary instrument instituted by the ACA to ensure states' implementation of the expansion—the withholding of all Medicaid funds to states that don't comply—was struck down; nevertheless, it is thought that most states will comply.

In March 2011, the Congressional Budget Office (CBO) and Joint Committee on Taxation (JCT) projected that, with the implementation of these measures, insurance coverage will reach an additional 32 million nonelderly residents by 2016, rising to about 34 million by 2021, meaning that 95 percent of the legal nonelderly population will be insured. In contrast, without the ACA, the projected share with insurance would only be about 82 percent.

Whatever the effects of the Supreme Court's Medicaid ruling, experts generally agree that these provisions will likely be successful in expanding coverage, but only if they are taken together as a package and even then there may be unintended consequences. This functional dependence largely relates to adverse selection, described by Neera Tanden and Topher Spiro in the Point of the individual mandate chapter: If insurers are required to expand coverage to sicker individuals, the risk pool must be broadened by mandate to cover healthy individuals as well. Assuming adequate risk pools can be attained, as Jason M. Hockenberry points out in his chapter on insurance regulations, the mandate also makes it possible for insurers to meet the new insurer requirements, such as the limit on rescission and prohibition on lifetime and annual limits. The insurance exchanges, as discussed by Alan C. Monheit and Joel C. Cantor, will provide a market mechanism for individuals to purchase insurance, though they caution that some believe government regulation and organization of such markets will weaken competition in the insurance industry. As always, the devil may be in the details. For instance, Thomas Miller, the author of the Counterpoint in the individual mandate chapter, argues that the specific design of the individual mandate provision alone will severely weaken its effects. For example, the penalties—reflected in an increase in the amount paid on tax returns—may likely be too small—in comparison to the premiums that individuals must pay—to incentivize the uninsured to buy insurance. Therefore, adverse selection may still weaken the system.

The employer mandate is also important to the coverage expansion and to the promise by the Obama administration that individuals will be able to keep their current plans. That is, the ACA aims to maintain the heavy reliance on an employment-based health insurance system—nearly 170 million Americans are covered by insurance purchased through an employer plan. The employer mandate takes the form of penalties on larger employers based on the use their employees make of federal subsidies to buy insurance on the exchanges. Again, the devil might be in the details. Much of the argument against the mandate, as put forth by Kathleen Carey in the Counterpoint of the employer mandate chapter, is based on the burdens placed on employers to keep track of their compliance with the mandate, as well as the increased cost due to new premiums or potential penalties. Although the employer mandate provisions do not appear to create significant changes in employer-sponsored coverage when taking an aggregated national view, the change could be significant at local levels, depending on such factors as the size of the firms involved. That said, using an employer mandate to help support the universal coverage goal makes use of the existing strength of employer-sponsored insurance (ESI), which Carey argues for in the Point side of this debate. The tax deductibility of ESI will continue under the ACA, thereby continuing the allowance for tax benefits to both employees and employers. Employers have considerable purchasing power given their size, and they offer natural risk pools to employers.

Paying for reform and bending the cost curve. The second collection of debates in this section revolves around the cost and financing of health care. Not only do the efforts to expand coverage—both in general and under the current ACA efforts—require funding but it is also vital to slow the acceleration of health care expenditures if the U.S. health care system is to be sustainable.

From the perspective of the federal government, health care costs appear to be a driving factor of the increasing federal debt. In fact, at times the political debate over health care reform seems to be more focused on reducing the deficit, without much regard for improving health or the health care system. Although it is a huge player in U.S. health care, the federal government is not the only payer affected by escalating costs. This burden is felt across the entire health care system by both public and private payers, including businesses and individual households. This raises the question of what role the federal government should play in health care reform. Focusing on deficit reduction runs the risk of simply shifting more of the burden onto other payers. Figuring out how to control national health spending (for all payers) while protecting the performance of an already compromised health care system should be the goal.

At the time of its passage, the CBO and JCT projected that the ACA will be able to cover the cost of the expansion (to the federal government) and even reduce the deficit by a modest amount—$124 billion from 2010 through 2019. In the chapter on deficit reduction, Kavita Patel, Shayla Nagy, and Mark Zezza question whether that savings estimate is too modest or whether the ACA is even likely to achieve that amount. It should be said that the Supreme Court's limitation of the federal government's ability to enforce the states' expansion of the Medicaid rolls has added more uncertainty concerning the federal costs for implementation of the ACA.

One aspect of the current U.S. system that receives relatively little attention compared to deficit reduction is the tax deductibility of employer-sponsored health insurance. To be sure, Medicaid and Medicare account for a large portion of federal government expenditures. However, the tax expenditure for ESI—that is, the loss of revenue to the federal treasury due to the tax exemption of ESI—also constitutes a considerable sum—over $170 billion in 2011—about one-fifth of the mandatory spending on all federal health care programs. As explored by Patricia Ketsche, William S. Custer, and E. Kathleen Adams, the advantages and disadvantages of the tax treatment for ESI need to be weighed against each other. The exclusion has helped solidify the status of ESI in our health care system for decades. But despite this long tradition, questions are raised not just about its effectiveness and equitableness as an instrument to increase health insurance coverage for U.S. workers but also about macroeconomic concerns. As was mentioned above, the tax expenditure is considerable, and that money might better be used to support a more universal approach to health care for all Americans, not just workers. However, is it wise to introduce such wholesale change? Would such change even be possible politically?

The ACA partially handles some of the concerns about the tax treatment for ESI with the excise tax on high-cost health plans, so-called Cadillac plans. Though viewed primarily as an effort to raise revenues to help fund health care reform and pay for expanded coverage, the provision, as Randy Haught describes in the Point of the chapter on taxing Cadillac plans, is also expected to help bend the cost curve by encouraging the use of more cost-efficient plans not subject to the tax. However, as discussed in the Counterpoint by Elise Gould, this potential may be thwarted by the possibility that lower-cost plans may lead to higher out-of-pocket expenses for individuals and families. In addition, it is not clear whether only Cadillac plans—plans that provide overly generous benefits—will be impacted. Thus many Americans may be left facing higher costs for needed care.

The ability of the excise tax on high-cost health plans to bend the cost curve is predicated on the notion of exposing consumers to the real price of health care. In the chapter on price transparency, Bianca Frogner considers the results of allowing more price transparency in all aspects of health care purchasing, including paying for services at the point-of-care, as well as when choosing insurance. Health care spending is the product of two basic factors: price and quantity. And the reason that increasing price transparency will help to reduce costs, many say, is that for consumers to act rationally in the health care market they need to know what their options are and what the cost and value of those options are. However, the current system is plagued with asymmetrical information: individual consumers don't have the expertise to analyze the quality of their providers or the comparative effectiveness of treatment options, and they are rarely made aware of the full cost of care. Therefore, proponents of increasing price transparency, as Frogner explains, argue that clearer options and pricing can make consumers smarter players in the health care market. However, as Frogner suggests in the Counterpoint, creating transparent health care markets is not an easy task: The complexity of the U.S. health care financing system and of medical care in general makes price transparency an elusive goal. Rather, controlling the other side of the equation—quantity—should be the trigger to reduce costs.

Indeed, controlling overconsumption—lowering the quantity side of the equation—is one avenue toward reducing costs. As David Howard and Cynthia Zeldin explore in the accountable care organizations (ACO) chapter, restructuring how providers are organized can incentivize them to deliver higher-value health care, achieving greater quality at lower costs. In fact, the ACA initiates a wide range of payment and delivery reform models aimed at creating systemic changes that can foster long-term financial sustainability while also generating improved health outcomes. However, these options remain largely unproven and, even if they are successful, it may take years before they achieve significant results.

If the ACA's various cost-control measures do not work, the reform act has inserted a stopgap instrument in the form of the Independent Payment Advisory Board (IPAB). Independent of Congress, consisting of individuals from various professions, the IPAB will develop annual recommendations to help ensure that payment and delivery efforts are successful at achieving a minimum level of savings. The goal is to keep the growth in per capita Medicare costs more aligned with general economic inflation, which has historically grown at much lower rates. The IPAB in its broadest outlines is a fairly simple mechanism: If Medicare costs are rising above targeted levels, and Congress does not pass a plan of its own that meets the level of savings projected under the IPAB's plan, the board's recommendations will automatically be enacted. As discussed by Jennifer M. Kerner in the IPAB chapter, the implicit legislative authority by a board of independent advisors is unprecedented. However, there are many reasons to believe that the IPAB will not be able to realize its goals, including the fact that the ACA severely inhibits the purview for IPAB recommendations and the possibility that Congress could undermine IPAB recommendations with subsequent independent legislation.

Even if the cost-control measures in the ACA prove to be effective, there is general agreement (even by the most ardent ACA cheerleaders) that more needs to be done to ensure long-term health care financing sustainability. One area commonly identified as a potential source of savings is Medicare drug pricing under the Part D program. Medicare Part D, which was implemented in 2006, closed the drug coverage gap for senior citizens, a much-needed reform. However, questions have arisen since the inception of the program about the right price for Medicare to pay for drugs. The debate surrounding Medicare Part D, as described by David W. Carlson here, focuses on legislation that forbids the federal government to negotiate drug prices with pharmaceutical companies, leaving that task to numerous private plan sponsors. Many feel that the federal government, negotiating on behalf of the entire Medicare population, would have greater leverage over the drug companies to set lower prices. However, some evidence supports the notion that the private-plan sponsors have had some success in keeping drug prices down and that the federal government would be hard pressed to achieve better prices without harming future access to innovative drugs.

Some politicians and policymakers, however, argue for less involvement by the federal government, hoping to increase focus on approaches to ensure deficit reduction and free up the private sector, states, and consumers to drive cost-efficiencies and value. One major effort along these lines is the proposal put forth in the Republican budget proposal of 2011by Representative Paul Ryan, whose plan was to turn Medicare into a voucher program and Medicaid into a block grant program. Currently, Medicare has an open-ended commitment to help states cover their Medicaid costs, but under the block grant model, the federal government would make lump-sum payments to the states. As R. Paul Duncan, Lilliana L. Bell, Allyson G. Hall, and Shenae K. Samuels describe in the chapter on Medicaid flexibility, giving states more flexibility in determining the best way to use federal funding for Medicaid could lead to a win-win situation. The federal government would be responsible for much more controllable and easier-to-budget annual amounts and states would be responsible for costs beyond the federal allotment, but free to run the program as they want. According to opponents, however, states already have a great deal of flexibility, which if increased too much, runs the risk of weakening the safety net provided by Medicaid—a safety net that will become even wider and more important with new eligibility provisions under the ACA, even with the limitation the Supreme Court placed on the federal government's ability to enforce the expansion.

Conclusion

While reading each of the debates, it may be worthwhile to consider certain thematic issues that run across them. The first is whether it is best to expand coverage or to focus on cost reduction first. While there is fairly strong consensus that the ACA can address the coverage problem, there is much uncertainty regarding the effectiveness of the ACA's cost control provisions. Even if the provisions are able to achieve the savings estimated by CBO, it is likely that much more will need to be done. This raises a second issue: finding the right balance between provisions that can achieve more immediate cost savings and deficit relief (e.g., payment cuts to Medicare or stronger limits on the tax exclusion for ESI) versus those that can help set up longer-term sustainability (e.g., payment and delivery reforms such as ACO initiatives). It should be emphasized that evidence for the effectiveness in achieving significant cost reductions of many of the longer-term strategies in the ACA are mixed at best. Another issue related to cost control is how to balance the efforts on the price and quantity side of the total cost equation. Furthermore, what should the appropriate role for the federal government be in these reform efforts? Of interest to this last issue is that, even when trying to use private market forces to achieve efficiencies in the health care system (e.g., such as the development of health insurance exchanges to promote competition), there appears to be a great deal of government regulation involved.

Assuming that the ACA does not get repealed or substantially weakened by future legal challenges or additional legislation, policy analysts, health economists, providers, payers, and other stakeholders will have their work cut out for them to determine what, if anything, about health reform is working well. Looking towards the future, if the ACA's efforts to bend the cost curve are not successful, how long can we go before asking what may be perhaps the ultimate question: Is it best to use an incremental approach, retaining the current system of employment-based insurance with multiple payers, or is more dramatic change needed?

Mark A. Zezza
The Commonwealth Fund

Individual Mandate

POINT: Short of a single-payer system, the best way to obtain universal, or near universal, coverage is through a mandate that individuals purchase insurance.

Neera Tanden and Topher Spiro, Center for American Progress

COUNTERPOINT: Individual mandates can only go so far in getting the U.S. health care system to universal coverage. Opponents find the mandate to be politically implausible, administratively challenging, constitutionally improper, and economically unnecessary.

Thomas Miller, American Enterprise Institute

Introduction

A major impetus behind the passage of the 2010 Patient Protection and Affordable Care Act (ACA) was to ensure that all Americans have adequate access to health care. According to the U.S. Bureau of the Census, some 50 million Americans lack health insurance, a little over 16 percent of the population. By January 1, 2014, the individual mandate in the ACA requires that nearly every legal resident of the United States obtain health insurance coverage. In general, compliance with the mandate means being enrolled in qualifying plans that provide minimum essential coverage. Noncompliance can lead to financial penalties of several hundreds of dollars to thousands, depending on one's income. The mandate was upheld in the June 2012 Supreme Court decision concerning the ACA on the narrow grounds that it fell under the Congress's taxing powers, since the penalty is collected through an individual's income tax returns.

A bevy of additional provisions are included in the ACA to support compliance and help meet the goal of universal coverage. These include requirements for states to create insurance exchanges through which individuals and small businesses can purchase coverage with pooled risk and therefore lower premiums. In addition, premium and cost-sharing assistance will be made available to substantially reduce the cost of purchasing insurance for those with incomes below 400 percent of poverty (which, in 2012, was about $44,000 for individuals and $92,000 for a family of four). Eligibility will also be greatly expanded for Medicaid to further support lower-income populations to obtain qualified coverage, although the extent of the planned expansion under Medicaid may be affected by the Supreme Court's limitation of the federal government's ability to enforce the expansion. In addition, larger employers (those with more than 50 employees) may face penalties for not offering coverage, and small employers can receive federal subsidies to help them offer coverage.

At the time the health-reform legislation was passed, the Congressional Budget Office (CBO) and Joint Commission and Taxation projected that the ACA will increase the number of nonelderly Americans with health insurance by about 32 million in 2016 and that about 95 percent of legal nonelderly residents will have insurance coverage in 2021, compared to only 82 percent in the absence of the ACA, although the CBO may adjust its estimates due to the Supreme Court's ruling on the Medicaid enforcement mechanism. In general, experts are in agreement that the ACA will significantly reduce the number of uninsured; however, there is considerable debate involving the philosophical, legal, and economic justifications of the individual mandate. In this chapter, the debate will primarily focus on the economic aspects.

Before getting into the debate, it is worthwhile to be reminded of two basic principles concerning the flow of funds that finance health care. First, the flow of funds ultimately always comes out of the pocket of individuals, with governments, employers, and private insurance plans acting as fiscal intermediaries. There are numerous ways that these intermediaries assist the flow of funds from consumers to providers. For the government, this predominantly occurs through the collection of taxes, which are used to fund programs such as Medicare, Medicaid, and eventually the subsidies for insurance purchased in the state health insurance exchanges. Private health insurance plans use premium payments from individuals to reimburse providers for health care. Businesses purchasing insurance for their employees are likely to recoup that money through reduced wages and higher prices on their products.

The second issue is that health care financing involves a significant transfer of funds from one population to another. Usually, this entails higher-income and healthier populations transferring funds to lower-income and less healthy populations. Taxes are an obvious mechanism to support this redistribution. The Medicaid program is perhaps the foremost example of a program that redistributes income (for the purpose of purchasing health care) to poorer and less healthy populations.

The transfer of funds occurring in the group market for private health insurance is of particular relevance when discussing the individual mandate, since this will be a primary platform for the coverage expansion. Premium amounts for groups (such as current employer groups or the group markets that will eventually become available in the exchanges for individuals and employees of small firms) are largely determined by the average health of the group. Thus, groups with greater risk for higher health care costs, such as coal miners or employers with predominantly older employees, are likely to face higher premium amounts in comparison to groups made up of younger, less risky individuals. By adding relatively healthier people to a risk pool, the average premium for that population will decrease as the average risk falls. The only way many sick or high-risk individuals can afford health insurance is if their risk is spread out with that of many healthier and less costly individuals. The key point is that premiums for the sicker individuals in the pool are essentially subsidized by those who are healthier and whose premiums are likely to be higher than the amount of health care they actually use.

Related to the flow of funds, another key point to keep in mind when evaluating the individual mandate is that the uninsured already use health care and that their costs result in a financial burden to others. Although the uninsured are forced to pay out of pocket for much of the care they receive, researchers at the Urban Institute have estimated that they are unable to pay for the majority of their care (see Jack Hadley et al.'s 2008 paper in *Health Affairs,* titled "Covering the Uninsured in 2008: Current Costs, Sources of Payment, and Incremental Costs"). This leaves other payers, predominantly the government, to pay for that care. Providers are also likely to shift some of the uncompensated costs to private payers in the form of higher prices, which in turn leads to higher premiums.

It can be argued that these existing health care funding flow attributes—as well as the fact that anyone, regardless of their ability to pay, can receive care in an emergency room or from other safety net providers—is evidence that we already have a universal health care system. Following this line of reasoning, the economic debate on the individual mandate in the ACA is really about whether it can lead to a more efficient and effective way of providing health care for all Americans relative to the current system. Moreover, is it better than other options for meeting that goal? In the Point, Neera Tanden and Topher Spiro provide insights to these questions.

On the pro side of the debate, arguments focus on why the individual mandate will help the most vulnerable Americans gain access to important health care services, while also doing so using a more-efficient allocation of health care funds. In general, economists argue that a universal mandate, at the very least, makes income transfers more visible; as such, it may have the potential of more precisely targeting transfers from those that can afford to pay for health insurance to those that cannot.

The current system for transfers is not very transparent and could result in inefficiencies. For example, Medicare provides additional payments to hospitals, through disproportionate share (DSH) and indirect medical education (IME) payment. These payments are meant to be directed to hospitals to treat a large number of low-income patients on the grounds that they are more costly to treat and may result in uncompensated care. However, these payments are not linked to specific patients or services and, hence, do not always end up aligned with the hospitals based on how much uncompensated care they deliver. In general, recordkeeping for uncompensated care is not especially good, as no specific payments are attached to that care. Even if it were possible to achieve better alignment of funds for uncompensated care, there are inefficiency concerns due to the notion that the uninsured are much more likely to avoid or postpone seeking care for treatable conditions. This can result in more costly care down the road when their conditions progress to a more complicated state. Having insurance may encourage more efficient use of care.

In general, the mandate is consistent with the notion that everyone assumes greater responsibility for their own health care by requiring everyone to obtain insurance, as well as for the societal costs associated with those who cannot afford insurance. The mandate, coupled with other insurance regulations, ensures that the implicit subsidies for higher-risk individuals come from a broader population of healthier patients. This helps combat the free-rider and adverse-selection problems inherent in the current system, as discussed in some detail by Tanden and Spiro. Of course, most people may eventually fall into the high-risk category, which is a point to keep in mind when considering the free-rider and adverse-selection issues.

On the con side, the argument focuses on the theoretical rationale for the individual mandate, as proposed in the ACA, and whether it can be translated into practice. As Thomas Miller argues, the mandate contains a lot of moving parts—definitions for required minimum benefits, determination of appropriate subsidy and penalty amounts, and administration through a multitude of exchanges and private plans—all of which will require continuous regulation and maintenance. In addition, the individual mandate is not especially popular either politically or even among the general public. Thus, it can be expected that there will be many problems in implementation.

Also, and perhaps most importantly, absent from the individual mandate (and ACA in general) are explicit and proven mechanisms to restrain health care costs—that is, to actually provide more efficient health care. Thus, even if the mandate is successful at reaching near universal health care coverage, there may be a great risk of compounding the already unsustainable levels of health care cost-growth. Already, as is discussed in the chapter on deficit reduction, government officials have serious concerns as to whether the subsidies can be sustained. No matter how one feels about the individual mandate, the ability to provide all Americans access to needed, high-quality care will ultimately always depend upon efforts to create a more efficient health care system.

POINT

In the U.S. health care system—until coverage is expanded in 2014—50 million people lack health insurance. Americans can be charged higher premiums when they are sick, and denied coverage because of preexisting conditions. All it takes is one illness or injury to send a family into bankruptcy. Sixty-two percent of all personal bankruptcies are caused by illness or medical bills, and a significant portion of medically bankrupted families lacked health insurance or experienced a recent lapse in coverage (Himmelstein, Thorne, Warren, & Woolhandler, 2009). In short, health insurance does not provide security to those who need it the most.

The uninsured also exact costs on society. They still receive health care, much of which is not paid for, at a cost of $57.4 billion in 2008 (Holahan & Garrett, 2010). That uncompensated care is paid for by taxpayers through public programs, by health care providers through lost profits, and by shifting costs to private insurers. In turn, private insurers may increase premiums; according to one estimate, this cost shifting increases family premiums by over $1,000 a year on average (Families USA, 2009). Though the uninsured still receive health care, they use much fewer health care services, and do not receive all of the health care they need, which adversely impacts their health. The poorer health and shorter lifespans of the uninsured is estimated to cost the economy $207 billion a year (Carpenter & Axeen, 2008).

Those who do have health insurance are at risk of losing it if they lose their jobs. Moreover, this risk may discourage employees from starting their own business or moving to a job in which they would be more productive—causing so-called job lock.

These problems have plagued the health care system for decades. If society wishes to solve them—but continue to rely on private health insurance markets—then the most effective solution involves a requirement to maintain health insurance coverage known as an "individual mandate." That is the approach taken by the national health-reform legislation signed into law in 2010, the Patient Protection and Affordable Care Act (ACA).

THE PROBLEM OF ADVERSE SELECTION

To guarantee access to health insurance at a premium rate that is affordable, reform must prohibit discrimination based on health status. That means requiring an insurer to enroll all individuals who apply for coverage, even if they are sick or have a preexisting condition—what is known as "guaranteed issue." It also means prohibiting an insurer from charging higher premiums for that coverage if an individual is sick or injured, and regulating how much premiums can vary based on age—what is known as "modified community rating." Otherwise, older, less healthy individuals would be priced out of the market, and the guarantee to enroll in coverage would do them no good. Finally, it means prohibiting an insurer from excluding from coverage preexisting conditions.

If these reforms were implemented by themselves, many individuals would wait to get health insurance until they need care, knowing that coverage will be guaranteed, at a premium rate that will not rise because they are sick or injured. Less healthy, more costly individuals would be more likely to enroll in coverage and would largely make up the insurance risk pool (American Academy of Actuaries, 2009). This "adverse selection" would drive up premiums, which in turn would cause even more healthy individuals to drop coverage, possibly leading to a so-called death spiral. Higher premiums would also significantly increase the cost to taxpayers of providing premium tax credits to make coverage affordable.

This adverse selection in the absence of an individual mandate is not theoretical, as there is substantial evidence from the actual experience of several states. A classic example is New Jersey (Monheit, Cantor, Koller, & Fox, 2004). In 1993 New Jersey implemented guaranteed issue and community rating in its direct-purchase market, where individuals buy health insurance directly from an insurer, not through their employer. Older, more costly individuals enrolled in coverage, and premiums rose by up to 155 percent from 1996 to 2000. Even the premium of the health maintenance organization (HMO) plan—which more aggressively manages costs—rose by 48 percent over this period. As a result, overall enrollment declined by 41 percent over the same period, consistent with a death spiral caused by adverse selection.

New Jersey was not the only laboratory for this experiment. Kentucky, Maine, New Hampshire, New York, Vermont, and Washington all enacted laws designed to guarantee access to health insurance, but without an individual mandate. In every state, the laws destabilized the direct-purchase market, increasing premiums, reducing enrollment, or causing insurers to exit the market. Some of these states, such as Kentucky, were ultimately forced to repeal the legislation. As could be expected, in states where community rating is currently in effect, premiums in the direct-purchase market are among the highest in the country (Chandra, Gruber, & McKnight, 2011).

OPTIONS TO MAXIMIZE PARTICIPATION

To address the problem of adverse selection—which is exacerbated by regulations that guarantee access—reform needs to maximize participation in the system, to ensure a broad insurance risk pool that includes young and healthy individuals. Of course, one way to ensure universal participation—common throughout the industrialized world—would be to adopt a so-called single-payer system. In these systems, premiums are in effect collected through the tax system, making participation mandatory.

In the United States, Medicare Part A—which pays for hospital care—is a good example. During their working years, individuals make contributions through a payroll tax, which pays for "free" insurance for hospital care after age 65. No sign-up is necessary because participation in this financing arrangement is mandatory. But, short of this approach, individuals could be required to pay premiums for their health insurance through an individual mandate. Indeed, the individual mandate was originally a conservative idea born as an alternative to a single-payer system or an employer mandate.

The Heritage Foundation, a conservative think tank, first proposed an individual mandate in 1989 (Butler, 1989). Conservative economists also proposed a mandate as part of a plan that "supports and makes use of competitive markets" and "avoids relying on the public tax or expenditure systems whenever possible" (Pauly, Damon, Feldstein, & Hoff, 1991, p. 7). In 1993 Senator John Chafee (R–RI)—along with 18 Republican cosponsors—introduced legislation that included a mandate as an alternative to President Bill Clinton's health-reform plan (S.1770, 1993). Notably, in 2007, 10 Republican Senators cosponsored the Healthy Americans Act (S.334), which also included an individual mandate.

These conservatives also recognized that individuals have a responsibility to pay for their own health care when they can afford to do so. An individual mandate was necessary to prevent individuals from being free riders who impose their costs on others. Thus, as the Heritage Foundation put it, "each household has the obligation, to the extent it is able, to avoid placing demands on society by protecting itself" (Butler, 1989, p. 6). Further, not having insurance "imposes a risk of delaying medical care; it may also impose costs on others, because we as a society provide care to the uninsured" (Pauly et al., p. 8).

Short of a single-payer system, it is not possible to achieve near-universal coverage in the absence of an individual mandate. Premium subsidies alone would increase participation, but would not come close to achieving universal coverage. Even generous premium subsidies would cover only 40 to 50 percent of the uninsured (Blumberg & Holahan, 2008). The nonpartisan Congressional Budget Office (CBO) estimates that in the absence of the mandate, the ACA would cover only half as many people (2010).

According to the American Academy of Actuaries, an individual mandate would be more effective than other types of incentives to increase participation, such as penalties for delayed enrollment or automatic enrollment (2009). Medicare Part B (for physician services) and Part D (for prescription drugs) use late-enrollment penalties and achieve high participation. But all enrollees are heavily subsidized, and seniors would likely enroll anyway because they know that they will need care. Available estimates indicate that such alternatives would cover substantially fewer people, while increasing premiums in the direct-purchase market as a result of adverse selection (Gruber, 2011).

EVIDENCE OF THE EFFECTIVENESS OF AN INDIVIDUAL MANDATE

Though the effectiveness of alternatives to an individual mandate is purely theoretical, there is substantial evidence from actual experience—both internationally and in the United States—that mandates are effective.

Both Switzerland and the Netherlands achieve near-universal coverage through an individual mandate (Leu, Rutten, Matter, & Rütschi, 2009). Both countries require insurers to enroll all individuals who apply for coverage, and both prohibit insurers from charging higher premiums based on health status. In Switzerland, which implemented a mandate in 1996, regional estimates indicate that the rate of uninsured is below 1 percent, and 1.6 percent of the population are enrolled in coverage but do not pay their premiums. In the Netherlands, which implemented a mandate in 2006, the rate of uninsured is about 1.5 percent, and 1.5 percent of the population is enrolled in coverage but do not pay their premiums. Of those who remain uninsured in the Netherlands, 54 percent are immigrants or their children.

The experience in Massachusetts. Here in the United States, health reform in Massachusetts contained the same basic building blocks as national health reform: regulations prohibiting discrimination based on health status, premium subsidies, a health insurance exchange, and an individual mandate. But the program in Massachusetts started almost a year before the mandate went into effect. As a result, the least healthy individuals were the first to enroll in coverage—as could be expected (American Academy of Actuaries, 2009). Those individuals were almost four years older, were almost 50 percent more likely to be chronically ill, and had about 45 percent higher health care costs than those who enrolled after the mandate was fully implemented (Chandra et al., 2011).

But once the individual mandate was fully effective, it worked as designed to bring healthy individuals into the insurance risk pool, and the program achieved near-universal coverage. Since 2006 over 411,000 individuals have enrolled, reducing the share of uninsured individuals to only 1.9 percent in 2010 (Massachusetts Division of Health Care Finance and Policy, 2011).

In Massachusetts, the individual mandate, combined with other reforms, has also strengthened employer-based coverage. If employees are obligated to have insurance, they increase their demand for their employers to offer it. Since 2005 the percentage of employers that offer coverage has actually increased in Massachusetts, from 70 percent to 77 percent (Long & Stockley, 2009; Massachusetts Division of Health Care Finance and Policy, 2011).

The individual mandate in Massachusetts is broadly comparable in scope and magnitude to the mandate under the ACA. Both mandates exempt low-income individuals. The mandate in Massachusetts exempts those with income below 150 percent of the federal poverty level (FPL), whereas the ACA's mandate exempts those with income below the federal income tax filing threshold (roughly 90 percent of the FPL). Both mandates also exempt individuals who cannot afford coverage. The mandate in Massachusetts exempts those for whom the premium of the lowest-cost plan exceeds an affordability threshold. The ACA's mandate exempts those for whom the premium of the lowest-cost plan exceeds 8 percent of income.

Under both individual mandates, even if a penalty would usually apply to an individual, the individual may claim an exemption due to financial hardship. In addition, both mandates exempt those who refuse to obtain health insurance because of their religious beliefs. Though the mandate in Massachusetts only applies to adults, the ACA's mandate applies to taxpayers and their dependents, requiring taxpayers to pay reduced penalties on behalf of their dependents.

In Massachusetts, the penalty for not having qualified insurance is 50 percent of the amount that an individual would pay for the lowest-cost plan, after taking into account any premium subsidy. Under the ACA, the fully phased-in penalty in 2016 will be the greater of $695 per adult (half of that for children), or 2.5 percent of the amount of income that exceeds the federal income tax filing threshold. However, the penalty may not exceed an overall cap equal to the national average premium of the lowest-cost plan.

Differences in design mean that the individual mandate under the ACA will be stronger for some individuals and weaker for others than the mandate in Massachusetts (Seifert & Cohen, 2010). Fewer people with income below 300 percent of the FPL will be exempt under the ACA's mandate. Moreover, the ACA's penalties are higher for people with income below 250 percent of the FPL. On average, the ACA's penalties, once fully phased in (in 2016), will be slightly higher than the penalties in Massachusetts—about $674 per person under the ACA, compared to $537 per person in Massachusetts (Frakt, 2010).

Given the experience in Massachusetts, then, there is reason to believe that the individual mandate will be effective nationally. Since the premium subsidies are smaller under the ACA than in Massachusetts, the ACA's mandate is that much more critical to bringing healthy individuals into the insurance risk pool.

INDEPENDENT ANALYSES OF THE AFFORDABLE CARE ACT

The experience in Massachusetts has informed analyses of the ACA. (Specifically, microsimulation models use the Massachusetts experience to make assumptions about the behavioral effects of individuals under an individual mandate.) According to the most recent estimates of the CBO, the ACA will cover 34 million people, a coverage rate of 95 percent (2011). (Note that these estimates were conducted before the Supreme Court ruled that the states could not be forced to participate in the Medicaid expansion. Hence, the estimates may be overestimated to the degree that states actually opt out.) Other independent analyses have produced similar results (Buettgens, Garrett, & Holahan, 2010; RAND Corporation, 2010). In particular, the RAND Corporation found that the individual mandate by itself is the provision that contributes the most to increasing coverage. Of those who will remain uninsured, one third will be undocumented immigrants, and one quarter will be eligible for Medicaid (CBO, 2011).

Given this significant reduction in the number of the uninsured, it is not surprising that the individual mandate will also significantly reduce the cost of uncompensated care. With the mandate, the ACA will reduce the cost of uncompensated care by $42.3 billion, compared to only $14.7 billion without a mandate (Buettgens et al., 2010). This indicates that the uninsured do shift costs to taxpayers, health care providers, and private health insurance—and a reduction in this cost shifting will save taxpayers money, increase provider revenue, and lower private health insurance premiums.

Moreover, estimates indicate that the individual mandate will work as intended to counter adverse selection. The CBO concluded that the mandate will "encourage a broad range of people to take up coverage in the exchanges" (2009). As a result, the CBO estimates that the influx of healthier enrollees will reduce average premiums by up to 10 percent in the direct-purchase market. Market reforms that reduce administrative costs and enhance competition will reduce premiums by up to an additional 10 percent. All told, premiums for the exact same coverage could be up to 20 percent lower under reform. Conversely, eliminating the mandate would result in adverse selection, increasing premiums by up to 20 percent in the direct-purchase market (CBO, 2010).

Similarly, in the market for employer-based coverage, the CBO concluded that the individual mandate will induce "younger and relatively healthy workers who might otherwise not enroll in their employers' plans to do so" (2009). In addition, the mandate will increase the percentage of small employers that offer coverage—and those employers that newly offer coverage will be more likely to have healthier employees. Both effects will reduce average premiums slightly. Overall, CBO estimates that premiums for employer-based coverage will remain stable.

As in Massachusetts, the individual mandate will also bolster private health insurance coverage. The CBO estimates that in the absence of the mandate, about 4 million to 5 million fewer people would be enrolled in employer-based coverage (CBO, 2010). The share of people covered by private health insurance would decline—and would actually be lower than under current law (Buettgens et al., 2010).

Importantly, the individual mandate yields the most "bang for the buck," increasing coverage by as much as possible for the least possible cost. By bringing healthy individuals into the insurance risk pool, the mandate lowers the average cost per person, reducing the cost of premium tax credits. With the mandate, many of the newly insured will gain private coverage, which also lowers the cost to the government. Government spending for each newly insured person will be slightly more than half of what it would be without a mandate (Buettgens et al., 2010). In other words, the mandate is essential to making reform cost-effective.

MUTUALLY REINFORCING REFORMS

To be sure, several components of the ACA are also important in achieving near-universal coverage and mitigating adverse selection. The ACA does the following:

- Offers significant federal funding support to states to expands Medicaid coverage to all individuals with income below 138 percent of the FPL

- Creates state-based health insurance exchanges, online marketplaces where individuals and small businesses can easily shop for and enroll in quality plans

- Provides premium tax credits to individuals, structured to guarantee that premiums will never exceed a certain percentage of income

- Provides tax credits to small businesses for up to 50 percent of their health insurance costs

- Collects payments from plans that have healthier enrollees and makes payments to plans that have less healthy enrollees, on average—known as "risk adjustment"

- Provides insurers with insurance against high-cost enrollees—known as "reinsurance"

The individual mandate complements these strategies and enables them to work effectively.

To reinforce the individual mandate, several reforms also help ensure broad participation among young people. Over 90 percent of young people enrolling through exchanges will be eligible for premium tax credits (Blumberg, Buettgens,

& Garrett, 2009). As of September 2010, young adults can remain on their parents' plans until age 26. This reform has already had a significant impact, covering an additional 2.5 million young adults (Department of Health and Human Services, 2011). In addition, young adults under the age of 30 will be able to enroll in a low-cost catastrophic plan (Affordable Care Act, Section 1303 (e)). CBO estimates the actuarial value of a catastrophic plan—the share of costs paid by the plan—to be less than 50 percent, compared to 60 percent for a Bronze plan.

Thus, empirical evidence and analysis show that the counterpoint—that young and healthy individuals will simply ignore the individual mandate—is false. What is more, the ACA includes several protections that are designed specifically to enroll young people, which are already working.

CONCLUSION

The individual mandate is the most controversial aspect of health care reform. If Americans are prepared to accept a system in which those who are sick or have a preexisting condition can be denied coverage, or charged exorbitant premiums, and shift their costs to others, then a mandate is not necessary. But if Americans want basic market reforms that eliminate discrimination based on health status, a mandate is essential to making the system work effectively. All known empirical evidence—both evidence of failure in several states, and evidence of success in Massachusetts—supports this conclusion.

Moreover, no other reform proposal has been estimated by independent analysts to achieve anywhere close to universal coverage. In every health care system that has achieved near-universal coverage, health insurance is mandatory. Some systems—such as Canada, Britain, Germany, and France—make it mandatory through the tax system. Others—Switzerland, the Netherlands, and Massachusetts—simply obligate individuals to maintain health insurance. As an alternative to a single-payer system, conservative economists and Republicans originally endorsed this latter approach.

Research and analysis indicate that the individual mandate will not only achieve near-universal coverage but will also significantly reduce the cost of uncompensated care, lower premiums in both the direct-purchase market and the market for employer-based coverage, increase the percentage of small employers that offer coverage, increase enrollment in employer-based coverage, and increase the cost-effectiveness of reform—its "bang for the buck." Several independent analyses consistently reach these results.

The individual mandate—and the participation that it encourages—affirms the nature of insurance. Insurance is protection against risks that are unknown, and involves the sharing of risk. At a given point in time, some will have higher costs, and some will have lower costs—and they will balance each other out. But over the course of a lifetime, the premiums that an individual pays should roughly reflect that individual's costs. Young and healthy individuals may not need health care at a given point in time, but insurance protects them and society against the financial catastrophe of an illness or accident. Moreover, their participation enables their continued participation over time as they age, and enables the sharing of risk, which is what makes insurance work in the first place.

Note: A version of this paper was published in February 2012 by the Center for American Progress as "The Case for the Individual Mandate in Health Care Reform: A Comprehensive Review of the Evidence" by Neera Tanden and Topher Spiro.

REFERENCES AND FURTHER READING

Affordable Care Act, U.S.C. §1303(e) (2010).

American Academy of Actuaries. (2009). *Critical issues in health reform: Individual mandate.* Washington, DC: Author. Retrieved from http://www.actuary.org/pdf/health/individual_mandate_may09.pdf

Blumberg, L. J., Buettgens, M., & Garrett, B. (2009). Age rating under comprehensive health care reform: Implications for coverage, costs, and household financial burdens. *Timely Analysis of Immediate Health Policy Issues* (pp. 1–9). Washington, DC: The Urban Institute. Retrieved from http://www.urban.org/publications/411970.html

Blumberg, L. J., & Holahan, J. (2008). Do individual mandates matter? *Timely Analysis of Immediate Health Policy Issues* (pp. 1–4). Washington, DC: The Urban Institute. Retrieved from http://www.urban.org/publications/411603.html

Buettgens, M., Garrett, B., & Holahan, J. (2010). *America under the Affordable Care Act.* Washington, DC: The Urban Institute. Retrieved from http://www.urban.org/publications/412267.html

Butler, S. M. (1989). Assuring affordable health care for all Americans. *The Heritage Lectures, 218*, 6. Retrieved from http://www.heritage.org/research/lecture/assuring-affordable-health-care-for-all-americans

Carpenter, E., & Axeen, S. (2008). *The cost of doing nothing: Why the cost of failing to fix our health system is greater than the cost of reform*. Retrieved from New America Foundation website: http://www.newamerica.net/publications/policy/cost_doing_nothing

Chandra, A., Gruber, J., & McKnight, R. (2011). The importance of the individual mandate—Evidence from Massachusetts. *The New England Journal of Medicine, 364*(4), 293–295.

Congressional Budget Office (CBO). (2009). *An analysis of health insurance premiums under the patient protection and affordable care act, report to U.S. Senator Evan Bayh*. Retrieved from http://www.cbo.gov/sites/default/files/cbofiles/ftpdocs/107xx/doc10781/11-30-premiums.pdf

Congressional Budget Office (CBO). (2010). *Effects of eliminating the individual mandate to obtain health insurance*. Retrieved from http://cbo.gov/sites/default/files/cbofiles/ftpdocs/113xx/doc11379/eliminate_individual_mandate_06_16.pdf

Congressional Budget Office (CBO). (2011, March 30). *CBO's analysis of the major health care legislation enacted in March 2010, Statement of CBO Director Douglas W. Elmendorf before Subcommittee on Health, Committee on Energy and Commerce*. Retrieved from http://www.cbo.gov/sites/default/files/cbofiles/ftpdocs/121xx/doc12119/03-30-healthcarelegislation.pdf

Department of Health and Human Services, Office of the Assistant Secretary for Planning and Evaluation. (2011). *2.5 million young adults gain health insurance due to the Affordable Care Act*. Retrieved from http://www.hhs.gov/news/press/2011pres/12/20111214d.html

Families USA. (2009). *Hidden health tax: Americans pay a premium*. New York, NY: Author. Retrieved from http://www.familiesusa.org/resources/publications/reports/hidden-health-tax.html

Frakt, A. (2010). *Dispatch from Massachusetts: The individual mandate is working*. Retrieved from Kaiser Health News website: http://www.kaiserhealthnews.org/Columns/2010/July/072210Frakt.aspx

Gruber, J. (2011). *Health care reform without the individual mandate*. Retrieved from Center for American Progress website: http://www.americanprogress.org/issues/2011/02/gruber_mandate.html

Health Equity and Access Reform Today Act of 1993, S.1770, 103rd Cong. (1993).

Himmelstein, D. U., Thorne, D., Warren, E., & Woolhandler, S. (2009). Medical bankruptcy in the United States, 2007: Results of a national study. *American Journal of Medicine, 122*(8), 741–746. Retrieved from http://www.amjmed.com/article/S0002-9343(09)00404-5/abstract

Holahan, J., & Garrett, B. (2010). *The cost of uncompensated care with and without health reform*. Washington, DC: The Urban Institute. Retrieved from http://www.urban.org/publications/412045.html

Leu, R. E., Rutten, F., Brouwer, W., Matter, P., & Rütschi, C. (2009). *The Swiss and Dutch health insurance systems: Universal coverage and regulated competitive insurance markets*. Washington, DC: The Commonwealth Fund. Retrieved from http://www.commonwealthfund.org/Publications/Fund-Reports/2009/Jan/The-Swiss-and-Dutch-Health-Insurance-Systems—Universal-Coverage-and-Regulated-Competitive-Insurance.aspx

Long, S. K., & Stockley, K. (2009). Massachusetts health reform: Employer coverage from employees' perspective. *Health Affairs, 28*(6), w1079–w1087. Retrieved from http://content.healthaffairs.org/content/28/6/w1079.abstract

Massachusetts Division of Health Care Finance and Policy. (2011). *Health care in Massachusetts: Key indicators, May 2011 edition*. Retrieved from http://www.mass.gov/eohhs/docs/dhcfp/r/pubs/11/2011-key-indicators-may.pdf

Monheit, A. C., Cantor, J. C., Koller, M., & Fox, K. S. (2004). Community rating and sustainable individual health insurance markets in New Jersey. *Health Affairs, 23*(4), 167–175. Retrieved from http://content.healthaffairs.org/content/23/4/167.abstract

Pauly, M. V., Damon, P., Feldstein, P., & Hoff, J. (1991). A plan for "responsible national health insurance." *Health Affairs, 10*(1), 5–25. Retrieved from http://content.healthaffairs.org/content/10/1/5.full.pdf+html

RAND Corporation. (2010, February). *Analysis of the Patient Protection and Affordable Care Act (H.R. 3590)*. RAND Policy Brief. Retrieved from http://www.rand.org/pubs/research_briefs/2010/RAND_RB9514.pdf

Seifert, R. W., & Cohen, A. P. (2010). *Re-forming reform: What the patient protection and affordable care act means for Massachusetts*. Retrieved from University of Massachusetts Medical School, Center for Health Law and Economics website: http://masshealthpolicyforum.brandeis.edu/forums/Documents/IssueBrief_ReportFINAL.pdf

Neera Tanden and Topher Spiro

COUNTERPOINT

The case for an individual mandate to purchase health insurance is built on false hopes, empty promises, and mistaken premises. It usually is presented as a necessary means to more popular ends—universal coverage, better access to care for those with preexisting health conditions, and lower health care costs for those already insured. However, the real evidence of the relationship between the mandate and the problems it purportedly could solve is tenuous and contradictory, at best. Opponents find the mandate to be politically implausible, administratively challenging, constitutionally improper, and economically unnecessary.

An individual mandate, in theory, should be universal, simple to administer, and widely accepted. After all, would not everyone agree that purchasing a basic level of health insurance constitutes a basic responsibility to oneself and the rest of society? Can't citizens agree on the level of insurance that everyone needs to have, what it should cost, and to what extent their society needs to assist less fortunate Americans in obtaining it?

It turns out that the type of individual mandate that the U.S. political economy and health care system is most likely to deliver in practice (such as the one recently authorized, but yet to be implemented, in the Patient Protection and Affordable Care Act [ACA]) is very different and more complicated than the one imagined above in theory. Defining and implementing a mandate requires many additional rules regarding exactly what it requires, how it is carried out, and who pays for it.

Once it is presumed that government is ultimately responsible for guaranteeing that every American has the health insurance that they are required to purchase, so, too, does society guarantee a permanent role for politicians and their favored interest groups in determining an accompanying set of issues that translate that goal into practice. The government must define what constitutes "adequate" insurance coverage for each person. It inevitably must specify the content of the insurance package that must be purchased. It then has to decide how mandatory health insurance can be provided to everyone in an "affordable" manner—in other words, how it will be subsidized and how its pricing will be regulated. The process of dictating how much, at what cost, to whom, and in what manner health insurance is bought and sold would severely hamper, if not preclude, treating health care as somewhat-varied bundles, types, and levels of goods and services that are distributed at least in part on the basis of individuals' different abilities and willingness to pay for them (as is done for most other goods and services, which not surprisingly are delivered more effectively, efficiently, and at lower costs). The longstanding bias of the U.S. political system—particularly when it comes to health benefits—is to promise more and deliver less, while blaming others for the resulting gap.

SHALLOW SUPPORT FOR A MANDATE

The greatest initial political support for an individual mandate primarily comes from people who already purchase or offer insurance, or expect to gain more paying customers for their health care services. Insured individuals want to believe political promises that the mandate will make someone else pay more for coverage, so that they can pay less. Some employers have supported an individual mandate as a way to avoid enactment of an employer coverage mandate. Providers of medical services hope that a mandate would ensure that more of their bills are paid. And insurers often find that the bitter pill of tighter political control of their operating rules becomes somewhat more palatable if they are promised more revenue from involuntary customers.

Many politicians also want to substitute "off-budget" mandated private funds in place of the far less popular taxes they would otherwise find hard to impose to meet their insurance coverage goals. Insurance mandates that conscript more individuals to pay for new, expanded coverage can act like a tax to help fund additional health spending, but they obscure the full political costs and visible "price-sticker shock" to taxpayers because mandated private spending is not officially treated as part of the federal budget. Instead, employers and insurers are enlisted as surrogate "tax collectors" through less transparent and politically accountable means.

Another political rationale for an individual mandate appears to be not only that it will guarantee universal insurance coverage but also that it will lead to lower overall health care costs. This argument defies the economic laws of (limited) supply and (over-stimulated) demand, the history of ever-expanding entitlement programs within the U.S. political economy, and even basic mathematics. Its vague promise of future savings comes close to adopting a "mutual hostage" theory that assumes once the political system has placed everyone in the same large but leaky (coverage) boat, someone on board will be more motivated to figure out a way to swim back to shore by providing health care at a lower cost (and perhaps with better quality) and show the way to safety for the rest.

Oft-stated rhetorical justifications for an individual mandate include that it actually will improve people's health or that everyone should have "equal" health care. However, neither the empirical evidence for the former proposition nor the political support for the latter one appears particularly strong within U.S. history. Other arguments occasionally advanced for such a mandate include leveling the playing field so that those using publicly funded health services pay their "fair share" of the costs of care, easing the concerns of private insurers about adverse selection aggravated by risk-rating restrictions, and forcing government bodies to commit to providing adequate subsidies for those citizens subjected to otherwise unaffordable mandates (Glied, Hartz, & Giorgi, 2007).

Not surprisingly, an individual mandate has the least support from those it is purported to help—people who currently do not enroll in public coverage or employer-sponsored insurance, or who do not purchase individual coverage. After all, coercion to get some people to do what they otherwise would not is the very point of a legal mandate.

FAILURE TO CLOSE A "BAD DEAL"

However, trying to force people to buy insurance that they cannot afford, or coercing them into paying more for coverage than it actually appears to be worth to them, remains politically difficult. Some may wonder why, if buying some kind of health insurance that is offered to them is such a good idea, they should have to be forced by law to buy it.

An individual mandate often promises, but never manages, to pay for itself. The facts are that taxpayers already face huge debt obligations of the present and future for existing political commitments to finance public spending for health care and other purposes. They really cannot "make up their losses on volume" by expanding even more health insurance offered at below-market prices that are heavily subsidized by taxpayers. Insurance mandates create a perpetual conflict between their escalating costs, limited public and private resources to pay for them, and the false guarantee of rich coverage. Hence, such mandates must recycle a large portion of any projected increases in new premium "revenue" to health care providers and health insurers through expanded coverage right back into additional taxpayer subsidies to reduce "net" premiums (or suppress the full premium costs of new health care services with tighter price controls). When such health benefits promises cost more than their immediate beneficiaries can afford, the difference is financed, one way or another, out of higher taxes, other reduced benefits, or higher premiums imposed on everyone else. Eventually, some of those hidden costs even are re-imposed on the initially more "fortunate" beneficiaries.

One way or another, the real costs to carry out an individual mandate outweigh the gains, and the identifiable losers outnumber the mythical winners once all the longer-term costs and consequences unfold and are calculated. Political demand for health care explodes, government budgets tighten, market supply of medical providers struggles to keep up, and overcharged private premium payers resist paying more for less. Eventually, a large critical mass of unhappy consumers and taxpayers resists having to underwrite the cost of an individual mandate that fails to pay for itself.

WEAK ENFORCEMENT OF "MANDATORY" INSURANCE

Hence, even though some modelers of the coverage take-up effects of an individual mandate appear to assume reflexively that its commands will be obeyed faithfully and executed flawlessly, actual proposals for enforcement of an individual mandate often provide more bark than bite. For example, the penalties for noncompliance with the mandate imposed under the ACA are weak and unlikely to drive much of a permanent purchasing response. One early indication is that the mandate does not even begin to apply until January 1, 2014—even though the law was enacted in March of 2010. Although the penalties are supposed to be enforced by the Internal Revenue Service (IRS) and collected through taxpayers' annual income tax returns, the agency will not be allowed to use many of its standard enforcement tools to ensure payment of taxes. The law provides that anyone who fails to pay in a timely manner any penalty imposed by the mandate "shall not be subject to any criminal prosecution or penalty" and that the Secretary of the Treasury shall not "file notice of lien" or "levy" on any property of a taxpayer by reason of such failure (Patient Protection and Affordable Care Act, 2010, 1501(g)(2)[(A) and (B)(i–ii)]—Public Law 111–148).

The amounts of the penalties for failing to comply with the insurance purchasing mandate under the ACA also are rather modest in proportion to the likely average premium cost of required coverage. The penalty will be either a flat-dollar amount or a percentage of one's income; whichever is greater. After the penalty amounts are phased in over three years (beginning in 2014), the flat-dollar version will equal $695, and the percentage-of-income version will equal 2.5 percent of income, in 2016. The likely result is that a significant percentage of lower-income individuals will calculate that it is less expensive to pay the penalty than to purchase mandatory insurance and consider doing so. The law's guaranteed-issue incentives for potential purchasers—enroll "just in time" when sick and "go bare" when healthy (and pay less in penalties than in total premiums)—further ensures limited and erratic mandate compliance. Moreover, the ACA's provisions for exemptions from the individual mandate—involving illegal immigrants, foreign nationals, religious prohibitions, and most importantly "unaffordability" (when one's required health premium costs would be greater than 8 percent of household income)—reveal how various political and economic factors limit the enforceable scope of any theoretically universal mandate. In addition, reliance on the federal income tax system and the IRS as primary enforcers of the mandate fails to reach the millions of nonfilers.

Other complex administrative hurdles also must be surmounted:

1. in determining whether a person is exempt from "unaffordable" mandated coverage;

2. if not, in estimating whether he or she is eligible for various levels of premium subsidies—either through Medicaid or via tax credits—based on their expected household income; and

3. in settling up later in the following tax year the final amount of subsidies versus premium payments to account for differences in *actual* household income reported to the IRS.

A comprehensive review of the likely efficacy of mandates for health insurance by Glied, Hartz, and Giorgi (2007) concluded that predicting a target population's response to a mandate is, at best, an inexact science. Performance of mandates varies greatly, with such important factors as the affordability of costs of compliance, the size of penalties, and the probability that penalties will be imposed in a timely manner. For example, the percentage of motorists who lack automobile liability insurance coverage, which is mandatory in almost all states, ranges from about 4 percent to 33 percent. Moreover, a 1995 study found that the average uninsured motorist rate was actually lower in states without such auto insurance mandates (Kelly, 2004). Glied, Hartz, and Giorgi also noted that even the best mandate is unlikely to affect the behavior of those who are transient (in terms of either residence location or employment status) and have few assets.

Ironically, even the strongest version of an individual mandate to purchase health insurance would be too weak to guarantee what should be its ultimate objective—improvements in people's health. Requiring that someone has health insurance in itself is not the same as ensuring that they actually receive all of the effective health care services they may need in a timely manner and comply with their physicians' advice, let alone that they will take the many other steps beyond the receipt of covered medical services that might do more to improve their current and future health (McGinnis, Williams-Russo, & Knickman, 2002; McGlynn et al., 2003). To do that, one might need to mandate not just the purchase of health insurance but also the delivery of the actual "treatment" itself. Yet somehow the image of closing the gap in delivering recommended care—which gets delivered only about half the time in current practice—with a mandate that all preventive and therapeutic "treatment" be received at the right time and right place, with no questions asked or informed consent required—suggests more vividly the limits of government coercion in achieving health goals.

A CONFLICT OF VALUES

The recent debate over the individual mandate and its underpinning of the ACA's other provisions for health insurance regulation, health care financing, and delivery system restructuring requires a more realistic understanding of the limits of high-level government commands within our political system, the balance of power between government and citizens in the Constitution, and the long-standing societal values that sustain both of them. The individual mandate touches exposed nerves and offends core principles in ways that other elements of the modern regulatory state do not.

Many Americans are troubled by Congress imposing a legal mandate on citizens to purchase something, regardless of their wishes. They worry that an individual mandate would operate as a gateway drug to even greater addiction to government control of health care. Implementing a mandate inevitably requires more and more rules regarding exactly what it requires, how it is carried out, and who pays for it.

Hence, the individual mandate has consistently remained the most intensely unpopular provision of the new health law since it first took shape. More than a year after enactment of the ACA, a clear majority of Americans continued to oppose the individual mandate and favored its repeal. For example, 67 percent favored repeal of the individual mandate in March 2011, and 54 percent still opposed it in June 2011 (CNN/Opinion Research Corporation Poll, 2011; Kaiser Family Foundation, 2011).

Because a fundamental part of those concerns is the view that an individual mandate violates core principles of economic freedom, personal choice, and limited government under the U.S. Constitution, the provision's constitutionality was challenged in a number of lawsuits filed shortly after the ACA was signed into law.

After more than two years of litigation, legal arguments, and conflicting rulings in a number of cases in the federal courts, the Supreme Court ultimately decided, in a controversial 5-to-4 ruling on June 28, 2012, that the ACA was constitutional in most respects (aside from its unconstitutional penalties for states that decline to participate in its proposed expansion of the Medicaid program). The majority opinion by Chief Justice John Roberts concluded that the law's individual mandate was not authorized under the U.S. Constitution as an exercise of the power of Congress to regulate interstate commerce. It also found that the mandate was not a "necessary and proper" means to carry out other enumerated powers of Congress. However, the Court determined that the individual mandate could be upheld as a "tax" rather than as a penalty. It therefore was interpreted as a valid exercise of the congressional power to lay and collect taxes to provide for the general welfare of the United States.

The four dissenting justices, and other critics of the individual mandate, may continue to assert that it is unconstitutional (Miller, 2012), but this issue of constitutional law is settled for the immediate future. The broader debate over the policy and political merits of the individual mandate will continue throughout the 2012 election season and into the next session of Congress in 2013.

COST-SHIFTING RATIONALES COME UP SHORT

The most frequently used argument to justify the individual mandate both on policy and legal grounds is that, without it, uninsured individuals will continue to receive lots of uncompensated care and private premium payers will pay for this free riding. When the costs of uncompensated care are shifted to those who already are insured and their average premiums increase, even more people will be unable to afford more costly insurance and will become (or remain) uninsured, according to the Secretary of Health and Human Services and Obama administration lawyers. They argue that decisions by the uninsured not to participate in the health insurance market have a collective effect on interstate commerce that poses a threat to a national market. Hence, the individual mandate is a "necessary and proper" measure under the Constitution to ensure the success of the larger health reforms in the ACA (such as guaranteed issue and adjusted community rating that ensure access to insurance for individuals with more costly preexisting health conditions), and it is "an integral part of the regulatory scheme" for the new health law's plan to increase insurance coverage and lower health care costs.

Congress even inserted a number of legislative findings (ACA, 2010, section 1501(a)) into the new health law designed to bolster the conclusion that a failure to regulate the decision to delay or forego buying insurance would shift the costs of that decision onto the larger health care system and undermine the law's comprehensive regulatory regime. Courts often defer to such congressional findings as long as there is some rational basis to support them. However, this "cost-shifting" argument remains exaggerated, misdirected, and short on convincing evidence.

President Obama himself has resorted to the cost-shifting rationale for an individual mandate on many occasions. For example, he told the American Medical Association in June 2009, "Each time an uninsured American steps foot into an emergency room with no way to reimburse the hospital for care, the cost is handed over to every American family as a bill of about $1,000 that is reflected in higher taxes, higher premiums, and higher health care costs; a hidden tax that will be cut as we insure all Americans" (Obama, 2009).

In 2009, this "hidden-tax" theory was stretched to its limits in a questionable advocacy paper by Families USA called "Hidden Health Tax: Americans Pay a Premium." Based on various federal data sources such as the Medical Expenditure Panel Survey (MEPS), it claimed not only that Americans without insurance received approximately $42.7 billion in net uncompensated care in 2008, but that this entire *amount* was shifted to the private insured population (but not to anyone covered by Medicare or Medicaid) at annual costs of $1,017 per insured family and $368 per insured single person.

These estimates, which provided the primary "empirical" foundation for the cost-shifting arguments made by Obama administration attorneys before the Supreme Court, conflict noticeably with a more thorough empirical analysis of uncompensated care costs and burdens developed by a group of Urban Institute researchers led by Jack Hadley and published by the Kaiser Family Foundation in August 2008 (Hadley, Holahan, Coughlin, & Miller, 2008). The authors refined and updated their earlier path-breaking work in 2003. They concluded that, under one method using MEPS-based estimates, uncompensated care received by the uninsured in 2008 amounted to $54.3 billion but only half of it ($27.8

billion) came from "implicitly subsidized" care, that is, funds potentially cost shifted to private insurance premiums. The rest ($26.5 billion) of that funding for uncompensated care represented payments from other public sources and other private sources.

However, the Urban Institute researchers also cross-checked their findings with an alternative method, based on independent data from other provider and government sources. The overall estimate of uncompensated care from those sources amounted to $57.4 billion in 2008, leading to Hadley and colleagues' conclusion that the total cost of uncompensated care received by the uninsured that year was roughly $56 billion. But they also calculated that federal, state, and local government funds accounted for $42.9 billion that was available to pay for that uncompensated care, even after adjusting for possible misallocation of funds spent in the name of the uninsured. Their study concluded that attributing increased private health insurance premiums to any expanded costs of treating the uninsured is a misperception, particularly when a net balance of only about $14.5 billion was arguably financed by the privately insured in the form of higher (cost-shifted) private payments for care and, ultimately, higher insurance premiums. Indeed, they estimated that the amount of uncompensated care potentially available for private cost shifting is most likely even lower, at about $8 billion in 2008, which was less than 1 percent of $829.9 billion in private health insurance costs (Miller, 2008).

The inflated findings by Families USA first undercounted other sources of payment for care received by the uninsured, in some cases arbitrarily dismissing better estimates by others. Second, they too crudely assumed that the costs of care for the part-year uninsured would be proportionate to the portion of the year that they were uninsured (unlike Hadley and colleagues, who adjust for the clustering of more health spending into periods of insurance coverage). Third, Families USA inflated MEPS health care costs for the uninsured by factors greater than those used by Hadley and colleagues, by overlooking the different rates of growth for insured versus noninsured health spending. Fourth, the Families USA figures evidently failed to adjust the 2006 MEPS numbers they report for total private insured spending ($557 billion) to their 2008 value under the National Health Expenditure accounting methods used annually by actuaries at the Centers for Medical & Medicaid Services (CMS) to provide the most definitive analysis of national health spending. Fifth, its estimates unconvincingly limited the entire amount of any possible cost shifting of uncompensated care only to the smaller base of privately insured health premiums, overlooking the difference between reimbursement fee levels under administered pricing in government programs and the behavioral offsets used by providers to increase reimbursed spending through greater volume and upcoding. By statistically suppressing the total size of the denominator, and inflating the numerator, the Families USA methods raised the resulting percentage in the cost-shifting equation. Sixth, one of the clinching arguments for Hadley and colleagues' view of cost shifting is their statistical demonstration that the *share* of hospitals' overall costs due to uncompensated care remained remarkably stable over time amidst rising levels of uninsurance—even as hospitals' cost-to-charge markup ratio for private payers (which might otherwise suggest different relative degrees of a cost-shifting response by hospitals in the form of higher or lower markups for privately insured patients) has fluctuated for other reasons in a completely uncorrelated manner.

In other words, the cost-shifting rationale used by the Obama administration to justify the ACA's individual mandate failed to distinguish accurately between uncompensated care costs financed by taxpayers and those financed by private premium payers. It also failed to acknowledge several inconvenient truths related to the ACA's other plans to expand Medicaid coverage substantially, which would aggravate problems of *undercompensated* care and the overuse of crowded hospital emergency rooms.

WHO REALLY IS CROWDING EMERGENCY ROOMS?

Ironically, the oft-stated, oversimplified political storyline for cost shifting, and why an individual mandate is needed to reduce or eliminate it, presumes that most, if not all, of it is due to free-riding uninsured people who postpone necessary medical treatment until they land in overcrowded and expensive emergency rooms of hospitals (as indicated, for example, in the 2009 remarks of President Obama cited above). However, the statistical reality is that among the under-65 population, the uninsured were no more likely than the insured to have had at least one emergency department (ED) visit in a 12-month period, but persons with Medicaid coverage were more likely to have had multiple visits to the ED than those other two categories of people under age 65 (Garcia, Bernstein, & Bush, 2010). ED visits by the uninsured were no more likely to be triaged as nonurgent than were visits by those with private insurance or Medicaid coverage. Adults with Medicaid accounted for most of the increase in ED visits from 1997 to 2007 (Tang, Stein, Hsia, Maselli, & Gonzales, 2010).

Medicaid beneficiaries currently are about 70 percent more likely than the uninsured to use hospital emergency department care. The uninsured represent only about 15 percent of all emergency department visits (Pitts, Niska, Xu, & Burt, 2008).

To the extent that free-riding and uncompensated care occurs in hospital emergency rooms, it is due largely to the requirements of another federal law—the Emergency Medical Treatment and Active Labor Act—enacted in 1986. It requires hospitals that participate in the Medicare program and accept Medicare patients and CMS payments (virtually all of them) to provide emergency care to anyone who needs it, regardless of ability to pay, citizenship, or legal status. This is an unfunded federal mandate to provide uncompensated care. However, emergency care as a whole (not just this federally mandated stabilization care for those entering hospital emergency rooms) still accounts for less than 3 percent of the total health care market, and only about half of that care goes uncompensated (American College of Emergency Physicians, 2012). Other forms of uncompensated hospital care account for most of the remaining amounts of uncompensated care, because physicians actually appear to earn more, on net, from their uninsured patients than their insured patients. Gruber and Rodriguez analyzed 2004–2005 survey data that took into account how much uninsured patients paid in higher, "undiscounted" prices for physician care. Even their most conservative estimates suggested that uncompensated care by physicians amounted to no more than $3.2 billion (Gruber & Rodriguez, 2007).

Thoughtful observers might reflect on such numbers and consider the possibility that increased ED visits primarily reflect broader health system delivery problems (e.g., physicians who don't do evening or weekend hours or answer e-mail, provider resistance to low-cost clinic competition) rather than increases in the number of uninsured Americans. They might also wonder whether the new health law's plan to increase coverage primarily through expansion of Medicaid (as an important supplement to the individual mandate imposed on Americans not eligible for Medicaid or other public health programs) will help or aggravate the emergency care overuse problem.

Early evidence from Massachusetts suggests that promises that its individual mandate would eliminate the need for most uncompensated emergency care by the uninsured (and provide sufficient savings to finance much of the cost of subsidies for increased insurance coverage) were overstated. The costs of the state's quite generous "uncompensated care pool" were indeed reduced by about 37 percent, but far from eliminated, after an individual mandate was implemented (from $661 million in fiscal year 2007 to $414 million in fiscal year 2009) and the percentage of the state population that was uninsured declined from 5.7 percent to 2.7 percent. On the other hand, hospitals' emergency visit volume actually increased 14 percent, and demand for payments to hospitals for emergency care rose 15 percent (state-administered payments increased less, but only due to a $70 million funding shortfall, otherwise known as "really uncompensated" care) from fiscal year 2009 to fiscal year 2010 (Massachusetts Division of Health Care Finance and Policy, 2010).

THE ADDED COSTS OF "UNDERCOMPENSATED" CARE

Moreover, the overall costs to Massachusetts and federal taxpayers for the state's experiment in increasing coverage through expansion of Medicaid and implementation of an individual mandate far exceeded the above modest savings in uncompensated care expenses (Klein, 2012). Because Medicaid consistently reimburses health care providers substantially below their actual costs to deliver care, its substantial expansion in Massachusetts (and in future years across the nation under the ACA) further increases the total costs of under-compensated care that is more likely to be shifted to taxpayers and private premium payers (Cogan, Hubbard, & Kessler, 2011). Even by estimates provided by actuaries at Milliman, Inc., the actual amount of estimated cost-shifting to private insurance by the low-paying Medicaid and Medicare program (to the extent that such cost shifting actually occurs) is nearly twice the amount of any purported cost shifting due to uncompensated care for the uninsured (Fox & Pickering, 2008).

The costs of being uninsured are indeed serious and significant. However, a relatively small portion of them are shifted to private insurance premiums. Instead, they show up primarily in poorer health, less adequate medical care and foregone subsidies for the uninsured.

HOW EFFECTIVE IS THE INDIVIDUAL MANDATE?

Various claims by advocates of the individual mandate include not only that it will substantially reduce uncompensated care costs but that it also will help ensure nearly universal coverage and lower future health insurance premiums. In reality, the individual mandate is projected, under relatively optimistic assumptions by the Congressional Budget Office

(CBO), to increase *privately purchased* (and highly subsidized) insurance coverage by about 16 to 17 million more people by 2021, about the same number of newly insured will receive their coverage through Medicaid, and about 23 million Americans will remain uninsured by that year. (These estimates date to before the Supreme Court ruled that the states could not be forced to participate in the Medicaid expansion.) Any such estimates of overall coverage effects remain approximations, subject to different assumptions and measurement times. Even more differences of opinion involve the effect of the individual mandate itself on future coverage increases. For example, a recent study by the Lewin Group estimates that, if the mandate were lifted, the ACA still would cover 23 million people who would have been uninsured without the law (in other words, about 8 million people would lose such future coverage without the mandate) (Sheils & Haught, 2011). Using different assumptions, the RAND Corporation concluded that, if the individual mandate were to be overturned by the Supreme Court or otherwise eliminated by Congress, the number of people covered through the ACA would drop from 27 million to 15 million as of 2016, but it would not send premiums into a death spiral that would make health insurance unaffordable for those not qualifying for new government subsidies (Eibner & Price, 2012).

Future effects of the individual mandate on health insurance premiums are more difficult to pinpoint, depending on which segments of the private health insurance one analyzes. However, the CBO's initial projections in November 2009 assumed that the greater amount of coverage (more benefits) required in the individual market—where the effects of the ACA's mandate would be greatest—would increase premiums by 27 to 30 percent above average premium levels otherwise expected in that nongroup market by 2016. Other CBO assumptions about the effects of new insurance rules and a different mix of insured people within that market would lower that premium hike to about 10 to 13 percent overall (Congressional Budget Office, 2009).

One overlooked characteristic of the individual mandate is that it would largely apply to the young, healthy, and voluntarily uninsured, who do not use much health care, do not account for more than a small fraction of the costs of uncompensated care, and therefore contribute little to any purported cost shifting. One recent estimate concluded that the individual mandate itself would affect no more than approximately $12.8 billion of the annual $43 billion uncompensated care figure often cited by its advocates. In 2010 the voluntarily uninsured (those not otherwise covered by Medicaid, not likely to gain coverage under new insurance rules providing greater access to private coverage for those with preexisting health conditions, and not poor enough to be exempted from the mandate) consumed, on average, only $854 in health care services. Hence, even though they generally *overcompensate* the market for their own care when they need it, because they generally are not able to obtain care at discounted prices negotiated by insurance providers or Medicaid programs, they remain more likely to decide to pay the penalty associated with the mandate as a more economically rational choice than paying much more for mandated health insurance that it is worth it to them (U.S. Supreme Court, 2012).

EVEN LESS SIGNIFICANT ARGUMENTS FOR AN INDIVIDUAL MANDATE

Individual mandate defenders often adopt a "throw in the kitchen sink" medley of lesser arguments to try to bolster their case, such as past support (several decades ago) from members of Congress and Republican-leaning think tanks, denials of coverage or higher premium charges for those with preexisting health conditions in "voluntary" insurance markets, and personal bankruptcies due to high medical costs and lack of health insurance.

Congressional Republicans dropped their misguided tactical dalliance with an individual mandate by the spring of 1994 and an overwhelming majority of Republicans at the grassroots level, plus right-of-center policy organizations, always opposed it before then and have ever since (Miller, 1994; Roy, 2012). Objections to the individual mandate as unconstitutional arose several decades later, when the Obama administration tried to justify it—for tactical reasons—as an unprecedented exercise of the power of Congress under the Constitution to regulate interstate commerce, rather than its power to tax and spend for the general welfare (Oliphant, 2011).

Insurance coverage problems for several million Americans with serious preexisting conditions are significant, but vastly exaggerated by the more extreme advocates of the ACA (Capretta & Miller, 2010; Herring, Song, & Pauly, 2008; Pauly & Herring, 2007). They can be dealt with much more effectively through policy mechanisms other than an individual mandate (see below). Similarly, a few published studies in recent years that are long on ideological advocacy and short on empirical methodology have misstated the underlying causes of rates of personal bankruptcies over the last decade as primarily due to lack of sufficient health insurance coverage, rather than other more important ones (Miller & Mathur, 2011).

CONCLUSION

There are other effective ways to ensure necessary health insurance coverage for more Americans that are less onerous and less unpopular. A better mix of policy reform ingredients would rely first on persuasive incentives rather than coercive commands. Part of this approach actually was proposed first in the House Republican alternative to Obamacare, back in November 2009 (H.AMDT.510 [A002] to HR 3962, 2009). The basic idea is to extend insurance portability rights and protection against new medical underwriting due to changes in health status (already provided since 1996 by the Health Insurance Portability and Accountability Act requirements for employer group health plans) to those entering, exiting, or remaining in the individual health insurance market—as long as they maintain continuous qualified insurance coverage. In short, the incentives to get insurance and maintain it would be strengthened. Switching between group and individual markets would become less complicated and stressful. However, those who delay obtaining coverage when healthy, or drop it and stay uninsured for too long, would run the risk of paying higher premiums in the future or facing restrictions for coverage of preexisting conditions they develop in the interim.

Second, it is necessary to redistribute and prioritize current insurance coverage subsidies. There just is not a sustainable line of credit ahead or enough tax revenue to keep financing the levels of tax expenditures and public program benefits that foster the illusion we can pay most, or at least a substantial share, of everyone's health insurance premiums with other people's money. The United States should not, and actually do not, need to bribe upper-middle-class and wealthier Americans to purchase and maintain insurance coverage. It could instead lower their other taxes to offset the net effects of reducing or even eliminating their access to current tax subsidies for the health insurance (like the tax exclusion for the value of health insurance paid by their employers). The latter would help make the full unsubsidized costs, and the real value, of their current coverage and care more transparent to them. The former would encourage them to make more efficient health care choices, but without raising their overall taxes.

However, that doesn't mean that additional subsidies (offset by other spending reductions in the health care portion of the federal budget) won't be needed to help other populations targeted on the basis of their lower-income and higher health-risk needs. Those dollars can help pay for some, and sometimes all, of the actuarially equivalent costs of their basic care. But almost everyone needs to start seeing more of the real price tags in more competitive and accountable health care markets again, instead of the fake ones at the government discount store.

Third, no system of coverage incentives and need-based subsidies is fool proof. The United States has to maintain a back-up system of safety-net protections for those who fall through the cracks or must be protected from the unbearable consequences of their less responsible behavior. Beyond a narrowed base of Medicaid assistance for the temporarily low-income and more permanently disabled, the next layer of taxpayer support should involve more sustainably financed, high-risk pools that are operated by states within basic federal parameters. Such subsidized coverage would still cost more than the conventional insurance for standard-risk customers, but its premiums would be capped in proportion to an enrollee's income and likely risk-related health costs (Capretta & Miller, 2010).

Designing a limited high-risk pool solution in the right way can also strengthen the rest of the private insurance market. Health researchers John Cogan, Glenn Hubbard, and Dan Kessler recently noted how a similar approach worked in the development of Medicare disability coverage in 1973. By publicly subsidizing the so-called tail of the health spending distribution involving higher-cost people with that condition, private insurance coverage for the rest of the market expanded. They found a 0.7 percent increase in parallel coverage for people who had some problems going to work relating to their health status but were not qualified for Medicare disability (Cogan, Hubbard, & Kessler, 2008).

Fourth, no matter how much money taxpayers decide they can afford to throw at the wall of insurance coverage problems, the real key to affordability is health care that is delivered quicker, simpler, cheaper, more consistently, and more effectively. An individual mandate tries to ignore that problem, because it cannot solve it. To fix it, better incentives are needed for more efficient health care. Less affordable health insurance is a secondary symptom, not the primary cause, of high-cost health care. Private purchasers and taxpayers should insist that insurers and health care providers find ways to offer different mixes and methods of care and coverage that cost less and are worth more.

Instead of trying to prop up a controversial and ineffective individual mandate, U.S. society should focus on the most important unmet tasks of true health reform: improving the value of health care (and its related insurance financing) that is delivered to patients so that more people can and will purchase it voluntarily, and investing in other, more effective ways to boost their lifetime health. Insurance coverage still can be increased through less intrusive means, such as higher premiums for those who delay, or fail to maintain, coverage; more targeted and equitable subsidies; and better products that customers will purchase voluntarily.

Note: A version of this chapter was published in March 2012 by the American Enterprise Institute in *Health Policy Outlook,* titled "The Individual Mandate: Ineffective, Overreaching, Unsustainable, Unconstitutional, and Unnecessary."

REFERENCES AND FURTHER READING

American College of Emergency Physicians. (2012). *Costs of emergency care fact sheet.* Retrieved from http://www.acep.org/content .aspx?id=25902

Capretta, J., & Miller, T. (2010). How to cover pre-existing conditions. *National Affairs, 4,* 110–126.

CNN/Opinion Research Corporation Poll. (2011, June 3–7). Retrieved from http://i2.cdn.turner.com/cnn/2011/images/06/09/ healthcare.pdf

Cogan, J., Hubbard, R., & Kessler, D. (2008). *The effect of Medicare coverage for the disabled on the market for private insurance* (National Bureau of Economic Research working paper no. 14309). Retrieved from http://www.nber.org/papers/w14309

Cogan, J., Hubbard, R., & Kessler, D. (2011, March 11). ObamaCare and the truth about "cost shifting." *The Wall Street Journal.* Retrieved from http://online.wsj.com/article/SB10001424052748703560404576189012255187694.html

Congressional Budget Office. (2009). *An analysis of health insurance premiums under the patient protection and affordable care act, report to U.S. Senator Evan Bayh.* Retrieved from http://www.cbo.gov/sites/default/files/cbofiles/ftpdocs/107xx/doc10781/ 11–30-premiums.pdf

Congressional Budget Office. (2011, March 30). *CBO's Analysis of the Major Health Care Legislation Enacted in March 2010, Statement of CBO Director Douglas W. Elmendorf before Subcommittee on Health, Committee on Energy and Commerce.* Retrieved from http:// www.cbo.gov/sites/default/files/cbofiles/ftpdocs/121xx/doc12119/03–30-healthcarelegislation.pdf

Eibner, C., & Price, C. (2012). *The effect of the affordable care act on enrollment and premiums, with and without the individual mandate.* Retrieved from RAND Corporation website: http://www.rand.org/content/dam/rand/pubs/technical_reports/2012/ RAND_TR1221.pdf

Families USA. (2009). *Hidden health tax: Americans pay a premium.* New York, NY: Families USA. Retrieved from http://www .familiesusa.org/resources/publications/reports/hidden-health-tax.html

Fox, W., & Pickering, J. (2008). *Hospital and physician cost shifting: Payment level comparison of Medicare, Medicaid, and commercial payers.* Retrieved from Milliman website: http://publications.milliman.com/research/health-rr/pdfs/hospital-physician-cost-shift-RR12-01-08.pdf

Garcia, T., Bernstein, A., & Bush, M. (2010). *Emergency department visitors and visits: Who used the emergency room in 2007?* (Centers for Disease Control and Prevention, NCHS Data Brief, No. 38). Retrieved from http://www.cdc.gov/nchs/data/databriefs/db38.htm

Glied, S., Hartz, J., & Girogi, G. (2007). Consider it done? The likely efficacy of mandates for health insurance. *Health Affairs, 26*(6), 1612–1621.

Gruber, J., & Rodriguez, D. (2007). How much uncompensated care do doctors provide? *Journal of Health Economics, 26*(6), 1151–1169.

Hadley, J., Holahan, J., Coughlin, T., & Miller, D. (2008). *Covering the uninsured in 2008: A detailed examination of current costs and sources of payment, and incremental costs of expanding coverage.* Washington, DC: Kaiser Commission on Medicaid and the Uninsured. Retrieved from http://www.kff.org/uninsured/upload/7809.pdf

Herring, B., Song, X., & Pauly, M. (2008). *Changes in coverage in the individual and group health insurance markets and the effect of health status.* Washington, DC: Office of Disability, Aging and Long-Term Care Policy, Office of the Assistant Secretary for Planning and Evaluation, U.S. Department of Health and Human Services. Retrieved from http://aspe.hhs.gov/daltcp/reports/2008/HIcover.pdf

House Amendment 510 (A002), Substitute Amendment to H.R. 3962. (2009). Retrieved from http://thomas.loc.gov/cgi-bin/bdquery/ D?d111:2:./temp/~bdDuVj::|/home/LegislativeData.php?n=BSS;c=111

Kaiser Family Foundation. (2011). *Kaiser health tracking poll.* Retrieved from http://www.kff.org/kaiserpolls/upload/8166-F.pdf

Kelly, G. (2004). Can government force people to buy insurance? *Council for Affordable Health Insurance, Issues and Answers, 123.* Retrieved from http://www.cahi.org/cahi_contents/resources/pdf/n123GovernmentMandate.pdf

Klein, P. (2012, January 30). Romney's Massachusetts mandate deception. *Washington Examiner.* Retrieved from http://campaign2012. washingtonexaminer.com/blogs/beltway-confidential/romneys-massachusetts-mandate-deception/348731

Massachusetts Division of Health Care Finance and Policy. (2010). *Health safety net 2010 annual report, December 2010.* Retrieved from http://www.mass.gov/eohhs/docs/dhcfp/r/pubs/10/hsn-2010-annual-report.pdf

McGinnis, J. M., Williams-Russo, P., & Knickman, J. (2002). The case for more active policy attention to health promotion. *Health Affairs, 21*(2), 78-93.

McGlynn, E., Asch, S. M., Adams, J., Keesey, J., Hicks, J., DeCristofaro, A., & Kerr, E. A. (2003). The quality of health care delivered to adults in the United States. *New England Journal of Medicine, 348*(26), 2635–2645. Retrieved from http://www.nejm.org/doi/full/10.1056/NEJMsa022615

Miller, T. (1994, June 13). *Cato Institute policy analysis, no. 210: Nickles-Stearns is not the market choice for health care reform.* Retrieved from The Cato Institute website: http://www.cato.org/pubs/pas/pa210.pdf

Miller, T. (2008, September 4). Covering the uninsured: Springing a leak in the "cost shifting hydraulic" [Health Affairs Blog]. Retrieved from http://healthaffairs.org/blog/2008/09/04/covering-the-uninsured-springing-a-leak-in-the-cost-shifting-hydraulic

Miller, T. P. (2012, June 29). The health care law fight isn't over. *Los Angeles Times.* Retrieved from http://www.aei.org/article/health/healthcare-reform/ppaca/the-health-care-law-fight-isnt-over

Miller, T., & Mathur, A. (2011, April 27). *Clarifying the research on medical bankruptcy: a response to Representative Kildee, House committee on education and the workforce.* Retrieved from http:www.aei.org/speech/economics/retirement/clarifying-the-research-on-medical-bankruptcy

Obama, B. (2009, June 15). Text of Obama's speech to the AMA. *Wall Street Journal: Health Blog.* Retrieved from http://blogs.wsj.com/health/2009/06/15/text-of-obamas-speech-before-the-ama

Oliphant, J. (2011, November 1). A long strange trip. *The American Lawyer.* Retrieved from http://www.law.com/jsp/tal/PubArticleFriendlyTAL.jsp?id=1202519697727

Patient Protection and Affordable Care Act of 2010. Pub. L. No. 111–148 (2010). Retrieved from http://www.gpo.gov/fdsys/pkg/PLAW-111pub1148/pdf/PLAW-111pub1148.pdf

Pauly, M., & Herring, B. (2007). Risk pooling and regulation: Policy and reality in today's individual health insurance market. *Health Affairs, 26*(3), 770–779.

Pitts, S., Niska, R. W., Xu, J., & Burt, C. W. (2008). National hospital ambulatory medical care survey: 2006 emergency department summary. *National Health Statistics Reports, 7.* Retrieved from http://www.cdc.gov/nchs/data/nhsr/nhsr007.pdf

Roy, A. (2011, February 2). Myths of the "Free rider" health care problem. *The Apothecary.* Retrieved from http://www.forbes.com/sites/aroy/2011/02/02/myths-of-the-free-rider-health-care-problem

Roy, A. (2012, February 7). The tortuous history of conservatives and the individual mandate. *Forbes.* Retrieved from The Apothecary blog: http://www.forbes.com/sites/aroy/2012/02/07/the-tortuous-conservative-history-of-the-individual-mandate

Sheils, J., & Haught, R. (2011). Without the individual mandate, the affordable care act would still cover 23 million; premiums would rise less than predicted. *Health Affairs, 30*(11), 2177–2185.

Tang, N., Stein, J., Hsia, R. Y., Maselli, J. H., & Gonzales, R. (2010). Trends and characteristics of U.S. emergency department visits, 1997–2007. *Journal of the American Medical Association, 304*(6), 664–670.

Turner, G.-M., Capretta, J. C., Miller, T. P., & Moffit, R. E. (2011) *Why ObamaCare is wrong for America.* New York, NY: HarperCollins.

U.S. Supreme Court. (2012). *Brief for* amici curiae *economists in support of respondents regarding individual mandate.* Retrieved from http://www.americanbar.org/content/dam/aba/publications/supreme_court_preview/briefs/11-398_respondents_amcu_economists.authcheckdam.pdf

Thomas Miller

Insurance Regulation

POINT: Regulation of the insurance industry is required to address egregious problems in the private insurance market, such as rescission, lifetime or annual limits, preexisting-condition clauses, essential benefits, and medical-loss ratios.

Jason M. Hockenberry, Emory University

COUNTERPOINT: Insurers do not oppose regulation in a blanket way; however, any regulatory pressure to expand coverage must be actuarially sound. Otherwise, insurers may compensate for increased costs with higher premiums across the board.

Jason M. Hockenberry, Emory University

Introduction

The 2010 Patient Protection and Affordable Care Act (ACA) includes provisions addressing what are perceived by some to be the most egregious problems in the private insurance market, including policy rescission, preexisting-condition clauses, and lifetime or annual limits on coverage. In addition, the ACA address two other areas of growing concern: the standard minimum benefits to be included in a plan (i.e., the essential benefit), and how much of a plan's premium actually goes to cover members' health care needs, (i.e., medical-loss ratio). At first glance, therefore, it might appear to be a wasted exercise to examine the debate concerning policies to address these practices by health insurers, given that they have already or will be addressed by January 2014 by specific provisions contained in the ACA. But there are at least three factors that make the study of these practices worthwhile, even in the era of ACA implementation and beyond.

First, the history of these practices is long, and differences in perceptions of their utility versus their negative effects have been around just as long—and these perceptions continue to inform public debates on health care. Second, it is not a given that the ACA's implementation will be carried out without modification or exception; there are, as of this writing, ongoing challenges to the existing ACA legislation, as many states lag in implementation of the private insurance reforms and threaten to not participate in the Medicaid expansion. In addition, there is the possibility that the ACA could be repealed and the possibility exists that it could be struck down by the courts or rendered meaningless by future counter-legislation. Third, though the ACA as written is poised to eradicate these certain insurance practices, it may not do so without other consequential effects. Developing an understanding of these practices—why they existed in the first place and why they were legislated away by the ACA—and the potential downstream effects is crucial for current and future policymakers. This chapter explores the need for, and value and potential impacts of, regulating specific insurance company practices.

Before one can consider the pros and cons of particular regulations, it is important to have a clear picture of the practices being regulated. *Rescission* is the practice by insurers of withdrawing an individual's coverage upon discovery of information that invalidates the original insurance contract into which the insurer and the covered individual entered. In practice, the discovery of this invalidating information often occurs when the insurer more closely reviews the claims of their higher-cost claimants. The information that leads to rescinding the policy is such that the insurer believes there was material misrepresentation. From a legal standpoint, this material misrepresentation does not always require intent to deceive (i.e., outright falsification), but rather could simply be an instance of inaccurate information provided by the insured at the time of contracting. But this misrepresentation, whether intentional or not, is considered material in that it impacted the pricing of the health risk during the underwriting process, which led to the insured's premiums being set too low given the underlying level of health risk. Several policy changes in most states now require some form of intent or stipulate a specific window after contracting called a contestability period (usually 2–3 years), within which rescission for reasons other than fraudulent misrepresentation must be taken.

The ACA defines *rescission* as cancellation or discontinuance of coverage with a retroactive component, which is in accord with the historical understanding of what the definition of rescission is. Prospective action that withdraws coverage from an individual is generally referred to as cancellation, and the ACA does not have specific provisions against that practice. The exceptions to the provisions against rescission in the ACA are in cases of failure to pay premiums or "fraud or intentional misrepresentation." Demonstrating that the insured fraudulently misrepresented material information is a substantial legal burden insurers would have to meet to rescind a policy.

Preexisting-condition clauses exclude from coverage treatments for any condition determined to be present at the time of the contracting for insurance. A key point to understand in the preexisting-condition exclusion provisions of the ACA is that the provision does not require coverage of treatment for conditions not included in a given plan. This provision stipulates that, if the plan covers treatment for a given condition, specific individuals enrolling in this plan cannot be restricted from coverage for these treatments based on the existence of the condition prior to their enrollment, nor can they be restricted from the plan entirely based on having these conditions.

Lifetime or annual limits on insurance benefits are maximum dollar amounts of the cost of coverage that a given insurance plan is contractually obligated to pay. (There is also a practice of visit limits for certain provider types, most notably mental health providers and chiropractors, but this chapter will focus on the more general issue of dollar limits.) Once the total amount the insurer reimburses care providers for an enrollee's care exceeds these amounts in a given plan year or across their lifetime, the insurer is not responsible for reimbursing any future care. The ACA has a phase-out plan for lifetime limits, ending them in 2014, at which point annual limits are prohibited as well.

The final two issues that will be discussed are the idea of essential benefits and medical-loss ratios. Essential benefits are those services that are required to be included in a health insurance plan for it to be offered. The rules on what is meant by essential benefits under the ACA are currently being developed, though initial indications are that it will be benchmarked by existing plans that each state indicates as containing the necessary benefits. A medical-loss ratio is the proportion of premiums a health insurance plan expends on health care for its beneficiaries, as opposed to profits and administrative costs.

POINT

Prior to the ACA, some regulatory efforts attempted to curb practices such as rescission and preexisting-condition clauses among insurers. For example, the Health Insurance Portability and Accountability Act of 1996 (HIPAA) and various laws enacted at the state level have attempted to address the issues of rescission and preexisting-condition exclusions. However, policy efforts to date have not been effective in restricting these practices. In failing to do so, policymakers have left vulnerable both those suffering the onset of new health conditions and those struggling with chronic conditions and long-term illnesses (Tu & Reed, 2002). These practices also have impacts on the employability and productivity and ultimately financial well-being of those who are exposed to them.

RESCISSION

From the standpoint of contractual law, the impetus for allowing rescission rests on the idea that contracts in which the individual parties made some misrepresentation prior to establishing the agreement should be rendered inapplicable with both parties being left in the state they were in prior to contracting. In legal jargon, this state is referred to as *status quo ante*. In many instances, the concept of rescinding a contract is generally acceptable and satisfying. For example, consider a situation in which an individual seeks automobile insurance coverage. Information that the individual recently had a traffic violation for speeding and running a red light would be of material interest to the insurer; individuals who speed are more likely to get in an accident. However, such information takes time to work its way through the legal and administrative systems, and therefore may not be available when the auto insurer provides the individual a quote for insurance. If, six months into the policy coverage, the information is discovered as a part of the auto insurer's review process, the insurer might decide that this driver no longer represents an insurable risk and rescind the policy, leaving the driver to reapply for insurance elsewhere. In this case, most reasonable people would agree that rescinding the contract was a satisfactory solution, given that the individual seeking auto insurance coverage had not disclosed information that may have led to the insurer refusing to cover him or her and had thus not been charged an appropriate premium. At this point, both the person seeking insurance and the insurer would be left in their original state, with neither much worse off than before.

The problem with rescission in health insurance is that achieving *status quo ante* is virtually impossible. (For a full legal view on this issue, see Lindsey, 2010.) The timing of the rescinding of an individual's health insurance policy is such that it usually occurs when the insured most needs it, when she is in the midst of the onset of a serious and costly illness. This happens because, when the insurer holds the option to rescind a policy based on material misrepresentation, said insurer only has an incentive to rescind that policy for material misrepresentation once a claim has been filed. Rescinding the policy of someone who has not had any claims would, from an economic standpoint, be absurd. This is because the insurer would not only forgo the income from the premiums paid by enrollees who might have their policies rescinded due to material misrepresentation but it would mean that the insurer would also need to be actively reviewing the files of all their enrollees and investigating the health claims made during the enrollment, a costly and time-consuming undertaking.

Instead insurers wait it out, effectively letting nature do the sorting for them. It is much less costly to focus the policy review on individuals with expensive treatment needs than it is to review the entire population, or to scrutinize more thoroughly during the initial underwriting process. The insurer effectively engages in a process of ex post underwriting in which it targets high-cost enrollees' initial contract materials, particularly the forms upon which enrollees are supposed to have disclosed their health history, for additional scrutiny. Operating this way, the insurer can continue to receive premiums from enrollees it might consider to be higher risk, knowing with some probability that it can successfully rescind some of those policies should they incur substantial treatment costs.

This practice of rescinding policies based on ex post underwriting is particularly heinous in the onset or discovery of conditions that require immediate and expensive care. At the time the individual most needs the policy she believed would cover her health care expenses, she is informed otherwise. In this instance, not only has she lost her current coverage but she is also left with little other options to finance her care. Other insurers are likely to refuse her application—she would almost certainly be categorized as a high-cost enrollee—or at a minimum-charge prohibitively expensive premiums. Though self-financed care is a theoretical possibility for such a person, the very fact that she sought insurance in the first place indicates that self-financing for this type of suddenly required and expensive care is beyond her means.

In this case, even if the insured individual wanted to legally challenge the rescission, the fact that rescission has been executed puts the individual in a difficult situation for a pair of reasons. First, to go ahead with treatment not knowing whether she will ultimately win what are often difficult and drawn-out legal battles puts her and her family at substantial financial risk. Second, finding alternate, affordable insurance in the interim will prove nearly impossible. A possible exception might be the case of a person whose spouse has coverage through his or her employer and this episode occurred just prior to the annual open enrollment period, though even then preexisting condition exclusions (which will be addressed below) might still make it difficult, if not impossible, to cover the current condition. Individuals who do not have access to coverage through an employed spouse will find attaining coverage to be highly unlikely indeed. Even a subsequent insurer willing to provide an individual policy would almost certainly charge a premium that was nearly equivalent to the actuarially fair cost of the needed care (even when a condition is certain, there is still substantial variation in the total care needed, and thus costs, to restore health), plus an amount equal to the expected cost of other as-yet-unrealized health conditions and administrative expenses. This would effectively result in an insurance premium that resembled prepaid health care for the current condition, plus true insurance for other possible illnesses, an option that would be even more cost-prohibitive than paying for the currently needed care.

Finding alternate coverage is also an issue for those individuals whose insurance rescission occurs at the diagnosis of a chronic condition. Insurers might target these conditions for rescission because, even though the immediate costs of care may not be especially high, the long-term costs can be. In cases in which rescission occurs at the onset of a chronic condition due to what the insurer might argue was material misrepresentation, individuals will still find it difficult to find other insurance options.

MATERIAL MISREPRESENTATION: WHO'S TO BLAME?

No general audit data are available as to the accuracy of statements made on enrollment forms or on the completeness of medical records. Insurers regularly cite the relatively small number of rescissions as evidence that the practice is not the problem. Rather, they argue, it helps combat a problem that, from their perspective, amounts to fraud. However, tallies of rescission per covered life understate the true proportion of individuals vulnerable to the practice because rescission is not usually undertaken until large expenditures on health care are incurred by an insured.

The complexity of health and medical information may lead to naïve misrepresentation that might later be construed as intentional. For instance, the individual applying for insurance may have, at some point, been given raw information by her physician without clearly understanding the clinical interpretation of a given medical test. Thus, when this individual proceeds to fill out a questionnaire, she may not realize that she (a) has a specific condition or (b) has indications of a condition. The patient could, in such cases, be confused by jargon, or she may simply be less medically literate than a health care professional. From her perspective, then, the applicant would have told the truth as she knows it, despite the fact this could later be construed as material misrepresentation.

One would assume that making it as easy as possible to fill out these enrollment forms would be in the best interest of the insurer; insurance forms are a primary source of information used for underwriting. However, closer scrutiny of the issue reveals that it may actually be advantageous for an insurer to make these forms vague and complicated. As long as the vagueness is not too overt so as to violate specific state laws and the information is accurate enough to underwrite the majority of risks, forms that are vague and induce some misrepresentation allow insurers to target high-cost enrollees for rescission. Insurers are thus able to rid themselves of the financial responsibility of some of the cases where actual outlays for beneficiary treatment exceed expectations without having to spend an excessive amount of effort gathering better information and potentially foregoing some premiums from individuals who may be relatively low cost despite having an indication that they are higher risk.

PREEXISTING EXCLUSION RESTRICTIONS

A second insurance industry practice in need of tighter regulation is preexisting condition clauses. Returning to the automobile insurance example, consider the driver who has had many accidents for which he has been deemed culpable.

This driver is now deemed too risky for any insurer to offer coverage. In that instance the individual has alternatives: He can use public transportation or arrange for friends and relatives to transport him to and fro. Further, it is likely that most people would agree that someone who has been at fault in many accidents deserves the inconvenience of finding alternative transportation.

This is not how health insurance works. For many who cannot find coverage due to preexisting conditions, there is no other option to obtain health insurance coverage if they remain in the labor force but do not have access to employer-sponsored coverage. And, contrary to the case of the bad driver, individuals in this situation are not entirely, if at all, culpable for their conditions. Even in the case of conditions where health behaviors might drive health status, it is not clear what the relative contribution of genetic, contextual, and institutional factors might drive these health choices.

IS HIPAA ENOUGH?

HIPAA has effectively limited the use of preexisting condition exclusions to those who have a break in insurance coverage or who seek coverage in the individual market. For employer group policies, HIPAA specifies that individuals who had creditable coverage (creditable coverage includes a broad array of insurance) during a recent period, and had a lapse of no more than 63 days of this coverage, cannot have any treatment exclusions based on existing conditions if these conditions are otherwise covered by the policy. Even if there was a longer lapse, the preexisting-condition exclusion is limited to a period of 12 months following enrollment in the group's plan. However, the use of these exclusions is still of concern because many individuals with chronic conditions lack adequate access to insurance to begin with, and lack this access for a variety of reasons. For individual policies there are no such provisions under HIPAA.

By limiting the HIPAA provisions to those with creditable coverage, it leaves the preexisting condition exclusion practice in place for those who arguably need the most protection from said practice. Those with severe health episodes or chronic disease are more likely to experience periods of unemployment. For example, individuals with cancer diagnoses may need to undergo treatments that preclude them from continuing employment in the near term, or those with chronic mental health conditions might suffer bouts of unemployment due to an inability to perform in the workplace. During these times, individuals could in theory enroll in Consolidated Omnibus Budget Reconciliation Act (COBRA) continuation coverage plans to maintain creditable coverage between access to group policies. The COBRA legislation was passed to ensure workers who lost coverage due to loss of employment could continue on their current insurance plan. The employer, however, is not required to subsidize this, so the enrollee bears the full premium cost, and the premiums for these plans are often above what an unemployed individual with a health condition is able to afford. Thus, there is a lapse in coverage that exceeds that allowed under HIPAA, and this subjects the individual to at least some period where she would not have coverage for her condition. That this period of being uninsured is limited of course assumes the person is able to return to the workforce in a position that offers group coverage.

Particularly for those with chronic conditions, then, the limited scope of HIPAA creates a vicious cycle of being uninsured, unemployed, and in worsening health. This cycle would likely eventually land the individual in the ranks of the disabled or leave her eligible for Medicaid. However, it is possible that had her condition not been excluded and she had timely access to treatment without financial distress, she would have remained relatively more healthy and productive and off the rolls of government entitlement programs. There has been little empirical examination into the relationship between chronic condition burden and remaining uninsured in post macroeconomic recession recoveries. However, according to economic theory, it is reasonable to assume that this vicious cycle of chronic health conditions, unemployment, and worsening health may be worsened as a result of macroeconomic downturns in the presence of preexisting-condition exclusions used by insurers.

RESCISSION AND PREEXISTING-CONDITION EXCLUSIONS: A COSTLY (AND POTENTIALLY DEADLY) COMBINATION

The interaction between preexisting conditions and rescission is particularly problematic. As was been discussed earlier, individuals who experience rescission of their insurance policy during an expensive health care episode are likely going to be viewed skeptically by subsequent insurers. Even with HIPAA in place, this combination of practices results in what is practically total exclusion from access to nongovernmental health insurance for at least a year at a time when individuals most need coverage (getting coverage for the condition within a year assumes those who had their individual policy rescinded are able to somehow gain employer-sponsored coverage, a rather difficult proposition in the midst of a severe episode of illness). Aggregate statistics on the treatment decisions and health outcomes for those who have their coverage rescinded are not readily available. Therefore we are left to examine overall rescission statistics to get a sense of the scope of this problem. One of, if not the leading, diagnoses used to rescind an insured's policy is the presence, previously diagnosed or not, of a mental health condition (NAIC, 2009). Substance abuse is also a leading candidate and is highly correlated with mental health. It is worth noting that those with untreated mental health conditions often have a hard time maintaining employment, often have or develop severe comorbidities as a result of their condition, and have a two- to four-fold increase in their risk of premature mortality (Druss & Walker, 2011).

In addition, the available data on reasons for rescission provide the diagnoses behind the rescission, not the diagnoses that triggered closer scrutiny of the insured's underwriting data in the first place. It is worth noting that cancers are not listed together in these data, despite being some of the most prominent cases of the effects of rescission (Girion, 2008). Individuals diagnosed with a life-threatening cancer who suddenly have their policy rescinded, and are practically uninsurable due to preexisting-condition exclusions, are left with a very difficult decision: to mortgage whatever financial security they have in an effort to extend their life, or to forego treatment and potentially shorten their lives by doing so. The continued allowance of the practice of rescission and employment of preexisting-condition exclusions is costly to those individuals subject to these practices, perhaps even in terms of life-years lost.

RAISING THE BAR FOR INSURERS: ACA RULES ON RESCISSION AND PREEXISTING EXCLUSIONS

The ACA limits rescission of health insurance policies to issues involving fraud for plans issued in September 23, 2010, and beyond. The plans themselves *must* contain language stipulating that rescission will be undertaken for fraudulent statements or actions in order for firms to maintain the option to rescind policies in these cases. Provided that the burden of proof of fraud remains high and insurers are not allowed to use misleading enrollment processes to induce more misstatements that are ultimately ruled fraudulent, this new policy gives necessary protections to health insurance consumers who otherwise might be subject to rescission.

The ACA also provides new regulations for preexisting-coverage exclusions. First, it strictly forbids *all* insurers from refusing coverage for particular conditions and their treatments for specific individuals if the plan otherwise includes coverage for these services. Thus those in the individual market will no longer be excluded from having their specific conditions covered. In addition, the ACA's rule goes one step further, insuring that an individual cannot be excluded from a plan based on a preexisting condition. Although this second point initially sounds encouraging for those in the individual market who are suffering from conditions which had excluded them previously, it is only going to be effective because of a second provision in the ACA, namely the medical underwriting rules. The ACA removes the ability of health insurers to medically underwrite, and also limits the premium differences charged between the oldest and youngest enrollees to a factor of three.

ESSENTIAL BENEFITS AND LIFETIME AND ANNUAL LIMITS

An area of health insurance practice that has received less attention, but may be just as devastating for those who are subject to it, is the use of lifetime limits on coverage. In these instances, individuals are likely either in the midst of an episode of expensive chronic disease or cancer care, or recovering from an organ transplant, and then they reach the insurer's predetermined spending limit. This leaves these rather ill individuals financially exposed to the high costs of continuing the treatment, and again virtually uninsurable other than by Medicaid.

As of 2009 lifetime limits are included in the policies of more than half of those with employer-sponsored coverage. It is estimated that between 20,000 and 25,000 individuals hit their lifetime limits in 2009 alone (PricewaterhouseCoopers & Raise the Caps Coalition, 2009). Although lifetime limits are usually in the range of millions of dollars for traditional employer-sponsored insurance plans that still have them, the rising cost of treatments would mean more individuals would be subject to these limits.

Annual limits are of a slightly different concern. Of particular concern are "mini-med" plans. These are often offered to hourly wage employees who have little income, and who may not understand the value, or lack thereof, that they actually provide. The median annual limit in these types of plans is $7,000. Although the firms offering these plans hail them as an affordable option for those who would otherwise go uninsured, they can hardly be considered insurance, as they are not generous enough to cover the costs of a serious illness or injury, nor are they a solution to high costs of care associated with chronic conditions.

Relatedly, some insurance plans exclude entire classes of medical treatment. The Health Maintenance Organization (HMO) Act of 1973 mandated the inclusion of an HMO in the choice of plans for employers with more than 25 employees, and included a clause that HMOs provide comprehensive benefits. Nevertheless, over time the face of medical care has changed substantially, and what plans include and define as comprehensive has diverged as is evident in the variation of what is included across plans. Indeed, patients who are choosing plans within their employer's offerings or trying to purchase insurance in the individual market are faced with a dizzying array of information on what is and what is not included in a given plan, the level of generosity of coverage for a particular set of services. Regulatory definition of what is an essential benefit would largely simplify this process and provide some degree of certainty for the insured.

The regulated implementation of an essential benefit package rule would offer an added benefit to insurers. If within this essential benefit package regulation a method for defining what is to be covered were laid out, insurers themselves would know with greater certainty what treatments had to be covered for a given condition from a legal perspective. Assuming this regulatory definition included a clause specifying that the definition of what was essential was based on treatments that scientifically demonstrated their efficacy, insurers would be less exposed to legal liability from patients who attempt to file claims to cover unfounded treatments.

Though an essential benefit plan would require insurance plans to cover more services, this additional coverage is not likely to raise premiums. In their review of the evidence on coverage mandates, Monheit and Rizzo (2007) noted that the increased costs of insurance resulting from mandates was modest. In fact, one of the difficulties of estimating such impacts is that many employers already cover the services that are specified in an insurance mandate, so testing the effects of policy becomes analytically challenging. While this raises concern for researchers, it is also evidence that group insurers demand coverage for these services, ostensibly because their employees value them. Mandating such benefits simply assures that all insurance purchasers have access to such coverage, and that certain classes of individuals do not lack this coverage because of the character of their occupations and employers.

The ACA lays out a plan for defining the essential benefit package, which is being determined as of this writing, and phases out lifetime limits, culminating in the eradication of these limits by 2014. The original drafting of the ACA was also supposed to end the mini-med plans. However, late lobbying by various parties claiming this would lead to low-wage employees facing premium increases that were too steep over such a short period, and would thus result in more individuals becoming uninsured, led to the creation of a waiver system. A waiver allows a firm to continue offering mini-med plans as insurance for their employees, provided that the value of those plans was clearly explained.

However, these plans will also be retired effective January 2014, assuming no further concessions are made to stave off their demise. At that point the health insurance exchanges and Medicaid expansions will be in place, and these will be subject to the essential benefit provision of the ACA. Although it is not entirely clear what will emerge from the current legislative process, it does appear that there will still be considerable flexibility within states to define what is essential, based on benchmark plans currently in existence. Though it sets a minimum, given the complex nature of health insurance benefit design, this lack of specificity does little to provide the clarity and assurance for consumers that would be the hallmark of a well-defined essential benefit package.

MEDICAL-LOSS RATIOS

The proportion of premiums that actually go to paying for beneficiaries' care has been a growing concern. Without regulatory mandates on the proportion of premiums that must be paid for beneficiaries' care, premiums can be used to support inefficient administration or increase profits for the insurer rather than spent on health care or simply used to reduce premiums.

Although some states have enacted policies on minimum medical-loss ratios for individual and small group plans, these are not universal, and the medical-loss ratios required in some states are relatively low. The ACA sets the loss ratio at 80 percent for small-market and individual plans, and at 85 percent for large group plans. This legislation will help keep the proportion of premiums being consumed by administrative expenses and insurer profits under control (Collins, 2010).

CONCLUSION

Comprehensive federal regulation is needed to address these insurance industry practices, inasmuch as the patchwork of state policies and industry best practices have failed to ensure all individuals have access to affordable health insurance. Enacting these regulations will provide much-needed access to care for those with chronic conditions and thus improve their health. Improved health potentially increases employment prospects, a positive spillover for the economy. Failure to enact these policies will perpetuate a system in which individuals lose health insurance coverage or cannot gain access at the time they most need it, and insurers profit as a result.

REFERENCES AND FURTHER READING

Collins, S. R. (2010). Medical loss ratio regulations good for consumers. *Commonwealth Fund Blog.* Retrieved from http://www.commonwealthfund.org/Blog/2010/Nov/Medical-Loss-Ratio-Regulations-Good-for-Consumers.aspx

Druss, B. G., & Walker, E. R. (2011). Mental disorders and medical comorbidity. *Research Synthesis Report, 21.* Robert Wood Johnson Foundation Synthesis Project. Retrieved from http://www.rwjf.org/pr/product.jsp?id=71883

Girion, L. (2008, February 23). Health Net ordered to pay $9 million after cancelling cancer patient's policy. *Los Angeles Times.* Retrieved from http://www.latimes.com/business/la-fi-insure23feb23,0,6265000.story

Health Maintenance Organization Act of 1973, Pub. L. 93–222, 42 U.S.C. § 300e (1973).

Lindsey, G. (2010). Why the rescission of health insurance policies is not an "equitable" remedy. *New Mexico Law Review, 40*(3), 363–390.

Monheit, A. C., & Rizzo, J. (2007). Mandated health insurance benefits: A critical review of the literature. *State of New Jersey Health Policy Brief.* Retrieved from http://www.cshp.rutgers.edu/Downloads/7130.pdf

NAIC: National Association of Insurance Commissioners. (2009). *Rescission data call of the NAIC Regulatory Framework (B) Task Force.* Retrieved from http://insurance.illinois.gov/hiric/RescissionDataCall.pdf

Patient Protection and Affordable Care Act, H.R. 3590 111th Cong. Pub. L. 111–148 (2010). Retrieved from http://www.gpo.gov/fdsys/pkg/PLAW-111pub1148/content-detail.html

PricewaterhouseCoopers, & Raise the Caps Coalition. (2009). *The impact of lifetime limits.* Retrieved from http://www.hemophilia.org/docs/LifetimeLimitsReport.pdf

Tu, H. T., & Reed, M. C. (2002). Options for expanding health insurance for people with chronic conditions. *Issue Brief, 50.* Retrieved from Center for Studying Health System Change website: http://hschange.org/CONTENT/412/412.pdf

Jason M. Hockenberry

COUNTERPOINT

Insurers are not opposed to the regulation of rescission and preexisting-conditions clauses, but legislators and the public should understand the consequences of these regulations, particularly the extent to which they will increase premiums. In general, any regulation that (1) limits an insurers' ability to accurately underwrite by either restricting how an insurer can gather information and determine or limiting the use of clauses requiring accurate disclosure of pertinent underwriting information, (2) mandates that insurers issue policies to all comers regardless of health status, or (3) mandates the services to be included in plans or levels of coverage provided will serve to raise premiums to all individuals or groups in a given insurance market.

Some demand increased regulation to eliminate the practices discussed above under the mistaken assumption that such practices increase the number of people without health insurance. However, the use of these practices is already substantially restricted by national and state-level policies enacted during the 1990s. Despite these existing policies, the ranks of the uninsured remained high, and may be higher than they otherwise would be, absent these restrictions on insurers' ability to control premiums. Indeed, because of rising premiums, many choose to forego insurance coverage because they cannot find a plan that provides them the level of coverage at a price they are willing to pay.

To understand this, one must first understand the fundamental roles that a health insurer plays in the system. The primary role of the health insurer is to pool the funds of the various enrollees in order to pay for future health care expenses. In this way, the insurers act as a financial intermediary, coordinating transactions for various parties who otherwise would pay large transaction costs to do so. Health insurance is different than most other financial intermediaries (e.g., banks) though, in that the purpose of coordination is not to transfer funds between parties who have excess funds available to those who would like to borrow those funds. Instead, the insurer coordinates the dispersion of funds among a pool of people who do not know their financial need with certainty. In this role the insurer also acts as a storer and investor of funds that will ultimately need to be transferred to those who incur a health-related financial liability.

In addition to coordinating financial activities, the insurer necessarily acts as an agent for the individual, or groups of individuals in the case of employers seeking to cover their workers, in multiple ways. The first agency role that most think of is the insurer's role in negotiating prices with service providers and potentially as a quality monitor. Although some may argue whether insurers can do this effectively and to what extent competition among insurers and the level of market power providers have may mitigate the ability of insurers to perform this role effectively, most of the regulation germane to this discussion have a relatively small impact on this agency role, with the exception of medical-loss ratios, which will be discussed below.

Instead, the role that insurers play that is often not considered in these policy discussions is that of getting those seeking insurance into pools where they receive the amount of financial-risk dispersion they are seeking at a price that is actuarially appropriate. Within this setting, individuals have budget constraints, so they may not be able to afford to disperse as much of the risk as they would like. Furthermore, simple economics says that, if people are able to purchase risk dispersion at a price below the actuarially fair price (i.e., the going market price), they will buy more risk dispersion within the constraints of their budget. Because determining the actuarially fair price of insurance requires information gathering, the insurer must expend effort and use techniques to ensure that those who wish to join the pool are being charged actuarially fair prices. Thus insurers have developed a variety of approaches to gathering accurate information in their role as agents helping individuals or groups decide what pools to enter.

RESCISSION: PROTECTING THE POOL FROM DECEPTION

Individual policy rescission in the group market for insurance does not occur due to existing policies governing employer-provided health insurance. As such, rescission is an issue that currently affects the individual-plan market. When health insurers undertake policy rescission, those in the individual health insurance market benefit, because these practices prevent high-cost individuals from staying in a pool. This may seem callous at first, but rescission addresses individuals who should not have been in a given insurance pool at the price they were paying had the person provided accurate information at the time of purchase.

Many are opposed to the practice of rescission because insurers target individuals for rescission after claims are filed, rather than performing extensive information-gathering exercises at the time of contracting. There are simple economic explanations for taking this approach, however. For the insurer to completely vet each applicant to minimize the risk that someone will enter the pool at an unfair price would be a considerably expensive undertaking. Said expense, in turn, would be passed on to all individuals in the plan in the form of higher premiums, and as such honest applicants will pay more than they otherwise would because they require protection against those who either intentionally falsify the information or are negligent in declaring all pertinent information. A less expensive approach that allocates more of the cost to those who are dishonest or negligent is to wait until claims are filed and to then review those specific applicants' information. The reason this is less expensive is it requires the review of a much smaller set of beneficiaries. Furthermore, the threat of rescission creates an incentive for truth-telling and individual effort in providing information during the application process. Not doing so means a dishonest or negligent individual's risk is not dispersed because her policy will likely be rescinded at the time she incurs the financial expense. Thus the threat of rescission acts as a deterrent against misrepresentation.

These points are often downplayed in popular press accounts of specific cases of rescission, which instead often highlight the profit motives of the insurer and invoke an emotional argument. Journalists frequently appeal to the individual's current health state and contrast this with the fact that health insurance executives earn what are admittedly large salaries. However, this tactic distracts from the fact that the individuals failed to provide accurate health information, and as such entered into a pool with thousands of other people at a price below what they should have paid. If society is concerned about issues like CEO salaries then regulation should address that issue. Removing insurers' ability to rescind policies, or substantially raising the legal hurdle to do so, simply passes the expense of additional monitoring on to other honest individuals and will in no way whatsoever affect CEO pay.

Another argument against allowing rescission is that insurers intentionally make forms misleading to leave open the door for rescission when and if a claim is filed. Indeed, this may be the case. However, other mechanisms and policies would prevent this practice at a much lower cost to individuals who are honest and otherwise able to fill out insurance forms accurately. Such regulation includes establishing a standard-language form, or mandating the inclusion of a plain-language warning that enrollees may want to discuss the form with their physicians to ensure that the information they provide is accurate lest the policy may later be deemed null and void.

PREEXISTING RESTRICTION EXCLUSIONS: MANDATING INCLUSION OF INDIVIDUALS WHO ARE CERTAIN TO BE COSTLY

Another feature of the U.S. health insurance system that raises concern is the practice of preexisting-condition exclusions. From the perspective of the insurer, the practice is a mechanism by which premium cost can be kept lower, which is part of the insurer's role as an agent for those in the pool. Furthermore, keeping the premium low allows the insurer to attract more individuals who would benefit from this agency relationship.

Actuarially fair prices are a function of both the potential cost of treatment and the probability of needing the treatment. If an individual already has a condition, the probability of consuming treatment for that condition is high. In a sense, insurance for such an individual is no longer functioning as insurance, but as prepaid health care. Pooling these individuals with others who were paying premiums based on the probability of developing conditions leads to healthy individuals subsidizing the care of those who had not purchased insurance prior to knowing their health state—those with the preexisting condition.

Further, existing policies allow individuals to avoid preexisting-condition exclusions by maintaining continuous insurance coverage in the period prior to developing a condition. In a system in which preexisting conditions cannot be used to exclude individuals from the market, those who choose to go without insurance until they develop a condition could simply free ride off of those who choose to pay premiums and maintain continuous coverage. Those who maintain continuous coverage would therefore wind up subsidizing that free-riding behavior through higher premiums, and more people would likely forego or delay purchasing insurance.

Given the emphasis on the role of preexisting conditions precluding individuals from getting coverage, one would assume that denials of coverage were common. To the contrary, however, current evidence suggests that approximately 10 percent of those under age 35 seeking insurance in the nongroup policy market are denied coverage (Harrington, 2010). This rate grows precipitously with age. This reveals two points of information. First, the risk of developing a preexisting condition grows with age. Second, and more important to the topic at hand, relatively few people who seek out insurance early in their adult lives are denied. So if these individuals would buy into the system at younger ages and maintain continuous coverage, they would not have to later face preexisting-coverage restrictions.

One might argue that cost is an issue especially for young people at a time when entrance into continuous coverage is established. This would be a legitimate concern if it were supported by the evidence. As Harrington (2010) shows, the annual health insurance premiums are relatively low at these younger ages. Figures on uninsured young adults in 2006 show that approximately half of uninsured in the 19–29 age range are in households that have income more than 200 percent of the federal poverty level (2/3 are above the federal poverty level) (Schwartz & Schwartz, 2008). Thus, for many of these uninsured, the affordability issue may not be the driving factor as much as individual preferences for insurance coverage versus other kinds of consumption and a willingness to take the risk of not having insurance later. Absent other regulation, restricting the use of preexisting-condition exclusions further incents individuals to wait to seek insurance until they develop a condition. At that point, the uncertainty of whether there will be a financial loss due to health care needs is much lower; they almost certainly require health care.

In an effort to reduce this delaying behavior, the ACA mandates that young adults be allowed to remain on their parents' health insurance until the age of 26 unless they have access to employer-based coverage. Though this will expand the coverage of young adults, it will still come at a cost. Family plan insurance premiums will rise in anticipation of more young adults staying on their parents' insurance plans. Furthermore, current data indicate that the rate of uninsurance is still high even among 27- to 34-year-olds.

The above arguments do not mean that other aspects of the U.S. health insurance system make it easy for those who develop conditions that start in childhood and carry through to adulthood to gain insurance coverage in adulthood. Children are often covered by their parents' policies, which cannot exclude them. These children, however, eventually age out out of eligibility for that coverage. Most states have dealt with this issue by coordinating and sub-sidizing high-risk insurance pools. From a social perspective, to the extent that a government insurer can coordinate negotiation of prices and improved care for this subpopulation, this approach may be more efficient than removing insurers' ability to exclude anyone with a preexisting condition. The latter incents free-riding behavior by the other segment of the population that qualifies for coverage medically and chooses not to purchase due to consumption preferences.

Given the other ACA reforms, one question that arises is whether free-rider problem is addressed by the individual mandate. The simple answer to the question, as stated, is yes: The individual mandate, if properly enforced, would allevi-ate the issue of free riding in a regulatory environment that does not allow preexisting exclusions. However, as discussed in the previous chapter that focuses on the individual mandate, that is a big "if."

TOO MUCH COVERAGE? REGULATIONS PROHIBITING ANNUAL AND LIFETIME LIMITS

As was mentioned at the beginning of this Counterpoint, the insurer acts as a financial intermediary, allowing policy-holders to disperse risk for a specified price. Regulations that eliminate dollar coverage limits force those seeking cover-age to purchase risk dispersion at levels of spending they otherwise would not have demanded. This increased level of coverage means that these individuals who would have been satisfied with a lower lifetime limit wind up paying a higher premium than they otherwise would have, or else foregoing insurance coverage entirely. The preferences of those who want access to the most expensive treatments are thus to some extent thrust upon those who would not otherwise want to pay for this access.

Not only does removing lifetime limits raise premiums but it also incentivizes the development of expensive tech-nology (Congressional Budget Office, 2008). This is because the market for said technologies would grow. Specifically, it would grow from only those who had more expensive policies that allow for this type of technology to nearly eve-ryone with insurance coverage. To understand why this expansion of technology would occur, consider that under a system with annual and lifetime limits in place the decision to have access to high-cost technology occurs prior to contracting, and individuals would face a price access trade-off, with the price being the increased premium to pur-chase increased levels of coverage. Once limits are forbidden by regulation, however, the decision to access these tech-nologies would likely not be governed by the price mechanism. Though many individuals have policies that include out-of-pocket limits, with these limits, the price is zero at the time the access to the most expensive technology has any positive health benefit. This is because the premiums have already been paid and the lead-up to the most expen-sive treatments resulted in the out-of-pocket maximum threshold being cleared prior to the decision to seek the most expensive treatments.

In theory, this technology development incentive effect would have a feedback mechanism in that it would further increase premiums. An enforceable individual mandate would make it impossible to choose to forego insurance rather than pay for access to the most expensive technology. As such, many individuals would either be forced to pay for the increased level of coverage, or be forced to purchase plans that do not have out-of-pocket maximums. The latter may not be likely, because even with moderately expensive treatments, out-of-pocket expenses due to coinsurance can rise quite quickly. Some would rather pay a higher premium to cap the out-of-pocket maximums. With more coverage of these services, and the incentive to develop them in place, the number of people receiving expensive treatments would rise, thus raising premiums. Finally, not only would this combination of no lifetime limits and a mandate raise premiums but it would also likely increase total national health spending as well as patients making use of the benefits that provide access to these treatments, which themselves would increase in number.

ESSENTIAL BENEFIT PLAN: DICTATING WHAT SERVICES ARE COVERED

Mandated coverage of specific health benefits is not a new idea, as many states have had various mandates on coverage ranging from obstetric services, to chiropractic care, and more recently to mental health services. Theoretically, increasing the scope of covered services may increase premiums, but it is not certain that this will occur inasmuch as employees and employers may change their behavior in response and thus mitigate these increases (Summers, 1989). In this instance, observers do not have to rely entirely on theory, as this is one area of health insurance where there is a large literature on the impacts of regulation.

Many studies do find an increased premium cost associated with a mandated benefit. It has been argued that the direct effects on premiums are modest (Monheit & Rizzo, 2007). However, some of the studies on this topic that find little effect examined mandated benefit policies that largely followed what was already being provided in the private sector, and as such that were likely demanded by most employers or their employees (Gruber, 1994b). Recent estimates of the effects on the nongroup health insurance plan market still suggest that premiums are impacted by benefit mandates (Kowalski, Congdon, & Showalter, 2008).

Well-executed empirical studies suggest that direct effects may not be the only relevant measure of the increased cost of benefit mandates. For instance Gruber's work on mandated maternity benefits has demonstrated fairly convincingly that women of childbearing age suffer a 5.4 percent reduction in wages as a result of mandated maternity benefits (Gruber, 1994a). Kaestner and Simon (2002) show that mandates increase hours worked, ostensibly to cover the increased cost of health insurance coverage. Finally, mandated benefits may also impact the effects on prevalence of coverage, though studies of this issue have yielded conflicting results (summarized in Monheit & Rizzo, 2007). With an effective individual purchase mandate in place, not buying insurance is one less dimension through which individuals can change their behavior.

REGULATING INSURERS' COSTS: SETTING MEDICAL-LOSS RATIOS

Consumer interest groups and policymakers have become interested in the proportion of premiums insurers actually spend on health care for their beneficiaries. Increasingly there have been calls to regulate this medical-loss ratio, as it is seen as a sign of a health plan's quality, though this may be misguided (Robinson, 1997). These calls appear to be driven by the perceived excessive compensation of insurance executives and the belief that insurers operate inefficiently with respect to administrative costs.

On its face, dictating a medical-loss ratio appears to be a reasonable approach to curbing and incenting the cutting of administrative costs by streamlining operations. However, empirical evidence suggests that the medical-loss ratios currently dictated by the ACA are already being met by many insurers in the nongroup market (Abraham & Karaca-Mandic, 2011). Also the trend in most states is that of an increase in the ratio spent on health care (see table 2 in Abraham & Karaca-Mandic, 2011), so the need for regulation may be questionable. In addition, enacting the medical-loss ratio puts individuals at risk of having to search for another plan, as some insurers will choose to discontinue plans rather than be subject to achieving the medical-loss ratio specified by the ACA (Abraham & Karaca-Mandic, 2011).

Using regulation to specify medical-loss ratios is also likely to actually raise premiums for a pair of reasons. First, is that insurers, as mentioned above, serve a dual agent function for their beneficiaries. The agent role not detailed above is that of negotiator of prices and monitor of provider quality (Robinson, 1997). If the dictated medical-loss ratio leads to less effort being expended on these activities, the prices will increase and quality monitoring may suffer as well. Second is that setting a ratio could actually concentrate the insurance market as a result of economies of scale in the administrative aspects of providing insurance. With a specified medical-loss ratio, and limited competition, insurers will have no incentive to keep down costs or try to restrict utilization, because allowing higher prices and more utilization will grow the total funds from which they can draw their administrative costs, allowing executive salaries to keep pace with where they were prior to medical-loss ratio regulation.

CONCLUSION

Insurers do not oppose federal regulation of the market for the sake of opposition. They do oppose regulation to the extent that it potentially impedes their ability to act as an effective agent for the large majority of their beneficiaries. Though these policies are intended to address facets of the health insurance market viewed as failures, enacting them will have negative consequences for some individuals, despite the benefits they may bring to others. Most apparent is that these policies do nothing to curb the growth in health care expenditures, and instead mandate increased coverage and access, which will simply increase the premium costs for many.

REFERENCES AND FURTHER READING

Abraham, J. M., & Karaca-Mandic, P. (2011). Regulating the medical loss ratio: Implications for the individual market. *American Journal of Managed Care, 17*(3), 211–218.

Congressional Budget Office (CBO). (2008). *Technological change and the growth of health care spending.* Retrieved from http://www .cbo.gov/ftpdocs/89xx/doc8947/toc.htm

Gruber, J. (1994a). The incidence of mandated maternity benefits. *American Economic Review, 84*(3), 622–641.

Gruber, J. (1994b). State-mandated benefits and employer-provided health insurance. *Journal of Public Economics, 55*(3), 433–464.

Harrington, S. E. (2010). The health insurance reform debate. *The Journal of Risk and Insurance, 77*(1), 5–38.

Kaestner, R., & Simon, K. (2002). Labor market consequences of state health insurance regulation. *Industrial and Labor Relations Review, 56*(12), 136–159.

Kowalski, A. E., Congdon, W. J., & Showalter, M. H. (2008). State health insurance regulations and the price of high-deductible policies. *Forum for Health Economics & Policy, 11*(2), 8.

Monheit, A. C., & Rizzo, J. (2007). Mandated health insurance benefits: A critical review of the literature. *State of New Jersey Health Policy Brief.* Retrieved from http://www.cshp.rutgers.edu/Downloads/7130.pdf

Robinson, J. C. (1997). Use and abuse of the medical loss ratio to measure health plan performance. *Health Affairs, 16*(4), 176–187.

Schwartz, K., & Schwartz, T. (2008). *Uninsured young adults: A profile and overview of coverage options.* Washington, DC: Kaiser Commission on Medicaid and the Uninsured. Retrieved from http://www.kff.org/uninsured/7785.cfm

Summers, L. H. (1989). Some simple economics of mandated benefits. *American Economic Review, 79*(2), 177–183.

Jason M. Hockenberry

Insurance Exchanges

POINT: Health insurance exchanges are essential to ensure that individuals have access to a choice among affordable health plans and to transparent information regarding the costs and quality of alternative coverage. They also help effectuate insurance market competition on the basis of price and quality, rather than on favorable risk selection.

Alan C. Monheit, University of Medicine and Dentistry of New Jersey

COUNTERPOINT: Health insurance exchanges are insufficient to solve the major problems in American health insurance markets; they may well add complexity, not reduce it; they will not dampen rising premiums, which are driven by health care inflation, and they will introduce new opportunities for adverse risk selection to undermine the major coverage expansion goals of the Patient Protection and Affordable Care Act.

Joel C. Cantor, Rutgers University

Introduction

Two perennial and interrelated concerns with the U.S. health care system have been the continuing increase in the number of Americans without health insurance and the rising costs of health care coverage. According to the U.S. Bureau of the Census, in the first decade of the new millennium, the number of persons without health care coverage increased from 36.7 million persons in 2000 to 49.9 million in 2010, or from 13.1 percent to 16.3 percent of the population. Over a similar period, data from the Kaiser/HRET Survey of Employer Sponsored Benefits reveal that health insurance premiums for employer-sponsored family coverage increased by 131 percent, from $5,791 in 1999 to $13,375 in 2009, with employee contributions increasing by 128 percent (from $4,247 to $9,860). The pronounced change in premiums over this period is certainly indicative of the increasing difficulty some Americans have in affording coverage during a period of relatively stagnant earnings. At the same time, attention has also focused on whether the behavior of insurers—especially a tendency to avoid offering coverage to high-risk individuals—has led to the failure of insurance markets to fulfill their important social role of protecting individuals against financial loss through risk pooling.

In the context of health-reform efforts, two reactions to the above concerns have emerged. On the one hand, some believe that insurance markets need to be purposefully organized and managed to ensure that consumers have transparent information on health plan costs and quality, a choice among competing and affordable health plans, and an ability to participate in markets with rules that constrain the favorable-selection practices of insurers. These advocates have envisioned the use of state or regional health insurance exchanges (HIEs) as a vital organizing structure to achieve such objectives. Alternatively, others believe that HIEs are unnecessary to oversee the dissemination of expanded consumer information on health plans, assure sufficient health plan choices, and promote efficient market competition. Instead, such individuals believe that state regulation of insurance markets, especially in the small-employer group and individual markets, prohibitions on the interstate selling of health plans, and state mandated health insurance benefits have stymied what otherwise could be effective insurance market competition that would yield access to affordable coverage. These advocates of a minimal regulatory approach argue that imposing the cumbersome and potentially costly administrative structure and rules necessitated by an insurance exchange will only discourage insurers from participating in an HIE and otherwise stifle effective market competition.

Barring repeal of the 2010 Patient Protection and Affordable Care Act (ACA), health insurance exchanges will become a reality in 2014. Although advocates of the HIE approach remain confident that implementation will achieve the goals necessary for insurance markets to enhance social welfare, among other observers the prospect of broad HIE implementation has raised numerous policy concerns. This chapter identifies several issues critical to the implementation of HIEs and uses these issues to stimulate a debate over the merits and shortcomings of such a policy approach. In doing so, Alan C. Monheit offers arguments in support of HIEs as a framework for organizing health insurance markets, while Joel C. Cantor takes the contrary view. Underlying this debate is a long-standing conflict between reform advocates who emphasize the need for regulation and government intervention and those that believe that the goals of reform can best be achieved by relying on the performance of relatively unconstrained private markets.

POINT

Ensuring access to affordable health insurance coverage and encouraging effective competition among health insurers has been a long-standing goal of health reform. To that end, reformers have proposed health insurance exchanges (HIEs) as a way to create organized health insurance markets that encourage the efficient and equitable provision of coverage. Among the goals of an HIE are to provide individuals with a choice among health plans, convey transparent information on health plan price and quality, effectuate health plan enrollment regardless of individual health status and ability to pay, and ensure health plan competition on the basis of cost and quality. Beginning in 2014 HIEs will play a prominent role in the implementation of the 2010 Patient Protection and Affordable Care Act (ACA).

THE CONCEPTUAL BASIS FOR HIEs

It is well established that health insurance markets enhance social welfare. They do so by creating the opportunity for risk-averse individuals to spread the potential financial loss associated with unexpected and costly medical events through the pooling of risks. In an ideal, efficient health insurance market, risk pools would have homogeneous actuarial risk profiles. As a practical matter, creating such risk pools is not possible because, compared to insurers, individuals know far more about their health status, past health problems, and perhaps even their genetic predisposition to illness. Such informational disparities put insurers at a disadvantage, leading to high-risk individuals being inappropriately grouped with those who have standard health risks. Over time, insurers lose money on such adverse health risks, and those in the insurance pool with more favorable risk profiles face rising premiums as the increased costs of insuring poor risks are realized. In the extreme, such asymmetric information between insurers and potential enrollees can threaten the stability of health insurance plans.

In response to the threat of such adverse selection in their health plans, insurers, particularly those in the individual and small-group markets, have sought ways to evaluate the health risk of potential enrollees. At best, they have applied tools such as medical underwriting to assign premiums and preexisting-condition exclusions or limitations on plan benefits to lessen the consequences of obtaining a "bad draw" from the pool of potential enrollees. At worst, insurers have been found to engage in more pernicious behavior that has included the redlining of industries and occupations perceived to be high risk; rescinding insurance contracts when claims are made; substantially increasing premiums when individuals or small groups file claims; imposing lengthy waiting periods prior to the onset of benefits; and favorably selecting enrollees through more subtle means such as excluding specific health benefits, strategically locating providers in areas less accessible to those likely to be health risks, and by selectively marketing to low-risk demographic groups.

The need to address the failures of health insurance markets to achieve an actuarially fair outcome is a prominent policy concern. However, some would go further, arguing that health insurance mechanisms should be explicitly designed to transfer resources from the well to the sick, regardless of differences in underlying health status. Adherents to this "social insurance" model argue that public policy intervention is needed to overcome the incentives of private markets that undermine the ability of health insurance to achieve this explicit transfer.

Whether directed at improving actuarial fairness and market efficiency or achieving a more egalitarian vision of the distribution of health care resources, state policymakers have spawned a patchwork of legislation to address exclusionary behavior by insurers. Such state legislation has been implemented in small-group and individual insurance markets and typically includes the following provisions: the guaranteed issue of health plans to all potential enrollees and the guaranteed renewal of coverage for those enrolled, constraints on premium variation by enrollee health status (through the use of full or modified community rating of premiums or narrowly defined premium rating bands), and limitation on the aggressive use of lengthy waiting periods before benefits become effective for those with preexisting health conditions. In voluntary health insurance markets, however, these efforts have not achieved the goals of enhancing enrollment, stabilizing premiums, or creating a more progressive distribution of resources.

A FRAMEWORK FOR HIEs

HIEs are largely a response to exclusionary practices used by insurers to avoid adverse risk selection, and represent an effort to foster a socially beneficial competition among health plans. This objective is to be accomplished through a number of provisions consistent with the managed-competition model of a health insurance market envisioned by Alain Enthoven. In this setting, insurer behavior is overseen by a "sponsor." The key responsibilities of the sponsor include establishing rules to govern access to the insurance market, such as by specifying open-enrollment periods, eliminating enrollment exclusion due to preexisting conditions, establishing premium-setting rules, guaranteeing continuous coverage, and determining which insurers can participate in the market. Within this framework, subsidies are available to ensure that individuals have access to the lowest-cost health plan, and the sponsor actively manages the enrollment process and administers enrollment changes. To further strengthen the environment for competition, the sponsor prepares information about health plan features and makes quality-related information available to enrollees. Finally, the sponsor addresses possible favorable risk selection by insurers by coordinating enrollee plan choice, communicating such choices to health plans, implementing risk-adjusted premiums, and monitoring enrollment patterns. Key features of this conceptual framework have been incorporated in the HIEs sanctioned under the ACA.

HISTORICAL PRECEDENTS

Although HIEs are a critical component of the ACA, they and their managed competition framework are not recent insurance-market innovations. Instead, both have historical antecedents, having served as the foundation for insurance-market reform in a number of policy proposals. Such proposals include Enthoven's own consumer-choice health plan proposal of the early 1980s, the health-reform proposals of the Jackson Hole group in the early 1990s, President Bill Clinton's 1993 proposed Health Security Act (where health insurance purchasing cooperatives were to act as regional HIEs) and more recently in Senators Ron Wyden and Robert Bennett's Healthy Americans Act (with Health Help Agencies taking on the role of HIEs). HIEs are presently a source of coverage for state employees in the California Public Employees Retirement System (CALPERS), for federal government employees and members of Congress in the Federal Employees Health Benefits Program (FEHBP), and are perhaps most prominent as the Commonwealth Health Connector, an essential component of health reform implemented in Massachusetts in 2006. The managed-competition and HIE framework is also represented by the participation of private health plans in the Medicare Prescription Drug program and in the Medicare Advantage program.

Observers such as Timothy Jost have noted that, to date, experience with HIEs has not been encouraging. HIEs, with few exceptions such as the FEHBP and CALPERS, have not successfully controlled rising health insurance costs, and efforts by some states to establish exchanges have not met with sustained success. The challenge for health reform is thus to create a viable exchange model that can meet a variety of objectives that include encouraging enrollment by diverse health risks, sustaining plan participation, controlling health plans costs, and addressing the objectives noted below.

HEALTH INSURANCE EXCHANGES IN THE ACA

State and regional insurance exchanges are essential components of the ACA. In this context, their purpose is essentially two-fold: first, to create organized health insurance markets that promote effective competition among insurers and create transparency for consumers regarding the price and benefits of coverage; and second, to ensure affordable coverage with a baseline of essential health benefits for eligible individuals seeking insurance in the individual and small-group insurance markets. HIEs—in concert with strict market conduct and premium rating rules in the ACA—play a direct role in assuring that insurer competition is not based on favorable risk selection, but rather on competition that seeks to attract enrollees through lower health plan costs and enhanced quality.

Persons eligible to obtain coverage through HIEs include U.S. citizens and legal immigrants and those without access to affordable employer-sponsored insurance and who are ineligible for Medicare. The framework for managed competition noted earlier serves as the foundation for the operation of HIEs. The HIE's sponsor must be a state or nonprofit entity established by a state or by the federal government should a state fail to set up an exchange before 2014. The sponsor can establish separate exchanges for the individual and small-employer markets, a combined exchange serving both, or a regional exchange. The sponsor can also allow multiple exchanges to operate within a state, provided that each serves a distinct geographic area. Participating plans must be certified as "qualified," defined as meeting marketing requirements (to assure that they will not discourage enrollment by those with significant health needs), ensuring a sufficient choice of providers (including those serving individuals with low income), being accredited on clinical quality measures, and using a standard format for presenting health benefits. In addition, qualified plans must abide by regulations relating to guaranteed issue, risk-adjusted premiums, and prohibitions on preexisting-condition exclusions.

The ACA mandates that most individuals obtain health insurance either through direct purchase or through their employers. Additionally, employers face a "play-or-pay" mandate that requires eligible employers to either provide coverage or face a financial penalty. Because such a requirement may create financial hardship for some workers and their families, HIEs assume the essential role of administering new income-related tax credits for premiums and cost-sharing subsidies for medical-care spending for those with HIE coverage. Exchanges also provide tax credits to eligible small employers that purchase HIE coverage, and will assist eligible individuals to enroll in expanded Medicaid coverage. Beginning in 2014, states will be required to establish HIEs for individual coverage, and for small employers with up to 100 employees through separate State Health Options Program (SHOP) exchanges. Prior to 2016, states can limit the SHOP exchanges to employers with fewer than 50 employees, and by 2017 can permit employers with more than 100 employees to obtain exchange coverage.

In addition to these activities, the exchange sponsor will monitor premium increases; require plans to provide a variety of information such as claims payment policies, denied claims, rating practices, financial status, and cost-sharing provisions for in- and out-of-network providers; rate each plan on the basis of their quality and price of benefits; and make available standardized comparison information, uniform enrollment forms, and a standardized presentation of health plan options. The sponsor will also inform individuals about their eligibility for public programs, coordinate enrollment with such plans, and engage in outreach to promote public knowledge about the exchange.

Finally, HIEs will offer four types of health plans (Bronze, Silver, Gold, and Platinum) that will provide specified "essential benefits" but differ with regard to coverage protection (e.g., the Bronze plan provides 60 percent of the benefit costs, and the Platinum 90 percent). HIEs will make available at least two multistate plans through the federal Office of Personnel Management, a response to the elimination of a public health plan as an option in the exchanges. HIEs will offer a catastrophic plan in the individual market for persons under age 30 and for those who qualify for an "affordability exemption" from the individual-coverage mandate, and states have the option to create a basic health plan for individuals who would be eligible for subsides through the HIE because their incomes are between 133 and 200 percent of the federal poverty line (FPL). For those with income between 100 and 400 percent of the FPL, the HIE will make available refundable and advanceable income-related premium credits.

Currently, a number of states have either implemented or are in the process of developing HIEs. To assist in these efforts, the federal government makes grants available to states. To date, 49 states and the District of Columbia have received planning grants, with Alaska the only state not to apply for such funds. According to the Center for Budget and Policy Priorities, as of November 8, 2011, ten states have enacted laws to fully establish exchanges, four states and the District of Columbia have legislation pending, and nine states have issued executive orders establishing or stating an intent to establish an HIE. Seven other governors have ordered the creation of exchange study commissions.

HIEs AND INSURANCE-MARKET COMPETITION

Current insurance markets lack an essential element for effective competition: transparency for consumers regarding the value and quality of coverage, out-of-pocket costs of coverage, and scope and breadth of benefits across plans. HIEs overcome these deficiencies by certifying plans as qualified to participate in the exchange; requiring plans to provide information on performance measures such as enrollment, denied claims, cost sharing, and rating practices among other information; requiring a baseline level of minimal health benefits and indicating the benefit costs that will be covered; rating each plan on the basis of quality and price of coverage; risk-adjusting premiums to reduce market risk segmentation; and reducing enrollment costs through a uniform enrollment form. By monitoring health plan enrollment practices and maintaining state insurance market rules regarding guaranteed issue and renewal, risk adjusting premiums and establishing temporary reinsurance protection during initial period of exchange implementation, HIEs will ensure that health plans compete on the basis of price and quality and not through favorable risk selection.

CONSUMER CHOICE

A frequent criticism of the predominately employment-based system of health insurance has been the limited choice of health plans typically available to employees within a given firm. Such a limitation has been alleged to compromise the ability of individuals to select health plans that are consistent with their preferences for coverage and out-of-pocket costs, thus compromising consumer satisfaction and welfare. By contrast, the individual-insurance market has been viewed as providing potential enrollees with a broad array of health plan choices that more effectively accommodate enrollee preferences. A fundamental purpose of HIEs is to more broadly apply this perceived advantage of the individual market in an environment of managed competition, and by doing so not only enhance consumer satisfaction but also encourage greater quality and cost competition on the part of insurance plans seeking to make their coverage more attractive to enrollees.

As discussed earlier, HIEs will present consumers with a broad array of health plan options. Such an expansion of health plan choices, together with more transparent information on plan costs and quality, will provide the basic elements for improved enrollee health plan selection. To ensure that an expanded choice of health plans also leads to more effective plan competition, HIEs will provide constraints on the favorable-selection practices by guaranteeing the issuance and renewal of plans, risk-adjusting premiums and constraining premium variation, and monitoring the enrollment practices of insurers. These measures, in tandem with more transparent information on insurance costs and quality, will contribute to the creation of a competitive health plan marketplace.

Finally, there remains the possibility—one that was rejected in congressional negotiations leading up to the passage of the ACA—that enrollee choice and health plan competition could be further enhanced through a publicly sponsored health plan. Such an option could re-emerge if private plans fail to provide effective price and enrollment competition. Apart from offering greater consumer choice—particularly for those who have had poor claims experiences with private insurers—public plans might also serve to keep private insurers honest and exert downward pressure on health plan costs. Proponents argue that this is the case because a public plan need only be self-sustaining, is not accountable to shareholders, may achieve economies in health plan administration, is exempt from state premium taxes, will have lower costs of capital than private plans, and exhibit greater bargaining power with providers, among other advantages.

FLEXIBILITY

Under the ACA's insurance mandate, HIEs will provide coverage to the employees of small firms, as well as to those seeking individual health insurance. Because those from small firms are actively working, such potential enrollees may be in better health than those who would obtain coverage from the individual market. Establishing an HIE that merges these disparate groups into a single market could have important consequences for the costs of coverage faced by each group. In particular, in a merged market, premiums for those in the small-group market will rise while premiums for those in the individual coverage market will fall, with the magnitude of the change depending on the representation of each type of enrollee in the merged market. As a result, the welfare of the relatively healthy employees in small groups may be reduced as they face higher premiums and indirectly subsidize the lower premiums faced by those with individual coverage.

To more closely conform to the principle of actuarial fairness, HIEs will have the flexibility to determine the market arrangement most appropriate to the risk profile of its enrollees. Under rules established by the ACA, states have the option of implementing a single HIE to accommodate both small businesses and individuals, or forming a separate small-business exchange (the SHOP exchanges noted earlier) and individual exchanges (the American Health Benefit Exchange). Such flexibility will enable states to determine whether enrollee welfare is best served by combined or separate exchanges and will thus help mitigate any unintended cost consequences and perceived inequities that may arise when groups with potentially disparate risk profiles are combined.

HIEs AND EMPLOYER-SPONSORED INSURANCE

In order to effectively compete in the labor market, and because it remains a valued employee benefit, employers will want to continue to provide health insurance to their employees. By offering their own coverage rather than steering employees to a state or regional HIE, employers can exercise greater control in tailoring benefits to the needs of their specific work force, and may be able to better monitor those health care costs that are unique to their workers. Under the ACA, employers will have the option of retaining health coverage that was in effect on March 23, 2010. Though such "grandfathered" plans must comply with certain ACA provisions, they are exempt from providing minimum essential health benefits, coverage of preventive services without cost sharing, and review of premium increases in excess of 10 percent, among other provisions. Employers will have to weigh the advantages of grandfathering prior coverage against the constraints imposed on those plans by the ACA in regards to adjustments to coinsurance, deductibles, employer contributions, and other plan features. To discourage employers from steering specific, high-risk employees to the HIEs, ACA imposes penalties on employers with more than 50 employees who encourage their workers to seek coverage and premium tax credits from the exchanges. Moreover, oversight by the HIE will identify whether employers are engaging in such selective behavior.

Finally, apart from the issue of penalties, the question remains whether large self-insured firms will cease providing health insurance benefits to their employees, thus adversely affecting the provision of employer-sponsored insurance (ESI). The plan benefit and premium rating requirements for HIEs, as well as the inclusion of required state-mandated benefits, could substantially alter the nature of health benefits and costs to such firms and their employees. Moreover, to the extent that large self-insured firms employ high-wage workers, many such employees may not be eligible for cost-sharing subsidies or premium tax credits. The prospect of having to abide by a specific new set of rules governing health insurance might compromise the value of this benefit to workers of self-insured firms, affect worker morale, and potentially create some workforce instability as some workers decide to seek alternative employment. However, projections by independent analysts suggest that any change in ESI enrollment in response to the ACA will be relatively moderate. In a survey of such estimates, Avalere Health LLC reports that compared to baseline projections of ESI coverage without the ACA, the impact of the ACA will yield a net change in ESI coverage ranging from a 0.3 percent decline to an 8.4 percent increase. Additionally, they note that surveys generally show employers are committed to the continued provision of ESI.

HIEs AND STATE INSURANCE REGULATIONS

HIEs' goals of access to affordable coverage and efficient market competition are consistent with the aims of current state small-group and individual-market regulations. Key ACA provisions (such as guaranteed issue and renewal, and limits on premium variation and the use of preexisting condition exclusions) are already in place in many states so that the transition to such requirements may be relatively costless with only modest changes required to some existing state regulations. For example, existing premium rating rules could be made consistent with the risk-adjusted premiums in the HIE. Under the ACA, states can also maintain existing benefit mandates in their HIE-sanctioned plans, many of which are likely to be valued by consumers. Because some states already provide Web-based information on benefits and premiums in their regulated markets, HIEs may avoid the unnecessary duplicative expense of disseminating such information to potential enrollees (although some start-up costs will necessarily be incurred). Consequently, HIE administrative costs may be mitigated to the extent that states already require private health plans to make such information available, as they also do information on enrollee satisfaction and the number and resolution of claims disputes.

HIEs AND RISK SELECTION

The ACA requires all eligible individuals to purchase health insurance and helps offset some of the costs of coverage by providing premium tax credits for those with incomes between 133 and 400 percent of the federal poverty line. With such a mandate in place, HIEs can avoid the adverse selection problem that arises for private health plans when individuals seek coverage because they are sick. As a result, plans within the HIE should not disproportionately enroll poorer health risks than do plans of comparable benefits issued outside the HIE. Because all qualified plans require a minimum set of essential benefits both inside and outside the HIEs, and because state benefit mandates are to be included in benefit packages, efforts by insurers to significantly differentiate their plan offerings to encourage favorable selection and avoid adverse selection will be minimized. Requirements of guaranteed issue and renewal, the use of age, location, and tobacco use to define permissible premium variation, reinsurance, and assessments on plans with a relatively large proportion of low-risk enrollees will also serve to ensure that plans with higher risks are compensated for disproportionately drawing high-cost enrollees, thus limiting incentives for favorable selection. The latter provision will apply to "nongrandfathered" plans and insurers, with high- or low-risk classification based on the average risk profile of all group health plans in the state that are not self-insured. Risk adjustment will be applied to plans both inside and outside of the HIE, and risk-adjustment methodology must be federally certified (either through the method developed by the federal government or through one devised by a state). Finally, oversight by the HIE's managing authority regarding enrollment patterns and plan switching should sound an early alert that will mitigate any systematic favorable risk selection by health plans.

CONCLUSION

By drawing upon well-regarded principles of managed health plan competition, HIEs represent a unique opportunity to achieve greater efficiency, transparency, and equity in the provision of health care coverage. HIEs will ensure the efficient provision of health plans to consumers by expanding their health plan choices; disseminating information on health plan benefits, costs, and quality; shielding insurers from the consequences of adverse enrollment selection through risk-adjusted premium provisions; monetary transfers to plans that draw high-cost enrollees; and close monitoring of enrollment and disenrollment patterns across plan types. As a consequence of such provisions, HIEs also will minimize health plan competition based on favorable risk selection, thus encouraging plans to seek enrollees through price and quality competition. The ACA's individual mandate along with tax credits to smaller firms will yield enrollment sufficient to achieve economies of scale in administration. Administrative costs will be further reduced through HIE measures such as uniform enrollment forms, taking responsibility for marketing, eliminating medical underwriting, and by simplifying the enrollment process. Recognizing that an individual mandate will cause financial hardship for some families, HIEs will provide tax credits for premiums and cost-sharing subsidies as well as a range of differentially priced health plans. HIEs will also be able to build on many existing state insurance market reform provisions. Finally, HIEs are unlikely to threaten the viability of the existing employment-related health insurance system, thus preserving a primary and long-standing source of coverage for most Americans.

REFERENCES AND FURTHER READING

Avalere Health, LLC. (2011). *The Affordable Care Act's impact on employer sponsored insurance: A look at the microsimulation models and other analyses.* Retrieved from http://www.avalerehealth.net/pdfs/2011-06-17_ESI_memo.pdf

Center on Budget and Policy Priorities. (2011). *Status of state health insurance exchange implementation, as of November 30, 2011.* Retrieved from http://www.cbpp.org/files/CBPP-Analysis-on-the-Status-of-State-Exchange-Implementation.pdf

Enthoven, A. C. (1993). The history and principles of managed competition. *Health Affairs, 12*(Supplement 1), 24–48.

Enthoven, A., & Kronick, R. (1989). A consumer-choice health plan for the 1990s: Universal health insurance in a system designed to promote quality and economy. *The New England Journal of Medicine, 320*(1), 29–37; *320*(2), 94–101.

Gruber, J. (2011). Massachusetts points the way to successful health reform. *Journal of Policy Analysis and Management, 30*(1), 184–192.

Jost, T. S. (2010). *Health insurance exchanges and the Affordable Care Act: Key policy issues.* New York, NY: The Commonwealth Fund.

Kaiser Family Foundation. (2010). *Explaining health care reform: Questions about health insurance exchanges.* Washington, DC: Kaiser Family Foundation. Retrieved from http://www.kff.org/healthreform/upload/7908-02.pdf

Kingsdale, J., & Berko, J. (2010). Insurance exchanges under health reform: Six design issues for the states. *Health Affairs, 29*(6), 1158–1163.

Stone, D. A. (1999). The struggle for the soul of health insurance. *Journal of Health Policy Politics and Law, 18*(2), 287–317.

Weil, A., & Scheppach, R. (2010). New role for states in health reform implementation. *Health Affairs, 29*(6), 1178–1182.

Alan C. Monheit

COUNTERPOINT

The purpose of this chapter is to debate the merits of organizing health insurance markets into state and regional health insurance exchanges (HIEs) consistent with the principles of managed competition. This counterpoint will demonstrate that HIEs—as currently conceived in the Patient Protection and Affordable Care Act (ACA)—will not be effective in creating market competition that will enhance consumer welfare through meaningful health plan choice and access to affordable coverage. As will be shown, the transition from current insurance markets to the structure imposed by an HIE will not be seamless or costless. Rules must be developed and administrative and informational structures and costs will be imposed on states, and in doing so, perverse incentives will be created that subvert the aims of the HIE. These incentives may constrain participation by insurers and cause some employers, especially those with bad risks, to drop coverage or steer their high-cost employees to the HIE, potentially undermining the composition of the exchange risk pool and significantly raising HIE premiums. The development of essential health benefits and possible addition of state-mandated benefits will do little to ensure that affordable coverage is available through the HIE, especially when the cost of medical care more generally continues to rise. At best, the HIE model will largely preserve and extend a cumbersome and inefficient regulatory structure for the provision of health insurance that has been unsuccessful in achieving reform objectives and controlling health insurance costs.

The goals of creating affordable coverage will require a stronger government hand than is contemplated in the ACA. Under current rules, HIEs are a halfway technology that will not solve, and may exacerbate, current flaws in health insurance markets. The strategy embedded in the ACA of preserving existing employer-sponsored coverage arrangements outside of exchanges while establishing HIEs only for the niche of families without access to adequate and stable employer-sponsored coverage which is offered mainly by large, high-wage firms, is fraught with risks. Single-payer advocates argue that the only way to eliminate the private insurance market's high overhead and risk-avoidance behavior is to eliminate private insurance in favor of a Medicare-like plan for everyone. Of course, a government-sponsored single payer for the United Statesis politically well out of reach at a time of partisan divisiveness and record low public confidence in government. Still, there are ways to structure and regulate private insurance to eliminate risk-avoidance behavior and tackle health care cost control. Achieving the goal of efficient administration of health coverage and broad risk pooling will require eliminating opportunities for individuals and firms to opt out of coverage and risk pools. Creating such a structure would be a significant departure from the managed competition paradigm that drove the design of HIEs under the ACA.

HIEs AND INSURANCE MARKET COMPETITION

That HIEs will see only limited participation by private insurers compromising the goal of effective insurer competition. The requirements for HIE plan certification and the cost of meeting information requirements unique to the HIE (such as information on plan quality and service-specific cost-sharing provisions) will discourage entry by insurers. Despite the requirements of open enrollment, limits on health-related premium variation by insurers, and efforts to monitor insurer behavior, entry by previously "uninsurable" individuals (e.g., from the ACA's temporary high-risk pools) will cause insurers to continue favorable-selection practices. Because HIEs will be responsible for checking the legal residency status of all participants and querying payroll databases for applicants for tax credits and subsidies, they will be unattractive to many market participants and may engender political backlash. Moreover, the high degree of complexity and short timeline available for states to tackle the technical challenges of establishing HIEs under health reform may serve to further undermine public confidence.

Ensuring sizeable enrollment is essential if HIEs are to capture the benefits of reduced administrative costs that can translate into lower premiums for consumers. Despite individual mandates, "pay-or-play" mandates for employers, and tax credits to encourage participation by small employers, the voluntary nature of insurer participation and the ability of individuals and employers to obtain coverage outside the exchanges can threaten the ability of HIEs to obtain significant administrative economies. The start-up administrative costs of HIE implementation are significant—including those associated with securing the necessary data to establish risk-adjusted premiums, developing the mechanisms to collect information on plan quality and consumer satisfaction, and assessing eligibility for tax credits and cost-sharing subsidies and overseeing their distribution, as well as other provisions—and will result in additional costs imposed on participating health plans, offsetting the administrative economies from increased enrollment.

HIEs AND EMPLOYERS

Given the likelihood that health care costs and insurance premiums will continue to increase faster than will the ability of businesses to pay, employers can be expected to seek ways to reduce their commitment to provide coverage to their employees. Individual coverage available through HIEs provide an alternative to employer-sponsored coverage, and some employers will steer their employees in that direction. Employers with fewer than 50 full-time-equivalent (FTE) workers are not subject to penalties for dropping coverage, and tax credit "carrots" are too weak to induce them to begin and continue to support coverage for their workers.

In addition, some employers subject to penalties for not providing coverage under the ACA may find it advantageous to drop coverage and have their employees obtain individual coverage through the HIE. The structure of ACA employer penalties makes this especially true for employers just above the 50-FTE threshold. Specifically, employers who do not offer creditable coverage and who have at least one worker receiving an exchange tax credit will be subject to a penalty of $2,000 per FTE, minus the first 30 workers. So an employer with 75 workers in this circumstance would face a penalty of $90,000, a sum that would cover the average employer-paid single premium for fewer than 25 workers. Other employers with high-cost employees may encourage such workers to obtain coverage through the HIE if they perceive that the cost savings associated with dropping coverage, not providing new coverage, or sending some employees to the HIE will exceed the penalties they will face for doing so. Other employers may find the minimum requirements for "qualified essential benefits" under the ACA to be prohibitively costly and encourage their employees to obtain insurance through the HIE. Small employers at the lower end of the firm-size requirement to offer coverage (50 employees) may adjust their number of full-time equivalent employees (e.g., by using more part-time labor) in order to fall below the size threshold. Additionally, some low- and moderate-income employees will find the premium tax credits available by obtaining coverage through the exchanges to be more attractive than employer contributions to their coverage. On this basis, they may opt for individual coverage through the exchanges, creating further incentives for employers to avoid providing coverage.

Such responses can crowd out available employer-sponsored insurance, thus threatening the viability of the employer-based insurance system. The pooling of health insurance risks is one of best-functioning features of the U.S. health care system, with low administrative costs, virtual elimination of adverse risk selection, and responsiveness to the needs of insured workers and their families.

HIEs AND STATE INSURANCE MARKET REFORMS

Although state insurance market reforms developed for the small-group and individual health insurance markets are to be integrated into HIEs, relying on such regulations to support reform goals will be insufficient and likely mimic the poor experience of states to date. Existing research on state regulation suggests that reform of the small-group and individual insurance market has not been effective in achieving the goal of affordable coverage. Instead, key provisions to be applied to HIEs—guaranteed issue and renewal and constraints on premium variation among others—have had the unintended effect of raising the risk composition of insurance markets and increasing premiums.

For instance, since the early 1990s, New Jersey has required guaranteed issue and used some form of community rating in its nongroup health insurance market, which has experienced premium increases in its standard health plans well above national averages and precipitous erosion in enrollment. Although such effects may be mitigated by the ACA's individual mandate and premium tax credits, these key elements of state reform legislation features could significantly affect the risk composition and costs of coverage provided through the HIE. Moreover, in the past, many states have relied on insurers to self-regulate their adherence to rules for these markets. Though doing so has raised issues in regard to effective enforcement, under the new regime these responsibilities would likely shift to the HIE sponsor, adding additional administrative costs that might translate into higher premiums.

HIEs AND RISK SELECTION

Because private insurers are not compelled to participate in HIEs, some carriers with relatively healthy enrollees may choose to stay outside the exchange. As a result, plans within the HIE may disproportionately take on greater health risks. This may be exacerbated by the elimination, in 2014, of ACA-sanctioned high-risk pools, whose enrollees will have to seek coverage through the HIEs. Eligible individuals of modest incomes (low income often reflects poor-health status) who can obtain HIE subsidies and face more favorable premiums also may be drawn to exchanges rather than to insurers who remain outside the HIE. Some small employers required to provide insurance may stop offering coverage so that their older and potentially sicker workers will have to obtain HIE coverage.

Employers with close to 100 workers are more likely to feel comfortable bearing the financial risk of their health plan offerings, a practice known as self-funding. Significant incentive will exist for employers with disproportionately healthy workforces to pull out of the small-group exchange by self-funding their benefits. This practice will increase average risk and cost within the exchange risk pool, further tempting employers to consider the self-funding option. An adverse risk spiral could be the result.

Another potential danger to the exchange risk pool comes from special provisions in the ACA having to do with adults in their 20s. Under the new law, young adults have two options, either of which may lead them to abandon the standard plan risk pool in the HIE. First, because young adults up to age 30 can obtain less expensive catastrophic coverage from individual insurers within an HIE, some insurers may choose to specialize in such coverage, further concentrating more costly enrollees in the HIE standard plan risk pool. Second, young adults up to age 26 may enroll as dependents on a parent's plan at no cost beyond standard family premiums. Many families attracted to this option are likely to have coverage through large employers outside of HIEs, further draining exchange plans of premiums from this young and comparatively low-risk population. Finally, regardless of the health insurance market environment, the possibility remains that private insurers will find subtle means to practice favorable risk selection. Despite the best intentions of HIE sponsors, risk-adjusted premiums will likely be insufficient to dissuade insurers from risk-selection practices.

HIEs AND RISING PREMIUMS

HIEs, as structured in the ACA, will do nothing to address the principle driver of rising premiums: the unchecked rise in the cost of health services. The ACA focuses on reducing the "loading" costs (e.g., the cost of administration, marketing, and profits) added by health insurers over the amount they pay to health care providers. The law does so by imposing minimum-loss ratios and by encouraging states to scrutinize large premium increases. The law also precludes most medical underwriting practices, such as evaluating applicants for preexisting conditions, which should reduce health insurance loading costs. These provisions may have a significant effect on premiums in states that had weak health insurance regulations prior to the passage of the ACA, but any savings will be of the one-time variety. It is clear that even the strongest forms of managed care have been unable to achieve sustained reductions in underlying health care costs, a dynamic that the HIEs are unlikely to change. With the prospect for continuing increases in premiums for plans within HIEs, the cost of federal tax credits and cost-sharing subsidies will also rise, creating a new unsustainable federal entitlement. Likewise, the level of premiums consumers will be required to pay, even after federal tax credits are applied, will continue to rise, over time leading many thousands to be excused from the individual mandate under the ACA's affordability exemption rules. Those applying for exemptions are most likely to be comparatively healthy (with a commensurate lower demand for coverage), which over time will further exacerbate the risk-selection problem discussed above.

CONCLUSION

HIEs represent a long-standing strategy to ensure access to affordable coverage, provide transparent information regarding health plan costs and quality, and promote effective insurance market competition. Despite the best intention of policymakers, however, HIEs are unlikely to meet these goals. Practical experience with HIEs among large public-employer groups at the federal and state levels, and in recently enacted health reform in Massachusetts, reveals that HIEs have had little success in controlling health care costs. The development of HIEs will place an enormous financial burden on states in order to implement the required administrative structures necessary to certify health plans, disseminate information, and oversee the performance of health plans and their compliance with HIE regulations.

The implementation of HIEs, as envisioned by the ACA, is not likely to address the serious problem of risk selection in health plans. The voluntary nature of HIE plan participation will create incentives for some health plans to shed high-cost cases to the HIE, and some employers will be willing to incur penalties to remove costly employees from their insurance plans in favor of the HIE. More generally, some employers will cease offering costly coverage should savings for doing so outweigh the penalties. Strategies such as merging the small-group and individual markets sanctioned by HIEs will not yield sufficient economies to compensate for the significant administrative costs, and the individual mandate and phase-out of the ACA's high-risk pool may result in higher-cost cases entering the exchanges, thus offsetting any administrative economies from the increased enrollment.

An effective regime for delivering health insurance with broad risk pools and minimum administrative costs will require stronger incentives for individuals and employers to participate in coverage, and must eliminate opportunities for low-risk persons and groups to exit the pool. Large employers (e.g., those with over 100 workers) achieve these goals, but the ACA does not create an HIE structure that will. It is essential that all individual, small- and medium-group coverage be moved into a single risk pool with no options to select out. Further, creating strict participation rules that do not permit risk segmentation for insurers would go a long way to making the system more equitable and efficient. Health insurance exchanges, as advanced in the ACA, do not adequately address flaws in the U.S. private health insurance system. As such, they are not likely to achieve the desired end. The first priority of health reform ought to be to fix this high-cost, risk-selection-prone system. Only then could a discussion of how to structure optimal health insurance exchanges be fruitful.

REFERENCES AND FURTHER READING

Cannon, M. F. (2011). *Should Missouri create a health insurance exchange?* Testimony before the Missouri Senate's Interim Committee on Insurance Exchanges. Retrieved from http://www.cato.org/pub_display.php?pug_id=13692

Enthoven, A. C. (1993). The history and principles of managed competition. *Health Affairs, 12*(Suppl. 1), 24–48.

Glied, S. A. (2005). The employer-based health insurance system: Mistake or cornerstone? In D. Mechanic, L. Rogut, D. Colby, & J. Knickman (Eds.), *Policy challenges in modern health care* (pp. 37–51). New Brunswick, NJ: Rutgers University Press.

Gruber, J. (2011). Massachusetts points the way to successful health reform. *Journal of Policy Analysis and Management, 30*(1), 184–192.

Holz-Eakin, D. (2011). Right analysis, wrong conclusions: Response to Jonathan Gruber. *Journal of Policy Analysis and Management, 30*(1), 192–194.

Jost, T. S. (2010). *Health insurance exchanges and the Affordable Care Act: Key policy issues.* New York, NY: The Commonwealth Fund. Retrieved from http://www.commonwealthfund.org/Publications/Fund-Reports/2010/Jul/Health-Insurance-Exchanges-and-the-Affordable-Care-Act.aspx

Kaiser Family Foundation. (2010). *Explaining health care reform: Questions about health insurance exchanges.* Retrieved from http://www.kff.org/healthreform/upload/7908-02.pdf

Kingsdale, J., & Berko, J. (2010). Insurance exchanges under health reform: Six design issues for the states. *Health Affairs, 29*(6), 1158–1163.

Monheit, A. C., & Cantor, J. C. (Eds.). (2004). *State health insurance market reform: Toward inclusive and sustainable health insurance markets.* International Health Economics Series. London, UK: Routledge.

Monheit, A. C., Cantor, J. C., Koller, M., & Fox, K. (2004). Community rating and sustainable individual health insurance markets: Trends in the New Jersey individual health coverage program. *Health Affairs, 23*(4), 167–175.

Stone, D. A. (1999). The struggle for the soul of health insurance. *Journal of Health Policy Politics and Law, 18*(2), 287–317.

Weil, A., & Scheppach, R. (2010). New role for states in health reform implementation. *Health Affairs, 29*(6), 1178–1182.

Joel C. Cantor

Employer Mandate

POINT: Under our current employer-based health insurance system, an employer mandate, sometimes referred to as "play or pay," is an efficient and effective tool to expand coverage.

Kathleen Carey, Boston University School of Public Health

COUNTERPOINT: The employer mandate is neither efficient nor effective, eliminating the flexibility employers have to structure benefits, increasing costs, and potentially leading employers to stop offering benefits entirely.

Kathleen Carey, Boston University School of Public Health

Introduction

The employer mandate, sometimes referred to as "pay-or-play," helps deal with one of the most fundamental concerns addressed in the Affordable Care Act (ACA)—getting to universal, or close to universal, coverage in the United States. This goal is desirable not just from a social value point of view. Indeed, getting to universal coverage is a key economic factor in health care reforms put forth by the ACA; it will create more stable and robust risk pools and therefore will make regulations concerning minimal levels of services required of insurance plans more palatable from an actuarial point of view. The implementation of the employer mandate, coupled with the individual mandate, according to the reasoning undergirding the ACA, will help shore up the insurance industry and equip it to deal with the enhanced requirements the law imposes.

The individual mandate, which requires nearly all individuals to have health insurance, is perhaps the most controversial of the ACA's provisions, exemplified by the constitutional challenges it has faced. That said, the mandate on employers is also worthy of debate, presented on both sides here by Kathleen Carey. The Point essay argues that an employer mandate is a wise and practical mechanism—both from an economic and political point of view—to assist in getting us close to universal coverage; and the Counterpoint outlines the ways in which the employer-sponsored insurance (ESI) has introduced distortions into the health insurance market, which will be aggravated when the mandate takes effect.

Strong cases can be made on both sides of this argument. The case for the mandate is the strength of ESI itself. As Carey argues in the Point essay, employers as insurers offer advantages now built into our system—companies' deep knowledge of the insurance market and their ability to negotiate with insurers, for instance—that should be capitalized on in our effort to maximize coverage. Employers offer insurers natural risk pools, they know their employees well and can work with insurers to develop plans that suit their workers, and they have much greater purchasing power than individuals in the marketplace. And the tax advantages given to ESIs—on both the employee and the employer side—bolster the ESI system now and will continue to do so under full implementation of the ACA.

The strength and prominence of ESI is clearly reflected in the numbers: Employers are the highest source of health insurance coverage in the country by far. According to a September 2011 report by the U.S. Census Bureau (*Income, Poverty, and Health Insurance Coverage in the United States: 2010*), approximately 55 percent of Americans had health insurance coverage through an employer sponsored plan in 2010. While the share of ESI-covered Americans has eroded over the last decade—dropping from about 65 percent in 2000—employer coverage is still, by far, the most prevalent source of insurance coverage for individuals in the United States: In 2010, the share of individuals with private coverage purchased directly, not obtained through an employer, was 10 percent, and the share of those with coverage under one of the three main government sources (Medicare, Medicaid, and veterans policies) was 31 percent. Building from this base to increase coverage seems to be a logical approach, according to many analysts. Indeed, the mandate, as Carey explains in the Point essay, will plant a backstop against the recent erosion of company insurance for its employees, especially given the per-employee penalty for companies with more than 50 employees face.

The analysis of the effects of the mandate becomes more complex, though, when you consider it against the backdrop of the insurance exchanges to be implemented at the state/regional level in conjunction with the other—individual—mandate. In one sense, the requirement for individuals to maintain insurance may help shore up ESI coverage since it will compel more people to buy into their employer's coverage when they might have opted out entirely from the health insurance market. On the other hand, the existence of the insurance exchanges may pull individuals into cheaper solutions to their health insurance needs and may offer small companies an alternative to buying, or continuing, their own ESIs.

Other unintended consequences may result as well. For example, for those employers hovering close to the cut-off of 50 employees, hiring decisions may indeed revolve around avoidance of potential penalties, as Carey argues in the Counterpoint essay. Since the employee count relates to full-time employees, will companies on the cusp hire part-timers to fulfill their growth needs? Another component also offers subsidies for small businesses to provide health insurance: Will these offer strong enough incentives to make the difference?

The Congressional Budget Office (CBO), not surprisingly, has studied the question of the effects of the ACA provisions on ESI, and reporting to Congress in March 2011 has projected a net loss, compared to projections under prior law, of about 1 million individuals from 2019 to 2021 (Elmendorf, 2011, p. 20). This net drop comprises three components: (1) 6 million to 7 million people will not be offered coverage under an ESI plan that would under prior law (i.e., without implementation of the exchanges and other provisions in the ACA); (2) an additional 1 million to 2 million will have coverage through the exchanges, even though they continue to be offered ESI covered; and (3) 7 million to 8 million currently uninsured will be covered under the new law by an ESI plan (this reflects the expectation that many employers who had not been offering an ESI plan prior to the ACA will be compelled by employees needing to comply with the individual mandate, the penalty for not offering coverage, and tax credits for small employers to begin doing so). In this same March 2011 testimony, the CBO commented on the reasons why the loss of ESI coverage is not greater, an effect that many had expected. It cites the fact that the substantial tax benefits of ESI remain in effect, even after the excise tax for high-premium plans goes into effect in 2018. Also at play, among other factors, are the subsidies to help individuals buy insurance on the exchanges, which are most generous to low-income individuals, with much smaller subsidies to middle-income and none at all to higher-income; but since most ESI plans are through big companies that have a mix of high- and low-income employees, those big companies would face considerable penalties if they dropped their insurance.

It is difficult to determine whether the relatively minor reduction—according to the CBO estimates—in the net number of people insured by employer-sponsored plans is a negative or positive. When viewed as one single component alongside the insurance exchanges, individual mandates, federal subsidies, as well as the expansion of Medicaid eligibility, proponents of the ACA would say that the ACA employer mandate works to help us get closer to universal coverage. As Carey says in the Point essay, the employer mandate "is a feasible strategy that has a wide reach," given that the politics surrounding it are easy compared to other forms of expanding coverage. Compared to the so-called Medicare for All approach (i.e., a single-payer system), an employer mandate is relatively benign politically in that it doesn't require as much government involvement.

The moderate changes in ESI enrollment also call into question whether the employer mandate is a "mandate." The fact is that small employers (with fewer than 50 employees) are exempt from any penalties if they do not offer insurance. Even larger employers may not have to pay any penalties if their employees do not use federal subsidies to buy insurance through the exchange.

That said, as the Counterpoint argues, the employer mandate will exacerbate problems that were instituted when the ESI system first developed during World War II, when employers facing a severe labor shortage and tight wage controls turned to ESI as a way to attract employees. Since then, this "accident of U.S. history," as Carey calls it in the Counterpoint essay, has introduced distortions and confusions into the health insurance market. Employees, as the end consumers, are shielded from the real cost of care and cushioned from the real cost of insurance. Perhaps most importantly, as the

Counterpoint argues, the distortions extend to wages, as employers trade off higher health insurance costs for lower, or smaller increases in, wages. Additionally, ESIs can tend to limit choice: Many employers offer only one plan, which then limits employees from shopping around for more suitable or desirable options.

Also, the effect of the employer mandate (as with most of the ACA provisions) will likely need to be evaluated at more local levels. For example, the impacts will obviously differ depending on the size of the employer and whether insurance was offered prior to passage of the health reform bill. Small employers seem to have the most to gain, as they face no financial requirements but can receive assistance in the form of tax credits to begin offering coverage to their employers. At the other end of the spectrum, most large employers already offer insurance to their workers and consequently may not be significantly affected. Although, as discussed earlier, employers near the threshold for facing penalties may have the most to think about when deciding whether to offer ESI.

There will also be a variety of impacts due to the mandate. While the mandate may significantly change the number of options for health insurance available to employees, it may also change the types of plans available and the premiums paid for coverage. New employer plan options will have to meet minimum benefit requirements that may provide more or less coverage in comparison to existing plan options. In addition, as more employees enter the risk pool for an insurance plan, the premium for those plans could change depending on the relative health status of the new enrollees compared to the existing enrollees (e.g., insurance could become more affordable as younger and healthier employees, who had previously avoided buying insurance, enter the risk pool). In general, the effects of the employer mandate will involve many complicated interactions, which may take years before they are fully understood.

POINT

The number of people without health insurance is one of the most pressing problems currently facing the United States. Although health expenditures per capita have tripled over the last two decades, the ranks of the uninsured have grown to roughly 50 million individuals. In recognition that most people inevitably will incur some medical expense, and in light of the high cost of health insurance, a general consensus has developed that coverage of all citizens should be a primary goal of health care policy.

A centerpiece of the 2010 Patient Protection and Affordable Care Act (ACA) is access to health insurance for all Americans. At the current political juncture, despite the widespread interest in reducing the number of uninsured, vociferous opponents are calling for a dismantling of various provisions of the law, if not its outright repeal. Yet many of the arguments against health care reform ignore a troublesome reality: An essential element of any universal health care system is that participation is mandatory.

This essay is premised on the principles that expanding health insurance coverage to all Americans is a social goal that ought to be pursued and that a requirement for reaching that goal is compulsory participation in the system. It follows that the overarching health policy challenge we now confront is finding the best way to achieve health insurance coverage for all. This is the primary concern, and it should frame any debate over where we go from here.

An important provision of the health care reform law is a play-or-pay mandate on employers to provide health insurance for their employees. Many people view this as an authoritarian government overreach that impinges on the personal liberties on which our society was founded. This is a shortsighted perspective. This essay argues that the employer-based health insurance system has a solid and proven foundation that is both economically compelling and politically feasible, and that a flexible mandate that builds on this system in order to expand coverage is wise public policy.

POOLING RISK

The idea of a health insurance mandate, whether imposed on employers or on individuals, is objectionable to many. Yet, once the social goal of universal health insurance coverage has been identified, mandatory participation in the system follows from fundamental economic principles.

Medical care is extremely costly and possibly unaffordable, so that in the event of sickness people face the danger of significant financial loss. Averse to such undesirable risk, they prefer to have insurance. Although the probability of illness for an individual is highly uncertain, the combined level of illness averaged over a large number of individuals is predictable. This is true because of the numbers involved, and holds despite the fact that it is impossible for an insurer to determine which individuals will suffer from which medical problems. Insurance brings about an efficiency gain because combining risk reduces the risk facing each individual.

If individuals want the financial security that health insurance provides, why in a market system do so many individuals choose to remain uninsured? And more importantly here, why is their decision to do so a problem? Leaving aside for the moment the reality that many poor people cannot afford health insurance, consider the following: Even though individual prospective buyers of health insurance are uncertain about their future medical expenditures, they know more than a potential insurer, from whom they can conceal knowledge about their health status and risk. This creates an information asymmetry between the insurer and the insured, such that those with significant medical problems tend to buy more expensive insurance that provides a lot of services, and many who are at low risk decide that they are better off taking their chances and choose to self-insure. This drives up the cost of premiums for those remaining in the risk pool. In a competitive insurance market, the higher cost drives other people to drop their policy in search of less expensive coverage elsewhere, and still others to opt out of insurance altogether, raising premiums even higher. This process of the bad risks driving out the good ones is known as adverse selection. In brief, including everyone in the risk pool is essential to the smooth functioning of the pool, and a mandate is needed to avert adverse selection.

In the United States, employer groups are the dominant form of health insurance risk pools. This is the case because, to the insurer, a group of people working for a company constitutes a convenient and efficient insurance risk pool. Because people generally accept jobs for reasons other than health coverage, insurers do not expect to attract a large proportion of high-cost workers. Insurers are willing to sell coverage for an employment group at a reasonable rate, because, in most cases, the group represents only an average level of medical risk.

According to Princeton University economist Uwe Reinhardt, employer-based health insurance is so far the most effective mechanism in the United States for avoiding adverse selection and for pooling health insurance risks in the private health insurance market. Adverse selection is minimized because many relatively healthy individuals who might otherwise go uninsured are willing to purchase health insurance when it is offered in the workplace. Two major incentives drive this behavior. First, the employer contributes the bulk of the premium cost. According to a survey of firms conducted in 2011 by the Kaiser Family Foundation, employers contributed 72 percent of the premium for a family plan and 82 percent for an individual plan. Second, under a tax benefit established in 1954, health insurance benefits are not taxable as income. Consequently, with employer-sponsored coverage, workers are not required to pay federal income or payroll taxes on either their contribution or the value of their employer's contribution to their health insurance.

CONTROLLING COSTS, IMPROVING QUALITY

The goal of health insurance coverage for all raises the thorny issue of financing, which heightens the critical challenge of controlling health care costs. Employers are well positioned to contribute to progress on this front. In the past, employers have been important players in controlling the cost of health insurance. They have been pivotal in promoting "managed competition," the market forces which drive down the price of health insurance through competition among plans for covered lives, by providing information to households on the quality of services covered by rival plans, and by motivating pressure from insurers on providers to lower costs. The significance of this role moving forward should not be under-estimated. Experienced employers are very sophisticated purchasers of health care who can respond to changes in the insurance market, and who are more adept at identifying high-quality health care plans than are people purchasing in the individual insurance market. Employers also are able to take advantage of economies of scale in buying insurance. Their administrative costs are curtailed, and their bargaining power is considerable because insurers ordinarily are willing to accept lower premiums in return for high volumes of covered lives. Indeed, as confirmed by Pricewaterhouse Coopers, the cost of health insurance on the individual market is 42 percent higher than on the large group market. Expansion of employer participation through the mandate will have considerable value as health reform progresses and we continue to wrestle with controlling cost.

Employers also have an inherent interest in the health of their workers for the simple reason that healthier workers are more productive and have fewer sick or disability days. This hails back to the days of the early industrialists, who recognized the need to provide health care as well as wages for their employees, and held sickness funds earmarked for medical care out of receipts. Today, employers play a positive role in promoting the health of their employees and increasingly are finding it worthwhile to provide incentives that encourage health-improving behaviors. These range from carrots such as offering reimbursement for gym memberships or discounts on insurance premiums conditional on meeting health standards, to sticks such as adopting policies of no tobacco use, on or off the job. Prodding workers to adopt healthier lifestyles is yet another function performed by employers that should not be underrated as we elect health policies for the future: A recent study conducted by Kenneth Thorpe of Emory University projected that, if current trends continue, over 40 percent of Americans will be obese by 2018 and that spending on the obesity epidemic will quadruple to $344 billion annually (United Health Foundation, 2009).

Some argue that the economic advantages of pooling risk though the employer-based system will diminish under health care reform once the health insurance exchanges are up and running and public subsidies are in place. But for the reasons cited above, employer-based coverage will remain a relative bargain. It is also important to bear in mind that the employer mandate is part of a reform effort that includes a penalty, federal subsidies to assist small employers to provide insurance, an individual mandate to encourage individuals to buy insurance, and a health insurance exchange to facilitate the process when employer coverage is not available or remains too expensive. This combination of provisions will protect employer flexibility and at the same time help the employer mandate to be a more effective lever in the objective of increasing coverage.

PROMOTING EQUITY

Much of the above discussion extols the economic advantages of the employer-based system itself, and emphasizes that by preventing the erosion of employer participation in the provision of health insurance, the mandate will expand these benefits. But the most compelling economic argument in favor of mandating employer participation is that it will extend coverage to many of the working uninsured by enabling low-wage earners who would otherwise have difficulty purchasing it. Many working Americans do not have health insurance coverage, and most of these workers have low incomes. According to research recently conducted by the Center for Economic and Policy Research (CEPR), in 2008, 21 million workers aged 18 to 64 did not have health insurance. For the lowest wage earners (the bottom quintile), approximately 37 percent (about 9.1 million people) had no coverage (Rho & Schmitt, 2010).

When uninsured Americans are asked why they do not purchase health insurance, the usual reply is that the premiums are unaffordable. Yet medical bills for those who must pay out-of-pocket are generally higher than those paid by health insurers, who receive discounts from the same providers for identical services. Insurance premiums are also more expensive on the individual market. This is not because insurers are trying to discriminate against the financially vulnerable, but rather because the average health risk that insurers anticipate when insuring employer groups does not carry over to the individual insurance market. Insurers know that people who expect to have higher-than-average medical costs are more likely to buy health insurance. To protect themselves from adverse selection, they price policies sold on the individual market much higher than the equivalent coverage sold to an employer group. Although perfectly rational from the business perspective of the insurer, the outcome is glaring inequity.

Other inequities are more subtle. That individuals do not have health insurance does not mean that they do not receive any health care. The uninsured receive tens of billions of dollars worth of uncompensated care annually in hospitals, clinics, and physicians' offices. Economist Jack Hadley and his colleagues at the Urban Institute estimated that nonelderly Americans who were uninsured for the entire year 2008 received $1,686 per capita in medical spending, compared to $4,463 per capita for those who were insured for the entire year. But only $583 per capita was paid out-of-pocket by the uninsured; the rest came from other sources of payment, including charity care, direct public-assistance programs, or indirect subsidies provided by government (e.g., the "disproportionate share" federal reimbursements to hospitals serving a high proportion of low-income patients) (Hadley, Holahan, Coughlin, & Miller, 2008).

The safety net is meant to inject equity into the system, and without doubt it achieves success on that score by providing a range of services in a variety of settings for those who cannot afford to pay. But the backup system also provides a disincentive for people to purchase health insurance, particularly if they are relatively young and healthy. For many of those individuals, affordability is not the issue; given their low risk, the wise economic choice is to self-insure. Consider the following case in point. In 1986 Congress enacted the Emergency Treatment and Labor Act (also known as the patient antidumping law) requiring that hospitals provide screening and stabilization for any individual needing emergency treatment, regardless of ability to pay. That means that under federal law, a local hospital must provide expensive trauma care to a healthy young man who presents in the emergency room following a bad automobile accident, even though he decided to pass up health insurance offered by his employer in favor of purchasing a new car.

At the core, it is unfair for some people to have to pay for their health care while others who could afford insurance receive care without paying. Without a mandate, millions of Americans will choose to remain uninsured yet will receive a substantial amount of medical care. This is in addition to the facts that these services are too often inefficiently delivered, and that the ultimate financiers are the taxpayers and subscribers to personal insurance in the form of higher premiums.

THE MIDDLE GROUND

Thus far, this chapter has made the economic case that mandatory participation is a requirement for achieving universal coverage, and has described the many economic advantages of the employer-based system. But why is a mandate on employers the right policy? The answer is that mandating employers to provide health insurance also prevails on the grounds of political feasibility.

Although U.S. employers have never before been required by law to provide health insurance for their workers, the employer mandate is neither a radical concept nor a new one. It dates back to the 1970s, when in curious contrast to the politics of today it was a Republican president, Richard Nixon, who espoused an employer mandate. Nixon was staunchly opposed by Democratic foes, including Senator Edward (Teddy) Kennedy, who regarded it as overly favorable to the insurance industry. The foremost recommendation of the 1990 United States Bipartisan Commission on Comprehensive Health Care (the Pepper Commission) was that all workers be entitled to health coverage in their jobs, just as they are entitled to a decent minimum wage or participation in Social Security. The employer mandate also was an inherent provision in the last major effort at national health insurance coverage, that of the Clinton administration, whose proposed national health insurance plan included the requirement that employers provide health insurance for employees and their dependents.

Although Americans generally agree on the core value of extending health care coverage to all, they have wide-ranging views on how to achieve that objective. On one end of the spectrum are liberals who have trust in strong government and would replace the entire private insurance system with government financing of health care for all—the so-called single-payer system, or sometimes the more euphemistic "Medicare for all." At the other end are conservatives who prefer to maintain the status quo of individually purchased insurance with a modicum of reform, such as providing tax subsidies to help individuals who either are not offered it in the workplace or cannot afford it.

Supplanting the current mixed system of job-based and public coverage with a single-payer system of coverage for all has consistently remained off the table of serious policy discussion in the United States. This is somewhat bewildering, given the unwavering popularity and guarded support of the government-financed, government-run Medicare program. Liberals on the other hand have been staunchingly unwilling to support voucher systems that would mandate individuals to purchase health insurance through tax-favored spending accounts. The challenge of a mixed system is to make it work. In policy debates, employer-mandated health insurance occupies the compromise position between a government-sponsored single-payer system and the market-oriented status quo. It falls within limits that are acceptable to most individuals by reinforcing the private-sector solution to the health care problem without relying on unfettered market forces.

The employer mandate is a vital component in the quest to achieve universal coverage. According to recent research conducted by the CEPR using the Current Population Survey (data collected monthly by the Bureau of Labor Statistics), employer-sponsored health insurance is eroding. Between 1979 and 2008, the share of workers with health insurance fell more than ten percentage points. In the absence of this fall, an additional 12.6 million workers would have had health insurance in 2008 (Rho & Schmitt, 2010). The mandate is needed to reverse this trend.

POPULARITY, PRAGMATISM, AND POLITICS

The employer mandate is not a comprehensive solution to the problem of the uninsured. But as a component in a mixed public-private system, it is a feasible strategy that has a wide reach. More than 160 million workers and their families, or almost three in five Americans under the age of 65, receive health insurance in the workplace. The vast majority of respondents to opinion polls declare themselves satisfied with that coverage; in a recent poll conducted by the Kaiser Family Foundation, 88 percent reported a somewhat or very positive experience with their employer-sponsored plan. That such policies automatically cover spouses and family members is a highly desirable feature. And, under health care reform, gone are the days when quitting a job meant that a worker had to endure a waiting period before becoming eligible to receive coverage from a new employer.

On the whole, the employer mandate is acceptable to employers; most firms offer it voluntarily. The nation's largest union federation, the AFL-CIO, has endorsed it, as has Walmart, the world's largest retailer. The mandate will level the playing field between those employers who offer coverage and those who do not, and the play-or-pay feature will provide employers with options, preserving flexibility for small businesses.

From the political perspective, the employer mandate is more acceptable than most other policies because even though it works like a tax, it does not flow through government accounts. Another political advantage is that by harnessing the private sector, it reduces the cost to the federal government in health insurance provision. A 2009 analysis of a preliminary version of the health-reform bill conducted by the Congressional Budget Office (CBO) estimated that in the absence of a mandate, 15 million individuals would shift from employer coverage to subsidized health insurance exchange coverage. When the model added a play-or-pay mandate, however, there was no net effect on employer coverage. The mandate also will ease pressure on the hard-hit state Medicaid budgets, helping alleviate the states' current fiscal problems.

A common critique of the employer mandate is that it would cause increases in unemployment, an ominous concern during times of major economic recession and large federal budget deficits. The CBO report also offers some reassurance on this point. Although the employment effects of the play-or-pay requirement have not yet been tested at the national level, the CBO judiciously argues that the impact of play-or pay on the employment of low-wage workers is similar to that of raising the minimum wage. The latter has been studied extensively, and the weight of evidence is that increases in the minimum wage have very small effects on employment.

THE TRACK RECORD

As debate over the ACA continues, it is useful to look to the experience of the states, which often can serve as laboratories for changes in public policy that might eventually be adopted at the national level. The prototype for the employer mandate is the state of Hawaii, where a play-or-pay policy has been in effect since 1975 and where repeal has never been a serious issue. The outcome has been consistently low rates of uninsured people in Hawaii. The results of a recent comprehensive analysis of the effects of Hawaii's mandate on coverage rates and labor markets conducted by Thomas Buchmueller and his colleagues (2011) at the University of Michigan are very positive. For the period of study 1979–2005, they found that the policy was highly successful in raising employer-sponsored insurance rates for workers with low coverage rates and that the burden of coverage was largely shifted from the public to the private sector. Moreover, they found no statistical support for the hypothesis that the mandate reduced either wages or employment probabilities.

The only state that currently has a higher coverage rate than Hawaii is Massachusetts, where in 2009 over 97 percent of the population was insured. Massachusetts passed major health-reform legislation in 2006 aimed at covering all residents, including a requirement that employers provide a "fair and reasonable" contribution to their employee's health insurance or else pay an annual fee per employee. Although the requisite was only one of a number of provisions contained in the law, it is interesting to note that in the period immediately following its implementation, the percentage of firms with three or more workers offering coverage increased from 73 to 79 percent. The Massachusetts program has been the target of a considerable amount of criticism on the basis of budgetary pressures that may be unsustainable. Yet changing the delivery system to produce high-quality health care at lower cost will be required, regardless of what financing mechanism is adopted, if Massachusetts or any other state is going to successfully eliminate the problem of the uninsured.

CONCLUSION

Record highs in both the number of uninsured Americans and the cost of health care is a dire combination that calls for a practical and immediate resolution. That individuals without health insurance have worse health status than those who do is a reality about which the clinical literature is very clear. A study published in the *American Journal of Public Health* reported that nearly 45,000 deaths in the United States each year are associated with lack of health insurance. In addition to health disparities is the loss of peace of mind tied to the constant threat to the uninsured of incurring unexpected and burdensome medical bills (Wilper et al., 2009).

The increasing number of Americans without health insurance has stimulated concern at the national level that now spans the entire political spectrum; it is now generally accepted that universal coverage should be a primary goal of U.S. health care policy. An essential element of any universal health care system is mandatory participation. Expansion of health insurance through the play-or-pay mandate enacted in the ACA is a key policy lever in a system of regulations aimed at achieving that goal. Employer-sponsored health insurance has been eroding in recent years. The mandate will turn this tide and move the nation closer to achieving universal coverage. And it will do so in the most acceptable of terms, a decidedly salient feature in the current climate of financial crisis and political divisiveness.

REFERENCES AND FURTHER READING

Buchmueller, T. C., DiNardo, J., & Valletta, R. G. (2011). *The effect of an employer health insurance mandate on health insurance coverage and the demand for labor: Evidence from Hawaii.* Federal Reserve Bank of San Francisco Working Paper Series. Retrieved from http://www.frbsf.org/publications/economics/papers/2009/wp09-08bk.pdf

Congressional Budget Office. (2009). *Effects of changes to the health insurance system on labor markets.* Retrieved from http://www.cbo.gov/ftpdocs/104xx/doc10435/07-13-HealthCareAndLaborMarkets.pdf

Gabel, J. R., Whitmore, H., Pickreign, J., Sellheim, W., Shova, K., & Bassett, V. (2008). After the mandates: Massachusetts employers continue to support health reform as more firms offer coverage. *Health Affairs, 27*(6), w566–w575.

Hadley, J., Holahan, J., Coughlin, T., & Miller, D. (2008). Covering the uninsured in 2008: Current costs, sources of payment and incremental costs. *Health Affairs, 27*(5), w399–w415.

Hand, L. (2009, Winter). Employer health incentives. *Harvard Public Health Review.* Retrieved from http://www.hsph.harvard.edu/news/hphr/winter-2009/winter09healthincentives.html

Henderson, J. W. (2005). *Health economics and policy* (3rd ed.). Mason, OH: Thomson South-Western.

Kaiser Family Foundation and Health Education and Research Trust. (2011). *Employer health benefits annual survey.* Retrieved from http://ehbs.kff.org/pdf/2011/8225.pdf

Pauly, M. V. (2004). Conflicts and compromise over tradeoffs in universal health insurance plans. *The Journal of Law, Medicine & Ethics, 32*(3), 465–473.

PricewaterhouseCoopers. (2009). *Potential impact of health reform on the cost of private health insurance coverage.* Retrieved from http://voices.washingtonpost.com/ezra-klein/PWC percent20Report percent20on percent20Costs percent20-percent20Final.pdf

RAND Corporation. (2011). *Analysis of employer mandate.* Retrieved from http://www.rand.org/pubs/technical_reports/TR562z2/analysis-of-employer-mandate.html

Reinhardt, U. (1999). Employer-based health insurance: A balance sheet. *Health Affairs, 18*(6), 124–132.

Rho, H. J., & Schmitt, J. (2010). *Health insurance coverage rates for U.S. workers: 1979–2008.* Retrieved from Center for Economic and Policy Research website: http://www.cepr.net/documents/publications/hc-coverage-2010-03.pdf

United Health Foundation, American Public Health Association, & Partnership for Prevention. (2009). *The future costs of obesity: National and state estimates of the impact of obesity on direct health care expenses.* Retrieved from http://www.americashealthrankings.org/2009/report/Cost percent20Obesity percent20Report-final.pdf

Weissman, J. S., & Bigby, J. A. (2009). Massachusetts health care reform—Near-universal coverage at what cost? *The New England Journal of Medicine, 361*(21), 2012–2015.

Wilper, A. P., Woolhandler, S., Lasser, K. E., McCormick, D., Bor, D. H., & Himmelstein, D. U. (2009). Health insurance and mortality in U.S. adults. *American Journal of Public Health, 99*(12), 2289–2295.

Kathleen Carey

COUNTERPOINT

Employer-based health insurance is an accident of U.S. history. It originated during the singular period of World War II, when firms were in desperate need of workers to carry out the war effort at home, civilian labor was in short supply, and government was managing war economy inflation with wage and price controls. Employers, unable to raise wages, found they could attract workers by offering a health insurance fringe benefit. Health insurance was a relatively new enterprise 70 years ago. But under ballooning employer sponsorship, private health insurance coverage grew seven-fold during the decade of the 1940s—from 20 million to over 140 million individuals.

Today, the U.S. health care sector is very unlike that of the mid-twentieth century. Cost has grown along an accelerated course, climbing from approximately $150 per capita in 1960 to over $8,000 in 2010. Mirroring this has been rapid escalation in the price of insurance premiums, placing many employer-sponsors on new and unsteady ground and causing the percentage of firms offering health care coverage to fall from 69 percent to 58 percent since 2000. More disturbingly, approximately one sixth of the population is uninsured, an unprecedented number. Despite clear signals that the employer-based system is no longer an effective private-sector mechanism for solving the growing problem of the uninsured, government is attempting a rescue by mandate: Under the 2010 Patient Protection and Affordable Care Act (ACA), beginning in 2014, businesses employing 50 or more workers are required to provide "adequate" health insurance for their employees or else face a financial penalty.

A majority of Americans still receive private insurance through their employers, and most of them are satisfied with it, so that expanding health insurance through an employer mandate has a decided political advantage. But a well-informed grasp of the effects of this unplanned and dated system of health insurance provision reveals serious shortcomings. As this essay will demonstrate, it has introduced a number of confusions, distortions, and inequities that have multiplied over time and that will be exacerbated if employer-based health insurance is extended through a mandate. Moreover, despite the appearance of a flexible "play-or-pay" approach, mandating employer coverage will introduce a number of undesirable new distortions into an already overly complex and increasingly dysfunctional health insurance system. Liberals and conservatives alike should oppose this precarious and ill-advised regulation.

WHO PAYS?

Ask a typical recipient of employment-based health insurance the question of who pays for his or her insurance premium and you will likely receive one of two answers. Either the employer pays for it fully, or the employer pays the bulk of it (perhaps 75 percent) and the recipient pays the rest. Ask an economist, and you will be told that neither answer is correct. In competitive labor markets, who actually bears the burden of health insurance cost is not necessarily the same party that purchases the premium; in fact, standard economic theory, supported by a large body of empirical evidence, shows that employers pass on or "shift" the cost of health insurance to their employees. This is best understood from the point of view of the employer, who sees the wage plus the cost of the insurance premium as the total price of hiring labor. Over time, faced with rising premiums, employers adjust wages downward to accommodate the higher cost that they face. And, if under the mandate an employer would choose to "pay" rather than "play," basic economics predicts that this "contribution" also would come out of what would otherwise be workers' wages.

Are employees simply naïve? Not really. To an individual subscriber who chooses not to take up insurance in the workplace, perhaps because he or she receives coverage through the spouse's employer, there is not a connection between that personal choice and earnings. That is, employers normally do not offer employees the option of receiving one salary plus a health insurance benefit or receiving a higher salary with no health insurance. So, from the perspective of the individual, it appears that the employer does indeed "pay" the premium. Yet, from the broader perspective, the insurance premium cost is reflected in a lower wage. Benefits and financing are not transparent to workers, and confusion plays an important role in sustaining the popularity of the employer-based system.

CONSUMER CHOICE

An economic principle that easily gets overlooked when judging the employer-based system is the importance of consumer choice. It is relatively clear that the menu of insurance plan options, which have been selected by employers, do not necessarily reflect employee preferences. Moreover, the set of choices is generally a very limited one. According to the 2011 Employer Health Benefits Survey conducted by the Kaiser Family Foundation, 84 percent of firms that sponsor health insurance offer only a single plan, such that nearly half of covered workers have no choice at all.

What is less obvious is that many employees would prefer to receive pure wages rather than a wage/benefit package. Payments in kind generally are worth less to recipients than payments in cash. Though it is true that middle- and high-income workers may prefer the convenience of obtaining their insurance in the workplace, the value of an additional dollar of wages is much greater to a low-income worker than to a middle- or high-income one. It follows that uninsured low-wage workers may be worse off if they are forced to change how they spend their limited income. Lower-income workers also are more likely to be employed by small businesses, where the choice of plan is most limited. Other parties also are worse off, such as employees who already receive coverage through working spouses and seniors who would like to continue working but are eligible to receive coverage through Medicare.

JOB MARKET DISTORTIONS

Employers are not always able to shift the cost of health insurance premiums to their workers. Again, it is at the low end of the income spectrum where the effects are felt. If workers are already at the minimum wage, employers' recourse in the face of rising premiums is to reduce the number of employees. Many other individuals earn close to the minimum wage, and employers may not find them worth hiring if they are required to offer health insurance coverage. According to research conducted by Katherine Baicker of Harvard University and Helen Levy of the University of Michigan, one third of uninsured workers earn within three dollars of the minimum wage and are at risk of unemployment if their employers are required to offer health insurance. Moreover, these workers are disproportionately likely to be high school dropouts, minority, or female (2008). The Congressional Budget Office (CBO) recently estimated the aggregate employment effects of the ACA mandate on employers: a labor reduction of about 700,000 jobs (2009).

Another misunderstood factor is labor-market mobility, which is constrained by the employer-based health insurance system. Many people believe that the problem of "job lock," the decision of employees to stay in jobs they would otherwise leave for fear of losing health insurance coverage, was solved in 1996 with the passage of the Health Insurance Portability and Accountability Act. But insurance is not fully portable; many employees are still unwilling to leave a job that offers health insurance for one that does not, or for a job that offers a plan that requires switching to different clinical providers. The job lock problem goes beyond the dilemma it presents for employed and insured individuals. Labor immobility restrains efficient market functioning and contributes to lower national labor productivity because many of the workers who remain in their jobs for the insurance are not the best long-term fit for the firms that employ them.

THE TAX SUBSIDY ISSUE

Since 1954, employer-based health insurance has been excluded from the determination of both federal and state income and payroll taxes. That this comes at a great cost in foregone government revenue is evident. Jonathan Gruber of the Massachusetts Institute of Technology estimates the amount at approximately $250 billion per year (2009). Also unambiguous, although less often discussed, is that the value of the tax subsidy rises with income, making it one of the more regressive features of the U.S. tax system. What is less obvious, however, is that the tax treatment of health insurance ends up providing a substantial discount on insurance coverage equal to an individual's marginal tax rate. For workers who pay both income taxes and payroll taxes, this generally ranges from about 25 percent to over 50 percent. As a consequence, the tax preference induces people to purchase more coverage than they otherwise would, and in the absence of a cap on the subsidy, it fails to restrict the generosity of insurance policies or to restrain the persistent annual growth in premiums.

SMALL BUSINESS HARM

As a careful consideration of key economic issues has demonstrated, it is low-income employee groups that stand to lose under an employer mandate. Among employers, it is small business. The rising cost of health insurance premiums has impacted employers across the board, but small businesses are experiencing its effects most acutely. Indeed, small employers cite the rising cost of health insurance as their most significant problem. By definition, even without a mandate, small business owners lack the benefits that come from economies of scale. Their smaller size puts them at a disadvantage in the purchase and administration of health insurance for their employees. While large firms can cost-effectively engage brokers or agents to recommend the best insurance options or hire full-time benefits staff to manage search efforts, the smallest firms must rely on owners, managers, or even employees to investigate insurance options. Higher administrative expense translates into considerably higher premium costs per employee for small businesses than for larger ones, and, in turn, into a proportionately greater toll on the bottom line. Mandating employers to provide insurance or else pay will only aggravate the handicapped position occupied by small businesses in a competitive insurance market.

The National Federation of Independent Business (NFIB), the nation's largest small business lobbying organization, provides strong evidence that pressure emanating from the imposition of a mandate on small business owners will result in substantial job loss. Computer simulation recently carried out by the NFIB Research Foundation predicted widespread firm closings, as well as contractions entailing layoffs and the elimination of positions. Under the conservative assumptions of a 50 percent employer premium contribution and no major reductions in health care cost, the macroeconomic model projected that a mandate would cause the loss of 1.6 million jobs within the first five years of program implementation, with a corresponding loss of $200 billion in gross domestic product (GDP). Small firms would experience the greatest adverse impact, accounting for 66 percent of all jobs lost. Nearly all sectors of the economy would be affected, with the exception of health care.

FURTHER CONSEQUENCES

Small businesses are not alone in the business community in their stance against the employer mandate. Staunch opposition also comes from the world's largest business federation, the U.S. Chamber of Commerce. The Chamber, which speaks for more than 3 million businesses and organizations of every size and sector, views the mandate as an expensive and complicated new barrier to the efficient functioning of businesses. An underlying cause for concern is the additional administrative effort that will be required of employers just to comply with the complex new layers of regulation. Under the play-or-pay feature, employers with 50 or more full-time-equivalent workers must offer health care coverage for their employees with a contribution of 60 percent of the premium, or else pay a tax penalty. However, this only applies if one of the full-time employees enrolls in health insurance coverage purchased through a state exchange and receives a premium tax credit or cost-sharing subsidy. But employers who do offer a 60 percent or greater contribution to coverage still incur penalties if the premium the employee is required to pay exceeds 9.5 percent of his or her income. Enforcement of the mandate requires that businesses submit additional information to the Internal Revenue Service each year; in filing tax returns, employers will need to include the names of all full-time employees, as well as pertinent information about the health insurance plans that they offer.

The intricacies of the mandate introduce a number of troubling new issues. Hiring and firing decisions at some firms will be affected because crossing the 50-employee threshold will prove extremely expensive. For example, a restaurant employing 49 full-time workers that wants to hire another full-time employee will face a $40,000 tax penalty ($2,000 annually, times the number of full-time workers, minus 30). But the penalty can be averted by hiring two part-time employees, by firing low-productivity workers, or by outsourcing. For businesses at or near the 50-worker threshold, estimating the costs of hiring and expanding will be complicated, and decisions will be driven by a government-mandated arbitrary cut-off, rather than the efficient and more productive market forces of price and quality competition.

Despite the fact that the mandate is intended to improve coverage rates, the play-or-pay feature introduces a perverse incentive on employers to drop coverage. Premiums have become so expensive that in most cases it will be much more economical for an employer to "pay" rather than to "play." According to the Kaiser Family Foundation 2011 Employer Health Benefits Survey, the average annual premium for employer-sponsored family coverage in 2011 was $15,073, an increase of 9 percent from the previous year. On average, 73 percent was paid by employers. Some employers may choose to drop coverage because the plans that they currently offer do not meet the qualifications specified in the ACA, even though many employees may be satisfied with the coverage. The presence of an incentive is not a prediction of outcomes; however, evidence from a 2011 survey commissioned by McKinsey & Company and fielded by Ipsos, the prominent market and opinion research company, suggests that a negative impact can be expected. Ipsos drew a sample of 1,329 U.S. private-sector employers, representing a cross-section of employer size, sector, and geographic location. According to survey results, 30 percent of employers said that because of the mandate they would definitely or maybe decide to no longer offer health insurance to employees. The disturbingly large negative response to this important survey question suggests that the mandate not only is unlikely to be successful in convincing employers to begin offering health insurance but also will lead numerous employers who currently offer insurance to drop it, triggering a disruption of coverage for many insured individuals who may be forced to buy coverage from a different insurance plan in the exchange. Moreover, if the firm simply pays, employers' positive incentive to control the health care costs of their workers will be lost.

Finally, the mandate raises awkward new privacy concerns, altering the relationship between employer and employee. In order to remain in compliance, employers will be required to obtain detailed personal information on each household, including family size and the income of other family members. For some firms, employers will face large penalties simply because of private changes in an employee's household. For example, loss of employment on the part of an employee's spouse (for whatever reason) could make the employer's coverage offer no longer "affordable" for that household, imposing thousands of dollars of unanticipated financial penalties on the employer.

THE BROADER ECONOMY

Employer-based health insurance raises many concerns for efficient operation of businesses, both big and small, and mandating employers to provide it will extend many negative consequences and introduce a host of new ones. But in a market system whatever impacts producers affects all players in the wider economy.

The mandate appears attractive from the perspective of government, because it relieves Medicaid burdens at the state level and low-income insurance subsidies at the federal level. But the impact on government is the net effect of many factors. It already has been noted that the tax exclusion on benefits is extremely costly to government in foregone taxes. Government budgets also are weakened by unemployment effects, due to the lost state and federal income tax revenue, as well as from Social Security and Medicare payroll taxes. Moreover, more subsidies are needed under health care reform to assist the unemployed in affording insurance through Medicaid or the exchanges.

Consumers also are indirectly affected. It is clear that the employer mandate will impose new costs on employers. Although many productive companies will manage to absorb the added expense associated with the mandate, many will not. As discussed, economic theory borne out by empirical evidence predicts that the higher cost of labor will lead to some reduction in wages or layoffs or reduced hiring. But for workers already at the minimum wage, lowering it further in order to offset the rising costs of benefits will not be an option for employers. Moreover, the mix between wages and health insurance is not fully flexible, particularly in the short run. Employers do have an additional recourse in the face of a rising price of labor—passing on the increased costs to consumers in the form of higher prices for goods and services.

THE NEW INEQUITY ISSUES: LOW-INCOME WORKERS

The penalty on employers only applies to businesses hiring 50 or more full-time employees, where full time is defined as 30 or more hours per week. This design does relieve pressure on the smallest businesses, but in doing so creates inequities among workers, the very groups for whom access to health care coverage is a key goal of the regulation. The 50-worker cutoff predominantly affects low-skilled, low-income workers, who are disproportionately employed in the smallest businesses. Richard Burkhauser of Cornell University and Kosali Simon of Indiana University applied data from the Current Population Survey, which is conducted by the Census Bureau and the Bureau of Labor Statistics, to a recent study of this issue. They estimated that the vast majority of those who stand to gain under a play-or-pay mandate have incomes at twice the poverty level or more, leaving a significant share of the working poor ineligible for such benefits because they work for smaller, exempt firms. These biases will be mitigated to some extent by subsidies that will become available for the lowest income groups. Small businesses will also be eligible for tax credits. However, the business tax credits are temporary and highly restricted. Only businesses hiring 25 or fewer employees who offer at least 50 percent of health insurance costs qualify, and the credits only apply in the cases of workers with relatively low incomes.

In accordance with the other major stipulation, part-time workers are left out altogether, creating an incentive for employers to replace full-time workers with part-time ones. This is precisely what happened in Hawaii, the one state that has legislated an employer mandate. Though coverage did rise in Hawaii following the implementation of the employer mandate in 1974, many employers began hiring workers for fewer than 20 hours per week, the cutoff for mandated insurance under the state regulation.

More finely tuned provisions of the law impose inequities on the working population in more subtle ways. Robert Greenstein and Judith Solomon of the Center on Budget and Policy Priorities explain how incentives introduced by the law can discriminate against hiring of individuals from low-income families. The provision requires employers who do not offer health coverage to pay substantial penalties for low- or moderate-income individuals who receive subsidized coverage in a health insurance exchange. But they are not required to pay anything for employees who do not receive subsidies because their family incomes are too high. The law also requires many employers who do offer coverage to pay these fines. Penalties would be imposed on such firms for full-time workers who receive subsidies because the benefits do not cover 60 percent of the cost of the plan or because the coverage that the employer offers is not considered "affordable" for them. In essence, these provisions tax firms for hiring workers from low-income families. They discourage employers from hiring such individuals in favor of hiring people with higher-income families—for the same jobs—simply because they do not qualify for the subsidies.

UNINTENDED CONSEQUENCES

Coverage is considered "unaffordable" if the premium share required from the employee exceeds 9.5 percent of income, in which case the employee qualifies for subsidized coverage through an exchange, and the employer is required to pay a penalty. At issue at the time of this writing is the unresolved question of whether the 9.5 percent "firewall" applies to the cost of individual coverage or to the cost of family coverage. The firewall provision of the law was intended to discourage employers from dropping coverage; however, it has larger and overlooked effects. If the firewall is gauged by the cost of individual coverage then many families for whom the more costly family plan offered by the employer is unaffordable will be denied subsidized coverage in an exchange. If the interpretation is the cost of family coverage then the cost of health care reform will be much higher than originally estimated. A recent study by the Employment Policies Institute has estimated that this will amount to an additional $50 billion per year in federal subsidy outlays. No matter how affordable coverage is finally codified into the ACA, there are potentially grave consequences that unfortunately received little attention prior to its passage.

Yet another inequity concern has been observed by Bradley Herring of Johns Hopkins University and Mark Pauly of the University of Pennsylvania. They demonstrate that given the structure of the subsidies, many lower-wage workers in firms that provide coverage can be worse off than comparable workers in firms that pay the penalty. Because each company will make the decision of whether to play or pay based on the average wage of their employees, heterogeneity of employee wage levels within companies will cause the subsidies for many individuals to be mismatched with their level of need.

CONCLUSION

A promise to Americans made by the architects of the ACA was that if they liked their employer-based health insurance plan, they would be able to keep it. Though true for the majority of workers, this sweeping assurance comes with many qualifications, and for low-income workers it is only a partial truth. The goal of reform is to increase health care access for low-income people, but the play-or-pay mandate on employers to provide insurance is laden with adverse incentives, unintended consequences, and new formulas for inequity. The provision is a government overreach that, contrary to the better judgment of businesses, will intrude needlessly, and in many cases harmfully, into the lives of individuals. The United States is the only country in the world where the health care of it citizens is directly tied to the fortunes of the specific enterprises where they happened to be employed. That employer-based health care is an anachronistic system is well expressed in the words of Princeton economist Uwe Reinhardt: "If we had to do it over again, no policy analyst would recommend this model." Yet, despite the considerable challenges facing the system today, the mandate slated to begin in 2014 will elevate them to a new level.

At the current juncture, public policy needs to optimize the opportunities for business to focus on the long-term goal which the U.S. economy is urgently calling for: job creation. Yet, while government is calling on the business sector to create jobs, at the same time it is erecting new regulatory barriers that will stand in the way of expanding and hiring. In the current climate of financial distress, the employer mandate is a dangerous public policy. It needs to be replaced with a plan for increased access to health insurance that is individual, portable, and in tune with a flexible and increasingly global economy.

REFERENCES AND FURTHER READING

Baicker, K., & Levy, H. (2008). Employer health insurance mandates and the risk of unemployment. *Risk Management and Insurance Review, 11*(1), 109–132.

Blaise, B. (2011). *Obamacare and the employer mandate: Cutting jobs and wages.* Retrieved from The Heritage Foundation website: http://www.heritage.org/Research/Reports/2011/01/Obamacare-and-the-Employer-Mandate-Cutting-Jobs-and-Wages

Blumenthal, D. (2006). Employer-sponsored health insurance in the United States—Origins and implications. *The New England Journal of Medicine, 355*(1), 82–88.

Burkhauser, R. V., Lyons, S., & Simon, K. I. (2011). *An offer you can't refuse: Estimating the coverage effects of the 2010 Affordable Care Act. Employment Policies Institute.* Retrieved from http://epionline.org/studies/110715_EPI_AnOfferYouCantRefuse_Final.pdf

Burkhauser, R. V., & Simon, K. I. (2008). Who gets what from employer pay or play mandates? *Risk Management and Insurance Review, 11*(1), 75–102.

Chow, M. J., & Phillips, B. D. (2009). *Small business effects of a national employer healthcare mandate.* Retrieved from National Federation of Independent Business Research Foundation website: http://www.nfib.com/Portals/0/PDF/AllUsers/NFIBStudy_HealthcareMandate.pdf

Congressional Budget Office. (2009). *Effects of changes to the health insurance system on labor markets.* Retrieved from http://www.cbo.gov/ftpdocs/104xx/doc10435/07-13-HealthCareAndLaborMarkets.pdf

Greenstein, R., & Solomon, J. (2009). *Finance committee makes flawed employer requirement in health reform bill still more problematic.* Retrieved from Center on Budget and Policy Priorities website: http://www.cbpp.org/files/9-16-09health3.pdf

Gruber, J. (2009). A win-win approach to financing health care reform. *The New England Journal of Medicine, 361*(1), 4–5.

Helms, R. B. (2005). Tax reform and health insurance. *American Enterprise Institute Outlook Series.* Retrieved from http://www.aei.org/outlook/21921

Herring, B., & Pauly, M. V. (2010). Play-or-pay insurance reforms for employers—Confusion and inequity. *The New England Journal of Medicine, 362*(2), 93–95.

Kaiser Family Foundation and Health Education and Research Trust. (2011). *Employer health benefits annual survey.* Retrieved from http://ehbs.kff.org/pdf/2011/8225.pdf

Kaiser Health News. (2009). *Checking in with James Gelfand, U.S. Chamber of Commerce.* Retrieved from http://www.kaiserhealthnews.org/Checking-In-With/Gelfand.aspx

McKinsey & Company. (2011). *Employer survey on US health care reform: Details regarding the survey methodology.* Retrieved from http://www.mckinsey.com/en/US_employer_healthcare_survey.aspx

Morrisey, M. A. (2008). *Health insurance.* Chicago, IL: Health Administration Press.

National Federation of Independent Business. (n.d.). *Health reform law: Timeline for small business.* Retrieved from http://www.nfib.com/Portals/0/PDF/AllUsers/IssuesElections/healthcare/Healthcarepercent20Reformpercent20Law_Timelinepercent20forpercent20Small percent20Business.pdf

Reinhardt, U. E. (2009, May 22). Is employer-based health insurance worth saving? *The New York Times.* Retrieved from http://economix.blogs.nytimes.com/2009/05/22/is-employer-based-health-insurance-worth-saving

Sommers, B. D. (2005). Who really pays for health insurance? The incidence of employer-provided health insurance with sticky nominal wages. *International Journal of Health Care Finance and Economics, 5*(1), 891–118.

U.S. Census Bureau. (2011). *Health insurance.* Retrieved from http://www.census.gov/hhes/www/hlthins/hlthins.html

Kathleen Carey

Deficit Reduction

POINT: The 2010 Patient Protection and Affordable Care Act (ACA) extends coverage to over 30 million previously uninsured individuals while reducing the deficit, and makes important steps toward long-term sustainability in national health expenditures by promoting the development of innovative care delivery and payment models.

Kavita Patel and Shayla Nagy, Engelberg Center for Health Care Reform, Brookings Institution
Mark A. Zezza, The Commonwealth Fund

COUNTERPOINT: The ACA will not reduce the deficit. The estimates showing reductions are full of accounting gimmicks. Once these are taken into account, as well as the fact that many of the provisions are not likely to be implemented as intended, it becomes clear that the reform act is more likely to increase the deficit.

Mark A. Zezza, The Commonwealth Fund
Kavita Patel and Shayla Nagy, Engelberg Center for Health Care Reform, Brookings Institution

Introduction

The Congressional Budget Office (CBO) reports that the federal budget deficit was nearly $1.3 trillion in fiscal year 2011 (federal fiscal years run from October 1 to September 30), raising the total debt held by the public to over $10.1 trillion. To help put that figure in perspective, CBO also reported that every dollar spent in the United States, as represented by the gross domestic product (GDP), amounted to nearly $15.0 trillion. Thus, about 70 percent of total U.S. spending (for both private and public consumption) would be needed to pay off the federal debt. Another way to consider the nation's public debt problems is to remember that, in 2011, interest payments on the debt alone amounted to $227.1 billion, money that could have paid more than 80 percent of all federal spending for the Medicaid program, the public health insurance program covering over 50 million low-income Americans.

CBO also develops projections for the federal deficit and total debt held by the public (which is largely driven by cumulative budget deficits). According to what CBO calls its "alternative fiscal scenario," which reflects likely changes to the current-law tax and federal spending policies, the total debt would climb to 94 percent of GDP in 2022, the highest figure since the unprecedented levels just after World War II. In order to prevent the federal debt to reach unsupportable levels, policymakers will need to make tough decisions to increase revenues (i.e., raise taxes) and/or decrease spending (i.e., cut important and popular public programs).

Health care reform is an area of particular focus during the policy debate on how to best avoid a deficit crisis. According to CBO, federal outlays in 2011 for Medicare, Medicaid, and other mandatory federal programs related to health care amounted to over $850 billion, just under 40 percent of all mandatory spending (see Figure 19.1). Over the next decade, due to the aging of the population and rising health care costs, federal health care programs are expected to account for an increasing share of the federal budget, reaching nearly half of the budget in 2022. This means that there

Figure 19.1 Share of Mandatory Federal Spending Accounted for by Social Security, Health Care Programs and All Other Programs: 2011 and 2022

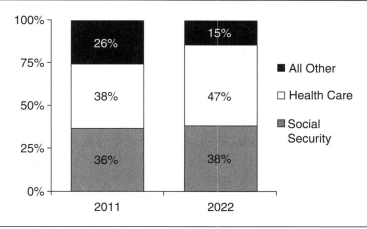

Source: Based on figures reported in Congressional Budget Office. (2012). *The Budget and Economic Outlook: Fiscal Years 2012 to 2022.* Retrieved from http://cbo.gov/ftpdocs/126xx/doc12699/01-31-2012_Outlook.pdf.
Note: Mandatory spending programs account for more than half of all federal outlays and are controlled by laws, but are not normally constrained by an annual appropriation process. That is, there are usually no specific budgeted amounts of spending.

will be less money for other programs. Although the share of the total budget accounted for by the Social Security program is expected to remain relatively stable during the projected period (increasing from 36 percent in 2011 to 38 percent in 2022), most of the decrease will be felt in other programs (decreasing from 26 percent in 2011 to 15 percent in 2022) including in unemployment compensation, Social Security income, the Supplemental Nutrition Assistance Program (SNAP), and military retirement programs, among many others. Moreover, growing debt and health care costs will make it difficult to appropriate additional discretionary (i.e., nonmandatory) funds that pay for federal employee salaries, transportation projects, military operations, and many other activities.

Nor will fiscal tightening be limited to nonhealth spending. If health care costs continue to rise at rates greater than the growth in the general economy, the states are likely to slash their Medicaid programs. In addition, federal actuaries already estimate that, since 2008, the trust fund used to provide hospital insurance for Medicare beneficiaries has paid more in benefits than it has taken in through revenues (which mostly come from the Medicare Hospital Insurance income tax). Under current projections, the trust fund is expected to be exhausted in 2024.

The Patient Protection and Affordable Care Act (ACA), as amended by the Health Care and Education Reconciliation Act of 2010, contains many provisions intended to reduce future federal health care program costs. Among these are provisions to encourage providers to reorganize themselves to deliver health care that is more cost-efficient and that produces better health outcomes, as well as provisions to expand antifraud and abuse efforts. In addition, taxes and fees are imposed to increase revenues for the Medicare program and reduce the federal deficit. Already, there is evidence that some of these initiatives have resulted in reduced federal health spending, particularly for the Medicare program.

The ACA also includes provisions that will create additional federal outlays in an attempt to reduce the number of uninsured. The most significant of these efforts entail federal subsidies for low-income Americans to buy health insurance through newly formed health insurance exchanges beginning in 2014. The ACA will also expand outlays for the Medicaid and the Children's Health Insurance Program (CHIP), and provide tax credits to help certain small employers afford health insurance for their employees. The CBO and Joint Committee on Taxation (JCT) have estimated that the ACA will increase the number of nonelderly Americans with health insurance by about 34 million in 2021, meaning about 95 percent of legal nonelderly residents will have insurance coverage, compared to only about 83 percent in the absence of that legislation.

At the time the legislation was passed, the CBO and JCT estimated the cost of the coverage expansion provisions to the federal budget to be about $938 billion for the 2010 through 2019 period. These will be additional mandatory spending costs to the federal budget. However, the CBO and JCT also estimated that the provisions to reduce health care costs and increase revenues will offset the costs of the coverage expansions, and in net the ACA will actually result in modest deficit reductions amounting to $124 billion during the 2010 through 2019 timeframe.

In this debate, Kavita Patel, Shayla Nagy, and Mark Zezza discuss whether those estimated savings to the federal deficit will in fact be realized and whether the ACA even represents a good starting point for controlling health care costs. As of this writing, the U.S. economy is recovering from a recent recession, and health care costs remain a primary target to achieve some savings for the federal budget. Though there appears to be consensus across the political spectrum that more work can and should be done to control health spending, major differences exist on how that can be accomplished.

From the perspective of ACA proponents, the ACA is seen as an effective tool for deficit reduction through its potential to significantly "bend the health care cost curve." A great deal of research has documented the wide variation in clinical practice patterns and resulting health outcomes across the country. Furthermore, it has been found that areas that tend to provide more services, and that consequently have higher costs, are not correlated with areas that have better quality of care. Some research has even found that lower-cost areas, which are also more likely to have more resources available for primary and preventive-care services, are actually associated with better quality. This mismatch between the variation in care and health outcomes can be seen as an opportunity to provide much more cost-efficient care (capable of producing better outcomes at lower costs). In fact, some experts have cited this variation as evidence that up to 30 percent of U.S. health spending is wasted on unnecessary and potentially harmful medical care. (For more, see the work of the Dartmouth Atlas Project.)

In the Point, provisions in the ACA are highlighted for their potential to improve the way care is delivered. From this perspective, it is argued that not only does the ACA achieve modest reductions in the deficit in the first decade after its passage but that it also sets the stage for deeper reforms that can achieve greater impacts in the long term. That is, the ACA does not view the health care cost problems as just a federal deficit issue, but instead aims to transform the entire health care system into one capable of producing greater value for less money. The Point aims to show that only through these systemic changes can there be any hope of putting health care spending on a more financially sustainable course in the long term, while maintaining and potentially even improving access to high-quality care. In the meantime, provisions in the ACA will help ensure at least some deficit relief in the short term.

The Counterpoint argues that provisions in the ACA are unlikely to achieve even modest deficit reductions. For starters, the savings projected by the CBO and JCT may be the result of accounting gimmicks. More concerning, though, is that there really is not much evidence that the delivery reforms in the ACA will be effective. In this sense, the notion that the ACA includes provisions to bend the cost curve may be more "hope-based" than "evidence-based." Also, it is likely that many of the provisions will not be implemented as intended, as Congress has had a long history of overturning, postponing and otherwise weakening legislation that could potentially reduce payments to providers or result in higher taxes and fees.

In addition, some provisions in the ACA may simply be based on unrealistic assumptions. For example, the Community Living and Assistance Services and Support (CLASS) Act has been deemed unsustainable by administration officials (who were its strongest supporters) even before it has started and consequently (as of the time this is written) is facing repeal legislation. The fear held by opponents of the ACA is that by focusing on provisions that may, at best, only have a marginal impact in the long term, the deficits will only continue to grow particularly as the coverage expansions require significant additional federal funding.

POINT

In the United States, growing fiscal concerns have pushed debt and deficit reduction to the top of the national agenda. In the context of federal government spending, *deficits* refer to the negative difference between revenues and spending over a given year. In contrast, *debt* reflects accumulated unpaid federal borrowing, the sum of all past deficits. The federal deficit and debt play a significant role in the U.S. economy, with tangible effects on inflation, interest rates, employment opportunities, and overall confidence in the U.S. dollar.

As legislators seek paths toward a sustainable future, the fiscal impacts of all federal government spending are called into question. Federal health expenditures, a major driver of increasing national deficits, remain a key area of focus in deficit-reduction efforts. Health expenditures consume a large and growing portion of the federal budget; federal health expenditures are currently the second-largest contributor to federal spending, trailing only interest paid on the debt.

In 2009 nearly 18 percent of the national gross domestic product (GDP) was spent on health care, up from 9.2 percent in 1980. Health costs have grown rapidly over the past three decades, exceeding GDP growth by an average 2.4 percent (Martin et al., 2011). Continued growth at pre-reform rates would lead to fiscally unsustainable health care expenditures. As nearly half of U.S. health expenditures are federally financed, controlling health care cost growth is imperative to containing the federal deficit.

However, it is important for policy leaders to keep in mind that rising health care costs are also an important issue for private payers, states, employers, and individuals. To implement draconian cuts to the federal budget for Medicare, Medicaid, CHIP, and other federal health programs is to run the risk of shifting an even greater burden to the nation's most vulnerable populations. Moreover, as the largest health care payer, the federal government is poised to play an integral role in fostering systemwide changes to transform the entire health care system into one that is capable of delivering better outcomes to patients at lower costs.

Proponents of the ACA would like to see the federal government play a more active leadership role in "bending the health care cost curve," while others have advanced proposals that would limit government intervention and shift responsibility for health spending to the private sector. However, the economic effects of the growing U.S. deficit cannot be mitigated by cost shifts to private payers, a move that would saddle individuals with the burden of high health spending that is detrimental to the economy as a whole.

Reductions in health spending are essential to avoiding a fiscal crisis, but slowing health care cost growth over the long term without draconian cuts to essential programs will require significant delivery reform. In the short term, policymakers must balance deficit relief with the need to lay a foundation for a higher performing, more sustainable health care system. The ACA was developed with that balance in mind.

In this half of the debate, at issue is the importance of focusing on improving the way health care is delivered in order to achieve long-term fiscal sustainability. Next, the ACA's impact on the deficit, as estimated by unbiased experts, is highlighted. This section will include detail on the role of specific payment and delivery system reform provisions, as well as certain revenue generating provisions that are part of the legislation. These provisions are discussed in the context of their ability to achieve short-term deficit relief along with setting the stage for longer-term sustainability.

THE IMPORTANCE OF MAKING SYSTEMWIDE CHANGES TO BEND THE COST CURVE

Rapid health-cost growth in excess of GDP growth has led health economists and policy leaders to call for a focus on "bending the cost curve" by making long-term adjustments in payment mechanisms and delivery systems. Although cost-cutting measures, such as reductions in administrative waste or health benefits, cause one-time downward shifts in health spending, they do little to alter the unsustainable trajectory of health spending. Critics refer to these efforts as "shifting," rather than "bending" the curve (see Figure 19.2). Instead, systemwide reforms are needed to slow the growth rate of health spending over time and preserve the sustainability of essential health programs.

Slowed cost growth or "bending the cost curve" can be achieved by changing the way we deliver and pay for health care, including the improved management of chronic conditions and the reduction of duplicative and unnecessary treatments. The movement toward accountable care organizations (ACOs) is one example of delivery system reform that can contain costs while improving quality. ACOs organize health care delivery to emphasize improved care coordination while reducing spending relative to prior expenditures. As will be discussed in more detail, ACOs are among several aspects of the ACA aimed at changing the delivery system with a view toward bending the cost curve.

Figure 19.2 illustrates the difference between bending and shifting the cost curve. Although there is little agreement on what level of health spending relative to GDP is sustainable, the figure sets spending of 25 percent of GDP as a hypothetical limit. The baseline (solid line) shows the growth trajectory of health spending extrapolated from historical growth rates. The dotted line shows the effect of a 15 percent cut in health spending, causing an immediate downward shift in health spending's share of GDP. However, the one-time cut fails to alter the unsustainable trajectory of health-cost growth, keeping spending below the 25 percent of GDP limit for only a few additional years relative to baseline spending. In contrast, the dashed line illustrates how bending the cost curve keeps spending below the limit for an extended period by achieving closer alignment of health spending and GDP growth.

THE ACA IMPACT ON THE FEDERAL DEFICIT AND NATIONAL HEALTH SPENDING

The ACA cuts the ranks of America's uninsured by nearly two-thirds while controlling health care costs and reducing the deficit. The bulk of the coverage expansion pertains to individuals newly eligible for Medicaid coverage and individuals purchasing private insurance through state-based exchanges with the assistance of federal subsidies beginning in 2014. As a result of these insurance reforms, the nonpartisan Congressional Budget Office (CBO) projected that by 2019 the share of non-elderly Americans with insurance would rise from 83 percent to 94 percent (Elmendorf, 2010). Note that these estimated were conducted before the Supreme Court ruled in June 2012 that the states could not be forced to participate in the Medicaid expansion. Hence, the estimates may be overestimated to the degree that states actually opt out. There are also implications that may impact the estimates of the effect of the ACA on the deficit.

The coverage expansion will contribute to short-term cost growth in federal health spending, but this investment will be more than offset by a number of revenue-raising mechanisms in the reform bill, including various new or increased taxes and fees. In addition, the ACA makes important inroads toward the development and piloting of payment innovations that incentivize efficient care delivery while slowing long-term growth in health spending. In fact, at the time the ACA was passed, the CBO and Joint Committee for Taxation (JCT) estimated that it would reduce the federal deficit by $143 billion over the 10-year period, fiscal years 2010 through 2019 (Elmendorf, 2010).

The ACA also begins the process of bending the cost curve and slowing health care cost growth. Figure 19.3 compares projected annual growth in national health expenditures before and after the passage of health reform. Note that, following a spike in spending growth during the coverage expansion period, projected growth under current law drops below projections under prior law (Foster, 2010). Although health reform's decreased cost growth relative to prior law may not appear substantial in Figure 19.3, as discussed earlier, slowed cost growth is essential to achieving long-term sustainability in national health spending.

It is important to note that, even though the rate-of-growth is projected to decrease, both private and public health expenditures will continue to rise each year following health reform. The benefits of this scenario can be easily understood: Imagine an annual purchase of some good, such as an apple. Last year, an apple cost $1. However, the cost of apples grows from year to year, so that this year you'll need to pay $2 for the exact same product, representing a growth rate of 100 percent. But if growth rates slowed to 50 percent, you'd only need to pay $1.50 for the apple. Though the apple still costs more than it did the previous year, you save 50 cents through slowed cost growth. The deceleration of spending-growth, rather than wholesale cuts, is consistent with the notion of supporting systematic changes to the health care system. That is, the goal is to continue supporting providers with appropriate levels of funding in order to deliver effective health care, while still attempting to achieve some cost control and to challenge providers to deliver higher-value (and more cost-efficient) care.

Cost-slowing delivery and payment reforms through the ACA will affect private health spending as well as public, making a significant impact on lowering overall national health expenditures. Between 2010 and 2019, average annual Medicare spending growth is expected to decline from 7.8 percent under prior law to 6.3 percent under current law (Foster, 2010). Meanwhile, the average annual growth rate in total spending for employer-sponsored health insurance is estimated to decline from 5.6 to 5.2 percent (Foster, 2010). At the family level, researchers have estimated that private

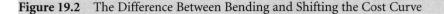

Figure 19.2   The Difference Between Bending and Shifting the Cost Curve

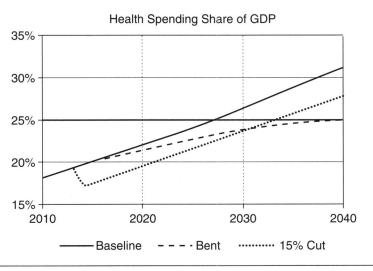

Source: Roehrig, C. S. (2011). Will the health care cost curve be bent? Where we stand at the start of 2011. *Business Economics, 46*, 159–162.

Figure 19.3   Projected Annual Growth Rates in National Health Expenditures (NHE) Pre- and Post-Reform: Calendar Years 2011–2019

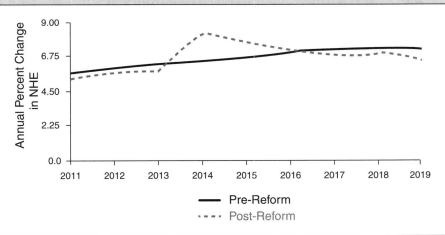

Source: Foster, R. S. (2010, April 22). *Estimated financial effects of the "Patient Protection and Affordable Care Act,"* as amended. Retrieved from https://www.cms.gov/Research-Statistics-Data-and-Systems/Research/ActuarialStudies/downloads//PPACA_2010-04-22.pdf.

premiums will be approximately $2,000 lower per family in 2019 because of provisions in the ACA (Cutler, Davis, & Stremikis, 2010).

Highlighted in the following text will be some of the health care reform bill's specific provisions for helping cover the costs of the coverage-expansion and lead to the aforementioned savings. These provisions can be characterized as revenue-generating mechanisms, which predominantly are in the form of new and modified taxes, and delivery reform initiatives, which are intended to create a higher-value health care system and lead to longer-term sustainability. In addition are some provisions that aim to ensure more immediate reductions in health spending, while also helping set the stage for delivery and payment reforms that can have a more significant longer-term impact.

REVENUE GENERATORS

The ACA includes a number of revenue-raising mechanisms to help offset the significant investments that must be made to extend coverage to approximately 32 million Americans. Increased outlays from the Medicaid and Children's Health Insurance Program (CHIP) expansion, premium subsidization for exchange-based coverage, and tax credits to help small employers offer insurance will be at least partially offset by Medicare hospital tax increases for affluent individuals, a "Cadillac tax" on high-cost health plans, taxes and fees on aspects of the medical device and pharmaceutical industries, and other revenue generators.

The JCT estimates that several new or modified tax provisions in the ACA will result in some $400 billion in revenues between 2010 and 2019 (Joint Committee on Taxation [JCT], 2010; Mulvey, 2010). High-income earners will bear the largest brunt of the tax provisions.

In 2012, the Medicare Hospital Insurance tax (the "HI tax") was 2.9 percent of wages and is split 50/50 between employees and employers. Beginning in 2013, an additional HI tax of 0.9 percent will be levied on earned income in excess of $200,000 for singles and $250,000 for families, with employees being responsible for the full 0.9 percent. Moreover, singles and families earning above those thresholds will face a 3.8 percent tax on unearned income (including capital gains, dividends, rents, and royalties), marking the first time that a nonwage tax will be used to fund Medicare. The JCT estimates that, from 2013 to 2019, these provisions alone will raise more than $200 billion in revenues.

Some revenue generators are aimed directly at the medical industry. For example, beginning in 2011, manufacturers and importers of branded drugs have paid an annual fee. Starting in 2013 medical device manufacturers must pay a 2.3 percent excise tax on medical-device sales. These provisions are expected to raise nearly $50 billion from 2011 through 2019 (JCT, 2010). An additional $60 billion is expected to be raised from health insurance providers via the imposition of annual fees, which will be apportioned by the companies' market shares (JCT, 2010).

Perhaps the most important revenue generator legislated by the ACA is an excise tax on insurers of high-cost insurance policies, known as "Cadillac plans." Beginning in 2018, a 40 percent tax will be levied on the portion of the premium for employer-based insurance plans that is in excess of certain thresholds. In 2018 the thresholds are set at $10,200 for individuals and $27,500 for families (some adjustments are made to increase the thresholds for certain populations that are expected to have greater health care needs, such as firefighters or employers with a preponderance of older workers).

By the end of 2019, the Cadillac tax is expected to generate over $32 billion in revenues to help cover the cost of coverage extension (JCT, 2010). What makes this tax an important health-reform provision is that at the same time it is raising revenues, the tax is also expected to decrease health spending by discouraging participation in the high-cost health plans often associated with overly generous benefit designs that can lead to the overuse of health care. Because insurance carriers are likely to pass along the tax to employers in the form of higher premiums, employers will be encouraged to switch to lower-cost plans that will likely have higher deductibles and co-pays. Thus, employees will be incentivized to use health care more efficiently, an eventuality that should lead to systemwide reductions in health spending.

The effects of the excise tax on high-cost insurance policies should magnify over time as the premium threshold for defining a high-cost plan is legislated to grow with the inflation rates of the general economy, rather than the cost growth of the health care industry. This should create further incentives to reduce future premiums and health spending, since general inflation rates typically grow at slower rates than does the health care industry. As employers respond to the Cadillac tax by reducing high-cost insurance offerings, Cadillac-tax revenue can be expected to fall; however, this decrease will be compensated for by increased payroll taxes as employees reap higher take-home wages as a result of lower insurance premiums (Zuckerman, 2010). Economists largely agree that, as employers reduce health insurance benefits to their employees, they will increase their wages and salaries to at least partially offset the loss in total compensation.

Other tax-related provisions include limitations on tax-advantaged health accounts (such as health savings accounts), eliminating certain Medicare tax deductions that employers can take on health care benefits and an excise tax on indoor tanning services. Additional revenues would come from the penalties collected from individuals who choose not to have insurance and employers who do not offer it, as well as through a number of non–health care revenue provisions in the bill.

PAYMENT AND DELIVERY SYSTEM REFORM

The revenue-generating provisions described previously are critical for ensuring that the coverage expansions are funded. The Cadillac tax also offers the promise of encouraging the delivery of higher-value health care along with more efficient health care choices by many consumers (e.g., employers and employees). However, the ACA includes many other provisions that are specifically aimed at addressing the underlying cost-drivers residing throughout the health care system, from the lack of coordinated care to the limited availability of information or financial support for patients and providers to make more value-based health care decisions.

As was outlined earlier, payment and delivery reforms to improve the efficiency and quality of care delivery are essential to bending the health care cost curve and making health spending sustainable over the long term. The ACA establishes several initiatives to encourage the development of more coordinated models of health care delivery, including incentives for providers to form ACOs that take responsibility for the quality and outcomes of their patients' care while reducing costs.

More specifically, beginning in 2012, the ACA establishes an ACO Medicare program that will build on a growing movement to transform the delivery system. By becoming ACOs, provider groups (which can include hospitals and other facilities, as well as physicians) will be reorganizing themselves and developing innovative new ways to deliver better managed care. This includes building up an infrastructure for rapid-cycle information sharing and evaluation in order to foster a culture of continuous improvement. The goal for the participating providers is to act as a coordinated team to manage the overall health of patients across a full spectrum of services. Duplicative and unnecessary tests should be reduced, and these efforts should better ensure that the right providers are delivering the right care at the right time.

The ACO program includes alternative provider reimbursement models that reward better outcomes and provide financial support for the health information technology infrastructure and other investments needed to develop information exchanges and delivery innovations. The ACO program is building on other similar federal and private initiatives, which should help align incentives and goals across the entire health system and lead to a quicker ramp-up of the requisite infrastructure for more effective and better coordinated care, increasing the chances for more significant systemwide improvements in care. Actuaries at the Centers for Medicare & Medicaid Services (CMS) have estimated that the program will save Medicare nearly $500 million over the period between 2012 and 2015 (Department of Health and Human Services, CMS, 2011).

Another provision in the ACA, and perhaps the most important in terms of promoting systemic changes in the health care industry, is the creation of a Center for Medicare & Medicaid Innovation (the Innovation Center). The Innovation Center provides a platform for developing new approaches to paying for health care that encourage greater quality and efficiency. In fact, its mission is to develop, implement, and evaluate innovative new delivery and payment models that have the potential to reduce costs and improve quality. After launching in November 2010, the Innovation Center has already announced several initiatives, such as the expanded use of bundled payments, patient-centered medical home models, and ACOs, including multi-payer initiatives (Zezza, Abrams, & Guterman, 2011).

The ACA also established the Patient-Centered Outcomes Research Institute (PCORI) with funding from the Medicare trust fund and a tax on private health insurance plans. PCORI, a nongovernmental entity, has the goal of investing those funds in comparative-effectiveness research to empower patients to make more informed decisions about the care they receive. Comparative-effectiveness research can improve quality while lowering costs by reducing unnecessary and often harmful treatments. In particular, patients can be directed to lower-cost and safer options of care that have similar outcomes to higher cost and, often times, more invasive and risky care.

None of these provisions was estimated by the CBO to achieve substantial savings. At a projected $5 billion in savings from 2010 through 2019, the ACO provision received the highest savings score (Elmendorf, 2010). However, such low estimates are more a reflection of the limited evidence available to determine their future impacts. There is wide agreement from health care industry experts that the types of payment and delivery reform initiatives being launched by the ACA are exactly those that are needed to set the stage for larger impacts going forward. It is also important to note that these are the same types of reforms being implemented in the private sector, which is conducting its own return-on-investment analyses.

In fact, having alignment across payers is critical. Although many of the ACA's initiatives focus specifically on the Medicare program, they are the type of initiatives that can help promote systemwide change, inasmuch as the same problems in Medicare (i.e., fragmentation, lack of information, and inappropriate financial incentives) also plague the private sector and other public payers. It is also important to realize Medicare's position in the health care system. In 2009, Medicare accounted for about 20 percent of U.S. national health expenditures for its almost 45 million beneficiaries (Martin et al., 2011). Thus, Medicare, as the major payer, can truly play a leading role in developing and spreading best practices for slowing systemwide health-spending growth.

BALANCING LONG-TERM SYSTEMATIC CHANGES WITH SHORT-TERM DEFICIT RELIEF

Though the delivery reform efforts discussed above represent a path to longer-term sustainability, the ACA also includes provisions to fortify the federal budget, particularly the Medicare Trust Fund, in the short term. These provisions focus on payment reductions both within the traditional Medicare fee-for-service (FFS) program and Medicare Advantage (i.e., the Medicare managed care program involving private health plans). While extending the viability of the Medicare Trust Fund and providing some federal budget relief, these provisions also hope to incentivize providers to transition to alternative models that better support more efficient care.

For example, the ACA reduces the growth in payment rates for services provided by hospitals and other facilities. Prior to the passage of the law, payments to providers were adjusted in accordance with the growth of input prices (e.g., nurse wages, medical equipment, and rent), but going forward updates will be made with regard to increases in productivity in the rest of the economy. CMS actuaries estimate that the provision will result in about a 1.1 percent reduction in Medicare payment rates, inasmuch as the costs of conducting business in the health care sector have historically grown faster than economy-wide productivity (Foster, 2011). Thus, this provision should create strong incentives for providers to better maximize efficiency. Moreover, providers in the traditional FFS program may find that the payment levels become increasingly uncomfortable and be more inclined to participate in alternative models that better reward more efficient care (such as the ACO model described above). CBO estimates that this reduction in payment-rate growth will save the deficit some $200 billion (Elmendorf, 2010).

The law will also lower payments to hospitals with high rates of hospital-acquired conditions or hospital readmissions. A recent study found that 20 percent of Medicare beneficiaries discharged from hospitals are readmitted within 30 days—an occurrence that often represents poor care, hardship for the patient, and avoidable costs (Jencks, Williams, & Coleman, 2009). These efforts should not only result in savings to the Medicare program while also further encouraging providers to consider delivering higher-value care but should also provide greater safety to Medicare beneficiaries.

Other provisions will also result in some savings to the Medicare program, such as refining payments for imaging services and implementing evidence-based coverage for preventative services. Taken all together, it is estimated that these provisions will result in annual reductions in coinsurance and premium payments that reach over $400 in 2019 for beneficiaries in the traditional FFS program (Foster, 2011).

One key provision that will help ensure these results are achieved (and potentially even greater improvements), is the one establishing an Independent Payment Advisory Board (IPAB). The IPAB is mandated to make recommendations for reducing Medicare spending if spending is projected by CMS actuaries to exceed certain targets. The recommendations would be made beginning in 2014 if Medicare per beneficiary growth-rates are projected to exceed targets based upon overall medical inflation. Starting in 2018, the Medicare spending target will be based upon the trend of the overall economy, which should place even greater pressure on the health care industry to reduce costs (because, as was discussed above, overall economic growth is typically lower than medical spending).

Although there are limitations on IPAB's jurisdiction (e.g., it is prohibited from changing beneficiary cost sharing or reducing hospital payment rates until 2020), the potential to control Medicare spending is significant, as Congress must act on all IPAB recommendations or develop provisions to create similar impacts. Because it does not have to face the political pressures of Congress, IPAB has the potential to be an effective vehicle to correct the misplaced incentives that currently reward providers for volume of services over value.

It has been estimated that, between 2015 and 2019, IPAB recommendations will save $15.5 billion (Elmendorf, 2010). Though these initial savings represent only a small fraction of Medicare spending, implemented changes are expected to accrue continued savings over the long term. Like the Innovation Center, the IPAB can become an important vehicle for recommending and implementing improvements in delivery systems that encourage better health outcomes through coordination of care and an emphasis on prevention and wellness. IPAB thus provides a means for the continued reform efforts necessary to bend the cost curve over the coming decades. The IPAB will also be required to make advisory recommendations for private health programs to help slow national health-spending growth. Unlike the mandatory Medicare recommendations, adoption of advisory recommendations pertaining to the private sector will require Congressional approval. However, private insurers could also choose to independently adopt these recommendations.

Another provision expected to yield significant savings involves changes to the way Medicare Advantage (MA) plans are paid. It is widely believed that MA plans have been overpaid for administering care that Medicare beneficiaries could have obtained through the traditional FFS program for much less (Biles et al., 2009). In 2011 the reform law effectively freezes Medicare payments to MA plans and in 2012 will begin reducing payments. However, MA plans that demonstrate that they are providing higher quality care to enrollees will be eligible for higher payments. Hence, these changes are consistent with efforts to align payments with better value. The CBO has estimated that, between 2010 and 2019, these payment changes will create over $130 billion in savings (Elmendorf, 2010).

Many other provisions in the ACA aim to stabilize the Medicare program and provide a measure of short-term deficit relief, including several antifraud and abuse initiatives, increases in premiums for higher-income Medicare beneficiaries, and administrative changes. All together, the CBO has estimated over $500 billion in Medicare payment reductions from 2010 through 2019. Medicare payments will still increase during those years, but the savings will help extend the solvency of the Medicare program by more than a decade.

CONCLUSION

The United States faces the challenge of providing deficit relief and reducing the cost of care in Medicare and Medicaid without simply shifting the responsibility to patients and other private payers like private insurance companies, employers, and individuals. Many health-reform alternatives, like Senator Paul Ryan's (R–WI) "Roadmap for America's Future," which proposed converting Medicare into a voucher system, would merely shift coverage costs to states, employers, and beneficiaries. If costs were simply shifted to patients through higher premiums and deductibles, individuals would still face the burden of high spending that is problematic for the economy.

The goal of health care reform is a fiscally sustainable health care system that provides equal access to high-performance care. This type of change will not happen overnight. The ACA extends coverage to two-thirds of America's uninsured at minimal cost to federal payers while mitigating cost shifts to states and the private sector. At the same time, the ACA is also expected to provide immediate deficit relief that has the potential to be even greater over the long term.

However, the passage of the ACA is just the beginning of the reform needed to fix America's broken health care system. Even though the ACA reduces the deficit and begins to lay the foundation for a more sustainable health care system, more work is needed to achieve the type of change that can truly bend the health care cost-curve and provide real relief to the federal budget.

Note: This chapter was authored to articulate both sides of a given argument. The views expressed in this Point–Counterpoint chapter are not necessarily the views of the authors.

REFERENCES AND FURTHER READING

Biles, B., Pozen, J., & Guterman, S. (2009). *The continuing cost of privatization: Extra payments to Medicare advantage plans jump to $11.4 billion in 2009.* New York, NY: The Commonwealth Fund. Retrieved from http://www.commonwealthfund.org/Publications/Issue-Briefs/2009/May/The-Continuing-Cost-of-Privatization.aspx

Cutler, D. M., Davis, K., & Stremikis, K. (2010). *The impact of health reform on health system spending.* New York, NY: The Commonwealth Fund. Retrieved from http://www.commonwealthfund.org/~/media/Files/Publications/Issue%20Brief/2010/May/1405_Cutler_impact_hlt_reform_on_hlt_sys_spending_ib_v4.pdf

Department of Health and Human Services, Centers for Medicare & Medicaid Services (CMS). (2011). Medicare program; Medicare shared savings program: Accountable Care Organizations, Final Rule. *Federal Register, 76*(212), 67802–67990.

Elmendorf, D. W. (2010). *Letter to Honorable Nancy Pelosi, March 20, 2010*. Retrieved from http://www.cbo.gov/ftpdocs/113xx/doc11379/AmendReconProp.pdf

Foster, R. S. (2010, April 22). *Estimated financial effects of the "Patient Protection and Affordable Care Act," as amended*. Retrieved from https://www.cms.gov/Research-Statistics-Data-and-Systems/Research/ActuarialStudies/downloads//PPACA_2010-04-22.pdf

Foster, R. S. (2011). *The estimated effects of the Affordable Care Act on Medicare: Testimony before the House Committee on Ways and Means*. Retrieved from http://waysandmeans.house.gov/UploadedFiles/Foster_Testimony_2-10_Hearing.pdf

Jencks, S. F., Williams, M. V., & Coleman, E. A. (2009). Rehospitalizations among patients in the Medicare Fee-for-Service program. *New England Journal of Medicine, 360*(14), 1418–1428.

Joint Committee on Taxation (JCT). (2010). Estimated revenue effects of the amendment in the nature of a substitute to H.R. 4872, the "Reconciliation Act of 2010," as amended, in combination with the revenue effects of H.R. 3590, the "Patient Protection and Affordable Care Act ('PPACA')," as passed by the Senate, and scheduled for consideration by the House Committee on Rules on March 20, 2010. Retrieved from http://www.jct.gov/publications.html?func=startdown&id=3672

Martin, A., Lassman, D., Whittle, L., Catlin, A., & the National Health Expenditure Accounts Team. (2011). Recession contributes to slowest annual rate of increase in health spending in five decades. *Health Affairs, 30*(1), 11–22.

Mulvey, J. (2010). *Health-related revenue provisions in the Patient Protection and Affordable Care Act (PPACA)*. Retrieved from http://www.nahu.org/legislative/resources/crs%20Health%20Revenue%20Tax%20provisions%20PPACA_May%203.pdf

Roehrig, C. S. (2011). Will the health care cost curve be bent? Where we stand at the start of 2011. *Business Economics, 46*(3), 159–162. Retrieved from http://www.palgrave-journals.com/doifinder/10.1057/be.2011.14

Sisko, A. M., Truffer, C. J., Keehan, S. P., Poisal, J. A., Clemens, M. K., & Madison, A. J. (2010). National health spending projections: The estimated impact of reform through 2019. *Health Affairs, 29*(10), 1933–1941.

Zezza, M., Abrams, M., & Guterman, S. (2011). The innovation center at one year: Much progress, more to be done [The Commonwealth Fund Blog]. Retrieved from http://www.commonwealthfund.org/Blog/2011/Nov/Innovation-Center-at-One-Year.aspx

Zuckerman, S. (2010). *What are the provisions in the new law for containing costs and how effective will they be?* Retrieved from Urban Institute website: http://www.urban.org/UploadedPDF/412194-ppaca-containing-costs.pdf

Kavita Patel, Shayla Nagy, and Mark A. Zezza

COUNTERPOINT

The passage of the Patient Protection and Affordable Care Act (ACA) and the Health Care and Education Reconciliation Act of 2010 in many ways represents the culmination of efforts started decades ago to give every American access to medical care. However, as written, the bill does little to control health care spending or improve the financial sustainability of the federal deficit.

The ACA includes many provisions that aim to improve the way health care is delivered, including various payment and delivery reforms and a comparative effectiveness research center to help identify the best practice patterns. However, there is little evidence that any of these efforts will lead to substantial cost savings. As will be discussed in more detail, this notion is reflected in the fairly nominal savings scored for these initiatives by the Congressional Budget Office (CBO) when estimating the impact of the reform act on the federal budget (Elmendorf, 2010a).

A small number of provisions in the ACA were scored with relatively high cost savings or revenue-generating potential. These include Medicare reimbursement rate-reductions to hospitals and other providers, as well as a tax on Cadillac insurance plans. However, even the effectiveness of these provisions has been met with a high degree of skepticism, as many experts believe they are either too weakly proposed to generate the intended impacts or so politically sensitive that future legislation will almost certainly mitigate their cost saving.

Given that health care spending continues to grow at unsustainable rates with no end in sight, health care reform remains a major political issue. Now more than ever, the debate centers on cost control and the federal budget. There is a great concern that, if something is not done now, Americans will faced the possibility of no longer being able to support federal insurance programs that are capable of providing meaningful benefits for the nation's elderly and low-income populations.

This half of the debate will outline the argument for why the ACA is not likely to reduce the deficit. It summarizes the critiques of the CBO score voiced by a number of experts and provides a detailed explanation as to why some of the provisions in the reform act that were estimated to provide the most substantial cost savings are not likely to attain those goals.

QUESTIONING THE REALITY OF THE CBO SCORE

Prior to the passage of the ACA, the CBO and Joint Committee for Taxation (JCT) estimated that the law would reduce the federal deficit by $143 billion over the ten-year period, in fiscal years 2010 through 2019 (Elmendorf, 2010a). This includes $124 billion in net reductions from health care and revenue provisions and $19 billion from education provisions. Note that these estimates were conducted before the Supreme Court ruled in June 2012 that the states could not be forced to participate in the Medicaid expansion. At the time of this writing, CBO is determining the impact of this ruling. If many states opt to not participate in the expansion, there could be nontrivial impacts on the deficit.

Several experts, including the former CBO director Douglas Holtz-Eakin are leery of the CBO estimate and believe that the health care reform law will widen the federal deficit (Holtz-Eakin & Ramlet, 2010). Even the current CBO leadership and other government agencies have underscored the vast amount of uncertainty involved in estimating the impacts of the reform bill. The critiques and concerns are highlighted below.

The back loading of high-cost provisions. The CBO score focuses on the first 10 years of the law's enactment. However, the costliest provisions (i.e., subsidies for the exchange and Medicaid expansion) do not go into effect until 2014, while many of the revenue-generating provisions, such as taxes and fees, are set to begin earlier than the major spending provisions.

The front loading of revenues and back loading of spending helps the health-reform bill meet the requirement of the pay-as-you-go (PAYGO) rule for deficit neutrality over a 10-year window. Holtz-Eakin and Ramlet attribute up to $66 billion of CBO's estimated $144 billion reduction in the deficit to what is essentially an accounting gimmick—the front loading of revenues and back loading of spending.

An example of this is the ACA's creation of a new long-term care insurance program, Community Living Assistance Services and Supports (CLASS). The CBO estimated that the CLASS provision would result in $70.2 billion in savings over the 10-year projection period (Elmendorf, 2010a). This program, if implemented, would be financed with participant premiums. The relatively high level of savings can be mostly explained by the fact that there is a five-year vesting period, so it would be at least 2016 before any benefits were paid out even though premiums are being accrued during that time. Hence, there is an inherent back-loading of costs and frontloading of revenues. (Note that 2015 would be the earliest that CLASS benefits could be incurred as of the time of the CBO score. Considering that, as of this writing, the program has not yet been implemented, this date would be pushed out much further if the CLASS program ever does reach implementation.)

Double counting. Another gimmick essentially involves double-counting dollars as both funding future program costs and current deficit needs. Again, the CLASS provision described above is a perfect example. The program is supposed to be completely funded using premiums paid by members. Thus, the premiums should be used to fund future benefits, instead of counting toward current deficit reduction. As a matter of fact, as will be discussed, it is unlikely that the new long-term care insurance program will even be implemented, meaning that the $70.2 billion the CBO counted toward deficit reduction would no longer be available.

Holtz-Eakin and Ramlet also identify $53 billion that the CBO earmarks for deficit reduction from anticipated increases in Social Security revenue. The additional revenues emanate from employers shifting payment for health insurance to higher wages, as workers drop (or are dropped from) their employer-sponsored plans and purchase insurance through the exchanges set to begin in 2014. Higher wages would indeed lead to more Social Security tax revenue. However, workers who earn higher wages will also qualify for additional Social Security benefits when they retire. Thus, the extra money should be earmarked to pay the future benefits rather than to lower the deficit.

Incomplete accounting of costs. Holtz-Eakin and Ramlet identify about $65 billion in additional spending during the 10-year projection period that future Congresses will need to approve, and which has not been included in the CBO score.

The unbudgeted spending includes about $15 billion for the Internal Revenue Service and the Centers for Medicare & Medicaid Services to administer the insurance coverage programs, and $50 billion to explicitly authorize various health care grant programs.

The CBO has also investigated these costs and estimated at least $115 billion in discretionary spending, spending that is funded through annual appropriations (Congressional Budget Office, 2010a; Elmendorf, 2010b). However, they point out that a significant portion of those costs are simply extensions of prior Congressional authorizations that they have taken into account in their baseline estimates. Thus, the estimates of incomplete accounting may not be as high as Holtz-Eakin and Ramlet estimate.

Inclusion of non-health-related provisions. As was mentioned earlier, $19 billion of the estimated $143 billion in deficit reduction is due to an education provision involving federally financed student loans. This provision has nothing to do with health care and seems to have been included in the bill simply to help score savings.

UNACHIEVABLE SAVINGS

The CBO has also estimated that a significant share of the projected savings come from provisions that are unlikely to ever be fully implemented. Other provisions were scored with savings even though there is little evidence to support those estimates. Below is a discussion of some of these provisions in more detail.

Medicare payment rate adjustments. The CBO estimated that the largest savings ($196.3 billion) will come from reducing the growth in Medicare payment rates for services provided by hospitals and other facilities. Prior to the passage of the law, payments to providers were adjusted in accordance with the growth of input prices (e.g., nurse wages, medical equipment, and rent), but going forward updates would be made with regard to increases in productivity in the rest of the economy. Because the costs of conducting business in the health care sector have historically grown faster than has economy-wide productivity, Medicare payment rates are expected to decrease.

However, and although such payment rate updates would create strong incentives for providers to maximize efficiency, both the CBO and the Chief Actuary of the Medicare program have expressed concerns about whether providers will be able to survive the payment reductions (Congressional Budget Office, 2010b; Foster, 2010). In fact, CMS actuaries estimate that approximately 15 percent of hospitals and other Medicare institutional providers would become unprofitable within the 10-year projection period as a result of the productivity adjustments (Foster, 2010). Providers with a large share of Medicare business can be expected to face the most difficulties. The problem is that many providers will have difficulty improving their productivity to levels achieved by the general economy, whose cost structure is largely unrelated to that of health care delivery.

Absent legislative intervention, providers experiencing the most difficulties might end their participation in the Medicare program, something that might jeopardize access to care for Medicare beneficiaries. Although the impacts of the payment rate adjustments could be monitored over time to avoid such adverse outcomes, changes would likely result in smaller actual savings. This is exactly what happened in the past when similar measures were taken to reduce Medicare payment rates.

For example, the Balanced Budget Act (BBA) of 1997 was introduced as a cost-saving measure that significantly cut Medicare reimbursements to hospitals, physicians, home health agencies, and skilled nursing facilities. After significant protests from industry representatives, Congress included provisions in the 1999 Balanced Budget Refinement Act (BBRA) and the 2000 Benefits and Improvement Protection Act (BIPA) to restore much of the reductions.

Perhaps the clearest example of the problem involves the Medicare physician fee schedule updates. Since 1998 the Medicare physician fee schedule has been updated using the statutorily mandated sustainable growth rate (SGR) system, established to serve as a restraint on spending. The basic idea of the payment system was that, if historical spending was less than target amounts for the period, physician payment rates were increased. In contrast, if spending exceeded the target, future updates would be reduced to bring spending back in line with the target. Each year since 2002, the SGR system indicated a reduction in the reimbursement rates. However, with the exception of 2002, when a 4.8 percent decrease was applied, Congress has passed a series of bills to override the reduction. More discussion on physician payment rates is provided in the following.

INDEPENDENT PAYMENT ADVISORY PANEL

The CBO scored $15.5 billion in savings for a provision in the ACA that forms an Independent Payment Advisory Board (IPAB). The IPAB is essentially mandated to act as a backstop to help ensure that a minimum threshold of health care cost control is attained. The IPAB would make recommendations to Congress beginning in 2014 if Medicare per beneficiary growth rates are projected, by CMS actuaries, to exceed targets based on overall medical inflation (which, as mentioned earlier, is typically lower than medical inflation). The IPAB's potential to control Medicare spending is significant as Congress must act on all of its recommendations or develop provisions expected to have similar impacts. Free of the political pressures of Congress, the IPAB has the potential to be an effective vehicle to push health care reform initiatives.

Again, there is a great deal of skepticism that the IPAB will be able to achieve the requisite savings. The ACA includes provisions that significantly limit the IPAB's jurisdiction; for example, it is prohibited from changing beneficiary cost sharing or reducing hospital payment rates until 2020. Given these and similar limitations, it is not clear what IPAB could recommend to realistically achieve its cost-reducing goals. Furthermore, the fact that the IPAB would need to make recommendations annually creates additional confusion over the types of recommendations the IPAB can make and the impacts that would result.

Also, as with the Medicare provider payment reductions described earlier, there is nothing in the law to assure that Medicare and its providers will be able to operate as effectively at lower budgetary costs. Thus, even if the IPAB recommendations are implemented, Medicare beneficiaries might possibly experience reductions in access to care or limitations in their benefits. It is likely that Congress would override such reductions.

Other provisions to bend the cost curve. Numerous provisions in the health care reform bill are designed to change the way doctors and hospitals are organized and provide services. Examples include the development of a Medicare accountable care organization program, and the Center for Medicare & Medicaid Innovation that will test various payment and delivery reform initiatives. The ACA also establishes the Patient Centered Outcomes Research Institute to help providers, patients, and other stakeholders make informed decisions more aligned with higher-value care. However, these provisions are mainly small and untested pilot projects unlikely to fundamentally change the cost structure of the U.S. health care system, at least not for many years to come.

UNACHIEVABLE REVENUE

Just as there are provisions in the ACA with questionable potential to achieve cost savings, so too are many of its revenue-generating instruments of dubious potential. Perhaps the best example is the imposition of an excise tax on high-premium insurance plans, known as the "Cadillac tax." According to the CBO and the Joint Committee on Taxation, the Cadillac tax is expected to raise some $32 billion in revenue over the 10-year projection period (Elmendorf, 2010a; Joint Committee on Taxation, 2010).

Economists widely agree that the exclusion of employer-sponsored insurance from taxable income represents a major distortion in the tax code that incentivizes overinsurance, which in turn contributes to overutilization of medical services and rising health care costs. Thus, the Cadillac tax, as a disincentive for overly generous insurance plans, is seen as an important tool to help control costs and generate revenues. Although there is strong support for such a tax in policy circles, implementing any new tax is extremely difficult politically. In fact, the Cadillac tax as passed in the ACA is already much weaker than it was initially construed. In earlier versions of the health-reform bill, the tax was supposed to start immediately. After intense lobbying by labor (which would essentially have to absorb the tax in its premium rates) and opposition by more conservative leadership, the start date was pushed back to 2018. As is purported by Holtz-Eakin and Ramlet (2010), this is a strong sign that the tax may prove to be politically infeasible and, indeed, may never be implemented at all.

SUSTAINABILITY OF NEW PROGRAMS

Another issue worth considering is the unsustainability of many of the ACA's provisions and programs. The sustainability of Medicare payment adjustments related to providers leaving the Medicare program and limiting access to care for

Medicare beneficiaries has already been outlined previously. Provisions such as these are likely to face future legislation restoring payment levels. Also discussed earlier is sustainability as it relates to pushing through additional taxes to help generate revenues.

The CLASS provision is also worth discussing in the context of sustainability. In fact, even the Obama administration itself has essentially decided that program, as proposed, is a nonstarter (Greenlee, 2011; Sebelius, 2011). The program was designed to be voluntary and have a minimal premium for students and low-income individuals (initially $5 per month). This would have left a high premium for other individuals, as there are no federal subsidies in place to help fund the program. Thus, those who anticipate using the benefit, who also tend to be the sickest and most costly, would be most likely to join. Premiums will have to be set at high levels to cover their costs, which will further discourage persons in better health from participating. This will lead to even higher premium levels in the future and to what some call the "insurance death spiral," as more people would be discouraged from joining and premiums continue to increase as only the sickest remain covered. For these reasons, many experts, as well as the Obama administration, have essentially concluded that the CLASS program would go bankrupt.

Another provision that will be difficult to sustain over time involves the growth of federal subsidies for health insurance bought through the exchange. From 2014 through 2018, the subsidies would be increased to help ensure that people with incomes below 400 percent of the poverty line do not have to pay an increasing share of the premium during that time. As a result, federal subsidies would grow at the same pace as per capita medical inflation. However, after 2018, if the federal share of the premium exceeds 0.504 percent of GDP, the share of the premium paid by low-income individuals would be increased so that the federal cost would remain at approximately 0.518 percent. Both CBO and CMS actuaries estimate that this threshold will be met and that the share of the premium covered by the subsidies will decline.

If so, after 2018, the share of the premium that enrollees have to pay will increase more rapidly, while the share of the premium covered by subsidies will decline. This has huge implications for the deficit and for the general public. On the one hand, policy leaders may be tempted to increase the aggregate premium thresholds so that subsidies could continue providing the same level of support on a percentage basis. Such action would increase the deficit. On the other hand, if the aggregate dollars available for premium supports are not adjusted, many individuals, states, and employers will face a greater burden.

Already health care costs are having a detrimental effect on the deficit and the economy in general. Legislating programs intended to help the situation, but which might not even be sustainable themselves, runs the risk of only making things worse. Moreover, valuable time is being lost that could be used to mitigate the problem.

Avoidance of Medicare physician payment rates. Another problem with the legislation as it relates to the deficit is that it avoided a key spending issue—Medicare payment rates for physician services. As discussed above, for years, these rates have been scheduled to receive reductions. However, Congress has continually postponed the cuts, to the point that the scheduled cuts have cumulated to nearly 30 percent (Centers for Medicare & Medicaid Services, 2012). Such payment cuts are unlikely to ever pass, but rather to be continuously postponed, until, eventually, more permanent action will be taken to fix the Medicare physician payment rates. Any fix will likely add significant costs to the federal budget—Holtz-Eakin and Ramlet cite one proposal of some $209 billion—and pose more problems for fiscal sustainability.

WHAT IS THE TRUE IMPACT OF THE REFORM BILL?

Holtz-Eakin and Ramlet conclude that the ACA will add $562 billion to the deficit in the first 10 years. This estimate is based on removing potentially unrealistic annual savings, incorporating the full costs of implementing the legislated programs (including a fix to the Medicare physician payment rates), acknowledging the unlikelihood of raising all of the promised revenues, and preserving premiums for the programs they are intended to finance.

Arguably, even if the rather modest reduction of $143 billion were to come to fruition, it would still not be enough to put the U.S. health care system on a sustainable path. In 2011, the federal deficit is estimated to be $1.3 trillion, with the total federal debt at approximately 70 percent of gross domestic product (GDP). Under a projection scenario that includes changes to laws that are expected to happen, such as the fix to Medicare physician payments, as well as the more optimistic impacts of the health-reform legislation (as described in the CBO and JCT score), the CBO estimates that the debt as a share of GDP would exceed its historical peak (during World War II) of 109 percent by 2023 and would approach 190 percent in 2035 (Congressional Budget Office, 2011).

Rising health care costs are a major driver of the increase in federal spending and the deficit problems. This rising trend is set to continue as the population ages, causing the cost of programs such as Medicare to soar. Adding additional entitlements to subsidize insurance in the exchange and expanding Medicaid runs the risk of hastening the arrival of an avoidable collapse, particularly as many of the deficit-reducing provisions of the ACA are either unrealistic or unsustainable.

In 2011, federal spending on Medicare, Medicaid, and the Children's Health Insurance Program (CHIP) amounted to 5.6 percent of the GDP, roughly $800 billion (Congressional Budget Office, 2011). Under the more realistic projection scenario (wherein changes to current laws that are expected to happen are factored into the calculations), Medicare's spending is expected to reach over 6 percent of GDP by 2035, with federal spending on Medicaid, CHIP, and the exchange subsidies reaching almost 4 percent. Thus, total federal spending on the major health care programs would be just over 10 percent of GDP. As shown in Table 19.1, the share of the federal budget accounted for by health care spending increased significantly over the last few decades and is expected to continue doing so moving forward. By 2035 federal spending for Medicare, Medicaid, and other major health care programs is expected to reach over 40 percent of all mandatory and discretionary federal spending (note that the data in Table 19.1 exclude federal net interest payments, an increasingly large share of the federal budget).

THE ACA DELAYS PROGRESS TOWARD REAL REFORM EFFORTS TO REDUCE THE DEFICIT

Some of the ACA critics have called claims that the legislation will reduce the deficit "irresponsible," largely because it will "delay meaningful action" (Capretta & Nix, 2011). Instead, they argue, realistic solutions that reform Medicare, Medicaid, and other entitlement programs are needed. The sooner this happens, the more time current beneficiaries will have to adapt to change and the less likely more dramatic cuts or reductions in benefits will occur in the future. In addition, more immediate action helps ensure that at least some level of meaningful benefits that are currently provided by federally funded programs will be maintained for future beneficiaries.

The ACA makes significant cuts to the Medicare program, but these cannot be used to both increase the program's solvency and pay for new spending. As described previously, accounting gimmicks, in concert with unachievable expectations, create an illusion of Medicare reform. Even worse, the highly questionable sustainability of many of the ACA's provisions creates nontrivial concerns about increased deficit burdens.

According to Douglas Elmendorf, CBO director, the kinds of policy changes required to control the deficit are those that will likely significantly reduce benefits from popular entitlement programs, such as Medicare, or increase people's tax payments, or both. That is, fiscal policy cannot be put on a sustainable path simply by eliminating waste and inefficiency. Counting on the provisions in the ACA aimed at "bending the cost-curve" by systematically changing the way that care is delivered and paid for is not going to be enough.

Table 19.1 Health Care Costs as a Major Federal Cost Driver

	1971	2000	2007	2011	2021	2035
	As a Percent of GDP					
Medicare, Medicaid, and other health programs	0.9	3.4	4.5	5.6	7.1	10.3
Social Security	2.9	4.2	4.1	4.8	5.3	6.1
Other mandatory spending (including defense) and nondefense discretionary spending	7.3	3.0	3.9	12.3	9.1	8.5

Source: Congressional Budget Office. (2011). *Long-term budget outlook.* Retrieved from http://cbo.gov/doc.cfm?index=12212.

Note: This chapter was authored to articulate both sides of a given argument. The views expressed in this Point–Counterpoint chapter are not necessarily the views of the authors.

References and Further Reading

Capretta, J. C., & Nix, K. (2011, January 21). Obamacare and the budget: Playing games with numbers. *WebMemo, 3114.* Retrieved from The Heritage Foundation website: http://thf_media.s3.amazonaws.com/2011/pdf/wm3114.pdf

Centers for Medicare & Medicaid Services. (2012). *Estimated sustainable growth rate and conversion factor, for Medicare payments to physicians in 2012.* Retrieved from https://www.cms.gov/SustainableGRatesConFact/Downloads/sgr2012p.pdf

Congressional Budget Office. (2010a). *Additional information on the potential discretionary costs of implementing the Patient Protection and Affordable Care Act (PPACA).* Retrieved from http://www.cbo.gov/ftpdocs/114xx/doc11493/Additional_Information_PPACA_Discretionary.pdf

Congressional Budget Office. (2010b). *The long-term budget outlook.* Retrieved from http://www.cbo.gov/ftpdocs/115xx/doc11579/06–30-LTBO.pdf

Congressional Budget Office. (2011). *CBO's 2011 long-term budget outlook.* Retrieved from http://cbo.gov/doc.cfm?index=12212

Elmendorf, D. W. (2010a). *Letter to Honorable Nancy Pelosi, March 20, 2010.* Retrieved from http://www.cbo.gov/ftpdocs/113xx/doc11379/AmendReconProp.pdf

Elmendorf, D. W. (2010b). *Letter to Honorable Jerry Lewis, May 11, 2010.* Retrieved from http://www.cbo.gov/ftpdocs/114xx/doc11490/LewisLtr_HR3590.pdf

Foster, R. S. (2010, April 22). *Estimated financial effects of the "Patient Protection and Affordable Care Act," as amended.* Retrieved from https://www.cms.gov/Research-Statistics-Data-and-Systems/Research/ActuarialStudies/downloads//PPACA_2010-04-22.pdf

Greenlee, K. (2011). *Memorandum on the CLASS Program to Secretary Sebelius, October 14, 2011.* Retrieved from http://online.wsj.com/public/resources/documents/Classdecision.pdf

Holtz-Eakin, D. (2010, March 21). The real arithmetic of health care reform. *The New York Times.* Retrieved from http://www.nytimes.com/2010/03/21/opinion/21holtz-eakin.html

Holtz-Eakin, D., & Ramlet, M. J. (2010). Health care reform is likely to widen the federal budget deficits, not reduce them. *Health Affairs, 29*(6), 1136–1141.

Holtz-Eakin, D., & Smith, C. (2010). Labor markets and health care reform: New results. *American Action Forum.* Retrieved from http://americanactionforum.org/files/LaborMktsHCRAAF5-27-10.pdf

Joint Committee on Taxation. (2010). Estimated revenue effects of the amendment in the nature of a substitute to H.R. 4872, the "Reconciliation Act of 2010," as amended, in combination with the revenue effects of H.R. 3590, the "Patient Protection and Affordable Care Act ('PPACA')," as passed by the Senate, and scheduled for consideration by the House Committee on Rules on March 20, 2010 (JCX-17-10). Retrieved from http://www.jct.gov/publications.html?func=showdown&id=3672

Kaiser Family Foundation. (2011). *Chartpack: Kaiser health tracking poll: February 2011.* Retrieved from http://www.kff.org/kaiserpolls/upload/8156-C.pdf

Sebelius, K. (2011). *Letter to the Honorable John Boehner, October 14, 2011.* Retrieved from http://capsules.kaiserhealthnews.org/wp-content/uploads/2011/10/boehner-.pdf

Mark A. Zezza, Kavita Patel, and Shayla Nagy

Tax Treatment of Employer-Sponsored Health Insurance

POINT: The tax deductibility of employer-sponsored health insurance is harmful to the level and distribution of health insurance benefits across individuals because it encourages overconsumption and unfairly favors group over individual purchase of coverage while providing the largest tax benefit to the highest-income employees.

Patricia Ketsche and William S. Custer, Georgia State University
E. Kathleen Adams, Emory University

COUNTERPOINT: The tax deductibility of employer-sponsored health insurance has positive effects in terms of increasing the number of insured persons, creating large viable risk pools independent of adverse selection, subsidizing health insurance for some low-income workers who could not otherwise afford it, and internalizing external benefits, such as increased productivity, of healthy workers within private worksites. Moreover, the net incidence of the tax expenditure favors middle-class workers.

William S. Custer and Patricia Ketsche, Georgia State University
E. Kathleen Adams, Emory University

Introduction

For every dollar they pay in employee wages, employers must also pay a payroll tax, of 7.65 percent, that is used to fund the Social Security and Medicare programs up to the Social Security taxable earnings ceiling, which in 2011 was $106,800. Beyond the ceiling, the tax reduces to 1.45 percent, which is the Medicare portion of the tax. The employee also pays a payroll tax in the same amount as the employer, as well as a personal income tax that varies based on his or her marginal tax rate. For example, an employee with a marginal tax rate of 25 percent would have a combined tax rate of 37.4 percent (7.65 [the employer payroll tax] + 7.65 [the employee payroll tax] + 25 [the employee personal income tax] = 37.4). As Henry Aaron and Leonard Burman describe in *Using Taxes to Reform Health Insurance,* this means that an additional $1 in earnings paid by the employer will pay for 62.6 cents (1 – 0.374) worth of goods and services other than health insurance premiums. Alternatively, because premiums for employer-sponsored health insurance (ESI) are excluded from both the income and payroll taxes, the $1 from the employer could pay for $1 in health insurance premiums.

The tax exclusions for ESI, which date back to World War II–era wage and price controls, effectively act as subsidies for employees' health insurance by lowering their tax liability and thus reducing their after-tax cost of health insurance coverage. According to the Employer Health Benefits Survey administered by the Kaiser Family Foundation and Health Research & Educational Trust, the average ESI premium for family coverage in 2011 was $15,073. Thus, for the employee with the 25 percent marginal tax rate, the tax subsidy for health insurance, relative to other consumption that would cost the same amount, is about $5,637 (15,073 × 0.374).

Taking into account that about 170 million Americans are covered by ESI, the value of the tax exclusion is quite high. According to annual budget estimates of the U.S. federal government by the Office of Management and Budget (OMB), the subsidy amounted to $173.8 billion in 2011. This subsidy is considered to be a federal government tax expenditure, which is defined by OMB as "revenue losses from special exemptions, credits, or other preferences in the tax code." These types of special tax treatments are considered tax expenditures because they essentially accomplish the same goals as direct outlay programs. In other words, a tax expenditure provision that provides $173.8 billion (essentially through lost tax revenue from the government's perspective) to encourage people to buy health insurance has the same effect on the national debt as appropriating $173.8 billion in grants or outlays directly to health insurance plans to reduce the cost of premiums.

There are many other types of tax expenditures, such as those that provide preferential tax treatment to people owning a home and having children. However, all told, the tax expenditure for ESI is the single largest tax expenditure, when both the employer and the tax-preferred employee-paid portions of the premium are taken into account. Therefore, to the extent that the debate on health care reform focuses on deficit reduction, this large tax expenditure is subject to increasing scrutiny.

The magnitude, incidence, and even the social goals inherent in the tax expenditure that result from excluding ESI premiums from income are all controversial and subject to ongoing debate. For example, many argue that the tax deductibility of ESI is harmful to the distribution of health insurance because it favors those who can buy group insurance over those who must buy individual health insurance. That is, people who cannot get health insurance at work must pay for their premiums with after-tax income. Opponents of the tax exclusion also point to the fact that the tax subsidization of ESI has a regressive nature to it because higher-income workers with higher marginal tax rates receive a greater tax benefit from the exclusion. Other arguments in favor of repealing the tax expenditure are that it promotes the purchase of "too much" insurance. Inasmuch as there is currently no limit to the amount of income that can be excluded, higher-cost plans result in larger subsidies.

Although there may be inefficiencies to the tax exclusion for ESI, there has also been staunch political opposition to any proposals to eliminate the preferential tax treatment from advocates of the employer-based health care system, who view the tax exclusion as a key feature for assuring that health insurance remains linked to employers. Also, limiting the tax exclusion would result in a direct increase in taxes for affected workers, as a greater proportion of their overall compensation would be shifted from health benefits (which are currently excluded from taxes) to taxable wages. Those in favor of the ESI tax exclusion also contend that it is integral to the formation and maintenance of more effective risk pools. That is, linking health insurance purchases with large employer groups mitigates problems of adverse selection that can lead to higher premium amounts. This can be particularly helpful for lower-income workers with higher health risks. Moreover, the optimal level of insurance (or the definition of "too much" insurance) depends in part upon the health status of the person obtaining coverage.

There are even those who would prefer to expand the preferential tax treatment to plans purchased by individuals (i.e., non-ESI plans), in addition to groups (ESI plans). Advocates for such a reform argue that individuals rather than employers should make decisions about the type of coverage they wish to purchase. Such a policy could also partially alleviate the inequity in the current formulation of the tax expenditure (because only people buying insurance from employers are eligible for the benefit); although, the expansion would likely increase, rather than decrease, the level of this expenditure.

In the following debate, the authors expand on the pros and cons of preferential tax treatments for ESI. Several questions naturally arise. Which employees could be better off if the tax deductibility for employer-sponsored coverage were expanded to non-employer based plans? Which might be worse off in that case? Would any groups be better off if the tax deductibility for ESI were eliminated altogether? Who gains and who loses from a change to refundable tax credits, as opposed to tax deductions, for all purchases of health insurance? Would other policies relating to health insurance need to be changed if the current tax treatment of health insurance were altered? Finally, those who argue for changing the current system of exempting employer-provided premiums from taxation should be able to demonstrate the superiority of an alternative system. Are any of the alternatives put forth here superior to the existing tax treatment of benefits?

POINT

Arguments for changing the current tax treatment or subsidization of employer-sponsored health insurance (ESI) reflect concerns about how the link between this type of insurance and employment disrupts the efficiency of labor markets, the possibility that the tax subsidy reduces the efficiency of health insurance markets, and that overinsurance in turn reduces the efficiency of the market for health care services. The latter source of inefficiency may actually undermine employer-sponsored insurance, as excess health care inflation makes it harder for employers to retain these benefits and remain globally competitive. Moreover, the greatest part of the tax subsidy flows to individuals who generally have sufficient resources to purchase insurance. This causes many to question, in addition to efficiency, the fairness or equity of the current tax treatment of ESI. (These arguments have been ongoing over many years; thus, some of the suggestions for further readings are for seminal papers that have formed the basis of this debate over several decades.)

The debate has recently become more salient: The budget constraints facing federal and state governments call into question the value of subsidizing private insurance to such a large extent when public programs designed for those with limited resources (Medicaid) or the greatest health needs (Medicare) are the potential targets of significant budget cuts. In addition, the 2010 Patient Protection and Affordable Care Act (ACA) includes a modest change to the tax treatment of employer-sponsored health insurance, a reform that is addressed in more detail as follows.

OVERVIEW OF THE TAX EXPENDITURE FOR EMPLOYER-SPONSORED HEALTH INSURANCE

Among developed nations, the United States is unique in its reliance on the employer as the primary purchaser of private health insurance plans that are then the dominant form of third-party payment for its citizens. Data obtained from the U.S. Census Bureau's Current Population Survey show that over 90 percent of individuals with private health insurance obtain it through an employer-sponsored plan, either through their own employer or as a dependent of an employee with insurance. As private coverage has declined in the United States over the past 20 years, reliance on employers as the primary sponsors of health insurance has remained strong.

David Blumenthal, a professor of medicine at Harvard University and formerly the National Coordinator for Health Information Technology under the presidential administration of Barack Obama, has written at length about the history of the current employer-sponsored system, which he has labeled an "accident of history" (2006). For decades, the leading private health insurance company was Blue Cross and Blue Shield, a provider-sponsored health insurance company that, from its inception in the 1920s, has marketed its products to employers. Other private insurance carriers marketed products to employers, but the growth of the employer-sponsored insurance market was understandably slowed during the Great Depression, given the prevailing high levels of unemployment and low wages. However, that changed during World War II, when a large share of the labor force shifted to the military, and President Franklin Roosevelt put into place wage and price controls. Employers responded by adding benefits such as health insurance to their compensation packages, and the market for such private coverage grew dramatically.

As the role of benefits in the employee-employer relationship grew, so too did the importance of determining whether such benefits should be counted as part of workers' income for tax purposes. The tax exclusion of employer-paid premiums from income was implicit in the beginning, but was codified in section 106 of the Internal Revenue Code (IRC), enacted in 1954. In addition, section 125 of the IRC, enacted in 1978, enabled employers to establish so-called cafeteria plans so that employees can pay their own portion of the premium with pre-tax dollars and set up flexible spending accounts to fund their out-of-pocket payments for health care services with pre-tax dollars.

As many have pointed out, a significant reduction in revenue to both federal and state coffers results from the exclusion from taxation of all employer-paid premiums, the majority of employee-paid premiums, and some out-of-pocket expenditures for health care. For example, in a report tracking the relative size of various tax expenditures over time, the Joint Committee on Taxation (JCT) suggests that between 2010 and 2014 the exclusion of employer contributions for health care, health insurance premiums, and long-term care insurance premiums will result in almost $660 billion in lost federal revenue, making it the largest single tax expenditure during that five-year period. Most of this amount is related to the exclusion of contributions for employer-sponsored health insurance. This estimate is nearly 10 times the largest tax expenditure related to corporations and nearly $200 billion more than the tax expenditure associated with the mortgage-interest deduction for the same five-year period. Moreover, the estimate does not include the lost payroll-tax revenue and the cost to state governments with an income tax. John Shiels and Randy Haught (2004) estimate a cost of $210 billion to the federal and state governments for 2004, and Tom Selden estimates over $200 billion in costs to all levels of government for 2006.

The JCT estimates assume that, were the tax deductibility of ESI to be repealed, individuals would still be able to include the value of employer-paid premiums with their total health care expenditures and, to the extent the value exceeds 7.5 percent of adjusted gross income and for those itemizing deductions, continue to deduct part of the premiums expended. Other estimates do not incorporate the ability of individuals to change how they complete the tax forms in their measure of the magnitude of the tax exclusion for ESI, or they vary other assumptions. For example, some analysts incorporate the assumption that the inclusion of health insurance benefits as taxable income would cause employees to purchase more of other tax preferred benefits (e.g., retirement savings plans or group life insurance) and this substitution effect makes sense if the cost of health insurance relative to other benefits were increased. The variability in the estimates, however, does not detract from the main message: The exclusion of employer-sponsored insurance premiums from taxation results in a large and growing tax expenditure with a significant effect on state and federal budgets and on the economic behavior of employers and employees.

WHY THE TAX EXCLUSION FOR EMPLOYER-SPONSORED HEALTH INSURANCE SHOULD BE CHANGED

For many years, some economists have argued for changing the current tax treatment of employer-sponsored health insurance. Many of these arguments focus on efficiency—the way in which the current tax exclusion alters the labor market, the health insurance market, or the health services market. Other arguments focus more on equity—the way in which the tax treatment of health insurance benefits higher- rather than lower-income citizens. Finally, some argue strictly from the perspective of fiscal affordability; in an era of significant budget pressures at every level of government, the tax base should be expanded by including the "in-kind" income that employees receive as benefits.

Labor market concerns. Tax preference for ESI has resulted in a strong link between employment and health insurance, especially for employment with larger firms. Indeed, employers offer health insurance in part to increase retention, and the tax exclusion is designed to encourage the provision of coverage by employers. However, the link between employment and health insurance carries with it some unintended and potentially negative consequences for how workers select their place of employment. In particular, discussion has focused on problems relating to reduced labor mobility (job lock) and employer discrimination against employees with greater risks of poor health.

When individuals make employment decisions in part to satisfy the demand for health insurance, or if they remain in less-than-satisfactory positions despite opportunities with higher total compensation elsewhere, then ESI results in a labor market inefficiency. In a literature review of the studies of job lock and health insurance, Jonathan Gruber and Brigitte Madrian (2002) suggest that the effects of ESI on labor market decisions and the resulting loss in efficiency is probably "modest" but that measurements of the magnitude of the loss are limited. Even a modest loss of labor efficiency is significant, but another, more important concern was identified in a more recent study by Robert Fairlie and coauthors (2011). They find evidence that the bundling of health insurance and employment may create an inefficient level of small-business creation by potential entrepreneurs. Business creation is a vital component of economic recovery after a recession, so such a limitation on entrepreneurship can have long-lasting negative effects on overall economic activity.

Employers who are able to identify individuals with high expected health care costs have an incentive to attempt to either avoid hiring such workers in favor of lower-cost employees, or to pay such workers less. Thomas Buchmueller (1995) found that workers with evidence of poor health are less likely to obtain employment positions with health benefits, and Jay Bhattacharya and Kate Bundorf (2009) found that the incremental costs for health care associated with obesity are passed on to obese workers through lower wages. Though, institutional and regulatory limitations constrain an employer's ability to either discriminate in hiring or adjust wages to reflect the true cost of insuring each employee, there is evidence that such practices persist.

Health insurance market concerns. The tax exclusion for ESI, and the resulting link between employers and health insurance, serves also to reduce the efficiency in the market for health insurance by reducing the price of insurance artificially and therefore promoting the purchase of excessively generous coverage. This is particularly true because individuals purchasing through a group are not able to pick the plan they would most like to buy. Because the insurance products available to a group of workers have to be selected by some form of group-choice mechanism, at least some of the workers will find that the offered coverage is different than the plans they would have chosen if they could take the same dollars and purchase their optimal insurance contract as an individual.

Several theories and various studies have attempted to explain how groups of employees make this decision. In a study of the relationship between employee preferences for health insurance and the availability of coverage in their chosen job, Alan Monheit and Jessica Vistnes (1999) provide evidence that at least some workers choose a job based on their stated perception of their need for coverage. If such sorting were perfect, individual choice would be the same as the group choice, and each worker would obtain a job with exactly the level of health insurance benefits he or she prefers.

However, sorting is not perfect, in particular because employers need diverse types of workers. As far back as 1976, Gerald Goldstein and Mark Pauly discussed alternative models for group decision making, such as the median worker model and the marginal worker model. They suggest that the generous level of coverage typically observed when unions negotiate health insurance benefit levels is evidence for the dominance of the median employee ("voter") model in cases where benefits are determined through collective bargaining. The marginal employee is presumed to be younger and hence to have a lower demand for comprehensive coverage. In both group choice models, some workers will have a demand for higher levels of coverage and may obtain less generous coverage than they prefer because of the group choice mechanism. In any case, the employer picks a plan (or a small set of plans) that is optimal for some worker or workers, and other workers will be forced to participate in a plan that is not optimal for them.

In a 2010 study of the implications of group choice for insurance benefits, Leemore Dafny and coauthors found that most employees are not enrolled in the kind of plan they would have chosen given a full menu of options. They found further that the average potential improvement in welfare if workers had comprehensive choices is worth about 20 percent of the premiums. That is the same as saying that the mean difference in plan value between the plan employees actually have and the plan they would have chosen if they had a full set of options is worth about 20 percent of the premium, a sizeable differential. However, the price differential that results from the tax preference available for group, but not individual, coverage and the workers' inability to take the employer contribution and apply it to the plan of their choice eliminates the potential for these workers to maximize their own welfare by choosing a different plan. These results suggest that many workers would be better off in a well-functioning individual market that could provide premiums with the same loading factor (i.e., the same level of administrative overhead and profit margin) as in the group market, which is subsidized through the tax system.

Health services market concerns. Although fostering the purchase of excess insurance is inefficient with respect to the insurance market, a related problem results from the implications of the generous coverage levels on consumer behavior related to the use of health care services. The high levels of generous coverage create additional moral hazards, such that the insured might be less likely to take care of themselves to prevent the need for care, be more likely to obtain care, and be less likely to seek cost-effective care than they would be if their insurance contracts were unsubsidized and thus less generous.

In a seminal study on the effects of insurance on care-seeking behavior conducted between 1974 and 1977—the RAND Health Insurance Experiment—a group of researchers led by Willard Manning found that individuals with very high deductibles (catastrophic coverage) spent 31 percent less on total care than did individuals with zero out-of-pocket costs. The important feature of this study is that individuals were randomly assigned to an insurance policy, thus minimizing the effect of selection on the outcome. These results support the contention that when individuals are responsible for a greater share of the cost of services, they obtain fewer services. Importantly, the study also finds that these delays in care do not increase the overall cost of care by shifting more care to the inpatient side.

It is important to note that the RAND Health Insurance Experiment did not find that the patients shopped for the lowest-cost provider or obtained care from primary care rather than specialty physicians. Instead, the identified cost savings are fully attributable to patients seeking fewer health care services. Today, proponents of consumer-directed health care hypothesize that price sensitivity is even greater, in part because consumers' ability to collect information about both prices and outcomes is vastly higher today than it was in the 1970s.

Authors such as Martin Feldstein (1973) and Mark Pauly (1986) have described these problems as contributors to inflation in health care costs, which for many years have exceeded the overall rate of inflation. Thus, the presence of extensive levels of coverage has a positive effect on the quantity of health care services consumed but negative effects on relative inflation. Proposals to limit the tax deductibility of health insurance have focused on this inefficiency in the health services market, created because of the moral hazard effects of high levels of insurance coverage (Pauly, 1986). The inefficiencies that Pauly describes arise both because of consumers' demand for excess services and providers' willingness to supply those services, especially in a fee-for-service environment, and because high levels of coverage reduce consumer sensitivity to provider prices that are above the competitive level. Payers have developed strategies to deal with both of these problems, such as utilization management, negotiated fee schedules, and prospective payment systems. However, when consumers have skin in the game through higher cost sharing (i.e., less generous coverage) or because they pay the full premium without the benefit of a tax subsidy, they can become partners with their health plan in working to control health care cost inflation by making more cost-conscious decisions.

Equity argument for changing the tax exclusion for ESI. The concept of equity is related to fairness. Although there is no single consensus as to how fairness should be defined, it is worth considering whether the tax treatment of employer-paid health insurance premiums is consistent with any concept of vertical equity: Do the benefits accrue to individuals proportionally to their spending on health care? Do they accrue to individuals proportionally to their income?

There is a long history of using the tax code to provide incentives to support socially desirable investments or purchases. In a tax system in which each individual faces the same marginal tax rate, such tax incentives are directly proportional to income for all individuals. However, when tax rates are progressive, the benefits of exempting income from taxation for certain purchases (such as the home-interest deduction) or to encourage certain behavior (such as charitable giving) increase as the tax rate increases. In that case, the benefits are distributed regressively across the population. Table 20.1 illustrates the implications of that tax treatment by considering three employees with different income levels but who all receive the same employer contribution for family coverage (and who file jointly).

In each case, the dollar value of the subsidy can be estimated by using the workers marginal tax rate and calculating what the additional tax liability would be if the employer contribution were taxed at that rate. For example, Worker B's marginal tax rate (both income and payroll) is 29.45 percent, so an additional $10,000 in income would result in an additional tax liability of $2,945.

This table uses tax rates in effect in 2010 and illustrates that the benefit of excluding the premium from taxation increases as family income also increases, such that the greatest benefit goes to families with the highest incomes. It is important also to note that families with higher incomes are almost universally insured. The demand for health insurance increases with income, so the social goal of expanding coverage to people who otherwise might forgo health insurance is not enhanced when the largest subsidies go to families that would have purchased the coverage even without the subsidy.

Two additional factors make this inequitable distribution even worse than is outlined previously. In the table, each of the three workers is presumed to receive comparable benefits from their employers. In reality, as family income goes up,

Table 20.1 Tax Subsidy for Health Insurance for Three Different Workers

	Worker A	Worker B	Worker C
Employer Contribution for Family Health Insurance	$10,000	$10,000	$10,000
Taxable Family Income	$60,000	$150,000	$400,000
Income Tax Rate	10%	28%	35%
Payroll Tax Rate*	7.65%	1.45%	1.45%
Benefit from the Tax Expenditure	$1,765	$2,945	$3,645

* Ignored in this case is the employer-paid portion of the payroll tax. Workers B and C are assumed to have wages that exceed the Social Security FICA cap. This simplified example also ignores behavioral changes, such as shifts in benefit preferences that might affect these workers differently.

so too does the likelihood of having any health insurance at all from an employer. Therefore, workers with lower incomes are much less likely to gain any benefit from this exemption because they are less likely to have any employer-paid health insurance. In addition, higher-income workers generally are able to obtain jobs with richer benefits (i.e., plans that cost more) and receive compensation where a greater share of the premium is paid by the employer. Therefore, the average benefit from the tax expenditure among the highest-earning families is likely to be even higher than the previous illustration demonstrates.

Because the employer-paid premiums are not counted as income, workers who receive compensation in the form of benefits rather than wages see their lifetime earnings reduced. This is irrelevant for workers who earn enough to reach the maximum Social Security benefit upon retirement. Workers B and C receive future Social Security payments that are largely unaffected by the tax exclusion because they have earnings that are above the level used to calculate benefits. However, Worker A's earnings records are lower each year that she is insured than they would be if her employer had paid wages instead of ESI, and the value of the ESI premiums were subject to the payroll tax. Therefore, Worker A's monthly Social Security payments are lower than they otherwise would be once she retires, and therefore, Worker A's annual benefit from the tax deductibility of ESI as shown earlier is considerably overstated.

Although such calculations are complex, the annual tax subsidy for health insurance is actually reduced by the current value of the future payments that a worker will *not* receive. Table 20.2 illustrates this by comparing Worker A, who is near retirement, to Worker X, who receives all of her income as wages. It is assumed that the lifetime difference in earnings varies because of patterns of enrolling in individual, spousal, or family coverage during different life stages. The table uses a near-retirement wage difference of $4,000 (rather than the $10,000 associated with family coverage used in Table 20.1) assuming that such an individual is currently enrolled in single or spousal coverage rather than in a package or family coverage. The expected monthly benefit for these individuals, assuming both were born in 1946 and retired at age 65 and 4 months, were arrived at using the Quick Calculator available through the Social Security Administration. Worker A's Social Security earnings would be reduced by over $800 per year, compared to Worker X who was without health insurance but had slightly higher wage-based compensation. If we assume both workers lived for 20 years and that the appropriate discount rate for that lost income is 3 percent, the value at retirement of that lost income is over $12,000. Over a 35-year career, the annual benefit from the tax expenditure would need to be reduced by at least $500 to account for the future lost income.

Budget argument for changing the tax exclusion for ESI. As discussed earlier, the cost to the federal and state governments in lost revenue from excluding ESI from income is high and increasing rapidly over time. The projections from the JCT cited previously suggest that, over the next decade, the typical timeframe for estimating programmatic costs and budgeting, the ESI tax exclusion will result in well over $1 trillion in forgone revenue. At a time of substantial debate about the sustainability of the Medicare and Medicaid programs, it may be wise to reconsider the efficacy of such a large tax expenditure for private insurance. In light of the importance of closing the federal budget gap, the sheer magnitude of this tax expenditure makes it difficult to ignore.

Table 20.2   Impact on Social Security Benefit From Tax Subsidy for Health Insurance

	Worker A (with insurance)	Worker X (without insurance)
Employer Contribution for Family Health Insurance	$4,000	$0
Taxable Family Income at Age 65	$60,000	$64,000
Projected Monthly Social Security Benefit	$1,456	$1,525
Annual Benefit	$17,472	$18,300
Present Value of Monthly Difference at Retirement*	($12,441)	
Annual Reduction in Tax Benefit Attributable to Health Insurance Exemption**	$579	

*Assumes 20-year life expectancy and a 3 percent annual discount rate compounded monthly.
**Assumes 35 work-years and a 3 percent annual discount rate compounded annually.

ALTERNATIVES TO THE CURRENT TAX EXCLUSION OF EMPLOYER-PAID PREMIUMS

The many arguments for changing the current tax treatment of employer-paid premiums must be considered in conjunction with the available alternatives. It is not enough to make a strong critique of the current system without some clarity about what the alternatives are and how those alternatives would resolve some of the problems discussed earlier.

Eliminate the current tax exclusion. One alternative is to simply eliminate the current exclusion without any other change to the tax code or any other spending change. This is the change estimated by the JCT, and it would represent an improvement over the current system in several ways. First, they would still be able to deduct premiums and health care expenditures that exceed 7.5 percent of family income, many families would continue to deduct some or all of the premium costs. In particular, families with either high health care expenditures (the sick) or low family incomes would then likely exceed the threshold for deductibility and would benefit from the tax exclusion. This focuses the tax preference on those in the greatest need of assistance, and addresses in part the equity concerns raised previously. Second, the change would indirectly equalize the treatment of individual and group insurance because individual premiums are already eligible for inclusion as itemized medical care expenses. As a result the demand for individually purchased private insurance could increase, potentially resulting in a more robust individual market. Third, because the overall level of subsidization would be reduced, it is likely that insurance plans with less generous coverage would flourish, resulting in a reduced demand for health services and a potential slowing in health care cost inflation. Finally, this approach would result in significant additional federal and state tax revenues in an era of concern about deficit spending.

Limit the tax exclusion. Another option for change is to limit or cap the tax exclusion so that plans are not subsidized above a certain level. This approach limits the total tax expenditure and reduces the budgetary impact, but the extent to which it achieves that goal depends on the level at which the exclusion is capped. For example, in 1984 President Ronald Reagan proposed replacing the open-ended deduction of health insurance premiums with a capped deduction that would have been generous at first but only grown over time with the rate of inflation.

Although a cap addresses some of the inefficiencies discussed earlier, for example by limiting the subsidy of plans with no cost sharing, it does not address other concerns. For example, a cap on the tax exclusion does not eliminate concerns about the inequity of the current subsidy but it could limit the regressive nature of the benefit by requiring those who purchase the most generous coverage (usually higher-income individuals) to pay the full, unsubsidized premium. In addition, a cap on the exclusion leaves in place the strong price advantage for group versus individual insurance plans with its potentially deleterious effects on the labor market and the health insurance market. Those like Alain Enthoven and Richard Kronick (1989), who favor enhanced competition between competing health plans, have long suggested that the tax preference for ESI should be capped at the contribution an employer makes to the most efficient (lowest cost for the given benefits) health plan. Doing so would serve to encourage enrollment in efficient plans and eliminate the subsidy for the additional costs associated with more generous and higher-cost plans.

Replace the tax exclusion with tax rebates/refundable credits. A proposal to replace the current tax deduction for employer-paid premiums with a tax credit was part of the health care reform platform of the 2008 Republican candidate for president, John McCain. Under his proposal, employer-paid premiums for health insurance would be treated as employee income and thus subject to income and payroll taxes. However, individuals purchasing any health insurance, including employer-paid health insurance, would receive a credit against their tax liability, typically designed to be refundable so as to benefit all individuals the same, regardless of their marginal tax rate. It is important to note that such a refundable credit would likely require everyone to file tax forms, even those without any income-tax liability. Moreover, in order to help low- and moderate-income families manage the cash flow requirements of purchasing coverage, such a plan might require that the credit be administered to provide monthly rather than annual subsidy payments.

As with other alternatives, the full effect of the McCain proposal on the labor, insurance, and medical-care markets and on equity depends upon the details. In general, such a system would reduce some of the inefficiencies noted earlier. It would minimize job lock by eliminating the preference for employment-based coverage over coverage in the individual market, although lower loading factors in group purchasing would still favor ESI. It would improve the efficiency of the health insurance market by expanding the demand for individual coverage and subsidizing choices at the individual rather than group level. It could be possible to design these credits to target those in greatest need by scaling them to income and thus address the equity concerns described here. However, the tax-credit alternative would continue to subsidize coverage and therefore fail to fully eliminate concerns about moral hazard, although a fixed rebate would provide incentives for people to choose lower-cost plans. This alternative would also reduce but not eliminate the overall budgetary impact of subsidizing health insurance through the tax code if the subsidies were designed to be less generous than the current tax expenditures and did not affect payroll-tax liabilities.

Equalize tax deductibility for individual and group insurance. In order to address the implications of the reliance on ESI for the labor market and improve the ability of individual insurance products to compete with ESI plans, it is conceivable that the tax preference could be extended to include individually purchased plans. It is important to note that, because it would still foster higher levels of insurance than are optimal by reducing its price, this option would not address the inefficiencies in the market for health services. It would not address the inequities that arise from subsidies based on marginal tax rates, and it would make the budgetary implications of the tax expenditure worse. It also would not remove the incentive to buy in a group plan, because the loading factor would still be markedly lower than in the individual market.

CONCLUSION

This essay has highlighted some of the significant concerns voiced by policy analysts, economists, and policymakers over years with respect to the heavy subsidies provided to ESI plans. At the same time, it is important to note that, although each of the outlined alternatives has the potential to address some of the problems associated with the current system, none of them is capable of resolving them all. The tax deductibility of ESI is harmful to the level and distribution of health insurance because it encourages overconsumption and unfairly favors group over individual purchase of coverage while providing the largest benefit to the highest-income employees. Yet any alternative could face significant political obstacles, require changes in regulation of the individual health insurance market, and might create transitional disruptions in health insurance coverage for the large number of Americans who rely on the employer-sponsored market.

REFERENCES AND FURTHER READING

Aaron, H., & Burman, L. (2008). *Using taxes to reform health insurance: Pitfalls and promises.* Washington, DC: Brookings Institution Press.

Bhattacharya, J., & Bundorf, M. K. (2009). The incidence of the healthcare costs of obesity. *Journal of Health Economics, 28*(3), 649–658.

Blumenthal, D. (2006). Employer-sponsored health insurance in the United States—Origins and implications. *New England Journal of Medicine, 355*(1), 82–88.

Buchmueller, T. (1995). Health risk and access to employer-provided health insurance. *Inquiry, 32*(1), 75–86.

Dafny, L., Ho, K., & Varela, M. (2010). *Let them have choice: Gains from shifting away from employer-sponsored health insurance and toward an individual exchange.* National Bureau of Economic Research Working Papers 15687.

Enthoven, A., & Kronick, R. (1989). A consumer-choice health plan for the 1990s. Universal health insurance in a system designed to promote quality and economy. *The New England Journal of Medicine, 320*(2), 94–101.

Farlie, R. W., Kapur, K., & Gates, S. (2011). Is employer-based health insurance a barrier to entrepreneurship? *Journal of Health Economics, 30*(1), 146–162.

Feldstein, M. S. (1973). The welfare loss of excess health insurance. *Journal of Political Economy, 81*(2), 251–280.

Goldstein, G., & Pauly, M. (1976). Group health insurance as a local public good. In R. Rosett (Ed.), *The role of health insurance in the health services sector* (pp. 73–114). New York, NY: National Bureau of Economic Research.

Gruber, J., & Madrian, B. C. (2002). *Health insurance, labor supply, and job mobility: A critical review of the literature.* National Bureau of Economic Research Working Papers 8817.

Joint Committee on Taxation. (2011). *Background information on tax expenditure analysis and historical survey of tax expenditure estimates* (JCX-15-11). Retrieved from http://www.novoco.com/hottopics/resource_files/jcx-15-11.pdf

Manning, W. G., Newhouse, J. P., Duan, N., Keeler, E. B., & Leibowitz, A. (1987). Health insurance and the demand for medical care: Evidence from a randomized experiment. *American Economic Review, 77*(3), 251–277.

Monheit, A., & Vistnes, J. (1999). Health insurance availability and the workplace: How important are worker preferences? *The Journal of Human Resources, 34*(4), 770–785.

Pauly, M. (1986). Taxation, health insurance and market failure in the medical economy. *Journal of Economic Literature, 24*(2), 629–675.

Pew's Tax Expenditure Database. (n.d.). *Subsidy scope.* Retrieved from http://subsidyscope.org/tax_expenditures/summary

Selden, T., & Gray, B. (2006). Tax subsidies for employment-related health insurance: Estimates for 2006. *Health Affairs, 25*(6), 1568–1579.

Shiels, J., & Haught, R. (2004). The cost of tax exempt health benefits in 2004. *Health Affairs, W-4,* 106–112.

Social Security Administration. (n.d.). *Calculators.* Retrieved from http://www.ssa.gov/planners/benefitcalculators.htm

Patricia Ketsche, William S. Custer, and E. Kathleen Adams

COUNTERPOINT

The current tax treatment of health insurance—that is, its exemption from federal and state income and payroll taxes—increases the level of health insurance coverage in the United States. This subsidization has positive benefits. Increasing the number of Americans with health insurance decreases health care costs, decreases the tax burdens for the publicly insured, and contributes to lower health insurance premiums. Increasing health insurance coverage through the private market also increases innovation in plan design and health care delivery, allows greater choice in coverage for individuals, and provides for greater flexibility in the public health insurance system. All of those benefits extend beyond those who directly benefit from the costs of the tax expenditure.

Arguments against the exclusion of employer contributions for health benefits from employee income for tax purposes generally focus on two aspects: It is regressive, in that higher-wage workers benefit more than lower-wage workers, and it creates moral hazard, in that individuals are incentivized to purchase too much insurance. The regressivity of the tax exclusion may be overstated. Estimates of its burden focus almost exclusively on taxes, leaving out the benefits of the tax expenditure. Moreover, the true effect of the tax expenditure on who pays must be calculated by considering both the effect of the tax treatment of health insurance on the premiums and the effect on who pays all other taxes to keep the government whole in terms of expenditures.

Important to the discussion is the fact that the moral hazard argument ignores the market failure that created the employment-based health care financing system in the first place. Market failure is a failure to efficiently allocate scarce resources among alternative uses. It can occur when one side in an economic transaction has more information than the other. In health insurance, this likely occurs because purchasers of insurance know more than the insurer about their health status and the probability that they will need to file a claim. For their part, insurers know that individuals with the greatest demand for health insurance are those with the greatest need for health care services. Because regulations in many states prevent full-risk adjustment of premiums, insurers cannot separate good risks from bad and are forced to offer coverage at high average premiums to cover the high-risk individual's claims. As a result, good risks drop (or never enter) the health insurance market, an effect known as adverse selection. If not mitigated, insurance plans that suffer from adverse selection enter a kind of death spiral in which better risks leave the plan. With each renewal period, the risk pool worsens, resulting in higher premiums that drive yet more good risks out of the pool. Ultimately, the plan becomes unsustainable. Insurers are increasingly using markers of health behavior, such as smoking, to adjust premiums, though these are not widespread or complete enough to remove the issue of adverse selection from the debate.

In the absence of the subsidy, large and viable risk pools may not form, and large numbers of Americans might find themselves struggling to obtain health insurance, especially those who are older, sicker, or in immediate need of care even if unrelated to health. Indeed, this was the case in the years prior to the early development of private insurance plans and markets.

THE HISTORY OF EMPLOYMENT-BASED HEALTH INSURANCE COVERAGE: A RISK-POOLING/ADVERSE SELECTION PERSPECTIVE

The current employment-based health insurance system is frequently called an accident of history. However, viewing the development of our current system through a lens of risk pooling makes it clear that the system is no accident. It is a rational response of the insurance market to the real problem of adverse selection and a result of policy specifically designed to deal with that problem.

Bundling the purchase of health insurance with employment helps to mitigate adverse selection. When health insurance is sold as part of a group's employment compensation package, good risks in the group help to keep health insurance premiums affordable. The insurance pool retains those good risks, lowering premiums and increasing coverage. This was the insight that led to the birth of the Blue Cross system starting with the faculty and staff at Baylor University in 1929. The offer of hospital coverage as part of employment induced good risks to remain in the risk pool, thereby reducing average premiums. This ability to induce good risks to stay in the risk pool was later enhanced by the tax treatment of insurance premiums paid by the employer.

The passage of the Sixteenth Amendment in 1913 clarified the ability of the federal government to tax income but left unsettled many of the details on how income should be defined. Accounting practice generally counted cash wages as income, but excluded other forms of compensation that were more difficult to quantify.

Marketed to employers, Blue Cross–type plans expanded slowly throughout the 1930s. Employers generally paid the entire premium. As a result, good risks had their coverage paid for with before-tax dollars, making insurance less expensive than if it had been purchased as individuals. For their part, poorer risks could purchase health insurance that would have been much more expensive or impossible to purchase as individuals.

World War II significantly expanded employment-based health coverage through two additional developments. In an effort to keep both unions and manufacturers from exploiting the war effort, in 1942, Congress enacted wage and price controls. Faced with increased demand for war materials and a rapidly decreasing labor supply as workers enlisted in the armed forces, employers sought ways to attract workers without increasing cash wages. Their solution was to increase noncash compensation in the form of health insurance, pensions, and childcare benefits. That last benefit was particularly attractive because of the increased participation of women in the workforce during the war.

The end of the war brought an end to wage and price controls, but pent-up consumer demand (long held in check by the war effort) contributed to an increased need for workers and an expansion of all types of compensation, including health benefits. (The exception was childcare benefits, which vanished as women dropped out of the labor force.) At the same time, the war debts incurred by the federal government created an incentive for Congress to reexamine tax policy and the definition of income for tax purposes.

After a long debate, Congress codified the practice of excluding employer contributions for employee health benefits from taxable income in the Taft-Hartley Act of 1948 and the enactment of the Internal Revenue Code of 1954. That debate centered on the revenue lost due to this exclusion, rather than on the expanded health insurance coverage resulting from that exclusion. As we see from the actions of Congress, the nation eventually decided that the value of the expansion of coverage was greater than the value of lost revenue.

After 1954 employment-based health insurance coverage expanded both in the numbers of people covered and the scope of that coverage until the early 1990s. Since the early 1990s, however, coverage in employment-based plans has been slowly eroding, especially for workers in small firms and low-wage workers. This trend has continued into the twenty-first century. In 2000, 69 percent of Americans under the age of 65 had employment-based coverage. By 2010 that percentage had fallen to 58 percent (see Figure 20.1).

THE TAX SUBSIDY, ADVERSE SELECTION, MEDICAL COST INFLATION, AND COVERAGE

The role of the tax subsidy in expanding coverage. This bundling of the decision to purchase health insurance with the attainment of employment mitigates the effects of adverse selection and allows for more complete risk pooling. In a system of employment-based health insurance, it is the employed group that determines how insurance is supplied to each individual. As the average tax rate of the group increases, the average price of insurance decreases due to the tax subsidy, and the group is more likely to prefer benefits to wages. Once a plan is offered, all high-risk employees are likely to participate, inasmuch as the premium is based on the pooled premium. However, some low-risk employees—those who perceive the value of insurance to be low—might choose to opt out of the benefit plan or might seek employment that does not offer health insurance as a benefit at all. The tax subsidy, by lowering the cost of group insurance, reduces the leakage of such good risks, and increases the general availability of health benefits. This effect of the tax subsidy would be even more important in determining access to coverage for high-risk individuals.

Figure 20.1 Health Insurance Coverage Among Non-Elderly Since 2000

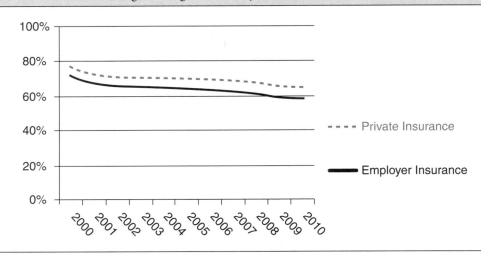

Source: Tabulations of the Annual Social and Economic Supplement to the Current Population Survey, 1999–2011.

In a study of how taxation affects the coverage of individuals in the employer-sponsored market, Ketsche and Custer (2000) found that the associated tax served to expand coverage for all workers, but it was more important in determining coverage for high-risk workers than for low-risk ones. This finding supports the relevance of the tax expenditure to moving entire groups into insurance, and thus ensuring that the poor health risks have access to insurance.

This expansion of risk pooling is even more important as medical cost inflation has continued to respond to market forces. The expansion of private health insurance coverage, coupled with the creation of the Medicare and Medicaid programs in 1965, led to a rapid increase in the demand for health care services. As a result, health care technology increased both the number of treatments available and the success of those treatments, in turn further building demand for health care services. The result has been rapid increases in the costs of health care and, subsequently, the cost of health insurance.

The rising costs of health insurance premiums have served to make employment-based health insurance—once a "fringe benefit"—a major component of total compensation. As health care costs have risen faster than wages, the employer's contribution to the health premium becomes an increasing share of total compensation even as it remains a constant share of the total premium. The result is that individuals increasingly take into account their own, or their dependents', health risks when weighing the attributes of competing job opportunities and compensation packages, thus reducing the ability of employment-based risk pools to mitigate adverse selection. This has led to an erosion of coverage, as some low-risk individuals opt for higher wages over benefits. However, this loss of coverage would have been much worse without the tax subsidy.

One study by Monheit, Nichols, and Selden (1995–1996) analyzed the distribution of net health insurance benefits in the employment-based market. These authors demonstrated that, without the tax subsidy, substantial negative net benefits could be anticipated for all but those in families with an insured member in fair or poor health or those in large families (five or more persons). Therefore, the tax subsidy reduces expected losses from insurance for the healthy and thus increases participation in the employment-based health insurance market by those who might otherwise choose not to participate.

It is reasonable to assume that removing the tax subsidy for health benefits significantly reduces the incentives for workers to continue in group coverage. Absent tax subsidies, low-risk individuals might leave insurance pools at a higher rate than would high-risk individuals because of the substantially negative net benefit they receive from group insurance. The result is an "adverse-selection death-spiral," in which rising premiums lead more good risks to leave the pool until the risk pool collapses. Without group coverage, good risks face higher premiums in the individual market, while higher-risk individuals may find it impossible to purchase coverage at any price.

The tax subsidy and welfare gains. Those who oppose the tax subsidization of health insurance suggest that the subsidy encourages the purchase of "too much" insurance, leading to the purchase of too much health care. It is a basic tenet of economics that any distortion of the price of a good or service will lead to an inefficient use of resources. That tenet rests on the assumption that in the absence of that distortion, in this case the tax subsidy, the markets would perform efficiently. As was demonstrated earlier, however, this is not the case.

The theory of second-best states that, in the presence of two distortions of the price system, removing one may not improve consumer welfare. In this instance, the tax subsidy, while clearly increasing the demand for health insurance and thus health care services, may be restoring demand for insurance to a level nearer it would be if all markets were operating efficiently.

The current employment-based system promotes a wealth transfer from those in good health to those in ill health, consistent with a pooled equilibrium. To the extent that such a reduction in the burden of the cost of illness contributes to social welfare, and to the extent that a stable employment-based system reduces risk of future uninsurability for those currently in good health, the estimates of welfare loss due to the tax subsidy may not only be overstated; there may actually be a welfare gain. The welfare gain from an increase in coverage may be larger for lower-income individuals, thereby counter balancing the regressivity of the tax subsidy itself.

The tax subsidy, individual preferences, and the scope of coverage. Opponents of the tax subsidy argue that many individuals would be better off if they could buy their preferred plan in the individual market. However, this presumes a well-functioning individual insurance market and ignores the problem of adverse selection. In fact, a review of enrollment in the individual market over time using data from the Current Population Survey reveals that, despite declines in coverage in the group health insurance market, there has been almost no change in enrollment in the individual market. This supports the notion that the individual market is not adequate to provide for widespread private coverage.

It is also difficult, if not impossible, for the individual or nongroup market to offer policies with the same benefits (e.g., deductibles and co-pays) as the group market at anywhere near the same price. This is largely due to the ability of large groups to obtain provider discounts and benefit from significant economies of scale. The effect of these economies is seen in the difference in offer rates between large and small firms. The latter cannot benefit from economies of scale and hence, cannot offer workers similar policies at prices that are available at larger firms.

Another argument put forward against the tax treatment of employment-based health benefits is that it encourages individuals to purchase more insurance than they would without the subsidy, leading to an inefficient use of health care services. This argument relies on the assumption that, absent the tax subsidy, the health insurance market would operate efficiently. As demonstrated earlier however, adverse selection due to asymmetrical information prevents health insurance premiums in the individual market from reflecting true risks. It is more likely that removing the tax treatment will lead to greater inefficiency in the insurance market.

An increase in insurance coverage clearly does mean an increase in demand for health care services above what it would have been without insurance. However, a good deal of evidence supports the conclusion that the uninsured purchase too little care, and have worse health outcomes when in need of care (Hadley, 2002). The tax subsidy of employment-based health insurance may increase coverage, increasing consumption of health services and increasing net consumer welfare.

The tax subsidy and the labor market. There has been an important stream of literature that argues that the tax preference given to employer-sponsored health insurance (ESI) reduces the efficiency of the labor market by reducing labor mobility. This phenomenon, called "job lock," refers to the inability of individuals to match their skills with jobs that would maximize their productivity if moving to those more productive jobs would mean the loss of their health insurance coverage.

One of the reasons an employer offers employee benefits in general, and health benefits specifically, is to retain workers who become more productive the longer they work for that employer. To the extent that an employee's productivity is greater at his or her current employer than at a competing firm, job lock may actually increase economic efficiency. In any case, the Health Insurance Portability and Accountability Act (HIPAA) Privacy Rule removed much of the aforementioned barrier on mobility by limiting the ability of employer plans to exclude coverage for preexisting conditions, clarifying opportunities to change coverage options outside the annual open-enrollment period, and prohibiting discrimination against employees or their dependents because of their medical history. HIPAA did not increase the number of firms that offered coverage, and so did not fully address all of the issues associated with job lock.

The actual magnitude of job lock is unclear. In a study of the phenomenon using more sophisticated economic models, Mark Berger and coauthors (2004) found that earlier estimates have likely overstated job lock. Moreover, their study was conducted using data from before the implementation of HIPAA.

Another reason employers offer health insurance benefits is because they recognize that the private consumption of health care services has numerous external benefits. These include long-run improvements in the health status of employees that translate into improved productivity. By ensuring that their labor force has access to health care services, employers are able to internalize those benefits.

The larger problem is why aren't health benefits offered by every employer. One of the factors affecting the provision of health insurance is firm size. Smaller employers face higher costs for providing health benefits than do larger firms for three reasons. First, their small size means that they are less able to spread risks. Second, their small size makes it harder for them to self-insure and avoid costly state mandates and taxes. Finally, because they are less likely to be able to devote staff to the management of health benefits, they face higher administrative costs. It should be noted that there are some provisions in the Affordable Care Act to help small employers offer insurance coverage to employees, including tax subsidies and the ability to offer insurance through exchanges that could, in all practicality, increase the risk pool for small employers.

EQUITY AND THE TAX SUBSIDY

The discussion up to this point has focused on concerns that subsidizing coverage through the employment-based system harms the overall efficiency of the market. The other primary source of opposition to the subsidy is that it is inequitably distributed because it reduces the price of coverage more for high- than for low-income workers. Although this argument seems to make sense when only the net price of coverage is taken into account, it is actually an inadequate measure of equity.

> ### Self-Insured Plans Under ERISA
>
> The Employee Retirement Income Security Act (ERISA) allocates the regulation of insurance to the states and the regulation of employee benefit plans to the federal government. The distinction for health insurance is the retention of risk. If an employer purchases insurance for his or her employees, the insurer bears the risk of paying claims, and the transaction is regulated by the state. If the employer pays claims out of employer-controlled funds, it is an employee benefit plan exempt from state regulation, and is regulated by the federal government under ERISA

It is true that the dollar value of the tax subsidy for employment-based health insurance increases as income goes up. The correct measure of vertical equity of taxes or of public benefits is the tax benefit expressed as a share of income. Table 20.3 illustrates that for workers with an employer contribution toward their health insurance, the benefit of the tax expenditure expressed as a percent of income declines with income. This occurs when premiums are constant for low- and high-wage workers. Though it's true that, on average, higher-wage workers with health benefits have more generous benefits than do their lower-wage counterparts, the difference is not enough to affect the result demonstrated in Table 20.3.

Some consider the inability or unwillingness of workers to take advantage of the benefit—for example, if their employer does not offer coverage or if they themselves view the benefit as unaffordable—yet another measure of the regressivity of the tax code, in particular because these workers tend to be younger and have lower incomes than workers with ESI. Including the workers who get a zero benefit from the tax preference in the lowest-income group exaggerates the pattern of regressive benefits illustrated in the previous example. However, this argument also ignores the benefits of the tax subsidy in stabilizing the group health insurance market. Jeske and Kitao (2009) find that removing the tax

Table 20.3   Health Benefits as a Percentage of Various Income Levels

	Worker A	Worker B	Worker C
Employer Contribution for Family Health Insurance	$10,000	$10,000	$10,000
Taxable Family Income	$60,000	$150,000	$400,000
Income Tax Rate	10%	28%	35%
Payroll Tax Rate*	7.65%	1.45%	1.45%
Benefit from the Tax Expenditure	$1,765	$2,945	$3,645
Benefit as a Percentage of Income	2.94%	1.96%	0.91%

* Ignored in this case is the employer-paid portion of the payroll tax. Workers B and C are assumed to have wages that exceed the Social Security FICA cap. This simplified example also ignores behavioral changes, such as shifts in benefit preferences that might affect these workers differently.

expenditure associated with employment-based coverage leads to a collapse in the group health insurance market. They find that not only individuals offered employment-based coverage "but also those with no access to the group insurance will face a welfare loss since the group insurance offer they may receive in the future is not so attractive anymore and they suffer from more future expenditure risks as well" (p. 219).

Equity arguments based on the face value of insurance ignore the potential differences in the real value of health insurance, which may also be greater for lower-income families than those with higher incomes. To understand this, we can compare health insurance to other types of insurance, such as homeowners' insurance. A family taking into consideration the risk of its home being destroyed by fire could envision several choices for financing the rebuilding of that home as alternatives to insurance. For example, a bank might provide financing for a majority of the costs on the condition that the rebuilt home serve as collateral. However, an uninsured family contemplating the costs of cancer treatments is likely to find no outside source of financing for that care. Although the high earners might be able to finance the care out of current income or from existing wealth, the low- and moderate-income family is unlikely to have that option. Thus, unlike other types of insurance that protect a consumer from a financial loss, health insurance also ensures access to otherwise unobtainable services. The improved access obtained through insurance is inversely related to income, meaning that the value of insurance is higher for low-income workers. (The role of insurance in improving access was the focus of a book by John Nyman in 2002.)

The value of the tax preference for ESI is also greater for those in poorer health. The ability to pool risks in group coverage means that the premium for group coverage is lower for those in poorer health than it would be for individually purchased coverage, if such a plan is available to high risks at all. The tax preference encourages the purchase of coverage in groups in which premiums are determined based on average rather than individual risk. Because poor health and income are inversely related, low-income and thus sicker individuals benefit more from obtaining group rather than individual (experience-related) coverage.

The argument that the tax preference for ESI is regressive also ignores the financing side of the preference. A study by Ketsche, Adams, and others (2011) examined the distributional effects of the subsidy, including its financing. If the subsidy is financed by all other tax sources (i.e., we assume constant government expenditures and that all other tax types are increased to finance the tax expenditure), although the lowest-income group also finances the tax expenditure to a greater degree than it benefits, the greatest burden of financing the tax subsidy is borne by those paying the greatest share of their income in taxes: the highest earners. In other words, the tax preference given to ESI is a middle-class benefit and, in conjunction with all other financing streams in the system, improves the vertical equity of the system overall.

CONCLUSION

The rise of the employment-based health insurance system is not an accident of history but a rather market innovation designed to overcome a specific and significant market failure: lack of substantial or complete risk pooling due to adverse selection. The tax treatment of compensation in the form of employer contributions to employee health insurance increases the demand among good risks for group coverage, thereby increasing the total number of Americans, both healthy and nonhealthy, with health insurance coverage and improving consumer welfare.

References and Further Reading

Berger, M. C., Black, D. A., & Scott, F. A. (2004). Is there job lock? Evidence from the pre-HIPAA era. *Southern Economic Journal, 70*(4), 953–976.

Custer, W. S., Kahn, C. N., & Wildsmith, T. F. (1999). Why we should keep the employment-based health insurance system. *Health Affairs, 18*(6), 115–123.

Cutler, D., & Reber, S. J. (1998). Paying for health insurance: The trade-off between competition and adverse selection. *Quarterly Journal of Economics, 113*(2), 433–466.

Feldman, R., & Dowd, B. (1991). Must adverse selection cause premium spirals? *Journal of Health Economics, 10*(3), 349–357.

Feldman, R., & Dowd, B. (1991). New estimate of the welfare loss of excess health insurance. *American Economic Review, 81*(1), 297–301.

Feldstein, M. S. (1973). The welfare loss of excess health insurance. *Journal of Political Economy, 81*(2), 251–280.

Hadley, J. (2002). *Sicker and poorer—The consequences of being uninsured: A review of the research on the relationship between health insurance, health, work, income and education.* Kaiser Commission on Medicaid and the Uninsured. Washington, DC: Kaiser Family Foundation.

Jeske, K., & Kitao, S. (2009). U.S. tax policy and health insurance demand: Can a regressive policy improve welfare? *Elsevier Journal of Monetary Economics, 56*(2), 210–221.

Ketsche, P., Adams, E. K., Wallace, S., Kannan, V., & Kannan, H. (2011). Lower income families pay a higher share of income toward national health spending than higher income families do. *Health Affairs, 30*(9), 1637–1646.

Ketsche, P., & Custer, W. (2000). The effect of the marginal tax rate on the probability of employment-based insurance by risk group. *Health Services Research, 35*(1.2), 239–251.

Monheit, A., Nichols, L., & Selden, T. (1995–1996). How are net health insurance benefits distributed in the employment-related insurance market? *Inquiry, 32*(4), 372–391.

Newhouse, J. P. (1996). Reimbursing health plans and health providers: Efficiency in production versus selection. *Journal of Economic Literature, 34*(3), 1236–1263.

Nyman, J. A. (2002). *The theory of demand for health insurance.* Stanford, CA: Stanford Economics and Finance.

Sanz-de-Galdeano, A. (2006). Job-lock and public policy: Clinton's second mandate. *Industrial & Labor Relations Review, 59*(3), 430–437.

Starr, P. (1982). *The social transformation of American medicine.* New York, NY: Basic Books.

William S. Custer, Patricia Ketsche, and E. Kathleen Adams

21

Taxing High-Cost (Cadillac) Plans

POINT: Taxing so-called Cadillac plans, which offer higher-than-average levels of benefits, will lead to more efficient health care spending and provide needed financing for health care reform.

Randy Haught, The Lewin Group

COUNTERPOINT: Such taxes will not lead to more efficient health care spending because lower premiums do not necessarily mean greater efficiency. Furthermore, plans with high-cost premiums are not necessarily overly generous; the tax could unfairly penalize plans in high-cost regions or that insure pools of older or other high-risk individuals.

Elise Gould, Economic Policy Institute

Introduction

The tax deductibility of employer-sponsored health insurance (ESI) has been a time-honored feature of the mixed public-private system of health care in the United States. What essentially started out as a way for employers to attract more workers during the World War II era of wage controls was eventually codified into the tax law in 1954. Now the tax deductibility of ESI is viewed as the key factor in enhancing insurance coverage for workers and for maintaining ESI as the predominant avenue for obtaining coverage in the United States. However, the tax deductibility for ESI is in effect a tax expenditure, inasmuch as it reduces tax revenues collected by the U.S. Treasury. The extent of the deductibility, along with its size, has raised more and more concern especially as the aggregate amount of the expenditure increases with the rising cost of health insurance. When efforts to overhaul the U.S. health care system gathered momentum in 2009, the deductibility of ESI came under even more scrutiny, especially for the so-called Cadillac Plans that offer high levels of coverage and nontaxable benefits to employees.

In a separate chapter the general tax deductibility of ESI is debated and the positive and negative aspects are summarized in that chapter's introduction, whereas in this chapter Randy Haught and Elise Gould consider the specific provision in the 2010 Patient Protection and Affordable Care Act (ACA) that deals with Cadillac plans. Although the provision and its implementation are somewhat complex, the basic approach involves a 40 percent excise tax to insurance plan administrators on the value of any employer health benefit that exceeds a certain threshold. The value that can be taxed will be determined by the insurance premiums paid, including both the employer and the employee contributions, as well as contributions for other health care related instruments that offer tax advantages (such as flexible-spending accounts). It should also be noted that some health care benefits are excluded from the calculation, such as those for stand-alone vision and dental plans.

The excise tax is imposed on plan administrators (which could be an insurance plan or even, in the case of those that self-insure, an employer) that offer a plan with a value in excess of the threshold amount. The plan administrator pays the value of the tax for each employee who enrolls in the high-cost plan; in other words, the total tax paid by the plan equals 40 percent of the excess cost of the plan, times the number of enrollees in the plan. For the first year of the tax, 2018, the threshold is set at $10,200 for individual coverage and $27,500 for family coverage. The provision allows for increases in the threshold to accommodate specific circumstances, such as for plans serving older individuals, for specific high-cost regions, and for high-risk occupations. Over time, the thresholds will be increased based on the growth of the general economy. Typically, health care costs grow faster than economy-wide costs; hence, it is likely that an increasing share of plans will be affected by the tax over time.

Economists have called for a reform to the tax exclusion for ESI based on several shortcomings. For example, some claim that the exclusion is poorly targeted, as it is most valuable to those with higher marginal tax rates and who generally need less help to buy insurance. It is also inequitable as those who do not purchase insurance through an employer do not receive as much of a tax subsidy for health care costs, if any. The exclusion is also unlimited, which does nothing to encourage people to choose more cost-efficient plans, because the subsidy increases as the cost increases. We have also already highlighted how the exclusion acts as a tax expenditure, essentially adding to the U.S. deficit burden.

Given these issues and others, a fairly wide range of reform proposals have been generated over the last few decades by both republican and democratic presidents and presidential candidates, such as capping the exclusion or eliminating it altogether and replacing it with a fixed deduction or tax credit for the purchase of health insurance. Each of those approaches has pros and cons. For example, any of those alternatives would solve the open-ended flaw of the tax exclusion, which would provide greater incentives to buy lower-cost plans. However the cap would still provide the most benefit to workers who purchase their insurance through an employer and also a greater benefit to workers with a higher marginal tax rate. Eliminating the exclusion altogether and having a fixed deduction for all health insurance costs (whether purchased through an employer or not) could solve those problems, but still may offer less value to tax filers that do not have enough income to take full advantage of the deduction. In addition, many employers may stop offering coverage since ESI would no longer enjoy the preferential tax treatment. A refundable tax credit could provide the same benefit to everyone no matter the income level, but does not avoid the potential for harming the politically popular employer-sponsored health insurance system. Also, all of these approaches would likely result in direct tax increases on businesses and employees, another politically difficult issue to pursue, as the income used to purchase health insurance becomes taxable.

Thus, it is no surprise that arriving at the specific elements of the ACA provision took quite a circuitous political route. As the health care reform debate heated up in the middle of 2009, several permutations were considered, beginning with simply a cap on the tax deductibility of ESI plans that was described in the 2008 Senate Finance Committee's "Call to Action" report. It was not soon after that the newly inaugurated President Barack Obama weighed in on the idea with a nod to the revenue-raising advantage of such a cap, but with ultimate opposition given the pledge President Obama made during his campaign not to raise taxes on low- and middle-income individuals. The Senate Finance Committee in May of that year put more options on the table including several versions of a cap on the exclusion and a conversion of the exclusion into a tax credit. Analysts weighed in and projections regarding the ESI cap included considerable savings over the long term. But the concern about the effect of the exclusion on workers and businesses grew (based on the direct tax increases they would face) and by July, Senator John Kerry (D–MA) had put forth the idea of a tax on high-cost plans to be paid by insurers. Indeed, the "Cadillac Plan Tax," viewed by some as an emasculated version of the more general and perhaps more potent cap to ESI tax exclusion, ultimately found its way into the ACA as a compromise fit.

Politics aside, do the provisions of the plan support its goals, which are primarily to help bend the cost curve and to help finance the expansion of health insurance coverage? In the Point side of this chapter, Randy Haught details how the tax on high-cost health plans will essentially act as a cap, except that the tax will indirectly impact employers and employees. That is, insurers who offer high-cost health plans will likely pass on the cost of the tax to the employer in the form of higher premiums, and consequently to the employee (who usually pays part of the premium for their coverage), leaving many employees to opt out of more expensive plans and move into more managed coverage, such as that provided by HMO-type plans. This effect will indeed help to reduce overuse of health care services and consequently help reduce health care spending in the long term. Regarding helping to finance the expansion of coverage under ACA, Haught cites the Joint Committee on Taxation, which projects that the increase in tax revenue resulting from the provision would be $12 billion in 2018 and $20 billion the following year. The committee's calculations are based on the assumption that employers, when faced with higher premiums, would reduce the scope of their health benefits packages and consequently compensate for the lost benefits by increasing the wages paid to workers, who will in turn pay more in federal income tax. This conclusion, Haught says, is supported by many economic and academic analyses. Also, because the threshold for the tax is indexed to economy-wide inflation rather than health care industry-specific growth, it is likely that the tax will have greater impacts moving forward as an increasing share of plans near the threshold of the tax.

In the Counterpoint, Elise Gould argues that the Cadillac plan provision is not only ineffective in bending the cost curve but it is also endangers quality of care. When insurers respond in the expected way to the provision—by raising premiums on high-value plans to cover the cost of the excise tax—employers are likely to redesign their benefits packages to offer less generous coverage in terms of higher deductibles and co-payments; this in turn will result in higher costs for individuals but, worse, may result in individuals forsaking the care they need, not simply care that is excessive. From a financial point of view, the cost shifting—from employers to employees—that may result from the tax provision may affect the revenue-generating side of the provision's equation. With increases in out-of-pocket expenses, Gould points out, the financial security of many individuals might be threatened. Gould also points to the work of several researchers that correlate rising out-of-pocket costs with financial distress and even bankruptcies. This will become increasingly problematic as the tax inevitably impacts an increasing share of lower- and middle-income workers as the relative value of the threshold decreases over time. Given these possibilities, the public might well wonder if the projected wage increases, from which additional federal taxes are estimated, are really an illusion.

Critics also point out that, even if the tax is mostly targeted to the Cadillac plans of affluent business executives and even if it were conceivable that employees are able to more efficiently utilize care so that their health did not suffer after choosing lower-cost health coverage, there is a great likelihood that the ACA provision will be further modified and limited before it is passed. Already, during the negotiations over the development of the provision, the implementation date was delayed by several years, the threshold was increased, and exceptions have been made so certain populations would not be affected. Given the track record of Congress to avoid tax increases, it would not be surprising if the tax provision was further weakened.

Clearly, the excise tax on high-cost employer-sponsored coverage is a complicated issue, both politically and practically. Though altering the tax deductible status of ESI should be an avenue, according to many economists, policymakers, and politicians, to help finance the expansion of coverage and bend the cost curve, no perfect model exists. The public is left to wonder whether this particular approach—taxing insurers who provide high-cost plans to companies and their employees—will deliver on such high aspirational goals without some unintended consequences.

POINT

The 2010 Patient Protection and Affordable Care Act (ACA) includes a number of revenue provisions to help finance the cost of the health insurance coverage expansions of the bill. One of these revenue sources is an excise tax on high premium health insurance plans, which have been labeled as "Cadillac" plans. The excise tax is designed to help reduce the growth in health care spending by discouraging insurers from offering and employers from purchasing overly generous health care plans. In fact the Cadillac plan tax is one of the few provisions of the ACA that attempts to reduce the future growth in health care costs.

Beginning in 2018, the ACA imposes a 40 percent excise tax on the aggregate value of health insurance plans that exceed certain thresholds. The annual thresholds are established as $10,200 for individuals or $27,500 for a family policy in 2018. The thresholds are increased by an additional annual amount of $1,650 for individuals and $3,450 for retired individuals over the age of 55 and for plans that cover employees engaged in high-risk professions (e.g., law enforcement, emergency medical, construction, and mining). The aggregate value of the health insurance plan includes the hospital and medical insurance premium (employer and employee contributions), reimbursements under a flexible spending account for medical expenses (health FSA) or health reimbursement arrangement (HRA), employer contributions to a health savings account (HSA), and coverage for supplementary health insurance coverage. However, dental and vision plans are not included in calculating the aggregate value of the benefit plans.

These threshold amounts may also be increased to reflect higher medical costs that may occur prior to 2018 and for firms that have higher costs due to the age and gender of their employees. The tax is imposed on the issuer of the health insurance policy, which in the case of a self-insured plan is the plan administrator or, in some cases, the employer.

Beginning in 2020 the threshold amounts are indexed for general inflation by the consumer price index for urban consumers (CPI-U) and not health care costs. So if health care costs continue to rise more than general inflation then more and more plans could exceed the thresholds and become subject to the excise tax.

WHAT ARE CADILLAC PLANS?

To put the thresholds into perspective, the average premium for employer-sponsored health insurance (ESI) in 2011 was $5,429 for single and $15,073 for family coverage (Kaiser Family Foundation, Health Research & Educational Trust, & NORC, 2011). The Centers for Medicare & Medicaid Services (CMS) predicts that per-capita health spending will increase by an average annual rate of 5.1 percent between 2011 and 2018. Assuming that employer premiums increase at this rate, average premiums in 2018 would be $7,695 for single and $21,364 for family coverage, which would be about 25 percent below the Cadillac plan thresholds. Thus only a small portion of plans will have premiums that exceed thresholds and are subject to the excise tax in 2018.

The tax was originally designed to target overly generous health care plans. Some of the highly publicized cases of Cadillac health plans are those like the plans provided to highly compensated executives at Goldman Sachs that cost in excess of $40,000 per year, which would generally include no deductibles or co-payments and no restrictions on which providers are seen or numbers and types of procedures and offer other benefits like gym memberships (Waye & Herszenhorn, 2009).

However, there are some problems with defining overly generous benefit packages based on price alone. It's often assumed that high-cost health insurance plans provide rich benefits to plan subscribers. However, an analysis of health plans offered by employers showed that only about 3.7 percent of variation in the employer health plan costs of family coverage could be explained by benefit design (actuarial value) and that benefit design plus plan type (HMO, PPO, POS, or high-deductible plans) explained only 6.1 percent of this variation (Gabel, Pickreign, McDevitt, & Briggs, 2010). Thus, the richness of benefits offered accounts for only a small difference in premium costs across employer plans.

Employer plan premiums can vary significantly from the average presented above due to factors other than rich benefit designs. Firms that employ a disproportionate share of older workers could observe higher premiums due to the fact that older people utilize more care than younger workers. Also smaller firms typically have higher premiums than larger firms due to the higher per-employee costs for administering health benefits. Studies have shown that the cost of administering health benefits for very small employers can average about 40 percent of medical costs compared to only about 5 percent for very large employers (Lewin Group, 2009).

Premiums will also vary for employers depending on their physical location due to geographic difference in health care costs for health care workers, property and rent expenses, differences in medical practice and competitiveness of the health care market in the area. Dartmouth Atlas of Health Care research found fee-for-service (FFS) Medicare spending on elderly beneficiaries can vary by as much as 2.5 times across different localities (Wennberg, Fisher & Skinner, 2002).

Although there may be some flaws in the initial specifications for how Cadillac plans are defined, this can easily be addressed by risk adjusting the thresholds. The thresholds are already increased for individuals over the age of 55 and for plans that cover employees engaged in high-risk professions. The premium thresholds subject to the tax could be adjusted for other factors that affect premium costs as well.

PURPOSE OF THE CADILLAC TAX

In addition to generating revenue to help fund the cost of coverage expansions under the ACA, the excise tax is designed to help reduce the growth in health care spending by discouraging insurers from offering and employers from purchasing overly generous health care plans. These types of plans are believed to encourage excess health care utilization and spending. The tax may also incentivize patients to move from fee-for-service or preferred provider organization (PPO) plans with fewer restrictions on which providers the patient can see to purchasing health maintenance organization (HMO) plans, which tend to be less expensive but include restrictions on which providers can be seen, requiring referrals for specialty services, and requiring pre-authorization for certain medical procedures. These types of plans tend to manage patient utilization and help lower costs.

Overly generous health plans may require little or no patient cost sharing. Studies have shown that patients without cost sharing have little or no financial disincentive to forgo care and can overutilize services. However, higher levels of cost sharing can induce patients to use care more efficiently once they bear some of the economic costs and are more likely to use only health care services that are worth the additional cost (Gruber, 2006). In addition, this higher utilization of care does not relate to better health outcomes. An analysis of costs for Medicare beneficiaries found substantial differences in the cost of health care per person across geographic areas and Medical Centers in the United States, with little or no statistical difference in outcomes. In fact, the study found that composite quality scores tended to be lower in geographic areas with higher health spending (Diamond, 2008).

Analyses of the ACA showed that health insurance premiums could be substantially lowered by changing patient cost sharing but still offering the same level of benefits. For example, there will be about a 30 percent difference in costs between the gold plan (90 percent actuarial value) and bronze plan (60-percent actuarial value). So lower-cost health insurance plans can be configured by increasing patient cost sharing. However, cost sharing amounts that are too high can lead individuals to avoid medical care that is actually necessary to their health or impose a substantial financial burden. Moreover, high co-insurance amounts place a financial burden on the poorest and sickest members of society.

ESTIMATING THE IMPACTS OF THE CADILLAC TAX

Modeling the impacts of the Cadillac health plan tax required making a number of assumptions about how workers with plans affected by this tax would behave. First, although the tax is levied on insurers and administrators of self-funded plans, assume that the tax will be passed on to employers and workers in the form of higher premium costs for those plans that exceed the thresholds. For the excise tax to have the desired effect, insurers would need to increase the price of only the high-cost policies to cover the cost of the tax. If insurers spread the cost of the tax across all their products then the effect would be diminished.

Second, assume that the change in premium price would cause some workers to switch to lower-cost health plans. The tax may incentivize patients to move from fee-for-service or PPO plans to purchasing less costly HMO plans or selecting a health plan with fewer covered benefits and more cost sharing. HMO plans have been shown to be about 12 percent less costly than other FFS plans, including PPOs and point-of-service (POS) plans (Stapleton, 1994). Other studies have shown that HMOs reduce costly hospital inpatient utilization by up to 30 percent or more, but that these savings are partially offset by an increase in hospital outpatient and physician visits (Miller & Luft, 1994). Also, studies have shown that higher levels of cost sharing can induce patients to use care more efficiently once they bear some of the economic costs.

Assume also that a portion of people who would face the excise tax would switch to lower-cost health plans and their employers would restructure high-cost benefit plans if a lower-cost alternative was not available in order to avoid the tax. Assume that those who switched into HMO plans or plans with higher cost sharing would reduce their utilization accordingly, which in turn would help reduce the rate of growth in national health spending in the future.

Similarly, the Congressional Budget Office (CBO) and Joint Committee on Taxation (JCT) estimated that most employers and households would *not* actually pay the excise tax but would modify their health plans to avoid paying the excise tax. And, in turn, the savings from reduced premium costs would be passed on to workers in the form of higher wages. In an analysis of the Senate version of the ACA, the JCT estimated that more than four-fifths of the revenue that the government would collect as a result of the excise tax would come from income and payroll tax revenue on the higher wages and salaries that employees would be paid.

The JCT estimated that the excise tax would generate about $12 billion in revenue in 2018 and $20 billion in 2019. In preparing their estimates the JCT assumed that employers would scale back their benefits packages to avoid the penalty and that the amount saved by employers in premiums would be passed on to workers in the form of higher wages, which would be subject to federal income tax. Most economists have concluded that by restraining the growth of health insurance premiums, the excise tax would allow larger wage increases. The trade-off between wages and health insurance premiums is strongly supported both by basic economic analysis and by extensive academic evidence, and has been confirmed by statements by labor unions in the past (Van de Water, 2010).

As mentioned, the threshold amounts will be indexed to general inflation plus one percentage point beginning in 2020. General inflation is projected to grow at about 2.1 percent compared to the increase in health care costs of 5.1 percent. So if health care costs continue to rise more than general inflation then more and more plans will exceed the thresholds and become subject to the excise tax over time, assuming there is no change in behavior of shifting to lower-cost plans. In this analysis, the number of people in affected firms is estimated to be about 60 million workers and dependents including retirees by 2019, a number that would grow to about 111 million people by 2029.

CONCLUSION

Unlike most employer benefits provided to workers, health benefits are not counted as taxable income. In addition, the employee's share of premiums can be tax exempt if his or her employer has established a "cafeteria plan." (Cafeteria plans were established under Section 125 of the IRS code, which allows employers to create a program for employees to pay for certain benefits with pre-tax earnings.) Therefore, there is a tax incentive for employees to purchase generous benefit packages with minimum cost sharing and rich benefits because the premiums for health care are purchased with pre-tax earnings, whereas direct payments for deductibles, co-payments, and noncovered services are paid for with after-tax dollars. Thus, there are tax incentives for employees to purchase generous benefit packages with low levels of cost sharing.

The concept of the Cadillac plan tax is not a new one. Some previous health reform plans looked to discourage the purchase of overly generous health plans by limiting the amount of the health care premium that employers could exempt from taxes. An example of this approach was a plan proposed by the Ronald Reagan administration in 1984 (American College of Physicians, 2009). This approach would have about the same effect as the Cadillac tax. Under the Reagan plan, the amount that the premium exceeds the specified threshold would be counted as income to employees and subject to income taxes. This option directly taxes employees for excessive premium amounts, whereas the Cadillac tax does it indirectly by taxing insurers which will then be passed on to employers and workers.

Other health reform plans looked at completely eliminating the current tax exclusion and replacing it with a tax deduction or tax credit. President George W. Bush's budget request included a proposal to replace the current tax exclusion for health insurance with a standard above-the-line deduction of $7,500 for single plans and $15,000 for family plans that would apply to either ESI or individual insurance coverage. Similarly, Senators Ron Wyden (D–OR) and Bob Bennett (R–UT) sponsored the Healthy America Act, which proposed to replace the existing tax exclusion for health insurance with a fixed income tax deduction for coverage and provided subsidies for lower-income workers who do not pay taxes. Senator John McCain's (R–AZ) health care proposal during his 2008 presidential campaign proposed to replace the current income tax exclusion with a refundable tax credit of $2,500 for individuals and $5,000 for families to purchase insurance from an employer or in the individual market.

These plans proposed a broader approach to changing the tax code so that people purchasing employer coverage or individual coverage would get the same tax benefit. Under the current tax code, those purchasing individual coverage do not get any tax advantage, unless they are self-employed. The tax deduction proposed by former President George W. Bush would provide a larger tax benefit to higher-income individuals since they have higher tax rates and virtually no benefit to people who did not file taxes. Senators Wyden and Bennett improved on this by also providing premium subsidies to lower-income people. The subsidies under the Healthy Americans Act were phased out as income rose and at the same time the income tax deduction was phased in as income rose. Senator McCain's refundable tax credit was the fairest option, because everyone received the same tax credit amount to help pay for health insurance, regardless of their income.

However, these plans proposed to completely eliminate the current tax exclusion system, which has the potential to greatly reduce the number of people who obtain health insurance through their employers. Some studies suggest that many employers would drop health benefits in response to a major change to the health insurance tax exclusion, which would alter the business case for offering benefits (Buchmueller, Glied, Royalty, & Swartz, 2008; Fronstin, 2007). Whereas, the Cadillac tax approach does maintain the current tax exclusion that could help preserve the employer-sponsored health insurance market.

REFERENCES AND FURTHER READING

American College of Physicians. (2009). *Reforming the tax exclusion for health insurance: Policy monograph.* Retrieved from http://www .acponline.org/advocacy/where_we_stand/policy/health_reform_tax_ex.pdf

Buchmueller, T., Glied, S. A., Royalty, A., & Swartz, K. (2008). Cost and coverage: Implications of the McCain plan to restructure health insurance. *Health Affairs, 27*(6), w472–w481.

Diamond, P. (2008, May 29). *Health care and behavioral economics: A presentation to the National Academy of Social Insurance.* Retrieved from CBO website: http://www.cbo.gov/sites/default/files/cbofiles/ftpdocs/93xx/doc9317/05-29-nasi_speech.pdf

Fronstin, P. (2007, December). The future of employment-based health benefits: Have employers reached a tipping point? *Issue Brief, 312.* Washington, DC: Employee Benefit Research Institute.

Gabel, J., Pickreign, J., McDevitt, R., & Briggs, T. (2010). Taxing Cadillac health plans may produce Chevy results. *Health Affairs, 29*(1), 174–181.

Gruber, J. (2006). *The role of consumer copayments for health care: Lessons from the RAND health insurance experiment and beyond.* Retrieved from Kaiser Family Foundation website: http://www.kff.org/insurance/7566.cfm

Kaiser Family Foundation, Health Research & Educational Trust, & NORC at the University of Chicago. (2011). *Survey of employer-sponsored health benefits, 2011.* Retrieved from Kaiser Family Foundation website: http://ehbs.kff.org

Lewin Group. (2009). *The health benefits simulation model (HBSM): Methodology and assumptions.* Retrieved from http://www.lewin .com/publications/Publication/357

Miller, R. H., & Luft, H. S. (1994). Managed care plan performance since 1980: A literature analysis. *Journal of the American Medical Association, 271*(19), 1512–1519.

Orszag, P. (2008, May 29). *Health care and behavioral economics: A presentation to the national academy of social insurance.* Retrieved from http://www.cbo.gov/ftpdocs/93xx/doc9317/05-29-NASI_Speech.pdf

Stapleton, D. (1994). *New evidence on savings from network models of managed care: A report to the Healthcare Leadership Council.* Washington, DC: Lewin Group.

Van de Water, P. N. (2010). *Changes to excise tax on high-cost health plans address criticisms, retain long-term benefits.* Retrieved from Center on Budget and Policy Priorities website: http://www.cbpp.org/cms/?fa=view&id=3060

Waye, L., & Herszenhorn, D. (2009, July 27). A bid to tax plans of executives. *The New York Times,* p. A15.

Wennberg, J. E., Fisher, E. S., & Skinner, J. S. (2002, April). Geography and the debate over Medicare reform. *Health Affairs.* Retrieved from http://content.healthaffairs.org/content/early/2002/02/13/hlthaff.w2.96.short

Randy Haught

COUNTERPOINT

Employer contributions to health insurance premiums are excluded, without limit, from workers' taxable income. Employee contributions are excluded if the employee works at a firm with a cafeteria plan, a plan that allows employees to choose between taxable and nontaxable fringe benefits (e.g., plans that offer flexible-spending accounts). Subsidizing compensation paid in the form of health insurance encourages employers to offer health insurance, increasing the number of insured workers. Nevertheless, some argue that limiting this tax exclusion would provide incentives for cost containment because it would make consumers more price sensitive, leading to reduced health expenditures, and it would raise tax revenue that could be used in part to pay for coverage expansions.

As part of the Patient Protection and Affordable Care Act (2010), also known as health reform, a 40 percent excise tax will be levied on employer-sponsored health care coverage if the total cost of that coverage—including contributions made by both employers and employees for premiums, and other tax-preferred health vehicles such as flexible-spending accounts and health savings accounts—exceed a particular threshold in 2018 ($10,200 and $27,500 for individual and family coverage, respectively). Though the excise tax on high premium plans will raise substantial revenue (an estimated $12 billion in 2018 and another $20 billion in 2019), this article points out several limitations of taxing benefits and reasons to doubt that doing so will be an effective cost-containment strategy.

First, it is a misnomer to call plans subject to the excise tax "Cadillac" plans. Premiums are higher for a variety of reasons (e.g., firm size, age of workforce, location) unrelated to the generosity or comprehensiveness of the health plan. And, because the threshold is indexed in future years at a growth rate that is expected to be slower than the growth of medical costs, it will capture more and more average or typical health plans.

Second, firms, workers, and insurers will most likely respond to this new tax by offering and selecting insurance plans with less comprehensive coverage (e.g., higher deductibles or co-pays) to avoid paying the excise tax (or eliminating the offer altogether). These types of changes could increase out-of-pocket costs, particularly for enrollees with high medical needs and use more services. Therefore, consumers are either burdened with paying higher medical costs for their care, or they may respond to increasing out-of-pocket costs by cutting back on care, some of which may be more or less medically indicated. Either way, they are increasing the likelihood of future financial risk due to less comprehensive coverage.

Third, the tax cap is not an effective cost-containment device. It misses the most expensive cost drivers in the U.S. health care system—80 percent of health dollars are spent by the top 20 percent of consumers. Further, when consumers respond by cutting back on medical care, some of which is cost-effective, they may in turn increase overall health costs, particular among those with chronic conditions or high medical needs. In addition, any cost containment from capping the tax exclusion is driven by reduced medical care, not reduced prices. Serious solutions to contain health costs may be found elsewhere (e.g., value-based insurance design, all-payer rates, better care coordination).

BACKGROUND

Employer-sponsored plans are the predominant from of health insurance in the United States. In 2010, 58.6 percent of Americans under 65 years old have employment-based coverage through the workplace, either as an employee, dependent, or retiree (Gould, 2012). One reason that employment-based insurance is so appealing is that workplaces pool large groups of people along dimensions unrelated to health, ensuring more predictable medical costs and allowing insurers to take advantage of the economies of scale. Legislated changes also have contributed to the dominance of the employment-based system.

Group policies expanded in response to tax changes in the 1940s and 1950s. An administrative tax ruling in 1943 that resulted in code clarifications in 1954 stated that an employer's contributions for its employees' groups medical and hospitalization premiums are tax exempt. As a results, employers' contributions to health insurance premiums were excluded from individuals' income and payroll taxes. Further, laws passed in the late 1970s and 1980s, including section 125 of the Internal Revenue Code, allow employee contributions to be excluded when the employer has a qualifying section 125 plan (often called a "cafeteria plan"). This combination of tax exemptions encourages the use of group policies through the employer. Effectively a government subsidy, those laws reduce after-tax insurance premiums, further encouraging healthy employees to enroll, forming stable and sustainable risk pools among employees and attracting insurance companies into the market.

EXCISE TAX PROVISION IN HEALTH REFORM

In March 2010, President Barack Obama signed into law the Patient Protection and Affordable Care Act (ACA), commonly known as health reform. As part of health reform, beginning in 2018, a 40 percent excise tax will be levied on health insurance policies with premiums in excess of $10,200 for individual policies and $27,500 for family coverage. The tax applies to the portion of premiums between the threshold and the total cost of the health policy. The premium thresholds are adjusted for workers in high-risk industries and for the age and gender of the workforce. In 2019 and beyond, the threshold above which premiums are taxed will be indexed to the overall rate of inflation plus one percentage point, not the growth of medical costs, which is expected to be higher.

According to the Congressional Budget Office's (CBO) Letter to the Honorable Nancy Pelosi dated March 20, 2010, the excise tax on high premium plans will raise $12 billion in 2018 and another $20 billion in 2019.

The excise tax would hit many workers with ordinary health plans, not exclusively those with high-value plans. Many health plans are expensive because the population is older or sicker than average, but they still do not provide more comprehensive coverage. Elise Gould and Alexandra Minicozzi (2009) have shown that some of the most-powerful predictors of a plan's high cost are the size of the firm and the age of its workers. Small firms and firms with older workforces tend to have less bargaining power with insurance companies. All else equal, this leads to higher prices for insurance coverage, which may be no more comprehensive than lower-priced coverage for larger firms or those with younger workers. Jon Gabel and co-authors (2006) have shown that small firms pay premiums 18 percent higher than do large firms for equivalent health coverage.

Another way to measure plan generosity is to use a health plan's actuarial value, that is, the share of average medical expenditures paid for by the insurance company (instead of by the policy-holder). Using actuarial value as a proxy for plan generosity, Jon Gabel and co-authors (2010) find that only a small percent (3.7 percent) of the variation in premiums for family plans is determined by a plan's generosity. This again exemplifies the fact that plan prices do not reflect plan value.

To some extent, the health-reform law recognizes this reality and specifically raises the threshold of the excise tax for selected groups of workers explicitly on the grounds that high cost is not synonymous with high value, for instance by increasing the threshold for health plans covering high-risk professions. It may not go far enough to account for the high prices some pay for coverage that is far from a Cadillac standard. Stan Dorn (2009) recognizes this problem and proposes an alternative solution to more clearly target the tax to high value plans by using actuarial value to measure benefit generosity. One solution he outlines taxes plans above the 75th percentile of actuarial value among all enrollees in employer-sponsored insurance plans, indexing this threshold by overall inflation over time.

In future years, 2019 and beyond, the threshold above which premiums are subject to the excise tax is indexed to the overall rate of inflation plus one percentage point (CPI+1). For instance, if overall inflation grows at an average rate of 2.5 percent while medical care costs rise at 4.0 percent, a growing wedge will be created between a CPI+1 of 3.5 percent and the growth of medical costs. The result is that more and more insurance plans would be subject to the excise tax, leading more employers and workers to demand lower-priced and less comprehensive coverage. As in the past, this growth rate *is* expected to be lower than the growth of medical costs, capturing more and more health plans in the future, an increasing number of which by any measure would not be "Cadillac."

Robert McIntyre (2009) makes the additional point that, as a share of income, taxing employer-sponsored health insurance does not unambiguously reduce the progressivity of the tax system across every segment of the income distribution. Though many low-income households do not enjoy access to employer-sponsored health insurance, high-income households are required to contribute only a small share of their income to pay the tax because there is a limit to how much any household would want to take income in the form of health insurance. For instance, compared to the home-mortgage deduction, the tax advantage given to health insurance is more tightly distributed as house prices vary more widely than do health premiums. McIntyre calculates the marginal federal income and payroll tax rate on converting a portion of tax-exempt wage (in this case, health insurance) into taxable wages. He finds that, if health premiums were taxed as wages, the tax rate would be relatively flat across income groups (including the payroll tax). Given the tight distribution of health premiums and relatively flat marginal tax rates, McIntyre estimates that the excise tax, as a share of income, would be 10–20 times as high on middle-income families as on the rich, reducing the overall progressivity of the tax system.

CONSEQUENCES: COST- AND RISK-SHIFTING MAY LOWER COVERAGE AND CARE

In response to the excise tax, a 2009 Mercer survey finds that nearly two-thirds of employers plan to cut health benefits to avoid the tax and a full 7 percent would eliminate their health plan altogether. The Joint Committee on Taxation (2009) revenue estimates assume that a small share of revenue would actually come directly from the excise tax (as opposed to the large share of revenue from taxed wages), implying that employers and employees alike will shy away from the more expensive plans. Among workers at firms that drop insurance coverage entirely, some workers will have no affordable alternative and become uninsured, risking their health and their financial stability. Others may become eligible for subsidized coverage in the state health exchanges.

For those employers choosing to just reduce benefits, the vast majority expect to increase deductibles and co-payments. Forcing people into less comprehensive plans would expose them to higher out-of-pocket costs and greater health-related financial shocks. People value insulation from these shocks—the reason people purchase insurance—so forcing them into less insulating plans has a cost.

Shifting health coverage costs onto workers and their families may hamper their ability to maintain and secure affordable health care. Such costs have already risen in recent years with increasing out-of-pocket burdens and difficulty in paying medical bills. Peter Cunningham (2010) finds growing financial burdens of health care across the socioeconomic distribution, not simply among the poor and uninsured. David Himmelstein and co-authors (2009) find a striking growth in bankruptcies associated with medical costs, even for those households covered by health insurance. Pushing insurance plans to be less comprehensive might make these financial problems worse.

This movement of people into less comprehensive coverage is often identified as a policy benefit of the excise tax—under the theory that when people have more "skin in the game" (i.e., face a higher share of total health spending), they will become more careful consumers of health care and will forego care that is unneeded and was only previously purchased because they were not facing its full cost—a problem often identified as moral hazard. John Nyman (2007) directly questions this theory by arguing that a large portion of moral hazard represents health care that sick consumers would not otherwise have access to without the income that it transferred to them through insurance. This aspect of moral hazard—the transfer of income—is efficient and generates a welfare gain. Raj Chetty (2008) makes similar arguments in the context of unemployment insurance, focusing on the fact that unemployment insurance benefits solve a liquidity problem rather than creating a disincentive to look for work. He suggests that this analysis could apply to the case of liquidity constraints in the purchase of health care. These arguments suggest that a tax on the health benefits of only high-income people might reduce some of these negative consequences for those at the lower end of the income scale while still raising revenue.

Because firms, workers, and insurers will most likely respond to this new tax by offering and selecting insurance plans with less comprehensive coverage (e.g., higher deductibles or co-pays) to avoid paying the excise tax, consumers will be faced with higher out-of-pocket costs when they decide whether to seek medical care. This effective price increase may lead some to cut back on medical spending. For vulnerable populations and those with chronic conditions, many interventions that are avoided may turn out to be health improving. Research has shown that higher cost sharing could lead families to cut back on medically indicated and effective health care. Dana Goldman and co-authors (2007) find that cuts in plan generosity can lead to reduced compliance with drug therapies for chronic disease and Melinda Buntin and co-authors (2011) find that enrollment in high deductible health plans leads to reductions in the use of preventive care. Both Jon Gruber (2006) and Hsu and co-authors (2006) demonstrate that higher cost sharing is detrimental to the health of the chronically ill.

Overall, the evidence shows that an optimal cost-sharing design may better serve consumers and the health care system when it takes all the considerations raised by different patient populations, therapies, and conditions into account. Consumers simply don't have the necessary information or wherewithal to make many health decisions, and various factors may keep prices from accurately signaling quality or effectiveness. Experts are required to makes these decisions and such methods can be instituted, for instance, in the form of the Independent Payment Advisory Board.

In short, efficient cost-sharing designs cannot be one-size-fits-all. A universally applied excise tax on health benefits does not create the right incentives for the creation of the most efficient insurance policy; in fact, it might be argued that it is a blunt instrument that creates no incentives except to purchase less expensive policies to avoid the tax. In doing so, it shifts costs onto workers and their families, hitting those with high medical needs especially hard.

Even so, proponents of the excise tax often note that if it encourages workers to take less compensation in the form of health insurance premiums, then this could raise other forms of compensation, especially cash wages. And, given that, in the long run, the excise tax will lead to nontrivial cuts in premiums, this means that cash wages may indeed rise. However, much of these wage increases may be used by workers to pay the high out-of-pocket costs they will incur with their less comprehensive coverage. Given the large variation in annual health spending (i.e., many families spend next to nothing on health costs in a given year, while some spend large amounts), many workers could see increases in out-of-pocket costs that far exceed the potential addition to cash wages that accompanies the imposition of the excise tax. On average, after-tax, after–health care wages will rise much less than proponents often claim. The characterization of the potential for cash wages to rise in response to the excise tax as a raise for American workers is not right. Even if there are rising cash wages in response, they will come as other forms of compensation are falling. Because some compensation previously subsidized through tax policy is now taxed, the result is a cut, not a raise to total after-tax compensation.

The excise tax will raise a fair amount of revenue—an estimated $32 billion in 2018 and 2019 alone—increasing as the tax hits more and more employer-sponsored health insurance plans into the future. Given that there are lots of potential ways to raise revenue, it is worth noting why it is favored over other methods. Many health policy experts claim that the excise tax could be a powerful tool in restraining the overall growth of U.S. health care costs. Given that these rapidly growing costs provide real strains on both the federal budget and family incomes, restraining them seems to be a worthy policy goal.

As it turns out, the excise tax has less reach in driving significant cost containment than is commonly recognized. First, the excise tax misses many of the most expensive costs in the health system. The sickest 20 percent of the population in any given year account for 80 percent of total health spending (Bivens & Gould, 2009). This includes people with chronic conditions, acute care needs, and end-of-life care. An increase in cost sharing among the big-ticket items of health care like transplants, major life-saving surgeries, or the management of chronic diseases like diabetes has not been explicitly suggested and is universally recognized as bad policy.

Katherine Swartz (2010) points out that it is often the health care providers and not the patients themselves who are the drivers of high health care spending. To the extent that moral hazard induced overconsumption of health care is a significant problem, patients already active in the health care system (e.g., those under the care of a physician) may be less sensitive to cost sharing. The corollary is that those less active in the health care system may be more sensitive to prices, meaning they are more likely to forego expensive care if they believe there is less of an immediate medical need for it. Efforts to bend the cost curve via the excise tax increasing costs paid by consumers would be limited to the relatively small share of total health spending borne by this population akin to the 20 percent of health dollars consumed by 80 percent of the population.

To the extent that consumers do cut back on care in response to increased cost sharing, there's little to suggest that they would only cut back on medical spending aimed at immediate needs; they may also cut medical spending that is cost-effective in the long run. The use of the word "Cadillac" presumes that the tax will force consumers to cut back on only luxury items. But, to the extent that people do not have overly generous coverage, the tax could hurt people who need to spend dollars to unambiguously improve their health and may actually cost the health system more later as the most cost-effective health interventions are delayed. There is a growing body of literature documents these relationships.

Michael McWilliams and co-authors (2011) find that cuts in plan generosity can lead to higher overall medical spending. Amitabh Chandra and co-authors (2009) find that there are substantial "offset" effects to broad increases in cost-sharing rates for physician visits and prescription drugs; spending on these categories fell with higher cost sharing but hospitalization costs rose substantially. In one related study, Goldman and co-authors (2007) find that higher cost sharing for pharmaceuticals is associated with an increased use of overall medical services, particularly for patients with greater needs (e.g., heart disease, diabetes, or schizophrenia).

Likewise, lower cost sharing is associated with a reduction in overall health spending, particularly for those with chronic diseases. For instance, Michael Chernew and co-authors (2008) demonstrate that cost sharing with lower costs for those for whom the intervention would be most cost-effective (generally the chronically ill) leads to higher compliance. Furthermore, Noem Muszbek and co-authors (2008) find that increased compliance with drugs for hypertension, diabetes, and a series of other ailments will lead to higher drug costs but lower nondrug costs, leading to overall cost savings. Mahoney (2005) also finds that lowered cost sharing for diabetes patients reduces health costs per plan.

The sum of this important research suggests that increased cost sharing in certain areas (e.g., prescription drugs or primary care) can lead to higher overall costs due to increased health services utilization in other areas (e.g., hospitalization) and that the optimal cost-sharing rate for many chronic conditions and large classes of prescription drugs is low or even zero. Therefore, the excise tax that leads to indiscriminate or misplaced cost-sharing changes (which is likely the case with the Cadillac tax, especially as plans struggle to keep premiums down) may be an ineffective and potentially harmful tool in making efficient cuts to health care utilization. A careful examination of the growing value-based insurance design literature may produce a more effective policy response.

To the extent that consumers respond by cutting back on medical care, it becomes clear that any cost containment from the excise tax on high priced plans is driven by the reduced quantity of medical care consumed, not reduced prices. If it works to contain costs to any significant extent, it does so by encouraging people affected by it to buy less health care. Gerard Anderson and co-authors (2003) would suggest that high medical spending in the United States, as compared to its industrial peers, is actually driven by high prices and not high utilization. To the extent this is true, the excise tax will not likely remedy this problem.

CONCLUSION

The excise tax on high-cost health insurance plans is likely to shift costs onto workers and their families. For those with high medical needs, it may cause them financial stress or medical sacrifice. For some, it may lead them to be even more costly consumers of health care. For that price, it may ease the federal budget, but research shows that it will do little to contain overall health spending. Furthermore, it puts all the burden of cost containment on consumers without giving them the tools to make qualified medical decisions.

Serious solutions to contain health costs may be found elsewhere. Among a series of alternatives John Holahan and co-authors (2011) estimate to contain health system costs, the one with the greatest effect on costs is the establishment of an all-payer rate-setting system, a system that would ensure that rates were controlled for all, regardless of how they received insurance. Miriam Laugesen and Sherry Glied (2011) offer ways to create incentives for the consumption of more medically and cost-effective care by reducing the payment disparities between physicians and specialists. Melinda Buntin and David Cutler (2009) explore alternative savings mechanisms such as investments in health information technology and payment system reforms. Furthermore, looking more closely at value-based insurance design, rather than using the blunt tool of a tax on high-priced plans, may provide a more effective incentive to rein in the high costs of the U.S. health care system.

REFERENCES AND FURTHER READING

Anderson, G. F., Reinhardt, U. E., Hussey, P., & Petrosyan, V. (2003). It's the prices, stupid: Why the United States is so different from other countries. *Health Affairs, 22*(3), 89–105.

Bivens, J., & Gould, E. (2009). House health care bill is right on the money: Taxing high incomes better than taxing high premiums. *Issue Brief, 267*. Retrieved from Economic Policy Institute website: http://www.epi.org/publication/ib267

Buntin, M. B., & Cutler, D. (2009). *The two trillion dollar solution: Saving money by modernizing the health care system.* Retrieved from Center for American Progress website: http://www.americanprogress.org/issues/2009/06/2trillion_solution.html

Buntin, M. B., Haviland, A. M., McDevitt, R., & Sood, N. (2011). Healthcare spending and preventive care in high-deductible and consumer-directed health plans. *American Journal of Managed Care, 17*(3), 222–230.

Chandra, A., Gruber, J., & McKnight, R. (2009). *Patient cost-sharing, hospitalization offsets, and the design of optimal health insurance for the elderly.* National Bureau of Economic Research, Working Paper No. 12972. Cambridge, MA: National Bureau of Economic Research.

Chernew, M. E., Shah, M. R., Wegh, A., Rosenberg, S. N., Juster, I. A., Rosen, A. B., & Fendrick, A. M. (2008). Impact of decreasing copayments on medication adherence within a disease management environment. *Health Affairs, 27*(1), 103–112.

Chetty, R. (2008). Moral hazard vs. liquidity and optimal unemployment insurance. *Journal of Political Economy, 116*(2), 173–234.

Cunningham, P. J. (2010). The growing financial burden of health care: National and state trends, 2001–2006. *Health Affairs, 29*(5), 1–5.

Dorn, S. (2009). *Capping the tax exclusion of employer-sponsored health insurance: Is equity feasible?* Retrieved from Urban Institute website: http://www.urban.org/publications/411894.html

Gabel, J., McDevitt, R., Gandolfo, L., Pickreign, J., Hawkins, S., & Fahlman, C. (2006). Generosity and adjusted premiums in job-based insurance: Hawaii is up, Wyoming is down. *Health Affairs, 25*(3), 832–843.

Gabel, J., Pickreign, J., McDevitt, R., & Briggs, T. (2010). Taxing Cadillac health plans may produce Chevy results. *Health Affairs, 29*(1), 1–7.

Goldman, D., Joyce, G. F., & Zheng, Y. (2007). Prescription drug cost sharing: Association with medication and medical utilization and spending and health. *Journal of the American Medical Association, 29*(8), 61–69.

Gould, E. (2012). *A decade of declines in employer-sponsored health insurance coverage.* EPI Briefing Paper, 337. Washington, DC: Economic Policy Institute.

Gould, E., & Minicozzi, A. (2009). *Who loses if we limit the tax exclusion for health insurance?* Retrieved from http://www.epi.org/publication/who_loses_if_we_limit_the_tax_exclusion_for_health_insurance

Gruber, J. (2006). *The role of consumer copayments for health care: Lessons from the RAND health insurance experiment and beyond.* Retrieved from Kaiser Family Foundation website: http://www.kff.org/insurance/7566.cfm

Himmelstein, D. U., Thorne, D., Warren, E., & Woolhandler, S. (2009). Medical bankruptcy in the United States, 2007: Results of a national study. *The American Journal of Medicine, 122*(8), 741–746. Retrieved from http://www.amjmed.com/article/S0002-9343(09)00404-5/abstract

Holahan, J., Blumberg, L. J., McMorrow, S., Zuckerman, S., Waidman, T., & Stockley, K. (2011). *Containing the growth of spending in the U.S. health system.* Washington, DC: Urban Institute Health Policy Center.

Hsu, J., Price, M., Huang, J., Brand, R., Fung, V., Hui, R., & Selby, J. V. (2006). Unintended consequences of caps on Medicare drug benefits. *The New England Journal of Medicine, 354*(23), 2349–2359.

Joint Committee on Taxation. (2009). *Letter from Thomas Barthold, staff director of the Joint Committee on Taxation, to the Honorable Joseph Courtney, U.S. House of Representatives, December 8, 2009.* Retrieved from http://files.cwa-union.org/healthcarevoices/12.8.09_JCT%20Report%20Response_to_Courtney_New_Thresholds.pdf

Laugesen, M., & Glied, S. (2011). Higher fees paid to US physicians drive higher spending for physician services compared to other countries. *Health Affairs, 30*(9), 1647–1656.

Mahoney, J. J. (2005). Reducing patient drug acquisition costs can lower diabetes health claims. *American Journal of Managed Care, 11*(5), S170–S176.

McIntyre, R. (2009). *Would the Senate Democrats' proposed excise tax on "high-cost" employer-paid health insurance benefits be progressive?* Retrieved from Citizens for Tax Justice website: http://ctj.org/ctjreports/2009/12/would_the_senate_democrats_proposed_excise_tax_on_high-cost_employer-paid_health_insurance_benefits.php

McWilliams, M., Zaslavsky, A., & Huskamp, H. (2011). Implementation of Medicare Part D and nondrug medical spending for elderly adults with limited prior drug coverage. *Journal of American Medical Association, 306*(4), 402–409.

Mercer. (2009, December 3). *Majority of employers would reduce health benefits to avoid proposed excise tax, survey finds.* Retrieved from http://www.mercer.com/press-releases/1365780

Muszbek, N., Brixner, D., Benedict, A., Keskinasian, A., & Khan, Z. M. (2008). The economic consequences of noncompliance in cardiovascular disease and related conditions: A literature review. *International Journal of Clinical Practice, 62*(2), 338–351.

Nyman, J. (2007). American health policy: Cracks in the foundation. *Journal of Health Politics, Policy and Law, 32*(5), 759–783.

Swartz, K. (2010). *Cost sharing: Effects on spending and outcomes, research synthesis.* Report No. 20. The Robert Wood Johnson Foundation Synthesis Project. Retrieved from http://www.rwjf.org/files/research/121710.policysynthesis.costsharing.rpt.pdf

Elise Gould

Price Transparency

POINT: Price transparency could be the single-most important factor in controlling rising medical costs.

Bianca K. Frogner, George Washington University

COUNTERPOINT: Price transparency is not the panacea that some policymakers believe. The health care industry is complex, which makes price comparison difficult to interpret. Equally important to price transparency, costs can be reduced with improved efficiency through better use of technologies and clear standards of care.

Bianca K. Frogner, George Washington University

Introduction

Health care spending is often summarized by the equation: *total expenditure* equals the product of *price* and *quantity* ($E = P \times Q$). Looking at this equation, it is clear that controlling health care expenditures means controlling the prices or quantity of care that is delivered. This debate focuses primarily on the opportunity available through prices to control health spending; in particular on the notion of having more price transparency.

According to basic economic theory, a market is transparent if, at the time of a transaction, the sellers and buyers know what products or services are available and at what price. Moreover, no intermediaries are involved. Price transparency helps assure that all market participants have equal access to prices quoted for the service or product and that the buyers have a good indication of the true value of that product.

In an ideal health care market that is price transparent, patients would be able to shop around in order to find the best value. This means knowing the prices of the service (e.g., surgery or lab test) or product (e.g., wheelchair or pharmaceutical) prior to delivery and also having the information on the comparative effectiveness of various treatment options, both of different types of services and from different providers (e.g., physicians, hospitals, and nurses). Not only can one provider, service, or product cost less than another but they can also be associated with different outcomes. With the information on prices and effectiveness of various treatment options, a choice could be made to optimize the value of care.

However, anyone familiar with the U.S. health care system would most likely consider it to be much more price-opaque than price-transparent. Prices are rarely available to patients prior to the delivery of care. Even if patients asked to know the price beforehand, providers may not be able to readily supply that information because prices for the same service from the same provider can vary substantially depending on the patient's health insurance coverage. In fact, the prices a health insurance plan negotiates with all of the providers within its network can vary significantly for the same service. For example, according to a 2008 publication by the New Jersey Commission on Rationalizing Health Services, the prices paid by a large New Jersey insurer for a colonoscopy to hospitals within its network ranged from $716 to $3,717 (a more than five-fold difference). The range for the same service was $443 to $1,395 (a more than three-fold difference) when comparing the insurer's reimbursement rates to ambulatory surgical centers.

Prices are further masked by the fact that patients with health insurance are usually only responsible for a small share (e.g., the co-payment, co-insurance, or deductible) of the total cost. This situation helps promote inefficient pricing as insured patients are already pre-paying for their health care in the form of a monthly premium and their co-pays are relatively marginal. Thus, there is little incentive for them to consider using health care more efficiently.

Even if the full price was known and faced by the patient prior to receiving care, there still would be the problem of whether the patient had the information necessary to determine the true value of care. In general, the field of medicine is fraught with uncertainty as the way that symptoms are exhibited in patients, even for the same illnesses of conditions, can vary substantially from one patient to the next. In addition, there are continuous advancements in biotechnology and comparative effectiveness research. This makes it difficult for trained doctors to determine the most appropriate treatment regimen, let alone the general public that does not have a clinical background.

Faced with these complexities and confusions, there may be a reliance on the notion that more care or more expensive (i.e., intensive) care is better. However, the evidence for such a correlation is mixed at best. In fact, research has even indicated the opposite, as the provision of lower-cost care, such as primary and preventive services, has been shown to lead to better health outcomes.

Given all of these concerns, a strong case can be made that increasing price transparency could help control health care costs. In the Point essay, Bianca Frogner argues that transparency is a critical first step toward more rational pricing that is better reflective of the true value to consumers. Achieving greater transparency will entail policy leaders to develop provisions that require better availability of data on prices and the comparative effectiveness of care. This information can empower consumers with the ability to make more efficient decisions, particularly if they were to face more of the costs as in high deductible health plans.

In general, policy solutions should be focused on helping to ensure that providers compete for patients based on the quality of care that they deliver. Instead, providers today often rely on anticompetitive forces to drive up prices, such as information asymmetries and monopolistic markets, which may have nothing to do with their ability to provide value to patients. Thus, some experts have pointed toward the use of all-payer payment systems (where providers are reimbursed the same price for a service, no matter who is paying) in order to "get the prices out of the way" so that the focus can be on quality. Frogner describes how other countries have used such approaches to help keep costs well below the levels in the United States.

However, to create a price-transparent health care market is easier said than done. In the Counterpoint, Frogner describes how some early efforts to increase price transparency has actually led to higher prices as lower-cost providers trend up to those with higher prices. Thus, price transparency alone may not be enough to control health care costs (i.e., medical price inflation). In fact, many other factors come into play such as the competitive balance between providers and payers determining pricing levels in a market and the ability for employers to offer a range of insurance plan choices to their employees. Even if those factors did not exist, as Frogner describes, it may be virtually impossible for consumers of health care to get access to all of the information needed to determine the true value of care and hence for anyone to set the "right price."

Instead, Frogner argues that efforts to reduce costs may actually be better spent on the quantity side of the expenditure equation, rather than on prices. According to researchers at Dartmouth University, if high-intensity providers could emulate practice patterns of their more efficient peers, who seem to be getting similar if not better health outcomes, up to 30 percent of health care spending could be saved at current prices. Though 30 percent of all health care seems almost unbelievable, several researchers have reached similar conclusions (e.g., see references in the Counterpoint essay, such as Farrell et al., 2008; Fisher, 2005; Fisher, Bynum, & Skinner, 2009; Kelly, 2009; NEHI, 2008; Skinner, 2011). Certainly, the evidence is fairly clear that wide variation exists in the way health care is delivered. The fact that there is a mismatch between the variation in intensity of care with the variation in outcomes also indicates that there are opportunities to achieve efficiencies. Thus, as Jonathan Skinner from Dartmouth points out in his 2011 debate "Understanding Prices and Quantities in the U.S. Health Care System" published in the *Journal of Health, Policy and Law*, even if only 15 percent could be saved, that would still amount to roughly 2.5 percent of the U.S. gross domestic product.

POINT

Transparency in medical pricing is arguably the single most important factor in "bending the cost curve." Medical expenditures grew faster than the gross domestic product (GDP) over the last few decades. Health care has become one of the largest sectors of the U.S. economy, and is projected to consume an increasing share of that economy. The danger is that increasing allocation to health care may divert resources away from other important nonhealth priorities. Each additional dollar spent on health care needs to be carefully examined in an era of tight budgets in a downturned economy. These allocation decisions require information about the value that each dollar buys.

The value of medical care is generally defined as the combination of medical prices and outcomes of medical services (e.g., quality of care or quality of life). Information about medical outcomes is increasingly available, but pricing information is often tightly held by providers and third parties. Arguably medical-outcomes information has limited utility without pricing information. Recognizing the importance of pricing information, 30 states proposed or enacted legislation to improve price transparency in medical care as of the end of 2011 according to the Government Accounting Office (GAO). But larger scale and consistent efforts to make medical prices transparent are necessary for optimal decision making.

Price transparency would vastly improve the interaction between patients, providers, and third-party payers. The medical system is complex and fragmented, which is often difficult for lay persons to understand and navigate. Transparent medical prices allow patients to become more informed consumers. Price transparency would also promote more competition among medical providers and third-party payer markets. Despite the important role of price information, price transparency largely does not exist in the U.S. medical system.

This essay argues why price transparency is one of the most important steps to bend the cost curve. The key point is that price transparency is critical to create a more competitive medical marketplace. A more competitive marketplace will result in more efficient allocation of resources and prevent unnecessary spending, both which reduce overall expenditures. The majority of the medical marketplace is filled with private firms such as health insurance companies. In a marketplace with many private entities, promoting a competitive environment is ideal to gain efficiency and prevent unnecessary excess costs. Health plans and providers are able to negotiate better reimbursement rates if they have full information on pricing, and patients are able to identify high-quality and low-cost care.

This essay opens with a discussion of why rising medical expenditures is a problem. The essay then gives a brief background on the role of prices in competitive versus noncompetitive markets. This includes a discussion of asymmetric information, product differentiation, price discrimination, and other characteristics of health care markets (such as having third-party payers) that prevent price transparency. This essay ends with lessons from other countries on how price transparency regulations impact medical expenditures.

THE PROBLEM WITH RISING MEDICAL EXPENDITURES

Medical expenditures grew from 12.5 percent of the gross domestic product (GDP) in 1990 to 17.6 percent in 2009. According to Martin and colleagues (2011), between 2008 and 2009 the growth in personal health spending (which is most of the total medical expenditures) was 60 percent attributable to price factors such as prescription drug prices. Price factors dominated over nonprice factors, such as the volume and intensity (i.e., using more services, more advanced and expensive services), in the growth of medical spending. This trend was in part due to people reducing consumption of health care during economically hard times. Also, medical prices were stable during the period of recession despite declining prices economy-wide.

Although the growth in medical expenditures decelerated in recent years, health care is projected to continue consuming a larger share of the economy. Medical expenditures are expected to reach 49 percent of GDP by 2082 according to the Congressional Budget Office. The growing demand from an aging population who have a high chronic disease prevalence combined with the growing cost of doing business in health care are expected to be the primary drivers of the medical care spending growth over the upcoming decades.

The problem with growing medical expenditures is the opportunity cost of spending one dollar more on medical care versus something else in the economy. Policymakers must make difficult decisions about whether an extra dollar spent on medical provides more value than an extra dollar spent somewhere else, such as education. The growing share of GDP allocated to medical care implicitly suggests that the United States values medical care and its outcomes more than it does other parts of the economy. Explicitly, Cutler and McClellan (2001) found quantifiable evidence of value in the increased medical expenditures especially in the area of heart disease.

Within health care itself, policymakers must decide whether a dollar spent on one medical service provides more value than one spent on another medical service. Inefficiency is reduced when spending on medical services is directed to the services that provide the most value. Unfortunately, the United States does not always make efficient decisions. Without efficient decisions, medical expenditures will likely increase and result in poor resource allocation within the economy.

THE ROLE OF PRICES IN RESOURCE ALLOCATION

When evaluating the various options available for medical care, consumers ideally would have all the necessary information including prices to make value judgments on each option. Value is the return on investment to a dollar spent; health economists often calculate value as the quality of life gained from a dollar spent on medical care. Quality of life is dependent on the quality of medical care and individual health outcomes. Metrics for quality of medical care are increasingly being standardized and made available as described below. Health outcomes have quantifiable measures, such as with the number of sick days, saved lives, number of initial or follow-up medical visits, life-expectancy gains, and changes in health status. Though these are quantifiable measures, they may not be the most meaningful. Meaningful measures may sometimes be difficult to quantify, such as quality of life and preferences.

Though to quantify the quality of medical care is challenging, efforts to make this information available are well ahead of those to make available pricing information. Before discussing the role of prices in allocation decisions, it is important to have a basic definition of prices for goods or services. A firm (or individual seller) sets a price that covers operational costs of producing a good or service, including (1) labor costs of producing the good or service, which is the product of the number of hours worked and wage rate per hour; (2) capital costs, for example, for buildings and equipment necessary to deliver the good or service; and (3) overhead costs such as for administration and profits. For consumers, price reflects their willingness to pay. Consumers are assumed to maximize their utility or "happiness" that they achieve in part by purchasing good health via medical care. According to basic microeconomic theory, consumers would purchase medical care up to the point when the last dollar spent on medical care would give them equal utility compared to the last dollar spent on any other good.

Ideally, many sellers and consumers naturally negotiate an equilibrium price. The equilibrium price would result in "market clearing," where the exact number of goods and services are produced and thus consumed. These conditions result in an efficient use of resources and reduce wasteful spending. If the price is higher than this equilibrium point, suppliers would want to produce more goods or services to gain more revenue, but buyers would prefer to consume less. At lower than equilibrium price, suppliers would produce fewer goods or services because suppliers would operate at a loss, but buyers would prefer to consume more. If prices are too low, the excess demand would lead to a shortage.

In the medical industry, the ideal situation does not often occur. More often, there is only one (monopoly) to a few (oligopoly) sellers. These sellers are able to take advantage of their situation to set prices higher than equilibrium, yet still sell the same number of goods or services as under a competitive scenario. In other words, the sellers gain excess profits. Lack of price transparency allows sellers to retain their status as a monopoly or oligopoly. Increased price transparency would allow new sellers to identify the opportunity (i.e., see the excess profits) and enter the market by out-pricing their competitor. With enough new entrants, a competitive market may ensue.

ASYMMETRIC INFORMATION, PRODUCT DIFFERENTIATION, AND PRICE DISCRIMINATION

A basic economic assumption of competitive markets is that the goods and services sold are identical. For example an X-ray of a person's foot done in one doctor's office should be a similar image to one done at another doctor's office. Also, durable medical equipment such as stents and orthotics are often nearly identical across sellers. There are also many pharmaceutically equivalent brand and generic drugs. On the other hand, medical care services (e.g., diagnostic testing, surgeries) can vary widely by such characteristics as the rendering medical provider, setting, or even the patient. For example, as a patient gains more co-morbidities and conditions become more complex, the "usual" treatment is difficult to define.

The lack of uniformity of medical services only adds to the difficulty that consumers face when making informed medical care decisions. Not only is the information difficult to gather but it is also difficult to understand given the highly technical nature of many medical decisions. In general, patients are not as well equipped to make medical decisions as the doctors that spend years training how to discern diagnoses and treatments. Thus, patients have difficulty differentiating the quality of care from one provider (e.g., physician or hospital) versus another. Patients tend to rely on the notion that their physicians are knowledgeable about all the treatments available for a condition, and trust the physician to act as their agent to make the best decision possible for their care plan. Also patients rarely feel comfortable challenging the physician in fear of appearing untrusting, upsetting the doctor and not receiving the best care, or out of respect that the physician may know more than the patient.

Providers can take advantage of this situation and charge higher than equilibrium prices. That is, medical providers (sellers) may know the true cost and value of their service, while the consumers (patients and other buyers of health care) do not. Providers can use this information asymmetry to induce greater demand from their patients. Providers may be able to justify a higher price (i.e., product differentiation) by arguing that (1) they deliver better quality services due to their higher pedigree or years of experience and (2) they open access for patients to a better and wider network of specialist providers and to the latest technologies. Hospitals may add further arguments that higher prices reflect the better aesthetics of the hospital environment and orientation toward customer service.

Similarly, sellers may also take advantage of different types of patients who may be willing to pay more or less for a service dependent on their situation (i.e., price discrimination). Patients may choose a physician because of built trust, familiarity, or convenience. Providers may raise prices to capitalize on the relationship knowing that the patient may not change to another provider despite the price increase. Another example could involve patients who are in urgent need for a service and may be willing to pay a high price for the convenience and immediacy of care.

Price discrimination in part occurs due to poor price transparency. With pricing information, patients would be better able to re-evaluate how much value they place on the relationship with their provider. Also, if patients have the choice of an urgent care facility a little further away, patients would be better able to comparison shop. This choice includes calculating (implicitly or explicitly) whether the savings of going to an urgent care facility a little further away is equal to the value of the extra transportation cost. These types of informed decision-making processes that are made possible with price transparency reduce inefficiencies and overall costs within society.

Asymmetry in knowledge and price discrimination is improving over time with the increasing availability of information. The advent of the Internet allows patients to self-educate on their condition using sources like webmd.com, mayoclinic.com, and other similar sites. Patients are then able to ask more directed and educated questions to their providers and be more of an active participant in their own care. Several groups (government and nongovernment) created websites to rate the quality of visits (subjectively and objectively) to doctors, hospitals, and health care plans. Websites such as ratemydoctor.com and hospitalcompare.hhs.gov provide quality metrics available to the public to help reduce this deficiency in knowledge.

Medical pricing, however, is still missing from most of these informational resources. With price transparency, patients would be better empowered to ask questions about why one physician's services are priced higher than another's. Eventually, more informed consumers can help narrow the variation in the service quality (and cost of care) provided by sellers.

SHELTERING PATIENTS FROM PRICES

According to economic theory, if individuals feel a direct impact of a purchase on their wallets, they may make more efficient choices. A primary reason why the health care market is not as efficient as it could be is because third-party payers (i.e., insurance companies) typically pay most of the medical bills. In fact, less than 15 percent of health care spending in the United States is paid by patients out-of-pocket (Martin et al., 2011) and, in fact, patients often purchase medical care before knowing the price of the service.

The price for a service is often not calculated until after the service is delivered. Prices are often revealed too late after the service was delivered in the form of the Explanation of Benefits or bill, rather than before the purchase of the service. Though patients may not have a choice in the services provided, upfront price transparency would help reduce the number of complaints, dissatisfaction, and appeals that often clog a system.

Even if medical care prices are available, patients typically focus on the out-of-pocket payments they are responsible for, such as the co-payments, deductibles, or co-insurance. Co-payments are a flat fee, typically around $10 to $40 for a physician visit. A deductible is a minimum amount that the patient has to spend first before insurance kicks in, and ranges from $100 up to as high as $2,500 for high-deductible health plans. Co-insurance is a percentage of a service, typically around 20 percent, and is usually for hospital visits or medical devices. Insurance companies pay for the rest of the medical bills through pooled premiums of individuals in a health plan.

Some would argue that health insurance shelters patients from the full price of medical care, particularly with low co-payments. The seemingly low price of care may result in moral hazard; moral hazard is an economic concept that suggests that patients may overutilize care even when it is medically unnecessary because they can easily afford to be overly aggressive in seeking treatments. For example, a patient covered by insurance is more likely to opt for extra diagnostic tests for peace of mind rather than out of medical necessity. On the other hand, a patient who pays the full price may limit the number of tests to only the most necessary.

Price transparency would help eliminate unnecessary overuse of medical care and free up providers to focus on more serious problems. Also, price transparency may make a patient more likely to consider the benefits of using preventive care rather than wait for the exacerbation of diseases, which could result in much more expensive care down the line.

Consumer directed health care (CDHC) plans (also known as high-deductible plans) are popular options as a mechanism to control unnecessary use of medical care by introducing more price transparency to consumers. CDHC plans are alternative health insurance options to the traditional employer-sponsored health insurance plans, such as indemnity plans and preferred provider organizations. CDHC plans provide less generous coverage with more restrictions. The main characteristic of a CDHC is a high deductible, which further exposes patients to the full price of care. CDHCs provide coverage for the unexpected and high-cost events. CDHCs are designed to incentivize patients to choose healthier lifestyles to prevent unnecessary use of medical care. Additional expectations are that patients will make the best use of preventative and primary care services. The direct impact of medical care on the patient's wallet gives patients pause prior to seeking expensive medical care and instead may motivate him or her to seek early, less costly preventive care. Yet CDHCs have not fully caught on, in part because patients do not have access to the price of care and other information that help to distinguish high-value care.

PUBLISHING PRICES

Reimbursement for delivery of medical services occurs in various ways. The dominant payment model is a fee-for-service model in which payment occurs on a per-service or per-unit basis. Under such arrangements, for each lab test, device, drug, or service delivered, a provider receives a fee. At the other end of the payment model spectrum are fixed upfront payments that cover a broad range of services. For example, providers can be paid for each patient on a capitation basis. In this case, a provider (or group of providers) would receive one payment to cover all the services for a particular patient during a given year. Another form of fixed-upfront payments for a broad range of services is bundled, or episodic, payments. In this case, the payment could cover all of the services (even if delivered by several providers in different settings) related to a patient's specific condition.

The different forms of payment add additional difficulties in defining the price of care. For example, payments that cover a broad range of services may make correct pricing of individual services less important. Also, extending different levels of services (from a single service to a broad range) as a basis for payment complicates the issues of value.

This is further complicated by the fact that there are different measures of prices and costs (i.e., the cost incurred by the provider in rendering the service or product). What is not clear is what is the most valuable to the patient (e.g., knowledge of the cost of providing the care, the amount that the provider charges the insurer, the amount that providers are allowed to charge, or the price charged without insurance). Though Medicare publishes its reimbursement rates, private payers are not required to do so. The information on how much it costs to deliver care is typically less available than prices (even within Medicare). Price and cost information could help consumers make better value judgments and eventually narrow the variation in pricing and costs. Consumers will gravitate toward the more efficient providers, who are likely to be providers that keep costs down and charge lower prices.

Some hospitals and clinics are pushed to publish the prices for their most common services to help patients make more informed decisions. In fact, providers such as those that are part of the Geisinger and Kaiser Permanente health systems created a pricing Web tool for patients to estimate the expense of their visit prior to its occurrence. Patients seem to value price transparency, as is evident from the popularity of acute-care clinics within commercial centers, including the most prevalent one, the Minute Clinics in CVS Pharmacies. Minute Clinics offer a set of minor acute care services, fairly consistent across stores, and provide a clear list of prices. To date, limited evidence exists on whether savings are achieved. With increased availability of prices, patients are able to make educated decisions about where to seek services.

PRICE TRANSPARENCY IN OTHER COUNTRIES

Health care funding in the United States typically flows from households to providers through a multitude of various taxes and third-party payers and administrators. This fragmentation, along with information asymmetries, the ability to price discriminate and other factors, results in little coordination of buying power in the United States. Hence, the United States is in a weaker position, relative to most other developed countries, to control health care prices.

In general, the health care systems of other countries tend to shift more of the market power over to the buyer's side, which is known as a monopsonistic approach. A single-payer system, such as the health insurance plans operated by the provincial governments in Canada, would be called a "pure monopsony" as there is only one buyer who leverages its market clout to essentially set whatever payment rates it is willing to pay. Even pure monopsonists are ultimately constrained by market forces on the supply side. That is, they cannot offer to pay below the minimally acceptable prices that providers would need to be willing and able to supply their services and goods (this minimal level is known as the "reservation price").

This leaves ample room for more monopsonistic countries to set prices well below the U.S. levels. For example, survey data from The International Federation of Health Plans (2010) showed that average U.S. prices for procedures are higher in comparison to 11 other countries surveyed for nearly all of the 14 common services and procedures analyzed. For example, total hospital and physician fees for delivering a baby were found to be $2,147 in Germany and $2,667 in Canada, while averaging $8,435 in the United States. The survey also found that the cost of a widely prescribed drug like Nexium can range from $30 in the United Kingdom to $186 in the United States.

In the paper by Anderson and colleagues (2003) titled "It's the Prices, Stupid: Why the United States Is So Different From Other Countries," the authors showed that prices are higher in the United States, which leads to the higher level of spending in that country. Compared to other Organisation for Economic Co-operation and Development (OECD) countries, the United States has similar and sometimes even lower quantity, or utilization, of services including rates for doctor consultations and hospital discharges (OECD, 2011). Yet health spending has been much higher in the United States. In fact, according to OECD data on 2009 spending, the United States spent more than 2.5 times per person than the average of all other countries in the OECD. If one assumes that total spending is a function of price and quantity, then prices must be driving up health care costs in the United States.

With high health spending in the United States, an important issue to consider is whether the United States is getting good value for that spending. Though data on the quality of care is always difficult to interpret, the preponderance of evidence seems to imply that the U.S. health care system is fairly mediocre. One report showed that the United States was equally likely to be in the top and bottom halves for 16 quality measures compiled by the OECD (Anderson & Frogner, 2008). Furthermore, life expectancy is lower than expected given the high-income levels in the United States. Also access to care has been limited relative to other countries. These findings only amplify the need to figure out why prices are so high in the United States and to determine whether such levels are warranted.

CONCLUSION

For a competitive market to exist in the medical care industry, price transparency is a must. Without price transparency, medical providers are able to price discriminate and take advantage of their asymmetric knowledge. Price transparency is crucial in order to begin to understand variations in care across the country. Without that piece of the puzzle, policymakers cannot begin to make judgments about the value for the dollar of health care. If the market works properly with clear prices, quality can become the focus.

The U.S. medical market is moving toward a more price transparent system. Laws are passed and more are being introduced to increase price transparency within hospitals. More needs to be done to increase price transparency at the physician-visit level. Medical insurers such as Medicare are increasing information about the reimbursement rates to providers. Private health insurance plans also need to do more to show their reimbursement rates so that providers can make informed decisions about who to contract with, and to ensure better regulation in the market.

Patients are becoming more savvy consumers of medical care, but as more information about quality is provided, patients need the other side of the equation to determine the value of their care. Patients need to be exposed to prices either through more information or by direct experience, such as through CDHC plans. The exposure will help patients make more educated choices. With each area of medical care aligned through improved transparency in medical prices, medical expenditures may have a better chance of coming down, while also encouraging higher quality and better value care.

References and Further Reading

Antos, J., Bertko, J., Chernew, M., Cutler, D., de Brantes, F., Goldman, D., & Shortell, S. (2010). Bending the curve through health reform implementation. *American Journal of Managed Care, 16*(11), 804–812.

Anderson, G. F. (2007). From "soak the rich" to "soak the poor": Recent trends in hospital pricing. *Health Affairs, 26*(3), 780–789.

Anderson, G. F., & Frogner, B. K. (2008). Health spending in OECD countries: Obtaining value per dollar. *Health Affairs, 27*(6), 1718–1727.

Anderson, G. F., Reinhardt, U. E., Hussey, P. S., & Petrosyan, V. (2003). It's the prices, stupid: Why the United States is so different from other countries. *Health Affairs, 22*(3), 89–105.

Austin, D. A., & Gravelle, J. G. (2008). *Does price transparency improve market efficiency? Implications of empirical evidence in other markets for the health sector* (Congressional Research Service Report). Retrieved from http://www.fas.org/sgp/crs/misc/RL34101.pdf

Centers for Medicare & Medicaid Services. (2011). *NHE summary including share of GDP, CY 1960–2009*. Retrieved from https://www. cms.gov/nationalhealthexpenddata/02_nationalhealthaccountshistorical.asp

The Commonwealth Fund. (2008). Minnesota: Payment reform and price transparency. *States in Action Newsletter*. Retrieved from http://www.commonwealthfund.org/Newsletters/States-in-Action/2008/Aug/August-September-2008.aspx?view=newsletter_print

The Commonwealth Fund. (2010). Medical price transparency: GOP sees it as a cost cutter. *Washington Health Policy Week in Review*. Retrieved from http://www.commonwealthfund.org/Newsletters/Washington-Health-Policy-in-Review/2010/Nov/November-1–2010.aspx?view=newsletter_print

Congressional Budget Office. (2007). *Technological change and the growth of health care spending*. Washington, DC: CBO.

Cutler, D. M. (1995). *Technology, health costs, and the NIH*. National Institutes of Health Economics Roundtable on Biomedical Research. Bethesda, MD: National Institutes of Health.

Cutler, D. M., & McClellan, M. (2001). Is technological change in medicine worth it? *Health Affairs, 20*(5), 11–29.

Docteur, E., & Oxley, H. (2003). *Health-care systems: Lessons from the reform experience* (OECD Health Working Papers). Retrieved from http://www.oecd.org/dataoecd/5/53/22364122.pdf

Glied, S. (2003). Health care costs: On the rise again. *Journal of Economic Perspectives, 17*(2), 125–148.

Government Accountability Office. (2011). *Health care price transparency: Meaningful price information is difficult for consumers to obtain prior to receiving care* (GAO-11-791). Washington, DC: U.S. Government Accountability Office.

Hall, R. E., & Jones, C. I. (2007). The value of life and the rise in health spending. *Quarterly Journal of Economics 122*(1), 39–72.

Hartman, M., Martin, A., Nuccio, O., Catlin, A., & the National Health Expenditure Accounts Team. (2010). Health spending growth at a historic low in 2008. *Health Affairs, 29*(1), 147–155.

Hsiao, W. C. (2011). State-based single-payer health care—A solution for the United States? *New England Journal of Medicine, 364*(13), 1188–1190.

Hsiao, W. C., Knight, A. G., Kappel, S., & Done, N. (2011). What other states can learn from Vermont's bold experiment: Embracing a single-payer health care financing system. *Health Affairs, 30*(7), 1232–1241.

International Federation of Health Plans. (2010). *Comparative price report: Medical and hospital fees by country*. Retrieved from http://www.ifhp.com/news56.html

Kastor, J. A., & Adashi, E. Y. (2011). Maryland's hospital cost review commission at 40: A model for the country. *Journal of the American Medical Association, 306*(10), 1137–1138.

Kyle, M. K., & Ridley, D. B. (2007). Would greater transparency and uniformity of health care prices benefit poor patients? *Health Affairs, 26*(5), 1384–1391

Laws, M., & Scott, M. K. (2008). The emergence of retail-based clinics in the United States: Early observations. *Health Affairs, 27*(5), 1293–1298.

Martin, A., Lassman, D., Whittle, L., Catlin, A., & the National Health Expenditure Accounts Team. (2011). Recession contributes to the slowest annual rate of increase in health spending in five decades. *Health Affairs, 30*(1), 11–22.

Murray, R. (2009). Setting hospital rates to control costs and boost quality: The Maryland experience. *Health Affairs, 28*(5), 1395–1405.

National Conference of State Legislatures. (2010). *State legislation relating to transparency and disclosure of health and hospital charge.* Retrieved from http://www.ncsl.org/default.aspx?tabid=14512

Organisation for Economic Co-operation and Development (OECD). (2011). *OECD health data 2011—Frequently requested data.* Retrieved from http://www.oecd.org/document/16/0,3746,en_2649_37407_2085200_1_1_1_37407,00.html

Pauley, M. V., & Burns, L. R. (2008). Price transparency for medical devices. *Health Affairs, 27*(6), 1544–1553.

Reinhardt, U. E. (2006). The pricing of US hospital services: Chaos behind a veil of secrecy. *Health Affairs, 25*(1), 57–69.

Shea, K. K., Shih, A., & Davis, K. (2007). *Data brief: Health care opinion leaders' views on the transparency of health care quality and price information in the United States.* The Commonwealth Fund, Commission on a High Performance Health System (Pub. No. 1078). Retrieved from http://www.commonwealthfund.org/usr_doc/Shea_HCOLtransparencysurveydatabrief_1078.pdf

Wallack, A. R. (2011). Single payer ahead–Cost control and the evolving Vermont Model. *New England Journal of Medicine, 365*(13), 584–585.

Bianca K. Frogner

COUNTERPOINT

Price transparency plays a role in reducing medical spending, but it is not a panacea. Early findings suggest that improving price transparency is not bringing about the expected results. The common culprit driving the medical cost curve is the advance of medical technologies, or the "march of science" according to Newhouse (1992). Patients demand the latest and greatest technologies. Providers are attracted to work in environments with cutting-edge technologies. Insurance reimbursement rates tend to be high for sophisticated technologies. Publicizing the price of care surrounding technologies may provide one piece of the puzzle. But the U.S. medical system is complex with many moving parts and players.

This essay begins with a discussion of the early evidence from price transparency legislation. It will then present the complex dynamic of competition in the medical care market place. Though patients consume health care from providers, health insurance rules and regulations prevent them from easily shopping for medical care. This essay will suggest that, before price transparency can be considered, guidelines for quality of care are necessary to establish the standard of care. Defining and comparing price across services may not be realistic given the wide array of conditions and treatments available. This essay will argue that large savings could be achieved through alternative ways by, for example, reducing duplication of services. For many, the first crucial step seems to be to develop a health information system to coordinate information, standardize care and eventually reduce costs rather than achieve price transparency. The last section discusses the need for more information to understand the reasons for the growth of medical expenditures before identifying a panacea solution.

POOR EVIDENCE FOR PRICE TRANSPARENCY

Farrell and colleagues (2010) simulated what would happen if an uninsured individual sought price information from hundreds of hospitals in California. The results suggest that an uninsured individual would have a hard time gaining sufficient information to make an educated decision. The current medical system is not designed to easily provide price information. Thirty states are trying to improve the availability of medical price information, but early evidence suggests that the efforts are not proving fruitful.

Beginning in 2007, New Hampshire tried a one- to two-year experiment of collecting and revealing price information for common services within medical facilities. Tu and Lauer (2009) found large variations in the cost of care for the same procedures, but the revelation did not cause a decrease in the variation in price. One reason for the lack of change is the high market concentration in some rural areas of New Hampshire. Unless there is a market with lots of sellers and buyers, the price of care is meaningless to many patients who have few, if any, other options for care. The only apparent benefit to collecting the data was an increase in referral requests by the patients to go to a slightly less expensive facility.

Love, Custer, and Miller (2010) evaluated the benefit of a database with all possible claims data sources to provide a full profile of a patient's care. Health insurance companies tried to use this type of information to better negotiate away the variation in hospital prices; yet hospitals argue that the data are incomplete or not up-to-date. Another downside of the data is that patients are not able to easily understand how to use the data to their advantage. With the high cost of developing and maintaining real time data, the question turns to who should bear the cost burden. The validity of the data is also questionable. Thus the cost-effectiveness of an all-claims data approach to reduce total medical expenditures needs more careful thought.

One state found success at bending the cost curve by controlling prices rather than having the goal of making prices transparent. The Maryland Health Services Cost Review Commission was established because medical costs were rising more rapidly than in other states. The commission collects data on hospital operations and finances to establish a hospital charge per case with adjustments for the type of patient. These rates are used for all payers in the state with the goal of promoting cost control, better access to care, and financial stability. This method controls costs but allows volume to vary from hospital to hospital. Despite the ability of hospitals to make up revenue by increasing volume for what they lose in charges, Maryland saw one of the slowest cumulative increases in cost per adjusted admission and the lowest charge level compared to other states (for further discussion, see Murray, 2009).

THE DANGERS OF PRICE TRANSPARENCY

Love, Custer, and Miller (2010) point out that, when patients have price information, they do not often know how to interpret the information. Patients may use prices as a proxy for quality of care, where higher prices indicate better quality of medical care and too-low prices may indicate poor quality of care. Several studies debunk the idea that higher prices are proxies for higher quality care.

Through a high deductible and less generous coverage, consumer directed health care (CDHC) plans expose patients more to the full price of medical care versus alternative health insurance options. As a result, patients are pushed to be proactive in understanding the price of care, and to make smarter choices in care by selecting earlier and lower-cost preventive care. LoSasso, Shah, and Frogner (2010) found that CDHC participation resulted in less medical spending, but mostly due to the reduction in elective medical visits. According to Manning and colleagues (1987), a general trend exists whereby, if a consumer has to pay more out of pocket for medical services, he or she may seek fewer services. The worry is that delayed treatments may result in that patient seeking care only when his or her condition becomes worse and therefore more expensive to treat.

Suppliers (including providers, insurance companies, medical manufacturers, and pharmaceutical companies) may react negatively to efforts to increase price transparency. For example price transparency may result in lower prices in some areas, so suppliers may not provide services in those areas. Altman, Shactman, and Eilat (2006) pointed out that when certain routes were not profitable, airlines discontinued service to certain areas. The danger is if medical providers do the same and not provide service areas, especially rural or low-income areas. Also, among insurance plans such as under Medicare Advantage, plans may enter market areas where they can gain the most profit and not serve areas where little profit may be made. These potential dangers would occur as long as there is a lack of uniformity in price transparency. With national standards to establish price transparency, prices would be stable across the country, which would lead to fewer opportunities for suppliers to move to another (more profitable) area.

MARKET CONCENTRATION

Many buyers and sellers need to be involved for a competitive market to exist. In a transaction of identical goods and services, buyers and sellers come together to determine equilibrium price under the somewhat mystical way of the "invisible hand" according to Adam Smith's *The Wealth of Nations* in 1776. Buyers get satisfaction (utility) from the good or service up to the point that the buyer gets more utility from purchasing another good or service. Sellers produce an item or good up to the point that the revenue from selling one more good or service covers the cost of producing the good or service.

Providers and insurance companies are competitive in some markets and dominant in others. The balance of market power between hospital and insurance companies considerably influences price setting. Hospitals, for example, provide services that insurance companies seek to contract and bundle into a plan to be sold to patients. Insurance companies, on the other hand, provide a potential customer base for hospitals. A strong health insurance company in a market of many hospitals may drive hospital prices down as hospitals compete to be listed in the health insurance network. Yet if one hospital is more dominant in the market with many health insurance companies, that hospital may demand higher prices. Using empirical evidence, Melnick and colleagues (1992) found that insurance providers were able to negotiate lower prices from providers in more competitive hospital environments. (For additional examples, see Dranove, Shanley, & White, 1993.)

The dynamics are even more complex when considering private versus public insurers. Medicare and Medicaid are typically more price transparent, but arguably less generous than other forms of health insurance. In fact, many hospitals are unable to recoup their costs from the relatively lower Medicare and Medicaid reimbursement levels. Robinson (2011) found that shortfalls from Medicare reimbursement resulted in higher prices to private health insurers in concentrated hospital markets. The notion behind this is that providers use private payers to cover their payment shortfalls from the public sector. In contrast, shortfalls from Medicare resulted in cost cutting in competitive markets. That is, providers are forced to increase their efficiency in more competitive markets as they do not have the market leverage to simply raise prices. Along those lines, Chernew and colleagues (2010) found that Medicare is not as effective in exploiting its market power compared to private insurers in competitive hospital markets. One key difference is that private insurers are able to negotiate while Medicare cannot. Price transparency is not going to solve these complex dynamics. Regulations such as price caps on private health insurance reimbursement (benchmarked to Medicare reimbursement rates) would be more likely to result in environments with lower medical prices.

One major downside to price transparency is that the information may reveal to the providers who charge lower prices that they could be charging more for their services. Providers may consider moving their prices closer to the higher price point if they realize customers are willing to pay this price. This phenomenon is more likely to occur in more concentrated markets.

Another potential danger is collusion when there is only one or two dominant hospitals and one or two dominant health insurance companies. In an oligopoly market, tacit collusion may occur between the dominant players, where the players create a silent agreement to set prices higher than equilibrium. When prices are published, cartels may form where the dominant players are clearly working together to keep prices higher than they would be in a more competitive market.

EMPLOYERS AND BENEFITS MANAGERS

Employers play a large role in the medical market. Three-fourths of individuals work in a large firm, and most large firms (200 employees or more) offer a private health insurance plan. A health benefits manager or specialist within a human resources department usually negotiates the price of plan options with a private health insurance company. Insurance companies set the premiums (e.g., price of health insurance) based on an evaluation of the likelihood of patients within an insurance plan to use or need medical care. Patients pay monthly premiums to insurance companies either directly or through payroll deductions if employed.

If employed, patients rely on a benefits manager to identify the choice of health plans with the best negotiated premium rate. The benefits manager and the employer become the *de facto* consumer on behalf of the patients. The goals of a company may be different than the goals of society; for example, an earlier study by Maxwell and Temin (2003) found that Fortune 500 companies based their purchasing and contracting of plans on the level of consumer satisfaction and customer service rather than quality of care. In a more recent study by Rosenthal and colleagues (2007), large companies were not engaging in purchasing plans based on quality of care (also known as value-based purchasing).

Though employers seem less concerned about quality or the value for the dollar, much evidence in the literature suggests that they are concerned with the increasing cost of insurance. To cope with the increasing costs, employers are passing the increasing costs to the employees. Employees are beholden to the choices made by their employer. Some would argue that this added layer between the consumer and the seller leads to inefficiency in the market; consumers are prevented from comparison shopping based on quality. Price transparency would be of little value to employees if they are limited to the selection of plans offered by their employer. Even within an employer, an increased selection of plans could allow employees to comparison shop, which has been proven to lower costs (Bundorf, 2010).

An advantage of working for a large company is that at least they may be able to negotiate a health insurance plan with lower rates than smaller companies. Large companies provide a larger customer base over which to spread the risk of disease. Health insurance companies also benefit from partnering with large employers, by substantially expanding their market share. Thus, they may be more likely to offer better deals to large employers for their business.

Small firms, self-employed, and unemployed individuals face less generous plans or CDHC plans, which place more of the cost burden on the employee. Price transparency would not change the fact that small firms, self-employed, or uninsured have little or no collective bargaining power to negotiate with health insurers. Under the Patient Protection and Affordable Care Act of 2010 (ACA), Health Insurance Exchanges (HIEs) will be developed to provide a market for small employers and other individuals. HIEs are expected to standardize benefits, improve regulation and rules across insurance companies (e.g., prevent denials), and build bargaining power.

PROVIDER SELECTION

Without sufficient information about how one provider differs from another, patients are often not able to identify and seek care from high-performing providers. Instead, because easily accessible quality of care information is lacking on medical providers (e.g., physicians and hospitals), patients are typically limited to basic information such as gender, location, and specialty when choosing providers. If possible, a patient may take the time to look up whether any Internet postings reveal more information about the physician, or else she might rely on referrals from friends, family, and physicians. This anecdotal evidence, however, may not provide meaningful comparative information to help the patient make more effective health care decisions.

If the price per visit was available in a standardized, easily accessible format to aid individuals in their physician selection decision making, patients may be influenced to pick a lower-priced doctor. Even with the information on prices, individuals would also need relevant information on the quality of care a physician provides in order to make the price data meaningful. In fact, many studies have shown that prices are not necessarily correlated with quality. Yet, as discussed earlier, patients may gravitate toward higher-priced care (particularly when their share of the cost is low) using price as a proxy for quality.

Quality-of-care information on providers is also not used when insurers select who to contract into their network. Insurers are more likely to contract with providers that accept a lower reimbursement rate, rather than those that provide the best value of care. Yet insurers, especially large insurers, are well positioned to demand contracts only with those that provide the best quality of care at a low price, given that insurers interface with a large number of providers. This action could greatly reduce health care costs by steering patients away from providers that deliver inefficient care.

STANDARDIZING DEFINITIONS OF VALUE

Even with pricing information, value is difficult to compare because at some point moral judgments are made. Patients may differ in how they value their health or life, where those who value their health more may be willing to pay more. Patients may place value on a personal relationship they have with a physician even if the physician provides slightly less quality care. Patients may rather pay for the comfort of seeing a physician they know rather than have the search cost of finding another physician. Patients may prefer to pay a little extra for convenience especially when tired or sick to see a physician that fit in the patient's time schedule and location.

Defining a service and its relevant market has been a struggle for researchers. Medicare is working toward bundling payments, which pays for a defined set of procedures and visits. The difficulty arises when a patient's set of conditions are complex and the need for service intensity increases. There is often a lack of consensus clinical guidelines for standardized care. As a result, physicians may treat the same condition differently. Until care is further standardized, price information provides little value when different services to treat a particular condition are compared.

PREVENTION AND INEFFICIENT USE OF RESOURCES

High cost of medical care could be in part mitigated by more appropriate use of medical care. For example, if health care systems like the Mayo Clinic and Intermountain Healthcare were used as benchmarks for efficient use of inpatient services, the United States could reduce hospital spending by 28 to 43 percent according to Wennberg and colleagues (2008). As an example of the inappropriate use of medical care, uninsured patients typically seek care in emergency rooms because they do not have an alternative source of regular care. Uninsured patients often seek care for minor acute conditions easily treatable in less expensive settings, such as their primary care physician's office. Also, without a regular source of care, patients often seek care too late.

Ultimately the way to keep medical expenditures low is to prevent patients from needing medical care in the first place. Many people do not encounter the health system until they are older or when an acute event takes occurs. Many of these individuals' medical expenditures are zero, and they may not see a need for much information to make medical choices because their encounters are rare.

In addition to improving the use of primary and preventative care, the need for better chronic disease management is a major issue in the United States. Studies show that chronic diseases are increasingly becoming the driver in health care spending (Thorpe et al., 2010). The aging of the population is likely to only intensify this effect. Implementing a system of early detection of and disease management for chronic disease patients is an important first step over price transparency for chronic disease care.

The recent push under the HITECH Act of 2009 is to incentivize providers to implement health information technology (HIT). HIT is expected to help facilitate chronic disease–management and the coordination of care, which will reduce duplication of services and thus reduce health spending. HIT would have benefits to the provider and reduce administrative hassles. Morra and colleagues (2011) calculated that U.S. physicians incur a time and labor cost by clinical staff of $82,975 per physician per year, four times higher than their Canadian counterparts, dealing with claims, coverage, and billing among multiple payers versus a single-payer system. These examples are only a few of the many possible scenarios of wasteful use of resources throughout the health system; price transparency would not fix these problems.

Waste also exists in a system with multiple payers that negotiate different prices with providers. The inefficiency resulting from this payer model is evident in the experiment taking place in Vermont, the first state to pass a single-payer system in 2011. The system provides insurance through a publicly funded program called the Health Benefits Exchange. The program works on a global budget, decouples coverage from employment, and provides a single system of payments and administrative rules. A public board is set up to control costs through rate setting, reviews of insurance rates and hospital budgets, and control over technology acquisition. The consolidation of payers is expected to reduce medical spending by 8 percent from administrative simplification and 5 percent by reducing fraud and abuse.

LACK OF THEORY TO UNDERSTAND MEDICAL-EXPENDITURE GROWTH

The United States already spends nearly one fifth of its overall economy on health care and is expected to continue growing at unsustainable levels. Health care spending is a primary issue in the debate over how to control the federal deficit and rebound the general economy. Thus, it is important to understand the determinants of medical-expenditure growth. One way to better understand why the United States has such high levels of health care cost growth is to look at the growth in health care input costs, such as investments needed to keep up with technological advances and also to pay for the workforce.

The health care workforce has been growing faster than all other sectors of the economy (Bureau of Labor Statistics, 2011). Other industries—in particular manufacturing and retail—downsized their workforce due to the economic downturn, outsourcing, and substitution of workers with technologies like information technology (IT). These laid-off workers sought work where people were still needed; health care is one of the most human capital–intensive industries that demand new workers, and has absorbed many of the laid-off workers. A slowdown in the growth of the health care workforce is subtly occurring though; while the reasons are unclear, it's possibly due to a constraint in the pipeline of workers coming from other industries combined with trends of individuals aging into and out of the health care workforce.

The growth in the health care workforce comes from the growth in administrative, and clinical and technical support occupations. The increase in administrative occupation is a reflection of the administratively complex nature of the U.S. medical system. The increase in clinical and technical support staff reflects the need for workers with technical skills to complement the delivery of services from the complex technologies and procedures. Reflecting the job trends, Frogner (2010) found that health care labor costs are higher in the United States than in other countries due to (1) a higher per capita ratio of administrative and clinical staff (excluding doctors and nurses), (2) the higher average education level of the health care workforce, and (3) a higher return from education generally in the United States compared to other countries.

Frogner shows that, although health care labor costs are higher in the United States than other countries, the rate of health care labor costs growth is similar to the growth of GDP in all countries. Generally, this finding can be interpreted to mean the prices (which are reflective of labor costs) are not driving the growth of medical expenditures. In other words, a cut in labor costs would only get a one-time reduction in medical expenditures, but would not change the trajectory of expenditures. Assuming that price (labor costs) multiplied by quantity (number of workers) roughly equals total expenditures, a slowdown in the growth of medical expenditures would need to come from a slowdown of the growth of the health care labor force. But as mentioned above, the health care work force may already be slowing down due to competing needs from other industries. A further slowdown may occur with effective adoption of HIT to reduce the administrative complexities and duplications in care, increased coordination of care, and more effective use of providers training (e.g., nurse practitioners delivers vaccinations rather than primary care physicians).

CONCLUSION

Price transparency is important, but it is not the panacea. Even when patients are armed with price information, that information often comes too late at or after the point of care. Uninsured individuals are often not empowered to negotiate with providers and insurers. Price transparency does not help in areas where there is a strong market concentration of either providers or insurers. Where oligopolies exist, collusion in pricing may occur and thus drive up prices rather than reduce prices.

Also much of medical care is preventable whereby early estimates suggest that 70 percent of the total disease burden and its associated costs is preventable (Fries et al., 1993) and over one third of deaths are due to preventable causes (Mokdad et al., 2004). Prevention and early detection to prevent people from entering the medical system is an important strategy to embrace in order to reduce medical spending. Health education could reduce claims by 20 percent (Fries et al., 1998), and increasing the use of preventive health services to 90 percent could save $3.7 billion in the health system (Maciosek et al., 2010).

Opinion leaders believe transparency will only bring down medical expenditures by a small amount; they believe quality of care and patient experience may be more important priorities in medical care. Several avenues exist to reduce medical expenditures and new ways are introduced by ACA, such as the proliferation of accountable care organizations and bundled payments. Further research is necessary to fully understand the mechanism by which to slow down the growth of medical spending.

REFERENCES AND FURTHER READING

Altman, S. H., Shactman, D., & Eilat, E. (2006). Could U.S. hospitals go the way of U.S. airlines? *Health Affairs, 25*(1), 11–21.

Anderson, G. F., & Frogner, B. F. (2008). Health spending in OECD countries: Obtaining value per dollar. *Health Affairs, 27*(6), 1718–1727.

Bundorf, M. K. (2010). The effects of offering health plan choice within employment-based purchasing groups. *Journal of Risk and Insurance, 77*(1), 105–127.

Bureau of Labor Statistics. (2011). *Current employment statistics: Employment, hours, and earnings—National.* Retrieved from http://www.bls.gov/data/#employment

Chernew, M. E., Hirth, R. A., & Cutler, D. M. (2003). Increased spending on health care: How much can the United States afford? *Health Affairs, 22*(4), 15–25.

Chernew, M. E., Sabik, L. M., Chandra, A., Gibson, T. B., & Newhouse J. P. (2010). Geographic correlation between large-firm commercial spending and Medicare spending. *American Journal of Managed Care, 16*(2), 131–138.

Cutler, D., & Dafny, L. (2011). Designing transparency systems for medical care prices. *The New England Journal of Medicine, 364*(10), 894–895.

Cutler, D. M., Rosen, A. B., & Vijan, S. (2006). The value of medical spending in the United States, 1960–2000. *New England Journal of Medicine, 355*(9), 920–927.

Davis, K., Schoen, C., Guterman, S., Shih, T., Schoenbaum, S. C., & Weinbaum, I. (2007). *Slowing the growth of US health care expenditures: What are the options?* (The Commonwealth Fund, Commission on a High Performance Health System Pub. No. 989). Retrieved from http://www.commonwealthfund.org/usr_doc/Davis_slowinggrowthUShltcareexpenditureswhatareoptions_989.pdf

Dranove, D., Shanley, M., & White, W. D. (1993). Price and concentration in hospital markets: The switch from patient-driven to payer-driven competition. *Journal of Law and Economics, 36*(1), 179–204.

Farrell, D., Jensen, E., Kocher, B., Lovegrove, N., Melhem, F., Mendonca, L., & Parish, B. (2008, December). *Accounting for the cost of U.S. health care: A new look at why Americans spend more.* Retrieved from McKinsey Global Institute website: http://www.mckinsey.com/Insights/MGI/Research/Americas/Accounting_for_the_cost_of_US_health_care

Farrell, K. S., Finocchio, L. J., Trivedi, A. N., & Mehrotra, A. (2010). Does price transparency legislation allow the uninsured to shop for care? *Journal of General Internal Medicine, 25*(2), 110–114.

Fisher, E. (2005). More care is not better care. *Expert Voices, 7.* Retrieved from National Institute for Health Care Management website: http://nihcm.org/pdf/ExpertV7.pdf

Fisher, E., Bynum, J., & Skinner, J. (2009). *The policy implications of variations in Medicare spending growth: A Dartmouth Atlas Project brief report.* Retrieved from http://www.dartmouthatlas.org/downloads/reports/Policy_Implications_Brief_022709.pdf

Fries, J. F., Koop, C. E., Beadle, C. E., Cooper, P. P., England, M. J., Greaves, R. F., & the Health Project Consortium. (1993). Reducing health care costs by reducing the need and demand for medical services. *The New England Journal of Medicine, 329*(5), 321–325.

Fries, J. F., Koop, C. E., Sokolov, J., Beadle, C. E., & Wright, D. (1998). Beyond health promotion: Reducing need and demand for medical care. *Health Affairs, 17*(2), 70–84.

Frogner, B. K. (2010). The missing technology: An international comparison of human capital investment in healthcare. *Applied Health Economics and Health Policy, 8*(6), 361–371.

Gilmer, T. P., & Kronick, R. G. (2011). Differences in the volume of services and in prices drive big variations in Medicaid spending among US states and regions. *Health Affairs, 30*(7), 1316–1324.

Ginsburg, P. (2007). Shopping for price in medical care: Insurers are best positioned to provide consumers with information they need, but will they deliver? *Health Affairs, 26*(2), w208–w216.

Hussey, P. S., Anderson, G. F., Osborn, R., Feek, C., McLaughlin, V., Millar, J., & Epstein, A. (2004). How does the quality of care compare in five countries? *Health Affairs, 23*(3), 89–99.

Kelly, R. (2009). *Where can $700 billion in waste be cut annually from the U.S. healthcare system?* Retrieved from http://thomsonreuters.com/content/healthcare/pdf/white_papers/TR-7261_WASTE_WHITE_PAPER.pdf

LoSasso, A. T., Shah, M., & Frogner, B. K. (2010). Health savings accounts and health care spending, *Health Services Research, 45*(4), 1041–1060.

Love, D., Custer, W., & Miller, P. (2010, September). All-payer claims databases: State initiatives to improve health care transparency. *Issue Brief.* The Commonwealth Fund.

Maciosek, M. V., Cofield, A. B., Flottemesch, T. J., Edwards, N. M., & Solberg, L. I. (2010). Greater use of preventive services in US health care could save lives at little or no cost. *Health Affairs, 29*(9), 1656–1660.

Manning, W. G., Newhouse, J. P., Duan, N., Keeler, E. B., & Leibowitz, A. (1987). Health insurance and the demand for medical care: Evidence from a randomized experiment. *American Economic Review, 77*(3), 251–277.

Maxwell, J., & Temin, P. (2003). Corporate management of quality in employee health plans. *Health Care Management Review, 28*(1), 27–40.

Medicare Payment Advisory Commission (MEDPAC). (2009). *Report to the Congress; Medicare payment policy.* Retrieved from http://www.medpac.gov/documents/Mar09_EntireReport.pdf

Melnick, G., Zwanziger, J., Bamezai, A., & Pattison, R. (1992). The effects of market structure and bargaining position on hospital prices. *Journal of Health Economics, 11*, 217–233.

Mokdad, A. H., Marks, J. S., Stroup, D. F., & Gerberding, J. L. (2004). Actual causes of death in the United States, 2000. *Journal of the American Medical Association. 291*(10), 1238–1245.

Morra, D., Nicholson, S., Levinson, W., Gans, D. N., Hammons, T., & Casalino, L. P. (2011). US physician practices versus Canadians: Spending nearly four times as much money interacting with payers. *Health Affairs.* doi: 10.1377/hlthaff.2010.0893

Murray, R. (2009). Setting hospital rates to control costs and boost quality: The Maryland experience. *Health Affairs, 28*(5), 1395–1405.

New England Health Care Institute (NEHI). (2008). *Waste and inefficiency in the U.S. health care system.* Retrieved from http://www.nehi.net/publications/27/clinical_care_a_comprehensive_analysis_in_support_of_system_wide_improvements

Newhouse, J. P. (1992). Medical care costs: How much welfare loss? *Journal of Economic Perspectives, 6*(3), 3–22.

Robinson, J. (2011). Hospitals respond to Medicare payment shortfalls by both shifting costs and cutting them, based on market concentration. *Health Affairs, 30*(7), 1265–1271.

Rosenthal, M. B., Landon, B. E., Normand, S. T., Frank, R. G., Ahmad, T. S., & Epstein, A. M. (2007). Employers' use of value-based purchasing strategies. *Journal of the American Medical Association, 298*(19), 2281–2288.

Sinaiko, A., & Rosenthal, M. (2011). Increased price transparency in health care—Challenges and potential effects. *The New England Journal of Medicine, 364*(10), 891–894.

Skinner, J. (2011). Understanding prices and quantities in the U.S. health care system. *Journal of Health Politics, Policy and Law, 36*(4), 792–801.

Thorpe, K. E., Ogden, L. L., & Galactionova, K. (2010). Chronic conditions account for rise in Medicare spending from 1987 to 2006. *Health Affairs, 29*(4), 718–724.

Tu, H., & Lauer, J. (2009). Impact of health care price transparency on price variation: The New Hampshire experience. *Issue Brief, 128.* Center for Studying Health System Change.

Wennberg, J. E., Brownlee, S., Fisher, E. S., Skinner, J. S., & Weinstein, J. N. (2008). An agenda for change: Improving quality and curbing health care spending: Opportunities for the Congress and the Obama administration. *Dartmouth Atlas White Paper.* Retrieved from http://www.dartmouthatlas.org/downloads/reports/agenda_for_change.pdf

Bianca K. Frogner

Accountable Care Organizations

POINT: There is growing consensus that the U.S. health care system could and should deliver better value—improved health outcomes and a slower cost-growth trajectory—through delivery system reform. Accountable care organizations (ACOs) are a central element of this reform and are designed to better align payment incentives to achieve more coordinated care and reduce medical spending.

David H. Howard and Cynthia Zeldin, Emory University

COUNTERPOINT: There is remarkably little evidence that integrated delivery systems, the antecedent to ACOs, reduce costs. By encouraging mergers between health care providers, ACOs may increase costs to private payers, who, unlike Medicare, must negotiate with providers over reimbursement rates.

David H. Howard and Cynthia Zeldin, Emory University

Introduction

A key strategy in the Affordable Care Act (ACA) for encouraging quality improvement efforts in the health care system and cost control is to promote the formation of accountable care organizations (ACOs), which can be defined as groups of providers that are held accountable for the cost and quality for a defined population of patients. This definition may appear overly simplistic, but, in actuality, there is a great deal of flexibility in how ACOs can be structured. For example, the number and mix of primary care providers and specialists within an ACO's provider network can look very different from one ACO to the next. The governance structure can also vary, ranging from a single entity that owns multiple physician groups and hospitals (typically known as an integrated delivery system) to loosely affiliated groups of providers, each independently owned, that may be sharing a health information exchange network.

There is also flexibility in terms of how ACOs will be held accountable for patient care and costs. In general, this is achieved by moving provider payment systems away from the predominant fee-for-service method, which rewards providers for delivering more care regardless of the value or quality of that care. Instead, ACO payments are based on predetermined budgeted amounts to encourage providers to become more efficient. Delinking payments from specific services also frees up money for providers to invest in potentially high-value services and products, such as telemedicine and other health information technology advancements, which may not be reimbursable under current fee-for-service arrangements. In addition, ACO payments will be linked to their ability to meet quality standards, helping ensure that ACOs are not stinting on necessary care in order to stay under budget and to encourage continuous quality improvement efforts.

In fact, providers participating in ACO contracts will be expected to continually evolve in how they are structured, with the goal of becoming increasingly proficient in achieving high-value outcomes and in their ability to take on fixed upfront payments with performance-based incentives. This means that the technical details of the contractual arrangements may need to change over time in order to best support providers depending on how far along they are in terms of investing and implementing innovative new ways to deliver care and building up an infrastructure for rapid-cycle information sharing and evaluation so that gaps in care can quickly and constantly be addressed.

In other words, the ACO framework is more about functional requirements rather than structural requirements. ACOs will need to show specific plans for how they will improve the way they deliver care, which includes being able to manage the full spectrum of patient needs and the ability to provide meaningful evidence that those plans are meeting high performance standards. This framework largely emanated from the work conducted by researchers at Dartmouth University, notably Elliot Fisher and Jonathan Skinner, who popularized the notion of ACOs. They used existing patterns in where Medicare patients were going for their care, to create "virtually" integrated organizations comprised of physicians and their associated local acute care hospitals. The key feature of the patterns is that the Medicare patients tended to stay within these virtual networks for most of their care. Note that these virtual organizations could be organized in a vast variety of ways and the providers within those organizations may not even have a formal legal relationship with each other (as they are empirically defined). However, the key feature shared by the providers within each network is that they treat a lot of the same patients over time. Hence, Fisher and colleagues contend these networks of providers are in a good position to take accountability for the care of those patients.

Fisher and colleagues describe the conceptual development of virtual organizations in a 2007 *Health Affairs* article titled "Creating Accountable Care Organizations: The Extended Hospital Medical Staff." Their aim was to find the right "locus of shared accountability" for the health of patients. They note that at the time of the paper, most pay-for-performance activities that aimed to make providers more accountable for the quality of care they delivered focused on individual providers and specific provider-patient interactions. Moreover, they contend that this focus is misplaced if the goal is to generate systemwide transformations in the way health care is delivered, in order to improve overall patient health while reducing their overall costs. Rather, high-performing care requires coordination across provider settings (e.g., primary care doctors, specialists, hospitals) as a patient makes his or her way through the health care system. Thus, some form of shared accountability by providers may be more appropriate.

Since that 2007 paper was written, the ACO concept has grown well beyond the notion of having providers organized based upon empirical analyses of patients' historical referral patterns. Today, hundreds of physician groups, hospitals, and other provider types are reorganizing themselves into more formal arrangements in order to participate in an ACO contract with a payer. The ACA has authorized a new Medicare program for ACOs, the Medicare Shared Savings Program, with multiple tracks to accommodate the varying degrees of provider readiness to participate in such models. In addition, a more advanced ACO program, the Pioneer Model, is being tested under Medicare that is geared towards provider groups that have already exhibited success with managing patient care across the full spectrum of services they need and with taking on payments that require managing care within a prospectively determined budget. Several private payers have also initiated ACO contracts. One of the largest examples is the Alternative Quality Contract (AQC) program administered by Blue Cross Blue Shield of Massachusetts. In 2011, there were 12 ACOs participating in the model, covering about 500,000 patients.

All of this activity is occurring even though there is little evidence about ACO impacts on cost and quality of care. The largest ACO initiative that has been evaluated to date is the five-year Medicare Physician Group Practice (PGP) Demonstration program, which featured 10 generally well-established, large and advanced multi-specialty group practices, such as Dartmouth-Hitchcock Clinic and Geisinger Health Systems. According to the July 2011 fact sheet on the PGP demonstration available on the Centers for Medicare & Medicaid Services website, all sites exhibited some quality improvements. However, their ability to reduce costs was more sobering as only half of the sites were able to reduce costs below budgeted amounts. It should be noted though that the experience was promising enough that all 10 sites have decided to continue participating in Medicare ACO activities.

The AQC program is still relatively new having started in 2009. As such, only first-year evaluation results have been published at the time of this writing. The results reported by Zirui Song and colleagues in their September 2011 *New England Journal of Medicine* article titled "Health Care Spending and Quality in Year 1 of the Alternative Quality Contract" seem to follow a similar pattern as the PGP demonstration. That is, modestly lower medical spending with slightly better evidence for quality improvement gains.

Thus, the ACO movement continues on but without much empirical evidence that it will work. Moreover, the flexibility in terms of structural requirements to participate in such programs works to encourage broad participation. This is leading to significant investments being made by providers and payers to participate in these programs. In this debate, David Howard and Cynthia Zeldin offer some additional insights on whether we should be concerned about the prospects of these investments leading to a good return in the form of health care quality improvements and cost control.

The Point begins with additional background on the rationale for ACOs and the need to encourage providers to practice more accountable care. While the ACO concept has not been well tested, the current system is obviously broken and the aims of the ACO appear to directly address the systemic problems of our health care system—fragmentation, lack of care coordination, lack of data to support care coordination and high-value decisions, and wrong payment incentives that reward inefficient care. From this perspective, even if the ACO model fails to achieve significant savings, it should at least help develop the foundation for the types of changes in the health care system that will eventually need to occur in order to "bend the cost curve."

The Counterpoint highlights the lack of evidence and the fact that similar movements to promote more coordinated and integrated care, such as with health maintenance organizations (HMOs), have failed in the past. In addition, there may be reasons to believe that not only will ACOs fail to reduce costs, but they may actually lead to increased spending. That is, the ACO movement may accelerate the already existing trend of provider consolidation. Instead of consolidating for the purpose of improving their ability to coordinate care, the main consequence may be to give them better leverage to negotiate higher prices with providers.

It will be critical to evaluate the progress and impacts of ACOs as quickly as possible to ensure that such unintended consequences are avoided. Given the large task at hand for ACOs—essentially requiring a complete culture change from how medicine is currently practiced—and the large number of ACO initiatives expected to occur in the near future, it will also be interesting to see how much time these initiatives will be given to prove themselves.

POINT

Over the past twenty years, the United States has seen an increase in the prevalence of chronic conditions such as diabetes, hypertension, and heart disease. Further, according to the U.S. Department of Health and Human Services, more than a quarter of Americans have multiple chronic conditions, and two thirds of Americans over age 65 have multiple chronic conditions. Primary care level intervention can help patients manage these conditions and allow them to function and remain productive. However, treatment is often condition specific, and a patient with multiple conditions may be under the care of multiple providers. If that care is not coordinated, a range of problems can result: Duplication, waste, and even harm to patients can occur if, for example, multiple drugs with negative interactions are prescribed.

With the exception of a handful of existing integrated delivery systems, health care delivery in the United States is characterized by fragmentation. Patients receive care from a range of providers, who may or may not communicate with each other. Although there have been recent efforts to employ electronic records, a patient-centered electronic medical record with information about a patient's treatment across multiple providers is the exception, not the norm. Providers may also order the same tests for the same patient because they don't have access to one another's results, leading to inefficiencies.

Compounding this fragmentation and duplication is the fee-for-service reimbursement system. Fee-for-service is the predominant form of physician payment in the United States and is characterized by a reimbursement system in which providers receive payment from third-party payers (such as Medicare or private health insurance companies) for the individual medical services they provide to their patients. Physicians receive a payment for each service they provide. As such, providers are rewarded financially for a higher volume and intensity of procedures and tests, creating a strong incentive for medical overutilization. Accountable care organizations (ACOs) are a vehicle for changing the way that hospitals and physicians are paid to encourage more cost-effective care without adversely affecting patient outcomes.

WHAT ARE ACCOUNTABLE CARE ORGANIZATIONS?

An ACO is a system of providers who are held accountable for meeting quality metrics and cost targets for a defined population of patients. ACOs must have the capacity to coordinate and deliver care across a range of conditions. They face payment incentives to reduce costs and are eligible for bonuses for improving various quality measures.

Unlike most managed care plans, which are essentially health insurers, ACOs are provider-driven organizations that treat large numbers of patients. ACOs can take a variety of forms (e.g., a multispecialty group practice, physician-hospital organization, independent practice association, or integrated delivery system), but, unlike an insurance plan that simply contracts with providers, an ACO must directly provide medical services or be able to arrange for those services, and it is accountable for their quality and cost even if the services are provided by physicians it does not directly employ.

ACOs adopt strategies, such as interoperable electronic medical records, the patient-centered medical home, and integrated delivery systems, to improve the quality of care for patients with complex chronic conditions. They do not focus on a single medical condition or body part. Instead, ACOs ensure that the medical interventions a patient receives are coordinated to maximize efficiency, patient safety, and health outcomes.

Under the ACO conceptual framework, groups of providers (including physicians, hospitals, and other provider types) voluntarily work together to better coordinate and manage care for a population of patients. While there is a great deal of flexibility in the types of providers that can participate and how they reorganize themselves in order to improve the way they manage care for their patients, several characteristics are to be expected. These include an infrastructure that makes available relevant patient information to all providers as the patient makes his or her way through the health care system. ACOs are also expected to have the ability to use that information to identify gaps in care, develop best practices, and, in general, continually improve the way care is delivered while also making it more cost efficient.

HOW DO ACCOUNTABLE CARE ORGANIZATIONS DIFFER FROM EXISTING PAYMENT ARRANGEMENTS?

The ACO model was developed with an eye toward the lessons learned from earlier, failed attempts at payment reform. According to a recent analysis by the Urban Institute, the three defining characteristics of ACOs are (1) shared savings (bonuses based on health care cost growth below projections based on their own historic spending), (2) accountability for quality based on metrics, and (3) free choice of providers by patients.

ACOs are not managed care plans. In the 1990s the dominant insurance model began to shift away from open-ended plans and toward managed care plans. The key features of managed care plans—such as utilization review, restricted physician networks, and capitation—restrained costs for a short period of time. However, a managed care backlash ensued in response to these restrictions—patients sensed the conflict between a drive to reduce costs and the quality of care—and they were subsequently loosened.

Policymakers, wary of upsetting consumers by encouraging the proliferation of tightly restricted managed care models but also faced with mounting evidence that fee-for-service encouraged overuse, began looking to payment-reform models that better aligned patient, provider, and insurer incentives to rein in cost growth and improve quality.

Unlike managed care plans, ACOs do not place restrictions on networks or restrict access to certain providers or procedures. ACOs are provider driven and are focused on improving quality of care. Tensions between costs and patient care are difficult to avoid, but ACOs do a better job of aligning providers' financial incentives with patient outcomes.

PREVIOUS EXPERIENCE WITH ACCOUNTABLE CARE ORGANIZATIONS

Although specific guidelines in the 2010 Patient Protection and Affordable Care Act (ACA) establish a framework for providers transitioning to an ACO model and encourage their rapid development, the concept underlying ACOs is not new. Some of the better known examples of ACO-like entities include Intermountain Healthcare in Utah, in which physicians are on salary, electronic medical records are utilized, and there is a systemwide focus on identifying and implementing evidence-based protocols; and Geisinger Health System in Pennsylvania, which has improved its outcomes through a focus on employing best practices as standard protocol and has implemented other payment reforms, for example a single bundled payment for certain episodes such as heart surgery. There is strong evidence that these systems are successful; however, whether they can be replicated on a widespread scale is unknown.

The inclusion of ACOs in the ACA also builds upon the Medicare Physician Group Practice Demonstration that offered bonus payments on top of regular fee-for-service payments to participating providers who were able to improve performance on defined quality metrics while lowering cost growth. Ten sites participated in the demonstration, and at the end of the fourth year, all of them had achieved targets in the vast majority of the measured areas. Five of the ten generated savings and received bonuses. However, a study of the project described in the *New England Journal of Medicine* (Iglehart, 2011) noted that some of the participating health systems were already on a trajectory that would lead to these favorable outcomes. This raises the issue of whether systems without a similar emphasis and commitment would find the incentive of the shared savings bonus payment sufficient to change course, or whether institutions predisposed to move toward a more value-based model would do so regardless of the bonus dollars on the table.

Further, there is some concern that, though the incentives to reduce overutilization within primary care may be attractive, ACOs may be less effective in curbing the use of costly care by specialists such as cardiologists. Incentives to reduce costs may not be sufficiently strong to offset the incentives that entice specialists to provide more care.

Although the Medicare program will serve as the primary vehicle for encouraging the formation of ACOs, many private payers are already establishing ACO-like agreements with providers. Many of these efforts are in their infancy, and so it is too early to judge whether they will be effective in reducing costs or improving quality. Still, the fact that private insurers and providers are forming ACOs on their own suggests that ACOs are not simply a regulatory creation of the ACA, imposed on an unwilling health system. They are a viable model for health care delivery.

ACCOUNTABLE CARE ORGANIZATIONS AND THE AFFORDABLE CARE ACT

The ACA authorizes the Medicare program to contract with ACOs. Given Medicare's clout as a payer, changes in the way Medicare operates have an effect on the entire health system.

The ACA sets out the basic requirements to qualify as an ACO: a legal structure; formal leadership and management; a commitment to and capacity for patient-centered care; inclusion of primary care providers with at least 5,000 Medicare beneficiaries; and agreement to terms of payment, primarily a "shared savings" approach (although other payment models, such as partial capitation, are allowed). The shared savings approach essentially builds on fee-for-service Medicare by grafting on top of it bonus payments for meeting certain criteria related to achieving quality benchmarks and financial targets. The law also created the Center for Medicare & Medicaid Innovation within the Centers for Medicare & Medicaid Services (CMS) to test and evaluate innovative payment and delivery models for Medicare, Medicaid, and the Children's Health Insurance Program.

In fall 2011, CMS issued its final rule on ACOs, addressing many of the concerns expressed about the proposed rule issued earlier that year. That rule, which had received extensive critical feedback (more than 1,200 formal comments), had laid out two possible models for the shared savings program for Medicare ACOs. ACOs that were not immediately prepared to take on the risk of sharing in the losses if they did not meet benchmarks right away could share in a smaller portion of savings in the first two years and move in the third year to accepting risk. ACOs could also opt to immediately take on the risk of sharing losses and larger shared savings.

The rule also proposed measures for ACO quality performance standards. These included care metrics associated with patient and caregiver experience, care transitions (for example, 30-day post-discharge physician visits), information systems for care coordination (such as the percentage of primary care providers meeting meaningful use requirements for health information technology), and patient safety (such as attempts to limit patients' exposure to hospital-acquired infections). They also included metrics aimed at improved health, such as preventive health (e.g., appropriate screenings) and the maintenance of chronic conditions such as diabetes, hypertension, and coronary artery disease.

The final rule made the following key adjustments: The requirement to accept risk by the third year was removed and providers allowed to participate in "shared savings" within Medicare without the risk of losing money; the proposed quality measures were reduced from 65 measures in 5 domains to 33 measures in 4 domains; electronic medical records are no longer a condition of participation but are weighted higher as a quality measure; and community health centers and rural health clinics will be allowed to lead ACOs.

CAUSE FOR OPTIMISM

Although the evidence that ACOs will transform the delivery system is mixed, the ACO model attempts to align provider and patient interests, addresses the growing issue of patients with multiple chronic conditions and the associated need for better integrated care, and aims to slow the rate of health care cost growth in a way that will not demonstrably harm consumers. It has become a common sentiment in health care policy that there is no silver bullet when it comes to reining in costs, and the hype surrounding ACOs could overstate their actual impact. Still, as a tool to make quality improvements in defined areas and modestly slow cost growth in some areas of health care, ACOs show promise.

REFERENCES AND FURTHER READING

Berenson, R. A., & Burton, R. A. (2011). *Accountable care organizations in Medicare and the private sector: A status update.* Retrieved from Urban Institute website: http://www.urban.org/publications/412438.html

Berwick, D. M. (2011). Launching accountable care organizations—The proposed rule for the Medicare shared savings program. *New England Journal of Medicine, 364,* e32.

Berwick, D. M. (2011). Making good on ACOs' promise—The final rule for the Medicare shared savings program. *New England Journal of Medicine, 365*(19), 1753–1756.

Dentzer, S. (2010). Geisinger Chief Glenn Steele: Seizing health reform's potential to build a superior system. *Health Affairs, 29*(6), 1200–1207. doi: 10.1377/hlthaff.2010.0517

Goldsmith, J. (2011). Accountable care organizations: The case for flexible partnerships between health plans and providers. *Health Affairs, 30*(1), 32–40. doi: 10.1377/hlthaff.2010.0782

Guterman, S., Schoenbaum, S. C., Davis, K., Schoen, C., Audet, A. J., Stremikis, K., & Zezza, M. A. (2011). *High performance accountable care: Building on success and learning from experience.* Retrieved from The Commonwealth Fund website: http://www.commonwealthfund.org/Publications/Fund-Reports/2011/Apr/High-Performance-Accountable-Care.aspx?page=all

Iglehart, J. K. (2011). Assessing an ACO prototype—Medicare's physician group practice demonstration. *New England Journal of Medicine, 364*(3), 198–200.

Leonhardt, D. (2009, November 3). Making health care better. *The New York Times.* Retrieved from http://www.nytimes.com/2009/11/08/magazine/08Healthcare-t.html?pagewanted=all

McClellan, M., McKethan, A. N., Lewis, J. L., Roski, J., & Fisher, E. S. (2010). A national strategy to put accountable care into practice. *Health Affairs, 29*(5), 982–990. doi: 10.1377/hlthaff.2010.0194

U.S. Department of Health and Human Services. (2010). *Multiple chronic conditions—A strategic framework: Optimum health and quality of life for individuals with multiple chronic condition, 126.* Washington, DC: Author.

David H. Howard and Cynthia Zeldin

COUNTERPOINT

Integrated delivery systems combine multiple physicians in a single organization with treatment protocols to improve the quality of care, electronic medical records to track patients' care and conditions, and other organizational innovations to improve quality and reduce costs. Although the Medicare program does not limit participation in accountable care organizations (ACOs) to integrated delivery systems, they are clearly the type of system that supporters have in mind when they tout the benefits of ACOs. The integrated delivery system is centered on characteristics similar to those envisioned for the ideal ACO.

Many health policy experts have promoted integrated delivery systems as the ideal model for delivering health care services. Examples of integrated delivery systems include Kaiser Permanente, which operates in multiple states, the Geisinger Clinic in Pennsylvania, and the Mayo Clinic in Minnesota. The assertion that integrated delivery systems deliver higher quality at lower cost has been repeated so often and by so many prominent figures in American medical care that it has taken on a life of its own. However, the evidence to back up these claims is relatively sparse. Only a few providers can correctly be classified as integrated delivery systems. Our knowledge of the impact of integrated delivery systems on costs is based on the experience of this small group.

Many studies have shown that patients at integrated delivery systems are more likely to receive recommended screenings and that integrated delivery systems are more likely to use electronic medical records and care protocols for patients with chronic diseases (Tollen, 2008). All of these factors are indirect measures of quality. They do not provide direct evidence as to whether patients treated at integrated delivery systems experience better outcomes or, more importantly, incur lower costs.

A handful of frequently cited studies have directly compared the costs incurred by patients in integrated delivery systems and patients treated in more traditional, nonintegrated settings (e.g., Agency for Healthcare Research and Quality 2008). Although the studies find that patients in integrated delivery systems incur lower costs, these findings should be viewed cautiously. Patients who enroll in integrated delivery systems may be healthier than those who chose traditional systems, and so the lower costs of integrated systems reflect differences in patient characteristics rather than the causal impact of integrated systems.

Regional differences in health care spending also make it difficult to compare integrated and nonintegrated delivery systems. Health care costs are determined by local practice patterns. For reasons not completely understood, physicians in some areas of the country practice a higher-cost style of medicine—they order more tests and perform more surgeries—than do physicians in other parts of the country. In this way, integrated delivery systems located in low-cost regions might create an inaccurate impression that integrated delivery systems reduce costs. For example, the Mayo Clinic in Rochester, Minnesota, is often held up as an example of a well-functioning, low-cost integrated delivery system. Yet, according to the Dartmouth Atlas of Health Care, Minnesota is a low-cost state, ranked 43rd out of 51 in terms of Medicare payments per enrollee (adjusted for geographic differences in reimbursement levels).

More recent evidence on the ability of ACOs to reduce costs is available from the Physician Group Practice Demonstration, a Medicare demonstration project to test the ACO concept with 10 large physician group practices. Many, like the Marshfield Clinic in Wisconsin, are cited as examples of the types of integrated delivery systems that providers will develop under the ACO program.

Participating practices were eligible to receive bonuses if they improved quality measures (e.g., the fraction of diabetics receiving routine eye exams) and held cost increases to two percentage points below a regional benchmark. For example, if costs in the regional benchmark increased by 7 percent and costs in the participating provider group increased by only 4 percent, a difference of three percentage points, the provider would be eligible for a bonus. The results, released in 2011 after the passage of the ACA, were mixed. At the end of the fifth year, all of the groups showed improvements in most of the quality measures. However, only half of the groups held costs below the regional benchmark, achieving savings of $134 million over the first five years, $110 million of which was paid in bonuses to the providers (the remainder was retained by Medicare) (Centers for Medicare & Medicaid Services, 2011; Iglehart, 2011). Although the savings were modest, all sites agreed to an extension.

The providers that participated in the demonstration were all large academic medical centers or well-known, large provider groups (e.g., the Marshfield Clinic in Wisconsin and the Everett Clinic in Washington state). These are the types of groups most expected to perform well as ACOs. However, as discussed above, several of the groups were not able to achieve savings. In addition, costs at these clinics may have increased at a lower rate than the regional average even in the absence of the bonus program, and so it is difficult to determine whether the Physician Group Practice Demonstration really reduced the rate of cost growth. The evaluators of the demonstration looked into this issue by simulating what the participants' performance would have been in the years prior to the demonstration (Centers for Medicare & Medicaid Services, 2009). They found evidence that the sites that actually achieved savings during the demonstration were likely to have achieved savings prior to the demonstration. Hence, the savings achieved in the demonstration simply may have been due to preexisting trends in those communities.

Even if existing integrated delivery systems are able to successfully reduce costs, it does not automatically follow that newly created integrated delivery systems will realize short-term cost savings. Most existing integrated delivery systems have been in place for decades. They have built up stable rosters of physicians and other providers who are invested in the system, its values, and its modes of operation. Physicians who believe in the benefits of primary, preventive care, and are skeptical about the benefits of high-tech specialty care, may be attracted to the type of low-pressure, collaborative environment offered by integrated delivery systems.

Some integrated systems, notably Kaiser Permanente and the Mayo Clinic, have opened satellite locations. Originally based in the Northwest, Kaiser Permanente now operates health plans in Hawaii and Atlanta, Georgia. The Mayo Clinic has expanded beyond its original Minnesota location to Jacksonville, Florida, and Phoenix, Arizona. Though there are few data with which to compare the performance of these new locations with that of the flagship sites, these examples suggest that the concept of integrated delivery systems are somewhat transferrable, at least within organizations. However, it may be difficult for newly created ACOs, which lack the long tradition of organized delivery and the panel of physicians to practice a low-cost style of medicine, to achieve the same level of success.

Blue Cross Blue Shield of Massachusetts (BCBS MA) recently started an ACO-like program, the "Alternative Quality Contract," for providers in that state. Again, participants in this program are fairly advanced in terms of their ability and experience with coordinating care. During its first year, the program achieved a modest reduction in the rate of cost growth. Quarterly costs per enrollee increased by $53 for providers subject to the Alternative Quality Contract, compared to $69 for a group of providers that continued to receive traditional fee-for-service reimbursement (Song et al., 2011). However, most of the savings were obtained by shifting patients to lower-cost providers, rather than through reductions in health care use, suggesting that these are one-time savings. Moving forward, it would be more impressive if the participants exhibit evidence for the type of system redesign that leads to long-term reductions in the rate of cost growth.

ACOs WILL INCREASE PRICES

Total health care spending equals price times quantity. Supporters hope that ACOs will lower the quantity of medical care consumed. By design, ACOs will not affect Medicare prices. The prices Medicare pays physicians and hospitals for medical care (i.e., reimbursement rates) are set via a complex set of formulas. Physicians and hospitals decide whether or not to participate in the Medicare program—and almost all do participate, given that over 47 million people are enrolled in Medicare—but once they have decided to participate they must accept Medicare's payment rates. Providers cannot bargain for higher reimbursement rates. The same is not true of private insurers, who, unlike Medicare, cannot simply dictate reimbursement rates to providers. Instead, prices are negotiated between private insurers and physicians and hospitals.

Insurers' ability to negotiate lower reimbursement rates depends on their bargaining power with providers. When there is a competitive market with lots of providers delivering comparable services, insurers can negotiate lower prices by threatening to exclude providers from their networks. Providers who face little competition and who provide unique services in the market are in a position to negotiate higher reimbursement rates.

Providers' negotiating power varies from market to market, but typically primary care physicians and family care physicians, who practice in small groups, are price takers. Insurers offer a standard contract and schedule of payment rates, and the physicians decide whether or not to accept patients from the insurer.

Specialist physicians, like interventional cardiologists, are in a stronger bargaining position. Large specialty groups may bargain with insurers for higher reimbursement rates. Large, university-affiliated teaching hospitals are also able to negotiate for higher payment rates. Teaching hospitals offer many services not available at other hospitals. Because of these offerings and their reputations as high-quality providers, teaching hospitals are "must haves" in insurers' provider networks. An insurer that tried to sell a plan that did not include the major teaching hospitals in a region would lose customers.

Provider consolidation increases providers' ability to negotiate higher payment rates. For example, Brigham and Women's Hospital and Massachusetts General Hospital are large teaching hospitals in Boston affiliated with Harvard Medical School. Prior to 1994 these hospitals operated independently. In 1994 the hospitals formed an entity, Partners Healthcare, to negotiate payment rates with insurers. Insurers could not realistically exclude these world-famous institutions from their provider networks, and so Partners Healthcare was in a strong position to negotiate higher payment rates. Insurers and consumer advocates have charged that prices and premiums have increased in the wake of the merger.

ACOs, by promoting integration between providers, will reduce the degree of competition between providers in the marketplace (Dranove, 2010; Goldsmith, 2011). Instead of bargaining with providers individually, insurance companies will have to bargain with the ACO, representing many physicians and possibly multiple hospitals in a community. As a result, private payers may have to pay higher reimbursement rates, and private insurers' costs will increase. These additional costs would be passed on to consumers in the form of higher premiums and coinsurance.

The Department of Justice (DOJ) and the Federal Trade Commission (FTC) share jurisdiction over federal antitrust cases. Antitrust laws are designed to prevent companies from gaining excess market power. In 2011 the DOJ and FTC released a joint statement describing how they will apply antitrust laws to ACOs (Federal Trade Commission & Department of Justice, 2011). ACOs with limited market shares will fall under a "safety zone" and will not be subject to antitrust enforcement except under "extraordinary circumstances." In brief, the ACO's share of clinical services in its primary services must be no larger than 30 percent. Hospitals must be non-exclusive to the ACO, meaning that private payers should be able to contract with an affiliated hospital without going through the ACO, if they so choose.

While no antitrust reviews are mandated, ACOs outside the safety zone will have a greater risk of being subject to antitrust review by the DOJ or FTC. During a review, either the DOJ or the FTC will apply the "Rule of Reason" in deciding whether the ACO violates antitrust laws. Under that rule, the DOJ and FTC weigh the benefits of integration (i.e., improved coordination) against the costs (i.e., reduced competition). The DOJ and FTC must also consider whether the ACO has taken steps to achieve clinical integration or whether it exists primarily as a mechanism to fix prices.

In trying to encourage integration without stifling competition, the federal government is engaged in a difficult balancing act. Already, anticipation of the growth of ACOs has accelerated a wave of mergers between health care providers. No provider wants to be behind the curve in forming integrated systems. Although the Rule of Reason sounds eminently *reasonable*, it is difficult to apply. As of this writing, the FTC is challenging the merger of two hospitals, ProMedica Health System and St. Luke's Hospital, both of Toledo, Ohio. The hospitals claim that the merger will allow them to provide more efficient care, while the FTC maintains that the combined hospital system could raise prices. At the end of the day, the FTC, the DOJ, and the courts have to decide whether the benefits of integration exceed the costs.

It is conceivable that ACOs will increase quality and prices simultaneously. Vigorous antitrust enforcement can help to blunt the impact of integration on prices, but the presidential administration of Barack Obama, which has a strong stake in the success of the ACO program, may pressure the FTC and DOJ to soft-pedal antitrust enforcement.

ACOs WILL REDUCE QUALITY COMPETITION

In most industries, firms use price and quality to compete for consumers. Though price competition has received a great deal of attention in debates over ACOs, few supporters or critics have addressed quality competition. Some health care experts are skeptical that hospitals and physicians compete over quality. They believe that patients are not informed consumers. Of course, patients can differentiate between a nice waiting room and a shabby one, but do they know which hospital does a better job of performing cardiac bypass surgery? Do they know which oncology group provides the best care for patients with colorectal cancer? Even experts struggle to measure quality in health care and rank providers based on quality.

Advocates for ACOs argue that consolidation and integration will improve quality in health care. Aside from the obvious advantages in terms of improved care coordination, ACOs may steer patients toward experienced providers. For many operations, patients treated by physicians and hospitals that perform more procedures experience better outcomes. For this reason, some health policy experts advocate "regionalizing" certain types of medical care so that patients are referred to a handful of high-volume hospitals and physicians. Although regionalization is not a primary or even a secondary goal of ACOs, the flagship hospitals spearheading the creation of ACOs in many cities clearly hope to increase referrals from community physicians.

But ACOs will reduce competition between providers, and a growing body of research suggests that providers do in fact compete over quality. The conventional view that patients are not good consumers is wrong. Studies of patient choice show that higher quality providers attract more patients. Some patients are sophisticated enough to figure out which providers offer higher quality care, and even unsophisticated patients now have access to a great deal of accessible, nontechnical information about provider quality. Internet "report cards," designed to help patients make informed choices, list provider-specific quality measures for many types of services.

Even if patients have trouble understanding quality measures, insurance companies do not. Insurers use provider networks to steer patients to low-cost, high-quality providers. Providers that don't maintain quality levels risk being dropped from insurers' preferred provider. If ACOs result in provider consolidation, both consumers and insurers will have fewer providers to choose from, and providers will feel less pressure to improve quality.

In summary, ACOs, which are usually justified by their ability to improve patient outcomes, may have the opposite effect if they reduce the degree to which providers compete over quality.

DISECONOMIES OF SCALE

ACOs are symbolic of the belief that, in health care, bigger is better. The benefits of larger providers are fairly obvious. Physicians in integrated delivery systems are able to share information about patients' medical conditions and the services they have received. Armed with this information, physicians can avoid ordering duplicate tests and improve how they coordinate treatment plans with other primary care providers and specialists.

There are also downsides to integration that, though somewhat less tangible than the benefits, are no less real. In economics and management, the terms "diseconomies of scale" and "diseconomies of scope" are used to describe the concept that once organizations reach a certain size, growing larger may actually reduce efficiency (Robinson, 2001). One of the advantages of the much-maligned individual and small-group medical practice—where individual or small groups of doctors essentially operate their own businesses—is that physicians in these types of practices have strong incentives to work hard and be productive. They are both the owners and employees of the practice, and so they will suffer financially from any reduction in their effort. In the case of ACOs, physicians will be part of an organization that employs hundreds or thousands of physicians and so may not work as hard because their impact on the organization's overall financial performance is minimal. Managerial oversight and the collection of quality measures can make up for some of this inevitable diminution in incentives, but it can be difficult for managers to determine which employees are working hard and which are not, especially in technical fields like medicine.

ACOs will offer many different clinical services. There is a risk that, by trying to do everything, ACOs will be good at nothing. Some management experts, such as Harvard Business School's Regina Herzlinger, argue that health care organizations should become "focused factories" that concentrate on a single service or disease. Though there are many examples in the current health system, including dialysis centers, in vitro fertilization clinics, and cardiac specialty hospitals, there are problems with this approach. Many patients require care for multiple conditions simultaneously, and the track record of single-service providers like dialysis centers hasn't always been stellar. Still, there is the risk that ACOs will become so large and unfocused that they have trouble maintaining quality and lowering costs. Many corporations get into trouble when they try to expand beyond their core business, and there is no reason to think that the same won't be true for health care.

THE KAISER QUESTION

Kaiser Permanente is a fully integrated provider and health plan. It uses integrated health care teams to deliver care and provide patients with "one-stop shopping." With the exception of a few services (e.g., liver transplantation), patients receive all the care they need within the Kaiser system. As a health plan, Kaiser receives payments directly from consumers and employers. If Kaiser spends more than it takes in, it loses money. In short, Kaiser seems to be the perfect model for ACOs. This raises the question: Why hasn't it been more successful? It's not that Kaiser is a failed delivery model—over 8 million persons receive care from the Kaiser system—but if integrated delivery systems are so much better than the "regular" health care system, why haven't consumers and employers flocked to Kaiser? Why do so many consumers and employers in Kaiser Permanente's service areas continue to patronize the supposedly inferior fragmented system that defines much of American health care? And why haven't other integrated delivery systems sprung up around the country to replicate the Kaiser model? This is the "Kaiser question."

It may be that the medical marketplace is so broken that providers that achieve higher quality and lower costs do not attract more customers. But this does not quite ring true. Employers and health plans are always looking for ways to save money. In all markets in which it operates, Kaiser Permanente competes for business against insurers that contract with traditional, nonintegrated providers. If integrated provider networks are so superior then traditional insurers should have long-since gone out of business.

One explanation is that patients like choice. Kaiser patients must, with a few exceptions, receive care from doctors employed by Kaiser. While this approach might work well for primary care, many patients do not want to be limited to a closed system for specialty care. They want to be able to go to the best provider for each type of service. Patients who receive care at ACOs will not be restricted from going outside it, but this feature of ACOs will limit their ability to coordinate care and reduce costs.

Another explanation is that integrated delivery models like Kaiser do not reduce costs, at least not enough to entice consumers to receive all of their care within a closed provider network. Kaiser physicians provide high-quality care, but the inability of Kaiser to dominate the markets in which it operates suggests that ACOs will not achieve quantum improvements in cost and quality compared to the existing health care system.

CONCLUSION

ACOs may deliver large savings while improving patient care and quality, but there is not enough evidence to conclude that integrated delivery systems are vastly superior to the present system. The greatest risk from ACOs is that they will result in massive provider consolidation, reducing price and quality competition. Vigorous antitrust enforcement can help avoid the worst side effects of consolidation, but the ACO program has already set off a wave of consolidation in the health care industry. We can shift from a fragmented system to ACOs, but if ACOs do not achieve reductions in cost or improvements in quality, it will be nearly impossible to reverse course. The government is placing all of its eggs in one basket in the belief that integrated delivery systems are *the* best model for delivering medical care.

REFERENCES AND FURTHER READING

Agency for Healthcare Research and Quality. (2008) *Cost of poor quality or waste in integrated delivery system settings.* Retrieved from http://www.ahrq.gov/research/costpqids/costpqids3.htm
Centers for Medicare & Medicaid Services. (2009). *Physician group practice demonstration: Report to Congress.* Retrieved from https://www.cms.gov/DemoProjectsEvalRpts/downloads/PGP_RTC_Sept.pdf
Centers for Medicare & Medicaid Services. (2011). *Medicare physician group practice demonstration: Physicians groups continue to improve quality and generate savings under Medicare physician pay-for-performance demonstration.* Retrieved from https://www.cms.gov/DemoProjectsEvalRpts/downloads/PGP_Fact_Sheet.pdf
Dranove, D. (2010). ACOs and the looming antitrust crisis. *Health Affairs Health Care Blog.* Retrieved from http://thehealthcareblog.com/blog/2010/10/14/acos-and-the-looming-antitrust-crisis
Federal Trade Commission, & Department of Justice. (2011). *Statement of antitrust enforcement policy regarding accountable care organizations participating in the Medicare shared savings program.* Retrieved from http://www.justice.gov/atr/public/health_care/276458.pdf

Goldsmith, J. (2011). Accountable care organizations: The case for flexible partnerships between health plans and providers. *Health Affairs, 30*(1), 32–40. doi: 10.1377/hlthaff.2010.0782

Iglehart, J. K. (2011). Assessing an ACO prototype—Medicare's physician group practice demonstration. *New England Journal of Medicine, 364*(3), 198–200.

Robinson, J. C. (2001). Organizational economics and health care markets. *Health Services Research, 36*(1 Pt 2), 177–189.

Song, Z., Safran, D. G., Landon, B. E., He, Y., Ellis, R. P., Mechanic, R. E., et al. (2011). Health care spending and quality in year 1 of the alternative quality contract. *New England Journal of Medicine, 365*(10), 909–918.

Tollen, L. (2008). *Physician organization in relation to quality and efficiency of care: A synthesis of recent literature.* Retrieved from The Commonwealth Fund website: http://www.commonwealthfund.org/Publications/Fund-Reports/2008/Apr/Physician-Organization-in-Relation-to-Quality-and-Efficiency-of-Care--A-Synthesis-of-Recent-Literatu.aspx

David H. Howard and Cynthia Zeldin

Independent Payment Advisory Board

POINT: As part of the 2010 Patient Protection and Affordable Care Act, the Independent Payment Advisory Board will reduce overall Medicare spending, improve the quality of care for Medicare beneficiaries, and create long-term solutions to the challenge of providing cost-effective health care.

Jennifer M. Kerner, University of New Mexico

COUNTERPOINT: The Independent Payment Advisory Board will not achieve the aims for which it was created. Instead, it will reduce the quality of care for seniors, introduce interest group–driven health care reforms, and negatively impact the private third-party payer sector.

Jennifer M. Kerner, University of New Mexico

Introduction

The 2010 Patient Protection and Affordable Care Act (ACA) includes numerous provisions aimed at controlling health care cost growth, particularly for the Medicare program. These provisions also cover a wide range of cost-controlling strategies. Among the provisions expected to have the most impact are alternative payment models to better encourage doctors and other health care providers to deliver more coordinated and efficient care. Other strategies are addressed through provisions to increase investments in activities to stop fraud and abuse, remove financial barriers to patients for receiving potentially cost-saving primary and preventative care, and align federal funding support for health care workforce training with the notion of team-oriented care.

As discussed in the debate on how the ACA will impact the deficit, at the time ACA was passed, the Congressional Budget Office (CBO) has estimated over $500 billion in Medicare savings from 2010 through 2019. One key provision in Section 3403 of the legislation is the authorization to create an Independent Payment Advisory Board (IPAB), which essentially acts as a backstop to help ensure those estimated savings (and potentially even more) are achieved. More specifically, the provision calls for an impartial, 15-member board that is tasked with recommending ways to keep Medicare's per capita spending growth below targeted amounts.

The task of determining whether Medicare spending growth is exceeding targeted amounts will fall to the Chief Actuary of the Centers for Medicare & Medicaid Services (CMS). The first year for this determination will be in 2013, with the goal of implementing recommendations, if needed, two years later (e.g., for the year 2013, this would be 2015). The Chief Actuary will make an annual determination in April of whether "expected" Medicare per capita growth rates will exceed a "target" growth rate. The expected Medicare per capita growth rate is defined as the projected average growth rate for the 5-year period ending two years after the determination year (e.g., this would be the 2011 through 2015 average rate for the 2013 determination). Until the 2017 determination calculation, the target growth rate will be calculated as the respective five-year average percentage increase of the average between the general economic and specific medical industry consumer price index (CPI). Afterward (2018 and beyond), the target growth rate will be based upon the five-year average percentage increase in the nominal gross domestic product (GDP) per capita plus 1 percentage point.

Historically, Medicare per capita spending has actually grown much faster than GDP (over 2 percentage points higher since 1990 according to data from the CMS Office of the Actuary). Hence, meeting targets linked to the rate of growth in the general economy (even plus 1 percentage point) can prove to be challenging. If the Chief Actuary determines that the expected Medicare per capita growth rate exceeds the target growth rate, the board must develop a proposal to reduce Medicare spending by the difference between the expected and target growth rate, up to a maximum percent (which starts at 0.5 percent for the first year and reaches 1.5 percent for the 2018 implementation year).

The ACA also includes a relatively expedited process for implementing the IPAB recommendations. If the Chief Actuary makes a determination by April 30 that the Medicare growth rate will exceed targeted amounts, the board's draft proposal to reduce the Medicare growth rate by the applicable savings target is due by September 1 to the Secretary of Health and Human Services. On January 15 of the following year (e.g., 2014 for the 2013 determination year), the board must submit a proposal, including implementing legislation, to Congress and the president. If the board fails to meet the deadline, the secretary must develop a proposal by January 25.

The secretary must implement the board's proposals by August 15 unless Congress acts to amend them, requiring Congress to consider the proposal under a "fast-track" process. In general, Congress cannot block the proposal or consider any amendment that does not meet the same cost-reduction goals as in the IPAB's proposal. Both houses of Congress must vote, including a super-majority in the Senate (i.e., three-fifths of the chamber), to waive this requirement. It should be noted though that Congress may not have to block the IPAB proposal to undermine it, as they could just pass independent legislation resulting in increased Medicare funding.

Also important to note is that there are fairly severe restrictions on the scope of recommendations that can be proposed by the IPAB. For example, according to the legislation, these mandatory recommendations must not "ration health care," "raise revenues or Medicare beneficiary premiums," restrict benefits, or modify eligibility criteria. Additionally, for implementation years 2015 through 2019, the IPAB cannot recommend reductions in payment rates for certain providers and suppliers of services. Those providers, most notably hospitals, were already singled out for substantial Medicare payment rate reductions by other ACA provisions.

Thus, IPAB may have to focus on expanding some of the payment reform efforts already being tested through other provisions in the ACA. This includes bundled payment, shared savings and other payment models that involve fixed, up-front payments covering a broad range of services. These types of models reward groups of providers that can work together to reduce costs for populations of patients. Proponents of the IPAB will point to these types of initiatives as consistent with a vision of care delivery that can achieve better patient outcomes and care experiences, as well as lower costs. Moreover, such delivery system transformation can be used to improve quality and reduce costs systemwide, not just for the Medicare population.

Proponents of the IPAB will also justify its existence by pointing out that relying on market forces alone to control costs does not appear to work. In addition, Congress may not have enough expertise or be too driven by special interests to identify the most appropriate methods to control costs. Probably the best example of Congress failing to generate a credible long-term solution to a health care cost problem is the current Medicare physician payment rate. As described in the deficit-reform chapter, Congress has been postponing a meaningful fix to the physician payment rate for several years, and if it continues to do so for the next couple years, perhaps the IPAB can be used to finally find a more sustainable approach for paying physicians to deliver services to Medicare beneficiaries.

Interestingly, the formation of an independent advisory board tasked with developing recommendations to help control Medicare spending is not an entirely new idea. Already, the Medicare Payment Advisory Commission (MedPAC) exists as an independent government agency that advises Congress on issues affecting the Medicare program. In June 2009, Senator Jay Rockefeller (D–WV) introduced legislation (S. 1380—"Medicare Payment Advisory Commission [MedPAC] Reform Act of 2009") that would have converted the MedPAC into an executive branch commission with specific savings targets and more formal regulatory authority. This bill became a precursor to the IPAB provision that was eventually adopted.

Also, it should be noted that even Republicans have proposed boards with private-sector representatives having regulatory authority. As Don Taylor, associate professor of Public Policy at Duke University, points out (see his blog "When did the IPAB become so controversial?" on the Incidental Economist website), Representative Paul Ryan (R–WI) introduced legislation (H.R. 2520 "Patients' Choice Act") to establish a Forum for Quality and Effectiveness in Health Care with private-sector representation having the authority to enforce comparative effectiveness guidelines. This includes the ability to recommend provisions allowing for penalties on physicians who do not follow the guidelines. As with the IPAB, the forum was proposed to be made up of 15 members representing views from medical providers, insurers, researchers, and consumers, and who could serve independently of any other employment.

Notwithstanding this prior history with similar concepts, skeptics of the IPAB point out that it may be hard to appoint and convince top candidates to participate. The fact remains that the idea of non-elected individuals essentially having congressional authority is a controversial political issue. Given that each member must be nominated and approved by the president along with the House of Representatives and Senate, there are likely to be disagreements and delays on making appointments. Also problematic is the fact that service on the IPAB is a full-time job with a six-year appointment, and members will be compensated about $165,300 to $179,700 (at 2010 levels). This means that candidates must be willing to give up their current jobs, research, practices, and teaching for six years, and potentially even take a cut in salary.

It is also not clear whether the IPAB would be able to focus on the types of reforms that could lead to systemwide changes in care that improves quality while also reducing costs. As Timothy Jost points out in his July 8, 2010, *New England Journal of Medicine* perspective entitled "Independent Payment Advisory Board," the IPAB is likely to be encouraged to focus on short-term payment fixes rather than long-term changes that might in fact bend the cost curve. The shorter-term focus may result due to the need to submit annual proposals. Thus, Jost lists cuts to Medicare Advantage plans, which are already slated for deep cuts under the ACA, or on prescription drug prices as more likely recommendations, as opposed to the alternative payment models discussed above which may take years to fully achieve the intended impacts.

Perhaps, most problematic are the severe restrictions on the IPAB purview, which will even limit the ability for the IPAB to achieve any short-term savings since the payment rates of many providers are off the table for several years. In addition, as Jost also points out, the IPAB can make only nonbinding recommendations regarding private payments. Any changes made to Medicare payment rates would likely have a much greater chance to achieve significant systemwide impacts if financial incentives were aligned in both the public and private payer markets.

Thus, the provision to create an Independent Payment Advisory Board is yet another strategy for cost control in the ACA that seems far from being certain to achieve its intended impact. In this debate, Jennifer Kerner provides more insights on the arguments both for and against the IPAB as a viable cost-controlling mechanism.

POINT

One of the prevailing issues in the U.S. health care industry is the cost of care versus quality of care. The rising cost of medical care is a result of a variety of factors, including an aging population, increased prevalence of multiple diagnoses, increased demand for specialty providers, and improved medical technology. The term *quality of care* is understood to mean necessary medical care—including procedures, treatments, and medications—administered in such a way that it optimizes the treatment outcomes per individual. Those who administer care must justify its application to the patient, as well as ensure that the treatment is administered with upmost efficiency. Neither the patient's health nor the cost-effectiveness of treatment should be compromised.

The idea that health care can be both effective and efficient informs the purpose of the Independent Payment Advisory Board (IPAB), considered one of the most important cost-reducing provisions of the 2010 Patient Protection and Affordable Care Act (ACA). The IPAB is tasked with reducing the overall cost of Medicare by proposing ways in which costs can be restrained.

Prior to the development of the IPAB, Congress was primarily responsible for keeping health care costs in check. The IPAB is an innovative solution to dealing with issues related to health care costs that will prove effective and sustainable. Specifically, the IPAB is the appropriate solution to the rising costs of Medicare for three reasons. First, the board will be composed of fifteen individuals from varied professional backgrounds. This eliminates bias in developing sustainable solutions to Medicare spending. Second, with membership diversity comes an opportunity for innovation. Third, the IPAB serves as a backstop in the event that programs already proposed by Congress do not meet their intended goals. Far from usurping Congress, the IPAB is a last resort in the event that current programs fail to achieve success. Fourth, the IPAB is, by law, restricted from rationing care, limiting benefits, or changing eligibility criteria. This ensures that the board is not given power and authority that might result in negative impacts related to access and quality of care.

THE ROLE OF THE INDEPENDENT PAYMENT ADVISORY BOARD

The need to halt the continuous increase in overall Medicare spending is imperative. The IPAB was created as a way to develop expert-driven, timely reform to meet target growth rates before Medicare costs become unsustainable. With the lengthy nature of congressional delegation, a separate advisory board was needed, one that could serve as a safety net if the growth rate for Medicare spending continued unabated. The IPAB is only required to develop cost-cutting proposals if programs developed by Congress fail to meet the established target for reducing Medicare spending within a certain time frame. Beginning in 2013, the Centers for Medicare & Medicaid Services (CMS) determine whether the actual Medicare growth rate is exceeding the established per capita growth rate. If the growth rate is exceeded, the IPAB must submit a proposal to Congress outlining ways in which the Medicare per beneficiary growth rate can be reduced. However, and although the proposed advisory board would have the freedom to develop Medicare spending reduction reforms, the IPAB is highly restricted in the types of recommendations it can make to Congress and has no power to make fundamental changes to the Medicare insurance program. This being the case, the IPAB will develop sound proposals to reduce Medicare spending while maintaining quality of care for Medicare beneficiaries.

SERVING AS A BACKSTOP

One concern raised by opponents of the IPAB is that the board will usurp Congress's health care policymaking power. By taking the power of health care reform out of the hands of Congress, opponents argue, the executive branch will, in effect, be ignoring the desires of U.S. citizens. However, these concerns are ill informed. Rather than serving as a policymaking institution, the IPAB will serve as a backstop or emergency brake in the event that other proposals for Medicare cost reduction fail to meet fiscal goals (Carroll, 2011). In other words, Congress is charged with developing and enacting policies to reduce Medicare costs.

However, if these policies should fail, the IPAB will make its own recommendations to Congress regarding Medicare cost reduction. The IPAB does not usurp congressional recommendations, nor does it have the power to veto or overturn congressional policies. If Congress does not create a program that matches or exceeds the spending cuts proposed by members of the IPAB then the U.S. Department of Health and Human Services (HHS) will automatically implement the IPAB's proposal. This backstop mechanism guarantees that at least some attempts to reduce Medicare spending will be made, regardless of whether members of Congress can come to a consensus. Not including the mechanism whereby the HHS automatically enforces the IPAB's recommendations could mean waiting years longer for a solution to the problem of increased Medicare spending.

RESTRAINTS AND LIMITATIONS

In order to reduce Medicare spending, changes must be made to the administrative procedures associated with Medicare billing; the mechanisms by which services are rendered to Medicare beneficiaries; or the way in which services, medical devices, and prescription drugs are priced. However, these changes must be proposed within the confines of rules and limitations. The IPAB has the ability to develop and recommend ways in which Medicare costs can be reduced, but it cannot dictate who will receive care and what care beneficiaries are eligible to receive. By law, the IPAB cannot draft proposals that "include any recommendations to ration health care, raise revenues or Medicare beneficiary premiums . . . , increase Medicare beneficiary cost-sharing (including deductibles, coinsurance, and co-payments), or otherwise restrict benefits or modify eligibility criteria" (Patient Protection and Affordable Care Act [ACA], 2010; Sec. 3403). This means that, although recommendations may be created to, for instance, ensure that magnetic resonance imaging (MRI) scans are provided only to those who really need them, the IPAB cannot dictate the provision of MRIs based on a patient's medical history or income. Additionally, the IPAB cannot change the way in which Medicare identifies who is eligible to receive benefits. As long as individuals meet the current eligibility requirements for Medicare assistance, they will continue to receive Medicare benefits. These examples address the concerns of those who oppose the IPAB out of fear that the board could potentially cut much-needed medical services to seniors. In addition, medical treatments and services not covered by Medicare will still be available to patients, although patients will be responsible for the extra cost. The rules imposed on the IPAB ensure that, even as efforts are made to reduce the cost of Medicare, beneficiaries still receive the quality care they need.

FOCUS ON REFORMING THE DELIVERY SYSTEM

Although the IPAB is expected to operate under many restrictions, the board can still be used as a tool to promote the delivery of better-coordinated and higher-value care. For instance, the IPAB may propose to develop a system for better physician communication, thereby reducing costly problems such as treatment overlap. For example, a patient who consults a primary care physician for a general checkup but then visits other specialty providers for health concerns such as diabetes, arthritis, and coronary heart conditions, might find that a lack of communication between his or her health care providers can lead to the provision of duplicative and otherwise unnecessary—and sometimes even harmful—services and costs. However, if the IPAB develops a proposal that creates a better system for physician communication across specialties, those extra costs and services would be reduced.

Other examples of how the IPAB can encourage providers to better coordinate and manage care include initiatives related to bundled payments and the creation of accountable care organizations (ACOs) (Carroll, 2011). Bundled payments (sometimes known as episode payments) are single fees attached to several treatments or medical expenses. An improvement over individual payments for individual services, a practice known as fee-for-service that rewards providers for delivering more care regardless of the impact on health outcomes, bundled payments encourage providers to be more efficient by reducing the provision of unnecessary care. In the bundled-payment model, health care providers are incentivized to better coordinate to make sure that higher-value care is being delivered within a bundle. The ACO model also includes payment mechanisms that offer providers better support and incentives to be more efficient in care delivery. In fact, ACOs are typically held accountable for keeping the total costs of patients below targeted amounts. Aside from financial incentives to become more efficient, initiatives such as bundled payments and ACOs include mechanisms that link payments to the quality of care delivered and patient outcomes. If a patient is treated for a particular medical condition, the health care provider is reimbursed, or paid, based on the quality of care provided and the health outcomes of the patient. These are just a few examples of the many ways that the structure and authority of the IPAB allows the board to develop effective means to reduce overall Medicare spending without compromising the care offered to Medicare beneficiaries.

The IPAB will propose sustainable, timely, and systemwide changes that will impact the health care system at multiple levels, potentially altering the ways in which providers are compensated and treatments are administered. Standards will be created whereby all Medicare beneficiaries will receive less costly care at every level of health care provision, including all specialty treatment areas. The IPAB's structure and proposal process will allow the board to make these changes in a timely manner. Relying on Congress to come to a consensus regarding the best way to reduce Medicare spending may mean waiting even longer for a solution. This paralysis is exemplified in the problems with the Medicare physician fee schedule (i.e., the payment rates that physicians are paid under Medicare), which has been scheduled to receive payment cuts for several years now. Though Congress has postponed those cuts to the point that the fee schedule is nearly 30 percent higher than it should be, the body still seems unable to arrive at a permanent solution. Because the IPAB can avoid political posturing and the influence of lobbying groups, and because it is more likely to propose smart payment system reforms aligned with higher-value care, rather than just payment cuts, it may be in a better position than Congress to improve the physician fee schedule. By ensuring that changes to Medicare costs are made across the health care system, IPAB proposals will not overburden any one area of the health care sector.

It is also important to note that, until 2020, the IPAB is prohibited from reducing payment rates for hospital, nursing home, home health, and other services. Such payment cuts are often proposed as across-the-board cuts, reducing payments for both necessary and unnecessary care. For example, from 2010 through 2019, the ACA includes several small percentage payment reductions (often less than one percentage point) for all services reimbursed to hospitals and other institutional providers (such as home health agencies, hospice providers, and skilled nursing facilities). Such payment cuts can create some immediate cost savings and federal deficit relief, as providers will be incentivized to become more cost efficient in delivering care to Medicare beneficiaries. However, there is also a risk that some providers who are no longer able to cover their costs for conducting Medicare business will simply decide to no longer offer access to Medicare beneficiaries. Thus, it is critical to consider policy solutions beyond simply cutting payments or reducing benefits and to embrace solutions aligned with the provision of high-quality care through viable business models for providers (e.g., ACOs and bundled payments).

Also, although payment cuts might result in savings to the federal government and reductions in the deficit, there is no guarantee that providers will in fact deliver less costly care. If they do not, private payers and individuals could end up bearing more of the costs as providers attempt to recoup reduced revenue. On the other hand, policies aimed at improving the health care system can translate into reduced spending for all payers, including individuals, as improvements in care that are incentivized through Medicare payment and delivery reform can be shared throughout the entire health care system.

MEMBERSHIP IN THE INDEPENDENT PAYMENT ADVISORY BOARD

Looking forward to the creation of an IPAB, it is important to determine the attributes most desired in potential candidates for membership. The group must be cohesive enough to come to a consensus regarding best practices for Medicare reform and diverse enough to offer fresh insights from various perspectives of health care provision. The board has the potential to embody both of these characteristics, because members of the IPAB are elected from a wide pool of candidates.

Two additional attributes of membership should also be taken into consideration. First, it is imperative that members of the board are unbiased and unprejudiced regarding best practices for reducing costs and maintaining quality of care. If they are to make fair and equitable decisions regarding an issue that affects a large number of individuals, those responsible for making recommendations must not harbor ulterior interests or motives. The members must focus primarily on the costs and benefits related to reducing Medicare spending, regardless of their personal or professional biases. Second, members must demonstrate their expertise in the relevant issue, reducing Medicare spending. Experts in the fields of health care provision, health care management, hospital administration, health care insurance, health economics, and other similar industries are preferred. With their knowledge of the intricacies of determining where and how Medicare spending reductions can occur, these experts will produce the most practical, cost-effective means of achieving the goals of the IPAB.

A PANEL OF EXPERTS

Potential board members, identified as having some expertise in the fields of health care and economics, will be nominated by the president of the United States. These individuals must accept or decline the offer to serve on the IPAB before going through the Senate approval process. Senate committee hearings, whereby members of the U.S. Senate interview each nominee to determine his or her qualification for the role of IPAB membership, can be grueling. Potential board members will be asked about their professional qualifications, their contributions to their field, and any professional or personal affiliations with interests groups that may play a part in how the individual approaches the task at hand. Once the candidate has been approved by the Senate committee hearing, that individual will be a member of the IPAB, serving a term that lasts six years, with a limit of two consecutive terms. Such lengthy tenure will allow members to leave their previous occupations (even temporarily) and concentrate fully on the goals of the IPAB.

It is important for several reasons that individuals who are experts and top contributors in the fields of health care provision, management, and economics be appointed to the IPAB. First, in order to effectively implement its proposed reforms, the IPAB must have the ability to convincingly justify them. IPAB members who have hands-on experience dealing with concerns related to the provision of health care services, and who understand the apprehension of how medical providers feel toward new rules and regulations, will determine the most effective and efficient means of reducing Medicare costs while taking into consideration the needs of those affected by such reforms. Once a proposal is made, IPAB members will be able to clearly and effectively explain to Congress, from a professional health care and health economics perspective, how the proposed program will reduce Medicare spending. Rather than having to rely on external expert opinions, as is the case with many congressional proposals, the IPAB exists as a single entity capable of developing sound, expert-led proposals. A second rationale for selecting experts for IPAB membership is that they are likely to be recognized as such by other members of the health care industry, and so their proposed reforms are less likely to meet with resistance.

The ACA clearly outlines the nomination requirements for IPAB membership. Under consideration will be "individuals with national recognition for their expertise in health finance and economics, actuarial science, health facility management, health plans and integrated delivery systems, reimbursement of health facilities, allopathic and osteopathic physicians, and other providers of health services, and other related fields, who provide a mix of different professionals, broad geographic representation, and a balance between urban and rural representatives" (ACA, 2010: Sec. 3403). Membership will also include "experts in the area of pharmaco-economics or prescription drug benefit programs, employers, third-party payers, individuals skilled in the conduct and interpretation of biomedical, health services, and health economics research and expertise in outcomes and effectiveness research and technology assessment." In addition, there will be "representatives of consumers and the elderly" (ACA, 2010: Sec. 3403). It is important to note that the "individuals who are directly involved in the provision or management of the delivery of items and services" mentioned above will "not constitute a majority of the appointed membership of the Board" (ACA, 2010: Sec. 3403). Though it remains to be seen exactly who will be nominated by the president and, subsequently, who will pass the Senate committee hearings for election to the board, it does seem reasonable to assume that the appointment of members from an array of health- and economic-related fields will help to ensure that recommendations are fair to all stakeholders.

The likelihood that members of the IPAB will possess all of these qualities is great considering the rigorous presidential selection and Senate confirmation processes they are required to pass. This group of unbiased, expert professionals will lead the way to reducing Medicare spending in a fair and sustainable manner.

ELIMINATING OUTSIDE INFLUENCES

Historically, health care policies in the United States have been created and passed by members of Congress, who are driven by the need for political survival. As a result, many health care policies and programs have been informed more by interest groups and the need to ensure votes than by the opinion of experts. By allowing a panel of carefully selected individuals to assist in developing solutions to the issue of Medicare spending, Congress will be inviting new ideas and innovations into the policymaking process. The diverse group of members that the IPAB promises to include will have the opportunity to pioneer new ways of managing Medicare spending. Unfettered by the need to satisfy constituents and informed by their diverse and rich experiences in the field of medicine, the members of the IPAB will be able to expand the current understanding of how to manage the Medicare program. Along with moving toward the use of empirical justification for creating certain Medicare reforms, the development of the IPAB demonstrates a dedication within the U.S. government to place matters of public welfare in the hands of individuals whose sole responsibility is to ascertain the most comprehensible solutions to curb Medicare spending without negotiating the well-being of Medicare beneficiaries.

CONCLUSION

In 2011 it is difficult to speculate as to what the actual outcome of the creation of the IPAB will be; at the time of publication, President Barack Obama had yet to make nominations for potential IPAB members. The debate continues as to whether the formation of the IPAB will have a significant impact on reducing Medicare costs and, therefore, on reducing the overall burden of health care on the federal budget. What is needed is an unbiased group of individuals qualified by years of professional experience to take on the task of Medicare reform. Who better to develop innovative and experientially informed solutions to the problem of increased Medicare spending than a select group of medical, public health, economic, and third-party payer professionals?

At the very least, the IPAB promises to take some much-needed action toward reducing Medicare spending. In addition, the IPAB's quality of membership and legitimacy of actions will be recognized by members of the health care industry, a recognition that will only serve to enhance and expedite the implementation process of IPAB's proposed Medicare spending reduction programs. The proposals that the IPAB puts forth will be informed by a group of presidentially nominated, Senate-approved experts in the fields of health care and economics. These members will be dedicated to the task of reducing Medicare health care costs and maintaining quality of care for Medicare beneficiaries. Without interest-group bias or the lengthy process of legislative delegation, the IPAB is sure to achieve meaningful changes in the Medicare program, leading to better quality of care, lower costs of health care per Medicare beneficiary, and a reduction in Medicare spending that will meet the targets set by the CMS.

REFERENCES AND FURTHER READING

Carroll, J. (2011). IPAB likely to put pressure on medicare advantage & part D. *Managed Care*. Retrieved from http://www .managedcaremag.com/archives/1106/1106.regulation.html

Center for Medicare Advocacy, Inc. (2010). *Health care reform does not cut Medicare benefits*. Retrieved from http://www.medica readvocacy.org/InfoByTopic/Reform/10_10.28.ReformDoesntCutBenefits.htm

DeParle, N. (2011). The facts about the Independent Payment Advisory Board [The White House Blog]. Retrieved from http://www .whitehouse.gov/blog/2011/04/20/facts-about-independent-payment-advisory-board

Enthoven, A. (2011). Reforming Medicare by reforming incentives. *The New England Journal of Medicine, 364*(21), e44. Retrieved from http://www.nejm.org/doi/full/10.1056/NEJMp1104427?ssource=hcrc

Haberkorn, J. (2011). Health policy brief: The Independent Payment Advisory Board. *Health Affairs*. Retrieved from http://www .healthaffairs.org/healthpolicybriefs/brief.php?brief_id=59

Kennedy, E. (1978). The Congress and national health policy: Fifth annual Matthew B. Rosenhaus lecture. *American Journal of Public Health, 68*(3), 241–244.

Kocher, R., & Sahni, N. (2010). Physicians versus hospitals as leaders of accountable care organizations. *New England Journal of Medicine, 363*(27), 2579–2582.

Newman, D., & Davis, C. (2010). *The Independent Payment Advisory Board* (Congressional Research Service Report No. 7-5700). Washington, DC: Congressional Research Service.

Office of Management and Budget. (2011). *Living within our means and investing in the future: The president's plan for economic growth and deficit reduction*. Retrieved from http://www.whitehouse.gov/sites/default/files/omb/budget/fy2012/assets/ jointcommitteereport.pdf

Patient Protection and Affordable Care Act (ACA), Pub. L. No. 111-148, §2702, 124 Stat. 119, 318–319 (2010).

Wilensky, G. (2011). Reforming Medicare—Toward a modified Ryan plan. *The New England Journal of Medicine, 364*(20), 1890–1892.

Jennifer M. Kerner

COUNTERPOINT

Although the U.S. population is aging and chronic diseases becoming more prevalent, regulating the way in which medical professionals administer care, as well as regulating the payment schedule of the benchmark for private insurers, is not a solution to the problem of Medicare spending growth. These are exactly the kinds of solutions to Medicare spending that the Independent Payment Advisory Board (IPAB) will impose. What is needed instead is empirically based policy reform that protects senior citizens and the rights of medical providers while addressing specific areas in which Medicare spending can be reduced.

The idea of the IPAB is misguided for several reasons. First, there is concern that the IPAB is not the best solution to the problem of Medicare spending. The process by which medical providers are compensated—in addition to issues concerning the cost of prescription drugs, hospital policies, and other considerations—contribute to overall Medicare spending. Second, any recommendation made by the IPAB can be overturned by Congress. Third, Medicare was created to assist seniors in receiving vital treatments and prescription medications. Through its proposals, the IPAB could fundamentally change the way seniors are treated, both in terms of short- and long-term care. Fourth, the 15-member board will be no less biased than a group of legislators. Members are selected from a wide range of fields, including third-party payers. These individuals may advocate for the interests of their former employers or affiliations. And, even if the board does manage to make unbiased recommendations, members of Congress may be weary of passing legislation proposed by former employees of third-party payers. For all of these reasons, the creation of the IPAB should be reconsidered. At the very least, stronger restrictions and legislative oversight are needed to ensure that the proposals introduced by the IPAB are beneficial to Medicare beneficiaries and the health care industry before they are put into practice.

The responsibility of the IPAB is to make recommendations to reduce the rising cost of Medicare spending. The causes of the continued increase in Medicare spending are many. It is likely that the IPAB will focus mainly on reducing the cost of care per Medicare beneficiary on a per-case basis. However, reforming aspects of Medicare spending on a per-beneficiary basis will not help reduce costs in the long run. Medicare costs are also associated with the way in which medical providers are paid, as well as how hospitals and hospices organize their provision of care to Medicare recipients. Therefore, rather than focus on the allocation of treatment per case, the board should concentrate on how providers are reimbursed for treating Medicare beneficiaries, in addition to how hospital and hospice payment structures affect Medicare spending.

COST OF CARE VERSUS QUALITY OF CARE

Any attempt to control the cost of health care should be undertaken with regard to how those changes might affect the quality of care delivered. It is possible to reduce costs without sacrificing quality, but since quality of care is not a primary focus of the IPAB, there is little to ensure that quality of care will not diminish. If, for example, the IPAB chooses to reduce provider compensation, it is possible that some providers would respond by accepting fewer Medicare patients, and some might refuse to accept any new Medicare patients at all. As a result, Medicare beneficiaries would experience a loss in access to care and be forced to seek emergency care. This, in turn, might overburden emergency departments, possibly reducing the quality of care for more than just Medicare beneficiaries. Developing cost-saving proposals, such as reducing provider compensation, may reduce overall Medicare spending. However, such proposals may also have the unintended consequence of negatively impacting quality of care.

A QUESTION OF IMPACT

As was discussed above, the cost of Medicare comes from many sources. Hospitals and hospices account for a large portion of Medicare spending. According to the Centers for Medicare & Medicaid Services (CMS), in the years 2006 through 2010, inpatient and outpatient hospital care have accounted for 47 to 49 percent of total benefit payments.

However, hospitals and hospices will not be subject to IPAB recommendations until 2019. This timeline calls into question the overall impact that the IPAB will have on Medicare cost reduction before that year. Another area where the IPAB's limited reach may be felt is in that of provider compensation. The IPAB may propose ways in which providers are compensated for certain services, as well as include measures to incentivize cost-effective care provision. The existing solutions to these problems, however, are less than empirically sound. Additionally, these solutions may not be easily implemented before the IPAB must conduct its first review on the programs' ability to carry out its primary charge.

To address the problem of rising Medicare spending without directly affecting hospitals and hospices, the IPAB has at its disposal accountable care organizations (ACOs), bundled payment, and medical homes. These provisions are not currently supported by a wealth of empirical evidence. Another issue related to the IPAB's recommendations is that many cost-reducing provisions take a year or more to develop and implement. If the IPAB is to accurately perform an annual review of the impact of a program on the overall cost of Medicare, the development and implementation of that program will have to take place within a shorter time frame.

THE IPAB'S RELATIONSHIP WITH CONGRESS

Prior to the creation of the IPAB, health care initiatives were mainly driven by legislation. Congress is the most appropriate institution for handling issues related to health care because each member of Congress represents constituents who are affected by health care policy. Congressional members are held accountable by those who vote for them. The IPAB, though designed to be composed of nonbiased health care professionals, does not answer directly to the people who will be affected by its Medicare spending reduction proposals. There is little accountability in allowing a select and small group of individuals to determine where Medicare costs should be reduced. This usurpation of Congress on issues pertaining to health care spending will cause costly disturbances in the process of implementing IPAB proposals. Health care providers may resist certain aspects of IPAB proposals, claiming that their particular patient demographic or economic situation will not allow for the full implementation of the proposed program. Additionally, Congress may decide to overturn IPAB proposals once they have been made. The extent to which the board is effective will depend on how Congress reacts to its recommendations, and on whether Congress can develop programs that match the spending reductions it proposes. However, members of Congress will do everything in their power to make certain that their constituents and the groups they represent are benefiting from the proposed changes. For example, members of Congress may, with the backing of interests groups and lobbyists, publicly decry IPAB proposals in an effort to garner support from other members of Congress to overturn such proposals. The IPAB will need to package its recommendations in such a way that Congress will see fit to act on those recommendations. As long as there is a conspicuous separation between the IPAB and Congress, the ability of the IPAB to push its proposals through Congress will be severely impaired.

MEMBERSHIP

The members of the IPAB will possess significant power to determine the fate of the Medicare program. According to ACA, board members will come from varied professional backgrounds and will be required to take on a six-year term. The length of that term may well become a factor as to what candidates are available for the president to choose from. Members who are professionals in their respective fields may be unwilling to leave their positions in order to pursue a six-year term on an advisory board created to reduce overall Medicare spending. Additionally, professionals that choose to sit on the board may be forced to take a pay cut.

Another issue concerning the professional background of potential members has to do with their professional affiliations and loyalties. Although members of the IPAB are, in theory, supposed to come from varied professional backgrounds and be free from the persuasion of special interest groups, it is nearly impossible to ensure that at least some members will not act on behalf of former employers or professional interest groups of which they have been a part. For instance, even though there is a limit on the number of health care providers that may serve on the board at a given time, if a majority of members are practicing medical professionals, it can be assumed that these individuals will lobby for proposals that do not damage the income or professional freedom of medical providers. Likewise, a member who is a former representative of a firm, such as a medical equipment producer or third-party payer, may be more likely to vote for proposals that favor the interests of that firm. The makeup of the IPAB will greatly impact the proposals it produces. This, in turn, could have a negative influence on the quality of care and availability of services to Medicare beneficiaries.

ADVERSE EFFECTS

Though there may be advantages to the formation of the IPAB and implementation of IPAB proposals, there are also obvious drawbacks. First, the IPAB's proposals to reduce Medicare spending may have an unintended negative consequence toward physician reimbursement. If the costs of medical treatment and services are reduced, physicians and other health care providers may see a significant decrease in their Medicare reimbursement, leading to declines in revenues. This may leave many providers unable to cover their costs and eventually to stop participating in the Medicare program, something that will reduce the availability of care in the private practices that serve Medicare beneficiaries.

Second, because Medicare is the nation's largest payer for health care and its payment systems often serve as the basis for the systems of other payers, changes in Medicare can cause adverse effects throughout the health care system. In particular, drastic reductions in Medicare payments could cause providers to attempt to make up for those reductions by increasing charges to non-Medicare payers. This effect is likely to result in increases to private health insurance premiums and out-of-pockets costs.

PROTECTING SENIOR CITIZENS

Perhaps one of the greatest concerns regarding the power and authority of the IPAB is that it has the potential to reduce services to seniors. Despite the fact that the IPAB is restricted from rationing care, the fear remains that cuts in Medicare spending will translate into fewer treatment options for seniors. Specifically, the IPAB cannot ration care, restrict benefits, or change eligibility criteria. The language in the ACA, however, is ambiguous regarding what is meant by "rationing," and "restricting." If the IPAB calls for programs that delineate the treatments available to patients with certain illnesses, they are, in fact, rationing care based on a patient's diagnosis. For example, the IPAB may develop proposals mandating that only individuals with certain symptoms and medical histories be allowed to have an MRI under their Medicare coverage. Any treatments or services a physician deems necessary in addition to what is allotted to the Medicare beneficiary will have to be paid by the patient either out of pocket or by a Medicare supplementary insurance package.

Another concern related to the provision of care for the elderly is that some services may be favored over others when the time comes to alter the Medicare fee schedule (Axelrod, Millman, & Abecassis, 2010). Some treatments and procedures are more expensive than others, in that they require both more technology and more expertise from the medical provider. If the IPAB makes recommendations based purely on the cost of services, hospitals may be required to hire fewer specialty physicians and forgo purchase of expensive, but necessary, medical equipment. This reduction could lead to longer waits for patients who require specialty treatments, as well as to higher costs to Medicare beneficiaries who elect to purchase services no longer covered by Medicare. In addition to this possible targeting of higher-cost services, the IPAB could potentially favor services and programs with which board members are affiliated. Although members must serve full time for at least one term of six years, the fact that the members will be chosen based on their past professional experience introduces considerable possibility for bias toward their original profession.

IMPACT ON MEDICAL PROFESSIONALS

Reducing the cost of Medicare spending means more than reducing the expense of medical treatment and health care services per Medicare beneficiary. Cuts in spending and costs may also mean reductions in the income of health care providers. Although some may argue that decreases in income for medical providers, particularly specialty physicians, are justified as part of a reform toward a more efficient means of health care provision, one must calculate the expertise and knowledge required to perform and provide particular medical treatments and services. If compensation to providers is decreased, so too might the number of individuals obtaining the proper credentials and training required to practice medicine. Likewise, medical practitioners may choose to forgo continuing education opportunities due to expense concerns. In general, lower reimbursement rates will likely cause providers to attempt to reduce their costs of conducting business. This could lead to reductions in training, investments in innovations, and even direct medical services, all of which could have detrimental effects on the health of patients in the future. A further concern related to reimbursement specifically concerns specialty providers. A large amount of money is spent in the specialty health care sector, making this area a prime target for IPAB recommendations. Likely IPAB proposals, such as bundling, could potentially reduce specialty reimbursements. This could mean fewer specialty providers and longer waiting periods for seniors seeking specialty treatments. Moreover, a reduction in medical providers' incomes may have adverse effects on physicians' practices, leading to unintended negative consequences related to health care provision (Jones & Amery, 2010). One negative impact of decreased physician reimbursement may be a reduction in the number of Medicare patients that physicians are willing to accept.

Another way in which medical professionals may potentially be impacted by IPAB spending-cut proposals is in each provider's ability to act autonomously to provide expert care to patients. Although the IPAB cannot, by law, ration care, restrict benefits, or change eligibility criteria, it could potentially restrict the ability of medical providers to prescribe treatment on a per-patient basis. By promoting payment systems based on prospective budgets, such as bundled payments, the IPAB could restrain the treatment choices of providers so much that patients would no longer receive personalized care. These types of payment systems put providers at risk for the costs of care that are above their budgeted amounts (particularly if they end up with patients who are sicker than expected); hence, there is a strong incentive to reduce the number of services used to treat patients. The fear is that necessary care may be limited in order to keep costs within budgets. As was the case with health maintenance organizations in the 1990s, such payment reforms could lead to health care decisions that focused more on cost management than on patient management. Moreover, physicians may feel constrained in the way they deliver care. In particular, they may be reluctant to deviate from standardized practices or to prescribe additional precautionary testing. This lack of individualized care not only puts patients at greater risk for misdiagnosed or underdiagnosed conditions but it also translates into a loss of the patient-provider relationship, creating more issues related to decreased quality of care and increased costs of Medicare spending. For example, patients of a physician allowed to provide only the services and treatments outlined within a confined set of rules may feel as though they are being treated not as individuals but, rather, as health issues. As a result, those patients may be less inclined to adhere to instructions for taking prescription drugs, or they may be less likely to follow up after an initial checkup or treatment. Clearly, physician autonomy is important, not just for allowing physicians to treat patients on a case-by-case level but also for decreasing overall Medicare spending (Kocher & Sahni, 2010).

CONCLUSION

The rising costs of health care and the continued increase in Medicare spending are due to many factors. These include the way in which physicians and medical providers are compensated, as well as the mechanisms for which health care providers pay and charge for their services. It is unlikely that the Independent Payment Advisory Board, with its limited focus, will be able to adequately and effectively tackle these baseline issues. In addition, some board members might have a predisposition to vote in favor of proposals that benefit their previous professions or institutions. Although the members of the IPAB have yet to be selected, it can be assumed that, if members are expert professionals in the fields of medicine and public health, they will maintain some bias toward the interests of the populations they represent. In addition to inviting possible bias into the creation of proposals, the IPAB may inadvertently have a negative impact on both the care of seniors and medical practices of physicians. If the IPAB proposes fundamental changes to the way in which seniors receive care under the Medicare plan, Medicare beneficiaries may experience a decline in quality of care, including a loss of a close patient-provider relationship. In addition, decreases in compensation for medical providers could also mean a decline in quality of care, as well as restrictions on the services available in providers' practices. As the IPAB develops changes to the services provided by Medicare, there is potential for a domino effect of reduced coverage and increased costs in the health insurance private sector. Although there may be some benefit to keeping the IPAB separate from legislation, allowing Congress to have a greater say in how Medicare spending should be constrained would introduce another element of accountability in the decision-making process. For all of these reasons, the construction and implementation of the IPAB should be seriously reconsidered.

REFERENCES AND FURTHER READING

Axelrod, D. A., Millman, D., & Abecassis, M. M. (2010). U.S. health care reform and transplantation, part II: Impact on the public sector and novel health care delivery systems. *American Journal of Transplantation, 10,* 2203–2207.

Carroll, J. (2011). IPAB likely to put pressure on medicare advantage & part D. *Managed Care.* Retrieved from http://www .managedcaremag.com/archives/1106/1106.regulation.html

DeParle, N. (2011). The facts about the Independent Payment Advisory Board [The White House Blog]. Retrieved from http://www .whitehouse.gov/blog/2011/04/20/facts-about-independent-payment-advisory-board

Haberkorn, J. (2011). Health policy brief: The Independent Payment Advisory Board. *Health Affairs.* Retrieved from http://health affairs.org/healthpolicybriefs/brief_pdfs/healthpolicybrief_67.pdf

Jones, E., & Amery, M. (2010). Health care reform: What it may mean for your practice. *Neurology Clinical Practice, 75*(Suppl. 1), S52–S55.

Kennedy, E. (1978). The Congress and national health policy: Fifth annual Matthew B. Rosenhaus lecture. *American Journal of Public Health, 68*(3), 241–244.

Kocher, R., & Sahni, N. (2010). Physicians versus hospitals as leaders of accountable care organizations. *New England Journal of Medicine, 363*(27), 2579–2582.

Newman, D., & Davis, C. (2010). *The Independent Payment Advisory Board* (Congressional Research Service Report 7-5700). Washington, DC: Congressional Research Service.

Patient Protection and Affordable Care Act, Pub. L. No. 111–148, §2702, 124 Stat. 119, 318–319 (2010).

Wilensky, G. (2011). Reforming Medicare—Toward a modified Ryan plan. *The New England Journal of Medicine, 364*(20), 1890–1892.

Jennifer M. Kerner

Medicare Negotiations of Drug Pricing

POINT: If it had the authority to negotiate drug prices with pharmaceutical manufacturers, Medicare would achieve significant savings.

David W. Carlson, PharmaMetrics, Inc.

COUNTERPOINT: The ability of Medicare to negotiate with drug companies directly will not substantially reduce drug costs and will, in fact, have detrimental indirect costs on both market innovation and the general economy.

David W. Carlson, PharmaMetrics, Inc.

Introduction

The Medicare Part D program was enacted as part of the Medicare Prescription Drug, Improvement, and Modernization Act of 2003 (MMA) and began operation in 2006. The new program filled a gaping hole in the Medicare benefit package, which up until that time had not covered outpatient prescription drugs. However, since Medicare was created in 1965, prescription drugs have evolved into a critical component of patient care, and the new drug benefit has allowed millions of elderly Americans to obtain drugs that are vital to their health.

The cost of supporting that access is substantial. In 2010 over 34 million Medicare beneficiaries were enrolled in Part D, up from nearly 28 million in 2006. Actuaries at the Centers for Medicare & Medicaid Services (CMS) project that, between 2011 and 2020, the federal government will spend more than $1 trillion on Part D. During this time, per capita drug costs are expected to grow much faster than the rate of increase in other categories of medical spending.

In 2010 federal spending on prescription drugs accounted for about 11 percent of total Medicare spending. By 2020 the number is expected to reach nearly 15 percent, with annual spending more than doubling from about $67 billion in 2011 to over $156 billion in 2020. Such spending growth will only add to existing federal deficit problems, particularly Medicare's long-term fiscal outlook, which raises the question of whether prescription drugs under Part D are being purchased in the most cost-effective manner.

Currently, the Part D program is delivered through private prescription drug plans (PDPs) and managed care plans participating in the Medicare Advantage program. These drug plan sponsors receive a monthly premium payment for each of their enrolled Medicare beneficiaries and share risk for the cost of the drug benefit with the government. That is, the drug plans are liable for a significant portion of the costs in excess of the premium amounts. Thus, plans have a clear incentive to control the costs of the benefit in order to offer lower and more attractive premiums to potential enrollees, as well as to protect their own bottom lines.

Drug plan sponsors employ a variety of tools, such as formularies and tiering, to manage costs and typically contract with pharmacy benefit managers (PBMs) to design and implement these tools. A drug formulary is a list of prescription drugs, both generic and brand name, that are preferred by the drug plan. The drug plan may cover more of the cost for drugs on the "preferred" list (i.e., tiering), providing an incentive to encourage the use of covered drugs. In some cases, formularies are closed, excluding coverage from drugs not on the list. The purpose of the formulary is to steer patients to the least costly medications with similar clinical effectiveness.

Although it appears that private plans have achieved some success at keeping costs down, some have called on the government to take a more active role in reining in Medicare drug spending. In particular, it is believed that, by regulating or directly negotiating prices with pharmaceutical manufacturers, the government could achieve significant savings by leveraging the Medicare program's large market share.

For the government to take such a step, however, would require the passage of new legislation. Current law precludes the government from negotiating or setting prices for drugs covered under Medicare Part D. More specifically, the MMA included a "noninterference" clause forbidding the Secretary of Health and Human Services from interfering with price negotiations between pharmaceutical manufacturers and Medicare drug plan sponsors. Furthermore, the secretary is forbidden from instituting a formulary or price structure for prescription drugs.

The noninterference clause is consistent with the notion that prescription price discounts are best achieved through private competitive market forces. In fact, many experts, including the nonpartisan Congressional Budget Office (CBO), have postulated that the federal government, if allowed to negotiate with drug manufacturers, would fail to achieve significant price reductions relative to the private sector.

Basic economic theory suggests that, when several drugs are available to treat the same medical condition, private plans should be able to effectively secure discounts from drug manufacturers by giving their drugs preferred status within formularies. Because plan enrollees are encouraged to use preferred drugs through lower cost sharing and other incentives, manufacturers are willing to offer discounts to obtain preferred status for their drugs and increase their market share.

The other side of the debate argues that, as a matter of basic economic theory, large buyers should be able to use their size and bargaining power to obtain price discounts. Other large government programs, such as the Department of Veterans Affairs (VA) and Medicaid, have put this theory into practice and pay substantially lower prices for drugs relative to Medicare. Moreover, because foreign governments typically make greater use of their ability to regulate price levels, drug prices tend to be much lower in other countries.

Even if the federal government could take a more active role in setting price levels, it is not clear what the right levels should be and through which mechanisms they should be set. For example, Medicare could negotiate prices directly with manufacturers or directly set maximum reimbursement levels based on prices of similar drugs in other countries or average prices paid in the private sector.

The effects of federal regulation on pharmaceutical prices, profits, and total spending are complicated and run the risk of creating adverse consequences. Though such regulations might in fact reduce short-term drug spending, they may also limit incentives for research and development (R&D), which could lead to the development of fewer life-improving pharmaceutical innovations. If the government were to regulate prices, it would require a method to determine the appropriate value of the drug, not only for its potential to improve human life but also to support future R&D to improve that drug and develop additional ones. Such a daunting task has led some experts to conclude that prices should not be regulated under Medicare Part D. Instead the federal government should focus on preventing pricing practices that are clearly inefficient or abusive, such as in cases where a lack of clear competitors for a certain drug has led to monopolistic pricing.

Regardless of one's perspective on the value of the intensified focus on drug prices, it is clear that, within the budgetary discussion of paying for health care, the effort to reform health care delivery in the United States is still a work in progress. Although the ability of Medicare to negotiate drug prices was part of neither the MMA nor the Patient Protection and Affordable Care Act (ACA), the topic is now back in play. During an April 2011 speech at George Washington University, President Barack Obama described how he intends to cut $200 billion over 10 years in government prescription drug spending. In part, this would be achieved by leveraging Medicare's purchasing power.

In the following debate, David Carlson offers more details on these issues and others involved with lifting the noninterference clause from Medicare Part D. The Point asserts that the health care cost curve can be bent substantially by allowing Medicare the ability to negotiate directly with drug companies. The argument states that the United States is the only developed nation that does not negotiate drug benefits on behalf of its citizenry. It argues further that the claims of stifled innovation are overplayed.

In the Counterpoint, the ability of Medicare to determine drug prices outside the short term is called into question. In fact, the costs would simply shift to the private sector and ultimately push prices up for Medicare as well, yielding few savings over the long run. In addition, innovation and access to novel therapies would be restricted creating both an economic drag on a major U.S. industry and costing lives.

In reading this chapter, consider the following questions. First, is price regulation at the expense of slower innovation a reasonable trade-off? Second, are significant cost savings at the risk of drugs reaching the market more slowly a reasonable trade-off? Both sides of the debate have data to back up their contentions and refute certain contentions of the other side. Much of what makes this a difficult question is that individuals may be susceptible to confirmation bias, selecting those studies or data points that align to their philosophy or perspective. The reader is invited to consider both perspectives and draw his or her own conclusions.

POINT

Although numerous issues contribute to the high cost of care in the United States, one of the seemingly most significant is the ability of Medicare Part D, the federal government–funded prescription drug program primarily for seniors, to leverage its size to negotiate drug prices directly with pharmaceutical and biologic manufacturers. This chapter outlines how similar approaches in other U.S. government agencies and in other countries have impacted costs and addresses the notion of reduced innovation.

HOW DRUGS ARE PRICED

Before any detailed debate can commence, it is important to understand what is meant by drug "pricing" and what are the underlying mechanisms of pricing for pharmaceuticals in the United States. One factor complicating any discussion of drug prices is that there really are two types of prices. There are "demand" prices, which are those paid by individuals, such as Medicare enrollees, and there are "supply" prices, which reflect the payments received by drug manufacturers. The demand prices can often be much lower than the true cost or value of a drug, such as when an individual is only responsible for a coinsurance rate, which is usually a small percentage of the cost of the drug (Newhouse, 2004).

In this debate, the focus will be on supply prices, which are those which determine a drug manufacturer's profitability as well as the overall cost to taxpayers, because higher supply prices will drive up Medicare costs (Newhouse, 2004). One of the most confusing aspects of this debate is the number of supply prices (henceforth "prices") that currently exist for prescription pharmaceuticals and biologics. Examples of different pricing levels are listed in Table 25.1.

In addition to the numerous pricing methods outlined above, multiple fees and rebates further complicate the issue of identifying the "true" price. As prescription drugs move from manufacturers to consumers, a complex set of market transactions involving prices, discounts, and rebates may be triggered (Congressional Budget Office, 2007). For example, the average manufacture price (AMP) reflects all rebates paid by manufacturers to wholesalers. Such rebates typically act as price discounts from manufacturers that are negotiated with the wholesalers in exchange for buying a large volume of drugs. (Manufacturers often offer rebates to health plans, pharmaceutical benefit managers, and other third-party payers, but those are not reflected in the AMP.) The AMP generates additional rebates as manufacturers are required to report the AMP to the federal government, which in turn uses it to calculate the rebates that manufacturers are required to pay state Medicaid programs for sales to Medicaid beneficiaries (Congressional Budget Office, 2007). An illustrative list of different types of fees and rebates that distort the price of drugs is included in Table 25.2.

Table 25.1 A Sample of Different Drug Price Types Within the U.S. Health System

Price Type	Description
Average Manufacturer Price (AMP)	The average price paid by wholesalers or retail mail-order pharmacies who buy directly from manufacturers. The AMP is used as the basis for Medicaid drug pricing.
Average Wholesale Price (AWP)	A published list price for a drug sold by wholesalers to retail pharmacies and nonretail providers. In practice the AWP is not the price paid by retailers and nonretail providers (e.g., hospitals, nursing homes, and federal facilities) but, rather, often serves as the basis of payment to pharmacies by pharmaceutical benefit managers and health plans.
Wholesale Acquisition Cost (WAC)	The manufacturer's list price (or published price) for sales of a drug to wholesalers; although, in practice, the WAC is not what wholesalers pay for the drug.
Federal Supply Schedule (FSS)	Pricing for federal entities such as the Department of Defense and the Department of Veteran Affairs.

Source: Congressional Budget Office. 2007. Prescription Drug Pricing in the Private Sector.

Table 25.2 A Sample of Different Drug Discounts Within the U.S. Health System

Discount Type	Description
Administrative Fee	Fee that is often a flat percent of Gross Sales paid by drug manufacturers to Group Purchasing Organizations (GPOs) to fund the bundling of purchase entities (such as hospitals and other institutional buyers).
Base Discount	A flat discount that is applied to the Gross Sales of a Drug regardless of product performance.
Best Price Discount	A form of discount given to Medicaid programs that represent the best pricing given for a drug in the commercial market.
Most Favored Nation Discount	An agreement where the drug manufacturer agrees to provide an entity with the best pricing and results in additional discounts when that pricing is exceeded.
Performance Discount	A variable discount that is applied to the Gross Sales of a Drug based on product performance. The performance discount is based on tiers or hurdle rates that must be achieved for the discount to be applied. The tiers are commonly based on the Drug's Market Share or the Drug's Market Share vs. National Market Share.
Price Protection Discount	An agreement where the drug manufacturer agrees not to increase prices beyond a certain percent results in additional discounts when that percent is exceeded.
Supplemental Discount	Discount paid to a single or group of state Medicaid programs that exceeds the federally prescribed level of discount (currently 23.1%).

Source: PharmaMetrics, Inc. September 2011.

All of this serves to illustrate how difficult it can be for someone who does not specialize in drug pricing to objectively gauge the true cost of a product, and thus contribute to a well-informed debate. As is made clear by the AMP example, even further complicating matters is the fact that many of these individual price types are not independent but, rather, have a direct impact on each other.

The supply chain is how drugs move from manufacturers to consumers. Consumers obtain about three-quarters of their prescriptions drugs from retail pharmacies (e.g., Rite-Aid) and the remainder from nonretail providers (e.g., hospitals, nursing homes, health maintenance organizations, and federal facilities). Retail pharmacies and nonretail providers purchase the majority of their drugs from wholesalers. Wholesalers help simplify the number of transactions a retailer or nonretail provider would have to initiate in order to obtain all of the different types of drugs needed from each of the many manufacturers. In some cases, a retailer or nonretail provider that is large enough to act as its own wholesaler, such as a large chain pharmacy, may purchase drugs directly from manufacturers (Congressional Budget Office, 2007).

Retail pharmacies and nonretail providers negotiate drug prices with wholesalers or pharmaceutical manufactures (in cases where drugs are purchased directly from the manufacturers). There are two additional negotiations in the retail pharmacy market: (1) between health plans or self-insured employers and the manufacturers and (2) between health plans and self-insured employers and retail pharmacies. The health plans and self-insured employers often contract out their negotiations to pharmacy benefit managers (PBMs). PBMs can negotiate on behalf of multiple health plans or self-insured employers, thus leveraging a large number of potential consumers to obtain rebates from manufactures, which are in turn shared with health plans and employers (Congressional Budget Office, 2007).

MEDICARE'S ROLE IN PART D

In the supply chain, Medicare essentially plays the role of a consumer in the Part D framework. This is so because Medicare outsources the Part D benefit to private health plans. Thus, Medicare has a passive role in determining the prices paid for drugs. This was done by design; included in the legislation that enacted the Part D program was a "noninterference clause" preventing the federal government from being a third party in price negotiations between pharmaceutical manufacturers and Part D drug plans.

Instead, Medicare focuses on ensuring some minimum standards for private plans to participate in the Part D program, as well as administering the monthly payments to the participating plans for each Medicare beneficiary that they enroll. The enrollees are responsible for paying a monthly premium and for making co-payments (which may be the entire price of the drug if the drug is not covered). However, Medicare highly subsidizes the premium, as well as covers a substantial share of the drug costs (Medicare Payment and Advisory Commission, 2011).

The subsidies include providing monthly capitated payments to plans, as well as covering 80 percent of costs once a beneficiary accrues above a certain out-of-pocket threshold for annual drug costs. By sharing in the drug costs, Medicare also shares in some of the financial risk that plan's take, as the monthly payments they receive for each enrollee (including both the enrollee and Medicare portions) may not be enough to finance higher than expected costs (i.e., enrollees may use more drugs than expected). Medicare also pays most of the cost sharing and premiums for low-income enrollees, which adds to the Medicare Part D costs (Medicare Payment and Advisory Commission, 2011).

In 2010 the federal government incurred about $62 billion in total Part D expenditures. Only about 10 percent of those costs are covered by Medicare beneficiary premium payments, leaving the vast majority to be financed by taxpayers. From 2011 to 2020 Part D expenditures are expected to reach well over $1 trillion (The Board of Trustees, 2011).

NEGOTIATIONS IN PART D

As a result of the way Part D was configured, Medicare currently directs nearly 1,500 private Part D drug plan sponsors. Each of these private insurers implements different benefit designs, formulary lists, and premium structures. To create a fractured buying group such as this defies normal purchasing logic and creates additional administrative costs. This has real consequences on the price paid for therapies by Medicare beneficiaries and U.S. taxpayers alike.

That so many private insurers administer the drug program means that there will be significant marketing, member acquisition, and member retention costs as plans compete for Medicare enrollees. Plan profits are additional costs that need to be financed by the Medicare Part D program. Providers (i.e., pharmacies, hospitals, and physicians) also face additional costs associated with having to deal with many insurers (instead of just Medicare) for drug reimbursements.

More critical, though, is the lost opportunity to leverage the size of the Medicare population to negotiate prices. In general, one of the key tenets of price negotiation for a product or service is that "size matters" and prices generally decline for a purchaser who commands a larger share of a market; consider Walmart, General Electric, or Microsoft. Each of these corporate titans uses its size to squeeze prices charged by suppliers who are eager to gain access to their large footprint, or conversely to negotiate higher prices for their products due, in part, to their influence within a market. Medicare, as a unit, is one of the largest purchasers of pharmaceuticals in the world and to not leverage that size for the benefit of the citizenry results in very real costs for the U.S. taxpayer and each Medicare Part D enrollee.

PHARMACEUTICAL PURCHASING SYSTEMS OF THE VA
AND OTHER FEDERAL GOVERNMENT AGENCIES

Those in favor of the federal government negotiating prices for the Part D program often point to the pharmaceutical purchasing system of the Department of Veterans Affairs (VA). One study by Families USA showed that seniors on Medicare pay about 58 percent more for major prescription drugs than do those that get their prescriptions through the VA. This is important because the VA acquires pharmaceuticals predominantly from the Federal Supply Schedule (FSS), a *negotiated* contract between the federal government and drug manufacturers. FSS prices for the pharmaceutical schedule are negotiated by the VA based on the prices that manufacturers charge their "most-favored" nonfederal customers under comparable terms and conditions.

Not only can the VA negotiate prices but it has the authority to create a national formulary, something Medicare is also prohibited from doing because of the "noninterference" clause. The VA uses that ability to develop a national formula to restrict the number of drugs that are covered, which gives them even more bargaining leverage with respect to drug plan manufacturers. A recent study by Frakt, Pizer, and Feldman (2011) suggests that Medicare could save about $14 billion per year (in 2009 prices) if it restricted its formularies to the level of generosity offered by the VA and obtained VA-like drug prices by doing so.

It should be noted, though, that the benefit of those savings would be at least partially offset by the fact that Part D enrollees would lose low-cost access to some drugs. Because each plan participating in Medicare Part D can have a different mix of drugs on their formularies and they are required to have a minimum amounts of drugs (usually at least two) in each drug class on their formulary (drugs are classified into a class by the chemical type of the active ingredient or by the way it is used to treat a particular condition), a fairly wide range of drugs end up covered under Part D. This improves the chances that Part D enrollees will be offered a plan that covers their preferred drugs. Again, Frakt, Pizer, and Feldman estimate that, on average, Medicare plans cover about 85 percent of the most popular 200 drugs (ranging from 68 percent to 93 percent); whereas the VA's national formulary includes only about 59 percent of the most popular 200 drugs. However, Frakt, Pizer, and Feldman also suggest that the savings achieved from being able to better negotiate drugs (estimated at $510 per enrollee) could be used to more than offset the loss of choice (the value of which the authors monetize at $405 per enrollee) experienced by the enrollees.

The VA is not the only federal agency to take advantage of its market leverage. Drug prices under Medicaid are also substantially lower than in Medicare. Although the federal government shares in the Medicaid costs by matching state expenditures, reimbursement levels for all Medicaid-covered services and items, including prescription drugs, are set by the states. However, prescription drugs are subject to federal upper limits (FULs) established by federal law to restrict the amount of federal matching payments available for those products. The FULs are typically set as a percentage of the AMP reported by pharmaceutical manufacturers. As was discussed above, the AMP is also used to help set the rebates that manufacturers must pay to the states. These rebates help ensure that states receive the "best price" for the drugs, something that is justified by the notion that Medicaid is the health-coverage program of last resort and consequently should have access to the lowest prices offered in the drug market (Jacobson, Panangala, & Hearne, 2007).

Interestingly, Medicare does use its leverage for drugs purchased under the Medicare Part B program, which covers the cost of a limited number of prescription drugs, including drugs furnished incident to a physician's service (e.g., injectable drugs used in connection with the treatment of cancer), drugs explicitly covered by statute (e.g., some vaccines and oral anticancer drugs), and drugs used in conjunction with durable medical equipment (e.g., inhalation drugs). Medicare beneficiaries receive drugs covered under Part B primarily in physician offices and hospital outpatient departments. For most Part B drugs, the Medicare provider actually acquires the drug (usually from a wholesaler) and then gets reimbursed by Medicare when the drug is administered.

Part B drug prices are determined using a reimbursement rate-setting approach; that is, Medicare acts as a price-setter and dictates the amount it will pay. More specifically, for most Part B drugs, Medicare is legislated to set the prices at 106 percent of their manufacturer reported average sales price (ASP), which is similar to the AMP in that it includes most rebates and discounts associated with drug sales. The extra 6 percent is meant to cover provider overhead costs to administer the drug. The idea behind using the ASP is to ensure that the Part B price for the product is tied to the actual (discounted) sales price available to nongovernmental entities.

THE GLOBAL CONTEXT

The United States is the only industrialized nation that does not negotiate preferential drug prices on behalf of its citizens. Ample research shows that, by nearly every measure, the United States spends significantly more on health care than any other Organization for Economic Cooperation and Development (OECD) country. At the same time, the data also show that the United States is no healthier than many of these same countries, which raises questions of the value delivered per health care dollar spent.

The disparity between drug prices in the United States and in other countries exemplifies why health care is so much more expensive in the former. One Congressional Budget Office (CBO) study in 2004 found that foreign countries pay 35 to 55 percent less for drugs. A separate study published in *Health Affairs* had similar findings: "In 2003 citizens of Canada, the United Kingdom, and France paid an average of 34 to 59 percent of what Americans paid for a similar market basket of pharmaceuticals" (Anderson, Shea, Hussey, Keyhani, & Zephyrin, 2004). A major driver for the elevated costs is the hesitance to put in place pricing restraints such as benchmark or reference pricing, price controls, or the use of negotiated formularies that enables Medicare to leverage its size to negotiate preferential drug pricing.

LITTLE IMPACT ON INNOVATION

Many who argue for the prohibition of direct negotiation for Medicare cite the impact on the pace of innovation within medical research and development (R&D). This concern is overstated, given that most true medical breakthroughs do not come out of the profits of the pharmaceutical industry, but rather emerge directly or indirectly (via grants) from the National Institutes of Health (NIH). Much of what comes out of major pharmaceutical company R&D relates to patent-extending coatings or enhancements to existing therapies, as such developments can have a much more predictable financial outcome for the company. In fact, the pace of innovation from the pharmaceutical industry has slowed to the point that the Obama administration authorized a new federal drug development center, the National Center for Advancing Translational Sciences, within NIH. These moves reflect actions to compensate for a steady decline in productivity of the drug industry over the past 15 years.

Furthermore, David Light suggested in a 2009 study in *Health Affairs* that the United States is not necessarily the innovative hub it often considers itself. Light shows that European manufacturers have actually been more innovative when it comes to drug development than their American counterparts, in spite of Europe's lower drug prices. This is further evidence that the true cost of more constrained pricing may not have nearly the impact often suggested.

CONCLUSION

The United States is the only industrialized nation to not negotiate preferential drug prices on behalf of its citizens. The United States is unique in mindfully reducing the leverage of a government insurance program by fracturing a singular entity (Medicare) into over a thousand separate entities (individual prescription drug plans), thus diluting the aggregate purchasing power. This is a major reason that the United States outspends other OECD countries on health care with little perceptible gain in the quality of that care. Furthermore, warnings about reduced innovation are overstated given the lagging levels of R&D discovery within the manufacturing community and the increasing role of government in this process.

Note: This chapter was authored to articulate both sides of a given argument. The views expressed in this chapter are not necessarily the views of the author.

REFERENCES AND FURTHER READING

Anderson, G. F., Reinhardt, U. E., Hussey, P., & Petrosyan, V. (2003). It's the prices, stupid: Why the United States is so different from other countries. *Health Affairs, 22*(3), 89–105.

Anderson, G. F., Shea, D. G., Hussey, P. S., Keyhani, S., & Zephyrin, L. (2004). Doughnut holes and price controls. *Health Affairs* (W4), 396–404.

Baker, D. (2006). *The savings from an efficient Medicare prescription drug plan.* Retrieved from Center for Economic and Policy Research website: http://www.cepr.net/documents/efficient_medicare_2006_01.pdf

The Board of Trustees. (2011). *2011 Annual report of the boards of trustees of the federal hospital insurance and federal supplementary medical insurance trust funds.* Retrieved from http://www.cms.gov/ReportsTrustFunds/downloads/tr2011.pdf

Cohn, J. (2006). Private lesson. *The New Republic.* Retrieved from http://www.tnr.com/article/pelosis-pet-issue-private-lesson

Congressional Budget Office. (2004). *Would prescription drug importation reduce U.S. drug spending?* Retrieved from http://www.cbo.gov/doc.cfm?index=5406&type=0

Congressional Budget Office. (2007). *Prescription drug pricing in the private sector.* Retrieved from http://www.cbo.gov/ftpdocs/77xx/doc7715/01-03-PrescriptionDrug.pdf

Davis, K., Schoen, C., Guterman, S., Shih, T., Schoenbaum, S. C., & Weinbaum, I. (2007). *Slowing the growth of U.S. health care expenditures: What are the options?* Washington, DC: The Commonwealth Fund.

Families USA. (2007). *Rhetoric versus reality: Comparing Medicare Part D prices to VA prices.* Retrieved from http://www.familiesusa.org/assets/pdfs/rhetoric-vs-reality.PDF

Frakt, A., Pizer, S. D., & Feldman, R. (2011). Should Medicare adopt the Veterans Health Administration formulary? *Health Economics.* doi: 10.1002/hec.1733

Harris, G. (2011, January 22). Federal research center will help develop medicines. *The New York Times.* Retrieved from http://www.nytimes.com/2011/01/23/health/policy/23drug.html?pagewanted=all

Jacobson, G. (2007). *Pharmaceutical costs: A comparison of Department of Veterans Affairs (VA), Medicaid, and Medicare Policies* (CRS Report for Congress). Retrieved from http://lieberman.senate.gov/assets/pdf/crs/vapharma.pdf

Light, D. (2009). Global drug discovery: Europe is ahead. *Health Affairs, 28*(5), w969–w977.

Medicare Payment and Advisory Commission. (2011). *Payment basics: Part D payment system.* Retrieved from http://www.medpac.gov/
documents/MedPAC_Payment_Basics_11_PartD.pdf

Newhouse, J. (2004). How much should Medicare pay for drugs? *Health Affairs, 23*(1), 89–102.

David W. Carlson

COUNTERPOINT

Many have claimed that allowing Medicare to directly negotiate with drug companies will reduce drug costs. This view ignores the basic structure of drug pricing within the United States, what drives costs in the pharmaceutical marketplace, and the broader definition of "cost" that one must consider if a holistic policy argument is to be made. The rationale for making this change to existing law is framed by two primary assertions: (1) that current drug costs are mispriced in the pharmaceutical marketplace and (2) that enabling Medicare to use its purchasing power to negotiate these prices directly would curb costs more than is possible under today's model. This side of the debate will outline why these assertions are based on false assumptions and how this approach endangers the spirit of innovation that has led to a major growth industry within the U.S. economy, an improvement in treatment options for patients, and the dramatic extension of life expectancy itself.

PRICES UNDER THE CURRENT MEDICARE PART D PROGRAM

Medicare Part D benefits are provided through one of two types of private insurance plans: (1) Prescription Drug Plans (PDPs), which provides coverage only for prescription drug costs, and (2) Medicare Advantage-Prescription Drug (MA-PD) plans, which insure all Medicare-covered services, including hospital care and physician services as well as prescription drugs. These plans contract with the Centers for Medicare & Medicaid Services (CMS) to offer services in defined regions across the United States.

Plans are financed through a combination of enrollee monthly premiums and subsidies from the federal government. Before the start of the year, each plan must submit to CMS an estimate, known as a bid, of the expected plan's average monthly revenue requirement for providing the basic benefit during the upcoming year (including administrative costs and profits, as well as drug costs). CMS uses these bids to calculate a national average bid, which is used to calculate the base monthly premium paid by enrollees. That is, the base premium is set as a percentage of the national average bid. For 2012 the national average bid amount is $84.50 and the base premium is $31.08 (Centers for Medicare & Medicaid Services [CMS], 2011).

If a plan's bid differs from the average bid, its monthly premium will differ from the base premium by the same amount. For example, if a plan's bid is above the national average by one dollar, the monthly premium for enrollees also would increase by one dollar. The government subsidy does not change. The goal of this system is to encourage plans to keep costs down through price competition, because plans with lower costs will be able to offer lower bids and consequently lower (and more attractive) premiums. When the Medicare beneficiary is making a choice between the plans available to him or her, monthly premiums, the drugs covered on the formularies, and drug prices (co-pays or the plan's negotiated drug prices for noncovered drugs) can all be expected to factor heavily into the decision.

Many experts believe that the current framework of the Part D system already leads to substantial price-reductions and that Medicare would be hard pressed to achieve greater savings without some unintended adverse effects (Congressional Budget Office, 2007; Duggan & Scott Morton, 2008; Duggan & Scott Morton, 2011; Holtz-Eakin, 2004). The ability of the plans to secure lower prices largely emanates from their ability to exclude certain drugs from their formulary and steer their enrollees away from certain drugs (a notion known as "control") in response to the prices of those treatments.

A formulary is a list of drugs approved by a drug benefit plan for coverage. Patients pay specific co-payments or co-insurance for the drugs on formulary. Patients typically pay the full cost for drugs not on a plan's formulary. Generally, the goal of a formulary is to reduce drug expenditures by steering members of the plan to specific drugs deemed to have a good cost-benefit ratio relative to competitive products. Plans encourage the use of preferred drugs by using such tactics as prior authorization or by having lower co-pays. This ability gives plans the leverage to negotiate price reductions from pharmaceutical manufacturers. Pharmaceutical manufacturers have the incentive to sell their drugs at lower prices in exchange for the market share the plan can deliver.

The development of formularies also often results in the use of generic drugs, as opposed to brand-name drugs. Generics may treat the same disease state as branded products and can have similar effectiveness, though branded products are often considered more advanced. Generics no longer enjoy patent protection, and this exposure to greater competition often drives down prices. These competitors are able to accept lower prices due, in part, to the fact that they did not have to finance the substantial investments required to develop the drug and bring it to market. DiMasi, Hansen, and Grabowski (2003) estimated the research and development costs for 68 randomly selected new drugs to be about $800 million (in 2000 dollars). Generic drugs are significantly lower in price compared to brand-name drugs. Hence, substantial savings can be achieved by encouraging consumers to use generics in the place of brand-name drugs.

MEDICARE AS A NEGOTIATOR

If Medicare were to be granted the authority to negotiate directly with drug companies, several major political and operational issues would need to be resolved before Medicare could achieve savings relative to the private sector, without creating unintended adverse effects. Some of those issues are discussed below.

"Negotiation" really means "regulation." First, it is important to better understand what is meant by the term "negotiation" in the context of the federal government's playing a larger role in Part D prices. In general, Medicare tends to set (or regulate) prices for covered medical services and products, such as hospital and physician care. The major exception is the way prices are currently determined for drugs under Part D, which also happens to be in stark contrast to how drugs are priced under other federal government programs, such as Medicaid, Veterans Affairs (VA), or Medicare Part B. In each of those cases, the government essentially uses a rigid formula to set the reimbursement amount of the drug. It can be expected that the government would use a similar approach with Part D if given the authority to "negotiate" prices with manufacturers.

Regulation that limits the ability of markets to develop organically from competition and other traditional market forces is typically viewed negatively by American society. From a political perspective, this explains the current configuration of the Part D program. Changing the system will likely require a lot of political capital and draw much scrutiny—particularly if there is not clear evidence of savings or if unintended consequences occur.

What are the right prices? The possibility of the government playing a larger role in setting drug prices also raises the question of what prices the government should pay for Medicare Part D drugs. Joseph Newhouse looks at this issue from an economic theory perspective, which states that the optimal price for a drug would be the level at which the last dollar spent provides as much value as that dollar would if it were used to buy any other good or service. This means being able to determine what the value of the drug is relative to its alternatives and includes considering the potential benefit of research and development that could be funded by the price of the drug (Newhouse, 2004). Given these goals, says Newhouse, it is difficult (if not impossible) to determine the "optimal price" for a drug.

As was mentioned above, there are enormous research and development costs associated with bringing a drug to market. Prices need to support those costs or pharmaceutical manufacturers will not continue to make those investments, a development that might serve to limit future medical innovation. It is also important to note that drug prices must support marketing costs so that pharmaceutical manufacturers can induce enough demand to remain profitable. However, if prices get too high, manufacturers may be incentivized to induce potentially abusive levels of utilization (Garber, Jones, & Romer, 2006; Newhouse, 2004).

Medicare negotiona is not likely to keep costs down. It is also important to understand that drug prices in the Medicare market have far-reaching implications for the prices experienced by other payers. The pharmaceutical industry has very real costs and investor expectations to contend with, which will force these companies to identify ways to "make up" any lost revenues. Assuming Medicare reduces its prices, the most straightforward way to make up for lost revenue is to increase pricing in the private sector. In fact, there is a great deal of variation in prices for the same drug across payers and countries, as pharmaceutical manufacturers deal with differing levels of negotiating leverage and price regulations while trying to remain profitable (Frank, 2001).

Should Medicare create a formulary? As discussed earlier, drug pricing, patient cost sharing, and other access barriers between a patient and product are very much part of a traditional negotiation between pharmaceutical manufacturers and insurers. Manufacturers are willing to pay large discounts to insurers to make sure access barriers between patients and pharmaceuticals are as shallow as possible. It is for this reason that the access barriers exist, as they are the "stick" that enables insurers to negotiate substantial discounts. Given the importance of formularies in reducing prices, two issues are worth bringing up in this debate: (1) whether Medicare Part D should have a national formulary and (2) whether Medicare could be as effective as private plans at developing a formulary.

A major challenge to the possibility that a restrictive Part D formulary could succeed as a cost-savings instrument is that much of the growth in pharmaceutical use is due to the financial savings offered by the drugs' ability to offset more costly and invasive medical techniques (commonly referred to as "medical offsets"). Thus, a problem with establishing a formulary system for Medicare beneficiaries is that any cost savings on drugs are often due to restrictions that can be placed on the drugs, which may in turn lead to more costly and invasive medical intervention. In fact, McWilliams, Zaslavksy, and Huskamp (2011) found that implementation of Part D was associated with significant reduction in non-drug health care spending for Medicare beneficiaries with limited prior drug coverage. Previous research has also found specific links between more restrictive formularies and increased physician office, emergency room, and inpatient hospital utilization (Horn et al., 1996). Because Medicare covers both medical and pharmacy benefits, the implementation of such an approach would run the risk of leading to additional costs, rather than creating savings. As Medicare beneficiaries are high users of pharmaceuticals and are susceptible to multiple chronic conditions, restrictive formulary may not be the best approach to achieving overall cost savings.

As for whether Medicare could be as effective in its use of a formulary to control drug costs, it is important to consider how private plans combine formularies with other mechanisms to achieve savings. There is the assumption that, aside from the product profile, the size of Medicare is the principle driver of net pricing (prices after discounts). This is false. Pharmaceuticals and biologics are not consumer packaged goods (CPG), among which size is often the most important driver of price negotiations after consideration of a product's core attributes. The most important factor considered by drug manufacturers is the notion of "control." Control is the insurance provider's ability to restrict or impact drug flows by erecting barriers between the patient and the product. A host of mechanisms can be used by an entity to make it more difficult for a patient to get a product and exert control. Some of the most common are found in Table 25.3.

The factors in Table 25.3 are of greatest concern to drug manufacturers when they determine the discounts paid to insurers. Private drug plans have spent decades developing these mechanisms of control, and there is little data to suggest that the government would do a better job in this regard. Furthermore, it is likely that some of these mechanisms of control would be politically difficult for a governmental agency to implement, such as an NDC (National Drug Code) Block, because there is a greater expectation that the government will provide complete care while insurance providers may face less "moral outrage."

Why does control matter so much to drug manufacturers? The mechanisms of control placed on a pharmaceutical or biologic product have a large impact on the drug's market share within the covered lives of the insurance provider. Many of the largest insurance providers have struggled to exert the mechanisms of control described in this section, while some smaller providers are able to completely lock a drug manufacturer out of their lives covered. Another way to think about this from a drug manufacturer standpoint is that the size of an insurer only indicates the number of lives that are likely to *need* drug therapy. Size in no way indicates how well the insurer is able to steer those lives to one therapy over another. It is largely that ability to steer therapy that incentivize drug manufacturers to pay large discounts.

A CHALLENGE TO INNOVATION AND ECONOMICS

In addition to the questionable cost impact of enabling Medicare to negotiate directly with drug companies, there is the question of how any cost savings would impact research and development. That is, even if the desired effect of a major impact on the cost curve of drug expenditures could be realized or if the undesired effect of a cost shift away from the

Table 25.3 Sample of Utilization Controls

Mechanism of Control	Description	Impact
Large Co-Pay Differentials	Co-pays represent the amount of money an insured person is expected to pay for a medical, pharmaceutical, or biologic treatment. An insurance provider's ability to create large differences in out-of-pocket costs for patients is seen as highly controlling because patients will gravitate to lower-cost alternatives rather than strictly what was prescribed.	Large co-pay differentials steer patients to lower out-of-pocket products, which invariably means some people will pay more for their presciptions and some less.
Rejections for Prior Authorization	Rejection for Prior Authorization is when an insurance provider blocks coverage for a patient's medication and requires a prescriber to contact the insurance provider to authorize the presciption.	This delays a patient getting the prescription by as little as 30 minutes or as much as several weeks.
Rejections for Step Edit	Rejection for Step Edit is when an Insurance provider blocks coverage for a patient's medication and requires the use of less expensive medications or therapies before allowing the prescription for the higher cost product to be approved.	This delays a patient getting the prescription by requiring the use of other therapies before the treatment recommended by the physician.
Rejections for NDC Block	Rejection for NDC Block (sometimes referred to as Rejection for Product Not Covered) is when an insurance provider blocks coverage for a patient's medication with no meaningful recourse. The patient is required to pay for the full cost of the medication out-of-pocket.	This is intended to push patients toward those drugs that are covered, thus preventing the patient from having to pay for the full cost of medication out-of-pocket.

Source: PharmaMetrics, Inc., September 2011.

pharmacy benefit to the medical benefit were to take place, would that produce unintended negative consequences? As implied, the answer is yes.

One such consequence would be a notable decline in R&D investments in innovative medications. This could have far-reaching implications on the rate of treatment discovery, given that the vast majority of innovation occurs within the pharmaceutical industry and the investments, both in terms of finances and time (it takes years to bring a drug to market), are so high (DiMasi et al., 2003). As an example of the importance of the biopharmaceutical industry, one National Institutes of Health (NIH) study (2001) claimed that only 4 out of 47 successful drugs (defined as having sales in excess of $500 million) had NIH involvement. This yields a host of impacts not typically addressed in cost discussions.

The most immediate impact of a reduced rate-of-cure is that patients will not have access to treatments that would otherwise exist. There is also good evidence from other nations, with much lower prices, that innovative products are slower to reach the market, potentially causing lower quality of care. The resulting reduction in treatment options and, potentially, life expectations for the U.S. population is surely a cost that should be considered.

In addition to the impact on innovation, the pharmaceutical and biotech industries are major contributors to the U.S. economy with "Pharmaceutical Preparations," defined as drugs intended for human or veterinary use presented in their finished dosage form, representing the fourth-largest export category of the United States. By no means is the argument that this industry should be indirectly subsidized via inefficient pricing, but rather that the costs associated with the lost revenues from decreased innovation should be included in policymakers' calculus.

CONCLUSION

There is clear and compelling evidence that allowing Medicare to negotiate with drug companies directly will not only fail to reduce overall health care costs in the long term but also that doing so will lead to a host of other unintended consequences often ignored in the cost debate. Although current drug costs are rising at a rapid rate, this rise is not due to mispriced products but rather the ability of therapies to replace more costly medical procedures. The impact is that more of the cost equation is falling into the drug-benefit category rather than that of a medical benefit.

In short, to allow Medicare to use its purchasing power to negotiate drug prices directly would simply shift costs to medical procedures and the private sector in the short term and in the long term yield no cost savings whatsoever. In addition, when one considers the lost industry productivity and export revenues from declining rates of innovation, the cost equation becomes even more negative. Lastly, lost innovation will have a debilitating impact on quality of care and treatment options for the American public, a qualitative cost that is no less real for being difficult to measure.

Note: This chapter was authored to articulate both sides of a given argument. The views expressed in this chapter are not necessarily the views of the author.

REFERENCES AND FURTHER READING

AMCP Task Force on Drug Payment Methodology. (2007). *AMCP guide to pharmaceutical payment methods.* Retrieved from http://www.amcp.org/data/jmcp/JMCPSUPPC_OCT07.pdf

Centers for Medicare & Medicaid Services (CMS). (2011). *Annual release of Part D national average bid amount and other Part C & D bid related information.* Retrieved from https://www.cms.gov/MedicareAdvtgSpecRateStats/Downloads/PartDandMABenchmarks2012.pdf

Congressional Budget Office. (2006). *Research and development in the pharmaceutical industry.* Retrieved from http://www.cbo.gov/ftpdocs/76xx/doc7615/10-02-DrugR-D.pdf

Congressional Budget Office. (2007). *Congressional Budget Office cost estimate: S.3 Medicare prescription Drug Price Negotiation Act of 2007.* Retrieved from http://www.cbo.gov/ftpdocs/80xx/doc8006/s3.pdf

Department of Health and Human Services Office of the Inspector General. (2001). *Medicare reimbursement of prescription drugs.* Retrieved from http://oig.hhs.gov/oei/reports/oei-03-00-00310.pdf

DiMasi, J. A., Hansen, R. W., & Grabowski, H. G. (2003). The price of innovation: new estimates of drug development costs. *Journal of Health Economics, 22*(2), 151–185.

Duggan, M., & Scott Morton, F. M. (2005). *The distortionary effects of government procurement: Evidence from Medicaid prescription drug purchasing* (National Bureau of Economic Research Working Paper No. 10930).

Duggan, M., & Scott Morton, F. M. (2008). *The effect of Medicare Part D on pharmaceutical prices and utilization* (National Bureau of Economic Research Working Paper No. 13917). Retrieved from http://www.nber.org/papers/w13917.pdf

Duggan, M., & Scott Morton, F. M. (2011). *The medium-term impact of Medicare Part D on pharmaceutical prices.* Retrieved from http://bpub.wharton.upenn.edu/documents/research/Duggan%20-%20PandP2011DugganScottMortonPaper.pdf

Frank, R. G. (2001). Prescription drug prices: Why do some pay more than others do? *Health Affairs, 20*(2), 115–128.

Garber, A. M., Jones, C. I., & Romer, P. M. (2006). *Insurance and incentives for medical innovation* (National Bureau of Economic Research Working Paper No. 12080). Cambridge, MA: National Bureau of Economic Research. Retrieved from http://www.nber.org/papers/w12080.pdf?new_window=1

Gorman, L. (2002). *Medicaid drug formularies* (Issue Paper No. 2-2002). Retrieved from Independence Institute website: http://www.i2i.org/articles/IP_2_2002.pdf

Hogberg, D. (2007). Letting Medicare "negotiate" drug prices: Myths vs. reality. *National Policy Analysis.* Retrieved from http://www.nationalcenter.org/NPA550MedicareDrugPrices.html

Holtz-Eakin, D. (2004). *Letter to Honorable William H. Frist, January 23, 2004.* Retrieved from http://www.cbo.gov/ftpdocs/49xx/doc4986/FristLetter.pdf

Horn, S. D., Sharkey, P. D., Tracy, D. M., Horn, C. E., James, B., & Goodwin, F. (1996). Intended and unintended consequences of HMO cost-containment strategies: Results from the Managed Care Outcomes Project. *The American Journal of Managed Care, 2*(3), 253–264.

McWilliams, J. M., Zaslavksy, A. M., & Huskamp, H. A. (2011). Implementation of Medicare Part D and nondrug medical spending for elderly adults with limited prior drug coverage. *Journal of the American Medical Association, 306*(4), 402–409.

National Institutes of Health. (2001). *NIH response to the conference report request for a plan to ensure taxpayers' interests are protected.* Washington, DC: U.S. Department of Health and Human Services. Retrieved from http://www.ott.nih.gov/policy/policy_protect_text.html

New York State Department of Health. (n.d.). *Definitions for Medicare/Medicaid dual eligibles and Medicare Part D information.* Retrieved from http://www.health.state.ny.us/health_care/medicaid/program/medicaid_transition/definitions.htm

Newhouse, J. (2004). How much should Medicare pay for drugs? *Health Affairs, 23*(1), 89–102.

David W. Carlson

26

Medicaid Program Flexibility

POINT: A block grant provision such as the one suggested by Representative Paul Ryan of Wisconsin would give states more flexibility to administer the Medicaid program, while also controlling the costs to the federal government.

R. Paul Duncan and Lilliana L. Bell, College of Public Health and Health Professions,
University of Florida

COUNTERPOINT: The current matching strategy used by the federal government to support state Medicaid programs is necessary to ensure that states are effectively providing access to care for some of the neediest and most at-risk populations, including children, pregnant women, low-income workers, and the disabled.

Allyson G. Hall and Shenae K. Samuels, College of Public Health and Health Professions,
University of Florida

Introduction

Medicaid is the core financing program that pays for the health and medical care of people without insurance or other means to pay for that care. The program has existed since the U.S. Congress passed Title XIX of the Social Security Act of 1965. Regulatory and management responsibility for Medicaid is jointly held by the federal and state governments.

In 2010 President Barack Obama signed the Patient Protection and Affordable Care Act (ACA), which in part authorized an increase in the number of people eligible for Medicaid. While the Supreme Court, in its June 2012 ruling, limited the ability of the federal government to force states to expand coverage, it is expected that most states will. This increase in enrollment raises concerns about the financial burden of Medicaid on both the federal and state budgets. Specifically, the current open-ended federal matching and entitlement structure makes the federal and state government legally obligated to provide benefits to those who qualify. Conservative commentators have advocated the use of block grants and increased state flexibility as a means to improve efficiency and reduce cost.

Each state manages its own Medicaid program within a cooperative framework overseen by the Centers for Medicare & Medicaid Services (CMS). Each state is responsible for program design, including eligibility requirements, covered services, implementation and management, and the appropriation of the state financial share. In general, the federal roles are (1) to establish core program guidelines and responsibilities (i.e., setting the minimum attributes and characteristics of the program that must be followed by all states) and (2) to manage the federal financial contribution to the program. The federal and state partnership aspect of Medicaid has long been touted as an important positive attribute that allows each state's program to vary somewhat in order to meet its unique needs, while ensuring a national foundation of minimum program characteristics and shared financial responsibilities.

Though state participation in Medicaid is voluntary, as of this writing each of the 50 states, the District of Columbia, and all U.S. territories operate their own Medicaid programs. In recent years, a few commentaries have raised the possibility of state withdrawal from the program, though it seems such suggestions are made mainly for polemic purposes.

No serious policy proposals to that end have been thoroughly developed. Certainly it is difficult to discern how savings achieved at the state level could possibly replace the federal dollars, so state withdrawal from the program would almost certainly mean much higher state costs (to maintain the existing level of service) or significant reductions in the medical care available for the most vulnerable.

States are legally obligated to provide benefits to those who qualify. Qualification is based on membership in an eligible category. These include families with dependent children, the elderly, those who are blind, and those who have other permanent disabilities of a serious nature. Individuals within these groups must also lack the income and resources insufficient to meet the costs of their medical care.

Medicaid currently covers 45 percent of all Americans with incomes below the Federal Poverty Level (FPL), which in 2012 was defined as $23,050 per year for a family of four. In 2011 the program served more than 69.5 million enrollees (Congressional Budget Office, 2011b). Under the entitlement structure, states are required to cover mandatory beneficiaries and can choose to expand coverage to optional beneficiaries. Mandatory beneficiaries include pregnant women and children under age six with family incomes below 133 percent FPL, children between ages 6 and 18 below 100 percent FPL, parents below states' July 1996 welfare eligibility cutoffs (below 50 percent FPL), and most elderly and individuals with disabilities who receive Supplemental Security Income (SSI) (Kaiser Commission on Medicaid and the Uninsured, 2011c). For states choosing to comply, the Patient Protection and Affordable Care Act (ACA) requires that, starting in 2014, the income eligibility level be expanded to 138 percent FPL; the ACA set state eligibility at 133 percent FPL but includes a stipulation to exclude the first 5 percent of an individual's income so the required FPL is effectively 138 percent. Consequently, low-income childless adults under age 65 will become eligible for Medicaid in 2014.

Medicaid is the nation's largest payer source for health care provided to children. Currently one in four children are enrolled in Medicaid, and receive a comprehensive array of benefits; this benefit package—known as the Early Periodic Screening, Diagnosis, and Treatment (EPSDT) program—emphasizes health development and assures that services are available to treat chronic and acute health care conditions (Kaiser Commission on Medicaid and the Uninsured, 2011a). The availability of Medicaid is linked to a child's ability to access and use health care services. A 2008 Kaiser Family Foundation Survey showed that only 4 percent of children with Medicaid or another public source of coverage had no regular source of care, compared to 30 percent of uninsured children (Kaiser Commission on Medicaid and the Uninsured, 2010a). Furthermore, Medicaid ensures that low-income women receive maternity and prenatal care. About 40 percent of all births are financed by Medicaid (Kaiser Commission on Medicaid and the Uninsured, 2011d).

At the other end of the age spectrum, Medicaid provides coverage for about 9 million low-income Medicare enrollees. These seniors are known as "dual eligibles" because they qualify for both programs. They are often extremely sick and very poor. More than half have annual incomes less than $10,000 (Kaiser Commission on Medicaid and the Uninsured, 2011d).

About 8 million people with disabilities also have Medicaid coverage. For many of these individuals Medicaid provides personal care assistance, transportation, and assistive devices that they need in order to function and perhaps work. The Kaiser Family Foundations' analysis of the 2004–2006 Medical Expenditure Panel Survey (MEPS) illustrates Medicaid's role in ensuring access for persons with disabilities. Approximately 9 percent of Medicaid enrollees with disabilities reported no usual source of care, compared to 14 percent with private insurance and 42 percent of uninsured individuals.

All told, Medicaid has emerged as the single most important medical safety net program in this country. By providing coverage for low-income seniors and for individuals living with a disability, Medicaid has become the largest payer for long-term care. Estimates are that 7 out of 10 nursing home residents are covered by Medicaid. Roughly one quarter of all mental health service funding comes from Medicaid. The program is also the largest source of funding for community health centers, public hospitals, and other entities that provide care to low-income persons (Kaiser Commission on Medicaid and the Uninsured, 2011d).

How Much Does Medicaid Cost?

Medicaid is an expensive program primarily because health care is expensive. According to the Centers for Medicare & Medicaid Services (CMS), national Medicaid expenditures now exceed $400 billion annually and continue to increase. The third-largest program in the federal budget after Social Security and Medicare, Medicaid accounts for 8 percent of federal spending. Despite a substantial federal share (generally close to half the total costs), state expenditures for the program can be quite high and are always among the top two or three largest single components of state budgets—typically, 16 percent of the total (Kaiser Commission on Medicaid and the Uninsured, 2011d). As a result, most state budget conversations begin and end with the line item associated with the Medicaid program. Beyond the sheer magnitude and dollar costs, states are concerned with the countercyclical nature of Medicaid expenditures. The number of enrollees increases in difficult economic periods when unemployment rises and incomes fall (Holahan, Clemans-Cope, Lawton, & Rousseau, 2011). These are precisely the times in which states are likely to experience declining tax revenues, which reduce their capacity to meet the increased needs.

Thus Medicaid's resource needs actually increase precisely when states are seeking ways to reduce expenditures. Because the program serves the most vulnerable, and provides support for critically important safety net organizations, it is highly charged with emotional advocacy. In the combination of these attributes, Medicaid has become the single most difficult budget issue facing many state governments.

How Is Medicaid Financed?

Medicaid's current financing mechanism is grounded in precedent and a belief about how federal assistance to disadvantaged groups should be structured. The basis for the federal government's provision of matching funds to states participating in Medicaid was established prior to 1965, primarily with reference to welfare and most clearly manifested in the Kerr-Mills legislation of 1960, which identified a new category of needy individuals to include persons who were elderly or blind, not receiving cash assistance, and medically needy. For these individuals, Kerr-Mills authorized the federal government to reimburse states for 50 to 80 percent of the cost of the program (Stevens & Stevens, 1970). The Medicaid legislation extended this federal/state funding mechanism beyond the aged and medically needy to include other categories of people receiving public assistance (i.e., those who are blind, individuals living with a disability, and single-parent families) (Newman, 1972).

The federal government's financial contribution to the Medicaid program is known as the Federal Medical Assistance Percentage (FMAP), a rate that is calculated for each state based on a specific formula of state and national per capita income. States with lower per capita incomes receive higher FMAPs, and those with higher per-capita incomes receive lower FMAPs. FMAPs vary annually, depending on states' Medicaid program characteristics, their economic and political climates, and federal policy changes through laws such as the American Recovery Act and the 2010 ACA. State FMAPs ranged between 50 and 75 percent in FY2011 (Baumrucker, 2010).

Medicaid is an entitlement program because individuals who meet the eligibility requirements are legally entitled to Medicaid coverage. Under Medicaid's entitlement structure, the federal government provides uncapped funding to states on an "as needed" basis as long as the state's expenditures meet the requirements of the program (Kaiser Commission on Medicaid and the Uninsured, 2004). In turn, states are not allowed to cap Medicaid enrollment nor to establish waiting lists, but those that offer more than minimum eligibility levels can reduce those levels in order to reduce enrollment (Kaiser Commission on Medicaid and the Uninsured, 2010b).

Furthermore, Medicaid is often referred to as an "open-ended entitlement program" because the federal government will pay the agreed FMAPs, no matter the cost. This creates a situation in which the federal share can only be estimated at the beginning of any budget cycle—the actual amount of the federal obligation will only become known as state decisions are made and state allocations spent. The total expenditures for the program will be whatever the states spend, plus the federal "match dollars" as determined by the FMAPs.

How Might Block Grants Affect Medicaid?

The Medicaid program is a clear manifestation of the nation's federalist approach to numerous issues. The program is funded and regulated with a mix of federal, state, and (sometimes) local resources. And although this mix produces a tension of sorts between the federal government and the states, that tension might be a good one. State involvement ensures that programs are designed to meet the unique needs of a region. Federal involvement assures that the program continues to serve as a safety net for the most vulnerable populations. Indeed, critiques of the program often fail to account for the fact that Medicaid serves millions of individuals who otherwise would not have access to health care, nursing home care, or other supportive services.

Changing circumstances in the nation's Medicaid program (and the 50-plus state/territorial operational versions thereof) are giving rise to a discussion of the relative merits of two major alternative approaches to financing and managing the program. Fundamentally, the issues are those of cost and access. Like other elements of medical care, Medicaid has experienced significant cost escalation over the past 45 years, reaching a level that creates great concern at both the state and federal levels. Beyond those general cost increases, it is estimated that the ACA could add 16 million to 18 million people to the program's total enrollment. The fiscal consequences of these increases in cost are also of great concern to both federal and state governments. At the federal level, Medicaid costs have become a central element in conversations about annual deficit spending and the growing national debt. For states, the primary concern is that, as Medicaid expenditures occupy an increasing share of state budgets, the capacity to pursue other needed activities (especially education and infrastructure initiatives) may well be curtailed.

One approach, discussed in the Point section, would modify the funding process to a block grant mechanism in which the federal contribution would be capped and hence predictable. This would limit, and might well reduce, the amount of federal funding received by each state. States would gain a new degree of flexibility in program design, development, and management. Proponents believe the improvements in effectiveness and efficiency that might flow from the increased flexibility would more than offset any losses in the actual dollar allocations.

As will be discussed in the Counterpoint section, however, others prefer to continue the basic structure as it currently exists. The current structure maximizes the capacity of states to cover eligible populations and, through the structure of federal matching, provides at least some level of relief from the counter cyclic nature of the program—a process that requires additional resource allocation during precisely the difficult economic times when governments are likely to experience declining tax revenues. With an open-ended federal obligation, states know that each increase in state allocation will be matched, providing approximately half of the additional resources needed to meet increases in need. Because of this, states are required to meet and maintain a variety of federally established program attributes. However, many analysts have argued that this constrains the flexibility and creativity that might lead the states to devise more efficient and effective ways to meet those needs.

POINT

Flexibility has long been a hallmark of the Medicaid program. Although Medicaid legislation mandated that participating states provide a required set of benefits (including physician services, inpatient and outpatient hospital care, nursing facility care, and laboratory and X-ray services), some flexibility was built into the program. States were given a general set of guidelines to govern their own Medicaid program, to establish their own eligibility standards and benefits beyond the required levels, and to determine the rate of reimbursement for services. States may choose to expand coverage to include certain optional benefits, such as prescription drugs, dental services, physical therapy, Tuberculosis-related services, home health care services, and inpatient psychiatric hospital services for individuals under 21 years old (Kaiser Commission on Medicaid and the Uninsured, 2010b). In fact, 60 percent of Medicaid expenditures go toward additional services provided to mandatory groups and mandatory services for optional groups (Kaiser Commission on Medicaid and the Uninsured, 2005).

Furthermore, states define and interpret federal rules about the Medicaid program differently, creating further variation across programs. For some, the federalist aspect of the program is a feature that might allow Medicaid to be even more flexible, adaptable, and innovative in the face of rapid changes in the organization and delivery of medical care. Ideally, the states would serve as laboratories, exploring different means of accomplishing program goals and learning lessons that can be applied (or avoided) in other states.

However, the same joint management and financing responsibilities that create such potential for flexibility introduce significant complexities in program administration and implementation. General actions taken by the federal government must be managed and implemented in all states, so proposals for change must be vetted with care. Similarly, individual states are constrained by the minimum program requirements and the fact that state-level changes may impact the federal fiscal obligations. Since the state and federal objectives may not always be fully congruent, a regulatory environment at both levels has evolved. Over the 40-plus years of the Medicaid program's life, this regulatory environment has become increasingly detailed and complex, adding a substantial layer of difficulty to the contemplation or enactment of changes, even those that seem to be quite reasonable.

WHY IS MORE STATE FLEXIBILITY NECESSARY?

For some states, increased flexibility has reflected a fundamental belief that the state could manage the program more effectively if federal constraints were looser. For others, increased flexibility is not so much a goal in itself, or even a means to program innovation. Rather, it is seen as a potentially valuable mechanism for coping with a feared reduction in the federal commitment. But regardless of underlying motivation, state interest in increased flexibility has existed to a substantial degree for much of the past two decades.

These longstanding views have become accentuated in recent months as states contemplate some possible consequences of the Patient Protection and Affordable Care Act (ACA). A key element of that health care initiative is to reduce the number of people without health insurance, in part by expanding Medicaid eligibility to all individuals under 65 with incomes up to 138 percent of the federal poverty level starting in 2014. While the Supreme Court did put limitations on the ability of the federal government to force states to accept the law's expansion, it can be expected that many states will comply. Before the decision (when it was assumed all states would comply), the Congressional Budget Office (CBO) and Centers for Medicare & Medicaid Services (CMS) estimated that this would initially result in 16 million to 18 million new Medicaid enrollees, which would amount to the largest expansion in the program's history, adding to the states' already strained Medicaid programs (Sommers, Swartz, & Epstein, 2011). These projections vary depending on the data sources of those estimates and the participation rates of newly eligible Medicaid enrollees, which will be influenced by the rigor with which states pursue those newly eligible to participate in the program. Of course, the decision for states to expand will also be a major factor in determining enrollment levels. For states that choose to expand their eligibility requirements, their financial burden will surely increase. Although the ACA provides increased Federal Medical Assistance Percentage (FMAP) rates to cover 100 percent of the necessary financing for those newly eligible for Medicaid from 2014 to 2016, those FMAPs will be incrementally phased down to 90 percent by 2020, which means that states will ultimately be responsible for financing a portion of the expansion.

Even before the ACA, many states were struggling to meet their Medicaid financial obligations. Some analysts propose that states receive additional flexibility to redesign their Medicaid programs, especially in light of the unknown and variable impact of the ACA on costs. It would be reasonable to expect that, with additional flexibility to redesign their Medicaid programs, states could cope better with a dramatic increase in Medicaid enrollment. The core argument remains that which existed prior to the passage of the ACA: States are more familiar with the dynamics and circumstances of their Medicaid enrollees and can better tailor the program to meet the needs of their enrollees within their current political and economic environments. The development of innovative strategies to improve the Medicaid program will also allow states to share best practices with other states and contribute to national efforts to reform the U.S. health care system (Coughlin & Zuckerman, 2008; Kaiser Commission on Medicaid and the Uninsured, 2009). Implicit in this argument is a contention that current mechanisms for state variation are insufficient.

How is state flexibility currently achieved? There are three principal mechanisms by which states can implement changes in their Medicaid programs, and thus pursue experimentation and innovation: comprehensive section 1115 waivers, the Health Insurance Flexibility and Accountability (HIFA) waiver initiative, and the Deficit Reduction Act (DRA) of 2005 (Coughlin & Zuckerman, 2008). Section 1115 of the Social Security Act was enacted in 1962 prior to the creation of Medicaid. In effect, the section acknowledges that there may be circumstances in which states should be granted the flexibility to modify their programs, even in a manner that might appear to diverge from the minimum federal standards, if the proposed modification shows promise for overall improvement in the program. Through section 1115 waivers, some states have increased eligibility thresholds, expanded benefits, and redesigned delivery and payment mechanisms (Coughlin & Zuckerman, 2008; Kaiser Commission on Medicaid and the Uninsured, 2009). As of April 2011, 30 states and the District of Columbia operated at least one comprehensive Section 115 Medicaid waiver (Kaiser Commission on Medicaid and the Uninsured, 2011b).

The HIFA waiver policy is a type of Section 1115 waiver that was introduced by the George W. Bush administration in 2001 (Coughlin & Zuckerman, 2008). HIFA enables states to model the Medicaid program after private health insurance, utilize employer-sponsored insurance, increase cost sharing, and expand coverage through an expedited application and review process (Engquist & Burns, 2002). As of March 2008, there were 14 approved HIFA waivers (Coughlin & Zuckerman, 2008).

In 2006 President George W. Bush signed the Deficit Reduction Act (DRA) that provided states with increased flexibility and ease to modify their Medicaid programs in pursuit of some identified improvement. The DRA allows states to redefine covered services based on a benchmark, increase cost-sharing for benefits and services, and enables up to 10 states to develop Health Opportunity Accounts based on health savings accounts. The DRA dramatically increased the ease with which states could modify their programs by allowing them to amend their state Medicaid plans and not requiring a full waiver (Coughlin & Zuckerman, 2008).

To date, the waiver mechanism has not been successful in achieving the degree, frequency, and diversity of program variation that would be necessary to discern potentially valuable fundamental changes that might provide a means for improving Medicaid or reducing the program's cost. In part this is because the federal government maintains oversight and restricts program flexibility (Waller, 2005). Waiver programs are only granted for a specific period and require extensive negotiations between CMS and the states. Section 1115 waivers also require independent evaluation of program outcomes, which greatly increase administrative burdens. Because these independent evaluations of program outcomes are often not publicly available and no specific source of the various evaluations are available, what observers are able to learn from the administration of the waiver programs is severely limited (Kaiser Commission on Medicaid and the Uninsured, 2011b).

FROM AN ENTITLEMENT PROGRAM TO A BLOCK GRANT PROGRAM

The fundamental element of a block grant is a cap on federal expenditures (Kaiser Commission on Medicaid and the Uninsured, 2004). The concept of block grants is not new and has generally been attractive to an ideological base that combines fiscal conservatism with preference for government interventions that are as local as possible, in this case vesting much greater managerial authority at the state level.

There have been four major attempts to implement Medicaid block funding. In 1981 Republican President Ronald Reagan proposed a block grant program in which the federal cap would be the sum of all state-specific caps. The state-specific caps would be based on the prior year's FMAP, plus 9 percent, with increases in subsequent years based on the previous year's cap and the gross national product (GNP) to account for economic growth. Although the proposal was passed in the U.S. Senate, it was dropped in the final budget conference for a policy to reduce the Medicaid growth rate (Lambrew, 2005).

In 1995 Representative Newt Gingrich (R–GA) proposed Medigrant, a type of block grant based on prorating each state's cap to sum to a specified federal cap using a complex formula adjusted for economic growth, state costs, case mix, and number of eligible Medicaid enrollees (Lambrew, 2005). The proposal was ultimately vetoed by Democratic President Bill Clinton.

In 2003 Republican President George W. Bush proposed a block grant program that would cap federal spending based on set state Medicaid budgets (Lambrew, 2005). These state budgets would be based on the previous year's state spending, plus medical cost inflation. A bipartisan gubernatorial committee could not agree on the proposal, however, and so it failed.

The fourth and most recent attempt was proposed by House Budget Committee Chair Paul Ryan (R–WI), which would repeal the ACA and convert Medicaid to a block grant program (U.S. House of Representatives Committee on the Budget, 2011). The amount available to states would be based on general inflation and population growth rate (Congressional Budget Office, 2011a). It was estimated that the budget plan could save $1.4 trillion between 2012 and 2022, $750 billion from changing Medicaid to a block grant (Holahan, Buettgens, Chen, Carroll, & Lawton, 2011). The FY 2012 budget proposal was approved in the Republican-dominated House of Representatives but ultimately blocked in the Democratic Senate (Barrett & Cohen, 2011; National Priorities Project, 2011).

All four attempts were unsuccessful for a variety of reasons, many having to do with strong ideological support for social justice and its tenet of caring for society's vulnerable populations. According to Lambrew (2005), the Reagan plan failed because the Social Security financing crisis and a presidential assassination attempt took precedence, and the Gingrich plan failed because it would result in substantial Medicare cuts and a de-emphasis on environmental policies, and went against President Clinton's ideology of social justice. The Ryan plan did not garner enough political and social support as people feared that the substantial cuts to federal Medicare and Medicaid programs would leave the nation's most vulnerable populations (elderly, disabled, and low-income) at too high of a risk for catastrophic medical expenses (Holahan, Buettgens, et al., 2011).

It is likely there will be more proposals. It can be argued that converting the Medicaid funding process from one based on an open-ended entitlement assumption to a program based on block-grant funding has the potential to accomplish two major policy goals simultaneously. First, it would essentially cap federal funding at a specified level. This would be of great value in terms of federal budget predictability and would serve the currently perceived need to reduce deficits and ultimately reduce the federal debt. Second, given a known cap on the federal contribution, states would be strongly motivated to control the costs of their Medicaid programs. Because a block grant mechanism would include a significant reduction in federal constraints, granting states the flexibility to contemplate fundamental Medicaid program redesign might achieve cost reductions *and* improve access and quality.

Budget predictability and reduced federal expenditures. Block grants would establish the amount of the federal obligation for the Medicaid program and create a baseline for future obligations. Previous block grant proposals linked the budgets to previous FMAPs with increases in subsequent years based on general economic indices, such as the GNP or Consumer Price Index, rather than medical inflation, which typically increases at a much higher rate. The lower increases from using a marketwide index would result in reduced federal obligations over time. The value of such certainty and potentially lower fiscal obligations for the federal government is clear. The value to states is less obvious. For some observers, eliminating the current motivation to add further programs or to retain existing activities simply because part of the costs is being borne by others would itself be a positive step. And certainly states that currently receive relatively lower federal matches (due to a lower FMAP) might obtain a short-term bump if block grants were set by a formula less favorable to poor states than the current FMAP process. Some observers argue that financing Medicaid using block grants would serve as an incentive for states, providers, and Medicaid enrollees to support, practice, and demand more efficient health care.

But, for states, the budgetary value of a block grant mechanism is indirect. It is obtained through the anticipated savings that may occur if the change in funding mechanism is accompanied by other changes in program requirements that will in turn provide a fiscal advantage.

Program innovation to control state costs and improve access and quality. Despite current avenues for Medicaid program flexibility, most state redesign efforts have been modest in both scope and magnitude, in part as a result of federal restrictions and the waiver-review process itself. Some administrative efficiencies would be achieved by reducing oversight and reporting burdens (Waller, 2005). Reduced federal restrictions would also enable states to be more proactive in ascertaining the needs of their Medicaid enrollees and redesigning the program to meet those needs in a simpler and more cost-efficient manner (Cannon, 2011). According to Cashin (1999), state flexibility would facilitate innovation for best practices that can be easily discerned and disseminated to other states.

Individuals who are elderly and disabled make up 25 percent of the Medicaid population and account for 67 percent of Medicaid expenditures (Kaiser Commission on Medicaid and the Uninsured, 2010b). Increased program flexibility through block grants might enable states to properly develop, test, and evaluate innovative delivery and payment models that provide greater focus on specific population subgroups where current costs are high and greater saving might be achieved.

States have historically tried to maximize the federal match for low-income enrollees through programs such as the Disproportional Share Hospital (DSH) and the Upper Payment Limit (UPL) programs (Cannon, 2005). The DSH program is intended to increase funding for hospitals that provide care to a high percentage of uninsured and underinsured individuals and the UPL program was developed to draw down federal matching dollars by increasing its payments to institutional providers (yet providers are required to return this money to the states, effectively causing the federal government to provide more state funding) (Coughlin, Zuckerman, & McFeeters, 2007). States have not always used these DSH and UPL payments to reimburse safety net providers but to fund other health programs and general state expenditures (Coughlin, Ku, & Kim, 2000). Therefore increased federal Medicaid expenditures have not necessarily equated to improved access and quality of health care. While federal oversight efforts have prevented states from collecting residual DSH funds, the accounting mechanisms which states use to fund uncompensated care to providers are complex and still in need of reform (Coughlin et al., 2007). Block grants eliminate state matching and thus the incentive for states to maximize federal funding with increased spending.

Other ways for block grants to promote state innovation. There are two other areas in which it is argued that a block grant mechanism would result in net improvements to Medicaid. The first is the issue of improper enrollment. For FY 2010, one of the most common reasons for improper Medicaid payments was errors in verifying eligibility (U.S. Department of Health and Human Services, 2010). This has two consequences. First, obviously, payments for medical care are made on behalf of individuals who are not eligible for program support. The amount of those payments is in turn "lost" to potential payments that might be made for eligible enrollees. Second, such improper enrollment may reflect "crowd-out," a phenomenon that occurs when individuals who could otherwise participate in private health insurance programs choose instead to enroll in Medicaid (Davidson, Blewett, & Call, 2004; Gruber & Simon, 2008). While estimates vary depending on data sources, assumptions, and methodological differences, crowd-out unnecessarily increases the cost of the Medicaid program by expanding Medicaid eligibility beyond what is truly necessary for the medically needy (Cannon, 2005; Davidson et al., 2004). Block grant financing would provide a strong incentive for states to better focus on enrolling those who are truly vulnerable.

Apart from the specific instance of improper enrollment, Medicaid is considered a high-risk program for fraud, waste, and abuse because of issues with preventing inappropriate spending (U.S. Goverment Accountability Office, 2011). The Department of Health and Human Services calculated that on average between FY 2008 and 2010, $22.5 billion were lost to improper Medicaid payments (U.S. Department of Health and Human Services, 2010). Improper payments resulted from errors in administration and documentation, authentication and medical necessity of services, and verification of eligibility and services. The complexities of state Medicaid programs have made efforts to curb fraud, waste, abuse, and improper payments at the federal level challenging. Furthermore, the legal and organizational processes that would be necessary to seriously impact the magnitude of the fraud problem would themselves have an unknown cost. It may be the case that states are better able to understand how fraud and abuse occur at their level and can implement improved management and oversight to significantly reduce Medicaid overpayments. It is argued that block grants would create a stronger incentive for states to reduce fraud and abuse, as they would retain 100 percent of the savings compared with sharing those savings with the federal government under the current system (Cannon, 2011).

Previous experience with block grants. The nation has at least two experiences for the block grant mechanism that might merit careful review. In 1996, the Personal Responsibility and Work Opportunity Reconciliation Act of 1996 converted the 60-year-old Aid to Families with Dependent Children welfare entitlement program to a block grant program under Temporary Assistance for Needy Families (TANF) (Cashin, 1999). It was part of Representative Newt Gingrich's Medicaid and Welfare block grant proposal, although only the Welfare portion was passed and enacted. The conversion did achieve lower federal costs but advocacy groups indicate the program is still very complex and ultimately ineffective in its primary goal of helping the poor achieve financial independence (Waller, 2005).

The second, more recent case study is the Rhode Island Global Consumer Choice Compact Medicaid Waiver, which was implemented on July 1, 2009. Rhode Island initially requested a block grant similar to TANF but the request did not garner sufficient support because of the extensive cap and flexibility the state would be awarded. Ultimately Rhode Island was granted a waiver that capped the amount of federal funding it would receive over five years at $12.075 billion in exchange for more flexibility in how it operates its Medicaid program. Initial reports indicate that the waiver saved the state more than $100 million in the first year and a half of its inception (Alexander, 2010). However there has been considerable controversy about whether or not the Rhode Island experiment is a true example of a block grant. Critics point out that the federal government is subsidizing health care programs it would not otherwise fund, that the cap is not provided as a lump-sum payment but as an FMAP over time, that the cap far exceeds what Rhode Island would spend on their Medicaid program within the period of the waiver, that the flexibility awarded varies, and that the waiver expires in 2014 with the option to terminate at any time (Roberts, 2011). Although it can be argued that the Rhode Island example lacks the basic tenets of block grant funding including a lump-sum payment, flexibility across the entire program, and permanency; lessons can be learned on how to facilitate a block grant.

OBJECTIONS TO MEDICAID BLOCK GRANTS

Critics have suggested that block grants will become acceptable to states only if the level of flexibility granted is effectively a *carte blanche* approach to take whatever steps they deem appropriate. Under strong budgetary pressure, and constitutional prohibitions against deficit spending, state Medicaid flexibility might result in an increased emphasis on reducing costs at the expense of quality and access. There is great concern that states would take steps, perhaps draconian steps, to reduce enrollment, decrease benefits, increase costs to enrollees, and lower provider payments (Angeles, 2011; Congressional Budget Office, 2011a; Holahan, Buettgens, et al., 2011). The extreme poverty, vulnerability and other marginalized attributes of Medicaid enrollees as a population would, in this view, provide little political basis for states to maintain a serious commitment to Medicaid. States that have difficulties meeting the budget challenges of their base Medicaid enrollment rolls would especially be unable to afford the consequences of increases in enrollment that might occur in turbulent economic times and state disasters.

Beyond concerns about access to care, the flexibility that would come with a block grant mechanism could reduce state accountability. The Federal government would have reduced capacity to raise questions or otherwise take steps to ensure that the program is succeeding in achieving one of its primary purposes—improved fairness, justice, and social equity in the availability and use of medical services.

Third, concerns have been expressed that when states are forced to achieve necessary savings in Medicaid they will do so in part by the device of reducing payments to providers—both physicians and hospitals (Holahan, Buettgens, et al., 2011; Park & Broaddus, 2011). Although there is much debate about payment rates, it seems certain that there exists a level at which providers would simply walk away from program participation. No matter how effective a program might be in theory, no matter how carefully designed the benefit package, and no matter how efficient might be its various services, no medical care will be delivered without the voluntary participation of providers; participation that cannot be assured if state flexibility results in payment rates that are insufficient. The potential impact on a state's traditional safety net providers is especially concerning.

Although careful research and simulation studies might answer some of the empirical questions manifested in these concerns, two realities must be acknowledged. First, the impact of block grants cannot be fully predicted. Measuring the effect of price, enrollment, and utilization on Medicaid costs is imprecise, and developing a block grant formula that would ensure appropriate federal spending without limiting access and quality would be challenging (Lambrew, 2005). Second, some elements of the debate are fundamentally ideological in nature. They reflect deeply held views about the appropriate role of government, the appropriate level at which governmental involvement should occur, issues of fiscal responsibility, our national commitment to fairness, justice and equality, and similar questions. The conversations also contain deeply ingrained suspicions about the motives, likely behaviors, and consequences that may occur if "the other" view prevails. Such circumstances do not facilitate thoughtful discussion about how the goals of block grants can be achieved without the potential adverse effects.

REFERENCES AND FURTHER READING

Alexander, G. D. (2010). *Rhode Island: Medicaid reform global consumer choice compact waiver.* Retrieved from The Galen Institute website: http://www.galen.org/topics/rhode-island-medicaid-reform-global-consumer-choice-compact-waiver

Angeles, J. (2011). *Ryan Medicaid block grant would cause severe reductions in health care and long-term care for seniors, people with disabilities, and children.* Retrieved from Center on Budget and Policy Priorities website: http://www.cbpp.org/cms/index.cfm?fa=view&id=3483

Barrett, T., & Cohen, T. (2011, May 25). *Senate rejects budget measure containing Medicare overhaul.* Retrieved from CNN website: http://articles.cnn.com/2011–05–25/politics/senate.medicare_1_medicare-overhaul-budget-plan-budget-proposal?_s=PM:POLITICS

Baumrucker, E. P. (2010). *Medicaid: The Federal Medical Assistance Percentage (FMAP).* Washington, DC: Congressional Research Service. Retrieved from http://aging.senate.gov/crs/medicaid6.pdf

Cannon, M. F. (2005). Medicaid's unseen costs. *Policy Analysis, 548.* Retrieved from http://www.cato.org/pubs/pas/pa548.pdf

Cannon, M. F. (2011). *Governors' letter show why Medicaid block grants are necessary.* Retrieved from Kaiser Health News website: http://www.kaiserhealthnews.org/Columns/2011/April/041811cannon.aspx

Cashin, S. D. (1999). Federalism, welfare reform, and the minority poor: Accounting for the tyranny of state majorities. *Columbia Law Review, 99*(3), 552–627.

Congressional Budget Office. (2011a). *Preliminary long term analysis of budget proposal by Chairman Paul Ryan.* Retrieved from http://www.cbo.gov/doc.cfm?index=12128

Congressional Budget Office. (2011b). *Spending and enrollment detail for CBO's March 2011 baseline: Medicaid.* Retrieved from http://www.cbo.gov/budget/factsheets/2011b/medicaid.pdf

Coughlin, T. A., Ku, L., & Kim, J. (2000). Reforming the Medicaid Disproportionate Share Hospital program. *Health Care Financing Review, 22*(2), 137.

Coughlin, T. A., & Zuckerman, S. (2008). State responses to new flexibility in Medicaid. *Milbank Quarterly, 86*(2), 209–240. doi: 10.1111/j.1468-0009.2008.00520.x

Coughlin, T. A., Zuckerman, S., & McFeeters, J. (2007). Restoring fiscal integrity to Medicaid financing? *Health Affairs, 26*(5), 1469–1480. doi: 10.1377/hlthaff.26.5.1469

Davidson, G., Blewett, L. A., & Call, K. T. (2004). *Public program crowd-out of private coverage: What are the issues?* (Robert Wood Johnson Foundation Research Synthesis Report, 5). Retrieved from http://www.rwjf.org/pr/synthesis.jsp

Engquist, G., & Burns, P. (2002). *Health insurance flexibility and accountability initiative: Opportunities and issues for states.* Retrieved from State Coverage Initiatives website: http://www.statecoverage.org/node/190

Gruber, J., & Simon, K. (2008). Crowd-out 10 years later: Have recent public insurance expansions crowded out private health insurance? *Journal of Health Economics, 27*(2), 201–217.

Holahan, J., Buettgens, M., Chen, V., Carroll, C., & Lawton, E. (2011). *House Republican budget plan: State-by-state impact of changes in Medicaid financing* (Report No. 8185). Washington, DC: Kaiser Commission on Medicaid and the Uninsured. Retrieved from http://www.kff.org/medicaid/8185.cfm

Holahan, J., Clemans-Cope, L., Lawton, E., & Rousseau, D. (2011). *Medicaid spending growth over the last decade and the Great Recession, 2000–2009* (Report No. 8152). Washington, DC: The Kaiser Commission on Medicaid and the Uninsured. Retrieved from http://www.kff.org/medicaid/8152.cfm

Kaiser Commission on Medicaid and the Uninsured. (2004). *Medicaid and block grant financing compared* (Report No. 7028). Retrieved from http://www.kff.org/medicaid/7028.cfm%20

Kaiser Commission on Medicaid and the Uninsured. (2005). *Medicaid: An overview of spending on "mandatory" vs. "optional" population and services* (Report No. 7331). Retrieved from http://www.kff.org/medicaid/7331.cfm

Kaiser Commission on Medicaid and the Uninsured. (2009). *The role of Section 1115 waivers in Medicaid and CHIP: Looking back and looking forward* (Report No. 7874). Retrieved from http://www.kff.org/medicaid/7874.cfm

Kaiser Commission on Medicaid and the Uninsured. (2010a). *Medicaid beneficiaries and access to care* (Report No. 8000-02). Retrieved from http://www.kff.org/medicaid/8000.cfm

Kaiser Commission on Medicaid and the Uninsured. (2010b). *Medicaid: A primer* (Report No. 7334-04). Retrieved from http://www.kff.org/medicaid/7334.cfm

Kaiser Commission on Medicaid and the Uninsured. (2011a). *Federal core requirements and state options in Medicaid: Current policies and key issues* (Report No. 8174). Retrieved from http://www.kff.org/medicaid/8174.cfm

Kaiser Commission on Medicaid and the Uninsured. (2011b). *Five key questions and answers about Section 1115 Medicaid demonstration waivers* (Report No. 8196). Retrieved from http://www.kff.org/medicaid/8196.cfm

Kaiser Commission on Medicaid and the Uninsured. (2011c). *Medicaid matters: Understanding Medicaid's role in our health care system* (Report No. 8165). Retrieved from http://www.kff.org/about/kcmu.cfm

Lambrew, J. M. (2005). Making Medicaid a Block Grant Program: An analysis of the implications of past proposals. *Milbank Quarterly, 83*(1), 41–63. doi: 10.1111/j.0887-378X.2005.00335.x

National Priorities Project. (2011). *One (bumpy) year in the life of the federal budget.* Retrieved from http://nationalpriorities.org/en/publications/2011/year-end-wrap-up/?gclid=CMDp78DkkK0CFUKR7QodHHQImA

Newman, H. N. (1972). Medicare and Medicaid. *Annals of the American Academy of Political and Social Science, 399*(1), 114–124.

Park, E., & Broaddus, M. (2011). *What if Ryan's Medicaid block grant had taken effect in 2000? Federal Medicaid funds would have fallen over 25% in most states, over 40% in some, by 2009.* Retrieved from Center on Budget and Policy Priorities website: http://www.cbpp.org/cms/index.cfm?fa=view&id=3466

The Republican Governors Public Policy Committee. (2011). *A new Medicaid: A flexible, innovative and accountable future.* Retrieved from Republican Governors Association website: http://www.rga.org/homepage/gop-govs-release-medicaid-reform-report

Roberts, J. (2011, May 15). Rhode Island's Medicaid experiment becomes a talking point for budget cutters. *The New York Times.* Retrieved from http://www.nytimes.com/2011/05/16/us/politics/16medicaid.html?pagewanted=all

Sommers, B. D., Swartz, K., & Epstein, A. (2011). Policy makers should prepare for major uncertainties in Medicaid enrollment, costs, and needs for physicians under Health Reform. *Health Affairs, 30*(11), 2186–2193. doi: 10.1377/hlthaff.2011.0413

Stevens, R., & Stevens, R. (1970). Medicaid: Anatomy of a dilemma. *Law and Contemporary Problems, 35*(2), 348–425.

U.S. Department of Health and Human Services. (2010). *FY 2010 agency financial report.* Retrieved from http://www.hhs.gov/afr

U.S. Goverment Accountability Office. (2011). *Medicare and Medicaid fraud, waste, and abuse: Effective implementation of recent laws and agency actions could help reduce improper payments* (Rep. No. GAO-11-409T). Retrieved from http://www.gao.gov/products/GAO-11-409T

U.S. House of Representatives Committee on the Budget. (2011). *The path to prosperity restoring America's promise: Fiscal year 2012 budget resolution.* Retrieved from http://www.gop.gov/indepth/budget/downloads

Waller, M. (2005). *Block grants: Flexibility vs. stability in social services* (Brookings Institution Policy Brief). Retrieved from http://www.brookings.edu/~/media/Files/rc/papers/2005/12welfare_waller/pb34.pdf

Weikel, M. K., & LeaMond, N. A. (1976). A decade of Medicaid. *Public Health Reports, 91*(4), 303–308.

R. Paul Duncan and Lilliana L. Bell

COUNTERPOINT

Critics of the current Medicaid program point out that as currently configured, Medicaid is too costly for both states and the federal government to operate (The Republican Governors Public Policy Committee, 2011). Indeed, the most recent estimates show that Medicaid spending on average has increased by 7.4 percent during fiscal year 2011 (Smith, Gifford, Ellis, Rudowitz, & Snyder, 2011, Figure 1, p. 5). In fiscal year 2009, total state spending on Medicaid was about $123 billion or about 34 percent of total spending. The federal share was $243 billion or 66 percent of total Medicaid spending (Kaiser Commission on Medicaid and the Uninsured, 2011f). Amid the current fiscal downturns, governors are saying that state funding of Medicaid is untenable and they are increasingly looking for ways to cut their share of Medicaid's cost (Iglehart, 2011).

It is important to note that spending growth in Medicaid is directly tied to growth in enrollment: as the rate of enrollment climbs, so too does the rate of increase in spending and vice versa. The most recent growth in enrollment is a direct result of a deepening recession. Nationally, however, growth in per enrollee Medicaid spending is slower than the growth in overall per capita health care expenditures and increases in private health insurance premiums (Holahan, Clemans-Cope, Lawton, & Rousseau, 2011).

Republican governors are also concerned that the expansion of Medicaid eligibility standards to or below 138 percent of the Federal Poverty Level (FPL) in 2014 as called for under the ACA will place a further burden on the states. Interestingly, the governors in their critique have not acknowledged that the ACA calls for the federal government to cover at least 90 percent of the costs associated with the expansion populations (The Republican Governors Public Policy Committee, 2011).

There is also worry that the program is structurally inept. One commentator noted that Medicaid provides an open-ended incentive for states to unnecessarily expand programs with little inducement for fiscal discipline; creates an misallocation of spending such that the wealthier states end up getting more federal money than poorer states; distorts the economy by setting price controls on medical services by discouraging individual savings, self-help, and work efforts and crowding out private efforts to provide health insurance coverage for low-income families; and fosters a significant amount of fraud and abuse, resulting in improper payments to providers (Edwards, 2010).

INCREASED PROGRAM FLEXIBILITY AND BLOCK GRANTS: A PROPOSED SOLUTION

Cost and structural concerns have resulted in renewed calls, mostly from political conservatives, to transform Medicaid into a block grant. In general, the federal government would transfer to each state a predetermined lump-sum amount. Although the proposed block grant amounts and growth factors provide budgetary safety for the federal government and might provide increased incentive for state governments to spend Medicaid dollars carefully, some caution also exists. For example, if increases in block-grant amounts over time are tied to a general inflation rate and medical inflation exceeds that general rate, states could find themselves with budget shortfalls that increase with each passing year. With block grants, states would have full flexibility to spend the money in a manner they see fit. Since federal funding would not be tied to state outlays, states would have a greater incentive to be more prudent with their Medicaid dollars. They could pursue these efficiencies unencumbered by federal rules and regulations (Lambrew, 2005).

The idea to move Medicaid to block grant funding is not a new one. Beginning in 1981 with President Reagan, Republicans in the White House and in Congress have proposed block grants for Medicaid. Reagan's proposal focused on placing a limit on federal support for Medicaid. Although there was support for his proposal in the Senate, it was eventually dropped in favor of a policy aimed at reducing spending growth but that retained the entitlement (Lambrew, 2005).

As speaker of the House of Representatives, Newt Gingrich proposed federal funding caps based on a predetermined formula that assessed each state's level of need. However, the sum total of all state allotments would have to meet a federal cap on spending. States would have seen a lower contribution to Medicaid. Although this proposal was approved by Congress, President Clinton vetoed the legislation. In 2003 President George W. Bush proposed giving states increased flexibility to manage their Medicaid programs in return for higher initial federal funding. The Bush proposal was to have been further developed by a bipartisan commission from the National Governor's Association. However, the commission disbanded before an agreement could be reached (Lambrew, 2005).

The most recent proposal was introduced by Representative Paul Ryan as part of a plan to reduce the nation's deficit. The House Budget Plan, which was subsequently passed by the House of Representatives in April 2011, would repeal the ACA and result in significant reductions in Medicaid spending. The House plan would shift current Medicaid financing to block grants. Federal funding for Medicaid would be capped annually and distributed across states based on a formula, as opposed to actual costs. Estimates are that $1.4 trillion savings in federal dollars over a 10-year period can be achieved by repealing health reform and converting the Medicaid program to a block grant (Holahan, Buettgens, Chen, Carroll, & Lawton, 2011).

BLOCK GRANTS AND FLEXIBILITY: NOT NECESSARILY THE ANSWER

Proponents of the block grant purport advantages such as reduced levels of federal funding, deficit reduction, and flexibility among states to administer Medicaid. However, the evidence does not suggest that such an approach will necessarily lead to a more efficient and effective system. At best, block grants will provide only a marginal increase in flexibility above what states already have, and at worst it can lead to reduced funding for states resulting in decreased access to care among vulnerable populations. Holahan and Weil (2003) argue that, although increased state flexibility might be of value to the states, it may have no impact on increasing Medicaid enrollment and health care inflation, which are the drivers of Medicaid's high costs.

Proponents of block grants have increasingly pointed to the success of Rhode Island's Global Consumer Choice Compact Medicaid Waiver. Implemented on July 1, 2009, the waiver was originally intended as a Medicaid block grant, but in its current form it does not include the typical elements of a block grant, such as capped federal funding provided as a lump-sum payment and flexibility. In fact, under the waiver, the state's Medicaid flexibility is limited, inasmuch as it still has to receive federal approval to make major changes (Roberts, 2011).

Significant flexibility already exists in the Medicaid program. As noted above, within the broad federal guidelines, states do have considerable flexibility in program design and implementation. Indeed, Medicaid is often described as a set of 50 different programs reflecting each state's unique approach. States, at their own option, have expanded eligibility to include nonmandatory populations. For example, 45 states including the District of Columbia have expanded coverage for pregnant women above the federally required minimum eligibility of 133 percent of FPL (Kaiser Commission on Medicaid and the Uninsured, 2011f).

States have also opted at times to increase benefits above the mandatory requirements and later to reduce such benefits when the need arises. All of the states do offer additional benefits, most typically prescription drug coverage, beyond that required by federal rule. In addition, for both mandatory and optional benefits, states can determine the amount, duration, and scope of such benefits (Kaiser Commission on Medicaid and the Uninsured, 2011a). This in effect determines how much or for how long a beneficiary can receive a benefit. States also have significant discretion in determining eligibility, enrollment, and renewal procedures. This can substantially impact the number of people in Medicaid. Thus, within the federal framework, states can vary the size of the enrolled population and the level of benefits they receive.

States also have considerable latitude in determining provider payment rates and methodologies. Some states use diagnosis-related groups based on the Medicare program, while others use per-diem amounts (Kaiser Commission on Medicaid and the Uninsured, 2011a). There is also considerable variability in fee-for-service payments to physicians across the states. In 2008 Florida's Medicaid fee-for-service reimbursement was about 63 percent of that of Medicare's. In contrast, Delaware and Nebraska's reimbursement levels are equivalent to Medicare's (Zuckerman, Williams, & Stockley, 2009).

The waiver process allows states to seek approval for additional flexibility in the delivery of care to Medicaid populations. Waivers are a process by which the federal government allows the states to make program changes otherwise not permissible under existing rules. Section 1115 waivers permit the Secretary of Health and Human Services to authorize states to use federal funds to engage in research and demonstration programs that have the potential to further the objectives of Medicaid (Kaiser Commission on Medicaid and the Uninsured, 2011a). These 1115 waivers generally allow broad changes in eligibility, benefits, cost sharing, and provider payments. However, narrower 1115 waivers focus on specific populations and services (Kaiser Commission on Medicaid and the Uninsured, 2011b). Longstanding administrative policy has required that waivers be budget neutral. That is, spending under the waiver must be less than or the equivalent of spending without the waiver. Thirty states and the District of Columbia have 1115 waivers, which fall into four broad categories: to implement managed care, to expand coverage with limited benefits, to restructure federal financing, and to expand coverage for low-income adults (Kaiser Commission on Medicaid and the Uninsured, 2011b).

Among the other kinds of waivers that states can seek are 1915(b) waivers, which allow mandatory managed care, and 1915(c) waivers, which expand home- and community-based services for individuals with disabilities (Kaiser Commission on Medicaid and the Uninsured, 2011e).

The Deficit Reduction Act of 2005 added new flexibility to the waiver process and gave states additional authority to make changes to their Medicaid programs (Coughlin & Zuckerman, 2008). This included allowing that certain beneficiaries pay a portion of their premiums and care costs; permitting states to offer a "benchmark benefit package" pegged to plans offered to federal or state employees, or the largest HMO option in the state; and allowing states to open up the equivalent of health savings accounts for their beneficiaries (Coughlin & Zuckerman, 2008).

Critics of the waiver process have argued that the associated paperwork is cumbersome and time consuming (Angle, 2011). Likely, there is truth to that statement and more attention needs to be devoted to streamlining the process. However, federal oversight of Medicaid assures that funds are appropriately used to support program's purposes in an efficient manner. Case in point is a recent negotiation between CMS and Florida state officials over the extension of Florida Medicaid's 1115 demonstration program. CMS wanted the Florida Medicaid agency to require that 85 percent of health plan revenues be spent on the provision of services and 15 percent on administration before the extension was granted (Lopez, 2011). In addition, further flexibility beyond that afforded by waivers may increase variability among state Medicaid programs. This may cause difficulty in the federal government's ability to hold states accountable for the administration of their Medicaid programs (Kaiser Commission on Medicaid and the Uninsured, 2011a).

Innovative programs do emerge under the current framework. As was noted above, the rate of Medicaid spending per capita is lower than the growth in per capita national health expenditures and increases in private insurance premiums (Holahan, Buettgens, et al., 2011). Part of this could be due to the fact that states take advantage of the flexibility already within the Medicaid program. As noted above, a significant amount of experimentation occurs within the current framework, and with some success. As such, states have been able to bend the cost curve as well as design more effective ways of care delivery.

One example of recent innovations are patient-centered medical home initiatives that have been launched within state Medicaid programs (Devers, Berenson, Coughlin, & Macri, 2011; Takach, 2011). Though these models are still in their infancy, reports thus far indicate that they can improve service delivery. For example, Colorado's medical home initiative has expanded access to care for children in Medicaid and the Children's Health Insurance Program (CHIP). Prior to implementation, 20 percent of pediatricians accepted Medicaid. After medical home implementation, that number increased to 96 percent. The increase in provider participation could in part be due to enhanced fee-for-service payments for certain kinds of primary care visits. In addition, median costs in Colorado's Medicaid program declined from about $215 per patient per year for children in medical homes, compared to children in control group practices (Takach, 2011).

Block grants can lead to increases in the number of the uninsured and limited access to care. Block grants can seriously jeopardize health care access. For example, due to capped federal funding, Medicaid coverage may be limited to a first-come-first-serve basis, thus increasing the number of uninsured individuals. CHIP is a block grant–funded program and federal funding is capped. One recent report showed that during times of recession when funding became limited, states cut enrollment in CHIP (Hill, Courtot, & Sullivan, 2007). Thus, when individuals are most likely to need public insurance (e.g., during an economic recession, epidemic, or disaster), block grants will limit their ability to acquire coverage. An analysis of the House Republican block grant proposal introduced in April 2011 shows that Medicaid enrollment could drop by about 19.4 million people (Holahan, Buettgens, et al., 2011).

Not having adequate health insurance coverage is linked to poor access to needed health care services. Individuals without health insurance have been shown to be less likely to have a usual source of care, to receive preventive care services, or to have timely physician contact (Kaiser Commission on Medicaid and the Uninsured, 2010).

Medicaid is an economic engine and provides state revenues. Not only does Medicaid serve as a major source of coverage for low-income individuals but it also provides millions to support health care jobs and infrastructure. The federal match is a significant source of revenue for states. In 2008 it represented 44 percent of all revenues to states (Kaiser Commission on Medicaid and the Uninsured, 2011c). This money is used in the provision of health care services and for payment to vendors. All of this translates into health care jobs. A cap on federal contributions to the Medicaid program will decrease the number of people with coverage, thereby reduce the demand for medical services, resulting in a decrease in the number of health sector–related jobs within states.

CONCLUSION

Concerns over the budget deficit have sparked renewed debate over the future of entitlement programs such as Medicaid. Indeed, health care spending in general, and Medicaid spending specifically represent significant portions of state and federal dollars. Understandably, policymakers need to find ways to make sure the health care dollar is spent efficiently and effectively. The core of the conversation, however, should not be just about cost. Providing quality health care to a population takes money, and it will always be costly. Rather, the conversation should be framed around how the government can best help individuals lead healthy and productive lives within a framework of resource efficiency.

The restructuring of Medicaid's program to a block grant structure has been proposed as a means to curb the nation's deficit while allowing states more flexibility in the administration of their programs. Certainly, a Medicaid block grant will save the federal government money by reducing spending (Lambrew, 2005). However, block grants will also shift the major burden of caring for the uninsured to the states. In turn, the states will be inclined (because of increased administrative flexibility) to limit enrollment reducing access to health care services for vulnerable populations. In this way, spending caps would undermine the original intent of the program.

A more reasoned approach will consider the primary role of Medicaid as a safety net for low-income populations. Such an approach would work within the current considerably flexible framework to experiment and test novel strategies and transform Medicaid. Continuing federal government oversight and involvement will ensure that the populations who are most in need of services will receive them.

References and Further Reading

Angle, J. (2011, June 13). *GOP Governors ask Washington to give states more flexibility on Medicaid.* Retrieved from Fox News website: http://www.foxnews.com/politics/2011/06/13/gop-governors-ask-washington-to-give-states-more-flexibility-on-medicaid

Coughlin, T. A., & Zuckerman, S. (2008). State responses to new flexibility in Medicaid. *Milbank Quarterly, 86*(2), 209–240. doi: 10.1111/j.1468-0009.2008.00520.x

Devers, K., Berenson, R., Coughlin, T., & Macri, J. (2011). *Innovative Medicaid initiatives to improve service delivery and quality of care: A look at five state initiatives* (Kaiser Commission on Medicaid and the Uninsured Report No. 8224). Retrieved from http://www.kff.org/medicaid/8224.cfm

Edwards, C. (2010). *Downsizing the federal government. Medicaid reforms.* Washington, DC: Cato Institute. Retrieved from http://www.downsizinggovernment.org/hhs/medicaid-reforms

Hill, I., Courtot, B., & Sullivan, J. (2007). Coping with SCHIP enrollment caps: Lessons from seven states' experiences. *Health Affairs, 26*(1), 258–268. doi: 10.1377/hlthaff.26.1.258

Holahan, J., Buettgens, M., Chen, V., Carroll, C., & Lawton, E. (2011). *House Republican budget plan: State-by-state impact of changes in Medicaid financing* (Kaiser Commission on Medicaid and the Uninsured Report No. 8185). Retrieved from http://www.kff.org/medicaid/8185.cfm

Holahan, J., Clemans-Cope, L., Lawton, E., & Rousseau, D. (2011). *Medicaid spending growth over the last decade and the Great Recession, 2000–2009* (Kaiser Commission on Medicaid and the Uninsured Report No. 8152). Retrieved from http://www.kff.org/medicaid/8152.cfm

Holahan, J., & Weil, A. (2003). *Block grants are the wrong prescription for Medicaid.* Retrieved from Urban Institute Health Policy Center website: http://www.urban.org/url.cfm?ID=900624

Iglehart, J. K. (2011). After midterm elections, changes are in store. *Health Affairs, 30*(1), 8–10. doi: 10.1377/hlthaff.2010.1165

Kaiser Commission on Medicaid and the Uninsured. (2010). *Medicaid beneficiaries and access to care* (Report No. 8000-02). Retrieved from http://www.kff.org/medicaid/8000.cfm

Kaiser Commission on Medicaid and the Uninsured. (2011a). *Federal core requirements and state options in Medicaid: Current policies and key issues* (Report No. 8174). Retrieved from http://www.kff.org/medicaid/8174.cfm

Kaiser Commission on Medicaid and the Uninsured. (2011b). *Five key questions and answers about Section 1115 Medicaid demonstration waivers* (Report No. 8196). Retrieved from http://www.kff.org/medicaid/8196.cfm

Kaiser Commission on Medicaid and the Uninsured. (2011c). *Implications of a federal block grant for Medicaid* (Report No. 8173). Retrieved from http://www.kff.org/medicaid/8173.cfm

Kaiser Commission on Medicaid and the Uninsured. (2011d). *State options that expand access to Medicaid Home and Community-Based Services* (Report No. 8241). Retrieved from http://www.kff.org/medicaid/8241.cfm

Kaiser Commission on Medicaid and the Uninsured. (2011e). *United States: Federal and state share of Medicaid spending, FY 2009.* Retrieved from http://www.statehealthfacts.org/profileind.jsp?cmprgn=2&cat=4&rgn=1&ind=636&sub=47

Kaiser Commission on Medicaid and the Uninsured. (2011f). *Where are states today? Medicaid and CHIP eligibility levels for children and non-disabled adults* (Report No. 7993-02). Retrieved from http://www.kff.org/medicaid/7993.cfm

Lambrew, J. M. (2005). Making Medicaid a Block Grant Program: An analysis of the implications of past proposals. *Milbank Quarterly, 83*(1), 41–63. doi: 10.1111/j.0887-378X.2005.00335.x

Lopez, A. (2011, September 22). GOP lawmakers angered over federal request for profit cap in state Medicaid reform. *The Florida Independent.* Retrieved from http://floridaindependent.com/48782/gop-legislature-medical-loss-ratio

The Republican Governors Public Policy Committee. (2011). *A new Medicaid: A flexible, innovative and accountable future.* Retrieved from Republican Governors Association website: http://www.rga.org/homepage/gop-govs-release-medicaid-reform-report

Roberts, J. (2011, May 15). Rhode Island's Medicaid experiment becomes a talking point for budget cutters. *The New York Times.* Retrieved from http://www.nytimes.com/2011/05/16/us/politics/16medicaid.html?pagewanted=all

Smith, V. K., Gifford, K., Ellis, E., Rudowitz, R., & Snyder, L. (2011). *Moving ahead amid fiscal challenges: A look at Medicaid spending, coverage, and policy trends. Results from a 50-state Medicaid budget survey for state fiscal years 2011 and 2012* (Kaiser Commission on Medicaid and the Uninsured Report No. 8248). Retrieved from http://www.kff.org/medicaid/8248.cfm

Takach, M. (2011). Reinventing Medicaid: State innovations to qualify and pay for patient-centered medical homes show promising results. *Health Affairs, 30*(7), 1325–1334. doi: 10.1377/hlthaff.2011.0170

Zuckerman, S., Williams, A. F., & Stockley, K. E. (2009). Trends in Medicaid physician fees, 2003–2008. *Health Affairs, 28*(3), w510–w519. doi: 10.1377/hlthaff.28.3.w510

Allyson G. Hall and Shenae K. Samuels

Quality Debates

Introduction

Compared to those in many other countries, health care debates in the United States have long been volatile, and in recent years have become something like flashpoints for broader ideological conflicts. This is not to say there have not been controversies in the past about the passage of major new health programs. At the time of the passage of Medicare in 1965, for example, major debates took place both between the political parties and with health-related organizations such as the American Medical Association (AMA). Once the Medicare program was implemented, however, it became clear that costs for the program were going to be higher than the initial estimates, leading to new controversies. As programs such as Medicare for the elderly and Medicaid for the poor became more accepted parts of the American approach to health care services, more of the discussion about health care focused on who had access to care, what to do about some groups who were not being covered, whether costs were becoming too high, and whether the quality of health care being delivered was appropriate. Often, the public discussion became part of a debate over whether there was a "crisis" in health care. Certainly, this was true of the public discussion surrounding President Bill Clinton's proposed health care plan, which eventually failed. During that time, any major push on health care reform ceased, and the sole major accomplishment of the Clinton administration in health care policy was the passage of the state child health insurance program (SCHIP), which expanded coverage for health care services to the children of the working poor.

In 2000 the Republican candidate George W. Bush won the presidency in an extremely close and hotly contested election that was eventually resolved by the U.S. Supreme Court. For the first time in more than 100 years, the United States had elected as president a candidate who had lost the popular vote. Initially, President Bush had not focused much in his campaign on health care, in contrast to his opponent, Al Gore, who proposed extensions to SCHIP and Medicare. When health care became part of the campaign in September 2000, Bush proposed a plan to convert Medicare into a system of competing private health insurance plans that would include prescription drug benefits, an important deficit in the original Medicare program. During his presidency, Bush focused on accomplishing that one part of his campaign platform, the creation of a prescription drug option for Medicare, and shied away from taking on any type of comprehensive health care reform. In 2004 the Medicare Prescription Drug, Improvement and Modernization Act, generally known as the Medicare Modernization Act, passed. This act had three separate parts, the prescription drug addition to Medicare, new provisions for private insurance coverage in Medicare, and tax incentives for health savings accounts. The part most anticipated by the public, the prescription drug addition, did not begin until January 1, 2006. Prior to that, in 2004, there had been a distribution of drug discount cards to the low-income elderly. Once the plan began, many of the elderly were initially confused by some of its details, since people had to pick among different private plans with different sets of drugs included. Some experts even think that confusion among the public about aspects of this plan may have played a role in the Republicans' loss of Congress in November 2006.

By early 2000, rising health care costs had returned. During the 1990s, the rise in costs had slowed somewhat, and there were some who hoped that the marketplace was playing a role in this effort to keep health care costs from rising as rapidly as it had in previous decades. As an example, from 2000 to 2006, average annual premiums for employer-sponsored family coverage rose by 87 percent, going from $6,348 in 2000 to $11,480 in 2006. As part of these rising costs, increasing numbers of employers decided to stop offering health insurance to their workers, and from 2001 to 2006 the number of firms providing health insurance declined from 69 to 61 percent. Even though in this same period there were some increases in coverage by Medicaid, the proportion of people who had a high financial burden from health care costs, defined as more than 10 percent of pretax income on insurance premiums and out-of-pocket expenses, rose 1 percentage point each year, up to 19 percent by 2006. Absolute numbers of people uninsured at any one time rose from 40 to 45 million, or about 15.3 percent of the population. Other indicators of how Americans were increasingly viewing health care as a concern were that in a Kaiser Family Foundation Survey in 2004, health costs ranked among Americans' major worries about the future.

Quality of care had become a focus of concern and of attention by some major health policy and health research groups during a similar time frame. Discussions of quality quickly become discussions also of the evaluation and measurement of health system outputs. Defining and examining quality is necessarily an evaluative process. As compared to the cost area, one difficulty in accessing quality is that measurement is less clear, and the United States health care system is less easily amenable to evaluation than are systems in some other countries, because it is not one unified system with an available database to use to understand quality issues. Quality is often defined as the degree of excellence or conformation to high standards, and it cannot be assessed without a clear understanding of the standards of excellence, which can present a challenge both to patients and to policymakers without a background in this complex field.

At times, researchers like Avedis Donabedian have defined quality, especially as it relates to patient care, in terms of three different components: structure, process, and outcome. Structure refers to such things as whether the right personnel or facilities are available, whether health care personnel are appropriately trained, and even whether facilities follow rules such as fire and safety codes. Process measures often reflect what was actually done to a patient, such as the numbers and types of procedures as well as laboratory tests. Another way to think about the process aspect of quality of care is that it is the *content* of care. One advantage of a focus on this level of quality assessment is that such issues are typically well documented in the medical record; certainly they are well recorded when compared to the third component of care, outcome, which may not be reflected in those documents and has been the most challenging aspect to assess. One way to think of outcome is as a net change that occurs in health status as a result of the medical care received. In health care today, the emphasis is on outcome measures of quality as the best types of measures.

Two important reports from the Institute of Medicine have dealt with quality concerns in the United States. The first was a 1999 report, *To Err Is Human,* which argued that, though physicians, nurses, and other health professionals were doing their best to provide quality care, the current system did not reward innovation and communication. This report documented that more people die each year in the United States from medical mistakes than from highway deaths, breast cancer, and AIDS combined. A second report focusing on quality issues was published in 2001, titled *Crossing the Quality Chasm.* This report argued that the current U.S. health care system is a tangled, highly fragmented web that often wastes resources with unnecessary services and duplicated efforts. Possible solutions would include revamping the system not only to deal with the needs and values of patients but also to develop greater teamwork among health professionals and greater use of information technology. Some suggested technological solutions, which are also included in the new health-reform legislation, are better medical information systems and more use of computers in the maintenance of medical records.

By the time of the election of President Barack Obama in 2008, problems with the availability of health care insurance, the overall rising costs of health care, and quality concerns again made health care an important campaign issue. Discussion about how to reform the health care delivery system in the United States was especially pronounced in the Democratic primary debates, with Obama and former First Lady Hillary Clinton each putting forward somewhat different proposals. By the general election campaign, Obama had made more comprehensive health reform a major promise in his election discussions. Once elected, accomplishing some of his goals in the area of health care reform became an important push, even though both the president and his advisers were all aware of the ways in which the failure of health care reform in the Clinton administration had been an important failure in Clinton's first term as president. Thus, with great difficulty and many compromises in the specifics of the plan, the Patient Protection and Affordable Health Care Act of 2010 (ACA) was eventually passed.

In reality, many of the provisions of this plan take place in different years, and some of the most important will not be put into place until 2014. This includes the creation of health exchanges to help make health insurance available to more people who do not have work-based health insurance available (either because their workplace does not offer it or because they are unemployed). Thus, the articles in this collection cannot really address how well the newest piece of legislation is working, inasmuch as many parts of that legislation are not yet implemented. In addition, issues of quality of care often take the most time to assess because the determination of quality of health care means that first the new policy must result in more people having insurance, then people must actually use the insurance to deal with a health problem or health-prevention concern, and only then can studies as to the longer-term outcomes of that care be conducted. Assessment of quality of health care services is not something that can occur quickly.

The 10 chapters collected in this section of the volume look at a variety of important issues. The first five explore issues related to health care providers: Are some types of providers better able to provide quality care than others? Crystal Wiley Cené, Dinushika Mohottige, and Diane Dewar discuss the question of whether primary care providers are more equipped to provide better care, or whether medical education should continue its current emphasis on specialists. In a related debate, Barbara Sheer discusses nurse practitioners and physicians' assistants, asking questions about the extent to which they can or cannot, in some circumstances, adequately shoulder the tasks of primary care physicians. Moving on from physician training to physician background, two chapters examine the questions of gender and ethnicity: Linda Grant and Aubrey Denmon debate whether female physicians are able to provide better care than their male counterparts, especially for female patients; Marsha Regenstein, Ellie Andres, and Dylan Nelson debate whether doctors of particular ethnic backgrounds are better able to care for patients of the same background. Finally, Brenda Ohta explores a debate about the location of care—is care in the home setting more efficient and of higher quality than institutional care?

Speaking of location, in a second section that looks at treatment methods and their impact on quality, Kevin Seitz and Marianne Udow-Phillips debate whether states and localities are best able to implement their own quality- and cost-control programs. Michael Hochman, Danny McCormick, and Elaine Morrato explore the fairly new field of comparative-effectiveness research, debating whether or not such research can make a positive impact on the quality of care. And finally Katy Mahraj and Kai Zheng debate the implementation of information technology systems in hospitals—are those high-tech solutions to quality control all they are cracked up to be?

Because health care costs are such an important animating factor in current health care debates, this quality section closes with two chapters that reflect on how cost-cutting measures may impact care. R. Tamara Konetzka, Marcelo Coca-Perraillon, and Sally Stearns debate whether proposed cuts to Medicare benefits will have a negative impact on patient outcomes, while Stephen Parente and David Randall debate the increasingly popular high-deductible insurance plans—do such plans encourage people to delay care, or do they help solve the "moral hazard" problem of overinsurance?

Jennie Jacobs Kronenfeld
Arizona State University

Primary Care Versus Specialization

POINT: The current U.S. health care system privileges specialization over general practice and therefore serves to fragment health care delivery and increase costs, as specialists tend to practice defensive medicine. The primary care physician oversees the health of the total patient, and without this oversight, interconnections between certain health factors can often be overlooked.

Crystal Wiley Cené and Dinushika Mohottige, University of North Carolina at Chapel Hill

COUNTERPOINT: Overdependence on primary care may create disincentives for entrance into important specialties, which is where cutting-edge medicine is practiced. Medical specialization—and the higher income–earning potential associated with various fields—is a driver not just of high-quality physicians entering medicine but also of innovation and advances in treatment and research.

Diane Dewar, School of Public Health, University at Albany, State University of New York

Introduction

A topic of much discussion in the U.S. health care system today is the role of primary care services as opposed to specialty services. One argument, the Point position in this chapter, is that specialty care services are privileged over primary care, and this can lead to greater fragmentation of care and higher costs. The Counterpoint argument, on the other hand, argues that too much emphasis on primary care will make physicians less likely to become specialists, yet it is from specialty care that many of the most important improvements and advances in patient care come. Thus, the current emphasis on physicians in primary care benefits both individual physicians with higher incomes and patients through innovation and advances in treatment and research.

What do health care experts mean by the term *primary care*? Generally, primary care is basic and routine health care, usually provided in an office or a clinic. Although primary care can be provided by a physician or by a nurse practitioner or physician's assistant, this chapter focuses more heavily on the issue of primary care as provided by physicians. A different chapter examines the role of nurse practitioners and physician's assistants as alternative primary care providers. Usually, a primary care provider takes responsibility for coordinating all aspects of a patient's health care. In this role, the primary care provider is often described as the patient's initial or first contact with the health care system. The types of care delivered by a primary care provider include those used to treat the most common health problems, as well as preventive services. This includes sore throats, sprained wrists, and infected ears, as well as screens and tests for hypertension and high cholesterol. Experts sometimes contrast primary care with secondary and tertiary care. Secondary care is provided for more specialized types of problems, such as setting a broken arm or leg or caring for a patient who has had a heart attack or stroke. Tertiary care is reserved for the most specialized and unusual health care problems, such as heart surgery or neurosurgery. Often, the contrast is simply expressed as one between primary care and specialty care (Kronenfeld, 1997).

Which physicians are considered primary care doctors? Generally, all family physicians are primary care providers. In addition, most pediatricians are, unless they are specialists in a particular subfield such as pediatric oncology. Many internists are also considered primary care specialists if they have a general internal medicine practice. Of course, many well-known specialties—for example, cardiology that deals with heart problems, pulmonology that deals with lung problems, and rheumatology (arthritis)—are all subspecialities within internal medicine, but physicians whose practice focuses on the narrow areas would not be considered primary care practitioners.

The large increases in the number of physicians that are specialists have mostly occurred in the past 60 or so years, although some trends in medicine along this direction started earlier. During World War II, physicians who were specialists were given higher ranks, higher pay, and preferred assignments. In the late 1940s and 1950s, financial incentives through the G.I. Bill of Rights encouraged physician veterans to receive specialty training. At the same time, the number of residencies expanded, and this also led to an increase in the numbers of physicians interested in subspecialty training. After 1965 the newly enacted Medicare law's payment system added to the growth of specialty training programs by providing direct and indirect payments to teaching hospitals to support residency slots.

Currently, specialists earn higher pay than do generalists (often more than twice as much), allowing these physicians to pay off loans more quickly, and many young physicians now have substantial college and medical school loans. This pushes even those who might be more interested in primary care to consider specialty care, as does the fact that, within the medical profession, specialists are often viewed as better trained and thus are given more prestige within medicine. This is a message that many students in medical school absorb; the majority of the teaching they are exposed to during their clinical years in medical school comes from specialists, rather than from primary care physicians (PCPs). Similarly, especially within the university hospital context, most of the patients with whom medical school students have contact are more seriously ill and often are using the services of many specialists. Even though medical schools in recent decades have added experience in outpatient clinics to the training of medical school students, more of the training still occurs in the context of the hospital and specialty oriented practice. This becomes a complicated issue, as the bulk of this chapter demonstrates, because there is evidence that primary care is associated with greater access to medical care, more provision of preventive services, and better recognition of patients' problems. The Point side of this chapter will discuss more studies linked to this position.

Part of the complexity, then, is also that specialty care is essential to the appropriate functioning of the health care system. Income gains are only one of the considerations that medical school students think about to help them plan what field of medicine should be their own focus after completion of medical school. Issues of flexibility in careers, prestige, and respect from other physicians are all factors. These are issues from the physician decision-making side. In addition, there are important external benefits to patients and to the overall health care system of having more care provided by specialists. Some studies find that specialists make more efficient use of medical technology through the increased utilization of procedure-based care, and display a greater ability to improve health outcomes through the appropriate utilization of advanced medicine. This is the position of the Counterpoint argument, and that section of this chapter points out many studies in support of this position and demonstrates why, as a society, it is necessary to make greater investments in the training of specialists relative to primary care practitioners.

POINT

The purpose of this chapter is to debate whether primary care or specialty care results in better health outcomes. Using the available scientific evidence, the authors of this paper emphatically answer that primary care results in better health outcomes and more equitable distribution of population health. In support of this stance, the authors will define primary care, summarize why there is a declining interest in primary care and a shift toward specialization, and review available evidence which generally supports the view that primary care results in better health outcomes at reduced costs. The chapter concludes with the authors' proposed strategies for attracting and retaining more primary care clinicians.

DEFINITION AND TYPICAL ROLES OF PRIMARY CARE

The public has varied ideas about what constitutes "primary care," but family physicians, general internists, and pediatricians are generally considered primary care clinicians. This section will use the term "clinicians" hereafter to refer to physicians and other health care providers, including "mid-level providers" (i.e., physician assistants and nurse practitioners) who also provide health care. The term *primary care* can also refer to a specified "set of functions" provided by one's usual source of care (USOC). Health policy expert Barbara Starfield defines four pillars of primary care: first contact or patient-centered "longitudinality," continuity of care, comprehensiveness or concern for the whole patient rather than one organ system, and coordination with other components of the health system (Smetana et al., 2007). She also describes six important mechanisms through which primary care improves population health. These include (1) increasing access to health care for marginalized populations, (2) delivering high-quality clinical care that addresses broad aspects of health, (3) improving health prevention efforts, (4) managing complex health problems, (5) creating overall improvements in care, and (6) reducing unnecessary or inappropriate costly specialty care (Sandy, Bodenheimer, Pawlson, & Starfield, 2009). Through these mechanisms, primary care is capable of achieving the efficiency, equity, and effectiveness that the U.S. health care system strives for.

HISTORY OF THE DECLINING INTEREST IN PRIMARY CARE

If primary care truly generates better health-related outcomes, why is the pursuit of primary care in the United States declining? This question is best answered by understanding the institutional, political, economic, and policy changes that shaped the field of medicine. Over a century ago, knowledge of physiology and the scientific basis of disease expanded, generating an ideological shift away from a sociobehavioral understanding of disease to a more "biomedical model" that conceptualized illness as physical and chemical alterations that primarily affect organ systems. This paradigm shift demanded greater understanding of disease processes *within* individual organ systems, thus paving the way for specialization (e.g., specialization in diseases of the heart or gastrointestinal system). In addition, efforts at medical education reform inspired by the Flexner report of 1910 (Davis et al., 2007) emphasized the creation of centers of excellence within teaching hospitals, which further set the stage for specialization and the creation of specialty and subspecialty boards (Sandy et al., 2009).

Changes to hospitalization costs and the emergence of third-party payers set the stage for the primary care–specialty income gap, which persists today as a significant contributor to the specialization trend among new medical graduates. Hospitals transformed in the early 1930s as a result of scientific advances. In an attempt to recruit practitioners, hospitals began offering incentives to surgeons, including the ability to set and collect fees for their services. However, when the country entered the Great Depression, hospitalization became unaffordable for the general public. The Depression limited patients' ability to pay their health care bills, and physicians began to rely more heavily on third-party reimbursement for their services. Blue Cross and Blue Shield insurance plans were especially promising because they ensured surgeons and hospitals payment for *inpatient* care (i.e., care delivered while the patient was in the hospital). Further boosting the primary-specialty income gap was the fact that most insurance plans allowed physicians to set their own fees so long as they were near the average fees charged by other local physicians, often called the "usual, customary, and reasonable" (UCR) payment system (Delbanco, Meyers, & Segal, 1979). The upshot was that insurance coverage for hospital-based services, such as surgery and radiology, grew much faster than insurance for office visits (Starr, 1982). Meanwhile, primary care services provided outside of the hospital were largely excluded from insurance coverage. Consequently, many of these providers were forced to decrease service fees so as to ensure affordability for their patients.

By the early 1940s policies and procedure growing out of World War II facilitated the trend toward specialization that continued into the postwar period. Specialists in the war received higher ranks, higher pay, and preferred assignments compared to general practitioners (Sandy et al., 2009). After the war ended, financial incentives offered through the G.I. Bill of Rights and the Veterans Affairs Department (VA) encouraged physician veterans to receive specialty training. Coincidently, during this postwar era, the number of residencies expanded dramatically, facilitating the pursuit of specialty and subspecialty training by medical graduates (Stevens, 1998).

In the 1950s the income gap between primary care physicians (PCPs) and specialists was exacerbated by the Relative Value Unit (RVU) scale, which essentially linked payment to procedures (Sandy et al., 2009). Amid concerns that insurers would abandon the "usual, customary and reasonable" system because of physician fee variability, the California Medical Association created a new system based on an *insurer-determined* fee schedule. Each service was assigned a "relative value unit" and payment was based on the RVU, multiplied by a "conversion factor" determined by each insurer. For example, a brief office visit might have an RVU of 1, though a comprehensive hospital visit might have an RVU of 7. Because patients tended to have insurance for procedures covered by specialists, fees for those specialists were already much higher than were the fees for primary care physician visits, which were rarely covered by insurance. Therefore, specialists benefited both from a rise in the conversion factor and from the creation of new services with higher RVUs. The RVU system, which became the prevailing "fee-for-service" payment model for physician services, including Medicare and most commercial insurance, was inherently biased toward specialty care.

In the early twentieth century, medical schools began affiliating with teaching hospitals, thus spawning the development of "academic medical centers" (Sandy et al., 2009). These centers became hubs for teaching, research, and specialty care. As medical schools' revenue increased, spending on medical research also increased by nearly 700 percent, as did reimbursement for hospital-based subspecialty surgery and procedures. The focus of medical education shifted away from everyday patient care and toward more highly technical procedures and treatments for relatively rare conditions. Specialists largely replaced generalists as clinical teachers, and research productivity (measured by publications) was valued over expert clinical teaching. These factors contributed to medical student interest in specialty-oriented fields.

Medicare's payment system fueled the growth of specialty training programs through direct and indirect payments to teaching hospitals to support residency slots instead of paying training programs directly (Rich, 2002). This "uncapped entitlement" increased hospital revenue, even though these institutions primarily trained residents to pursue specialty careers and provide specialty-oriented services. Financial support for primary care training initiatives, such as that provided through the U.S. Public Health Service Act, was miniscule (about 1%) compared to what Medicare provided hospitals (Mullan, 1996). The U.S. government's decision to allow academic medical centers and hospitals to determine the proportion of generalist and specialist physicians, instead of instituting a national policy that served the best interest of the nation's health, further shifted the balance toward the pursuit of specialization over primary care. Not surprisingly, the leadership of academic medical centers and hospitals—often dominated by specialists—chose to expand specialty-oriented research, training, and clinical care.

In the 1980s and 1990s, the rising health care costs, exponential growth of specialty services, and primary care workforce shortage created an economic environment ripe for health care reform that would reduce costs and revive primary care. Two strategies emerged to achieve this goal. One involved using primary care physicians as "gatekeepers" to specialty care, and the other provided physicians with a fixed payment per patient regardless of the service rendered (i.e., capitation). Although these strategies successfully lowered costs and helped revive interest in primary care, their effects were short lived due to the backlash against managed care and the notion of the primary care provider as gatekeeper. Consequently, the income gap between primary care providers and specialists continued to widen, in accordance with rising specialist volume and fees, as well as the increasing orientation toward specialist-performed medical procedures.

EVIDENCE FOR THE EFFECTIVENESS OF PRIMARY CARE VERSUS SPECIALIZATION ON VARIOUS HEALTH-RELATED OUTCOMES

An extensive scientific literature examines the relative merit of primary and specialty care in providing accessible, high-quality, safe, and efficient health care. The vast majority of studies show that primary care best achieves these outcomes. The sections that follow will offer a summary of the evidence comparing primary care to specialty care for the following health-related outcomes: access to and continuity of care, utilization of care, preventive care, mortality, quality of care, and cost of care.

Access to and continuity of care. Primary care has been associated with better access to and continuity of care, both of which lead to better health outcomes. Patients have fewer barriers accessing primary care provided by generalists compared to care by specialists who act as primary care providers. As a result, generalists provide more first-contact care. Indeed, a regular relationship with a physician is a better predictor for health care access than is insurance status. Enhanced access to and continuity of health care are associated with better self-reported general and mental health. Patients who report better primary care (as assessed by the health delivery characteristics of primary care) were less likely to report depression and poor health.

In a meta-analysis of 40 studies addressing the relationship between interpersonal continuity and outcomes of care, continuity improved the majority of outcomes (Saultz & Lochner, 2005). The same study also examined 41 cost variables associated with interpersonal continuity and found that expenditures were significantly less for 35 of the outcomes. The authors also concluded that interpersonal continuity and improved preventive care were likely associated with reduced hospitalization. Other studies support this conclusion with their findings that provider continuity of care is associated with reduced resource utilization and costs for patients with a range of medical conditions. These conclusions also apply to adolescent and veteran populations. Not having a consistent provider for prevention and disease management is associated with greater use of emergency services, and having a different source of care for preventive and illness care nearly doubled the likelihood that adolescents had used emergency services. Data from the VA revealed that reorganizing care to emphasize primary and ambulatory care resulted in enhanced continuity, higher rates of preventive service provision, reduced hospitalizations, and lower death rates.

Health care utilization. Extensive evidence from a range of populations suggests that having a primary care provider or having better continuity of care is associated with lower health care utilization in terms of hospitalizations and emergency department (ED) use. In a national random sample of 78,000 Medicare beneficiaries aged 66 and over who died in 2001, having made primary care visits in the preceding year was associated with fewer hospital days at the end of life and lower costs (American College of Physicians, 2008). A similar study conducted among Medicaid patients who made at least three ambulatory physician visits in a two-year period found that patients with better provider continuity in year one of the study had significantly lower rates of hospitalization in year two (Gill & Mainous, 1998). More primary care visits also resulted in less in-hospital deaths and fewer preventable hospitalizations for those with congestive heart failure and chronic obstructive pulmonary disease. Studies of Medicare patients have also shown that patients with principal care physicians (64% of whom were generalists) were much less likely to use the ED for every category of disease severity (Parchman & Culler, 1999). AIDS patients with a primary care physician or a primary care clinic as their USOC were less likely to use emergency department services than were patients whose USOC was an AIDS-specialty clinic (Mauskopf et al., 1994).

The availability and accessibility of primary care services also impacts health care utilization. Across all U.S. counties, a greater proportion of primary care physicians are associated with significantly fewer hospital admissions, visits, and total surgeries, even after controlling for patient and community factors. Studies of certain conditions (such as congestive heart failure and asthma) commonly managed in ambulatory settings have revealed that hospitalization rates and health expenditures are higher in areas with fewer primary care physicians and limited access to primary care. Finally, a survey of Medicare beneficiaries found that beneficiaries with "fair" or "poor" self-rated health were about twice more likely to experience a preventable hospitalization if they resided in a primary care shortage area (PCSA). Thus, living in a PCSA is an independent risk factor for preventable hospitalization, even after accounting for other factors, such as age, income, and race that are associated with preventable hospitalizations and that influence how people rate their own health.

Preventive care. Improving health prevention efforts is one of the main functions of primary care. Scientific literature supports this claim and suggests that having a PCP or generalist is associated with greater provision of behavioral counseling, immunizations, cancer screening, and other tests. Generalists are more likely than specialists to counsel and offer persistent counseling about smoking, exercise, alcohol use, and seat belts. For example, Medicare beneficiaries with primary care generalists as their USOC had higher odds of immunization than did those with a specialist USOC.

Another concern is that patients who use a specialist as their USOC may not reliably receive indicated preventive services. For example, one study showed that cardiologists and pulmonologists were less likely to be knowledgeable about breast cancer screening guidelines than general internists, who are more likely to screen their patients for breast cancer. Having a primary care generalist versus a specialist as one's USOC was also associated with higher odds of colorectal screening.

In general, primary care providers offer more preventive care than specialists (American College of Physicians, 2008). These preventative services play a pivotal role in reducing hospitalization rates and associated costs. Yet it is unclear whether patients are aware of this important fact. Further, there is legitimate concern that patients and physicians often have different expectations about a health care visit and the physician's role. In fact, one study designed to examine the extent to which specialists incorporate elements of primary care into their clinical practice found that, though a considerable proportion of patients only sought care from specialists, most specialists did not assume responsibility for patients' primary care needs. It is important for patients to not only understand that their primary care needs may go unmet when specialists are their sole providers of health care, but they should also be aware of the overarching implications for health outcomes.

Mortality. Primary care is associated with longer life and reduced mortality from all causes, as well as from specific conditions. A majority of data from 35 separate studies showed that states with higher ratios of primary care physicians to the population had decreased mortality from cancer, heart disease, or stroke (American College of Physicians, 2008). The majority of these findings were "statistically significant"—that is, unlikely to be due to chance. In contrast, the ratio of specialists to the population was generally associated with higher mortality. Based on findings from a state-level analysis, the authors concluded that an increase of 1 PCP per 10,000 population was associated with a 6 percent decrease in all-cause mortality and nearly 3 percent decreases in infant, low-birth weight, and stroke mortality.

Finally, an increase in the number of PCPs per 10,000 persons was associated with a reduction in the incidence and death from cervical cancer. The same pattern emerged for colorectal cancer incidence and mortality. On the contrary, the supply of specialists has no correlation with a range of health outcomes, including mortality. One might ask, "how much life expectancy a person gains from having a primary care provider and whether these benefits are equally distributed among all groups?" One study showed that primary care was associated with a reduction in 14.4 deaths per 100,000 people, with blacks benefitting more in terms of reduced mortality than whites.

Quality of care. Quality of care has been defined by the Institute of Medicine as "the degree to which health services for individuals and populations increase the likelihood of desired health outcomes and are consistent with current professional knowledge" (1994, p. 3). In essence, quality refers to whether people get the care they need, whether the care is appropriate, and whether it is effective. Researchers identify two primary dimensions of quality of care for individuals: access and effectiveness (Campbell, Roland, & Buetow, 2000). In a study examining the differences between general internists and cardiologists in approaches to treating patients with unstable angina in a community hospital, researchers found significant differences in patterns of care by provider type. General internists were less likely to give aspirin, heparin, and beta-blockers in the initial treatment of patients with chest pain. General internists had a tendency to use exercise testing for risk stratification and diagnosis, whereas cardiologists performed revascularization procedures two to four times as often. Yet there were no significant differences in myocardial infarction or mortality between the two groups. A study by Mahajan and colleagues in 1996 followed more than 300 patients scheduled for open-access esophagogastroduodenoscopy (EGD) and colonoscopy by nongastroenterologist physicians over a nine-month period to examine whether nongastroenterologist physicians scheduled patients for appropriate indications based on American Society for Gastrointestinal Endoscopy guidelines. It found that family practitioners and general internists performed better in scheduling for appropriate indications than did internal medicine subspecialists and surgeons.

It is important to note that many studies demonstrate that specialist physicians are able to deliver higher quality care within the narrow, specific areas of their specialty than generalists (Ayanian, Guadagnoli, McNeil, & Cleary, 1997; Chin, Friedmann, Cassel, & Lang, 1997; Go, Rao, Dauterman, & Massie, 2000; Harrold, Field, & Gurwitz, 1999; Jollis, 1996). However, Smetana and colleagues found that studies favoring specialty care over generalist care had methodological flaws including inadequate case-mix adjustment and failure to address physician practice settings. These studies also tended to exclude data regarding information technology, physician volume and experience, and care management programs, among other factors, as compared to studies that show no difference or that favor generalists in terms of health care outcomes for patients with a single discrete condition (Smetana et al., 2007).

When assessing quality, it is important to also consider interpersonal outcomes (e.g., patient satisfaction and experiences) in addition to clinical effectiveness. Researchers in Massachusetts conducted a study to examine whether characteristics of primary care (accessibility, continuity, comprehensiveness, integration, clinical interaction, trust) are associated with important quality outcomes, including adherence to physician's advice, patient satisfaction, and improved health status (Safran et al., 1998). They found patients who rated physician's comprehensive scores in the ninety-fifth percentile had almost three times higher adherence to physician advice compared to patients who rated physician comprehensiveness in the fifth percentile.

An increase in the number of primary care physicians may result in better quality at lower cost. An increase of one PCP per 10,000 in a state was associated with a rise in that state's quality rank by 10 places and in a reduction in overall spending by $684 per Medicare beneficiary (Baicker & Chandra, 2004). By comparison, an increase of one specialist per 10,000 in a state was estimated to reduce the overall quality rank nine places and increase overall spending by $526 per Medicare beneficiary.

Data from international studies support the claim that primary care enhances health care quality, outcomes, efficiency and access to care. Data from a 2007 survey comparing adults' health care experiences in the United States, Germany, Australia, the Netherlands, New Zealand, the United Kingdom, and Canada revealed that positive patient experiences were associated with having an accessible "medical home" that coordinated care (American College of Physicians, 2008). These data further substantiate cross-national studies that found associations between accessible, well-integrated, comprehensive primary care and better health outcomes and lower costs. It also lends support to numerous U.S. studies showing that adults with a primary care USOC are more likely to receive preventative care, are less likely to have care coordination challenges, and are less likely to experience care disparities compared to individuals lacking a USOC (Schoen et al., 2007). In a similar 2004 survey of adults' primary care experiences in Australia, Canada, New Zealand, the United Kingdom, and the United States, the authors (Davis et al., 2006) found that the U.S. primary care system ranked lower in access, coordination, physician-patient experiences, and other dimensions of patient-centered care.

Cost of care. Primary care has been associated with a better cost-benefit ratio, compared with specialist care (American College of Physicians, 2008). Data based on a nationally representative sample of Americans 65 and older with a USOC who participated in the Medicare Current Beneficiary Survey revealed that longer patient-physician relationships were associated with fewer costs. For example, compared with patients who had a relationship with their physician for one year or less, patients with relationships of 10 years or more incurred $317 less in Part B Medicare costs, even after accounting for key demographic and health factors. This finding makes clear the numerous benefits of longitudinal care relationships with patients—a key tenet of primary care. A similar notable study by Carey and others (1995) compared outcomes and costs in the management of acute low-back pain provided by different provider types, including primary care physicians, chiropractors, and orthopedic surgeons. Though the time required for functional recovery, return to work, and complete recovery from back pain was similar among the different provider types, costs were significantly lower for primary care physicians. Studies focused on diabetes and hypertension illustrate a similar theme; namely, that primary care providers deliver a similar quality of care as specialists, despite using fewer resources.

The health of the nation and the complex realities of its current health care practice environment impact the nature of primary care visits, and thus the relative cost and quality of primary care. In a 2009 paper exploring whether the U.S. health care workforce is equipped to manage and prevent chronic disease, Bodenheimer and colleagues noted that of the 133 million patients with chronic illnesses, 47 percent have more than one diagnosis. The average family physician manages three problems per visit, increasing to 3.8 problems for elderly patients, and 4.6 for patients with diabetes (Beasley et al., 2004). In a population characterized by multiple comorbidities, multiple specialists would be required to address the numerous illnesses a primary care provider manages during a single encounter, which would further exacerbate rising health care costs (Bodenheimer, 2009b).

CONCLUSION

Primary care physicians provide high-quality, efficient, comprehensive care that rivals that provided by specialists for general health concerns. An abundance of evidence corroborates this claim by demonstrating that primary care is associated with greater access to medical care, more accurate diagnosis, better disease prevention, better recognition of patient's problems, better coordination of care for chronic illnesses, better quality of care, fewer avoidable hospitalizations, decreased ED use, longer life, and other health-related outcomes, all at lower costs (American College of Physicians, 2008).

Although the evidence is clear, most studies comparing generalist to specialist care focus on a single condition that usually falls within the narrow domain of the specialist. Few studies have evaluated the outcomes of care for people with multiple conditions (Smetana, 2007); the lack of data in this area is particularly troubling given that the number of patients with multiple chronic diseases is increasing. Currently, about 23 percent of Medicare beneficiaries have 5 or more chronic conditions, and this group accounts for two thirds of all Medicare spending. These patients will likely require and benefit from the coordination and comprehensiveness of care provided by primary care physicians who receive training to appropriately care for medically complex patients. Though the benefits of primary care are obvious, specialty care remains essential and vitally important to patient care, clinical teaching, and research. Efforts to strengthen collaboration and communication between primary care providers and specialists should continue, particularly in light of an aging population where the number of medical and psychiatric co-morbidities is increasing and medical care is becoming more complex.

Primary care, and thus the health of the nation, is in grave trouble. Although primary care physicians account for nearly one third of the physician workforce, the percentage of U.S. medical students entering residencies in family medicine, internal medicine, OB/GYN, and pediatrics has declined. Inevitably, the demand for primary care will exceed the supply. The U.S. population will increase by 18 percent to 349 million from 2005 to 2025, with an increasing proportion of people over age 85. As the population ages and the proportion of people with multiple chronic illnesses increases, so too will the demand for ambulatory (or outpatient) visits. Yet there has been a dramatic decline in the number of graduating medical students entering primary care.

The reasons for this movement toward specialization are complex but largely related to financial incentives that allow recent graduates to pay off student debt sooner and earn higher long-term incomes. Additionally, the high work-related stress in overloaded primary care practices is unattractive to recent graduates who perceive primary care as more work for less pay. Consequently, many primary care physicians are retiring early or have left the workforce for other reasons. An increasing proportion of new primary care providers are women who tend to work fewer hours secondary to additional demands on their time (e.g., child rearing), further reducing the effective workforce. By 2025 half of all primary care physicians will be female. Finally, most graduate medical education largely favors training in nonprimary care fields. Sixty-five million Americans live in what are called "primary care shortage areas" (Rieselbach, Crouse, & Frohna, 2010). A 2008 study predicted that the United States will experience a shortage of 35,000 to 44,000 adult primary care physicians by 2025. Without substantial reforms to the current health care system, the United States will continue to rely on international medical graduates to fill primary care needs, especially in rural and underserved areas (Steinbrook, 2009).

So what can be done to revitalize interest in primary care? Numerous scholars have proposed strategies, the cornerstone of which is physician-payment reform, to address the adult primary care shortage and increase training of primary care physicians in the United States (American College of Physicians, 2008; Bodenheimer, 2009b). Primary care physician reimbursement may be improved by (1) decreasing existing Medicare payment gaps between primary care physicians and specialists, (2) providing financial relief for new medical graduates choosing primary care careers via expanded funding of the National Health Service Corps, and (3) appropriately reimbursing care-coordination activities that improve health care quality in patient-centered medical homes and other primary care practices. In addition to payment reform, a national investment in health information technology and technical assistance for primary care practices may decrease the financial and time burden associated with coordinating care in primary care settings. Finally, increasing funding to primary care residencies and residency programs that train physicians in community-based practices and other ambulatory settings may enhance the recruitment and quality of primary care physicians. The U.S. health care system is broken. Improving and strengthening the primary care system and incentivizing careers in primary care may be a critical fix.

References and Further Reading

American College of Physicians. (2008). *How is a shortage of primary care physicians affecting the quality and cost of medical care?* (White Paper, Report No. 501281700). Philadelphia, PA: Author.

Ayanian, J. Z., Guadagnoli, E., McNeil, B. J., & Cleary, P. D. (1997). Treatment and outcomes of acute myocardial infarction among patients of cardiologists and generalist physicians. *Archives of Internal Medicine, 157*(22), 2570–2576.

Baicker, K., & Chandra, A. (2004). Medicare spending, the physician workforce, and beneficiaries' quality of care. *Health Affairs,* pp. 184–197.

Beasley, J. W., Hankey, T. H., Erickson, R., Stange, K. C., Mundt, M., Elliott, M., et al. (2004). How many problems do family physicians manage at each encounter? A WReN study. *Annals of Family Medicine, 2*(5), 405–410.

Bodenheimer, T., Chen, E., & Bennett, H. D. (2009a). Confronting the growing burden of chronic disease: Can the U.S. health care workforce do the job? *Health Affairs, 28*(1), 64–74.

Bodenheimer, T., Grumbach, K., & Berenson, R. A. (2009b). A lifeline for primary care. *New England Journal of Medicine, 360*(26), 2693–2696.

Campbell, S. M., Roland, M. O., & Buetow, S. A. (2000). Defining quality of care. *Social Science and Medicine, 51*(11), 1611–1625.

Carey, T. S., Garrett, J., Jackman, A., McLaughlin, C., Fryer, J., Smucker, D. R., & North Carolina Back Pain Project. (1995). The outcomes and costs of care for acute low back pain among patients seen by primary care practitioners, chiropractors, and orthopedic surgeons. *New England Journal of Medicine, 333*(14), 913–917.

Chin, M. H., Friedmann, P. D., Cassel, C. K., & Lang, R. M. (1997). Differences in generalist and specialist physicians' knowledge and use of angiotensin-converting enzyme inhibitors for congestive heart failure. *Journal of General Internal Medicine, 12*(9), 523–530.

Davis, K., Schoen, C., Shoenbaum, S. C., Audet, A. J., Doty, M. M., Holmgren, A. L., & Kirss, J. L. (2006, April 4). *Mirror, mirror on the wall: An update on the quality of American health through the patient's lens* (The Commonwealth Fund Report, vol. 12).

Delbanco, T. L., Meyers, K. C., & Segal, E. A. (1979). Paying the physician's fee: Blue Shield and the reasonable charge. *New England Journal of Medicine, 301*(24), 1314–1320.

Gill, J. M., & Mainous, A. G. (1998). The role of provider continuity in preventing hospitalizations. *Archives of Family Medicine, 7*(3), 352–357.

Go, A. S., Rao, R. K., Dauterman, K. W., & Massie, B. M. (2000). A systematic review of the effects of physician specialty on the treatment of coronary disease and heart failure in the United States. *The American Journal of Medicine, 108*(3), 216–226.

Harrold, L. R., Field, T. S., & Gurwitz, J. H. (1999). Knowledge, patterns of care, and outcomes of care for generalists and specialists. *Journal of General Internal Medicine, 14*(8), 499–511.

Institute of Medicine. (1994). *American's health in transition: Protecting and improving quality.* Washington, DC: National Academy Press.

Jollis, J. G., DeLong, E. R., Peterson, E. D., Muhlbaier, L. H., Fortin, D. F., Califf, R. M., & Mark, D. B. (1996). Outcome of acute myocardial infarction according to the specialty of the admitting physician. *New England Journal of Medicine, 335*(25), 1880–1887.

Kronenfeld, J. J. (1997). *The changing federal role in U.S. health care.* Westport, CT: Praeger

Mahajan, R. J., Barthel, J. S., & Marshall, J. B. (1996). Appropriateness of referrals for open-access endoscopy: How do physicians in different medical specialties do? *Archives of Internal Medicine, 156*(18), 2065–2069.

Mauskopf, J., Turner, B. J., Markson, L. E., Houchens, R. L., Fanning, T. R., & McKee, L. (1994). Patterns of ambulatory care for AIDS patients, and associations with emergency room use. *Health Services Research, 29*(4), 489–510.

Mullan, F. (1996). Powerful hands: Making the most of graduate medical education. *Health Affairs, 15*(2), 250–253.

Parchman, M. L., & Culler, S. D. (1999). Preventable hospitalizations in primary care shortage areas: An analysis of vulnerable Medicare beneficiaries. *Archives of Family Medicine, 8*(6), 487–491.

Rich, E. C., Liebow, M., Srinivasan, M., Parish, D., Wolliscroft, J. O., Fein, O., & Blaser, R. (2002). Medicare financing of graduate medical education. *Journal of General Internal Medicine, 17*(4), 283–292.

Rieselbach, R. E., Crouse, B. J., & Frohna, J. G. (2010). Teaching primary care in community health centers: Addressing the workforce crisis for the underserved. *Annals of Internal Medicine, 152*(2), 118–122.

Safran, D. G., Taira, D. A., Rogers, W. H., Kosinski, M., Ware, J. E., & Tarlov, A. R. (1998). Linking primary care performance to outcomes of care. *Journal of Family Practice, 48*(3), 213–220.

Sandy, L. G., Bodenheimer, T., Pawlson, L. G., & Starfield, B. (2009). The political economy of U.S. primary care. *Health Affairs, 28*(4), 1136–1145.

Saultz, J. W., & Lochner, J. (2005). Interpersonal continuity of care and care outcomes: A critical review. *Annals of Family Medicine, 3*(2), 159–166.

Schoen, C., Osborn, R., Doty, M. M., Bishop, M., Peugh, J., & Murukutla, N. (2007). Toward higher-performance health systems: Adults' health care experiences in seven countries. *Health Affairs, 26*(6), w717–w734.

Smetana, G. W., Landon, B. E., Bindman, A. B., Burstin, H., Davis, R. B., Tjia, J., & Rich, E. C. (2007). A comparison of outcomes resulting from generalist vs. specialist care for a single discrete medical condition: A systematic review and methodologic critique. *Archives of Internal Medicine, 167*(1), 10–20.

Starr, P. (1982). *The social transformation of American medicine.* New York, NY: Basic Books.

Steinbrook, R. (2009). Easing the shortage in adult primary care—Is it all about money? *New England Journal of Medicine, 360*(26), 2696–2699.

Stevens, R. (Ed.). (1998). *American medicine and the public interest* (Updated ed.). Berkeley, CA: University of California Press.

Crystal Wiley Cené and Dinushika Mohottige

COUNTERPOINT

Though many health care workers are relatively unskilled, the U.S. health sector also requires large numbers of highly trained professionals to provide increasingly technological medical care. Through education and training, medical students make investments in their human capital, with the training required for specialties being substantially greater than that for primary care. Economists treat the decision to invest in human capital with the same tools they use to analyze investment made by businesses in the physical world. Given the high investment costs of medical education, students will naturally wish to maximize the return on their educational investment by choosing a medical field that yields the highest expected income (or return). The return from an education that focuses on a medical specialty is much higher, on average, than that which focuses on primary care. Given the income differential between specialty care and primary care, most physician specialists obtain years of postgraduate education past their medical school education in order to have sufficient return on their investment in education and training. These specialists then produce not only quality medical care but also advances in the science of medicine, with most being trained in procedure-based medicine. The result is that the United States has the most technologically advanced medical-care system in the world.

THE MARKET FOR PHYSICIANS

Most physician specialists obtain years of postgraduate education past their medical school education. As part of their postgraduate education, many physicians choose to select specialties that enhance their income opportunities and allow them to pursue more advanced, often procedure-based medicine. Physicians come from a large number of medical specialties rather than a homogeneous group. About 50 percent of physicians are in office-based practice in primary care, and 20 percent are in general surgery or the surgical specialties, with the remainder having other specialties.

Concerns about specialization as well as about uneven distributions between rural and urban areas have long been heard in the United States. These concerns include the fact that there are too few primary care practitioners relative to specialists, creating problems in care coordination and access to care for even routine conditions. For example, specialists only treat specific body systems, not the more general health of the patient. This may result in uncoordinated care, given that the overall health and interactive effects of medical conditions and multiple treatments for more than one body system may go unrecognized.

Studies of physician specialty selection are especially important because of widespread beliefs that quality health care requires access to an appropriate mix of specialists. These beliefs hold that specialists are better able to coordinate diagnostic and treatment services related to specific conditions of specific body systems better than the general primary care physician, who cannot be expected to know intricate details of every body system. Specialists may also have better outcomes and higher quality of care for specific treatments of the body systems under their care due to the greater chance of having a greater volume of patients and more opportunities to treat patients with specific conditions. This increased exposure to patients with conditions leads to greater experience for the specialists and improved outcomes for the patients relative to treatment for the same conditions by a primary care physician who may only see occasional patients with such conditions.

Though changes in supply can take place relatively quickly for those health care occupations requiring minimal education or training, for physicians the change in supply can be seen as having long and variable lags between primary care and specialist areas. For physician specialists and others requiring the highest levels of education and training, the number of new professionals is determined by the admission decisions of medical schools as well as the decisions of applicants made many years earlier. Physicians must be licensed by a state in order to practice in that state. Requirements for licensure include graduating from an accredited medical school, passing a licensure examination, and completing one to two years of internship or residency in an accredited graduate medical education program. Many graduates, nevertheless, complete three- to four-year residency programs. Many physicians also become board-certified specialists. The requirements typically include advanced training for periods of three to six years, practice in the specialty, and passing the board examination. These investments in training result in large opportunity costs in terms of foregoing immediate income-generating opportunities and other lifestyle choices similar to those made in the investment in physical capital.

THE SPECIALIST'S INVESTMENT IN HUMAN CAPITAL

Through education and training, medical students make investments in their human capital. As was expressed above, economists treat such decisions as similar to those made by businesses. The decision maker will consider the avenues associated with investment, along with all financial and economic costs, including any opportunity costs. For example, for medical students in training, the foregone earnings associated with the time it takes to complete their medical education is an important opportunity cost, but monetary values must also be imputed to nonpecuniary gains, such as satisfaction from helping the ill and the prestige associated with being a physician. Prospective medical students, in principle, will compare the return, or expected income potential from medical education, with those of other possible occupational choices and select the occupation with the highest return or expected lifetime income. This results in more students gravitating to specialty areas, which are associated with greater returns on education.

Economists also recognize the role that nonpecuniary rewards, such as status and social responsibility, may play in the decision to specialize. Nevertheless, the economic focus is usually the degree to which physicians respond to financial incentives. Because decisions to specialize are normally made early in the physician's education and training career, Nicholson (2005) became curious about medical students and their knowledge of physician incomes. He examined surveys of the first- and fourth-year students conducted annually by large medical schools and found systematic biases in the responses. The students overestimated incomes in the 1970s but underestimated incomes by about 25 percent in more recent years. The estimates were also more accurate for a specialty that a student was more likely to select. For physicians who had been practicing in their specialty for more than one year, the U.S. Department of Labor reported 2005 median earnings of $322,000 for anesthesiologists and $283,000 for general surgeons, compared to $161,000 for pediatricians and $156,000 for family practitioners. Economic theory suggests that a rational decision, that which maximizes the return on investment in education, ought to be based on expected lifetime income, not simply the current earnings within a specialty. For example, lifetime income potential is a better measure of earnings than the fluctuating yearly income measure. This has been shown in the work of Nicholson, who illustrated that the choice between training for primary versus specialty care is substantially responsive to the expected lifetime income of the various fields.

Estimated elasticities of entry into specialties with respect to changes in expected lifetime earnings are usually greater than one, leaving little doubt that physicians respond to income when making their specialty decision. This means that for every percentage change in expected lifetime earnings with the movement from primary to specialty training, there is a more than proportional likelihood that the student will choose specialty training over primary care. This means that the rational medical student is more attracted to specialty care fields relative to primary care, controlling for other characteristics of the student such as gender, location, and other demographic or occupational characteristics. Bhattacharya (2005) describes four possible explanations for the wide income disparities across specializations: (1) differences in hours worked, (2) differences in length of residency and other required training, (3) differences in attributes and skills needed to perform in a specialty, and (4) barriers to entry into some specialties. The first three possibilities, which reflect competitive labor-market forces, account for only one half of the observed differences in lifetime earnings. The remaining differences can be seen as variations due to discrimination in the labor market, suggesting that some specialist fees, or charges imposed on medical students to enter into the specialty upon graduation, are excessive relative to competing fees. From a policy perspective, a strong case can be made to pressure those specialty boards that impose relatively high entry barriers in order to increase their number of residency slots if these barriers are not associated with other determinants of the higher wage, such as differential training needed to advance the science of medical care delivery.

THE SPECIALIST'S ROLE IN ADVANCING CUTTING-EDGE MEDICINE

More importantly, though, these specialty training areas also are associated with a more efficient use of higher medical technology and hence improved health outcomes. This is partially due to the fact that many specialties are procedure based, and specialists by nature have access to more advanced medical technology than do generalists, and therefore a higher volume of procedures performed than the latter. This increased volume leads to improved health outcomes through greater opportunities to practice with and refine the technology at hand.

A recent example of the incremental benefit of the use of specialists in the improvement of health outcomes can be seen in the work of Majumdar and colleagues (2001) in that specialists' use of pharmaceuticals in the treatment of cardiac conditions yielded much improved health outcomes for patients than was the case with general practitioners. Further, in the treatment of stroke, Mitchell and colleagues (1996) found that neurologists were significantly more expensive than other specialties, but were associated with much better health outcomes, confirming that even with the increased investment in specialists, the return on investment in terms of improved health status is superior to other physician classes.

Specialists also create major demand for new technology and are best trained to efficiently utilize cutting-edge medicine to improve health outcomes in a variety of settings. Both Freiman (1985) and Escarce (2005) found that the rate of adoption of new procedures by specialists far outweighed that of other physicians, with better health outcomes associated with the more intense utilization. These results show that even with the cost-increasing investment in human capital for specialists coupled with the use of more advanced technology, the returns in health far outweigh the initial investment. Therefore, the increased training and utilization of specialists in health care appear to be an efficient use of resources in the improvement of population health.

CONCLUSION

Though the individual physician in training may appear to seek out specialties in order to maximize personal income, the external benefit of this behavior is that specialists have a more efficient utilization of high medical technology through the increased utilization of procedure-based care, and greater ability to improve health outcomes through the appropriate utilization of advanced medicine. Therefore, as a society, we should invest in the training of specialists relative to primary care practitioners due to the greater external benefits gained from this investment. Specialists are a vital component of the U.S. medical system, and further investment in the specialties should be encouraged due to the higher quality of the care delivered for specific body systems. However, this investment in specialties should be monitored and selectively encouraged in order to address shortages geographically and among the specialties. The overall distribution among the specialties needs to better reflect the demand for such services nationally and in regards to smaller geographic areas. Without the preservation of specialists, advanced quality medicine would not be available.

REFERENCES AND FURTHER READING

Bhattacharya, J. (2005). Specialty selection and lifetime returns to specialization within medicine. *Journal of Human Resources, 40*(1), 115–143.

Escarce, J. J. (1996). Externalities in hospitals and physician adoption of a new surgical technology: An exploratory analysis. *Journal of Health Economics, 15*(6), 715–734.

Freiman, M. P. (1985). The rate of adoption of new procedures among physicians: The impact of specialty and practice characteristics. *Medical Care, 23*(8), 939–945.

Majumdar, S. R., Inui, T. S., Gurwitz, J. H., Gillman, M. W., McLaughlin, T .J., & Soumerai, S. B. (2001). Influence of physician specialty on adoption and relinquishment of calcium channel blockers and other treatments for myocardial infarction. *Journal of General Internal Medicine, 16*(6), 351–359.

Mitchell, J. B., Ballard, D. J., Whisnant, J. P., Ammering, C. J., Samsa, G. P., & Matchar, D. B. (1996). What role do neurologists play in determining the costs and outcomes of stroke patients? *Stroke, 27*(11), 1937–1943.

Nicholson, S. (2005). How much do medical students know about physician income? *Journal of Human Resources, 40*(1), 100–114.

Diane Dewar

Nurse Practitioners and Physician Assistants

POINT: Primary care as a gateway to specialized care is a cost-effective way to focus on prevention, diagnosis, and treatment. Nurse practitioners (NPs) and physician assistants (PAs) have a history of providing competent, cost-effective care. Nurse practitioners are independently licensed in each state and could serve as the point of contact for patients. Physician assistants are also in a position to provide competent primary care at the entry level.

Barbara Sheer, University of Delaware

COUNTERPOINT: New models of health care delivery should be explored. Multidisciplinary groups can provide quality care for a lower cost. The government should alleviate the current shortage of physicians by instituting policies to make primary care a more attractive area, in addition to training NPs and PAs. To ensure high-quality, cost-effective, coordinated care, physicians are needed to direct the multidisciplinary effort.

Barbara Sheer, University of Delaware

Introduction

Because primary care is generally viewed as a cost-effective way to focus on prevention, diagnosis, and treatment, finding the best delivery model for that care is a topic of considerable importance in U.S. health care today. Most discussions of primary care models include some role for non-physician practitioners, such as nurse practitioners (NPs) and physician assistants (PAs). In addition, other new models of health care delivery discuss the development of multidisciplinary groups, such as groups of physicians across different primary care–oriented specialties that together make primary care services of high quality at a lower cost than some current models and may make primary care careers more attractive to physicians than is currently the case. In this chapter, Barbara Sheer considers whether an increase in NPs, PAs, and multidisciplinary groups would represent a useful model to increase the quality of primary health care.

The American Nursing Association defines nurse practitioners, sometimes referred to as non-physician practitioners or as "physician extenders," as individuals who have completed a program of study leading to competencies as a registered nurse in an expanded role. According to the American Academy of Nurse Practitioners, in 2010, there were almost 140,000 nurse practitioners in the United States. About 6,000 new NPs are trained each year. Although in the past, some programs for NPs involved a simple nine-month certificate program, today most NPs complete a master's degree program of two additional years of full-time study beyond the bachelor's degree in nursing. Some nursing schools even offer a doctoral program in the NP areas. Most NPs work in primary care, although there are some who focus on specialty care. (In addition, there are other specialized non-physician providers, such as certified nurse midwives who work in maternity and obstetrical care and certified nurse anesthetists who deliver anesthesia, but these groups are not part of this discussion about how to modify primary care.)

Physician assistants serve as a part of the health care team but work in a dependent relationship with a supervising physician. Currently in the United States, there are around 65,000 PAs in practice. The number of PA programs has been increasing, and now stands at more than 140. Initially, many PA programs awarded certificates or bachelor's degrees; however, today most programs award a master's degree and take an average of 26 months to complete.

NPs and PAs have certain differences in how they practice and what procedures they are licensed to perform. For instance, PAs are licensed to perform medical procedures only under the supervision of a physician, while in some states NPs can practice more independently. NPs can prescribe medications in almost all states and can receive direct reimbursement as providers under Medicare and most Medicaid programs. There are other differences, as well: NPs mostly work in primary care, whereas about half of PAs work in specialty care settings. NPs are more oriented toward health promotion and education, while PAs are often more focused on diseases.

Among other new approaches to delivering primary care are convenient care clinics, also known as retail clinics. Many of these are located in retail stores, often drugstore chains such as Walgreen's and CVS and also in some Walmarts. They are most often staffed by nurse practitioners and physician assistants but may also be staffed by physicians. Their operating hours are longer than a typical physician practice, and usually no appointment is required. Typically, these clinics provide acute and episodic treatment, preventive services, physical examinations, screenings, and immunizations. They do not provide continuous care, however, nor are they a good choice for managing chronic illnesses.

Another much discussed concept in primary care today is the medical home. Though this idea originated as an aspect of pediatric care, today it can refer to patient-centered comprehensive primary care for children or adults. Often, this involves a partnership between the patient, family, and clinicians in which the care is accessible, family centered, comprehensive, continuous, and culturally sensitive. In contrast to the retail clinic, a medical home is an appropriate source of care for people with ongoing health problems, such as chronic health conditions, and is believed to be an important way to improve the overall quality of health care services for many patients.

This idea of a medical home means more than just the presence of a primary care physician to serve as a gatekeeper to specialized services, as was the case in some of the managed care organizations in the United States in the 1980s and 1990s. In that case, a financial relationship between the primary care provider and the managed care group involved the use of incentives to discourage primary care physicians from using too many specialty services. This aspect of managed care became unpopular with many patients; thus it is important to differentiate the current discussion of a medical home, which should help patients integrate care and receive higher quality care, from the concerns about quality that the gatekeeping approach and its limitation of specialty care access raised in the 1990s.

One of the issues between the two positions outlined in this chapter is the question of whether NPs and PAs can provide the best quality of care if, in the future, they come to serve as primary care practitioners, or whether it is important to retain physicians as the main provider in medical homes, with NPs and PAs playing a more supplemental role. Though it may seem obvious that a physician, who has undergone a longer period of training than an NP or a PA, would be the ideal provider, in practice it is not that simple. For one thing, for physicians to play the major role as primary care providers will require an increase in the number of physicians who choose primary care as a specialty. The recent trend, however, has been in the opposite direction, and the number of physicians choosing primary care specialties has been dropping. Though there are many explanations as to why this is the case, it seems clear that the lower salary earned by primary care physicians—compared to those who choose other specialties—is an important factor. In practical terms, these lower salaries mean that physicians as the major providers of primary care are likely to be more expensive. More, the retirements of primary care physicians in the next few decades will contribute to physician shortages. In addition, physicians are often reluctant to locate to more isolated geographic areas, and to urban areas with underserved populations, but NPs and PAs may be more willing to live in these places. Assuring care to people in difficult-to-serve areas might be another challenge for a physician-centered primary care model. These factors must be addressed if a physician-centered primary care model is the recommend approach for the future, rather than a model that makes greater use of NPs and PAs.

POINT

The Patient Protection and Affordable Care Act (ACA) signed into law by President Barack Obama on March 23, 2010, is a monumental step toward reforming the U.S. health care system. The law provides for increased health care access for children and young adults, and provides recommended preventive services. Health care reform has been a heavily debated topic for decades, polarizing the stakeholders. The overall goal is to have affordable, accessible, quality health care for all. Is this a realistic concept or an impossible dream? While the debate continues, costs increase, and more and more of the population go uninsured.

COST

Any attempt to balance health care services and costs requires the consideration of several key issues. The first is what exactly constitutes health and health care. The World Health Organization (WHO) defines health as "a state of physical, social and mental well-being not merely the absence of disease or infirmity." In the United States, the question of health and health care has moral implications. The country's multitier system means that those with the most income can afford healthy lifestyles and health insurance. A growing number of Americans are experiencing unemployment, homelessness, and other significant life changes due to the economy. They are caught in the middle without resources and most often without health care insurance or the means to obtain it. Young, healthy individuals often opt out of expensive insurance in the belief that nothing catastrophic will occur. The remainder of the population is covered by national and state programs such as Medicare, Medicaid, and Children's Health Insurance Program (CHIP). There are racial disparities in health care and outcomes. There is a disconnect between lifestyle choices, prevention, health, and health care. Responsibility for health and health care is not shared by consumers and the health care system.

The United States spends approximately 17 percent of its gross national product on health care, more than any other nation. Despite this, the country's health outcomes are poor. The United States falls behind other industrialized nations in almost every measure, including life expectancy and infant mortality. According to WHO, the United States ranks twenty-third out of 23 developed nations in universal coverage. The United States is the only developed country where insurance coverage can be denied, resulting in bankruptcy for many Americans. The Kaiser Family Foundation (2009) found that more than half of Americans said they limited their medical care due to cost concerns. Some were weighing health care costs against their need for food, clothing, and shelter.

Most of the health care costs are related to the diagnosis and treatment of disease, with little emphasis on prevention. Spending is not associated with outcomes. There is wide variation in the costs of care from region to region with little evidence of improved outcomes. Chronic disease expenditures account for 75 percent of health care costs. As the population ages, the percentage of chronic disease such as hypertension, heart disease, stroke, cancer, and diabetes will increase. More children and adults are susceptible to a growing epidemic of obesity, asthma, and diabetes.

FINANCING

A short overview of the history of health care financing is helpful in understanding the challenges prevalent today. In his 1998 book *Not What the Doctor Ordered*, Jeffrey Bauer discussed the changes that occurred after World War II when wage controls were in place and health insurance was offered to employees as a benefit. Initially, physicians were opposed to the third-party payment, fearing it would interfere with the doctor-patient relationship; as a direct result of the new payment system, the patient no longer paid directly for services. With the advent of Medicare and Medicaid, the federal and state governments became the largest insurers of health care. As more complex payment systems emerged, insurers were able to negotiate different payment rates. Today the United States has a system in which neither the patients nor the providers are aware of the cost of a service, and the same service has a wide range of costs depending on the insurance-negotiated contracts. The downside is that it is almost impossible to compare costs and make decisions based on the cost and effectiveness of the service. In the process, those who do not have insurance and pay out-of-pocket bear an increased burden of the cost. As long as health care bills were being paid by a third party, both patients and providers were complacent about costs. As technology advanced and litigation increased, doctors began to practice defensive medicine and utilize the expensive technological tools. Patients began to expect that, if a treatment or technology was possible, access was a right and should be paid by a third party.

As the health care costs escalate, patients are denied service or are required to accept more of the cost burden. Providers spend more and more time with administrative issues associated with payment and have less time for patient care. Providers are frustrated, and patients not satisfied with their care. The frustration has led to a boutique or concierge model of health care where providers limit the number of patients, and the patients pay out of pocket for the services. The initial satisfaction rates are high for both physicians and patients. The system favors the wealthy and places an additional burden on providers who treat higher-risk, lower-income patients.

THE AFFORDABLE CARE ACT

At the one-year anniversary of the ACA, Secretary of Health and Human Services Kathleen Sebelius stated that the reform had given new rights and benefits to the American people. Among the ACA's accomplishments: More children have access to health care; young adults can stay under their parents policies until age 26; most annual and lifetime coverage limits were eradicated, and access to prevention services were extended to more patients. Other provisions include a "patient bill of rights," Medicare screenings, donut-hole rebates, and small business tax credits. The bill was not without controversy. Thirty percent of Medicare expenditures occur in the last year of life. Some of the care is palliative, but a large portion of the cost is on aggressive treatment and therapy. A provision of the bill was reimbursement for end-of-life counseling. Many patients and families are not aware of the ramifications of end-of-life treatments and would opt out of some treatment if they fully understood the options. This provision was contested in the media, erroneously, as the establishment of "death panels," bureaucratic committees that would supposedly assess—and either approve or deny—treatment based on that treatment's expense and likelihood of success. Ultimately, provisions for end-of-life counseling was dropped from the final bill.

The law provides for a new Center for Medicare & Medicaid Innovation that will begin to test new ways of delivering care. The emphasis will be on improving quality and decreasing cost. Models of care will differ from region to region, from urban and rural, and will differ in provider make up.

Primary care and patient-centered care can increase efficiency by providing coordinated care and preventive services. The concept of each patient having a medical home is gaining acceptance. How this will be accomplished is, once again, controversial. Testing innovative models and measuring cost-effective outcomes present an opportunity for health care providers and patients to work together to bring about fundamental change in the health care system. It takes a village to build a healthy community.

Nurse practitioners, physician assistants, and physicians will work with multidisciplinary groups to reach the goal of accessible, affordable care for all. How this is accomplished differs from each perspective. Below is a presentation of a point and counterpoint related to each of the differing perspectives. Nurse practitioners and physician assistants are in a pivotal position to deliver primary care. Physicians deliver primary care, work in multidisciplinary groups, and believe health care can succeed with the physician coordinating the care efforts.

Primary care as a gateway to specialized care is a cost-effective way to focus on prevention, diagnosis, and treatment. Nurse practitioners have a history of providing competent, cost-effective care. They are independently licensed in each state and could serve as the point-of-contact for patients. Physician assistants are also in a position to provide competent primary care at the entry level.

EDUCATION

Nurse practitioner education began in 1965 as a demonstration project at the University of Colorado. It was believed that nurses with skills such as advanced health assessment, advanced pathophysiology, and advanced pharmacology could care for 80 percent of the primary care needs of children. The program was successful, and expansion into other areas such as women's health and adult and family health soon followed. The initial programs in the late 60s were offered to registered nurses as continuing education, often in conjunction with medical schools. By the 1980s knowledge was expanding, and most of the programs were at the master's level. By 2015 nurse practitioner education may be at the doctoral level.

The National Organization of Nurse Practitioner Faculties (NONPF) developed guidelines for the family and adult programs. These were first published in 1990 and subsequently updated with the latest release in 2011. Accreditation of the university programs is accomplished by the National League for Nursing Accrediting Commission (NLNAC) or the Commission on Collegiate Nursing Education (CCNE). The curriculum must meet national standards and contain core courses: advanced health assessment, pathophysiology, pharmacology, and specialty clinical courses. Clinical courses include content on assessment, management, and evidence-based practice guidelines. Didactic content is combined with extensive precepted clinical hours. Precepted clinical hours involve direct supervision by a licensed professional, usually a nurse practitioner or physician. As the student progresses, he or she is given additional responsibilities for the care of the patient. Evaluation by faculty and preceptors is included in each clinical course.

Graduates from accredited programs are eligible to take a national certifying examination. A master's degree is a requirement to sit for the examination. Two certification exams are available for family, adult, and geriatric nurse practitioners. These are offered by the American Nurses Credentialing Center (ANCC) and the American Academy of Nurse Practitioners (AANP). Pediatric and women's health nurse practitioners also have the option of taking one of two examinations. These certifying examinations are offered by ANCC and the Pediatric National Certification Board (PNCB) for pediatrics and the National Certification Corporation (NCC) for women's health.

Upon satisfactory completion of the certifying examination, nurse practitioners are eligible to apply for licensure at the state level. In every state, the nurse practitioner must be a registered nurse to apply for advanced licensure. Prescriptive privileges vary from state to state, with all 50 states granting privileges. To maintain licensure, certification must be current and must be renewed every five years. The requirements for renewal include clinical practice and continuing education with designated pharmacology hours.

To summarize, nurse practitioners are registered nurses with additional education at the master's or doctoral level who provide patient care in a variety of settings. They are independently licensed and can prescribe medications in all 50 states.

SCOPE OF PRACTICE

Nurse practitioners practice in all settings ranging from clinics to hospitals in rural and urban areas. They are frequently found as the only health care provider in rural areas and working with underserved populations. They can be found in all specialties. Ninety percent of NP's credentialed to practice are currently practicing. Almost 89 percent are prepared in a primary care area. According to the American Academy of Nurse Practitioners, the majority of family and adult nurse practitioners treat patients over 66 years of age. Over 88 percent accept Medicare patients and over 80 percent accept Medicaid patients. Almost 60 percent accept charitable or uncompensated patients. Nurse practitioners are more likely than are other disciplines to practice in rural settings.

The scope of practice includes the assessment, diagnosis, and management of acute and chronic conditions. Their services include, but are not limited to, ordering, conducting and interpreting diagnostic and laboratory tests, prescribing pharmacologic and non-pharmacologic therapies, teaching, and counseling. Their care is holistic and places an emphasis on health promotion and disease prevention.

Nurse practitioners have been providing patient-centered care to patients of all ages for over 45 years. Extensive research has been done on the quality, and cost-effectiveness of service. In all studies their care was equal or better in quality and more cost-effective than other disciplines. More research has been done on this group than any other discipline.

The 2011 Institute of Medicine (IOM) report *The Future of Nursing: Leading Change, Advancing Health* makes the following recommendations: (1) ensure that nurses can practice to the full extent of their education, (2) improve nursing education, (3) provide opportunities for nurses to assume leadership positions and to serve as full partners in health care redesign, and (4) improve data collection for workforce planning and policymaking.

The ACA provides an opportunity for nurse practitioners to be part of envisioning the future of health care. In many places, nurses have developed an infrastructure of nurse-managed health care clinics and convenient markets to address the primary care needs of the population.

NURSE-MANAGED CENTERS

Nurse-managed centers are not a new concept: the first nurse-managed center was established in the early 1970s. They differ from the traditional concept of health care center in that they are managed by nurses, rather than by physicians. Nurse practitioners provide necessary care and refer patients to physicians or hospitals only when necessary. Most of the centers provided a safety net for vulnerable populations that are underinsured or uninsured. Approximately 58 percent of the patients are uninsured, on Medicaid, or self-pay. The centers are community based and can be found throughout the nation in housing projects, blighted areas, senior centers, community centers, and store fronts. They can be found wherever the need is greatest.

An analysis of studies done by Coddington and Sands (2008) on the cost of health care and quality outcomes of patients at nurse-managed clinics demonstrate positive outcomes. The centers provide accessible care with an emphasis on health promotion and disease prevention, and a focus on the role of the family unit and community in shaping health. Patient satisfaction remains high, with patients citing their relationship with the nurse practitioner as a positive aspect of their care. It is probably no surprise that nurse practitioners in these centers tend to spend more time with individual patients.

Positive outcomes include better management of acute and chronic conditions leading to fewer visits to urgent care centers and the emergency room. The cost savings are substantial. For example, the average cost of a visit to a nurse-managed center is $40 to $70. The same patient visit in an urgent care facility would cost about $115 to $175, and in an emergency room $569. Although the cost for service is lower, most of the centers are not profitable because of restrictive reimbursement policies from state, federal, and third-party payers.

In an effort to support the continued development of nurse-managed centers, the Independence Foundation in Philadelphia has invested millions of dollars in 12 nurse-managed health centers. These centers provide primary care, health promotion, and disease prevention, and help to manage the current health problems of underserved populations. With the support of Governor Ed Rendell, Pennsylvania has made 49 changes in regulatory and statutory barriers to assist NPs to practice to the full extent of their scope of practice. The support in Pennsylvania serves as a model for an alternative health care delivery system on a national scale.

According to the National Nursing Centers Consortium (NNCC), nurse-managed centers are effective because they focus on and understand their community's needs. As part of the neighborhood, they are positioned to link to social services to provide necessary care for the social welfare of the population, and they aim to create leadership in the community to strengthen its ability to address and solve its problems. They not only provide health care but are also part of an effort to develop a health community.

There are, however, a number of policy challenges that will need to be addressed if nurse-managed centers are to make a significant contribution to improving primary care on a larger scale. In 2009 the NNCC developed a white paper discussing a five-point plan for innovation. Included in the plan is investment in nurse-managed care centers, many of which do not qualify for the resources available to Federally Qualified Health Centers (FQHCs). Nurse-managed centers have the infrastructure to manage and coordinate care for aging patients and for those with chronic disease, and they need to be included in the Medicare Medical Homes Demonstration Project. A more efficient infrastructure for health care administration needs to be adopted. Currently there is no unified approach for insurers to credential health care providers. Each insurer has a different credentialing process and may or may not recognize nurse practitioners as independent providers. The process may take as long as one year, and needs to be duplicated for each insurer. The process takes considerable administrative time and must be duplicated if the provider moves to another state. Unifying the process would save administrative time and money. Nurse-managed centers must have access to the same incentives as physician-led practices to implement new information technology (IT) initiates and improve quality of care. Nurse practitioners need to be included in the health-reform discussion as they are in a position to implement interdisciplinary innovative models of health care.

CONVENIENT CARE CLINICS

A relatively new model of care is the convenient care clinic, also known as the retail clinic. These clinics are housed in retail stores, such as Walmart, and pharmacies. They are staffed by nurse practitioners and physician assistants but may also be staffed by physicians. They are open 8 to 12 hours a day, 7 days a week. No appointment is necessary, and the usual wait is 30 minutes. Patients can go online to see actual wait-times at their nearest clinic.

Services provided include acute and episodic treatment, preventive services, physical examinations, screenings, and immunizations. Such clinics may serve as collection points for laboratory testing. The number of clinics continues to expand due to the convenience and quality of care they offer. Studies of these clinics have shown high patient satisfaction, and quality equal to primary care offices at a lower cost.

A cost-comparison of matched episodes of three common illnesses demonstrated the cost-effectiveness of retail clinics (Ateev et al., 2009). The cost for care at the retail clinic was $110, compared to $166 for physician offices, $156 for urgent care, and $570 for emergency departments. The cost of prescriptions was higher in the emergency department and the receipt of preventive care lower in that setting.

Screening tests and medications are available on-site. An increasing number of insurers are covering the costs, which are transparent and are posted in the waiting area. The clinics utilize IT to store and share patient records with primary care providers. They also provide a list of referral sources to patients who do not have a primary care provider.

The disadvantage of such clinics is their limited scope of practice. The clinics focus on the management and treatment of common illnesses and minor injuries. Patients with serious conditions are sent to an urgent care center or emergency room. The patients who are best served are those who are reasonably healthy or who have stable chronic diseases.

Early opposition to convenient care clinics was mounted by physician groups. The American Medical Association (AMA) spoke against retail clinics, citing potential poor quality care, fragmented care, and inadequate preparation of providers. It urged regulatory oversight. The American Academy of Pediatrics (AAP) opposed the use of the convenient clinics for care involving infants, children, and adolescents. The concerns cited included fragmentation of care, inadequate care for children with special needs, lack of access to health records, and lack of appropriate follow-up. In response, some states have required physicians to oversee the clinics, while others have suggested Joint Commission on Accreditation of Healthcare Organizations (JACHO) approval, or that the scope of the care offered by the clinics be limited to wellness and prevention.

The convenient care market offers cost-effective, quality care on a walk-in basis. It is a market that will continue to expand; already there are plans to increase the scope of services for chronic care, injection, and infusion. Some clinics are coordinating services with hospital systems and plan to expand into dentistry and other specialties.

MEDICAL HOME

The concept of a "medical home" was introduced by the AAP in 1967 as a central location for children's medical records. AAP expanded the concept in a 2002 policy statement to be an accessible, comprehensive, family centered, and coordinated system of health care delivery. Other physician groups, including the American Academy of Family physicians (AAFP) and the American College of Physicians (ACP), developed their own models of the medical home. The medical home provides patient-centered comprehensive primary care for children and adults. It is a partnership between the patient, family, and clinicians in which the care is accessible, family centered, coordinated, comprehensive, continuous, compassionate, and culturally effective. The purpose is to provide better access to health care, improve satisfaction with care, and improve health.

The physician groups identified several principles guiding the implementation of the medical home in a 2007 policy statement. The principles begin with the personal physician. Each patient has an ongoing relationship with a personal physician trained to provide first contact, continuous, and comprehensive care. The physician leads a team of providers who collectively take responsibility for ongoing care. The personal physician is responsible for providing for all of the patient's health care needs or for arranging care with other professionals. Care is coordinated with other agencies. Evidence-based medicine assures quality and safety and that the patient is an active participant in decision making. Access is accomplished by means such as expanded hours, open scheduling, and additional communication measures. The payment for services should reflect the value of the work

Primary care is foremost in this model. The model differs from the "gatekeeper" concept that is often utilized by Health Maintenance Organizations (HMO). In the gatekeeper model, access to any specialist needed a referral from the primary care provider. In this capitated model, the gatekeeper has incentives and is rewarded for a lower referral rate. When it was first instituted, many patients expressed concern that they could not access their specialists, such as their gynecologists and ophthalmologists. All care had to be provided within the system. In the medical home model, patients have a choice of primary provider. The medical home primary care provider is a coordinator of specialty care. The medical home may involve an individual or a group providing care. The primary provider coordinates patient care. This is based on a fee-for-service system, rather than capitation. A key to the system is the electronic medical record that will provide all care providers with patient information. The concept helps to ensure accessible, continuous, and cost-effective care. By providing coordination of care, the system eliminates costly duplication and fragmentation, creating a seamless integration with better outcomes.

In 2006 the Medicare Improvement and Extension Act provided for the initiation of the Medicare/Medical Home Demonstration project. This rewarded primary care providers for coordination of care for patients with complex chronic conditions. At the time, the definition of a primary care provider was restricted to mean a physician. In 2008, however, nurse practitioners and other non-physicians were included in an extension of the project (Schram, 2010).

In 2006 the American College of Physicians published a policy monograph endorsing the inclusion of nurse practitioner–led practice to test different patient-centered medical home models. In its statement, the organizations urged that both physician and NP models be held to the same eligibility requirements and evaluation standards, with payment based on the types of patients that are seen.

For its part, the ACA establishes a grant program for community-based interdisciplinary teams to support primary care practices. Medical homes were defined as practices focusing on primary care with a primary care clinician to oversee and coordinate care. The primary care clinician is defined as a physician, nurse practitioner, or physician assistant.

RECOMMENDATIONS

Envisioning the future of nursing, the IOM (2011) recommends that nurse practitioners practice to the full extent of their education, achieve higher levels of education, be full partners in redesigning the future of health care, and improve data collection for workforce planning and policymaking. This cannot be done by nurses in isolation. The transformation will call for policymakers on the state and national levels, payers, professional organizations, educational institutions, and all other stakeholders to work together to remove regulatory and statutory barriers.

CONCLUSION

The United States is facing a health care crisis. The population is aging, chronic disease is increasing, and the need for expensive technology is expanding. Health care has focused on cures, neglecting health promotion and disease prevention. Health care costs are spiraling with no transparency. Neither patients nor providers are aware of individual costs, which vary by region and insurer. More and more of the population cannot afford insurance and so join the ranks of the uninsured. Many Americans have been bankrupted by medical costs.

Although the United States spends more on health care than any other nation, the outcomes are poor. Patients and providers are frustrated. Care is not always accessible and is fragmented. The system is looking toward new and innovative models.

Primary care is patient-centered care with a focus on disease management, health promotion, and disease prevention. Care can be coordinated to improve quality and outcomes in a cost-effective way.

Nurse practitioners are educated at the master's or doctoral level. They are credentialed professionals who are licensed in every state and can prescribe in all states. They have a long history of providing safe, quality care with a focus on heath promotion and disease prevention. They provide holistic patient-centered care. Several models have evolved with nurse practitioners as the primary care provider. The nurse-managed centers, convenient care clinics, and the medical home model are some examples.

Nurse practitioners, as the primary care providers working with a health care team, can provide cost-effective, competent, patient-focused care at a cost saving. New innovative models need to include the nurse practitioners as the primary coordinator of care. This is a time of significant change. Nurse practitioners are visionary and are positioned to be a leading force in creating the health care model for the future.

References and Further Reading

AANP American Academy of Nurse Practitioners. (2011). *Comments on the IOM report: The future of nursing: Leading change advancing health.* Retrieved from http://aanp.org/AANPCMS2/publicpages/AANPIOMResponse92Date8_4_11.pdf

ACA Affordable Care Act, Pub. L. No. 111–148, 111th Cong. (2010).

American Academy of Nursing. (2008). *The health care home debate: Opportunities for nursing.* Retrieved from http://www.aannet.org/files/public/health_home_paper_FINAL.pdf

American Academy of Pediatrics. (2008). *"Every child deserves a medical home" training curriculum.* The National Center for Medical Home Initiatives for Children with Special Needs. Retrieved from http://www.medicalhomeinfo.org/training/index.html

American College of Physicians. (2006). *The advanced medical home: A patient centered, physician guided model of health care: Policy monograph*. Retrieved from http://www.acponline.org/advocacy/where_we_stand/policy/adv_med.pdf

American College of Physicians. (2009). *Nurse practitioners in primary care: Policy monograph*. Retrieved from http://www.acponline.org/advocacy/where_westand/policy/adv_pc.pdf

Ateev, M., Hangsheng, L., Adams, J. L., Wang, M. C., Lave, J. R., Thygeson, N. M., et al. (2009). Comparing costs and quality of care at retail clinics with that of other medical settings for 3 common illnesses. *Annals of Internal Medicine, 151*(5), 321–328.

Ateev, M., Wang, M. C., Lave, J. R., Adams, J. L., & McGlynn, E. A. (2008). Retail clinics, primary care physicians, and emergency departments: A comparison of patients' visits. *Health Affairs, 27*(5), 1272–1282

Bauer, J. C. (1998). *Not what the doctor ordered: How to end the medical monopoly in pursuit of managed care*. New York, NY: McGraw-Hill.

Coddington, J., & Sands, L. P. (2008). Cost of health care and quality outcomes of patients at nurse managed clinics. *Nursing Economics, 26*(2), 75–84. Retrieved from http://www.medscape.com/viewarticle/575312

Freudenberg, N., & Olden, K. (2011). Getting serious about the prevention of chronic diseases. *Preventing Chronic Disease, 8*(4), A90. Retrieved from http://www.cdc.gov/pcd/issues/2011/jul/10_0243.htm

Institute of Medicine. (2001). *Crossing the quality chasm: A new health system for the 21st century*. Washington, DC: National Academies Press.

Institute of Medicine. (2011). *The future of nursing: Leading change, advancing health*. Washington, DC: National Academies Press.

Kaiser Family Foundation. (2009). *Kaiser Health Tracking Poll—February 2009*. Retrieved from http://www.kff.org/kaiserpolls/posr022509pkg.cfm

Mundinger, M. O. (2004). Advanced practice nurses: The preferred primary care providers for the 21st century. In J. Showstack, S. Hasmiller, & A. Rothman (Eds.), *The future of primary care* (chap. 7). San Francisco, CA: Jossey-Bass.

Mundinger, M. O., Kane, R. L., Lenz, E. R., Totten, A. M., Tsai, W. Y., Cleary, P. D., et al. (2000). Primary care outcomes in patients treated by nurse practitioners or physicians. *Journal of the American Medical Association, 283*(1), 59–68.

National Nursing Centers Consortium. (2009). *White paper executive summary: Maximizing our existing health care resources: A five-point plan for innovation*. Retrieved from http://www.nncc.us/site/pdf/NNCC%20White%20Paper%202009.pdf

Reid, T. R. (2009). *The healing of America*. New York, NY: Penguin.

Schram, A. P. (2010). Medical home and the nurse practitioner: A policy analysis. *Journal for Nurse Practitioners, 6*(2), 132–139. Retrieved from http://www.medscape.com/viewartilce/717463

Shi, L. (1992). The relationship between primary care and life chances. *Journal of Health Care for the Poor and Underserved, 3*(2), 321–335.

Barbara Sheer

COUNTERPOINT

There is agreement that the health care system has serious flaws, and that new models of health care delivery need to be explored. However, there is a lack of agreement on how this is to be accomplished. Primary care is seen as a way to reduce health care costs by coordinating care for patients with chronic diseases and increasing the focus on health promotion and disease prevention. Physicians are taking up the challenge and see this as an opportunity to create a seamless system benefiting all. Nurse practitioners (NPs) and other health care providers will be a part of this system. But physicians are in the best position to coordinate the care and work together with other providers to offer quality care.

EDUCATION

There is a significant difference in the education of physicians and nurse practitioners. Nurse practitioner education is at the master's level, though by 2015 it will transition to the doctoral level (PhD). The preparation requires a minimum of 1,000 hours of postbaccalaureate clinical experience.

Physicians are required to have four years of premedical college education, four years of medical school that includes two years of clinical rotations, and three or more years of residency. Fellowships and subspecialty education may continue for additional years, depending on the specialty.

The Doctor of Nursing Practice (DNP) education is not equal to a medical doctor (MD). The nurse practitioner has a holistic approach and incorporates prevention and promotion into the management of disease. The physician approach is geared to diagnosis and the management of the disease process. The professions have complementary perspectives.

Most agree that nurse practitioners provide quality, cost-effective care. They are able to diagnose and treat common primary care acute problems and can manage chronic stable conditions. Their scope includes health education, health promotion, and disease prevention. The issue of concern is that, without years of experience, they may not recognize more serious conditions. Physicians, with their broader education and experience, are better positioned to recognize and coordinate care at this level. Physicians are prepared to diagnose and treat advanced diseases and complex disorders. Health care teams of physicians, physician assistants, and nurse practitioners can offer the patient a higher quality of care.

Another issue of concern is the titling of nurse practitioners. When the nurse practitioner has a DNP or a PhD, he or she may use the title of doctor. In the medical profession, the title of doctor has always meant physician. The use of the title by nurse practitioners may prove confusing to patients, who may not be aware of the educational distinction between the terms. The patient has the option of selecting a provider but needs to be informed of the difference in credentialing.

PHYSICIAN ASSISTANTS

Physician assistants (PA) are health care professionals who practice as part of a medical team. Their educational program requires four years of college and is 24 to 36 months in length. PAs can practice and have prescriptive authority in all 50 states. They must pass the Physician Assistant National Certifying Exam. They must obtain licensing, registration, or certification from the state licensing authority. They must practice in conjunction with a physician in a variety of primary care and specialty areas. To maintain certification, PAs must complete 100 hours of continuing education every two years and pass a recertification examination every six years. Today, there are more than 81,000 PAs in the United States.

PHYSICIAN SHORTAGE

Primary care can significantly reduce health care costs. With the passage of the 2010 Patient Protection and Affordable Care Act (ACA), as many as 32 million more Americans will have access to medical insurance and 36 million to Medicare. It is estimated that many of these Americans will access health care that they may have been putting off for lack of insurance. Another factor to be considered is the aging population. Baby boomers are turning 65 and will further stress the system with more complex medical conditions and chronic disease.

The Association of American Medical Colleges (AAMC) warns that there will not be enough physicians to accommodate the influx of new patients. The physician shortage is particularly acute in primary care, especially in rural areas. It is estimated that by 2015 there will be a shortage of about 63,000 physicians, and greater shortages in the future. The shortage of physicians means decreased access, longer waiting times, and shorter visits.

The annual number of medical students going into primary care has dropped by more than half since 1997. The cost of medical school leaves most students with a substantial debt that can be more than $200,000. In order to pay off their debt and lead a comfortable lifestyle, graduates tend to opt for specialty practices. The average salary for primary care physicians is around $150,000 per year, while specialty practices have much higher salaries.

The coming wave of physician retirements will only serve to compound the shortage. It is estimated that one third of currently active physicians plan to retire within the next 10 years. With the promise of a lower salary, and fewer physicians meaning higher patient loads, efforts to recruit new physicians into primary care practices will have a daunting task ahead of them, especially in rural areas where the needs will be even more acute. Some medical schools have developed innovative programs to introduce students and residents to primary care in the community. These programs sometimes offer financial enticements. For its part, the federal government has programs such as the National Health Service Corps to assist with loan repayment in return for service in a designated shortage area. Some states also offer financial incentives for physicians who agree to practice in rural areas.

To meet the needs of the population, the AAMC offers some possible solutions to the physician shortage. One of these is to increase federal support of residency programs through Medicare, a primary source of medical education funding. The Balanced Budget Act of 1997 froze the number of available residency slots at 100,000, and it has remained frozen at that number ever since, despite increasing demand. Teaching hospitals accept additional residents for the community but need to pay out of pocket. Increasing funding by 15 percent would add about 4,000 physicians a year. Raising reimbursement rates for some primary care services would also help to increase the income of the primary care physicians, but if it comes at the expense of specialists there would be resistance from within the profession. Changing the reimbursement to include more preventive services would also have some positive outcomes. With appropriate reimbursements and an increased number of physicians, practices could be expanded to larger teams and include other health care providers, such as nurse practitioners and physician assistants. This model would expand practices and enable the physician to coordinate patient care, offering the quality of medical assistance patients deserve without relinquishing care to providers who are educationally less prepared.

TURF WARS

Organized physician groups have a long history of opposing any expansion of the scope of practice for nurse practitioners. American Medical Association (AMA) lobbyists work on the state and national levels to monitor legislative and regulatory reform. Nurse practitioners are governed by nurse practice acts that are different for each state. Some states allow NPs to function to the full extent of their education, while others do not allow specific acts such as prescribing a certain class of medications or performing certain physical examinations. In every state, nurse practitioners lobbying for expansion of practice acts, third-party reimbursement, and prescriptive authority have faced opposition. The result is inconsistent regulation that often prevents nurse practitioners from practicing where the need is greatest. Time and energy is spent on activities like signing for disability placards to allow the disabled to park in designated parking places or conducting physicals for school systems and state agencies. In some states, only a physician can sign a death certificate. In others, nurse practitioners are allowed to practice independently in rural or urban areas not served by physicians, but are prohibited from independent practice in districts in the same state where there is no physician shortage. With regulatory changes and physician-coordinated care, nurse practitioners as part of a multidisciplinary team could continue to practice in rural areas.

Over the years, the focus of physician groups has been on the scope-of-practice rather than the needs of the community, state, and nation. Restrictive regulation may include physician oversight, direct supervision by physicians of a limited number of nurse practitioners, requirements that physicians be onsite a certain percentage of the time, and review of a certain percentage of patient records. Some states restrict nurse practitioners' prescriptive authority, resulting in a delay of patients accessing needed medications. Those opposed to expanded nurse practitioner care argue that nurse practitioners lack the requisite knowledge to operate independently of physicians. These restrictions not only increase the cost of care but also affect its quality by decreasing access and by delaying access to needed medications.

Physician assistants are regulated or licensed to work under the supervision of the physician, rather than independently. Because of this relationship, turf wars have been avoided, and instead there has been acceptance and support for physician groups. A resolution to the problems of turf wars and the inconsistent scope of practice is for nurse practitioners and physician assistants to work together under the direction of physicians. In this way, the physician can assure that the right provider delivers care to the right patient.

REIMBURSEMENT

Reimbursement is erratic. Medicare reimbursements to nurse practitioners, if billed under the NP provider number, are only 85 percent of the physician fee. When a nurse practitioner is employed by a physician, however, Medicare will reimburse the physician 100 percent of fee schedule. Physician assistants are employed by physicians and bill under the physician number, thus receiving 100 percent of the fee schedule. This is called "incident to" billing, and it requires that certain conditions be met. The physician does the initial workup and devises a plan of care for a given patient. For subsequent visits, the nurse practitioner or physician assistant sees the patient under the direct supervision of the physician. It is not necessary that the physician be onsite, but he or she must see the patient at least once a year. Medicaid reimbursement varies by state at rates from 50 percent to 100 percent. If Medicaid is a managed care plan, to be reimbursed the provider must be enrolled. Enrollment may be restricted to physicians. Other third-party insurers require enrollment in the provider panel. When the plan is restricted to physician providers, the nurse practitioner is employed by the physician and becomes an invisible provider. Payment-driven databases are often linked to physician provider numbers and do not reflect the contributions of the nurse practitioner. When statistics are gathered from these sources, they do not reflect the total picture. As the U.S. health care system moves toward coordinated care, the best option is physician-coordinated care. Physician-coordinated care will have a consistent fee scale. The physician-based practice can be reimbursed 100 percent of the fee schedule for the patients seen by nurse practitioners and physician assistants within the group.

COLLABORATIVE EFFORTS

In 2009 the American College of Physicians (ACP) developed a policy paper urging physicians and nurse practitioners to work together to improve primary care. The paper recognizes the importance of a multidisciplinary team to meet the challenges of providing health care. Bridging the gap between professions, the paper acknowledges the contributions of nurse practitioners.

The policy developed in response to physician shortages and the development of DNP programs acknowledges that both professions are complementary and are committed to providing quality care. There are differences and similarities. The educational preparation of the professions differs in approach. Nurse practitioners' focus on holistic care with an emphasis on prevention and health promotion is well suited to the primary care needs of the nation. On the other hand, physicians' focus on diagnosis and disease management is suited to the treatment of complex diseases, though at a higher cost.

Patients have the right to choose the providers with the skills that best meet their needs. Patients need to understand the provider's credentials, experience, and skills. The ACP also advocates for research to develop effective systems of consultation between nurse practitioners and physicians and payment systems that provide sufficient reimbursement for coordination of care and collaboration.

The policy is in sharp contrast to the 30-year turf wars. It acknowledges that nurse practitioners provide quality, cost-effective care with a holistic primary care approach and supports research on physician and nurse-led medical homes.

MEDICAL HOME

The patient-centered medical home (PCMH) model is best served by a multidisciplinary team. ACP advocates for a team that is physician led but believes that different demonstration projects should evaluate the effectiveness of nurse- and physician-led practices. The demonstration projects need to meet the same eligibility requirements, be subject to the same recognition standards, and be held to the same standards of evaluation. Patients selecting the PCMH for their care need to be informed whether it is physician or nurse led. Further research can identify effective models for collaboration, referral, and co-management of patients between and among nurse practitioners and physicians.

According to the policy, opportunities for professional multidisciplinary training and team development should be incorporated into the education and training of all health professionals. Multidisciplinary education has been effective over the years. In some academic institutions, nurse practitioners and physicians take the same basic sciences, pathophysiology, physical assessment, and pharmacology courses. Faculty have joint appointments and teach across disciplines. At many clinical sites, multidisciplinary professionals and students work together. As multidisciplinary professionals learn together and work together, they will embrace their differences and learn to work as a team, which will be beneficial to all.

AMERICAN MEDICAL ASSOCIATION STRATEGIES

To address the rising cost of health care, the AMA identified a number of broad strategies: reduce the burden of preventable disease, make health delivery more efficient, reduce nonclinical health system costs, and promote value-based decision making at all levels.

Chronic diseases—such as heart disease, cancer, hypertension, stroke, and diabetes—account for 80 percent of the deaths and 75 percent of the health care costs (Freudenberg & Olden, 2011). Many of the diseases can be prevented through certain lifestyle changes. The morbidity rates of those that are not preventable can be reduced through early diagnosis and close management. Programs that emphasize healthy lifestyles through, for example, smoking cessation, nutritional counseling, weight reduction, stress reduction, and exercise promotion can make a significant difference. Likewise, working within the community to reduce motor-vehicle accidents and gun violence will lead to a healthier community. Within minority and underserved populations, there is a higher incidence of chronic disease and community issues. The AMA calls for additional education for physicians to focus on health promotion and disease prevention. Because nurse practitioners incorporate these aspects into their practice, a team approach that includes a physician to coordinate care will increase quality.

Inefficiencies in the health care system add to the cost of health care. Costs vary widely from region to region and are not related to outcomes. Universal utilization of evidence-based practice protocols can produce better outcomes. Comparative effectiveness research (CER) will be needed. Currently, multiple guidelines are published by a variety of resources. Often the information is conflicting.

Fragmented care accounts for increased costs and increased morbidity. Coordinating specialty care through a primary care provider will eliminate duplication of services and costly diagnostic testing. Medications can be streamlined and medication interactions avoided. Management by a primary health care provider can save a significant amount by preventing unnecessary visits to the urgent care center and emergency room. Access to streamlined electronic medical records will assist in seamless care and provide a coordinated record when urgent care or emergency services are needed.

Administrative costs account for approximately 7 percent of health care spending, and the number increases each year. The funding system in the United States is complex and includes both public and private payers. Many patients are covered by more than one plan, increasing the administrative costs for the both the patient and provider. Because administrative costs are calculated in a different way for each system, direct comparisons are not accurate. The United States spends more than any other nation on administrative costs. A standardized system would aid in the reduction of administrative costs and reduce health care spending.

Health care decisions need to be cost-effective. Decisions regarding medications and treatments can be based on value, even as the overall quality of care is improved. Patients and providers can work together to develop a cost-effective quality plan. An example is end-of-life care. Every year, billions of dollars are spent on care that is delivered during the last two months of patients' lives at no benefit and often at the cost of considerable discomfort for the patients. Most patients would like to die at home or in a quiet environment, but without advance planning they are admitted to the hospital, see a multitude of specialists, and are kept alive through the use of technology. In effect, their lives are not saved, only their deaths prolonged. Meanwhile, Medicare spends $50,000 a day for a patient in the intensive care unit (ICU). Patients need to understand their options and make informed decisions.

NEW INCENTIVES FOR COLLABORATION

The Department of Health and Human Services announced new incentives for primary care doctors, specialists, and hospital and other care providers to coordinate care under the ACA. The Medical Shared Savings Program offers eligible providers who meet quality standards to share in cost savings. Program eligibility encompasses physicians in group practices, networks of individual practitioners, and hospitals partnering with or employing eligible physicians, nurse practitioners, physician assistants, and specialists. Each group must be accountable for at least 5,000 beneficiaries annually and include health care providers and Medicare beneficiaries on their governing boards. The Advance Payment Model is offered to physician-owned practices and rural providers in the Medicare Shared Savings Program. Both of these programs will provide incentives for physicians to coordinate cost-effective care utilizing the expertise of multidisciplinary providers.

CONCLUSION

Traditional models of health care are no longer viable. Health care has become a complex system of fragmented care and outdated reimbursement. Payment is circuitous and arbitrary, adding administrative time at the expense of patient care. The relationship of provider and patient has eroded into a series of 15 minute visits. Satisfaction is at an all-time low for both patients and providers. Patients are becoming sicker, communities unhealthy. Health care spending is out of control, and health outcomes are poor. The traditional focus has been on diagnosis and treatment of disease at the expense of health promotion.

Primary care is a way to coordinate complex care, focus on health promotion and disease prevention, and reduce cost. Primary care providers include nurse practitioners, physician assistants, and physicians. Their educational focus is different. Nurse practitioners focus on holistic care, with an emphasis on health promotion and disease prevention. Physician assistants focus on medical issues, and physicians have extensive clinical training and are attuned to the diagnosis and management of disease.

Medical schools are experiencing decreased enrollments, leading to a physician shortage. Medical education is expensive, and there is little incentive for students to elect to practice in primary care. The shortage of physicians renewed the option for nurse practitioners and physician assistants to provide primary care. After many years of turf battles, the American College of Physicians developed a policy paper urging physicians and nurse practitioners to work together to improve primary care. Their skills and expertise are complementary. There is support for exploring new innovative models of care. It is recommended that continued research explore the outcomes of nurse-led and physician-led primary care models. The most important outcome is cost-effective, quality care. In the future, the U.S. health care system must focus on the needs of the population and the communities in which they live. Providers, patients, insurers, and government need to work together to create a healthier community.

REFERENCES AND FURTHER READING

Agency for Healthcare Research and Quality (AHRQ). (2008). *Medical expenditure panel survey household component data: Household emergency room visits event file.* Retrieved from http://www.meps.ahrq.gov/mepsweb/data_stats/download_data_files_results.jsp?cboDataYear=All&cboDataTypeY=2%2CHousehold+Event+File&buttonYearandDataType=Search&cboPufNumber=All&SearchTitle=Emergency+Room+Visits

American Academy of Family Physicians. (2008). *Joint principles of the patient-centered medical home.* Retrieved from http://www.medicalhomeinfo.org/downloads/pdfs/jointstatement.pdf

American Medical Association (AMA). (n.d.). *Strategic issues: Getting the most for our health care dollars.* Retrieved from http://www.ama-assn.org/ama/pub/about-ama/strategic-issues/health-care-costs.page

Association of American Medical Colleges (AAMC). Retrieved from http://www.aamc.org

Center for Medicare & Medicaid Innovation. (n.d.). *About us.* Retrieved from http://innovations.cms.gov/about-us/our-charge

Center for Workforce Studies. (2011). *Recent studies and reports on physician shortages in the U.S. Association of American Medical Colleges.* Retrieved from https://www.aamc.org/download/100598/data/recentworkforcestudiesnov09.pdf

Devi, S. (2011). U.S. nurse practitioners push for more responsibilities. *The Lancet, 377*(9766), 625–626. Retrieved from https://www.aamc.org/newsroom/reporter/april11/184178/addressing_the_physician_shortage_under_reform.html

Freudenberg, N., & Olden, K. (2011). Getting serious about the prevention of chronic diseases. *Preventing Chronic Disease, 8*(4), A90. Retrieved from http://www.cdc.gov/pcd/issues/2011/jul/10_0243.htm

Litow, M. E. (2006). *Medicare vs. private health insurance: The cost of administration.* Retrieved from http://www.cahi.org/cahi_contents/resources/pdf/CAHIMedicareTechnicalPaper.pdf

Matthews, M. (2006). *Medicare's hidden administrative costs: A comparison of Medicare and the private sector.* Retrieved from Council for Affordable Health Insurance website: http://www.cahi.org/cahi_contents/resources/pdf/CAHI_Medicare_Admin_Final_Publication.pdf

Yong, P. L., Saunders, R. S., & Olsen, L. A. (Eds.). (2010). *The health care imperative: Lowering costs and improving outcomes: Workshop series summary.* Washington, DC: National Academies Press.

Barbara Sheer

29

Female Physicians

POINT: Women and men often need different types of care and want different types of relationships with their health care providers. It would be better for women, and perhaps for men, too, if there were more women providers of care; women providers may spend more time with patients, are more interested in having close relationships with patients, and are more interested in serving underprivileged populations.

Linda Grant and Aubrey Denmon, University of Georgia

COUNTERPOINT: There is no quantifiable improvement in the quality of patient care that is provided by a female physician. Women physicians do not fill positions of high need and, in fact, are less productive than are male physicians. They are also limited in their ability to improve the quality of patient care due to their relatively restricted positions in managed care organizations and poor distribution in policy- and decision-making organizations.

Aubrey Denmon and Linda Grant, University of Georgia

Introduction

Although 50 years ago, medicine was an overwhelmingly male profession, in the twenty-first-century women make up almost half of most medical school classes. However, beginning in the 1970s, the number of women in medical school began to increase and continued to do so throughout the decade. Though the percentage of women in practice currently constitutes only one third of the total field, the trends in medical school enrollment guarantee that the percentage will continue to increase as more men retire from the profession and are replaced by cohorts with a greater proportion of women. One of the interesting issues this raises is whether the matching of physicians and patients based on gender is an important example of the issue of concordance in health care between the patient and physician, an issue that is also discussed in this volume in terms of ethnic concordance. In the case of ethnic concordance, one assumption is that the patient and physician will share a common culture, place of origin, or native language, the essence of what is meant by *concordance* as a term. In the case of matching of patients and physicians by gender, there is also some assumption that unique aspects of health are linked to being a male or a female that will make that matching helpful in the delivery of health care services. In health care services research, the importance of gender concordance in a patient-physician relationship has not received as much discussion as the topic of ethnic concordance, although there has been an assumption for the past decades that for some types of care, especially maternity care, patients increasingly are interested in having a woman provider. The argument holds that patients may feel an increased sense of comfort with another woman, especially for care related to obstetrics and gynecology. Some of the other arguments in favor of increasing the number of female physicians are not based so much on concordance, however, but rather on the concept that women bring some special attributes to the practice of medicine that will impact quality of care.

In this chapter, Linda Grant and Aubrey Michelle Denmon take on the debate of whether or not an increase in the number of female physicians will bring with it an improvement in the quality of care. Some data show that women are more likely to fill the most critical primary care positions in medicine and thus are more likely to provide service to medically needy patients. In addition, researchers have found that women bring distinctive, altruistic values to medical practice, and are likely to establish stronger and better communication with their patients. Another argument as to why the increasing numbers of women in medicine will be good for quality of care is that women doctors are also more likely to emphasize preventive care and to practice medicine in a responsible manner that avoids complaints and malpractice suits. Additionally, women physicians may improve care by serving as advocates for women's health, children's health, and the medical needs of the medically underserved. Studies have shown that women physicians spend more time with patients than do men, and this can lead both to higher quality of care and greater patient satisfaction.

Arguments can also be made for the other side; that is, that the increase in the number of women will *not* improve quality of care for most patients. Not all researchers agree that women bring distinctive or more altruistic values to medical practice, nor do they agree that women are better at patient communication than are their male counterparts.

Further, some experts argue that female physicians are less productive than are male physicians, both because they tend to work fewer hours per week (although still more than the typical 40-hour workweek of most Americans) and because women physicians also take time away from their jobs to have babies or to fulfill family responsibilities. So, even if there are more female doctors in primary care (which few dispute), this alone may not increase the amount of hours of physician time available to patients. In addition, it may be the case that women physicians lack the opportunities and influence to create substantial improvements in quality of patient care, because, at least so far in the U.S. health care system, they do not tend to hold positions of influence and control over the structure of health care practices. This being the case, the argument goes, it is highly unlikely that women doctors will do much, if anything, to affect the quality of patient care in the United States. As you read this chapter, consider the arguments on both sides and determine which of them is stronger and which of them reflects the ways in which you view the world.

POINT

The influx of women into careers as physicians is a positive trend, one that will enhance the quality of medical care for patients. According to the Association of American Medical Colleges (AAMC), women now constitute about 47 percent of new entrants into U.S. medical schools, and in 2009–2010 they reached a peak of 48 percent of newly graduated MDs. As of 2012, about one third of practicing physicians in the United States were women, but these proportions will grow substantially in the next decade. An increase in the total number of female physicians will improve quality of care in a number of ways. Women are more likely to fill the most critical primary care positions in medicine and provide service to medically needy patients. Women bring distinctive, altruistic values to medical practice, and they are more likely to establish strong and effective communication with patients (McMurray et al., 2002; Riska, 2001). Female doctors are also more likely to emphasize preventive care, practicing medicine in a careful and responsible manner that avoids complaints and malpractice suits (Bertakis, 2009). Female physicians also improve care by satisfying the preference of many women and men for treatment by a woman doctor and by serving as advocates for women's health, children's health, and the medical needs of the medically underserved (Phillips et al., 2009).

A BRIEF HISTORY OF WOMEN IN MEDICINE

Women practitioners have always had a presence in medical practice and patient care in the United States. Women served patients as healers and midwives and dispensers of herbal medicines, with knowledge passed down cross-generationally in communities of women. As the historian Mary Roth Walsh has demonstrated, women's social role as "healer" was deliberately and systematically discredited when medicine was professionalized in the late 1800s and early 1900s. Apprentice-type learning programs that were not attached to formal medical schools lost credibility, and women healers lost prominence as the primary providers of medical care. Economic competition was often at the core of these struggles for dominance, as can be seen in battles between women midwives and men obstetricians for control of childbirth (Katz-Rothman, 2007). Men obstetricians won that battle and succeeded not only in monopolizing obstetrical care but also in effectively transporting childbirth out of private family homes and into hospital settings. In the process of professionalization, women lost access to medical education through outright bans on female students at many co-ed medical schools and through the closing of women-only medical schools. Women's prestige as healers within their communities was further eroded as their bases of knowledge and lay training were labeled "unscientific." The increasing proportion of women physicians in contemporary times promises to revive some of the valuable, patient-oriented practices characteristic of women in medicine that declined during this period of professionalization.

WOMEN DOCTORS' PLACEMENT IN MEDICINE: A PENCHANT FOR PRIMARY CARE

Access to a regular, trusted primary care physician is one of the strongest predictors of better health for patients. Starfield, Shi, and Macinko (2005) found that having a regular primary care physician significantly reduced the five-year mortality rate for patients, with other factors controlled, and the presence of larger numbers of general practitioners on hospital staffs reduced hospital mortality rates. Furthermore, they report that in international comparisons, countries with higher ratios of primary care doctors enjoyed better health outcomes for their populations. One reason to anticipate improved quality of patient care as women make up larger shares of the physician workforce is that women have always had proportionally greater representation than men physicians in the critical primary care fields: internal medicine, family practice, pediatrics, public health, and preventive medicine. As men doctors have turned away from these primary care specialty areas, women have entered them in large proportions, preventing an even worse shortage of primary care doctors.

Currently, the United States faces a serious maldistribution of physicians across specialty areas, with too many specialists and too few primary care doctors (Phillips et al., 2009). Unlike in many other countries, in the United States specialty choice is the prerogative of the individual physician, and the federal government does not regulate allocation of doctors to particular specialty areas. Two important factors will only intensify the need for primary care physicians in the future. First, the population of the United States is aging, and elderly patients visit the doctor—usually primary care physicians for the management of ongoing, chronic conditions—more often than do other age groups. The second factor is the

2010 Patient Protection and Affordable Health Care Act (ACA), which, by enlarging the pool of citizens with some health insurance coverage, will thereby increase the demand for primary care providers, with a very real potential to exacerbate the existing shortage. In addition to providing continuity of care for patients with chronic conditions, access to primary care physicians helps to reduce costly and unnecessary emergency room visits. Had women not become doctors in rapidly increasing proportions in the past three decades, the crisis in primary care would be even worse than it is today.

GENDER AND DOCTORS' MOTIVATIONS

In a 2010 article in *Academic Medicine,* Donna Jeffe and colleagues reported that women doctors' greater likelihood of entering primary care areas of medicine can be linked to the extent to which they cite values of altruism and social responsibility as motivations for entering medicine. Whereas men may be attracted to high-paying specialties such as radiology and orthopedic surgery because of prestige and earnings that are often double or triple those of primary care providers, women tend to enter medical school less concerned about prestige and money and maintain these orientations at the specialty selection point. Women medical students and doctors also seem to be more concerned than are their male counterparts about the equitable distribution of medical resources (Levinson & Lurie, 2004). Altruistic orientations and concerns about social responsibility may also account for women's doctors' willingness to treat many underserved populations—the poor, minorities, immigrants, the elderly, and the uninsured. According to a recent report from the Macy Foundation (Phillips et al., 2009), female doctors treat proportionally more of these population groups than do their male counterparts.

PRACTICE EXPERIENCES OF WOMEN DOCTORS

Women doctors, more so than men, have a history of working in third-party, salaried positions rather than in entrepreneurial practices (Phillips et al., 2009). Although many women doctors choose these types of practices because they provide greater predictability of work hours and on-call responsibilities, many also express a preference for managed practices because they allow them to devote their energies to patient care, rather than to finances or practice management. Women doctors thus have more experience with the forms of medical practices likely to predominate in the United States in the years ahead.

Although research by Julia McMurray and colleagues (2002), investigators in the massive Physician Worklife Study, shows that women doctors are skeptical about some of the transformations in medical care delivery brought about by managed care, they have nevertheless been powerful advocates within these organizations for maintenance of the quality of patient care. For example, within managed care–affected practices, women doctors have resisted the imposition of productivity quotas on physicians that discourage them from spending ample time with each patient. Further, women often have more experience than do their men colleagues working in interdisciplinary teams with non-physician health providers. They therefore may be more savvy advocates for patients within this system.

WOMEN'S DISTINCTIVE ORIENTATIONS TOWARD PRACTICE

To their medical practices, women bring distinctive orientations and practice styles that provide high-quality care for patients. Julia McMurray and her colleagues' report suggests also that women place a high value on close and extended relationships with their patients. Women doctors report greater overall satisfaction with their practices, particularly as it pertains to encounters with patients, compared with men doctors. In the eyes of both patients and colleagues, women doctors are more empathic than their men counterparts. The patient-centered orientation of female physicians affects not only their choices of medical specialty areas but also the way they practice medicine on a day-to-day basis.

TIME WITH PATIENTS

In all types of practices, women doctors spend more time with each patient in comparison to men physicians. Pauline Chen, a prominent transplant surgeon and *New York Times* columnist, noted in her May 10, 2010, column that women physicians spend about 10 percent more time with patients than do their male counterparts. Similar patterns have been reported for women physicians worldwide (Boulis & Jacobs, 2004; Riska, 2001). More time with patients provides clear benefits for quality of care. Not only does it lead to a more thorough medical encounter but it also engenders higher levels of trust between patient and physician. Patients are more willing to confide in women doctors, and studies have shown that they experience higher levels of satisfaction from treatment by women doctors.

WILLINGNESS TO WORK WITH UNDERSERVED PATIENTS

Even when one takes into account the types of practices women are apt to enter, they are still more likely than men doctors in comparable positions to treat underserved patients (Phillips et al., 2009). Although women doctors practice in rural communities less often than men do, in all other regions they are more likely to serve medically needy, uninsured, elderly patients and patients with more complex medical needs. Women's willingness to serve such patients is evident as they enter medical school, surveys from the AAMCs suggest. From entry into medical school onward, women show greater concern about altruism and social responsibility than do their male classmates. Women doctors contribute more to meeting the health care needs of these underserved populations, whose circumstances have worsened under the recent recession and its accompanying losses of jobs and medical insurance coverage. Even though women doctors are less likely than men physicians to hold positions in medical administration, they are overrepresented as administrators of institutions and programs serving needy populations, such as migrant health clinics (Levinson & Lurie, 2004). Women doctors are significantly less likely to be members of the tradition-bound American Medical Association (AMA) (about 24 percent to men's 36 percent), according to the medical sociologist Rose Weitz (2010), but women doctors are represented within the ranks of progressive organizations such as Doctors without Borders/Médicins Sans Frontières and Physicians for Social Responsibility.

EMPATHY AND COMMUNICATION

Female doctors have a tendency to be more empathic practitioners than do male doctors, and they show stronger communication skills in encounters with patients (Hall, Irish, Roter, Ehrlich, & Miller, 1994). They are more encouraging and reassuring toward their patients; inquire more often about psychosocial issues that might be affecting patients; and are more likely than men physicians to establish collaborative, shared decision-making relationships with patients (Levinson & Lurie, 2004). For example, studies reviewed by Elianne Riska show that in their initial encounters with new patients, women doctors ask more questions about current life circumstances, whereas men physicians devote more time to taking formal medical histories. The women doctors' approach appears to create stronger rapport with patients of both genders. Fellow physicians, patients, and other health care coworkers such as nurses and medical technicians all rate women physicians as the more empathic practitioners and judge them to have better communication skills in encounters with patients.

Indeed, across a broad range of studies, women doctors emerge as better communicators. They manage encounters with patients differently, and more effectively, than do men doctors (Hall et al., 1994). According to Klea Bertakis, women physicians provide patients with more information in medical encounters. Patients of both genders find women doctors more approachable, and as a result patients ask women doctors more questions during medical visits and are more apt to contact them with follow-up questions (Riska, 2001). As a result of these interchanges, patients gain better understandings of their medical conditions and recommended treatments and become motivated to cooperate with the doctor. Levinson and Lurie report that women doctors establish more egalitarian relationships with their patients, and that these types of relationships are especially beneficial for the long-term treatment of patients with chronic illnesses or conditions. In the United States and other developed countries, patients with chronic conditions make up an ever larger share of the typical physician's patient load, a trend that will only escalate in the coming decades.

Shared decision making, trusting bonds between patient and physician, and effective communication are particularly important for patients with chronic conditions, where the quality of the physician-patient relationship is an important predictor of a positive outcome. Women physicians are more likely than men to discuss treatment options with patients, and the choice of strategy is more likely to be a shared decision (Levinson & Lurie, 2004). Patients feel a stronger sense of commitment to the treatment strategy and a greater sense of control over their health status, a valuable orientation when managing a chronic condition. Successful management of chronic conditions requires that patients take on high levels of responsibility for their own care. They need to be knowledgeable enough about their situations to monitor symptoms, self-administer medications and treatments, recognize when they need to contact the doctor, and feel comfortable in contacting the doctor when the need arises.

Men physicians have benefitted from working with women physicians and observing their styles of interacting with patients. In 2010–2011, several U.S. medical schools announced plans for new courses in patient communication, so that all of the physicians they train—women and men—can become more proficient in these skills. The New Pathways curriculum instituted at Harvard Medical School, requiring course work over three years focused on patient-physician communication, is but one example. Developing effective models of patient communication is a distinctive contribution that women doctors have made to contemporary medical practice. The growing presence of women doctors in medical practice thus has had a positive effect on the practice styles of all doctors.

AUTHORITY AND CONTROL

In addition to establishing better channels of communication with patients with chronic conditions, women doctors show greater forbearance when coping with such patients (Scholle et al., 2001). Women doctors are less likely than men physicians to become frustrated when they do not have a definitive answer and cannot immediately resolve a patient's problem. They are more likely to admit the limits of their knowledge, to seek consultations or referrals, and to engage in further research about a particular condition. They are less defensive about requests for second options and listen more carefully to suggestions for treatment offered by patients. Research suggests that women physicians are more effective in working with multidisciplinary teams, and this form of medical practice tends to benefit patient outcomes (Levinson & Lurie, 2004).

ATTENTION TO PSYCHOSOCIAL ISSUES

Female doctors are more attentive to the psychosocial needs of patients, and they treat more patients with multiple health problems or psychosocial needs that coexist with physical health problems. These are patients that many male doctors do not particularly care to treat, and within group practices that include doctors of both genders, they may be disproportionately assigned to women physicians. Because even when they see patients with physical ailments women doctors are more likely than men physicians to ask about social milieu and psychosocial concerns, they are more apt than men doctors to uncover issues that can generally affect patients' health and well-being (Bertakis et al., 2001). Women doctors make more referrals for mental health and social services, where indicated. Women doctors' greater willingness to grapple with complex emotional issues is consistent with a generalized cultural image of women as emotional and relationship specialists. Women doctors may be more willing than men to take on the role of the psychosocial specialist, but within large practice groups such patients seem also to be steered more frequently to women doctors. Women's focus on the whole person, and not just the particular physical complaint, harkens back to historical roles played by women healers before they were driven out of practice as medicine became professionalized.

Female doctors also tend to be the psychosocial experts in relation to their colleagues and coworkers. Within the context of multi-physician practices, women are called upon more frequently than men to resolve interpersonal disputes in practice settings. (Male doctors, in contrast, are called on more to resolve financial, management, or technological issues.) Pringle (1996) reports that nurses, including male nurses, prefer to work with women doctors, whom they believe to be more appreciative of their distinctive skills and more likely to treat them with respect. Thus, the stronger relationship skills of women doctors benefit not only their contacts with patients but also their interactions with coworkers.

MORE CAREFUL PRACTITIONERS?

A 2010 report from the AMA, based on its 2007–2008 Physicians' Practice Information survey, revealed that men doctors were nearly twice as likely than women doctors to have been sued. Women physicians worry less than men doctors about malpractice suits and thus may be less likely to practice defensive medicine, ordering expensive and unnecessary tests primarily to avoid the risk of malpractice suits. Studies from countries such as New Zealand, Australia, and Canada also show that, even accounting for differences in practice locales and specialties, women doctors receive fewer patient complaints, are disciplined less by medical boards, and are sued for malpractice far less often.

A number of factors may make women safer practitioners. More time spent with patients might reduce the chance of error. Better communication with patients may result in fewer disgruntled patients who become angry enough to file a complaint or to sue. Finally, although nearly all women physicians work at least a 40-hour week, women doctors are less likely than men to work extremely long hours. The risk of medical error increases sharply as overtime work hours accumulate. Jeremy Laurance, writing in 2009 in the British medical journal *Lancet*, proposed that women doctors faced fewer malpractice suits and drew fewer complaints than men doctors because they were more meticulous and less error-prone in their everyday practices. The influx of women into medical practice in the Unites States should help to counter skyrocketing medical malpractice insurance premiums and the unnecessary costs to patients and insurers associated with defensive medicine.

WOMEN DOCTORS AND LIFE BALANCE

As women's share of the physician workforce has increased, some have raised concerns about decreases in physician productivity (or the number of hours worked) that might exacerbate the existing physician shortage in the United States. Women doctors, on average, work about 4.5 fewer hours a week than men, although nearly all work at least a 40-hour week, and some women doctors take short maternity leaves early in their careers (Arnst, 2008). Claims about low levels of productivity by female physicians are misleading, masking the fact that the majority of women doctors for most of their careers practice a full-time or greater schedule (Dacre & Shepherd, 2010; McMurray et al., 2002). However, women doctors do place greater emphasis on a balanced life with time for family or other personal concerns. As Dacre and Shepherd note, the minimization of overwork by women doctors may have positive consequences, reducing the risk of medical error traceable to fatigue and integrating women doctors more thoroughly into the communities they serve. Furthermore, as Levinson and Lurie (2004) have proposed, the presence of greater proportions of women in positions as physicians encourages the profession to devise more flexible working conditions, an outcome that can benefit both women and men doctors.

Women doctors have challenged traditions of "trial by fire" as a mark of competence and professionalism in medicine (DelVecchio Good, 1985). There is some evidence that women have had an impact on men doctors who are their contemporaries, as younger men doctors seem to be rejecting the notion that extremely long hours at work are the mark of competence and commitment, instead limiting their extensive overtime hours in favor of a balance of medical work and other interests (Arnst, 2008).

APPROACHES TO MEDICAL TREATMENT: AN EMPHASIS ON WOMEN'S HEALTH?

As studies reviewed by Boulis and Jacobs (2004) and Riska (2001) have shown, there are many commonalities in the treatment strategies recommended by women and men doctors of similar ages and training. Furthermore, some differences in practice styles attributed to gender may in fact reflect generational differences among physicians, inasmuch as women have made up much larger shares of recent graduating medical school classes. Nonetheless, some important gender differences are relatively consistent across studies. In their encounters with patients, women doctors stress the importance of preventive care for both women and men patients (Henderson & Weisman, 2001). Women doctors are more likely than men to advocate interventions such as changes in diet or exercise patterns, smoking cessation, treatment for alcohol or drug abuse, or the integration of alternative therapies into conventional medical treatment. They are also more likely to recommend immunizations and counseling to both women and men (Flock & Gilchrist, 2005). Women are more likely to value teamwork and to work closely with non-physician health professionals, such as nutritionists, massage therapists, or acupuncturists, and they generally are more open than their male colleagues to incorporating nonconventional and alternative treatments into their practices (Levinson & Lurie, 2004). Rather than viewing alternative medical practitioners as competitors—the typical response of men physicians—women doctors are more favorably disposed toward cooperation and inclusion.

Within group practices, women devote more of their time to women patients and women's health. Even as internists or family practitioners, women doctors have proportionally more women patients and do more reproductive health care. Men, by contrast, handle more cardiovascular and muscular-skeletal cases. Women doctors have been somewhat less likely to recommend potentially dangerous hormone replacement therapy (HRT) to women patients as they approach menopause. Instead, women doctors have been more likely to follow what now are AMA guidelines to consider such therapy only for women who are experiencing disruptive symptoms, to use it for the least amount of time possible, and to carefully discuss risks and benefits with patients. Women doctors also have been more likely than men doctors to recommend that women try less dangerous alternative treatments for menopausal symptoms, such as yoga, meditation, exercise, or dietary changes.

Although, overall, male doctors spend more time on cardiovascular cases, it is worth noting that female doctors are more attentive to cardiac problems and other gender-specific health conditions in their women patients (Henderson & Weisman, 2001). Cardiac disease is the leading morbidity among women, although this fact is not always recognized within the medical community. Symptoms of cardiac distress can present differently in women and men. Because most medical research on cardiac problems has been carried out on men and doctors in medical school learn more about cardiac symptoms as they affect men rather than women, physicians are less apt to diagnose cardiac problems in women at early, treatable stages. Whereas men doctors often overlook or trivialize symptoms in women patients, women doctors tend to take them more seriously and diagnose and treat symptoms as aggressively in women as in men patients (Gunilla et al., 2010). Women doctors therefore provide a higher quality of care for women patients, without compromising the quality of care provided to men. As Ellen More (1999) documented in her historical study of women physicians, at the policy level women physicians have been advocates for greater inclusion of women in medical research and greater research attention to medical conditions affecting women. As a result, in the future, all physicians will benefit from increased knowledge of women's health conditions.

ACCOMMODATING PATIENT PREFERENCES

Especially when it comes to intimate care, women patients express a preference for women physicians, and the influx of women into careers as physicians gives them opportunities to satisfy that preference in ways that were not previously possible. Women patients frequently prefer a woman doctor in fields such as obstetrics/gynecology because they believe she has firsthand experience with health issues unique to women. These preferences recall earlier eras in the United States when most women were attended in childbirth by women midwives. With victims of rape, sexual assault, or domestic abuse who require medical attention, treatment by a woman doctor can be extremely important to women's well-being and recovery.

Another way women doctors make a significant contribution to the quality of patient care is by treating women, many of whom are recent immigrants, whose religious and cultural beliefs do not permit treatment by a male provider. When women doctors are unavailable, many such women go without medical care altogether. For example, some, when pregnant, get no prenatal care, and give birth without a medical attendant. Women doctors are uniquely suited to provide high-quality care to these distinctive population groups.

Women physicians are preferred by a majority of women and men, according to an experimental study conducted by Barbara Gerbert and her colleagues. The study presented male and female respondents with photos and brief video portrayals of potential physicians who differed in race and ethnic characteristics. Although women patients tended to prefer female doctors, they found no evidence that men would resist treatment by a woman for most types of medical problems. Both women and men anticipated that women doctors would be more empathetic. Thus, it seems likely that, in most medical situations, men patients will not be resistant to treatment by a woman doctor, and under some circumstances they may even prefer it.

WOMEN DOCTORS AS ADVOCATES FOR WOMEN'S HEALTH CARE

An important, but sometimes overlooked, reason that women doctors will improve the quality of patient care is the role that many of them have played in putting the health needs of women, children, and families on research and policy agendas. Women doctors have been on the forefront of this activism for decades. As More's (1999) historical study of women in medicine reveals, women physicians have been on the forefront of campaigns for improved medical care for women and children, championing campaigns for better quality prenatal care, family-centered childbirth, promotion of breast-feeding, less medicated treatment of menopausal symptoms, and more medical research on women's health needs. Women doctors have also been prominent advocates of public health initiatives in the United States and abroad, such as improved sanitation and nutrition, childhood vaccination campaigns, and provision of medical care to the poor. In psychiatry, a specialty area into which women doctors have entered in large proportions in recent years, women doctors have challenged diagnoses and treatment of women psychiatric patients and developed a subfield of feminist psychiatry as an alternative to sexist and insensitive psychiatric treatment provided to some women patients. With demand for mental health services on the rise, greater representation of women physicians in psychiatry should provide better quality of care, especially for women physicians.

Women doctors have made contributions to the women's health movement. Many have contributed to publications such as *Our Bodies, Ourselves,* which have been aimed at demystifying medical conditions and empowering women as health care consumers. More recently, women doctors have become media spokespersons on issues of women's health, writing columns in major newspapers and magazines and appearing on television as experts on women's health. Under the leadership of the late Dr. Bernadine Healy, its first woman director, the National Institutes of Health issued new guidelines for medical research that required incorporation of women and minorities into federally funded health research, unless researchers made a compelling case as to why this would be inappropriate. The policy change helped to correct a long-standing pattern of exclusion of women subjects and a lack of attention to conditions especially relevant for women's health from federally funded research. Also under the direction of Dr. Healy, the NIH also launched a massive longitudinal study of women's health (the Women's Health Initiative) that has yielded valuable new information on many health conditions affecting women, such as the risks and benefits of HRT, identification of cardiac symptoms in women, origin and treatment of fibroid tumors, osteoporosis, and improved techniques of mammography and treatment of breast cancer. Women physicians continue to contribute to the quality of patient care as advocates for greater knowledge about and improved treatment plans for women patients and conditions affecting women.

CONCLUSION

The increase in proportions of women doctors already has benefited the quality of patient care in the United States. The projected increase in the proportions of practicing women physicians in the future promises to enhance these benefits. Women doctors improve the quality of patient care by practicing in areas of critical need and providing care to underserved populations, by developing practice styles that are patient centered, and by advocating on behalf of the health care needs of women and others who have been marginalized from quality medical care in the past. Finally, women doctors have the potential to influence in positive ways the practices of the men physicians with whom they work.

REFERENCES AND FURTHER READING

American Medical Association. (2010). Medical liability. Retrieved from http://www.ama-assn.org/amednews/2010/08/16/pr120816.htm

Arnst, C. (2008, April 17). Are there too many women doctors? *Bloomberg BusinessWeek.* Retrieved from http://www.businessweek .com/magazine/content/08_17/b4081104183847.htm

Association of American Medical Colleges. (2012). *U.S. medical school applicants and students 1982-1983 to 2011-2012* (Chart 2, p. 2). Retrieved from https://www.aamc.org/download/153708/data/charts1982to2012.pdf

Bertakis, K. D., Helms, L. J., Callahan, E. J., Azari, R., Leigh, J. P., & Robbins, J. A. (2001). Patient gender differences in the diagnosis of depression in primary care. *Journal of Women's Health & Gender-Based Medicine, 10*(7), 689–698.

Bertakis, K. D., Helms, L. J., Callahan, E. J., Azari, R., & Robbins, J. A. (1995). The influence of gender on physician practice style. *Medical Care, 33*(4), 407–416.

Bertakis, K. D. (2009). The influence of gender on the doctor-patient interaction. *Patient Education and Counseling, 76*(3), 356–360.

Boulis, A., & Jacobs, J. (2004). An analysis of the impact of gender on physician practice patterns. *Journal of Health and Social Policy, 18*(1), 57–87.

Chen, P. (2010, May 6). Do women make better doctors? *The New York Times.* Retrieved from http://www.nytimes.com/2010/05/06/ health/06chen.html

Dacre, J., & Shepherd, S. (2010). Women and medicine. *Clinical Medicine, 10*(6), 544–547.

DelVecchio Good, M. (1985). Discourses on physician competence. In R. A. Hahn & A. Gaines (Eds.), *Physicians of western medicine: Anthropological perspectives on theory and practice.* Boston, MA: D. Reidel.

Flocke, S. A., & Gilchrist, V. (2005). Physician and patient concordance and the delivery of comprehensive clinical services. *Medical Care, 43*(5), 486–492.

Gerbert, B., Berg-Smith, S., Caspers, N., Danley, D., Herzig, K., & Brand, R. (2003). Video study of physician selection: Preferences in the face of diversity. *Journal of Family Practice, 52*(7), 552–559.

Hall, J. A., Irish, J. T., Roter, D. L., Ehrlich, C. M., & Miller, L. H. (1994). Gender in medical encounters: An analysis of physician and patient communication in a primary care setting. *Health Psychology, 13*(5), 384–392.

Henderson, J. T., & Weisman, C. S. (2001). Physician gender effects on preventive screening and counseling: An analysis of male and female patients' health care experiences. *Medical Care, 39,* 1281–1292.

Jackson, I., Bobbin, M., Jordan, M., & Baker, S. (2009). A survey of women urology residents regarding career choice and practice challenges. *Journal of Women's Health, 18*(11), 1867–1872.

Jeffe, D., Whelan, A. J., & Andriole, D. A. (2010). Primary care specialty choices of United States medical graduates, 1997–2006. *Academic Medicine, 85*(6), 947–958.

Katz-Rothman, B. (2007). Laboring then: The political history of maternity care in the United States. In W. Simonds, B. Katz-Rothman, & B. M. Norman (Eds.), *Laboring on: Birth in transition in the United States* (pp. 3–28). New York, NY: Routledge.

Laurence, J. (2009). On reflection: Are women safer doctors? *The Lancet, 374*(9697), 1233.

Levinson, W., & Lurie, N. (2004). When most doctors are women: What lies ahead? *Annals of Internal Medicine, 141*(6), 471–474.

McMurray, J. E., Angus, G., Cohen, M., Gavel, P., Harding, J., Horvath, J., et al. (2002). Women in medicine: A four-nation comparison. *Journal of the American Medical Women's Association, 57*(4), 185–190.

More, E. S. (1999). *Restoring the balance: Women physicians and the profession of medicine, 1850–1995.* Cambridge, MA: Harvard University Press.

Phillips, R. L., Dodoo, M. S., Petterson, S., Xierali, I., Bazemore, A., Teevan, B., et al. (2009). *Specialty and geographic distribution of the physician workforce: What influences medical student and resident choices?* Report of the Josiah Macy Foundation. Washington, DC: The Robert Graham Center.

Pringle, R. (1996). Nursing a grievance: Women doctors and nurses. *Journal of Gender Studies, 5*(2), 157–169.

Riska, E. (2001). Does gender matter? Women as medical practitioners. *Medical careers and feminist agendas: American, Scandinavian, and Russian women physicians* (pp. 87–102). New York, NY: Aldine de Gruyter.

Riska, E., & Wegar, K. (1993). Women physicians: A new force in medicine? *Gender, work and medicine: Women and the medical division of labor* (pp. 77–94). Newbury Park, CA: Sage.

Scholle, S. H., Gardner, W., Harman, J., Madlon-Kay, D. J., Pascoe, J., & Kelleher, K. (2001). Physician gender and psychosocial care for children: Attitudes, practice characteristics, identification, and treatment. *Medical Care, 39*(1), 26–38.

Starfield, B., Shi, L., & Macinko, J. (2005). Contribution of primary care to health systems and health. *Milbank Quarterly, 83*(2), 457–502.

Walsh, M. R. (1977). *Doctors wanted: No women need apply: Sexual barriers in the medical profession, 1835–1975.* New Haven, CT: Yale University Press.

Wear, D., & Keck-McNulty, C. (2004). Attitudes of female nurses and female residents toward each other: A qualitative study in one U.S. teaching hospital. *Academic Medicine, 79*(4), 291–301.

Weitz, R. (2010). *The sociology of health, illness, and health care: A critical approach* (5th ed.). Boston, MA: Wadsworth.

Linda Grant and Aubrey Denmon

COUNTERPOINT

The recent influx of women into the field of medicine will not result in a significant improvement in the quality of medical care. Although one third of practicing physicians and one half of medical students are women, the increasing presence of women will not drastically affect the quality of care patients receive from physicians. Despite considerable speculation to the contrary, research has shown few gender-based distinctions in the practice and quality of care received. Where gender-based distinctions in practice do exist, they tend to be small or in areas that are irrelevant to quality of care. Because of differences relative to men physicians in levels of productivity and location within medical hierarchy, women physicians lack the opportunities and influence to create substantial improvements in quality of patient care, even if they do hold distinctive preferences for the provision of patient care. Therefore, it is highly unlikely that women doctors will do much, if anything, to affect the quality of patient care in the United States.

Women physicians respond differently than men to the challenges of the lifestyle and professional demands of a career in medicine, particularly related to women physicians' productivity, work-life balance, approach to medicine, satisfaction with medical practice, and gender differences in both medical treatment and patient interaction.

PRODUCTIVITY ISSUES

Women doctors will not improve the quality of patient care because they are less productive than men in terms of hours worked and time devoted to practice. Women doctors tend to work 20 to 25 percent fewer hours than men in an average week, and they see 10 percent fewer patients (Chen, 2010). Women physicians also take more time off early in their careers than do their male counterparts. These interruptions usually come early in their careers and tend to be related to family and child rearing. American women physicians retire earlier than men physicians, and they are more likely to be listed as "inactive" than men physicians (McMurray et al., 2002). Women as physicians, then, are less able to provide the same continuity of care than are their male counterparts.

Because women physicians work fewer hours than men and choose specialties with regular hours and limited call, they will be less helpful than many people hope in alleviating the projected physician shortage. The immediate inability of women physicians to maintain full-time positions will result in the expensive and time-consuming training of additional primary care physicians. Although some studies suggest that both women and men doctors are exploring a more balanced approach to their work and nonwork lives, and physicians of both genders are expected to move away from the 80-hour workweeks of the past. But in the meantime, the "shirking" of professional responsibilities by women physicians tends to create resentment among co-workers, especially if a woman is a partner in a private practice. It has even led to suggestions in the United States, Scotland, England, and other countries that it might be necessary to reduce the proportion of women admitted to medical school, so that patient needs are not compromised by the typically fewer weekly work hours and more early career interruptions of full-time work by women doctors (Arnst, 2008; McKinstry, 2008).

WORK-LIFE BALANCE

Though men medical students generally choose a specialty and a practice type based upon their personal academic and professional interests, women medical students often choose specialties based on the anticipated fit with work-family plans (Phillips et al., 2009). Many female medical students choose primary care specialties in part because they have shorter residency training periods than most other specialties. As medical school and residencies occur at the same general phase in the life course when other couples are finishing college and starting families, it is much more common for women than men to pass up elite opportunities for residency and postdoctoral work if it interferes with their desire to have children and establish a home. Specialty areas such as family practice or public health and group or clinic-based practice settings promise more regular work hours and less on-call time, and women are predictably concentrated there.

Female doctors are more likely than male doctors to be married to other doctors, and conversely, male physicians are more likely to have a partner who is not employed full-time or whose career is secondary to his (Hinze, 2004). Although the two-doctor career can provide certain advantages, research suggests that the woman's career is often subordinated to the needs of her often more senior spouse (Leserman, 1981). The division of household labor in two-physician households still tends to fall along gender lines, with mothers being responsible for childcare and housework, or for making arrangements so that childcare and housework are covered, while fathers are responsible for household and childcare tasks that are less rigidly scheduled, such as lawn or automobile maintenance or recreational activities with children. The attention given to daily housekeeping tasks by women physicians allows for the neglect of those tasks by their physician spouses as well as the privilege of focusing completely on career matters, including networking activities and projects that lead to career advancement. Whether or not women and men physicians consciously choose this division of labor, it is nonetheless true that women physicians tend to choose specialties and work schedules that allow for a decreased workload and fewer call hours, or at least flexibility in those areas.

SATISFACTION WITH PRACTICE OF MEDICINE

Although some studies have suggested that women experience greater satisfaction with patient interaction aspects of medical practice, other aspects of medical practice are particularly dissatisfying for them (McMurray et al., 2002). Women doctors continue to earn significantly less than do their male counterparts, and pay inequity is a major source of dissatisfaction. Additionally, McMurray and colleagues show that, though women physicians are more likely to report that they are satisfied with their specialty and with the relationships they maintain with colleagues and patients, they generally experience burnout earlier in their careers, possibly due to a dissatisfaction with their autonomy, pay, resources, and relationships with the medical community.

Unfortunately, women physicians experience challenges in the workplace related to sexual harassment at higher rates than do men. Women physicians report more experiences of sexual harassment and sexist behaviors from professors, patients, and colleagues, both in training and in practice, than do their male colleagues (Grant, 1989). One study has shown that the presence and influence of women mentors and maternal role models does not protect women physicians from the career dissatisfaction that follows an incident of sexual harassment (Shrier et al., 2007). If women feel threatened by their work environment, their talents can be lost. Responsibility for incidents of workplace sexual harassment can rightly be placed on the perpetrators; nevertheless, a woman physician who experiences sexual harassment is likely to be less productive and satisfied in her work environment than one who does not.

MALDISTRIBUTION INTO FAMILY PRACTICE

Research focusing on medical students has revealed that students' motivations and academic interests in medicine do seem to vary somewhat along gender lines. In the United States, the social role of physician has many accompanying benefits, including money, prestige, and success. Some medical students are motivated to study medicine because of peer or family pressure, while some have a genuine desire to improve people's lives or a genuine interest in scientific topics. The only significant gender-based motivation for entering medical school is that more women medical students report reasons having to do with altruism, suggesting that they bring a distinctive orientation to medical practice.

However, medical students do express well-distributed interests regarding specialization and options for residency, which ought to manifest in relatively equal distribution of men and women physicians into research, academics, and practice. The reality, though, is that women and men physicians have diverged widely—and somewhat predictably—into career paths upon completion of their medical school education, as is documented by data on specialty choices from the Association of American Medical Colleges (2008). Men physicians are overrepresented in surgery, ophthalmology, radiology, and many internal medical subspecialties, women are overrepresented in family medicine, obstetrics/gynecology, pediatrics, preventive medicine, and public health. Though women recently have begun filling the ranks of most subspecialties, numerous disincentives discourage them from entering traditionally male-dominated fields.

Boulis and Jacobs (2008) suggest several explanations for this divergence through an examination of the mechanisms of systematic gender discrimination within medical education. They argue that, during the 1970s, when the first significant wave of women applicants to medical school appeared, gender-based differences in specialty choice were vulnerable to factors such as gender stereotypes among faculty and students, women students' attempts to avoid conflict and harassment and to seek out social support, biases in the process by which residency candidates were selected, gender differences in academic experiences, differences in the growth-rate of particular medical specialties, and a long-standing tradition of women physicians limiting themselves to specialties related to the care of women or children in order to avoid facing explicit discrimination and hostility from other medical students. Because of their relatively anomalous position, women students in medical schools sought to minimize their own ability to influence the field of medicine as a concession to gender-based discrimination, allowing them to complete their medical education and practice without creating additional conflict by overtaking traditionally male roles. The necessary adaptation to occupational norms established by upper-class white men reinforced the channeling of women medical students into certain proper and expected specialty choices: family medicine, pediatrics, and obstetrics/gynecology. In the same way that medical specialty choices were highly influenced by men mentors among men students, women faculty and mentors guided those women students who sought their support, often leading to a career path similar to the mentors' career path. Because highly paid, prestigious and influential specialty positions were more often held by men than by women, the drafting of students into those same specialties reinforced a gender-based division.

Women students may also face the unique challenge of choosing a mentor based on rank over gender. In their 1989 study, Ochberg, Barton, and West found that women students with high-ranking male mentors reported greater amounts of career sponsorship, while women students with lower-ranking women mentors reported receiving greater amounts of career advice. The researchers concluded that the mentor's academic rank, rather than his or her gender, was a greater determinant of the effectiveness of the mentor's sponsorship. Clearly, both aspects of career counseling are helpful for women students, since women report more concern than men about combining personal life with developing a satisfying career. However, with women physicians filling lower-ranking positions, their efforts at mentoring women students regarding career planning and advancement may be less effective than those of men physicians.

LACK OF GENDER DIFFERENCE IN MEDICAL TREATMENT

As research has revealed that women and men physicians approach medicine with similar philosophies, motivations, and intentions, it is no surprise that research has found few gender-based differences in physician interactions with patients and in treatment strategies. Where differences do exist, they are likely explained by a difference in training and education, not gender. In terms of treatment protocols for medically recognized conditions, there is little evidence that women doctors treat their patients differently than do men doctors.

Some women doctors are somewhat more conscious of the need to temper potential harmful treatments for "women's health issues," as in the use of hormone replacement therapy (HRT) to manage uncomfortable qualities of menopause. However, a 2011 study of Canadian obstetricians found that the physician's likelihood to pursue a Caesarean section was correlated much more with the physician's age than the physician's gender (Klein et al.). Older physicians (defined in the study as those 40 and up) diverged from younger physicians in their beliefs about women's agency during childbirth and the need for medical intervention, with older physicians favoring less intervention and greater participation by laboring women. In this study, distinctive beliefs about treatment protocol were associated with the age cohort of the physician, not with gender. Literature on this topic is not conclusive and acknowledges the complexity in isolating specific gender-based outcomes in any situation.

PATIENT INTERACTION

In the United States, the nature of family practice is one of gatekeeping and health maintenance. Patients experiencing a minor, acute condition, like a sore throat, usually see a family practitioner first, who may refer them to a specialist if the patient's symptoms indicate a severe condition, or if the symptoms become chronic. Some patients with generous health insurance can bypass the gatekeeper and seek care directly from a specialist without a referral from their family practitioner. The traditional patient-physician relationship operates on a hierarchy and is based on patient compliance with physician recommendations.

Women physicians probe more into patients' social and emotional health than do men physicians, and their style of communication more often reflects a desire for patients to ask questions and act as collaborators in their own health care. Current trends toward patient-centered care aim to promote this type of communication in all patient-physician interactions, but it may not be effective for all patients or for all physicians. Patients who are accustomed to traditional medical relationships, or whose cultural propensities are strongly oriented toward deference to authority, and who expect the doctor to take charge may be put off by collaborative approaches to medical care and may even be suspicious of their quality of care when their physician asks them, "How should we approach this problem?" Collaborative approaches may be ineffective in certain types of medical situations, such as a critical emergency. Traditional gender roles attribute leadership and decision-making skills to men, and those skills may be lacking or overlooked when displayed by women in emergency settings.

Although there has been considerable speculation that women patients prefer a collaborative style of treatment, such a conclusion is oversimplified, as factors such as patient age and type of medical issue influence preferences. A woman physician may be more likely than a man to inquire after the patient's support system and other psychosocial influences in their patients' lives, including the amount of stress experienced by the patient. Although some patients may appreciate this approach, others may view it as intrusion and interference. In fact, physician inquiries about stress and emotional health could seem counterproductive, given the inability that most people in the United States have to make significant changes in their work schedules, family life, and financial circumstances. In short, women physicians might make a contribution to improving the quality of patient care through a distinctive style of communication. However, communication skills are highly valued in any occupation, and the extent to which improved physician-patient communication actually enhances quality of care is unknown. Conversely, research shows that, regarding the actual provision of medical treatment, there are only minor differences between men and women physicians.

PATIENT PREFERENCE FOR SAME-SEX PHYSICIANS

In the past, men patients have been privileged by the availability of same-sex physicians for physical exams and interviews related to medical services of an intimate nature. The discomfort and embarrassment experienced by patients in such a situation can be a deterrent to medical care. Men as patients do not utilize medical care at the same high rates as women, and men generally wait until a medical condition becomes serious or particularly troublesome before seeking the intervention of a medical professional. If women physicians are to provide the majority of general practice care, including physical exams for diagnostic purposes, men patients are apt to be more reluctant to seek comprehensive treatment for medical conditions. It is important to note, though, that studies of patient interaction may be oversimplified, and in reality these interactions may be more complicated and involve any number of physician-patient gender matches and mismatches.

Furthermore, studies have not shown that men and women as patients prefer different types of relationships with their medical providers. A patient's preference for a specific type of physician-patient relationship has been associated, though, with specific types of medical conditions, such as the presence of a chronic condition. Patients with chronic conditions requiring regular consultation with their physician do tend to prefer a collaborative approach to their care, in which decisions are made mutually, and with regard to the social and psychological milieu of the patient, but this preference is based on the patient's condition, not his or her gender.

ABSENCE FROM AREAS OF HIGH NEED

Women physicians will not improve the quality of patient care because, contrary to what many assume, they are less likely than men physicians to fill positions of high need. It is true that, according to the American Association of Medical Colleges, women physicians are more likely than men to enter primary care fields, and this trend is projected to continue. The 2010 Patient Protection and Affordable Health Care Act (ACA) will insure as many as 35 million Americans for basic health care services and will increase the demand for primary care physicians, already in short supply in the United States. However, these projections overlook the evolution of the age structure of the United States, in which baby boomers (as of this writing, those 60 years old and up) constitute the largest population of citizens needing medical care. Therefore, in the near future, a substantial need will exist for specialists in fields of particular relevance for older Americans, including cardiologists, gerontologists, orthopedists, oncologists, and nephrologists. The physician shortage, in other words, will not be limited to primary care doctors. Women doctors are significantly less likely to enter these specialty areas than are men. Thus, women patients who prefer to receive medical treatment from a same-sex physician may be unable to satisfy that preference if they require the services of specialists.

GEOGRAPHIC LOCATION: SCARCITY IN RURAL AREAS

Communities in rural areas of the United States are experiencing physician shortages at substantially higher rates than urban areas, establishing rural regions as areas of high need (Phillips et al., 2009). Women are particularly unlikely to affect the quality of health care in rural areas due to several unique challenges faced by women physicians in those locales. Rural doctors are more likely to practice alone or in small groups, lacking ready access to consultants and referral specialists. Women doctors seem to be less comfortable practicing under such circumstances, and they, more so than men, object to the difficulties of separating personal and professional life in small rural communities.

The report by Phillips and colleagues, issued by the Macy Foundation, shows that male physicians are more likely than women to begin and remain in practice in rural areas. Rural health care is a critical need for the United States and most other developed countries. The isolation of rural practice is a greater barrier to women physicians than men. Women physicians report a greater desire than do men for significant amounts of social support, among both professional colleagues and personal friends. Women physicians who have delayed marriage until after medical school are unlikely to move to rural areas to begin a practice because of a quantifiable lack of potential romantic partners. Women doctors may also face a limited pool of similarly educated professional women friends in such locales. Spouses of married women physicians often face difficulty in rural areas finding employment related to their training and education, and rural areas lack support services such as daycare centers, dry-cleaning services, and meal preparation and delivery services, which are disproportionately important for women physicians in balancing work and family life (McGuire, Bergen, & Polan, 2004).

JOB STRUCTURES AND AUTONOMY

Women physicians tend to fill salaried positions within an established practice or hospital, leaving them less freedom to act upon distinctive orientations toward medical practice, even if such gender-based orientations exist. The types of entrepreneurial medical practices that allow that type of freedom are disappearing as an increasing proportion of physicians affiliate themselves with managed care organizations, and women doctors—typically seeking more regularity in their work hours and on-call responsibilities—have affiliated with such organizations more readily than have men doctors (Phillips et al., 2009). In such a practice setting, women physicians lack autonomy and their practice behaviors are highly regulated, limiting their ability to substantially transform medical practice in ways that benefit patient care.

When primary care physicians operate as gatekeepers, as they usually do under their terms of association with managed care organizations, referrals to specialists are made after an initial exam and consultation with a patient's primary care physician. Referral networks in any field operate on personal and professional connections; women specialists whose skills are devalued due to their gender, or who are not on the professional radar of their primary care colleagues will receive fewer referrals for new patients, creating difficulties for a woman physician to maintain a specialty practice by relying on referrals from networks from which she might be excluded or marginalized. In fact, a 2004 study listed seven major factors that influenced the choice of a specialist by a primary care practitioner; of these seven factors, five are highly subjective, including the perceived medical skill of the specialist, the primary care practitioner's previous experience with the specialist, the quality of specialist communication, the specialist's efforts to return the patient to the primary physician for care, and the likelihood of good patient-specialist rapport (Kinchen, Cooper, Levine, Wang, & Powe, 2004). (The other two factors were related to insurance coverage and appointment timeliness.) In networks where women are alienated or whose skills are devalued due to their gender, these factors operate against women specialists relying on referrals.

ABSENCE FROM POSITIONS OF POWER AND INFLUENCE

Women physicians will not improve the quality of patient care because they are not represented in positions of influence. Judith Lorber, in her 1984 book *Women Physicians,* demonstrates the subtle but powerful ways in which women are marginalized from powerful positions in medicine, regardless of their competence. Linda Pololi, in *Changing the Culture of Academic Medicine* (2010), shows how the culture of academic medical institutions continues to devalue women and constrain their influence. Even when women in medicine do have distinctive ideas about how medical practice might affect patient care, they often lack the clout in important institutions to influence how patient care is delivered beyond their own practices.

Women doctors are less likely than men to hold positions of influence and prestige within the medical community, including as university faculty and administrators, and medical researchers. A cohort study of women in academic medicine shows both that women's career development lags behind that of their men counterparts, and that the number of women being hired as assistant professors is increasing while fewer women physicians than expected are being hired as associate and full professors (Nonnemaker, 2000). According to the Association of American Medical Colleges, women faculty in medical schools are more likely than men to fill assistant and associate professor positions and are more likely than men to be untenured or off the tenure track. They also are scarce in top administrative positions: In 2001, only 11 deans of 126 medical schools in the United States were women (Darves, 2005). Men doctors fill a disproportionately large share of the more stable, more prestigious, and better compensated full professor positions (Ash, Carr, Goldstein, & Friedman, 2004). Most women therefore are excluded from making important policy decisions affecting admission, curriculum, instruction, and personnel decisions in medical schools.

Moreover, since women are disproportionately located in junior faculty positions, they have faced greater competition for research funding, which is essential to the advancement of careers of medical researchers but has become significantly more difficult to obtain as a result of recent recession-based cutbacks in federal and private funding for medical research. Women doctors are less likely than men to serve as principal investigators on research grants, signifying that women doctors have less influence than men over the central focus of medical research. Therefore, if women doctors have special skills and interests that might be related to improvement in the quality of patient care, such as particular concerns about women's health topics, their lack of influence within the medical community limits the potential impact they would exert.

Women in medicine are also susceptible to what Judith Lorber (1984) calls "the Salieri phenomenon," in which a gatekeeper exploits an individual's marginalization within a professional community in order to deprive the individual of recognition for her talents and accomplishments. This exploitation occurs unbeknownst to both the individual and the figure of authority for whom the gatekeeper maintains access. The Salieri phenomenon demonstrates that an individual who remains socially disconnected from persons in positions of authority and influence within their professional or personal community will lack the access needed to promote oneself and one's accomplishments.

In a practical sense, the Salieri phenomenon constrains the careers of women physicians in several ways. Medical careers, especially in the most influential positions, are highly structured, with established professionals wielding an incredible amount of influence on careers of younger aspirants. Women doctors are frequently marginalized from mentorship at all stages of their careers, and they are unlikely to gain access to the most influential positions in medical education or medical administration. Because of this estrangement, women doctors may lack understanding of the politics of medical organizations. Worse, women who put in fewer hours at the office, or on office-related tasks, may be contributing to their own marginalization; if other physicians in their practice question women's professional commitment, women's professional rewards will be reduced, and the cycle of marginalization and estrangement will be perpetuated (Bickel, 2000).

Women professionals also tend to be less professionally connected than men. The act of networking, whether it includes attendance at national conferences or drinks after work with the rest of the staff, has been less of a priority for women professionals than for men. Whether women have only recently learned the importance of networking and self-promotion, whether they lack the time, the inclination, or the childcare for it, or whether the male-dominated networks explicitly exclude them, women's traditional lack of engagement in this nonwork, work-related activity has been implicated in the failure of women professionals to reach the heights of success and prestige in their fields.

Moreover, traditional gender roles encourage men to assume that their qualifications are adequate for the tasks they desire to undertake, while women tend to base evaluations of their qualifications on their actual qualifications and experiences. Understanding the political machine in an organization becomes less urgent to women than proving that they can accomplish the tasks they undertake. These same gender roles have conditioned women to downplay their own accomplishments and to deny any interest in promotion, authority, power, and influence, as well as to deny expectations of equal attention and available resources.

LACK OF POLITICAL CLOUT BEYOND PRACTICE

Women physicians also are poorly represented in professional associations and policymaking organizations, although overall they are more politically active than their men counterparts. Women physicians are more likely than men to express support for organized labor in the form of unions, and many of the special interests championed by women physicians as women's health advocates are politically charged. However, because women physicians are not in positions of decision-making authority within their organizations and administrations, they are limited in their abilities to pursue their unique research agendas, introduce innovations in curriculum, or champion particular political causes.

CONCLUSION

Although it is generally supported that physicians of different genders communicate differently with patients, research literature regarding approaches to medicine and actual administration of care has not revealed significant gender-based differences. If gender-based differences in doctors' practice behaviors exist that will improve the quality of health care, these improvements can only be realized on a small scale, in one-on-one interactions between women physicians and their patients. Women's lack of representation in positions of influence and authority in areas such as medical academia and administration, which has been fairly resistant to change, limits their potential to create widespread change in physician-patient relationships or the conventions that govern medical practice. This pattern is perpetuated when women physicians are more likely than men physicians to enter medical specialties with regular hours, lower wages, and less prestige in an effort to maintain a more accommodating work-family balance.

With an increase in the number of women physicians providing family practice–type care, the aging population may find that they are unable to satisfy their preferences for same-sex physicians. The lesser productivity of women physicians, especially women who are mothers, remains an important policy issue for meeting projected future needs for physician services in the United States. The social perception of women physicians also reinforces long-held stereotypes about women in medicine that could actually disadvantage their patients. Thus, an increase in proportions of doctors who are women is unlikely to result in fundamental change in the delivery of medical care and the quality of care for patients.

REFERENCES AND FURTHER READING

Arnst, C. (2008, April 17). Are there too many women doctors? *Bloomberg BusinessWeek.* Retrieved from http://www.businessweek.com/magazine/content/08_17/b4081104183847.htm

Ash, A. S., Carr, P. L., Goldstein, R., & Friedman, R. H. (2004). Compensation and advancement of women in academic medicine: Is there equity? *Annals of Internal Medicine, 141*(3), 205–212.

Association of American Medical Colleges: Center for Workforce Studies. (2008). *Physician specialty data.* Retrieved from https://www.aamc.org/download/47352/data/specialtydata.pdf

Bickel, J. W. (2000). *Women in medicine: Getting in, growing, and advancing.* Thousand Oaks, CA: Sage.

Boulis, A. K., & Jacobs, J. A. (2008). *The changing face of medicine: Women doctors and the evolution of health care in America.* New York, NY: Cornell University Press.

Chen, P. (2010, May 10). Do women make better doctors? *The New York Times.* Retrieved from http://www.nytimes.com/2010/05/06/health/06chen.html

Darves, B. (2005, April). *Women in medicine force change in workforce dynamics.* Waltham, MA: NEJM Career Center. Retrieved from http://www.nejmjobs.org/career-resources/women-in-medicine.aspx

Grant, L. (1989). The gender climate of medical school: Perspectives of women and men students. *Journal of the American Medical Women's Association, 43*(4), 109–110, 115–119.

Hinze, S. W. (2004). Women, men, career and family in the U.S. young physician labor force. In N. Ditomaso & C. Post (Eds.), *Research in the Sociology of Work* (Diversity in the Workforce, Vol. 14, pp. 185–217). London, UK: Emerald Group Publishing.

Kinchen, K. S., Cooper, L. A., Levine, D., Wang, N. Y., & Powe, N. R. (2004). Referral of patients to specialists: Factors affecting choice of specialist by primary care physicians. *Annals of Family Medicine, 2*(3), 245–252.

Klein, M. C., Liston, R., Fraser, W. D., Baradaran, N., Hearps, S., Tomkinson, J., et al. (2011). Attitudes of the new generation of Canadian obstetricians: How do they differ from their predecessors? *Birth: Issues in Prenatal Care, 38*(2), 129–139.

Leserman, J. (1981). *Men and women in medical school: How they change and how they compare.* New York, NY: Praeger.

Lorber, J. (1984). *Women physicians.* London, UK: Tavistock.

McGuire, L. K., Bergen, M. R., & Polan, M. L. (2004). Career advancement for women faculty in a U.S. school of medicine: Perceived needs. *Academic Medicine, 79*(4), 319–325.

McKinstry, B. (2008). Are there too many female medical graduates? Yes. *British Medical Journal, 336*(7647), 748.

McMurray, J. E., Graham, A., Cohen, M., Gavel, P., Harding, J., Paice, E., Schmittdiel, J., & Grumbach, K. (2002). Women in medicine: A four-nation comparison. *Journal of the American Medical Women's Association, 57*(4), 185–190.

McMurray, J. E., Linzer, M., Konrad, T. R., Douglas, J., Shugerman, R., & Nelson, K. (2000). The work lives of women physicians: Results from the physician work life study. *Journal of General Internal Medicine, 15*(6), 372–380.

Nonnemaker, L. (2000). Women physicians in academic medicine—New insights from cohort studies. *New England Journal of Medicine, 342*(6), 399–405.

Ochberg, R. L., Barton, G. M., & West, A. N. (1989). Women physicians and their mentors. *Journal of the American Medical Women's Association, 44*(4), 123–126.

Phillips, R. L., Dodoo, M. S., Petterson, S., Xierali, I., Bazemore, A., Teevan, B., et al. (2009). *Specialty and geographic distribution of the physician workforce: What influences medical student and resident choices?* (Report of the Josiah Macy Foundation). Washington, DC: The Robert Graham Center.

Pololi, L. (2010). *Changing the culture of academic medicine: Perspectives of women faculty.* Hanover, NH: Dartmouth University Press.

Shrier, D. K., Zucker, A. N., Mercurio, A. E., Landry, L. J., Rich, M., & Shrier, L. A. (2007). Generation to generation: Discrimination and harassment experiences of physician mothers and their physician daughters. *Journal of Women's Health, 16*(6), 883–894.

Aubrey Denmon and Linda Grant

30

Ethnic Background of Physicians and Patients

POINT: When a physician and a patient are of matching ethnic backgrounds, the patient is more comfortable, and the care ends up being of higher quality. Minority providers spend more time with patients and care more about them; they are also more interested in the underprivileged.

Marsha Regenstein, Ellie Andres, and Dylan Nelson, George Washington University School of Public Health and Health Services, Department of Health Policy

COUNTERPOINT: The ethnic backgrounds of the physicians are not relevant to the quality of care they provide. Quality of care relates to understanding the needs of different patient groups, and understanding the special needs of racial/ethnic minorities is possible whatever the background of the provider. Minority providers want career paths similar to other providers.

Marsha Regenstein, Ellie Andres, and Dylan Nelson, George Washington University School of Public Health and Health Services, Department of Health Policy

Introduction

When a patient and physician share a common culture, place of origin, or native language, they are said to be ethnically *concordant.* In health care services research, the importance of racial or ethnic concordance in a patient-physician relationship has been a topic of discussion for many years. Some experts argue that concordance may provide a sense of harmony, comfort, or shared understanding through the common experience of ethnic heritage (or, in the case of those who speak a foreign language, a common experience through being able to understand that language and the nuances of differences in description of bodily complaints). Patients may feel an increased sense of comfort with a racially or ethnically concordant physician, who they believe understands their background and will provide care in a way that makes sense to them.

This is not a new concern in American society. Over 100 years ago, when people from a variety of different European ethnic backgrounds were migrating to the United States, there was a growth of new hospitals created by those ethnic groups. Catholic hospitals brought both nurses connected with Catholic nursing orders and physicians from first Irish, and then Italian and Polish backgrounds, along with the presentation of more ethnic foods for patients. Similarly, Jewish hospitals, according to Charles E. Rosenberg in his 1987 book *The Care of Strangers: The Rise of the American Hospital System,* were also created to have a place for both Jewish physicians to practice and for Jewish patients to be sure that Jewish dietary restrictions were carefully followed. Newer immigrant groups that arrived later, such as Asians and Latinos, have largely not tried to build hospitals to cater to their specific group. The concern about having a health care provider either with a similar background or who understands cultural issues remains a concern for some, but certainly not all, patients.

In the past few decades, a growing concern has been racial and ethnic disparities in health and use of health care services (Kronenfeld, 2009; Williams & Sternthal, 2010). Scholars from many different disciplines, including many of the social sciences and public health, have participated in these discussions and pointed out several issues linked to concordance that have not been covered well in the past. In their 2010 article "Understanding Racial and Ethnic Disparities in Health: Sociological Contributions," published in *Journal of Health and Social Behavior,* which summarizes sociological contributions to understanding racial and ethnic disparities in health, Williams and Sternthal discuss four major contributions from a sociological perspective. One is the challenge to a biological definition of race. The second is an emphasis on the primacy of social structure and context as determinants of racial and ethnic differences in disease. The third is a more developed understanding of the ways in which racism has impacted health. The fourth is a focus on how migration history and status have impacted health. Writing from this approach, other researchers, such as David T. Takeuchi, Emily Walton, and Man Chui Leung, in "Race, Social Contexts and Health: Examining Geographic Spaces and Places," published in the *Handbook of Medical Sociology*, have focused on social contexts linked to geography and residence and their impact on health and health care use. These researchers have pointed out that residential segregation of racial and ethnic groups have led to certain problems, but have also sometimes helped with creation of health care settings with greater cultural congruence between some workers and people receiving care.

Work from both of these approaches has also pointed out how lack of racial and ethnic concordance, at some points in history, has been an important factor in use of health care services, although many social scientists would argue this is of less importance in recent years, as there has been an emphasis across the health care system on increasing the cultural sensitivity of providers. In health professions' education today, future physicians and nurses are taught about cultures different from their own and about the importance of understanding cultural variability in dealing with issues of health, illness, and death. In addition, both medical and nursing schools are more concerned with having students from a diversity of racial and ethnic backgrounds, something which was not common 50 years ago when the most typical medical student was a white man, often without any strong ethnic identification.

The debate in this chapter addresses whether or not it is important for patients and health care providers to be of matching ethnic background. Some of the reasons why concordance is positive are factors such as the amount of time spent with patients and ease of communication. Communication is so important because most patient visits begin with interaction and communication between the patient and physician, as in the taking of a medical history and the discussion of the problems the patient is having. In addition, it can be important for communication to occur in both directions, and when patients are comfortable with their physicians, they are more likely to ask questions and share details. Being able to communicate in one's native language is another factor. Although most health care facilities will bring in interpreters if the health care provider does not speak the language of the patient, not everyone agrees on whether a third-party interpreter is sufficiently able to communicate on behalf of a patient.

The Counterpoint argues, however, that there are many complex aspects of what we define as quality care, and concordance on race/ethnicity is not the most critical factor in the determination of quality of care. Though paying attention to equity of care is important as is the care being patient centered, there are a variety of ways to meet those goals other than concordance on race/ethnicity, and the Counterpoint reviews some of those approaches. In addition, the chapter points out that proposed changes are underway within the health care delivery system, especially some linked to new regulations that stem from the Patient Protection and Affordable Care Act of 2010. Some of those changes may lead to linking the amount of payments the government makes to hospitals to their performance on publicly available performance scores, as well as the adoption of related policies for physician payments, and these could provide other aspects of assuring quality of care to all patients, including racial and ethnic minorities even without concordance of patients and providers on racial/ethnic characteristics.

POINT

When patients and physicians have the same ethnic or racial heritage or background, they are said to be ethnically or racially *concordant*. A patient and physician who are ethnically concordant may share a common culture, place of origin, or native language. Racial or ethnic concordance in a patient-physician relationship may provide a sense of harmony or shared understanding through the common experience of ethnic heritage. Patients may feel an increased sense of comfort with a racially or ethnically concordant physician, who they believe understands their background and will provide care in a way that makes sense to them. The concept of concordance applies to other characteristics beyond race and ethnicity, such as gender, age, language, sexual orientation, and social class.

Racial and ethnic concordance in health care is not a new concept. Historically, many patients and their physicians have been racially concordant by default, largely as a result of the long and regrettable history of slavery and racial segregation in the United States. Whites have commonly been treated by white physicians and blacks, if treated at all, have often been treated by black physicians trained primarily in a small number of medical schools associated with historically black colleges and universities. Hospitals were not officially desegregated until the passage of Medicare in 1965, which required health care organizations that received any federal funding (including payments from the newly passed Medicare and Medicaid programs) to comply with civil rights legislation barring discriminatory practices. Black students were barred from admission to most medical schools in the United States until after 1865, when several medical schools for blacks were established, leading to a host of inequities in the care of blacks that have persisted to this day.

RATIONALE FOR PATIENT-PHYSICIAN ETHNIC CONCORDANCE

Many studies have shown that racial and ethnic minorities tend to receive lower-quality health care and have poorer health outcomes than do nonminorities (Smedley, Stith, & Nelson, 2003). Factors such as income, education, and insurance coverage may contribute in part to these discrepancies in health and health care, as minorities generally have lower incomes, less education, and less access to health insurance coverage. Yet, studies suggest that these differences in health and health care, known as health disparities, persist even after accounting for other socioeconomic or health-related factors. For example, blacks are much more likely to have a chronic disease or disability than whites, regardless of income level. Additionally, infant mortality rates, which measure the number of deaths at birth and through the first year of life, are much higher among blacks despite equal access to prenatal care (due to concerted efforts to improve access for black mothers). Although infant mortality declined by 45.2 percent for all races from 1980 to 2000 (from 12.6 to 6.9 deaths per 1,000 live births), the decline was greater for whites than for blacks; infant mortality among whites declined 47.7 percent (from 10.9 to 5.7 deaths per 1,000 live births) and infant mortality among blacks declined 36.9 percent (from 22.2 to 14.0 deaths per 1,000 live births) (CDC Morbidity and Mortality Weekly Report, 2002). Despite substantial improvements over two decades, infant mortality rates for blacks remained more than double the rate of whites. Striking disparities are evident in virtually all areas of health care.

There are complex reasons for these disparities and no one factor can fully account for the extent to which quality of care differs between racial and ethnic groups. However, over the last two decades many scholars have come to the conclusion that a key contributor to overall quality is the relationship that is formed between patients and physicians. These relationships require effective communication and are built on trust, respect, and a commitment to create a partnership to advance health and well being. Providing patients the option to select racially and ethnically concordant physicians is an important strategy to reduce disparities between different racial and ethnic groups. By providing patients the opportunity to select physicians with similar racial and ethnic backgrounds, patients feel more comfortable with their health professional. If patients are comfortable with their physicians, the patient-physician relationship is enhanced and is less likely to contribute to disparities in care.

For many patients, particularly minorities, sharing the same ethnicity as their physician is a matter of comfort and is similar to the way a patient might prefer to see physicians of the same gender. Selection of physicians in part based on gender concordance is common among female patients seeking primary care providers such as physicians in internal medicine, family practice, obstetrics and gynecology, and pediatrics (Garcia, Paterniti, Romano, & Kravitz, 2003). Choosing one's doctor based on the doctor's gender has become routine for certain patients and does not carry with it the controversy that may arise in making race- or ethnicity-based decisions in terms of physician preference. Yet the same issues are at play in both of these situations; just as patients should have the ability to select physicians based on gender, so too should they be able to select physicians based on race or ethnicity. In practice, when given a choice of physician, minority patients are more likely than are white patients to indicate that they took the race or ethnicity of the physician into consideration.

Much of the information that is known about minority patients' sentiments related to racial and ethnic concordance with physicians comes from two surveys conducted by the Commonwealth Fund, a health foundation that has tracked issues related to quality of care for minorities over the past two decades (Cooper & Powe, 2004; Cooper et al., 2003). Among other findings, one of the surveys found that about one in four black patients prefer a black physician, one in five Hispanic or Latino patients prefer a Hispanic physician, and about one in 20 white patients prefer a white physician. Two overarching concerns have been identified as influencing those preferences—trust and understanding.

TRUST

At the heart of a strong patient-physician relationship is the belief that the physician will act in the patient's best interests (Blanchard & Lurie, 2004). A patient who trusts his or her physician is more likely to believe that the physician has his or her best interests in mind. Trust has critically important implications for quality of care and is a dimension of the physician-patient relationship that transcends patient preference alone. Research shows that patients who trust their physicians are more likely to accept diagnosis and follow the doctor's recommended course of treatment (Keating et al., 2002; Trachtenberg, Dugan, & Hall, 2005). This includes taking recommended medicines and making lifestyle changes related to diet and exercise, all of which are necessary to improve health (Cooper & Powe, 2004; Cooper et al., 2003). Trust in a patient-physician relationship is essential for patient comfort and willingness to engage in a productive partnership to improve health.

Trust is a particularly important consideration for minorities, who have lower levels of trust in providers overall and report less involvement in and satisfaction with care. Racial and ethnic minorities are less likely to feel respected as full partners in the decision-making process with their physicians, and compared to white patients, minority patients experience greater difficulty communicating with physicians and report being treated with disrespect more frequently (Collins et al., 2002). Racial or ethnic concordance in a patient-physician relationship essentially removes the potential for distrust associated with racial or ethnic discrimination from the patient-physician relationship. Similarly, distrustful or negative perceptions of members of different ethnic groups based on stereotypes or other historical tensions are irrelevant in concordant patient-physician relationships. Even though patients or providers may not actually harbor discriminatory thoughts, perceptions of what the other thinks could negatively impact the relationship. Allowing patients the opportunity to select concordant physicians enhances trust and the productivity and partnership of the patient-physician relationship.

CULTURAL UNDERSTANDING

Race and ethnicity is closely related to culture for many Americans. Culture is a significant predictor of patients' decisions about their health, as well as the barriers they may encounter as they seek to make lifestyle changes prescribed by their physicians to improve health. Culture can affect foods eaten, gender roles, preferences for family involvement in care, and countless other issues that affect health.

For example, different cultures are distinguished by traditional foods, cultural expectations related to food, and gatherings around food. Given this strong focus, it is often difficult for patients to change their diets to improve health. It can be particularly challenging if the patient's health care provider does not share or understand their culture and suggests courses of action that are unrealistic or unfamiliar to the patient. Physicians may be unaware of food preparation techniques or specific types of foods that contribute to unhealthy diets. Ironically, merely suggesting to patients that they eat more vegetables or lean meats could also inadvertently increase intake of unhealthy fats, salt, and sugar, which are used to prepare certain goods. Patients may feel more comfortable seeing physicians with the same ethnic backgrounds who are more likely to understand cultural norms related to food and can help craft plans of action with these considerations in mind.

Similarly, different cultures may have distinct understandings of illness or disease and particular notions of what constitutes appropriate care. Patients from certain cultures may not feel comfortable taking certain medicines, or undergoing a diagnostic test or procedure, based on their cultural understanding of illness and disease. For example, patients from some cultures interpret seizures or other conditions as signs of spiritual or other afflictions that cannot be cured with medication. Many cultures regularly use herbs or other alternative therapies instead of the treatment plans their physicians prescribe. Physicians from the same cultures are familiar with cultural practices that are unknown to physicians who are not members of that ethnic group. Often, patients do not tell physicians from different ethnic groups about these practices, either because they do not consider them relevant to the physician-patient encounter, or because they believe they will be judged by the physician as inappropriate for care. These gaps in communication can be quite dangerous for example, if the physician prescribes medications that have unsafe interactions with the therapies or alternative medicines that the patient is using. Racial or ethnic concordance in the patient-physician relationship may help to bridge gaps in knowledge about the sources of illness and the appropriate treatment strategies.

Physicians must understand and respect cultural expectations or constraints and develop skills in the area of *cultural competence,* a term that refers to "the ability of health systems and health professionals to provide care to patients with diverse values, beliefs and behaviors, including tailoring delivery to meet patients' social, cultural, and linguistic needs" (Betancourt, Green, & Carrillo, 2002, p. 3). For many patients, assumptions about the physician's level of cultural competence may affect their decisions about seeking care. If patients think doctors will not accept or accommodate their culture and practices, they may delay or avoid care altogether. Often, patients will seek out physicians of their own culture or background as a way of enhancing the likelihood of finding a culturally competent practitioner.

THE EFFECTS OF PATIENT-PROVIDER CONCORDANCE

Given the many reasons that patients may have for choosing a physician of their own race or ethnicity, it should be no surprise that minority patients who are given a choice of provider often exercise their ability to receive care from a minority physician.

The patient-provider relationship is enhanced when patients see themselves as similar to their physicians in personal beliefs, culture, values, and communication based on shared ethnic background. A number of positive effects accrue to patients when they are able to choose concordant physicians, including enhanced patient-physician partnerships, better communication, more time with physicians, access to health professionals who are dedicated to improving minority health, and higher satisfaction (Cooper et al., 2003).

PARTNERSHIP WITH PROVIDERS

Not only do many patients choose concordant providers when they are available but they are also more likely to feel they are full partners in their care with concordant providers. Partnership in the patient-physician relationship is essential for obtaining patient buy-in and involvement in improving health and ensuring that care appropriately reflects the patient's needs and concerns. In concordant patient-physician relationships, patients are more likely to report taking an active, participatory role in their care. For example, Cooper-Patrick and colleagues surveyed approximately 1,800 patients between 1996 and 1998 and found that patients in race-concordant relationships rated their physicians as significantly more likely to involve patients in important decision making related to their care than patients in race-discordant relationships (1999). The sense of partnership patients feel with concordant physicians carries over and reaps benefits after they leave the doctor's office as well. Patients with concordant physicians are more likely to report following their doctor's recommendations, including taking their medications and making suggested lifestyle changes (van Wieringen, Harmsen, & Bruijnzeels, 2002).

MORE TIME MAKES BETTER COMMUNICATION

The adage "time is money" is particularly true in health care. Most physicians are paid on a "fee-for-service" basis, which means that the more patients a physician treats, the more money the physician can earn. In primary care settings composed mostly of checkups and examinations, physicians have a major financial incentive to make visits as brief as possible to maximize the number of patients they are able to see. Spending more time with one patient reduces physician compensation if it keeps them from seeing additional patients. Interestingly, research shows that physicians spend more time with patients of their own race. This is especially true for minority patients and physicians.

Not only do patients with concordant physicians spend more time with their physicians, but they are also likely to communicate more within the same amount of time (Cooper-Patrick et al., 1999; Gordon, Street, Sharf, & Souchek, 2006). Robust communication is a cornerstone of the patient-physician relationship. A standard part of any interaction between patient and physician, whether for a checkup or an emergency room visit, includes the physician asking the patient questions about how he feels, why he came in, the level of pain, medical history, whether or not he takes medications or has any allergies, and so on. This information exchange, commonly referred to as "taking the patient's history," is critical for ensuring the physician (or other health professional) has the appropriate level of understanding to provide effective treatment. Additionally, for effective communication to take place, patients need to be able to ask questions of their physicians.

When patients are comfortable with their physicians, they are more likely to ask questions and share details about their health. On average, minority patients communicate more with physicians of the same race, which leads to more complete information (Johnson et al., 2004). Patient-physician communication is also improved in concordant relationships. Studies have demonstrated that patients show higher levels of engagement, interest, friendliness, and responsiveness and physicians show higher levels of interest, friendliness, responsiveness, sympathy, and patience in concordant relationships than in discordant relationships (Cooper et al., 2003).

Additionally, many racial or ethnic minorities are immigrants who do not speak English proficiently to interact with their providers in English. Ethnically concordant physicians are more likely to speak the same language as their patients and are better able to communicate with those patients who cannot speak English. When physicians and patients do not speak the same language, interpreters are often used to facilitate communication and there is a significant body of research indicating that interpreters improve the quality of care (Flores, 2005). However, a one-on-one conversation between patients and physicians is clearly the preferred vehicle for communicating, especially when sensitive medical issues arise.

CARE FROM PHYSICIANS DEDICATED TO THE UNDERPRIVILEGED

As discussed above, in the United States minorities are much more likely to be affected by a number of diseases, to have inferior access to care, to be poor or homeless, and to have worse health outcomes when compared to whites (Smedley, Stith, & Nelson, 2003). Minority physicians are more likely to have come from communities with high populations of minorities and therefore are more likely to have witnessed firsthand the detrimental effects of poverty, poor health, and discrimination faced by their peers.

Many of these physicians feel the need to "give back" to the communities that produced them. Minority physicians are more likely to practice medicine in communities with high minority populations. This is beneficial for minority patients seeing concordant providers, because their physicians are more likely to "go the extra mile" for them. There are numerous challenges associated with taking care of impoverished patients, including seeing patients who lack health insurance, or whose insurance provides lower payment rates than other, more affluent patients. Also, patients who live in poor neighborhoods, who lack health insurance, who have lower levels of education, or who have less stable employment, tend to have higher rates of chronic health conditions that require more time from physicians when the patient comes in for a clinic or office visit. Research shows that minority physicians stand out in terms of caring for minority patients, particularly those who are underprivileged (Smedley, Stith, & Nelson, 2003).

SATISFACTION WITH CARE

Given all of the above benefits of receiving care from concordant providers, it is not surprising that patients are also more likely to be satisfied with care delivered by concordant providers. Regardless of race or ethnicity, patients are more satisfied with their care if their physician is a member of their own racial or ethnic group. Higher satisfaction with race-concordant physicians is particularly strong among African American patients who prefer a race-concordant physician. In a 2005 study, African Americans who preferred an African American physician who ended up receiving care from an African American were almost three times as likely to rate the physician as excellent, compared to African Americans who had a preference for race concordance but had a non–African American physician (Chen, Fryer, Phillips, Wilson, & Pathman, 2005). Overall, patients tend to indicate high satisfaction with their physicians, but satisfaction is higher in situations with racial or ethnic concordance.

CONCORDANT CARE IS PATIENT-CENTERED CARE

All of the effects of racial or ethnic concordance on care and health outcomes relate directly to the quality of health care that people receive. One particular dimension of quality centers around *patient-centered care,* a concept that crosses all categories of race, ethnicity, gender, or other characteristics but one that is particularly relevant to the discussion about concordance and culturally competent caregivers. The concept of patient-centered care is built on the notion that patients who feel comfortable in a health care setting are far more likely to feel empowered, satisfied with their care, receive high-quality care, follow their doctors' recommendation, and have improved health. To provide health care that is patient-centered, the physician and care setting must be oriented to the needs and wishes of the patient. Patients must be comfortable with both seeking care from their physician and discussing the intimate details of their medical history. When patients feel that their needs are being met, they are also more likely to feel empowered to take charge of their health, as well as trust that their care providers are doing all that they can to attain the best outcomes.

It is clear that racial and ethnic concordance between patients and physicians can assume critical importance in terms of the ability of the patient to receive—and the ability of the physician to deliver—patient-centered care. For a sizeable group of patients, a physician of the same race or ethnicity is what will make them feel most comfortable interacting with their physician and what will reassure them that their physician understands their lifestyle and culture. This sense of comfort with their concordant provider empowers them to become an active participant in their care.

CONCLUSION

Physicians of the same racial or ethnic background as their patients are able to develop deeper relationships than noncordant physicians can provide. A sense of shared experience allows for a bond that has been shown to have a number of positive effects on the provision of care for concordant patients. Conclusive evidence suggests that promoting the ability to see physicians of their same race has significant, positive effects for minority patients.

Patients must have the ability to choose their own physician, a practice recognized and supported by many health plans that provide information on the race, ethnicity, gender, and language(s) spoken by physicians in their provider networks. Racial or ethnic concordance is clearly not a magic bullet for eliminating racial and ethnic disparities in health and health care, but it should be supported as one important component of a larger strategy that will begin to close the gap in health outcomes and access between minorities and whites in America. Policymakers and health care leaders would be wise to heed the available evidence and use the common sense conclusions found with them to support greater diversity in the health care workforce and ensure that all patients are able to make informed decisions about which doctors they choose to see.

REFERENCES AND FURTHER READING

Beach, M. C., Price, E. G., Gary, T. L., Robinson, K. A., Gozu, A., Palacio, A., & Cooper, L. A. (2005). A systematic review of health care provider educational interventions. *Medical Care, 43*(4), 356–373.

Betancourt, J. R., Green, A. R., & Carrillo, J. E. (2002). *Cultural competence in health care: Emerging frameworks and practical approaches.* Washington, DC: The Commonwealth Fund.

Blanchard, J., & Lurie, N. (2004). R-E-S-P-E-C-T: Patient reports of disrespect in the health care setting and its impact on care. *The Journal of Family Practice, 53*(9), 721.

CDC. (2002, July 12). Infant mortality and low birth weight among black and white infants—United States, 1980–2000. *Morbidity and Mortality Weekly Report, 51*(27), 589–592.

Chen, F. M., Fryer, G. E., Phillips, R. L., Wilson, E., & Pathman, D. E. (2005). Patients' beliefs about racism, preferences for physician race, and satisfaction with care. *Annals of Family Medicine, 3*(2), 138–143.

Collins, K. S., Hughes, D. L., Doty, M. M., Ives, B. L., Edwards, J. N., & Tenney, K. (2002). *Diverse communities, common concerns: Assessing health care quality for minority Americans.* Washington, DC: The Commonwealth Fund.

Cooper, L. A., & Powe, N. R. (2004). *Disparities in patient experiences, health care processes, and outcomes: The role of patient-provider racial, ethnic, and language concordance.* Washington, DC: The Commonwealth Fund.

Cooper, L. A., Roter, D. L., Johnson, R. L., Ford, D. E., Steinwachs, D. M., & Powe, N. R. (2003). Patient-centered communication, ratings of care, and concordance of patient and physician race. *Annals of Internal Medicine, 139*(11), 907–915.

Cooper-Patrick, L., Gallo, J. J., Gonzales, J. J., Vu, H. T., Powe, N. R., Nelson, C., & Ford, D. E. (1999). Race, gender, and partnership in the patient-physician relationship. *The Journal of the American Medical Association, 282*(6), 583–589.

Duke University Medical Center. (1999). Black history month: A medical perspective. *History of Medicine Exhibit.* Retrieved from http://www.mclibrary.duke.edu/hom/exhibits/blkhist

Flores, G. (2005). The impact of medical interpreter services on the quality of health care: A systematic review. *Medical Care Research and Review, 62*(3), 255–299.

García, J. A., Paterniti, D. A., Romano, P. S., & Kravitz, R. L. (2003). Patient preferences for physician characteristics in university-based primary care clinics. *Ethnicity & Disease, 13*(2), 259–267.

Gordon, H. S., Street, R. L., Sharf, B. F., & Souchek, J. (2006). Racial differences in doctors' information-giving and patients' participation. *Cancer, 107*(6), 1313–1320.

Johnson, R. L., Roter, D. L., Powe, N., & Cooper, L. A. (2004). Patient race/ethnicity and quality of patient–physician communication during medical visits. *American Journal of Public Health, 94*(12), 2081–2090.

Keating, N. L., Green, D. C., Kao, A. C., Gazmararian, J. A., Wu, V. Y., & Cleary, P. D. (2002). How are patients' specific ambulatory care experiences related to trust, satisfaction, and considering changing physicians? *Journal of General Internal Medicine, 17*(1), 29–39.

Kronenfeld, J. J. (2009). Social sources of disparities in health and health care: An introduction to the volume. In J. J. Kronenfeld (Ed.), *Social sources of disparities in health and health care and linkages to policy, population concerns and providers of care.* Bingley, UK: Emerald Press.

Rosenberg, C. E. (1987). *The care of strangers: The rise of the American hospital system.* New York, NY: Basic Books.

Smedley, B. D., Stith, A. Y., & Nelson, A. R. (Eds.). (2003). *Unequal treatment: Confronting racial and ethnic disparities in health care.* Washington, DC: National Academies Press.

Takeuchi, D. T., Walton, E., & Leung, M. C. (2010). Race, social contexts and health: Examining geographic spaces and places. In C. E. Bird, P. Conrad, A. M. Fremont, & S. Timmermans (Eds.), *Handbook of medical sociology* (6th ed.). Nashville, TN: Vanderbilt University Press.

Trachtenberg, F., Dugan, E., & Hall, M. A. (2005). How patients' trust relates to their involvement in medical care: Trust in the medical profession is associated with greater willingness to seek care and follow recommendations. *The Journal of Family Practice, 54*(4), 344–352.

Van Wieringen, J. C., Harmsen, J. A., & Bruijnzeels, M. A. (2002). Intercultural communication in general practice. *European Journal of Public Health, 12*(1), 63–68.

Williams, D. R., & Sternthal, M. (2010). Understanding racial and ethnic disparities in health: Sociological contributions. *Journal of Health and Social Behavior. 51*(S): s12–s27.

Marsha Regenstein, Ellie Andres, and Dylan Nelson

COUNTERPOINT

Racial and ethnic disparities are a common, persistent, and dangerous reality of health care in America. In virtually every aspect of health and health care—whether the amount, quality, or appropriateness of care a person receives—minorities fare worse than whites. For example, over the past few decades numerous research studies have documented disparities related to heart care, with clear evidence that blacks are more likely to suffer from serious heart disease, less likely to manage heart problems effectively, less likely to receive sophisticated interventions or therapies for heart disease, and more likely to die prematurely from the disease (Smedley, Stith, & Nelson, 2003). Similar mountains of evidence document disparities in diabetes, cancer, and asthma; they also document disparities in primary care and preventative services, mental health care, and many other areas.

Understanding why racial and ethnic disparities exist is no simple task. A major contributor to disparate care is the design and structure of the U.S. health care system, in which the majority (62 percent) of non-elderly adults receive health care through their employment. The employer-based system favors full-time employees in larger businesses, where employees are more likely to participate in health insurance in a shared-cost arrangement with their employers. Unemployed, part-time, seasonal workers, or individuals who work in small businesses, may face substantial difficulties obtaining affordable health coverage. Because disproportionately high numbers of minorities are among this second group, disparities in health and health care are certainly rooted in the access barriers that are endemic to the employer-based insurance market.

The U.S. health care system offers certain low-income individuals the ability to enroll in Medicaid, a federal-state entitlement program that in 2010 provided health services to more than 60 million Americans (Kaiser Commission of Medicaid and the Uninsured, 2010). By virtue of having higher rates of poverty, minorities are overrepresented in the Medicaid program. Thus, millions of minority Americans gain access to the health system through Medicaid. However, Medicaid pays physicians far less for seeing Medicaid patients than physicians receive for privately insured patients or patients covered by Medicare, the public health insurance program for the elderly. This creates a disincentive for physicians to see Medicaid patients, and hence, it is often difficult for Medicaid patients to find primary care or specialty physicians who will see them.

These structural and access barriers undoubtedly contribute to disparate care in America, but a 2003 landmark report by the Institute of Medicine challenged the notion that they are the only driver of disparities (Smedley et al., 2003). In its 2003 report, *Unequal Treatment: Confronting Racial and Ethnic Disparities in Health Care,* the Institute of Medicine (IOM) conducted an extensive review of the evidence on disparities and concluded that disparities in care persist even when controlling for issues related to systemic factors, such as health insurance and access, or patient characteristics, such as poverty or education.

Since the IOM report, substantial research and policy focus has shifted from merely documenting disparities to determining the causes of disparities and identifying strategies to eliminate them. Chief among these strategies, and included as one of the IOM's recommendations for future action, was growing and expanding a diverse workforce to provide minority patients the opportunity to receive care from an ethnically or racially concordant physician. This recommendation was rooted in the belief that many of the manifestations of disparities can be eliminated through interactions with patients and physicians in concordant relationships. The belief was supported by evidence suggesting that patients are more satisfied with concordant physicians, that they have higher levels of trust in concordant physicians, and that they will become more engaged and active participants in their health care when in a trusting relationship with a physician who acts as a supportive partner (Saha, Komaromy, Koepsell, & Bindman, 1999).

The notion of concordance between patient and provider has gained popularity as a potential mechanism to reduce racial and ethnic disparities in America. This essay does not argue against this approach, per se. Many studies have shown that minorities are more likely than whites to indicate a preference for a concordant physician; the strongest indications for satisfaction and trust within a patient-physician relationship occur when a patient who prefers a racially or ethnically concordant physician actually receives care from a physician from that racial or ethnic group.

Nevertheless, focusing on concordance as a vehicle for reducing racial and ethnic disparities will result in unacceptably low levels of improvement in care for minority Americans. In a survey of public perceptions of medical care related to race and ethnicity, only about one in five blacks indicated a preference for a black physician and about one in four Latinos preferred a Latino physician (Kaiser Family Foundation, 1999). The vast majority of patients—regardless of race or ethnicity—want a physician who is available to them, who is skilled and knows how to care for them, who can communicate effectively with them, who will give them the time they need, who will treat them with respect (both for their person and their time), and who provides a clean, safe space for an office visit. In short, people want to see a good doctor who will give them the care they need when they need it.

WHAT IS HIGH-QUALITY CARE?

Much progress has been made over the past decade in defining, measuring, and developing strategies around health care quality. The IOM has also served a key role in consolidating information around quality and developing policy and practice recommendations to advance quality in the United States. In 1999 the IOM created a committee of leaders in health, business, policy, and ethics to study issues related to health care quality in the United States and offer recommendations to create a better functioning health system. As part of that process, the IOM proposed six aims for improvement, targeting areas that, according to the committee's assessment, were functioning at "far lower levels than they can and should." These six aims were published in one of the committee's reports in 2001, *Crossing the Quality Chasm: A New Health System for the 21st Century,* and have served as a guidepost and road map for quality-related initiatives throughout the decade.

Health care should be:

- *Safe,* avoiding injuries to patients from the care that is intended to help them;
- *Effective,* providing services based on scientific knowledge to all who could benefit and refraining from providing services to those not likely to benefit (avoiding underuse and overuse, respectively);

- *Patient centered,* providing care that is respectful of and responsive to individual patient preferences, needs, and values and ensuring that patient values guide all clinical decisions;

- *Timely,* reducing sometimes harmful delays for both those who receive and those who give care;

- *Efficient,* avoiding waste, including waste of equipment, supplies, ideas, and energy; and

- *Equitable,* providing equally high levels of care to all patients.

The IOM domains of quality address many of the core values inherent in patient-physician concordance, but add elements that embed evidence-based medicine and processes for effective practice into routine patient care. It is only through the pursuit of these six domains of quality—as well as ensuring access to health care and other health programs—that real progress will be made to reduce or eliminate racial and ethnic disparities.

Each of the domains of quality requires the same types of skills, experience, and commitment to care envisioned in the concordant relationship. For example, the safety domain involves creating systems of care and practices to reduce medical errors, to eliminate negative outcomes in treatments, and to provide the safest possible experience to all patients. Hundreds of studies have been published indicating that medication-related errors are common, with the effects ranging from negligible to severe, and with some resulting in the death of the patient. Clearly, effective communication between patients and physicians is a critically important aspect of safety. The ability of the patient and physician to understand each other, clarify allergies or other reasons that a particular medication should not be prescribed, communicate freely and openly, and explain the correct dosage or administration of a medication will reduce the chances that dangerous medication errors will occur. But so, too, will "systems" that take some judgment and the possibility of memory lapses out of the equation. Physicians who use electronic health records that document a patient's medication history and have the ability to match the patient's history and current medication use with safety information can receive alerts when dosage instructions are not appropriate for the particular patient and can flag situations where patients have been prescribed medications with unsafe or potentially troublesome interactions. Likewise, widespread initiatives to reduce the rate of hospital-acquired infections—an event that is responsible for more than 99,000 deaths each year—revolve around systems of improvement that draw upon the best scientific evidence to determine safe care and how it can be routinely incorporated into daily practice. Hand-washing campaigns in hospitals are an example of a simple intervention that has required extraordinary efforts to embed into everyday care. Such simple techniques, however, are helping to significantly reduce hospital-acquired infections. The safer the care provided to all patients across-the-board, the less likely that racial and ethnic disparities related to safety will persist.

The same situation applies to *effective* care, which strives to provide the right services to any and all individuals who can benefit from that care. This is an especially important quality concern when it comes to racial and ethnic disparities, because minorities frequently receive less care compared to white patients. But minorities are not the only people who do not get the care they need. A 2003 study by Elizabeth McGlynn and colleagues from the RAND Corporation identified a set of services that were considered necessary for a variety of health conditions and also included services associated with routine primary care and prevention. McGlynn found that on average, people in the United States received about half of the care they needed; minorities received what they needed even less often, only about 40 percent of the time (McGlynn et al., 2003). The fact that Americans receive half or less of the care they need is particularly troublesome in light of the fact that they pay far more for their health care than any other nation in the world. It does not matter how the numbers are calculated, the United States spends more—more per person, and more as a percent of its total economy, compared to other countries. And yet Americans get less of the health care they need.

The figures suggest vast opportunities to improve quality for millions of Americans, including racial and ethnic minorities. Clearly, health system redesign and new ways of providing care are needed to transform the U.S. health care system into one that provides effective care to everyone. Racial and ethnic concordance may be an important component among many aspects of the patient-physician relationship, but it is only one aspect. More fundamental changes are necessary to ensure higher quality care for all patients.

PATIENT-CENTEREDNESS AND EQUITY

The IOM included two domains of quality that speak directly to the concerns of patients who may prefer and benefit from a concordant relationship with their physician. To be high quality, care must be patient centered and equitable.

Patient-centered care may best be summed up as care that respects the patient and all considerations that flow from that respect. It cannot exist without effective communication between the patient and physician; the physician must understand the patient's preferences and beliefs and incorporate them into all aspects of patient care. It is in this regard that concordance may appear to be a superior model, inasmuch as patients and physicians who are racially or ethnically concordant may be better able to understand each other's backgrounds, communicate more effectively, and be less likely to judge differences that stem from ethnic or racial traditions, beliefs, and practices.

From a practical perspective, however, concordance may not always be possible or preferred, and even in the absence of concordance, the IOM's construct places a requirement on the health system and the health professionals who occupy it to practice patient-centered care. One positive development over the past decade or so has been substantial training programs and other activities designed to promote cultural competence in health care settings. Though the evidence on the effectiveness of these programs is mixed (they result in greater awareness but may not translate to better care), they provide the promise of advancing patient-centered care for all patients, regardless of race or ethnicity, and regardless of patient-physician concordance (Beach et al., 2005).

The IOM's inclusion of the equity domain is particularly interesting, because it places the aim of equity squarely within a quality context. Simply stated, care that is not equitable is not high quality. This value was clearly articulated in a quality improvement project designed to improve care and reduce disparities for African American and Latino patients with heart disease. The project, known as "Expecting Success: Excellence in Cardiac Care," tracked measures of quality performance for patients with heart disease in 10 hospitals in the United States and worked with teams of health professionals at the hospitals to develop ways to improve care for all patients (Siegel, Bretsch, Sears, Regenstein, & Wilson, 2007). The project ran from 2005 to 2009. The 10 hospitals agreed to share information on their performance with the other hospitals in the project and all tracked performance data for white, black, and Latino patients. Hospitals saw remarkable progress in terms of the care they provided to their patients, creating systems of equitable care and following established protocols for certain care or treatment that is considered to be high quality. For example, when patients come to the hospital with chest pain, or a heart attack is suspected, the hospital should provide the patient an aspirin upon arrival. By working to improve performance, hospitals were able to meet this measure nearly 100 percent of the time. Since all participating hospitals had high minority populations, the improvements in quality accrued to minority patients as well, and the hospitals were able to identify any gaps in care by race/ethnicity since they tracked performance data for the different groups. The project demonstrated that equitable care is an achievable outcome and one that is not necessarily dependent on patient-physician concordance.

TIMELINESS AND EFFICIENCY

Two additional domains of quality involve timeliness and efficiency of care, both of which can reduce disparities that have been demonstrated to exist for racial and ethnic minorities. Black and Latino patients receive critically important health services later than white patients, causing delays in prevention, diagnoses, and treatment. Black women, for example, are more likely to receive cancer diagnoses later in the course of their disease; they also receive treatment at a much later stage, resulting in greater disease burdens and higher mortality rates. For people who seek care in the emergency department (ED), a commonly accepted measure of poor quality is the percent of patients who leave the hospital "without being seen." Presumably, people seek care at emergency departments for conditions that are serious and require immediate attention. Though much debate over the years has focused on patients' use of EDs for non-emergent needs, it is fair to assume most patients believe they need immediate attention when they present to the ED. If a patient registers in the ED, waits to see a physician, but ultimately leaves without being seen, a dangerous gap in care can occur. Black patients consistently have higher rates of leaving the ED without being seen, compared to white or Latino patients.

Hundreds of emergency departments across the country have developed quality improvement strategies to reduce waits in the ED and correspondingly, to reduce the numbers of patients who leave without seeing a health professional. These strategies tend to be system related—for example, creating a fast track to move low-risk patients through the ED more quickly and designing systems to improve patient flow and expedite the admissions process for patients who are admitted to a hospital bed from the ED. Real advances in reducing disparities in the ED may be associated with these more comprehensive quality improvement interventions rather than efforts to ensure concordance in these or other health care encounters.

At times, however, the most efficient use of health resources does involve patient-physician concordance. Patients who seek care from physicians who do not speak their languages can face enormous challenges obtaining high-quality care. Interpreters are not always available and when available, they involve costs to the health care organization or physician. An efficient solution is to match a patient with a physician who speaks his or her language. Many studies indicate these situations facilitate more efficient use of resources and can result in fewer unnecessary or repeat tests—a common occurrence when a physician cannot determine whether the patient has had certain diagnostic tests in previous encounters.

CHOOSING A HIGH-QUALITY PHYSICIAN

As was stated above, when given a choice of physician, the majority of individuals do not indicate a preference related to the race or ethnicity of the physician. Individuals place greater emphasis on the language spoken by the physician (about 35 to 42 percent of people say they take language into consideration), which may reflect the practical need to converse with the physician, rather than a preference rooted in the ethnicity of the individual (Saha, Taggart, Komaromy, & Bindman, 2000).

How, then, should individuals decide when it comes to choosing a physician? Current practice generally provides very little information about a physician and rarely any useful information about the quality of care the physician provides. Health plans provide their members basic information about physicians in their networks, including their names, medical specialty, and practice location. Some plans also list the languages spoken by the physicians and their educational background. A few include pictures of physicians on their websites or may list the race, ethnicity, or gender if provided by the physician. Thus, race and ethnicity may be two of a few characteristics patients are given to consider when deciding whom to see. Still, relatively few patients indicate that they take race or ethnicity into consideration.

The lack of information about the quality of care provided by medical practices or individual physicians makes selection of physician based on quality an impossible task. If patients were able to obtain comprehensive physician performance information on certain quality-related measures such as health outcomes and patient satisfaction that could be compared to local averages or national benchmarks, patients would be able to choose physicians based on far better barometers of quality of care than are currently available.

Data on physician performance has been collected by health plans for years. Originally used to monitor physician productivity, more and more it is also used to track physician performance on various quality measures and identify areas for physician improvement. With few exceptions, this data has not been made public, although this trend is changing. Health care quality performance scores are slowly becoming more transparent. Several national private and public initiatives have developed programs to increase transparency in health care provider performance measurement. For example, two multicommunity initiatives, the Robert Wood Johnson Foundation's Aligning Forces for Quality program, and the U.S. Department of Health's Agency for Healthcare Research and Quality Chartered Value Exchanges, have spurred communities to include publicly available Web-based information on quality of physician care, using common performance measures related to heart care, diabetes, asthma, prevention, women's health, and many other areas (Agency for Healthcare Research and Quality, 2010; Aligning Forces for Quality, n.d.). Furthermore, new regulations that stem from major health-reform legislation passed in 2010, known as the Patient Protection and Affordable Care Act of 2010 (ACA), will begin to tie the amount of payments the government makes to hospitals to their performance on publicly available performance scores. Other policies also link physician payments directly to performance on selected quality measures.

Greater transparency in terms of physician quality and performance information could result in one of two trends when it comes to patient-physician concordance. Because it is known that only about one fourth or one fifth of minority patients choose doctors based on race or ethnicity, it can be assumed that decision making for most people is either random or based on other known factors, such as location, gender of the physician, service hours, or the courteousness and helpfulness of the person answering the phone when the patient calls to inquire about an appointment. Because most minorities do not indicate a preference for a physician based on race or ethnicity, it is possible that some or all of these factors are important. If information on the quality of care delivered by the provider were accessible and added to these other pieces of information, minority patients might be more likely to choose a concordant physician. Patients might seek out a concordant physician who they believe provides an equal or higher level of quality than other physicians. If most patients do not associate quality of care with race or ethnicity, they may change their minds about the importance of concordance if they can choose a minority physician with an established record of excellence. In this case, concordance would be a consideration, secondary to quality information. An alternative scenario is that patients would pay even less attention to race and ethnicity, instead taking quality scores into greater consideration.

PATIENTS ARE NOT THE ONLY ONES MAKING A CHOICE

Underlying this discussion is an assumption that racially and ethnically concordant physicians are available to see minority patients if they prefer that arrangement. Though minorities represent an increasing proportion of medical students and physicians, they are severely underrepresented overall. Blacks, Latinos, and American Indians represent 28 percent of the population, but only 8.5 percent of the physician workforce. Although the numbers and proportions of minority Americans continue to grow, with projections that the United States will become a "majority, minority" nation by 2050 (meaning that more than half of U.S. residents will be members of racial or ethnic minority groups), growth in the minority physician population has not moved ahead at a comparable pace. The reality is that the U.S. physician workforce woefully underrepresents its minority population and therefore choice related to physician concordance is often a luxury rather than a standard option. This is true in all aspects of medicine but especially so in certain medical specialties and certain areas of the country.

As mentioned in the previous essay, minority physicians are more likely to practice in areas with high minority populations and are much more likely to serve lower-income, disadvantaged patients (Smedley et al., 2003). That being said, many minority physicians, like whites or other groups of physicians who are not underrepresented relative to their population groups, do not prefer to practice in low-income areas or to serve primarily low-income patients. Expecting minority physicians to take on the challenges associated with treating poor populations (regardless of the racial or ethnic composition of those populations) places an unfair burden on a group of medical professionals who have the same training and professional aspirations as any other physician group.

The Patient Protection and Affordable Care Act includes several provisions designed to strengthen the health care workforce and promote training of a more diverse workforce (Patient Protection and Affordable Care Act, 2010). For example, the health-reform law greatly expands the budget of the National Health Service Corps, a program that provides medical school loan repayment in exchange for service in certain underserved communities, often with high proportions of minority patients. The Corps is open to physicians regardless of race and ethnicity but many of its graduates are minority physicians.

In general, however, progress on developing a more diverse workforce, especially for African American and Latino physicians, has been slow and disappointing. Policy efforts to encourage minorities to enter health careers in medicine, nursing and other clinical areas should be supported and expanded.

CONCLUSION

For many patients, racial or ethnic concordance is an important consideration when choosing a physician. Disparities in care are ubiquitous and there is evidence that concordant relationships result in higher patient satisfaction, better communication, and a stronger overall relationship between a patient and physician. As such, providing information on physicians to facilitate informed patient choices may result in reductions in some health disparities.

Concordance is but one of many strategies that should be employed to improve care. Quality improvement strategies that seek to transform care, framed around the six domains of quality articulated by the Institute of Medicine, provide substantial opportunities to advance care for minorities and other populations. Because minority Americans have received, overall, lower quality care than others in the country, special attention should be paid to tracking quality of care for minority groups and implementing improvement interventions. The recent health-reform law is likely to advance disparities reduction activities for at least two important reasons: (1) more information will be collected and reported at the state and federal levels, including patient demographics such as race, ethnicity, and language spoken, allowing comparisons of quality and access across different racial and ethnic groups; and (2) payment policies will increasingly link payment to quality of care. Thus, the information to identify disparities, and the incentives to decrease them, can provide a platform for meaningful disparities reductions.

REFERENCES AND FURTHER READING

Agency for Healthcare Research and Quality. (2010). *Overview: AHRQ learning network for chartered value exchanges.* Rockville, MD: U.S. Department for Health and Human Services. Retrieved from http://www.ahrq.gov/qual/value/lncveover.htm

Aligning Forces for Quality. (n.d.). *About.* Retrieved from http://www.forces4quality.org/about-af4q

Beach, M. C., Price, E. G., Gary, T. L., Robinson, K. A., Gozu, A., Palacio, A., & Cooper, L. A. (2005). A systematic review of health care provider educational interventions. *Medical Care, 43*(4), 356–373.

Kaiser Commission of Medicaid and the Uninsured. (2010). *Medicaid: A primer.* Washington, DC: Kaiser Family Foundation.

Kaiser Family Foundation. (1999). *Kaiser Family Foundation survey of race, ethnicity, and medical care: Public perceptions and experiences.* Storrs, CT: Roper Center, University of Connecticut.

McGlynn, E. A., Asch, S. M., Adams, J., Keesey, J., Hicks, J., DeCristofaro, A., & Jerr, E. A. (2003). The quality of health care delivered to adults in the United States. *The New England Journal of Medicine, 348*(26), 2635–2645.

Patient Protection and Affordable Care Act, H.R. 3590, 111th Cong. (2009–2010).

Saha, S., Komaromy, M., Koepsell, T. D., & Bindman, A. B. (1999). Patient-physician racial concordance and the perceived quality and use of health care. *Archives of Internal Medicine, 159*(9), 997–1004.

Saha, S., Taggart, S. H., Komaromy, M., & Bindman, A. B. (2000). Do patients choose physicians of their own race? *Health Affairs, 19*(4), 76–83.

Siegel, B., Bretsch, J., Sears, V., Regenstein, M., & Wilson, M. (2007). Assumed equity. *Journal for Healthcare Quality, 29*(5), 11–15.

Smedley, B. D., Stith, A. Y., & Nelson, A. R. (Eds.). (2003). *Unequal treatment: Confronting racial and ethnic disparities in health care.* Washington, DC: National Academies Press.

Marsha Regenstein, Ellie Andres, and Dylan Nelson

31

Home Care

POINT: The encouragement of home-based care in place of nursing home care allows the elderly and the disabled to remain independent longer and experience an overall higher quality of life and thus quality of health care.

Brenda Ohta, New York University Hospitals Center

COUNTERPOINT: Although many elderly people wish to remain independent and in their homes, the nature of care provided—often by overburdened family caregivers or poorly trained individuals with limited supervision—as well as the limitations in insurance coverage and access, threatens the overall quality of care for this population.

Brenda Ohta, New York University Hospitals Center

Introduction

Care for the elderly, and what is sometimes called long-term care services, is not a new concept, but the numbers of people now living long enough to need these types of services has been on the increase in the United States since the 1950s. Among the specialized aspects of long-term care services are home- and community-based services. The debate in this chapter focuses on home-based care and whether it can be provided in an appropriate and efficient manner, preserving quality of care for the elderly and others in need.

Before examining home-based care, it is useful to review the demographic underpinnings of the need for such care, especially among the elderly. In 1900, only 4.1 percent of all Americans were 65 years of age or older, but by 2000, that figure was 12.4 percent. Even more significantly for home-based care, gerontologists, scientists who focus on the study and social aspects of aging, point out that the most rapidly increasing age group in the United States is the oldest of the old, those 85 years of age and above. Between 1950 and 2000, the proportion of people in the 85-and-older age group increased over 300 percent. If we look toward the future, by 2030, over 20 percent of all Americans will be 65 and older, and researchers estimate that, by 2040, there will be 14 million people 85 and older, versus the 4.2 million in 2000.

Numbers such as these tell only part of the story. Also important to understand is the relationship, within the elderly, of people's age and their corresponding need for assistance. Jill Quadagno's 2011 book, *Aging and the Life Course,* points out that most of the "younger old" do not need assistance, and less than 50 percent have disabilities. For those age 65 through 69, while almost 40 percent have a disability, only 8 percent need help. For those 75 to 79 years of age, 54 percent have some type of disability, but 16 percent need assistance. For those 80 years of age and older, about 72 percent have some type of disability, and 30 percent need assistance.

Providing health care at home is certainly not a new idea. Indeed, prior to the twentieth century, home was where most care was received, typically delivered by relatives with some help from formal caregivers. Eventually, more formal settings—which in time evolved into what we now know as nursing homes—became a care option for many elderly people. These developed alongside such places as county poor homes, which extended care to the poor elderly. With the passage of Medicare and Medicaid in 1965, the nursing home industry grew, even though Medicare only covers a limited amount of nursing home services following an acute illness. Medicaid in many states has now become the major payer to nursing homes for the elderly poor, including many who were not poor throughout their lives but became poor as their medical expenses increased due to serious illnesses. One of the issues with nursing home care that quickly emerged was the preference of people to be in their own homes, if possible, or at least in more home-like settings than was typical of nursing homes.

Today, home-based care usually involves skilled nursing and therapy services provided by a licensed home health care agency, often combined with nonskilled home attendant, personal care, and homemaker services. These services are paid for mostly through Medicare or other health plan coverage for time-limited skilled services, through Medicaid and other assistance plans for home attendant services, and by out-of-pocket expenses incurred by individuals who do not qualify for Medicaid or other assistance plans. In the twenty-first century, assisted-living facilities and the supportive care those provide have emerged as another option, and serve often as an interim place of care between a person's original home and a nursing home setting. Home- and community-based services including a range of services: personal care, such as bathing, dressing, feeding, and grooming; housekeeping including meal preparation and planning, and grocery shopping; transportation to medical services; bill paying; and case management. Case management is often provided by a social worker who assists frail elderly persons and their families in obtaining the medical, social, and personal services they need. In some communities, additional services are available, such as respite care, adult daycare, and hospice services for people with terminal illnesses. Many of these services are not covered by Medicare, and although more services are covered by Medicaid (depending on the state), the evidence that home-based services reduce the overall costs or nursing home care is mixed.

One of the concerns is that, because the costs for delivery of health care services to Medicare recipients is growing, it has become more important to find delivery models that provide the highest-quality services at the lowest cost. There are some conflicting findings on this, particularly if the researcher also tries to factor in issues such as the preferences of individual people as they age and a variety of different types of family circumstances. Certainly, there is research to support the contention that home-based services for older adults can provide for a high quality of life at a potentially lower cost than traditional nursing home or long-term care facilities. Home-based services for older adults can better support their functional capacity, aid in recovery from illness or injury following a hospitalization, improve mental health, and support patients' sense that they control their own lives. This is the argument made in the Point section of this chapter.

In the Counterpoint, issues are raised about the potential problems facing older adults who wish to remain in their homes to receive care. Some of these involve the transition to value-based payment, in which health care providers increasingly see reimbursement linked to the level of quality care provided. Patients with advanced, progressing illnesses may experience difficulty even finding home care providers, because providers may have less incentive to care for elderly whose severity of illness and disability increase their likelihood of hospitalization. Currently, home care services are variable by geographic region, race, ethnicity, and socioeconomic status, leading to accessibility issues for some patients. This is especially true because the success of a home-based plan of care often depends on the availability and ability of a family caregiver. Current public policy is not especially supportive of the needs of these family caregivers. In addition, some observers have expressed concerns that older people in these situations will be exposed to improper care, whether delivered by family members or paid providers.

POINT

Prior to the twentieth century, home-based care was the primary mode of delivery for most health care needs, and particularly so in the case of elderly individuals. Their care was often delivered by family members and supplemented by physician or nurse visits to the home. In more recent decades, with the emergence of the mobile, nuclear family structure, the increasing longevity of the population, technological and pharmaceutical advances in medicine, and health care policy directives regarding funding and service-delivery models, the very core of traditional family-based home care services has been challenged. An elaborate continuum of services has subsequently emerged whereby individuals may receive their rehabilitative, skilled nursing, or long-term care in a variety of settings, including acute rehabilitation, subacute nursing, chronic or long-term care settings, assisted-living facilities, small group homes, or through professional and informal caregiving services in the home. Home-based care in this modern context usually involves skilled nursing and therapy services provided by a licensed home health care agency, and may be combined with nonskilled home-attendant, personal-care, and homemaker services. These services are paid largely through Medicare and other health plan coverage for time-limited skilled services, through Medicaid and other assistance plans for home attendant services, and by out-of-pocket costs incurred by individuals who do not qualify for Medicaid or other assistance plans.

The cost for delivery of health care services to Medicare recipients is growing exponentially and the impetus is on finding the delivery model that provides the highest-quality services at the lowest cost. In general, research has found that home-based services continue to provide for a higher quality of life, and at potentially less cost, than do traditional nursing home and long-term care facilities. Home-based services for older adults better support their functional capacity, improve recovery from illness or injury after hospitalization, and enhance the individual's mental health and sense of control.

THE HISTORY OF HOME-BASED CARE

Since the early nineteenth century, health care was primarily delivered within the domestic setting by a visiting physician or nurse and supported extensively by the contributions of family members and neighbors. The growing class of urban poor in the United States through the ensuing decades (e.g., immigrants and factory workers), however, lacked the financial ability or supportive family resources to acquire needed care; with the rising awareness of the link between poverty and illness, the concept of public health began to emerge, and with it the job of visiting home care nurse. Originating from a foundation created by the Ladies Benevolent Society in Charleston, South Carolina, the concept took hold throughout major metropolitan areas within the United States. Primarily charitable in nature, these services were run not as a business, but rather as a means to address the public health needs within cities. In time, companies such as Metropolitan Life Insurance recognized the "cost-effective social investment" of sending a visiting nurse to the home with the mission of returning their beneficiaries to health and productivity. From the insurers' perspective, preventing premature death equated to longer beneficiary life expectancies, fewer death claims, and more policyholders. Thus, the nature of home-based nursing services evolved toward a professional model, reimbursable through major establishments such as Metropolitan Life, John Hancock, Aetna, and others (Buhler-Wilkerson, 2007).

Metropolitan Life's contribution to the development of home health services was notable not only for its reimbursement of home care nursing but also for its monitoring of home care utilization and patient outcomes. It concluded that the greatest value was derived from limited nursing visits for acute conditions that would allow for quick recovery or a discharge to the care of family. Home care for the chronically ill was also of concern; evaluations into the efficacy and cost-effectiveness of such services ensued, and efforts were made to develop a model for reimbursement "stringent enough to avoid paying for long-term personal care . . . elastic enough to care for patients with the potential to recover, and humane enough to cover the care of patients requiring skilled care to minimize suffering" (Buhler-Wilkerson, 2007, p. 617). The findings revealed that both limited and unlimited nursing care in the home produced the same results—patients either recovered within a number of visits, or their progress plateaued. In terms of a return on the investment for paying for home care services, the most gain was derived, therefore, from time-limited services for patients with conditions that were episodic in nature or for whom families could continue care once the patient achieved a certain level of functioning. Essentially, payers were willing to cover expenses for home care services that would improve a patient's condition to the point of relative independence, but could not justify an investment in services that would be unlimited for those for whom illness was chronic, not curative. Over subsequent decades, with shifting patterns from acute illness to chronic disease, availability of institutional care, and research unable to support a positive, cost-effective impact for management of chronic disease in the home, companies such as Metropolitan Life discontinued their home care reimbursement benefit.

Since the early days of reimbursement, support for the funding of home-based services has waxed and waned. At the federal level, funding was initiated with the advent of the Social Security Act and Older Americans Act. Rising costs coincided with growing demand, the increasingly chronic nature of illness, and an aging population. This, in turn, brought about intermittent periods of curtailment of support. By 1965, through the establishment of the Medicare and Medicaid programs, home-based services were recognized as essential, and a "golden age" of fee-for-service reimbursement commenced. History, however, serves as a strong predictor, and funding was again followed by periods of curtailment, expansion, and curtailment related to policy and reimbursement changes (Choi & Davitt, 2009).

The relevance of this history to the argument in favor of home-based services is linked to the enduring need for Americans to secure an alternative to hospital and institution-based care. Additionally, the changing nature of disease, the aging demographics of the nation, and the inexorable battle against rising health care costs are crucial elements that serve to shape reimbursement and health policy, ultimately affecting the public's access to and the availability of services.

Throughout this history, family and other informal means of support (e.g., neighbors, friends, nonskilled paid home care aides) remained the cornerstone of an effective model of home-based care, and in concert with the enduring desire of older adults to remain at home, home-based services continue as a fundamental, though at times underfunded, component of the care continuum. According to Murkofsky and Alston (2009), the goal of home care can be described as two-fold: (1) to provide treatment for an illness or injury, helping patients regain their independence and become as self-sufficient as possible, and (2) to maintain the highest level of ability or health while learning to live with a long-term illness or disability. When provided at home, care is generally less expensive and more convenient than is the care in a hospital or nursing facility, and with the advent of new technologies and pharmaceutical advances, home-based care is genuinely preferred by older adults over hospital or nursing-facility care (Murkofsky & Alston, 2009).

WHY CARE AT HOME? OUTCOMES IN SUPPORT OF HOME-BASED SERVICES

Especially for older adults, home is intimately linked with identity, autonomy, and security. Home creates a strong sense of control and offers the comfort of familiar surroundings. According to Butler, Lewis, and Sunderland (1998), some older adults insist on remaining home, regardless of the cost to their physical and emotional health. For them, the prospect of hospital and nursing home is associated with dependence and the loss of contact with familiar places, possessions, and people; the very notion of a nursing home conjures images of a place "where old people go to die" (Butler et al., 1998, p. 272). Thus, a principal advantage of home care is that it allows older adults to remain in the setting they most prefer.

The attachment to home is of tremendous benefit to older adults in terms of retaining a sense of control and emotional well-being. This has been well noted throughout the classic literature within the gerontological field. As discussed by Rodin (1986), aging is associated with both biological and environmental changes that can impact emotional and physical health. In particular, relocations and transfers from one setting to another have been found to have deleterious effects on older adults. Even when the change is one away from a deteriorating neighborhood to better housing and environment, some older people respond by presenting a higher incidence of disease such as stroke, more hospitalizations, and a greater likelihood for transfer to nursing homes. Further, Rodin has noted that older persons vicariously exposed to dependent elderly in nursing home settings have also been found to show a decline in their own judgment of self-efficacy and control. In contrast, interventions that promote control over daily routines and enhance responsibility have been shown to have positive health outcomes, including greater adherence to medical regimes and an engagement in positive self-care activities. As a result, it appears that services that promote an older person's care needs within their preferred setting of home will likely foster more positive outcomes, both medically and psychologically.

Consistent over the decades, and necessary for ensuring greater self-reliance among the elderly, is a call to promote alternatives to institutionalization and to curtail a medicalized approach to aging. Unfortunately, aging and health-related services are currently pathology based and acute care or institutionally biased. Patients with conditions that limit their independence at home, but who could remain independent with supportive-care services—for example, home health aid or housekeeping—will find that such services, considered "social" in nature, are not covered by insurance. Such "artificial distinctions" between the health and social needs of the elderly serve as a fundamental barrier to "aging in place," as funding is skewed toward the medical and institutional venues in which technical quality overrides quality-of-life concerns (Blum & Minkler, 1980; Estes & Binney, 1997; Kane, 2001). As such, plans for the care of older people as inpatients are less likely to be individually tailored, and are more likely to fail to recognize the impact of social-psychological dynamics on health and recovery and to fall short of supporting individual autonomy, self-reliance, and self-efficacy. Blum and Minkler have described the nursing home setting as "care in place of caring" (1980, p. 150). From this perspective, home-based services, broadly defined, are critical as an alternative to impersonal inpatient and institutional care. They also serve to foster health and promote and support individual dignity and autonomy in the setting most preferred by older adults.

Impact on cost and patient functioning. Positive results have been demonstrated for models of home-based care for patients with a variety of needs and conditions. A meta-analysis of 20 studies identified a positive impact of home care in reducing hospital days. This study found that in a six-month period, patients who received home care used up to six fewer hospital days than did those who did not receive home care. Given the high cost of hospitalization, this translates to substantial cost savings without compromising patient outcomes (Hughes et al., 1997). A more recent meta-analysis of 18 trials conducted in the United States and Europe also confirmed that, for individuals age 65 to 80, home-based interventions were effective in reducing functional decline and mortality (Stuck, Egger, Hammer, Minder, & Beck, 2002).

The continuing trend toward rapid hospital discharge necessitates an array of posthospital services that provide patients with ongoing nursing and therapy services. Research has demonstrated that home-based rehabilitation, for example for stroke patients, reduces the use of more costly acute-rehabilitation beds while ensuring a comparable level of quality services as measured at six months after discharge from the hospital. In a randomized, controlled trial conducted by Anderson and colleagues (2000), early hospital patient discharge coupled with home-based rehabilitation, in comparison to patients receiving inpatient rehabilitation, showed no difference in patient outcomes. Reduction in hospital bed days, however, was significant. Patients who received the home-based services had, on average, 15 bed days, while those receiving inpatient services had an average of 30 hospital days on average per patient receiving the home-based service in comparison to those receiving the inpatient rehabilitation service.

Despite variation in the specific models of home-based service, research findings are highly supportive of the value of such approaches to care for older adults. Importantly, within these findings is the promise of adaptability of services, which is perhaps the hidden strength of home care.

The needs of older adults and their families are in and of themselves variable due to the very nature of disease and a wide variety of psychosocial and economic factors. Not all patients require around-the-clock care. Services at home may be supplemented by community services, such as adult day health care. Families have various degrees of skill and comfort in supporting the needs of elders at home. Service needs may include nursing and physical therapy coupled with private-duty home health aides, as well as social workers and other behavioral health professionals. Protocols can target specific disease and treatment pathways for conditions such as heart failure, diabetes, wound care, or pulmonary issues. Hours of care may be expanded or reduced based on changes in patient condition and his or her pace of recovery. No two individuals will need exactly the same kind of care, and home-based care allows for this individualization. In short, home-based service is a concept with many variants that enable flexibility to help caregivers to meet the targeted needs of the patients and population being served.

Heart failure and cardiac surgery patients are examples of subgroups that require flexibility in home-based service design, including specific nursing and clinical pathways, supplementation of nursing services via telehealth monitoring, cardio-pulmonary rehabilitation in the home or outpatient setting, and targeted patient and caregiver assessment and education regarding nutrition, medication management, and recognition of worsening signs and symptoms. Home-based services that include intensive and comprehensive visits at least weekly by specially trained teams have been found to be effective at reducing rehospitalization rates (Kornowski et al., 1995). Rogers and colleagues (2007) demonstrated that "front loading" home care services (i.e., increasing the frequency of visits in the first couple of weeks following hospital discharge) reduced hospital readmissions by over 50 percent. At the University of California, San Francisco (UCSF), 30-day and 90-day readmissions for heart failure patients were reduced by 30 percent through a specially trained heart failure team that helps ensure patient success at home through education and support after discharge. By preventing 40 patient readmissions a year, UCSF estimates cutting $1 million annually from its Medicare billing, while freeing up hospital beds for other patients and, more importantly, increasing the opportunity for patients to remain at home. Positive results have also been obtained by enhancing traditional home-based care with telephonic care management, which simply involves a health provider, generally a nurse, making contact with patients via telephone after a hospital discharge to ensure that patients are taking their medications, understand their instructions for self-care, and are following up with their physicians. For patients with heart failure or coronary artery bypass surgery, studies have shown that a telephonic home care program has the potential to reduce readmissions and disease-related symptoms and problems, including depression (Barnason, Zimmerman, Nieveen, & Hertzog, 2006; Dimmick et al., 2003; Wakefield et al., 2008).

The most challenging task in evaluating home care efficacy is sorting through the field of oftentimes mixed results. The strength that is home care's flexibility and adaptability is at times its Achilles' heel in terms of comparative effectiveness research. As was discussed above, there is variation in delivery models and targeted approaches based on disease-specific needs (e.g., acute versus chronic, orthopedic surgery versus heart failure), making effective comparisons across studies challenging. The host of studies attesting to outcomes such as improved patient perceptions of health status, reduced hospital use, improved patient satisfaction, and recovery at the same level as more costly hospital-based rehabilitation are, however, highly consistent. Accordingly, as previously discussed, reports indicate that the effective use of home-based services could dramatically reduce the cost of patient care and rehospitalization. In the case of heart failure alone, Dimmick and colleagues (2003) estimate that the use of an effective home-based care/telehealth program could reduce the cost of hospitalization by nearly 50 percent, equating to millions in annual cost reductions. National, state, and local funding and support for larger comparative-effectiveness studies is needed; however, given such an allocation of resources toward more research, there is every confidence that home-based services will continue to demonstrate their crucial role in supporting and advancing the health and wellness of older adults within the community.

HOME-BASED SERVICES FOR PATIENTS NEAR THE END OF LIFE

Research into the direct impact of home-based services on the elderly near the end of life has likewise been favorable. It has demonstrated the potential for improved quality of life through better adherence to individuals' specific goals for care and their preference to die at home. In a study by Hughes and others (1992), patient survival, activities of daily living, and cognitive functioning and morale showed no difference for terminal patients supported through a specialized in-home program in comparison to a similar cohort of patients without the benefit of the program. Yet patient and caregiver satisfaction improved, hospital days were fewer, and there was an associated significant per capita savings in hospital costs.

Further, home-based services established through the Program for All Inclusive Care of the Elderly (PACE) have historically demonstrated positive results including improved patient satisfaction, fewer acute hospital days, and lower per capita health care costs. In terms of end-of-life care, though surveys of older adults reveal that the majority of seriously ill elders would prefer to die in their homes, 53 percent of older adults experience a hospital death. In comparison, 21 percent of PACE program participants die in hospitals. The authors express that, although some believe that society "is unlikely to decide to take our dying older people back into our homes," the PACE experience indicates the potential and the method to do otherwise (Temkin-Greener & Mukamel, 2002, p. 125).

CHANGING DEMOGRAPHICS AND HAZARDS OF HOSPITALIZATION AND NURSING HOME CARE

There is no denying that the U.S. population is aging—both in terms of absolute numbers entering the ranks of 65 and above, and in terms of increased longevity (Administration on Aging [AOA], 2011; Lee & Tuljapurkar, 1998; Yang, Norton, & Stearns, 2003). According to the AARP Public Policy Institute (2009), the Medicare population is projected to grow to 79 million by 2030, more than double the enrollment in the year 2000. With regard to health care, the greatest needs and resource utilization will be among individuals age 75 to 84 and even more so by those age 85 and above, the fastest growing segments of the population. As reported by the Administration on Aging (2011), the number of disabled elderly at all levels of disability will grow rapidly through 2040, and those with moderate or severe disability will more than triple. The number could grow from what was about 5.1 million in 1986 to 22.6 million in 2040, a 350 percent increase. These anticipated demographic changes over the next 30 to 50 years will challenge national and state policy to identify alternatives to current models for payment and service delivery.

If the U.S. health care system is to rely on institutionally based rather than home-based care for the elderly, the potential impact on the costs of long-term care is staggering. The cost of a semi-private nursing home room has continued to rise and currently stands at approximately $75,000 per person, per year according to a report issued by John Hancock Financial (2011). The impact of the increase in overall numbers of disabled elderly in conjunction with the $104 billion per year nursing home industry are indeed startling and the cost incurred by Medicare, Medicaid, and private individuals and families will pose a severe economic burden. As a result, alternatives to nursing home care that promote patient care that is less costly and that is of equal if not higher quality are of paramount importance. This fact has not gone unrecognized at the federal level and was addressed in the 2010 Patient Protection and Affordable Care Act. This law promotes the development of models for effective community and home-based care to reduce the reliance on and need for hospital and nursing home–based services. Simply stated, in the coming years "the need and cost of support of dependent elderly can be mitigated by substituting home care for nursing home care" (AOA, 2011, p. 2).

According to the Institute of Medicine (2001), one in seven patients will experience an adverse event related to hospitalization. Adverse events might include a hospital-acquired infection, medication error, surgical error, or some other event that negatively affects patient health. Some events have been fatal, while others have left patients with increased disability, illness, and excessive out-of-pocket health care expenses. Regardless of the initial reasons for a hospital or nursing home stay—whether for cure, repair, recovery, or rehabilitation—inpatient stays can result in complications unrelated to the original reason for admission. Among frail elders, such settings contribute to enforced immobilization, sensory deprivation, and accelerated bone loss, all of which can lead to an irreversible decline (Creditor, 1993).

Though adverse effects are most commonly reported in association with acute care hospitalization, nursing facilities are not immune to such events. In fact, older adults with long-term care needs are particularly vulnerable to hospitalization and other adverse health effects related to nursing home placement. As reported by Konetzka and colleagues (2008), more than 25 percent of nursing home patients are hospitalized in any given six-month period. Nursing Home Acquired Pneumonia (NHAP), for example, is the leading cause of rehospitalization and death among nursing home patients (Polverino & Torres, 2009). In contrast, the risk of hospitalization and death due to pneumonia is substantially less among elderly residing in their homes. Recommendations by researchers include improving the hospital-to-home transition and substituting home health care for selected hospital and nursing home admissions in order to prevent such adverse events (Konetzka et al., 2008).

Home care–quality improvement efforts. Although legitimate concerns exist about the consistency of home care, quality monitoring of key aspects of services is a growing expectation on the part of home health care operations. Ensuring patient satisfaction with services, reducing rehospitalization, and improving immunization rates for the prevention of pneumonia are examples of measures that agencies either have or will soon have in place to ensure the quality of services provided (Rosait, 2009). Improving patient safety in the home through fall prevention, reduction of adverse medication reactions or errors, and reduction of pressure ulcers are key measures for benchmarking against other agencies and ensuring progress in quality improvement goals. Use of patient high-risk screening tools and resources such as patient risk assessments, home-safety assessments, and telehealth are additional methods that can help ensure high-quality care and reduce hospital readmission rates. Though much has been done to develop and improve the delivery of services within the home, further improvements will serve to strengthen the track record of this important component within the continuum of services for the elderly.

TRANSITIONAL CARE AND HOME-BASED SERVICES

Given that one in five Medicare beneficiaries is rehospitalized within 30 days, the management of the transition from hospital to home or hospital to other setting is of critical importance (Jenks, Williams, & Coleman, 2009). Post-acute care that is not well coordinated is prone to breakdowns in the handoff of health-provider communication, and patient limitation in the management of self-care can lead to medication management errors, infection, and other adverse events resulting in hospital readmission. The toll that hospital recidivism takes on older adults cannot be overstated, nor can the associated economic costs, which could be reduced by millions of dollars annually through a lessening of preventable hospital readmissions alone (Centers for Medicare & Medicaid, 2011).

According to Naylor, "more than any other segment of health care services, home health care practitioners are uniquely poised to address the challenges and capitalize on the opportunities to ensure that these patients and their caregivers do not fall through the cracks" (2006, p. 48). Research over the past decade has yielded a consistent pattern of interventions that, when focused on the patient transitioning from hospital to home, are highly effective in improving patient outcomes and reducing recidivism. These strategies include screening to identify high-risk patients in need of transitional-care services, identification of patients' and caregivers' goals and preferences for care, effective communication between providers and across settings to ensure a consistent plan of care, patient and caregiver education to identify and respond to worsening health problems, and the availability of highly skilled nurses to ensure continuity of services (Coleman & Berenson, 2004; Naylor, 2006; Naylor et al., 2004). Although these approaches have not previously been part of the traditional home care repertoire, they once again demonstrate the adaptability and malleability of a home-based methodology to respond to the changing needs of the population served and to provide a model for quality and cost-effective health care services.

CONCLUSION

For many people, security, familiarity, and identity are closely linked. This is no less true for individuals as they age and experience illness and disability—and, indeed, it may become more true with age. As Lanspery and colleagues wrote, "Home is a place to take one's ease, a refuge, a center, a treasure chest of memories and of valued . . . belongings . . . an extension and reflection of oneself" (Lanspery, Callahan, Miller, & Hyde, 1997, p. 1). Within the home, family and formal care providers can offer a higher quality of life and more personalized care than can be found within an institutional setting. So strong is the desire among older adults to remain within this refuge that, despite declining health, they often cling to home. And, if the argument for reimbursement for home care services based on the dignity and comfort it affords the older adult is not enough, then the potential and promise for home care to deliver on cost savings, reductions in hospital days, prevention of hospital readmissions, reduction in mortality, and slowing of functional decline should be. The alternative is both unpleasant and costly.

References and Further Reading

AARP Public Policy Institute. (2009). *The Medicare beneficiary population.* Retrieved from http://www.aarp.org/health/medicare-insurance/info-01-2009/fs149_medicare.html

Administration on Aging (AOA). (2011). *Aging into the 21st century.* Retrieved from http://www.aoa.gov/AoARoot/Aging_Statistics/future_growth/aging21/health.aspx

Anderson, C., Rubenach, S., Mhurchu, C. N., Clark, M., Spencer, C., & Winsor, A. (2000). Home or hospital for stroke rehabilitation? Results of a randomized controlled trial. *Stroke, 31,* 1024–1031.

Barnason, S., Zimmerman, L., Nieveen, J., & Hertzog, M. (2006). Impact of a telehealth intervention to augment home health care on functional and recovery outcomes of elderly patients undergoing coronary artery bypass grafting. *Heart & Lung, 35*(4), 225–233.

Blum, S. R., & Minkler, M. (1980). Toward a continuum of caring alternatives: Community-based care for the elderly. *Journal of Social Issues, 36*(2), 133–152.

Buhler-Wilkerson, K. (2007). Care of the chronically ill at home: An unresolved dilemma in health policy for the United States. *The Milbank Quarterly, 85*(4), 611–639.

Butler, R. N., Lewis, M. I., & Sunderland, T. (1998). *Aging and mental health: Positive psychosocial and biomedical approaches* (5th ed.). Boston, MA: Allyn and Bacon.

Centers for Medicare & Medicaid. (n.d.). *Strengthening Medicare: Better health, better care, lower costs.* Retrieved from http://www.cms.gov/apps/files/medicare-savings-report.pdf

Choi, S., & Davitt, J. K. (2009). Changes in the Medicare home health care market: The impact of reimbursement policy. *Medical Care, 47*(3), 302–309.

Coleman, E. A., & Berenson, R. A. (2004). Lost in transition: Challenges and opportunities for improving the quality of transitional care. *Annals of Internal Medicine, 141*(7), 533–536.

Creditor, M. C. (1993). Hazards of hospitalization of the elderly. *Annals of Internal Medicine, 118*(3), 219–223.

Dimmick, S. L., Burgiss, S. G., Robbins, S., Black, D., Jarnagin, B., & Anders, M. (2003). Outcomes of an integrated telehealth network demonstration project. *Telemedicine Journal and E-Health, 9*(1), 13–23.

Estes, C. L., & Binney, E. A. (1997). The restructuring of home care. In D. M. Fox & C. Raphael (Eds.), *Home-based care for a new century* (pp. 5–22). Malden, MA: Blackwell.

Hughes, S. L., Cummings, J., Weaver, F., Manheim, L., Braun, B., & Conrad, K. (1992). A randomized trial of the cost effectiveness of VA hospital-based home care for the terminally ill. *Health Services Research, 26*(6), 801–817.

Hughes, S. L., Ulasevich, U., Weaver, F. M., Henderson, W. L., Manheim, L., Kubal, J. D., & Bonarigo, F. (1997). Impact of home care on hospital days: A meta analysis. *Health Services Research, 32*(4), 415–432.

Institute of Medicine, Committee on Quality of Health Care in America. (2001). *Crossing the quality chasm: A new health system for the 21st century.* Washington, DC: National Academy Press.

Jenks, S. F., Williams, M. V., & Coleman, E. A. (2009). Rehospitalization among patients in the Medicare Fee-for-Service Program. *New England Journal of Medicine, 360*(14), 1418–1428.

John Hancock Financial. (2011). *John Hancock announces results of 2011 national Long-Term Care (LTC) cost study.* Retrieved from http://www.johnhancock.com/about/news_details.php?fn=apr2011-text&yr=2011

Kane, R. A. (2001). Long-term care and a good quality of life: Bringing them closer together. *The Gerontologist, 41*(3), 293–304.

Konetzka, R. T., Spector, W., & Limcangco, M. R. (2008). Reducing hospitalization from long-term care settings. *Medical Care Research and Review, 65*(1), 40–66.

Kornowski, R., Zeeli, D., Averbuch, M., et al. (1995). Intensive home-care surveillance prevents hospitalization and improves morbidity rates among elderly patients with severe congestive heart failure. *American Heart Journal, 129*(4), 762–766.

Lanspery, S., Callahan, J. J., Miller, J. R., & Hyde, J. (1997). Introduction: Staying put. In S. Lanspery & J. Hyde (Eds.), *Staying put: Adapting the places instead of the people* (pp. 1–22). New York, NY: Baywood.

Lee, R., & Tuljapurkar, S. (1998). Uncertain demographic futures and social security finance. *American Economic Review, 88*(2), 237–241.

Murkofsky, R. L., & Alston, K. (2009). The past, present, and future of skilled home health agency care. *Clinical Geriatric Medicine, 25*(1), 1–17.

Naylor, M. D. (2006). Transitional care: A critical dimension of the home healthcare quality agenda. *Journal for Healthcare Quality, 28*(1), 48–54.

Naylor, M. D., Brooten, D. A., Campbell, R. L., Maislin, G., McCauley, K. M., & Schwartz, J. S. (2004). Transitional care of older adults hospitalized with heart failure: A randomized controlled trial. *Journal of the American Geriatrics Society, 52*(5), 675–684.

Polverino, E., & Torres, A. (2009). Current perspective of the HCAP problem: Is it CAP or is it HAP? *Seminars in Respiratory and Critical Care Medicine, 30*(2), 239–248.

Rodin, J. (1986). Aging and health: Effects of the sense of control. *Science, 233*(4770), 1271–1276.

Rodin, J. (1989). Sense of control: Potentials for intervention. *Annals of the American Academy of Political and Social Science, 503*, 29–42.

Rogers, J., Perlic, M., & Madigan, E. A. (2007). The effect of frontloading visits on patient outcomes. *Home Healthcare Nurse, 25*(2), 103–109.

Rosait, R. (2009). The history of quality measurement in home health care. *Clinical Geriatric Medicine, 25*(1), 121–134.

Rush-Monroe, K. (2011). *UCSF medical center program cuts heart failure readmission rate by 30 percent.* Retrieved from University of California, San Francisco website: http://www.ucsf.edu/news/2011/07/10166/ucsf-medical-center-program-cuts-heart-failure-readmission-rate-30-percent

Stuck, A. E., Egger, M., Hammer, A., Minder, C. E., & Beck, J. C. (2002). Home visits to prevent nursing home admission and functional decline in elderly people: Systematic review and meta-regression analysis. *Journal of the American Medical Association, 287*(8), 1022–1028.

Sui, A. L. (1997). The effect of home care on hospital days: What is the take home message? *Health Services Research, 32*(4), 385–389.

Temkin-Greener, H., & Mukamel, D. B. (2002). Predicting place of death in the program of all-inclusive care for the elderly (PACE): Participant versus program characteristics. *Journal of the American Geriatric Society, 50*(1), 125–135.

Wakefield, B. J., Ward, M. M., Holman, J. E., Ray, A., Scherubel, M., Burns, T. L., et al. (2008). Evaluation of home telehealth following hospitalization for heart failure: A randomized trial. *Telemedicine and E- Health, 14*(8), 753–761.

Yang, Z., Norton, E. C., & Stearns, S. C. (2003). Longevity and health care expenditures: The real reasons older people spend more. *Journal of Gerontology: Social Sciences, 58*(1), S2–S10.

Brenda Ohta

COUNTERPOINT

Any evaluation of the efficacy of health services must take into full account issues of quality, access, and cost; the simple fact that a service is inexpensive does not in itself make it worthy. Research on the quality of home-based services has produced mixed findings. For specific conditions, for limited durations of time, for individuals with resources that allow supplementation of covered Medicare services, the quality of care has been deemed high. But for individuals without resources to supplement those services not covered by insurance, without a willing and able family caregiver, with unlicensed or undertrained paid caregivers, or for whom the clinical and psychosocial needs exceed the current array of available services, the quality of home-based services has been found lacking. An additional consideration, beyond the impact on the care recipient, is the quality of life for the family caregiver: Research has shown a negative impact on caregivers' mental health due to the burden of their role. Lack of licensure and training for home health attendants likewise raise questions as to whether some older patients are being put at risk. The media and popular press have no shortage of stories about elder abuse at the hands of overburdened family caregivers or unlicensed personal-care attendants.

In addition to quality concerns, access to services may be hindered by geographic location, availability of service providers in a given area, cultural and racial disparities, or cultural incompetency in service delivery, and the reimbursement rules governing Medicare and Medicaid services. The rules, in and of themselves, restrict access to in-home services because reimbursements are dependent on factors such as available family caregiver, being "homebound," demonstrating a measurable degree of progress over a selected period of time, and limitations on coverage for nonskilled services (i.e., personal care and homemaker/chore services). Finally, the rising cost to Medicare and Medicaid of home-based services threatens to change reimbursement policy such that a greater share of the financial burden will shift to the patient and family.

CHALLENGES OF COST AND ACCESS

Cost and coverage for home-based services. The type and duration of home care services received by older adults is most directly related to the payer source; Medicare is the largest single-payer for home care. For qualifying patients, Medicare covers in-home medical and personal-care needs for time-limited episodes, and payment is based on the degree of medical complexity. The care must be part-time, intermittent, skilled nursing care, physical therapy, or speech therapy that is based on a physician's order and provided by a certified home health agency participating in Medicare. In addition, it is required that patients meet the definition for "homebound" status—a patient is considered homebound if trying to leave home would require a considerable and taxing effort (Centers for Medicare & Medicaid Services [CMS], 2011a).

Medicare serves as the primary payer for a sizeable portion of home-based services. As such, its reimbursement methodology strongly acts to shape the type and degree of services accessible to older adults. From its inception through the mid-1990s, Medicare reimbursed on a fee-for-service basis, thereby creating financial incentives for long lengths of service and more home visits. Put simply, the more services provided to older adults, the more an agency was able to bill. Due to dramatic growth in Medicare home health utilization—between 1990 and 1996 usage increased by 350 percent—as well as a high degree of regional variation in service utilization, Congress took action to change the reimbursement structure for home care services, efforts that, in turn, were expected to curtail the growth and reduce variation across providers (Murkofsky & Alston, 2008). First, Operation Restore Trust was established in 1995 to address billing fraud and abuse in the home care industry (CMS, 2011b; Fitzgerald, Boscardin, & Ettner, 2009; Welch, Wennberg, & Welch, 1996). Then, in 1997, the Balanced Budget Act fundamentally changed the payment methodology for home care services with the creation of the Home Health Interim Payment System, followed in 2000 by the Home Health Prospective Payment System. The new methodology no longer reimbursed on a fee-for-service basis but rather through a fixed payment for a 60-day episode of care that was based on patient acuity (e.g., clinical severity and functional status), not agency costs (Choi & Davitt, 2009).

This change had a marked impact on reducing the cost and utilization of home care services. Fewer home health aide and therapy or social work visits were provided, and patients were discharged from home care more quickly as the agencies were now incentivized to provide less service over shorter periods of time (Murkofsky & Alston, 2009). The effect on Medicare home health agencies was substantial, resulting in agency closures and curtailment of services, more so in some service areas than others. Unfortunately, there was a corresponding rise in unmet home-based needs among disabled and chronically ill elders. Furthermore, studies have found that the cutbacks led to a notable decline among supportive services that are often required for a successful home care plan: social work services, medical equipment, transportation services, home health aide and homemaker hours, companion services, and nutrition/meal services (Lee, 2007; Thomas & Payne, 1998). Among those older adults needing and receiving home health care, these additional supportive service needs were found to be unmet at least 50 percent of the time (Thomas & Payne, 1998). Essentially, older adults whose service needs are deemed to be too costly under the present reimbursement structure may be denied needed services outright, leaving them more vulnerable to rehospitalization or other adverse outcomes.

In addition to Medicare, there are a host of other funding sources for home-based care, including state and local governments, Medicaid, private insurance, and patient and family out-of-pocket payments. A shift in payer sources from traditional Medicare to Medicare-managed care plans, as well as splitting payment for services among different payers (e.g., Medicare plus Medicaid), further complicates how services are paid (Grabowski, 2007). At the Medicaid and local levels, there may be more flexibility for coverage of nonskilled and supportive services and more or less restriction on interpretation of the definition of homebound status (Coffey, 2009). With this mix of funding sources and varying rules and guidelines for covered services, the benefit package and authorization process can be confusing and complicated, consequently challenging agencies, patients, and families to effectively navigate the system and maximize service benefits for patients. Consequently, the degree to which elders access and maximize their home care benefits depends in large part on their ability to navigate the payment system and qualifying guidelines. The level of service accessed appears to depend more on the sophistication of the elder consumer than on his or her actual health and supportive-care needs.

Finally, despite the rising costs and utilization of home care services, there remain unmet home-based needs among disabled and chronically ill elders that are not consistently reimbursed by Medicare, Medicaid, and other payers. Among these are supportive services that are often required for a successful home care plan but which lack sufficient funding, especially under Medicare Prospective Payment System (PPS), to ensure social work services, medical equipment, transportation services, home health aide and homemaker hours, companion services, and nutrition/meal services (Lee, 2007; Thomas & Payne, 1998). The payment structure for home-based services, therefore, acts to curtail and inhibit elderly consumers' access to needed care and support, not only for skilled services but also for supportive services that are essential in addressing the psychosocial and functional needs of older adults.

Disparity in home care access. In the last decade, a curious shift in the racial and ethnic composition of the nursing home population has taken place. Once disproportionately white, the balance is now tipping. At a cursory glance, this may appear to signal improved access for older minorities in receiving nursing-home care. In fact, however, it may signal a disparity in minority access to alternatives to nursing-home care. According to a study by Feng and colleagues (2011), factors related to whites' comparative ease in affording alternatives to nursing-home care, along with changing minority family patterns, have limited the ability of minority patients to remain at home when assistance is required for medical and personal-care needs. With changes in family patterns, work demands, and limited financial resources, immigrant and minority families that traditionally cared for aging parents at home may now be less able to do so.

Disparity in home care access for minorities is also historically rooted in health care policy. In the mid- to late 1990s, the point at which the Balanced Budget Act of 1997 dramatically decreased Medicare home health funding, African American and other minority patients were found to experience greater decreases in home-based services than did white patients. Minority elders are less likely to have the financial resources for out-of-pocket supplemental in-home services, and African American elders especially rely to a larger extent on public programs to fund their long-term care needs. Such circumstances increase their vulnerability to changes in reimbursement policy and cutbacks, which in turn affect their access to needed care at home. Such findings indicate that race and ethnicity do have a differential effect on determining service use, and "health policy has a disparate impact on minority older adults" (Davit & Kay, 2010, p. 591).

Unscrupulous business practices and service cutbacks. The industry for home-based care that has emerged in recent decades has ventured far from the altruistic foundation established in the 1800s by the Ladies Benevolent Society and the services of the settlement houses of the inner city (Buhler-Wilkerson, 2007; Murkofsky & Alston, 2009). Today, accusations of billing fraud for payment of services not provided, or for the provision of services not needed, add to the concern about the rising costs of home-based care that are being reimbursed through government programs, as well as to the quality of care provided to older consumers. The federal government and law enforcement agencies, in response to growing concerns, have heightened their surveillance and subsequent prosecutions in recent years. The media is ripe with accounts similar to "111 charged in Medicare scams worth $225 million" (Kennedy, 2011). Further, the Office of the Inspector General (OIG) has uncovered disturbing trends, such as the fact that one in three Medicare claims paid for durable medical equipment have been erroneous—that is, the billed-for services never reached their intended consumer. According to the OIG, growth in home health care services relative to the number of eligible beneficiaries in a particular service area is one indicator of possible fraud. Case in point: In 2008 Miami-Dade County accounted for more than half of the approximately $1 billion in outlier home health payments paid by Medicare nationally, while only 2 percent of all Medicare beneficiaries receiving home health services reside in Miami-Dade County.

This abuse of the Medicare system entails schemes whereby home care providers file claims for non-existent patients, or do not provide the services they claim to be providing to frail elders, resulting in a fraudulent-claims industry that earns $60 billion to $90 billion annually (Kennedy, 2011). Beyond the obvious waste of resources, this fraudulent activity threatens future levels of federal and state home care funding and reimbursement, as governments are increasingly looking for methods to limit expenditures.

Growing demand, fraudulent billing activity, and consequent decreases in government funding coupled with service cutbacks may prompt a shift to greater reliance on family caregivers or on unlicensed, less costly home care professionals. This, in turn, adds to the level of concern pertaining to the quality and safety of home-based care.

QUALITY OF CARE: RISK TO FRAIL ELDERS

Quality of the workforce. The current supply of qualified home-based and long-term care workers is challenged to meet current demand. Additionally, the training standards for nonprofessional staff are often insufficient to the task of managing the increasingly complex care regimens required by ill and disabled elders at home (Institute of Medicine [IOM], 2008; Seavy, 2010). Aging-services work is undervalued and offers noncompetitive compensation and benefits. In fact, home care aide jobs are one of the top 25 worst-paying occupations in America (Maidment, 2007). By 2030 the number of Americans age 65 and older will nearly double, and with it the demand for home-based and long-term care services will increase (CMS, 2011c; Department of Health and Human Services [DHHS], 2011; IOM, 2008). The critical challenge now and in the future is for the available nonprofessional workforce (i.e., home health aides or personal-care aides) to meet the demand for quality home-based care. This challenge is heightened by the current lack of adequate standards for training and oversight, coupled with the undervalued nature of the work.

Home care work is physically and emotionally challenging, requiring a high degree of responsibility, autonomy, judgment, and skill. And yet home health aide positions in most states carry only minimal requirements for training. As required by federal law, they receive only 75 hours of training, a level that has remained the same for the last 20 years. Though some states require more than 75 hours, most fall short of the 120 hours of training recommended by the IOM (2008). Seventeen percent of home care aides are self-employed, meaning that they have no agency oversight for training, or assurance for competency, quality, and safety. These jobs entail low wages, poor benefits, high levels of stress, clients with complex and challenging physical and cognitive needs, long work hours, and high injury rates (Dale, Brown, Phillips, & Carlson, 2005; DHHS, 2011). The occupational category of nursing aides, among which include home care aides, is cited as one of the most dangerous occupations, placing in the top three for nonfatal illness and injury rates among all occupations (Bureau of Labor Statistics, 2009).

This workforce is disproportionately minority and approximately one quarter are foreign born. Over half have a high school diploma or less, and wages are often below 200 percent of the federal poverty level, making the workers themselves eligible for public assistance such as food stamps and Medicaid (DHHS, 2011; PHI, 2011; Seavy, 2010). The irony of placing our most vulnerable and disabled elders in the care of one of our most vulnerable and undervalued workforces is striking and threatens the overall efficacy and quality of care delivered in the home for this population.

Impact on family caregivers. Family caregivers are an important part of the home-based services equation. In fact, 80 percent or more of the care for the elderly in the home is provided by family members. Although the literature consistently reports that home care is preferred by older adult recipients, the satisfaction results regarding the older adult's family caregiver suggest that home may not be best for everyone involved. Though some studies indicate a boost to patient satisfaction or functioning as a result of receiving home care services, a host of studies pinpoint the serious toll taken on the family caregiver, not to mention the family finances (Emanuel, Fairclough, Slutsman, & Emanuel, 2000; Stuck, Egger, Hammer, Minder, & Beck, 2002; Temkin-Greener & Mukamel, 2002; Zarit, Reever, & Bach-Peterson, 1980).

A study by the United Hospital Fund found that family caregivers provide three quarters of the care for stroke and brain injury patients, even when professional home care staff were employed. These family caregivers also reported feelings of isolation, anxiety, and depression. Emanuel and colleagues (2000) interviewed terminally ill patients and their caregivers from across the United States. They found significant levels of both economic burden and caregiver depression related to caring for patients with substantial needs in the home.

Caught between trying to sustain their work and family lives while tending to the care needs and safety of their elder loved one, family caregivers suffer physically and psychologically (Buhler-Wilkerson, 2007; Houser & Gibson, 2007; Zarit et al., 1980). This can lead to caregivers neglecting their own physical and mental health or that of the family members in their care.

Additionally, there is the economic burden. One in three family caregivers must tap into their own savings or cut back on their own health care expenditures in order to assist the older relative with their care needs (Ness, 2011; Houser & Gibson, 2007; Buhler-Wilkerson, 2007). As discussed by Buhler-Wilkerson, "Despite two centuries of experimentation, however, no agreement exists concerning the balance between the public and private resources to be allocated" (p. 611). At this juncture, for families with limited funds and a chronically/seriously ill elder at home, there are profound choices to be made, both personal and fiscal, between continuing care at home and seeking nursing-home placement. The correct balance between public and private funds and professional and family caregivers has yet to be appropriately addressed.

For those whose home-based health need is truly part time, intermittent, uncomplicated, and episode based—for example, in-home rehabilitation for a relatively healthy older adult following elective hip surgery—payment and service allocation is fairly straight forward. Home care, as currently modeled and reimbursed, is effective primarily for these types of short-term episodic conditions. It is not, however, an effective delivery model for those with longer-term needs. For the burgeoning population of elderly chronically ill and disabled, the fragmentation and tension is magnified in terms of who pays, for what level of services, and for what duration of time. What is the correct balance between public funding and private out-of-pocket costs, between clinical/medical services and supportive social services, and between services to ensure caregiver support and families managing on their own? Ongoing efforts to resolve this dilemma "reflect the unavoidable tensions between fiscal reality and legitimate need" (Buhler-Wilkerson, 2007, p. 612).

Additional concerns arise when considering the payment for such needed care. Given that there is minimal insurance/government reimbursement for this type of care, the direct labor cost and out-of-pocket expenses are borne largely by family caregivers. An estimated 34 million private family caregivers provide care to frail and disabled elders at home, at an economic value of $375 billion (Houser & Gibson, 2007). In essence, this is a cost-shifting framework: The long-term care of elders at home is reliant on family members' unpaid labor, most often provided by female members of the household (Buhler-Wilkerson, 2007; Houser & Gibson, 2007). Furthermore, while in-home services may seem to require a low degree of technical skill, elder care has evolved into a high-tech, high-skill endeavor. Caregiving requires increasingly complex skill acquisition, as older patients are discharged from hospitals earlier than ever with a high level of nursing-care needs: wound care, intravenous antibiotic infusion, parenteral nutrition, pain and diabetes management, and anticoagulation therapy, to name just a few.

Even for patients with access to professional in-home service providers, the role of the family cannot be understated. In fact, patient success at home is more likely to reflect the level of involvement and care delivered by the family caregiver than it is that of the employed home care worker or agency directly. Though many argue for increasing funding for agency based home care services, the unseen critical success factor, the role of the family and how they are supported, continues to go unaddressed. According to Buhler-Wilkerson, "it remains very difficult to resolve whether care of the sick at home is a publicly funded civic duty or a private family responsibility. . . . The history of homecare suggests . . . it seems unlikely that home care will become the cornerstone of delivery of care" (2007, p. 632).

Risk of abuse and neglect. "Death of 91-year-old spotlights line between care and killing." "Pearl Harbor survivor found living in filth; caretaker arrested on suspicion of abuse." So read two 2011 headlines from the *Los Angeles Times*. Each of these stories, in different ways, spotlight the very real risk faced by vulnerable adults seeking to live out their wish to be cared for in their own homes. In the first scenario, the neglect and abuse were at the hands of a loved family member—a 26-year-old, ill equipped to manage the multiple health and functional needs of her elderly aunt. The niece's defense stated that she was providing care according to her aunt's wishes, which included not to be taken to the hospital or doctor. The aunt was found in her home amidst filth and was extremely medically compromised, dying soon after being admitted to the hospital. In the second scenario, the abuse was at the hands of an unlicensed home care worker not affiliated with a home care agency. Although this worker had been caring for her older client for three years, the bank began to notice irregularities in his account. When the authorities went to the home to check on him, they found him among mounds of garbage, overflowing toilets, and rat feces. He was disoriented and dehydrated. When and how does caring devolve into abuse?

Elder abuse refers to the mistreatment of an older adult that threatens his or her health or safety. According to the best available estimates, between 1 and 2 million Americans age 65 or older have been injured, exploited, or otherwise mistreated by someone on whom they depended for care or protection. For the abused, there is a significantly increased risk of depression, functional decline, and mortality (Dong et al., 2009; National Research Council, 2003).

Abuse may come from paid in-home caregivers as well as from family members. Even among trusted family members and paid caregivers, and even if the abuse or neglect is not intentional, the greater the care needs of the elderly individual and the more limited the caregiver's resources for support, the greater the risk for abuse or neglect. A longitudinal study found that one half of family members caring for a relative with dementia reported abusive behavior at the beginning of the study (Cooper, Blanchard, Selwood, Walker, & Livingston, 2010). After one year, those reports rose to three quarters of the caregivers. Among caregivers who received fewer hours of in-home social care at baseline, more anxiety and depression was found and was also associated with increases in abuse at the one-year follow-up. Clearly, the greater the care needs of the older adult, the more cognitive impairment and the greater the burden perceived by the caregiver, the higher the risk factors for abuse and neglect (Lachs, Williams, O'Brien, Hurst, & Horwitz, 1997; Mathias & Benjamin, 2003; Zarit et al., 1980). Although abuse is a risk faced by the elderly regardless of their residential settings, the abuse of an older adult in an isolated home setting may go longer without detection. Furthermore, within the home, there are no requirements for caregiver training, no limitations on caregiver hours imposed as means of reducing stress and fatigue, and no assurance of regular oversight by professional nurses or administrators as would be available in a facility.

CONCLUSION

Although older adults consistently voice their preference for receiving their health and long-term care needs at home, a number of forces converge to make this increasingly difficult and risky. First, under the Patient Protection and Affordable Care Act (ACA) and a transition to value-based payment, health care providers will increasingly see their reimbursement linked to the level of quality care provided. Patients with advanced, progressing illnesses may find that their home care providers have less incentive to care for them when the severity of their illness and disability increase their likelihood of hospitalization. Under this "pay-for-performance" methodology, reimbursement will be negatively impacted for agencies whose clients are readmitted to the hospital, thereby potentially affecting an agency's ability or desire to take on the risk posed by individuals with a progressive illness and increased odds of hospitalization.

Second, home care services, though often effective for short-term episodic health care needs, are not in their present state the panacea to the chronic care and long-term care needs of older adults. Highly subject to variation by geographic region, race, ethnicity, and socioeconomic status, home care services are not readily accessible to all. At times, they appear to be less about meeting the true medical, functional, and psychosocial needs of frail and disabled older adults than they are about minimizing business risk and maximizing revenue. Moreover, as cutbacks in reimbursement continue, the business approach for home-based services will make "gaming the system" and selectivity in accepting patient referrals more the rule than the exception.

In addition, the true success of a home-based plan of care is often reliant on the willingness, ability, and availability of a family caregiver. Regardless of the amount of professional in-home services, without the caregiver's ability to effectively manage their needs, the quality of care for the frail elder will be seriously compromised. Unfortunately, public policy as it now stands does not sufficiently support or address the needs of these family caregivers or their sacrifice on behalf of their elder loved ones.

Last, older adults who require assistance to manage their health and functional needs in the home are a highly vulnerable group. At a time in their lives when they are struggling to remain in their communities and as independent as possible, they are confronted by a health care system that funnels more resources toward institutional care than home care. They are reliant on the support and services of family members who have family demands and economic burdens of their own. When they are able, they pay for assistance, the quality of which may be questionable due to the limited training and oversight standards for home care workers. They may also be subject to exploitation by unscrupulous businesses or possibly to abusive behavior at the hands of overburdened caregivers. Given this myriad list of challenges, without progressive change to the current system in terms of reimbursement policy, family support, and improvements in wages and training for the direct-care workforce in the home, the overall quality of home-based care for the frail and disabled elderly will continue to be threatened.

REFERENCES AND FURTHER READING

AgingStats. (2010). *Older Americans 2010: Key indicators of well-being*. Retrieved from http://www.agingstats.gov/agingstatsdotnet

Buhler-Wilkerson, K. (2007). Care of the chronically ill at home: An unresolved dilemma in health policy for the United States. *The Milbank Quarterly, 85*(4), 611–639.

Bureau of Labor Statistics. (2009). *Economic news release: Nonfatal occupational injuries and illnesses requiring days away from work*. Retrieved from http://www.bls.gov/news.release/osh2.nr0.htm

Centers for Medicare & Medicaid Services (CMS). (2011a). *Chart series: Overview*. Retrieved from https://www.cms.gov/thechartseries/01_Overview.asp#TopOfPage

Centers for Medicare & Medicaid Services (CMS). (2011b). *Home Health Agency Center*. Retrieved from https://www.cms.gov/center/hha.asp

Centers for Medicare & Medicaid Services (CMS). (2011c). *Home Health PPS*. Retrieved from http://www.cms.gov/HomeHealthPPS

Choi, S., & Davitt, J. K. (2009). Changes in the Medicare home health care market: The impact of reimbursement policy. *Medical Care, 47*(3), 302–309.

Coffey, G. (2009). *To be or not to be homebound: The limits of states' discretion in Medicaid's coverage for the home health services*. Retrieved from National Senior Citizens Law Center website: http://www.nsclc.org/wp-content/uploads/2011/07/Home-Health-Brief.pdf

Cooper, C., Blanchard, M., Selwood, A., Walker, Z., & Livingston, G. (2010). Family carers' distress and abusive behaviour: Longitudinal study. *The British Journal of Psychiatry, 196*, 480–485.

Dale, S., Brown, R., Phillips, B., & Carlson, B. L. (2005). How do hired workers fare under consumer-directed personal care? *The Gerontologist, 45*(5), 583–592.

Davit, J. K., & Kaye, L. W. (2010). Racial/ethnic disparities in access to Medicare home health care: The disparate impact of policy. *Journal of Gerontological Social Work, 53*(7), 591–612.

Department of Health and Human Services (DHHS). (2011). *Understanding direct care workers: A snapshot of two of America's most important jobs: Certified nursing assistants and home health aides*. Retrieved from http://aspe.hhs.gov/daltcp/reports/2011/CNAchart.pdf

Dolansky, M. A., Xu, F., Zullo, M., Shishehbor, M., Moore, S. M., & Rimm, A. A. (2010). Post-acute services received by older adults following a cardiac event: A population-based analysis. *Journal of Cardiovascular Nursing, 24*(4), 342–349.

Dong, X., Simon, M., Mendes de Leon, C., Fulmer, T., Beck, T., Hebert, L., & Evans, D. (2009). Elder self-neglect and abuse and mortality risk in a community-dwelling population. *Journal of the American Medical Association, 302*(5), 517–526.

Emanuel, E. J., Fairclough, D. L., Slutsman, J., & Emanuel, L. L. (2000). Understanding economic and other burdens of terminal illness: The experience of patients and their caregivers. *Annals of Internal Medicine, 132*(6), 451–459.

Feng, Z., Fennell, M. L., Tyler, D. A., Clark, M., & Mor, V. (2011). Growth of racial and ethnic minorities in U.S. nursing homes driven by demographics and possible disparities in options. *Health Affairs, 30*(7), 1358–1365.

Fitzgerald, J. D., Boscardin, W. J., & Ettner, S. L. (2009). Changes in regional variation of Medicare home health care utilization and service mix for patients undergoing major orthopedic procedures in response to changes in reimbursement policy. *Health Service Research, 44*(4), 1232–1252.

Grabowski, D. C. (2007). Medicare and Medicaid: Conflicting incentives for long term care. *The Milbank Quarterly, 85*(4), 579–610.

Hartman, L., Jarosek, S. L., Virnig, B. A., & Durham, S. (2007). Medicare-certified home health care: Urban- rural differences in utilization. *National Rural Health Association, 23*(3), 254–257.

Houser, A., & Gibson, M. J. (2007). Valuing the invaluable: A new look at state estimates of the economic value of family caregiving (data update). *Insight on the Issues, 13*.

Institute of Medicine [IOM], Board on Health Care Services. (2008). *Retooling for an aging America: Building the health care workforce*. Washington, DC: National Academies Press.

Kennedy, K. (2011, February 17). 111 charged in Medicare scams worth $225 million. *Associated Press*.

Lachs, M. S., Williams, C., O'Brien, S., Hurst, L., & Horwitz, R. (1997). Risk factors for reported elder abuse and neglect: A nine-year observational cohort study. *The Gerontologist, 37*(4), 469–475.

La Ganga, M. L. (2011, June 2). Death of 91-year-old spotlights line between care and killing. *Los Angeles Times*. Retrieved from http://articles.latimes.com/print/2011/jun/02/local/la-me-elderly-homicide-20110602

Lee, J. S. (2007). The unmet needs of the elderly with diabetes in home health care. *Social Work in Health Care, 45*(3), 1–17.

Maidment, P. (2007, June 5). America's best- and worst-paying jobs. *Forbes.* Retrieved from http://www.forbes.com/sites/jacquelynsmith/2011/05/17/americas-best-and-worst-paying-jobs

Mathias, R. E., & Benjamin, A. E. (2003). Abuse and neglect of clients in agency-based and consumer-directed home care. *Health & Social Work, 28*(3), 174–184.

Murkofsky, R. L., & Alston, K. (2009). The past, present, and future of skilled home health agency care. *Clinical Geriatric Medicine, 25*(1), 1–17.

National Research Council. (2003). *Elder mistreatment: Abuse, neglect, and exploitation in an aging America* (R. J. Bonnie & R. B. Wallace, Eds.). Washington, DC: The National Academies Press.

Ness, D. L. (2011). Women, caregivers, families, and the Affordable Care Act's bright promise of better care. *Generations, 35*(1), 38–44.

Office of the Inspector General. (n.d.). *Office of Evaluations and Inspections.* Retrieved from U.S. Department of Health and Human Services website: http://oig.hhs.gov/reports-and-publications/oei/h.asp

Perry, T. (2011, January 26). Pearl Harbor survivor found living in filth; Caretaker arrested on suspicion of abuse. *Los Angeles Times.* Retrieved from http://latimesblogs.latimes.com/lanow/2011/01/a-93-year-old-pearl-harbor-survivor-was-founddirty-disoriented-and-living-in-filth-at-his-home-outside-el-cajon-the-san-d.html

PHI. (2011). Who are direct-care workers? *PHI Facts,* No. 3. Retrieved from http://www.directcareclearinghouse.org/download/NCDCW%20Fact%20Sheet-1.pdf

Seavy, D. (2010). Caregivers on the front line: Building a better direct-care workforce. *Generations, 34*(4), 27–35.

Stuck, A. E., Egger, M., Hammer, A., Minder, C. E., & Beck, J. C. (2002). Home visits to prevent nursing home admission and functional decline in elderly people: Systematic review and meta-regression analysis. *Journal of the American Medical Association, 287*(8), 1022–1028.

Thomas, C., & Payne, S. (1998). Home alone: Unmet need for formal support services among home health clients. *Home Health Care Services Quarterly, 17*(2), 1–20.

Welch, H. G., Wennberg, D. E., & Welch, W. P. (1996). The use of Medicare home health care services. *New England Journal of Medicine, 335*(5), 324–329.

Wilensky, G. (2000). *The Balanced Budget Act of 1997: A current look at its impact on patients and providers.* Testimony before the Subcommittee on Health and Environment, Committee on Commerce, U.S. House of Representatives. Retrieved from http://pages.stern.nyu.edu/~jasker/BBA1.pdf

Yamada, Y. (2001). Profile of home care aides, nursing home aides, and hospital aides: Historical changes and data recommendations. *The Gerontologist, 42*(2), 199–206.

Zarit, S. H., Reever, K. E., & Bach-Peterson, J. B. (1980). Relatives of the impaired elderly: Correlates of feelings of burden. *The Gerontologist, 20*(6), 649–655.

Brenda Ohta

Centralized Versus Decentralized Control

POINT: There is little doubt that centralized authority is needed for health care quality improvement and effective cost control. The alternative decentralized approach that relies exclusively on local innovation and private-sector solutions is based mostly on ideology rather than fact, experience, and research.

Kevin Seitz, Health Policy Consultant
Marianne Udow-Phillips, Center for Healthcare Research & Transformation

COUNTERPOINT: Health care quality and cost-containment programs should be led at the state and local level. Centralized, federal programs do not adequately take into account local conditions and differences in available structures and resources. State and local leadership can move more quickly and be more responsive to local needs.

Marianne Udow-Phillips, Center for Healthcare Research & Transformation
Kevin Seitz, Health Policy Consultant

Introduction

It is difficult to find an issue that is more politically contentious than health care, particularly the policy changes and programs that are needed to assure that Americans have access to needed care. Similar refrains are heard in a wide variety of debates over reforming the private health market, guaranteeing access to insurance coverage, and fixing the Medicare and Medicaid programs. In political terms, the liberal position tends to see health care as a right and seeks a strong, centralized public role in creating programs and safeguards that assure equity of benefits and access for all Americans. The conservative position usually sees fiscal and personal responsibility as the top priorities and tends to favor decentralized, private-market solutions.

These liberal and conservative inclinations can be plotted along a continuum. The ultimate liberal position favors a tax-financed system with federally controlled provider networks and federally designed reimbursement and quality control systems. As one moves along the continuum, authority moves from federal to state governments, then to a regulated private market, and finally to what might be considered the ultimate conservative position: an unregulated private market. Similarly, financing moves from tax-based, to mandatory private financing, and finally to a voluntary, privately financed system. Along the same liberal-to-conservative continuum, benefits shift away from defined-benefit packages and toward defined-contribution approaches, in which consumers have fixed, public-dollar support and purchase the benefit packages that best fit their needs.

There is little doubt that the liberal position does a better job of assuring coverage equity with a defined set of benefits. This is most evident in the Veterans Administration (VA) health system and Medicare, both of which have uniform, national benefit packages. It is handled less perfectly in Medicaid, where limited state discretion has led to multiple approaches for covering (and not covering) the medically needy, and each state has its own take on covering optional benefits. Then, in the private sector, which is much more decentralized, insurers are asked to administer thousands of different benefit designs as employers and groups are able to craft their own individualized benefit packages.

It is less clear whether centralized or decentralized authority is preferable in terms of health care quality improvement and cost control. Health care quality improvement is often cited as important, not only to improve patient outcomes but also to control health care spending. Repeated lab and radiology tests, unnecessary surgery, and hospital-acquired infections and complications all reduce health care quality and increase spending. Policy analysts and practitioners alike agree that focusing on improving health care quality is an important underpinning of the goal of reducing the rate of increase in spending.

This chapter will explore both sides of the quality/cost issue, focusing on the arguments and evidence that support—or refute—the claims of each perspective. The Point position will highlight how centralized authority has facilitated the Veterans Administration and Medicare's track records in controlling cost. It will also argue that centralized approaches to administration maximize the percentage of each health dollar that pays for actual medical care (higher medical-loss ratios) and the importance of establishing national expectations relative to the practice of medicine. The Counterpoint position will highlight the innovation that occurs through decentralized approaches to cost control and quality improvement. It will argue that, because most health care is delivered locally, practice improvement only happens one physician at a time.

Most other developed countries have chosen largely centralized approaches to addressing cost and quality. And, though these systems still face increasing health care spending and considerable opportunities to improve population health, overall these centralized approaches have worked relatively well where they have been implemented, predominantly in Europe and Japan. Indeed, compared to these countries, the United States spends considerably more on health care, covers fewer individuals, and has worse health outcomes on many key measures. The relative global performance of the United States would seem to be an indictment of the generally decentralized, pluralistic approach that currently governs most of the nation's health care benefit design, quality improvement, and cost-management approaches. The reality, however, is that American politics and temperament are such that it is unlikely that a fully centralized approach akin to that in other developed countries will ever be implemented. Therefore, the question is really less about whether federal or state/local structures do better at leading improvements in quality and cost, and more about determining the most important prerequisites for either entity to function optimally in the United States.

The case argued in the Point demonstrates that centralized (federal) approaches have been shown to be most effective with regard to both cost and quality when they have total control of all elements of the health system—payments, rewards, data, and structure—as in the Veterans Administration. In systems where they have partial control (e.g., Medicare, which is reliant on a generally private health care system of independent practitioners or on locally based managed care entities), they do best when setting overall goals, ensuring accountability, and encouraging local collaboration. The patient-centered medical home demonstration project is the best example of the intelligent use of federal authority: Key principles were identified, multi-payer collaboration required, and the financial and quality goals to be achieved by the end of the demonstration were made clear.

When acting directly alone, federal systems like Medicare that have only partial control of the system can do an excellent job of developing provider-reimbursement methodologies that foster greater uniformity and accountability, and are often emulated by private payers. Medicare also outperforms the private sector in controlling unit price (which is a significant component of total cost) but it must be careful that lower fees do not come at the expense of either access to health care (too many providers choosing not to participate) or costs shifting to the private sector.

Although state approaches to price control have shown that they can effectively help constrain spending (in Medicaid), these programs have serious problems with providing access to needed care because their provider fees are often significantly lower than Medicare fees. And Medicaid doesn't have the clout of the federal Medicare program because the population covered is not as core to most providers as is the senior population.

As illustrated in the Counterpoint discussion, local initiatives can be effective in focusing on quality improvement and better controlling utilization of services. Prospects for success of these efforts are enhanced if they are implemented in higher-cost communities (generally more room for improvement), and if the environment encourages collaboration with other payers so that incentives to providers are aligned. Indeed, with intelligent centralized guidance and support, locally designed quality standards and administrative structures, as were seen in the patient-centered medical home demonstration program, can play a key role in obtaining widespread support from providers, which can significantly improve the opportunities for success.

In the end, improvements in quality and cost can be led by either realm—each has certain strengths and limitations. Indeed, most such efforts are done as partnerships between the public and private sector and the federal, state, and local level. The challenge for health care reformers is to get the mix right: building on the strengths of each and minimizing the limitations.

POINT

THE VETERANS ADMINISTRATION HEALTH SYSTEM

The U.S. Department of Veterans Affairs is perhaps one of the best examples of the value of providing health benefits and managing quality and costs at the federal level. With its roots in the 1600s, when the Pilgrims pledged the support of Plymouth Colony for soldiers disabled in the Indian wars, the modern Veterans Administration (VA) was established in 1930 to provide a range of services to returning veterans. At that time, there were 54 VA hospitals; as of 2011, the VA comprised 171 medical centers; more than 350 outpatient, community, and outreach clinics; and 126 nursing home care units. In 2006 the Veterans Health Administration employed more than 200,000 full time–equivalent employees and provided services to more than 5 million veterans and 400,000 other individuals throughout the country.

Recent analyses of the care provided by the VA have documented that its overall quality is better—and cost of care lower—than either the Medicare system or the private sector. Indeed, adjusting for the changing mix of patients, the Congressional Budget Office (CBO) estimated that Veterans Health Administration's budget authority per enrollee grew by 1.7 percent in real terms from 1999 to 2005 (0.3 percent annually). In that same period, Medicare's real rate of growth was 29.4 percent in cost per capita (4.4 percent per year). In these years, private health insurance premium increases ranged from a low of 5.3 percent (1999) to a high of 13.9 percent (2003). Though the private sector data was not adjusted for changes in benefit design, there is little doubt that real cost-growth in the private sector was higher than the VA's for the same period.

The VA has advantages that other health systems do not. For example, federal law enables the VA to purchase pharmaceuticals at lower prices than those paid by virtually any other payer. In addition, because the VA is a single system with defined benefits, there is less need for administrative complexity than in the private sector, which is highly pluralistic.

In the 1990s VA leadership began a concerted effort to improve quality, adopting key tenets proposed by the Institute of Medicine and disseminating them throughout their facilities and programs. By the mid-2000s, the VA came to be recognized as a leader in health care quality and safety. A 2003 study published in the *New England Journal of Medicine* showed VA patients receiving quality of care better than the Medicare fee-for-service system. A study reported in the *Annals of Internal Medicine* the following year noted that 67 percent of VA patients received the care specified by key quality indicators, compared with 51 percent of the patients in the national sample.

Though there are many potentially confounding variables when analyzing the VA's performance in relation to the private sector or Medicare (e.g., different benefit designs, patient populations, and geographic distribution), the data clearly demonstrate that a fully federally funded and run entity can provide high-quality care at a lower cost than the private sector. In looking at the reasons behind this performance, the Congressional Budget Office concluded that the "VA's structure as a vertically integrated system that operates on an appropriation may have helped the system to focus on providing the best quality of care possible for a given amount of funds." This finding is consistent with what has been found with health care internationally: Strong, centralized systems have generally outperformed the United States with both lower per capita health spending and better population health performance. And, though some believe that a centralized, federally run system could not work in the United States, the VA presents a clear, real-life demonstration that this belief is simply not true.

MEDICARE

Medicare demonstrates the advantages of centralized authority in terms of cost control. The Kaiser Family Foundation tracked Medicare per capita costs from 1998 to 2008 and compared the annual rate of increase to private insurance. It found that Medicare per capita costs increased at an average annual rate of 6.8 percent, compared to a private health insurance increase of 7.1 percent. It went on to say:

> [T]his overstates Medicare cost growth, since a new drug benefit was added during that period. Based on figures from the actuaries that compare costs on a "common benefits" basis, Medicare per capita cost grew at an average rate of 4.9 percent per year over the period, substantially less than the 7.1 percent rate for private insurance. (Altman, Levitt, & Claxton, 2010)

This occurred primarily because of Medicare's ability to set provider fees, while maintaining participation by the overwhelming majority of providers. The market share held by any one private insurer is generally too low to exercise the same market clout as Medicare and achieve the same favorable provider prices. Therefore, private insurance usually pays higher rates to providers than does Medicare.

Medicare has innovated in the development of reimbursement methodologies that promote provider efficiency, quality improvement, and greater accountability. In 1983 Medicare implemented a hospital-based diagnostic-related groups (DRG) reimbursement system. This led to an approximate 20 percent reduction in the average length of inpatient hospital stays. In subsequent years, this innovation, which pays fixed prospective fees based on diagnostic categories, was adopted by many Medicaid plans and larger private insurers. Other payers have continued to reimburse inpatient services based on negotiated per diems or at a percentage of charge, two systems with significantly less predictability and accountability.

In the late 1980s Medicare adopted a revised physician reimbursement system, setting a payment value for each procedure based on a number of factors including work effort, needed training, associated practice expense, and malpractice exposure. This resource-based relative-value reimbursement system has been copied by many payers, and it moved most payers away from a prevailing charge methodology, thereby promoting greater predictability and uniformity in the business relationship between payers and physicians.

Medicare was the first payer to take a clear stand on refusing to pay for hospital-based "never events"—situations in which physicians and hospitals provided the wrong service or botched the service they intended to provide. Once Medicare took the stand not to pay for never events, the private sector got a dose of courage and adopted similar policies. Most would agree that this action by Medicare was largely symbolic, doing little to impact cost and quality; nevertheless, many private insurers adopted virtually the same policy following Medicare's action, emphasizing the power of the centralized, federal approach to affect the country as a whole.

Medicare has also been involved in sponsoring local demonstration programs to test and encourage improvements in the organization and delivery of care. The intent of these demonstrations is to reward providers for managing the health of a defined population and to gradually move away from the fee-for-service reimbursement system, which financially incents providers to provide more and more service. The findings from these demonstrations will be used to design future reimbursement and product options in Medicare.

The list of Medicare innovations created to lower cost and improve quality goes on and on. This is not to say that Medicare is problem-free. It faces ongoing issues involving provider overbilling and cost growth, raising concerns about long-term financial viability. But compared to the private sector, Medicare is the gold standard. It usually establishes the systems and sets the provider rates that others scramble to emulate. This point can be illustrated through a comparison between Medicare and private Medicare Advantage plans.

Currently, Medicare Advantage plans cover some 25 percent of Medicare beneficiaries. They are the private-sector option to traditional Medicare coverage, combining Medicare various parts and supplemental coverage into a single plan. Though authorized by Congress to give Medicare beneficiaries a private-sector option for Medicare coverage, in reality these plans are simply not competitive with the traditional program. They receive premium payments from the federal government that average about 10 percent more than the traditional Medicare program; much of this additional funding goes to support profit and administrative expense. The Government Accountability Office (GAO) estimated that Medicare Advantage plans budget about 13 percent of premium to profit and administrative expense, although some estimate that the percentage of premium that actually goes to fund profit and administration is higher, averaging a little over 15 percent. This compares to an administrative expense for traditional Medicare of around 3 percent.

The competitive imbalance of Medicare Advantage plans goes further than higher administrative expense and extra federal premium subsidies. Most private Medicare Advantage plans simply do not have the market leverage to negotiate contracts with hospitals and physicians at Medicare rate levels. Therefore, the federal government has stipulated that providers must accept Medicare rates from these plans if the providers currently participate in the traditional Medicare program. These Medicare Advantage plans would not exist without this rate protection afforded by the centrally controlled Medicare program.

Medicare Advantage plans also receive premiums that are adjusted based upon the case mix (severity) of the population they cover. This has helped spur growth in vendors who comb through medical records to document any diagnoses that could be used to justify higher premium payments from Medicare. This in some ways is a logical extension of private-insurer practices in the individual market to maximize its advantages from risk selection. In this case, however, the function is reversed, with vendors trying to make their membership look sicker than other Medicare beneficiaries.

In summary, Medicare outperforms the private sector in terms of cost performance and quality improvement. It tends to set the base level of provider reimbursement and establishes programs that promote quality improvement and greater accountability. The private sector generally cannot match Medicare's performance, but instead rushes to copy the policies and systems that Medicare implements.

PRACTICE VARIATION: A FUTURE OPPORTUNITY

Advocates for decentralized control argue that health care is delivered locally, and so change must be implemented on a community-by-community basis. It is true that, to date, the responsibility for quality improvement has largely rested at the local level. But though there have been some examples of success, in general local discretion has not resulted in significant improvement toward adoption of best practices, and significant unwarranted variation in physician practice persists from community to community. To be fair, attempts to reduce this variation and move toward an expectation of best practice have not yet been actively promoted by Medicare, either. Historically, Medicare has not focused on best practice, but has instead set a priority on promoting open access to most licensed providers. This represents an area of future opportunity for central authority.

Dr. John Wennberg has spent much of his professional life studying variations in the way medicine is practiced from community to community. He periodically publishes the *Dartmouth Atlas,* which charts variations in practice by hospital referral regions for Medicare beneficiaries throughout the United States. He has found that communities tend to have patterns of care delivery that persist over time. For example, communities with a greater availability of hospital beds per capita tend to have higher hospitalization rates for acute and chronic medical conditions. In some communities, physicians are more prone to perform hysterectomies, while others have higher-than-average rates of tonsillectomies or prostatectomies. These higher rates tend to reflect local physician treatment preferences: the "favorite" treatment of local physicians selected from a number of treatment options for different medical conditions.

These variations in patterns of care have both a quality and a cost impact on the health system. Atul Gawande, in a 2009 article that appeared in *The New Yorker,* demonstrated some of these impacts by comparing Dartmouth Atlas Medicare data for two communities in Texas. Using 2006 Medicare data, he contrasted McAllen, Texas, with El Paso. The McAllen Medicare cost per beneficiary was second nationally only to Miami, Florida, at $15,000 annually per beneficiary. This compared to a cost in El Paso of $7,500 per beneficiary. The per capita cost in El Paso approximated the national average cost per Medicare beneficiary. Gawande chose these two communities because of the noticeable difference in cost, but also because they are demographically similar, so differences could not be attributed to disease burden, socio-economic status, or other factors. He found that

> [b]etween 2001 and 2005, critically ill Medicare patients received almost fifty per cent more specialist visits in McAllen than in El Paso, and were two-thirds more likely to see ten or more specialists in a six-month period. In 2005 and 2006, patients in McAllen received twenty per cent more abdominal ultrasounds, thirty per cent more bone-density studies, sixty per cent more stress tests with echocardiography, two hundred per cent more nerve-conduction studies to diagnose carpal-tunnel syndrome, and five hundred percent more urine-flow studies to diagnose prostate troubles. They received one-fifth to two-thirds more gall bladder operations, knee replacements, breast biopsies, and bladder scopes. They also received two to three times as many pacemakers, implantable defibrillators, cardiac-bypass operations, carotid endarterectomies, and coronary-artery stents. And Medicare paid for five times as many home-nurse visits. The primary cause of McAllen's extreme costs was, very simply, the across-the-board overuse of medicine. (Gawande, 2009, n.p.)

The comparison between McAllen and El Paso is an extreme example, but it serves to highlight that practice variations can be quite large and can significantly affect the quality of care that is delivered. The disparities simply cannot be justified as reasonable and acceptable, even if one affords physicians wide discretion on their treatment decisions. But this degree of variation is to be expected from a system that relies heavily on community standards of care and locally based peer review. Decentralized authority leads to a health system where treatment choices can be disproportionately impacted by provider supply, misinformation, income maximization, and subjective bias.

It is recognized that quality improvement occurs one physician at a time. Implementing changes in physician practice occurs locally. But these local physician-led efforts should be guided by national standards. There should be clear protocols for the treatment of different conditions. Best practice should be the same in McAllen as it is in Newark and Seattle. These best-practice standards can and should be determined nationally. Also, there should be a national methodology and process for assessing physician compliance with these standards. In effect, centralized authority is required in order to move the expectation on physician practice from a relative, local barometer to an objective, science-based approach that consumers and other providers can trust. In this regard, the comparative-effectiveness provisions of the 2010 Patient Protection and Affordable Care Act (ACA) hold some promise toward achieving more of a national consensus regarding best practices.

A MIXED MODEL: STATE AUTHORITY AND MEDICAID

State-based authority represents a variation on the central-authority theme. Control is vested with each state, allowing policies and programs to vary from state to state. State-level authority may be comprehensive when a function is fully delegated to state decision making. It may also be mixed when the federal government prescribes certain standards that must be followed, and individual states have discretion over a more limited set of decisions. This mixed-authority model generally does not perform as well as federally centralized authority in terms of health care cost and quality, but it tends to outperform decentralized authority, particularly in relation to cost control.

Historically, states have exercised authority over numerous facets of the health care system. They have traditionally licensed providers, regulated the private insurance market, set malpractice policy, and assumed responsibility for the uninsured. An individual state's approach reflects the political culture of the state, and can lead to sharp differences in policies and programs from state to state. Also, each state tends to feel a touch of pride about its own unique approach. As a result, observers often hear about state-based innovations that have implications for national programs. Unfortunately, most state-initiated innovations have little applicability beyond the borders of individual states. Observers hear about innovation that has occurred in Massachusetts through its health-reform initiative, or the single-payer system planned for Vermont, or Hawaii's success in reducing its rate of uninsured. But these glowing stories of success gloss over the fact that these are the exceptions: In aggregate they affect less than 5 percent of the U.S. population and have little or no chance of being adopted by other states.

Even when the federal government partners with the states to meet a policy objective (i.e., a mixed model), states tend to take advantage of any area of discretion, thereby creating state-to-state differences based more on fiscal ability and political priority than on variations in local need. Take Medicaid as an example. The differences from state to state in eligibility criteria and access to care for Medicaid recipients can be significant. These differences impact who is eligible, who gets access to care, and the quality of care that is received.

A 2011 study from the Commonwealth Fund highlights this issue. The study looked at Medicaid managed care and compared the performance of publicly traded health plans with the performance of nonpublicly traded plans (mostly provider owned). It found that publicly traded plans tended to devote a higher percentage of premium dollar to administrative expense (including profit) and tended to receive lower scores for quality of care related to preventive care, treatment of chronic conditions, members' access to care, and customer service. Again, this leads to variations between states because for-profit plans tend to be concentrated in certain states.

Also, a 2011 study conducted in Cook County, Illinois, suggests that children covered by Medicaid and the Children's Health Insurance Program (CHIP) are less likely to receive specialty care than are children covered by commercial insurance. The study involved calling specialty care providers to schedule appointments. The researchers found that 66 percent of the callers reporting Medicaid-CHIP coverage were denied an appointment for specialty care, as compared with 11 percent of the callers reporting Blue Cross Blue Shield insurance coverage. It is important to note that states have a good degree of discretion in the setting of Medicaid physician fee screens. Illinois is one of the lower Medicaid rate states, paying less than 70 percent of the Medicare fee level. Lower Medicaid rates generally equate to lower provider participation in Medicaid and reduced access to care for Medicaid recipients.

State to state variations in Medicaid can affect access to care and quality of care. But, it does appear that Medicaid is reasonably effective in controlling costs compared to the private insurance sector. The Kaiser Family Foundation compared per capita Medicaid spending increases for covered families (not including the aged and the disabled) to per-capita private insurance spending from 2000 to 2008. They found that Medicaid per capita spending increased by 5.2 percent per year, compared to a 7.2 percent private-sector increase. Medicaid may have outperformed the private sector because of a trend in Medicaid programs of mandating recipient participation in managed care and tight controls on provider rates (though such controls can result in significant reductions in access to the provider community).

The major reasons for Medicaid's profile on cost and quality performance involve two interrelated factors: states' political cultures and fiscal capacities. The states with the largest proportionate poverty populations tend to have less fiscal capacity than do more affluent states. When these poorer states are asked to match federal dollars, they simply do not have the tax base to afford more generous benefits and higher eligibility thresholds. Second, Medicaid is not a popular program in most states. Legislators would rather allocate incremental tax dollars to other purposes, such as elementary and secondary educations, higher education, or tax relief. Even though two thirds of Medicaid dollars go to fund care for the elderly and the disabled, these dollars are generally viewed as going into the pockets of providers, who are thought to be well off and not a priority for incremental state spending. As a result, in most states there is not an effective political constituency to advocate for the Medicaid program.

In summary, state-based accountability tends to result in programs with wide, and sometimes unjustified, disparities from state to state. There are some success stories, but these tend to occur in the more progressive and affluent states and represent the exception and not the rule. Yes, state accountability is better than no accountability, but it is not the way to develop equitable and effective coverage or to improve quality of care. State control can be more effective than fully decentralized models in cost control, but because cost control often becomes the overriding policy priority, that success sacrifices quality, access to care, and breadth of coverage.

CONCLUSION

Americans have a somewhat irrational, negative response to centralized authority. This may generally serve them well as they promote private, competitive solutions to market problems. However, such an approach does not serve Americans well in health care, because the health care market has certain imperfections that mitigate the impact of competition on efficiency and quality improvement. Most notably, consumers will always have a knowledge gap relative to providers and cannot be expected to make clinical decisions without disproportionate influence from the people who stand to economically benefit from certain decisions. Also, because most communities are not large enough to support multiple competing hospital systems, consumer choice is often limited, and the principle that competition drives continued improvement is simply not applicable.

There is a need for centralized authority in health care. The VA health system and Medicare strongly suggest that such an authority can and does result in cost savings relative to the private sector. Moreover, centralized authority helps assure equity in coverage for needs that really do not vary appreciably from one locale to another. Finally, there exists a clear need for an expansion of central authority in the quality area to move practice improvement from a local assessment of local practice to an objective assessment based on national standards. The example of Medicaid proves that state authority is an imperfect substitute for central, federal control. States tend to perform reasonably well on the cost control, but often sacrifice access and quality in the process.

There is a reason why virtually every other country has implemented health finance and delivery systems with a strong emphasis on central authority. They have learned that cost control, quality improvement, and equity of treatment depend on it.

REFERENCES AND FURTHER READING

Altman, D., Levitt, L., & Claxton, G. (2010). *Pulling it together: An actuarial Rorschach test.* Retrieved from Kaiser Family Foundation website: http://www.kff.org/pullingittogether/021610_altman.cfm

Asch, S. M., McGlynn, E. A., Hogan, M. M., Hayward, R. A., Shekelle, P., & Kerr, E. A. (2004). Improving patient care: Comparison of quality of care for patients in the Veterans Health Administration and patients in a national sample. *Annals of Internal Medicine, 141*(12), 938–945. Retrieved from http://www.annals.org/content/141/12/938.full.pdf+html

Bisgaier, J., & Rhodes, K. V. (2011). Auditing access to specialty care for children in public insurance. *New England Journal of Medicine, 364*(24), 2324–2333.

Cassidy, A., Berenson, R., Gold, M., Lemieux, J., Agres, T., & Dentzer, S. (2011). Health policy brief: Medicare advantage plans. *Health Affairs.* Retrieved from http://www.healthaffairs.org/healthpolicybriefs/brief.php?brief_id=48

Committee on Energy and Commerce. (2009). *New report highlights Medicare Advantage insurer's higher administrative spending.* Retrieved from http://democrats.energycommerce.house.gov/index.php?q=news/new-report-highlights-medicare-advantage-insurers-higher-administrative-spending

Congressional Budget Office. (2007). *The health care system for veterans: An interim report.* Retrieved from http://www.cbo.gov/ftpdocs/88xx/doc8892/MainText.3.1.shtml

Gawande, A. (2009, June 1). The cost conundrum. *The New Yorker.* Retrieved from http://www.newyorker.com/reporting/2009/06/01/090601fa_fact_gawande

Government Accountability Office. (2008). *Report to congressional requestors: Medicare Advantage—Increased spending relative to Medicare fee for service may not always reduce beneficiary out of pocket costs* (GAO-08-359). Retrieved from http://www.gao.gov/new.items/d08359.pdf

Jha, A. K., Perlin, J. B., Kizer, K. W., & Dudley, R. A. (2003). Effect of the transformation of the Veterans Affairs Health Care System on the quality of care. *New England Journal of Medicine, 348*(22), 2218–2227. Retrieved from http://www.nejm.org/doi/full/10.1056/NEJMsa021899#t=article

Kaiser Family Foundation. (2007). *Health care costs: A primer, key information on health care costs and their impact.* Retrieved from http://www.kff.org/insurance/upload/7670.pdf

Kaiser Family Foundation. (2011). *Average annual growth rates for nominal NHE and GDP for selected time periods.* Retrieved from http://facts.kff.org/chart.aspx?ch=855

Kaiser Family Foundation. (2011). *Distribution of personal health care expenditures by source of payment, 1999 and 2009.* Retrieved from http://facts.kff.org/chart.aspx?ch=1349

Latta, V. B., & Keene, R. E. (1990). Cost of short-stay hospital services under Medicare, 1988. *Health Care Financing Review, 12*(1).

McCue, M. J., & Bailit, M. H. (2011). Assessing the financial health of Medicaid managed care plans and the quality of patient care they provide. *Issue Brief No. 11.* Retrieved from The Commonwealth Fund website: http://www.commonwealthfund.org/~/media/Files/Publications/Issue%20Brief/2011/Jun/1511_McCue_assessing_financial_hlt_Medicaid_managed_care_plans_ib_FINAL.pdf

U.S. Department of Veterans Affairs. (2012). *History—VA history.* Retrieved from http://www.va.gov/about_va/vahistory.asp

Wennberg, J. E. (2010). *Tracking medicine.* New York, NY: Oxford University Press.

Zuckerman, S., Williams, A. F., & Stockley, K. E. (2009). Trends in Medicaid physician fees, 2003–2008. *Health Affairs, 28*(3), w510–w519. doi: 10.1377/hlthaff.28.3.w510

Kevin Seitz and Marianne Udow-Phillips

COUNTERPOINT

Health care in the United States is delivered through a complex set of payers, providers, and purchasers. Though most countries in the developed world have expanded health coverage through strong, centralized approaches, the United States has a long tradition of health care coverage delivered through a mix of private and public structures and local and state efforts. According to a Kaiser Foundation study, in 2009 47.4 percent of total health expenditures were publicly funded, and 52.6 percent were privately funded. Most of the publicly funded portion of health care was accounted for by Medicare and Medicaid (22.5 percent and 16.5 percent of total spending, respectively). Most privately funded health care was funded by private insurance (34.1 percent of total expenditures), with most of the remainder being funded by personal out-of-pocket spending (14.3 percent of total spending). Come 2014, the Patient Protection and Affordable Care Act (ACA) will change this mix somewhat, mostly by decreasing out-of-pocket spending and increasing both Medicaid and private insurance spending. The fundamental mix of payers in the American health insurance landscape will not change under the ACA.

Given this pluralism—or, some might say, fragmentation—of the U.S. approach to financing of health care, it is extremely difficult to rely on centralized, federal authority as the core approach to addressing critical issues in health care. And the issues are fundamental. Again, according to the Kaiser Foundation, the United States spends the most of any country in the world on health care per capita, and the rate of increase in spending has been consistently higher than real growth in the economy. Advocates for central authority may have theoretically compelling arguments. But these arguments largely ignore the realities of the nation's hybrid public-private system: a structure with deep roots that will not change due to the latest health-reform strategies embodied in the ACA. The idea of a system relying entirely on a federal approach in the United States is simply politically unrealistic.

LOCAL PRACTICE VARIATION

Health care is delivered at the local level by teams or individual practitioners working with patients. The work of Dr. John Wennberg and his colleagues, as reported by the Congressional Budget Office (CBO), has shown for more than 30 years that there is tremendous variation in the use of health care services by community. Indeed, in their published works, these researchers have noted that otherwise similar groups of Medicare beneficiaries received 60 percent more services in high-spending areas of the country than in low-spending ones. In their most recent reports, Jonathan S. Skinner and his colleagues at Dartmouth noted that Medicare expenditures per beneficiary ranged from a low of approximately $6,200 in Rapid City, South Dakota, to a high or $15,571 in Miami, Florida, in 2008. (These data were adjusted for race, age, gender, and price variation between regions.) Though some of this variation can be explained by other demographics for which the data are not adjusted, much of it remains unexplained by any inherent differences in the population. For their part, Wennberg and colleagues estimated that, were variation to be reduced to the low-spending region levels, Medicare could save 29 percent of total spending. Although the Dartmouth team focused its work on the Medicare population, other studies have shown that this same variation occurs within the Medicaid and private-sector populations.

A core question is why are these variations evident and what can be done about variation that is not warranted by patient characteristics? Many believe that the differences in utilization are based on the different local conditions (e.g., the supply and structure of providers) and local physician practice patterns. As such, it is extremely difficult to take a centralized approach to addressing these issues. Rather, it seems that the most important strategy is to focus on interventions at the state and local level.

FEDERAL VERSUS LOCAL APPROACHES TO MEDICARE

Private health plans have been providing services to Medicare beneficiaries essentially since the beginning of the Medicare program in 1965. In the early years, their role was quite small, and private-sector options were provided to minimize disruptive changes in coverage for seniors. The scope of private plans in the Medicare program grew in the 1980s with the Tax Equity and Fiscal Responsibility Act of 1982 (TEFRA). The payment formula used in the program, however, was unstable and many plans began exiting the Medicare market in the 1990s. The Balanced Budget Act of 1997 (BBA) introduced a new approach to payment for private plans in Medicare, called Medicare + Choice. The Medicare Modernization Act of 2003 (MMA) expanded on the Medicare + Choice concept and modified the payment approach thereby adopting the Medicare Advantage Program. A major intent of the MMA was to expand access to private plans geographically.

Medicare Advantage plans provide an option to Medicare enrollees: They offer a private health plan alternative to the traditional federal fee-for-service program. They often expand benefits relative to the traditional Medicare program. The plans are popular with senior citizens, and some plans demonstrate innovations to care management for Medicare beneficiaries. In 2011 somewhat more than one fourth of all eligible Medicare beneficiaries were enrolled in Medicare Advantage plans. Medicare Advantage enrollment has steadily increased from fewer than 6 million in 2005 to more than 11 million in 2011. Many seniors are now getting coverage for vision and dental care, as well as for health maintenance services (including gym memberships), and they enjoy lower co-payments and deductibles than do those in traditional Medicare. This expanded coverage has been of particular importance to low-income seniors, who cannot afford to purchase supplemental Medicare coverage. In addition, this coverage has provided expanded benefits in many rural areas where access to health care has been difficult. It should be noted that many Medicare Advantage plans have been able to offer additional benefits because they receive premium payments that exceed traditional Medicare costs. These plans will face challenges in continuing to provide these benefits as Medicare Advantage rates are reduced as part of the ACA.

Although Medicare Advantage programs have not yet demonstrated overall savings compared to traditional Medicare, there are some promising trends. Specifically, a 2009 study reported by America's Health Insurance Plans' Research and Policy group reported positive findings of the impact of Medicare Advantage in California and Nevada. The researchers found that, in 2006, risk-adjusted rates of inpatient days per patient were 30 percent lower for Medicare Advantage enrollees than for fee-for-service (FFS) enrollees in California, and 23 percent lower in Nevada. Readmissions were 15 percent lower among Medicare Advantage patients in California and 33 percent lower in Nevada. These are important data points that signal that private, locally designed health plans may have a positive impact on cost and use trends, in contrast to a uniform federal structure of benefits and cost control. The future direction for Medicare Advantage should consider the role that it can play in providing services tailored to the local populations.

HEALTH CARE QUALITY AND COST

Recognizing the complexity of the U.S. system and that quality and cost improvement will require changes in how individual providers practice, numerous promising strategies have been developed. Major approaches include the following:

- Pay for performance: providing incentives to hospitals, doctors, or other providers based on health, quality, or cost outcomes

- Disincentive approaches: reductions in payments based on outcomes to be avoided (e.g., not paying for wrong-site surgery)

- Care/disease-management/wellness programs: approaches to working with individual patients to improve patient compliance in follow-through care or in strategies to improve health and reduce the need for future medical care

- Reimbursement structures: payment systems designed to reward efficiency and caring for defined populations, such as capitation, global budgeting, and per-case payments, among others

- Provider-based continuous-improvement programs to enhance quality of care

Because health care is delivered locally, it is difficult to structure these approaches in a centralized, top-down approach. Success will require buy-in by the provider community and an ability to customize payments and judgments based on case-mix and other factors reflecting provider performance.

ACCOUNTABLE CARE ORGANIZATIONS

Perhaps the most vivid example of the challenge is the initially proposed federal rules for accountable care organizations (ACOs). The concept behind ACOs came into focus beginning in 2006 with a paper published by Elliot Fisher at Dartmouth. The concept behind ACOs grew from the Dartmouth research on variation and builds off the observation that integrated health systems perform better than do individual providers in terms of per-case cost and outcomes (as compared to per-unit cost alone). Building on this observation, Fisher and others recommended that incentives be developed to encourage a strong linkage between primary care, specialists, and hospitals. In effect, the concept is to try to create an integrated system of care within the current fragmented system of financing. The idea is similar to the foundational principles of all managed care organizations, especially health maintenance organizations (HMOs). However, there are some important differences.

In HMOs, patients must choose or are assigned to specific primary care providers. Referrals are required from these primary care providers, and the providers are compensated through some form of risk-based payment. The HMO generally takes insurance risk—that is, sets a premium for employers—and will take a loss if costs come in at a rate higher than that premium. The founding principles of HMOs were that care could be better coordinated and, therefore, more efficient if the primary care practitioner was in charge and had financial incentives either as an individual practitioner or as a group to provide more efficient quality care. In contrast, preferred provider organizations (PPOs) generally pay practitioners on a fee-for-service basis and do not require patients to select a particular primary care provider to coordinate all their care. Instead, there is a network of practitioners and patients have broader benefits if they go to practitioners within that network. Practitioners often have incentives for achieving certain quality/cost outcomes. Insurers who run these networks either take insurance risk (for insured groups) or else the risk is borne by self-funded employers (other than for high-cost cases which is usually covered by stop-loss coverage).

As described conceptually (to date, there are no operational ACOs, per se), ACOs are closest to PPO structures. That is, there is no requirement for patients to select a particular practitioner to coordinate all of their care, and practitioners are generally paid on a fee-for-service basis with incentives tied to performance. ACOs can be led by hospital or physician groups (or by a joint hospital/physician organization). The providers do not assume insurance risk; rather, they contract with an insurer, self-funded employer, or public payer (Medicare or Medicaid) and the cost trends' risk stays with the purchaser. Not much is known about whether or not these systems will have an impact on health care cost and quality trends. There are some cautionary data, however, based on experiences with managed care plans in the 1990s. Research shows that managed plans that were tightly structured showed some evidence of cost savings but no consistent picture of quality improvement. Further, provider-structured entities evidenced considerable challenges, especially because the goals of physician groups and hospitals were often at cross-purposes.

Despite the historical experience with managed care, the ACA placed significant emphasis on ACOs as a concept that might have a positive impact on quality and cost trends. The framers of the act were informed both by the literature on health care variation and the experience of the Medicare Physician Group Demonstration project. Even in advance of the publication of the draft regulations, and with no commonly agreed upon definition, providers across the country were labeling themselves "Accountable Care Organizations," and hospitals went back to a strategy they had first employed in the 1990s: purchasing physician practices so that physicians would be more closely tied to hospitals.

On March 31, 2011, the Department of Health and Human Services (HHS) published its proposed ACO rules and encountered a firestorm of a response. Academic journals published articles such as "Overweight and Out of Shape" to describe the proposed rules. Major health systems, which were considered the poster children for already arrived ACOs (e.g., Mayo Clinic and the Cleveland Clinic system), stated they would not participate in this pilot unless the rules were fundamentally changed.

Criticisms of the proposed rules centered on the perceived heavy-handedness of the regulations, the uncertainty inherent in the ACO structure, and the questionable design of the financial model. For example, the draft regulations called for approved ACOs to report on 65 different quality measures. Though these measures are generally agreed to be good quality indicators, the reporting requirement is such that many providers would need to build complex data systems capable of capturing information at the patient level without any additional financial support.

The regulations also envisioned a system whereby incentives (i.e., shared savings) would be paid to ACOs based on retrospective data analysis. In effect, providers would only know after the fact which patients affected their incentive payments increasing the measurement complexity and the risk to providers.

Finally, the design of this program is such that it will require significant upfront investment in data systems, medical records, and care-management processes with uncertain returns. Though HHS built the ACO model from the Physician Group Demonstration Program, it is important to know that that demonstration program included only 10 provider groups across the country. Even in that structure, only two demonstrated consistent savings throughout the program and only half achieved net savings by the end of the four-year demonstration period—and the ways those savings were achieved is still not fully understood.

The ACO draft regulations illustrate the problems that can occur with a top-down, federally designed cost-and-quality improvement program. In an attempt to establish a uniform approach across the country, regulations were architected in ways that don't take advantage of local circumstances. Unfortunately, the draft regulations tended to reflect an amalgamation of input from different interests but lost touch with the requirements and flexibility in design needed for successful adoption in the real world.

PATIENT-CENTERED MEDICAL HOME

There are many examples of the stifling nature of federal approaches to cost and quality control. Policies around never-events, readmissions, and the sustainable growth formula all evidence problems similar to the ACO regulations: All reach for the lowest common denominator to address complex problems that would be better addressed at the local level. In contrast, the federal government got it right in the Medicare/Medicaid Multipayer Advanced Primary Care Demonstration Project, which stands in sharp contrast to the ACO strategy and presents an interesting approach that builds on the strengths of the state and local environment. The Multipayer Advanced Primary Care Demonstration Project is founded in the principles of the patient-centered medical home (PCMH).

The PCMH framework is a long-standing idea in health care with its origins in pediatrics. The term appears to have been first coined in 1967 by pediatricians who were treating patients with multiple and complex health care needs. These pediatricians noted the importance of coordinated and comprehensive medical records for these children, and specifically the importance of each child having a primary care practitioner who was principally responsible for his or her care.

Thus, the term "patient-centered medical home." The concept grew to include specific principles and support recognized practices to assure better coordinated and integrated medical care for these children.

At the same time pediatricians were expanding and reinforcing their commitment to the PCMH concept, family practitioners were engaging in considerable discussion about the future of primary care. In 2002 the concept became formalized, and in 2007 the joint principles were adopted. The seven principles state that patient care should be delivered with

1. a personal physician as the point-of-contact,

2. physician-directed medical practice,

3. a whole-person orientation,

4. coordination and integration of care,

5. quality and safety emphasis,

6. enhanced access to care, and

7. payment that reflects the unique attributes of primary care.

These principles have been widely embraced by physician groups, health plans, and purchasers, and now by the federal government. In 2010 the Centers for Medicare & Medicaid services (CMS) released a solicitation for a demonstration project on the PCMH concept. In contrast to the ACO demonstration project, the Medicare and Medicaid Advanced Primary Care Practice Demonstration was designed to build on state models and allow for experimentation. The PCMH demonstration outlined key principles that were couched in a nonprescriptive model, enabling the federal government to partner with state and local entities that were already experimenting with this approach to determine its merits and capabilities.

The framework for the Medicare PCMH demonstration project recognized the extent and variability of local efforts underway to embed the principles in an operational structure. Medicare selected eight states with sufficiently advanced patient centered medical home initiatives to participate in the demonstration project. The eight states were Maine, Vermont, New York, Rhode Island, Pennsylvania, North Carolina, Michigan, and Minnesota. Though many of these initiatives have not been in effect long enough to evaluate, there are some early signs that these efforts are having an impact on quality and other outcomes.

One example of promising state and local models is the Vermont Blueprint for Health, a statewide PCMH model in effect since 2006. Under the blueprint, advanced primary care practices act as medical homes with support from community health teams and integrated technology. The community health teams typically include nurses, social workers, and behavioral-health counselors. The teams augment the work of primary care physicians by providing individual-care coordination, health-and-wellness coaching, and connections to appropriate community resources. The information technology focus is to make patient registries available to all participating practitioners. Providers in the pilot are paid fee-for-service with a bonus based on quality scores as determined by the National Committee on Quality Assurance. In the summer of 2011, the program was expanded to include specialists who will get enhanced payments based on both quality and cost performance.

All payers in the state are participating in the pilot and Vermont was selected by Medicare as one of the state demonstration project sites. Early qualitative evaluations of the program showed increases in patient and provider satisfaction and patient compliance with recommended care. A review of the first site in the pilot also showed significant reductions in hospital admissions and emergency visit costs with overall reported cost savings of more than 11 percent per person year over year. As of March 2011, about 10 percent of the Vermont population (60,000 people) was included in the pilot, with plans in place to expand statewide with a goal of reducing statewide health care spending by more than 25 percent over the next several years. The Vermont initiative is an important underpinning to the broader system reforms it plans to undertake: to create a single-payer financing mechanism and fundamentally change payment structures for providers, moving away from fee-for-service financing into more global/bundled payment approaches.

Another example of promising PCMH models is the experiment going on in the state of Michigan with its foundation in the Blue Cross and Blue Shield of Michigan (BCBSM) Physician Group Incentive Program (PGIP). The PGIP began in 2004 as an approach to improve chronic disease management and promote the use of generic drugs. The program was expanded over time to include many more initiatives focused on both improving quality and reducing health care spending. Individual physicians participate in the PGIP through a physician group, which are able to earn incentives based on their participation and taking into account certain performance measures. As of February 2011, more than 100 groups of physicians were participating, representing more than 11,000 physicians and including 1.8 million patients statewide.

The PCMH designation is one component of the PGIP initiative. PCMH-designated practices are those that have met specific criteria inherent in the core PCMH principles originally established by physician organizations: assuring after-hours access, use of patient registries, tracking of tests, and establishing a patient-provider partnership, among others. As of June 2010, approximately 2,500 physicians in 770 practices had achieved designated status. Data reported by Blue Cross and Blue Shield of Michigan showed that PCMH-designated practices had lower rates of ambulatory care–sensitive inpatient admissions, lower rates of high-tech radiology use, lower rates of certain emergency services, and higher rates of generic-drug use than did practices that were not so designated.

Like Vermont, Michigan was selected as one of the states to participate in the Medicare and Medicaid Advanced Primary Care Initiative. Michigan's selection was in part based on the fact that the BCBSM PCMH initiative is the largest in the country and a key participant in the Michigan Primary Care Transformation initiative (MiPCT). The MiPCT will include Medicaid, Medicare, Blue Cross Blue Shield of Michigan, and many health maintenance organizations across the state. This multi-payer initiative includes health plans that pay providers on a capitated basis as well as plans that pay using fee-for-service methodologies. Lean learning collaboratives, care-management initiatives, quality incentives, a patient registry and provider data reporting, and increased primary care fees for designated providers are all core to the MiPCT. The Blue Cross and Blue Shield of Michigan strategy and initiatives with the PGIP program and the PCMH initiatives have created the underlying infrastructure to enable the next evolution of financing and care-delivery models: organized systems of care (OSCs). The OSC has the same goals as the ACO concept and also includes hospital providers but unlike the federally designed ACO strategy, the BCBSM OSC strategy was designed in partnership with local providers and builds on the successes of the existing PGIP/PCMH models. Though different in the specifics from the Vermont model, the goals of the Michigan model parallel those of Vermont and the other states similarly testing patient centered medical home ideas.

CONCLUSION

Though it is still too early to tell what the response to the ACO shared-savings program will be, it is fair to say that the initial reaction by providers and health plans was quite different between the ACOs and the PCMH model. The PCMH concept was allowed to grow organically from local efforts, while to date the Medicare approach to ACOs has taken a more tightly structured federal approach. Whereas the PCMH initiatives have been embraced by providers, provider feedback on the ACO rules thus far has been lukewarm at best.

Vermont and Michigan both demonstrate that innovations developed at the local level, based on the culture and practice structure of communities is the strongest approach to sustained quality and cost improvement. In both cases, the PCMH strategies are leading to a broader vision, with the potential to have even bigger impacts on the cost and quality of care.

Similarly, the Medicare Advantage programs show that locally based health plans can offer benefit designs that attract members and may have the potential to help control the use of services. Early results show innovations built into these programs can produce results in ways that have not been as successful in the fully federally structured traditional Medicare program. The birth of all of these strategies at the local level is fundamental to their success and likely growth over the longer term.

Although policy made at the federal level can reduce cost and improve quality, it can also discourage or hamper effective efforts at the state and local level. Among providers, payers, and states throughout the country, vibrant efforts already in place are showing results on the cost-and-quality continuum. Many of these efforts are characterized by collaboration and partnership between entities within the state and local environment. Such initiatives contrast to some federal efforts that try and prescriptively dictate change in ways that are intended to be applied uniformly across the board. These prescriptive federal initiatives will simply not achieve much success when confronted with the realities of local implementation, priorities, and preferences.

References and Further Reading

America's Health Insurance Plans, Center for Policy & Research. (2009). *Reductions in hospital days, re-admissions, and potentially avoidable admissions among Medicare advantage enrollees in California and Nevada, 2006*. Retrieved from http://www.ahipresearch .org/pdfs/CAvsNV.pdf

Berenson, R. A., & Dowd, B. E. (2009). Medicare advantage plans at a crossroads—Yet again. *Health Affairs, 28*(1), w29–w40. Retrieved from http://content.healthaffairs.org/content/28/1/w29.full.pdf+html

Bielaszka-DuVernay, C. (2011). Innovation profile: Vermont's blueprint for medical homes, community health teams, and better health at lower cost. *Health Affairs 30*(3), 383–386. Retrieved from http://content.healthaffairs.org/content/30/3/383.full.pdf+html

Blue Cross Blue Shield of Michigan. (2011). *Blue Cross Blue Shield of Michigan designates approximately 2,500 physicians in nation's largest patient-centered medical home program*. Retrieved from http://news.bcbsm.com/news/2011/news_2011-06-27-08096.shtml

Cassidy, A. (2011). Health policy brief: Medicare advantage plans. *Health Affairs*. Retrieved from http://www.healthaffairs.org/ healthpolicybriefs/brief.php?brief_id=48

Congressional Budget Office. (2008). *Geographical variation in health care spending*. Retrieved from http://www.cbo.gov/ftpdocs/89xx/ doc8972/MainText.3.1.shtml

Fisher, E. S., Staiger, D. O., Bynum, J., & Gottlieb, D. J. (2007). Creating Accountable Care Organizations: The extended hospital medical staff. *Health Affairs, 26*(1), 44–57. Retrieved from http://content.healthaffairs.org/content/26/1/w44.full

Gilmer, T. P., & Kronick, R. G. (2011). Differences in the volume of services and in prices drive big variations in Medicaid spending among US states and regions. *Health Affairs 30*(7). Retrieved from http://content.healthaffairs.org/content/30/7/1316.full.pdf+html

Gold, M. (2010). *Policy brief: Accountable care organizations: Will they deliver?* Retrieved from http://www.mathematica-mpr.com/ publications/pdfs/health/account_care_orgs_brief.pdf

Iglehart, J. K. (2011). Perspective: The ACO regulations—Some answers, more questions. *New England Journal of Medicine, 364*(17), 1316–1324. Retrieved from http://healthpolicyandreform.nejm.org/?p=14218

Jaffe, S. (2009). Health policy brief: Medicare advantage plans. *Health Affairs*. Retrieved from http://www.healthaffairs.org/healthpolicybriefs/ brief.php?brief_id=1

Kahn, N. (2004). The future of family medicine: A collaborative project of the family medicine community. *Annals of Family Medicine, 2*(Suppl. 1), S3–S32. Retrieved from http://www.annfammed.org/cgi/reprint/2/suppl_1/s3

Kaiser Family Foundation. (2011). *Average annual growth rates for nominal NHE and GDP for selected time periods*. Retrieved from http://facts.kff.org/chart.aspx?ch=855

Kaiser Family Foundation. (2011). *Distribution of personal health care expenditures by source of payment, 1999 and 2009*. Retrieved from http://facts.kff.org/chart.aspx?ch=1349

Kaiser Health News. (2011). *Disappointment abounds regarding ACO regs*. Retrieved from http://www.kaiserhealthnews.org/ daily-reports/2011/june/01/acos.aspx

Klar, R. (2011). Overweight and out of shape: ACO regs need a major makeover [Health Affairs Blog]. Retrieved from http://healthaffairs .org/blog/2011/04/07/overweight-and-out-of-shape-aco-regs-need-a-major-makeover

Patient Centered Primary Care Collaborative. (2007). *Joint principles of the patient centered medical home*. Retrieved from http://www .pcpcc.net/content/joint-principles-patient-centered-medical-home

Sia, C., Tonniges, T. F., Osterhus, E., & Taba, S. (2004). History of the medical home concept. *Pediatrics 113*(4). Retrieved from http:// pediatrics.aappublications.org/content/113/Supplement_4/1473.10ng

Skinner, J. S., Gottlieb, D. J., & Carmichael, D. (2011). *A new series of Medicare expenditure measures by hospital referral region: 2003–2008*. Retrieved from Dartmouth Atlas Project website: http://www.dartmouthatlas.org/downloads/reports/PA_Spending_ Report_0611.pdf

Takach, M. (2011). Reinventing Medicaid: State innovations to qualify and pay for patient-centered medical homes show promising results. *Health Affairs, 30*(7), 1325–1334.

Udow-Phillips, M., Ogundimu, T., Ehrlich, E., Kofke-Egger, H., & Stock, K. (2010). *CHRTBook: Health care variation in Michigan*. Ann Arbor, MI: Center for Healthcare Research & Transformation. Retrieved from http://www.chrt.org/publications/price-of-care/ chrtbook-2010-09-health-care-variation-in-michigan

Wallack, A. R. (2011). Single payer ahead—Cost control and the evolving Vermont model. *New England Journal of Medicine, 365*(7), 584–585. Retrieved from http://healthpolicyandreform.nejm.org/?p=14965&query=TOC

Wennberg, J. E., Fisher, E. S., & Skinner, J. S. (2002). Geography and the debate over Medicare reform. *Health Affairs*. Retrieved from http://content.healthaffairs.org/content/early/2002/02/13/hlthaff.w2.96.short

Marianne Udow-Phillips and Kevin Seitz

33

Comparative-Effectiveness Research

POINT: Comparative-effectiveness studies, which aim to determine the best treatment protocols for conditions and diseases, will lead to higher-quality care and should be applied to all medical treatment.

Michael Hochman, University of California, Los Angeles
Danny McCormick, Harvard Medical School

COUNTERPOINT: Comparative-effectiveness studies cannot replace the individual experience, knowledge, and judgment of physicians and other health care professionals.

Elaine Morrato, University of Colorado Denver

Introduction

Comparative-effectiveness research (CER) is a term that refers to side-by-side studies that compare the effectiveness of different health care services or health care products and help doctors use existing health services more effectively. In 2009 the Institute of Medicine (IOM) defined CER as

> The generation and synthesis of evidence that compares the benefits and harms of alternative methods to prevent, diagnose, treat, and monitor a clinical condition or to improve the delivery of care. The purpose of CER is to assist consumers, clinicians, purchasers, and policy makers to make informed decisions that will improve health care at both the individual and population levels.

Although early studies often focused on comparing different medications, the IOM's expanded definition highlights the fact that CER can encompass a broader array of studies that address fundamental questions in medical decision making, not only medication studies. Though many researchers, and especially clinicians, think of CER as something new, linked to some new trends in health services research, studies comparing different approaches to the treatment of health problems have occurred for the past 50 years. However, until more recently, the ideas underpinning these studies were not systematized. Studies in the 1970s that led to the rejection of the radical mastectomy are examples of earlier research similar to what we now call CER. Drug companies have also conducted studies comparing the effectiveness of new medications to older, existing ones as part of the process of bringing new products to market. However, commercially funded research typically focuses on the development and approval of new products; if CER is to expand beyond that limited role, it will have to address the challenge of developing broader funding sources, such as nonprofits and governmental agencies that will look more broadly at determining which interventions are best.

One important factor in the expansion of CER is increased federal funding. Two recently passed pieces of legislation have included federal funding to support CER. The 2009 American Recovery and Reinvestment Act provided over $1 billion in funding for CER, most of it allocated to the National Institutes of Health with a smaller amount for the Agency for Healthcare Research and Quality. This act provided a one-time increase in funding, but 2010's American Recovery and Reinvestment Act included a more permanent focus on CER, with the establishment of the Patient Centered Outcomes

Research Institute (PCORI). The law sets up PCORI as an independent nonprofit organization and gives the organization the task of establishing priorities for CER through its own Board of Governors and Methodology Committee.

The roots of CER research are complex. CER is linked to what has become a major trend both in medical education in the United States and in clinical care, the evidence-based medicine (EBM) approach. At its core, EBM argues that all clinicians need to learn to use scientific evidence as the basis for their medical decisions, rather than just relying on what the clinician learned in medical school or at recent continuing-education meetings, or through more casual contacts with clinical colleagues. Some of the early research that has led to the acceptance of EBM—first in medical education and later in nursing and other types of clinical education, as well—included studies over the past 40 years examining significant geographic variation in the rates of use of medical services, including hospital admissions and surgical and diagnostic procedures. Wennberg and colleagues at the Dartmouth Institute for Health Policy and Clinical Practice, who began work in the early 1970s, called this line of research "studies in small area variation." They argued that a lack of consensus about the diagnosis and treatment of conditions leads to a wide variation in health care utilization and to what are considered the best ways to treat certain health problems. The research culminated in what is often called the Dartmouth Atlas Project, which again focuses on variations in medical practices and outcomes across geographic areas, looking at both small areas as well as across states and major metropolitan areas. Some of this research was cited in the congressional debates over the passage of health care reform in 2010 and was cited as an example of why greater attention to variations in clinical practices has the potential both to improve health care services and to lower the costs of care.

In the twenty-first century, CER has become easier to conduct (and thus more easily expandable) partially due to advances in health information technologies. The wider availability of electronic medical and health record systems, linked to health care reform and payment-modification approaches, has led to those systems being adopted by larger numbers of medical providers and health care systems. Point-of-care clinical data will make studies of medical effectiveness even more likely, as will the development of formal organizations such as health information exchanges that could share health care information electronically between providers, hospitals, and public health systems. In this chapter, Michael Hochman and Danny McCormick provide data and a review of past studies that lead to the conclusion that comparative-effectiveness studies should be applied to all medical treatment and will lead to higher quality care. In the Counterpoint section, Elaine Morrato argues that these studies cannot replace the individual experience, knowledge, and judgment of physicians and other health care professionals and their critical role in delivery of high-quality patient care.

POINT

In the 1980s, several new types of medications were approved in the United States to treat high blood pressure. The new medications were introduced with considerable fanfare and zeal. Soon, with the help of pharmaceutical industry marketers, the new medications became widely used.

Some doctors and health care policymakers, however, had concerns about the new medications. For one thing, the new drugs commanded a high price—in some instances, 30 times that of the older medications. In addition, there were only limited data about how well the new medications worked. But when these experts asked the medication manufacturers to conduct head-to-head studies comparing the new medications with older ones, the companies balked. Such studies were risky to these companies because it might turn out that the older, less expensive medications were just as effective.

It was at this point that the National Heart, Lung, and Blood Institute (NHLBI)—a division of the National Institutes of Health (NIH)—decided to fund the research itself. The study, which began in the early 1990s and was published in 2002, was known as the antihypertensive and lipid lowering treatment to prevent heart attack trial (ALLHAT). In the end, this large and well-conducted study with long-term follow-up confirmed what skeptics had suspected: An inexpensive, well-established medication—chlorthalidone—proved to be at least as good, and in some cases better, than the expensive new blood pressure medications. Following the publication of ALLHAT, most major medical guidelines began endorsing thiazide diuretics (the class of medications that chlorthalidone represents) as the appropriate first-line medication for treating high blood pressure.

In addition to answering the question about which of the numerous existing blood pressure medications is best, ALLHAT stimulated interest in a type of research frequently referred to as comparative-effectiveness research (CER). In a nutshell, CER refers to research like ALLHAT that compares the effectiveness of different health care services and helps doctors use existing services more effectively.

Before advocates of comparative-effectiveness research could celebrate too much, however, new data emerged to add a wrinkle to the ALLHAT story: Despite ALLHAT's clear findings, many doctors continued to use medications other than thiazides as first-line treatment for high blood pressure. "[ALLHAT] should have more than doubled [the use of thiazides]," said Dr. Curt D. Furberg, a Wake Forest professor and the former chairman of the steering committee for ALLHAT. But the study did not have this effect. According to a 2008 report in *The New York Times*, after the publication of ALLHAT's findings, the percentage of patients with high blood pressure treated with a thiazide increased from 30 to 35 percent to only about 40 percent.

Multiple factors likely explain ALLHAT's limited impact. One might simply be that doctors do not stay up-to-date on the medical literature and therefore might not have been aware of ALLHAT's results (or the current treatment guidelines). Another potential factor is that the pharmaceutical industry's marketing successfully convinced some doctors that its products were superior to thiazides, despite ALLHAT's findings. Yet another possible reason is that, since ALLHAT began, even newer blood pressure medications have been approved, and the makers of these newer medications argue that they are more effective than thiazides despite the lack of comparative data.

Overall, the story of ALLHAT illustrates both the possibilities and challenges of conducting and funding comparative-effectiveness research. In this chapter, these possibilities and the challenges will be examined in more detail. In addition, this section will argue that, despite the challenges, further investment in comparative-effectiveness research will be critical for improving the U.S. health care system.

DEFINITION OF COMPARATIVE-EFFECTIVENESS RESEARCH

When most lay people think about CER, they envision studies like ALLHAT that directly compare two or more medications. However, in 2009 the Institute of Medicine (IOM) defined CER more broadly as

> The generation and synthesis of evidence that compares the benefits and harms of alternative methods to prevent, diagnose, treat, and monitor a clinical condition or to improve the delivery of care. The purpose of CER is to assist consumers, clinicians, purchasers, and policy makers to make informed decisions that will improve health care at both the individual and population levels.

Table 33.1   CER Priorities From the Institute of Medicine

Topic	Goals
Atrial fibrillation (a common cardiac abnormality)	To determine whether patients with atrial fibrillation are best treated with medications, surgery, or a procedure known as catheter ablation in which the abnormal cardiac tissue is destroyed with an electrical impulse
Hearing loss	To determine whether patients with hearing loss are best treated with hearing aids, cochlear implants (replacement of the nerve tissue responsible for hearing), or therapy aimed at teaching patients to read lips and use sign language
Falls in the elderly	To determine the best treatments (such as balance training or exercise) to prevent falls in the elderly
Heartburn	To determine which patients with heartburn should undergo a procedure called upper endoscopy in which a camera is inserted into the throat to help determine the cause and to rule out the possibility of throat cancer
Research dissemination	To determine the best ways to disseminate the results of medical research to patients, medical practitioners, and insurance companies
Care coordination	To determine whether programs to promote coordination of care (e.g., hiring case managers to provide logistical assistance to patients with chronic diseases) leads to substantial improvements in patient outcomes, compared to usual care
Childhood obesity	To compare the effectiveness of school-based programs (e.g., meal programs, policies to remove vending machines, and physical activity programs) in preventing obesity in children

This broader definition highlights the fact that CER encompasses an array of studies that address fundamental questions in medical decision making, not just medication studies. Table 33.1 provides examples of high-priority CER studies as identified in a recent report from the IOM. The list includes studies that compare surgical and nonsurgical treatments, studies that evaluate the effectiveness of diagnostic tests, and studies that evaluate health system changes such as care-coordination programs. In addition, the list includes studies evaluating programs that do not even directly involve the health care system, such as school-based obesity prevention strategies. The IOM report also emphasizes that CER encompasses research aimed at determining which groups of patients are most likely to benefit from health care services—for example, which medications are most effective in elderly patients or patients with a particular genetic makeup.

It is also important to note that, although CER most commonly involves a comparison of two or more tests, treatments, or strategies, this is not always the case. Studies aimed at determining the appropriate use of existing health care services might also be classified as CER even when multiple services aren't directly compared. For example, the IOM listed research evaluating a diagnostic test called upper endoscopy (in which a camera is inserted into the throat to look for abnormalities) in patients with heartburn as a CER priority topic, even though such studies would simply compare patients undergoing endoscopy to those who do not receive the test. The IOM presumably classified this study as CER because endoscopy is an existing and widely used service and additional research is needed to clarify its appropriate use. By contrast, a study that compared a novel test or treatment involving the use of a placebo to no treatment at all would likely not be classified as CER.

Though the definition of CER has only been clearly articulated in recent years, the concept of CER has been discussed for decades, and several successful examples of CER have led to important changes in clinical practice. Below are a few commonly cited examples:

- Women with breast cancer once were almost uniformly treated with a surgical procedure called total mastectomy in which the entire breast and surrounding tissue are removed. Well-designed studies showed that a less invasive procedure called lumpectomy, in which only the cancer and immediate surrounding tissue are removed, could be just as effective. Now, many women with breast cancer are treated effectively without the complete removal of their breasts.

- Shortly after effective treatment for HIV/AIDS was developed, it became clear that doctors did not know how to use the medications optimally. For example, should patients begin treatment before they developed symptoms of the disease? Should the medications be given continuously or only intermittently when immune markers decreased or symptoms developed? Over the past two decades, a number of important studies have helped to better define the appropriate use of these medications and patients with HIV/AIDS to receive much more effective therapy.

- Patients with abnormal heart rhythms after heart attacks frequently received medications to suppress these abnormalities. Eventually, however, studies demonstrated that these medications were actually harmful. Now, patients rarely receive these dangerous medications after heart attacks.

THE SHORTCOMINGS OF EXISTING CLINICAL RESEARCH

The need for a greater investment in CER is underscored by the shortcomings of existing clinical research. Analyses of recently published medical studies have demonstrated the following:

- Fewer than half of studies published in top medical journals compare active treatments against each other (the majority compare active treatments with placebo or no therapy).

- Only 3 percent of studies published in top medical journals compare medications with other types of treatments, such as lifestyle changes or surgery.

- Just 1 percent of studies published in top medical journals include formal cost analyses.

- Existing medical research disproportionately focuses on white male patients.

- Few studies focus on health system changes (e.g., care-coordination programs) or public health programs (e.g., school-based obesity prevention programs).

In addition, there is a growing recognition that clinical research has focused too much on studying patients under experimental settings rather than under "real-world" conditions. As an example, a complicated medication that requires frequent monitoring may be effective in a research study in which study nurses regularly check in with the patients. However, when that medication is used in real-world clinical practice without close monitoring, it is likely to cause a higher rate of complications; under such conditions, the adverse effects may outweigh the benefits.

Because of the limitations of existing CER, clinicians do not have answers to many important medical questions. For example, considerable uncertainty exists about the appropriate treatment for early-stage prostate cancer, despite the fact that the main treatment options for this common condition (surgery, radiation, and close monitoring) have been around for decades. Similarly, because of a dearth of research, doctors still do not know what blood sugar levels to aim for when they treat patients with diabetes. Moreover, doctors don't know how many of the treatments and strategies that have proven effective under research conditions are effective in real-world settings.

FUNDING FOR EXISTING CLINICAL RESEARCH

Some of the shortcomings of existing clinical research may be a consequence of how such research is funded in the United States. A large proportion of funding for clinically oriented medical research in the United States comes from commercial entities such as pharmaceutical companies and device makers. One obvious concern with commercially funded research is that it could be biased in favor of products made by the sponsor. Indeed, numerous studies have documented that commercially funded research is considerably more likely to generate studies with positive results.

Another, less appreciated concern with commercially funded research is its scope. Commercial entities—which have a fiduciary responsibility to generate profits—fund research primarily for the purpose of winning regulatory approval for new products, or to expand indications for existing products. One might expect that commercial entities would want to favorably compare their new products against those of their competitors. But often it does not happen this way. Instead, commercially funded studies disproportionately compare new products against placebos. Upon closer examination, this strategy makes commercial sense: In order to win approval for new products, companies frequently only need to prove that those products are better than nothing (i.e., a placebo), which is often easier than showing that new products are better than existing products that have already demonstrated their effectiveness. Once the new products are approved, the companies can use marketing to gain market share.

In addition, commercial entities don't have incentives to fund other types of studies that physicians and policymakers need. Why, for example, would a company fund a study evaluating a care-coordination or public health program that doesn't involve the use of a commercial product? Why would a company fund a study to determine the optimal use of a treatment strategy among patients from an underrepresented minority group? Why would a company fund a study to evaluate a new diagnostic test in a real-world setting if the test has already won regulatory approval based on research in a more favorable experimental setting?

Because most commercially funded research focuses on the development and approval of new products, the responsibility for funding CER most often falls to noncommercial entities (nonprofits and governmental agencies). In other words, noncommercial entities must fund the studies that help doctors use existing medical interventions more effectively and that determine which interventions are best. Because noncommercial research funding is limited so, too, is the amount of CER produced in the United States.

LOST IN TRANSLATION

In order for CER to have a positive impact on the health care system, the findings must be disseminated and implemented in regular clinical practice. But it does not always happen this way, as the story of ALLHAT illustrates. Other prominent examples of CER that has not yet been widely adopted in routine clinical practice include the following:

- The COURAGE trial demonstrated that medications should be the first-line treatment for most patients with stable blockages in the arteries feeding the heart. Despite these findings, most patients with this condition continue to receive an invasive procedure aimed at opening up the blockages.

- Many patients with a heart condition known as heart failure do not receive the appropriate medications.

- A substantial number of hospitals do not follow protocols proven to reduce the risk of hospital-acquired infections.

The discordance between what the research shows and what actually happens in clinical practice is pervasive. One widely cited study suggests that Americans receive only about half of the health care services that they should receive when they visit the doctor. Another suggests that there is a lag of almost 20 years between the time that knowledge is generated through research and the time it is widely incorporated into clinical practice.

Thus, it is clear that generating high-quality CER alone is not sufficient to bring about changes in clinical practice. To ensure that research leads to better health care for patients, there must be concurrent efforts to ensure the appropriate dissemination and implementation of new research findings into clinical practice. (See the following for further discussion.)

NEW COMPARATIVE-EFFECTIVENESS RESEARCH INITIATIVES

Interest in CER has burgeoned in recent years in response to two important new federal initiatives to support this type of research: the American Recovery and Reinvestment Act and the Patient Protection and Affordable Care Act (ACA).

The Recovery Act, which was signed into law in February 2009, provided $1.1 billion in funding for CER, $400 million of which was allocated to the Department of Health and Human Services, $400 of which was allocated to the National Institutes of Health, and $300 million of which was allocated to the Agency for Healthcare Research and Quality. These funds were used to support a variety of CER studies by researchers from around the United States (including academic institutions, nonprofit organizations, and for-profit companies). Most of these studies are ongoing. In addition, some of the funding supported programs aimed at compiling, organizing, and disseminating research findings, as well as the production of the IOM report outlining CER priorities.

The Recovery Act provided only a one-time infusion of CER funds, however. Congress made a longer-term commitment to CER in 2010 when it passed ACA. The new law established the Patient Centered Outcomes Research Institute (PCORI), an independent nonprofit organization similar to the National Academy of Sciences that will ultimately receive more than $500 million annually to support CER. The PCORI—which has its own Board of Governors and Methodology Committee—will establish priorities for CER (likely similar to the priorities recommended by the IOM) and will coordinate federal CER funding. Eventually, the PCORI will either fund CER directly or will appropriate its funds to federal agencies, academic institutions, or private organizations to manage the funding. The Agency for Healthcare Research and Quality (AHRQ) and the National Institutes of Health—both federal agencies that sponsor much of the existing federally funded CER—will receive preference for such funding contracts (i.e., it is likely that PCORI's funding will ultimately be distributed to researchers through AHRQ or the NIH).

Because of the new funding opportunities resulting from the Recovery Act and the ACA, there will likely be a considerable increase in investment in CER.

COST-EFFECTIVENESS RESEARCH

Most of the public discussion about CER has focused on determining which health care services are best for individual patients. CER can also provide information about the relative costs of different health care strategies. Such information can guide policymakers and developers of medical practice guidelines. (This information should not be used by clinicians when treating individual patients, however.)

As an example, imagine that strategy A is as effective as strategy B, but strategy A is less expensive. This information might allow physicians who are developing a treatment guideline to recommend strategy A over strategy B. Similarly, policymakers at an insurance organization might decide to cover strategy A but not strategy B as first-line therapy. Such a coverage decision would likely be appropriate, particularly if strategy B was also covered for patients who did not respond adequately to treatment A (or in subgroups of patients for whom strategy B was known to be more effective than strategy A).

Cost-effectiveness data may also be helpful in circumstances in which a health care service is marginally effective but extremely expensive. For example, a new treatment for advanced prostate cancer was recently found to extend life by an average of four months; however, the new treatment costs $93,000. A panel of medical experts might use such information to reasonably recommend that insurance organization and Medicare not cover this treatment simply because the small benefit is not worth the cost.

As part of its recent legislation to increase funding for CER, however, Congress made the unfortunate decision to ban the PCORI from funding research that uses a common method of cost analysis in which a monetary threshold is employed to determine whether health care services are cost-effective. Though the language is somewhat ambiguous, many have interpreted the rule to indicate that the PCORI cannot fund any research involving cost analyses at all. In addition, a 2010 article in the *New England Journal of Medicine* noted that the legislation states that CER findings "may not be construed as mandates, guidelines, or recommendations for payment, coverage, or treatment or used to deny coverage" (Neumann & Weinstein, 2010) These stipulations were inserted in response to political pressure from advocates (led by pharmaceutical companies and medical-device manufacturers) who were concerned that CER findings might lead to the denial of insurance coverage for treatments that proved to be ineffective or not cost-effective (i.e., the benefit-to-cost ratio is low).

Although concerns about cost analyses must be taken seriously, such limitations on cost-effectiveness research could greatly undermine the usefulness of federally funded CER. In the coming years, policymakers will need to make important decisions to slow the growth in health care spending. Such decisions will be difficult, and should be made with input from the public in a transparent, equitable, and thoughtful manner. Without cost-effectiveness data, however, policymakers will be greatly limited in their ability to make well-informed decisions.

A VISION FOR COMPARATIVE-EFFECTIVENESS RESEARCH

In an ideal system, CER would be driven by the need to answer and address the uncertainties that doctors face in everyday medical decision making. It would be conducted by unbiased researchers whose primary motivation was to answer clinically relevant questions under real-world conditions, and it would be funded by responsive noncommercial agencies whose primary motivation was to improve health care. These funding agencies would target CER topics that would not otherwise receive support. Such research would evaluate not only the safety and effectiveness of different health care services but also cost. In addition, CER would help identify which groups of patients are most likely to benefit from which health care services, enabling more personalized health care (e.g., which medications are most effective in elderly patients).

Just as importantly, once CER results became available, the findings would be conveyed to clinicians in a clear and useable way and in a timely fashion. In addition, clinicians would be given tools, such as easy-to-follow guidelines that would promote the use of evidenced-based services, as well as the resources to implement the findings (e.g., support for an effective smoking-cessation program). CER would also be used by policymakers and panels of experts to develop clinical guidelines. These groups would use the results of CER studies to recommend which services are effective and should be widely adopted. In some cases, these groups might need to make difficult decisions involving cost with input from the public in a transparent, equitable, and thoughtful manner.

Lastly, clinicians should never be put in a situation in which they are expected to use cost data to make decisions about individual patients. A physician who considers cost when treating a patient could create a significant conflict of interest in the physician-patient relationship, betray the accepted professional obligations of physicians, and undermine a patient's confidence in the health care system.

Under the system described above, it is easy to envision how CER could directly lead to higher quality and more efficient care for patients. While an idealized system like this might seem impossible to achieve, this vision should serve as the ideal to which we should strive.

CHALLENGES AHEAD

The new initiatives contained in the Recovery Act and ACA represent important steps toward making the vision for CER described above a reality. The creation of the PCORI in particular provides a mechanism for ongoing support for CER. However, important challenges for CER remain.

First, as discussed above, PCORI should be enabled and encouraged to fund cost analyses, including those involving a monetary threshold for determining which services are cost-effective. Such studies provide crucial information for policymakers.

Second, policymakers must be enabled to use CER results to generate guidelines and recommendations. As noted above, the ACA legislation states that CER findings "may not be construed as mandates, guidelines, or recommendations for payment, coverage, or treatment or used to deny coverage"; however, the language is ambiguous and how it will be interpreted remains uncertain. Though CER findings should not dictate guidelines or recommendations, physicians and policymakers must be empowered to implement CER findings if CER is to maximally benefit patients.

Third, because CER in isolation will not necessarily bring about changes in clinical practice, it is essential that policymakers institute concurrent strategies to promote dissemination, adoption, and implementation of new research findings. For example, many successful health systems have developed easy-to-use programs to assist doctors and other providers with clinical decision making. Such programs—which ideally would be incorporated into an electronic medical record system, but also could be paper based—would assist doctors in following the evidence. This programs might, for example, remind and encourage a doctor who is about to prescribe a blood pressure medication that he or she should select a thiazide diuretic as first-line therapy. Further research aimed at identifying programs that promote the dissemination and implementation of CER findings is sorely needed (and was identified as a CER priority area in the recent IOM report).

RESPONSES TO COMMON CRITIQUES OF COMPARATIVE-EFFECTIVENESS RESEARCH

Some critics have suggested that, because CER findings are often not effectively disseminated or adopted into clinic practice, conducting these studies is a waste of time. It is true that identifying more effective strategies for disseminating and promoting the implementation of CER findings is critical. However, the fact that CER findings aren't always effectively translated into clinical practice is not a reason to limit CER funding. As was outlined above, there are numerous examples of how CER has led to important improvements in the U.S. health care system already.

Another argument against CER is that money allocated to such studies could be better spent in other ways (e.g., by directly paying for health care services). This is a shortsighted viewpoint. Although it may take several years before the benefits of investing in CER become apparent, CER is likely to reap dividends over time. Had previous generations not invested in medical research, the U.S. health care system would be considerably worse off today.

Some critics worry that CER may provide ammunition for insurance companies to deny coverage for costly services, or that it could result in the rejection of new treatments and technologies by regulatory agencies, limiting patients' access to new services. But the only way to determine what works and what doesn't is through research. Effective treatments, tests, and services should fare favorably in CER studies, while those that are ineffective likely will not. In fact, CER may provide ammunition for health care professionals to justify the use of effective services to insurance companies. Likewise, regulatory agencies such as the Food and Drug Administration (FDA) understand that, because not every patient responds to standard therapies, they should have access to multiple treatment options. In fact, the FDA frequently approves medications that may be inferior to existing therapies in order to provide additional options for patients.

Finally, critics of CER worry that, citing data from cost-effectiveness analyses, doctors and other health care providers might select less effective tests and treatments for their patients to save money. But cost-effectiveness analyses are intended for use by policymakers, not individual doctors. Though it is theoretically possible that health care providers might use cost data inappropriately, this is unlikely because health care providers shouldn't have any motivation to do so. On the contrary, since because companies and Medicare pay for health care services, doctors are frequently unaware of the cost of the services they recommend.

CONCLUSION

Comparative-effectiveness research refers to research aimed at determining which of multiple health care services—including diagnostic tests, treatments, public health programs, or other health care delivery strategies—is best. Generally speaking, CER studies focus on existing health care services rather than novel services. In the United States today, there is a dearth of CER, in large part because most medical research is funded by commercial entities that focus on winning regulatory approval or expanding indications for novel tests and treatments.

In 2009 and 2010, the American Recovery and Reinvestment Act and the ACA expanded governmental funding for CER. The CER funds authorized in the ACA will be administered by the PCORI. The new funds should provide a much-needed boost to CER; however, several challenges loom. In particular, the legislative language that established the PCORI appears to indicate that PCORI funds should not be used to support cost-effectiveness research. Such a limitation—strictly followed—is unfortunate since cost-effectiveness data provide critical information for policymakers. Second, the legislative language seems to suggest that CER findings should not be used to develop guidelines, recommendations, or coverage decisions. If this language is strictly adhered to, it could greatly limit the usefulness of CER data. Finally, and perhaps most importantly, CER findings have not always been widely disseminated and implemented into clinical practice; it will be critical to identify more effective strategies for achieving these key goals in the years ahead.

Despite such challenges, CER is crucial for improving the U.S. health care system. Investing in CER now will surely reap dividends in the years to come.

REFERENCES AND FURTHER READING

ALLHAT Officers and Coordinators for the ALLHAT Collaborative Research Group. (2002). Major outcomes in high-risk hypertensive patients randomized to angiotensin-converting enzyme inhibitor or calcium channel blocker vs diuretic: The antihypertensive and lipid-lowering treatment to prevent heart attack trial (ALLHAT). *Journal of the American Medical Association, 288*(23), 2981–2997.

Bekelman, J. E., Li, Y., & Gross, C. P. (2003). Scope and impact of financial conflicts of interest in biomedical research: A systematic review. *Journal of the American Medical Association, 289*(4), 454–465.

Borden, W. B., Redberg, R. F., Mushlin, A. I., Dai, D., Kaltenbach, L. A., & Spertus, J. A. (2011). Patterns and intensity of medical therapy in patients undergoing percutaneous coronary intervention. *Journal of the American Medical Association, 305*(18), 1882–1889.

Clancy, C., & Collins, F. S. (2010). Patient-centered outcomes research institute: The intersection of science and health care. *Science Translational Medicine, 2*(37), 37cm18.

Committee on Comparative Effectiveness Research Prioritization, Institute of Medicine. (2009). *Initial national priorities for comparative effectiveness research.* Washington, DC: National Academies Press.

Contopoulos-Ioannidis, D. G., Alexiou, G. A., Gouvias, T. C., & Ioannidis, J. P. (2008). Life cycle of translational research for medical interventions. *Science, 321*(5894), 1298–1299.

Hochman, M., & McCormick, D. (2010). Characteristics of published comparative effectiveness studies of medications. *Journal of the American Medical Association, 303*(10), 951–958.

McGlynn, E. A., Asch, S. M., Adams, J., Keesey, J., Hicks, J., DeCristofaro, A., & Kerr, E. A. (2003). The quality of health care delivered to adults in the United States. *New England Journal of Medicine, 348*(26), 2635–2645.

Neumann, P. J., & Weinstein, M. C. (2010). Legislating against use of cost-effectiveness information. *New England Journal of Medicine, 363*(16), 1495–1497.

Pollack, A. (2008, November 27). The minimal impact of a big hypertension study. *The New York Times,* p. B1.

Szabo, L. (2010 April 30). FDA approves $93K prostate cancer vaccine. *USA Today.* Retrieved from http://www.usatoday.com/news/health/2010–04–30-prostatevaccine30_ST_N.htm

Wennberg, J. E., & Fisher, E. S. (Eds.). (2006). *The care of patients with severe chronic illness: A report on the Medicare program by the Dartmouth Atlas Project.* Hanover, NH: The Center for the Evaluative Clinical Sciences and Dartmouth Medical College.

Wennberg, J. E., Fisher, E. S., Stukel, T. A., & Sharp, S. M. (2004, October). Use of Medicare claims data to monitor provider-specific performance among patients with severe chronic illness. *Health Affairs.* Retrieved from http://content.healthaffairs.org/cgi/content/full/hlthaff.var.5/DC1

Wennberg, J. E., & Gittelsohn, A. (1973). Small area variations in health care delivery. *Science, 182*(4117), 1102–1108.

Michael Hochman and Danny McCormick

COUNTERPOINT

A key premise underpinning health care reform in the United States is that public investment in comparative-effectiveness research (CER) will result in lower health care costs through better health care decision making and quality of care resulting in better outcomes. The purpose of this chapter is to debate the question of whether America's focus on the use of CER evidence to standardize medical care will supplant the patient-provider relationship. Or, in other words, can comparative-effectiveness studies replace patient preferences and the individual experience, knowledge, and judgment of physicians and other health professionals? The answer is no. This essay argues that CER evidence is necessary for informed decision making, but insufficient on its own. Provider experience and patient preferences will still play a vital role in clinical-care decisions and in establishing health policy. Lessons learned from the evidence-based medicine movement and from other nations that have enacted health care technology assessment programs will be summarized to support the necessity of patient and health provider engagement when establishing and implementing medical guidelines. The Patient-Centered Outcomes Research Institute (PCORI) in the United States will also be discussed, specifically its congressionally mandated mission to conduct CER through a process that emphasizes patient and provider engagement.

THE MEDICAL NECESSITY OF COMPARATIVE-EFFECTIVENESS RESEARCH

The Institute of Medicine (a nongovernmental, nonprofit organization which provides authoritative advice to decision makers and the public on issues of health and health care) defined CER as the "generation and synthesis of evidence that compares the benefits and harms of alternative methods to prevent, diagnose, treat, and monitor a clinical condition or to improve the delivery of care." The recent and substantial public investment in comparative-effectiveness research has emerged from several converging factors.

First, U.S. health care costs have risen at rates that are financially untenable. The Centers for Medicare & Medicaid Services report that national health expenditures grew 4.0 percent to $2.5 trillion in 2009, or approximately $8,000 per person, and accounted for 17.6 percent of gross domestic product (GDP). The health share of GDP is projected to reach 19.3 percent by 2019. The Kaiser Family Foundation reports that "rising costs coupled with an overall economic slowdown and rising federal deficit is placing greater strains on the systems used to finance health care, including private employer-sponsored health insurance coverage and public insurance programs such as Medicare and Medicaid." As a result, the containment of health care costs has become a major policy priority in the United States as health care has become an increasingly large component of government, employer, and individual budgets (Kimbuende, 2010).

Second, evidence-based medicine (EBM) has become a major driving force in many health care organizations offering the promise of delivering better and more consistent quality while reducing costs. EBM advocates the use of current best scientific evidence from health research as the basis for medical decisions. High health care costs have been attributed, in part, to significant geographic variation in the rates of use of expensive (and possibly unwarranted) medical services, including hospital admissions and surgical and diagnostic procedures. Wennberg and colleagues at the Dartmouth Institute for Health Policy and Clinical Practice have called variation in medical-service utilization "small-area variation." They argue that a lack of consensus on the diagnosis and treatment of many conditions leads to wide variation in health care utilization. To decrease unwarranted variation in medical practice is a target of health reform because higher spending on health care in certain geographic areas has not always translated into better outcomes (2002). The Kaiser Family Foundation quotes experts who claim that up to 30 percent of health care is unnecessary. Therefore, the need for evidence-based prevention and treatment strategies to inform medical decisions is high.

Third, high-quality evidence is lacking for many important health decisions affecting the nation's health. The gold standard of comparative-effectiveness evidence has been randomized controlled trials. Such trials often compare medical products or medical-treatment strategies, and sometimes compare medications with nonpharmacologic approaches. Pharmaceutical manufacturers will conduct comparison trials to support a market claim or to justify pricing and prescription drug reimbursement. Public agencies, such as the National Institutes of Health and the Veterans Administration, have funded comparison trials in specific priority disease areas, such as the prevention and treatment of diabetes, cardiovascular disease, and cancer. However, rigorous clinical trials are expensive, time consuming, and challenging to conduct. In addition, manufacturers may be less likely to sponsor comparison trials given the inherent uncertainty and the economic consequences for the manufacturer if their drug or product is not shown to be superior. Indeed, Hochman and McCormick reported that just one third of comparative-effectiveness medication studies (34 out of 104) published in leading medical journals during 2008–2009 received commercial funding. As a result, there are more unanswered medical questions than rigorous clinical trials to answer them. Moreover, randomized clinical trials are often conducted at academic research centers with strict controls and eligibility requirements, and therefore are generally viewed as nonrepresentative of real-world patients and clinical settings.

The American Recovery and Reinvestment Act of 2009 (ARRA) called on the Institute of Medicine (IOM) to recommend a list of priority topics to be the initial focus of national investment in real-world CER. One hundred initial national priorities were selected from more than 2,600 proposed topics submitted by the public. Approximately half of the final list of priorities involved questions comparing the effectiveness of different treatment and diagnostic strategies; the other half involved comparing the effectiveness of different health-delivery models.

Advances in health information technologies have enabled comparative-effectiveness studies to be conducted more cost-effectively in real time. Electronic medical and health-record systems have become more broadly adopted by medical providers and health care systems. Point-of-care clinical data represents real-world health care utilization. Because the data are already collected and available electronically, observational studies can be conducted relatively quickly and efficiently. Formal organizations are now emerging to develop health information exchanges to share health care information electronically between providers, hospitals, and public health systems. These organizations have been enabled and supported financially by statewide grants funded through ARRA and its HITECH provisions.

Several research initiatives and collaborations have formed to pool resources and data from large, established electronic databases in order to conduct CER among diverse health care settings and patient populations. These include the HMO Research Network; the HealthCore Integrated Research Database using WellPoint Blue Cross, Blue Shield, and Anthem data; the DARTNet practice-based research network among primary care practices; the Medicaid Medical Directors Learning Network; the Veterans Health Administration quality improvement initiatives; and the Food and Drug Administration Sentinel Initiative for monitoring medical product safety. Moreover, about 40 percent of the $1.1 billion in ARRA funding was spent to improve America's capacity to conduct CER through data, infrastructure, and methods development. Benner and colleagues noted in their review of ARRA funding that "these investments will enhance the ability to use observational data routinely collected during health care delivery to learn about the safety, effectiveness, and costs of interventions in real-world populations."

In summary, several factors have collectively contributed to the rising importance and ability to conduct CER on a large scale in the United States. More comparative evidence is needed to adequately address many of the unanswered clinical questions facing health providers and patients today. The passage of the 2010 Patient Protection and Affordable Care Act (ACA) provided the political opportunity to hardwire in financial support for comparative-effectiveness research as part of health reform.

However, comparative-effectiveness evidence alone is insufficient for medical decision making. Patient preferences and the knowledge and experience of health professionals are essential. The IOM asserts that the purpose of CER is "to assist consumers, clinicians, purchasers, and policy makers to make informed decisions that will improve health care at both the individual and population levels." Furthermore, consumers, patients, and health care providers must be involved in all aspects of CER to ensure its relevance to everyday health care delivery. For example, public input is essential in the development of research priorities that address societal needs. In addition, the IOM asserts that comparative-effectiveness evidence is insufficient without effective strategies for engaging the public in the dissemination of the research and promoting the adoption of the findings into clinical practice.

Americans have had mixed opinions about the use of CER for medical decision making and remain skeptical. Strong public concern has been expressed regarding the use of comparative-effectiveness evidence as justification for cost cutting and the resulting denial of care for critically ill individuals—the so-called death panels rumored in the health-reform debates. A 2009 national survey of about 1,000 Americans published in *Health Affairs,* more than 40 percent of respondents were convinced that "the government and insurance companies will use treatment guidelines as a way to control costs and ration care." Gerber and colleagues reported that the majority of survey respondents believed that "no outside group should come between doctors and patients in making treatment decisions." In the same survey, only a minority of respondents (less than 15 percent) found the argument that "requiring doctors to follow evidence-based guidelines will improve care for most patients" to be very convincing. Instead, most respondents were convinced that research-based treatment guidelines could not keep pace with medical innovation. Proponents in favor of using comparative-effectiveness evidence in the United States to determine treatment guidelines must address these concerns before they will be able to secure broad and sustained public support.

Another challenge in translating comparative-effectiveness research into clinical practice is the inherent conflict of trying to optimize health care at both the individual and population levels. Population-level evidence reflects the average patient. Patient preferences reflect individual values. Given the same population-based evidence, different individuals might select different treatment paths after weighing the pros and cons of the alternatives. This is particularly true when the evidence does not clearly delineate a single best solution for all patients. The value an individual places on different benefits and harms will guide which path he or she chooses.

Recent controversies over cancer screening guidelines illustrate the challenge in balancing population- and individual-level considerations in the application of comparative-effectiveness evidence. For example, in 2011 the U.S. Preventive Services Task Force (USPSTF) recommended against routine prostate-specific antigen (PSA) screening for prostate cancer in men; in other words, the task force's suggestion for practice is to "discourage the use of this service." The annual cost of PSA screening in the United States exceeds $3 billion, with the majority of the costs paid by the publicly funded Medicare and the Veterans Administration. Approximately 3 percent of men with prostate cancer will succumb to the disease. However, complications of prostate cancer treatment are common and include partial or total urinary incontinence and sexual dysfunction, both of which can significantly impair a man's quality of life. The concern is that the PSA test is poor in predicting lethal disease, and the risks of unnecessary treatment from "false positives" is costly to the patient and society. After carefully weighing the evidence, the task force concluded that at a population level, PSA screening results did little to reduce prostate cancer–specific mortality.

From a strictly societal perspective, the evidence did not support PSA screening for the general population. Physicians have applauded the USPSTF for providing a definitive synthesis of the data to help them in discussions with their patients. However, the American Cancer Society and other have stopped short of recommending that screening be prohibited. Instead, they recommend individualized decisions after doctors discuss with their patients the benefits and risks of testing. Some informed men may select to proceed with screening. As McNaughton-Collins and Barry have written, "who is to decide what constitutes a 'small' benefit and whether it outweighs the potential harms?" Secondary endpoints from the European prostate screening study indicate that screening reduces the relative risk of metastatic disease by 41 percent. Nevertheless, some men may conclude that the potential psychological and physical harm resulting from unnecessary cancer treatment do not outweigh the possible benefits of screening. Given the need to facilitate informed choices, Schröder has been a proponent of risk-based stratification using a number of readily available clinic-risk modifiers—for example, results from digital rectal examination—and recommends using the Prostate Cancer Risk Calculator (www.prostatecancer-riskcalculator.com) developed using the European findings.

In the debate surrounding prostate screening, the research evidence is being used to inform national guidelines, but not to dictate care at the individual level. In other words, the evidence did not replace patient preferences and the individual knowledge and judgment of physicians in the translation of the evidence into individual decisions. It is noteworthy that the USPSTF acknowledged that "clinical decisions involve more considerations than evidence alone" and "clinicians should understand the evidence but individualize decision making to the specific patient or situation."

Figure 33.1 provides a conceptual framework for showing the over-arching role that patients and health professionals play in the continuum of CER. Evidence synthesis, generation, and translation are necessary foundational requirements. However, patients and health professional involvement is vital for the ultimate interpretation and use of the evidence for medical decision making.

LESSONS LEARNED FROM EVIDENCE-BASED MEDICINE

The debate over the incorporation of patient preferences and provider experience in the application of medical evidence is not unique to CER. For the past two decades, physicians have been taught that clinical decisions should be made based on the systematic use of clinical evidence, rather than on expert opinion. Adversaries of this approach have stated that an over-reliance on scientific evidence results in "cookbook medicine" and negates the skill and experience of the health care practitioner. Rather, EBM champions Sackett and colleagues have argued that evidence-based medicine is not "cookbook" because it "requires a bottom up approach that integrates the best external evidence with individual clinical expertise and patients' choice. . . . External clinical evidence can inform, but can never replace, individual clinical expertise." The reality is that, at any given point in time, a range of scientific evidence exists for any medical question. Grading systems have been developed to evaluate the relative strengths and weaknesses of the evidence for informing guidelines, for example the A, B, C, D grading scale and levels of certainty regarding net benefit developed by the USPSTF. However, the amount of scientific evidence can be daunting. Previous estimates suggest that it would take reviewers two decades to produce the 10,000 systematic literature reviews required to summarize and synthesize existing evidence. Ultimately, Sackett and colleagues contend that medical expertise is necessary to decide whether an individual guideline and available evidence apply to an "individual patient at all and, if so, how it matches the patient's clinical state, predicament, and preferences, and thus whether it should be applied."

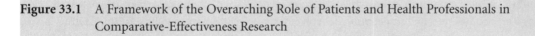

Figure 33.1   A Framework of the Overarching Role of Patients and Health Professionals in Comparative-Effectiveness Research

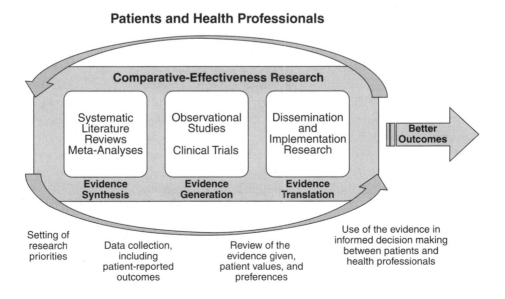

Perhaps, the greater challenge in the application of EBM has been ensuring that medical decisions remain aligned with the values of the patients. Guyatt and colleagues have noted that the values and personal choices of health professionals often differ from those of their patients. Eliciting patient values and preferences in a time-constrained clinic visit is a difficult communications challenge. The authors further ask, "How can clinicians quickly and accurately ascertain patient values? And how should they convey efficiently complex information that includes appreciable uncertainty . . . [when] clinicians often barely have time to do the necessary history and physical exam." Patient decision aids (e.g., pamphlets and iPad applications) have been developed to provide structured presentations of options and outcomes for many common medical conditions. Decision aids enhance knowledge transfer and help establish realistic patient expectations of the benefits and risks of their choices so that better alignment between patient values and treatment choices can occur.

Despite this interest in incorporating patient preferences, evidence suggests that few guidelines incorporate preferences into their recommendations. One review of 51 evidence-based clinical practice guidelines found only minimal reference to patient preferences. Krahn and Naglie have argued that patient-centered medicine has been at odds with evidence-based medicine because the former emphasizes outcomes of "patient experience"; whereas, the latter emphasizes objective clinical endpoints. Not all guidelines are necessarily sensitive to patient preferences either. A medical decision may be preference-sensitive if the evidence about benefit is unclear or conflicting, or subjective trade-offs exist between risks and benefits, or financial considerations vary widely between options.

When recommendations are preference sensitive, guidelines should endorse the acceptability and rationality of basing treatment decisions on patient preferences. Importantly, they conclude that "getting guidelines right means not only rolling out science, but also taking seriously what matters to patients, in finding evidence, making recommendations, and integrating these recommendations into clinical practice."

LESSONS LEARNED FROM OTHER NATIONS

Although evidence-based medicine focuses on the individual patient, the term "evidence-based health care" has been used to describe the application of evidence-based approaches at the population level. Muir Gray has noted that decisions about groups of patients or populations are based on a combination of three factors: (1) the evidence, (2) values, and (3) resources. Again, evidence is necessary, but not sufficient, for making societal health care choices. Several countries with national and provincial health coverage have had substantial experience in engaging health providers and the public in the development of national medical guidelines and clinical translation within the local community. Coverage decision making is inherently political, and who and how those decisions are made is of profound societal interest.

Australia, Canada, and the United Kingdom have implemented evidence-based health care on a national scale. Each has published guidelines and toolkits for including public involvement in health care policy setting. Health Canada states that it is particularly important to engage the public in the formation of medical guidelines involving complex, value-laden issues. The need for engagement is perceived most acutely for vulnerable populations, particularly those who have been historically excluded from the policy process, for example minority groups and the economically disadvantaged. The Australian Institute of Health Policy Studies published a report which investigated best approaches for more effective consumer participation in Australian health policy. The report identified four levels for engaging with consumers within health care: individual care, service, organizational, and broad policy. The institute concluded that consumer engagement at the broad-policy level is both feasible and successful. All three nations agree with the premise that consumer engagement is a mindset, not a technique. Engagement means that patient and health professional feedback is genuinely acknowledged and addressed when policy is shaped, and not just solicited for the sake of solicitation alone. The United Kingdom's National Institute for Health and Clinical Excellence (NICE) values patient and caregiver input because these groups add insights into "practical, physical and emotional challenges associated with living with, or supporting someone with, a particularly medical condition," "how acceptable different options for care and treatment are to people," and whether "different groups of patients may have different views or needs, for instance, with regard to age, ethnicity, sex or disability." An analysis of NICE decisions by Dakin and colleagues found that patient opinions and advocacy were among the most important factors determining NICE decision making. The general lesson has been that in a democracy, health agencies are accountable to the public and must incorporate patient preferences and provider experience when developing guidelines and policy lest the public begins to question their institutional legitimacy.

THE FUTURE DIRECTION OF CER IN THE UNITED STATES

Lessons learned from the implementation of evidence-based medicine and the importance of incorporating patient preferences have shaped the comparative-effectiveness research in the United States. A key provision of the Patient Protection and Affordable Care Act was the establishment of PCORI, a private, nonprofit corporation empowered to develop and fund comparative-effectiveness research. Starting in 2013, Medicare and every private health insurance company will pay a tax on each of their insured lives. Revenues from this tax will be held in a trust fund and used to support research. PCORI funding should increase to approximately $350 million in 2013 and $500 million annually from 2014 through 2019. PCORI is governed by a 21-member Board of Governors with broad stakeholder representation, including individuals representing patients and health care consumers; clinicians; private payers; manufacturers and developers of drugs, devices, and diagnostics; independent health service researchers; and leaders in federal and state health programs and agencies. The directors of two federal research agencies, the National Institutes of Health (NIH) and the Agency for Healthcare Research and Quality (AHRQ), are also members.

The PCORI describes its mission as one to "help people make informed health care decisions—and improve health care delivery and outcomes—by producing and promoting high integrity, evidence-based information that comes from research guided by patients, caregivers and the broader health care community." Since PCORI was established, patient-centered outcomes research (PCOR) has become synonymous with comparative-effectiveness research. The term *patient-centered* reinforces the idea of patient engagement as central to the research process such that the patient's "voice [is] heard in assessing the value of health care options." Both CER and PCOR generate evidence to support the effectiveness of giving the right treatment at the right time to the right patient through the right health-delivery mechanism. Both types of research should result in better health outcomes, and better health outcomes should, in the long run, yield cost-savings. However, because of public concern that patients could be denied coverage or hospitals denied reimbursement based on CER evidence, limits have been placed on PCORI's ability to conduct cost-effectiveness studies. Specifically, "[i]n releasing its research findings, PCORI will ensure that its research is not construed as mandates for practice guidelines or coverage recommendations."

PCOR is designed to address the following types of questions, asked from a patient's perspective:

1. Given my personal characteristics, conditions, and preferences, what should I expect will happen to me?

2. What are my options and what are the benefits and harms of those options?

3. What can I do to improve the outcomes that are most important to me?

4. How can the health care system improve my chances of achieving the outcomes I prefer?

PCOR compares benefits and harms, as does CER, but PCOR more explicitly and transparently incorporates the "individual's preferences, autonomy and needs" into the research design and investigates "optimizing outcomes while addressing burden to individuals, resources, and other stakeholder perspectives." Patient-centered outcomes are measures that matter to people, including survival, physical function, symptoms, and health-related quality of life. Patient-reported outcomes have been included unevenly in previous clinical studies, but they can help establish a more meaningful definition of the concept of effectiveness.

The demand for the collection of patient-reported outcome measures is growing. Wu and colleagues offer the example of the Centers for Medicare & Medicaid Services (CMS) and proposals for it to pay for episodes of care, rather than just individual services as it does today. For instance, providers with the best risk-adjusted patient outcomes (e.g., functional status 90 days after discharge for surgical procedures) could be designated as "preferred" providers and receive financial incentives. To encourage clinical use of patient-reported outcomes, Wu and colleagues suggest that payers could pay for the collection of patient-reported outcomes data in the same way they pay for laboratory data. Another data-collection strategy for patient-reported outcomes would link insurance coverage with a requirement that patients participate in relevant research, called "coverage with evidence development" by CMS. This CMS mechanism was "designed to be applied when promising findings suggested that patients might benefit from a new technology, but additional evidence was needed to determine this with confidence."

In 2012 PCORI began funding pilot projects to develop and evaluate the best approaches for generating national comparative-effectiveness priorities and for identifying gaps in evidence that most affect vulnerable populations. Once national priorities have been drafted, and vetted with the public, PCORI will begin to fund larger projects. A variety of outcomes research studies is envisioned, including randomized trials, observational studies using registries or electronic databases derived from clinical care, and data syntheses. In the meantime, PCORI's methodology committee is reviewing and summarizing state-of-the-art standards for comparative-effectiveness study designs, statistical analyses, and conduct of patient-centered outcomes research, including the integration of patient engagement into the research design.

CONCLUSION

This essay has argued that comparative-effectiveness evidence is essential for informed health care decision making, but insufficient alone. Significant national investment in comparative-effectiveness research is necessary for addressing many important, yet unanswered, medical decisions faced by patients and health professionals. However, patient preferences and provider knowledge and expertise will remain central to the application of the evidence for everyday decision making.

REFERENCES AND FURTHER READING

Australian Institute of Health Policy Studies. (2009). *Consumer engagement in australian health policy.* Retrieved from http://www .healthissuescentre.org.au/documents/detail.chtml?filename_num=280548

Benner, J. S., Morrison, M. R., Karnes, E. K., Kokot, S. L., & McClellan, M. (2010). An evaluation of recent federal spending on comparative effectiveness research: Priorities, gaps, and next steps. *Health Affairs, 29*(10), 1768–1776.

Chong, C., Chen, I., Naglie, G., & Krahn, M. D. (2007). Do clinical practice guidelines incorporate evidence on patient preferences? *Medical Decision Making, 27*(4), E63–E64.

Chou, R., Croswell, J. M., Dana, T., Bougatsos, C., Blazina, I., Fu, R., Gleitsman, K., et al. (2011, October 7). Screening for prostate cancer: A review of the evidence for the U.S. Preventive Services Task Force. *Annals of Internal Medicine.* Retrieved from http://www.annals .org/content/early/2011/10/07/0003-4819-155-11-201112060-00375.full#cited-by

Committee on Comparative Effectiveness Research Prioritization. (2009). *Initial national priorities in comparative effectiveness research.* Washington, DC: Institute of Medicine, National Academies Press.

Corporate Consultation Secretariat, Health Policy and Communications Branch, Health Canada. (2000). *Health Canada policy toolkit for public involvement in decision making.* Ottawa, ON: Minister of Public Works and Government Services Canada. Retrieved from http://www.hc-sc.gc.ca/ahc-asc/pubs/_public-consult/2000decision/index-eng.php

Dakin, H. A., Devlin, N. J., & Odeyemi, I. A. (2006). "Yes," "no," or "yes, but"? Multinomial modelling of NICE decision-making. *Health Policy, 77*(3), 352–367.

Gerber, A. S., Patashnik, E. M., Doherty, D., & Dowling, C. (2010).The public wants information, not board mandates, from comparative effectiveness research. *Health Affairs, 29*(10), 1872–1881.

Guyatt, G. H., Cook, D. G., & Haynes, R. B. (2004). Evidence based medicine has come a long way: The second decade will be as exciting as the first. *BMJ, 329*(7473), 990–991.

Hochman, M., & McCormick, D. (2010). Characteristics of published comparative effectiveness studies of medications. *Journal of the American Medical Association, 303*(10), 951–958.

Kimbuende, E. (2010). *U.S. health care costs: Background brief.* Menlo Park, CA: Kaiser Family Foundation.

Krahn, M., & Naglie, G. (2008). The next step in guideline development. *The Journal of the American Medical Association, 300*(4), 436–438.

Muir Gray, J. (2001). *Evidence-based healthcare.* Edinburgh, UK: Churchill Livingstone.

National Institute for Health and Clinical Excellence. (2011). *Patient and public involvement policy.* Retrieved from http://www.nice.org .uk/getinvolved/patientandpublicinvolvement/patientandpublicinvolvementpolicy/patient_and_public_involvement_policy.jsp

Patient-Centered Outcomes Research Institute. (2011). *Patient-centered outcomes research.* Retrieved from http://www.pcori.org/ patient-centered-outcomes-research

Sackett, D. L., Rosenberg, W., Gray, M., Haynes, R. B., & Richardson, W. (1996). Evidence based medicine: What it is and what it isn't. *BMJ, 312*(7023), 71–72.

Schröder, F. H. (2011). Stratifying risk—The U.S. Preventive Services Task Force and prostate-cancer screening. *New England Journal of Medicine, 365*(21), 1953–1955.

Torpy, J. (1992). Evidence-based medicine. *Journal of the American Medical Association, 268*(17), 2420–2425.

Washington, A. E., & Lipstein, S. H. (2011). The Patient-Centered Outcomes Research Institute—Promoting better information, decisions, and health. *New England Journal of Medicine, 365*(15), e31.

Wennberg, J. E., Fisher, E. S., & Skinner J. S. (2002, February). Geography and the debate over Medicare reform. *Health Affairs.* doi:10.1377/hlthaff.w2.96

Wu, A. W., Snyder, C., Clancy, C. M., & Steinwachs, D. M. (2010). Adding the patient perspective to comparative effectiveness research. *Health Affairs, 29*(10), 1863–1871.

Elaine Morrato

Information Technology Adoption

POINT: Health information technology has great potential to reduce costs, enhance efficiency, and improve quality of care and patient safety. These systems are instrumental to enabling a powerful transformation of health data and providing support for evidence-based medicine and patient-oriented applications.

Katy Mahraj and Kai Zheng, University of Michigan, Ann Arbor

COUNTERPOINT: Health information technology has failed to reduce costs, improve quality of care and patient safety, or enhance efficiency. Poor usability, conflicts with workflow and culture, and lack of standards significantly hinder the ability of health information technology to transform health care.

Katy Mahraj and Kai Zheng, University of Michigan, Ann Arbor

Introduction

Over the past decades, the development and use of information technology (IT) in health care in the United States have been driven by the rising costs of care coupled with persistent inefficiency and low quality. From the 1980s to the mid-1990s, development focused on artificial-intelligence technologies with the capacity to make diagnosis and treatment decisions. These technologies failed to gain widespread support due to their frequent inaccuracy and because providers felt that they threatened their own roles as expert, autonomous decision makers. Following this first wave of attempts, attention shifted to electronic billing systems and homegrown technologies such as electronic health records (EHR), clinical decision support systems (CDSS), and computerized provider-order entry (CPOE), designed to be attuned to the needs of specific health care organizations. EHR systems support electronic recordkeeping and communication. CDSS draw upon EHR data in combination with information such as drug interaction data and evidence-based guidelines to alert providers to potential dangers and to suggest certain preventative, diagnostic, and treatment regimens. CPOE enables providers to order medications and laboratory tests electronically, provide alerts such as drug allergy and drug-interaction warnings, and facilitate communication between providers and pharmacies. In their homegrown iterations, these technologies demonstrated encouragingly positive results, leading to a burgeoning of vendor-designed counterparts. Recent years have witnessed a proliferation of vendor-designed systems and the slow but steadily increasing adoption of health IT by health care organizations across the country.

Continued need for an effective, comprehensive solution has manifested in widespread hope that these technologies will serve as a solution to the U.S. health care crisis. Former President George W. Bush spoke in 2004 about the capacity of health IT to reduce costs and improve the quality and safety of care. The following year, the RAND Corporation released a report predicting potential savings of $81 billion or more annually from the effective implementation and use of interoperable electronic medical records to improve safety, efficiency, and the management of chronic diseases. Hope for health IT has increased since that time and extends from national and institutional levels to the opinions of individual patients and practitioners, many of whom, according to a 2010 survey by the Markle Foundation, strongly believe in the ability of health IT to improve patient care.

In 2009 the U.S. government passed the Health Information Technology for Economic and Clinical Health (HITECH) Act to promote the rapid, nationwide implementation of health IT. The act provides $23 billion in funding for research, education, and incentives to pay health care providers for implementing IT in accordance with criteria for "Meaningful Use," which specify the functions that health IT systems must provide and the rate at which those functions must be employed. The HITECH Act supports numerous components of health IT adoption and development. First, the act has created an incentive program of financial awards and penalties for health care organizations that respectively adopt or fail to adopt officially certified health IT systems according to the Meaningful Use criteria. The act has also funded research on topics including health information exchange, software development, secondary use, and privacy and data security. Finally, the act has funded new health IT training and curriculum and initiated a network of Regional Extension Centers that provide decision-making, implementation, and training support for health care practices.

The Point essay included in this chapter details the argument in favor of health IT as a potential tool to transform the health care system in the United States. This section discusses the potential and documented positive impacts of health IT on reducing costs, improving the quality and safety of care, and enhancing efficiency. It also explores the powerful transformation in health data and the support for patient-empowering, consumer-oriented applications enabled by computer-mediated communication technologies. The section concludes by emphasizing the importance of implementing health IT systems sooner rather than later to accelerate the maturing of the design and standardization of these technologies.

The Counterpoint essay, on the other hand, details the argument against the ability of the current generation of health IT systems to transform health care in the United States. This section begins by exploring three major failures of health IT, namely the failure to reduce cost, to improve the quality and safety of care, and to increase efficiency. The section concludes by examining three motivating factors behind these struggles: poor usability, conflicts with workflow and culture, and lack of standards. This section emphasizes the paucity of clear and conclusive evidence in support of health IT, while examining the documented negative impacts of these technologies.

As you read, keep in mind the tension between the benefits and risks of implementing health IT systems in their current form. Do the benefits outweigh the risks or vice versa? Second, what are the benefits and costs of waiting to implement these systems until further research and development can be completed? Third, what strategies could be effective to resolve the conflicts with workflow, communication, and culture?

POINT

Health information technology (IT) has the ability to transform health care in the United States, offering benefits in four primary areas—cost, efficiency, quality, and safety. Health IT has demonstrated the capacity to reduce medication errors, speed prescription and laboratory ordering, and support evidence-based medicine, among other improvements. IT systems are powerful tools for data gathering, information management, collaboration, and communication, and will revolutionize the ways in which health care organizations capture, share, and use data to improve quality of care and patient safety. Increased data transparency can also enhance patients' decision making, broaden patients' choices, and create a foundation for Internet-based and mobile consumer health applications. A growing body of evidence demonstrates the potential of properly designed and implemented health IT systems to improve health care, new privacy and security regulations in place to safeguard electronic health data, and a growing level of financial investment to support these systems' development and widespread use.

REDUCING COSTS

According to the Centers for Medicare & Medicaid Services (CMS), from 1997 to 2006, health care costs consumed on average approximately 15 percent of the nation's gross domestic product (GDP) (CMS, 2010b, p. 1), a percentage that is predicted to reach 19.4 percent by 2019 (CMS, 2010a, p. 4). A 2008 comparison by Anderson and Frogner found that health care expenditures in other industrialized countries from 1996 to 2005 represented an average of only 9 percent of GDP. There is widespread agreement across the political spectrum that health care costs are not sustainable. Health IT has the potential to reduce these growing costs. For example, a technology called computerized prescriber order entry (CPOE), which computerizes order management and generates safety alerts and prescription guidance, provides several mechanisms for cost reduction. A 1998 study by Bates and colleagues found that widespread adoption of CPOE systems could save approximately $1 million per hospital per year. In 2006 Brigham and Women's Hospital in Boston, Massachusetts, reported a cumulative net savings of $16.7 million through CPOE usage over a 10-year period (Kaushal et al., 2006). First, CPOE systems can help providers avoid duplicate and unnecessary medication orders and laboratory or radiology tests. Second, CPOE systems can recommend cheaper but equally effective drugs in the form of generic equivalents or drugs preferred by the patient's insurance company. Third, CPOE systems can alert providers to safety issues such as drug allergies and drug-drug interactions and thus help to avoid the costs associated with preventable medication errors. Indeed, two studies at LDS Hospital/Intermountain Health Care in Salt Lake City, Utah, documented statistically significant reduction in adverse drug events following CPOE implementation, while a third study at Brigham and Women's Hospital documented a large decrease in nonintercepted serious medication errors following CPOE implementation (Chaudhry et al., 2006). By preventing such incidents, CPOE systems can significantly reduce spending caused by adverse drug events and other types of medication errors, the cost of which has been estimated at $37.6 billion per year (Ginzburg, Barr, Harris, & Munshi, 2009). The reduction of adverse drug events clearly has a significant impact on improving quality of care, and the safety benefits of health IT will be discussed in further detail in later parts of this essay.

Health IT can also reduce costs by enabling more comprehensive and timely exchange of health information, a goal known as health information exchange (HIE) and interoperability. Currently, systems often work as silos. That is, when patients are moved from one hospital to another, there is no simple way for their records to transfer as well. This creates gaps and inaccuracies in patient records that can lead to reduced quality of care and patient safety. HIE and interoperability mean that health IT systems can work together, sharing data such as medical histories, current and previous orders, allergies, and test results. HIE can occur between health IT systems and applications run by hospitals, pharmacies, radiology units, payers, patients, and other organizations involved in health care delivery and management. It can be achieved by developing software interfaces, compliant with terminology standards and data exchange protocols, that allow systems to talk to each other. HIE results in more complete patient records, meaning that providers can have a more informed understanding of patients' conditions and existing treatments and thus avoid duplicate and unnecessary orders and tests in addition to drug allergies and drug interactions. HIE also allows providers and payers to communicate more efficiently, for example by speeding chart requests. A comprehensive cost-benefit analysis conducted by Walker and colleagues

(2005) estimated a net benefit of $77.8 billion per year from fully implemented HIE and interoperability, and smaller but still considerable savings from partially implemented HIE and interoperability.

IMPROVING EFFICIENCY

Health IT systems have the potential to increase clinical efficiency by streamlining and accelerating patient-care processes. In turn, increased efficiency can lead to reduced costs and more time available for clinicians to care for patients and devote to other aspects of patient care, including quality and safety improvement initiatives. Numerous examples exist of health IT adoption resulting in improved efficiency. A study conducted by Guss and colleagues (2008) reported shorter medication order turnaround time between prescribers and pharmacies as one of the most significant benefits of CPOE. CPOE can speed order turnaround through several mechanisms. For example, these systems eliminate the need to manually process orders. In addition, they can automate order prioritization and distribution (Prince & Herrin, 2007). Moreover, they provide order sets, or pre-defined bundles of medication commonly ordered together, thus speeding routine prescribing activities. Barcode administration and robotic order dispensing in pharmacies further accelerate order processing. In addition to CPOE and other order-management technology, electronic health record (EHR) systems can improve efficiency. EHR systems can enable concurrent access to patient records by multiple users, in addition to providing faster chart search and retrieval capabilities. EHR implementation corresponded with increased efficiency in ambulatory care at the Kaiser Permanente Colorado and Northwest systems, which together serve over 817,000 members (Garrido, Jamieson, Zhou, Wiesenthal, & Liang, 2005). In part through more ready access to comprehensive patient data, EHR usage enabled clinicians to identify and resolve patient issues with fewer appointments and resolve more issues via telephone in lieu of in-person appointments.

IMPROVING QUALITY OF CARE AND PATIENT SAFETY

Health IT possesses great potential to enhance quality of care and patient safety through enabling evidence-based medicine (EBM), which has been defined as the "conscientious, explicit, and judicious use of current best evidence in making medical decisions about the care of individual patients" (Sackett, Rosenberg, Gray, Haynes, & Richardson, 1996, p. 71). To increase clinicians' adherence to EBM has been an ongoing challenge in health care but has proven difficult to implement because of the overwhelming volume of patient data and constantly evolving medical evidence that must be considered to effectively practice EBM. Health IT facilitates EBM practice by providing automated means to assemble and analyze large volumes of patient data that can contain years of content including vital signs, problem lists, medications, family and social history, lab tests, drug allergies, and adverse drug reactions. Furthermore, health IT incorporates evolving knowledge from current medical literature and from authoritative sources such as the National Guideline Clearinghouse for the generation of case-specific alerts, reminders, and other forms of decision-support recommendations. As a result, health IT is capable of facilitating finding, selecting, and applying appropriate EBM knowledge at the point of medical decision making, making it possible to provide the right information, at the right time, for the right person.

Computerized clinical decision support systems (CDSS) are a prime example of health IT facilitating the practice of EBM. Such systems work to address information overload by automating the integration, analysis, and updating of data from multiple sources, including patient records, drug lexicons, and evidence-based clinical guidelines. By applying knowledge to data through sophisticated inference engines, CDSS generates clinician-directed decision support advisories. A systematic review by Chaudhry and colleagues (2006) documented four benchmark studies that demonstrate the positive impact of health IT on quality, especially through the capability of CDSS to increase clinician adherence to evidence-based preventative-care guidelines. For example, CDSS can be particularly useful to assist clinicians in managing the abundance of information necessary to provide comprehensive and timely care for patients with chronic diseases. At least two studies have examined this potential in the context of disease management among type 2 diabetics (Bu et al., 2007; Grant, Lester, Meigs, & Chueh, 2006). These studies leveraged CDSS to enhance the identification of patients needing hemoglobin A1c and LDL-cholesterol testing, eye and foot exams, aspirin prescriptions, and other preventative-care routines. Such interventions are essential and immensely timely: From 1990 to 2002 the incidence of type 2 diabetes increased 61 percent in the United States, and the cost of diabetes-related complications skyrocketed likewise and is expected to reach $200 billion per year by 2020 (Wyne, 2008). Health IT systems in general and CDSS in particular have great potential to improve the quality of life for people suffering from diabetes and other chronic illnesses—a significant proportion of the population.

In addition to enhancing chronic disease management, CDSS can also enhance EBM education by supporting the unique needs of trainees in medicine. For example, van Dijk and colleagues (2010) identified limited time, knowledge, skills, and attitude as the main barriers to residents' application of EBM on a daily basis. CDSS could help to address such barriers by performing the time-intensive work of gathering evidence and providing that evidence at the appropriate moment, thus supporting experiential learning and reducing knowledge gaps. Nurses are another group of clinicians who have struggled to achieve EBM practice, frequently due to the lack of time and knowledge (Simpson, 2006). Anderson and Wilson (2008) reviewed numerous CDSS applications that support EBM practice in nursing, such as systems that offered decision support for emergency triage, prevention and management of pressure ulcers, warfarin dosage, and telephone helplines.

Health IT has great potential to improve patient safety by reducing preventable medical errors—the fifth leading cause of death in the United States (Kohn, Corrigan, & Donaldson, 2000). As simple as it seems, electronic records immediately eliminate errors stemming from illegible handwriting (Smith, Dang, & Lee, 2009). CPOE systems provide significant safety benefits by reducing adverse drug events through detecting and alerting for abnormal drug dosage, drug allergies, and drug interactions. Barcode administration of medication in combination with the use of advanced tracking technology such as radio-frequency identification tags (RFID) further help eliminate medication errors due to misidentification of patients or drugs. For example, RFID tags are small electronic tags that can be embedded in patient wristbands and medication packaging to confirm patients' identity, match patients to correct medications, and log medication administration (Peris-Lopez, Orfila, Mitrokotsa, & Van Der Lubbe, 2011). The impact of health IT on improving patient safety has been documented in numerous studies. For example, Ginzburg and colleagues (2009) examined the benefits of using a weight-based prescribing system with pediatric patients to prevent acetaminophen and ibuprofen dosage errors, including incorrect strength and regimen and unclear directions. Medication errors dropped by over 50 percent following system implementation.

In a systematic review of the impact of health IT on quality, safety, and efficiency, Chaudhry and colleagues (2006) reported three other studies documenting reduced dosage errors for antibiotics and anticoagulants following CPOE implementation. These reductions ranged from 12 to 21 percent. In a subsequent systematic review, Ammenwerth and colleagues (2008) confirmed these findings. They analyzed 25 studies on the impact of CPOE on medication error rates and found considerable relative risk reduction in 23 studies, with reduction rates ranging from 13 to 99 percent. In the future, this positive impact may expand beyond medication errors to include diagnostic errors. Schiff and Bates (2010) have begun this work by identifying criteria for redesigning health IT systems to prevent diagnostic errors.

The potential of health IT to improve quality of care and patient safety stems from its ability to change how data are managed and used in health care. Health IT systems record and store electronic data that can be analyzed more effectively at an unprecedented scale. These systems are also a critical vehicle for enforcing data standards so that providers and organizations describe the same observations, diagnoses, treatments, and outcomes in the same or interoperable ways. Better data-capture and interoperability—that is, the improved ability to collect and share data—yield increased data transparency. Greater transparency could enable health care organizations to compare performance, identifying areas for improvement and empowering the health care system as a whole to institutionalize pay-for-performance initiatives that directly link incentives to achievement of goals for quality, efficiency, and other domains. Health IT provides the computational capacity to generate performance feedback reports for providers and organizations, and thus fuel other types of continuous quality improvement initiatives. To protect this growing body of electronic health information, especially as it moves between providers and organizations, the federal government added new measures to secure patient privacy and data handling and more stringent penalties for mishandling patient information to the Health Insurance Portability and Accountability Act in 2009 (Devin & Vinson, 2011).

Many studies have documented the use of data stored in health IT systems for quality improvement initiatives. The improvements in diabetes management and medication errors described above both stem from better data gathering and analysis enabled by the use of health IT. Similar work has been performed to improve quality of care in fields such as anesthesia. Egger Halbeis and Epstein (2008) reported that information management systems in anesthesia could introduce numerous benefits, including more complete documentation than is possible with paper-based operations, improved clinician adherence to guidelines, and more analyzable data for quality improvement initiatives and clinical research. Miller and West (2007) analyzed EHR adoption in community health centers (CHCs), a major setting providing primary care in the United

States, particularly for disadvantaged populations. They found that CHCs are more likely to use EHRs for quality improvement than private practices because of these centers' focus on preventative care and chronic illnesses. In addition to clinical practice, public health organizations such as the U.S. Centers for Disease Control and Prevention can use data recorded in health IT systems to speed the early detection of disease outbreaks at a national level. For example, Overhage and colleagues (2001) documented a 29-point increase in cases of shigellosis identified during an outbreak and a 2.5-day decrease in identification and public health reporting time using an electronic reporting system. Such fundamental, powerful changes in data gathering, sharing, and use justify the investments and efforts dedicated to implementing health IT systems.

Changes in the way that data are gathered and shared also have additional benefits for consumers of health care, such as patients and families, beyond the improvements that can be achieved in medical settings. First, increased data transparency allows consumers to become more informed about cost-effective treatments and better performing hospitals and providers, which not only empowers consumers to make more cogent purchasing decisions but also stimulates competition among health care providers that could ultimately drive down costs. Second, health information exchange and interoperability enables consumers to move more freely from one provider to another (or across health care organizations) because their medical records have become more portable, in effect reducing the switching-costs for consumers to choose other, potentially better performing or more cost-effective health care providers. Third, patient records being shared electronically between systems enable consumer-oriented applications such as personal health records, patient portals, and other types of Internet-based and mobile applications. These applications allow consumers to access their information typically stewarded by health care organizations and utilize that information for the purposes of self-management of chronic diseases, health risks, and other health issues. When practiced on a population level, these changes have the potential to reduce health care costs and improve quality of life on a much broader scale.

THE CASE FOR IMMEDIATE IMPLEMENTATION

Opponents of health IT often argue that the widespread deployment of health IT systems should wait until systems become more mature and the evidence of immediate and long-term benefits grows more conclusive. However, managing risk to achieve the best possible outcome is a daily reality in medicine. Surgeons do not shy away from performing potentially life-saving but delicate operations. Rather, they seek to understand the risks and how to manage them, select a trustworthy team with whom to work, and proceed carefully and thoughtfully to achieve the hoped-for benefits as consistently as possible. The same philosophy can be applied to health IT.

Though the current generation of commercial health IT systems needs significant improvement and may introduce unintended risks under certain circumstances, many studies have documented these systems' positive impact on cost, quality, safety, and efficiency. In a systematic review of the literature on health IT outcomes, Buntin and colleagues (2011) state that 92 percent of studies from July 2007 to February 2010 reach conclusions that are positive overall, confirming that expanded health IT adoption is worthwhile. Furthermore, many health IT systems have been closely inspected through federally regulated certification processes, for example by the Certification Commission for Health Information Technology, which assure they are technologically and functionally sound. Indeed, poorly planned implementation processes, rather than the technology itself, are more fundamental and more frequently cited reasons for failures and adverse consequences. Numerous studies and reviews emphasize the centrality of implementation-related decisions in determining the outcomes of health IT adoption and describe decisions that yielded positive and negative results (e.g., Buntin, Burke, Hoaglin, & Blumenthal, 2011; Gruber, Cummings, LeBlanc, & Smith, 2009; Harrison, Koppel, & Bar-Lev, 2007; Ozdas & Miller, 2007; Sittig, Ash, Zhang, Osheroff, & Shabot, 2006). In other words, health care organizations now have the capacity to achieve the benefits of health IT by selecting appropriate, officially certified systems and carefully managing the implementation process according to evidence.

In addition to positive impacts on cost, efficiency, quality, and safety, implementing health IT systems sooner rather than later has the potential to create a critical mass of investment and demand to stimulate faster progress toward improved designs and standards. There is considerable government funding for health IT adoption and research at this time, creating an opportunity that should not be squandered (Blumenthal, 2009). As more organizations adopt health IT, there will be even greater incentives for the government to heighten benefits and cut costs by improving standards, information exchange, and privacy and security measures across systems. Vendors will also be more motivated to improve systems to gain a competitive edge. Overall, expanding the demand for health IT development fuels a burgeoning area for economic growth and innovation that has the potential to push computing to a more sophisticated level. More health IT systems being deployed in the field will foster opportunities to conduct *in-situ* evaluation of system design. A booming, competitive market for health IT also has the capacity to motivate broader technological advances in natural language processing, information exchange, privacy, security, and ubiquitous computing. In short, implementing these systems now, using evidence to guide implementation and government investment to enable adoption, can yield considerable benefits both immediately and into the future.

CONCLUSION

There are many reasons to support the implementation of health IT in a variety of settings. A growing body of evidence documents the impact of health IT on reducing costs, boosting efficiency, and improving quality of care and patient safety. Health IT has demonstrated an ability to reduce medical errors, facilitate information exchange, speed order processing, and enhance chronic disease management. Furthermore, health IT systems will form a cornerstone of health care reform in the United States by providing an unprecedented capability to effectively gather and analyze data. These systems are critical enablers of the long sought-after advantages of widespread evidence-based medicine and will capture data invaluable to quality and safety improvement initiatives. The financial and human costs of current deficiencies in health care are too great, and rising too fast, to ignore a tool with so much potential for immediate and future benefits. The opportunities available now to adopt health IT should not be wasted.

References and Further Reading

Ammenwerth, E., Schnell-Inderst, P., Machan, C., & Siebert, U. (2008). The effect of electronic prescribing on medication errors and adverse drug events: A systematic review. *Journal of the American Medical Informatics Association, 15*(5), 585–600.

Anderson, G. F., & Frogner, B. K. (2008). Health spending in OECD countries: Obtaining value per dollar. *Health Affairs, 27*(6), 1718–1727.

Anderson, J. A., & Wilson, P. (2008). Clinical decision support systems in nursing: Synthesis of the science for evidence-based practice. *Computers, Informatics, Nursing, 26*(3), 151–158.

Bates, D. W., Leape, L. L., Cullen, D. J., Laird, N., Petersen, L. A., Teich, J. M., & Seger, D. L. (1998). Effect of computerized physician order entry and a team intervention on prevention of serious medication errors. *Journal of the American Medical Association, 280*(15), 1311–1316.

Blumenthal, D. (2009). Stimulating the adoption of health information technology. *New England Journal of Medicine, 360*(15), 1477–1479.

Bu, D., Pan, E., Walker, J., Adler-Milstein, J., Kendrick, D., Hook, J. M., et al. (2007). Benefits of information technology-enabled diabetes management. *Diabetes Care, 30*(5), 1137–1142.

Buntin, M. B., Burke, M. F., Hoaglin, M. C., & Blumenthal, D. (2011). The benefits of health information technology: A review of recent literature shows predominantly positive results. *Health Affairs, 30*(3), 464–471.

Centers for Medicare & Medicaid Services (CMS). (2010a). *National health expenditure projections 2010–2010.* Retrieved from https://www.cms.gov/NationalHealthExpendData/downloads/proj2010.pdf

Centers for Medicare & Medicaid Services (CMS). (2010b). *National health expenditure web tables.* Retrieved from https://www.cms.gov/nationalhealthexpenddata

Chaudhry, B., Wang, J., Wu, S., Maglione, M., Mojica, W., Roth, E., et al. (2006). Systematic review: Impact of health information technology on quality, efficiency, and costs of medical care. *Annals of Internal Medicine, 144*(10), 742–752.

Devin, D., & Vinson, J. D. (2011). No more paper tiger: Promise and peril as HIPAA goes HITECH. *Journal of Healthcare Risk Management, 30*(3), 28–37.

Egger Halbeis, C. B., & Epstein, R. H. (2008). The value proposition of anesthesia information management systems. *Anesthesiology Clinics, 26*(4), 665–679.

Garrido, T., Jamieson, L., Zhou, Y., Wiesenthal, A., & Liang, L. (2005). Effect of electronic health records in ambulatory care: Retrospective, serial, cross sectional study. *British Medical Journal, 330*(7491), 581–585.

Ginzburg, R., Barr, W. B., Harris, M., & Munshi, S. (2009). Effect of a weight-based prescribing method within an electronic health record on prescribing errors. *American Journal of Health-System Pharmacy, 66*(22), 2037–2041.

Girosi, F., Meili, R., & Scoville, R. (2005). *Extrapolating evidence of health information technology savings and costs.* Santa Monica, CA: RAND Corporation.

Grant, R. W., Lester, W. T., Meigs, J. B., & Chueh, H. C. (2006). New models of population management for patients with diabetes—using informatics tools to support primary care. *Diabetes Research and Clinical Practice, 74*(2 Suppl), S220–S224.

Gruber, D., Cummings, G. G., LeBlanc, L., & Smith, D. L. (2009). Factors influencing outcomes of clinical information systems implementation: A systematic review. *Computers, Informatics, Nursing, 27*(3), 151–163.

Guss, D. A., Chan, T. C., & Killeen, J. P. (2008). The impact of a pneumatic tube and computerized physician order management on laboratory turnaround time. *Annals of Emergency Medicine, 51*(2), 181–185.

Harrison, M. I., Koppel, R., & Bar-Lev, S. (2007). Unintended consequences of information technologies in health care: An interactive sociotechnical analysis. *Journal of the American Medical Informatics Association, 14*(5), 542–549.

Kaushal, R., Jha, A., Franz, C., Glaser, J., Shetty, K., Jaggi, T., et al. (2006). Return on investment for a computerized physician order entry system. *Journal of the American Medical Informatics Association, 13*(3), 261–266.

Kohn, L. T., Corrigan, J. M., & Donaldson, M. S. (Eds.). (2000). *To err is human: Building a safer health system.* Washington, DC: Institute of Medicine, National Academy Press.

Markle Foundation. (2010). *Markle Survey on health in a networked life 2010.* Retrieved from http://www.markle.org/sites/default/files/20110110_HINLSurveyBrief_0.pdf

Miller, R. H., & West, C. E. (2007). The value of electronic health records in community health centers: Policy implications. *Health Affairs, 26*(1), 206–214.

Overhage, J. M., Suico, J., & McDonald, C. J. (2001). Electronic laboratory reporting: Barriers, solutions, and findings. *Journal of Public Health Management and Practice, 7*(6), 60–66.

Ozdas, A., & Miller, R. A. (2007). Care provider order entry (CPOE): A perspective on factors leading to success or to failure. *International Medical Informatics Association Yearbook of Medical Informatics,* 128–137.

Peris-Lopez, P., Orfila, A., Mitrokotsa, A., & Van Der Lubbe, J. (2011). A comprehensive RFID solution to enhance inpatient medication safety. *International Journal of Medical Informatics, 80*(1), 13–24.

President's Information Technology Advisory Committee. (2011). *Report to the President: Revolutionizing health care through information technology.* Retrieved from http://www.itrd.gov/pitac/meetings/2004/20040617/20040615_hit.pdf

Prince, S. B., & Herrin, D. M. (2007). The role of information technology in healthcare communications, efficiency, and patient safety: Application and results. *Journal of Nursing Administration, 37*(4), 184–187.

Sackett, D. L., Rosenberg, W. M., Gray, J. A., Haynes, R. B., & Richardson, W. S. (1996). Evidence based medicine: What it is and what it isn't. *British Medical Journal, 312*(7023), 71–72.

Schiff, G. D., & Bates, D. W. (2010). Can electronic clinical documentation help prevent diagnostic errors? *New England Journal of Medicine, 362*(12), 1066–1069.

Simpson, R. L. (2006). Evidence-based practice: How nursing administration makes IT happen. *Nursing Administration Quarterly, 30*(3), 291–294.

Sittig, D. F., Ash, J. S., Zhang, J., Osheroff, J. A., & Shabot, M. M. (2006). Lessons from "Unexpected increased mortality after implementation of a commercially sold computerized physician order entry system." *Pediatrics, 118*(2), 797–801.

Smith, M., Dang, D., & Lee, J. (2009). E-prescribing: Clinical implications for patients with diabetes. *Journal of Diabetes Science and Technology, 3*(5), 1215–1218.

Van Dijk, N., Hooft, L., & Wieringa-de Waard, M. (2010). What are the barriers to residents' practicing evidence-based medicine? A systematic review. *Academic Medicine, 85*(7), 1163–1170.

Walker, J., Pan, E., Johnston, D., Adler-Milstein, J., Bates, D. W., & Middleton, B. (2005). The value of health care information exchange and interoperability. *Health Affairs, 24*(Web Suppl.), W5-10–W15-18. Retrieved from http://content.healthaffairs.org/content/suppl/2005/02/07/hlthaff.w5.10.DC1

Wyne, K. (2008). Information technology for the treatment of diabetes: Improving outcomes and controlling costs. *Journal of Managed Care Pharmacy, 14*(2 Suppl.), S12–S17.

Katy Mahraj and Kai Zheng

COUNTERPOINT

There is no doubt that the field of information technology (IT) has been transformative in American and indeed global society. Indeed, positive results from the first wave of homegrown health IT systems, developed and implemented in-house by health care organizations, provided strong support for electronic health records, computerized clinical decision support, and computerized provider order entry. Yet the field of health IT has shifted dramatically from the era of homegrown systems, with health care organizations now investing significant time and money in a proliferation of unproven vendor systems. Health IT as it is currently being implemented nationwide is not a panacea for the many problems plaguing the U.S. health care system. Despite the excitement about the potential of health IT in some quarters, in reality this generation of health IT is still immature. This section critiques not the benefits of health IT as it may become, but rather the failings of health IT as it currently exists. There is little to no clear evidence that these systems have the power to reduce costs, improve quality of care and patient safety, or enhance efficiency. Three major factors contribute to these struggles: poor usability, conflicts with workflow and culture, and lack of standards. Substantial additional research and development must be conducted to improve these systems across multiple domains, from safety and efficiency to usability, interoperability, and implementation. More health IT systems should not be widely deployed in situations of patient care until the positive impacts of this technology can be guaranteed and negative impacts predicted and controlled.

FAILURE TO REDUCE COSTS

The first strike against health IT systems are their ongoing struggle to reduce costs. To begin with, this technology is highly expensive to implement. Initial costs include hardware and software purchase, configuration, pre-loading of historical data, and staff training. System maintenance incurs ongoing costs for hardware and software repair and upgrades, data backup, and continued staff training. The costs of meeting future federal standards for health IT will be particularly significant for organizations whose systems must be upgraded to meet expectations, especially if those organizations' contracts with vendors do not contain explicit ties to federal criteria. According to Blumenthal (2009), a former National Coordinator for Health Information Technology, there were many health IT systems on the market in 2009 that lacked ability to improve efficiency and quality of care, even among systems approved by the federally authorized certifying commission. Furthermore, considerable investment in purchasing and configuring a health IT system often creates a lock-in effect that renders it difficult to change vendors when a better price or product appears on the market. The cost of migrating to a new system includes a new round of expenditures on hardware and software, configuration, staff training, and data migration on top of the learning curve and productivity drop associated with mastering a new system.

In addition to expenditure on system implementation, maintenance, and migration, there is limited and inconclusive empirical data to demonstrate that health IT systems diminish costs. Two systematic reviews by Black and colleagues (2011) and Chaudhry and colleagues (2006) observe that data on cost and cost-effectiveness of health IT is very limited in the literature. In fact, health IT systems may *increase* costs for numerous reasons. First, especially in the few years immediately following implementation, these systems can raise costs by reducing efficiency while health care workers become acclimatized to new systems and the radical changes these systems introduce into clinical practice. For example, Devine et al. (2010) observed that computerized provider order entry (CPOE) usage in three primary care clinics increased prescribing time by 25 seconds per prescription event compared to handwritten prescribing; relocating computer stations from offices and workstations into examination rooms further increased electronic prescribing time by 24 seconds. Second, while these systems can also motivate increased monitoring of chronic health conditions and health risks, this heightened vigilance does not always reduce costs (Sidorov, 2006). For example, Welch and colleagues (2007) found that electronic health records (EHR) had no impact on short-term cost per visit for patients with diabetes, hypertension, hyperlipidemia, or selected heart conditions. Third, negative impacts on safety, discussed in greater detail below, inhibit the cost-reducing power of health IT by increasing medical errors and error risks. Responding to medical errors is a costly endeavor that can involve longer hospital stays, hospital readmissions, and even mortality. The lack of definitive evidence supporting the positive impact of health IT on patient safety also limits the impact of health IT adoption on reducing malpractice insurance premiums (Sidorov, 2006).

The costs and tasks outlined above have distinct impact based on the size of the organization. In small practices without dedicated IT staff, the burden of adopting health IT falls on providers and managers. These individuals must select systems, negotiate contracts, train themselves and other staff, and oversee system implementation and maintenance. In larger practices, these challenges may be addressed by a group of providers, administrators, and IT staff. These organizations must identify an appropriate committee for decision making to ensure buy-in of remaining personnel and select and implement systems that fit the needs, workflows, and cultures of diverse departments. This variety of situations means that the burden of health IT costs can impact different organizations in different ways. Though some health care practices are able to recoup costs in subsequent years of usage, in other cases adoption of health IT places a continued drain on organizations. Rural hospitals, community health centers that provide care to disadvantaged patients, and small and solo practices that provide the majority of the country's primary care may especially struggle to manage the financial and technological demands of health IT adoption (Miller & West, 2007; Miller, West, Brown, Sim, & Ganchoff, 2005; Ohsfeldt et al., 2005). Health care costs will not be contained through the implementation of systems that cause organizations to expand their budgets or, even worse, close from lack of funding.

FAILURE TO IMPROVE QUALITY AND SAFETY

In addition to failing to reduce costs, health IT has demonstrated limited improvements in quality of care or patient safety. In a systematic review of the literature on EHR and quality of care, Jones and colleagues (2010) found that adoption of EHR had no significant impact on quality of care for patients with heart attack, heart failure, or pneumonia. Similarly, computerized clinical decision support systems (CDSS) and CPOE—two health IT applications key to the realization of quality and safety goals—have demonstrated limited ability to improve overall quality of care or reduce prescribing errors in numerous analyses (e.g., Black et al., 2011; Reckmann, Westbrook, Koh, Lo, & Day, 2009). Romano and Stafford (2011) found no consistent connection between EHR, CDSS, and improved quality of care.

There are many possible reasons for this lack of impact on quality and safety: for example, problems stemming from flawed system design, poor implementation, inadequate staff training, or limited use of system features. Regardless of the cause, the widespread, costly adoption of health IT to enhance quality and safety of care is unjustified until systems and implementation methods advance. The potential of health IT to improve quality and safety should not just be predicted but proven by empirical evidence gathered by organizations that have already adopted these systems.

More alarming than the lack of positive impact is the documented role of health IT in diminishing quality of care and patient safety through a range of unintended adverse consequences. These negative outcomes demonstrate continued inadequate understanding of the systems' design and implementation. Problems with CPOE are particularly concerning. These systems create numerous risk factors for medication errors that can result in increased adverse drug events, especially in the first few years following implementation. For example, CPOE use at Brigham and Women's Hospital led to an increase of 200 percent in actual serious adverse drug events in the first two years following implementation (Berger & Kichak, 2004). CPOE implementation was believed to result in an increased mortality rate at the Children's Hospital of Pittsburgh (Han et al., 2005). There are many ways in which CPOE creates medication errors and error risks (see Campbell, Sittig, Ash, Guappone, & Dykstra, 2006; Koppel et al., 2005). For example, confusing system displays cause uncertainty during medication ordering and difficulty tracking patients' medications. New procedures required by CPOE systems, such as additional steps to cancel and reapprove medications, can lead to incorrect and uncompleted orders.

Another significant issue is the high rate of alert overriding. CPOE systems issue alerts to providers regarding potential medication problems such as drug allergies, drug interactions, and drug dosage errors, a key promise held by such systems for improving patient safety. However, according to a systematic review by Van der Sijs and colleagues (2006), clinicians override active or pop-up alerts issued by CPOE systems at a rate of 49 to 96 percent. Though these overrides may be justified in some situations when medication risks are known, necessary, and managed, the high level of alerts in general and the high level of inappropriate alerts more specifically can lead to alert fatigue, a mental state in which an overwhelming number of alerts drains time and mental energy. Alert fatigue can cause providers to ignore not only unimportant alerts but also important ones. Concern about alert fatigue inspired system designers to develop more customized alert mechanisms. Unfortunately, studies of customized and noninterruptive alerts have not demonstrated any more consistent, positive impact on measures of quality of care (e.g., Lo, Matheny, Seger, Bates, & Gandhi, 2009; Tamblyn et al., 2008). Such poorly designed systems, which demonstrate inconclusive impact on quality while placing patient safety at risk, should not be made integral to the provision of health care. Further standards and procedures are needed to measure and ensure positive outcomes. There should be zero tolerance for potential threats to patient safety introduced by the deployment of immature systems.

Not only is health IT intended to improve quality and safety for individual patients but these systems are also expected to provide data to support quality and safety improvement initiatives at the population level. It remains unclear whether health IT will provide data robust enough to achieve this goal. Although EHR generally makes it easier for providers to locate a patient's record, the layout of individual electronic records can make it more difficult to glean an overview of patient history and to locate information from earlier visits (Christensen & Grimsmo, 2008). Moreover, data captured by EHR systems, particularly that entered in a codified format, may introduce severe quality issues that adversely affect the reuse value of the data (Tang, Ralston, Arrigotti, Qureshi, & Graham, 2007). For example, providers may vary their method of data entry, recording the same data in different ways. This diversity makes it difficult to combine and compare data across providers or organizations. Furthermore, a great deal of EHR content is still captured in narrative, free-text format. This content requires extensive processing similar to paper records to be useful for research (Rosenbloom et al., 2011). This processing may take the form of manual coding, a labor-intensive endeavor, or natural language processing, a computer-driven analysis of human language that still lacks adequate sophistication for this purpose. In short, electronic data is not necessarily higher quality or more easily usable than data captured on paper. The goal of improving population health through technology would be better served by developing standards that improve the quality and usability of captured data before these systems are implemented.

FAILURE TO IMPROVE EFFICIENCY

Finally, health IT has not achieved its goal of increasing efficiency. Rather than speed documentation or workflow, health IT systems frequently slow work, create more and new work, and interrupt workflow. A systematic review on the impact of EHR on physician and nurse time efficiency by Poissant and colleagues (2005) indicated that, though bedside and centralized computer systems reduced documentation time for nurses, these systems increased documentation time for physicians. Impacts on efficiency are some of the strongest barriers to EHR use during patient visits. In a survey of 255 primary care providers conducted by Linder et al. (2006), 52 percent of respondents reported falling behind schedule as a barrier to EHR use during patient visits. Linder and colleagues (2006) observed that these responses were not necessarily linked to age or self-reported EHR experience, indicating that problems with efficiency are related to the technology itself and not to providers' familiarity with it.

Even if overall documentation time does not increase, health IT systems often fragment workflow, interrupting tasks and attention; this fragmentation can increase cognitive load, stress, and errors while decreasing efficiency and continuity (Zheng, Haftel, Hirschl, O'Reilly, & Hanauer, 2010). Many of the barriers to improving efficiency result from the contributing factors discussed below such as poor usability and implementation decisions that fail to understand the impact of health IT on local workflow and culture. Yet again, this failure of health IT stems from inadequate understanding of the potential impacts and effective design and implementation of this new technology and demonstrates the continued need for further testing and development before encouraging widespread health IT adoption.

POOR USABILITY

Health IT systems are marred by usability deficiencies, particularly those originating in the mismatch between software design and health care workers' day-to-day activities. Many systems' user interfaces are not intuitive or user-friendly and lack necessary consideration of clinical realities. For example, current design often fragments and hides information in layers of tabs and menu trees, hindering fast and complete viewing, assembly, and comprehension of data (Ash, Berg, & Coiera, 2004). Navigation may be unclear or disjointed, requiring frequent jumps to different tabs or areas of the screen. Sometimes it may even be unclear where to find a desired function within the application. There is often no search functionality or spelling correction or suggestion support. Other documented usability problems include inability to access a patient's record simultaneously at different computer stations, slow system response, complex processes for ordering, cumbersome structured forms, and no ability to enter free-text data (Niakhani, Pirnejad, Berg, & Aarts, 2009).

Not only do these flaws undermine user satisfaction but they also more seriously result in many unintended adverse consequences such as reduced efficiency and increased medical error risks that threaten patient safety and quality of care (Ash et al., 2004; Koppel et al., 2005). Poorly designed systems take more time to navigate. A crowded presentation of information is incompatible with fast-paced, collaborative clinical work in which computer users are frequently interrupted (Ash et al., 2004). For example, several studies document juxtaposition errors in which users select the wrong option, such as an incorrect medication, due to the dense proximity of those options (Ash et al., 2004; Campbell et al.,

2006). Interface deficiencies can also lead prescribers to order medication for the wrong patient (Ash et al., 2004). Too little work has been done to understand and remedy these issues, even as systems are already being deployed for clinical use.

CONFLICTS WITH WORKFLOW AND CULTURE

A second problem causing many of the unintended adverse consequences documented in the health IT evaluation literature is the conflict between this technology and the workflows and cultures of the organizations in which they are adopted. Introducing health IT changes the dynamics of clinical care, and too frequently those changes can compromise communication and coordination. Overall, health IT systems are not adequately adaptable or flexible for the demands of clinical care. These systems often require providers to perform data entry and order processing at fixed desktop stations, sometimes installed a distance from the point of care. This configuration can cause inefficiency and remove providers from the bedside in situations such as intensive care units, compromising patient safety and reducing opportunities for communication and collaboration (Sittig, Ash, Zhang, Osheroff, & Shabot, 2006).

On a deeper level, technology processes information in less flexible ways than humans do. Providers must be and can be highly adept at handling novel situations such as exceptions (Zheng et al., 2011), but current health IT design responds inflexibly to situational demands (Ash et al., 2004). For example, Kuehn (2009) describes a potentially problematic CPOE use policy which dictates that medication orders must not be placed until after the patient's weight has been documented in the system. Although this policy is meaningful in many respects (e.g., so that computerized algorithms preventing overdose errors can be activated), weighing the patient may not always be operationally possible. Workflow may then be disrupted or clinicians forced to enter an estimated value to temporarily disable this constraint to execute the pending medication-ordering task. In either case, unintended patient safety events could occur. In summary, health IT is not ready for implementation until it can be configured by the organization or department using it to adapt to its specific needs. Furthermore, these configurations should be supported by adequate testing to demonstrate their safety, efficiency, and usability.

Achieving the benefits of health IT is further impeded by provider resistance stemming from personal unfamiliarity with technology, cultural incompatibilities between new technology and traditional approaches to clinical care, and anticipated if-not-realized changes in the power structure within organizations and professions (Ford, Menachemi, Peeterson, & Huerta, 2009). Providers must struggle with the challenges that health IT places on workplace culture, including relationship with patients and sense of autonomy. Providers may also be concerned about replacement and de-skilling due to perceptions that computerized decision support systems will one day provide diagnostic capability and reduce the training and expertise required to practice medicine.

First, several studies document that computer terminals interrupt the interaction and relationship between providers and patients (e.g., Linder et al., 2006). Providers must turn their focus from the patient to the terminal to enter data and complete orders. Second, there is a fundamental tension between documentation and communication styles (Rosenbloom et al., 2011). On the one hand, providers are trained to write in the form of a narrative, describing patients' stories. On the other, computers work best with structured data recorded via check boxes and drop-down lists. Additionally, providers lose the benefit of paper's flexibility and the extra information that paper can efficiently and effectively convey through color, size, and placement. The persistence of paper following health IT implementation, found in many studies, demonstrates the inability of these systems to serve the same functions (Dykstra et al., 2009). Third, the lack of flexibility discussed above can make it seem as though the systems, rather than the providers, are controlling patient interactions. The provision of computerized decision support may appear to undermine the providers' role as skilled, autonomous decision makers. All these issues serve to create powerful and, frequently, negative emotions for providers. And negative experiences can create even greater resistance to these systems. These experiences can also serve as barriers to implementation of future generations of improved technology and may become a factor in staff turnover, especially due to increased stress.

Poorly planned implementation of health IT exacerbates conflicts with workflow and culture. For example, some organizations decide to take a "big bang" approach, launching new technology systemwide in too short a time, overwhelming staff and increasing the likelihood of unpredicted complications (Sittig et al., 2006). Other organizations fail to secure buy-in of nurse leadership or provide adequate end-user support, such as preliminary and ongoing training (Gruber et al., 2009). Negative experiences are too often plentiful for providers as well as patients, whose quality of care can seriously suffer due to flawed implementation. As providers become increasingly dependent on technology to access and process patient data, decision support, and order entry, technical issues such as system downtime can also severely impact the delivery of care.

Studies of local workflow, communication patterns, and culture should precede health IT implementation, and the results should be used to guide that process. Providers within the organization should be consulted for insight into their needs and concerns, and influential figures in the organization should be recruited into the adoption effort to increase overall staff support. The success of homegrown health IT systems demonstrates the importance of configuring health IT for local needs. Homegrown systems benefited from substantial attention to the unique environments in which they were used. These systems held out the promise that health IT could be a method for cutting costs and improving quality, safety, and efficiency. Instead, the rush to implement a new generation of technology largely neglected the lessons and best practices that should have been learned from this history.

LACK OF STANDARDS

Until the recent release of the Health Information Technology for Economic and Clinical Health (HITECH) Act's Meaningful Use criteria, health IT in the United States developed as a fragmented landscape without clear standards to ensure quality or interoperability (Blumenthal & Tavenner, 2010). Even Blumenthal, a former National Coordinator for Health Information Technology, observed that the first phase of the Meaningful Use criteria were themselves a shifting target, modified due to considerable initial resistance (Blumenthal & Tavenner, 2010). The relative immaturity of health IT and health data standards has resulted in the adoption of highly diverse and inadequately tested systems with significantly varied design and functionality. Lack of interoperability is a central problem arising from the dearth of commonly agreed upon and widely implemented standards. Currently, health IT systems cannot consistently or easily communicate with each other, additional IT systems, or electronic resources such as databases within or across organizations. Systems must often be configured to interoperate on a case-by-case basis at considerable financial cost to the adopting organization. As a result, organizations cannot harness the full power of health IT to collaborate in patient care or quality improvement initiatives. Patient records continue to be fragmented and incomplete despite the growing use of EHR. Among other drawbacks, such gaps present a risk for undetected drug allergies and drug interactions and may lead to unnecessary, duplicate tests.

Lack of standards for data privacy and security are also a continuing concern. Information policy for the digital era is still in its infancy, and the federal government, providers, researchers, and other parties are still striving to understand the implications of electronic health records and information exchange for privacy and security. Concerns over data security are a significant barrier to increased health information exchange (Edwards, Hollin, Barry, & Kachnowski, 2010). Auditing access of patient records may track and deter unauthorized access but will not necessarily prevent such access. Moreover, information is increasingly easy to share through the growing prevalence of mobile devices, social networking, email, and chat (Danis, 2010).

Even de-identified data drawn from health IT systems to support research can be re-identified in numerous ways, compromising patient confidentiality (Rothstein, 2010; Gellman, 2010). When data is de-identified, information such as names, zip codes, and social security numbers are removed as a means to prevent data being linked back to specific individuals. However, federal standards for de-identification remain inconsistent, and, once de-identified, information is exempt from regulation (Rothstein, 2010). The process of re-identification, linking data back to an individual, is not impossible. For example, Malin and colleagues (2010) documented re-identification attacks on hospital discharge records and genome databanks: This data had been stripped of personally identifiable information but could be traced back to individuals by combining records and databanks with other sources such as voter registration lists and obituaries, as well as through more complex strategies. Health IT systems should not be implemented until data privacy and security policies are further developed and research into the privacy and security implications of EHR has been completed and applied to system design.

CONCLUSION

Many factors influence the promotion of health IT as a solution to this country's struggles with health care costs, quality, safety, and efficiency. Commercial interests have played a role in creating the belief that CPOE systems in particular have the power to improve health care (Berger & Kichak, 2004). Positive results from the first wave of homegrown health IT systems provided strong support for EHR, CDSS, and CPOE. Yet the field of health IT has shifted dramatically from the era of homegrown systems, with health care organizations investing significant time and money in a proliferation of unproven vendor systems. There is little to no clear evidence that these systems have the power to reduce costs, improve quality of care and patient safety, or enhance efficiency. On the contrary, due to poor usability, conflicts with workflow and culture, and lack of standards, many of these systems increase costs, decrease efficiency, and place patient safety and patient data at serious risk.

The next step for improving health care in the United States is greater investment in the research and development of a new generation of health IT systems that are built on a set of common usability and data standards. Among other factors, these standards should enhance the consistency of user interactions, coordination of care, and data interoperability. Systems developed from these standards should be robustly tested for quality, safety, efficiency, and usability and carefully configured and implemented according to best practices to meet the needs of each unique instance. These systems may then achieve the potential of health IT to transform health care. Until then, patients are risking their lives and organizations are investing precious resources to serve as a testing ground for immature technology.

REFERENCES AND FURTHER READING

Ash, J. S., Berg, M., & Coiera, E. (2004). Some unintended consequences of information technology in health care: The nature of patient care information system-related errors. *Journal of the American Medical Informatics Association, 11*(2), 104–112.

Berger, R., & Kichak, J. P. (2004). Computerized physician order entry: Helpful or harmful? *Journal of the American Medical Informatics Association, 11*(2), 100–103.

Black, A. D., Car, J., Pagliari, C., Anandan, C., Cresswell, K., Bokun, T., McKinstry, B., et al. (2011). The impact of eHealth on the quality and safety of health care: A systematic overview. *PLoS Medicine, 8*(1), e1000387. doi:10.1371/journal.pmed.1000387

Blumenthal, D. (2009). Stimulating the adoption of health information technology. *New England Journal of Medicine, 360*(15), 1477–1479.

Blumenthal, D., & Tavenner, M. (2010). The "meaningful use" regulation for electronic health records. *New England Journal of Medicine, 363*(6), 501–504.

Campbell, E. M., Sittig, D. F., Ash, J. S., Guappone, K. P., & Dykstra, R. H. (2006). Types of unintended consequences related to computerized provider order entry. *Journal of the American Medical Informatics Association, 13*(5), 547–556.

Chaudhry, B., Wang, J., Wu, S., Maglione, M., Mojica, W., Roth, E., et al. (2006). Systematic review: Impact of health information technology on quality, efficiency, and costs of medical care. *Annals of Internal Medicine, 144*(10), 742–752.

Christensen, T., & Grimsmo, A. (2008). Instant availability of patient records, but diminished availability of patient information: A multi-method study of GP's use of electronic patient records. *BMC Medical Informatics and Decision Making, 8*(12). doi:10.1186/1472-6947-8-12

Danis, M. (2010). How to plan for the new era of data management. *Health Management Technology, 31*(12), 24–25.

Devine, E. B., Hollingworth, W., Hansen, R. N., Lawless, N. M., Wilson-Norton, J. L., Martin, D. P., et al. (2010). Electronic prescribing at the point of care: A time-motion study in the primary care setting. *Health Services Research, 45*(1), 152–171.

Dykstra, R. H., Ash, J. S., Campbell, E., Sittig, D. F., Guappone, K., Carpenter, J., et al. (2009). Persistent paper: The myth of "going paperless." *American Medical Informatics Association Annual Symposium Proceedings*, pp. 158–162.

Edwards, A., Hollin, I., Barry, J., & Kachnowski, S. (2010). Barriers to cross—institutional health information exchange: A literature review. *Journal of Healthcare Information Management, 24*(3), 22–34.

Ford, E. W., Menachemi, N., Peterson, L. T., & Huerta, T. R. (2009). Resistance is futile: But it is slowing the pace of EHR adoption nonetheless. *Journal of the American Medical Informatics Association, 16*(3), 274–281.

Gellman, R. (2010). Why deidentification fails research subjects and researchers. *American Journal of Bioethics, 10*(9), 28–30.

Gruber, D., Cummings, G. G., LeBlanc, L., & Smith, D. L. (2009). Factors influencing outcomes of clinical information systems implementation: A systematic review. *Computers, Informatics, Nursing, 27*(3), 151–163.

Han, Y. Y., Carcillo, J. A., Venkataraman, S. T., Clark, R. S., Watson, R. S., Nguyen, T. C., et al. (2005). Unexpected increased mortality after implementation of a commercially sold computerized physician order entry system. *Pediatrics, 116*(6), 1506–1512.

Jones, S. S., Adams, J. L., Schneider, E. C., Ringel, J. S., & McGlynn, E. A. (2010). Electronic health record adoption and quality improvement in U.S. hospitals. *American Journal of Managed Care, 16*(12 Spec No.), SP64–SP71.

Koppel, R., Metlay, J. P., Cohen, A., Abaluck, B., Localio, A. R., Kimmel, S. E., & Strom, B. L. (2005). Role of computerized physician order entry systems in facilitating medication errors. *Journal of the American Medical Association, 293*(10), 1197–1203.

Kuehn, B. M. (2009). IT vulnerabilities highlighted by errors, malfunctions at veterans' medical centers. *Journal of the American Medical Association, 301*(9), 919–920.

Linder, J. A., Schnipper, J. L., Tsurikova, R., Melnikas, A., Volk, L. A., & Middleton, B. (2006). Barriers to electronic health record use during patient visits. *American Medical Informatics Association Annual Symposium Proceedings,* 499–503.

Lo, H. G., Matheny, M. E., Seger, D. L., Bates, D. W., & Gandhi, T. K. (2009). Impact of non-interruptive medication laboratory monitoring alerts in ambulatory care. *Journal of the American Medical Informatics Association, 16*(1), 66–71.

Malin, B., Karp, D., & Scheuermann, R. (2010). Technical and policy approaches to balancing patient privacy and data sharing in clinical and translational research. *Journal of Investigative Medicine, 58*(1), 11–18.

Miller, R. H., & West, C. E. (2007). The value of electronic health records in community health centers: Policy implications. *Health Affairs, 26*(1), 206–214.

Miller, R. H., West, C., Brown, T. M., Sim, I., & Ganchoff, C. (2005). The value of electronic health records in solo or small group practices. *Health Affairs, 24*(5), 1127–1137.

Niazkhani, Z., Pirnejad, H., Berg, M., & Aarts, J. (2009). The impact of computerized provider order entry systems on inpatient clinical workflow: A literature review. *Journal of the American Medical Informatics Association, 16*(4), 539–549.

Ohsfeldt, R., Ward, M., Schneider, J., Jaana, M., Miller, T., Lei, Y., & Wakefield, D. (2005). Implementation of hospital computerized physician order entry systems in a rural state: Feasibility and financial impact. *Journal of the American Medical Informatics Association, 12*(1), 20–27.

Pirnejad, H., Niazkhani, Z., Van der Sijs, H., Berg, M., & Bal, R. (2008). Impact of a computerized physician order entry system on nurse-physician collaboration in the medication process. *International Journal of Medical Informatics, 77*(11), 735–744.

Poissant, L., Pereira, J., Tamblyn, R., & Kawasumi, Y. (2005). The impact of electronic health records on time efficiency of physicians and nurses: A systematic review. *Journal of the American Medical Informatics Association, 12*(5), 505–516.

Reckmann, M. H., Westbrook, J. I., Koh, Y., Lo, C., & Day, R. O. (2009). Does computerized provider order entry reduce prescribing errors for hospital inpatients? A systematic review. *Journal of the American Medical Informatics Association, 16*(5), 613–623.

Romano, M. J., & Stafford, R. S. (2011). Electronic health records and clinical decision support systems: Impact on national ambulatory care quality. *Archives of Internal Medicine, 171*(10), 897–903.

Rosenbloom, S. T., Denny, J. C., Xu, H., Lorenzi, N., Stead, W. W., & Johnson, K. B. (2011). Data from clinical notes: A perspective on the tension between structure and flexible documentation. *Journal of the American Medical Informatics Association, 18*(2), 181–186.

Rothstein, M. A. (2010). Is deidentification sufficient to protect health privacy in research? *American Journal of Bioethics, 10*(9), 3–11.

Sidorov, J. (2006). It ain't necessarily so: The electronic health record and the unlikely prospect of reducing health care costs. *Health Affairs, 25*(4), 1079–1085.

Sittig, D. F., Ash, J. S., Zhang, J., Osheroff, J. A., & Shabot, M. M. (2006). Lessons from "Unexpected increased mortality after implementation of a commercially sold computerized physician order entry system." *Pediatrics, 118*(2), 797–801.

Tamblyn, R., Huang, A., Taylor, L., Kawasumi, Y., Bartlett, G., Grad, R., & Pinsonneault, A. (2008). A randomized trial of the effectiveness of on-demand versus computer-triggered drug decision support in primary care. *Journal of the American Medical Informatics Association, 15*(4), 430–438.

Tang, P. C., Ralston, M., Arrigotti, M. F., Qureshi, L., & Graham, J. (2007). Comparison of methodologies for calculating quality measures based on administrative data versus clinical data from an electronic health record system: Implications for performance measures. *Journal of the American Medical Informatics Association, 14*(1), 10–15.

Van der Sijs, H., Aarts, J., Vulto, A., & Berg, M. (2006). Overriding of drug safety alerts in computerized physician order entry. *Journal of the American Medical Informatics Association, 13*(2), 138–147.

Welch, W. P., Bazarko, D., Ritten, K., Burgess, Y., Harmon, R., & Sandy, L. G. (2007). Electronic health records in four community physician practices: Impact on quality and cost of care. *Journal of the American Medical Informatics Association, 14*(3), 320–328.

Zheng, K., Haftel, H. M., Hirschl, R. B., O'Reilly, M., & Hanauer, D. A. (2010). Quantifying the impact of health IT implementations on clinical workflow: A new methodological perspective. *Journal of the American Medical Informatics Association, 17*(4), 454–461.

Zheng, K., Hanauer, D. A., Padman, R., Johnson, M. P., Hussain, A. A., Ye, W., & Diamond, H. S. (2011). Handling anticipated exceptions in clinical care: Investigating the clinical use of "exit strategies" in an electronic health records system. *Journal of the American Medical Informatics Association, 18*(6), 883–889.

Katy Mahraj and Kai Zheng

Medicare Benefit Cuts

POINT: Given the skyrocketing increases in health care expenses projected over the next few decades, Medicare cuts must be on the table. As long as they are targeted toward inefficient care, Medicare benefit and service cuts can be fair, cost saving, and without adverse consequences for the health of beneficiaries.

R. Tamara Konetzka and Marcelo Coca-Perraillon, University of Chicago
Sally C. Stearns, University of North Carolina at Chapel Hill

COUNTERPOINT: Reductions in Medicare benefits will restrict seniors' access to quality health care. Waste in the system, ranging from outright fraud and abuse to more subtle causes such as administrative costs and misaligned provider incentives, should be the priority targets to reduce aggregate health care spending.

R. Tamara Konetzka and Marcelo Coca-Perraillon, University of Chicago
Sally C. Stearns, University of North Carolina at Chapel Hill

Introduction

Medicare, first passed in 1965 and signed into law by President Lyndon B. Johnson, has become one of the best-known programs in the U.S. government. Along with Social Security, the main program that provides income support for the elderly, Medicare has become a cornerstone for the elderly in the United States through its provision of health insurance for people over the age of 65. As originally created, Medicare consisted of two parts, A and B. Part A is the hospital insurance component that covers certain amounts of inpatient care, home care, hospice care, and care in a skilled nursing facility. Part A is financed by a compulsory matching payroll tax, which in 2011 was 1.45 percent of an employee's wages, matched by an equivalent payment by the employer. (Discussions in policy papers of a Medicare "trust fund" refer to these funds.) Part B is the supplementary health insurance portion that provides coverage for physician services, home health services, and a variety of other outpatient services. The financing for this part of Medicare is not linked to a payroll tax and does not have a trust fund component. Part B is financed by a combination of monthly premiums levied on current recipients of Medicare and federal general revenues (tax revenues). Parts C and D of Medicare were added later: Part C, now known as the Medicare Advantage Program, provides a choice for the elderly to enroll in private plans such as health maintenance organizations; Part D, which went into effect in 2006, subsidizes prescription drugs.

Until recently, in most major U.S. political campaigns since 1965, the continuance of both Medicare and Social Security has been seen as essential to secure not only the votes of the elderly, but many younger U.S. citizens as well, since many have parents or other older relatives who rely upon these programs. Thus, Medicare has come to be known as the "third rail of American politics," meaning that no politician wants to "touch" it. Cutting Medicare or privatizing it has been until recently viewed as politically impossible.

This is not to say that Medicare has existed for nearly 50 years without controversy. There was great opposition to its passage in 1965, and opposition has continued over the years as costs have risen. A number of important attempts have been mounted to deal with those costs, both by increasing the program's revenue and by controlling the rising costs of health care. Medicare has been changed in many ways since its initial passage and the range of services covered has been expanded, most recently with the passage of the Medicare Prescription Drug Improvement and Modernization Act of 2003. With this legislation, the George W. Bush administration created through private health insurance plans a drug coverage option, known as Medicare Part D, paid by individual recipients. The health care reform modifications passed in 2010 and known as the Patient Protection and Affordable Care Act (ACA) have helped remove some of the missing coverage from the drug portion of Medicare (known as the donut hole), added more coverage for preventive services, and modified some other provisions in the Medicare Advantage plans (the managed care option for Medicare) to help extend the life of the Medicare Trust Fund for Part A hospital costs. That act does have some additional provisions to try and control rising health care costs, which would benefit the trust funds and other parts of Medicare. The legislation estimates about $500 billion in savings over the next 10 years.

Since the 1990s some critics have suggested that the program could be improved through privatization, meaning that the program would no longer be run by the government but rather would become part of private health insurance, as with the current option C under Medicare. In some of the discussions, the amount of money given to people to purchase this health insurance would be capped or would increase with the general costs of living; however, over the past 50 years, health care insurance costs have generally increased at a higher rate than have the general costs of living. Some of the problems with that type of approach are that costs for private health insurance in individual policies are high as people reach their 50s and beyond and begin to develop chronic health problems. The high costs of health care coverage on their own would return if Medicare were privatized.

It is often claimed that the Medicare trust fund is running out of money. As mentioned earlier, the program has a trust fund only for Part A, the hospital insurance component, which is financed by a compulsory matching payroll tax. In this way, the current working generation pays for the care of the current elderly, on the assumption that workers younger than themselves will pay for them with future payroll tax income. As initially set up in 1965, it was clear that the trust fund potentially could run out of money at some point as the ranks of the retired became larger than the number of working people. In 26 of the past 30 years, there has been a predicted long-range trust fund deficit, and from 1974 to 1994 there was no positive actuarial balance. It is actually difficult to project this trust fund, because doing so involves estimating the cost of medical care needs over time and how quickly those expenditures will increase. However, it is clear that the current income and outgo for Medicare is not sustainable in the short term as the large Baby Boom generation retires and the younger working-age groups are smaller; however, this population trend could be reversed over time.

Several different solutions to these problems present themselves. Two relate to increased taxes. One is to increase the Medicare tax rate. Another is simply to make up deficits from general tax revenues, resulting in increased taxes from sources such as the income tax. Although the United States is currently in the grip of an anti-tax fever, in reality U.S. taxation rates are lower than in many other countries and are currently lower than in much of the second half of the twentieth century—in other words, using tax increases to pay for Medicare is actually a practical, realistic solution, but one that would require political courage. The other solution is to control health care costs. There is no trust fund for Part B, the supplementary health insurance portion that covers physician services, home health services, and a variety of other outpatient services. Part B is financed by a combination of monthly premiums paid by enrollees and federal general revenues. In the past few years, one change to bring more funds to the program has been to charge higher premiums for those with higher incomes.

This chapter contains two different positions on Medicare benefit cuts. The first is that Medicare cuts must be on the table and should not hurt the quality of care for the elderly as long as the cuts are targeted at reducing inefficient care. This position involves such approaches as raising the age of eligibility, means-testing Medicare, and requiring more cost sharing, especially for inefficient services. The other position argues that reductions in Medicare benefits could restrict seniors' access to quality health care. The argument in this position focuses on the need to identify waste in the system, which could include outright fraud and abuse or more subtle causes such as administrative costs and misaligned provider incentives, and use this as an approach to reduce Medicare costs in future years.

POINT

The Medicare program has been applauded for its success in increasing access to health care for the nation's elderly—access that has been associated with increased well-being and increased equality of health care in a population that, a century ago, suffered high rates of poverty and illness. However, when the program was designed in the 1960s, the currently dramatic rates of growth in health care costs could not have been anticipated. Medicare is now straining the federal budget in such a way that the status quo is unsustainable. Furthermore, much of the increased spending is thought to be either unnecessary or not worth the cost. Because increasing taxes at the rates that would be needed to support Medicare growth under current projections would be politically infeasible, benefit cuts must be considered. However, benefit cuts should be designed to target inefficient spending while maintaining access to necessary care.

THE MEDICARE PROGRAM

Medicare was created in 1965 as an addition to the Social Security Act with the aim of providing health insurance to individuals 65 and older, many of who did not have access to health insurance after retirement. Insurance companies were reluctant to offer insurance to the elderly, and the policies offered were not affordable or did not provide comprehensive coverage. At the time of its enactment, more than half of the elderly did not have health insurance, and most of the insured only had coverage for inpatient hospital services. When Medicare became effective, it provided insurance coverage for inpatient hospital services (Part A) and offered coverage for doctor visits and other related outpatient services through a voluntary component (Part B). Similar to Social Security, Part A of Medicare was designed to be financed mostly by employers and employees through payroll taxes (which are entered into a trust fund). As of 2010 employers and employees each paid a tax of 1.45 percent on the employee's earnings, while the self-employed paid the combined 2.9 percent. However, as part of the Patient Protection and Affordable Care Act (ACA) of 2010, high-income workers will pay an additional 0.9 percent tax starting January 1, 2013. Part B is financed by general tax revenues and premiums paid by beneficiaries or, in some cases, Medicaid programs (public insurance for low-income individuals). Over the years, Medicare eligibility was expanded to include permanently disabled individuals and those with end-stage renal disease, regardless of age.

Medicare has two additional parts, C and D. Part C, established under the Balanced Budget Act of 1997 and now referred to as Medicare Advantage (MA), is administered through private insurers. Medicare pays the insurance companies a per-capita payment for the care of beneficiaries who enroll in a MA plan. The insurance companies use various incentives to control the use of resources. Most offer plans that require enrollees to receive care from a network of eligible physicians and institutions. Services are managed by primary care doctors who coordinate care and refer beneficiaries to specialists. Other private plans have fewer restrictions and function much like traditional Medicare. In general, MA plans charge smaller co-payments and deductibles than traditional Medicare but subscribers might pay higher premiums if additional services are offered. In 2011 approximately 24 percent of Medicare beneficiaries had some form of MA plan coverage.

The Medicare Prescription Drug Improvement and Modernization Act of 2003 created Part D to cover outpatient prescription medications through private insurance companies. Prior to Part D, coverage of pharmaceuticals was limited to inpatient prescriptions under Part A and specific pharmaceuticals such as chemotherapy provided under Part B in physician clinics. Enrollment in Part D is voluntary. Part D plans are required to offer a standard benefit that is determined by law or a similar plan of equal actuarial value. One defining characteristic of Part D is that the plans' beneficiaries can choose from significant variations in benefits, drug formularies, premiums, and co-payments. Part D is financed through beneficiary premiums, general revenues, and transfers from the states.

Medicare beneficiaries have other options to supplement their coverage, in particular Medigap policies. Medicare enrollees can buy additional insurance for defined sets of services from private insurers to cover a portion of Medicare deductibles and coinsurance or other services not covered (or only partially covered) by Medicare. A beneficiary must be enrolled in Parts A and B to be eligible to enroll in a Medigap plan. For low-income Medicare beneficiaries who are "dually eligible" for Medicare and Medicaid, supplemental coverage is provided by Medicaid. Finally, some elderly may supplement or replace Medicare through retirement plans that provide health insurance.

MEDICARE AND COST GROWTH

Since its creation, Medicare has provided increased access to health care at reduced prices to the elderly and the disabled. In doing so, it has been considered a successful program, widely supported by the general public and its users. Yet Medicare, which covers more than 95 percent of the elderly, has also been a major source of strain on the federal budget. Though the funding of Parts A and B may have been adequate at the time of the program's inception, the increase in health care costs and the expansion of coverage have been significant. At the time of Medicare's enactment, health care cost accounted for only 5 percent of Gross Domestic Product (GDP). The former director of the Congressional Budget Office (CBO) Peter Orszag, in testimony to Congress in 2008, stated that spending per-capita grew, on average, around 4.9 percent per year in real terms from 1965 to 2005, while per capita GDP grew by only 2.1 percent per year during the same period. As a consequence, health care spending is now about 15 percent of GDP. Furthermore, the United States spends more on health care per person than does any other country. As the primary payer of health care for the nation's elderly, Medicare plays a substantial role in this cost growth, and a role that is most relevant to public spending. Although the rate of growth in Medicare expenditures has slowed somewhat recently (e.g., according to the 2010 Medicare Statistical Supplement, the annual average rate of increase in expenditures was only 5.6 percent in 2008–2009, compared to an annual average rate of 17.2 percent during 1967 to 1983), the rate has generally exceeded the growth in GDP as well as total health expenditures.

No single factor is responsible for the increase in health care costs. But one consensus among health service researchers is that a major reason for the increase in costs is the emergence and widespread adoption of new medical technologies. Medicine has seen remarkable advances in the last four decades, in new treatments, medications, and diagnostic tools, and many of these are extremely expensive. In the same testimony to Congress, Orszag mentioned that by some estimates approximately half of all long-term growth in health care spending has been associated with the expanded capabilities created by technological advances. These advances, such as new technologies for cardiovascular care, have generally been especially relevant to the elderly.

Another commonly cited factor that has contributed to the increase in Medicare spending has been the aging of the population. Health care spending increases with age, and an aging population increases the absolute number of Medicare beneficiaries, as well the proportion of the population represented by the elderly. Although the aging population explains some of the past growth in spending, most economists consider it to be a small factor compared to the growth of medical technology. The aging population, however, will be a more relevant factor in the future, due to increases in what economists call the dependency ratio—the ratio of the number of people using benefits from taxes and no longer paying in to the number of people in the labor force and paying taxes. An increasing dependency ratio means that the tax revenue that funds part of Medicare will shrink relative to Medicare spending increases.

Other factors driving past and future health care spending growth are the increase in the number of people with long-term chronic conditions and obesity, the increase in administrative costs, payment policies that encourage overuse of more expensive specialty care at the expense of primary care, a legal system that encourages doctors to practice "defensive medicine," and fraud and abuse of the system.

The ever-increasing costs of providing health care and the lack of sufficient dedicated funding for Medicare are forcing the program to rely more on general revenues, government funds that are collected primarily through income taxes and that must support a broad range of government functions. The Board of Trustees of the Federal Hospital Insurance and Federal Supplementary Medical Insurance Trust Funds forecasts that the Part A trust fund will be exhausted in 2024, at which point either benefits will have to be reduced or more revenue allocated to the fund. The other parts of Medicare with no direct funding will continue to use a larger portion of general revenues in a time when the federal budget faces unprecedented long-term fiscal deficits.

MEDICARE BENEFIT CUTS MAY BE FAIR AND EFFICIENT

Many consumers of Medicare believe that they have paid an actuarially fair amount in Medicare taxes, so that a cut in benefits would be analogous to a private insurer charging a fair premium and then refusing to pay the promised benefits. However, Medicare was not designed to be subject to the constraints of private insurers. In reality, the average Medicare beneficiary receives far more in Medicare benefits than she paid in through Medicare taxes. According to Medicare's 2011

Trustee Report, the dedicated payroll taxes and premiums charged to beneficiaries were a major source of funding around 1966, but they are becoming a smaller and smaller portion of funding. Future projections indicate that, by 2060, general tax revenue will need to contribute more than half of Medicare's funding. This imbalance is at the root of Medicare's sustainability problems, as new benefits and technologies have been added over the years without commensurate increases in taxes, a problem that is exacerbated by rising health care costs that also are not balanced by increased taxes.

To solve the problem, at least one of three approaches should be used: Medicare taxes need to be increased; general tax revenues allocated to Medicare need to be increased; or benefits or services need to be cut, either directly through non-coverage of services or indirectly through increased cost sharing on the part of consumers. In an age of strong resistance to additional taxes, cutting benefits may be the most feasible option. If benefits are cut in efficient and equitable ways, benefit cuts need not be viewed as unfair.

Fairness aside, Medicare benefit cuts may also make sense from an efficiency perspective. It is a well-known phenomenon in health insurance that insured individuals consume more health care than is socially efficient (i.e., benefits equal costs) because consumers do not face the full price of services at the point of purchase; economists call this phenomenon a "moral hazard." An individual with insurance may, for example, see a doctor for a minor issue because the visit is not subject to out-of-pocket costs, but that same individual would forgo the visit if she had to pay out-of-pocket. Health care that one would not choose to pay for when faced with the full price (assuming sufficient income) is generally considered socially inefficient, as those resources could be used for more valuable care. The health care may not even be individually efficient, as patients may not understand the limited value or health gains from some services. This understanding of moral hazard has led to decades of evolution in insurance design to include deductibles, co-payments (a set dollar amount that must be paid by the consumer per visit or type of service), and co-insurance (a percentage of the reimbursement amount that must be paid by the consumer), all of which are intended to restore a sense of value in health care use and thereby discourage overuse on the part of consumers. Although these design features cannot eliminate moral hazard entirely, they may serve to reduce it. The remaining moral hazard becomes a cost to the insurer that either gets translated into higher premiums or, in the case of Medicare, is passed on to the government.

Medicare, like other insurance systems, is subject to moral hazard effects in terms of consumer behavior. For example, as newer and more expensive technologies become available, consumers who are insured under Medicare are likely to see only the potential benefit and not the potential cost of using them, and are therefore likely to overuse these technologies. However, Medicare is different from private insurers in key ways. A private insurer would set premiums to be equal to the value of the expected outlays; this premium would be the actuarially fair price. Some administrative costs and profit, known as the "administrative load," are generally added to the actuarially fair price, which consumers are usually willing to pay in order to reduce their risk and smooth consumption over time in the face of uncertain health care costs. If use of health care is higher than expected—whether due to moral hazard or other reasons such as incomplete information, uncertainty, or patient risk aversion—a private insurer would likely raise premiums or cut benefits the following year in order to return to a sustainable operating balance. Under Medicare, the amount people pay in while they are working is not tied to expected benefits; thus, ongoing reconciliation of expected costs and expected benefits is more complex, and the fiscal effects of moral hazard accumulate over time.

Medicare spending is also unique due to the existence of supplemental coverage, which the majority of Medicare beneficiaries have through Medicare Advantage, employer-based retiree plans, or privately purchased Medigap policies. Similarly, for Medicare beneficiaries who are simultaneously covered by state Medicaid programs (i.e., dually eligible individuals), Medicaid supplies supplemental coverage for Medicare-covered services. Supplemental policies are designed to wrap around Medicare and pay for what Medicare does not—specifically, co-payments and co-insurance. Thus, the very features used by private insurers to discourage wasteful use of health care by consumers are blunted among most Medicare beneficiaries. This blunting occurs regardless of whether the supplemental coverage is paid for by beneficiaries (e.g., Medigap) or the government (e.g., Medicaid).

Research by Fang, Keane, and Silverman (2008) shows that, controlling for health status, individuals with Medigap policies spend thousands of dollars more each year than do those without such policies. Although some of this higher spending may be due to selection (e.g., less healthy individuals may be more likely to buy supplemental coverage), much of it is unlikely to be efficient. Importantly, although the private Medigap policies induce the moral hazard in this case, the Medigap policies themselves bear only a fraction of the costs associated with the additional use of health care. Medicare itself bears the majority of the costs, costs associated with health care that may not be an efficient use of resources or, at the extreme, may have no value at all in terms of health. Thus, benefit cuts, depending on what form they take, may be efficient.

ACROSS-THE-BOARD APPROACHES: RAISING THE AGE OF ELIGIBILITY

The simplest approaches to cutting benefits under Medicare are across-the-board measures that affect eligibility and premiums. One option is to raise the age of eligibility, currently set at 65. The arguments for this approach parallel those recently used to raise the age of eligibility for full Social Security benefits. As longevity has increased and age-specific levels of disease and disability have decreased, it no longer makes sense for many individuals to retire at age 65. That individuals should work several years longer, while still potentially living a similar number of years in retirement, may be a reasonable expectation in terms of public policy, and this premise has been largely accepted by the public. Similarly, as the health of the average 65-year-old is now better than the health of the average 65-year-old when Medicare was first passed, delaying the years of Medicare eligibility may not impose a substantial burden. Presumably, individuals who continue working until the age of eligibility for Social Security and Medicare would continue to participate in employer-sponsored health insurance if available.

Though, at first glance, raising the age of eligibility may seem to be an equitable and simple solution, several valid arguments against it have been raised. First, increases in life expectancy and decreases in age-specific disability are applicable to the higher end of the income spectrum but not to the poor. Thus, for the poor, who are also less likely to have employer-sponsored coverage, raising the age of eligibility for Medicare simply extends the problems associated with lack of insurance into an age when the need for health care increases. Second, it is not clear whether delaying eligibility would substantially solve the Medicare cost problem, as the early years of Medicare eligibility are relatively inexpensive, and foregone care may result in higher costs later. (Indeed, a reasonable argument exists that *lowering* the eligibility age could improve the Medicare risk pool overall and potentially lower spending per beneficiary while reducing the number of uninsured among the near-elderly who may have chronic conditions and substantial need for health care.) Finally, costs during the additional years of ineligibility may simply be shifted to others—to private payers or to high-cost emergency care. The shift might still help Medicare but exacerbate health spending by the nation as a whole.

ACROSS-THE-BOARD APPROACHES: MEANS-TESTING

A second conceptually simple approach to cutting Medicare benefits is means-testing. In general, means-testing refers to determining eligibility to receive benefits based on income or wealth. The objective is to provide assistance to those who need it the most. Means-testing is used, for example, to evaluate eligibility for bankruptcy and some student loans. Medicare historically has avoided means-testing, and that avoidance has contributed to the broad popularity of the program. Medicare payroll taxes are assessed at an equal percentage for all taxpayers, and Part B premiums are currently the same for all Medicare beneficiaries, regardless of their ability to pay. Thus, one might think of Medicare as a regressive program (i.e., those with more means pay a lower proportion of their income or wealth than do individuals with less). Wealthier individuals could simply pay more for Medicare-covered services or receive less in Medicare-covered benefits. Although many people would still receive more in Medicare benefits than they have paid in Medicare taxes and premiums, means-testing could eliminate this subsidy for wealthy individuals who arguably do not need it. A similar concept on a much smaller scale is already embedded in Part D, as the extent to which premiums are subsidized depends on income.

The means-testing approach may be more equitable and less disadvantageous to the lower end of the income spectrum than would raising the age of eligibility. However, means-testing also has its drawbacks. First, depending on the structure, it is unclear how much money would actually be saved by means-testing, especially under Part A. The costs of the most expensive types of health care—inpatient hospital stays, for example—are high enough that substantial cost sharing may not be feasible for most. But perhaps the most important disadvantage of both of these fairly blunt approaches is that they do not differentiate between efficient and inefficient spending. Approaches that target inefficient spending on Medicare benefits have the potential to reduce costs with little effect on health outcomes.

TARGETED APPROACHES TO MEDICARE BENEFIT CUTS

An alternative to across-the-board cuts in benefits should consider that any increases in the cost of health care, or more specifically, Medicare spending, should be evaluated in terms of the value and benefits gained from that care. Health care should be used if benefits equal or exceed costs; if costs exceed benefits then those resources could be better used elsewhere where the benefits are greater. Yet Medicare historically pays for health care based on services used rather than outcomes achieved. Such a system, combined with low or zero out-of-pocket prices for services, creates the incentive to use health care as long as there is any potential benefit, a level of benefit that may be substantially smaller than the cost. Over the last few decades, research conducted in association with the Dartmouth Atlas of Health Care has demonstrated wide geographic variation in treatment rates (often referred to as "small-area variation") that seems to be associated with physician practice patterns rather than underlying need. In particular, beneficiaries living in areas with higher levels of spending do not have, on average, better outcomes or greater satisfaction with care. The researchers conclude that Medicare spending in recent years could be reduced by approximately 20 to 30 percent with no impact on mortality. In other words, much could be saved if service provision in all areas is at the level of low-spending areas.

In response, clinicians, health services researchers, and government agencies such as the Agency for Healthcare Research and Quality have focused attention on determining the value of medical treatments by advocating and conducting comparative effectiveness research (CER). CER seeks to generate information on the benefits and harms of alternative treatments in order to improve the delivery of care and help ensure that health resources are not being used on treatments with little value at either the individual or population level. CER by itself does not invoke specific limits on services based on the cost per outcome achieved, as happens in several Commonwealth or European countries, and avoiding this contentious approach in the United States is probably well advised. As the economist Amitabh Chandra and colleagues explain:

> In light of charges about "death panels" in the debate surrounding the healthcare reform bill of 2010, Congress explicitly forbade the use of cost-effectiveness analysis in government programs (Sections 1182(b)(2), 1182(c)(1), 1182(e) of the Patient Protection and Affordable Care Act) . . . In this context, comparative effectiveness research emerged as an alternative strategy to understand better what works in health care . . . Costs are much easier to measure, and can be appended at a later date as financial Armageddon draws closer. (Chandra, Jena, & Skinner, 2011, pp. 28, 34)

Despite the appeal of CER, a caveat to its usefulness and acceptance is the fact that most medical treatments rarely have the same health effects for all patients. This situation (sometimes referred to as "heterogeneity of treatment effects") means that some medical treatments that might not improve health on average for the whole population could still be extremely beneficial for certain individuals. Failure to provide the treatment to patients whose benefit is worth the cost at the individual level means that resources are not being used efficiently. CER methods are evolving in their ability to capture heterogeneous effects, but this caveat is likely to remain.

Two additional major challenges exist to using CER to make Medicare services more efficient. First, researchers need to determine, to the extent possible, which services are beneficial and for whom. Well-meaning physicians generally guide their patients to the services they believe will be most helpful; this "patient selection" complicates the determination of both the individual and population benefits from medical treatment. Second, even without using arbitrary limits (e.g., without requiring that treatments produce an additional year of quality-adjusted life for less than $100,000), Medicare must determine how to encourage use of services by patients who will benefit from them while discouraging or prohibiting use by patients whose health is not improved or may be harmed by those same treatments.

Obtaining valid estimates of the relative effectiveness of treatments for different types of individuals entails vast statistical challenges, especially inasmuch as most of these assessments must be done using observational (and often limited) data. Yet many economists and health services researchers are currently focused on exactly this problem. Furthermore, the data are becoming much more complete with the development of registries, longitudinal surveys, expanded administrative data systems, and, ultimately, with greater use of electronic health records. Some uncertainty in knowledge of the impact of treatments on health outcomes and resource use will always remain because of underlying random factors. Yet innovations in areas such as genetics may help pave the way for increasingly personalized medicine in which patients and providers can avoid fruitless and potentially harmful interventions and instead maximize outcomes with fewer total resources.

INSURANCE REDESIGN

In addition to universal decisions by Medicare about what to cover and what not to cover based on the comparative effectiveness of particular services and treatments, consumers themselves have a role to play in achieving the most efficient use of services. This role depends on the existence of the appropriate incentive structure. The improved understanding of treatment effects that should come with advances in CER must be accompanied by innovations in payment systems that capitalize on this knowledge and provide corresponding incentives. Proposed innovations such as value-based insurance design are based on the premise of patient heterogeneity in treatment response and on capitalizing on that knowledge. As the economist Michael Chernew and colleagues explain:

> Unlike most current health plan designs, Value-Based Insurance Design (VBID) explicitly acknowledges and responds to patient heterogeneity. It encourages the use of services when the clinical benefits exceed the cost and likewise discourages the use of services when the benefits do not justify the cost. (Chernew, Rosen, & Fendrick, 2007, p. w195)

In other words, cost sharing should be used to decrease moral hazard and the use of inefficient services. Yet applying cost-sharing uniformly to all services (e.g., the 20% co-insurance charged for many Medicare services) ignores key differences among services and patients. Some services have greater clinical benefit than others, for example, and benefits may differ by patient type. In addition, co-insurance may in some cases discourage the use of highly beneficial services due to short-run affordability concerns—even if such services could reduce total costs over a longer period. Value-based insurance design is an approach that takes these issues into account and sets different cost-sharing requirements depending on the type of service and, ideally, depending on patient characteristics. The approach, which is clearly a complex undertaking in practice, is consistent with evidence from the RAND Health Insurance Experiment, a large randomized trial conducted in the 1970s and still a fundamental reference on insurance design. The RAND study showed that cost sharing can substantially reduce use of health care services without adversely affecting health outcomes, but that coinsurance can sometimes encourage underuse of beneficial services, especially for low-income individuals.

The effectiveness of value-based insurance design in targeting inefficient use of services for reduction clearly depends on cost sharing as a tool, and yet, as noted earlier, the effects of cost sharing are blunted by the pervasiveness of supplemental coverage under Medicare. Without reforms to the extent and design of supplemental coverage, the principles of value-based insurance design would be impossible to implement in Medicare. Several possibilities for reform exist. One is a regulatory approach: Medicare could require that beneficiaries forgo supplemental coverage in order to qualify for Medicare benefits. The second is a market-based approach: Medicare could charge an additional fee to beneficiaries with supplemental policies, in order to make up for the additional spending induced by the supplemental coverage—that is, the spending associated with moral hazard. For low-income Medicare beneficiaries who are "dually eligible" for Medicare and Medicaid, Medicaid either would have to introduce cost sharing, perhaps at a scaled-down level and only for less efficient services, or implement constraints on use of certain services. However, the latter approach proved to be not only extremely unpopular but also easily circumvented when attempted by Medicaid in Oregon in the mid-1990s. Though the details of implementing either change would be politically challenging, some reform of this type is crucial in designing Medicare cuts that preserve personal choice and maximize the value of Medicare spending to individuals with heterogeneous characteristics.

CONCLUSION

The current growth rates in Medicare spending are unsustainable. Given political resistance to increases in taxes and given that most beneficiaries pay far less in Medicare taxes and premiums than they receive in benefits, cuts to Medicare benefits may be the most feasible and reasonable approach to solving the problem. However, some approaches to benefit cuts are more desirable than others. Blunt approaches such as raising the eligibility age and means-testing have the benefit of apparent simplicity and fairness, but when one digs deeper they are neither simple nor fair and, moreover, do not differentiate between efficient and inefficient spending. On the other hand, more targeted measures such as CER combined with insurance redesign can help avoid wasteful use of services, particularly because variations in both the use and effects of treatments may be greatest when evidence about their relative effectiveness is absent. More specifically, CER can improve the overall quality of health care by raising demand for treatments that work and by lowering demand for treatments that don't, thereby avoiding waste and arbitrary limits on patient and physician choice of treatments. Realistically, to control Medicare spending, benefits may need to be cut, but it matters a great deal how they are cut. Targeted approaches to benefit cuts, such as redesigning cost-sharing incentives and using CER to selectively reduce spending on services of little comparative benefit, have the potential to reduce inefficient spending while maintaining efficient spending, thereby containing costs without adversely affecting the health outcomes of Medicare beneficiaries.

REFERENCES AND FURTHER READING

Annual report of the boards of trustees of the Federal Hospital Insurance and Federal Supplementary Medical Insurance Trust Funds. (2011). Washington, DC: Government Printing Office. Retrieved from https://www.cms.gov/reportstrustfunds/downloads/tr2011.pdf

Baicker, K., & Chernew, M. E. (2011). The economics of financing Medicare. *The New England Journal of Medicine, 365*(4), e7(1)–e7(3). doi:10.1056/NEJMp1107671

Basu, A. (2011). Economics of individualization in comparative effectiveness research and a basis for a patient-centered health care. *Journal of Health Economics, 30*(3), 549–559.

Basu, A., Jena, A. B., & Philipson, T. J. (2011). The impact of comparative effectiveness research on health and health care spending. *Journal of Health Economics, 30*(4), 695–706. doi:10.1016/j.jhealec0.2011.05.012

Binstock, R. H., George, L. K., Cutler, S. J., Hendricks, J., & Schulz, J. H. (2006). *Handbook of aging and the social science* (6th ed.). Boston, MA: Academic Press.

Centers for Medicare & Medicaid Services. (2011). *Choosing a Medigap policy: A guide to health insurance for people with Medicare.* Retrieved from www.medicare.gov/publications/pubs/pdf/02110.pdf

Chandra, A., Jena, A. B., & Skinner, J. S. (2011). The pragmatist's guide to comparative effectiveness research. *Journal of Economic Perspectives, 25*(2), 27–46. doi:10.1257/jep.25.2.27

Chernew, M. E., Rosen, A. B., & Fendrick, A. M. (2007). Value-based insurance design. *Health Affairs, 26*(2), w195–w203. doi:10.1377/hlthaff.26.2.w195

Congressional Budget Office. (2008, January). *Technological change and the growth of health care spending* (CBO Paper). Retrieved from http://www.cbo.gov/ftpdocs/89xx/doc8947/01-31-TechHealth.pdf

Cutler, D. M. (2004). *Your money or your life: Strong medicine for America's health care system.* New York, NY: Oxford University Press.

Cutler, D. M., & Berndt, E. R. (2001). *Medical care output and productivity.* Chicago, IL: University of Chicago Press.

Cutler, D. M., McClellan, M., Newhouse, J. P., & Remler, D. (1998). Are medical prices declining? Evidence from heart attack treatments. *The Quarterly Journal of Economics, 113*(4), 991–1024.

Davis, K., & Collins, S. R. (2005). Medicare at forty. *Health Care Financing Review, 27*(2), 53–62.

Davis, P. A. (2010). *Medicare primer.* Washington, DC: Congressional Research Service. Retrieved from http://aging.senate.gov/crs/medicare1.pdf

Fang, H., Keane, M. P., & Silverman, D. (2008). Sources of advantageous selection: Evidence from the Medigap insurance market. *Journal of Political Economy, 116*(2), 303–350.

Fisher, E. S., Wennberg, D. E., Stukel, T. A., Gottlieb, D. J., Lucas, F. L., & Pinder, E. L. (2003a). The implications of regional variations in Medicare spending. Part 1: The content, quality, and accessibility of care. *Annals of Internal Medicine, 138*(4), 273–287.

Fisher, E. S., Wennberg, D. E., Stukel, T. A., Gottlieb, D. J., Lucas, F. L., & Pinder, E. L. (2003b). The implications of regional variations in Medicare spending. Part 2: Health outcomes and satisfaction with care. *Annals of Internal Medicine, 138*(4), 288–298.

Fuchs, V. R. (2011). *Who shall live?: Health, economics, and social choice* (2nd ed.). Hackensack, NJ: World Scientific Publishing.

Garber, A. M., & Tunis, S. R. (2009). Does comparative-effectiveness research threaten personalized medicine? *The New England Journal of Medicine, 360*(19), 1925–1927. doi:10.1056/NEJMp0901355

Kaiser Family Foundation. (2011). *Medicare fact sheet: Medicare spending and financing.* Retrieved from http://www.kff.org/medicare/upload/7305-05.pdf

Kaiser Family Foundation. (n.d.). *Raising the age of Medicare eligibility: A fresh look following implementation of health reform.* Retrieved from http://www.kff.org/medicare/8169.cfm

Kessler, D., & McClellan, M. (1996). Do doctors practice defensive medicine? *The Quarterly Journal of Economics, 111*(2), 353–390. doi:10.2307/2946682

King, K. M. (2011, June 15). *Medicare waste and abuse: Challenges and strategies for preventing improper payments.* General Accounting Office Testimony before the House Subcommittees on Health and Oversight, Committee on Ways and Means, House of Representatives. Retrieved from http://www.gao.gov/new.items/d10844t.pdf

Manning, W. G., Newhouse, J. P., Duan, N., Keeler, E. B., & Leibowitz, A. (1987). Health insurance and the demand for medical care: Evidence from a randomized experiment. *The American Economic Review, 77*(3), 251–277.

Newhouse, J. P. (1996). *Free for all? Lessons from the RAND Health Insurance Experiment.* Cambridge, MA: Harvard University Press.

Orszag, P. R. (2008). *Growth in health care costs.* Congressional Budget Office Testimony before the Senate Committee on the Budget. Retrieved from http://www.cbo.gov/ftpdocs/89xx/doc8948/01–31-HealthTestimony.pdf

Pauly, M. V. (1968). The economics of moral hazard: Comment. *The American Economic Review, 58*(3), 531–537.

Sox, H. C., & Greenfield, S. (2009). Comparative effectiveness research: A report from the Institute of Medicine. *Annals of Internal Medicine, 151*(3), 203–205. doi:10.1059/0003-4819-151-3-200908040-00125

Triplett, J. E. (1999). *Measuring the prices of medical treatments.* Washington, DC: Brookings Institution Press.

Waldron, H. (2007). Trends in mortality differentials and life expectancy for male Social Security-covered workers, by socioeconomic status. *Social Security Bulletin, 67*(3), 1–28.

R. Tamara Konetzka, Marcelo Coca-Perraillon, and Sally C. Stearns

COUNTERPOINT

Although rising health care costs are a problem that must be addressed, a great portion of the increases in health care spending are not as big a problem as some of the current public debate implies. Some of the growth in spending that has occurred over the last few decades represents an appropriate and rational response to increases in societal wealth reflected by the growth of income per person. Nonetheless, given that Medicare is a government program subject to budgetary concerns and constraints, public policy action to constrain costs is warranted. Rather than focusing on cutting eligibility or increasing the cost sharing required by beneficiaries, which may have adverse consequences for access to care, cost containment efforts should focus on the provider and payment side, reducing fraud and abuse and making the provision of services more efficient.

Reductions in benefits through increases in the Medicare eligibility age or means-testing threaten the underlying goals (and successes) of the Medicare program. Social security and Medicare have often been credited with dramatically improving the quality of life for senior citizens in the United States relative to a century ago and, through universal coverage, with reducing the extent of health care disparities by race and ethnicity. Satisfaction with Medicare is generally high, and administrative costs are relatively low. Studies by eminent scholars such as David Cutler, Amy Finkelstein, and colleagues show that Medicare benefits substantially improved the health and well-being of the elderly in the United States. Medicare also enables payment for new technologies that improve outcomes, such as those for patients with cardiovascular disease. Cutting Medicare benefits blindly, without attention to the value of the services, could lead to adverse consequences in terms of access and health, and could even increase health care costs over time—for example, if beneficial preventive care is foregone due to lack of coverage. And although Medicare payroll taxes and premiums are insufficient to fund current services, Medicare was never designed to exist on dedicated taxes alone. From the beginning, the benefits to the nation of insuring the elderly and facilitating access to necessary but often expensive services were thought to warrant the use of general tax revenues. Similar to spending on infrastructure and educational subsidies, ensuring access to health care for the elderly produces benefits for the population that cannot be achieved through individual purchase of insurance, so Medicare should not be thought of as a private insurer where premiums must cover expected outlays. Rather, the growth in Medicare costs should be controlled in recognition of the fact that general revenues must fund myriad programs in addition to health care that provides benefits to society.

More targeted approaches to Medicare benefit cuts may also be problematic. For example, approaches that focus on increased cost sharing by consumers, which are designed to reduce demand for services that are not worth the cost, are good in theory but can have adverse consequences when it comes to access to care and health outcomes. Some services are more beneficial than others, and the extent of benefit may vary by person. Because cost-sharing arrangements cannot possibly be tailored to reflect these differences from person to person, increased cost sharing may result in reduced access to necessary and beneficial services for some people. Furthermore, the effectiveness of cost sharing is blunted by the popularity of supplemental coverage that pays co-payments and co-insurance. Finally, simply increasing the extent of cost sharing raises issues of equity. Low-income elderly whose assets are not quite low enough to qualify for Medicaid and who cannot afford private Medigap coverage are most likely to feel the effects of Medicare cost-sharing provisions; they are the most vulnerable to any increases in deductibles, co-payments, and co-insurance, which can be expected to have negative repercussions for their access to needed care.

Using targeted methods to eliminate coverage of specific services rather than increasing cost sharing presents different problems. Although it is desirable to facilitate seniors' access to quality health care by using CER to identify effective services that are worth the cost, CER is unlikely to substantially constrain Medicare spending. Elders with relatively complete coverage (e.g., through dual Medicaid eligibility or Medigap/retiree supplemental policies) may demand treatments with benefits that are minimal or highly uncertain. Furthermore, physicians have little reason to discourage the use of minimally beneficial services, especially under fee-for-service reimbursement arrangements, which continues to dominate ambulatory care.

Therefore, when it comes to constraining Medicare spending, waste and inefficiency in the system present the best targets. In contrast to efforts aimed at the demand side (changing eligibility, coverage, and the choices made by Medicare beneficiaries), these targets can be characterized as those relating to the supply side of care (i.e., to providers). Waste or inefficiencies may arise from

- fraud and abuse,

- defensive medicine and medical errors,

- prices that are higher than costs, and

- provider reimbursement methods that do not offer incentives for cost containment.

Efforts to address these sources of expenditure growth will require concerted actions to generate new information, enact legislative changes, reconfigure existing systems, or even increase criminal investigations (e.g., for fraud and abuse). Current as well as potential strategies for each component are discussed separately in the remainder of this chapter.

FRAUD AND ABUSE

Fraudulent service claims constitute an important and surprisingly large target for reductions in Medicare spending. The National Health Care Anti-Fraud Association, which is composed of private insurers and government agencies, estimated the rate of fraudulent claims in 2009 at 3 percent of spending, though the rate for Medicare may be higher. Though all parties can agree that billing by bogus providers for services that are never delivered should be stopped, the realities of the processes required are much more complex, as the same administrative processes that promote efficient billing and payment make it difficult to identify even these extreme cases. Furthermore, the Medicare program already denies payment for services that are not medically necessary; although such denials may be appropriate if the services were not medically necessary, determination of medical necessity may be subject to some controversy, can require fairly burdensome documentation, and may lead to nonpayment for services that in some cases are beneficial.

The level of fraud has been a concern for some time, and the Centers for Medicare & Medicaid Services (CMS) expanded fraud identification operations substantially in 2009 when the Recovery Audit Contractors (RAC) program was initiated to analyze paid claims and identify overpayments. Under the RAC program, CMS sets performance targets to reduce the rate of improper payments for fee-for-service as well as managed care; performance measure targets for Part D are being developed. The 2010 baseline payment error rate was 10.5 percent for fee-for-service and even higher (14.1 percent) for Part C, and one estimate puts improper payments for Part D at $5.4 billion. These high percentages and large dollar amounts show the potential for reductions in spending, yet these amounts do not translate into pure savings, inasmuch as the identification and recovery of inappropriate payments require considerable resources. Recognizing that preventive actions may also be valuable, CMS is implementing other efforts, such as increased provider enrollment requirements to discourage fraudulent providers from participating in Medicare, and a Center for Program Integrity to identify and address components of the Medicare and Medicaid programs that make them vulnerable to improper payments.

Although CMS is hopeful that its multipronged approach will reduce fraudulent claims, even the largest estimates of the problem mean that total elimination of improper payments would not address the bulk of Medicare spending. In addition, reducing fraud and abuse cannot counter cost *growth* for legitimate services. Attention to fraud and abuse therefore is likely to be an important but insufficient approach to controlling Medicare expenditures.

REDUCING DEFENSIVE MEDICINE AND IMPROVING SAFETY

Different issues pertain to the practice of what is known as "defensive medicine," in which providers use services (especially diagnostic tests) with little expected benefit other than reducing the risk that a patient may later sue. Defensive medicine is not like fraud in the sense that the services are performed and do provide information; the problem is that the information gained is likely not worth the cost. At issue, however, is the contribution of defensive medicine to growth in Medicare expenditures. If the contribution is substantial, policymakers need to consider the effects of tort reform (changing laws to reduce the potential rewards from suing) or other approaches to constraining health care costs related to defensive medicine or medical errors.

Estimates of defensive medicine as a proportion of total health care costs as well as growth in this proportion over time offer some perspective on the magnitude of the problem. Those who believe that defensive medicine is a major problem estimate that services related to defensive medicine and medical malpractice may account for up to 15 percent of medical costs. In reality, direct tort costs represent less than 2 percent of those costs—this percentage, as well as the total number of cases of medical malpractice, have remained fairly constant over time. Estimates of the indirect costs of the threat of litigation—those stemming from defensive medicine practices to avoid litigation—are naturally more difficult to calculate. Darius Lakdawalla and Seth Seabury estimate that defensive medicine costs accounted for at most 5 percent in cost growth during the late 1980s and the 1990s, a fraction of the total cost growth in health care expenditures during the same period.

Even if estimates of the magnitude of the problem are somewhat exaggerated in popular discourse, policymakers are interested in knowing the extent of cost reductions that might occur as a result of tort reform. Using data on Medicare beneficiaries with heart disease, a seminal study by Daniel Kessler and Mark McClellan (1996) showed that malpractice reforms to reduce provider liability pressure were associated with a reduction in medical expenditures of 5 to 9 percent without increasing the rates of medical complications or mortality. Lakdawalla and Seabury, however, examining all types of Medicare patients, concluded that reducing malpractice costs would be unlikely to have a major impact on either health care costs or outcomes; a 10 percent reduction in malpractice costs would reduce total health care expenditures by at most 2 percent.

Although some level of tort reform could contribute modestly to reductions in Medicare expenditures, additional mechanisms could further reduce defensive medicine or malpractice cases. First, evidence from CER can be used to develop or refine guidelines for care. Physicians who provide care consistent with guidelines accepted by professional associations may not only be able to improve health outcomes for their patients but would also have support for decisions not to pursue treatments or tests that have little demonstrated effect. Second, the high rate of medical errors identified in a 1999 Institute of Medicine report titled *To Err Is Human* represents a major source of unnecessary costs and malpractice risk. Many medical errors occur in systems with insufficient safety checks or processes to prevent providers from making human mistakes. Although systems involving more extensive checks and scrutiny can be expensive, they can reduce malpractice concerns, improve health outcomes, and in some cases reduce total costs.

DO PRICES REFLECT COSTS?

The cost-based reimbursement methods used by Medicare during the first few decades of the program were thought to contribute to large increases in Medicare expenditures because providers were able to pass on costs with relatively little scrutiny. Under a fee-for-service or cost-based reimbursement model, medical providers are paid for the procedures and services they perform (based on provider cost, plus some markup), not for the outcome or by type of ailment they treat. Thus, medical providers have strong monetary incentives to provide the largest possible number of procedures. Since the 1980s Medicare has moved away from cost-based reimbursement to pricing based on units of care (e.g., Diagnosis-Related Group payment for hospital stays, Resource Utilization Group payment per day for skilled nursing care, or reimbursements based on the Resource-Based Relative Value Scale for physician visits). At the federal level, these prices have been set administratively by CMS with congressional oversight. Prices are based on analysis from the Medicare Payment Advisory Commission and its contractors, using historical claims to determine a reasonable amount of resources required to treat a particular event or condition.

An important alternative to administrative pricing is to set prices competitively, for example through competitive bidding by providers. The U.S. Department of Veterans Affairs (VA) uses competitive bidding for a number of services (e.g., durable medical equipment) and pays prices that are substantially lower than the those paid by Medicare. Congress has approved demonstrations for competitive bidding for Medicare services such as procedures (e.g., bundled payments for cataract surgery or coronary artery bypass graft [CABG]), durable medical equipment, and clinical laboratory services. Yet Medicare has taken little advantage of this approach. Congress legislated competitive bidding by health care plans under Part C as part of the 2010 Patient Protection and Affordable Care Act (ACA), but the provision was quickly removed under subsequent legislation. Medicare Part D incorporates some degree of competitive bidding in that individual plans must compete with each other for members and negotiate drug prices with suppliers.

At a practical level, one important concern about competitive bidding pertains to whether quality could decline if providers compete on price. Doug Coulam and colleagues argue that the implementation of minimum quality standards as a component of competitive bidding might improve the overall level of quality and would institute some important oversight of quality that does not currently exist. They also argue that the failure to use competitive bidding to bring Medicare prices in line with costs for services of sufficient/appropriate quality may be due to the vested interests of provider groups, who lobby against the idea of having to compete on price for services that they have long provided in either a cost-based system or unit prices based on historical costs. The passage of competitive bidding among prescription drug plans under Medicare Part D provides support for this argument, as it was a new benefit without longstanding provider interests in a particular payment system. Although it is difficult to assess the impact of competitive bidding on pharmaceutical costs without a control group or information on the counterfactual, Part D expenditures have grown less than predicted. In total, the extent to which administrative pricing under congressional oversight is less effective in constraining costs than is an approach like competitive bidding is unresolved but intriguing.

PROVIDER PAYMENT: INCENTIVES AND METHODS

Although greater use of competitive bidding has the potential to reduce the price of services and therefore restrain cost growth, it does not address the issue of overuse of services. As noted above, traditional fee-for-service payment encourages overuse, as health care providers have the financial incentive to supply as many services as possible, regardless of whether the benefit of the services is worth the cost. In the extreme, the additional services or tests may be burdensome or even harmful for the patient, with little or no expected benefit. In recognition of this problem, Medicare has implemented "prospective payment systems" for many of its provider types, including hospitals, skilled nursing facilities, home health care agencies, and hospital outpatient service providers; many of these were mandated under the Balanced Budget Act of 1997. Under prospective payment, providers are paid a set amount per admission, per day, or per condition, with the set amount determined by average historical costs for similar cases. Although adjustments can be made for extreme (outlier) cases, under prospective payment providers are generally not reimbursed more for providing more services. Rather, they have an incentive to provide care as efficiently as possible, because if they spend less than the prospective payment amount they can keep the difference. Under such a system, instead of Medicare bearing the entire financial risk of health care costs for beneficiaries, providers take on some of that risk, thus internalizing the incentive to contain costs.

Medicare's prospective payment systems have generally been credited with holding down costs relative to fee-for-service and cost-based reimbursement, and in the absence of these systems Medicare costs might long ago have reached a crisis level. Although providers in theory have an associated incentive to skimp on care, researchers have generally not found significant adverse consequences for health outcomes, possibly because competition on quality and reputation rather than price is common in health care.

However, the potential for prospective payment to constrain overall Medicare costs has been limited by several factors. First, not all types of services are covered by these systems. Physician payment under Part B, for example, is subject to a fee schedule (the Resource Based Relative Value Scale) rather than prospective payment. Although the fee schedule is also intended to enable Congress to maintain control over costs, it does not incorporate the risk-sharing attribute that is key to the success of prospective payment systems in reducing use of unnecessary services. Relatedly, the fee schedule has also been blamed for rewarding specialty care over primary care, encouraging the overuse of high-cost technologies and specialty care while discouraging the use of potentially more cost-effective primary care. Second, prospective payment systems tend to become less prospective over time as new payment categories are added for new technologies—again, this reduces the amount of risk sharing and thus the incentive for cost containment.

A final and significant challenge regarding Medicare's prospective payment systems is that they are setting-specific, which produces unintended incentives for inefficiencies across settings. The so-called silos of care—created in part by separate payment systems—have received substantial attention associated with the ACA. Transitions between hospitals, post-acute care settings, and long-term care settings have long been known to be problematic. Hospitals often discharge patients to nursing homes or to home health care for post-acute care without adequate documentation and communication, and those post-acute care settings often transfer patients back to the hospital when issues arise that are costly or complicated to treat. Transfers are inherently risky for seriously ill individuals, and hospitalizations are expensive, and yet the current payment incentives make such transfers largely inevitable. Under prospective payment, hospitals receive a per-admission payment, so discharging patients to post-acute care as soon as possible is financially prudent. Hospitals are not at risk for poor post-acute outcomes, so the incentive to provide a smooth transition and adequate communication with the post-acute setting is absent. (This is changing under provisions included in the ACA whereby hospitals will be penalized in payment for excessive readmissions.)

Post-acute care providers, on the other hand, have little incentive to ensure that these patients do not return to the hospital. Under prospective payment, post-acute care providers are paid based on categories of patient condition and severity, but if the patient turns out to be among the more complicated patients within a particular category, the provider could lose money. Rehospitalizing that patient, however, both relieves the post-acute care provider of needing to address a complicated case and incurs little or no financial risk to the post-acute care provider, as Medicare pays for the rehospitalization. In the long run, the nursing home has little incentive to invest in the resources required to address more complicated cases, even if avoiding transfers would be better in terms of health outcomes. Regardless of the efficiencies created within settings by prospective payment, substantial inefficiencies remain across settings that are in fact exacerbated by the incentives under setting-specific prospective payment. Under these incentives, each participating entity working in its own best interest does not add up to the best interest of the whole. These inefficiencies are major contributors to high health care spending as well as to adverse health outcomes.

Recognition of this problem is inherent in several models of payment under Medicare that have existed for much longer than the ACA. For example, Evercare is a Medicare Advantage model in which the insurer is at financial risk for both nursing home care and hospital admissions for its members. The insurer pays nurse practitioners to provide more intense primary care to nursing home residents, thereby avoiding adverse events or addressing adverse events in the nursing home, and reducing the need for hospital admissions. The Program of All-Inclusive Care for the Elderly (PACE) is another model in which providers take on financial risk across multiple types of care, in this case all types of health care for dual Medicare/Medicaid beneficiaries who enroll. PACE providers address needs of their members in a service delivery model based on adult day care in a community setting; much of the care is available at a single site to avoid referrals to more costly care such as nursing homes and hospitals. If placement in a nursing home becomes necessary, PACE providers generally follow up with additional primary care to avoid hospital admissions, much like in Evercare. Although these models are both fairly small programs and there is some uncertainty as to whether they could be scaled up effectively, they hold some promise for breaking down the silos of payment and care delivery.

The ACA recognizes the problem of inefficiencies across settings and establishes (as permanent features or demonstrations) several models of payment and delivery designed to address the problem. One is payment bundling across hospitals and post-acute care. Bundling is similar to prospective payment, but the payment is combined across settings. For example, for a hip fracture or hip replacement patient, one entity (e.g., the hospital) would receive a payment intended to cover both acute and post-acute care and would be responsible for arranging delivery of both types of care. If just one entity takes on the financial risk of both acute and post-acute care for a patient episode, that entity acquires the incentive to use both hospital care and post-acute care in a way that produces the best health outcomes at the lowest cost. Another is accountable care organizations (ACOs), a model in which one entity takes on financial risk for not only acute and post-acute care but also for primary care. A key assumption in these models is that the delivery system will adapt to the incentives inherent in the payment arrangement.

Many of the specific details of these programs are yet to be worked out and will evolve over years, if not decades. Adverse indirect effects will likely evolve and have to be countered in some way. For example, bundling acute and post-acute care may simply shift and exacerbate the boundary of the inefficiencies elsewhere—perhaps between post-acute and long-term care or post-acute and primary care. The appropriate bundles and associated payment rates may be elusive, such that efficiencies are not gained or providers refuse to participate. Risk adjustment, always a challenge, may prove a particular impediment in a model like ACOs, where patients will not be required to use care within the ACO system of providers. Finally, delivery systems may not adjust quickly enough, such that efficiencies in payment across settings and providers will not be matched by smoother transitions in care delivery across settings and providers. Other issues, such as physician ownership (direct or indirect) of sophisticated equipment, laboratory/testing services, and even facilities provide additional challenges in that financial incentives to the individual physician may outweigh financial incentives built into the broader payment system; some provisions known as Stark laws try to address these incentives directly by prohibiting physicians from referring patients for some services to entities in which they have a financial interest. Nonetheless, given the enormous inefficiencies created by setting-specific payment, models of payment that spread risk to those making the care recommendations (i.e., health care providers themselves) and that break down the boundaries between settings hold substantial promise for addressing the cost containment challenge. These are models where, at least in concept, what is in the provider's best interest is also in the best interest of the patient and of cost containment, a confluence of interests that minimizes inefficiencies and waste. Perhaps most importantly, when these payment incentives align with delivery system incentives to reduce fragmentation of care, they have the potential to simultaneously improve care and reduce spending.

CONCLUSION

The identification of four key areas for reducing waste in the provision of Medicare services was a relatively straightforward task. Attention to these areas, both separately and jointly, could be more efficient in ensuring quality health care at affordable costs than approaches such as broad benefit cuts, changes in eligibility, or targeted measures aimed at reducing consumer demand for inefficient services, such as increased cost sharing and the use of CER. The effects of increased cost sharing may be blunted by the prevalence of supplemental coverage and may have adverse consequences for access to beneficial care for some segments of the population. CER offers a hopeful path for identification of beneficial services, but in and of itself, CER is unlikely to constrain Medicare spending sufficiently. Thus, increased attention to approaches aimed at reducing waste and inefficiency on the provider side is warranted.

Some approaches are already underway but may need to be expanded (e.g., investigations of fraud), while others are being considered through government-sponsored demonstrations (e.g., accountable care organizations, bundling of payments). An increased focus on all areas is likely essential to enable access to quality health care for elders and Medicare non-aged beneficiaries with acute or chronic conditions. Even with solutions or progress in each area, Medicare spending will most likely continue to grow at an absolute level. The goal is to constrain the rate of spending increases using mechanisms to ensure that the spending is worthwhile.

REFERENCES AND FURTHER READING

Baicker, K., & Chernew, M. E. (2011). The economics of financing Medicare. *New England Journal of Medicine, 365*(4), e7(1)–e7(3). doi:10.1056/NEJMp1107671

Baker, T. (2005). *The medical malpractice myth.* Chicago, IL: University of Chicago Press.

Cassidy, A. (2011, September). Health policy brief: Putting limits on Medigap. *Health Affairs.* Retrieved from http://healthaffairs.org/healthpolicybriefs/brief_pdfs/healthpolicybrief_52.pdf

Coleman, E. A., & Berenson, R. A. (2004). Lost in transition: Challenges and opportunities for improving the quality of transitional care. *Annals of Internal Medicine, 141*(7), 533–536.

Coleman, E. A., Min, S.-J., Chomiak, A., & Kramer, A. M. (2004). Posthospital care transitions: Patterns, complications, and risk identification. *Health Services Research, 39*(5), 1449–1465. doi:10.1111/j.1475–6773.2004.00298.x

Coleman, E. A., Parry, C., Chalmers, S., & Min, S.-J. (2006). The care transitions intervention: Results of a randomized controlled trial. *Archives of Internal Medicine, 166*(17), 1822–1828. doi:10.1001/archinte.166.17.1822

Coulam, R. F., Feldman, R. D., & Dowd, B. E. (2011). Competitive pricing and the challenge of cost control in Medicare. *Journal of Health Politics, Policy and Law, 36*(4), 649–689. doi:10.1215/03616878-1334677

Cutler, D. M. (2004). *Your money or your life: Strong medicine for America's health care system.* New York, NY: Oxford University Press.

Finkelstein, A., & McKnight, R. (2008). What did Medicare do? The initial impact of Medicare on mortality and out of pocket medical spending. *Journal of Public Economics, 92*(7), 1644–1668. doi:10.1016/j.jpubec0.2007.10.005

Fuchs, V. R. (2004, October 7). Perspective: More variation in use of care, more flat-of-the-curve medicine. *Health Affairs.* doi:10.1377/hlthaff.var.104

Fuchs, V. R. (2011). *Who Shall Live? Health, economics, and social choice* (2nd ed.). Hackensack, NJ: World Scientific Publishing.

Hall, R. E., & Jones, C. I. (2007). The value of life and the rise in health spending. *The Quarterly Journal of Economics, 122*(1), 39–72.

Institute of Medicine. (1999). *To err is human: Building a safer health system.* Retrieved from http://www.iom.edu/Reports/1999/To-Err-is-Human-Building-A-Safer-Health-System.aspx

Kaestner, R., & Silber, J. (2010). Evidence on the efficacy of inpatient spending on Medicare patients. *Milbank Quarterly, 88*(4), 560–594. doi:10.1111/j.1468-0009.2010.00612.x

Kastor, J. A., & Adashi, E. Y. (2011). Maryland's hospital cost review commission at 40. *The Journal of the American Medical Association, 306*(10), 1137–1138. doi:10.1001/jama.2011.1311

Kessler, D., & McClellan, M. (1996). Do doctors practice defensive medicine? *The Quarterly Journal of Economics, 111*(2), 353–390. doi:10.2307/2946682

King, K. M. (2011, March 2). *Medicare program remains at high risk because of continuing management challenges.* Government Accounting Office Testimony before the House Subcommittee on Oversight and Investigations, Committee on Energy and Commerce. Retrieved from http://www.gao.gov/new.items/d11430t.pdf

Konetzka, R. T., Spector, W., & Limcangco, M. R. (2008). Reducing hospitalizations from long-term care settings. *Medical Care Research and Review, 65*(1), 40–66.

Lakdawalla, D. N., & Seabury, S. A. (2009). *The welfare effects of medical malpractice liability.* National Bureau of Economic Research (Working Paper No. 15383). Retrieved from http://www.nber.org/papers/w15383

Levinson, D. R. (2009, June 25). *Health care reform: Opportunities to address waste, fraud and abuse.* U.S. Department of Health and Human Services Testimony before the House Subcommittee on Health, Committee on Energy and Commerce. Retrieved from http://oig.hhs.gov/testimony/docs/2009/06252009_testimony_health_reform.pdf

Newhouse, J. P. (1996). *Free for all? Lessons from the RAND Health Insurance Experiment.* Cambridge, MA: Harvard University Press.

Schuck, P. H., & Zeckhauser, R. J. (2006). *Targeting in social programs: Avoiding bad bets, removing bad apples.* Washington, DC: Brookings Institution Press.

Sox, H. C., & Greenfield, S. (2009). Comparative effectiveness research: A report from the institute of medicine. *Annals of Internal Medicine, 151*(3), 203–205. doi:10.1059/0003-4819-151-3-200908040-00125

R. Tamara Konetzka, Marcelo Coca-Perraillon, and Sally C. Stearns

High-Deductible Health Insurance Plans

POINT: Employers and individuals continue to gravitate toward high-deductible health plans as a means of controlling escalating health care costs. Evidence suggests that these plans reduce utilization of health care and costs by giving employees direct choices of which health care service to use for their own health and benefit.

Stephen T. Parente, Carson School of Management, University of Minnesota
David Randall, Consumer Driven Health Care Institute

COUNTERPOINT: The use of high-deductible health plans has almost tripled since 2004, but concerns are mounting about how the plans may affect the health status and quality of care, especially for low-income and vulnerable populations. The result may be to actually increase overall costs, due to the social costs of a sicker, underserved population.

Stephen T. Parente, Carson School of Management, University of Minnesota
David Randall, Consumer Driven Health Care Institute

Introduction

One of the trends in the U.S. health care system today is the increase in high-deductible health care plans (HDHP). These plans have been growing because of a desire by both employers and employees to reduce the costs of health care insurance. From the employer's perspective, these plans have also been viewed as a way to restrain the growth in utilization of services. HDHPs are reversing what had been a trend over the previous decades of declines in the amount of deductibles people pay under their health insurance plans. (A deductible is the amount a person must pay out-of-pocket when he or she uses health care services.) In these newer, high-deductible plans, deductibles are generally at least $1,000 a year per person insured under the plan. In some plans, the deductible may be as high as $5,000 a year.

One of the reasons for this increase in HDHPs is the growth of health savings accounts as a benefit funded by employers. These types of savings accounts received some initial support under the Health Insurance Portability and Accountability Act of 1996 (HIPAA), which provided for a trial of 750,000 medical savings accounts for people in small firms or the individual market. Based on that legislation, the trend got started in some smaller U.S. companies around 2001; over the next few years these types of accounts were added to the benefit programs of more and more employers. These types of insurance options gained much greater attention as part of the passage of the Medicare Modernization Act of 2003, which created tax-advantaged Health Savings Accounts (HSAs), which are open to anyone under the age of 65. This legislation included subsidies for such accounts that some experts estimate cost around $174 billion. These accounts were linked to high-deductible private insurance plans. Though these plans had not attracted much attention as demonstration plans under the 1996 legislation, Congress nevertheless expanded them in a variety of ways in the 2003 legislation. If people bought health insurance with a deductible of at least $1,000 for an individual and $2,000 for a family, they could have a tax-advantaged savings plan. Part of the argument for these plans was that, if consumers had more of their own money at stake to pay for health care services, it would increase their incentive to look more closely at overall medical costs and to shop around for the best bargains in attaining health care services. At times, some referred to this as "consumer-driven" health care, in contrast to managed care.

The idea that different levels of cost sharing for different people might impact the use of health care services is not new. In fact, one well-known study conducted by the RAND Corporation in 1973 tested the effects of increased cost sharing with employees. The RAND Health Insurance Experiment (HIE) was designed to test the effects of higher coinsurance and deductibles on consumer utilization of health care services. This was a large study that included over 7000 individuals who were randomly assigned to participate across distinct geographic areas in the United States. People were assigned different cost-sharing amounts, with a range from no out-of-pocket costs or free health care services to varying coinsurance and deductible amounts from 25 to 95 percent. These amounts were also subject to an overall out-of-pocket cost limit of $1,000 per individual as well; this may seem lower than figures being talked about currently, but one must consider the impact of inflation on costs over this almost 40-year period. A quick summary of the findings of this important study by Karen Davis in "Concluding Commentary: Consumer Directed Plans: Will it Improve Health System Performance?" published in *Health Services Research* in August 2004, showed that individuals subject to higher deductibles and coinsurance amounts tended to consume fewer health insurance services.

The rest of this chapter will provide newer information on this topic, but it is always useful to know the results of classic studies in the field. Though there are arguments both in favor of and against the utility of HDHPs in impacting the use and quality of health care services, as covered in greater detail in the rest of this chapter, there are some generally accepted relationships between background characteristics of people and their interest in enrollment in these types of plans. Higher deductibles and account-based plans are generally favored by individuals and families in higher income brackets. By contrast, individuals and families in lower income brackets are often more price- and cost-sensitive. One of the concerns is whether people in these groups will have a greater tendency to forgo necessary health care services. If this were to be true, then it could have an indirect effect on overall health status. There has been some evidence that, at least in the past, these types of plans have not been as popular with most employees as plans that provide coverage for more of the costs of health care utilization. This seems to be true for many types of employees, and perhaps even more so for those with serious health problems such as those with chronic illnesses.

POINT

The use of high-deductible health plans (HDHPs) has increased in the last decade as a result of both employer and employee desiring to reduce both costs and utilization of health care services. As a result of this trend, the typical health plan enrollee has seen her deductible (or amount she must pay out-of-pocket for the utilization of health care benefits) increase to over $1,000 per year (Haviland, Sood, McDevitt, & Marquis, 2011; RAND, 2011). Employers of all sizes as well as individuals have increasingly turned to HDHPs as a solution to confront rising costs. Researchers have found that health care utilization and thus health care costs are reduced by the use of HDHPs (Parente, Feldman, & Christianson, 2004b). A principal critique of HDHPs is that they create an incentive to delay or forgo health care services as a result of potentially high out-of-pocket costs and thus indirectly affect health status. The empirical evidence suggests that this claim is not valid, and, in fact, the use of these plans has no material effect on health status. Indeed, HDHPs can assist in providing consumers of health care services price awareness and transparency, thus reducing utilization and costs.

The increased use of HDHPs can be traced to 2001 when several start-up insurance companies began offering new products that featured a HDHP paired with a health savings account that was funded by the employer (Christianson, Parente, & Taylor, 2002). These plans, called Health Reimbursement Arrangements (HRAs), were added to the benefit programs of a relatively small number of employers over the next two years. However, by 2004, they were included in the product portfolios of almost all major insurance companies. The visibility of this type of insurance arrangement was heightened by the passage of the Medicare Modernization Act of 2003, which created tax-advantaged Health Savings Accounts (HSAs), which are open to anyone under the age of 65.

The goal of account-based plans such as HSAs is to make individuals responsible for routine care such as doctor visits, prescription drugs, and recurring diagnostic tests. The hope is that, by exposing individuals to these routine expenses, consumers will become aware of the actual costs of health care, thus introducing a measure of price transparency. Similar to HRAs, an HSA is a high-deductible health insurance plan of at least $1,200 for individuals and $2,400 for families, combined with a medical savings account. The 2010 maximum out-of-pocket amount that an individual or family is responsible for in an HSA is $5,950 and $11,900 respectively and can be adjusted annually by the Treasury Department (U.S. Department of the Treasury, 2011). In an HSA, both the employer and employee can contribute pre-tax dollars to pay for medical expenses not covered by the insurance policy. Money left in the account can be carried forward to pay for future medical expenses. In contrast to HRAs, HSA accounts are fully portable, meaning that individuals who leave their current jobs or change health plans retain control of account dollars. These dollars can be used to pay for nonmedical expenses, although the money becomes subject to taxes and a 10 percent penalty, which is waived after age 65. Also, after age 65, any remaining balance in the account can be used to pay Medicare premiums without being taxed.

Consumer-driven health plans (CDHP), a term that encompasses both HRAs and HSAs, are viewed by many large employers as a critical piece in a larger "consumerism" strategy for dealing with increasing health care costs (Herzlinger, 2004). Under this strategy, employers use HDHPs and health insurance plans with high deductibles to increase the share of medical care costs borne directly by employees at the point-of-care. Health insurance plans include Preferred Provider Organizations (PPOs) that have a restricted network of health care providers, including physicians and hospitals. Enrollees in HDHPs and PPOs are expected to play a greater role in managing their own health care expenditures, becoming more sensitive to cost and quality differences among providers. It is hoped that this, in turn, will increase consumers' demands for cost and quality information, in effect creating a "retail market" for health care, in which providers compete for consumers by keeping costs down and improving quality.

For this scenario to be realized, employers must replace existing health plans with CDHPs or high-deductible PPOs, or these plans must attract a significant portion of enrollees in multiple-choice benefit offerings. To date, relatively few employers have adopted a "total-replacement" strategy, with most opting to offer HDHPs as additional choices for employees. A small number of studies have examined health plan choices of enrollees in this situation (reviewed below), but to date no study has examined the choice of an HSA versus an HRA when both are options available to employees. There are significant differences in the designs of these HDHPs, which suggest they could attract employees with different characteristics such as health status and price sensitivity. It is critical for employers and government programs adding HDHPs to multiple-choice benefit plans to have a better understanding of these differences.

Some analysts believe that HSAs will be more attractive to consumers because HSAs can be used for nonmedical purposes and are fully portable (Greene et al., 2006). On the other hand, HSAs are less flexible in some ways (e.g., in 2010 the sum of the annual deductible and other out-of-pocket expenses in an HSA may not exceed $5,950 for an individual or $11,900 for a family, and there are limits on the annual contribution to the account) and this could make them less attractive to some consumers. No analysis of the factors affecting the choice of an HSA versus an HRA in a multiple-choice benefit situation has been published to date. However, a small amount of literature has examined the choice of a HDHP versus other more traditional health plans. In the first study of this type, researchers looked at the effects of health plan choice with employees of the University of Minnesota in 2002 by examining health status of enrollees who chose a traditional PPO plan with high deductibles versus a HDHP. Self-reported chronic illness of the employee or family members had no effect on choice of the HRA, but such employees tended to choose the PPO. Higher-income employees were more likely to choose the HRA (Parente, Feldman, & Christianson, 2004a).

A study by Parente, Feldman, and Christianson examined claims data from a large employer that introduced an HRA plan in 2001, in addition to differing types of traditional PPO health plans. Using claims from 2000, they found that the employees who used the HDHP reported the lowest incidence of illness. The traditional plans that used lower deductibles had a higher rate of illness incidence. The research also confirmed that there was no apparent change in health utilization among employees with chronic health care conditions that used HDHPs versus traditional health plans (2004b).

Additional research also found similar selection results from a HDHP design where the amount left in the account could not roll over. They examined prior claims data from Humana, Inc., which introduced two CDHPs with health-reimbursement arrangements to employees at its headquarters in Louisville, Kentucky, in July 2000. Data from this study showed that the employees enrolled in HDHPs had 60 percent fewer claims, thus confirming the theoretical goals that HDHPs help to reduce health care utilization. However, the CDHPs attracted only 600 of 10,000 covered employees and dependents (Tollen, Ross, & Poor, 2004).

A 2005 survey of privately insured adults, ages 21 to 64, found HDHP enrollees more likely to be in excellent self-reported health than those in a comprehensive plan (less than $1,000 deductible for an individual or $2,000 for a family) (Fronstin & Collins, 2005). There was no difference in the prevalence of self-reported chronic conditions, but HDHP enrollees were less likely to be obese or smoke cigarettes and more likely to exercise regularly. The study did not report whether HDHP enrollees held individual or employment-based policies, had a choice of plans, or were enrolled in an HRA or HSA. In general, the data from various studies suggest that enrollees in HDHPs are generally healthier with fewer chronic conditions.

High-deductible health plans with Health Savings Accounts were offered by the Federal Employees Health Benefits Plan (FEHBP) in January 2005. The Government Accountability Office (GAO) compared demographic characteristics of enrollees in the HSA plan with those in a national preferred provider organization (PPO) plan that was recently introduced (Government Accountability Office [GAO], 2006). The study found that HSA enrollees, though similar in age to those enrolled in traditional PPO plans, earned more than the population enrolled in the FEHBP.

Building on the initial research on the impact of HDHP benefit designs, a 2006 study examined a large employer that introduced two HRA plans in 2004, in addition to several preferred provider organization (PPO) options; the HRA plans differed only in the deductible and out-of-pocket premium. The high-deductible HRA plan was less popular, with 13 percent of total enrollment compared with 23 percent of employees enrolled in the low-deductible HRA. Statistical analysis of the employee's choice of the high deductible did not predict plan choice for either salaried or hourly employees, but hourly employees with chronic illnesses were less likely to join both HRA plans compared with the PPO. Employees with higher-than-average pharmacy and medical claims and costs were less likely to enroll in a HDHP than in traditional plans. In addition, researchers found that those enrollees in the high-deductible HRA (HDHP) were substantially healthier than PPO enrollees (Green, Hibbard, Dixon, & Tusler, 2006).

Using five years of claims data collected from multiple employers, researchers observed per-member-per-year expenditures among five cohorts of employees: members switching voluntarily (optional plan) or involuntarily (full replacement plan) from traditional plans to either HRAs or HSAs, and members staying voluntarily in traditional managed care plans (Parente, Feldman, & Christianson, 2010). This study compared the effects of optional HRA/HSA cohorts with those of the optional traditional plan cohort, and the effects of full replacement HRAs/HSAs with those of optional HRAs/HSAs. The findings suggest that enrolling in optional HRAs was associated with a higher level of spending compared with staying in traditional plans. Enrolling in optional HSAs was associated with a level of spending comparable with continuous enrollment in traditional plans, though higher spending was observed in some years. This research found that full replacement HRAs are cost-neutral to optional HRAs, while full replacement HSAs saved costs over optional HSAs.

These results were not surprising, given the relatively generous plan benefits in HRAs compared with HSAs. The different account ownership arrangements in consumer-driven health plans could also explain the different spending behaviors associated with them. Because the employer-owned HRA accounts are not portable across employers or health plans, even though the funds can be rolled over from year to year, members may prefer spending now rather than saving for later. In contrast, HSAs are portable with members, who can decide to use the funds at any time. The so-called benefit rush that might occur in HRAs is less likely to be observed in HSAs. Benefit rush refers to situations in which one wants to spend all the money in the account when she starts looking for a new job or worries about losing a job, faces retirement, or changes plans at the same employer.

Though enrolling in all HDHP plans appeared to be associated with much higher member-paid amounts, it should be noted that the increased member-paid amounts would be absorbed on a pre-tax basis by the spending account. In 2006, the average employer contribution exceeded the average member-paid amounts in all CDHPs, suggesting that members' out-of-pocket expenses were on average fully covered by the employer contribution. This means that employee contributions to their HDHP HSA were enough to cover the routine out-of-pocket health care costs.

Additional research has found that benefit design characteristics, such as free preventive care and cost sharing, were associated with lower health plan insurance premiums as well as total expenditures. Higher employer contributions, on the other hand, were associated with higher plan-paid and total expense. The price elasticity of demand was only –0.01 when coinsurance increased from 10 percent to 20 percent. Although this elasticity is smaller than the one reported by Manning and colleagues in 1987 using RAND HIE data (–0.2), the absolute value for both was much less than one, implying inelastic demand with respect to the price change (Manning et al., 1987). This finding suggests that, as employees are asked to contribute more to their health plan in the form of higher deductibles and greater out-of-pocket expenses, there is little change in the demand for the consumption and utilization of health care services.

As more employers are offering HDHPs to their employees, HSAs seem to provide better control of costs than HRAs. Meanwhile, as many employers are looking at full replacement HDHPs, research suggests that full replacement may not be worthwhile because there may be no saving (in HRAs), or the saving is relatively small (in HSAs). In fact, a trend in favor of HSAs has been observed in one health insurer's member population. While HSA members accounted for 37 percent of the HDHP members in 2006, the first follow-up year of this study, HSA market penetration increased to 52 percent of the HDHP population in 2010 (Parente et al., 2010). This shift toward HSA enrollment suggests that employers adding HDHPs are mostly adding HSAs, existing HRA employers are switching to HSAs, and more employers are offering full replacement HSAs. This research offers evidence that employers are switching to HSAs as part of a strategy to reduce overall health costs.

The HSA appears to experience considerable favorable selection, attracting a population of relatively healthy employees. Equally striking is the unfavorable selection into the high-option HRA. Previous studies of health-risk selection in consumer-driven health plans have produced mixed results. The most complete data for addressing the issue of risk selection and HDHP choice were provided by Parente, Feldman, and Christianson (2004a) with a mix of survey and claims data and a nearly identical econometric approach conducted in previous research. The authors found little evidence that the HRA plan experienced favorable selection compared with a health maintenance organization (HMO), a PPO, and a tiered-network design somewhat similar to a point of service (POS) plan. Other researchers found more evidence of favorable selection, but did not account for income or premiums in their plan choice analysis. Greene and colleagues (2006) found more compelling evidence of favorable selection in HRAs by looking at prior medical claims and chronic conditions. The collective evidence from this research suggests that employers and employees are selecting HSAs at a greater rate that HRAs, even when the employer offers employees a more generous contribution. HSAs are generally viewed more favorably by employees because they retain ownership of the account and because the accounts are portable from employer to employer.

In contrast to earlier literature, other research includes HSA and HRA choices along with more traditional PPOs and HMOs. Though this analysis suggests that the high-option HRA and the HSA represent nearly the extremes of risk selection, the low-option HRA has an employee risk profile more similar to the HSA than does the high-option HRA. One possible explanation for this finding is that the low-option HRA had deductible and coinsurance benefits much like the HSA. The only real difference was that the HSA was truly an employee asset contrasted to the HRA, which operates as a "notional" account and is owned by the employer, not the employee. It should be noted that health-risk selection is not limited to HSAs. Measured in terms of chronic illness, favorable selection was experienced by the PPO and the staff HMO as well (Parente et al., 2010).

With respect to price sensitivity, analysis suggests that employees who choose HMOs may have a strong "brand preference" for these designs. This could be a preference for low out-of-pocket medical cost that is not completely measured by benefit coverage variables such as co-payments or coinsurance, but that is due to the HMO's care-management style. In contrast, there is greater out-of-pocket premium elasticity in the consumer-driven health plans than among any other health plans. This might be expected in a new market that is in the early stages of product diffusion. In other words, those most likely to "try the new brand" may have greater price sensitivity. Interestingly, there appears to be a more elastic response with the more established HDHP design, the HRA, than with the relatively new HSA design.

The research suggests that there is a favorable selection associated with the HSA plan and substantial unfavorable selection in a generous HRA, meaning that employees are more likely to choose the HSA option with a HDHP. In addition, premium sensitivity for consumer-driven health plans is significantly higher than other plan choices, and changes in the out-of-pocket premiums of other plans have little impact on the probability that consumers will choose a consumer-driven health plan. This research has implications for the overall quality and health status of individuals who are enrolled in CDHPs and on whether their choices have an impact.

Healthy and sick employees may place different values on the two types of CDHP plans offered by this employer. A healthy enrollee should view the HSA account as almost fungible with tax-free saving because she owns the account and can use it to pay for current or future medical bills including future Medicare premiums. In contrast, a healthy enrollee with the same employer contribution to an HRA account should have less incentive to save because the employee does not own the account and will lose it if she leaves the plan or the firm. This is a form of moral hazard that will reduce the value of the HRA for the healthy enrollee.

Sicker employees should view the consumer-driven plan choices as more similar, especially if they anticipate spending more than the deductibles in the HRA or HSA plans. These employees should see the accounts as a tax-free method of paying their annual out-of-pocket medical bills. However, plan choice might be influenced by differences in cost sharing after the deductible is met. In the CDHPs offered by this employer, expenses greater than the deductible were subject to 10 percent coinsurance in the generous HRA and 20 percent in the "stingy" HRA and HSA. These considerations suggest that healthy enrollees will be more likely to select the HSA plan. Sicker enrollees might perceive the plan types to be more equal in value, except for the cost-sharing requirements that would attract them to the generous HRA.

CONCLUSION

Health care consumers should take numerous considerations into account when they assess the impact of high-deductible health plans. Price considerations are found to be an important determinant in the selection of high-deductible health plans. In addition, the evidence from the research literature also suggests that individuals with HSAs have a greater likelihood of being healthy than does a similar cohort. However, HRAs were found to allow individuals that were sicker to utilize services at the same level as individuals in comparable traditional health benefit designs. The use of high-deductible health plans, coupled with an account-based mechanism, suggest little impact on health status and an accompanying decreased utilization of service and a reduction in aggregate benefit costs to employers and employees.

REFERENCES AND FURTHER READING

Christianson, J. B., Parente, S. T., & Taylor, R. (2002). Defined contribution health insurance products: Development and prospects. *Health Affairs, 21*(1), 49–64.

Dowd, B., Feldman, R., Maciejewski, M., & Pauly, M. V. (2001). The effect of tax-exempt out-of-pocket premiums on health plan choice. *National Tax Journal, 44*(4), 741–756.

Fishman, P. A., Goodman, M. J., Hornbrook, M. C., Meenan, R. T., Bachman, D. J., & O'Keeffe Rosetti, M. C. (2003). Risk adjustment using automated ambulatory pharmacy data: The RxRisk model. *Medical Care, 41*(1), 84–99.

Fronstin, P., & Collins, S. R. (2005, December). Early experience with high-deductible and consumer-directed health plans: Findings from the EBRI/Commonwealth Fund Consumerism in Health Care survey. *EBRI Issue Brief*, 288. Retrieved from http://www.common wealthfund.org

Greene, J., Hibbard, J. H., Dixon, A., & Tusler, M. (2006). Which consumers are ready for consumer-directed health plans? *Journal of Consumer Policy, 29*(3), 247–262.

Haviland, A. M., Sood, N., McDevitt, R., & Marquis, M. S. (2011). How do consumer-directed health plans affect vulnerable populations? *Forum for Health Economics & Policy, 14*(2), 1–23.

Herzlinger, R. E. (2004). *Consumer-driven health care: Implications for providers, payers, and policymakers.* San Francisco, CA: Jossey-Bass.

Manning, W. G., Newhouse, J. P., Duan, N., Keeler, E. B., Leibowitz, A., & Marquis, M. S. (1987). Health insurance and the demand for medical care: Evidence from a randomized experiment. *American Economic Review, 77*(3), 251–277.

Parente, S. T., & Feldman, R. (2007). *Continuation of research on consumer directed health plans: HSA simulation model refinement.* Draft Technical Report for DHHS Contract HHSP23320054301ER, January 21, 2007.

Parente, S. T., Feldman, R., & Christianson, J. B. (2004a). Employee choice of consumer-directed health insurance in a multiplan, multi-product setting. *Health Services Research, 39*(4), 1091–1111.

Parente, S. T., Feldman, R., & Christianson, J. B. (2004b). Evaluation of the effect of a consumer-directed health plan on medical care expenditures and utilization. *Health Services Research, 39*(4), 1189–1209.

Parente, S. T., Feldman, R., & Christianson, J. B. (2010). *Impact of health status and price on plan selection in a multiple-choice health benefit program including HRA and HSA options.* Unpublished manuscript.

RAND Corporation. (2011). *Largest study of high-deductible health plans finds substantial cost savings, but less preventive care.* Retrieved from http://www.rand.org/news/press/2011/03/25.html

Tollen, L. A., Ross, M. N., & Poor, S. (2004). Risk segmentation related to the offering of a consumer-directed health plan: A case study of Humana, Inc. *Health Services Research, 39*(4), 1167–1187.

U.S. Department of the Treasury. (2011). *Health savings accounts indexed deductible and out of pocket amounts.* Retrieved from http://www.treasury.gov/resource-center/faqs/Taxes/Pages/HSA-2010-Indexed-Amounts.aspx

U.S. Government Accountability Office (GAO). (2006, January). *Federal employees health benefits program: First-year experience with high-deductible health plans and health savings accounts* (GAO Report 06-271). Retrieved from http://www.gao.gov/new.items/d06271.pdf

Stephen T. Parente and David Randall

COUNTERPOINT

Health insurance deductible amounts have increased steadily in recent years as employers, seeking to reduce costs, have shifted more payment responsibility to their employees. A principal rationale for the increased level of employee cost sharing is that increased responsibility will lead to reduced utilization of services and thus a reduction in the overall cost of health care. A new wave of products and benefit design configurations has emerged since the 2003 passage of the Medicare Modernization Act created Health Savings Accounts (HSAs). HSAs are coupled with high-deductible health plans (HDHPs) and are commonly referred to as consumer-driven health plans or CDHPs. Higher deductibles and account-based plans such as health savings accounts (HSAs) are generally favored by individuals and families in higher income brackets. However, those in lower income brackets are more price- and cost-sensitive and thus may tend to forgo necessary health care services and thus have an indirect effect on overall health status. In the future, other methods, incentives, and policy tools beyond high-deductible health plans should be pursued to curb the overutilization of service to reduce costs and improve the overall health status of individuals.

Cost-sharing mechanisms are not a new tool. In fact, there is little debate about their effectiveness, inasmuch as it has generally been found that employees (patients) who pay more for their health care services will consume less. The price of health insurance has the effect of reducing the price of health care services; therefore, the net price paid by the consumer is reduced. The utilization of health care services increases when patients pay less for the service (Davis, 2004).

The effects of increased cost sharing with employees were tested in a large study conducted in 1973 by the RAND Corporation. The RAND Health Insurance Experiment (HIE) was designed to test the effects of higher coinsurance and deductibles on consumer utilization of health care services. The HIE is noteworthy because a large population of over 7,000 individuals were randomly assigned to participate across distinct geographic areas in the United States. Individuals who participated were assigned different cost-sharing amounts, ranging from no-cost or free health care services to varying coinsurance and deductibles from 25 to 95 percent. These amounts were also subject to an overall out-of-pocket cost limit of $1,000 per individual (Newhouse, 1981).

The findings from the RAND HIE confirmed that, if individuals are subject to higher deductibles and coinsurance amounts, they will consume fewer health insurance services. These results were not surprising to economists because patients with "free" care were found to consume over 60 percent more than were individuals subject to higher cost sharing under the HIE (Davis, 2004). Importantly, the HIE also excluded individuals who were over the age of 62 and those that were disabled. This exclusion is the source of a principal criticism of the RAND HIE, inasmuch as individuals in these categories would have skewed the results toward higher utilization; thus, the RAND HIE did not measure the impact of health status as a result of greater levels of cost sharing.

Additional research into the effects of higher deductible amounts and cost sharing found that low-income families were more likely to forgo care. In an examination of data from the RAND HIE, researchers found that low-income children were far more likely to not see a physician than were children who were enrolled in the free plan (Lohr, 1986). At-risk individuals with preexisting conditions were also found to have better care as a result of the free plan option under the HIE and a reduced risk of major health issues, including death (Rasell, 1995). These results raise many questions about the effects of low-income and at-risk populations and about how HDHPs result in potentially adverse health statuses among those populations.

One concern about the impact of HDHPs and CDHPs is that a reduction in physician visits may result in less use of preventive care. The assumption behind this concern is that the CDHP benefit design provides a disincentive to pay for preventive services because of the high out-of-pocket financial exposure. In a recent examination of vulnerable populations and HDHPs, researchers found that children were particularly affected by these plans. The study focused on the effect of switching to HDHPs, and attempted to determine whether children with chronic health conditions were affected if they enrolled in these plans. The results showed that children with chronic health conditions were more likely to be enrolled in HDHPs if they were part of a small-employer group that had little choice of health plan available (Galbraith et al., 2009). The implication of this research is that families with children that have chronic health issues may be adversely affected by enrolling in HDHPs since they may be prone to postpone preventative care because of the cost-sharing burden associated with HDHPs.

Health benefit design affects the demand for medical care, including preventive services. Increased patient cost sharing acts as a price increase to reduce medical-care demand. Therefore, patients in high-deductible health plans should use fewer services and spend less on medical care than do those in plans with low cost sharing (Newhouse & The Health Insurance Group, 1993). To mitigate this effect, CDHP designs often exempt preventive care partially or totally from the cost-sharing requirements imposed on other services. A partial exemption might specify a dollar limit for covered spending on preventive care; a full exemption would waive this limit on all preventive services covered by the policy.

Despite this exemption, patients in CDHPs might use fewer covered preventive services if there are strong linkages or "complementarities" between acute and preventive medical care services. For example, patients seen in nonpreventive physician visits may be advised to use preventive services, and the reduced frequency of the former could lead to reduced use of the latter. Evidence supports the association between the number of nonpreventive physician visits and the probability of using preventive care; for example, the number of nonpreventive physician visits has been found to be associated with the likelihood of influenza vaccinations among diabetic adults (Egede, 2003). These studies suggest that CDHP enrollees might still use fewer preventive services than those in comparison to traditional insurance benefits such as Preferred Provider Organization (PPO) plans, despite the CDHP exemption of preventive services from cost sharing.

As the HDHP market matured, researchers began to focus more on the effect of benefit design and how preventive services are utilized. One study compared the use of preventive services among employees in a traditional health plan who experienced a change in plan design—lower cost sharing for preventive services and higher cost sharing for other services—with that of a control group from the same company whose benefits did not change. Health care costs for the affected employees fell 5 percent, while those for the control group rose 4 percent (Busch, Barry, Vegso, Sindelar, & Cullen, 2006). There were no changes in the rates of preventive care use, but caution is warranted about the effect on vulnerable populations.

Other research compared the use of preventive, cancer screening, and diabetic monitoring services among continuous enrollees in a CDHP for three years and a matched group of PPO enrollees who had free preventive and screening services. The research concluded that CDHP plan enrollees did not underuse preventative services (Rowe, Brown-Stevenson, Downey, &

Newhouse, 2008). Additional research on the effects of HDHPs on the use of preventative care services examined physicians' recommendations for colorectal cancer screening. This research found that patients with low socioeconomic status (SES) received inappropriate recommendations more often than those with high SES, but there were no differences in inappropriate recommendations for patients of either SES group in low- and high-deductible plans. The researchers also found that if a patient had a low level of funds ($700) in her health savings account, physicians were less likely to recommend health care services that were deemed inappropriate (Pollack, Mallya, & Polsky, 2008).

The findings from this collective research have several implications about the effectiveness of HDHP and CDHP benefit designs. The research conducted showed that preventive care decreased in at least one firm as a result of employees using a HDHP. Half of the firm combinations had a significant decrease, and five more had a decrease but not a significant effect. The irony is that, in all of the firms, prevention was covered at 100 percent reimbursement with no cost sharing. Therefore, it appears that the overall reduction in medical care use has implications for decreased preventive care, despite this 100 percent coverage.

The recent research about HDHP and CDHP benefits on the question of whether they affect the ability of enrollees to receive preventive care has implications for not only employers but also employees. This body of research finds that if an employer fully replaces a traditional insurance plan (PPO) with a HDHP plan that there is a small reduction in preventive services. As employers and policymakers consider the value of CDHPs, these results offer evidence that plan design can reduce the growth of health care inflation. With respect to prevention, there are concerns that warrant further attention. In particular, multiple years of full replacement data are required to test the impact of preventive services that are not required annually. The evidence suggests that the full replacement development is worthy of future investigation and that employers contemplating austerity in light of the 2008 financial crisis will find CDHPs a reasonable cost-control alternative to not offering any employer-sponsored insurance.

A key aspect of HDHPs and CDHPs is that their goal is to induce price sensitivities in the utilization of health care services. In theory, plans with higher deductible amounts will cause individuals with higher deductible amounts to be cost-conscious shoppers and thus spend only on health services that they deem are necessary. However, the price sensitivities associated with CDHP plans are associated with higher income brackets. In short, lower-income employees were less likely to participate in HDHPs (Parente et al., 2004).

HDHPs and accompanying HSAs are also associated with higher-income employees and tend to attract healthier and wealthier enrollees. The adverse selection of a specific demographic groups have recently found that lower-income individuals are less likely to enroll in these plans, and if they do enroll they are more likely to suffer adverse health status. Employees with chronic health conditions are more likely to be price sensitive and thus choose plans with lower out-of-pocket costs. However, research has shown that higher income employees that selected the CDHP option with an HSA were not found to have adverse chronic health conditions as a result of the HSA selection (Christianson, Parente, & Feldman, 2004).

Another critique of HDHPs and CDHPs is that, to effectively use the products, consumers must have a high amount of information and data. Researchers have found that, as a result of the information requirements, consumers are often overwhelmed by the scope of data they must process in order to make decisions. CDHPs and HSAs have high information requirements so that individuals can make cost-effective choices about specific health care services. Information overload is an often-used term that describes the volume of information that consumers must process to make a decision about which health care service to utilize. Additionally, quality and cost data are often not available when consumers make decisions about which health care provider to visit (Rosenthal & Milstein, 2004). This problem is also cofounded by lack of information readily available about inpatient and outpatient hospital services. The information gap is an important criticism of HDHPs and CDHPs because the use of these plans presupposes that consumers will have ready access to information about both prices and quality of health care services they consume. Though the companies associated with HDHPs and CDHPs have made progress in making price and quality information available, there is still work to be done to ensure that enrollees have all the information they need to make informed decisions.

CONCLUSION

The evidence suggests that HDHPs, CDHPs, and accompanying account-based plans (HRAs and HSAs) have many positive attributes. Most notably, the research shows that the plans that encompass the HDHP universe do have an effect on the utilization of services and thus the cost of health care services. Spurred by rising costs, employers have been eager to try these new plans in the last decade, and the early evidence suggests that the plans are achieving their intended goals of reducing health care utilization. However, another emerging body of research suggests that these results are suspect due to the potential adverse effects on vulnerable populations.

HDHPs are favored by individuals in higher income brackets because of their lack of price sensitivity to out-of-pocket health care costs. In contrast, lower-income employees enrolled in HDHPs were found to be very price sensitive to higher deductible levels, which supported the findings of the RAND Health Insurance Experiment. Evidence also suggests that, as a result of the price sensitivity associated with HDHPs, there is an adverse selection bias toward higher-income employees using the plans. This may lead to risk segmentation and HDHPs and CDHPs favoring only the healthy and wealthy. Importantly, adverse-risk selection may lead to traditional health plans having a disproportionate share of poorer and sicker enrollees, leading to a so-called death spiral that causes traditional plans to have greater-than-anticipated costs as wealthier and healthier individuals instead select HDHPs.

Vulnerable populations, such as children and those with chronic health conditions, also have been found to be potentially adversely affected when enrolled in HDHPs. Evidence suggests that these populations are not well suited to using HDHPs due to the fact that they have greater tendency to postpone and even forgo care as a result of the high out-of-pocket costs associated with the plans. In addition, an emerging body of research evidence finds that there may be negative health consequences for vulnerable populations enrolled in HDHPs as the result of high out-of-pocket costs and the potential that individuals will forgo care. The research also confirms the finding of the RAND study that shows that price sensitivity disproportionally affects those in lower income brackets.

As an alternative to the tools and benefit designs associated with HDHPs and CDHPs, there are a variety of methods to deal with the systematic cost issues associated with the U.S. health care system. Several scholars believe that the goal should be the fostering of high-performing health systems and providers that are rewarded for offering high-quality and cost-effective care. This would include the establishment of best practices and the additional public reporting of quality and health outcome data for all providers and health systems. By establishing best practices, insurers and government payers can reward high-performing health care providers and systems with pay-for-performance. Many of these initiatives are currently being implemented as a result of the passage of the Patient Protection and Affordable Care Act of 2010 (ACA). An additional tool would be a greater investment in information technology to make a more efficient system to achieve the goals of a high-performing health care system across all health care providers (Davis, 2004).

Employers continue to gravitate toward HDHP plans, with an estimated 12 million enrollees in CDHP-type plans (Employee Benefits Research Institute, 2011). It is expected that these plans will continue to grow in popularity as a result of the documented cost savings to employers. However, as research suggests, caution should be noted about the effect of these types of plans on those in lower income brackets, children, and those with chronic health conditions. The impact of enrolling individuals in these socioeconomic categories in HDHPs, though potentially showing short-term savings, could have the unintended consequence of increasing long-term costs to society in general, due to a sicker, underserved population.

References and Further Reading

Busch, S. H., Barry, C. L., Vegso, S. J., Sindelar, J. L., & Cullen, M. R. (2006). Effects of a cost-sharing exemption on use of preventive services at one large employer. *Health Affairs, 25*(6), 1529–1536.

Christianson, J., Parente, S. T., & Feldman, R. (2004). Consumer experiences in a consumer-driven health plan. *Health Services Research, 39*(4), 1123–1140.

Davis, K. (2004). Concluding commentary: Consumer-directed plans: Will it improve health system performance? *Health Services Research, 39*(4), 1219–1233.

Egede, L. E. (2003). Association between number of physician visits and influenza vaccination among diabetic adults with access to care. *Diabetes Care, 26*(9), 2562–2567.

Employee Benefits Research Institute (EBRI). (2011). *Annual survey of consumer driven health care plans.* Retrieved from http://ebri .org/publications/ib/index.cfm?fa=ibDisp&content_id=4958

Galbraith, A., Ross-Degnan, D., Soumerai, S. B., Miroshnik, I., Wharam, J. F., Kleinman, K., & Lieu, T. A. (2009). High deductible health plans: Are vulnerable families enrolled? *Pediatrics, 123*(4), e589–594. doi:10.1542/peds.2008-1738

Lohr, K. N. (1986). Use of medical care in the RAND HIE. *Medical Care, 24*(9, Suppl.), S1–S87.

Newhouse, J. P. (1981). Some interim results from a controlled trial of cost sharing in health insurance. *New England Journal of Medicine, 305*(25), 1501–1507.

Newhouse, J. P., & the Health Insurance Group. (1993). *Free for all? Lessons from the RAND health insurance experiment.* Cambridge, MA: Harvard University Press.

Parente, S. T., Feldman, R., & Christianson, J. B. (2004). Evaluation of the effect of a consumer-directed health plan on medical care expenditures and utilization. *Health Services Research, 39*(4), 1189–1209.

Pollack, C. E., Mallya, G., & Polsky, D. (2008). The impact of consumer-directed health plans and patient socio-economic status on physician recommendations for colorectal cancer screening. *Journal of General Internal Medicine, 23*(10), 1595–1601.

Rasell, M. E. (1995). Cost sharing in health insurance: A re-examination. *New England Journal of Medicine, 332*(17), 1164–1168.

Rosenthal, M., & Milstein, A. (2004). Awakening consumer stewardship of health benefits: Prevalence and differentiation of new health plan models. *Health Services Research, 39*(4, pt. 2), 1055–1070.

Rowe, J. W., Brown-Stevenson, T., Downey, R. L., & Newhouse, J. P. (2008). The effect of consumer-directed health plans on the use of preventive and chronic illness services. *Health Affairs, 27*(1), 113–120.

Schoenbaum, S. C., Audet, A. J., & Davis, K. (2003). Obtaining greater value from health care: The roles of the U.S. government. *Health Affairs, 22*(6), 183–190.

Stephen T. Parente and David Randall

INDEX

Aaron, Henry, 285
AARP Public Policy Institute, 451
Aarts, J., 503
Abortion and reproductive health services
    abortion, taxpayer support and, 175, 186–187
    ACA, cost sharing for contraceptive services and, 175
    ACA, subsidies for abortion services and, 3–4, 143, 176, 186
    Church Amendments and, 187
    conscientious objections to taxpayer funding of, 3–4, 175, 176, 181–183
    constitutional limits to abortion and contraception and, 3–4, 176, 183–184
    contraceptive services and, 3–4, 175, 183–184, 187
    definitions regarding, 177
    Eisenstadt v. Baird and, 179, 183
    employer-sponsored insurance and, 175
    Fourth World Conference on Women and, 178
    Griswold v. Connecticut and, 179, 183
    Harris v. McRae and, 175, 179, 183
    Hyde Amendment and, 175, 176, 183, 186
    individual conscience in U.S. law and, 181–182, 185–186
    international human rights law and, 176, 177, 184–185
    international reproductive health perspective and, 178, 182
    Maher v. Roe and, 179, 183, 184
    male reproductive health and, 181
    Medicaid funding and, 175, 177, 180–181, 187
    Nelson Amendment and, 176
    No Taxpayer Funding For Abortion Act and, 176
    Planned Parenthood and, 179, 181, 183, 186, 187
    Planned Parenthood of Southeastern Pennsylvania v. Casey and, 179
    point/counterpoint summaries of, 175–176, 177, 182, 183, 187
    positive vs. negative rights and, 176, 184–185
    poverty factor in, 19
    pregnancy related care and, 177, 178–180
    privacy rights and, 179
    religious liberty vs. gender equality issues and, 3–4
    reproductive health care importance and, 175, 177
    reproductive medicine issues and, 144
    rights against government interference issue and, 179
    Roe v. Wade and, 175, 179, 183, 186
    sexually transmitted infections and, 177, 178, 180, 187
    societal benefits of, 180–181
    sterilization procedures and, 143
    Title X of Public Health Service Act funding and, 177, 179
    unintended pregnancies data and, 177
    Universal Declaration of Human Rights (UDHR) of UN and, 178
    unsafe abortions and, 180
    U.S. fundamental rights and, 178–180
    women's equality and, 176, 177, 179, 180

Abramyam, H., 194
ACA (Affordable Care Act). *See* Patient Protection and Affordable Care Act (ACA)
Academic Medicine (Jeffe), 418
Accessing health care. *See* Racial disparities in health status and accessing health care
Accountable care organizations (ACOs)
    ACA and, 69, 93, 103–104, 206, 271–272, 275, 329, 333–334
    Alternative Quality Care (AQC) program of Blue Cross Blue Shield and, 330, 336
    antitrust laws and, 337, 339
    Center for Medicare & Medicaid Innovation and, 334
    Centers for Medicare & Medicaid Services (CMS) and, 334
    characteristics and functions of, 332–333
    costs debate regarding, 335–337, 339
    deficit reduction and, 271–272, 275
    definition of, 329, 332
    diseconomies of scale and, 338
    electronic medical records element of, 334, 335
    examples of, 333, 335–336
    existing payment arrangements vs., 333
    vs. fee-for-service systems, 329
    as "focused factories" danger, 338
    free choice of providers element of, 333
    functional vs. structural focus of, 330
    health care fragmentation in U.S. and, 332
    HHS rules governing, 473
    high-value outcomes element of, 206, 329
    HMOs vs., 331, 472–473
    increased prices and, 331, 336–337
    Independent Payment Advisory Board (IPAB) and, 345, 350
    information technology advances and, 329, 330, 334, 335
    integrated health systems focus of, 472
    the IPAB and, 345
    Kaiser Permanente example of, 335, 336, 339
    "locus of shared accountability" element of, 330
    vs. managed care systems, 333
    Medicare ACOs and, 275, 330, 335, 336
    Medicare Physician Group Practice (PGP) Demonstration program and, 330, 333, 335, 336, 473
    Medicare Pioneer Model and, 330
    Medicare Shared Savings Program and, 330
    mergers between providers and, 337
    optimism regarding, 334
    origins of, 472
    point/counterpoint summaries of, 329–331, 332, 335–336, 339
    previous experience with, 333
    quality competition reduction and, 337–338, 339
    quality performance standards and, 329, 333, 334, 335, 337–338